Mental Deficiency
The changing outlook

Fourth edition

Mental Deficiency
The changing outlook

Fourth edition

Edited by
ANN M. CLARKE, ALAN D. B. CLARKE
and JOSEPH M. BERG

METHUEN AND CO. LTD
London

First published in 1958 by
Methuen & Co. Ltd
11 New Fetter Lane, London EC4P 4EE
Reprinted 1961
Second edition 1965
Third edition 1974
© 1958, 1965, 1974 Ann M. Clarke and Alan D.B. Clarke
© 1985 Ann M. Clarke, Alan D.B. Clarke and
Joseph M. Berg

Typeset by Graphicraft Typesetters Limited
Printed in Great Britain at the
University Press, Cambridge

British Library Cataloguing in Publication Data

Mental deficiency: the changing outlook. —4th ed.
1. Mental retardation
I. Clarke, Ann M.   II. Clarke, Alan D.
III. Berg, Joseph M.
616.85'88   RC570

ISBN 0–416–38160–X

Dedicated to the memory of
Lionel S. Penrose, F.R.S. 1898–1972
and
Jack Tizard 1919–79
Pioneering, humane scientists

Contents

Plates and figures

PLATES

FIGURES

Contributors

Joseph M. Berg, M.B., B.Ch., M.Sc., F.R.C.Psych., F.C.C.M.G., Director of Genetic Services and Biomedical Research, Surrey Place Centre, Toronto, and Professor of Psychiatry and Medical Genetics, University of Toronto, Canada. Formerly Clinical Research Consultant, Kennedy-Galton Centre, Harperbury Hospital, Hertfordshire.

Michael Berger, Ph.D., F.B.Ps.S., Top Grade Psychologist, St George's Hospital, London.

Janet Carr, B.A., Ph.D., F.B.Ps.S., Regional Tutor in the Psychology of Mental and Multiple Handicap, Department of Psychology, St George's Hospital Medical School, London.

Alan D.B. Clarke, C.B.E., Ph.D., F.B.Ps.S., Professor of Psychology, University of Hull. Formerly Consultant Clinical Psychologist, The Manor Hospital, Epsom, Surrey.

Ann M. Clarke, Ph.D., F.B.Ps.S., Professor of Educational Psychology, Department of Educational Studies, University of Hull. Formerly Principal Psychologist, The Manor Hospital, Epsom, Surrey.

Jane A. Evans, B.Sc., Ph.D., F.C.C.M.G., Assistant Professor, Division of Human Genetics, Faculty of Medicine, The University of Manitoba, Winnipeg, Canada.

Ronald Gulliford, C.B.E., B.A., Dip.Ed.Psych., A.B.Ps.S., Professor of Education, Department of Special Education, Faculty of Education, The University of Birmingham.

Bengt Hagberg, M.D., Professor of Pediatrics, Department of Pediatrics II, University of Göteborg, East Hospital, Göteborg, Sweden.

Gudrun Hagberg, B.A., M.C., Research Assistant, Department of Pediatrics II, University of Göteborg, East Hospital, Göteborg, Sweden.

John L. Hamerton, D.Sc., F.C.C.M.G., Professor of Pediatrics, Division of Human Genetics, Faculty of Medicine, The University of Manitoba, Winnipeg, Canada.

Chris C. Kiernan, Ph.D., F.B.Ps.S., Professor and Director, Hester Adrian Research Centre, The University of Manchester. Formerly Deputy Director, Thomas Coram Research Centre, University of London, Institute of Education.

Helene Koller, B.A., M.S., Research Associate, Department of Pediatrics, Albert Einstein College of Medicine, Yeshiva University, New York, USA.

Steven Lovett, B.Sc., Senior Clinical Psychologist, Hull District Health Authority, North Humberside.

Peter Mittler, C.B.E., M.A., M.Ed., Ph.D., F.B.Ps.S., Professor of Special Education, University of Manchester. Formerly Director of the Hester Adrian Research Centre, University of Manchester.

Andrew H. Reid, M.D., F.R.C.P., F.R.C.Psych., Consultant Psychiatrist, Dundee Psychiatric Service, Honorary Senior Lecturer in Psychiatry, University of Dundee.

Stephen A. Richardson, Ph.D., Professor of Pediatrics and Community Health, Albert Einstein College of Medicine, Yeshiva University, New York, USA.

Robert Serpell, D.Phil., Professor of Psychology, University of Zambia, Lusaka, Zambia. Formerly Director, Institute for African Studies, University of Zambia.

Jan Stern, Ph.D., F.R.C.Path., Consultant Clinical Biochemist, Queen Mary's Hospital for Children, Carshalton, Surrey.

Edward Whelan, Ph.D., Senior Lecturer, Hester Adrian Research Centre, University of Manchester.

William Yule, Ph.D., F.B.Ps.S., Reader in Clinical Psychology, Institute of Psychiatry, Maudsley Hospital, London.

Acknowledgements

The contributors and editors have drawn heavily upon the publications of many workers in this field, to all of whom they wish to express their gratitude. Specific acknowledgements are made by the following authors:

Professor Ann M. Clarke and Professor Alan D.B. Clarke
Her Majesty's Stationery Office for quotations from the Warnock Report in Chapter 2. The Editors, *Educational Psychology*, for permission to base part of Chapter 12 on an article by the first author, 4 (1984), 5–19.

Dr Jane A. Evans and Professor John L. Hamerton
The National Health Research and Development Programme, Canada, for support of the first author as a National Health Research Scholar. The Medical Research Council, Canada, for support of Professor Hamerton's research activities.

Professor Bengt Hagberg and Mrs Gudrun Hagberg
The Sävstaholm Foundation, Sweden, for support.

Professors Peter Mittler and Robert Serpell
Chapter 19 was written while the second author was on sabbatical leave from the University of Zambia and held the position of Visiting Professor in the Department of Psychology, University of Hull.

Dr Andrew H. Reid
The Editor, *Medicine International*, for permission to base part of Chapter 8 on the article 'Diagnostic problems in the mentally handicapped', 1 (1983), 1554–7.

Professor Stephen A. Richardson and Ms Helene Koller
The preparation of Chapter 10 was made possible by financial support from the Foundation for Child Development. Drs Mervyn Susser and Ernest W. Gruenberg for their helpful comments. Drs G. Innes, A.W. Johnston and W.M. Millar, and the Scottish Home and Health Department, for permission to reproduce Figure 1 from *Mental Subnormality in North-East Scotland: A Multi-Disciplinary Study of Total Population* (1978) (Figure 10.1). Dr Innes also allowed reproduction of Figure 3 from the *Proceedings of the Third Congress of the International Association for the Scientific Study of Mental Deficiency* (1975), p. 199, as did the Association (Figure 10.2). Pergamon Press Limited agreed to the reproduction of Figure 3 from S.A. Richardson, H. Koller, M. Katz and J. McLaren (1984a), 'Career paths through mental

retardation services: an epidemiological perspective', *Applied Research in Mental Retardation*, 5, 58 (Figure 10.3).

Dr Edward Whelan
The preparation of Chapter 18 was made possible by research support from the Department of Health and Social Security.

Foreword to the first edition

Traditionally mental deficiency has been a neglected field of study, with the exception of some aspects of neuropathology and genetics. Here some outstanding work has been done, although extremely rare conditions have often assumed relatively greater importance than their numbers might warrant, in comparison with much more common but less clear-cut manifestations of mental subnormality. The fact that there is no 'cure' for the vast majority of clinical conditions subsumed under the wide legal-administrative category of mental deficiency seems to have rendered this aspect of mental handicap the least attractive to therapists and research workers alike. The possibility of capitalizing on the defective's limited assets by the application of learning theories has not yet been sufficiently explored; too often textbooks have concentrated upon his deficits. Moreover, the relative complexity of subnormal personalities has all too often been overlooked. Fortunately, however, such pioneers as Binet, Burt and Wallin have laid firm foundations for subsequent work.

Early this century an extreme and oversimplified genetical theory raised profound fears that national degeneracy was imminent; it is nowadays realized, of course, that inheritance does not take place in the simple manner then postulated, and, as Burt has recently stated, it must be supposed that heredity produces differences as often as resemblances. Moreover, the pattern of differential fertility which originally gave rise to alarm is itself changing. Nevertheless, from this original and largely inaccurate premise, a logical belief arose that *custodial care* was the correct solution, on both humanist and scientific grounds, to the social and genetic problems of mental deficiency. This was further reinforced by unemployment between the two world wars, and the overall effect, among others, prevented any real evaluation of the certified defective's prospects in the community. Similarly, the equally extreme behaviourist view originating from the work of J.B. Watson also had its adherents in the field of mental deficiency research. Nowadays, however, better experimental controls and more sophisticated techniques are beginning to give us more accurate, if less sensational, information about environmental influences. Moreover, much of the earlier work concerned children only, and as this book will endeavour to indicate, the mentally deficient child may in some cases show a different picture in adult life, and certainly his problems will be different.

Mental deficiency is a social-administrative rather than a scientific concept, varying in different countries and within a given country at different times. With the major social and economic changes which have occurred during the last fifteen years, a re-evaluation of the problem has become possible. It is clear that advances have occurred in our understanding of the nature, causes, and treatment of the many conditions which we term mental deficiency, resulting in a steadily changing outlook. Much new research in this country, the United States and Scandinavia has been completed and there has also been increased public interest and understanding, culminating in Britain in the recent Royal Commission. It is being increasingly appreciated that this is a rewarding and often exciting field of study.

In the present volume we have three main aims: first, to summarize as comprehensively as possible the literature on psychological and social aspects of mental deficiency (particularly that of the last decade) against a background of genetics and neuropathology. Second, we have tried to show the intimate, reciprocal and enriching relationship between theory and practice, and the use of experimental method in both areas; and third, an attempt has been made to indicate in a practical manner how the learning difficulties and social problems posed by the subnormal may be ameliorated. We would like to express our gratitude to the contributors who have willingly fitted in with this general plan, and who have patiently tolerated editorial interference over a long period.

Dr Vernon Hamilton read the original manuscript and made many useful suggestions, and Mr Roy Brown provided valuable help at the proof stage; we are very much indebted to them. We are also glad to record our thanks to Dr J.F. MacMahon who has taught us so much and over many years provided facilities for, and encouraged us in, our endeavours to apply scientific method to the problems of mental deficiency; our debt to him is great. We are also grateful to Professor C.A. Mace, General Editor of the Methuen Manuals of Modern Psychology series, for his interest and assistance.

May 1958   A.M.C.

A.D.B.C.

Preface to the second edition

When the first edition of this book was published in 1958 it was necessary to include a short section on the neglect of mental deficiency. Even so, the trends initiated during that decade enabled us to justify our subtitle: 'The Changing Outlook'. Between 1958 and 1964, however, many developments have occurred, and the pace of change has been greatly accelerated. It may, therefore, be worth reviewing the immediate background in England and in the United States.

In England, the development of the Welfare State in the postwar years sensitized public awareness of deprived members of the population, and this led to particular concern for the conditions of those in mental and mental deficiency hospitals. In the early 1950s it became obvious that custodial care for mildly subnormal persons was no longer appropriate on either humane or economic grounds, and survey and other findings helped to identify the necessary bases for reform.

Public unease about the mental health services undoubtedly played a large part in bringing into being the Royal Commission on Mental Illness and Mental Deficiency, 1954–7, and ultimately the passing of the Mental Health Act, 1959. The main principles now were, first, an emphasis on voluntary rather than compulsory admission, and second, a shift from hospital care, often in remote isolated areas, to community provisions for the mentally subnormal. Local health authorities were empowered to build training centres for the severely subnormal, as well as hostels for these and for others of higher grade. A great expansion of community services is thus now in progress (Ministry of Health, *Health and Welfare: The Development of Community Care*, Cmnd 1973, London, HMSO, 1963).

In the United States, a similarly accelerated development has taken place during the last decade. This has been well reviewed by D. Gibson (Psychology in mental retardation: past and present, *Amer. Psychol.*, 1964, **19**, 339–41). Between 1946 and 1960, according to this writer, changing social conditions brought sharply increased community expectations for improved educational and other services. This renaissance in public and professional concern reached its peak in 1962 with the Report of the President's Panel on Mental Retardation. Indeed, it is clear that the Kennedy family's personal interest in these problems did much to focus attention on the whole field. And before his untimely death in November 1963, President Kennedy was able to sign two major pieces of legislation relating to mental retardation.

The trends outlined have, of course, not merely been confined to Britain and the United States; similar changes have occurred, or are in process of occurring, in many other countries. Indeed, this heightened interest was reflected in the 1960 London Conference on the Scientific Study of Mental Deficiency, attended by nearly 700 delegates coming from twenty-seven countries. During this, the first multidisciplinary international conference, a provisional committee was set up with the aim of fostering an international organization. This latter was inaugurated as a permanent body at The International Copenhagen Conference on the Scientific Study of Mental Retardation in August 1964, with national committees in many countries. Its aim is to encourage research and disseminate scientific information.

Mental deficiency poses two main problems; first, the task of primary prevention of these conditions, whether they be of biological or sociocultural origin. The second problem is the amelioration of existing mental deficiency wherever possible, again whether by biological, social or educational means. There have been recent important theoretical advances in the first sphere, even though, as yet, little immediate practical outcome can be expected, and it is very unlikely that, in the immediately foreseeable future, mental deficiency will be substantially reduced in incidence. In the second, however, the increased awareness of mental deficiency as a special problem in learning has already borne practical fruit. Although not wishing to minimize our continuing ignorance, it is now obvious that much can be done to use, develop, and indeed sometimes to create, limited assets in a way thought impossible a mere ten or fifteen years ago. The ground has thereby been cleared and the way is now open for behavioural scientists to explore in depth the details of learning and other processes. Perhaps the most important recent development in the field of mental retardation is the increasing concern by experimental scientists with perception, attention, memory, speech, and concept attainment. Work of this nature takes time to yield applicable knowledge; it seems to us, however, that the foundations of adequate educational programmes for the future will be laid on the basis of research carried out under conditions sufficiently controlled to indicate causes of behavioural deficits and precise methods of overcoming them.

Mental deficiency is a meeting point of a very large number of disciplines; neurology, sociology, biochemistry, psychology, genetics, education and psychiatry all have some part to play. Work in this field is not only rewarding for its immediate theoretical interest, or practical implications for the handicapped person, but also for its bearing upon the wider study of mankind. As Penrose has put it, 'these unfortunate mentally handicapped individuals can reveal, unwittingly, information of the utmost value to the rest of the human community, and we may well be grateful to them for this service'.

In this, the second edition, we have been fortunate to retain the help of our original contributors. In addition, we welcome Dr J.M. Berg to our numbers, and are very grateful for his masterly overview of aetiological principles in pathological deficiency. We have found no reason to alter the general outline of the book, but all chapters have been revised, in some cases considerably. Advances in various fields also made it necessary completely to rewrite and restructure Chapters 1, 6 and 13. And with the greatly increased output of research, all contributors have been forced into a greater selectivity than was necessary in the first edition. Nevertheless, we hope that the student or research worker will find this book reasonably comprehensive, and that our 1200 or so references will enable him to follow up his particular interests without major difficulty.

Mrs M. Phillips prepared the author and subject indexes and references with the assistance of Mr A.S. Henney; we are very grateful to them for undertaking this time-consuming task.

December 1964

A.M.C.

A.D.B.C.

Preface to the third edition

Advances in research on mental retardation in all disciplines have been immense during the last decade. The outlook since the second edition of this book was prepared in the mid-1960s has changed so considerably that a complete restructuring and virtually complete rewriting of the volume has proved necessary, together with a great extension of coverage. The first and second editions comprised eighteen chapters each; the present one has been increased to twenty-five. Earlier editions were both made up of three sections; we have now found it more logical to delete the distinction between theoretical and applied work and divide the book into sections according to research area.

Although this book has altered almost beyond recognition, its general message remains the same: that careful empirical work in all disciplines pays off in both the short and long term. It has implications for prevention and amelioration of subnormality, as well as a more general understanding of man as a biosocial organism. We have not, however, changed the book's title. It is amusing now to recall that in 1958 we were criticized for using 'The Changing Outlook' as part of it. Our critic felt that this would date the book, particularly if there were to be future editions, for although the outlook had then changed, it could not continue to do so. Happily, such pessimism was unjustified. We prefer the term 'Mental Retardation' to its synonyms but have been urged to retain 'Mental Deficiency' in the title because of its familiarity.

In Chapter 1 we refer, among other things, to the recent pronouncement of the President's Committee on Mental Retardation (1972) that, using present techniques in the biomedical and behavioural sciences, it is possible to reduce the incidence of mental retardation by half by the end of the century. It is, of course, significant that the word 'possible' has been chosen. Whether a possibility will become a probability depends very largely upon the resources which society will allocate to the problems. So far as the culturally disadvantaged, a very large group, are concerned, it is not enough to intervene effectively to break the cycle of deprivation. Society must learn to understand and overcome its own pathology which currently allows the cycle ever to start. Similarly, so far as biological factors are concerned, now is the time to focus attention upon such problems as malnutrition and high maternal age in the aetiology of handicapping conditions.

In this, the third edition, we have been fortunate in retaining our 1958 and 1965 teams of contributors. We welcome to their numbers Mr R. Blunden, Dr Janet Carr, Messrs D.F. Clark and R. Fawcus, Mrs Gail Hawks, Drs Beate

Hermelin, C.C. Kiernan, B.H. Kirman, A. Kushlick and Professor P.J. Mittler. Their assistance has been invaluable.

Finally, we must again express gratitude to Mrs Moira Phillips who prepared the index and assisted with the compilation of references and the checking of proofs.

July 1973　　　　　　　　　　　　　　　　　　　　　　　　　A.M.C.

　　　　　　　　　　　　　　　　　　　　　　　　　　　　　A.D.B.C.

Preface to the fourth edition

A decade has passed since the publication of the third edition, a period which has witnessed further advances in the understanding of the nature of mental retardation and in the development of preventive and ameliorative measures. Indeed, the statement in the third edition that 'this book has altered almost beyond recognition, [yet] its general message remains the same: that careful empirical work in all disciplines pays off in both the short and long term', remains valid for the fourth.

Some readers and reviewers may be surprised that we have retained in the title the unfashionable term *Mental Deficiency*, particularly since these words appear nowhere in the text except in a historical context. We have once again debated seriously the issue of a possible change, particularly as the designation is virtually unused in this book. An alternative, *Mental Retardation: The Changing Outlook*, might have been preferable, but this has already been pre-empted by an American author. Previous editions are, however, so familiar that this has weighed heavily with us, and we note that we remain in good company. The American Association on Mental Deficiency and the *American Journal of Mental Deficiency*, after much debate, have kept their names unchanged, as have the younger *Journal of Mental Deficiency Research* and the International Association for the Scientific Study of Mental Deficiency, founded in 1957 and 1964 respectively.

Although the title has not changed, the design and organization are completely new. The first edition published in 1958 contained, as a matter of deliberate policy, no input from a medical scientist. In Britain, prior to that date, mental deficiency research and practice were dominated by the medical profession, and behavioural scientists were accorded a minor role, often confined to giving in somewhat routine fashion intelligence tests to aid those responsible in 'diagnosis', according to the medical model with which they had been brought up. Contributors to this book saw themselves as part of a revolution in thinking and practice, a belief which motivated the choice of our subtitle: *The Changing Outlook*.

For the second edition, in 1965, a medical investigator provided a chapter on pathological factors in the aetiology of mental subnormality. Nine years later, in 1974, two additional medical colleagues joined the team of authors for the third edition. Now, in this fourth edition, further substantial extension of this multidisciplinary focus has resulted in the initial biomedical contributor (J.M.B.) joining the original editors (A.M.C. and A.D.B.C.) as co-editor.

Readers will note not only the extended multidisciplinary character of this edition but also, as an essential and major feature, the interweaving of biomedical, psychological and educational contributions. The increasing awareness of the need for a multidisciplinary approach to both research and practice in the field of mental retardation has caused us to organize our text in such a way that no behavioural scientist should be unaware of important advances in biomedical areas, while the biomedical scientist will have at his disposal contributions from the behavioural sciences which are germane to discussions of aetiology, prevention and amelioration as they arise.

We wish to express our gratitude to all the contributors to earlier editions, whose work helped to give the books their distinctive character. Many have now retired, or moved into different fields of research, and a new generation is to be found among our present collaborators.

Pamela Brown prepared the Name Index, and Moira Phillips undertook the demanding task of producing the Subject Index, as she has for the two previous editions. Professor Michael Rutter provided constructive suggestions on the penultimate draft of the book. To all of these we are most grateful.

We must also refer here with great sorrow to the deaths during the 1970s of two exceptional and admirable scientists, Professors Lionel S. Penrose and Jack Tizard, active in the biomedical and psychosocial spheres, respectively. Both these pioneers were gentlemen in the original sense, and both were practising advocates of multidisciplinary approaches to human problems; this book is affectionately dedicated to their memory.

November 1984

A.M.C.

A.D.B.C.

J.M.B.

PART ONE
Introduction

I

The changing outlook

Joseph M. Berg, Ann M. Clarke
and Alan D.B. Clarke

INTRODUCTION

This volume is offered as a wide-ranging analysis of the present state of knowledge in the field of mental retardation.[1] It assesses the advances and achievements of the past decade, and it examines those areas in which uncertainties persist and problems, often new ones, arise. In this introductory chapter, rather than presenting a synopsis of the contributions that follow, we wish to focus on the major changes in outlook and practice that have taken place in the past decade Underlying those changes is the shift to an interdisciplinary approach to the aetiology, prevention and amelioration of handicap, an approach that this book reflects in its assumption of both the equal importance of psychosocial and biomedical issues, and their interrelationship.

CHANGING PERSPECTIVES

From a social perspective, perhaps the greatest change that has occurred recently is a fundamental and pervasive alteration in official attitudes to handicap, reflected in new laws and new practices. As argued in Chapter 2, during the period spanning the first three editions of this book (1958–74) changes in attitude towards, and definitions of, retarded people were regularly advocated, together with evidence suggesting why and how these innovations might be effected. The gradual shift in perspective has gathered momentum, culminating in fairly revolutionary changes to regulations relating to the

---

1. Useful reviews on various aspects of mental retardation are to be found in the Proceedings of the International Association for the Scientific Study of Mental Deficiency, four sets of which have appeared in print (Primrose, 1975; Mittler, 1977, 1981; Berg, 1984) since the last edition of this book. The March 1984 issue of the *American Journal of Mental Deficiency* offers a valuable account of the work of the thirteen major research centres in the United States.

retarded. There is now a greater regard for the civil rights of handicapped persons, recognition that legally enforced provision is unnecessary for the majority, and a more widespread awareness of the complexity of aetiology, assessment of functioning and prediction in individual cases.

An example of how this change in outlook has affected practice is afforded by the English Warnock Committee's recommendations and the 1981 Education Act discussed in Chapters 2 and 17, in which *children's educational needs* become the focus of attention, and no reference is made to different degrees of intellectual retardation.

Society generally no longer assumes that persons with IQs below 75 represent a potential threat, but rather considers them to be, at least in the milder ranges, part of the normal variation between humans, unless a particular problem arises. Several influences thus converge upon a growing readiness to accept and treat the retarded in a more humane way than in the past. The concept of normalization arose both from pioneer research in the 1950s and from the influence of parental pressure groups. It is a concept which frequently needs explanation; it applies not only to enhancing the development of processes to the highest possible levels in the individual, but also to promoting a life context which is as ordinary and 'normal' as possible. It also requires acceptance of and support for handicapped persons on behalf of individual members of any community in which those with handicaps live and work. Empirical research on community attitudes is discussed in Chapter 19.

As is well known, the mildly retarded are several times more numerous than the more severe cases. Behavioural research in the past was particularly concerned with this large group. There has been a radical shift in emphasis in the last decade, which justified Haywood's (1979) paper entitled 'What happened to mild and moderate retardation?' He indicates that a major change has taken place in the relative distribution of services, the levels of research interest and the flow of research with respect to mild and moderate versus severe and profound mental retardation. Throughout the 1960s the emphasis in most areas has been on the former; research reports in the social and behavioural sciences and in education were largely confined to work on the milder grades. What little research was undertaken with the more severely impaired lay primarily within the operant school. At that time the imbalance was obvious and many called for more emphasis on the severely handicapped. Instead of achieving a balance, resources in the United States have shifted to the other extreme, such that 'it is frequently impossible to obtain public funds to support both research and services in this important area unless one promises to give primary emphasis to those individuals who are severely or profoundly handicapped' (p. 429). This is especially regrettable, writes Haywood, when considering the far greater number of individuals in the upper levels of retardation. On the other hand, it could be argued that the mildly retarded have largely melted away, merging into the general community where their problems, if any, are viewed and researched in a wider context.

By contrast, biomedical research has been overwhelmingly focused for many years on those with severe and profound retardation because it was apparent that nearly all such persons had organic pathology which lent itself to exploration. Ironically, perhaps, in view of the drift of behavioural research away from the mildly retarded, mentioned above, biomedical studies recently have been giving increasing attention to this group. A stimulus for this has been the growing awareness that many biomedical causes of mental retardation of both genetic and environmental origin can have, as indicated later in this and other chapters, relatively subtle as well as more marked and obvious effects on mental function.

The social context of handicap

It appears that there has been some movement away from laboratory-type research using mentally retarded persons to systematic assessments of individuals in defined social contexts, and to the evaluation of defined interventions. This approach has necessitated new research techniques and often complex programmes of statistical analysis in order that valid conclusions may be drawn. A distillation of much of the best empirical work in both laboratory and field settings appears regularly in the *International Review of Research in Mental Retardation* edited by Norman R. Ellis. A recent example of the sophisticated approaches now being advocated is provided by Heal and Fujima (1984) who consider the methodological requirements of valid research on residential alternatives for the developmentally disabled. They emphasize that many issues in applied social science are ideological rather than empirical, a point which applies to the strong move away from large institutions as a means of providing support for the retarded. But not all institutions are equally inadequate, and some community homes might well embrace the same uncaring, depersonalized attitudes which have often been associated with large residential settings (see also Chapter 19). Heal and Fujima consider with great clarity the issues underlying *external validity* (in terms of population, referent and ecological validities), *validity of measurement* (operationism and features of measurement validity), as well as *internal validity* (quasi- and true experiments, analyses and inferences, hypothesis discovery and other extra-experimental research methodologies). Finally they discuss *social validity* and the *ethics of research*.

The authors deplore the lack of research on important issues concerning residential alternatives. It is rare for a survey to be able to report responses from 100 per cent of its target sample and, indeed, they are aware of only two sets of studies with this level of achievement. A second major flaw is the almost complete lack of true experiments. Only a handful of studies indicate random allocation of subjects to experimental and control conditions, thus adding a further potential and, we would add, a possibly quite powerful distorting influence upon evaluation. It is clear that we know very well what is methodologically necessary, but have failed to employ these criteria in most cases. So the changing outlook here is an increasing knowledge of the necessities of truly scientific work on many complex social issues, yet a failure to practise them. By the time our fifth edition has been produced, we hope to report their wider implementation.

The change in official attitudes towards greater integration of the retarded into schools and the community has been dictated by the finest of motives, in the hope that the best interests of handicapped persons may thus be served. However, the philosophical and political issues inherent in this changing outlook require close examination, a task undertaken by Rose-Ackerman (1982) in an outstanding paper on the ethics and politics of normalization.

The author suggests that in certain advanced societies an earlier consensus on desirable changes is falling apart, with problematic implications for activists in the normalization movement. She examines four philosophical positions, the choice-based, class-based, respect-based and happiness-based theories, pointing to inconsistencies between and within these attitudes. For example, a class of philosophical work stresses each individual's right to equal respect as a person, but the understanding of this position depends on definitions and also on the criteria to be used in determining the basis for respect. Some would argue that fairly minimal standards of autonomy or rationality would suffice to include most (but not all) retarded persons in the category of being respect-worthy. However, problems arise with the concept of 'equal respect'. One interpretation emphasizes legal equality, which leaves the logical consequence that the mentally retarded have the same right to fail as other citizens. By contrast, another approach is concerned with 'effective autonomy', seeking to avoid situations where people feel they have no personal control over their own lives, a position which leads logically to the idea of controlled environments in which serious failure, embarrassment or shame can be avoided.

The retarded are a minority in society, and in order to change policy the minority must generate support from the majority. A simple message is more easily used as a rallying cry than a balanced and complicated evaluation of the relative merits of alternative policies, and the normalization movement faces the problem of all successful reforms in translating slogans into policy. A common problem is that activists may argue for changes in the law to emphasize legal equality, but at the same time demand large earmarked subsidies for the retarded, often to be used for social service programmes which purport to raise the happiness of the retarded, without empirical support for the contention. The author isolates four kinds of conflict between principles:

> an individual may hold internally inconsistent or poorly articulated positions, or people may disagree with each other on which principles should guide policy. The second is a conflict between private interests and moral principles, and the third is the conflict between opposing private interests. The final conflict is an internal tension that activists face when their principles clash with the realities of political life. Should they hold out

for their principles, or should they compromise in order to obtain money for services?

To the warnings issued by Rose-Ackerman, an additional one might be added. As we have many times indicated, a slogan by its very nature tends to oversell its product. By the time this becomes clear, a counter-reaction sets in. However, as Rose-Ackerman herself points out, 'One can at least hope to discover which claims require a stronger empirical basis, which depend upon basic beliefs, and which further a private interest.' Her paper should be required reading for all those concerned with the betterment of the conditions of life for the retarded.

The integration of retarded children into mainstream education settings is another aspect of normalization. In Chapter 17, Gulliford concludes that a major aim in the future must be to increase such integration. Dangers exist, however, in an uncritical enthusiasm for reform. Pointing to the methodological problems inherent in research in this area, Begab (1977) concludes that we cannot as yet state with certainty that the move to integrate retarded children will be more beneficial than harmful (a different point of view, expressed by Madden and Slavin (1983), is discussed by Gulliford). Philosophical issues and concern with existing services, Begab argues, have precipitated massive and ill-researched programmes. Proper evaluation together with experimental studies of new models of care are essential. Gulliford quotes Crowell (1980), who found that over a four-year period only 18 articles out of a total of 822 in three journals devoted to the education and training of mentally retarded people were concerned with programme evaluation. Clearly this is a vast area for carefully monitored and sophisticated research endeavour, bearing in mind that both outcome and process variables need to be considered.

ASSESSMENT

The mentally retarded are a vastly heterogeneous group of people. The identification of those in need of special services is a complex matter, requiring a combination of medical, behavioural and social assessment.

Mental testing has come under attack in the last decade, as much for ideological as for technical reasons, and often by persons who have little comprehension of the complex technology underlying the standardization and administration of tests. Lately the question of test bias has exercised many critics, and a useful pooling of professional opinion was published in *The Behavioral and Brain Sciences* (1980) as a peer review of Jensen's *Bias in Mental Testing* (1980). Although various issues were addressed by the thirty-two reviewers, there was substantial agreement that, leaving aside the question of the origins of individual differences (on which tests are, of course, neutral), mental tests remain useful tools which should not be discarded lightly. In the hands of the ignorant, however, they may be considerably abused and misused.

It has become increasingly clear that once-and-for-all, single-shot assessment is seldom justified; evaluation of the individual should be an ongoing process. The notion that the development of human characteristics is necessarily constant across time is no longer tenable. There are both constancies and changes during growth, and the variabilities can be of considerable importance in many mildly retarded persons (Clarke and Clarke, 1984). Behavioural measurement may thus reflect individual development, progress or lack of this, and programme effectiveness, and it may also be important for 'pure' scientific knowledge. As an example of many of these aspects, the nature of the widely reported deceleration of cognitive development in Down's syndrome children may be cited; can this be prevented (see Chapter 12)? The use of IQ tests in the assessment of retarded persons is discussed in greater detail in Chapter 3.

Mentally retarded people are identified administratively because of behavioural differences compared with the rest of the population (Belmont, 1971). In the past, such concepts as 'social incompetence' have been used in an entirely vague manner, with the result that many social unfortunates have been labelled retarded and institutionalized, even though of normal potential. In recent years attempts have been made to assess more precisely the attributes of competence and the AAMD Adaptive Behavior Scale is the best known of these measures (see Chapter 2). Further work is clearly needed, however, and there remain some intrinsic problems. Adaptive behaviour is to some extent situationally specific; a person may be competent in a situation he knows well but totally maladaptive to a new one. Moreover, ratings themselves are susceptible to extraneous influences such as negative or positive 'halo effects'.

PSYCHOSOCIAL INTERVENTION

High hopes for effective prevention of retardation were echoed in the United States by the President's Committee (1972) which stated that: 'Using present knowledge and techniques from the biomedical and behavioral sciences, it is possible to reduce the occurrence of mental retardation by 50 per cent before the end of the century.' At that time pre-school psychosocial intervention was perceived as a key to the solution of environmentally engendered backwardness and retardation. A spirit of unbridled optimism pervaded American society during the 1960s, ably and expressively documented by Edward Zigler and colleagues in several important statements (Zigler and Valentine, 1979; Zigler and Berman, 1983). According to these authors there was an overreaction against the hereditarian view of child development; environmentalism became the *Zeitgeist*. Bloom's (1964) belief that there was a

> brief critical period in which intervention could be accomplished filled program planners with a sense of urgency. The ensuing rush to produce programs to enrich the environments of the poor through education

overrode the need for research data on which to base these intervention strategies .... Great expectations and promises were based on the view that the young child was a plastic material to be molded quickly and permanently by the proper school environment. Over a decade later, Head Start is still recovering from the days of environmentalism run amok. (Zigler and Valentine, 1979, p. 9)

They go on to say: 'In retrospect it is hard to believe that so much confidence could have been placed in one isolated year of intervention at one "magic period" in a child's life' (p. 13).

The essential features of evaluation research were frequently ignored in assessing outcomes, resulting in delayed recognition of how relatively small the real benefits of such programmes were likely to be. When it became apparent that early intervention could not raise disadvantaged children at risk for mental retardation to average intellectual growth and school achievement there was inevitably a counter-reaction of some pessimism.

Chapter 12 is devoted to considering lifespan development and psycho-social intervention, and no synopsis is offered here. Instead, we will merely note that a more sober attitude to the prospects of altering retarded development within socially disadvantaged life settings is now beginning to emerge from recent studies and evaluations.

The changing outlook on Skeels's classic study

Future historians will trace the development of the intervention theme from the work of the Iowa school in the 1930s, 1940s and even later. The widely quoted study of Skeels and Dye (1939) together with Skeels's (1966) follow-up have had a profound and often uncritical influence on past and current thinking. For this reason the evidence is examined fairly extensively here. The study indicated that mentally retarded infants from a very austere orphanage for 'normal' children made rapid IQ gains when transferred, as the only young children, to a mental retardation colony. Most were adopted and their outcome in adulthood was entirely normal. A contrast group showed, apart from one specially treated child, a deceleration of development and very poor adult status.

Even in the first edition of this book, we expressed some modest reservations about Skeels's first report, offering four criticisms of its methodology. First, the initial assessments were undertaken at ages when their predictive power is very limited. Second, the two groups were by no means matched even for IQ and, moreover, the evaluation periods were markedly different. Third, the inclusion of a contrast group was clearly an afterthought, indicative of poor planning. Fourth, although members of both groups had the same orphanage experiences, they were not identically impaired, so that factors other than environmental influences were clearly operating.

These criticisms were elaborated in a paper presented in Vermont in 1980 and published later (Clarke, 1982, pp. 62–4) in which attention was drawn to selective factors favouring the experimental group, members of which were mostly eligible for adoption in Iowa at that time by comparison with the contrast group who were not so favoured. Moreover, among the twelve contrast children there were more with possible cerebral damage than among the experimental children.

The most succinct and devastating critique has, however, been provided by Longstreth (1981) who points out that the 1966 follow-up is quoted in many textbooks without reservations and in glowing or dramatic terms. He recapitulates the results showing that the treatment group improved an average of 53.7 IQ points relative to the contrast subjects, 'over a period of 18.9 months'. Equally dramatic were the differences in adult status.

The contrast group was obtained from a 'control group' in an earlier study, and so it was known in advance that a 26.1 point decline in IQ had already occurred over a $2\frac{1}{2}$-year period. 'Had the treatment group not changed at all, Skeels was still guaranteed a 26.1 relative improvement.' However, the contrast group subjects did not constitute the total earlier 'control group'; they were only those who had not been adopted. Hence they were unrepresentative of the orphanage children, but were those with the lowest IQs. The total group lost a mean of 4.6 IQ points, instead of the 26.1 points of the reconstituted contrast group. 'What it means, to state it baldly, is that the contrast group *had* to show a deterioration in IQ because otherwise they would have been adopted.'

A further problem is that the contrast subjects initially scored much higher than their own mothers, but treatment children did not. 'So either the initial scores of the contrast children or the IQ scores of their natural mothers are off the mark.' Longstreth calculates from Skeels's data that the former are implicated; hence the decrements are meaningless.

Similar problems apply to the treatment group. The initial scores are unreliable, so that gain scores are equally so. Among several calculations, Longstreth shows that length of 'treatment' is negatively associated with IQ gain! So dramatic rises in IQ scores may have been due to uncertain initial status. Longstreth concludes that Skeels's study, commendable as it was from a humanitarian point of view, is worthless scientifically. We would suggest, however, that the case-studies of the experimental children (in conjunction with case 19, the only fortunate member of the contrast group) may be seen as useful evidence for the effect of late adoption on the fortunes of children who had had several changes of environment in early life (see Clarke, 1984), and who had displayed at least some evidence of early developmental delay.

Advances in technology and communication

Turning now to the more severely handicapped, who as already indicated are commanding increasing attention in the behavioural sciences, we note two developments during the last decade, not even envisaged in previous editions of this book. The first, recorded in Chapter 15, concerns the use of electronic devices as aids to stimulating those who in the past have remained passive and immobile, receiving basic care but interacting little with their environments. The full potential of these methods remains to be established, but a start has been made.

The second development, discussed in Chapter 16, concerns the effective extension of sign language from communication with deaf persons to the severely handicapped. The author argues convincingly for a broader approach to the use of signs in communication. Both writers stress the need for careful evaluation research.

COST–BENEFIT ANALYSES AND THE INVERSE CARE LAW

Cost–benefit analyses of various forms of medical, educational and other services are not new, but they have increased in frequency and sophistication during the last decade. There are two major reasons for this trend. First, at a time of diminishing resources, such evaluations are clearly necessary. Second, it is important for the research worker to have some feedback about programmes with which he or she is associated. Analyses of this kind should, wherever possible, be conducted by independent agencies without an obvious vested interest in a particular type of intervention.

Akehurst and Holterman (1978) conclude that policies for the prevention of mental handicap are most appropriately analysed using a mixture of monetary and nonmonetary measures of outcome. It is important to specify the alternatives to the policy being analysed. They offer a paradigm in which Gross Monetary Benefits (savings from reduced institutional care, special education, lost working time of parents) are deducted from Gross Monetary Costs (equipment, staff time, time lost by parents for screening, patients' travel costs). Nonmonetary Benefits include reduction in births of the severely handicapped, and of the mildly handicapped, and Nonmonetary Costs include false positives.[1]

Some unusually good pre-school programmes (e.g. Schweinhart and Weikart, 1980, 1981) have been evaluated for long-term effects (reduction in allocation to special education) in the Report of the Consortium for Longitudinal Studies (Lazar and Darlington, 1982), considered in Chapter 12. These include a substantial number of mildly retarded children, and cost–benefit analyses are included.

One of the problems in cost–benefit studies which predict benefits from particular interventions (e.g. screening, special programmes or services) is to

---

1. The Ciba Foundation has devoted a symposium to the methods and costs of preventing severe mental handicap, and the book which emerged is a mine of information on this topic (Ciba Foundation, 1978).

estimate the take-up of such interventions. An estimate, for example, that Down's syndrome could be reduced by a very significant amount if all pregnant women aged thirty-five or more were screened prenatally for fetal chromosome abnormality must also make it clear that only a proportion of mothers in the relevant age group in fact offer themselves for screening. It must, of course, be borne in mind that not all pregnant women would wish to be screened, and some would be perfectly prepared to have and rear a handicapped child.

A continuing problem is that too often those most in need of help are least likely to seek it, or be offered it, or if offered it to accept and benefit from it. This has been referred to as the Inverse Care Law, and applies as much to medical services as to social and educational assistance for the handicapped. Too often, services originally designed with the disadvantaged primarily in mind have been maximally used by the more advantaged sections of the population for a variety of reasons, some of a purely social and economic kind, others of a subtler cultural and intellectual kind; such services are therefore under-used by those for whom they were originally intended. The question of how best to approach those families known to be at greatest risk and how best to help them remains an important area of social research, and one in which volunteer groups may prove to be effective agents.

A growing awareness that parents have a vital role in assisting the development of their children is reflected in many places in this book. Parents who undertake the task of rearing their handicapped children should expect the fullest support from society. It must be recognized, however, that not all will be prepared to shoulder this responsibility, and as indicated by Carr in Chapter 14 the recognition of their potential role in teaching must allow that not all will wish to be involved at the level of detailed collaboration that some professionals are now demanding. One might once again invoke the Inverse Care Law: some parents will fail to be offered the help they need or be unable to use it by virtue of the manifold problems which impinge upon their lives.

BIOMEDICAL DEVELOPMENTS AND RAMIFICATIONS

Alongside and overlapping developments in psychosocial fields, outlined above, have been those in biomedical spheres. Dramatic technological advances which have had an impact on human disease and disability in general have at least partially illuminated previously obscure aspects of mental retardation as well. Progress in the sciences of epidemiology, genetics, teratology and perinatology, to name in broad terms but a few relevant disciplines, has made inroads into hitherto unexplained biomedical facets of mental retardation in ways hardly considered realistic in earlier decades of this century, let alone previous ones. Probably the most significant achievements have been those concerned with aetiological delineation, with early recognition of those actually or potentially affected or at risk of producing affected offspring, and with the capacity for preventive and ameliorative intervention.

Although the optimistic tone above seems justified, much remains to be unravelled and elucidated before aspects of mental retardation are well and comprehensively understood in a manner which could have a major expanded impact on incidence and prevalence (i.e. prevention) and on improving the function of those affected (i.e. amelioration). Furthermore, the gaps which exist, to a varying extent in different countries, between preventive and ameliorative knowledge and its application in practice for these purposes urgently require narrowing, a process closely dependent on socioeconomic realities and ideological values as well as on developments in the psycho-behavioural and biomedical sciences.

It is necessary to add also that the technical advances referred to raise new concerns and ethical questions which require airing and debate. For instance, what, if any, degree and extent of the increasing array of prenatally detectable abnormality justifies termination of viable pregnancy?; how much effort and resources should be devoted to improving the survival prospects of infants born very prematurely and/or very small who may have severe mental and physical disabilities later, and where, if anywhere, is the dividing line?; when, if ever, should medical and surgical life-saving measures be withheld from those with grave concomitant handicaps not amenable to improvements?

Many of the developments mentioned and the issues they raise are discussed in this and other chapters of this book. We hope that these observations reasonably reflect the current status of the changing outlook in mental deficiency. That there is a continuing process of such change, generally advantageous, is perhaps the best overall indication that prospects for prevention and amelioration will become increasingly brighter.

AETIOLOGICAL DELINEATION AND CLASSIFICATION

Classification always serves a purpose, and different purposes may yield different classifications. Chapter 2 is concerned with legal and administrative definitions, and subclassifications in terms of intelligence, social competence and educability. Here, however, we consider the important problem of aetiological classification, with some emphasis on methodological pitfalls in research which may claim to establish causes (as opposed to correlates) in mentally retarded populations. Some of these are further considered in Chapter 7.

The time has passed, though it was not all that long ago (see Chapter 11), when mental retardation was viewed as a more or less unitary entity in causal or other terms and when even relatively specific diagnostic designations like 'cretinism' were often applied to mentally handicapped persons in general. Distinct biomedical syndromes, recognizable by clinical appraisal and/or other technical investigative procedures (see Chapters 4, 5 and 6), now abound and continue to be delineated phenotypically and aetiologically. The large majority of these syndromes are usually associated with relatively severe mental retardation whereas, in many instances of mild retardation, a distinct biomedical basis for the mental defect cannot be established in the present state of knowledge. Furthermore, the severely retarded (say, IQ below 50) show a high frequency of associated physical abnormalities (for example, microcephaly, epilepsy, neuromotor disorders and visual impairment), whereas such abnormalities are less common (though not rare) in the mildly retarded. Neuropathologically this approximate dichotomy is evidenced by the usual presence of detectable cerebral involvement in those with severe mental impairment (Crome and Stern, 1972) but, though data are scanty, in seemingly relatively few of those with mild impairment.

These kinds of distinctions between nearly all persons who are severely retarded and many who are mildly retarded led Lewis (1933) to categorize these two groups as 'pathological' and 'subcultural' respectively, the former being composed of individuals with definite organic pathology and the latter, not apparently showing such pathology, being regarded as constituting the lower ranges of normal variation of mental endowment. A somewhat modified elaboration of this concept, influenced by changing outlooks consequent on more recent biomedical advances, is presented in its simplest form here, as elsewhere (Berg, 1985), in Table 1.1, with the terms 'specific' and 'general' approximating to Lewis's 'pathological' and 'subcultural' respectively. However, the 'general' category is not confined only to instances of mental deficit which are normal nonpathological variants of the general population in Lewis's sense (see below). Furthermore, the subdivision into 'genetic' and 'environmental' factors is not intended to suggest a rigid demarcation between these two groups of aetiological variables. Apart from the rather trite and obvious generalization that both nature and nurture have an impact, to a greater or lesser extent, on the mental and physical characteristics of individuals (be they normal or handicapped), comments in the Introduction and other sections of Chapter 4 serve to illustrate further the interrelationship between genetic and environmental influences. Attributing a primary role to one or the other tends to be comparatively easy with regard to the 'specific' aetiological factors in Table 1.1 and, as Chapter 7 indicates, often substantially more difficult and controversial with regard to the 'general' factors in that table. The difficulty often is dealt with semantically, though not resolved, by applying the term 'multifactorial' to an apparent combined effect of those 'general' genetic and environmental influences.

Many of the aetiological factors in the 'specific' category of Table 1.1 have been considered in other chapters of this book. In particular, physical determinants of environmental origin (Chapter 4) and chromosomal aberrations (Chapter 6) have been reviewed comprehensively, as have single gene defects with a recognizable biochemical basis (Chapter 5), most of which are transmitted, in Mendelian terms, in an autosomal recessive manner. There are, in addition, an increasing number of conditions, generally or relatively frequently associated with mental deficit of different degrees, which are also autosomal recessive, and others which are autosomal dominant or X-linked,

TABLE 1.1   Aetiological classification of mental retardation

Aetiological factors	Specific[1]	General[2]
Genetic	Harmful single genes and aberrant chromosomes	Deleterious polygenic influences
Environmental	Particular physical hazards before, during and after birth	Adverse domestic and social circumstances

Source: This table from Berg (1985) is reproduced with permission from J. Wortis (ed.), *Mental Retardation and Developmental Disabilities Review*, vol. 14, New York, Elsevier, in press.

Notes: 1 *Specific*: usually circumscribed single factors relatively easier to identify and delineate precisely.
   2 *General*: usually less circumscribed multiple factors relatively harder to identify and delineate precisely.

which can be recognized on the basis of morphological and other phenotypic manifestations without evidence of a distinct biochemical defect. Several examples are listed in Table 1.2. Interested readers will find succinct accounts of these and many others in, for instance, a number of photographically well-illustrated atlases or compendia concerned particularly with mental retardation entities (e.g. Gellis and Feingold, 1968; Holmes *et al.*, 1972), or with a wider array of syndromes and malformations (e.g. Nyhan and Sakati, 1976; Smith, 1982; Baraitser and Winter, 1983). For those inclined to delve further into these matters, McKusick's (1983) catalogues of Mendelian inheritance in man, now in its sixth edition, is a veritable mine of invaluable information and references.

The conditions listed in Table 1.2 serve to illustrate two generalizations applicable to them as well as to other syndromes due to specific biomedical causes considered in the chapters referred to above. First, though the mental deficit and additional phenotypic characteristics in these conditions are often relatively severe, a good deal of variability occurs; for instance, though most cases of Bourneville disease reported in earlier years had marked mental defect, it is now apparent that a substantial proportion are only mildly retarded and some not at all (Gomez, 1979). Second, as more precise methods of examination develop, some entities previously considered to be discrete turn out to be heterogeneous; for instance, acrocephalosyndactyly, frequently designated in the past by the single eponymous title of Apert syndrome, has been shown to consist of several morphological types not necessarily trans-mitted in the same way – as exemplified by Carpenter syndrome in which, unlike classical Apert syndrome, poly- as well as syndactyly occurs and transmission is in an autosomal recessive manner (Temtamy, 1966). Thus, and

TABLE 1.2 Examples of genetic conditions without known biochemical basis usually or relatively frequently associated with mental retardation

Certain or probable mode of transmission	Syndrome[1]
Autosomal recessive	Seckel (bird-headed dwarfism)
	Carpenter (acrocephalopolysyndactyly)
	Smith−Lemli−Opitz
Autosomal dominant	Bourneville (tuberous sclerosis)
	Apert (acrocephalosyndactyly)
	Crouzon (craniofacial dysostosis)
X-linked	Bickers−Adams (aqueductal stenosis with hydrocephaly)
	Norrie
	Coffin−Lowry

Note: 1 Eponymous names are listed, with other commonly used designations in brackets.

in ways described more extensively in other chapters, delineation of the 'specific' aetiological factors in Table 1.1, and the range of their phenotypic manifestations, continues with ramifications in the spheres of prognostic expectations, management and prevention.

In considering biomedical causes of mental retardation, some attention must be given also to the 'general' factors in Table 1.1, especially presumed deleterious polygenic influences. The intricate relationship of such influences with social adversity in the home and wider environment in producing apparent, though usually mild, mental deficit has been discussed in Chapter 7. Whatever the final definitive outcome (if there will be such an outcome) of the continuing, often emotional, debate regarding the respective roles of natural and nurtural factors in various circumstances, it seems as evident today as when Lewis (1933) wrote of 'subcultural' deficit over fifty years ago that such deficits are often 'normal' in the sense of not being associated with detectable organic cerebral pathology − though some of the many persons presumed to be in this category will almost certainly continue to be found to exhibit such pathology as investigative techniques, particularly at the submicroscopic level, advance. It has yet to be established to what extent subtle biochemical aberrations in the central nervous system, in contrast to grosser anatomical or structural alterations, contribute to cerebral pathology and subsequent mental deficit.

Apart from such considerations, polygenic influences have been proposed to account for, or contribute substantially to, the causation of various malformations or diseases, some of which are not connected with mental deficit (e.g. pyloric stenosis) and others which are (e.g. neural tube defects). Here too, as mentioned above with the example of the acrocephalosyndactyly group of conditions, similar combinations of manifestations do not necessarily have the same cause. Thus it has been argued, though not widely accepted, that exogenous hormones used in pregnancy tests, ingestion of blighted potatoes by mothers, and maternal exposure to hyperthermia are each aetiologically significant in some instances of neural tube defects (see Chapter 4). Other evidence of aetiological heterogeneity of these defects, in addition to their periodic presence in individuals with various chromosomal aberrations, is reports of possible autosomal recessive (Christakos and Simpson, 1969; Fuhrmann *et al.*, 1971) or X-linked (Toriello *et al.*, 1980) transmission in particular families. Such heterogeneity does not, of course, exclude a causal role for multiple genes in other cases and, indeed, such a role seems likely (Smith and Aase, 1970; Carter, 1976). The prospect of occurrence of various forms of organic cerebral pathology with consequent mental retardation, as illustrated by neural tube defects, is thus not limited in causal terms only to the 'specific' factors in Table 1.1.

CAUSALLY UNDIFFERENTIATED MENTAL RETARDATION OF BIOMEDICAL ORIGIN

A distinction is often made between retarded persons with IQ at or below 50 and those with IQ above 50. For convenience, the adjectives *severe* and *mild* are used in the following discussion of biomedical aetiology to designate each of these groups respectively.

Severe mental retardation

Despite the detectable presence of organic pathology, including central nervous system abnormality, in most individuals with severe retardation, the cause of the pathology and concomitant mental deficit can be established, in the present state of knowledge, in only a proportion of such persons. Our discussion here of certain aetiological surveys, analysed in Table 1.3, indicates the need for much caution in accepting uncritically figures regarding the proportion of persons with severe mental retardation who may be claimed to be aetiologically delineated. The surveys presented in Table 1.3 were each undertaken in different countries and published since the beginning of the 1970s.

There are a number of factors which account for discrepancies in the percentages with and without diagnoses shown in the table. Among these are differences in selection processes, and hence in composition, of the surveyed samples (resulting in, for instance, different age ranges and IQ levels), and variability in availability of investigative resources and perhaps also of diagnostic acumen. Much more significant, however, are variations in criteria for regarding aetiology as established. In our opinion there is a tendency, particularly marked in series in which the large majority of subjects are said to

TABLE 1.3 Aetiological surveys of severely retarded samples

Investigators	Location	No. surveyed	Source	Ages	Mental levels	% with diagnoses[1]	% undiagnosed[1]
Moser and Wolf (1971)	Massachusetts, USA	1378	Institution	All ages	Most IQ < 50	61	39
Iivanainen (1974)	Southern Finland	338	Institution	1–49 yrs (mean = 17 yrs)	93% with IQ < 50	±80	±20
Turner (1975)	New South Wales, Australia	1000	Out-patient clinic	1–40 yrs (nearly all children)	All IQ ≤ 50	35 (78)[2]	65 (22)[2]
Gustavson et al. (1977)	Väster-botten, Sweden	161	Community	1–16 yrs	All IQ < 50	78	22
Laxova et al. (1977)	Hertford-shire, England	146	Private homes (mostly) and other residences	Children aged ≤ 10 yrs	All IQ ≤ 50	63	37
Czeizel et al. (1980)	Budapest, Hungary	304	Institution	7–14 yrs	Most IQ < 50	84	16
Hunter et al. (1980)	Manitoba, Canada	406	Institutions	< 20 yrs	All IQ ≤ 50	58	42
Elwood and Darragh (1981)	Northern Ireland	4701 (401)[3]	Community and institutions	All ages (children aged ≤ 10 yrs)	All IQ < 50	49 (64)[3]	51 (36)[3]

Notes:
1 The term diagnosis is used here to indicate attribution by the investigators of definite, supposed or suspected causes or causal factors, and/or recognition of distinct syndromes.

2 The figures outside and inside the brackets are percentages based on definite diagnoses and definite plus 'possible' diagnoses, respectively.

3 The figures in brackets concern that portion of the total sample of 4701 individuals who were children aged up to about 10 years at the time of the survey.

be aetiologically accounted for, to minimize or even ignore a distinction between *causes* and *associations*.

For example, in Iivanainen's (1974) admirably meticulous and comprehensive investigation of a selected sample of 338 persons, 106 (31 per cent) were considered to owe their retardation to 'unknown prenatal influences'; despite this, however, they were classified in the aetiologically diagnosed category because they had cerebral pathology which was thought to be a likely 'cause' of the retardation. It seems reasonable to say that, although mental retardation in the 106 cases would almost certainly not have occurred in the absence of the detected cerebral pathology, the causes of the retardation were the unknown causes of this associated neuropathology.

In a somewhat different respect, of the 304 institutionalized, mainly severely retarded children in Czeizel *et al.*'s (1980) study, over 80 per cent were said to have an aetiological diagnosis; these included 95 children (31 per cent of the total of 304) whose retardation was attributed to perinatal hypoxia. It would be extraordinary, to say the least, if almost one-third of the children in this Hungarian survey owed their retardation to perinatal hypoxia in comparison, for instance, with the 5.3 per cent and 4.2 per cent in Iivanainen's (1974) and in Hunter *et al.*'s (1980) approximately comparable Finnish and Canadian samples respectively. An *association* between various types of perinatal distress and subsequently observed mental retardation does not, in itself, prove that the former *caused* the latter, and in many cases both might well be due to antecedent aetiological circumstances. In the absence of convincing evidence, the exceptionally high proportion of children in Czeizel *et al.*'s survey thought to be retarded because of perinatal hypoxia must be regarded with considerable scepticism.

The requirement for caution is further reinforced by the fact that, in one or more of the surveys summarized in Table 1.3, there are some individuals in the diagnosed category in whom factors like prematurity, postmaturity and toxaemia of pregnancy are considered to be causal; it is arguable whether such factors, *per se*, are specific causes of mental retardation in many instances. Furthermore, in some surveys, *established* and *suspected* causes are pooled in providing percentages of aetiologically diagnosed cases. Finally, phenotypically identified syndromes of obscure aetiology (see p. 21) are sometimes allocated to a causally differentiated category, thus boosting percentages in that category.

Readers are encouraged to examine independently such texts as those listed in Table 1.3 and to judge for themselves what proportion of published series of severely retarded persons can be regarded as having been convincingly, and reasonably precisely, elucidated in causal terms. In our view, such elucidation seems to have been achieved in, on average, about 50 per cent of individuals in series documented in recent years – even if one counts the usually substantial contribution of detectable chromosomal aberrations (particularly trisomy 21) in the aetiologically delineated proportion, despite general uncertainty about causation of these aberrations.

These perceptions are not intended to convey what may seem like a rather pessimistic outlook with respect to biomedical aetiology of severe mental retardation, given that such an aetiology, whether currently clearly ascertainable or not, certainly exists in the overwhelming majority, if not in all, of these cases. On the contrary, there are grounds for optimism. The capacity for aetiological delineation has improved substantially in the last decade or two, with greater appreciation of relevant interrelated influences. As attested in various chapters of this book, important advances have been made in that period in the elucidation of the many genetic and environmental causal factors resulting in mental retardation. It seems entirely realistic to believe that this process will continue and that growing understanding of causation will further extend the scope for prevention.

Mild mental retardation

Distinct biomedical causes of mental deficit are substantially less often detectable, and presumably less frequently present, in mildly than in severely retarded persons. However, as mentioned on page 5, the former are receiving increasing attention in that regard. To a considerable extent, this has resulted from the realization that specific biomedical causes of mental retardation, which in the past were often elucidated largely through studies of severely retarded individuals or groups, can frequently have a wide range of phenotypic consequences including mild or minimal mental deficits; indeed, some aetiological factors, commonly resulting in mental handicap, have *no* apparent adverse mental effects in some instances. This is so for both genetic and environmental influences. Bourneville disease (tuberous sclerosis) was referred to earlier as an example, among a large number of others, in the former category, and careful follow-up of persons exposed to various physical hazards of environmental origin, described in Chapter 4, shows too that adverse mental consequences can persist in comparatively subtle as well as grosser forms. It is now well known also that certain biological aberrations, perhaps best exemplified by the sex chromosome disorders (Stewart, 1982; see also Chapters 6 and 8), characteristically are associated with milder, rather than more marked, mental deficits, compounded in some instances with behavioural disturbance.

Recent studies in Sweden (Blomquist *et al.*, 1981; Hagberg *et al.*, 1981) have addressed the question of biomedical causes of mild mental retardation, and further observations on these data by two of the investigators are presented in Chapter 9. Biomedical causes or causal factors were considered traceable in about half of the total of 262 children with IQs of 50–70 in the two studies mentioned. Among these children were some in whom aetiology was not listed as 'untraceable' because the time of causal occurrences (pre-, peri- or postnatal) was thought to be established, even though the cause itself was not apparent – for instance, a number of children with abnormality of prenatal onset but of unknown causation. This consideration, together with questions raised on pages 17–19 regarding causes and associations, leads one to suggest that definite causes are uncertain in a substantial proportion of the children listed as having a traceable aetiology. However, the undoubted importance of the investigations does not depend on the exact proportions of mildly retarded persons in whom precise biomedical causation could be found, but on the clear demonstration that considerably more mildly retarded individuals than is often realized owe their mental deficit primarily or largely to biomedical hazards (singly or in combination) of the kinds that are frequently associated with severe mental handicap. That this is so underlines the fact that the scope for biomedical intervention, with preventive or ameliorative objectives, is by no means limited to severe retardation only.

Syndromes of obscure origin

The term *syndrome*, derived from Greek, is widely used in medicine to refer to a concurrence of clinical and/or other phenotypic manifestations which, despite some variability, result in a resemblance between affected persons. As many causes of mental retardation produce rather characteristic physical, as well as mental, effects, it is not surprising that a large number of syndromes have been recognized among the mentally retarded, some long years ago and many others recently. They are often designated with greater or lesser justification by eponymous or descriptive names which, in their profusion, can be somewhat confusing.

Many syndromes considered in the biomedical chapters of this book have been aetiologically delineated, whereas others are of uncertain or obscure causation. A number of examples currently in the latter category are shown in Table 1.4. Each of these, like many with a known cause, shows variability in physical features and in the degree of mental deficit. Even when fairly homogeneous and distinctive phenotypically, aetiological heterogeneity may be found; for instance, in a small minority of recorded examples of de Lange syndrome, a chromosomal anomaly, in particular duplication of a portion of the long arm (q25 → q29) of chromosome 3, has been observed (Wilson *et al.*,

TABLE 1.4 Examples of aetiologically undelineated syndromes[1] with mental retardation as a commonly reported feature

Syndromes described prior to 1970s	*Syndromes described since* 1970
de Lange	Cohen
Rubinstein–Taybi	Marshall–Smith
Sotos	Ruvalcaba
Sturge–Weber	Ruvalcaba–Myhre
Williams	Weaver

Note: 1 Accounts of these conditions, with photographic illustrations, are available in Smith (1982) under the eponymous designations shown in this table.

1978). Further, especially with recently described syndromes of which comparatively few examples have been reported to date (see right-hand column of Table 1.4), it is very likely that, as new instances come to light and as investigative techniques advance, revision of a list such as that in Table 1.4 will be necessary on phenotypic and/or aetiological grounds. Thus, for instance, the Cohen syndrome may be firmly shown to be due to a specific gene defect, and the Marshall–Smith and Weaver syndromes may be found to be related to each other (Smith, 1982).

Even when aetiologically obscure, continued phenotypic delineation of mental retardation syndromes is of practical value because useful clues related to prognosis and medical management in a given instance can often be culled from accumulated knowledge of similarly affected persons. Furthermore, empirically derived recurrence risks, though not as precise as the statistical odds applicable to, say, specific gene defects with a known Mendelian pattern of inheritance (see Chapter 11), can be helpful to families containing an individual with a syndrome of unknown origin.

CONCLUSIONS

There is ample evidence in this book to justify its subtitle (*The changing outlook*) and, indeed, that the continuing process and rate of such change in the sphere of mental retardation calls for new editions at fairly frequent intervals. Particular features of the present volume are the equal attention given to both psychosocial and biomedical issues and to their consideration as interrelated topics. It is for the latter reason that chapters concerned with each of these subjects are not sectionally separated but deliberately intermingled. The book, though intended to be reasonably comprehensive in its review of the current state of knowledge and endeavours in mental retardation, is not designed to be encyclopaedic. Although many details are provided throughout, this is not primarily done for its own sake but to illustrate principles, advances which have occurred and uncertainties which persist.

In general, the changing outlook in mental retardation in recent years has been salutary. More humane and rational attitudes to those with such handicaps have resulted in their being accorded a greater dignity and better opportunities than usually attained in the past; increased knowledge about their developmental and functional potentials and the application of novel ways to foster these have been advantageous; and improved understanding of aetiology has enhanced prospects for prevention in many instances.

At the same time, many questions remain unresolved in the areas of, for instance, causation and intervention strategies. Indeed, new and controversial problems arise, often ethical and moral in nature, as techniques advance (see Chapter 11). In the commendable enthusiasm to accelerate progress and to improve the outlook, through better appreciation of the complex aetiological variables that determine mental deficit and through development of more effective social, educational, medical and biological preventive and ameliorative measures, there is some danger that the desire becomes parent to the conclusion; in other words, the wish for beneficial attainments sometimes results in over-optimistic claims not entirely borne out by careful scientific scrutiny.

All in all, however, the balance sheet indicates distinctly favourable recent gains, and a consequently better outlook is apparent. It may be added that what has thus been learned in all these ways not only benefits those with mental handicap and their families, but also contributes to the greater understanding and appreciation of the needs of the human species as a whole.

REFERENCES

AKEHURST, R.L. and HOLTERMAN, S. (1978) 'Application of cost–benefit analysis to programmes for the prevention of mental handicap', in CIBA FOUNDATION, *Major Mental Handicap: Methods and Costs of Prevention*, Ciba Foundation Symposium 59, Amsterdam, Oxford, New York, Elsevier, Excerpta Medica, North-Holland.

BARAITSER, M. and WINTER, R.M. (1983) *A Colour Atlas of Clinical Genetics*, London, Wolfe Medical Publications.

BEGAB, M.J. (1977) 'Closing session address: some priorities for research in mental retardation', in P. MITTLER (ed.), *Research to Practice in Mental Retardation*, vol. 1, Baltimore, University Park Press, 21–30.

The Behavioral and Brain Sciences (1980) Multiple book review of A.R. JENSEN, *Bias in Mental Testing*, The Behavioral and Brain Sciences, 3, 325–71.

BELMONT, J.M. (1971) 'Medical-behavioral research in retardation', *Rev. Res. Ment. Retard.*, 5, 1–81.

BERG, J.M. (ed.) (1984) *Perspectives and Progress in Mental Retardation*, vols I and II, Baltimore, University Park Press.

BERG, J.M. (1985) 'Etiology update and review: I. Biomedical factors', in J. WORTIS (ed.), *Mental Retardation and Developmental Disabilities Review*, vol. 14, New York, Elsevier.

BLOMQUIST, H.K.:SON, GUSTAVSON, K.-H. and HOLMGREN, G. (1981) 'Mild mental retardation in children in a northern Swedish county', *J. Ment. Defic. Res.*, 21, 169–86.

BLOOM, B. (1964) *Stability and Change in Human Characteristics*, New York, Wiley.

CARTER, C.O. (1976) 'Genetics of common single malformations', *Brit. Med. Bull.*, 32, 21–6.

CHRISTAKOS, A.C. and SIMPSON, J.C. (1969) 'Anencephaly in three siblings', *Obstet. Gynec.*, 33, 267–9.

CIBA FOUNDATION (1978) *Major Mental Handicap: Methods and Costs of Prevention*, Ciba Foundation Symposium 59, Amsterdam, Oxford, New York, Elsevier, Excerpta Medica, North-Holland.

CLARKE, A.D.B. and CLARKE, A.M. (1984) 'Constancy and change in the growth of human characteristics', *J. Child Psychol. Psychiat.*, 25, 191–210.

CLARKE, A.M. (1982) 'Developmental discontinuities: an approach to assessing their nature', in L.A. BOND and J.M. JOFFE (eds), *Facilitating Infant and Early Childhood Development*, Hanover, NH, University Press of New England, 58–77.

CLARKE, A.M. (1984) 'Early experience and cognitive development', *Rev. Res. Educ.*, 11, 125–60.

CROME, L. and STERN J. (1972) *Pathology of Mental Retardation*, 2nd edn, Edinburgh, Churchill Livingstone, 121–91.

CROWELL, F.A. (1980) 'Evaluating programs for educating mentally retarded persons', in J. GOTTLIEB (ed.), *Educating Mentally Retarded Persons in the Mainstream*, Baltimore, University Park Press.

CZEIZEL, A., LÁNYI-ENGELMAYER, A., KLUJBER, L., MÉTNEKI, J. and TUSNÁDY, G. (1980) 'Etiological study of mental retardation in Budapest, Hungary', *Amer. J. Ment. Defic.*, 85, 120–8.

ELWOOD, J.H. and DARRAGH, P.M. (1981) 'Severe mental handicap in Northern Ireland', *J. Ment. Defic. Res.*, 25, 147–55.

FUHRMANN, W., SEEGER, W. and BOHM, R. (1971) 'Apparently monogenic inheritance of anencephaly and spina bifida in a kindred', *Humangenetik*, 13, 241–3.

GELLIS, S.S. and FEINGOLD, M. (1968) *Atlas of Mental Retardation Syndromes: Visual Diagnosis of Facies and Physical Findings*, Washington, DC, US Department of Health, Education and Welfare.

GOMEZ, M.R. (ed.) (1979) *Tuberous Sclerosis*, New York, Raven Press.

GUSTAVSON, K.-H., HOLMGREN, G., JONSELL, R. and BLOMQUIST, H.K.:SON (1977) 'Severe mental retardation in children in a northern Swedish county', *J. Ment. Defic. Res.*, 21, 161–80.

HAGBERG, B., HAGBERG, G., LEWERTH, A. and LINDBERG, U. (1981) 'Mild mental retardation in Swedish school children', *Acta Paediat. Scand.*, 70, 445–52.

HAYWOOD, H.C. (1979) 'What happened to mild and moderate retardation?', *Amer. J. Ment. Defic.*, 83, 429–31.

HEAL, L.W. and FUJIMA, G.T. (1984) 'Toward a valid methodology for research on residential alternatives for developmentally disabled citizens', in N.R. ELLIS (ed.), *International Review of Research in Mental Retardation*, 12, New York, Academic Press, in press.

HOLMES, L.B., MOSER, H.W., HALLDÓRSSON, S., MACK, C., PANT, S.S. and MATZILEVICH, B. (1972) *Mental Retardation: An Atlas of Diseases with Associated Physical Abnormalities*, New York, Macmillan.

HUNTER, A.G.W., EVANS, J.A., THOMPSON, D.R. and RAMSAY, S. (1980) 'A study of institutionalized mentally retarded patients in Manitoba: I. Classification and preventability', *Develop. Med. Child Neurol.*, 22, 145–62.

IIVANAINEN, M. (1974) *A Study on the Origins of Mental Retardation*, Clinics in Developmental Medicine, no. 51, London, Heinemann Medical.

JENSEN, A.R. (1980) *Bias in Mental Testing*, London, Methuen; New York, Free Press.

LAXOVA, R., RIDLER, M.A.C. and BOWEN-BRAVERY, M. (1977) 'An etiological survey of the severely retarded Hertfordshire children who were born between January 1, 1965 and December 31, 1967', *Amer. J. Med. Genet.*, 1, 75–86.

LAZAR, I. and DARLINGTON, R. (1982) 'Lasting effects of early education: a report from the consortium for longitudinal studies', *Mongr. Soc. Res. Child Develop.*, 47, 2–3.

LEWIS, E.O. (1933) 'Types of mental deficiency and their social significance', *J. Ment. Sci.*, 79, 298–304.

LONGSTRETH, L.E. (1981) 'Revisiting Skeels' final study: a critique', *Develop. Psychol.*, 17, 620–5.

MCKUSICK, V.A. (1983) *Mendelian Inheritance in Man: Catalogs of Autosomal Dominant, Autosomal Recessive, and X-linked Phenotypes*, 6th edn, Baltimore, Johns Hopkins University Press.

MADDEN, N.A. and SLAVIN, R.E. (1983) 'Mainstreaming students with mild handicaps: academic and social outcomes', *Rev. Educ. Res.*, 53, 519–69.

MITTLER, P. (ed.) (1977) *Research to Practice in Mental Retardation*, vols I, II and III, Baltimore, University Park Press.

MITTLER, P. (ed.) (1981) *Frontiers of Knowledge in Mental Retardation*, vols I and II, Baltimore, University Park Press.

MOSER, H.W. and WOLF, P.A. (1971) 'The nosology of mental retardation: including the report of a survey of 1378 mentally retarded individuals at the Walter E. Fernald State School', *Birth Defects Original Article Series*, 7, 117–34.

NYHAN, W.L. and SAKATI, N.O. (1976) *Genetic and Malformation Syndromes in Clinical Medicine*, Chicago, Year Book Medical Publishers.

PRESIDENT'S COMMITTEE ON MENTAL RETARDATION (1972) *Entering the Era of Human Ecology*, Washington, DC, DHEW publ. no. (05) 72–7.

PRIMROSE, D.A.A. (ed.) (1975) *Proceedings of Third Congress of International Association for Scientific Study of Mental Deficiency*, Warsaw, Polish Medical Publishers.

ROSE-ACKERMAN, S. (1982) 'Mental retardation and society: the ethics and politics of normalization', *Ethics*, 93, 81–101.

SCHWEINHART, L.J. and WEIKART, D.P. (1980) *Young Children Grow Up: The Effects of the Perry Preschool Program on Youths through Age 15*, Ypsilanti, Mich., High/Scope Press.

SCHWEINHART, L.J. and WEIKART, D.P. (1981) 'Perry preschool effects nine years later: what do they mean?', in M.J. BEGAB, H.C. HAYWOOD and H.L. GARBER (eds), *Psychosocial Influences in Retarded Performance*, 2, Baltimore, University Park Press, 113–25.

SKEELS, H.M. (1966) 'Adult status of children with contrasting early life experiences', *Monogr. Soc. Res. Child Develop.*, 31 (3), no. 105.

SKEELS, H.M. and DYE, H.B. (1939) 'A study of the effects of differential stimulation on mentally retarded children', *Proc. Amer. Assoc. Ment. Defic.*, 44, 114–36.

SMITH, D.W. (1982) *Recognizable Patterns of Human Malformation: Genetic, Embryologic and Clinical Aspects*, 3rd edn, Philadelphia, Saunders.

SMITH, D.W. and AASE, J.M. (1970) 'Polygenic inheritance of certain common malformations: evidence and empiric recurrence risk data', *J. Pediat.*, 76, 653–9.

STEWART, D.A. (ed.) (1982) *Children with Sex Chromosome Aneuploidy: Follow-up Studies*, March of Dimes Birth Defects Foundation, Original Article Series, vol. 18, no. 4, New York, Alan R. Liss.

TEMTAMY, S.A. (1966) 'Carpenter's syndrome: acrocephalopolysyndactyly. An autosomal recessive syndrome', *J. Pediat.*, 69, 111–20.

TORIELLO, H.V., WARREN, S.T. and LINDSTROM, J.A. (1980) 'Possible X-linked anencephaly and spina bifida – report of a kindred', *Amer. J. Med. Genet.*, 6, 119–21.

TURNER, G. (1975) 'An aetiological study of 1000 patients with an IQ assessment below 51', *Med. J. Austr.*, 2, 927–31.

WILSON, G.N., HIEBER, V.C. and SCHMICKEL, R.D. (1978) 'The association of chromosome 3 duplication and the Cornelia de Lange syndrome', *J. Pediat.*, 93, 783–8.

ZIGLER, E. and BERMAN, W. (1983) 'Discerning the future of early childhood intervention', *Amer. Psychol.*, 38, 894–906.

ZIGLER, E. and VALENTINE, J. (eds) (1979) *Project Head Start: A Legacy of the War on Poverty*, New York, Free Press.

2
Criteria and classification
Ann M. Clarke and Alan D.B. Clarke

SOME HISTORICAL ASPECTS OF CLASSIFICATION

The need to classify is deeply embedded in human beings; indeed, it appears to be a fundamental basis of cognitive activities. As Bruner once put it, categorization allows the complexity of stimuli to be reduced by treating phenomena as equivalent when indeed they can be differentiated from each other in a variety of ways. It is thus important to recognize that the tendency to classify, either implicitly or explicitly, is part of the biological basis of all persons.

The categories which will be created are intimately related to the overall society in which persons develop, and to their roles in that society. For example, the 'man-in-the-street' and the architect will 'see' a given building in terms of very different selective categories. Moreover, the degree of selective categorization itself tends to change during individual development, as more and more knowledge is gained. Thus the young child's concept of a kangaroo will differ markedly from that of a zoologist, even though both have a clear and overlapping concept of this animal.

There is a close parallel between the use of classifications by the individual and those used by society. Different classifications of the same phenomenon serve different purposes and themselves change as the purposes change. This in turn is intimately related to prevailing social orientations at a given point in time. For example, the word 'cretin' is derived from the French *chrétien* (Christian) and is testimony to the fact that in early times the severely handicapped were cared for by monastic communities.

Classification involves 'labelling' and there is a constant act of changing labels as new knowledge is acquired or as society's view of the concept changes. Langdon Down first described in 1866 the condition of mongolism, a label based upon the physical appearance of a particular clinical type, together with the aetiological notion of 'atavistic regression' which itself really implied that the 'Mongolian race' was inferior. In the mid-twentieth century, as world biological science expanded, it became necessary to reject this archaic label in the interests of scientific precision, and to oppose the perpetuation of an offensive racist label. 'Down's syndrome' was thus invented, and the word 'syndrome' of course rightly underlines the constellation of possible symptoms in this condition. With even more recent cytogenetic discoveries, subclassifications of Down's syndrome such as regular, mosaic and translocation 'trisomy 21' became necessary.

Lables for a given concept may also change in response to popular feeling. Thus, in Britain, the terms 'mental deficiency', 'feeble-mindedness', 'imbecility' and 'idiocy' were dropped, in favour of 'subnormality' and 'severe subnormality', in the 1959 Mental Health Act, as being less pejorative. Similarly, in the United States the words 'mental retardation' are seen as less offensive than 'mental deficiency'. And now 'mental handicap' has become a more favoured label. Finally, it should be pointed out that a given label carries with it different connotations for different people, and may lead to great confusion in discussion if the number or quality of assumptions underlying the same label differs between two communicators (e.g. between a geneticist and a teacher, or a paediatrician and a relatively naïve parent).

Historical documents provide an insight into the varying social reasons why certain members of society have been classified as mentally subnormal. Early in history, the reasons for classification were clearly linked with administrative matters. In England, statutory mention of the mentally subnormal dates as far back as the reign of Edward I (1272–1307), when the distinction was made for the first time on record between the born fool and the lunatic. In the Statute of Prerogatives in the reign of Edward II, a similar division is recorded, between 'born fool' (*fatuus naturalis*) and the person of unsound mind who may yet have certain lucid intervals (*non compos mentis, sicut quidam sunt per lucida intervalla*). The purpose of this distinction in feudal times was to facilitate the disposal of property: thus, if a man were found by questioning to be a lunatic, the Crown took possession of his belongings only during the period of his illness; whereas, if a man were found to be an idiot, his property reverted permanently to the Crown, subject only to an obligation to provide for his person and estate.

Biological views, however, began from the beginning of this century to make a larger impact upon administrative and social concepts. Thus oversimple and confused genetic theories, in the context of a type of social Darwinism, began to emerge with the work of Goddard (1912) and others. From then on one can perceive an interplay between social and biological concepts.

Sarason and Doris (1969) have given extended consideration to this interplay between the development of biological science and social attitudes towards mental subnormality. They traced the origin and consequences of the degeneration theory, the confusion between insanity and mental subnormality, the impact of social Darwinism, the development of the eugenics movement and the role of the intelligence testing movement, among other topics. Their book is essential reading for all those interested in the origins of different forms of provision and changing social attitudes. Here, however, space forbids little more than the briefest excursion into this area.

We propose to trace very briefly the changing use of the word 'idiot', a word derived from the Greek and meaning 'a private person'. It has also been used to denote 'layman' (1660), and professional fool or jester, as in Shakespeare ('a tale told by an idiot'), or an ignorant, uneducated person. For a considerable period of time the word idiot appeared to denote anyone who was mentally subnormal, and it is of course impossible to know what level of impairment was then defined. John Locke (1623–1704) was fully aware of the distinction between insanity and subnormality: 'Madmen put wrong ideas together, and so make wrong propositions, but argue and reason right from them; but idiots make very few or no propositions, and reason scarce at all.' In the late eighteenth century, Blackstone mentions that the 'idiot or natural fool is one that hath had no understanding from his nativity; and therefore is by law never likely to attain any'. At the beginning of the nineteenth century, Pinel considered idiocy as being a variant of the general class of psychosis, involving a partial or total abolition of the intellectual powers. The idiots' natural indolence and stupidity might, however, be obviated by engaging them in manual occupations, suitable to their respective 'capacities'.

Esquirol (1772–1840) wrote that 'Idiocy is not a disease, but a condition in which the intellectual faculties are never manifested; or have never been developed sufficiently to enable the idiot to acquire such an amount of knowledge, as persons of his own age, and placed in similar circumstances as himself, are capable of receiving.' In the United States, Howe in 1848 referred to the difficulty of distinguishing dementia from idiocy. He contrasted those whose understanding is undeveloped, or developed to a very feeble degree, with those who have lost their understanding, the demented: 'by far the greater part of the idiots are children of parents, one or both of whom are of scrofulous temperaments, and poor flabby organization.' Alcoholism was seen as a major aetiological factor; however, Howe began to distinguish between idiots, fools and simpletons.

The classic book by Seguin (1866), *Idiocy: Its Treatment by the Physiological Method*, perpetuated for a while the use of idiocy as a generic term. But increasing awareness of differences within the broad group, as well as differing prognosis, was fully recognized terminologically by the Idiots Act of 1886. Here lunacy, on the one hand, and idiocy and imbecility, on the other, are distinguished. Idiots and imbeciles from birth or from an early age would be placed in any registered hospital or institution for the care and training of such persons. In using the term imbecile, it indicated that a class of subnormal persons existed, less retarded than the idiot. It also recognized that the idiot might be trained. Before long the Education Act of 1870 showed that there existed yet other groups, the 'educable imbecile and the feeble-minded'. In 1897 a Departmental Committee was set up, among other things, to 'report particularly upon the best practicable means for distinguishing on the one hand between the educable and non-educable children'. In turn this led to the Elementary Education (Defective and Epileptic Children) Act of 1899 with its distinction between those who could, and those who could not, be sufficiently educated to become at least partially self-supporting in later life. Within a few years, Binet was to be faced with objectifying this same distinction.

The Royal Commission of 1904 reported in 1908, and as a result the Mental Deficiency Act of 1913 was passed. In this, idiots, imbeciles, feeble-minded persons and moral imbeciles were for the first time clearly defined: 'Idiots; that is to say, persons so deeply defective in mind from birth or from an early age as to be unable to guard themselves against common physical dangers.'

We need take this survey of 'idiocy' no further, for the 1913 definition, perpetuated in the amending Act of 1927, to all intents and purposes is synonymous with the 'profound retardation' of the World Health Organization today. It has been clear that a specific meaning in Greek gave way to a number of alternatives in 'plain English'. It took on a pathological connotation in the seventeenth century, was seen in the nineteenth century variously as a form of psychosis, or the result of alcoholism and degeneration, or as the most severe degree of defect, as well as being used as a generic term for all grades of defect. Only at the end of the century was the more recent diagnostic synonym foreshadowed, while latterly the term has been omitted from the new vocabulary of scientists and administrators.

Even in the simplest of societies from the beginning of history there have probably been those who perceived that some of their fellow men were socially incompetent and very stupid, and reasoned that these factors were causally connected. During the nineteenth century the 'disease model' became basic to a consideration of this population, for society placed those in need of care in the hands of the medical profession. At first, such persons seem to have been predominantly fairly severely retarded but, by the end of the century, as legislation developed, a wider range of persons became designated as mentally deficient. As our brief considerations of the development of attitudes will show, the subnormal were regarded as a race apart in the early years of the present century. The social problems which some of them posed in a developing, complex, urban society were 'explained' by reference to an oversimple genetic model, in the context of social Darwinism. This is well exemplified by Goddard's (1912) work on the Kallikak family which had very wide social and legislative repercussions both in the United States and in this country. Both Goddard and Walter E. Fernald found themselves members of the same committee of the American Breeders' Association, and it is probably no accident therefore that through this connection Fernald (quoted by Sarason and Doris, 1969) was able to express such views in an alarming and succinct form to the Massachusetts Medical Society in 1912:

> The social and economic burdens of uncomplicated feeble-mindedness are only too well known. The feeble-minded are a parasitic, predatory class, never capable of self-support or of managing their own affairs. The great majority ultimately become public charges in some form. They cause unutterable sorrow at home and are a menace and danger to the community. Feeble-minded women are almost invariably immoral, and if at large usually become carriers of venereal disease or give birth to children who are as defective as themselves. The feeble-minded woman who marries is twice as prolific as the normal woman.

We have only begun to understand the importance of feeble-mindedness as a factor in the causation of pauperism, crime and other social problems. Hereditary pauperism, or pauperism of two or more generations of the same family, generally means hereditary feeble-mindedness. In Massachusetts there are families who have been paupers for many generations. Some of the members were born or even conceived in the poor house.

Every feeble-minded person, especially the high-grade imbecile, is a potential criminal, needing only the proper environment and opportunity for the development and expression of his criminal tendencies. The unrecognized imbecile is a most dangerous element in the community.

Until fairly recently (the 1950s) such an analysis as that of Fernald, albeit in an attenuated form, underlay much thinking about subnormality. No doubt humane attitudes also played a part in legal provision, but basically legislation was conceived as protecting society. In the United Kingdom, until 1959, the procedure was thus of 'certification as mentally deficient' provided the individual could be proved as 'subject to be dealt with'. Periodic reassessment or alleged reassessment took place, with visits of justices of the peace, followed in some cases by trial in daily employment, trial in residential employment and ultimately, if the 'patient' was fortunate, 'discharge from care'.

In any consideration of the classification of the mentally subnormal two elementary but, none the less, important general points must be made. Classification always has a purpose. Its function has often been to allow some administrative action to be taken, sometimes investing it with a precision and scientific flavour it does not possess. Second, while no doubt boundaries do exist in nature, these are seldom as sharply defined or as rigid as we seek to make them. It is generally agreed that intellectual abilities, and also social competence, form graded continua, so that any dividing line must, in effect, be arbitrary.

Within the subnormal group, subclassification equally has a purpose: sometimes the bias may be educational, sometimes aetiological or prognostic, and here again boundaries are often arbitrary, although those conditions in which the biological basis is fairly well understood (e.g. Down's syndrome) may be more precisely delineated than those in which it is not (e.g. autism).

During the latter half of the present century several factors have combined to alter considerably society's view of the mentally retarded and therefore of appropriate provisions for them. These include: (1) an awareness that genetic variation is a much more complex matter than was formerly realized; (2) evidence that the national degeneracy earlier predicted by certain prophets of doom was not taking place; (3) indications that nutritional and social factors may be implicated in some forms of subnormality; (4) the success of programmes of remediation undertaken in a few institutions which yielded hopeful results; and (5) a more humane and tolerant attitude towards at least mild forms of social deviation. It followed that the subnormal person should not be shut away in remote hospitals, but community care and integration became the watchwords, with plans for ultimately a very large number of hostel places. Moreover, in the 1970s the belief that half the inmates of mental subnormality hospitals could and should find a place in the community was generally accepted. At the same time, voluntary admission as opposed to 'certification' caters for the vast majority, and legislation has shifted from primarily protecting society to primarily protecting the rights of handicapped individuals.

PURPOSES OF CLASSIFICATION

The different purposes of modern classification will now be briefly described.

Administrative

Some specific action may be needed on behalf of an individual or, in rare cases, on behalf of society. It may be necessary to have defined categories of disabilities in order to provide statistical data on the basis of which educational, medical and social facilities are made available for persons of various ages. Indeed, it has been suggested that for some less advanced societies the act of labelling persons mentally handicapped might be an important method of ensuring that their needs might be catered for within limited national budgets. Although nowadays a legally arranged deprivation of liberty, so common in the past, is unusual, it is clearly essential that if a person is to be detained compulsorily for his own protection or that of society, clear definitions specifying criteria for both inclusion and exclusion should be used.

Scientific

(a) *Diagnostic*

The social deviant (of whatever form) stands out as different from his peers. Natural curiosity suggests that the nature of this difference should be described – 'What is wrong with this person?' is the usual question in response to a grossly deviant appearance or grossly deviant behaviour. Then comes the question 'What is the cause or what are the causes of the condition?' and a diagnostic assessment may in itself suggest the approach to remediation, whether medical, educational or psychological (e.g. behaviour modification).

(b) *Prognostic*

Close on the heels of the question 'What is wrong?' comes the query 'What are his prospects?' Prognostic evaluation may often be linked with diagnosis, and can include an assessment of the likely contribution, and interaction, of biomedical and soical factors in determining the handicap. It is appreciated, for example, that some children, drawn from very adverse social conditions, whose behaviour is indistinguishable from others, in terms of their present personal characteristics, mature later, and during adolescence or early adult life show marked improvement in behavioural characteristics. Or again, some pathological conditions carry with them a prognosis of deterioration and early death. The complex question of prediction has been considered by Clarke and Clarke (1972, 1973, 1984).

(c) *Research*

Classification, using well-defined criteria, allows scientists at different periods or from different areas to compare findings and communicate with each other. Is the survival rate for Down's syndrome increasing? Is the incidence of severe subnormality decreasing? Is encephalitis an equally frequent cause of subnormality in Africa as in India? Do adults originally suffering from mild subnormality continue to improve after the age of twenty, or indeed forty? These are but a few of the innumerable questions which can only be asked validly if the classification method and the constituent population are clearly defined.

CRITERIA OF SUBNORMALITY

Medico-legal criteria

Significant social and economic changes taking place in the 1950s and 1960s led to an emphasis on both civil rights and also integration of disabled people of all kinds within the community. Previous editions of this book have, we believe, contributed to this process, both by authors' advocacy of community care and special education for the retarded, and also by indicating how handicapped people might be enabled to learn the skills required to place them above the threshold of community tolerance. The approach to an ideal has been gradual, and there remains a great deal to be done. However, in Britain, within the frameworks of both psychiatry and education, important advances have recently been made which are likely to have a profound influence upon the future well-being of the mentally retarded.

The Mental Health Act, 1983

The English Mental Health Act of 1983 defined the generic term 'mental disorder' as meaning 'mental illness, arrested or incomplete development of mind, psychopathic disorder and any other disorder or disability of mind and "mentally disordered" shall be construed accordingly'. Within this framework two subcategories of arrested or incomplete development of mind to cover those to be compulsorily detained are defined as follows:

> In this Act *'severe mental impairment'* means a state of arrested or incomplete development of mind which includes severe impairment of

intelligence and social functioning and is associated with abnormally aggressive or seriously irresponsible conduct on the part of the person concerned.

In this Act *'mental impairment'* means a state of arrested or incomplete development of mind (not amounting to severe mental impairment) which includes significant impairment of intelligence and social functioning and is associated with abnormally aggressive or seriously irresponsible conduct on the part of the person concerned. (Authors' italics)

The terms 'severe mental impairment' and 'mental impairment' replace the terms 'severe subnormality' and 'subnormality' used in the 1959 Act, thus introducing descriptions with a less explicit normative reference. It is difficult to believe that these synonyms will in the end prove any less (or more) offensive. Of greater significance, however, is the following specific instruction:

Nothing in this section shall be construed as implying that a person may be dealt with under this Act as suffering from mental disorder or from any form of mental disorder described in this section, by reason only of promiscuity or other immoral conduct, sexual deviancy or dependence on alcohol or drugs.

The result of this change in legislation is to make it exceedingly difficult for the mentally retarded to be compulsorily detained, with numerous additional safeguards to their civil rights, and specifically to exclude as grounds for detention the personal characteristics so feared by those in the early part of this century. The vast majority of mentally handicapped persons will no longer be dealt with under a Mental Health Act, and for those not needing compulsory detention the term mental handicap is retained, *impairment* being kept only for those requiring compulsory admission to hospital.

Thus, within the English National Health Service, mental deficiency (1913, 1927) became mental subnormality in 1959 (just too late for the first edition of this book) which in turn became mental handicap, and in 1983, for purposes of detention, mental impairment or severe mental impairment. The changes in nomenclature are depicted in Fig. 2.1.

In commenting on the 1983 Mental Health Act Spencer (1983) has noted that: 'The new terminology has the laudable aim of differentiating from the majority of mentally handicapped people a minority group who present particular problems which may require special management or treatment, and who may be the subject of compulsory powers.' He goes on to say that within his own hospital some 20 per cent were classified as coming within the definition of severe mental impairment, a proportion reported elsewhere. The term mental impairment 'has the merit that it is not applicable to all mentally handicapped people purely on the basis of "retarded" or "subnormal" intelligence, as was the category of "severe subnormality" used in the Mental Health Act of 1959'.

World Health Organization classifications

The World Health Organization (1969), in its eighth revision of the *Manual of the International Statistical Classification of Diseases, Injuries and Causes of Death*, offered IQ criteria for mental retardation as follows:

Borderline	68–85
Mild	52–67
Moderate	36–51
Severe	20–35
Profound	under 20

This wide range, including the borderline category, put at risk of being labelled mentally retarded some 16 per cent of the population, a point strongly taken up in the preceding year (WHO, 1968), too late to affect the *Manual*. In the former Report (with which the present writers were associated) mild retardation was taken to relate to from − 2.0 to − 3.3 standard deviations from the IQ mean (100, s.d. 15); moderate, from − 3.3 to − 4.3 standard deviations; severe, from − 4.3 to − 5.3 standard deviations below the mean. The Report went on to indicate:

> It should again be stressed that these are not exact measurements, nor should they be considered the sole criteria; in practice the categories will tend to overlap, but the IQ has some value within the range of mental retardation, both as a diagnostic and as a prognostic guide.

These considerations clearly influenced those who produced the ninth revision of the *Manual*. Here mental retardation was described as a condition of

> arrested or incomplete development of mind which is especially character-ized by subnormality of intelligence. The coding should be made on the individual's *current* level of functioning . . . the assessment should be based on whatever information is available, including clinical evidence, adaptive behaviour and psychometric findings. The IQ levels are based on a test with a mean of 100 and a standard deviation of 15 − such as the Wechsler scales. They are applied as a guide and should not be applied rigidly.

Borderline mental retardation was then totally omitted, and the ranges given as:

Mild	50–70	
Moderate	35–49	
Severe	20–35	
Profound	under 20	(WHO, 1977)

So far, classification has been considered solely in terms of inclusion/exclusion, or in functioning levels within the retarded population, whether in intelligence or in social adaptation. There is, of course, far more to retarded individuals than this. For scientific or treatment purposes, a classificatory coding requires additional information. For example, aetiological factors, current stressors, physical or psychiatric problems may be implicated. 'Mental retardation often involves psychiatric disturbances and may often develop as a result of disease or injury. In these cases, an additional code or codes should be used to identify any associated condition, psychiatric or physical. The Impairment and Handicap codes should also be consulted' (WHO, 1977). Each of these variables constitutes an axis.

The ICD itself is organized in seventeen major sections, relating to the whole range of diseases. Each section is subdivided and identified by three digits (000 to 999). These categories are further subdivided by a fourth digit (0.0 to 0.9) to provide greater detail. As the *Glossary* (WHO, 1978) indicates, the axes of classification are not consistent across the seventeen sections. In some, the primary axis is topographical (e.g. diseases of the respiratory system); less often it is aetiological (e.g. infectious diseases) or situational (e.g. complications of pregnancy). Two supplementary sections provide for classification of external causes of injury and poisoning (the E code) and for factors influencing health status and contact with health services (the V code), respectively. Both provide items of relevance to psychiatric and related mental health services and facilities.

The primary axis for mental retardation (317–319) relates, as noted, to current level of functioning, regardless of nature or causation. Mild mental retardation, IQ 50–70, is coded as 317. Other specified mental retardation uses a four-digit code: moderate mental retardation, 318.0, IQ 35–49; severe mental retardation, 318.1, IQ 20–34; profound mental retardation, 318.2, IQ under 20. Finally, unspecified mental retardation is coded 319. Greater precision is attained by the addition of codes derived from other sections of the ICD.

The WHO scheme for retardation is, of course, merely part of a much wider classification system, as is DSM III (American Psychiatric Association, 1980). In contrast, the AAMD system (Grossman, 1983), which has some compatibility with both, was developed for those scientists primarily interested in mental retardation and the various associated syndromes and diseases. This third system of classification is discussed on pages 46–9.

The advantages of multi-axial classification have been stressed by Rutter *et al.* (1975) who played a very significant role in the WHO ninth revision of the Mental Disorders Section. Werry (1985) offers a useful comparison of ICD-9 with DSM III, arguing that the former is 'conservative' and the latter more 'imaginative', though more complicated and more error-prone. He also draws attention to the 'justifiable cynicism' of those 'who actually work with children, as opposed to those who study them' where detailed classification systems are involved. However, Werry notes the views of Rutter and Shaffer (1980) who rightly argue that 'ordering information and . . . grouping phenomena [are] not only basic to all forms of scientific enquiry but also . . . essential as a code of communication between clinicians'. Werry adds (p. 2) that there is an additional value to classification:

> parents often obtain significant relief from a label with its consequent probabilistic statements about aetiology and prognosis, even when the latter is unfavourable, because they are led to believe that the doctor understands what their child is like and that there are other children in the world like them. A diagnostic label also relieves anxiety and uncertainty that is often more intolerable than a stated unfavourable prognosis.

Educational criteria

The changing outlook is nowhere more clearly apparent than in the field of education, in both Britain and the United States.

Categories of pupils requiring special educational treatment in England and Wales were defined in the Handicapped Pupils and Special Schools Regulations 1959, as amended. Definitions of ten types of disability, including problems relating to vision, hearing, maladjustment and various physical handicaps were offered. For example:

(a) blind pupils, that is to say, pupils who have no sight or whose sight is likely to become so defective that they require education by methods not involving the use of sight;

(d) partially hearing pupils, that is to say, pupils with impaired hearing whose development of speech and language, even if retarded, is following a normal pattern, and who require for their education special arrangements or facilities though not necessarily all the educational methods used for deaf pupils;

(e) educationally subnormal pupils, that is to say, pupils who, by reason of limited ability or other conditions resulting in educational retardation, require some specialized form of education wholly or partly in substitution for the education normally given in ordinary schools;

(i) pupils suffering from speech defect, that is to say, pupils who on account of defect or lack of speech not due to deafness require special educational treatment.

At that time there was also a category of children excluded from school altogether on the grounds of ineducability. The law was altered to include them within the education system as from 1 April 1971, necessitating the creation of a new category of schools, Educationally Subnormal (Severe), distinguished from schools covering pupils defined in (e) above for Educationally Subnormal (Moderate).

As in the United States, increasing disquiet concerning the somewhat rigid categorization and labelling of young children was expressed. A committee under the chairmanship of Lady Warnock was set up, which reported in 1978, and recommended important changes, as will be apparent from the following very brief extracts:

3.22   It is generally accepted that in the early post-war years the list of statutory categories helped to focus attention on the existence and needs of different groups of handicapped children and offered a broad framework for planning special school provision which was generally found useful by local education authorities. There are some who believe that categorization is still a valuable safeguard of the rights of a handicapped child to an education suited to his needs. They would probably accept that categories add nothing of substance to the existing general legal safeguards ... but they argue that categories nevertheless underline the duties of local education authorities towards handicapped children.

3.23   These considerations have some force, but the use of statutory categories also has a number of disadvantages, as was pointed out by contributors to the written evidence, of whom a majority, although not an overwhelming one, favoured their abolition. First, their use pins a single label on each handicapped child and each special school. Many children suffer from more than one disability and this can present intractable problems of classification, especially as the major disability from a medical point of view may not, as we have pointed out already, be the most significant educationally; it also means that a wide variety of schools is required, with some catering for combinations of disabilities. Moreover, labels tend to stick, and children diagnosed as ESN(M) or maladjusted can be stigmatized unnecessarily for the whole of their school careers and beyond. More important, categorization promotes confusion between a child's disability and the form of special education he needs. The idea is encouraged that, say, every child with epilepsy or every maladjusted child requires the same kind of educational regime. The confusion is heightened by the fact that only two categories – blind and deaf pupils – are defined in terms of educational methods positively required, whereas the other categories are defined in terms of disability which makes the pupils unsuited to the normal regime of ordinary schools. Moreover, although most local education authorities provide special help for children who in their opinion need it, even if these children do not readily fit into any of the statutory categories, a strict construction of Section 33 (1) of the 1944 Act, or in Scotland Section 62 of the Education (Scotland) Act 1962 as amended, would prevent a child from being regarded as handicapped unless he came within one of the categories defined in regulations. However carefully a scheme of categorization of handicaps is drawn up, there are always likely to be some children in need of special educational provision who will be excluded because they do not fit into any of the categories.

3.24   Whatever the weight attached to the preceding arguments, we believe that the most important argument against categorization is the most general one. Categorization perpetuates the sharp distinction between two groups of children – the handicapped and the non-handicapped – and it is this distinction which we are determined, as far as possible, to eliminate.

(Warnock, 1978)

The committee recommended that statutory categorization of handicapped pupils should be abolished, while recognizing that for the sake of convenience descriptive terms will be needed for particular groups of children who require special educational provision. They went on to say (para. 3.26):

While the continued use of the existing forms of description of children with physical or sensory disabilities seems acceptable, we consider that it would be preferable to move away from the term 'educationally sub-normal' or in Scotland 'mentally handicapped', terms which can unnecessarily stigmatize a child not only in school, but when he comes to seek employment. 'Educationally sub-normal' is, in any case, open to criticism on the grounds that it is imprecise and assumes agreement on what is educationally normal with regard to ability and attainment. It also suggests that a child so described suffers from an intrinsic deficiency whereas often the deficiency has been in his social and cultural environment. *We recommend that the term 'children with learning difficulties' should be used in future to describe both those children who are currently categorized as educationally sub-normal and those with educational difficulties who are often at present the concern of remedial services.* Learning difficulties might be described as 'mild', 'moderate' or 'severe'. Children with particular difficulties, such as specific reading difficulties, might be described as having 'specific learning difficulties'. It will be argued that the practical effect of our proposal will be only to replace one label by another. We believe, however, that the term we have proposed, which will be used for descriptive purposes and not for any purpose of categorization, is preferable to the existing label because it gives more indication of the nature of the child's difficulties, and is less likely to stigmatize the child.

In England and Wales, the Education Act (1981) Chapter 60 follows quite closely the philosophy of the Warnock Committee. A child has 'special educational needs' if he has a 'learning difficulty'. The Act also provides a number of important safeguards for the child, the parents and local education authorities.

The committee suggested that the largest single category of children in need of special educational provision would be pupils with mild learning difficulties, around 9 per cent. These children should attend normal schools, but would probably require special attention and/or some degree of segregation in remedial classes. 'Children with moderate learning difficulties' was the term proposed to describe pupils at present attending special schools for the mildly/moderately subnormal (ESN(M)). They indicated (para. 11.51) that children showing these difficulties constitute the largest group at present in special schools and a large proportion of children in ordinary schools for whom special education is needed. 'Children with severe learning difficulties' was the preferred description of those who were commonly referred to as being mentally handicapped and defined as severely educationally subnormal (para. 11.57).

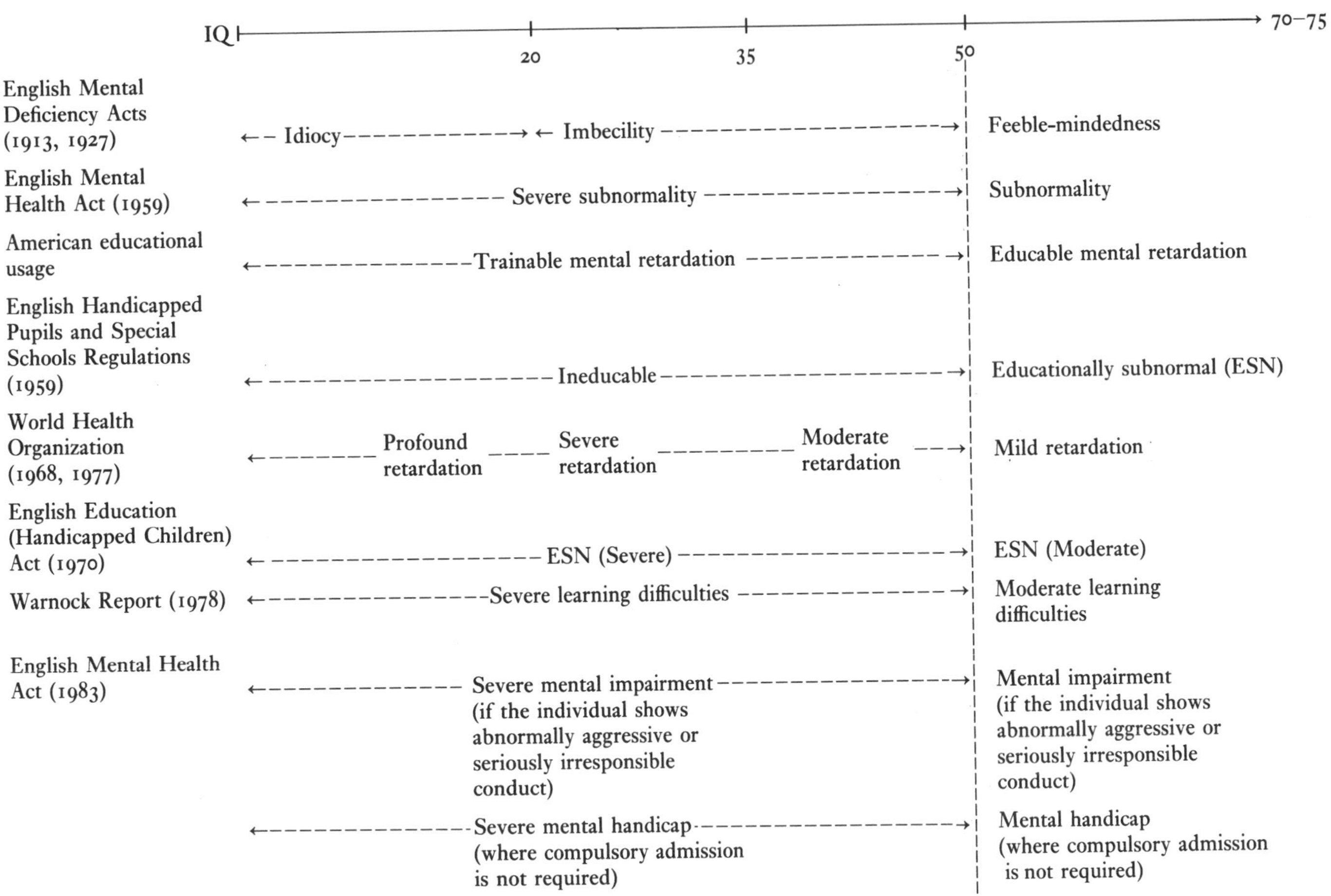

IQ |———————|———————|———————|——————————————→ 70–75
             20   35   50

English Mental Deficiency Acts (1913, 1927)
Idiocy ——————→ ←—— Imbecility ————→ | Feeble-mindedness

English Mental Health Act (1959)
Severe subnormality ————→ | Subnormality

American educational usage
Trainable mental retardation ————→ | Educable mental retardation

English Handicapped Pupils and Special Schools Regulations (1959)
Ineducable ————→ | Educationally subnormal (ESN)

World Health Organization (1968, 1977)
Profound retardation —— Severe retardation —— Moderate retardation | Mild retardation

English Education (Handicapped Children) Act (1970)
ESN (Severe) | ESN (Moderate)

Warnock Report (1978)
Severe learning difficulties | Moderate learning difficulties

English Mental Health Act (1983)
Severe mental impairment (if the individual shows abnormally aggressive or seriously irresponsible conduct) | Mental impairment (if the individual shows abnormally aggressive or seriously irresponsible conduct)

Severe mental handicap (where compulsory admission is not required) | Mental handicap (where compulsory admission is not required)

FIGURE 2.1 Changing terminology in relation to IQ levels, as used in practice (subcategories only)

The changes proposed in nomenclature (outlined in Fig. 2.1), methods of assessment, educational needs and curriculum development to meet those needs amount to a very significant change in outlook, including a substantial emphasis on integrating as many children as possible within ordinary schools. It is hoped that the intelligent idealism which informed this report will survive the translation of its recommendations into action. Gulliford elaborates the specific educational proposals in Chapter 17.

However, it should be noted that, despite the seductive arguments put forward by apologists for greater equality of educational opportunity, the available evidence does not suggest that labelling *per se* makes much difference to teachers' expectations for retarded pupils. After examining the literature on labelling and finding it contradictory and somewhat confusing, Aloia and MacMillan (1983) conducted an experiment with 1114 regular classroom elementary teachers, who had taught for an average of eleven years. The study was designed to examine three factors assumed to influence teacher expectations: (1) the particular domain in which the label is viewed, e.g. academic versus social/behavioural; (2) the amount and type of information presented in conjunction with the label; and (3) varying levels of child characteristics such as attractiveness and school-related competencies. It was anticipated that the 'educable mentally retarded' label would exert differential expectations in different domains and, for example, be greater for academic tasks than for success in athletics.

Teacher expectations were examined in relation to four areas: the child's behavioural/social capabilities; the child's academic capabilities; the teacher's ability to work with the child; and the teacher's general attitudes concerning EMR pupils. The information presented was designed to elicit teacher expectation for an EMR child with whom they had no previous contact but who was being considered for placement in their classroom. The information presented and the experimental design allowed for manipulation of the EMR label, attractiveness and behavioural characteristics and a multivariate analysis of responses to a 54-item questionnaire presented.

The results highlight the complexity of the label *per se* on the initial expectations of teachers, which, although significant on three out of four dependent variables, had no effect on the behavioural subscale, and in any case accounted for a minute proportion of the variance ($R^2 = 0.05$). By contrast the multivariate analysis of variance on the child's vignette describing academic, behavioural and social traits accounted for a substantial part of the variance ($R^2 = 0.75$). There seems to the present authors no way of teaching children or adults in which *no* information about their personal characteristics percolates to the teacher, whether or not a label is attached, which, of course, it is likely ultimately to be. Wise teachers react to the child, with all his complexities, but this does not preclude classification and personal labelling.

By the same token it should not be assumed that integrating pupils into ordinary schools or mainstreaming into regular classrooms will necessarily and automatically result in enhanced achievement, adjustment and self-concept.

This topic is dealt with extensively by Gulliford in Chapter 17. Gottlieb (1981), in a careful overview of research relating to the major objectives of mainstreaming, concluded that academic achievement was uniformly low for both segregated and integrated pupils, with no significant benefit accruing to either type of placement. Handicapped children who were partially main-streamed and partially segregated had on average higher self-concept ratings, but when it came to sociometric status contact with more normal children this led to rejection of the EMR child (although not invariably) unless active steps were taken to overcome the social problem. The observable behaviour of retarded children was the reason for social nonacceptance, rather than the use of a label, and children of this kind may suffer ostracism more in mainstreamed than in segregated classes because their inappropriate behaviour is more visible. Gottlieb joins Warnock in urging research in curriculum development and special courses for teachers as well as further monitoring of the progress of integration. His paper serves as a timely reminder that merely changing labels or educational contexts may serve no useful purpose, unless considerable human resources are made available to ensure that children with learning difficulties are indeed enabled to learn. Madden and Slavin (1983) outline the essential components for successful integration (see pages 647–8).

PSYCHOMETRIC MEASUREMENTS AS CRITERIA

Intelligence test scores

In previous editions of this book we have offered critical evaluations of the criteria most commonly used internationally in identifying and labelling individuals as mentally deficient, mentally subnormal or mentally retarded (depending on which term was most prevalent at the time or place of writing) and also used for subclassifications. We challenged the imprecision of the concept of social incompetence as a medico-legal term in Britain, and argued that at the very least intelligence must be low in order to qualify for inclusion within the framework of this book. We also had many criticisms to make of the IQ as a *sole* criterion. These, briefly stated, were:

1. The IQ is liable to some degree of measurement error, either because of imperfect standardization or because of individual cognitive or motiva-tional fluctuations possessing no long-term significance.
2. The same IQ on different tests may not, for reasons of standardization, mean the same thing. In practice this may be overcome with the use of standard scores but this is seldom undertaken by clinicians or administrators.
3. Intellectual growth over long periods of time (and particularly among some of the mildly subnormal) does not necessarily proceed in a constant fashion with reference to age peers. Like physical growth, intellectual growth may change, sometimes markedly, in its rate of increase. This does not lead to

error in the sense defined in (1) above; rather it indicates that IQ changes may reflect real growth changes.

Unfortunately, in our view, the IQ has in some quarters come under savage attack, often by people who have little knowledge either of psychometrics or of the extensive literature concerning the external validity of mental measurements. In an attempt to restore the balance, we have commissioned for this edition Berger and Yule's Chapter 3. It is our belief that intelligence testing continues to have a major and constructive role to play in clinical and educational practice and in developmental research.

Social competence and adaptive behaviour scales

So far as social competence is concerned we have argued that incompetence, a commonly used criterion of mental retardation, is self-evidently vague, and has been used in the past to label a variety of social deviants. Standards of competence differ in different places, at different times and within different social classes. Social difficulties are not confined to the mental subnormal; nor are all the latter, with IQs below 70, in social difficulties. Thus in a survey carried out for our last (1974) edition we were able to identify rather less than one-third of those with IQs below 70 as being specially dealt with administratively. A more recent survey by one of our students yielded a similar picture. We suggested, therefore, that to have an IQ below 70 does no more than put the individual at risk of social problems and of being labelled mentally subnormal. The lower the IQ, the greater the risk, which becomes almost a certainty below IQ 50. So far as learning difficulties at school are concerned, an IQ below 70 is, of course, a rather accurate predictor.

We accept, however, that it is the perception by the authorities of social or educational incompetence, or its predicted appearance in an individual, that is the presenting problem. We note, too, that the new English Mental Health Act (1983), already referred to, specifically excludes certain behaviour (e.g. sexual promiscuity) as demanding compulsory legal action. It was behaviour of this sort which was so commonly used up to the end of the 1950s for administrative intervention.

Attempts have been made to produce objective assessments of social competence, especially by Balthazar (Balthazar and English, 1969) and by the American Association on Mental Deficiency (AAMD) which produced an Adaptive Behavior Scale (ABS) arising from the work of Nihira *et al.* (1974).

Bortner (1978) offers an excellent early review of the 1974 revision. The ABS represents an important attempt to objectify the concept of social competence, covering between twenty-one and twenty-four areas of functioning, ranging from ratings of self-direction, responsibility and socialization to withdrawal, inappropriate interpersonal manners, hyperactive activities and sexually aberrant behaviours. It is appropriate for ages between three years and adulthood. Part I relates to personal independence and Part II measures maladaptive behaviour. Percentile norms were based on 4000 institutionalized retarded persons, but a public school version offers norms on 2600 children in grades 2–6. Inter-rater reliabilities for Part I range from 0.71 to 0.93, with a median 0.86 for the ten domains of the scale. Reliabilities for the fourteen domains of Part II range from 0.37 to 0.77 with a median of 0.57.

Bortner points out that various studies suggest the existence of meaningful factors or aspects of adjustment, and the ability of different parts of the scale to discriminate successfully between variously labelled groups. However, since adaptive behaviour can only be defined in terms of a particular setting, and since there is a variety of settings to which individuals may differentially adapt, it will be important to evaluate the diagnostic validity of the scale in terms of the variety of criteria that are applicable to such settings. This is an important point, and indeed an earlier paper by Bortner and Birch (1970) argues forcefully for the evaluation of skills in the retarded against the demands of the particular environments to which they are exposed. It is possible that the correlations between behaviour of institutionalized persons and their adaptation in the wider context of the community after proper training may not be very high. It is important, too, to recognize that scores may represent current levels of functioning without possessing a necessary predictive validity for individuals, especially in the upper ranges of intelligence. Bortner maintains that, as a descriptive tool, the scale has many uses. Scores may help to define a programme or objectives, and the states and changes in an individual may be evaluated.

During the last decade, research on adaptive behaviour has burgeoned. In an important recent book Grossman (1983) points out that adaptive behaviour scores yield information that is sometimes closely correlated with IQ, especially at levels of low functioning, but this close correlation is not always present. The differences between the two types of measurement are outlined. First, intelligence tests seek to determine an individual's highest potential, whereas adaptive behaviour scales seek to establish a person's common and typical performance. Second, intelligence tests emphasize language, reasoning and abstract abilities; everyday proficiencies in self-care, communicating needs and meeting ordinary social responsibilities are reflected in adaptive behaviour scores. Third, intelligence tests are administered in a controlled clinical testing interview, while adaptive behaviour information is generally secured through interviews with informants. Grossman indicates that the quality of everyday adaptation is mediated by level of intelligence, and, one should add, the experiences and demands placed upon the individual. But adaptive behaviour measurement is more concerned with everyday coping than the abstract potential implied by intelligence measures. It clearly possesses a high concurrent face validity.

There is a growing consensus that the ABS is useful both for diagnostic and prognostic purposes (e.g. Futterman and Arndt, 1983). There is in most studies a moderately strong relationship between adaptive behaviour and IQ (e.g. MacEachron, 1983), but some have argued that ABS scores might well prove more useful than IQ as a single measure for predicting programme placement and for classifying retarded persons (Futterman and Arndt, 1983). However, single predictors are clearly unlikely to be as effective as combined predictors, with several intercorrelated measures, each of which possesses a significant association with outcome. The use of the ABS for studying lifespan development of the retarded, whether in institutional or community settings, has also been demonstrated (Eyman and Arndt, 1982).

Huberty *et al.* (1980) have discussed the use of adaptive behaviour and adaptive behaviour scores in the definition of mental retardation. Pointing out that in the United States the methods by which mentally retarded children are placed in special education have become a source of controversy, especially since Public Law 94–142 (The Education of All Handicapped Children Act, 1975) was enacted, the authors indicate that the IQ has been emphasized as the primary, if not single, criterion for placing children in special classes. They surveyed the practices in allocation to special education of state education agencies, indicating that nine elaborated on the IQ concept in a way suggesting poor understanding of its meaning. Of the twenty-seven states that did not use the AAMD definition, twenty-six made some reference to adaptive behaviour without any necessary definition or method of measurement. While many listed appropriate IQ scales, few indicated how adaptive behaviour should be measured. Various rather vague formulations were offered, but without standards or criteria.

Data analysed from the authors' survey suggested that there were some serious inconsistencies between states in their definitions of mental retardation. It seemed possible for a child in one state to be classified as retarded and that same child not to be so categorized in another, if IQ is used as a sole criterion, for different states used different borderlines. Two children with the same IQ might not be so classified if their adaptive behaviour levels were dissimilar. However, although adaptive behaviour is regarded as a necessary consideration in diagnosis, it is all too frequently ignored. If specialists cannot agree on criteria, how can they make comparisons, compile incidence figures and evaluate the effectiveness of educational programmes? write Huberty *et al.* (1980)

Bean and Roszkowski (1982) indicate that adaptive behaviour is part of the definition of mental retardation, and that its assessment has often been recommended as a basis of individual programme planning and as an outcome measure following habilitation. They indicate that reliability studies are still rather scarce and thus they decided to establish the degree of internal consistency and to undertake item analyses of the ABS, using all persons in a university-affiliated state residential facility for the retarded.

The internal consistency of the ABS Part I was above 0.80 for all domains other than physical development where it was 0.65. The median coefficient was 0.91. For Part II, only six of the fourteen domains had reliabilities of 0.80 or above. Three showed reliabilities of less than 0.70 (unacceptable vocal

habits, 0.65; self-abusive behaviour, 0.64; and use of medications, − 0.06).
Item analysis indicated that some of the Part I domains measured essentially
the same thing, and appeared to be influenced by general cognitive ability. For
Part II, item analysis showed that some 39 per cent possessed undesirable
psychometric characteristics. Two main implications follow: first, users of the
ABS should be aware that some subscales have internal consistencies that are
too low for decision-making about individuals. Second, profile interpretations
suggested in the ABS Manual should be undertaken with extreme caution.
Clearly, future work must attempt to refine the ABS still further.

Grossman (1983) warns that the scaling of adaptive behaviour is more
recent than the development of intelligence testing, resulting in less experience
both in the evaluation of these measures and in the interpretation of results.
Moreover, he reports 'some history of less than careful use of such scales'.
While early test instruments (e.g. Vineland) yielded a single score, most new
scales yield multiple subscores, each for a particular 'domain'. The reasons for
distrust of single scores reside first in an awareness that many facets of
competence are involved, and second that there is more within-subject
variability than with intelligence scores, so that reporting of different
components of adaptive behaviour may be advantageous. Profiles of results
may also assist in programme planning. For a discussion of the methodology of
behavioural measurement, the reader is referred to Chapter 3.

The safest conclusion is that the use of these measures reflects the perceived
level of the handicapped person's present functioning, possessing therefore
good concurrent validity, and that the scores so derived may assist the
identification of areas of strength or weakness and thus assist programme
planning for the individual. The extent to which such scores possess a longer-
term predictive validity may depend on a number of factors:

1. Prediction will be much more accurate if the initial level of functioning is
   very low, and associated also with low IQ.
2. The lifespan context of the individual. The institutionalized person may
   remain perfectly adapted to his restricted environment, but grossly
   maladapted to the wider community if deinstitutionalized without proper
   preparation.
3. The objectivity of assessment by the informants.
4. The individual's responsiveness or otherwise to training opportunities.

THE AAMD SYSTEM OF CLASSIFICATION

The most comprehensive contributions to definition and classification have
been provided by the American Association on Mental Deficiency. The eighth
revision of its views has recently become available (Grossman, 1983). Four
considerations have prompted the current recommendations. First, it has been
increasingly recognized that clinicians must be aware that the standard error of
measurement varies with different intelligence tests, depending on reliability

and standard deviation. Second, there is an increasing awareness of variability in individuals of similar levels of intellectual functioning. Such variability precludes the setting of precise cut-off points in diagnosis. Third, available measures of adaptive behaviour are necessarily somewhat imprecise. Since evaluation of intellectual level and adaptive behaviour define mental retardation, sound judgement is necessary. Once diagnosis has been made, however, adaptive behaviour scales are useful in further specification. Fourth, no classification system can provide for the unique needs of individuals who require services. It is suggested that it is important to determine diagnosis prior to, and independently of, assessing the service needs of individuals.

The definition arrived at is as follows:

> Mental retardation refers to significantly subaverage general intellectual functioning existing concurrently with deficits in adaptive behavior and manifested during the developmental period.

'Significantly subaverage' is defined as 'approximately IQ 70 or below'. 'Adaptive behavior' relates to 'the effectiveness or degree with which individuals meet the standards of personal and social responsibility expected for age and cultural group' and 'developmental period' relates to ages between birth and eighteen years.

In discussing the purposes of classification, the book advances views close to our own. First, it contributes to an acceptable system to be used world-wide and ensures reasonable compatibility with the two other major schemes: the WHO's (1977) ninth revision of the *International Classification of Diseases* (ICD-9), and the American Psychiatric Association's (1980) *Diagnostic and Statistical Manual* (DSM III). Second, it facilitates prevention efforts by identifying the causes of mental retardation. The book also emphasizes what has been a feature of all our previous editions. An evaluation of *current* functioning only is implied in diagnosis.

With increasing awareness of the complexity of aetiologies and of different aspects of functioning, as well as the developments and availability of computer analysis and information storage, all three modern contributors to problems of classification (WHO, AAMD and APA) have, as noted earlier, adopted multi-axial coding systems, excellently reviewed by Grossman (1983). The AAMD system, for example, which is close to the others in important ways, provides for a diagnosis by level, by aetiology, and by an evaluation of the individual's concurrent problems. However, change to the ICD-9 system is encouraged and, as an example of a four-axial description, a case is presented of mild mental retardation (Axis 1); aetiology, lead poisoning (Axis 2); with concurrent problems of sensorineural hearing loss (Axis 3); and with a psychosocial stress of death of parent (Axis 4). Other case-histories illuminate problems of classification and diagnosis.

The AAMD system of classification is, however, not without its critics. Zigler *et al.* (1984), in an important review, have argued that the concept of social adaptation is simply too elusive and ill defined to be a criterion of mental retardation. 'The AAMD definition appears to have created as many problems as it has solved' (p. 218).

These authors argue for a classification system based on aetiology (organicity/nonorganicity) and IQ. The latter 'is probably the most theoretically and practically important measure yet devised. Over seventy-five years of sound work have gone into its development. The result is that the IQ has more correlates than any other known measure . . . and has predictive power across a wide array of situations' (p. 225). Zigler *et al.* point out that, given the nature of intelligence tests, a definition based solely on a single IQ would not be problem free. With additional confirmatory assessments, however, the IQ should become the primary criterion for inclusion (below 70) into the mentally retarded group. Aetiology within the population thus defined must, however, be given clear recognition. Differences in various characteristics (e.g. SES, motivational-personality traits) between organic/nonorganic persons, 'possibly extending to a difference in the structure of intelligence, lead us to champion aetiology as a classificatory system' (p. 227).

To drop social adaptation from the definition of mental retardation does not, the authors maintain, suggest that the concept is unimportant, merely that currently it is too imprecise. Making IQ central to the definition of mental retardation is determined by their view that the behavioural sciences have no better measure to assess low intellectual functioning, which is the common feature of retardation.

To some extent, differences between these authors and the AAMD are understandable in the light of different aims of classification. If true prevalence is to be studied, then IQ assessment of a representative sample of a total population, or of a total population of a given age, is appropriate. However, a proportion of the mildly retarded, the major group, do not require special services (see Chapter 10) and their social adaptation may be entirely satisfactory, albeit at a below-average level. Practitioners, on the other hand, are required to exercise their function only when the person below IQ 70 presents difficulties. They define the latter as problems of social adaptation, wide though this concept may be. Two different estimates of prevalence may be obtained: prevalence of those in, say, the school years, who obtain an IQ more than two standard deviations below the mean, or prevalence of those similarly impaired for whom society offers, or ought to offer, particular facilities or services because they have problems of social adaptation. The latter will always be lower than the former (see Chapter 10).

The AAMD Medical Etiological Classification is coded under ten headings, each of which is further subdivided, in some areas many times. These major headings are: infections and intoxications; trauma or physical agent; metabolism or nutrition; gross brain disease (postnatal); unknown prenatal influence; chromosomal anomalies; other conditions originating in the perinatal period; following psychiatric disorder (specify); environmental influences; and other conditions. The use of these codings will enhance the collection and comparison of aetiological data.

An important chapter in Grossman's book outlines the application of the AAMD system to the delivery of services and research. Five primary applications are offered. First, the study of the history of mental retardation and the efficacy of preventive measures by analysis of changes in incidence and prevalence over time, in overall terms as well as in specific syndromes. Second, an analysis of the extent and nature of mental retardation in specific communities or geographic areas, with associated conditions or factors peculiar to them. Third, evaluation of service efficiency as indicated by intellectual or behavioural change in clients, as well as in preventing conditions and diseases related to retardation. Fourth, the study of the natural history of disease states and the identification of populations at risk. Fifth, the identification of causes by studying the incidence in different groups in terms of demography, heritability, experiential factors, behaviour and environment.

CONCLUSIONS

In this chapter an outline has been presented of some of the alterations in the criteria and classification of mental retardation in Britain across the centuries, and more recently in the World Health Organization and the United States. During the period spanning the first three editions of this book (1958–74) changes in attitude towards, and definitions of, subnormal people were regularly advocated, together with evidence suggesting why and how these innovations might be effected. The gradual shift in perspective has gathered momentum culminating in fairly revolutionary alterations to laws relating to the retarded. There is now a greater regard for the civil rights of handicapped persons, recognition that legally enforced provision is unnecessary for the majority, and a more widespread awareness of the complexity of aetiology, assessment of functioning and prediction in individual cases.

As we have argued for years, the mentally retarded are an enormously heterogeneous group of people with varying needs and prospects. Depending upon definition, a very large number require little or no special assistance, and it is desirable that they should not be identified as deviant, although this inevitably depends to some extent on their social context. Thus an adolescent with an IQ of 75 may (and to our knowledge sometimes does) appear handicapped within a community of university teachers and their families while the same young person would pass virtually unnoticed in a less incompatible social setting. While we assume that there will be in any society (perhaps particularly those which increasingly rely on complex cognitive skills) those whose individual qualities appear less adequate than others, we also take for granted that a constellation of problems (sometimes intrinsic to the individual and sometimes residing in his family or school) will have to be present before anything more than regular services are required. In identifying these, a combination of biomedical, behavioural and social assessments may be warranted, and in the second category both intelligence tests and also properly standardized measures of adaptive behaviour are likely to be important in a majority of cases. Low IQ alone was never an adequate criterion for diagnosis, although an important component (but see Zigler *et al.*, 1984).

These points are illustrated by the considerable differences in administrative prevalence of mental retardation, and prevalence on the single criterion of IQ. We have shown in one of our estimates that less than one-third of those with IQs of 70 or below in England and Wales are in receipt of special services. Most of those for whom we had statistical records would have been severely retarded (i.e. below IQ 50). The mildly retarded in terms of IQ, then, are only 'at risk' of being labelled as such, of having serious problems or of being dealt with in some special way. This can occur during the school years because of educational difficulties, or at any other time when they exhibit behavioural characteristics which exceed the limits of community tolerance.

The development of scales designed to measure adaptive behaviour is to be welcomed, although coupled with the warning that there is still plenty of room for their further refinement. Some aspects of the ABS, for example, overlap too strongly with others, or have poor internal consistency. However, these scales at the very least mark a major advance from the vague and often unreliable statements concerning 'social incompetence' which we have so often criticized in the past. Moreover, profile analysis may yield valuable insights into necessary planning for individual training, as well as baselines for later evaluation of progress or lack of it.

An important question which arises in these circumstances is how to arrive at a sensible taxonomy for scientific use which will enable research workers and others to communicate. This has as yet not been fully achieved, although the AAMD has taken important steps in this process. Multi-axial classification, pioneered by WHO, is to be commended.

Difficulties in classification will occur, especially at borderlines, and where there are doubts about whether an individual should be labelled and offered special services, such dilemmas must always be resolved in the interests of the individual. This constitutes a further problem, since the interests of the person can be very difficult to determine: integration versus segregation, the probable persistence of labelling effects, the possibly greater value of specialist help versus normal services – the effects of all these are not always clear. If one word sums up the issues, especially for the brighter individual, it is 'complexity'. The growing recognition that this is so is perhaps one important aspect of the changing outlook.

REFERENCES

ALOIA, G.F. and MACMILLAN, D.L. (1983) 'Influence of the EMR label on initial expectations of regular-classroom teachers', *Amer. J. Ment. Defic.*, 88, 255–62.

AMERICAN PSYCHIATRIC ASSOCIATION (1980) *Diagnostic and Statistical Manual* (DSM III), 3rd edn, Washington, DC, APA.

BALTHAZAR, E.E. and ENGLISH, G.E. (1969) 'A system for the social classification of the more severely mentally retarded', *Amer. J. Ment. Defic.*, 74, 361–8.

BEAN, A.G. and ROSZKOWSKI, M.J. (1982) 'Item-domain relationships in the Adaptive Behavior Scale (ABS)', *Appl. Res. Ment. Retard.*, 3, 359–67.

BORTNER, M. (1978) 'AAMD Adaptive Behavior Scale, 1974 revision', in O.K. BUROS (ed.), *The Eighth Mental Measurements Yearbook*, Highland Park, NJ, The Gryphon Press.

BORTNER, M. and BIRCH, H.G. (1970) 'Cognitive capacity and cognitive competence', *Amer. J. Ment. Defic.*, 74, 735–44.

CLARKE, A.D.B. and CLARKE, A.M. (1972) 'Consistency and variability in the growth of human characteristics', in W.D. WALL and V.P. VARMA (eds), *Advances in Educational Psychology*, I, London, University of London Press.

CLARKE, A.D.B. and CLARKE, A.M. (1973) 'Assessment and prediction', in P. MITTLER (ed.), *Assessment for Learning in the Mentally Handicapped*, Edinburgh and London, Churchill Livingstone.

CLARKE, A.D.B. and CLARKE, A.M. (1984) 'Constancy and change in the growth of human characteristics: the first Jack Tizard Memorial Lecture', *J. Child Psychol. Psychiat.*, 25, 191–210.

EYMAN, R.K. and ARNDT, S. (1982) 'Lifespan development of institutionalized and community-based mentally retarded residents', *Amer. J. Ment. Defic.*, 86, 342–50.

FUTTERMAN, A.D. and ARNDT, S. (1983) 'The construct and predictive validity of adaptive behavior', *Amer. J. Ment. Defic.*, 87, 546–50.

GODDARD, H. (1912) *The Kallikak Family*, New York, Macmillan.

GOTTLIEB, J. (1981) 'Mainstreaming: fulfilling the promise?', *Amer. J. Ment. Defic.*, 86, 115–26.

GROSSMAN, H.J. (ed.) (1983) *Classification in Mental Retardation*, Washington, DC, American Association on Mental Deficiency.

HUBERTY, T.J., KOLLER, J.R. and TEN BRINK, T.D. (1980) 'Adaptive behavior in the definition of mental retardation', *Except. Children*, 46, 256–61.

MACEACHRON, A.E. (1983) 'Institutional reform and adaptive functioning of mentally retarded persons', *Amer. J. Ment. Defic.*, 88, 2–12.

MADDEN, N.A. and SLAVIN, R.E. (1983) 'Mainstreaming students with mild handicaps: academic and social outcomes', *Rev. Educ. Res.*, 53, 519–69.

NIHIRA, K., FOSTER, R., SHELLHAAS, M. and LELAND, H. (1974) *AAMD Adaptive Behavior Scale*, Washington, DC, American Association on Mental Deficiency.

RUTTER, M. and SHAFFER, D. (1980) 'DSM III: a step forward or back in terms of the classification of child psychiatric disorders?', *J. Amer. Acad. Child Psychiat.*, 19, 371–94.

RUTTER, M., SHAFFER, D. and SHEPHERD, M. (1975) *A Multi-axial Classification of Child Psychiatric Disorder*, Geneva, World Health Organization.

SARASON, S.B. and DORIS, J. (1969) *Psychological Problems in Mental Deficiency*, 4th edn, New York, Harper.

SEGUIN, E. (1866) *Idiocy: Its Treatment by the Physiological Method*, New York, William Wood.

SPENCER, D. (1983) 'Classification of "Severe Mental Impairment"', *Ment. Handicap*, 11, 174.

WARNOCK, H.M. (1978) *Special Educational Needs. Report of the Committee of Enquiry into the Education of Handicapped Children and Young People*, Cmnd 7212, London, HMSO.

WERRY, J.S (1985) 'Annotation: ICD-9 and DSM III classification for the clinician', *J. Child Psychol. Psychiat.*, 26, 1–6.

WORLD HEALTH ORGANIZATION (1968) *Organization of Services for the Mentally Retarded*, Fifteenth Report of the WHO Expert Committee on Mental Health, *WHO Tech. Rep. Ser. 392*, Geneva, WHO.

WORLD HEALTH ORGANIZATION (1969) *Manual of the International Statistical Classification of Diseases, Injuries and Causes of Death, Eighth Revision*, Geneva, WHO.

WORLD HEALTH ORGANIZATION (1977) *International Classification of Diseases* (ICD-9), Geneva, WHO.

WORLD HEALTH ORGANIZATION (1978) *Mental Disorders: Glossary and Guide to their Classification in Accordance with the Ninth Revision of the International Classification of Diseases*, Geneva, WHO.

ZIGLER, E., BALLA, D. and HODAPP, R. (1984) 'On the definition and classification of mental retardation', *Amer. J. Ment. Defic.*, 89, 215–30.

3
IQ tests and assessment
Michael Berger and William Yule

INTRODUCTION

Anyone familiar with the historical and contemporary controversies surrounding the use of intelligence tests may well question their advocacy and continued use. Our support of IQ testing is qualified and based on two major grounds: empirical evidence of the validities of IQ tests, and their usefulness in individual clinical assessment and research.

IQ testing has both a history and a historically derived technology, both of which exert a profound influence on contemporary practice and attitudes about such practice. We begin, therefore, by identifying a number of major historical influences that have shaped the development of IQ tests and reactions to them.

HISTORICAL BACKGROUND

The influence of early tests

The publication of what is generally regarded as the first test of intelligence in 1905 was not a fortuitous event. The time at which it appeared and its characteristics were the expression of several historical developments: the search by Binet and others for a procedure that would enable a reliable discrimination between the medical grades of 'mental deficiency'; philosophical and theoretical speculations about the nature and origins of human intelligence; attempts to measure psychological phenomena in pursuit of scientific rigour; and an increasingly influential humanitarian philosophy directed at improving the quality of the lives of disturbed or otherwise handicapped people.

At the turn of the century mental testing was in crisis, and in so far as the psychology of intelligence was concerned, ready for change. The aura of crisis is well illustrated by Spearman's (1904b) review of the early attempts to relate mental test scores to various criteria of academic performance:

> Thus far, it must be confessed, the outlook is anything but cheerful for experimental psychology in general. There is scarcely one positive conclusion concerning the correlation between mental tests and independent

practical estimates that has not been with equal force flatly contradicted; and amid this discordance, there is a continually waxing inclination – especially among the most capable workers and exact results – absolutely to deny any such correlation at all. (Spearman, 1904b)

The early crisis was helped towards resolution by a number of important papers, two published by Spearman (1904a, b) and one by Binet and Simon (1905). Together, these had a number of ramifications, perhaps the most important being the foundations that they laid for applied intelligence testing, for psychometrics, for the various theories of intelligence associated with correlational psychology, and for the split they fostered between the 'scientific' study of intelligence and applied testing. Most of the tests used in the early period were, apart from those employed by Binet and Ebbinghaus to study 'higher mental processes', single tests, homogeneous in content, directed mainly at measuring sensory and motor processes and memory. These tests were derived from experimental psychology laboratories and were used in the study of inheritance (exemplified in the work of Galton), in the prediction of academic success, or in other aspects of research on individual differences (Freeman, 1939; Boring, 1957). In this early period the tests were not organized into scales, and if a number of them were administered concurrently, the scores were not combined (Freeman, 1939). The development of a scale that produced a summated total score probably originated in the set of tests used by Blin and Damaye for the diagnosis of subnormality (Wolf, 1973).

The central idea of the 1905 Binet–Henri scale was that individuals of different degrees of 'intelligence' at the same level of maturity (chronological age) would be distinguished by the number of tests passed. The novelty in the 1905 scale was the combination of various features and, particularly, the provision of explicit instructions for administration and scoring.

In the 1908 version and later editions of the scale, mental age was computed by first finding the basal age (the age level below which all items were passed) and then adding one year for each five items passed above that level. This procedure of adding together disparate items to produce an agglomerate score is of paramount importance because it represents an approach to quantification that has characterized the scoring of psychological tests ever since.

The history of intelligence testing prior to the advent of the 1905 scale, and subsequently, and the circumstances that led to the proliferation of tests and testing and the many technical developments in IQ testing are amply documented (Wolf, 1973; Berger, 1982; Sutherland, 1984). In the next section we consider some of the reasons for the negative reactions to the use of IQ tests.

The negative ethos of the IQ

The explicit purpose of the 1905 Binet test was to identify children unlikely to benefit from the then current French state education system. The intention was to provide them with an education more suited to their needs: Binet's immediate motivation for publishing the 1905 scale can, with some justification therefore, be seen as an expression of an essentially humanitarian or 'enlightened' social tradition (see Wolf, 1973; Anastasi, 1982).

Galton's intentions, by contrast, emerge among other things as eugenic in the worst sense of that term. He was primarily concerned in his research and writings with 'hereditary genius' – 'grand human animals, of nature preeminently noble, of individuals born to be kings of men. . . . I have not cared to occupy myself much with people whose gifts are below the average' (see Wiseman, 1967, p. 25). The Eugenics Society, founded in 1907, was established to further views that 'Galton had been propounding for over twenty years' (Hearnshaw, 1979, p. 20).

The history of the nineteenth-century theory of degeneracy, the emergence of the eugenics movement and the use of intelligence testing in pursuance of anti-humanitarian social and political ideologies is well documented by Sarason and Doris (1969).

The study of genius and a concern with intellectual purification of the human race were the themes propagated by Lewis Terman in the USA. He was pre-eminent among those who adapted and developed the Binet–Henri tests, published by him as the Terman–Merrill–Binet, later the Stanford–Binet tests. Terman's Galtonism and his bastardization of Binet's intentions are clearly illustrated by the following statement made by him in 1917:

> If we could preserve our state for a class of people worthy to possess it, we must prevent, as far as possible, the propagation of mental degenerates . . . curtailing the increasing spawn of degeneracy. (Terman, quoted in Kamin, 1977, p. 21)

It is indeed ironic that it was Terman's adaptation of the Binet test that was to be the means for realizing his intentions. This is abundantly clear in the opening chapter of the 1916 book that presented his Americanized version of the Binet (Kamin, 1977). It is perhaps fitting, therefore, that this test, because of its metric and other inadequacies (Kaufman and Reynolds, 1983; Frank, 1984), is now best confined in museums of psychometric technology.

The social philosophy of the eugenicists was tied to a conception of the genetic basis of intelligence that conceded little to environmental influences. Much of the reaction to Jensen's (1969) paper in the *Harvard Educational Review*, for instance, was an expression of the hostility of many towards the assumption of a high heritability of IQ extending to all populations, including socially disadvantaged minorities.

These historical influences have, we believe, been very powerful in creating the negative ethos of IQ testing. Whether or not this will be dispelled by the reconsidered evidence of the genetics of the IQ (Vernon, 1979; Wilson, 1983) and the recent reconceptualizations of genetic influence (Scarr, 1981; Plomin, 1983; Wilson, 1983) remains to be seen. At least these recent trends, while supporting a nontrivial dynamic genetic influence, point increasingly to a more refined appreciation of the equally nontrivial significance of experience (Plomin, 1983).

Not unrelated to the above but contributing with some potency to the unpopularity of IQ testing were those applications of tests directed at educational and other forms of selection and streaming:

> When Civil Service examinations were introduced in the 19th century in the West, the inspiration came again from the mandarinate examinations conducted for 2000 years previously in China. (Needham, 1970, pp. 379–80)

Discriminating people on the basis of their ability is not new. The introduction of competitive examinations in the civil services, both colonial and home-based, and in educational streaming has been described by Sutherland (1984). Hearnshaw (1979) also provides a detailed account of the history of selective education in the UK and includes an assessment of the role of Burt in this history (see pp. 111–21). IQ tests, thinly disguised and euphemistically labelled, were the main instruments for selection and a major focus of the attack from those who held anti-selection views. The underlying issues were and remain empirical as well as political and social; the politicization of IQ testing continues, both in Britain and in the USA, to be a major source of the negative ethos.

Other qualms stem from the misuse of intelligence tests, mainly through a failure to appreciate their psychometric strengths and limitations in the interpretation of individual test scores. Although objective procedures have long been available for guiding interpretations (Payne and Jones, 1957; Field, 1960), few psychologists in our experience understand or exploit these. Evidence for this assertion is based in part on the appearance from time to time of articles in professional journals that remind readers of their existence (e.g. Silverstein, 1981) or point out the continuing misunderstanding and misapplication of particular techniques (Dudek, 1979). For instance, Silverstein's (1981) paper in the *Journal of Clinical Psychology* re-presents techniques described by Payne and Jones (1957) in that journal.

The importance of using such techniques has been reiterated (Berger and Yule, 1972; Berger, 1977) and is now emphasized in guides to individual assessment (Kaufman, 1979; Sattler, 1982; Berger, 1984). Failure to employ them perpetuates the misinterpretation of test scores and leads to questionable decisions that can have adverse and enduring repercussions on the lives of testees and their relatives.

Some of the techniques and their appropriate use are described in a later section of this chapter.

IQ testing in applied settings

For many years psychological and, particularly, IQ testing were the mainstay of applied psychology. Clinical and other psychologists devoted much of their time generating and interpreting test scores which, while seemingly useful for clinical and educational diagnosis, had little other practical relevance. It was mainly through the reconceptualization of the role of clinical psychologists, as envisaged for instance in the pioneering writings of Shapiro (1957, 1962) and others, and the emergence of behaviour therapy in the UK (and the USA – Barrett and Breuning, 1983), that the preoccupation with testing diminished. Behaviour therapy in particular gave psychologists something that appeared to be more relevant to the immediate needs of their clients and opened the way for many to direct involvement in treatment that required the expertise of a trained psychologist. These developments, we believe, were of great significance in diminishing the perceived relevance of IQ and other forms of testing in clinical practice, particularly in mental handicap services.

The decline in IQ testing and the impact of behavioural interventions might not have been so marked had the ground not been well prepared for such activity by the policy innovations relating to mentally handicapped people that were emerging at that time. The research and writings of the late Jack Tizard, of Neil O'Connor, and of the Clarkes, contributed substantially to laying the foundations for national policies aimed at improving the quality of life for mentally handicapped individuals. Given the radical changes that were and still are required, particularly for people who are institutionalized, it is not surprising that diagnosing mental retardation, as opposed to involvement in identifying and developing skills for living in the community, would come to be regarded as a trivial if not irrelevant exercise.

The decreased use of IQ tests with handicapped people has not, in our view, been general. Rather, it appears to have been mainly confined to clinical practice in services for adult clients. Psychologists working with infants, children and adolescents, while actively engaged in behaviour therapy and its associated developments, have also continued to use IQ tests as an integral part of their assessment procedures. We do not claim to have direct evidence to support these contentions, but base them, among other things, on the observation that almost all of the individual intelligence tests that have been revised, most of the new scales, as well as the textbooks concerned with IQ testing, have been geared to pre-adult ages. The reasons for this may not be too obscure. Questions about current and future developmental status, educational difficulties and the like inevitably arise in the early years of a person's life. It is, therefore, not surprising that systematic procedures for responding to such questions would be more readily available and commonly used in the assessment of younger people.

In so far as we are correct in the view that there has been a differential decline in the use of IQ tests, we suggest that it is a consequence of several influences that in combination have led to the emergence of a preponderant negative ethos surrounding IQ tests. Further, we believe that, in relation to mental handicap, IQ testing tends to be regarded as irrelevant to the needs of these people. Our task is to challenge this stance. To prepare the way, we begin by introducing a number of basic concepts.

PSYCHOLOGICAL MEASUREMENT WITH SPECIAL REFERENCE TO IQ TESTS

Some basic concepts

Cronbach (1970) has defined a test as 'any systematic procedure for observing a person's behaviour and describing it with the aid of a numerical scale or category system'. Following this definition, any procedure that is rule-governed (systematic) and satisfies the criteria for quantification can be classed as a test. (The advantages of such a definition are discussed by Berger, 1984.) Hence an interview that is systematic and yields a categorical conclusion (e.g. depressed versus not-depressed) falls within the compass of this definition, as does a direct observation schedule that enables recording the frequency of certain classes of behaviour.

The creation of an IQ test that conforms to the minimal requirements for use in individual applications (American Psychological Association, 1974) is a complex, time-consuming and expensive task. Most tests, however, are essentially variations of a number of basic ideas, and it is these which are presented here.

Commonly, psychological characteristics (intelligence, personality and the like) are not directly observable but are inferred on the basis of public be-haviours: the child solves a logic problem and we infer that she is 'intelligent'; someone cries a lot and the inference is made that he is depressed or emotional. A psychological test (device for measurement) is a procedure, with or without bits of apparatus, contrived so as to provoke the operation of particular internal or mental functions and their overt expression. Underlying this task is the goal of identifying and quantifying individual differences in the attribute.

In order to provoke particular classes of behaviour, rather than any reaction, the test designer must have some idea, usually in the form of theoretical preconceptions, of what behaviours to encourage. In this sense, all tests are to varying degrees theory-inspired with regard to content and structure.

One or more options are available to quantify the test-provoked behaviours. The numbers directly representing performance (e.g. correct answers, time taken) are called *raw scores* and the single task an *item*. Intelligence tests are made up of items devised to provoke and quantify the operation of 'intelligence'. The organization of items within tests varies according to the particular instrument. Some tests have several different sets of items of homogeneous content (such as defining words) grouped together (a *subtest*). Some IQ tests comprise several different types of subtest (e.g. the Wechsler tests); others may consist of only a single-item type (Raven's matrices), and some mix items of different types (Merrill–Palmer). Further, sets of subtests may also be grouped into more general categories. The Verbal section of the Wechsler tests combines into a *subscale* subtests presumed to require the operation of verbal aspects of intelligence. The entire collection of items and/or subtests is called a *scale*, the term itself being a vestigial allusion to kinship with other measuring devices.

Psychological measurement involves comparison with some standard or unit, as do all forms of measurement. The metre, for instance, was at one time the length of a platinum bar stored under controlled conditions in Paris. There are no such exact units in psychological measurement, for a variety of reasons. Instead, measurement is accomplished by comparing the performance of an individual on a test, represented by his/her total raw score, with the performance of similar individuals on the same scale. Most recent tests of intelligence transform the individual score to a *deviation IQ*. In essence, this represents the distance above or below the group average of the individual's raw score. The distance from the average or mean is measured in standard deviation units, the mean and standard deviation of the raw score distributions having first been transformed to an arbitrary standard such as 100 and 15 (or 16, depending on the scale) respectively. These manipulations are introduced for reasons of statistical convenience and do not distort the original raw test scores. The tester does not have to be concerned with the intricacies of conversion as the test constructor usually provides an appropriate set of tables for that purpose.

Data on the performance of a comparison group constitute the *norms* of the test, and procedures that accomplish measurement by comparing individual performance with group norms are known as *norm-referenced* tests.

There are several ways of expressing individual performance on an IQ (or other test). *Mental age* (MA) can be computed in different ways. One way to do so might be to give the test to groups of different-aged individuals, and obtain an index of the group performance (mean, median or mode) at each age. For instance, if 6-, 7- and 8-year-olds on average obtain total raw scores of 20, 35 and 48 respectively, and a testee scores 38, closest to that of 7-year-olds, he or she would be given a *test age* of 7 years. If the test was thought to tap intelligence, the test age would be called *mental age*. If it were a test of reading, the child is said to have a *reading age* of 7 years. MAs are sometimes useful in communication but, because they have certain technical limitations, are not commonly used (Anastasi, 1982).

The MA has been used in the past for computing a form of IQ, the *ratio quotient* (IQ = MA/CA × 100), but, because of the limitations of the MA, ratio IQs are no longer used.

The term *standardized test* is commonly used to refer to procedures for which there are explicit instructions for administration and scoring, as well as normative data. Following Cronbach (1970), we prefer a usage which entails only the former, namely procedural rules. One of the reasons for restricting the term in this way is that many tests have clearly specified administration rules but are not normed, for instance, structured or semi-structured interviews, direct observation schedules and the like, and there are no other concepts currently in use that encompass such procedures.

The degree of standardization varies between tests as does the adequacy of the norms. No test can be completely standardized. Each depends to a greater or lesser extent on the judgements of the tester because test constructors, try as they might, cannot anticipate all the possible ways individuals will respond to test items.

There is, we believe, no absolute criterion for the degree of standardization. Much depends on the purpose of the test and the circumstances in which it is intended to be used. A screening procedure need not be as standardized as one intended for individual measurement, as only relatively crude decisions are likely to be made from the former; for group testing it may be difficult or uneconomic to create highly controlled conditions for testing, and therefore only approximate guidelines are given. Group test IQs should not be used for drawing conclusions about individuals; they are far too crude (see Berger, 1982, pp. 24–5), although they may be useful for preliminary screening.

Scaling, measurement error and reliability

Conceptually and mathematically, psychological measurement as used in many tests is modelled on natural science measurement theory. (One of the major contributions of Binet, as Kaufman and Reynolds (1983) point out, was to draw the problem of error (inherent in all measurement) to the attention of those engaged in mental measurement.) However, measuring psychological phenomena is more complex because of the nature of what is to be measured. Whereas most physical measurement is nonreactive (e.g. the length of a line does not change during measurement) or, if it is, is easily replicable (e.g. destructive testing – as in measuring the breaking strength of a rivet, the measurement can be repeated on other rivets) almost all psychological testing is reactive and nonreplicable. People learn how to solve problems in the process of solving them; an anxious child may become more or less anxious during testing, or if the test is readministered; attributes also change as part of normal growth and development.

Problems of error of measurement are comparable, but less often freely recognized, in most aspects of medical practice. Thus blood pressure and heart rate are both highly sensitive to the conditions under which they are measured. Psychological factors, such as empathy with the examiner, and physical factors, such as immediately prior exercise, can distort readings, apart altogether from the human error that inevitably occurs when busy professionals have to read thermometers, count pulses and talk to patients simultaneously. Even 'harder' measures inevitably encompass errors. While it is quite easy to train people to take a sample of blood, to do so in such a way that the sample is not contaminated by extraneous pollutants might be a major technical problem. In measuring the amount of lead (in parts per million) in children's blood, for instance, dirty hands contain many times that concentration and can easily pollute the sample. It is little wonder that a recent World Health Organization calibration exercise took over two years before different laboratories could agree on the amounts of lead contained in standard samples (Vahter, 1982).

Theoretical divergences, disagreements over definition and other reasons (Angoff, 1971; Green, 1981) lead to special difficulties in developing units and scales for psychological attributes that would enable measurements in the form, and with the implications, of scales such as a ruler or thermometer. Psychological scaling has to be contrived in a more circuitous manner than is the case with physical scales, and the resulting units have more arbitrary and circumscribed properties. Hence, according to the canons of conventional measurement theory, the scales constructed for IQ tests constitute a lower-level *ordinal* form of measurement. That is, they enable only comparisons of order of magnitude of the phenomenon (B more than or less than C) but cannot specify by how much. Some writers (e.g. Jensen, 1969) argue that IQs show some of the properties of *interval* scales, a higher level of measurement allowing more refined quantitative comparisons and a more complex form of statistical manipulation.

With interval scales, the distance between two points can be measured in equal units: going from 5 to 10 would be the same as going from 15 to 20, i.e. the difference of 5 would be the same for any part of the scale. The same assumptions cannot be made for measures such as IQs, i.e. the difference between IQs of 70 and 80 is not the same as the difference between IQs of 100 and 110. All that can be strictly concluded from such differences is that an individual with an IQ of 70 performed better on the test than an individual with an IQ of 60. Similarly, someone with an IQ of 100 is not twice as intelligent as someone with an IQ of 50.

The fact that IQs are expressed as numbers increasing by 1 (110, 111, 112, etc.) or that the average IQ of a group is 97.56 gives the IQ an aura of precision it does not merit. No well-informed test user would argue that there was a real difference in 'intelligence' between two individuals who respectively obtained IQs of 90 and 95. (An average difference of 5 points between two populations might, however, have major implications – see Jensen (1969), pp. 23–5; Yule and Rutter (1985) discuss this in relation to the effects of low levels of lead on children's intelligence.)

Implicit in the above discussion is the idea that the 'thing' being measured by an IQ has the property of 'magnitude' and that this can be quantitatively expressed. These are, of course, theoretical notions open to question. Nevertheless, this assumption forms the basis of a major theory of psychological measurement known as *classical test theory* (Gulliksen, 1950; Novick, 1966; Green, 1981) and provides the technical foundation for much of contemporary IQ test construction, measurement and error estimation. For various reasons, it is not possible in psychological measurement to determine directly the amount of error in a single measurement or set of measurements. Classical test theory is a circuitous, mathematically complex approach to deriving error estimates, its complexity being a consequence of the reactive and intrusive nature of psychological measurement.

On the basis of classical theory equations, it is possible to derive a quantitative estimate of the *reliability* or accuracy of a test, expressed in the form of a number not unlike a correlation coefficient. Tests with reliability coefficients in the range of about 0.70 or more (theoretical range 0–1.0) are usually accepted as being suitable for individual use. Given a reliability coefficient, it is possible to compute an index of the *error of measurement* (the standard error of measurement – SE) associated with a particular test, and by further computation (see Dudek, 1979) an estimate of the degree of precision associated with a single test score can be derived. We suspect that the use of the SE is infrequent in applied testing and that even when employed is likely to be misunderstood and misinterpreted (Dudek, 1979).

The axiom of error in measurement highlights the inappropriateness of attaching to an IQ the precision suggested by its numerical form. This view is further reinforced by the evidence (see Kaufman, 1979, p. 191) that experienced testers can make many small errors in calculating IQs. In one study, a single test protocol was marked by 64 experienced psychologists who obtained Full Scale IQs ranging from 78 to 95 (Miller and Chansky, 1972).

The nature of IQ tests is such that errors in scoring and administration can and do intrude themselves. That they need not do so to the gross extent described by Miller and Chansky (1972) is evidenced by the very few errors found by Clarke *et al.* (1958) in their rescoring of several hundred Wechsler test protocols. The problem, in our view, is not so much to do with the test but rather with the quality and rigour of training in test administration and scoring that testers receive, plus the degree of responsibility they choose to exercise when using tests.

Psychometrically, reliability has a specific technical meaning defined through classical theory and can be estimated in a variety of ways. Each produces a somewhat different estimate of test reliability. The outcomes of reliability studies have been used to designate a test as 'reliable' (or not). More recently, however, it has come to be recognized that general statements about any test (reliable or unreliable) are inappropriate, mainly because changing one aspect of a reliability estimation study can lead to marked variations in the coefficient and hence the error of measurement. In effect, any reliability coefficient is *specific* to the sample, test, circumstances of testing *and computational procedure*. A test cannot, therefore, be regarded as 'reliable' in a generic sense. Rather, it becomes necessary to determine how reliable a measure it is for a particular purpose when used in a particular way and with a clearly defined group. This caveat applies whether or not a test is used for research or in clinical testing, and can only be removed if there is evidence from a variety of studies that the reliability coefficient is robust despite variations in sampling or other procedural changes. All too often researchers and clinicians assume, incorrectly, that because someone else found the test to be reliable they need not justify its use in the particular circumstances of their study or application.

The problem of the instability of reliability coefficients, as well as other considerations, has led Cronbach and his colleagues (1972) to a reconceptualization of reliability, presented in the form of *generalizability* theory. This theory recognizes that tests do not have the property of 'reliability' outside the context in which the reliability coefficients are determined. Rather, the question becomes one of discovering the extent to which it is possible, on the basis of careful empirical investigation, to make generalizations about the robustness of test scores.

It is worth noting, too, that a 'reliable' test, judged as such on the basis of systematic study, will not inevitably lead to a 'reliable' IQ for an individual. People who are anxious, who do not comprehend test instructions or who have incompetent examiners can produce a performance which may not reflect what they might have done in other circumstances. There are many sources of 'error' in individual testing that can intrude their effects to produce an 'unreliable' test result. The practical implications of this will be developed later.

Validation

Test scores in the first instance are a quantification of aspects of performance at the time of testing. Their meaning or interpretation depends on evidence that they measure what they are supposed to and how well they do so, that is, their validity (Anastasi, 1982). A fundamental problem in psychological testing is that test *performance* is an amalgam of many influences that can affect the score. It is very unlikely that the magnitude of a score will be in one-to-one correspondence with the attribute measured, even excluding error. Scores on tests of language development are likely to be influenced by cognitive factors. Tests of motor competence require comprehension of the task and may also tap spatial abilities. The task in test validation is to gather the evidence that a test of a particular attribute 'measures' that attribute and little else.

Although there are a number of established procedures for validating a test (see Anastasi, 1982), the process of validation is more complex than is perhaps generally appreciated and is as much a matter of theory and theory testing as it is of the technical procedures for gathering validity data (Cronbach, 1971). For instance, the question 'Does intelligence test X measure intelligence?' depends on what is meant by intelligence. The meaning of the concept is in turn given in the context of the theory of intelligence that inspired the form and content of the test. The use of the test in research provides data relevant to the veracity of the theory; the relationship between test and theory is one of reciprocity where each contributes to the refinement of the other over time. Ideally, both should be modified as a consequence of feedback from validity studies although in practice this rarely happens, at least in the short term.

Current views of test validation have come to recognize that tests are not valid in an inherent or absolute sense. Rather, each will have different *validities* for different purposes and may not be valid for others, or for use with individuals dissimilar to those involved in studies of validity. An IQ test may be a good predictor of examination performance for individuals in the average ability range but poor as a predictor for high-ability individuals. Further, if a test has not been validated on groups of mentally handicapped individuals, it should not be used for discriminating individual differences in this group, although it can be useful for comparing such individuals with nonhandicapped people.

It needs to be emphasized that the quality and acceptability of validation data are dependent on the methodological adequacy of the studies that gave rise to them and, as a minimum, require that conclusions be supported by independent replication.

The paramount importance of validity will emerge when we consider the question of test selection and interpretation of individual test data.

Conceptually and technically, reliability and validity have in the past been regarded as distinct aspects of a test. With the advent of generalizability theory the boundaries have blurred – both can be encompassed within the conceptual and statistical framework of this theory and are subsumed by the generic question, 'What generalizations can be made from scores on a given test?' Answers depend on appropriate studies. However, generalizability theory in its mathematical form is essentially a variant of classical test theory and there are good grounds, as Lumsden (1976) argues, for discarding classical test theory and its derivatives. Whether or not Lumsden's arguments come to be more widely accepted, the conceptual aspects of generalizability theory are a helpful orientation in individual testing.

INTELLIGENCE MEASUREMENT: A CRITICAL APPRAISAL

IQ tests as 'measuring' instruments

The metric and other inadequacies of intelligence tests have been commented on for decades (Spearman, 1927; Thorndike *et al.*, 1927; Furneaux, 1961; Eysenck, 1967, 1973). Spearman (1927), for instance, criticized the 'hotch-potch' approach to scoring tests – 'the prevalent procedure of throwing a miscellaneous collection of tests indiscriminately into a single pool' (p. 71).

A more fundamental issue is that of unidimensionality – that measurement involves the quantification of one characteristic and, as Lumsden (1976) points out, the 'whole conception of psychological testing as measurement depends on it' (p. 266). There is no evidence that what is tested by IQ tests is unidimensional, and the major tool for attempting to demonstrate this, factor analysis, is regarded on its own as inadequate for the purpose (Vernon, 1979, p. 61). For instance, subtests with apparently homogeneous content when examined via factor analysis are shown to tap several dimensions rather than a unidimensional ability (see Kaufman's (1979) discussion of subtest specificity on the WISC-R, pp. 111–15, for example).

A problem with factor analytic decomposition of test scores is that it will only identify those aspects that are attributable to the influence of variables included in the initial analysis. Kaufman's (1979) assessment of subtest specificity examines only those aspects of a particular WISC-R subtest that are tapped by other subtests in the battery. It does not, for instance, indicate the extent to which, say, the vocabulary subtest is influenced by social class, motivation or by non-WISC-R indices of verbal ability.

In terms of the available evidence, however, it is clear that few if any subtests or IQ scales are unidimensional.

Classical test theory, virtually from the time it began to be elaborated, was known to be deficient. Since then, many efforts have been made to sustain it as a viable approach to reliability, either by reconceptualizing it statistically (Novick, 1966; Lord and Novick, 1968) or in the form of generalizability theory (Cronbach *et al.*, 1972). These attempts, according to Lumsden (1976), have been unsuccessful to the extent that he asserts that 'reliability theory in its present forms should be abandoned' (p. 265), that the 'reliability coefficients and statistics calculated from it have no useful application. They should not be used to select tests, to estimate true scores, to estimate confidence limits for either true or obtained scores, in the correction for attenuation or for anything else' (p. 261).

The absence of evidence for unidimensionality and the inadequacy of the classical theory of reliability together undermine any pretensions there may be that IQ tests 'measure' in the usual sense of that term. The implications of this conclusion are considered below.

IQ tests and theories of intelligence

With few notable exceptions (Piaget and the approaches to intelligence inspired by information theory), much of the theoretical work in intelligence has been more concerned with the organization or structure of abilities than with explaining why people behave intelligently.

There are several structural theories, an indication that there is as yet no generally accepted conceptualization of how human abilities are organized. The influence that structural theories have had has been mainly centred on the notion of *g* or general ability and two or more subgroups of ability such as verbal and spatial. In IQ tests this is manifested by the production of a single summary score as a measure of *g* with a variety of different names (Full Scale IQ – Wechsler; General Cognitive Index – McCarthy, 1972) as well as sub-scale IQs (the Verbal and Performance scale IQs of the Wechsler test). Differences between structural theories are concerned with whether or not *g* should be split (such as Cattell's (1971) *gf* and *gc* – fluid and crystallized general abilities respectively), or disregarded. Some American psychologists prefer a model with several equally important abilities (Thurstone's (1938) primary mental abilities or the 120 elements proposed in Guilford's (1967) 'structure of intellect' model.

There are yet other variations. Some tests (e.g. Uzgiris and Hunt, 1975) are based on Piagetian theory whereas others incorporate a few Piaget-inspired subtests, the remainder being of a conventional type (British Ability Scales, Elliott *et al.*, 1983).

Overall, the simple fact is that most of the commonly used tests of intelligence lack a 'foundation in theories of intelligence, whether these theories be based on research in neuropsychology, cognitive information processing, factor analysis, learning theory, or other domains' (Garcia 1981; Kaufman and Reynolds, 1983). Even when tests show some kinship with a particular approach to intelligence, alternative explanations of test results can make equally good sense. Furneaux (1961) has suggested that certain ability patterns, such as the differentiation between visuospatial and arithmetic abilities on Thurstone's PMA battery, arose because the tests differed in the extent to which each measures speed and accuracy of performance, and not because they reflected the different underlying abilities proposed by Thurstone.

Another major problem in the relationship between theory and test emerges in individual test interpretation. The types of ability supposed to be measured by a test are ascertained from the analysis of group data or, in the case of Piagetian tests, on the basis of theoretical dictates and observation. It is possible that an individual who obtains a high score on a test of spatial ability, or who passes a test of conservation of number, has done so by virtue of some other capacity or via some other route. Similarly, someone with a low score is not necessarily deficient in that ability. Low scores could be a consequence of, for example, poor motivation, partial hearing loss or poor vision. Many of the tasks in IQ tests may implicate different forms of competence, and in individual testing it is virtually impossible to know which of these or what combination has been responsible for the observed score.

Conclusions

The first IQ test was introduced essentially as an empirical solution to a practical problem. Following this, both the original test and its derivatives became invested with theoretical and technical properties that they do not merit. Some of the problems of IQ tests and their application have been described in earlier parts of this chapter. We believe, however, that the most fundamental failings of such tests reside in their metric inadequacy and theoretical poverty. On these grounds alone, we suggest that psychologists abandon any inclinations they may have towards regarding IQ tests as instruments for measuring intelligence.

Does this mean that we should abandon the IQ? Certainly not. Continued use of the IQ, at least in applied settings, depends on its ability to provide information that is clinically useful. Whether or not it does this is an empirical question that can only be answered in the light of evidence from validation studies. These studies provide data on the concurrent and predictive value of the IQ and, to the extent that they provide clinically relevant information, constitute the basis for the continued use of IQ tests. Of equal importance is how validation data, derived as they are from group studies, can be used in individual assessment. In later sections we outline an approach which enables the clinician to exploit such data in ways that do not depend on the status of IQ tests as measures of intelligence or on the classical test theory approach to measurement.

The use of IQ tests in clinical settings provides standardized opportunities of observing both the individual and the nature of his or her performance. Further, information of potential relevance to assessment and management can be derived from a proper analysis of the scores produced. (For many reasons, some of which we detail later, test-derived information should be regarded as hypothesis-generating or as hypothesis-supporting, rather than as conclusive, as Shapiro (1970) and others have argued (Kaufman, 1979).)

We consider the information-producing potential of IQ tests to be the second major reason for their continued use. In the sections which follow we present the evidence and arguments in support of IQ testing. Before doing so, it is necessary to provide a conceptual and technical framework. This is the task of the next section.

SOME ISSUES IN VALIDATION

Specificity of test scores

> a validation study examines the procedure as a whole. Every aspect of the setting ... and every detail of a procedure may have an influence on performance and hence on what is measured. (Cronbach, 1971, p. 449)

Concepts such as intelligence, competence, personality, extraversion and the like refer to general attributes which have diverse behavioural manifestations that can be quantified using different techniques.

Accumulating evidence, however, shows that test scores derived from different procedures are not readily interchangeable. Mechanical counts or other indices of physical activity have only moderate correlations with direct observations of activity (Barkley, 1981). Hence a high score on one index does not mean that person is 'active' in a general sense; he or she may get low scores on other indices of activity. Similarly, 'successful treatment' as defined by one procedure may not be so regarded when indexed by a different device (Agras *et al.*, 1979).

In the realm of mental and educational testing there has been a move away from unsupported generalizations about the meanings and implications of test scores as a consequence of the findings of validation studies.

Test scores thus allow only such interpretations as can be empirically supported. Unless there are findings to the contrary, they must be assumed to have only specific relationships with other criteria, and to have interpretations restricted to the sample and procedural characteristics of the validation study.

Hence if there is a strong correlation between IQs on a particular test administered at a ten-year interval, it cannot be assumed that a similar correlation will be found between this test and another IQ test administered after ten years, or between the initial IQ and other criteria (such as academic performance, or teacher ratings of ability, or interview-based measures of mental ability). Nor can we assume that an IQ test at one age samples the same competencies as it does at a later age, even though the test content remains similar. This follows from what is known about developmental changes in mental functioning across the lifespan and from the restricted generality of test scores. Each interpretation of a test score requires justification, and, in the absence of such support, only limited onces are permissible.

Another important constraint on interpretation is the adequacy of the criterion measure. Criteria in concurrent and predictive studies are themselves specific performance-based indices of more global concepts. Academic achievement, social competence and the like have also to be operationalized for discovering correlational links. In principle, the problems of developing suitable criteria do not differ from those of validating predictors such as IQ as indices of intelligence; good criteria derive from clear conceptualization and careful research that lead to an accumulation of evidence that the index is an adequate representation of the criterion. For instance, in examining the relationship between IQs and 'social competence' or 'self-help' skills, it is important to ensure that the indices of these characteristics have appropriate validities.

Special attention needs to be drawn to criteria that are derived from direct observation of behaviours or are indirect reports such as interviews. It may sometimes be assumed that because the criterion measure is a sample of the actual behaviour, questions of validity do not arise. This, as Johnson and Bolstad (1973) point out, is a false assumption. For instance, some patterns of behaviour are situational or task-specific. Someone who can brush her teeth may only do so when given toothpaste and brush; the man who can dress himself only does so because his clothing requires the use of zips and studs but not buttons; people asked to report on the skills possessed by a client using a behavioural checklist may not have had the opportunity for observing the person across situations or may not interpret questions in the way intended by the designer of the checklist.

The practical implications of these observations are far-reaching. In essence it means that, unless there is strong evidence to the contrary, information-gathering procedures are not interchangeable. The interview, direct observation, the IQ test and other procedures each produce at least some unique information. To generalize from one without recourse to a search for other forms of supporting and contradictory evidence before drawing a conclusion constitutes an unjustifiable practice. It is for these and other reasons that there is increasing advocacy of multi-method assessments (Nay, 1979; Beck, 1983), a theme to which we return later.

Decisions and descriptive interpretations

Cronbach (1971) makes an important distinction between two forms of interpretation of validity data as a function of their use. *Decisions* involve interpretations which help to make a choice between alternative courses of action. Using tests to guide decisions presupposes that they will reduce the number of incorrect judgements. The use of tests for decision-making also presupposes evidence for the validity of each decision and by implication adequate indices of the criteria. For instance, directing someone to a school for moderately mentally handicapped children, as opposed to a mainstream school, should be based on particular forms of evidence. These include data that show that children with a particular level of IQ perform better in one school than in the other. This in turn requires that notions such as 'perform better' have been carefully operationalized and that such criteria have been shown to hold for the children so selected throughout their special school years. Providing such evidence is very complex methodologically, and we doubt that appropriate data exist for this purpose. Instead, most decisions in conventional practice are based on *descriptive interpretations*, such as 'he or she is mentally retarded'.

As Cronbach (1971) puts it, 'A description is more than an adjectival phrase; it pulls behind it a whole train of implications. To say that a child is mentally retarded is to call up a great number of expectations about what he will do in response to certain demands' (p. 448). If the IQ is to be interpreted descriptively, the empirical task is to discover how much confidence can be placed in each of the implications. To use an IQ as the major diagnostic criterion of mental retardation presupposes that all or most of the connotations of mental retardation, when expressed operationally, correlate strongly with the IQ. Ensuring that this is so is particularly important when a descriptive interpretation is to be used for decision-making, as commonly happens in clinical practice. The distinction between these two uses of interpretation is a logical one; in practice most tests can be used for both purposes (see Cronbach 1971, p. 448).

'Mental retardation' (like its progenitor, intelligence) is a general concept difficult to define precisely. It cannot be defined by IQ alone because low IQs can be a consequence of a particular test, the tester, the circumstances of testing and characteristics of the individual other than low intelligence (e.g. language handicap) acting alone or interacting to produce the low score. If analysed carefully, mental retardation turns out to be very much like its progenitor, namely, what Waddington (1977) calls a 'fuzzy entity' – a concept with a soft core and an indefinite boundary. As such, it carries with it all the problems of conceptualization and operationalization associated with 'intelligence'. However, we can examine a number of properties that it shares with intelligence and consider the implications of these for assessing the available validity data. Some of these issues have been elaborated in Chapter 2.

As normally understood, mental retardation as a general condition of an individual on the whole implies that many aspects of concurrent and future functioning will be limited. Empirically, a low IQ should be associated with low criterion scores on tests of other aspects of mental functioning as expressed in performance. Another important implication is predictive outcome. Mentally retarded people are often anticipated to remain much the same over time. Empirically, their current IQ should predict their future IQs. More importantly, *current* IQs should predict performance on other criteria of mental functioning *at later times*. We would argue that there is little point in IQ at time 1 being a good predictor of IQ at time 2 unless it can be demonstrated that IQ at time 2 has already been shown to have a strong relationship with other criteria (apart from the IQ score) at time 2. Further, in obtaining such evidence it is important that the outcomes at time 2 are not a consequence of selection at time 1. For instance, IQ at time 2 may correlate with IQ at time 1 and other criteria at time 2 because the individual has been institutionalized following IQ testing at time 1. To demonstrate the predictive value of IQ at time 1 it is necessary to include individuals who have undergone a wide range of experiences following testing at time 1 and that all those who were 'poorly adapted' (for want of a better phrase) at time 2 also had low IQs at time 1. Again, when secondary schooling was largely determined by the results of group IQ tests administered at age ten to eleven years, it should not be surprising that children who 'passed' the eleven-plus test did better at public examinations some five or six years later – the ones who 'failed' followed a less academic syllabus and were not entered for the examinations: a tragic example of a self-fulfilling prophecy.

These we consider to be some of the major implications in attempting to use IQ as a basis for descriptive interpretations.

The task of establishing the descriptive validity of IQ in relation to mental retardation is not one that can be accomplished by a single study or even several studies, even if they are methodologically acceptable. Instead, credibility emerges over time through the accretion of evidence from various sources, including good research.

Some validity implications of a developmental perspective

The problem of validating descriptive interpretations of the IQ in relation to mental retardation (or intelligence) is compounded by what we may loosely call the 'nature of mental or cognitive development'. If the IQ is to be evaluated as an index of 'cognitive development', it is necessary to begin to identify what is meant by cognition and its developmental manifestations.

Most current tests were constructed without regard to contemporary views of cognitive functioning. Tests such as the Wechsler scales have a standard set of subtests which span an age range from 4 to 74; they implicitly assume that the underlying pattern of organization of ability does not change over this span and that the major form of change is quantitative. Developmental psychologists are much less certain about the nature of what happens over time and basic issues continue to be debated. For instance, there is a legacy in western psychology that seeks and sees developmental continuities. Changes are regarded as superficial in the sense that, while overt behaviours may change, they are the expression of underlying continuities. The possibility of new structures (radical changes) emerging in the course of development only recently began to intrude itself in the thinking of developmentalists (see Brim and Kagan, 1980, and Kagan, 1980, for a detailed consideration of the issues). Further, qualitative transitions are increasingly being accepted as part of the phenomenology of mental development (see McCall, 1979, for instance).

Apart from such basic issues, there is as yet little clear description let alone understanding of the phenomenology of cognitive development; nor is there any clear evidence that cognitive development in mentally handicapped people is delayed (quantitatively less), qualitatively different or both, depending on which aspects are being considered.

While these are fundamental issues, the demands of clinical practice cannot be stayed while they are being elucidated. Further, from an applied viewpoint, the concerns of developmentalists could be regarded as interesting but irrelevant if it could be shown that IQs correlated substantially with indices of cognitive functioning derived from more recent views of cognitive development.

Restriction of range

The statistical procedure of correlation is the empirical essence of validation. The magnitude of correlation coefficients – the numbers that express the covariation, or association between two variables (bivariate) or between two sets of variables (multivariate) – is sensitive to *restriction of range* in either, both or any of the variables used. Range refers to the range of scores (lowest to highest) used to compute the correlation. Restriction of range effects are a particular problem in research in mental handicap for reasons that will become apparent.

The magnitude of r is dependent on several major factors, the actual strength of the relationship between the two variables, the sensitivity of the measuring devices, and the respective ranges of the variables in the sample. If the range of either or both variables is restricted in some way, the r will be reduced below the value that would have been obtained had the range not been restricted. For instance, in a sample heterogeneous as to IQ it might be found that the correlation between IQ and reading skills is $+0.6$. In a sample relatively homogeneous on IQ (with a narrower range of IQ), the correlation may come out at $+0.2$. The reasons for this are a consequence of the technicalities of computing r and are discussed in detail in Kaufman (1972), Anastasi (1982) and other sources.

In studies involving people with low IQs, only the lower portion of the IQ range is used. Hence relationships between IQ and other measures indexed by *r* would be weaker, and thus less predictable, than would be the case if the full IQ range were represented in the sample. Consequently, it may sometimes appear that low IQ is a poor predictor of performance on another variable and this can lead to erroneous conclusions. For instance, using the above example, if only low IQ people were used in a study of the relationship between IQ and reading attainment, it might be concluded that low IQ does not predict reading skill to any great extent. Had the full range of IQs been used, a quite different conclusion would be reached. It is therefore essential when examining data on the relationship between IQ and other variables to consider this in conjunction with studies that provide data from samples heterogeneous with respect to the two measures. Obviously, if the correlation in such samples does not differ significantly from 0, then range restriction in either or both may not matter, but fortuitous correlations greater than 0 may still occur.

Range can also be influenced by two particular effects known as *floor* and *ceiling* effects. The former arises when the competencies of a group are below the lowest score possible on the test. Some items may be passed by chance and individuals attain scores on the test that are higher than they might have obtained had the test floor been lower. The test in effect makes the range more homogeneous. Ceiling effects occur when the abilities of the group are above the top scores possible on the test. Testees can only get the maximum score, and the group again appears as more homogeneous than it is. The resulting correlations would thus be lower than if tests with higher ceilings were used. These effects can be detected if there tends to be a bunching of scores at the extremes of the score distribution. As these distributions are rarely published, such effects may be difficult to detect.

THE VALIDITIES OF IQs

Introduction

With the hindsight of history, it becomes possible to identify a fundamental failing in the application of IQ tests: it was *assumed* that such tests measured intelligence. From this, testers proceeded to decisions and descriptive interpretations.

If the IQ test were invented today, the future course of such testing might develop differently. The basic questions would be focused around the issue of 'What are the developmental and other consequences for people with IQs of different magnitudes and with different preceding or subsequent life experiences?' In this section of the chapter, research on IQ testing is examined from this perspective, with a focus on studies of people with low IQs. We do not begin with the assumption that IQ tests measure intelligence, but examine the associations and consequences of low IQs.

In keeping with this pragmatic, empirical approach to IQs, we must seek evidence for the validities of IQs from studies of the relationships between IQ scores and other measures. In particular, we are interested in the *concurrent* validity of IQ (how well it relates to other measures taken at the same point in time) and in its *predictive* validity. The evidence on such validity within the majority of the population with IQs above 70 is well reviewed elsewhere (Vernon, 1979; Jensen, 1980; Madge and Tizard, 1980; Anastasi, 1982) and is only briefly summarized.

IQ and developmental assessment

During the first one and a half to two years of life, children's development is assessed in a more naturalistic way than at later ages. Infants' reactions to everyday stimuli are carefully observed and recorded. The Gesell Developmental Schedules (Knobloch and Pasamanick, 1974) and the closely similar scale devised by Griffiths (1954) collate information on a wide range of behaviours – motor development, language, adaptive behaviour and personal-social behaviour. These scales concentrate on providing good descriptions of current functioning and have obvious face validity. They have also been found useful in detecting severe mental handicap within the first year of life (Illingworth, 1971), although the rate of misclassification remains high (Clarke and Clarke, 1974).

The Bayley Scales of Infant Development (Bayley, 1969) require the infant to interact more actively with test-like material provided by the examiner. They provide separate standardized scores for mental and motor development from 2 to 30 months. Very low scores on these scales indicate poor current functioning and a high risk of continuing mental retardation (see p. 75) but, contrary to the general finding, Carr (1975) reports that the prediction of later individual development was more accurate in a group of normal infants than in a group of infants with Down's syndrome. Carr raises the interesting possibility that there is something unusual about the motor development of children with Down's syndrome that makes it dangerous to generalize findings from studies of normal development to children with specific handicapping conditions. She notes that the Down's syndrome group – as a group – was indeed scoring significantly lower than the normal controls on the Bayley scales at six weeks of age and that the discriminative power of the test increased over the next few years.

Carr's study underlines two methodological points. First, developmental tests can discriminate *groups* of mentally handicapped children from *groups* of normal infants. Second, the short-term predictive validity for *individuals* within the handicapped group is not necessarily very good.

IQ and educational attainment

After the age of two years, IQ tests include many more verbal items. From age five onwards, IQ test scores correlate moderately highly (generally correlations of around +0.6) with scores on reading, spelling and mathematical achievement. Knowledge of these empirical relations is useful in identifying schoolchildren who are performing markedly less well than expected on the basis of their apparent general ability (Rutter and Yule, 1975; Yule *et al.*, 1982), but this is not to deny that academic progress also depends on many other factors.

In one study of a total school population (Rutter *et al.*, 1970), it was found that there were as many children with measured IQs below 70 doing reasonably well in ordinary primary schools as there were children with IQs above 70 who were in a special school for slow learners. This was as it should be in a properly integrated educational system. The former group was coping with the educational demands of ordinary school, whereas the latter needed extra help. However, for those with IQs below 50, with a rapidly increasing incidence of physical and neurological handicaps, there is a closer relationship between measured IQ and the identification of 'special educational needs'.

Ordinal scales

It is widely recognized that traditional IQ tests are not very useful in leading directly to prescriptions for intervention. This is particularly true in the case of the severely mentally handicapped, where far too few such individuals have been studied during the standardization of the test (Hogg and Mittler, 1980). This objection has less force when considering ordinal scales such as those developed by Uzgiris and Hunt (1975). They developed their tasks from Piagetian theories of development, attempting to find ones that reflected a consistent order in the development of behavioural competencies. Assuming that severely retarded individuals nevertheless develop skills in the same sequence as normal children, these tasks are applicable irrespective of chronological age.

Kahn (1975) was one of the earliest investigators to demonstrate that, within a severely retarded population, scores on the object permanence subscale were highly predictive of children's language development. This was independently observed in an unpublished study by Hillier and Yule (1978) in which it was found that severely retarded children who performed at or above stage VI on the object permanence scale responded better to an operant language programme than did children who scored below this cut-off. More generally, Kahn (1983) provides evidence that, within a group of severely retarded children, scores on the Uzgiris–Hunt scale add significantly to information on CA and MA in predicting concurrent levels of adaptive behaviour.

Clearly, the relevance of Piagetian views on very early cognitive development, discussed by Woodward (1963) in earlier editions of this book, are beginning to have an important influence on the assessment of severely retarded individuals.

Stability and change of IQ scores

It is now widely accepted (Madge and Tizard, 1980) that developmental quotients (DQs) of children tested before expressive language is testable bear little relationship to scores on later IQ tests. After the age of two, correlations begin to be higher, and, after the age of six years, successive assessments seem more consistent. Correlational studies generally point to two general conclusions (Clarke and Clarke, 1984): first, that measures of infant behaviour scarcely predicted later ordinal position within a group; and, second, that the longer the period between assessments, the lower will be the correlation. Generally, over a ten-year interval the correlation between two sets of IQ scores is in the region of $+0.5$, although recent studies using the Wechsler scales have produced correlations of $+0.67$ (Wilson, 1983) and $+0.86$ (Yule *et al.*, 1982) with normal children, and of $+0.92$ (Tew and Laurence, 1983) with a group of children with spina bifida.

Clarke and Clarke (1984) have reiterated their argument that high correlations tell little about the stability of the level of individual children's IQ scores. Correlation is a statistic that applies to a *group* of scores. There are now a number of longitudinal studies that indicate that, during the course of childhood, IQ scores will change by 15 points or more in about one in three of the children (Vernon, 1979; Madge and Tizard, 1980). The latest results which confirm this come from Hindley and Owen (1978) who followed 84 children from 6 months to 17 years. Comparing standardized IQ scores at ages 3 and 17, they found that 50 per cent of children's scores changed at least 10 points, while some 25 per cent of scores shifted by 22 points or more. The correlation between the two sets of scores obtained 14 years apart was $+0.53$, a dramatic example that within a normal sample a moderately high correlation between successive IQ scores is compatible with a large degree of change.

But what of the stability of scores of mentally handicapped children? In general, the lower the IQ, the greater the stability but, as within normal samples, the relation between IQ and other parameters is far from fixed. Changes in IQ do occur (Madge and Tizard, 1980). Goodman and Cameron (1978) obtained repeated estimates of IQ on 289 retarded children initially assessed before the age of 5 years. For those who originally scored 80 or above, the retest correlation was 0.32 for boys and 0.17 for girls; the group that originally scored between 48 and 79 had a retest correlation of 0.70; the group which scored below 48 achieved a retest correlation of $+0.86$. In other words, the lower the initial IQ, the higher the test–retest correlation, and in general these IQ scores are more stable than those of normal children during preschool years. Silverstein (1982) studied the Stanford–Binet scores of 101 'educable mentally retarded' children tested yearly for 4 years, starting when they were, on average, 10.85 years old. The average IQ at each testing remained stable and the average correlation between sets of test scores was 0.85. The median change in IQ was 3.89 points and less than 8 per cent of the sample altered their IQ scores by 10 or more points in either direction.

While the evidence is consistent with the conclusion that IQ scores change less among retarded people, two things have to be emphasized. First, as mentioned earlier, substantial changes do occur in a substantial minority of cases where there has been no deliberate attempt to improve the social environment. Second, as is well documented by Clarke and Clarke (1984), where the social environment has been deliberately improved dramatic increases in measured IQ have been reported (see in particular Chapters 7 and 12).

In summary there is, we believe, sufficient evidence from group studies to support the view that individuals with low IQs may not be able to respond to the demands of our educational and social systems, that they may not develop the competencies expressed by people with higher IQs, and that they may therefore require special provision. IQ tests are a quick, standard and fairly reliable way of alerting us to this, not as an inevitability, but as a possibility. Because of the profound and far-reaching implications of such a conclusion, it is essential that the tests are used and interpreted properly. These are the topics we address next.

IQ TESTING IN CLINICAL PRACTICE

Introduction

The administration and scoring of tests are technical skills best acquired under close supervision. The integration of testing and test data in clinical and educational practice and research demands more.

Clinical assessment is concerned with individuals whereas validity data are derived from group studies. A major task in assessment is thus the translation of group data into information that is relevant to individual needs. In this section are identified a number of important aspects of practical testing with special reference to individual assessment.

Performance, the IQ and competence

There are sufficient grounds for assuming that what individuals do during testing – their behaviour – is the expression of a multiplicity of influences, some emanating from the testee directly, some from the test situation mediated through the testee (such as the influence of the situation), and some from the specific demands of the test (e.g. the physical manipulation of objects). The IQ itself is in part a reflection of aspects of performance, but includes effects contributed by the tester, for instance through lax or stringent interpretation of scoring criteria, computational errors and the like.

For some purposes, such as making concurrent or predictive statements, the complex determination of the IQ score is of no great significance provided such statements are constrained by what is known about the empirical accuracy of the score. Techniques for interpreting data in this way (expectancy tables and regression models) are presented below.

If the purpose of testing is to identify and describe characteristics or attributes of the individual, the complex determination of the IQ, the fact that it is a 'noise-laden' form of information, becomes a major issue. In this context it is useful to make a distinction akin to that in psycholinguistics or social learning theory, between 'competence' and 'performance' or 'learning' and 'performance', respectively (Bandura, 1977). Making statements about the 'abilities' or 'competencies' of the individual from an IQ test performance poses special problems in interpretation, something we consider in a later section. For the present, all that is necessary is to note distinctions between the IQ, performance during testing, and the abilities or competencies of the individual.

Tests and testing as sampling

It is also helpful in individual testing to exploit the concepts of sampling theory. IQ tests can be regarded as devices for sampling from the population of competencies. A fundamental question then arises: do they provide a representative sample that is also unbiased? Given the variations in the conceptualization of the structure of human abilities (e.g. *g* plus group factors versus Primary Mental Abilities versus Guilford's (1967) structure of intellect model), or given that we do not as yet have an established comprehensive scheme of human abilities, we cannot know if IQ tests, via their content, representatively sample the mental population of competencies. Further, most forms of competence can be expressed in different ways (knowledge of word meanings could be shown by oral definition, appropriate use in spoken or written sentences, or through manual communication), and they can be systematically tested in various ways (oral definition, multiple choice, identifying word–picture correspondence). The equivalence of particular tactics for sampling an area of competence, however, is not known (see below). We cannot, therefore, be certain about the representativeness of specific test procedures for sampling within each area of competence.

It has been pointed out, for instance, that tests such as the WISC and WAIS do not have item content that corresponds to what is know about the functional properties of the left and right cerebral hemispheres (Kaufman, 1979). The Stanford–Binet is known to be verbally biased. Different tests sampling verbal abilities show only some overlap, as indexed by their intercorrelations. These empirically based conclusions support the contentions in the preceding paragraph.

Sampling concepts can also be applied to the conceptualization of test performance. Hence a single test score can be regarded as a biased index in that, for example, the time, circumstances of testing and tester, are not usually chosen at random from the population of options potentially available. Nor can it be assumed that the health, motivations and other state aspects of the testee at the time of testing are representative of the population of such features within the individual.

This sampling conceptualization makes explicit the inherently tenuous nature of tests and testing, for instance in making inferences about present or future competence from test performance. Given this conceptualization, it is more readily appreciated that at best scores can only have the status of tentative statements or hypotheses that require corroboration from other sources; or they can provide support or suggest a contradiction of hypotheses generated on other grounds.

Techniques for exploiting validity data

> wise test users ... have chosen tests in terms of their superior validity.
> (Lumsden, 1976, p. 269)

An IQ (or any psychological test) is given not because we want to know the IQ, but because knowing the IQ enables certain statements to be made. These statements – interpretations of the test score – have to be both relevant to the purpose of testing and justifiable on the basis of empirical evidence. Not all psychologists may agree with an empirical stance such as this, but we regard its acceptance in principle and in practice to be the keystone of clinical assessment.

The data that suggest hypotheses or contribute evidence for a particular interpretation are derived initially from research using the test, for instance correlating IQ test scores with performance on a reading test. The test user should, therefore, have an appreciation of research design and methodology so as to be able to evaluate the empirical data that are to be used for test interpretation. In this section, two basic procedures for the use of validity data, expectancy tables and linear and other regression procedures, are outlined.

Consider a study in which an IQ test has been given on two occasions, X and Y, separated by an interval of ten years. At time X all individuals in the sample were given a test and obtained a particular score. When retested, some produced the same score, others did better or worse. From the retest data it is possible to draw up a table which has rows representing the scores at time X and columns representing the range of scores at time Y. The values within this table are the empirically observed data. Such a table, called an *expectancy table*, is illustrated in Table 3.1.

From a table such as this it is possible to identify the expected outcome ten years later for someone with a given initial score. The *expectation* is based

TABLE 3.1 An expectancy table

		Y scores					
		71–75	76–80	81–85	86–90	91–95	96–100
X scores	71–75	0	2	4	1	1	0
	76–80	1	3	5	4	2	0
	81–85	1	3	10	15	20	0
	86–90	0	1	4	8	15	0
	91–95	0	0	0	0	0	0

directly on what was actually observed when the study was carried out. For instance, individuals with an initial score of 76 would be expected (because it has happened to similar individuals in the past) under similar conditions to obtain scores between 71 and 95 or, most commonly, between 76 and 90, and would not be expected to score 71 or less, or more than 95.

Note that the data in the table could be expressed as frequencies, percentages or probabilities without distorting the observed relationships. Note, too, that X could be a score on any categorical or continuous variable, that the Y scores could be from similar variables, and that the intervals between the administration of the tests could range from very short intervals onwards. Hence such a table could contain the conjoint or bivariate distributions from the same test administered at an interval of five minutes or twenty years, or it could refer to scores from two different IQ tests administered one after the other or at an interval of five months, or an IQ and a reading test at any interval.

The advantages of such tables are that they make no assumptions about the statistical properties of the data, and that they are easily used. However, certain preconditions need to be taken into account. The individual tested should be similar to the sample. The tests and circumstances of testing should also be similar. The greater the dissimilarity between the testee and the sample, the more qualified conclusions must be.

Expectancy tables have a wide range of uses and illustrate the irrelevance of computing reliability coefficients from classical test theory procedures. In individual testing, for instance, the client's scores can be compared with those obtained from similar individuals under similar circumstances. Assume someone gains an X score of 87 when first tested, and we are interested in knowing whether or not over a ten-year interval he has shown a deterioration in functioning, having obtained a retest (Y) score of 72. From Table 3.1 it can be seen that no one in the research sample obtained a retest score of 72 having had an original score of 87. Hence the retest score is unusual and it *suggests* a deterioration in functioning or perhaps failure to progress at the same rate as similar individuals. If other information is consistent with one or other of these specific test-based hypotheses, there are strong grounds for drawing such a conclusion.

If the two variables in the table represented a retest interval of, say, one week, and it is assumed that the attribute is stable, such a table would enable some conclusions to be drawn regarding the stability of measures (analogous to retest reliability). If the data are scores on the same individuals determined by two different testers, we have the equivalence of an inter-observer agreement measure. Or if the two variables were supposed to be scores on equivalent forms of the test, the data would enable inferences about the comparability of the measures.

The research literature on tests is replete with studies examining bivariate relationships although they do not commonly publish the bivariate distribution which could be used for creating expectancy tables. It should, however, be possible to obtain such data from authors for the more common clinical applications.

With sufficiently large samples, it is possible to derive equations which both summarize bivariate or multivariate relationships and enable more refined conclusions. By means of such techniques, given certain assumptions, it is possible to estimate an *outcome* (*expected/criterion*) score for a given *initial* (*predictor*) score. The difference between the *obtained* and *expected* score can then be tested for statistical significance (a likelihood that it is due to chance). For example, on the basis of large sample data it is possible to use *regression* equations, as they are termed, to estimate a score on a second test for a given score on an initial test, if the means and standard deviations of both sets of scores and their intercorrelation are known, and if the bivariate distribution is normal. Regression equations in effect allow the computation of the most likely value on the second test (its mean if the distribution is normal) for a given level of score on the first. A *standard error of estimate or prediction*, the standard deviation of the distribution of scores on the second variable, can also be computed. From this information it is then possible to calculate how far above or below the mean an obtained score is. If the obtained score is, say, more than two standard deviations above or below the expected value, the difference might be regarded as statistically significant and of potential clinical significance.

Multiple regression procedures enable several predictors to be combined in estimating a particular outcome. Further discussion of these techniques can be found in Payne and Jones (1957) and Cronbach (1971). Rutter and Yule (1975) provided an illustration of the use of multiple regression procedures for identifying individuals with specific reading problems.

INTERPRETING TEST SCORES

Statistical significance and psychological importance

For those techniques that enable statistical evaluation of test data, it is important to distinguish between statistical significance and psychological importance. The former means simply that the findings were unlikely to be due to chance; *very low* probability levels mean only that the results are *very* unlikely to be due to chance and not that they are *very important* psychologically. Psychological importance or relevance does not automatically follow from even highly improbable statistical outcomes although, in the normal course of events, test interpretation would proceed only from those findings that had low probabilities of being due to chance. Psychological importance derives primarily from studies that show that particular patterns of results have empirically supportable consequences or implications. For instance, differences between two measures may be of low probability but the interpretation of the psychological importance of that difference depends on, among other things, replication of the findings and research linking the occurrence of differences of that magnitude with particular psychological consequences.

A distinction should also be made between differences that are statistically significant and those that are statistically frequent or infrequent. It is, for example, possible to have a difference between scores that is unlikely to be due to chance but that can be observed frequently in a population. Differences unlikely to be due to chance are sometimes called *reliable* differences, whereas differences that occur infrequently in the population are termed *abnormal* or atypical in the statistical sense. This distinction and its implications are discussed more fully by Payne and Jones (1957) and Silverstein (1981).

The importance of the distinction between a *reliable* difference and an *abnormal* difference, as well as the distinction between *statistical* and *psychological* significance, can be easily illustrated with reference to data relating WISC IQ scores to independent indices of CNS dysfunction – an issue often encountered in the assessment of mentally handicapped children. Putting aside altogether the very real objection to using tests to diagnose 'brain damage' (Herbert, 1964), and accepting for the purposes of argument that differences between Verbal and Performance IQs are believed to indicate cerebral dysfunction where the Verbal IQ is depressed, the problem is how does the clinician use such data in reaching a clinical decision?

From previous discussion it is clear that both Verbal and Performance IQs must be regarded as potentially fallible. Each has an error component. It would be foolish to say that a Verbal IQ of 63 was really lower than a Performance IQ of 65. So how large must a (V–P) difference be before it is regarded as reflecting a real difference in cognitive function? Put another way, how large must the differences be to be regarded as *reliable*? As Sattler (1982) shows, a difference of 12 points is needed before it can be confidently (P < 0.05) accepted as not being due to random fluctuations.

However, differences of 12 points are very common. They are found in between 25 and 50 per cent of ten-year-olds. A difference of 29 points in the direction V lower than P is found in less than 5 per cent of the standardization sample of ten-year-olds (one-tailed, i.e. in the direction V lower than P). Such a large difference could fairly be described as *statistically abnormal*.

But what does it mean in psychological terms? To answer this we turn to some of the findings from the Isle of Wight epidemiological studies (Rutter *et al.*, 1970). All children with identifiable brain disorder were tested. Out of 84 cases, 13 (or 14 per cent) were found to have a significant Verbal–Performance discrepancy, compared with only 7.5 per cent of a control group. This difference was itself statistically significant, thereby lending some credibility to the hypothesized link between Verbal–Performance discrepancies and brain disorder. Does this mean that where a psychologist finds a child with a Verbal IQ some 25 points higher than Performance IQ that a diagnosis of brain disorder should be made? To answer this, yet another important concept must be introduced – that of *base rate*.

In the Isle of Wight studies, *all* the children with brain disorder were tested, but only a sample of the remainder of the population was tested to act as a control group. The total population consisted of 11,865 children. Thus the true relationship between abnormal (V–P) discrepancies and brain disorder can be seen in Table 3.2.

TABLE 3.2   Relationship between abnormal (V–P) discrepancies and brain disorder

	Normal	*Brain disorder*	*Total*
No discrepancy	10,897	71	10,968
Abnormal (V–P) discrepancy	884 (7.5%)	13 (15%)	897
Total	11,781	84	11,865

Source: Rutter, Graham and Yule (1970).

From this it can be seen that whereas *proportionally* twice as many children with identifiable brain disorder as controls have an abnormal (V–P) discrepancy, none the less for every one child with brain disorder with such a discrepancy there are about 68 with an equally large discrepancy who are perfectly normal. (In passing, it should also be noted that only a minority of the brain disorder group share this famous sign, showing how useless it is, on its own, as a diagnostic index.)

Thus interpreting data from even as well known a test as the WISC-R demands a high level of knowledge and statistical sophistication. Children in difficulties deserve such skilled professional advice. It is doubtful how often they receive it when appreciation of psychometric subtleties is at such a low ebb as it is today.

Types of interpretation: statistical and psychological

A test score permits two basic types of interpretation, those that are translations of the numerical properties of the score (*statistical*) and those that additionally depend on validation (*psychological*).

For tests that have either numerical norms or that enable comparison with some behavioural criterion, it is possible to make interpretations that simply translate the score in terms of its relationship with the criterion. It is not commonly appreciated that a statement such as 'below-average intelligence' has two elements – 'below-average' and 'intelligence', both of which require appropriate grounds for interpretation. Whereas the former is dependent on measurement theory and sampling of individuals to provide test norms, the latter is more closely linked with test validation.

On a test that has a known mean and standard deviation, an individual's score can be presented in terms of its distance from the sample average in units of the standard deviation, provided that the distribution is normal. There are also various ways of expressing this relationship, all of which are interchangeable. Hence an IQ of 115 on a test with a mean of 100 and a standard deviation of 15, is one SD above the mean (above average statistically). Such a score has a *percentile* value of 84 and could be presented as a *z score* of +1, etc. (see Anastasi, 1982, p. 84). All these scores simply indicate the relationship between the obtained score and the average score obtained by the particular normative sample. That is, on this particular test, the testee obtained a score above the average for the normative group. Extensions of statistical interpretations are dependent on the characteristics of the normative group, the correspondence between individual and group characteristics, and the procedures used. If the sample represents a population of like-aged individuals in London, then it is possible to assert that an individual's score is above the London average, and so on. If the norms were, say, stages in the development of a particular skill, generalizations about an individual performance would be similarly tied to sample, test, testee and setting characteristics.

Another form of statistical interpretation, again subject to the constraints on generalization noted above, translates relationships between two tests. These interpretations take the form of 'low score on test X is likely to be associated with low score on test Y'. Such interpretations are essentially empirical and may refer to concurrent or future performance depending on the data on which they are based. Their certainty depends, too, on the magnitude of the statistical criterion, a correlation or chi-square value, the two indices being conceptually interchangeable.

Psychological interpretations require increasingly complex forms of justification as a function of the degree of abstraction of the underlying concept; verbal fluency or academic attainment appear as less complex concepts than do intelligence or personality.

One form of psychological interpretation relates test scores to a narrow class of performances, such as educational attainment. To assert that low IQ means that an individual is likely to fail educationally (now or in the future) is an illustration of this; to do so presupposes good empirical grounds as well as valid criteria, as was noted on p. 73.

Interpretations that link test scores to the more abstract concepts such as intelligence are also psychological. As should by now be apparent, we regard the jump from a statement such as 'below-average IQ' to 'below-average *intelligence*' as being of the nature of a quantum leap not to be negotiated in a cavalier fashion.

Psychological interpretations of validity data also pose a separate set of problems because they extrapolate group data to the individual. One way of illustrating this is in the interpretation of subtest scores from a test such as the WISC-R. (Whether or not a score is worth interpreting is a statistical decision, various grounds for which are discussed in greater detail by Kaufman (1979).) If a very low score has been obtained on the vocabulary subtest in the context of high ones on the other subtests, does the low score imply poor word knowledge, assuming that the subtest has been correctly administered and scored?

In analyses of group data for vocabulary, there is some evidence that it has a degree of uniqueness. That is, scores on the subtest are only moderately influenced by other skills on the WISC-R. While this may be true for group data, an individual obtaining a low score may do so not because he or she is deficient in that particular skill, but for a host of other reasons, such as a high-frequency hearing loss, or because of the particular form in which word knowledge was tested, and so on.

A central problem is that in group data idiosyncrasies tend to cancel each other; in individual data they may not.

The task confronting the clinician is to decide what to interpret and how to do so, on the basis of observations during testing, knowledge of the characteristics of the test, and what is known about the effects of being tested. Expectancy tables, regression equations or other statistical techniques serve only as *guides* to interpretation.

Such is the nature of individual testing and test data that scores should not be expected or allowed to carry the absolute significance that is often attributed to them. Rather, test data need to be absorbed in the broader context of clinical assessment in which they can inspire hypotheses or lend support to hypotheses developed on other grounds. On the next page we present a distinction between assessment and testing and consider its implications.

Profile analysis

A particularly problematical approach to the differences between scores is 'profile analysis', in which the *pattern* of scores on a battery of tests is interpreted and is closely associated in practice with *diagnostic-prescriptive* remediation. In theory, the pattern of cognitive strengths and weaknesses should be reflected in the pattern of scores; and, in turn, knowledge of the cognitive pattern should guide the therapist to the appropriate intervention strategy.

As noted elsewhere (Berger and Yule, 1972; Kaufman, 1979; Sattler, 1982), most subtests in a battery contain only a few items, and are thus less reliable than tests with more items. Caution is necessary in interpreting scores on subtests, and differences between them have to be correspondingly large before any 'real' differences can be inferred. Further, without information on the temporal stability of a difference, the clinical significance of the findings may be highly questionable.

To date, the diagnostic-prescriptive approach has not proved of much practical value even in such an extensively researched area as that of reading difficulties (Bateman, 1969; Hammill and Wiederholt, 1973). But this approach must be carefully distinguished from one which adapts a criterion-referenced approach to assessment. For example the use of the Portage materials (see Chapters 13, 14 and 17) pinpoints the skills and skill-deficits of individual children (Shearer and Loftin, 1984). Specific programmes are geared to improving each skill, working within a developmental-learning framework. As discussed later in this book (see Chapter 13), the Portage programmes have reasonably good evidence of success with handicapped children. Whether this is a consequence of the diagnostic-prescriptive approach *per se* is an open question.

Testing and assessment

Psychological testing is the application of a set of procedures that enable aspects of performance to be expressed quantitatively. An *assessment* (evaluation is the American equivalent) is a set of statements about an individual and his or her circumstances in relation to some clinical problem. Assessment as a *process* is the bringing together of information from a variety of sources that is relevant to the problem. As Sundberg and Tyler (1962) put it, assessment is the 'systematic collection, organization and interpretation of information about a person and his situations' which may be used for 'the prediction of his behaviour in new situations' (Jones, 1970). Standardized norm-referenced tests may be included as part of the assessment process, but not inevitably.

Considerations of test-score specificity detailed earlier, the sampling limitations of tests and testing and of statistical techniques themselves lead us to differentiate testing and assessment, and to assert that all individual assessments must be multimethod, with IQ and other tests being used if they are relevant to the clinical problem.

The fundamental techniques of clinical assessment, in our view, are not the narrow range of conventional tests but the interview and direct formal and informal observation, a view we share, at least with regard to interviewing, with Korchin and Schuldberg (1981).

The task of quantifying all aspects of behaviour that are relevant to clinical problems, even if tests were available to do so, would be so time-consuming as to be impracticable. The flexibility of interviewing combined with interview techniques that can yield replicable results (Rutter and Brown, 1966) give it an information-producing power that no test or collection of tests on their own can achieve.

Observation is very much more than 'looking at or listening to'. Rather, we use it in the sense of the clinically educated eye and ear, that is, observation guided by a knowledge of psychological theory and research, and the phenomenology of clinical disorders. Both enable us to make and label discriminations that are not made by the untrained observer; they require a conceptual framework for observation and a direction for looking and listening. It is the trained clinician who is alert to the possibility of Down's syndrome or other chromosomal abnormalities when encountering certain physical signs (e.g. epicanthic fold) rather than concluding that the child appears unusual. Parents may be concerned that their child who does not speak is 'backward'. Those who know about the theory and research in language development will probe for alternative modes of communication and comprehension as part of their investigation, their actions being guided by a knowledge of language development and its disorders.

Because a single technique might lead to a technique-specific conclusion, supportive evidence must be sought by other means. IQ data should be consistent with findings from interviews and focused observation before the assessment is crystallized. Major discrepancies between findings using different techniques need to be resolved before any action is taken.

Some practical issues

'Deterioration'

A commonly posed clinical problem with mentally handicapped people is whether cognitive functioning has deteriorated. Like many apparently simple questions, answering requires sophisticated knowledge of test construction and psychometrics.

Let us say that a boy obtained a Full Scale WISC-R IQ of 65 at age nine and a Full Scale IQ of 53 two years later. His 'IQ' has dropped by 12 points over this short period. Does this indicate some deterioration in his cognitive ability? Does it indicate some degenerative neurological condition? Before jumping to conclusions, frightening the parents or demanding expensive EEGs or CT scans, consider what questions need to be asked.

IQs can fluctuate dramatically, so the first question is – is this a *real* change in score? Put more formally, how often is such a change of scores observed in the normal population? The assumption is that if the change is seen in at least 5–10 per cent of the sample, it is unlikely that anything other than random variation is at work. Note that this is a probabilistic statement, and it is possible for a loss of function both to be within normal limits and to be 'caused' by a neurological disorder. Such are the uncertainties operating in the real world.

Other factors have been taken into account. By definition, when working with mentally handicapped individuals, their initial IQ scores will be well below the mean. On average, the expectation from statistical theory is that on retest their scores will regress towards the mean. In practice, they do so less than expected (Silverstein, 1982). Moreover, on retesting on the same test such as the WISC-R, practice effects occur and over the whole range an increase of 4 points in Verbal IQ and 9 points in Performance IQ can be expected (Kaufman, 1979). Thus the sophisticated assessor might argue that, on the grounds of regression and practice, very low scores should increase; therefore a drop of 12 points is even more notable.

However, all this argument forgets that at very low IQ scores at age 9–10 the child is being tested on very few items. Indeed, as reference to the test manual will show, even when the child does not score at all on a particular subtest, the raw score of zero is often transformed into a scaled score considerably above zero. Thus the resulting 'IQ' scarcely reflects the child's performance. Rather, it reflects the test's normative inadequacies. An apparent lowering of IQ score can sometimes mean that the child is performing more adequately on a subtest even though less adequately *in comparison with his or her* peers. Let us illustrate with this concrete example:

TABLE 3.3   Retest scores on WISC-R: a hypothetical example

	First test		*Second test*	
Chronological age	9 years		11 years	
Full Scale IQ	65		53	
Verbal Scale IQ	60		55	
Performance Scale IQ	73		60	
	Scaled score	*Raw score*	*Scaled score*	*Raw score*
Information	3	6	1	6
Similarities	5	6	3	6
Arithmetic	4	6	3	6
Vocabulary	1	0	1	14
Comprehension	5	7	3	7
Picture completion	5	8	3	9
Picture arrangement	6	10	4	10
Block design	6	8	4	9
Object assembly	8	13	5	13
Coding	5	20	3	24

In this case, while it is true that the boy's IQ score was lower at the second testing, none the less there is evidence that on most subtests his scores remained static and on a few he actually increased. In no case did he lose any raw scores. The answer to the simple question – does he show signs of deterioration on the test? – has to be 'no'. He has lost no skills and continues to develop slowly.

Similar problems have to be considered when dealing with older children and adults. The tester must be familiar with the way the test converts the subject's behaviour into abstract scores. Lack of such familiarity leads to inexcusable misinterpretation of data.

The same effect can be seen in longitudinal studies of the cognitive development of mentally handicapped individuals. For example, in both Carr's (1975) and Cunningham and Mittler's (1981) longitudinal studies of infants with Down's syndrome, radically different conclusions can be reached depending on whether IQ or MA is used as the dependent variable. Where IQ is plotted, it appears that children with Down's syndrome 'deteriorate' on this test performance. When MA is plotted, it is immediately apparent that the children are continuing to develop, but at a much slower rate than their normal peers. However, the psychological impact of the scores on parents and teachers is quite different.

Clinical utility

Assessing 'deterioration' is one illustration of the usefulness of IQ tests in clinical practice. There are others of equal relevance.

1. Such tests provide an index of cognitive functioning that has concurrent and prognostic implications.
2. They sample areas of functioning that are easily accessible by other means and, properly used and interpreted, do so in a reliable manner.
3. They enable a discrimination between general and circumscribed strengths and weaknesses, pointing to differential abilities in the individual. Given the high incidence of language disorders in children with mental retardation (Rondal, 1985), this property of IQ tests is of particular value in assessment.
4. Not uncommonly, in our experience, these tests provide the first indication that a person's abilities are being misconstrued. For instance, the child in a mainstream school, referred because of difficult behaviour, who turns out to be less able, or on occasion very much more able, than believed; or the noncommunicating or autistic child who turns out to have good nonverbal skills.
5. Test results, depending on their magnitude, can reduce or increase the number of alternative 'hypotheses' or explanations the clinician needs to invoke in attempting to understand presenting problems.
6. Tests provide a systematic baseline for monitoring aspects of progress, or the lack of it.
7. IQ data facilitate the interpretation of other forms of information, derived from other tests or other sources.
8. The process of testing, particularly for the experienced examiner, provides an opportunity for structured observation that can be useful in providing hypotheses about stylistic aspects of the person's functioning that may be clinically or otherwise relevant (e.g. impulsivity, poor error checking, motor slowness, mild or gross incoordination). Even when the individual produces wrong solutions, the astute examiner may on occasion spot that these are rule-governed rather than random.
9. Cognitive data also need to be collected for research purposes – for use both in *describing* the samples investigated and in matching *groups* and individuals. Problems in the use of intelligence test data in matching samples are discussed by Hogg and Mittler (1980) and cogently illustrated by a recent carefully controlled study undertaken by Hogg and Moss (1983). Two groups of infants, one with Down's syndrome,

the other normal, were matched on MA and other variables. It was then found that, although of equal MA, the two groups achieved the same score by quite different routes. Infants with Down's syndrome failed more of the motor items and fewer of the language items on the Bayley scales.

There are few if any other techniques available to psychologists that serve such a diversity of purposes, with the degree of reliability and economy of IQ tests, and none that has an equivalent empirical data base to guide their interpretation. Ultimately, however, the clinical value of IQ tests depends on the care, knowledge and skill of the test user and her or his ability to relate what is known about tests and testing to the needs of the individual and the purposes of testing.

CONCLUSIONS

In this chapter we have attempted to put forward a view about IQ tests and their use, particularly with regard to their contribution to the assessment of mentally handicapped people. There are many other issues that we have been unable to address (for instance, clinical *v.* statistical prediction), the length of the present chapter having already stretched the tolerance of our editors and no doubt that of readers who have got this far. Nor have we been able to describe some of the newer developments, such as the use of physiological measures that correlate strongly with IQ, or the implications of advances in the study of artificial intelligence.

There is no doubt that IQ tests have been misused, misinterpreted and abused, and that they will continue to be so used, in the hands of some, in the future. But this should not divert us from employing them if such use can be justified with regard to the clinical and other needs of handicapped people and on the basis of adequate empirical evidence.

the intelligence test is one of the major achievements of psychology. It is objective, reliable and valid. Although it is not perfect, can be misused, and does not provide a real definition of intelligence, it is the best working definition that we have of intelligence regarded as a trait. (House, 1977, p. 537)

REFERENCES

AGRAS, W.S., KAZDIN, A.E. and WILSON, G.T. (1979) *Behavior Therapy: Toward an Applied Clinical Science*, San Francisco, Freeman.
AMERICAN PSYCHOLOGICAL ASSOCIATION (1974) APA, American Educational Research Association and National Council on Measurement on Education, *Standard for Educational and Psychological Tests*, Washington, DC, American Psychological Association.
ANASTASI, A. (1982) *Psychological Testing*, 5th edn, New York, Macmillan.

ANGOFF, W.H. (1971) 'Scales, norms and equivalent scores', in R.L. THORNDIKE (ed.), *Educational Measurement*, 2nd edn, Washington, DC, American Council on Education.

BANDURA, A. (1977) *Social Learning Theory*, Englewood Cliffs, NJ, Prentice-Hall.

BARKLEY, R.A. (1981) 'Hyperactivity', in E.J. MASH and L.G. TERDAL (eds), *Behavioral Assessment of Childhood Disorders*, New York, Guilford Press.

BARRETT, R.P. and BREUNING, S.E. (1983) 'Assessing intelligence', in J.L. MATSON and S.E. BREUNING (eds), *Assessing the Mentally Retarded*, New York, Grune & Stratton, 87–114.

BATEMAN, B. (1969) 'Reading, a controversial view: research and rationale', in L.TARNOPOL (ed.), *Learning Disabilities: Introduction to Educational and Medical Management*, Springfield, Ill., C.C. Thomas.

BAYLEY, N. (1969) *Bayley Scales of Infant Development: Birth to Two Years*, New York, Psychological Corporation.

BECK, S. (1983) 'Overview of methods', in J.L. MATSON and S.E. BREUNING (eds), *Assessing the Mentally Retarded*, New York, Grune & Stratton, 2–26.

BERGER, M. (1977) 'Psychological testing', in M. RUTTER and L. HERSOV (eds), *Child Psychiatry: Modern Approaches*, Oxford, Blackwell, 306–33.

BERGER, M. (1982) 'The scientific approach to intelligence: an overview of its history with special reference to mental speed', in H.J. EYSENCK (ed.), *A Model for Intelligence*, Berlin, Springer-Verlag.

BERGER, M. (1984) 'Psychological assessment and testing', in M. RUTTER and L. HERSOV (eds), *Child and Adolescent Psychiatry: Modern Approaches*, 2nd edn, Oxford, Blackwell.

BERGER, M. and YULE, W. (1972) 'Cognitive assessment in young children with language delay', in M. RUTTER and J.A.M. MARTIN (eds), *The Child with Delayed Speech*, London, Heinemann Medical.

BINET, A. and SIMON, T. (1905) 'Méthodes nouvelles pour le diagnostic du niveau intellectuel des anormaux', *L'Ann. Psychol.*, 11, 191–244.

BORING, E.G. (1957) *A History of Experimental Psychology*, New York, Appleton-Century-Crofts.

BRIM, O.G. and KAGAN, J. (eds) (1980) *Constancy and Change in Human Development*, Cambridge, Mass., Harvard University Press.

BROOKS, P.K. and BAUMEISTER, A.A. (1979) 'A plea for consideration of ecological validity in the experimental psychology of mental retardation', *Amer. J. Ment. Defic.*, 81, 407–16.

BROWN, G. and DESFORGES, C. (1977) 'Piagetian psychology and education: time for revision', *Brit. J. Educ. Psychol.*, 47, 7–17.

CARR, J. (1975) *Young Children with Down's Syndrome*, London, Butterworth.

CATTELL, R.B. (1971) *Abilities: Their Structure, Growth and Action*, Boston, Mass., Houghton-Mifflin.

CLARKE, A.D.B. and CLARKE, A.M. (1974) 'The changing concept of intelligence: a selective historical review', in A.M. CLARKE and A.D.B. CLARKE (eds), *Mental Deficiency: The Changing Outlook*, 3rd edn, London, Methuen.

CLARKE, A.D.B. and CLARKE, A.M. (1984) 'Consistency and change in the growth of human characteristics', *J. Child Psychol. Psychiat.*, 25, 191–210.

CLARKE, A.D.B., CLARKE, A.M. and REIMAN, S. (1958) 'Cognitive and social changes in the feebleminded – three further studies', *Brit. J. Psychol.*, 49, 144–57.

CLAUSEN, J. (1966), *Ability Structure and Subgroups in Mental Retardation*, London, Macmillan.

CRONBACH, L.J. (1970) *Essentials of Psychological Testing*, 3rd edn, New York, Harper & Row.

CRONBACH, L.J. (1971) 'Test validation', in R.L. THORNDIKE (ed.), *Educational Measurement*, 2nd edn, Washington, DC, American Council on Education.

CRONBACH, L.J., GLESER, G.C., NANDA, H. and RAJARATNAM, N. (1972) *The Dependability of Behavioral Measurements*, New York, Wiley.

CUNNINGHAM, C.C. and MITTLER, P. (1981) 'Maturation, development and mental handicap', in K. CONNOLLY and H.V. PRECHTL (eds), *Maturation and Development: Biological and Psychological Properties*, London, Heinemann Medical.

DE VRIES, R. (1974) 'Relationships among Piagetian, IQ and achievement assessments', *Child Develop.*, 45, 746–56.

DUDEK, F.J. (1979) 'The continuing misinterpretation of the standard error of measurement', *Psychol. Bull.*, 86, 335–7.

ELLIOTT, C., MURRAY, D.J. and PEARSON, L.S. (1983) *The British Ability Scales*, new edn, Windsor, NFER/Nelson.

EYSENCK, H.J. (1967) 'Intelligence assessment: a theoretical and experimental approach', *Brit. J. Educ. Psychol.*, 37, 81–98.

EYSENCK, H.J. (ed.) (1973) *The Measurement of Intelligence*, Lancaster, MTP Press.

FIELD, J.G. (1960) 'Two types of table for use with Wechsler's intelligence scales', *J. Clin. Psychol.*, 16, 3–7.

FISHER, M.A. and ZEAMAN, D. (1970) 'Growth and decline of retarded intelligence', in N.R. ELLIS (ed.), *International Review of Research in Mental Retardation* vol. 4, London, Academic Press.

FRANK, G. (1984) *The Wechsler Enterprise*, New York, Pergamon Press.

FREEMAN, F.N. (1939) *Mental Tests: Their History, Principles and Applications*, New York, Harrap.

FURNEAUX, W.D. (1961) 'Intellectual abilities and problem-solving behaviour', in H.J. EYSENCK (ed.), *Handbook of Abnormal Psychology*, New York, Basic Books.

GARCIA, J. (1981) 'The logic and limits of mental aptitude testing', *Amer. Psychol.*, 36, 1172–80.

GOODMAN, J.F. and CAMERON, J. (1978) 'The measuring of IQ constancy in young retarded children', *J. Genet. Psychol.*, 132, 109–19.

GREEN, B.F. (1981) 'A primer of testing', *Amer. Psychol.*, 36, 1001–11.

GRIFFITHS, R. (1954) *The Abilities of Babies*, London, University of London Press.

GUILFORD, J.P. (1967) *The Nature of Human Intelligence*, New York, McGraw-Hill.

GULLIKSEN, H. (1950) *Theory of Mental Tests*, New York, Wiley.

HAGEN, J.W., BARCLAY, C.R. and SCHWETHELM, B. (1982) 'Cognitive development of the learning-disabled child', in N.R. ELLIS (ed.), *International Review of Research in Mental Retardation*, vol. 11, New York, Academic Press.

HAMMILL, D.A. and WIEDERHOLT, J.L. (1973) 'Reviews of the Frostig Visual Perception Test and the related training program', in L. MANN and D. SABATINO (eds), *The First Review of Special Education*, Philadelphia, Buttonwood Farms.

HEARNSHAW, L.S. (1979) *Cyril Burt: Psychologist*, London, Hodder & Stoughton.

HERBERT, M. (1964) 'The concept and testing of brain damage in children: a review', *J. Child Psychol. Psychiat.*, 5, 197–216.

HILLIER, J. and YULE, W. (1978) 'Object permanence as a prerequisite for language acquisition through operant training in severely mentally handicapped children', unpublished study, London, Institute of Psychiatry.

HINDLEY, C.B. and OWEN, C.F. (1978) 'The extent of individual changes in IQ for ages between 6 months and 17 years, in a British longitudinal sample', *J. Child Psychol. Psychiat.*, 19, 329–50.

HOGG, J. and MITTLER, P.J. (1980) 'Recent research in mental handicap: issues and perspectives', in J. HOGG and P.J. MITTLER (eds), *Advances in Mental Handicap Research*, vol. 1, Chichester, Wiley.

HOGG, J. and MOSS, H.A. (1983) 'Prehensile development in Down's syndrome and non-handicapped preschool children', *Brit. J. Develop. Psychol.*, 1, 189–204.

HOUSE, B.J. (1977) 'Scientific explanation and ecological validity: a reply to Brooks and Baumeister', *Amer. J. Ment. Defic.*, 81, 534–42.

ILLINGWORTH, R.S. (1971) 'The predictive value of developmental assessment in infancy', *Develop. Med. Child Neurol.*, 13, 721–5.

JENSEN, A.R. (1969) 'How much can we boost IQ and scholastic achievement?', *Harvard Educ. Rev.*, 39, 1–123.

JENSEN, A.R. (1980) *Bias in Mental Testing*, London, Methuen.

JOHNSON, S.M. and BOLSTAD, O.D. (1973) 'Methodological issues in naturalistic observation: some problems and solutions for field research', in L.A. HAMERLYNCK, L.C. HANDY and E.J. MASH (eds), *Behavior Change: Methodology, Concepts and Practice*, Champaign, Ill., Research Press.

JONES, H.G. (1970) 'Principles of psychological assessment', in P. MITTLER (ed.), *Psychological Assessment of Mental and Physical Handicaps*, London, Methuen.

KAGAN, J. (1980) 'Perspectives on continuity', in O.G. BRIM and J. KAGAN (eds), *Constancy and Change in Human Development*, Cambridge, Mass., Harvard University Press.

KAHN, J.V. (1975) 'Relationship of Piaget's sensorimotor period to language acquisition of profoundly retarded children', *Amer. J. Ment. Defic.*, 79, 640–3.

KAHN, J.V. (1983) 'Sensorimotor period and adaptive behavior development of severely and profoundly mentally retarded children', *Amer. J. Ment. Defic.*, 88, 69–75.

KAMIN, J. (1977) *The Science and Politics of IQ*, Harmondsworth, Penguin.

KAUFMAN, A.S. (1972) 'Restriction of range: questions and answers', *Test Service Bulletin*, no. 59, New York, Psychological Corporation.

KAUFMAN, A.S. (1979) *Intelligent Testing with the WISC-R*, New York, Wiley.

KAUFMAN, A.S. and REYNOLDS, C.R. (1983) 'Clinical evaluation of intellectual functioning', in I.B. WEINER (ed.), *Clinical Methods in Psychology*, New York, Wiley.

KNOBLOCH, H. and PASAMANICK, B. (1974) *Gesell and Amatruda's Developmental Diagnosis: The Evaluation and Management of Normal and Abnormal Neuropsychologic Development in Infancy and Early Childhood*, 3rd edn, Hagerstown, Md, Harper & Row.

KORCHIN, S.J. and SCHULDBERG, D. (1981) 'The future of clinical assessment', *Amer. Psychol.*, 36, 1147–58.

LORD, F.M. and NOVICK, M.R. (1968) *Statistical Theories of Mental Test Services*, Reading, Mass., Addison-Wesley.

LUMSDEN, J. (1976) 'Test theory', *Ann. Rev. Psychol.*, 27, 251–80.

MCCALL, R.B. (1979) 'Qualitative transitions in behavioral development in the first two years of life', in M.H. BORNSTEIN and W. KOSSAR (eds), *Psychological Development from Infancy: Image to Intention*, Hillsdale, NJ, LEA.

MCCARTHY, D.A. (1972) *Manual for the McCarthy Scales of Children's Abilities*, New York, Psychological Corporation.

MADGE, N. and TIZARD, J. (1980) 'Intelligence', in M. RUTTER (ed.), *Scientific Foundations of Developmental Psychiatry*, London, Heinemann Medical.

MILLER, C.K. and CHANSKY, N.M. (1972) 'Psychologists' scoring of WISC protocols', *Psychol. in the Schools*, 9, 144–52.

NAY, W.R. (1979) *Multimethod Clinical Assessment*, New York, Gardner Press.

NEEDHAM, J. (1970) *Clerks and Craftsmen in China and the West*, Cambridge, Cambridge University Press.

NOVICK, M.R. (1966) 'The axioms and principal results of classical test theory', *J. Math. Psychol.*, 3, 1–18.

PAYNE, R.W. and JONES, H.G. (1957) 'Statistics for the investigation of individual cases', *J. Clin. Psychol.*, 13, 115–21.

PLOMIN, R. (1983) 'Developmental behavioral genetics', *Child Develop.*, 54, 253–9.

RONDAL, J.A. (1985) 'Language development and mental retardation', in W. YULE, M. RUTTER and M. BAX (eds), *Language Development and Communication Problems in the Handicapped*, London, Spastics International Medical Publications.

RUTTER, M. and BROWN, G. (1966) 'The reliability and validity of measures of family life and relationships in families containing a psychiatric patient', *Soc. Psychiat.*, 1, 38–53.

RUTTER, M., GRAHAM, P. and YULE, W. (1970) *A Neuropsychiatric Study in Childhood*, London, Heinemann Medical.

RUTTER, M., TIZARD, J. and WHITMORE, K. (eds) (1970) *Education, Health and Behaviour*, Harlow, Longman.

RUTTER, M. and YULE, W. (1975) 'The concept of specific reading retardation', *J. Child Psychol. Psychiat.*, 16, 181–97.

SARASON, S.B. and DORIS, J. (1969) *Psychological Problems in Mental Deficiency*, 4th edn, New York, Harper & Row.

SATTLER, J.M. (1982) *Assessment of Children's Intelligence and Special Abilities*, 2nd edn, Boston, Mass., Allyn & Bacon.

SCARR, S. (1981) 'Testing *for* children: assessment and the many determinants of intellectual competence', *Amer. Psychol.*, 36, 1159–66.

SCHLOTTMAN, R.S. and ANDERSON, V.M. (1982) 'Developmental changes of institutionalized mentally retarded children: a semi-longitudinal study', *Amer. J. Ment. Defic.*, 87, 277–81.

SHAPIRO, M.B. (1957) 'Experimental method in the psychological description of the individual psychiatric patient', *Internat. J. Soc. Psychiat.*, 3, 89–103.

SHAPIRO, M.B. (1962) 'Clinical approach to fundamental research with specific reference to the single case', in P. SAINSBURY and N. KREITMAN (eds), *Basic Research Techniques in Psychiatry*, Oxford, Oxford University Press.

SHAPIRO, M.B. (1970) 'Intensive assessment of the single-case: an inductive-deductive approach', in P. MITTLER (ed.), *The Psychological Assessment of Mental and Physical Handicaps*, London, Methuen.

SHEARER, D.E. and LOFTIN, C.R. (1984) 'The Portage Project: teaching parents to teach their pre-school children in the home', in R.F. DANGEL and R.A. POLSTER (eds), *Parent Training: Foundations of Research and Practice*, New York, Guilford Press, 93–126.

SILVERSTEIN, A.B. (1970) 'The measurement of intelligence', in N.R. ELLIS (ed.), *International Review of Mental Retardation*, vol. 4, London, Academic Press.

SILVERSTEIN, A.B. (1981) 'Reliability and abnormality of test score differences', *J. Clin. Psychol.*, 37, 392–9.

SILVERSTEIN, A.B. (1982) 'Note on the constancy of the IQ', *Amer. J. Ment. Defic.*, 87, 227–8.

SILVERSTEIN, A.B., PEARSONS, L.B., COLBERT, B.A., CORDEIRO, W.J., MARVIN, J.L. and NAKAJI, H.J. (1982) 'Cognitive development of severely and profoundly mentally retarded individuals', *Amer. J. Ment. Defic.*, 87, 347–50.

SPEARMAN, C.E. (1904a) 'The proof and measurement of association between two things', *Amer. J. Psychol.*, 15, 72–101.

SPEARMAN, C.E. (1904b) "General intelligence" objectively determined and measured', *Amer. J. Psychol.*, 15, 201–93.

SPEARMAN, C.E. (1927) *The Abilities of Man*, London, Macmillan.

SUNDBERG, N.D. and TYLER, L.E. (1962) *Clinical Psychology*, New York, Appleton-Century-Crofts.

SUTHERLAND, G. (1984) *Ability, Merit and Measurement*, London, Oxford University Press.

TEW, B.J. and LAURENCE, K.M. (1983) 'The relationship between spina bifida children's intelligence test scores on school entry and at school leaving: a preliminary report', *Child: Care, Health, Dev.*, 9, 13–17.

THORNDIKE, E.L., BREGMAN, E.O., COBB, M.V. and WOODWARD, E. (1927) *The Measurement of Intelligence*, New York, Teachers College of Columbia University.

THURSTONE, L.L. (1938) 'Primary Mental Abilities', *Psychomet. Monogr.*, 1.

UZGIRIS, I.C. and HUNT, J.M.V. (1975) *Assessment in Infancy: Ordinal Scales of Psychological Development*, Urbana, Ill., University of Illinois Press.

VAHTER, M. (ed.) (1982) *Assessment of Human Exposure to Lead and Cadmium through Biological Monitoring*, Stockholm, National Institute of Environmental Medicine and Karlinska Institute.

VERNON, P.E. (1979) *Intelligence, Heredity and Environment*, San Francisco, Freeman.

WADDINGTON, L.M. (1977) *Tools for Thought*, London, Paladin.

WILSON, R.S. (1983) 'The Louisville Twin Study: developmental synchronies in behavior', *Child Develop.* 54, 298–316.

WISEMAN, S. (1967) *Intelligence and Ability: Selected Readings*, Harmondsworth, Penguin.

WOLF, T.M. (1973) *Alfred Binet*, Chicago, University of Chicago Press.

WOODWARD, M. (1963) 'The application of Piaget's theory to research in mental deficiency', in N. ELLIS (ed.), *Handbook of Mental Deficiency*, New York, McGraw-Hill.

YULE, W., GOLD, R.D. and BUSCH, C. (1982) 'Long-term prediction validity of the WPPSI: an eleven-year follow-up study', *Person. Indiv. Diff.*, 3, 65–71.

YULE, W., LANSDOWN, R. and URBANOWICZ, M.A. (1982) 'Predicting educational attainment from WISC-R in a primary school sample', *Brit. J. Clin. Psychol.*, 21, 43–6.

YULE, W. and RUTTER, M. (1984) 'Reading and other learning disabilities', in M. RUTTER and L. HERSOV (eds), *Child and Adolescent Psychiatry: Modern Approaches*, 2nd edn, Oxford, Blackwell.

YULE, W. and RUTTER, M. (1985) 'Effect of lead on children's behaviour and cognitive performance: a review', in K.R. MAHAFFEY (ed.), *Dietary and Environmental Lead, Human Health Effects*, Amsterdam, Elsevier.

PART TWO

Characteristics, causes
and distribution

4
Physical determinants of environmental origin
Joseph M. Berg

INTRODUCTION

The distinction between environmentally and genetically determined varieties of mental retardation is not always as clear-cut as might appear at first sight. The time frame of reference can be relevant to such a distinction, for example when genetically determined maternal hyperphenylalaninaemia constitutes an environmental hazard to the fetus (see page 106) and when irradiation results in harmful gene mutation. In addition, the individual's genetic constitution may significantly affect the response to, and the outcome of, a deleterious environmental event, and environmental influences and interventions, be they medical, psychosocial or educational, can substantially modify the effects of genetic adversity and thus have an impact on the mental status attained. Bearing such considerations in mind, it is nevertheless useful to try to distinguish between forms of mental retardation which are primarily of environmental or of genetical origin, most particularly because such differentiation can have important preventive implications.

The present chapter is concerned with environmental hazards of essentially physical kinds (in contrast to psychosocial ones, considered comprehensively in Chapter 7) which have been firmly established, or postulated, as causal factors in the production of mental deficit. There has been extensive documentation and speculation about a wide array of such actual or supposed factors operating before, during or after birth. A detailed account of each of these is well beyond the bounds of a single chapter. It is hoped, however, that the overview presented, with illustrative examples, provides a reasonable indication of the substantial progress achieved in the elucidation of environ-awaiting resolution in this sphere. (See Chapters 5 and 9 for further comments.)

PRENATAL HAZARDS

A vast literature has accumulated on deleterious influences on the fetus which can demonstrably or hypothetically lead to miscarriage, stillbirth or abnormality in the live-born child. Propositions on the subject have existed since antiquity and indicate something of the seemingly boundless flights of fancy which the human imagination can undertake. Thus, for example, wrathful visitations by both godly and devilish beings of extraterrestrial origin and by their minions on earth have been invoked to explain deviations from normality, and aetiological significance has been attributed to sights witnessed by parents-to-be or to thoughts harboured by them. Though some such ideas persist in certain quarters, increased understanding of fetal development combined with more rational scientific enquiry have largely separated myth from reality, and many of the environmental factors which produce fetal damage and subsequent disability have been elucidated to a considerable extent. A wide variety of these factors, operating during intrauterine life, are exemplified below in relation to their roles as known or suspected causes of mental deficit in survivors.

Congenital syphilis

Infection of the fetus by the spirochaete *Treponema pallidum*, transmitted by the mother and resulting in congenital syphilis, is a very long-known example of a prenatal hazard to mental development (Berg and Kirman, 1959). It may be of historic interest to mention here that the disease acquired its name, in the sixteenth century, from that of a legendary shepherd called Syphilus, who is said to have been stricken with it by Apollo as punishment for disobedience (Nabarro, 1954).

With the establishment of the therapeutic efficacy of penicillin, the incidence of congenital syphilis has fallen dramatically. Budell (1984) indicated that reported cases in the United States declined from 17,600 in 1941 to only 331 in 1979. This trend is reflected in aetiological surveys of mentally retarded populations born in the earlier part of this century compared to those born in more recent years. Sizeable numbers of congenital syphilitics are common in the former groups, with substantially fewer or even none in the latter.

Manifestations in infected children are protean because many tissues can be affected. The central nervous system is frequently involved, though clinical signs may not be apparent. Those that are include mental retardation, behaviour disturbances, seizures, functional limb abnormalities and visual and hearing impairments. Presence of the classic triad of manifestations (peg-shaped, notched incisors, interstitial keratitis and labyrinthine disease with deafness), described over a century ago by Sir Jonathan Hutchinson, a relative of one of the editors of this book (A.M.C.), is practically proof of the infection. A recent informative review of manifestations following central nervous system involvement was provided by Wiggelinkhuizen and Mason (1980).

Congenital rubella

Rubella in early pregnancy was first shown by Gregg (1941) to be a cause of congenital abnormalities in the offspring of infected mothers, and a large number of reports on the subject have been published since then. In contrast to postnatal infection, which is usually asymptomatic or mild, effects on the fetus of maternal infection, especially but not only in the earlier stages of the first trimester, are often devastating. Death in utero or soon after birth can occur and, among survivors, many tissues can be affected (Krugman and Katz, 1981). In addition to cerebral involvement with consequent mental retardation of different degrees, other effects which could significantly hamper developmental progress include cataracts, deafness and congenital cardiac anomalies. An instructive study of the consequences of confirmed maternal rubella at successive stages of pregnancy was published by Miller *et al.* (1982).

Instances of congenital rubella have been fairly common in most aetiological surveys of mentally retarded populations undertaken since Gregg's observations were published. However, the development of effective rubella vaccines and their widespread application can be expected to significantly reduce, if not yet entirely eliminate, the occurrence of such cases.

Congenital cytomegalovirus infection

Because of its relative frequency, ranging from about 0.5 to 2.5 per cent in screened infants in various parts of the world (Hanshaw, 1983), congenital cytomegalovirus infection is now almost certainly an even greater potential viral hazard to the fetus than that due to rubella. Stagno *et al.* (1983) estimated that in the United States alone at least about 2700, and perhaps as many as 7600, infants currently born each year are at risk for developmental abnormalities caused by congenital cytomegalovirus infection. A minority of congenitally infected individuals show, in infancy, distinct evidence of disease, including cerebral involvement in the form of, for instance, microcephaly, periventricular calcification and psychomotor delay. Though about 90 per cent are symptom-free at birth (Peckham *et al.*, 1983), there is evidence that more subtle mental impairment in later childhood can be a consequence of the original infection (Reynolds *et al.*, 1974; Hanshaw *et al.*, 1976). With the ability to recognize clinically asymptomatic infected infants by means of serological and other laboratory tests, further careful psychological follow-up studies, in comparison with suitably matched uninfected controls of like socio-economic status, should help to clarify the as yet uncertain extent and prevalence of mental delay and related handicaps (such as visual and hearing impairment) due to this infection. Hanshaw (1983) stated that no specific therapy for congenital cytomegalovirus infection has been shown to be clearly helpful and, indeed, that certain antiviral drugs may actually be harmful in terms of effects related to bone marrow depression. Effective vaccination is a prospect for the future, though it appears uncertain whether live cytomegalovirus vaccines produced to date can prevent congenital infection (Editorial, *Lancet*, 1983).

Congenital toxoplasmosis

The protozoon parasite, *Toxoplasma gondii*, is now a well-established cause of prenatally determined disability. About 3300 (that is, about one per 1000) infants born annually in the United States in recent years are said to have been congenitally affected (Remington and Desmonts, 1983). The infection may occur at different stages of pregnancy and with variable consequences. Characteristic signs in an affected infant are chorioretinitis, hydrocephaly or microcephaly, and intracranial calcification (Couvrier and Desmonts, 1962). However, these features are not necessarily present and most congenitally affected babies are asymptomatic at birth, though subsequently intellectual deficit and various sensory and neurological abnormalities may develop. In a series of 24 children with subclinical infection neonatally, who were followed-up to mean age of $8\frac{1}{2}$ years, low IQ scores were common and substantially reduced (IQ below 65) in several instances (Wilson *et al.*, 1980); a disturbing feature was a downward IQ trend in 6 of 7 children tested more than once, with the mean falling from 97 to 74 over an average of $5\frac{1}{2}$ years. The extensive cerebral pathology which underlies substantial mental and neurological sequelae in congenital toxoplasmosis was recently reviewed comprehensively by Weber (1983) on the basis of an analysis of 9 personal cases and 61 from the literature of affected individuals who died between birth and 9 years of age.

Irradiation

Man-made radiation has become an increasingly ubiquitous hazard as the twentieth century has advanced. In addition to its potential, before conception, to produce harmful gene mutations and perhaps certain chromosomal aberrations, its direct effect on the developing embryo and fetus in utero is well established from both human and animal investigations (Kriegel *et al.*, 1982). Early observations on the effects of X-ray irradiation during pregnancy include those of Zappert (1926) and Murphy (1929). A couple of decades later, such findings were supplemented by those from a less benignly motivated source of irradiation – the atomic bomb explosions in Hiroshima (Plummer, 1952) and Nagasaki (Yamazaki *et al.*, 1954).

The consequences of prenatal irradiation depend largely on time of exposure and dosage, and include both nonviable and viable pregnancy outcomes (Brent, 1980). Among characteristic manifestations in live-born children are mental retardation, microcephaly and ophthalmological defects such as microphthalmia. Radiation procedures for diagnostic and therapeutic purpose are widely, and usually appropriately, undertaken in clinical practice. For both the protection and the peace of mind of pregnant women or those contemplating a pregnancy, competent advice should be available to them regarding the safety or otherwise of any such procedures.

Prenatal malnutrition

As with postnatal malnutrition, discussed on page 119, many associated variables and confounding influences are a daunting consideration in attempting to assess the precise effects, particularly long-term mental effects, of prenatal nutritional deficiency. In addition to methodological concerns considered in Chapter 1, it is likely that the child of a mother undernourished during pregnancy will continue to be exposed to postnatal undernutrition also, thus making it very difficult to distinguish between later effects of each. Furthermore, the fetus of a malnourished mother may very well be at increased risk for concomitant noxious prenatal influences, such as alcohol, drugs and infections, each of which can contribute to adverse postnatal outcome.

Formidable as these and related problems may be in interpreting the effects of prenatal maternal malnutrition, many publications have attested to adverse physical and mental consequences of such undernutrition (Shanklin and Hodin, 1979). An important encouraging note in what is otherwise largely a catalogue of disturbance and disability emerged from the methodologically careful and scholarly study by Stein *et al.* (1975) of the effects of the Second World War famine in Holland consequent on the Nazi occupation of that country. Despite many adverse early results of the famine, a follow-up study of a large sample of young adult male survivors at military induction showed no effects on mental performance of the prenatal exposure to famine. Furthermore, an analysis of the prevalence of both mild and severe mental retardation showed no famine effect either. The authors appropriately pointed out that these findings on poor *prenatal* nutrition in an *industrial* society did not exclude the possibility of adverse mental effects from the combined influences of poor pre- and postnatal nutrition, especially in pre-industrial societies.

Apart from general nutritional inadequacy, lack of specific dietary ingredients is either firmly or possibly linked with distinct deleterious consequences. Iodine deficiency is a long-known example, particularly in relation to endemic goitre and cretinism (Stanbury and Hetzel, 1980). Despite the availability of relatively simple and effective eradication measures, iodine deficiency remains remarkably common in various countries. Disorders connected with such deficiency, of both prenatal and postnatal origin, include significant and often severe impairments of mental function (Hetzel, 1983). Considerable experimental animal evidence is also available of harmful effects on the fetus, including skull and central nervous system abnormalities, of maternal dietary deficiency of manganese, zinc and copper (Hurley, 1981). In general, however, as Hurley's comprehensive review indicates, possible adverse physical or mental consequences in human offspring of such deficiencies do not appear to have been extensively or conclusively explored. A comparatively recent example of specific dietary deficit which may be related to cerebral development is the possibility that relatively small deficiencies of one or more vitamins may contribute to the causation of neural tube defects (Smithells, 1980), with the prospect therefore that maternal vitamin supplementation could reduce the risk of occurrence or recurrence of these defects. Smithells *et al.* (1981, 1983) have published strong presumptive evidence of the protective effect of periconceptual multivitamin supplementation against neural tube defect recurrences in mothers with a previous history of affected births.

Effects of alcohol

Views that parental alcohol consumption could be disadvantageous to the unborn child date back to ancient times and include, Abel (1983) points out, perceptions in this regard by both Plato and Aristotle. Present-day observations on the subject are probably best exemplified in reports of what has become known as the fetal alcohol syndrome. Since the introduction of that term by Jones and Smith (1973), and the descriptions by them and others at about that time, many hundreds of human and animal studies have been published on the increased likelihood of intrauterine death and on the effects in live-born offspring resulting from alcohol intake by the mother during pregnancy. Readers are referred to comprehensive and instructive recent accounts of the issues and evidence provided by Abel (1983) and in the proceedings of an important Ciba Foundation symposium (Porter *et al.*, 1984).

A major finding in the fetal alcohol syndrome, or alcohol embryopathy as Majewski (1981) preferred to call it, is mental deficit of different degrees, associated with a characteristic, though variable, pattern of physical abnormalities which include growth reduction, craniofacial anomalies and cardiac defects. There is an association between decreased intellectual performance and increased severity of physical manifestations (Streissguth *et al.*, 1980). However, mental impairments and behavioural disturbances, particularly mild ones, can occur in the absence of distinct physical peculiarities. It seems probable, at least in some instances, that this could be due to associated psychosocial disadvantage in an alcoholic household rather than to the alcoholism as such.

There appears to be a definite relationship between the amount and time of maternal alcohol consumption and subsequent pregnancy outcome and manifestations in the live-born child, with some controversy as to what quantity consumed, and when, may be innocuous. It is understandable in these circumstances that many advocate total abstinence during pregnancy, though care must be taken in that case to do so in a thoughtful and sensitive manner. The present writer had occasion to counsel a pregnant woman who had been advised that her consumption of a small glass of wine on a couple of social occasions during the first, and early part of the second, trimester could well have seriously harmed her unborn baby; her consequent agitation and anxiety led her seriously to contemplate pregnancy termination. An interesting demonstration project concerning alcohol consumption during pregnancy was undertaken in a metropolitan United States community (Little *et al.*, 1984). It included public and professional education, an information and crisis telephone line, screening for alcohol problems in selected prenatal clinics, and treatment and support for women concerned about their drinking during pregnancy. The considerable effectiveness of the programme should be a stimulus for setting up similar endeavours in other communities.

The mechanisms of the action of alcohol on the fetus are not well understood (Henderson *et al.*, 1981) and, indeed, there may well be several mechanisms originating at different stages of antenatal development with each producing effects of different severity, ranging from early spontaneous abortion to ill-defined behavioural problems and general growth deficit (Pratt, 1984). As with many other demonstrable associations between a specific noxious substance and subsequently recognized mental and/or behavioural defects, the possible roles of related environmental variables (for example, concomitant nutritional or other chemical intake status), as well as of genetically determined susceptibility, need further exploration.

Effects of tobacco

Notions about possible harmful effects on the fetus of maternal smoking predate current widespread interest in the subject by several hundred years. Early in the seventeenth century, Francis Bacon equated tobacco with alcohol, in this respect, with the observation that each 'endangereth the childe to become lunaticke, or of imperfect memory' (Abel, 1983). More data-based concerns are of relatively recent origin. There is now general agreement that, whatever the mechanism may be, maternal smoking during pregnancy is associated with reduction of birth weight – on average, Johnston (1981) states, by 170–200 grams, with approximately twice as many babies, compared to those of nonsmoking mothers, weighing less than 2500 grams. Rather less clear is the precise link of smoking with such variables as length of gestation, pre- and perinatal mortality and congenital anomalies, and even more uncertain is the issue of whether smoking mothers are more prone than nonsmoking ones to have children with mental impairments.

Butler and Goldstein (1973) reported between 3 and 5 months' retardation in reading, mathematics and general ability among 7- and 11-year-old children of mothers who smoked 10 or more cigarettes per day after the fourth month of pregnancy, in comparison with the children of nonsmoking mothers; the discrepancies existed after allowing for possible influences of several socio-biological factors. Dunn *et al.* (1977) also found slightly less satisfactory intellectual maturation by the age of about $6\frac{1}{2}$ years in children of mothers who smoked during pregnancy compared to children of nonsmoking mothers, and felt that this could not be entirely explained by social status differences between the two groups. Though these investigations gave attention to the possible role of associated influences in determining the results, the crucial question remains as to whether such relatively subtle long-term psychological effects as those noted are a consequence of the smoking or of other undifferentiated characteristics of the smoker and her milieu.

Maternal phenylketonuria and hyperphenylalaninaemia

This circumstance is a striking example, referred to in the Introduction, of a genetically determined disorder constituting an environmental hazard to an unborn child of an affected mother. Phenylketonuria, originally described by Fölling (1934), is an autosomal recessive metabolic disease, with a number of variants, in which treatment with a reduced-phenylalanine diet has enabled some affected individuals to reach adulthood with substantially enhanced mental competence compared to what would otherwise have been likely in most of them. Among these are women with raised phenylalanine levels who have become pregnant, with a very high probability of giving birth to children with microcephaly and mental retardation, many of whom also have congenital heart defects (Lenke and Levy, 1980; Levy and Waisbren, 1983). Though the precise cause of these effects is not clear, their extent is positively correlated with increasing levels of maternal phenylalaninaemia. This had led to the prophylactic use of phenylalanine-free or -low diets for phenylketonuric women already pregnant or preferably before conception. Though it is difficult to institute and maintain this literally rather unpalatable measure (O'Connor and Mulcahy, 1984), there seems little doubt about its potential advantage.

Other adverse prenatal influences

As exemplified in this section, many other prenatal occurrences or circumstances have been implicated or postulated from time to time as environmental causes of mental deficit.

A considerable number of infections, in addition to the extensively documented ones reviewed above, can be transmitted to the fetus but few of these have been convincingly shown to cause mental retardation. Maternal Asian influenza had been noted by Coffey and Jessop (1959, 1963) to be associated with an increased incidence of central nervous system abnormalities in offspring, but Doll *et al.* (1960) did not find such an association. On rare occasions, herpes simplex virus, either type 1 (Florman *et al.*, 1972) or type 2 (South *et al.*, 1969), may infect the fetus in utero, rather than the infant at or after birth as indicated on page 116, and result in intracranial calcification and other cerebral pathology with mental defect in survivors. Occasionally, too, convulsions and psychomotor retardation have been reported as a result of intrauterine varicella-zoster virus infection (Dudgeon, 1976). Bacteria can also infect the fetus prenatally, as well as perinatally, as a result of amniotic fluid infection. Cerebral damage may thus ensue with consequent psychomotor and sensory impairments; however, the mechanism by which the brain is damaged and whether this happens before or after birth is uncertain (Naeye, 1981).

Malaria, like the other parasitic infection discussed earlier (toxoplasmosis), can be transmitted to the fetus and was found by Archibald (1958) and more recently by Macgregor and Avery (1974) to be associated with a reduction in birth weight, but no specific long-term follow-up data appear to be available. Even though more than 150 million persons are said currently to be infected with malaria (Quinn *et al.*, 1982), it is perhaps not surprising that little consideration has been given to the question of postnatal consequences of prenatal exposure. In regions where malaria is still widespread, a multitude of additional environmental torments could well make it unrealistic to attempt to distinguish the precise mental effects of each and, indeed, devoting scarce available resources to reduce the hazards seems a much more important undertaking.

Congenital infections with other parasites have also been identified, particularly in tropical countries (Reinhardt, 1980). Examples are the trypanosomes *T. cruzi* (Chagas' disease) and *T. brucei gambiense* and *rhodesiense* (African trypanosomiasis). Considering the frequency of such conditions in various parts of the world, relatively little data have been published on fetal effects, and even less on long-term consequences in live-born children, some of which may well have a bearing on delayed mental development. Establishing mental effects specifically due to any of these parasitic infections is complicated by the multiple other adversities often prevailing in the environments in which the infections are rife.

Concerns about drugs and other chemicals possibly being teratogenic were greatly increased as a result of the tragic consequences to the unborn child, particularly involving limb defects, following maternal exposure to thalidomide (Leck and Millar, 1962). Many observations regarding proven or possible harmful effects of chemical substances on the fetal central nervous system, among other tissues, have now been published, as indicated by the following examples in addition to those reviewed more fully above.

Besides alcohol and tobacco, discussed earlier, other ubiquitous substances to which there is frequent exposure during pregnancy, such as caffeine (widely consumed in, for instance, such beverages as coffee, tea and colas), have received some attention. Soyka (1981) concluded, from his review, that there was suggestive evidence of such fetal consequences of maternal caffeine consumption as intrauterine growth retardation, and that the possibility of prolonged effects cannot be dismissed. To avoid a possible impression that caffeine is necessarily hazardous to the unborn child, it may be added that Martin (1982) regarded the available evidence for caffeine damage as neither compelling nor consistent, with the fetus probably not at risk unless a woman ingests 'extremely large quantities daily'.

Worries about deleterious effects on the fetus of maternal anti-epileptic medication are best exemplified by what has been termed the fetal hydantoin syndrome. Hydantoin anticonvulsants used during pregnancy have been noted to be associated relatively frequently with mental deficit of different degrees and a fairly typical, though variable, pattern of physical anomalies including microcephaly (Hanson *et al.*, 1976). Trimethadione is another anticonvulsant which has been linked with delayed mental development and a considerable range of physical defects in some offspring of treated mothers (Feldman *et al.*, 1977). It is not entirely clear whether the association is a directly causal one or whether other factors in the epileptic mother are aetiologically relevant – for instance, the epilepsy itself, as suggested by Shapiro *et al.* (1976).

Coumarin derivatives, especially warfarin, prescribed as anticoagulants during pregnancy, have from time to time been reported to be associated with variable degrees of mental retardation in offspring, as well as rather characteristic nasal hypoplasia and stippled epiphyses (Shaul and Hall, 1977). The nasal and epiphyseal changes appear to be a consequence of relatively early first trimester ingestion, whereas central nervous system abnormality with subsequent mental deficit may result from later ingestion by a different mechanism secondary to fetal bleeding (Hall, 1976). The sequelae of anticoagulation therapy during pregnancy were more recently analysed in a comprehensive review by Hall *et al.* (1980).

A number of examples have been reported to date, for instance by Fernhoff and Lammer (1984) and by Lott *et al.* (1984), of congenitally malformed infants born to mothers taking isotretinoin early in pregnancy as a treatment for cystic acne. Anomalies noted include craniofacial ones with severe involvement of the central nervous system, as well as congenital cardiac defects. Isotretinoin (13-*cis*-retinoic acid) is a vitamin A analogue, and Hall (1984) has underlined a concern that large doses of other vitamins may also be teratogenic. The issue is an important one in an era when substantial vitamin supplementation is often encouraged and undertaken.

There have been suggestions, initially by Gal *et al.* (1967), that hormonal pregnancy tests early in gestation may produce central nervous system abnormalities, notably neural tube defects. However, other studies, for example by Laurence *et al.* (1971), Oakley *et al.* (1973) and Michaelis *et al.* (1983), have not confirmed such a possible link. The aetiology of neural tube defects is essentially obscure, and other environmental causes, besides exogenous hormones in the pregnancy tests referred to above, have been postulated from time to time. These include such varied influences as maternal ingestion of potatoes blighted by fungus and exposure of mothers to hyperthermia. Though deserving further exploration, serious doubt has been cast on the validity of these propositions (Smithells, 1976; Editorial, *Lancet*, 1978).

Failed attempts at abortion using chemicals may sometimes be responsible for cerebral damage and consequent sequelae in live-born children. A recent example of this possibility was recorded by Collins and Mahoney (1983). In this instance, a mother who received intravaginal prostaglandin seven weeks after conception was delivered at thirty-four weeks of a live-born infant with hydrocephaly and digital anomalies. No other explanation for the abnormalities was apparent and it was felt that the prostaglandin could have been responsible. The report illustrates the difficulty of drawing firm aetiological conclusions from single-case reports alone. A number of earlier accounts of sequelae of the folic acid antagonist, aminopterin, and its methyl derivative (methotrexate), unsuccessfully used in early pregnancy to procure abortion, have indicated teratogenic effects including a variety of dysmorphic features affecting the head and facies (Milunsky *et al.*, 1968; Howard and Rudd, 1977). Surprisingly perhaps, in view of these features, surviving children can fare well in terms of mental function as the years advance.

Observations concerning methadone, used in recent years to treat heroin addiction, illustrate the difficulties that can arise in attempting to distinguish between causes of, and associations with, mental and/or physical impairments. Rosen and Johnson (1982) found reduced head circumference and developmental delay, among other abnormalities, in follow-up to eighteen months of infants born to mothers on methadone treatment. Despite the use of a control group matched for a number of variables, including socioeconomic class, many other confounding factors, as the authors themselves and Aylward (1982) noted, could have influenced the outcome, making it injudicious to conclude that methadone, *per se*, was the specific cause of the abnormalities reported.

The fetus can be harmed by metallic poisons accidentally ingested by the mother during pregnancy, with serious implications for the mental and neurological prospects of children thus exposed in utero. Comparatively recent tragedies of this kind occurred in Japan and Iraq as a result of extensive consumption of fish in the former country (Tsubaki and Irukayama, 1977) and of bread in the latter (Amin-Zaki *et al.*, 1979) which had been contaminated with methyl mercury (see also page 121).

Reference is made to postnatal exposure to leaded gasoline on page 119. The possibility of maternal gasoline inhalation during pregnancy having a teratogenic effect, including marked mental retardation among subsequent manifestations, was raised by Hunter *et al.* (1979). However, the available findings did not permit definite conclusions. In more general terms, Bellinger *et al.* (1984) recently published observations which they considered compatible with the hypothesis that low levels of lead delivered transplacentally are toxic to infants.

Though nearly all data on the effects of drugs and other chemicals on the fetus are concerned with maternal exposure, some information is accumulating regarding paternal exposure at or near the time of conception (Pearn, 1983) and the possibility that the fetus may then be disadvantaged by a variety of mechanisms. There is no firm indication at present that mental deficit in offspring thus ensues. However, experimental evidence from various animal species showing decreased litter size and birth weight and increased neonatal mortality (Joffe, 1979; Joffe and Soyka, 1982; Pearn, 1983) cannot be dismissed lightly in terms of possible relevance to human progeny, including their developmental prospects. In this connection, it is of interest that Brady *et al.* (1975) found, in the rat, that offspring of fathers ingesting lead acetate prior to conception were less efficient in a black–white discrimination water T maze test than offspring of unexposed parents; curiously, perhaps, the results following maternal-only exposure were similar to those from paternal-only exposure and better than those obtained when both parents had ingested lead.

The main prenatal environmental dangers to the fetal central nervous system are infections and chemicals. However, other occurrences sometimes are linked with, and/or blamed for, subsequent mental retardation. Observations are periodically made, for instance recently by Costeff *et al.* (1981), of an increased frequency of pregnancy complications, such as antepartum haemorrhage and toxaemia, in the mothers of children with mental retardation of obscure causation. However, the precise aetiological role, if any, of such complications remains unclear. Maternal fever *per se*, of whatever origin, has been considered as a possible cause of cerebral pathology in the fetus. In humans, the evidence seems inconclusive. A prospective study by Clarren *et al.* (1979) did not establish that maternal hyperthermia during the first trimester was responsible for mental deficit in the children surveyed. A postulated role of such hyperthermia in the production of neural tube defects is mentioned on page 108. Though difficult to establish conclusively, physical trauma to the pregnant abdomen may, on rare occasions, cause fetal central nervous system damage with subsequent mental retardation in the child. An instance where this seems distinctly possible was reported by Hinden (1965) and, in an aetiological survey of a large series of mentally retarded children in Budapest, Hungary, Czeizel *et al.* (1980) stated categorically, though without details, that the cause of cerebral damage in two of the children was 'severe abdominal trauma of the pregnant mother'.

In addition, alterations of head shape due to fetal head constraint in utero can occur due to such circumstances as abnormal or unusual fetal lies and presentations (Graham, 1983). Graham, in his review of the subject, indicated that most such cases resolve within a few days of postnatal life. In the absence of such resolution, the question of possible adverse effects on the otherwise normal brain, and consequent mental impairment, arises. There appears to be little, if any, good evidence of such effects, but perhaps further consideration of well-controlled follow-up studies in that regard is indicated.

PERINATAL HAZARDS

Traditionally, there has been a particular focus on two circumstances at birth, namely asphyxia or hypoxia and mechanical injury, as causes of cerebral pathology and hence of subsequent mental and neurological handicaps. Observations bearing on the subject which deservedly attracted wide attention were published more than a century ago by Little (1862).

Impaired oxygenation and physical trauma to the central nervous system, in relationship to the birth process, are often closely associated, and the neonatal distress together with other immediate consequences may be clinically similar with each of these eventualities or with a combination of both. In surveys of mentally retarded persons some investigators have attempted to distinguish the aetiological role of each, whereas others have considered them together under the general designation of birth injuries. Whichever approach has been adopted, there have been marked discrepancies in the proportion of retarded populations in whom perinatal asphyxia/hypoxia and/or trauma have been considered to be causally significant. For instance, in two recently published aetiological studies (Czeizel *et al.*, 1980; Hunter *et al.*, 1980) of what appear to be comparable samples of moderately or more markedly retarded individuals in institutional settings in Budapest and Manitoba, respectively, perinatal asphyxia/hypoxia was considered to be the cause in 95 out of 304 persons (31.3 per cent) in the Hungarian series and in 17 out of 406 (4.2 per cent) in the Canadian series. Differences in the composition of the two samples or in diagnostic acumen or resources of the respective investigators cannot explain this remarkable discrepancy, leading to the virtually unavoidable conclusion that the discrepancy largely reflects different perceptions as to what constitutes aetiology. Methodologically, it is very difficult to distinguish the effects of perinatal asphyxia *per se* in surviving children because of the many confounding variables often associated with it, and reported findings are further affected by different definitions of asphyxia and of its severity. Taking these considerations into account, Peters *et al.* (1984) found, in their extensive study of respiratory delay at birth as one measure of asphyxia, that delay in onset of regular respiration from less than one minute to over three minutes was not in itself related to apparent mental deficits or deviant behaviour in surviving children at the age of five years.

Interestingly, the perceived frequency of birth trauma, as opposed to hypoxia or asphyxia, as the cause of mental retardation was fairly similar in the Czeizel *et al.* and Hunter *et al.* studies referred to above – that is, 1.0 per cent and 2.2 per cent respectively. Going back several decades to Penrose's (1938) renowned Colchester survey of an institutionalized population of retarded persons, of a wider age and mental-level range than in the two investigations referred to above, it is notable that he concluded that only 11 of the 1280 cases surveyed (0.9 per cent) could be regarded with reasonable certainty as owing their mental defect to birth injury, though he cautiously added that trauma may have been an unrecognized aetiological factor in a number of other instances.

The role of birth injury as a cause of mental deficit may well have changed markedly in the approximately fifty years since Penrose's survey was undertaken, at least in populations with general access to sophisticated present-day obstetric and perinatal monitoring and management facilities. There have been rapid and remarkable recent developments in these spheres with the prospect of substantial further advances in the immediately foreseeable future. These developments include sophisticated new diagnostic brain-imaging techniques involving such procedures as ultrasonography, computed tomography (Rumack and Johnson, 1984) and nuclear magnetic resonance (Steiner and Radda, 1984); and innovative treatment approaches, with a bearing on decreasing the likelihood of mental deficit, which are reviewed in such recent works as those edited by Cohen and Friedman (1983) and by Warshaw and

Hobbins (1983). Details about these undertakings are beyond the scope of this chapter, but readers can find ample information in such well-documented texts as those mentioned.

There is no doubt about the advantages to many infants of the attention referred to, though perinatal injury to the brain remains a significant contributory factor to mental deficit in surviving children despite investigative, prophylactic and therapeutic advances. Indeed, concern is sometimes expressed that vigorous modern resuscitative measures and neonatal intensive care may result in the saving of life at the price of serious mental and neurological sequelae in survivors. Without dwelling here on ethical and moral aspects of this issue (see Chapter 11 for a consideration of these aspects), it should be mentioned that the prognostic outlook of many may be substantially better than has often been supposed. For example, in a 5- to 10-year follow-up of 31 infants with severe birth asphyxia, 29 showed no serious mental or neurological handicap and all of these seemed to be progressing normally (Thomson *et al.*, 1977).

It is encouraging also that babies at risk for birth injury and its sequelae, because they were born sooner and/or smaller than desirable, now have prospects of progressing more favourably than was formerly the case. For instance, asphyxiated pre-term infants in a follow-up study to a mean age of 4.8 years during the past decade (Mulligan *et al.*, 1980) had the same chance for what the authors called 'intact survival' as asphyxiated term infants, reflecting, it was felt, recent advances in neonatal care. The possibility of a similar explanation was raised by Hagberg *et al.* (1973) as a result of their findings of a decreased incidence of low birth weight diplegia from 1964 to 1968, compared with 1959 to 1963, in a specific Swedish geographic region. An analysis by the same investigators (Hagberg *et al.*, 1982) of more recent Swedish data, related to survival following intensive neonatal care measures, indicated that the incidence of cerebral palsy had increased to some extent in the 1970s, but not that of severe multiple handicaps including mental retardation.

Reference was made above to 'small babies', a subject of much relevance in a consideration of perinatal causes of mental deficit, particularly as modern technology has greatly reduced the neonatal mortality of these babies, including 'very small' ones with birth weights below 1500 and even 1000 grams (Bennett, 1984). In the past, the term 'prematurity' was often used with regard to infants who were small, usually on the basis of a birth weight below a rather arbitrarily designated amount. The substantially increased frequency of low birth weight among mentally retarded populations, especially severely retarded ones, quite commonly resulted, and occasionally still does, in an uncritical listing of 'prematurity' as a specific cause of mental defect. In recent years the term appears to have been applied less generally in considerations of unduly small newborn infants, and such infants have been divided into various categories in accordance with, for instance, whether they showed intrauterine growth retardation and were small for gestational age, or whether they were pre-term births.

The small infants mentioned can be further subdivided, for purposes of prognosis and management, in various ways, for instance according to the presence or absence of intracerebral haemorrhage. In this regard, the brain-imaging techniques referred to on page 111 enable much more accurate detection and grading of different degrees of germinal matrix and intra-ventricular haemorrhage during life than was possible previously. Such haemorrhages are common in small pre-term infants (Papile *et al.*, 1978; Shankaran *et al.*, 1982), and even lesser grades may result in less favourable neurodevelopmental outcome than might otherwise have been the case (Scott *et al.*, 1984). Nevertheless, in careful investigations of a series of very preterm infants, Stewart *et al.* (1983) found that adverse neurodevelopmental sequelae at follow-up appeared more often to be attributable to cerebral ischaemia and infarction than to periventricular haemorrhage.

There are, of course, many ramifications in all these respects, embraced within the specialized territories of obstetrics and perinatology. Some of these ramifications have been comprehensively reviewed recently in, for instance, a text edited by Howie and Patel (1984) devoted to a consideration of small babies. For the present purpose suffice it to say that, despite improvements in developmental prognosis, small, underweight babies, particularly if sub-stantially below normal expectations, are more likely than their better-developed newborn peers to show mental and physical handicaps at various ages. The reasons for this association are manifold and include preconceptual genetic influences and environmental factors of both physical and psychosocial kinds. In that sense, it is very difficult to envisage smallness at birth as such as a cause of mental defect; the association is much more likely to exist because preceding circumstances were responsible for both manifestations and/or because small infants are more vulnerable (and in some instances more exposed) to peri- and postnatal environmental hazards of various kinds.

As illustrations of the many problems, besides hypoxia and mechanical trauma, connected with subsequent mental development which can arise at birth in babies who are unduly small for whatever reason, hyperbilirubinaemia and hyperoxia may be referred to here.

Hyperbilirubinaemia is operative perinatally though usually determined earlier than during the birth process. It can result in central nervous system effects, sometimes designated as bilirubin encephalopathy, which may be fatal, particularly if bilirubin staining and damage of the basal ganglia and other areas of the brain (kernicterus) occurs; among survivors, mental retardation combined with motor and sensory disorders is a prospect. A situation in which this took place with relative frequency was haemolytic disease of the newborn due to rhesus, or sometimes ABO, blood group incompatibility between mother and fetus. Advances in prophylaxis and treatment (Frigoletto and Umansky, 1979) have reduced this likelihood, and hyperbilirubinaemia is now encountered more often due to different circumstances, particularly in low-birth-weight infants. The exact role and extent of hyperbilirubinaemia, however caused, in producing mental deficits in such infants is not entirely clear, at least partly because they frequently have associated perinatal central nervous system involvement such as those due to injuries and infections. Cashore and Stern (1982) recently provided a well-documented review of these issues, and some are also discussed in Chapter 5.

Hyperoxia, as a result of the therapeutic use of oxygen in the neonatal period, can also be hazardous. Its association with retrolental fibroplasia and subsequent blindness is well known (Wester, 1981), and there have been some indications as well that hyperoxia might be a significant factor in the production of certain types of cerebral pathology (Phelps, 1982). Hyperoxia might have been considered just as suitably in the postnatal, as in the present, section of this chapter, so that reference to it here was for convenience rather than principle. By the same token, comments in the previous and next section of the chapter on infections occurring near the time of birth could have been included in this section. The point is made to emphasize that, although the short and crucial period during which labour and birth takes place is fairly well demarcated, adversity to the brain at that time is not neatly separable from preceding or succeeding occurrences. To underline this interrelationship, the adjective 'perinatal' rather than 'natal' has been used to designate the period in question.

Most of the observations on perinatal hazards in this chapter, as elsewhere, relate particularly to children who are small at birth. Much less research attention, with respect to subsequent outcomes, has been given to large (heavy) babies. A comparatively early study by Babson *et al.* (1969) of a parental low-income group in Portland, Oregon, found that 23 per cent of infants with a birth weight of over 4000 grams had an IQ below 80 at four years, compared to 10.6 per cent of infants who were of usual birth weight. Data on many of the relevant variables which might have accounted for this difference were not available. Recently, a more extensive investigation by Ousted *et al.* (1983) of a probably representative sample of births in Oxford, England, did not show an excess of mental retardation, or of neurological and medical problems, in a four-year follow-up of large-birth-weight-for-dates, compared to average-birth-weight-for-dates, children. Indeed, though not propounding the notion that 'bigger at birth is better at follow-up', and recognizing the great diversity in postnatal growth patterns, the authors remarked that large-for-dates infants who remain large are possibly developmentally advanced compared to those who revert to the median after birth. A subsequent follow-up by the same investigators (Ousted *et al.*, 1984) of the children to the age of seven years appears, in general, to have revealed findings in keeping with the earlier ones.

POSTNATAL HAZARDS

Postnatal physical causes of mental retardation, particularly if occurring when there was earlier evidence of a child's normal development and no prior reason to suspect that this would not continue to be so, are often easier to recognize and delineate than pre- or perinatal causes operating when previous developmental status was uncertain. The simplest scenario is of a normally developing child who survives an acute illness or accident but with obvious mental and related impairments. It is not, of course, always as straightforward as that. Thus the aetiological agent may not be operating as an acute episode in a circumscribed time frame, but chronically with slowly cumulative effects over a considerable period. Furthermore, even with a single dramatic environmental occurrence, relatively mild mental consequences may not be apparent without careful prolonged follow-up of supposedly fully recovered individuals. In addition, exposure and susceptibility to some potential environmental causes of mental defect may be more likely among those who are genetically and/or psychosocially at a disadvantage, with consequent difficulties in distinguishing between the interrelated variables.

The examples of postnatal hazards described or mentioned below illustrate the extensive range of these hazards as well as the above-mentioned methodological issues often involved in their delineation.

Meningitis and/or encephalitis

Neonatal infections of the central nervous system are a comparatively frequent cause of mental deficit. Meningitis due to a variety of organisms is the commonest suppurative intracranial infection in the neonatal period, with the pathogens concerned being most often acquired from the mother's birth canal (Bell and McGuinness, 1982). Low-birth-weight infants are at particular risk (Overall, 1970). Frequent sequelae among survivors include hydrocephaly, sensory and motor defects, seizures and mental retardation. Similar sequelae occur with infection in post-neonatal age groups, though the distribution of bacteria producing meningitis differs in older infants and children from that in the neonatal period (Baumgartner *et al.*, 1983; Sell, 1983). A comprehensive Finnish survey of the early and late outcome of 249 treated cases of nontuberculous purulent meningitis, due to a number of organisms, was provided by Sillanpää *et al.* (1977), and data of an equivalent kind for 79 instances of tuberculous meningitis in Canada were presented by Delage and Dusseault (1979). Both studies demonstrate the persisting mortality and overt morbidity tolls of such infections. In present-day populations of retarded children there are undoubtedly postmeningitic individuals who would have died without modern chemotherapy and associated treatments. These measures, though curative in many, are still inadequate to prevent mental and neurological defects in some.

Mental impairment is probably more frequent than is often recognized because of the relative paucity of long-term follow-up data with emphasis on such considerations. An indication that this could be so was provided by Sell *et al.* (1972). In one of their studies, survivors of treated bacterial meningitis contracted before the age of three years, who had been considered to be entirely normal, were found at school age to function at significantly lower levels than their nonmeningitic classroom peers when examined on

standardized psycholinguistic abilities, visual perception and picture vocabulary tests. It should be realized, however, that slight mental impairments in
follow-ups of postmeningitic children (or, for that matter, children who have
had other ailments) are not necessarily due to the original illness. For instance,
in a four-year follow-up of children who had had H. influenzae meningitis
(Tejani *et al.*, 1982), poor IQ, reading and arithmetical performance scores
evident in some of them were also found in their siblings, suggesting factors
other than meningitis as the explanation.

Encephalitis due to viral infections can also have serious consequences. For
example, of 12 instances of herpes simplex encephalitis reported by Schauseil-
Zipf *et al.* (1982) in children aged 6 months to 13 years, two succumbed in the
acute phase of the illness, and another two died 20 months and $3\frac{1}{2}$ years later,
respectively; none of the survivors showed normal psychomotor development
and most of them were severely retarded. Nearly all the children had been
admitted to hospital within a few days of the onset of symptoms, but the
nonspecific and variable symptomatology noted by the authors may have
prognostic relevance in that treatment with antiviral drugs, or other specific
medical intervention, could thus be delayed. In numerical terms, the problem
seems to be becoming more urgent than in the past because of accumulating
evidence that neonatal herpes simplex virus infection has been showing an
increasing incidence in the United States and in several other countries
(Sullivan-Bolyai *et al.*, 1983).

Less marked or consistent mental consequences than those noted above
with herpes simplex encephalitis have been reported as a result of enterovirus
(Coxsackie and echo viruses) infections of the central nervous system, though
relatively mild deficits in, for instance, receptive language functioning and
speech development have been described in children several years after
infection in early life (Sells *et al.*, 1975; Wilfert *et al.*, 1981).

Encephalitis or meningo-encephalitis complicating infectious fevers can also
result in neurological complications and mental defect of varying degrees.
Examples noted in several aetiological surveys of mentally retarded populations (McDonald, 1973; Iivanainen, 1974; Elwood and Darragh, 1981) are
whooping cough, measles and chicken pox. At least in the case of whooping
cough, cerebral damage may be due to mechanisms other than inflammatory
ones, for instance haemorrhage and anoxia, in some affected persons (Berg,
1959).

Head injury

Parents quite frequently attribute mental impairment in their children to
postnatal head injury. However, such an explanation is established with
reasonable certainty in only a small minority (often of the order of about 1 per
cent) of children with substantial mental retardation. In a recent study,
Mahoney *et al.* (1983) found that, even in children with prolonged coma
following severe head trauma, many survivors progressed well and returned to

normal or near-normal function. Less severe post-traumatic effects than frank mental retardation, including behaviour and personality disturbances and poor adjustment in school, seem more common and were reported in, for instance, 10 and 20 per cent of groups of head-injured children studied by Rowbotham *et al.* (1954) and by Newell (1937), respectively. More recently Shaffer *et al.* (1980) found that one-third of a sample of school-age children who had previously sustained a compound depressed fracture of the skull, resulting in damage to the cerebral cortex, had a reading age at least twenty-four months behind their chronological age. Though confounding factors which the authors considered, such as a socially disadvantageous background, are relevant in determining the precise causal role of the head injuries *per se* in producing these results, it seems virtually certain that these injuries did have aetiological significance.

It is often said that adults tolerate head injuries less well than children (Blau, 1936; Mahoney *et al.*, 1983), so that harmful mental consequences of cerebral trauma in adulthood may be more frequent than indicated above for children. On the other hand, as Shaffer *et al.* (1980) noted, it has been suggested that brain injury may adversely affect new skills rather than already acquired ones, and, they add: 'One might also expect that children who are injured at a time when they are acquiring literacy skills would be especially vulnerable to any disruption of cognitive processes or to absence from school.'

In evaluating the role of head injuries in the production of mental retardation, it is important to bear in mind that such injury may be a consequence rather than a cause of mental deficit in that a retarded individual could be relatively incautious or incompetent in avoiding accidents. Furthermore, some retarded persons exacerbate already existing cerebral pathology, of whatever origin, because of repeated head trauma resulting from epileptic fits or deliberate head banging (Akuffo and Sylvester, 1983).

It is, of course, also important for prognostic and therapeutic purposes to distinguish the nature and extent of head injuries and their immediate physical effects (for example, skull fractures and intracranial haemorrhage at various sites). Imaging techniques, referred to earlier in relation to the perinatal brain, provide much improved diagnostic scope. The presence or absence of associated injuries in other parts of the body can also have a bearing on prognosis. Mayer *et al.* (1981), in an investigation of ninety-five children with severe head injury (unconsciousness greater than six hours duration), found that the mortality and morbidity outcome was substantially worse in those with concomitant multiple injuries at other sites compared to those with injuries confined to the head. Shock, refractory hypoxaemia and sepsis were contributing factors worsening the outlook in the former group.

With preventive considerations in mind, it is notable that in a number of relatively recent aetiological studies of substantially retarded persons from various countries, traffic accidents figured rather prominently in head injuries leading to the retardation; for instance, see Pitt *et al.* (1972), Iivanainen (1974), Laxova *et al.* (1977), Hunter *et al.* (1980), and Elwood and Darragh (1981). In

Bruce *et al.*'s (1978) series of severely head-injured children, and in that of
Mayer *et al.* (1981) referred to earlier, well over half the patients sustained
their injuries in vehicular accidents. By no means all head injuries are
accidental, of course, and a growing literature on so-called 'battered children'
provides extensive testimony of that disturbing fact. To take but one example,
inflicted trauma was diagnosed at the Children's Hospital of Los Angeles in
263 cases over an 8-year period, and 138 of these (52 per cent) involved head
trauma, often with persisting mental and neurological sequelae in those
surviving (Apthorp, 1970). These findings are in keeping with Klein's (1981)
more recent observation that trauma to the central nervous system accounts
for most of the disability and death associated with physical child abuse.
Inflicted cerebral trauma is not only due to direct and relatively readily
recognizable blows to the head. Caffey (1974) has described another distressing
variety (the whiplash shaken infant syndrome) consequent on manual shaking
and jolting of infants with resultant intracranial damage which can be severe
enough to be fatal or result in mental and sensory deficits of varying degrees.
Abuse of this kind, whatever its motivation, is difficult to recognize because of
the absence of evidence of external trauma to the head.

Lead poisoning

Lead as a hazard to man (refer also to Chapters 5 and 7) has long been known,
and many reports attest to the fact that severe mental and neurological
sequelae can occur in children who survive an acute lead encephalopathy.

More controversial is the question as to what levels of lead absorption can
reasonably be considered not to be deleterious to a child's mental prospects.
An admirable review of the evidence has been presented by Rutter (1980), who
concluded that persistently raised blood lead levels in a range above 40 µg/
100 ml may cause, in some otherwise asymptomatic children, slight cognitive
impairments and perhaps also increase the risk of behavioural difficulties; he
considered that the evidence of psychological risks below the 40 µg level was
inconclusive. Among other methodological issues highlighted by Rutter in
interpreting existing data is that, as lead exposure is not randomly distributed,
many living in areas exposed to it may also be socially disadvantaged; hence an
association between some lead exposure and cognitive/behavioural deficit may
not be causally related but may both be a consequence of social disadvantage.
This issue arises as well in a recent study by Yule *et al.* (1981) of 6- to 12-year-
old children living near a lead works in outer London. They were found, on a
single blood lead measurement, to have levels between 7 and 33 µg/ml.
Although, on psychological testing 9–12 months later, the children scored
within the normal range of educational attainment and intelligence, there were
significant associations between the blood lead levels and attainment scores on
tests of reading, spelling and intelligence – the tendencies being for the higher
lead levels to be associated with lower criterion scores. With commendable
caution, the authors mention a relationship between lower socioeconomic

status on the one hand, and higher blood lead levels plus poorer performance on reading, spelling and IQ tests on the other, so that the lower scores found may have been associated with, rather than causally related to, the lead levels.

Generally, there have been many sources of lead in the environment (Piomelli *et al.*, 1984) and pica has often been related to its ingestion in young children (Berg and Zappella, 1964; Gallacher *et al.*, 1984). A comparatively recent and somewhat bizarre form of exposure has been deliberate inhalation of leaded gasoline, for amusement or pleasure, as a fairly widespread practice in certain communities (Seskia *et al.*, 1978). These authors reported a considerable array of neurological manifestations after such exposure; though generally reversible, the question of possible persistent effects on mental function remained unresolved. That exposure to lead from gasoline can occur in ubiquitous ways, other than as in the instance mentioned, is apparent from Mielke *et al.*'s (1983) estimate that between 5000 and 10,000 metric tons of lead were emitted by vehicular traffic into one (presumably fairly typical) urban United States environment (Baltimore City) during the past forty to fifty years.

Prevention of harm from lead is best achieved, of course, by vigorous steps to remove or minimize its presence as an environmental pollutant. When lead poisoning has occurred, valuable treatment, using chelating (binding) agents to enhance lead excretion in association with concomitant measures, exists. These management procedures of children affected in various degrees have been precisely described by Piomelli *et al.* (1984).

Postnatal malnutrition

Among the most distressing widespread disadvantages from which human beings suffer is malnutrition, ranging from the iniquity of outright starvation to specific dietary deficiencies. It is, of course, belabouring the obvious to state that inadequate nourishment is deleterious to those exposed to it, from whatever vantage point the situation may be viewed. The precise effects on mental development and function are extremely difficult to delineate for a variety of reasons, but mainly because undernourishment is generally intricately linked with many other adverse circumstances, including socioeconomic, psychological and biomedical ones, which hamper mental progress. Nevertheless, many studies have been undertaken to examine these effects, with strong indications that nutritional factors contribute significantly to depressed intellectual level and learning failure (Birch, 1972).

The question as to whether such effects necessarily persist over the years or not is a vexed one. Hoorweg and Stanfield (1976), for example, concluded that chronic undernutrition 'exerts a permanent impairment of intellectual ability and motor development', whereas Stein *et al.* (1975) felt that evidence was lacking that the effects of nutritional deprivation persist into adulthood and prevent full realization of mental competence. It is likely that different perceptions on these issues will long continue to be voiced. However, no one other than the most bigoted would dispute that, both in the interests of individuals exposed to undernourishment and of society as a whole, inadequate nutrition and the wide range of environmental adversity usually related to it deserve vigorous attention (see also Chapters 5 and 7).

In addition to malnourishment in general, deficiencies in the diet of specific ingredients are also a matter of concern. Reference has been made to iodine lack on page 103. Another important example is iron deficiency, a very common occurrence and one with adverse consequences which can include behavioural and cognitive ones (Pollitt and Leibel, 1982). Even short-term iron therapy may have beneficial mental effects in iron-deficient infants (Oski and Honig, 1978; Walter *et al.*, 1983), though findings in this regard have not always been consistent (Lozoff *et al.*, 1982), perhaps partially due to different environmental circumstances.

Other adverse postnatal influences

A large number of other physical hazards of environmental origin, in addition to those reviewed above, can operate postnatally to produce mental deficit. The examples outlined below provide an indication of the wide variety of such hazards. Some are unusual everywhere, whereas others differ considerably in frequency of occurrence in different milieux, depending on prevailing circumstances of many kinds, including social and economic ones.

Gastroenteritis, particularly when severe and accompanied by marked dehydration, can result in cerebal pathology (Crome, 1952). Various mechanisms may be involved, including electrolyte disturbances and cerebral haemorrhages, thromboses and oedema. Gastroenteritis is periodically mentioned as the aetiological basis of substantial mental defect, and in various surveys of mentally retarded populations in 'developed' countries several instances were noted in recent years by, for example, McDonald (1973), Turner (1975), Hunter *et al.* (1980) and Elwood and Darragh (1981). Such occurrences, though unusual in socioeconomically advantaged countries, are bound to be more frequent, albeit relatively poorly documented, in impoverished societies with grossly inadequate food, housing, hygiene and community services like medical ones.

Whooping cough was referred to on page 116 as a possible cause of mental and neurological defects. Immunization against this infection has occasionally also resulted in similar adverse consequences (Berg, 1958). Reports of affected children during the past decade (Kulenkampff *et al.*, 1974) have led to much debate, particularly in the United Kingdom, on the comparative benefits and dangers of whooping cough immunization (Robinson, 1981).

Otitis media is a good example of a common occurrence in childhood which may lead to actual or apparent developmental delay, but which is infrequently mentioned in surveys of the causes of such delays. When persistent or recurrent, otitis media includes among its sequelae conductive hearing loss, delayed speech and language development, and reduction in IQ scores (Howie,

1980). As such chronic infection is more likely to occur in depressed socioeconomic circumstances, where its presence may be less readily recognized or treated, it is an illustration of the caution required in drawing conclusions about the aetiological role of psychosocial disadvantage, *per se*, in impairing mental function.

Chemicals are a matter of concern as possible postnatal, as well as prenatal, hazards. With industrialization, man-made chemical pollution of the environment has increased dramatically as illustrated, for instance, by recent United States Environmental Protection Agency data, quoted by Slone *et al.* (1980), indicating that about 35 million metric tons of industrial wastes judged to be hazardous are produced annually in that country. Furthermore, the increased use of chemicals in relation to food production and distribution may not always be entirely beneficial and/or innocuous. Among chemicals potentially harmful to the central nervous system and hence to mental development are the metals lead (described above) and mercury. Methyl mercury was mentioned on page 109 with respect to its harmful effects in utero. Its potential as a postnatal danger was most extensively revealed in a disaster in Iraq in 1971–2 when over 6500 cases of poisoning were admitted to hospitals as a result of consumption of bread prepared from seed wheat treated with a methyl mercurial fungicide (Bakir *et al.*, 1973). Follow-up reports provided all-too-ample confirmation of cerebral involvement with mental retardation of varying degrees in postnatally (Amin-Zaki *et al.*, 1978), as well as prenatally, exposed children.

The issue of possibly harmful effects on the suckling infant of drugs ingested by the mother and excreted in breast milk has been receiving increasing attention. A recent review by Lewis and Hurden (1983) concluded that, with a number of exceptions, cause for concern is far less than some have maintained. Among the exceptions referred to, in so far as they have a bearing on adverse mental consequences, are the potential for thiouracil to cause hypothyroidism and for sulphonamides to precipitate kernicterus in jaundiced infants, even mildly jaundiced ones.

Reference has been made to well-established and widely known dangers of preconceptual and prenatal radiation on page 102. More recently, evidence has accumulated that postnatal cranial radiation, with or without other therapy, undertaken for the treatment in childhood of acute lymphocytic leukaemia and some cerebral tumours, can have adverse effects on intellectual function and behaviour (see, for example, Meadows *et al.* (1981), Duffner *et al.* (1983), Kuhn *et al.* (1983) and Whitt *et al.* (1984)). Reported neuropsychological results have varied – not surprisingly, since methodological approaches and evaluation methods have not been uniform in measuring the relatively subtle mental characteristics concerned, and because many different influences can affect outcome. Among these influences are the radiation dose used, age at and duration of the treatment, concomitant medication such as intrathecal chemotherapy, and the possible medical and psychological effects of the underlying neoplastic process itself. There is a recognized need by researchers in this field for further careful investigations to supplement earlier ones, taking account of such variables as those mentioned, in order to achieve the most effective therapy while at the same time eliminating or reducing the possibility of disadvantageous mental consequences of the treatment.

Water immersion accidents are frequent in childhood, with many deaths at the time and soon afterwards. Though a high proportion of near-drowned survivors appear to have a favourable prognosis, anoxic brain damage with grave mental and neurological sequelae occurs in some (Kruus *et al.*, 1979). The latter numbers may be substantially greater than in the past as a result of what Peterson (1977) referred to as 'a conversion of death by drowning to near-drowning anoxic encephalopathy' through the use of sophisticated cardiopulmonary resuscitative measures. Other occasionally observed sudden catastrophes resulting in cerebral anoxia and grave mental retardation include temporary cardiac arrest and partial strangulation.

Excessive exposure to heat in some circumstances can result in heatstroke with a fatal outcome or mental and physical sequelae of varying gravity. Wadlington *et al.* (1976) noted that in adults heatstroke is usually associated with strenuous exercise, whereas in children it is more often produced by increased environmental temperature and/or poor fluid intake. These authors and Roberts and Roberts (1976) reported instances of children aged 16 and 19 months who were thus affected because of exposure to heat in the confined surroundings of parked cars. Subsequently, Bacon *et al.* (1979) published data on a group of 5 infants between 3 and 8 months of age in whom apparent excessive wrapping or warming in their cots during mild infection was considered to be the possible principal cause of encephalopathy; 4 died with postmortem findings which included cerebral oedema, and the remaining child survived with gross retardation in development, cortical blindness and partial spasticity. Bacon and Bellman (1983) were able to trace a number of seemingly similar cases from different areas of the United Kingdom. There is obvious scope for prevention of this relatively infrequently recognized potential hazard.

Finally, central nervous system involvement with persisting mental deficits is sometimes described as a relatively rare consequence of an occurrence which, in itself, may be fairly common. The following are examples. Ashworth (1964) reported encephalopathy of uncertain pathogenesis as a result of insect stings in two adults who continued to show mental impairment six months and two years, respectively, after the original incident. Electrical injuries whether from currents (Halpérin *et al.*, 1983) or lightning strikes (Myers *et al.*, 1977) can result in severe central nervous system damage with major long-term neurological and mental dysfunction in survivors.

CONCLUSIONS

Though no attempt has been made in this chapter to describe, or even to refer to, every possible physical determinant of mental deficit in the environment, it is hoped that the many examples outlined or mentioned provide a reasonably comprehensive indication of the wide array of such factors which can contribute to developmental delay and impaired mental function. Reference was made in the Introduction to the interdependence of these factors with others, both genetical and psychosocial, in determining the ultimate outcome in a given individual.

In trying to delineate environmental causes of mental defect, significant additional considerations arise concerning the interpretation of findings, as illustrated in the present chapter. Perhaps the most important of these is the problem of distinguishing between causes and associations. Thus the fact that there is an increased frequency of, for instance, neonatal difficulties or distress among those subsequently found to be mentally retarded does not demonstrate that the former necessarily caused the latter; indeed, it is often more likely that each was due to the same preceding causal factors, whether recognizable or not. Different perceptions regarding such distinctions account, to a considerable extent, for substantial discrepancies in different surveys as to the proportion of mentally retarded persons considered to have an established aetiology.

Another difficulty can occur with respect to possible relatively mild long-term mental effects of an environmental hazard. Most of the existing data on teratogens, for example, concern physical malformations comparatively easily noticeable at birth or in infancy; when associated with distinct cerebral pathology and relatively severe developmental delay, this is often readily apparent. Much less well documented are the more subtle effects on mental development which may be missed without careful follow-up studies for years after the original environmental exposure. Furthermore, as many hazards to the fetus, newborn infant and young child are not randomly distributed throughout the population as a whole, the possible role of confounding variables in producing such subtle effects can be very difficult to evaluate. Given the complexity and interrelationship of many of the influences determining mental function, it may often be unduly simplistic to consider a particular occurrence as the definitive cause of mental deficit (especially when of mild degree) rather than as a contributory factor acting in combination with others.

Despite methodological dilemmas of the kind mentioned above, much has been learned in recent years about physical influences in the environment which can impair mental function, and many that are primarily responsible for intellectual deficit have been identified and delineated from various perspectives, including epidemiological, neuropathological and clinical ones. The challenge that remains is not only to continue to make such inroads but, more importantly, to achieve widespread application of this knowledge for preventive purposes. That there are inequities, often glaring, in the latter respect both within countries and between them should be a matter of serious concern not only to biomedical and social scientists and practitioners but to society as a whole.

REFERENCES

ABEL, E.L. (1983) *Marihuana, Tobacco, Alcohol, and Reproduction*, Boca Raton, Florida, CRC Press, 73 and 137.

AKUFFO, E.O. and SYLVESTER, P.E. (1983) 'Head injury and mental handicap', *J. Roy. Soc. Med.*, 76, 545–9.

AMIN-ZAKI, L., MAJEED, M.A., CLARKSON, T.W. and GREENWOOD, M.R. (1978) 'Methyl mercury poisoning in Iraqi children: clinical observations over two years', *Brit. Med. J.*, 1, 613–16.

AMIN-ZAKI, L., MAJEED, M.A., ELHASSANI, S.B., CLARKSON, T.W., GREENWOOD, M.R. and DOHERTY, R.A. (1979) 'Prenatal methyl mercury poisoning: clinical observations over five years', *Amer. J. Dis. Child.*, 133, 172–7.

APTHORP, J.S. (1970) 'The battered child', in C.R. ANGLE and E.A. BERING (eds), *Physical Trauma as an Etiological Agent in Mental Retardation*, Washington, DC, US Dept. of Health, Education and Welfare, 283–5.

ARCHIBALD, H.M. (1958) 'Influence of maternal malaria on newborn infants', *Brit. Med. J.*, 2, 1512–14.

ASHWORTH, B. (1964) 'Encephalopathy following a sting', *J. Neurol. Neurosurg. Psychiat.*, 27, 542–6.

AYLWARD, G.P. (1982) 'Methadone outcome studies: is it more than the methadone?', *J. Pediat.*, 101, 214–15.

BABSON, S.G., HENDERSON, N. and CLARK, W.M. (1969) 'The pre-school intelligence of oversized newborns', *Pediatrics*, 44, 536–8.

BACON, C.J. and BELLMAN, M.H. (1983) 'Heatstroke as a possible cause of encephalopathy in infants', *Brit. Med. J.*, 287, 328.

BACON, C., SCOTT, D. and JONES, P. (1979) 'Heatstroke in well-wrapped infants', *Lancet*, 1, 422–5.

BAKIR, F., DAMLUJI, S.F., AMIN-ZAKI, L., MUSTADHA, M., KHALIDI, A., AL-RAWI, N.Y., TIKRITI, S., DHAHIR, H.I., CLARKSON, T.W., SMITH, J.C. and DOHERTY, R.A. (1973) 'Methyl mercury poisoning in Iraq: an interuniversity report', *Science*, 181, 230–41.

BAUMGARTNER, E.T., AUGUSTINE, R.A. and STEELE, R.W. (1983) 'Bacterial meningitis in older neonates', *Amer. J. Dis. Child.*, 137, 1052–4.

BELL, W.E. and MCGUINNESS, G.A. (1982) 'Suppurative central nervous system infections in the neonate', *Sem. Perinat.*, 6, 1–24.

BELLINGER, D.C., NEEDLEMAN, H.L., LEVITON, A., WATERNAUX, C., RABINOWITZ, M.B. and NICHOLS, M.L. (1984) 'Early sensory-motor development and prenatal exposure to lead', *Neurobehav. Toxicol. Teratol.*, 6, 387–402.

BENNETT, F.C. (1984) 'Neurodevelopmental outcome of low-birth-weight infants', in V.C. KELLEY (ed.), *Practice of Pediatrics*, revised edn, vol. 2, chap. 28, Philadelphia, Harper & Row, 1–24.

BERG, J.M. (1958) 'Neurological complications of pertussis immunization', *Brit. Med. J.*, 2, 24–7.

BERG, J.M. (1959) 'Neurological sequelae of pertussis with particular reference to mental defect', *Arch. Dis. Childh.*, 34, 322–4.

BERG, J.M. and KIRMAN, B.H. (1959) 'Syphilis as a cause of mental deficiency', *Brit. Med. J.*, 2, 400–4.

BERG, J.M. and ZAPPELLA, M. (1964) 'Lead poisoning in childhood with particular reference to pica and mental sequelae', *J. Ment. Defic. Res.*, 8, 44–53.

BIRCH, H.G. (1972) 'Malnutrition, learning and intelligence', *Amer. J. Publ. Hlth*, 62, 773–84.

BLAU, A. (1936) 'Mental changes following head trauma in children', *Arch. Neurol. Psychiat. (Chic.)*, 35, 723–69.

BRADY, K., HERRERA, Y. and ZENICK, H. (1975) 'Influence of parental lead exposure on subsequent learning ability of offspring', *Pharmacol. Biochem. Behav.*, 3, 561–5.

BRENT, R.L. (1980) 'Radiation teratogenesis', *Teratology*, 21, 281–98.

BRUCE, D.A., SCHUT, L., BRUNO, L.A., WOOD, J.H. and SUTTON, L.N. (1978) 'Outcome following severe head injuries in children', *J. Neurosurg.*, 48, 679–88.

BUDELL, J.W. (1984) 'Syphilis', in V.C. KELLEY (ed.), *Practice of Pediatrics*, revised edn, vol. 3, chap. 103, Philadelphia, Harper & Row, 1–18.

BUTLER, N.R. and GOLDSTEIN, H. (1973) 'Smoking in pregnancy and subsequent child development', *Brit. Med. J.*, 4, 573–5.

CAFFEY, J. (1974) 'The whiplash shaken infant syndrome: manual shaking by the extremities with whiplash-induced intracranial and intraocular bleedings, linked with residual permanent brain damage and mental retardation', *Pediatrics*, 54, 393–403.

CASHORE, W.J. and STERN, L. (1982) 'Neonatal hyperbilirubinemia', *Pediat. Clin. N. Amer.*, 29, 1191–203.

CLARREN, S.K., SMITH, D.W., HARVEY, M.A.S., WARD, R.H. and MYRIANTHOPOULOS, N.C. (1979) 'Hyperthermia – a prospective evaluation of a possible teratogenic agent in man', *J. Pediat.*, 95, 81–3.

COFFEY, V.P. and JESSOP, W.J.E. (1959) 'Maternal influenza and congenital deformities: a prospective study', *Lancet*, 2, 935–8.

COFFEY, V.P. and JESSOP, W.J.E. (1963) 'Maternal influenza and congenital deformities: a follow-up study', *Lancet*, 1, 748–51.

COHEN, W.R. and FRIEDMAN, E.A. (eds) (1983) *Management of Labor*, Baltimore, University Park Press.

COLLINS, F.C. and MAHONEY, J.J. (1983) 'Hydrocephalus and abnormal digits after failed first-trimester prostaglandin abortion attempt', *J. Pediat.*, 102, 620–1.

COSTEFF, H., COHEN, B.E., WELLER, W. and KLECKNER, H. (1981) 'Pathogenic factors in idiopathic mental retardation', *Develop. Med. Child Neurol.*, 23, 484–93.

COUVRIER, J. and DESMONTS, G. (1962) 'Congenital and maternal toxoplasmosis: a review of 300 congenital cases', *Develop. Med. Child Neurol.*, 4,

519–30.

CROME, L. (1952) 'Encephalopathy following infantile gastro-enteritis', *Arch. Dis. Childh.*, 27, 468–72.

CZEIZEL, A., LÁNYI-ENGELMAYER, A., KLUJBER, L., MÉTNEKI, J. and TUSNÁDY, G. (1980) 'Etiological study of mental retardation in Budapest, Hungary', *Amer. J. Ment. Defic.*, 85, 120–8.

DELAGE, G. and DUSSEAULT, M. (1979) 'Tuberculous meningitis in children: a retrospective study of 79 patients, with an analysis of prognostic factors', *Canad. Med. Ass. J.*, 120, 305–9.

DOLL, R., HILL, A.B. and SAKULA, J. (1960) 'Asian influenza in pregnancy and congenital defects', *Brit. J. Prev. Soc. Med.*, 14, 167–72.

DUDGEON, J.A. (1976) 'Infective causes of human malformations', *Brit. Med. Bull.*, 32, 77–83.

DUFFNER, P.K., COHEN, M.E. and THOMAS, P. (1983) 'Late effects of treatment on the intelligence of children with posterior fossa tumors', *Cancer*, 51, 233–7.

DUNN, H.G., MCBURNEY, A.K., INGRAM, S. and HUNTER, C.M. (1977) 'Maternal cigarette smoking during pregnancy and the child's subsequent development: II. Neurobiological and intellectual maturation to the age of $6\frac{1}{2}$ years', *Canad. J. Publ. Hlth*, 68, 43–50.

Editorial (1978) 'Hyperthermia and the neural tube', *Lancet*, 2, 560–1.

Editorial (1983) 'Congenital cytomegalovirus infection', *Lancet*, 1, 801–2.

ELWOOD, J.H. and DARRAGH, P.M. (1981) 'Severe mental handicap in Northern Ireland', *J. Ment. Defic. Res.*, 25, 147–55.

FELDMAN, G.L., WEAVER, D.D. and LOVRIEN, E.W. (1977) 'The fetal trimethadione syndrome – report of an additional family and further delineation of this syndrome', *Amer. J. Dis. Child.*, 131, 1389–92.

FERNHOFF, P.M. and LAMMER, E.J. (1984) 'Craniofacial features of isotretinoin embryopathy', *J. Pediat.*, 105, 595–7.

FLORMAN, A.L., GERSHON, A.A., BLACKETT, P.R. and NAHMIAS, A.J. (1972) 'Diffuse brain damage, microcephaly, intracranial calcifications, and "owl eye" inclusion bodies associated with intrauterine infection with herpes simplex virus, type 1', *Pediat. Res.*, 6, 422.

FÖLLING, A. (1934) 'Über Ausscheidung von Phenylbrenztraubensäure in den Harn als Stoffwechselanomalie in Verbindung mit Imbezillität', *Hoppe-Seyler's Z. Physiol. Chem.*, 227, 169–76.

FRIGOLETTO, F.D. and UMANSKY, I. (1979) 'Erythroblastosis fetalis: identification, management and prevention', *Clin. Perinatol.*, 6, 321–30.

GAL, I., KIRMAN, B. and STERN, J. (1967) 'Hormonal pregnancy tests and congenital malformation', *Nature (Lond.)*, 233, 495–6.

GALLACHER, J.E.J., ELWOOD, P.C., PHILLIPS, K.M., DAVIES, B.E. and JONES, D.T. (1984) 'Relation between pica and blood lead in areas of differing lead exposure', *Arch. Dis. Childh.*, 59, 40–4.

GRAHAM, J.M. (1983) 'Alterations in head shape as a consequence of fetal head constraint', *Sem. Perinat.*, 7, 257–69.

GREGG, N.M. (1941) 'Congenital cataract following German measles in the mother', *Trans. Ophthalm. Soc. Aust.*, 3, 35–46.

HAGBERG, B., HAGBERG, G. and OLOW, I. (1982) 'Gains and hazards of intensive neonatal care: an analysis from Swedish cerebral palsy epidemiology', *Develop. Med. Child Neurol.*, 24, 13–19.

HAGBERG, B., OLOW, I. and HAGBERG, G. (1973) 'Decreasing evidence of low birth weight diplegia – an achievement of modern neonatal care?', *Acta Paediat. Scand.*, 62, 199–200.

HALL, J.G. (1976) 'Warfarin and fetal abnormality', *Lancet*, 1, 1127.

HALL, J.G. (1984) 'Vitamin A: a newly recognized human teratogen. Harbinger of things to come?', *J. Pediat.*, 105, 583–4.

HALL, J.G., PAULI, R.M. and WILSON, K.M. (1980) 'Maternal and fetal sequelae of anticoagulation during pregnancy', *Amer. J. Med.*, 68, 122–40.

HALPÉRIN, D.S., OBERHÄNSLI, I. and ROUGE, J.C. (1983) 'Cardiac and neurological impairments following electric shock in a young child', *Helv. Paediat. Acta*, 38, 159–66.

HANSHAW, J.B. (1983) 'Cytomegalovirus', in J.S. REMINGTON and J.O. KLEIN (eds), *Infectious Diseases of the Fetus and Newborn Infant*, 2nd edn, Philadelphia, Saunders, 104–42.

HANSHAW, J.B., SCHEINER, A.P., MOXLEY, A.W., GAEV, L., ABEL, V. and SCHEINER, B. (1976) 'School failure and deafness after "silent" congenital cytomegalovirus infection', *New Engl. J. Med.*, 295, 468–70.

HANSON, J.W., MYRIANTHOPOULOS, N.C., HARVEY, M.A.S. and SMITH, D.W. (1976) 'Risks to the offspring of women treated with hydantoin anticonvulsants, with emphasis on the fetal hydantoin syndrome', *J. Pediat.*, 89, 662–8.

HENDERSON, G.I., PATWARDHAN, R.V., HOYUMPA, A.M. and SCHENKER, S. (1981) 'Fetal alcohol syndrome: overview of pathogenesis', *Neurobehav. Toxicol. Teratol.*, 3, 73–80.

HETZEL, B.S. (1983) 'Iodine deficiency disorders (IDD) and their eradication', *Lancet*, 2, 1126–9.

HINDEN, E. (1965) 'External injury causing foetal deformity', *Arch. Dis. Childh.*, 40, 80–1.

HOORWEG, J. and STANFIELD, J.P. (1976) 'The effects of protein energy malnutrition in early childhood on intellectual and motor abilities in later childhood and adolescence', *Develop. Med. Child Neurol.*, 18, 330–50.

HOWARD, N.J. and RUDD, N.L. (1977) 'The natural history of aminopterin-induced embryopathy', in D. BERGSMA and R.B. LOWRY (eds), *Natural History of Specific Birth Defects*, Birth Defects Original Article Series, vol. 13, no. 3c, New York, Alan R. Liss, 85–93.

HOWIE, P.W. and PATEL, N.B. (eds) (1984) *The Small Baby*, Clinics in Obstetrics and Gynaecology, vol. 11, no. 2, London, Saunders.

HOWIE, V.M. (1980) 'Developmental sequelae of chronic otitis media: a review', *Develop. Behav. Pediat.*, 1, 34–8.

HUNTER, A.G.W., EVANS, J.A., THOMPSON, D.R. and RAMSAY, S. (1980)

'A study of institutionalized mentally retarded patients in Manitoba: I. Classification and preventability', *Develop. Med. Child Neurol.*, 22, 145–62.

HUNTER, A.G.W., THOMPSON, D. and EVANS, J.A. (1979) 'Is there a fetal gasoline syndrome?', *Teratology*, 20, 75–80.

HURLEY, L.S. (1981) 'Teratogenic aspects of manganese, zinc and copper nutrition', *Physiol. Revs.*, 61, 249–95.

IIVANAINEN, M. (1974) *A Study on the Origins of Mental Retardation*, Clinics in Developmental Medicine, no. 51, London, Heinemann Medical.

JOFFE, J.M. (1979) 'Influence of drug exposure of the father on perinatal outcome', *Clin. Perinat.*, 6, 21–36.

JOFFE, J.M. and SOYKA, L.F. (1982) 'Paternal drug exposure: effects on reproduction and progeny', *Sem. Perinat.*, 6, 116–24.

JOHNSTON, C. (1981) 'Cigarette smoking and the outcome of human pregnancies: a status report on the consequences', *Clin. Toxicol.*, 18, 189–209.

JONES, K.L. and SMITH, D.W. (1973) 'Recognition of the fetal alcohol syndrome in early infancy', *Lancet*, 2, 999–1001.

KLEIN, D.M. (1981) 'Central nervous system injuries', in N.S. ELLERSTEIN (ed.), *Child Abuse and Neglect – A Medical Reference*, New York, Wiley, 73–93.

KRIEGEL, H., SCHMAHL, W., KISTNER, G. and STIEVE, F.E. (eds) (1982) *Developmental Effects of Prenatal Irradiation*, Stuttgart, Gustav Fischer.

KRUGMAN, S. and KATZ, S.L. (1981) *Infectious Diseases of Children*, 7th edn, chap. 25, St Louis, C.V. Mosby.

KRUUS, S., BERGSTRÖM, L., SUUTARINEN, T. and HYVÖNEN, R. (1979) 'The prognosis of near-drowned children', *Acta Paediat. Scand.*, 68, 315–22.

KUHN, L.E., MULHERN, R.K. and CRISCO, J.J. (1983) 'Quality of life in children treated for brain tumors: intellectual, emotional, and academic function', *J. Neurosurg.*, 58, 1–6.

KULENKAMPFF, M., SCHWARTZMAN, J.S. and WILSON, J. (1974) 'Neurological complications of pertussis inoculation', *Arch. Dis. Childh.*, 49, 46–9.

LAURENCE, M., MILLER, M., VOWLES, M., EVANS, K. and CARTER, C. (1971) 'Hormonal pregnancy tests and neural tube malformations', *Nature (Lond.)*, 233, 495–6.

LAXOVA, R., RIDLER, M.A.C. and BOWEN-BRAVERY, M. (1977) 'An etiological survey of the severely retarded Hertfordshire children who were born between January 1, 1965 and December 31, 1967', *Amer. J. Med. Genet.*, 1, 75–86.

LECK, I.M. and MILLAR, E.L.M. (1962) 'Incidence of malformations since the introduction of thalidomide', *Brit. Med. J.*, 2, 16–20.

LENKE, R.R. and LEVY, H.L. (1980) 'Maternal phenylketonuria and hyperphenylalaninemia: an international survey of the outcome of untreated and treated pregnancies', *New Engl. J. Med.*, 303, 1202–8.

LEVY, H.L. and WAISBREN, S.E. (1983) 'Effects of untreated maternal phenylketonuria and hyperphenylalaninemia on the fetus', *New Engl. J. Med.*, 309, 1269–74.

LEWIS, P.J. and HURDEN, E.L. (1983) 'Drugs and breast feeding', in D.F. HAWKINS (ed.), *Drugs and Pregnancy – Human Teratogenesis and Related Problems*, Edinburgh, Churchill Livingstone, 204–28.

LITTLE, R.E., YOUNG, A., STREISSGUTH, A.P. and UHL, C.N. (1984) 'Preventing fetal alcohol effects: effectiveness of a demonstration project', in R. PORTER, M. O'CONNOR and J. WHELAN (eds), *Mechanisms of Alcohol Damage in Utero*, Ciba Foundation Symposium 105, London, Pitman, 254–74.

LITTLE, W.J. (1862) 'On the influence of abnormal parturition, difficult labours, premature births, and asphyxia neonatorum, on the mental and physical conditions of the child, especially in relation to deformities', *Trans. Obstet. Soc. Lond.*, 3, 293–344.

LOTT, I.T., BOCIAN, M., PRIBRAM, H.W. and LEITNER, M. (1984) 'Fetal hydrocephalus and ear anomalies associated with maternal use of isotretinoin', *J. Pediat.*, 105, 597–600.

LOZOFF, B., BRITTENHAM, G.M., VITERI, F.E., WOLF, A.W. and URRUTIA, J.J. (1982) 'The effects of short-term oral iron therapy on developmental deficits in iron-deficient anemic infants', *J. Pediat.*, 100, 351–7.

MCDONALD, A.D. (1973) 'Severely retarded children in Quebec: prevalence, causes, and care', *Amer. J. Ment. Defic.*, 78, 205–15.

MACGREGOR, J.D. and AVERY, J.G. (1974) 'Malaria transmission and fetal growth', *Brit. Med. J.*, 3, 433–6.

MAHONEY, W.J., D'SOUZA, B.J., HALLER, J.A., ROGERS, M.C., EPSTEIN, M.H. and FREEMAN, J.M. (1983) 'Long-term outcome of children with severe head trauma and prolonged coma', *Pediatrics*, 71, 756–62.

MAJEWSKI, F. (1981) 'Alcohol embryopathy: some facts and speculations about pathogenesis', *Neurobehav. Toxicol. Teratol.*, 3, 129–44.

MARTIN, J.C. (1982) 'An overview: maternal nicotine and caffeine consumption and offspring outcome', *Neurobehav. Toxicol. Teratol.*, 4, 421–7.

MAYER, T., WALKER, M.L., SHASHA, I., MATLAK, M. and JOHNSON, D.G. (1981) 'Effect of multiple trauma on outcome of pediatric patients with neurologic injuries', *Child's Brain*, 8, 189–97.

MEADOWS, A.T., MASSARI, D.J., FERGUSSON, J., GORDON, J., LITTMAN, P. and MOSS, K. (1981) 'Decline in IQ scores and cognitive dysfunctions in children with acute lymphocytic leukaemia treated with cranial irradiation', *Lancet*, 2, 1015–18.

MICHAELIS, J., MICHAELIS, H., GLÜCK, E. and KOLLER, S. (1983) 'Prospective study of suspected associations between certain drugs administered during early pregnancy and congenital malformations', *Teratology*, 27, 57–64.

MIELKE, H.W., ANDERSON, J.C., BERRY, K.J., MIELKE, P.W., CHANEY, R.L. and LEECH, M. (1983) 'Lead concentrations in inner-city soils as a factor in the child lead problem', *Amer. J. Publ. Hlth*, 73, 1366–9.

MILLER, E., CRADOCK-WATSON, J.E. and POLLOCK, T.M. (1982) 'Consequences of confirmed maternal rubella at successive stages of pregnancy', *Lancet*, 2, 781–4.

MILUNSKY, A., GRAEF, J.W. and GAYNOR, M.F. (1968) 'Methotrexate-induced congenital malformations, with a review of the literature', *J. Pediat.*, 72, 790–5.

MULLIGAN, J.C., PAINTER, M.J., O'DONOHUE, P.A., MACDONALD, H.M., ALLEN, A.C. and TAYLOR, P.M. (1980) 'Neonatal asphyxia: II. Neonatal mortality and long-term sequelae', *J. Pediat.*, 96, 903–7.

MURPHY, D.P. (1929) 'The outcome of 625 pregnancies in women subjected to pelvic radium or roentgen irradiation', *Amer. J. Obstet. Gynec.*, 18, 179–87.

MYERS, G.J., COLGAN, M.T. and VAN DYKE, D.H. (1977) 'Lightning-strike disaster among children', *J. Amer. Med. Ass.*, 238, 1045–6.

NABARRO, D. (1954) *Congenital Syphilis*, London, Edward Arnold.

NAEYE, R.L. (1981) 'Fetal infection and its sequelae', in J.A. DAVIS and J. DOBBING (eds), *Scientific Foundations of Paediatrics*, 2nd edn, London, Heinemann Medical, 1023–44.

NEWELL, H.W. (1937) 'The effect of head injury on the behavior and personality of children: a study of 20 cases', *Med. Clin. N. Amer.*, 21, 1335–65.

OAKLEY, G.P., FLYNT, J.W. and FALEK, A. (1973) 'Hormonal pregnancy tests and congenital malformations', *Lancet*, 2, 256–7.

O'CONNOR, S. and MULCAHY, M. (1984) 'Maternal phenylketonuria in the Republic of Ireland', in J.M. BERG (ed.), *Perspectives and Progress in Mental Retardation*, vol. 2, Baltimore, University Park Press, 85–92.

OSKI, F.A. and HONIG, A.S. (1978) 'The effects of therapy on the developmental scores of iron-deficient infants', *J. Pediat.*, 92, 21–5.

OUSTED, M.K., MOAR, V.A. and SCOTT, A. (1983) 'Large-for-dates babies at the age of four years: health, handicap and developmental status', *Early Hum. Develop.*, 9, 9–19.

OUSTED, M.K., MOAR, V.A. and SCOTT, A. (1984) 'Children of deviant birth weight at the age of seven years: health, handicap, size and developmental status', *Early Hum. Develop.*, 9, 323–40.

OVERALL, J.C. (1970) 'Neonatal bacterial meningitis. Analysis of predisposing factors and outcome compared with matched control subjects', *J. Pediat.*, 76, 499–511.

PAPILE, L., BURSTEIN, J., BURSTEIN, R. and KOFFLER, H. (1978) 'Incidence and evolution of subependymal and intraventricular haemorrhage: a study of infants with birth weights less than 1500 grams', *J. Pediat.*, 92, 529–34.

PEARN, J.H. (1983) 'Teratogens and the male: an analysis with special reference to herbicide exposure', *Med. J. Austr.*, 2, 16–20.

PECKHAM, C.S., COLEMAN, J.C., HURLEY, R., CHIN, K.S., HENDERSON, K. and PREECE, P.M. (1983) 'Cytomegalovirus infection in pregnancy: preliminary findings from a prospective study', *Lancet*, 1, 1352–5.

PENROSE, L.S. (1938) *A Clinical and Genetic Study of 1280 Cases of Mental Defect*, Medical Research Council Special Report Series no. 229, London, HMSO.

PETERS, T.J., GOLDING, J., LAWRENCE, C.J., FRYER, J.G., CHAMBERLAIN, J.V.P. and BUTLER, N.R. (1984) 'Delayed onset of regular respiration and subsequent development', *Early Hum. Develop.*, 9, 225–39.

PETERSON, B. (1977) 'Morbidity of childhood near-drowning', *Pediatrics*, 59, 364–70.

PHELPS, D.L. (1982) 'Neonatal oxygen toxicity – is it preventable?', *Pediat. Clin. N. Amer.*, 29, 1233–40.

PIOMELLI, S., ROSEN, J.F., CHISOLM, J.J. and GRAEF, J.W. (1984) 'Management of childhood lead poisoning', *J. Pediat.*, 105, 523–32.

PITT, D., ROBOZ, P. and SEIDURS, E. (1972) 'The spectrum of severe mental deficiency: experiences with 1400 cases', *Aust. J. Ment. Retard.*, 2, 40–6.

PLUMMER, G. (1952) 'Anomalies occurring in children exposed in utero to the atomic bomb in Hiroshima', *Pediatrics*, 10, 687–93.

POLLITT, E. and LEIBEL, R.L. (eds) (1982) *Iron Deficiency: Brain Biochemistry and Behavior*, New York, Raven Press.

PORTER, R., O'CONNOR, M. and WHELAN, J. (eds) (1984) *Mechanisms of Alcohol Damage in Utero*, Ciba Foundation Symposium 105, London, Pitman.

PRATT, O.E. (1984) 'What do we know of the mechanisms of alcohol damage in utero?', in R. PORTER, M. O'CONNOR and J. WHELAN (eds), *Mechanisms of Alcohol Damage in Utero*, Ciba Foundation Symposium 105, London, Pitman, 1–7.

QUINN, T.C., JACOBS, R.F., MERTZ, G.J., HOOK, E.W. and LOCKSLEY, R.M. (1982) 'Congenital malaria: a report of four cases and a review', *J. Pediat.*, 101, 229–32.

REINHARDT, M.C. (1980) 'Effects of parasitic infections in pregnant women', in K. ELLIOT, M. O'CONNOR and J. WHELAN (eds), *Perinatal Infections*, Ciba Foundation Symposium 77, Amsterdam, Excerpta Medica, 149–63.

REMINGTON, J.S. and DESMONTS, G. (1983) 'Toxoplasmosis', in J.S. REMINGTON and J.O. KLEIN (eds), *Infectious Diseases of the Fetus and Newborn Infant*, 2nd edn, Philadelphia, Saunders, 143–263.

REYNOLDS, D.W., STAGNO, S., STUBBS, K.G., DAHLE, A.J., LIVINGSTON, M.M., SAXON, S.S. and ALFORD, C.A. (1974) 'Inapparent congenital cytomegalovirus infection with elevated cord IgM levels: causal relation with auditory and mental deficiency', *New Engl. J. Med.*, 290, 291–6.

ROBERTS, K.B. and ROBERTS, E.C. (1976) 'The automobile and heat stress',

Pediatrics, 58, 101–4.

ROBINSON, R.J. (1981) 'The whooping-cough immunization controversy', *Arch. Dis. Childh.*, 56, 577–80.

ROSEN, T.S. and JOHNSON, H.L. (1982) 'Children of methadone-maintained mothers: follow-up to 18 months of age', *J. Pediat.*, 101, 192–6.

ROWBOTHAM, G.F., MACIVER, I.V., DICKSON, J. and BOUSFIELD, M.E. (1954) 'Analysis of 1400 cases of acute injury to the head', *Brit. Med. J.*, 1, 726–30.

RUMACK, C.M. and JOHNSON, M.L. (eds) (1984) *Perinatal and Infant Brain Imaging: Role of Ultrasound and Computed Tomography*, Chicago, Year Book Medical Publishers.

RUTTER, M. (1980) 'Raised lead levels and impaired cognitive/behavioural functioning: a review of the evidence', *Develop. Med. Child Neurol.*, Supplement No. 42, 1–26.

SCHAUSEIL-ZIPF, U., HARDEN, A., HOARE, R.D., LYEN, K.R., LINGAM, S., MARSHALL, W.C. and PAMPIGLIONE, G. (1982) 'Early diagnosis of herpes simplex encephalitis in childhood: clinical, neurophysiological and neuroradiological studies', *Europ. J. Pediat.*, 138, 154–61.

SCOTT, D.T., MENT, L.R., EHRENKRANZ, R.A. and WARSHAW, J.B. (1984) 'Evidence for late developmental deficit in very low birth weight infants surviving intraventricular haemorrhage', *Child's Brain*, 11, 261–9.

SELL, S.H. (1983) 'Long-term sequelae of bacterial meningitis in children', *Pediat. Infect. Dis.*, 2, 90–3.

SELL, S.H.W., WEBB, W.W., PATE, J.E. and DOYNE, E.O. (1972) 'Psychological sequelae to bacterial meningitis: two controlled studies', *Pediatrics*, 49, 212–17.

SELLS, C.J., CARPENTER, R.L. and RAY, C.G. (1975) 'Sequelae of central-nervous-system enterovirus infections', *New Engl. J. Med.*, 293, 1–4.

SESKIA, S.S., RAJANI, K.R., BOECKX, R.L. and CHOW, P.N. (1978) 'The neurological manifestations of chronic inhalation of leaded gasoline', *Develop. Med. Child Neurol.*, 20, 323–34.

SHAFFER, D., BIJUR, P., CHADWICK, O.F.D. and RUTTER, M.L. (1980) 'Head injury and later reading disability', *J. Amer. Acad. Child Psychiat.*, 19, 592–610.

SHANKARAN, S., SLOVIS, T.L., BEDARD, M.P. and POLAND, R.L. (1982) 'Sonographic classification of intracranial hemorrhage: a prognostic indicator of mortality, morbidity, and short-term neurologic outcome', *J. Pediat.*, 100, 469–75.

SHANKLIN, D.R. and HODIN, J. (1979) *Maternal Nutrition and Child Health*, Springfield, Ill., C.C. Thomas.

SHAPIRO, S., HARTZ, S.C., SISKIND, V., MITCHELL, A.A., SLONE, D., ROSENBERG, L., MANSON, R.R., HEINONEN, O.P., IDÄNPÄÄN-HEIKKILÄ, J., HÄRÖ, S. and SAXÉN, L. (1976) 'Anticonvulsants and parental epilepsy in the development of birth defects', *Lancet*, 1, 272–5.

SHAUL, W.L. and HALL, J.G. (1977) 'Multiple congenital anomalies associated with oral anticonvulsants', *Amer. J. Obstet. Gynec.*, 127, 191–8.

SILLANPÄÄ, M., PELTONEN, T. and NURMIKKO, T. (1977) 'Social and medical prognosis of children with acute nontuberculous purulent meningitis', *Acta Paediat. Scand.*, Supplement 265, 1–28.

SLONE, D., SHAPIRO, S. and MITCHELL, A.A. (1980) 'Strategies for studying the effects of the antenatal chemical environment of the fetus', in R.H. SCHWARZ and S.J. YAFFE (eds), *Drugs and Chemical Risks to the Fetus and Newborn*, New York, Alan R. Liss.

SMITHELLS, R.W. (1976) 'Environmental teratogens of man', *Brit. Med. Bull.*, 32, 27–33.

SMITHELLS, R.W. (1980) 'The nutrient intake of pregnant women in a British industrial city', in N. AEBI and R. WHITEHEAD (eds), *Maternal Nutrition during Pregnancy and Lactation*, Bern, Hans Huber, 117–26.

SMITHELLS, R.W., SELLER, M.J., HARRIS, R., FIELDING, D.W., SCHORAH, C.J., NEVIN, N.C., SHEPPARD, S., READ, A.P., WALKER, S. and WILD, J. (1983) 'Further experience of vitamin supplementation for prevention of neural tube defect recurrences', *Lancet*, 1, 1027–31.

SMITHELLS, R.W., SHEPPARD, S., SCHORAH, C.J., SELLER, M.J., NEVIN, N.C., HARRIS, R., READ, A.P. and FIELDING, D.W. (1981) 'Apparent prevention of neural tube defects by periconceptual vitamin supplementation', *Arch. Dis. Childh.*, 56, 911–18.

SOUTH, M.A., TOMPKINS, W.A.F., MORRIS, C.R. and RAWLS, W.E. (1969) 'Congenital malformation of the central nervous system associated with genital type (type 2) herpes virus', *J. Pediat.*, 73, 13–18.

SOYKA, L.F. (1981) 'Caffeine ingestion during pregnancy: in utero exposure and possible effects', *Sem. Perinat.*, 5, 305–9.

STAGNO, S., PASS, R.F., DWORSKY, M.E. and ALFORD, C.A. (1983) 'Congenital and perinatal cytomegalovirus infections', *Sem. Perinat.*, 7, 31–42.

STANBURY, J.B. and HETZEL, B.S. (eds) (1980) *Endemic Goiter and Endemic Cretinism*, New York, Wiley.

STEIN, Z., SUSSER, M., SANGER, G. and MAROLLA, F. (1975) *Famine and Human Development: The Dutch Hunger Winter of 1944–1945*, London, Oxford University Press.

STEINER, R.E. and RADDA, G.K. (eds) (1984) 'Nuclear magnetic resonance and its clinical applications', *Brit. Med. Bull.*, 40, 113–206.

STEWART, A.L., THORBURN, R.J., HOPE, P.L., GOLDSMITH, M., LIPSCOMB, A.P. and REYNOLDS, E.O.R. (1983) 'Ultrasound appearance of the brain in very preterm infants and neurodevelopmental outcome at 18 months of age', *Arch. Dis. Childh.*, 58, 598–604.

STREISSGUTH, A., LANDESMAN-DWYER, S., MARTIN, J.C. and SMITH, D.W. (1980) 'Teratogenic effects of alcohol in humans and laboratory animals', *Science*, 209, 353–61.

SULLIVAN-BOLYAI, J., HULL, H.F., WILSON, C. and COREY, L. (1983) 'Neonatal herpes simplex virus infection in King County, Washington: increasing incidence and epidemiologic correlates', *J. Amer. Med. Ass.*, 250, 3059–62.

TEJANI, A., DOBIAS, B. and SAMBURSKY, J. (1982) 'Long-term prognosis after H. influenzae meningitis: prospective evaluation', *Develop. Med. Child Neurol.*, 24, 338–43.

THOMSON, A.J., SEARLE, M. and RUSSELL, G. (1977) 'Quality of survival after severe birth asphyxia', *Arch. Dis. Childh.*, 52, 620–5.

TSUBAKI, T. and IRUKAYAMA, K. (eds) (1977) *Minimata Disease*, Amsterdam, Elsevier.

TURNER, G. (1975) 'An aetiological study of 1000 patients with an IQ assessment below 51', *Med. J. Austr.*, 2, 927–31.

WADLINGTON, W.B., TUCKER, A.L., FLY, F. and GREENE, H.L. (1976) 'Heat stroke in infancy', *Amer. J. Dis. Child.*, 130, 1250–1.

WALTER, T., KOVALSKYS, J. and STEKEL, A. (1983) 'Effect of mild iron deficiency on infant mental development scores', *J. Pediat.*, 102, 519–22.

WARSHAW, J.B. and HOBBINS, J.C. (eds) (1983) *Principles and Practice of Perinatal Medicine: Maternal–Fetal and Newborn Care*, Menlo Park, Calif., Addison-Wesley.

WEBER, F. (1983) 'Les lésions cérébrales de la toxoplasmose congénitale', *Helv. Paediat. Acta*, Supplement 48, no. 1, 1–51.

WESTER, J.J. (1981) 'Retrolental fibroplasia: an unsolved problem', *New Engl. J. Med.*, 305, 1404–6.

WHITT, J.K., WELLS, R.J., LAURIA, M.M., WILHELM, C.L. and MCMILLAN, C.W. (1984) 'Cranial radiation in childhood acute lymphocytic leukemia: neuropsychologic sequelae', *Amer. J. Dis. Child.*, 138, 730–6.

WIGGELINKHUIZEN, J. and MASON, R. (1980) 'Congenital neurosyphilis and juvenile paresis: a forgotten entity?', *Clin. Pediat.*, 19, 142–5.

WILFERT, C.M., THOMPSON, R.J., SUNDER, T.R., O'QUINN, A., ZELLER, J. and BLACHARSH, J. (1981) 'Longitudinal assessment of children with enteroviral meningitis during the first three months of life', *Pediatrics*, 67, 811–15.

WILSON, C.B., REMINGTON, J.S., STAGNO, S. and REYNOLDS, D.W. (1980) 'Development of adverse sequelae in children born with subclinical congenital toxoplasma infection', *Pediatrics*, 66, 767–74.

YAMAZAKI, J.N., WRIGHT, S.W. and WRIGHT, P.M. (1954) 'Outcome of pregnancy in women exposed to the atomic bomb in Nagasaki', *Amer. J. Dis. Child.*, 87, 448–63.

YULE, W., LANSDOWN, R., MILLAR, I.B. and URBANOWICZ, M. (1981) 'The relationship between blood lead concentrations, intelligence and attainment in a school population: a pilot study', *Develop. Med. Child Neurol.*, 23, 567–76.

ZAPPERT, J. (1926) 'Über röntgenogene fötale Mikrozephalie', *Arch. Kinderheilk.*, 80, 34–50.

5
Biochemical aspects

Jan Stern

INTRODUCTION

Evidence of metabolic disturbances before or after birth is found in the histories of many mentally retarded patients. Their contribution to the pathogenesis of the mental defect is often difficult to assess. It may be decisive, significant or trivial. In neuronal storage diseases it is usually the deficiency of a single enzyme which leads inexorably to the destruction of the cells affected and to progressive intellectual deterioration. Here the metabolic factor is decisive. In an infant with antenatal brain damage caused, for example, by a virus infection, consequent loss of intellectual potential is often compounded by perinatal anoxia, hypoglycaemia and jaundice. Here biochemical abnormalities may play a significant albeit not decisive part in determining intelligence. In phenylketonuria, there is a clear causal connection between the metabolic defect and the mental retardation (p. 173). This does not mean that for any amino acid abnormality in a mentally retarded patient a causal relationship can safely be assumed. For several aminoacidopathies such an assumption has proved unfounded (p. 178). Quite often, then, a biochemical abnormality either has no bearing on an observed intellectual deficit or is but one of several pathogenetic factors. Among the tasks of the physician and psychologist is the identification, with the aid of the laboratory, of patients with biochemical abnormalities, assessment of the role of these abnormalities in the pathogenesis of the mental defect, and exploration of the possibilities of treatment and prevention.

BRAIN METABOLISM – INBORN ERRORS

The brain is the most specialized of all human organs. Its functional unit is the excitable nerve cell, the neuron, with its anatomical and biochemical connections, the synapses. Synaptic contact is mediated by chemical molecules, the neurotransmitters, which ensure the propagation of nerve impulses. The metabolic processes which provide the necessary energy are not peculiar to the nervous system, in contrast to the mechanisms of neurotransmission which are. The unique capability of nerve cells to conduct electrical impulses over long distances rests on the possession of semi-permeable excitable membranes capable of undergoing rapid changes in permeability to small molecules and cations. To support this function efficient production of energy is required (Table 5.1). This energy, largely stored as adenosine triphosphate (ATP), is essentially derived from glucose, although neonates also utilize ketone bodies to a significant extent. Of all organs, the brain is most sensitive to an interruption of a regular supply of glucose.

TABLE 5.1   Energy requirements of the brain

Function	*Metabolic process involved*
Neurotransmission	Synthesis, storage, release and catabolism of neurotransmitters
Maintenance of excitability of neurons	Nucleotide synthesis, active cation transport by sodium pump
Maintenance of molecular structures	Synthesis and disposal of membrane constituents

Source: Eadie and Tyrer (1983); McIlwain and Bachelard (1985).

Glucose is anaerobically metabolized to pyruvate via the *glycolytic pathway* operating in the cytoplasm of the cell. In anoxia, pyruvate may be reduced to lactate, but normally it is converted in the mitochondria to acetyl CoA ('active acetate'). Complete oxidation requires oxygen, generates ATP and requires the integration of several mitochondrial systems: the *pyruvate dehydrogenase complex*, the *citric acid cycle* and the *electron transport chain*. Lactate can either be oxidized to pyruvate or it can serve as a precursor for *gluconeogenesis* which takes place in liver and kidney and regenerates glucose by a pathway which shares some and differs in other steps of glycolysis.

Amino acids of dietary or endogenous origin are involved in biosynthetic processes yielding proteins, nucleic acids and derivatives, porphyrins, coenzymes and, of particular importance in brain metabolism, neurotransmitters. Essential amino acids like phenylalanine or the branched chain amino acids cannot be synthesized by man and must be ingested in the diet. Amino acids are catabolized through pyruvate and the citric acid cycle which they enter via their keto acid analogues. Build-up of toxic levels of ammonia is prevented by its transformation to urea, mainly in the liver, by the chain of reactions which make up the *urea cycle*.

Fatty acids, derived from lipid stores, are transported as acyl CoA derivatives into the mitochondria with the aid of carnitine and there metabolized by β-oxidation to acetyl-CoA which then enters the citric acid cycle or, if the capacity of the cycle is exceeded, gives rise to ketone bodies. Both carbohydrate and fat can serve as a source of energy, and their utilization is integrated and controlled both at the cellular and at the organ level. In starvation, ketone bodies are an important source of energy in peripheral tissues. Lipids, carbohydrates and amino acids, then, together provide fuel for the energy requirements and the components for building the physical structures of cells. The necessary biochemical reactions are mediated by enzymes, proteins which act as biochemical catalysts. Some enzymes require nonprotein cofactors. In many instances these cofactors cannot be synthesized by man; they or their precursors are taken in the diet as vitamins.

The major metabolic pathways are closely linked and involve many steps. Interruption of these chains of reaction may occur due to toxic substances produced endogenously or derived from the environment, or due to failure to synthesize an enzyme. More than seventy years ago A.E. Garrod (1909) coined the term *inborn errors of metabolism* to describe a metabolic disorder in which clinical, biochemical and pathological manifestations are the consequence of a genetically determined deficiency of a specific enzyme. In general, such a mutation leads to a build-up of metabolites immediately preceding the block. Significant amounts of these metabolites may be diverted into pathways which, in the normal organism, are of only minor importance, and excessive amounts of 'abnormal metabolites' may be found in the body fluids. Often there is a deficiency of metabolites subsequent to the block. Sometimes this may be made good from the diet or via alternative pathways. Occasionally, failure to form compounds subsequent to the block may invoke *feedback mechanisms* increasing the flow of metabolites up to the block and aggravating the biochemical abnormalities. Transport of substances across cell membranes is in some cases mediated by specific carrier proteins which possess the characteristics of enzymes and are also genetically controlled. Mutations occur which give rise to inborn errors involving transport processes and these can affect the organism by depriving it of essential nutrients. Inborn errors associated with mental handicap have been identified in virtually all major pathways of metabolism (Table 5.2).

TABLE 5.2   Major pathways of metabolism implicated in mental retardation syndromes

Glycolysis and gluconeogenesis
Galactose metabolism
Pyruvate, acetyl-CoA and Krebs cycle interrelationships
Mitochondrial electron transport and oxidative phosphorylation
Amino acid transport and metabolism
Intermediary metabolism of fatty acids
Purine and pyrimidine metabolism
Porphyrin and bilirubin metabolism
Cofactor transport, synthesis and utilization
Disturbance of cation equilibrium and trace metal deficiencies

The enzyme defect has now been characterized in over three hundred inborn errors of metabolism (McKusick, 1983). Only a minority are associated with mental handicap. All are rare, some very rare (Table 5.3). Collectively, they nevertheless make a significant contribution to the prevalence of mental retardation.

TABLE 5.3   Approximate estimates of the birth frequencies of some disorders associated with mental handicap

Monogenic disorders	
Dominant disorders	
Huntington's chorea	1 : 10,000
Neurofibromatosis	1 : 2500
Myotonic dystrophy	1 : 5000
Tuberous sclerosis	1 : 30,000
Autosomal recessive disorders	
Phenylketonuria	1:7000–17,000
Homocystinuria	1 : 50,000
Histidinaemia	1 : 15,000
Maple syrup urine disease	1 : 250,000
Argininosuccinic aciduria	1 : 250,000
Galactosaemia	1 : 75,000
Mucopolysaccharidoses I and III	1 : 30,000 (combined)
Tay–Sachs disease	1 : 150,000 (higher in Jews)
Metachromatic leucodystrophy	1 : 50,000
X-linked disorders	
Mucopolysaccharidosis II	1 : 100,000
Fabry's disease	1 : 100,000
Menkes' syndrome	1 : 100,000
Duchenne muscular dystrophy	1 : 7000
Endocrine disorders	
Neonatal hypothyroidism	1 : 4000–6000
Chromosomal disorders	
Down's syndrome	1 : 650
Sex chromosomal disorders	1 : 550
Congenital malformations	
Spina bifida	1 : 300–1500

PATHOGENETIC FACTORS

Genetic or environmental factors will impair intelligence if they act at the molecular level to produce structural or metabolic defects in the brain which preclude normal function. Both genetic disorders, such as tuberous sclerosis or untreated phenylketonuria, and conditions of environmental aetiology such as rubella embryopathy or lead poisoning may present a whole spectrum of severity of mental defect ranging from virtual normality to the grossest handicap. A distinction between 'pathological' and 'subcultural' mental subnormality as initially enunciated by Lewis (1933) does not commend itself to the pathologist or biochemist. When mentally retarded patients die it is found at postmortem examination that biochemical disturbances sufficiently severe to result in permanent intellectual handicap are almost invariably associated with identifiable structural changes in the nervous system. The distribution of these changes is often topologically uneven, and most observed neuropathological changes are nonspecific, as the repertory of structural changes in the nervous system is rather limited in relation to the great variability of adverse metabolic factors, endogenous or environmental, to which it may be exposed. Genetic and environmental factors may act via common pathological pathways. For example, a high level of unconjugated bilirubin in the blood may occur in a premature infant in whom the enzyme which normally conjugates bilirubin with glucuronic acid, making its excretion possible, has not yet formed. High levels may also occur in cases of blood group incompatibility when so much bilirubin is formed from haemoglobin that the conjugating enzyme system is overwhelmed, or in the Crigler–Najjar syndrome in which there is hereditary absence of the enzyme. Brain damage with kernicterus (yellow staining of certain formations of the brain) may be seen in all three situations (p. 157).

Severe mental handicap may result from the effects of a single gene or a well-defined environmental hazard such as meningitis or head injury. Often, the aetiology of the mental defect is multifactorial, as a result of the interaction of several genetic and environmental factors, and such interactions are, indeed, the basis of biological variation. What matters is not to argue the relative importance of heredity and environment but to identify pathogenetic factors, be they genetic or environmental, and to counteract their harmful effects.

The vulnerability of the brain at critical periods of its development has been stressed by Dobbing (1981). On this view, it is the severity and duration of growth-restricting factors and, crucially, the developmental stage of the brain which determine the extent of the ultimate intellectual deficit rather than the precise nature of the insult. Early in pregnancy metabolic upsets or teratogens may produce malformations, and in mid-trimester neuronal multiplication is at risk. The period from the last trimester of pregnancy to eighteen months or two years after birth has been called by Dobbing (1981) the 'brain growth spurt'. This is the period of glial multiplication, dendritic arborization and synaptogenesis, and of a high rate of myelination when the brain is particularly vulnerable to malnutrition, to endogenous and environmental poisons, and to hormonal imbalance.

The timing of the pathogenetic process from clinical and biochemical observations is not always unequivocal. Damage sustained by the brain during early development may only become apparent months or even years later, as demands on the nervous system increase and ability for abstract reasoning is tested. On the other hand, the effects of an early metabolic insult may be mitigated if the infant is subsequently reared in a favourable environment (Eisenberg, 1977, 1984).

The genetic make-up of an individual may affect, for better or for worse, the effects of drugs or poisons, and the clinical manifestations of an inborn error are influenced by the environment and by other genes. Of great importance in shaping the disease pattern of hereditary disorders is the phenomenon of *genetic heterogeneity*. For mutant genes of large effect this has nearly always been found when looked for. It means that more than one mutation may occur at the locus involved in an inborn error. Often this results in variable residual enzyme activity. In general, the higher this residual activity the milder the disorder, and the lower the risk to the nervous system. In some cases a mutation may alter the stability of an enzyme, in others its kinetics or cofactor requirement.

Sometimes enzyme activity is reduced to a small fraction of normal, but this residual activity may be sufficient for normal development. However, those affected may exhibit enhanced vulnerability to environmental hazards such as infections, in whose presence the underlying defect may be unmasked. These intermittent inborn errors of metabolism present a difficult problem to both clinician and laboratory staff, as often only prompt, specific treatment prevents death or mental deterioration. Between attacks the disorder may or may not be detectable by examination of the body fluids, but it should always be demonstrable by assay of the affected enzyme.

Determinants of pathogenesis in inborn errors are listed in Table 5.4, and some mechanisms by which metabolic defects can affect the brain are shown in Table 5.5. Because of the multiplicity of factors involved it is seldom possible to identify a unique pathogenetic process. It must be stressed that the fact that a plausible pathogenetic mechanism exists does not mean that it is operating in patients, the fact that it has been found to operate in one affected patient that it will also operate in another whose environment or genetic make-up, apart from the mutation involved, may be entirely different. In general, it is the task of workers in basic research to single out possible pathogenetic factors and to study them, as far as possible, in isolation. The clinician's role is to utilize the knowledge gained in assessing the significance and contribution of interacting pathogenetic factors in individual patients.

DETECTION OF METABOLIC DISORDERS

Most disorders causing mental retardation are diagnosed by presymptomatic screening of the newborn or by investigation of high-risk groups (Table 5.6). The logistics, techniques and ethics of mass screening have been discussed by Chitham *et al.* (1976) and Bickel *et al.* (1980). In many countries neonatal mass screening has been introduced for phenylketonuria and hypothyroidism. Antenatal detection of Down's syndrome in the fetuses of mothers aged thirty-

TABLE 5.4 Determinants of pathogenesis in inborn errors of metabolism

Nature of defect	Disorder generally more serious if enzyme deficiency is on major metabolic pathway, or if synthesis or metabolism of neurotransmitters or neuropeptides is affected
Genetic heterogeneity	Disorder generally more serious if deficient enzyme occurs in more than one organ or if more than one isoenzyme is affected, more benign if enzyme deficiency only partial
Effect of other genes	Effects of an inborn error may be mitigated by operation of alternative pathways
A multiplicity of environmental factors	Anoxia and hypoglycaemia, infections, malnutrition or inappropriate diet, drugs, lack of stimulus in environment
Developmental stage of the brain	Brain particularly vulnerable in early pregnancy and during the 'brain growth spurt' from last trimester of pregnancy to end of second year of life

TABLE 5.5   Some mechanisms by which metabolic defects can affect the brain

Function affected	Examples
Interference with neurotransmission	Anoxia-ischaemia, hyperammonaemia, nonketotic hyperglycinaemia, malignant phenylketonuria
Interruption of energy supply to cells	Anoxia-ischaemia, hypoglycaemia, pyruvate dehydrogenase deficiency, some organic acidaemias
Inhibition of synthesis of low molecular weight molecules	Untreated phenylketonuria, maple syrup urine disease, urea cycle disorders
Failure of synthesis or degradation of macromolecules	Glycogen synthetase deficiency, most lysosomal disorders
Failure to maintain blood brain barrier	Anoxia-ischaemia, many organic acidaemias, Reye's encephalopathy
Failure to maintain integrity and function of membranes or intracellular organelles	Reye's encephalopathy, Duchenne muscular dystrophy
Impairment of uptake, transport or renal conservation of essential metabolites	Some variants of methylmalonic acidaemia, Menkes' disease, Wilson's disease
Failure of detoxication of products of metabolism, drugs or poisons	Bilirubin encephalopathy, galactosaemia, urea cycle disorders, fetal alcohol syndrome

Note: Several mechanisms may operate simultaneously and synergistically.

five years and over and antenatal detection of neural tube defects probably also meet the criteria for mass screening laid down by the World Health Organization (Wilson and Jungner, 1968). For most other conditions a convincing case has not yet been made. Often, not enough is known about the range of clinical manifestations or natural history of the disorder, or there is no reliable diagnostic test or effective treatment.

TABLE 5.6 Detection of inherited metabolic diseases

Presymptomatic mass screening of the newborn
Investigation of patients with disorders of the central nervous system
Investigation of mothers of retarded children
Investigation of infants with life-threatening metabolic disturbances
Antenatal detection by examination of amniotic fluid or fetal cells or tissues

---

Most cases of neurometabolic disorders are diagnosed in children seen because of acute or chronic signs of nervous system involvement, or when they are referred because of delayed physical and mental development, with or without congenital malformations. The probability of a metabolic disorder is enhanced if certain clinical signs are present.

Ocular findings are common in severely retarded children. Nystagmus, strabismus, optic atrophy and microphthalmus do not suggest specific biochemical investigations, nor does retrolental fibroplasia, but metabolic disorders may be associated with the signs listed in Table 5.7.

Deafness is probably as prevalent as blindness in the severely retarded, but in most cases a significant role for biochemical factors in the aetiology has not been established. Exceptions include Hunter's syndrome (Table 5.23) and the Pendred syndrome in which nerve deafness and an iodination defect in the synthesis of thyroxine is often associated with mental retardation. Disorders in which mental retardation is associated with abnormalities of *skin* and *hair*, or with *peculiar odours*, are shown in Tables 5.8 and 5.9 respectively.

Ataxia must be distinguished from the immature co-ordination often seen in mentally retarded patients. Blass (1979, 1980) noted that a number of inborn errors may be accompanied by spinocerebellar disorders and in some cases by ataxia and neuropathy (Table 5.10). It is important to remember that ataxia may be a sign of toxicity of certain drugs such as phenytoin, often prescribed for epileptic mentally retarded patients. Hagberg *et al.* (1979) commented on the frequent association of *dyskinesia*, abnormal movements, and *dystonia*, defective control of muscle tone, with neurometabolic disorders. This may reflect more stringent metabolic requirements or enhanced vulnerability of the basal ganglia relative to other areas of the CNS. Examples of the 'dyskinetic/dystonic syndrome' are shown in Table 5.11.

Of special interest in this field is the infant or child with *hypotonia* (Dubowitz, 1978). Hypotonia and weakness may result from a disorder of the

TABLE 5.7 Ocular findings in some metabolic disorders associated with mental retardation

Sign	Disorder	Comment
Cataracts	Galactosaemia	Cataracts also seen in galactokinase deficiency
	Mannosidosis	Seen in severe, infantile variant
	Lowe's syndrome	Other signs include glaucoma and buphthalmus
	Pseudohypoparathyroidism	Not always associated with mental retardation
	Dystrophia myotonica	Abnormality in IgG turnover
Corneal clouding	Many mucopolysaccharidoses	See Table 5.23
	Fabry's disease	Most patients not mentally retarded
	Wilson's disease	Kayser–Fleischer rings rarely seen before age seven years
Retinal changes	Many lipidoses	See Table 5.22
	Abetalipoproteinaemia	Preventable by vitamin E therapy
	Laurence–Moon–Biedl syndrome	Associated with abnormalities of sex hormones
Optic nerve involvement	Some lipidoses	See Table 5.22
	Some leucodystrophies	See Table 5.24
	Menkes' disease	See p. 202
Dislocation of lens	Homocystinuria	See p. 183
	Sulphite-oxidase deficiency	More severe course than homocystinuria
Conjunctiva	Ataxia telangiectasia	Telangiectasia of conjunctiva, immune deficiency

TABLE 5.8 Abnormalities of skin and hair in mentally retarded patients

Disorder	Abnormality	Comment
Menkes' disease	Pili torti and trichorrhexis nodosa	Pathognomonic, see p. 202
Argininosuccinic acidaemia	Brittle hair	Wide spectrum of severity, see Table 5.27
Homocystinuria	Hair sparse and brittle, malar flush	See p. 183
Hartnup disease	Pellagra-like rash	Sign of nicotinamide deficiency, most patients not retarded
Holocarboxylase synthetase deficiency	Extensive skin rash, alopecia	Patients generally respond to biotin therapy
Phenylketonuria	Eczema, dry skin, dilution of hair colour	Only in untreated patients with classical phenylketonuria
Tyrosinosis II (Richner–Hanhart)	Hyperkeratotic plaques on palms, soles, elbows	About half the cases seen have been mentally retarded
Gaucher's disease	Yellow coloration of skin	Some cases, see Table 5.22
Niemann–Pick disease	Yellow coloration of skin	Some cases, see Table 5.22
Farber's disease	Brown desquamating dermatitis	See Table 5.22

motor unit, but may also be secondary to disorders affecting levels above the motor neuron. Relationships between muscle weakness, hypotonia and mental retardation are summarized in Table 5.12.

Growth disorders are common in mental retardation. *Primary growth deficiency* may be caused by teratogens as in the fetal alcohol, phenytoin, thalidomide, aminopterin and rubella syndromes, by chromosomal aneuploidy and by mutant genes which may affect brain and skeleton in parallel as, for example, in the mucopolysaccharidoses. *Secondary growth deficiency* is also common in mentally retarded children but in contrast to primary growth deficiency can sometimes be reversed by appropriate management. Examples are malnutrition and psychosocial deprivation still seen in some old-fashioned institutions. Renal disease, heart disease, respiratory problems, often exacerbated by a deficient cough reflex, and above all chronic infection, also retard growth.

TABLE 5.9 Metabolic disorders associated with peculiar odours

Disorder	Smell	Compound	Comment
Phenylketonuria	Musty	Phenylacetic acid	Noticeable in some older, untreated patients
Maple syrup urine disease	Burnt sugar	Branched chain ketoacid derivatives	Many variants, in classical form a neo-natal emergency
Isovalericacidaemia	Sweaty feet	Isovaleric acid	Smell diagnostically helpful in acidotic sick neonate
Glutaric acidaemia II	Sweaty feet	Organic acids	May be associated with acidosis and hypoglycaemia
3-Methylcrotonyl glycinuria	Cat's urine	3-Hydroxyisovaleric acid	Clinical presentation variable
Oasthouse disease	Musty	2-Hydroxybutyric acid	Very rare, due to defect in methionine malabsorption
Tyrosinosis I	Cabbage	Methionine	Only in a few severely affected cases with high blood methionine
Trimethylaminuria	Fishy	Trimethylamine	Not associated with mental retardation

TABLE 5.10   Ataxia in the mentally retarded

Aminoacidopathies
    Urea cycle defects, hyperlysinaemia, γ-glutamyl cysteine synthetase deficiency
Organic acidurias
    Pyruvate carboxylase and pyruvate dehydrogenase deficiency, glutaric acidaemia I, intermittent maple syrup urine disease, pyroglutamic aciduria
Other metabolic disorders
    Ataxia telangiectasia, Lesch–Nyhan disease, Wilson's disease
Neurodegenerative disorders
    Juvenile variants of some lipidoses, mucolipidoses and metachromatic leucodystrophy, adrenoleucodystrophy
Environmental aetiology
    Subacute sclerosing panencephalitis, anticonvulsants, phenothiazine, lead intoxication

---

TABLE 5.11   The dyskinetic–dystonic syndrome in various neurometabolic disorders

---

Aminoacidopathies
    Malignant phenylketonuria, homocystinuria (rare complication), Hartnup disease (rare complication)
Organic acidurias
    Propionic acidaemia (some cases), glutaric acidaemia I (frequent complication), 3-methylglutaconic aciduria (see Table 5.33 (2)), pyruvate dehydrogenase deficiency (rare complication, see also Table 5.33(1))
Lysosomal disorders (see Tables 5.21–5.24)
    Krabbe's disease, metachromatic leucodystrophy, Gaucher's disease, some gangliosidoses (rare complication)
Miscellaneous metabolic disorders
    Lesch–Nyhan disease, hypoparathyroidism and pseudohypoparathyroidism (a few cases), Wilson's disease, galactosaemia (rare complication), Huntington's chorea, xeroderma pigmentosum (some cases), Crigler–Najjar syndrome

---

Source: adapted from Hagberg *et al.* (1979).

Mild stereotyped *self-injurious behaviour* occurs in over 10 per cent of mentally retarded patients; self-injurious behaviour severe enough to result in irreversible brain injury in about 0.1 per thousand of the total mentally handicapped population (Corbett and Campbell, 1981). Biochemical factors may be involved as certain drugs, for example, the 5-hydroxytryptamine precursor 5-hydroxytryptophan or the GABA analogue Baclofen (lioresal)

TABLE 5.12 Hypotonia and muscle weakness in mentally handicapped children

Disorder	Comment
Hypotonia without significant weakness	
Nonspecific mental retardation	Very common in unclassified mental retardation. Often variable and tends to get less severe with age
Down's syndrome	Treatment of the hypotonia with 5-hydroxytryptophan produced no lasting benefits. Other trisomies may show increased tone
Aminoacidurias	Hypotonia is marked in hyperlysinaemia and nonketotic hyperglycinaemia
Organic acidurias	Hypotonia is seen in a number of organic acidurias resulting from defects in the metabolism of pyruvate and of the derivatives of the branched chain amino acids
Prader–Willi syndrome	Adiposity, short stature, hypogenitalism with severe hypotonia, endocrine abnormalities, high risk of diabetes
Zellweger's syndrome	Cerebrohepatorenal syndrome; severe hypotonia, convulsions, hepatic cirrhosis; serum pipecolate level raised, abnormal bile acids in urine
Other metabolic disorders	Hypotonia is found in hypercalcaemia of infancy, and untreated hypothyroidism
Muscle weakness with incidental hypotonia	
Congenital myopathies	May affect nervous system in addition to muscle. See Table 5.33 (3)
Mitochondrial myopathies	Serum CPK may be elevated; other glycogenoses not associated with mental retardation if carefully managed
Pompe's disease (glycogenosis type II)	
Congenital myotonic dystrophy	Mental retardation common but nonprogressive; serum CPK and CSF protein normal; electro-myogram shows 'dive bomber' effect
Congenital muscular dystrophy	Often associated with mental retardation; serum CPK raised in early stages, later normal; condition nonprogressive
Duchenne muscular dystrophy	Nonprogressive mental retardation found in some patients; serum CPK grossly elevated in presymptomatic and early stages of the disease
Peripheral neuropathies	Lower motor neuron affected in the leucodystrophies, in some other lysosomal disorders, in abetalipoproteinaemia, familial dysautonomia, Leigh's encephalopathy and in infectious polyneuropathies

Note: Werdnig–Hoffmann disease, myasthenia gravis, Refsum's disease and most congenital myopathies are not normally associated with mental retardation.

affect this behaviour at least temporarily. Self-mutilation is a diagnostically useful sign in the rare Lesch–Nyhan syndrome (p. 198).

Behaviour problems are common in mentally retarded patients; often they amount to little more than behaviour appropriate to the patient's mental age. Severe behaviour problems have been noted in two out of three patients with γ-glutamyltranspeptidase deficiency so far described (Wright *et al.*, 1979), and overproduction of phenylethylamine has been reported in aggressive psychopaths (Sandler *et al.*, 1978). *Autistic features* are on rare occasions seen in some metabolic disorders, for example, in untreated phenylketonuria, homocystinuria and some lipidoses. On the whole, biochemical approaches have not been rewarding in childhood autism, which is probably not a disease entity.

Chromosomal disorders, antenatal infections and drugs or poisons ingested in early pregnancy are well-known causes of *congenital malformations* (see chapters 4 and 6). While most inborn errors, in contrast, exert their effects postnatally, some may act as teratogens by restricting the energy supply available to the developing embryo for cell division and growth (Editorial, *Lancet*, 1984). Examples are multiple acyl CoA dehydrogenase deficiency, β-hydroxyisobutyryl CoA deacylase deficiency and the cerebrohepatorenal syndrome of Zellweger (Table 5.30).

Maternal phenylketonuria (pp. 106, 176) is a frequently quoted example of a *maternal neurometabolic disorder* which, if untreated, carries a high risk of mental retardation in the offspring. Most phenylketonuric women of childbearing age are known. The very small and decreasing numbers of undiagnosed women in the community who are mildly or moderately retarded and able to bear children do not justify mass screening of pregnant women. Tests for phenylketonuria should be considered in a woman of childbearing age who (1) is mentally retarded or, while of near-normal intelligence, has other neuropsychiatric symptoms; (2) has a family history of phenylketonuria, mental retardation or microcephaly; or (3) has one or more children with intrauterine growth retardation or congenital malformation. Maternal hereditary metabolic disorders are a rare cause of mental retardation in the offspring compared to environmental factors acting on the fetus via the mother.

Hereditary disease severe enough to produce a *life-threatening crisis* usually manifests itself in the first few days or weeks of life, but may present at any age (Haan and Danks, 1981; Holton, 1982). Examples are some organic acidaemias (p. 189), urea cycle disorders (p. 180) and galactosaemia (p. 196). Symptoms are often preceded or accompanied by viral or bacterial infection and may include acid base disturbance, often metabolic acidosis, hypotonia, persistent vomiting, lethargy, fits and coma. Most of these signs are, of course, nonspecific, and more commonly the result of severe infections or some cerebral pathology. When the patient dies undiagnosed, body fluids and tissues should be preserved for metabolic studies as recommended, for example, by Kronick *et al.* (1983).

For many neurometabolic disorders *antenatal detection* is now possible. Accurate diagnosis is the indispensable foundation on which subsequent

TABLE 5.13   Techniques used in prenatal diagnosis

Technique	Sample	Comments
Amniocentesis (15th–16th week)	Cell-free fluid	Useful for glycosaminoglycans (p. 164) and, for example, some organic acids by GC/MS
	Uncultured cells	Unsuitable for enzyme assays; but has been used for EM studies in lysosomal disorders (p. 164)
	Cultured cells	Time delay a drawback; cells used for enzyme assays or in situ studies of incorporation of labelled precursors
Chorionic biopsy (1st trimester)	Chorionic villi	Less delay; suitable for recombinant DNA techniques, probably for lysosomal enzyme assays
Fetoscopy (18th–21st week)	Fetal blood	Somewhat higher risk to fetus; lymphocytes have been used to detect inborn errors
	Fetal liver	Has been used for diagnosis of OCT deficiency (p. 180); possible application to liver-specific enzymes
	Fetal skin	Feasibility has been demonstrated

Source: adapted from Rodeck and Nicolaides (1984).
Notes: EM: electron-microscopy; GC/MS: gas chromatography/mass spectrometry; OCT: ornithine carbamoyl transferase.

medical intervention is based. Precise knowledge of the biochemical abnormality for which the fetus is at risk is therefore mandatory, as is an accurate and specific assay for its detection on an appropriate fetal specimen. Enzyme assays in current use will, for many autosomal recessive disorders, also reliably identify heterozygotes; this may help when the index case has died or is not available for other reasons. In a few X-linked disorders the female carriers can also be reliably identified. Whenever antenatal diagnosis is undertaken, close co-operation with the obstetricians is essential and there must be ready access to expert genetic counselling. All diagnoses must be confirmed for both affected and unaffected fetuses. Some techniques currently used for antenatal diagnoses are listed in Table 5.13, and metabolic disorders in which they have been successfully applied in Table 5.14 (see also Chapter 11).

Laboratory investigations

Problems in the detection of neurometabolic disorders may arise because of shortcomings in the methodology in some laboratories, often due to lack of experience of what are mostly very rare disorders, or through failure to appreciate the relevance or lack of relevance of a biochemical finding. Clinical signs may not be acted upon when those in charge do not realize their possible association with a metabolic disorder, or do not know how and of whom to request appropriate laboratory tests. A 'blunderbuss' approach of ordering large numbers of investigations on every patient in the hope that something will turn up is nowadays ruled out on grounds of cost, if for no other reason. The techniques of thin layer chromatography, gas chromatography and high pressure liquid chromatography often used in metabolic studies are widely available, but interpretation of the results is often extremely difficult in a field in which artefacts and false trails abound. It must be emphasized that nearly all the clinical signs listed in this chapter are nonspecific and more often than not occur in the absence of a specific neurometabolic disorder. They may assume significance only if, for example, their intensity and failure to respond to routine treatment appear inappropriate in their clinical context. A high index of suspicion and continued alertness on the part of all those dealing with mentally handicapped patients in whatever capacity is as helpful as any clue. A scheme for the detection of neurometabolic disorders is shown in Table 5.15.

It must be remembered that biochemical abnormalities detected in mentally retarded patients, particularly those in institutions, are more often caused by malnutrition, chronic infections or adverse reactions to drugs than by neurometabolic disorders. Often, hormone assays show a wider than normal scatter; inappropriate responses to stress and inadequate homeostasis are frequent findings. Mostly, such abnormalities are the consequence of the way mentally retarded patients live, and they play no part in the aetiology of the mental defect. They are found less frequently as the living conditions of retarded patients improve.

As in other branches of medicine, biochemical investigations should start

TABLE 5.14   Some hereditary disorders associated with neuropsychiatric handicap detectable prenatally

Disorder	Diagnostic assay
Aminoacidurias	
Phenylketonuria	DNA probe (some families)
Homocystinuria	Cystathionine synthase
Nonketotic hyperglycinaemia	Liver enzyme assay
Ornithine transcarbamylase deficiency	Liver enzyme assay
Citrullinaemia	Argininosuccinate synthase
Argininosuccinic aciduria	Argininosuccinase
Tyrosinaemia type I	Succinyl acetone
Disorders of carbohydrate metabolism	
Galactosaemia	Galactose-1-phosphate uridyl transferase
Pompe disease	α-1,4-Glucosidase
Pyruvate carboxylase deficiency	Pyruvate carboxylase
Organic acidurias	
Propionic acidaemia	Propionyl-CoA carboxylase
Methylmalonic acidaemia	
(1) B_{12} responsive	Defects in cobalamine synthesis
(2) nonresponsive	Methylmalonyl-CoA mutase
Maple syrup urine disease	Branched chain keto acid decarboxylase
Glutaric acidaemia type I	Glutaryl-CoA dehydrogenase
Glutaric acidaemia type II	Defect in β-oxidation of fatty acids
Lipidoses and leucodystrophies	
Gaucher disease	β-Glucosidase
Tay–Sachs disease	Hexosaminidase A
Sandhoff disease	Hexosaminidase A and B

TABLE 5.14 cont.

Disorder	Diagnostic assay
Niemann–Pick disease	Sphingomyelinase
Fabry's disease	α-Galactosidase A
Farber's disease	Ceramidase
Wolman disease	Acid lipase
Adrenoleucodystrophy	C_{26} fatty acid esters
Metachromatic leucodystrophy	Arylsulphatase A
Krabbe leucodystrophy	Galactocerebrosidase
Mucopolysaccharidoses and mucolipidoses	
MPS IH (Hurler)	α-Iduronidase
MPS II (Hunter)	Iduronate sulphatase
MPS IIIA (Sanfilippo)	Heparin sulphamidase
G_{M1}-gangliosidoses	β-Galactosidases
Mucolipidosis I (sialidosis)	Neuraminidase
Mucolipidosis II (I-cell disease)	Multiple lysosomal enzymes
Mucolipidosis IV	Storage bodies by electron microscopy
Neuraminidase-β-galatosidase deficiency	Neuraminidase and β-galactosidase
Mannosidosis	α-Mannosidase
Other disorders	
Lesch–Nyhan syndrome	Hypoxanthine–guanine phosphoribosyl transferase
Menkes' disease	^{64}Cu uptake by amniotic cells
Acid phosphatase deficiency	Lysosomal acid phosphatase
Xeroderma pigmentosum	Abnormal DNA excision-repair
Ataxia telangiectasia	Clastogenic factor in amniotic fluid

Source: abridged from Patrick (1984).

TABLE 5.15 Scheme for the investigation of mentally retarded patients

Clinical presentation ──→ Nonmetabolic investigations
  Chromosomes
  Imaging techniques
  Electrophysiological techniques
  Biopsies

Acute crisis
See p. 149

Stable condition
See p. 143

First-line investigation
  Acute infection screen
  Haematology screen
  Drugs and poison screen
  CSF (save some for further tests)
  Blood: electrolytes, blood gases,
    glucose, ammonia, lactate
  Urine: sugars, ketones
  Renal function tests
  Liver function tests

First-line and routine investigations
  Screening tests on blood and urine
  Biochemical profile
  Haematology screen
  Infection screen

Specialized tests
  Amino acids
  Organic acids
  Mono-, di- and oligosaccharides
  Glycosaminoglycans
  Purines and pyrimidines
  Enzyme assays on body fluids,
    biopsies on cultured cells

Diagnosis
  Genetic counselling
  Antenatal diagnosis
  Heterozygote detection

from the clinical signs noted in the patient and proceed via first-line tests to specialized studies. Local resources will determine where the line between first-line and specialized tests is drawn. When samples are referred, only centres with first-hand experience of the disorder looked for should be approached. In the United Kingdom, lists of centres are published and regularly updated by several scientific societies. For fuller accounts of the role of the laboratory in the detection of neurometabolic disorders see Rundle (1979), Stern (1983) and Hammond and Stern (1984).

ENCEPHALOPATHIES OF ENVIRONMENTAL ORIGIN

Hypoxia and ischaemia, hypoglycaemia, ventricular haemorrhage

Hypoxic-ischaemic brain injury is the most important single cause of mental handicap originating in the perinatal period. The brain can be deprived of oxygen by *hypoxaemia*, a diminished oxygen level in the blood, or *ischaemia*, a reduced perfusion of the tissues. Both may occur as the result of *asphyxia*, impairment of the respiratory exchange of oxygen and carbon dioxide. Hypoxaemia is associated with accelerated uptake of glucose by the brain, increased glycolysis and production of lactate, and diminished production of high-energy phosphates. Neurotransmitter synthesis, notably that of acetylcholine, is so sensitive to hypoxia that brain function may be severely affected before major changes in energy metabolism have occurred. The biochemical effects on the brain of ischaemia are similar to those of anoxia; commonly both occur together, before and during birth, rather than after birth.

The brain has an absolute requirement for glucose and *hypoglycaemia* has long been recognized as an important cause of mental retardation (Table 5.16). There is a margin of safety in the supply of glucose to the brain at normal blood levels, but if its minimum requirements cannot be met, hypoglycaemic coma will ensue. During fasting, glucose is mobilized from liver glycogen, glycerol, and fatty acids from fat. Glycerol and the glycogenic amino acids may serve as a source of glucose by gluconeogenesis (p. 136). Excess fatty acids are oxidized to the ketone bodies acetoacetic and 3-hydroxybutyric acid which, if availability of carbohydrates is reduced, become a major source of energy for the brain, particularly in infants. However, an uncontrolled increase in the level of the ketone bodies, as indeed of lactic acid and many organic acids (p. 189), can produce an acute metabolic crisis with severe tissue acidosis leading to a breakdown of the blood brain barrier, tissue oedema and destruction of brain tissue. In general, however, risk of brain damage is greater in hypoglycaemia without ketosis. Thus the chances for normal intellectual development are not good in hyperinsulinism due to nesidioblastosis, a condition in which no ketone bodies are present (Aynsley-Green, 1981).

Hypoglycaemia in the neonate is not uncommon and must be promptly treated if the intellectual development of the infant is not to be prejudiced. Before feeding is established, the infant depends on endogenous glycogen and

TABLE 5.16 Some aetiological factors in hypoglycaemia in infants

Environmental
   Asphyxia, anoxia, hypothermia
   Shock, haemorrhage
   Septicaemia, meningitis, Reye's encephalopathy
   Intrauterine malnutrition
   Alcohol, salicylate, paracetamol
Endocrine
   Hyperinsulinism (maternal diabetes, nesidioblastosis)
   Hypopituitarism
   Adrenal insufficiency
   Congenital adrenal hypoplasia
Hereditary
   Defects in gluconeogenesis
   Defects in glycogenolysis
   Galactosaemia, fructose intolerance
   Some organic acidaemias

Source: abridged from Leonard (1984a).

fat. Low-birth-weight infants, and particularly infants who are small for gestational age, may have low glycogen and fat reserves, and production of ketone bodies is reduced because of the slow maturation of the enzyme systems involved. This increases the demand for glucose at a time when the transport system carrying glucose into the brain is not yet fully developed. Infants with antenatal brain damage are often of low birth weight and are burdened with a host of perinatal problems which include a tendency to become hypoglycaemic. Pre-existing brain damage may then be made worse by episodes of hypoglycaemia.

In the newborn, particularly in the pre-term infant, *ventricular haemorrhage* not only results from trauma and circulatory disturbance but is also often a consequence of perinatal or postnatal hypoxia, particularly in the respiratory distress syndrome. The association between *low birth weight* and mental handicap has long been known. Infants of low birth weight due to intrauterine growth retardation (small-for-dates infants) must be distinguished from those who are pre-term but of normal weight for gestational age. The respiratory distress syndrome and intraventricular haemorrhage are more common in true pre-term babies, hypoglycaemia in those small for gestational age. The chances of normal intellectual development are generally less good for small-for-dates infants than for genuine pre-term infants of comparable birth weight. The former group includes infants with severe intrauterine malnutrition, chromosomal disorders and congenital malformations; the low birth weight and perinatal problems may then be the consequence of an abnormal brain rather than its cause. Prematurity with a birth weight appropriate for gestational age is often associated with uterine or placental abnormalities.

For the past thirty years paediatricians have striven to prevent mental handicap in these infants, by active management. Prevention of perinatal trauma, asphyxia, stabilization within the normal range of physiological parameters (Po_2, Pco_2, blood pressure, haematocrit) which affect cerebral blood flow and cerebrovascular transmural pressure help to reduce the incidence of ventricular haemorrhage (Szymanowicz *et al.*, 1984). Hypothermia and infections must be prevented and adequate nutrition provided by the appropriate route. In many low-birth-weight infants, administration of oxygen to prevent hypoxia was followed by retrolental fibroplasia which was generally attributed to 'excessive' use of oxygen. A critical reappraisal of the evidence by Lucey and Dangman (1984) suggests that excess of oxygen is but one of many factors which can disturb the delicate retinal circulation of the pre-term infant and interact to produce retinal damage.

Modern techniques which include CT scans, ultrasound and nuclear magnetic resonance imaging, positron emission tomography, and cerebral blood flow studies by xenon clearance or transcutaneous Doppler ultrasound have furnished windows for observing the brain, to localize lesions and monitor their evolution during life. There have been concomitant advances in electrophysiological and neurological assessment. A sound basis exists, therefore, for prospective studies. Any prognosis based on perinatal risk factors and observations of biochemical or clinical complications must be guarded. The quality of the environment in which an infant grows up following an insult to the brain may also profoundly affect the outcome (Eisenberg 1977, 1984; Siegel, 1982; Dubowitz *et al.*, 1984). Death or permanent handicap often ensue from the cumulative effect of several adverse factors each of which, acting on its own, might have been withstood. Yet some children escape in spite of perinatal problems, unresponsive care-giving and poor living conditions.

A nationwide high-technology service for the intensive care of low-birth-weight infants can reduce infant mortality and the prevalence of mental handicap, although the fight to prevent, for example, the respiratory distress syndrome and intraventricular haemorrhage is by no means won (Barson *et al.*, 1984). Provision of services of ever-increasing complexity and cost to care for smaller and smaller infants increases the stress experienced by family and staff, and faces the community with resource-allocation problems. Ultimately, medical care, no matter how excellent, is no substitute for inadequate maternal nutrition, low income, poor housing and lack of education, all prime determinants of low birth weight (Bloom, 1984; Stahlman, 1984).

Bilirubin encephalopathy

Severe jaundice of the newborn may damage widely scattered areas of the brain, classically the basal ganglia, brain stem and cerebellum, and the spinal cord. The early lesions are bright yellow, hence the term kernicterus (*Kern* is

German for nucleus). Clinically, classical kernicterus is characterized by athetosis, deafness and mental retardation. In the full-term infant with haemolytic disease it will often occur when the level of unconjugated bilirubin exceeds about 340 μmol/l (20 mg/100 ml). Exchange transfusions have been effective in preventing brain damage by reducing the blood bilirubin level until it acquires the capacity to detoxicate bilirubin by conjugation with glucuronic acid. Phototherapy with ultraviolet light is often sufficient in mild cases. Unconjugated bilirubin occurs in plasma free or bound to albumin; the level of free bilirubin is much lower than the total bilirubin. Nevertheless, it is free bilirubin which is believed to be responsible for kernicterus, and factors such as anoxia, acidosis and certain drugs which reduce the binding of bilirubin to albumin increase the risk of kernicterus.

The pathogenesis of the brain damage is poorly understood. In vitro bilirubin inhibits many enzymes of respiration, glycolysis, lipid and protein metabolism, but this may not be relevant to in vivo events. While Rh haemolytic disease in the newborn has been all but eliminated by administration of anti-D gammaglobulin at the birth of their first infant to Rh-negative primiparae, bilirubin encephalopathy continues to occur in low birth weight infants, whose immature liver fails to conjugate bilirubin. In many cases the bilirubin level at no stage exceeds 170 μmol/l. The pattern of lesions in the brain in these infants may be unlike that seen in classical kernicterus. In one series, the thalamus was predominantly involved in more than half the infants (Sherwood and Smith, 1983). The decisive factor in bilirubin toxicity in low birth weight infants may be a breakdown of the blood brain barrier rather than the bilirubin level. Many of the low birth weight infants have intracranial haemorrhages, known to produce hyperbilirubinaemia. The haemorrhages may also contribute to the handicap. In neonates, attempts to relate a single plasma biochemical parameter to later poor intellectual development and to define 'safe' or 'critical' levels have, in general, been conspicuously unsuccessful. Bilirubin is no exception (Lucey, 1982).

Epilepsy

In the mentally retarded, fits may be the primary cause of handicap; seizures and retardation may both be the result of an underlying disease process such as a storage disease or other inherited metabolic disorder, or they may be iatrogenic, caused, for example, by withdrawal of an anticonvulsant or administration of other drugs which interfere with the metabolism of anticonvulsants (Table 5.17). The view that convulsions harm the brain is deep-rooted. Many believe that fits or their consequences, such as hypoxia, asphyxia or vascular disturbance and associated biochemical changes, may cause permanent brain damage. This can occur in a previously well or retarded child. Sometimes a vicious circle is set up, the lesions caused by fits producing further fits.

TABLE 5.17 Disorders and events which may be associated with convulsions and mental retardation

---

Predominantly environmental

Anoxia, septicaemia, intra- and periventricular haemorrhage, electrolyte and acid base disturbance, hypocalcaemia, hypoglycaemia, bilirubin encephalopathy, narcotic withdrawal, poisons, drugs

Inborn errors

Urea cycle defects, organic acidaemias, nonketotic hyperglycinaemia and some other aminoacidurias, disorders involving the pathways of gluconeogenesis and pyruvate oxidation, lysosomal storage disorders and some other neurodegenerative disorders, Menkes' disease, Lesch–Nyhan disease (some cases)

Recently it has been recognized that the ingress of calcium ions into some neurons plays an important part in the genesis of paroxysmal depolarization, shifts which underly seizures at the cellular level. Within the cell, excessive accumulation of calcium ions during prolonged fits results in mitochondrial failure and activation of hydrolytic enzymes which fatally injure the cell and produce the appearance of ischaemic cell change (Rose, 1983). However, cognitive deterioration in retarded patients may be the consequence of injudicious anticonvulsant therapy rather than of seizures. There is also a well-recognized link between folate deficiency, intellectual deterioration and psychiatric disorder in patients on long-term anticonvulsants.

About one-third of the severely retarded have fits, compared to 0.5–1.0 per cent of the general population. Monotherapy, monitoring of anticonvulsant levels and possible toxic effects, and careful attention to nutritional status to prevent vitamin D and folate deficiencies, should greatly benefit these patients. This field has recently been reviewed by Rose (1983) and Aird *et al.* (1984), and further observations are provided in Chapter 8.

Nutrition

The adult brain can withstand even extreme and prolonged starvation without irreversible effects on intelligence. Recently, the vulnerability of the developing brain to malnutrition has been demonstrated in animal experiments and this has stimulated epidemiological studies in humans. Malnutrition is most dangerous during the 'brain growth spurt' from about mid-gestation to the second birthday (Balázs *et al.*, 1979; Dobbing *et al.*, 1984; p. 139).

A major difficulty has been to isolate the effects of malnutrition as a specific cause of mental handicap from the many other adverse environmental factors with which it is almost invariably associated. In animals, malnutrition results in reduced brain size, in itself not of great significance, but certain formations, for example the cerebellum, are selectively affected. Biochemical analyses have shown a reduction in myelin lipids, brain protein and mucopolysaccharides. The reduction in cell number as reflected by DNA analysis is not striking but synaptic ultrastructure is affected, as are many enzymes, including some involved in neurotransmitter synthesis. The major part of the brain growth spurt takes place after birth. Intrauterine malnutrition should, therefore, be correctable to some extent in the postnatal period. The effects of perinatal malnutrition will persist if the damage is sufficiently severe, or compounded by postnatal malnutrition or if biological deficits are reinforced by a poor environment and lack of stimulation (Eisenberg, 1977, 1984; Dobbing *et al.*, 1984).

Malnutrition during pregnancy may, in some cases, result in low birth weight infants and supplementation of the diet of pregnant women in poor populations has at times been recommended. This field has recently been reviewed by Campbell and Gillmer (1983). Results of protein and calorie supplementations have been variable and difficult to interpret. The importance of vitamins and trace metals is increasingly recognized. Deficiency or imbalance could result in fetal anomaly or low birth weight, both threats to normal intellectual development. Marginal differences could be significant as one of a number of interacting factors in causing abnormalities.

Vitamins, teratogens and poisons

Vitamins are involved in enzyme systems as co-enzymes and a deficiency may therefore result in severe metabolic disturbance. Beriberi caused by thiamine deficiency may present in infants as an acute encephalopathy; pellagra, nicotinic acid deficiency may result in dementia; hypocalcaemic tetany with convulsions may complicate vitamin D deficiency; folate deficiency may result in dementia or organic brain syndrome, vitamin B_{12} deficiency in sub-acute degeneration of the cord. Vitamin E deficiency is responsible for the neurological lesions in abetalipoproteinaemia (Table 5.10).

The teratogenic effects of vitamin deficiencies in the fetus have been extensively studied in animals, by both selective elimination of vitamins from the diet and the administration of vitamin antagonists. For a review of this topic see Crome and Stern (1972) and Vinken and Bruyn (1976). Postnatally, in advanced countries, inadequate intake is probably rare as a cause of vitamin deficiency except in alcoholics, psychiatric and particularly psychogeriatric patients. In most cases, supplementation of the diet to the recommended vitamin intake will correct any deficiency state. In some mentally retarded patients malabsorption is responsible for low blood vitamin levels in spite of adequate dietary intake.

A few individuals have a constant specific requirement for a particular vitamin and may need up to several hundred times the recommended intake: they exhibit *vitamin dependency*. Vitamin dependency is found in a minority of patients with inborn errors which untreated carry a high risk of death and mental retardation. For them, a simple, specific and safe treatment is available which is usually at least as effective as any alternative (Bartlett, 1983). Vitamin-dependent individuals form only a minute section of the population. There is, therefore, no justification for massive and indiscriminate vitamin supplements, but there is every reason to encourage diets with vitamin contents close to recommended norms. An adequate vitamin intake may be an important factor in reducing the incidence of neural tube defects in susceptible individuals (Dobbing, 1983). Lejeune (1982) has suggested that folinic acid supplements may reduce the fragility of the X chromosome in the fragile X syndrome in vivo as well as in vitro. Tetrahydrobiopterin plays a key role in malignant phenylketonuria (p. 174). Hydroxycobalamine and folinic acid enhance the in vivo synthesis of this cofactor (Leeming *et al.*, 1982). Tetrahydrobiopterin metabolism is disturbed in a number of neuropsychiatric disorders (Aziz *et al.*, 1982; Leeming *et al.*, 1982).

Drugs and poisons can interfere with prenatal development by disturbing embryogenesis giving rise to *malformations* or by exerting their toxic actions on developing fetal organs resulting in *deformities*. A single teratogen can be responsible for a wide spectrum of defects; identical malformations may result from diverse pathogenetic processes. Almost any pharmacologically active drug can be teratogenic given a sufficiently unfavourable environment, but conclusive proof is often difficult and requires laborious investigations. The timing of the insult may determine the form of the malformation as much as the agent responsible. Anticonvulsants, particularly phenytoin and barbiturate, increase the incidence of malformations in the offspring of pregnant epileptic women. Some effects on the intelligence of these offspring have been observed, but failure to control the fits may be more dangerous to the fetus than the anticonvulsant. Antimitotic drugs may be teratogenic. on the other hand, a small number of women who have had renal transplants and who routinely receive steroids, athothioprine and folic acid antagonists throughout pregnancy do not appear to have an increased incidence of malformed babies (Campbell and Gillmer, 1983).

The possibility that *maternal alcoholism* might harm the fetus was considered by a Select Committee of the House of Commons in 1834 but it is only in the past few years that the role of alcohol as a teratogen has been firmly established (p. 104). The nature of the pathogenetic process is not known but acetaldehyde, an oxidation product of alcohol, zinc and tryptophan pyrrolase deficiency have been implicated. Alcohol abuse in pregnancy is nearly always associated with other factors which have adverse effects on the fetus. The mothers tend to be heavy smokers and some are on psychotropic or addictive drugs. Trying to tease out the effects on learning or behaviour of only one of these variables at a time is virtually impossible. Current opinion is that in pregnancy one or two drinks a day will do no harm to the fetus of a healthy nonsmoker (Campbell and Gillmer, 1983). For a review of recent work on the mechanism of alcohol damage in utero, see Pratt (1984).

It is extremely difficult to decide to what extent *pollutants*, *food additives* and *allergens* adversely affect psychological development (Edwards and Owens, 1984). Up to 20 per cent of the population are atopic; allergic disorders of varying severity are, therefore, extremely common. Very rarely, severe food allergy plays a decisive role in the aetiology of neuropsychiatric disorders, for example in some children with severe migraine (Egger *et al.*, 1983) and some with intractable behaviour disorders. In general, however, food allergies do not appear to play an important part in the aetiology of psychiatric or psychosomatic disorders (Lessof, 1983; Pearson *et al.*, 1983), although, if present, they may well interact synergistically with a concomitant psychiatric illness. Retarded children as a group show no adverse behavioural or cognitive reactions to artificial food colourings although a few individuals may do so (Taylor, 1984; Thorley, 1984). Occasionally, parents wrongly believe that their children have severe disease due to food allergies. Parental obsession with allergen avoidance may then result in bizarre lifestyles and dangerous attempts to treat with oligoantigenic diets (Warner and Hathaway, 1984).

Mental retardation following an acute lead encephalopathy is rare in Britain. There is, however, considerable concern that children may be adversely affected by *low-level lead exposure* at body burdens well below the threshold for frank poisoning. Blood lead estimation is the most suitable test for detecting mildly increased exposure to lead. In the United States, assay of red cell zinc protoporphyrin is also widely used as a screening test (Table 5.18). Blood lead levels reflect recent exposure, while measurement of the lead content of teeth, widely used in epidemiological studies, probably reflects the body burden averaged over a period of time.

TABLE 5.18   The assessment of exposure to lead

Radiological examination	Gut, long bones
Haematological investigations	Anaemia, punctate basophilia
Biochemical tests	Lead in blood, urine, teeth
	Protoporphyrins in red cells, urine
	δ-Aminolaevulinic in urine
	δ-Aminolaevulinic dehydratase in red cells

Needleman *et al.* (1979) compared the intelligence of children with high and low lead exposure as reflected by the lead content of dentine and found a significant difference of about 5 IQ points. These findings were not universally accepted. More recent studies in Britain were specifically designed to eliminate methodological difficulties which abound in this field and to account for confounding variables. Uniformly, only small effects attributable to lead were found and where initially there were significant differences, they became nonsignificant when account was taken of confounders (Harvey, 1984). For a recent discussion of this topic see Dobbing *et al.* (1984). Toxic metals may interact with essential elements (Magos, 1981). Excess of iron decreases the toxicity of lead, while lead poisoning is aggravated by diets low in calcium and iron. Secondary deficiencies may be caused by a toxic metal when the supply of an interacting essential element is barely adequate. Even if allowance is made for social factors, epidemiological studies in behavioural toxicology in which a single biochemical parameter is measured are most unlikely to yield meaningful results. Further details on environmental hazards are provided in Chapter 4.

DEGENERATIVE DISEASES OF THE NERVOUS SYSTEM: LYSOSOMAL STORAGE DISORDERS

A significant proportion of degenerative disorders are genetic and presumably therefore have a biochemical basis. Often it is difficult to decide whether or not a condition is progressive. Clinical signs may narrow the diagnostic options but in some cases longitudinal observations over months or longer, supplemented by psychological assessments and electroencephalographic studies, are necessary to demonstrate first slowing, then arrest of acquisition of skills, and finally regression. Pathological processes may be active before birth, resulting in perinatal complications which can mask the progressive deterioration. It must be remembered that even collectively the contribution of inborn errors to neuropsychiatric symptomatology is relatively small compared to, say, antenatal and perinatal injury. Loss of previously acquired milestones is seen not only in storage disorders but also in many other encephalopathies (see Table 5.19).

TABLE 5.19   Some examples of disorders of the nervous system associated with intellectual deterioration

---

Tumours
Infections (subacute sclerosing panencephalitis)
Auto-immune and post-infectious disorders (Schilder's disease)
Chronic poisoning (lead, organic mercury)
Heredodegenerative disorders
    Neurocutaneous disorders (tuberous sclerosis, Sturge–Weber disease)
    Spinal and spinocerebellar degenerations (Friedreich's disease)
    Storage disorders (sphingolipidoses, mucopolysaccharidoses, leucodystrophies)
    Leucodystrophies (Krabbe's disease, metachromatic leucodystrophy, adrenoleucodystrophy)
    Huntington's chorea
    Wilson's disease
    Childhood autism (some cases)

In suspected degenerative disorders every attempt should be made to arrive at a firm diagnosis, even if this is unlikely to help the patient, so that the parents can be informed of the chance of a subsequent child being affected.

The incidence of rare recessive disorders is increased in consanguineous marriages, and some rare genes have a much increased frequency in certain ethnic groups. Thus, in Tay–Sachs disease the mutant gene frequency is a hundred times higher in Jews of eastern European origin than in other populations. Aspartylglucosaminuria and Salla disease occur almost exclusively in Finns. Awareness of the nonrandom distribution of rare genes may be of help in diagnosis.

Traditionally, storage disorders have been classified by the composition of the substance stored. In the *sphingolipidoses* the stored substance is a sphingolipid. Its basic structural unit is ceramide, an ester of the amino alcohol sphingosine. Ceramide may be linked to phosphorylcholine to form sphingomyelin or to one, two, three or four hexoses, and up to three residues of sialic acid (N-acetyl neuraminic acid), giving rise to gangliosides. The chief lipids of myelin are the phospholipids, sphingomyelin, cerebrosides (ceramide with one hexose residue) and cholesterol; nerve cells and their processes contain less phospholipid and more ganglioside. Sphingomyelin is also a constituent of subcellular organelles and the plasma membrane. The acid glycosaminoglycans (acid mucopolysaccharides), the substances stored in the *mucopolysaccharidoses*, are macromolecules consisting of repeating units of sulphated hexosamine and hexuronic acid. They are found in various tissues, particularly the cornea, blood vessels and cartilage, where they are an important constituent of ground substance. Some disorders combining the biochemical and clinical features of lipidosis and mucopolysaccharidosis have been termed *mucolipidoses*.

A definitive classification has been possible in many cases with the identification of the affected enzymes in these disorders. Invariably, these enzymes are located in lysosomes. These cytoplasmic organelles normally possess a full range of specific acid hydrolytic enzymes for the stepwise degradation of sphingolipids and glycosaminoglycans. Loss of activity at any of the catabolic steps is followed by intralysosomal accumulation of the molecule which cannot be broken down, with on occasion an overspill into the cytoplasm, and almost invariable hypertrophy of the lysosomes. The rate of accumulation of stored material depends on the turnover of the substance that has to be degraded in the course of cellular activity, and this varies from organ to organ. The stored material will be heterogeneous if the bond resistant to hydrolysis occurs in more than one type of molecule. In the brain, storage leads to mechanical distortion of cells, interferes with their metabolic activity and ends with their destruction.

In inborn lysosomal disorders, as in other errors of metabolism, the enzyme deficiency may be virtually complete in some cases; in others some enzyme activity may be preserved (Lloyd, 1984; Tables 5.21–5.24). In general, low enzyme activity is associated with early onset and rapid deterioration. Heterozygotes are clinically normal and usually have mean enzyme levels midway between those for normal and affected homozygotes. Some enzymes occur as isoenzymes which differ in activity and organ specificity and utilize different substrates. They may be under independent genetic control, in which case distinct clinical entities are associated with mutations affecting each isoenzyme. If, as sometimes happens, one mutation affects several isoenzymes the resultant disorder will combine the clinical and pathological features of the individual deficiencies. Examples are arylsulphatase A deficiency, metachromatic leucodystrophy, and arylsulphatase B deficiency, Maroteaux–Lamy disease, a mucopolysaccharidosis. Mucosulphatidosis, multiple sulphatase deficiency, presents both as a leucodystrophy and as a mucopolysaccharidosis.

Diagnosis

Although individually rare, the overall incidence of lysosomal storage disorders is probably between 1 in 5000 and 1 in 10,000 births in European populations. The clinical presentation is variable and in many cases does not conform to classical textbook descriptions. Disturbance of ganglioside metabolism is often associated with nerve cell destruction expressed by psychomotor retardation, fits, a cherry-red spot on the macula and later spasticity and paralysis. Disorders of the metabolism of sulphatide or cerebroside, which are important constituents of myelin, affect the peripheral as well as the central nervous system giving rise to signs of peripheral neuropathy, spasticity and ataxia. Seizures may occur, but usually in the later stages. In the mucopolysaccharidoses, storage in the skeletal system gradually results in a characteristic appearance and bony changes. When a stored substance has a high turnover in liver or spleen, visceromegaly occurs.

In the mucopolysaccharidoses (Table 5.21) and some mucolipidoses (Table 5.23) a collection of skeletal abnormalities referred to as *dysostosis multiplex* produces striking radiological changes. Electron microscopy supplemented by histochemical studies is particularly helpful where the biochemical defect is ill defined or unknown, as in some late-presenting variants of amaurotic family idiocy, the cerebroretinal degenerations. Skin biopsies which contain axons and Schwann cells can be used, obviating the need for brain biopsies. Reduced nerve conduction velocities are seen in disorders with segmental demyelination which include the leucodystrophies (Table 5.24). Electroretinograms and visual evoked potentials are helpful in suspected neurolipidoses (Table 5.22). Metachromatic inclusions and vacuoles occur in lymphocytes, and abnormal cells in bone marrow, in a number of lysosomal disorders. Biochemical investigations must form part of a multidisciplinary approach to diagnosis.

Most clinical laboratories offer screening tests for the detection of excess urinary glycosaminoglycans in the mucopolysaccharidoses and oligosaccharides in the mucolipidoses. In many cases, characteristic patterns are seen on thin-layer chromatography (TLC) or thin-layer electrophoresis. In the sphingolipidoses, quantitative analysis by high-pressure liquid chromatography (HPLC) of glycolipids in urinary deposits or plasma will identify, for example, cases of Gaucher's, Fabry's and Farber's disease. It is known that

TABLE 5.20 Genetic risks for carriers of monogenic disorders

Mendelian inheritance	Risk to offspring of carrier	Carrier detection
Autosomal dominant	50 per cent chance of transmission; risk of overt disease variable	Valuable but often beset by technical and ethical problems
Autosomal recessive	Very low unless (1) gene is very common (2) there is consanguinity in parents (3) same disorder occurs in spouse's family	Only advised for population of high gene frequency for certain disorders
X-linked recessive	50 per cent of male offspring affected	Valuable but results not always unequivocal

Disorder	Enzyme defect	Clinical features
MPS IH (Hurler)	α-L-iduronidase	Corneal clouding, visceromegaly, dysostosis multiplex, coarse facies, heart disease, severe mental retardation
MPS IS (Scheie)	α-L-iduronidase	Corneal clouding, stiff joints, aortic valve lesions, mental retardation mild or absent
MPS II (Hunter)	L-iduronosulphate sulphatase	Clear cornea, deafness, otherwise like MPS IH, mental retardation; mild and severe variants occur
MPS IIIA (Sanfilippo)	Heparan sulphate sulphamidase	Somatic features mild initially, may be more pronounced in late stages of disease, severe mental retardation
MPS IIIB (Sanfilippo)	α-N-acetylglucosaminidase	Clinically indistinguishable from MPS IIIA
MPS IIIC (Sanfilippo)	Acetyl-CoA: α-glucosaminimide N-acetyl transferase	Clinically indistinguishable from MPS IIIA
MPS IIID	Heparan sulphate acetylglucosamine-6-sulphate sulphatase	Clinically indistinguishable from MPS IIIA
MPS IVA	N-acetylgalactosamine-6-sulphatase	Corneal clouding, severe bone changes, aortic valve disease, mental retardation mild or absent
MPS IVB	Keratan sulphate β-galactosidase	Corneal clouding, mild dysostosis multiplex, mental retardation mild or absent
MPS VI (Maroteaux–Lamy)	Arylsulphatase B	Corneal clouding, dysostosis multiplex, no mental retardation
MPS VII (Sly)	β-Glucuronidase	Bone deformities, ? corneal clouding, dysostosis multiplex, visceromegaly, mental retardation
MPS VIII (DiFerrante)	Keratan sulphate acetylglucosamine-6-sulphate sulphatase	Mild dysostosis multiplex, visceromegaly, coarse hair, mental retardation.

Source: adapted from McKusick (1983).

TABLE 5.22 Neurolipidoses

Disorder	Enzyme defect	Clinical features
Tay–Sachs disease B variant	Hexosaminidase A	Fits, hyperacusis, dementia, paralysis, cherry-red spot on macula, early or late infantile onset, milder forms occur
Tay–Sachs disease O variant (Sandhoff)	Hexosaminidase A and B	Similar to B variant
Tay–Sachs disease AB variant	Hexosaminidases inactive with natural substrate	Similar to B variant
Gaucher's disease	Glucocerebrosidase	Hepatosplenomegaly, early and late onset variants, brain affected in early variants only
Niemann–Pick disease Type A, C, D (Nova Scotia)	Sphingomyelinase in Type A, C and ?D	Hepatosplenomegaly, neurological deterioration, cherry-red spots, less severe forms occur
Niemann–Pick disease Type B (E)	Sphingomyelinase in Type B and ?E	Visceral involvement only
Fabry's disease	Ceramide trihexosidase	Skin, eyes and kidney affected, peripheral neuropathy, most cases mentally normal, mild symptoms in female carriers
Farber's disease	Acid ceramidase	Hoarse cry, joint deformities, skin nodules, extent of mental retardation varies
Wolman's disease	Acid lipase	Hepatosplenomegaly, adrenal calcification, psychomotor retardation, steatorrhea
Pompe's disease	Acid α-1,4-glucosidase	Cardiomegaly, hypotonia, large tongue, infantile, childhood and adult forms

Note: Mode of inheritance autosomal recessive in all disorders except Fabry's disease.

TABLE 5.23 Mucolipidoses and related disorders

Disorder	Enzyme defect	Clinical features
GM₁ gangliosidosis (Landing)	β-galactosidase	Similar to Hurler syndrome, cherry-red spot, onset at birth, rapid deterioration
GM₁ gangliosidosis (Delly)	β-galactosidase	Mental and neurological deterioration, fits, no resemblance to Hurler syndrome
Mannosidosis	α-mannosidase	Similar to Hurler syndrome, dementia, less severe cases occur
Fucosidosis Type I	α-fucosidase	Similar to Hurler syndrome
Fucosidosis Type II	α-fucosidase	Milder course than Type I, skin lesions as in Fabry's disease
Mucosulphatidosis (Austin)	Multiple sulphatase deficiency	Features of mucopolysaccharidoses and metachromatic leucodystrophy, severe course
Mucolipidosis I (sialidosis)	α-N-acetylneuraminidase	Similar to Hurler syndrome, myoclonus, cherry-red spot
Mucolipidosis II (I-cell disease)	N-acetylglocosaminylphosphotransferase	Similar to Hurler syndrome, rapid course
Mucolipidosis III	As for mucolipidosis II but milder	As for mucolipidosis II, but milder
Mucolipidosis IV	? Ganglioside sialidase	Psychomotor retardation, clouding of cornea
Aspartylglucosaminuria	Aspartylacetylglucosamine amidase	Hurler-like appearance, psychomotor retardation, fits

TABLE 5.24 Leucodystrophies

Disorder	Enzyme defect	Clinical features
Adrenoleucodystrophy	?C_{26}–C_{30} fatty acid oxidation	Ataxia, fits, adrenal insufficiency, X-linked recessive, schizophrenic features in some older patients
Metachromatic leucodystrophy	Arylsulphatase A	Motor loss, ataxia, spasticity, fits, paralysis, late infantile, juvenile or adult onset, autosomal recessive, at least four genotypes identified, schizophrenic features in some older patients
Krabbe's leucodystrophy	Galactocerebrosidase	Progressive paralysis, fits, dementia, optic atrophy, hyperacusis, autosomal recessive

fibroblasts growing in culture incorporate ^{35}S-sulphate into acid glycosamino-glycans. This accumulation is greatly enhanced in fibroblasts from patients with mucopolysaccharidoses. This excessive accumulation, due to inability to degrade the glycosaminoglycan, can be prevented by supplying secretions from any genotypically different fibroblasts. Genotypes can therefore be identified by cross-correction experiments even if the precise defect is unknown. The correction factors in the secretions are the lysosomal enzyme deficient in the patient.

However, in all lysosomal disorders, identification, characterization and assay of the deficient enzyme are the definitive ways to establish the diagnosis and in favourable circumstances the heterozygous state of a sibling or other relative. Experimental details will be found, for example, in Galjaard (1980) and Glew and Peters (1977). Enzymes are usually assayed in leucocytes or fibroblasts, occasionally in serum or urine. The effect of deficiency of a lysosomal enzyme on other lysosomal enzymes is variable: in some cases activity is reduced; in others it may be increased several fold. Deficient activity of a lysosomal enzyme is more likely to be significant if other lysosomal enzymes are shown to be present in adequate amounts. Most lysosomal disorders can be diagnosed antenatally (see Table 5.14).

Approaches to treatment

In the storage disorders both substrate and enzyme are located within the lysosomes, which are the scavenger organelles of the cell, programmed to ingest extraneous as well as endogenous material. Cells can take up enzymes by endocytosis into pinocytotic vesicles which fuse with the lysosomes. An exogenous enzyme can then take part in the degradation of stored substances. Lysosomal enzyme deficiencies are therefore prime candidates for enzyme replacement therapy. Active enzymes can be delivered by infusion of plasma or leucocytes from a normal donor, but the short half-life of the enzymes necessitates frequent transfusions with all their attendant problems. Purified human placental enzyme has been used in Gaucher's disease with preponderant storage in the reticuloendothelial system. The placental enzyme can be modified by linking it to mannose or mannose oligosaccharides. The enzyme is thereby 'targeted' to the storage cells in the reticuloendothelial system which carry galactose-recognizing receptors on the plasma membrane. Preparation of adequate amounts of enzyme is costly and difficult, but production of lysosomal enzymes by recombinant DNA technology should be possible in the near future. This field has been reviewed in a recent symposium (Crawfurd *et al.*, 1982).

An alternative approach is to provide patients with a continuous source of enzyme by tissue or organ graft. Organ transplants have been carried out for Gaucher's, Niemann–Pick and Fabry's disease but, while biochemically effective, clinical results have been disappointing. Initial results have been encouraging with transplants of skin fibroblasts, bone marrow and placental epithelial cells. However, at least for fibroblasts, early optimism has not been justified by later studies (Gibbs *et al.*, 1983). Bone marrow transplants (Krivit *et al.*, 1983) have the advantage that many centres have extensive experience of this technique, gained from treating patients with leukaemia and immunodeficiency disorders. Amniotic epithelial cells have in their favour that they are not immunogenic and are, therefore, not rejected when transplanted. They produce the enzyme deficient in many lysosomal disorders (Adinolfi *et al.*, 1982). The results of long-term studies with these techniques will be of great interest.

Additional problems arise where storage occurs primarily in the brain as in Tay–Sachs disease. In animal experiments, infusion of hypertonic mannitol into the external carotid altered the permeability of the blood brain barrier and allowed exogenous lysosomal enzymes to enter the brain. Cerebral oxygen emboli have been used to alter brain permeability in cats, to allow enzymes to enter the brain and degrade substrate (Crawfurd *et al.*, 1982). Such approaches are unlikely to be used in patients in the foreseeable future. More hopeful is the evidence, from animal experiments, that the reticuloendothelial cells of the brain originate in bone-marrow-derived cells; there would then be a potential mechanism for enzymes to pass into the brain following bone marrow transplants (Krivit *et al.*, 1983). There is evidence that in some lysosomal disorders, for example Tay–Sachs disease, the pathogenetic progress is active in utero. For treatment to be effective we must assume not only that the enzyme will degrade stored ganglioside, but that no irreversible changes have occurred in the fetal brain.

In the foreseeable future the emphasis will rightly be on early diagnosis, genetic counselling and prevention. For example, in Tay–Sachs disease heterozygotes may be detected by assay in serum of the affected enzyme, hexosaminidase A. Screening is offered to high-risk populations in some countries, together with antenatal diagnosis for at-risk pregnancies.

Finally, dietary treatment has a place in hereditary neurological disorders. Refsum's disease (heredopathia atactica polyneuritiformis) presents with polyneuritis, retinitis pigmentosa, ataxia and progressive paralysis. The disorder is caused by a defect in α-oxidation of fatty acids. This results in failure to metabolize phytanic acid, which is largely of dietary origin. Patients benefit when placed on a phytol-free diet. A severely restricted diet may, however, lead to weakness and weight loss. A moderately restricted diet in conjunction with plasmapheresis carried out at two- to four-week intervals appears more promising. Plasmapheresis has also been used in Fabry's disease (Moser, 1981). Adrenoleucodystrophy is probably caused by a defect in the metabolism of C_{26} fatty acids which are also exclusively of dietary origin. This suggests that the cause of this disorder might also be favourably affected by dietary treatment (Moser, 1981). Neurological deterioration in abetalipoproteinaemia can be prevented by vitamin E therapy (Muller *et al.*, 1983; see p. 160). For full reviews of this field see Adams and Lyon (1982), Stanbury *et al.* (1983) and Brett (1983).

THE AMINOACIDURIAS

Many inherited and acquired disorders of amino acid metabolism have been described, and in some of these mental retardation is a constant or frequent manifestation. While in the storage disorders obvious disruption of cellular and subcellular organization provides a ready explanation for neurological and intellectual deterioration, the pathogenetic processes in the aminoacidopathies have proved more elusive despite accumulation of a formidable body of biochemical and clinical observations.

Phenylketonuria (PKU)

The discovery fifty years ago that mental retardation could be the result of a well-defined biochemical abnormality constitutes a landmark in the history of mental deficiency. PKU was also the first disease of intermediary metabolism to yield in large measure to specific treatment. The disorder is transmitted as an autosomal recessive trait. Heterozygotes are free from symptoms. In European populations the incidence is not uniform, but in most countries it lies between 1 in 5000 and 1 in 20,000 births. The disease is much rarer in non-European populations.

The enzymatic block in PKU is in the hydroxylation of the essential amino acid phenylalanine to form tyrosine, catalysed by an enzyme complex consisting of phenylalanine hydroxylase, a cofactor, tetrahydrobiopterin, and dihydropteridine reductase. The reductase is required to recycle the cofactor by reducing dihydrobiopterin back to tetrahydrobiopterin. Normally hydroxylation of phenylalanine serves as a safety valve which prevents the accumulation of this amino acid when intake exceeds requirements. As a result of the block in PKU, phenylalanine accumulates in the body fluids and is diverted into pathways which, in unaffected individuals, are of only minor importance, and gives rise to a urinary excretion pattern characterized by phenylpyruvic acid and other aromatic metabolites. In normal infants, the blood phenylalanine may rise temporarily to reach levels of two to three times the mean adult normal. This occurs particularly in premature or sick babies. By contrast, in PKU the level climbs steadily to settle at more than ten times the mean normal, the actual value depending on protein intake. *Classical PKU* is defined biochemically by a blood phenylalanine level persisting above 1.2 mmol/l on a free diet with a low or normal tyrosine level and the presence in the urine of characteristic metabolites.

In more than 97 per cent of phenylketonurics the mutation affects the phenylalanine hydroxylase moiety of the enzyme which is present in the liver in the form of several isoenzymes. Very low activity is found in classical PKU but variants with some residual enzyme activity and blood levels usually of 1 mmol/l or lower are not uncommon, about one case being found in many mass screening centres for every two cases of classical PKU. Transient PKU, apparently with slow maturation of the enzyme system, also occurs. Patients

Mental Deficiency

with deficiency of phenylalanine hydroxylase respond to a diet low in phenylalanine. Phenylalanine is an essential amino acid. Sufficient must be provided for growth and synthesis of essential metabolites, but not so much that dangerous levels can build up. A strict, onerous diet which includes a rather unpalatable mixture of amino acids as a protein substitute is prescribed in classical PKU, while less stringent regimens are often possible in milder variants. Most paediatricians will not treat infants with blood levels below 0.6 mmol/l. Infants with levels below 1.2 mmol/l on a free diet are often referred to as cases of *atypical PKU* or hyperphenylalaninaemia (a term which strictly speaking should include the classical variant), and those with lower levels, typically in the range 0.5–0.25 mmol/l, often also as *benign hyperphenyl-alaninaemia*. In treatment, a blood level of 0.2–0.5 mmol/l is aimed for but not always achieved. Overtreatment must be avoided as it can lead to deficiency states, which are particularly dangerous during the brain growth spurt.

To be effective, treatment of classical PKU must be started early. Most countries, therefore, operate neonatal mass screening schemes. Blood is collected on filter paper, usually four to eight days after birth, and blood phenylalanine assayed in screening centres which typically handle from 20,000 to 100,000 cases a year. Infants with elevated levels are referred for further investigations and treatment, if appropriate.

In up to 3 per cent of phenylketonurics the mutation affects the dihydropteridine reductase or cofactor synthesis. The reductase and cofactor are also involved in the hydroxylation of tyrosine and tryptophan. In classical PKU due to hydroxylase deficiency, symptoms other than mental retardation (dilution of hair and iris colour, skin problems, occasionally epilepsy) are usually not striking. Life expectation is good. Patients with mutations involving the reductase or cofactor are much more severely affected. They do not respond to a phenylalanine-low diet. In spite of normalization of the blood phenylalanine level, patients present progressive neurological deterioration, fits, dystonia and dysphagia. The neurological signs have been attributed to the failure to form dihydroxyphenylalanine (dopa) and 5-hydroxytryptophan, the precursors of the neurotransmitters dopamine, adrenaline, noradrenaline and 5-hydroxytryptamine (5-HT). The catecholamines and 5-HT are in fact reduced in the body fluids. These variants are often referred to as *malignant PKU*, and by some authors confusingly as atypical PKU. Most affected infants appear to respond to neurotransmitter replacement therapy with dopa, carbidopa and 5-hydroxytryptophan (see Table 5.25). It is, therefore, important to identify infants with malignant PKU early, before the brain is irreversibly damaged. In the United Kingdom blood spots from all infants who have persistently raised blood phenylalanine levels are now routinely assayed for cofactor level and reductase activity; assay of urinary pterins is also widely used and is equally effective (Dhondt, 1984; Leeming *et al.*, 1984).

Neonatal screening followed by dietary treatment has dramatically reduced

TABLE 5.25 Variants of hyperphenylalaninaemia

	Phenylalanine hydroxylase deficiency	Dihydropteridine reductase deficiency	Defects in dihydropteridine synthesis
Tryptophan and tyrosine hydroxylation	Mildly affected	Severely affected	Severely affected
Phenylalanine-low diet	Normal development	Progressive neurological deterioration	Progressive neurological deterioration
Dopa, carbidopa, 5-hydroxytryptophan	Does not respond	Most cases respond	Most cases respond
Effect of tetrahydrobiopterin	No effect	Lowers blood phenylalanine	Lowers blood phenylalanine

the number of phenylketonurics who are retarded. Unsolved problems include the nature of the pathogenetic process, the role of factors other than dietary control which may affect the outcome, the risks of relaxing the diet in the older child when brain development is assumed to be complete, and the management of pregnancies in phenylketonuric mothers. Considering the large number of publications on the biochemistry of PKU, it is surprising how little is known about the pathogenetic process (Gaull *et al.*, 1975). Persistently high phenylalanine levels, greater than 1.2 mmol/l in early infancy, almost invariably lead to moderate to severe retardation; no harmful effect of levels below 0.25 mmol/l has been demonstrated. Beyond that we know very little for certain. Myelination is disturbed in untreated PKU. In high concentration, phenylalanine interferes at some stages of protein synthesis and inhibits the entry of other essential amino acids into the brain. Some metabolites present in abnormally high concentration have been shown in vitro to inhibit some enzymes of glycolysis and pyruvate metabolism, and particularly neurotransmitter synthesis. There is a much more severe course in malignant PKU where neurotransmitters are more immediately affected. Tyrosine, the metabolite subsequent to the block, is for phenylketonurics an essential amino acid. In general, however, the dietary intake is sufficient to prevent significant deficiency. So far, positive evidence is lacking that postulated pathogenetic processes demonstrated in vitro actually operate in the brain of patients (see p. 140).

Very little is known about the effect on patients of intermediate blood phenylalanine levels (0.5–1.2 mmol/l) as seen in infants with milder atypical variants of PKU and with some residual enzyme activity, particularly as these infants are deliberately excluded from some of the most extensive clinical trials (Koch *et al.*, 1982). These infants may show dramatic increases in blood phenylalanine levels, for example during a febrile illness, or when their protein intake is increased on weaning. The decision whether or not to treat may be difficult, particularly if the infant is developing normally, as neither course is free from risk. The management of various types of PKU has been reviewed by Walker *et al.* (1981), and details of dietary management will be found in Francis (1986).

There is now substantial, though perhaps inconclusive evidence that in PKU high, uncontrolled blood phenylalanine levels are harmful in late childhood, although less so than in early childhood during the brain growth spurt of the first one to two years after birth. Paediatricians, therefore, mostly continue dietary treatment beyond eight years, although some relaxation of the diet is usually allowed (Smith *et al.*, 1978; Koch *et al.*, 1982).

The phenylketonuric fetus of a heterozygote mother is not exposed to elevated phenylalanine levels during gestation and the phenylketonuric infant is essentially normal at birth. In the reverse situation, the heterozygous fetus of a phenylketonuric mother is at risk from high maternal phenylalanine levels. During the first trimester phenylalanine is teratogenic and cardiac and skeletal malformations are seen in some affected infants. Intrauterine growth is retarded and affected infants are microcephalic and mentally retarded with a characteristic facies (Lenke and Levy, 1980; Levy and Waisbren, 1983). To minimize risks to the fetus, it is now recommended practice to control maternal blood phenylalanine carefully, starting if possible before conception, and to maintain blood levels not higher than 0.5 mmol/l throughout pregnancy (see also p. 106).

Phenylketonuric mothers diagnosed by mass screening as neonates are likely to be used to the low-phenylalanine diet and will be of normal intelligence. For them, chances of effective treatment are good. There are also still in the community a small number of undiagnosed phenylketonuric women, born before screening was introduced. Unlike over 95 per cent of untreated phenylketonurics they are not severely retarded, although most have some handicap, often with additional psychiatric problems. These women are not used to the diet and when diagnosed during pregnancy or after having given birth to an affected child they are often unwilling or unable to co-operate in treatment. A third group are mothers with atypical variants, whose blood phenylalanine levels in infancy were not high enough to require treatment yet are too high for the safety of the fetus. They are confronted with the restricted and rather unpalatable diet for the first time as adults. Often, however, these women are strongly motivated and if sympathetically counselled readily accept treatment.

The success of treatment and the progress of patients has usually been assessed by monitoring changes in blood phenylalanine levels and IQ, taking account where possible of genotype by assay of the phenylalanine hydroxylase in liver biopsies and by taking into account pre-treatment levels of blood phenylalanine and the results of dietary challenges. In practice, the situation is rather complex. IQs do not necessarily adequately describe intellectual attainments. Some well-treated patients do not maintain at school the progress expected from psychometric assessment. Problems of language development and behaviour are not uncommon (Stevenson *et al.*, 1979). Able, caring parents who provide a stimulating environment are also likely to succeed with the diet, and good performance by the child may reflect a favourable home background as well as good dietary control. Conversely, dietary failure often goes hand in hand with unsatisfactory home conditions. Failure to maintain progress at school when the diet is relaxed at age eight may be attributable to the increased phenylalanine intake but may also, at least in part, reflect damage to the nervous system sustained much earlier, or even before birth.

The benefits of dietary treatment in classical PKU cannot be disputed. However, the extent of these benefits relative to other factors affecting intellectual development which must operate in these patients is uncertain. In particular, comparison between treatment groups will be falsified if, unbeknown to the investigators, they contain different proportions of milder cases who might escape major brain damage without treatment, and are better able to tolerate dietary indiscretions. Paediatricians do not always agree at what elevation of blood phenylalanine treatment should be given. Many err on the side of caution, on the not unreasonable assumption that any deficits in an untreated child will be attributed to failure to treat, while deficits in a treated child will, perhaps unjustifiably, be ascribed to insufficiently rigorous treatment rather than to adverse nutritional or psychosocial side effects of treatment which is, *a priori*, also possible. We must resist the temptation to accord overriding importance to any one factor. Treatment of inborn errors like PKU has to be long term, and it is difficult and not without risks. It should never be embarked upon without adequate back-up for the clinician from laboratory, dietician, psychology and EEG departments.

Early-treated phenylketonurics are of normal intelligence and will often want to marry and have children. At present, antenatal diagnosis is not offered, but detection of affected fetuses probably will become available soon by methods utilizing recombinant DNA technology (Cederbaum *et al.*, 1984), although the technique may not be applicable in all families. Enquiries of parents suggest that a substantial proportion have sufficient confidence in the treatment and their ability to cope to be willing to face the risk of another affected child. Many such parents state that they will not avail themselves of an antenatal diagnostic service when offered. Heterozygotes may be identified, in most cases, by phenylalanine load tests or, more simply, by the plasma phenylalanine/tyrosine ratio determined on a sample collected in carefully defined conditions (Rosenberg and Scriver, 1980). Care in interpretation is necessary as the ratio is affected in pregnancy, in women taking oral contraceptives, and by drugs affecting folate metabolism such as cotrimoxazole. Surprisingly, at least in the United Kingdom, there has been little demand for genotyping. For detailed reviews of PKU the reader is referred to Bickel (1980), Rosenberg and Scriver (1980) and Stanbury *et al.* (1983).

Histidinaemia

In this aminoaciduria there is a block at the first step in the catabolism of histidine, its transformation to urocanic acid. As a consequence histidine accumulates in the body fluids and there is excessive urinary excretion of imidazole pyruvic acid and other imidazoles. As the metabolic phenotype has many analogies with PKU, and as the first few cases described had neuropsychiatric deficits including in some cases delayed language development, the biochemical abnormality was assumed to be responsible for the clinical finding. Mass screening of neonates and treatment with a diet low in histidine was introduced in some centres. As more cases were found a discrepancy emerged between retrospective and prospective studies. Retrospective analysis of published reports, corrected for bias in selection, suggested that histidinaemia has an adverse effect on the development of the nervous system; prospective evaluation of cases discovered by newborn screening that the condition is benign.

Scriver and Levy (1983) reassessed the evidence and concluded that the reported frequency of handicapped individuals in the histidinaemic population is no higher than that in the normal population. However, histidinaemia may result in a lowered seizure threshold and enhanced vulnerability of the nervous system to adverse factors. Neonatal screening or dietary treatment for this condition is not recommended. Children born to histidinaemic mothers are generally normal (Tada *et al.*, 1982). Blood histidine levels in histidinaemia tend to be considerably lower on a molar basis than blood phenylalanine levels in PKU, due perhaps to the lower histidine content of our diet and the higher renal clearance of histidine relative to phenylalanine. This may at least in part explain the benign nature of this disorder.

Nonketotic hyperglycinaemia

In man, persistent hyperglycinaemia occurs with ketosis in some organic acidaemias (see p. 191). This form of hyperglycinaemia is referred to as *ketotic hyperglycinaemia*. Hyperglycinaemia without ketosis, *nonketotic hyperglycinaemia*, is associated with deficiency of the glycine cleavage system which transforms glycine and tetrahydrofolate into ammonia, carbon dioxide and 5,10-methylenetetrahydrofolate. The enzyme is present in liver and brain and it is the almost complete absence of the brain enzyme which results in extreme hypotonia, myoclonic fits, apnoeic episodes and a characteristic EEG with paroxysmal bursts on an almost flat record. Symptoms usually start within hours or days of birth and more than half the infants die in the first thirty days; survivors are nearly always severely retarded, as are some patients with a somewhat less acute course who may present at a later age. A significant biochemical finding is a marked increase in the CSF/plasma glycine ratio.

TABLE 5.26 Therapeutic measures proposed for nonketotic hyperglycinaemia

---

Protein restriction
Exchange transfusion
Insertion of ventricular shunt
Glycine conjugation with sodium benzoate or sodium salicylate
Pyridoxine, folate and lipoic acid (cofactor supplementation)
Supply of one-carbon units (N^5-formyltetrahydrofolate, methionine)
Supply of N^5, N^{10}-methylenetetrahydrofolate
Strychnine treatment (competition for glycine receptor sites)
α-Aminoisobutyrate administration (to increase glycine excretion)
α-Methylserine administration (to inhibit endogenous glycine formation from serine)

The role of glycine as an inhibitory neurotransmitter is well established. In mammals, both the influx of glycine into the brain and its neurotoxicity are strongly age dependent, being much greater in the newborn. The higher influx is required for the highly active protein synthesis in the developing brain. The glycine cleavage system presumably operates as a safety valve to prevent undue accumulation of glycine, particularly where it might interfere with neurotransmission. Toxic levels will build up if the delicate balance is upset between dietary intake, the active transport systems for influx and efflux of the amino acid, and the cleavage system. Treatment has generally proved disappointing, but some improvement in neurological state has been claimed for a few infants who survived the perinatal crises and who were treated with the glycine antagonists, strychnine, or γ-aminobutyric acid together with folate, lipoic acid and pyridoxine, the cofactor of the cleavage system (see Table 5.26).

Reliable heterozygote detection is not possible, but the disorder has been diagnosed antenatally by measurement of the enzyme in fetal liver biopsies. The syndrome has been reviewed recently in a symposium (Carson, 1982) and by Stanbury *et al.* (1983).

The hyperammonaemias

Ammonia is a major product of the catabolism of nitrogen compounds. It is formed endogenously by deamination of amino acids and the breakdown of purines and pyrimidines or it may be absorbed from the alimentary or urinary tracts where it can be produced by bacterial action. Ammonia is constantly produced in the brain, in increased amounts during convulsions and electroshock. High levels are extremely toxic, particularly to the nervous system. Detoxication occurs mainly in the liver by transformation to urea by the urea cycle enzymes (see Table 5.27). The cycle does not operate effectively in the brain due to the virtual absence there of the mitochondrial enzymes carbamyl phosphate synthetase and ornithine transcarbamylase (ornithine carbamyl transferase, OCT). Ammonia can also be metabolized by the formation of glutamate from oxoglutarate and glutamine from glutamate. This mechanism does operate in the brain but its scope is limited as it diverts oxoglutarate from the citric acid cycle and thereby jeopardizes energy availability and synthesis of high-energy phosphate compounds. Nearly all ammonia formed in the brain must be transported to the liver for conversion into urea.

The mechanisms whereby ammonia exerts its toxic action on the brain are still conjectural. While energy metabolism and changes in high-energy phosphate compounds are pronounced in the late stages of severe ammonia poisoning associated with coma, functional disturbances are observed well before measurable effects on the energy metabolism of the brain. Ammonia has an excitant effect exerted by interference with both post- and presynaptic inhibition and a depressant action on nerve cell excitability associated with reduced levels of the neuroexcitory compounds glutamate and aspartate. Interpretation of neurological signs is rendered more difficult by the possibility of selective depletion of energy stores in vulnerable regions of the brain and compartmentation of ammonia within the cell. Overall levels of brain ammonia

TABLE 5.27 The hyperammonaemias

Primary deficiencies of urea cycle enzymes
  N-acetyl glutamate synthetase
  Carbamoylphosphate synthetase (ornithine carbamoyl transferase)
  Ornithine transcarbamylase (ornithine carbamoyl transferase)
  Argininosuccinate synthetase (citrullinaemia)
  Argininosuccinate lyase (argininosuccinic aciduria)
  Arginase (argininaemia)
Other hereditary disorders
  Ornithinaemia with homocitrullinuria
  Familial protein intolerance (dibasic amino acid transport defect)
  Some organic acidaemias
  Nonketotic hyperglycinaemia
  Lysinaemia with hyperammonaemia (one case only)
Secondary hyperammonaemias
  Reye's encephalopathy
  Hypoxia-ischaemia (particularly in neonates)
  Shock
  Intravenous feeding
  Diffuse liver failure (poisons, infections, biliary obstruction)
  Sodium valproate therapy
  Transient (in neonates)

---

and overall oxygen consumption may be poor guides to an understanding of pathogenesis.

Hyperammonaemia may occur as a primary event due to an inborn error of one of the urea cycle enzymes, as a secondary phenomenon in liver disease, or in any disorder, hereditary or acquired, which prejudices the metabolic integrity of the mitochondrion in which some reactions of the urea cycle take place (see Table 5.27).

Complete blocks in the urea cycle are probably incompatible with life. Severely affected patients present in the neonatal period with lethargy, fits, vomiting, coma and death; patients with less severe disease and some residual enzyme activity develop symptoms in infancy or childhood. Persistent vomiting, failure to thrive and mental retardation are common. Symptoms may be triggered by an infection and exacerbated by high protein intake. Even mildly affected patients may have episodes of acute illness with ataxia, alterations in consciousness and other neurological signs. Some patients have died during such acute episodes owing to the development of cerebral oedema. Hyperammonaemia should be excluded in any mentally retarded child who develops an encephalitis-like illness or similar encephalopathy.

Among environmental causes of hyperammonaemia is Reye's encephalopathy. This syndrome usually follows a viral infection, but a similar clinical pattern is seen in some inborn errors (see p. 191) as a rare complication of treatment with some drugs (e.g. valproate) and after ingestion of some toxins. Signs include vomiting, stupor, hyperventilation and, in severe cases, coma, opisthotonus and cerebral oedema. With best treatment survival is close to 90 per cent, but some survivors are left with neurological and mental handicap. Reye's syndrome probably is the combined result of hepatic mitochondrial injury and hyperammonaemia (DeLong and Glick, 1982).

Clinically, it is difficult to distinguish hyperammonaemia from conditions such as intracranial haemorrhage or septicaemia, which also present with vomiting, lethargy and coma. To complicate matters, hyperammonaemia due to enzyme deficiency is often associated with intracranial haemorrhage. Nor are biochemical investigations straightforward. The concentration of ammonia in blood is normally low, and its estimation technically difficult (Leonard, 1984b). Abnormal amino acid patterns help in the diagnosis of deficiencies of the cytosolic enzymes argininosuccinic acid synthetase, argininosuccinase and arginase. Carbamoyl phosphate accumulates in all urea cycle disorders except carbamoyl phosphate synthetase and acetylglutamate synthetase deficiency and leads to excessive urinary excretion of pyrimidines which are diagnostically useful, as are the urinary ammonia/urea and ammonia/creatinine ratios. For the definitive diagnosis of deficiency of the mitochondrial enzymes in particular, enzyme assays on a liver biopsy are strongly recommended. Here, too, interpretation may be difficult as urea cycle enzymes show adaptive changes to dietary protein intake. The mitochondrial enzymes in particular are labile, making their assay difficult, and besides are low in conditions of mitochondrial injury caused by environmental as well as inherited factors, for example, in Reye's syndrome. In this syndrome liver function tests are abnormal and hypoglycaemia is frequent.

Secondary hyperammonaemia is treated by dealing, where possible, with the underlying cause, correcting metabolic derangements and, in Reye's syndrome in particular, controlling intracranial pressure. Therapy of urea cycle disorders was until recently confined to low protein diets. This was effective in some mildly affected patients but was often inadequate to promote normal growth. Matters are improved by supplements of essential amino acids or their keto-analogues and in particular arginine, which for these patients is virtually an essential amino acid, and, besides, in citrullinuria and argininosuccinic aciduria facilitates removal of ammonia via ornithine by excretion as citrulline and argininosuccinate respectively. Most effective for the removal of ammonia are the recently introduced promoters of the excretion of nitrogenous compounds, phenylacetic acid and benzoic acid (see Table 5.28). Treatment of comatose hyperammonaemic patients with benzoic acid has led to clinical improvement and a return of plasma ammonia levels towards normal in some cases (Koch, 1981; Leonard, 1984b). Even so, the outlook for most patients who present neonatally is poor, but the chances of preventing mental retardation in the less severely affected by timely and vigorous treatment of hyperammonaemic episodes are better (Lingam *et al.*, 1984).

TABLE 5.28   Treatment of urea cycle disorders

Low protein diet
Arginine supplements
Essential amino acid mixtures
Nitrogen-free analogues of essential amino acids
Oral citrate
Sodium benzoate
Sodium phenylacetate

All urea cycle disorders are inherited as autosomal recessive traits, except ornithine transcarbamylase which is X-linked. Female carriers can be detected by protein load tests. Symptoms in female heterozygotes vary widely as a result, presumably, of the extent to which normal or deficient chromosomes are inactivated (Lyon hypothesis). Even the most mildly affected carriers may have slight reduction in intelligence. Antenatal detection of several of the urea cycle disorders has been achieved (see Table 5.14). Recent reviews of this topic are by Koch (1981), Stanbury *et al.* (1983) and Leonard (1984b).

Homocystinuria

Excess of homocystine in urine is found in several inborn errors of metabolism (Rosenberg and Scriver, 1980; Bremer *et al.*, 1981; Stanbury *et al.*, 1983). Of these, cystathionine β-synthetase deficiency is the most important. This enzyme catalyses the formation of cystathionine from homocystine in the trans-sulphuration pathway from methionine to cystine. Patients usually have a malar flush, sparse and brittle hair, long thin limbs and other skeletal abnormalities reminiscent of Marfan's syndrome. The most distinctive clinical sign is dislocation of the lenses. Symptoms develop with age; they are absent in the newborn or young infant. Dislocation of the lenses usually presents by two to three years. In cystathionine synthase deficiency, excess of methionine and homocystine (formed by the condensation of two molecules of homocystine) is found in the blood, and there is increased urinary excretion of homocystine, methionine and other sulphur amino acids. Most patients are diagnosed clinically as the levels of methionine and homocystine in the blood and urine are usually not sufficiently elevated to permit detection by neonatal screening tests currently available, particularly in neonates who are breastfed or on low-protein milks.

Less than half the patients with homocystinuria are severely retarded, but many of the remainder who are mildly retarded, of normal or even of superior intelligence, have abnormal EEGs, epilepsy and various psychotic disorders. The pathogenesis of the mental defect is uncertain. Homocystine interferes with the formation of the normal cross-links of collagen, resulting in damage to the intima of arteries, platelet adhesion to the damaged surface and thromboembolic accidents. At autopsy, multiple infarcted areas have been found in the brains of some patients and these can account for at least some intellectual deficits seen in this disorder and for intellectual deterioration observed over the years in some patients. Roth (1969) pointed out that organic and functional psychiatric disorders occur together with a frequency well beyond chance expectation. Cerebrovascular accidents in homocystinuria may well trigger psychotic breakdowns in predisposed patients. This does not necessarily imply a causal relationship between the inborn error and psychiatric illness.

The disorder is genetically heterogeneous, as shown by in vitro studies on the properties of the enzyme in cultured fibroblasts, and a variable response in patients to treatment with pyridoxine: nearly half respond to pharmacological doses (100-500 mg/day) of the vitamin both biochemically and clinically. Homocystine disappears from plasma and urine and the blood amino acid pattern is normalized. Pyridoxal phosphate is the cofactor of cystathionine synthase. The mechanism whereby cofactor supplementation restores or preserves some enzyme activity is unclear. A diet low in methionine and supplemented with cystine, which for affected patients is an essential amino acid, will correct the biochemical abnormality in all variants of the disorder, and is the only effective treatment available for patients not responding to pyridoxine. Treatment has resulted in normal or near-normal somatic and intellectual development in some cases, but long-term follow-up is required for full evaluation of its benefits.

As important as the transulphuration pathway from methionine to cystine via homocystine are the remethylation pathways from homocystine to methionine. Inborn errors are known affecting two of the enzymes involved, N^5-*methyltetrahydrofolate transferase* and N^5,^{10}-*methylenetetrahydrofolate reductase*. In these disorders increased excretion of homocystine is accompanied by normal or decreased blood methionine levels. Transferase deficiency has been described in several patients with a wide spectrum of clinical manifestations. The deficiency may be caused by defective vitamin B_{12} transport or intracellular metabolism of cobalamine, the cofactor of this enzyme. In severe forms of this variant, CNS lesions resemble those seen in B_{12} deficiency with subacute combined degeneration of the cord. As in B_{12} deficiency, methylmalonic acid is excreted in urine. Cobalamine supplements may benefit some patients. Reductase deficiency is also associated with a wide range of symptoms. Folate administration was followed by dramatic biochemical and clinical improvement in a mildly retarded patient with a schizophrenia-like psychosis. The three forms of homocystinuria are outlined in Table 5.29.

Other aminoacidurias

Selected aminoacidurias are listed in Table 5.30 in their relationship to mental handicap. For detailed treatment of these and other aminoacidurias the reader is referred to Bremer *et al.* (1981). Of especial interest here are disorders in which nervous function appears directly affected. The most likely site of the

TABLE 5.29 Three forms of homocystinuria

	Synthase deficiency	Transferase deficiency	Reductase deficiency
Clinical manifestations			
Mental retardation	Common	Common	Common
Retarded growth	No	Common	No
Bone deformities	Common	Rare	No
Dislocated ocular lenses	Common	No	No
Thromboembolic tendency	Common	No	Rare
Laboratory findings			
Megaloblastic anaemia	No	Rare	No
Methylmalonic aciduria	No	Yes	No
Plasma and urinary homocystine	Increased	Increased	Increased
Plasma methionine	Increased	Normal or decreased	Normal or decreased
Plasma and urinary cystathionine	Decreased	Normal or increased	Normal or increased
Serum folate	Normal or decreased	Normal or increased	Normal or decreased
Treatment			
Response to vitamin	B_6 helpful	B_{12} harmful	Folic acid harmful
Severe methionine restriction			

Note: Synthase, cystathionine synthase; transferase, N^5-methyltetrahydrofolate–homocystine methyltransferase; reductase, $N^5, {}^{10}$-methylenetetra-hydrofolate reductase.

TABLE 5.30 Selected aminoacidurias

Disorder	Enzyme affected	Comment
Generally associated with mental defect		
Phenylketonuria	Phenylalanine hydroxylase complex	See p. 173
Homocystinuria	Cystathionine synthase	See p. 183
Nonketotic hyperglycinaemia	Glycine cleavage system	See p. 179
Hyperammonaemia	Urea cycle enzymes	See p. 180
Tyrosinosis type II	Cytoplasmic tyrosine amino transferase	Mental retardation seen in Richner–Hanhart syndrome; see Table 5.8
Hyperlysinaemia	Saccharopine dehydrogenase (lysine forming)	Clinical signs variable, may include hypotonia, laxity of joints, growth retardation; some patients mentally normal
Saccharopinuria	Saccharopine dehydrogenase? (glutamate forming)	Two cases, both retarded, one with cerebral palsy
Pipecolic acidaemia	L–Pipecolate dehydrogenase?	Progressive neurological deterioration, hepatomegaly; elevated levels of pipecolate seen in Zellweger's syndrome
2–Aminoadipic aciduria	2–Ketoadipate dehydrogenase?	2–Aminoadipic aciduria also seen in some organic acidurias and Reye's syndrome
Glutathionuria	γ–Glutamyl transpeptidase	Behaviour disorder, see p. 188
β–Alaninaemia	β–Alanine aminotransferase	Somnolence, fits; excess GABA in body fluids
Carnosinaemia	Carnosinase	Progressive neurological deterioration; occasionally benign; carnosine is a neuropeptide
Homocarnosinosis	?	Homocarnosine elevated in CSF only; ? dominant inheritance; spastic paraplegia

TABLE 5.30 cont.

Disorder	Enzyme affected	Comment
Hypervalinaemia	Valine aminotransferase	Distinct from branched chain ketoaciduria
Hyperleucinaemia	Leucine/isoleucine amino transferase	Distinct from branched chain ketoaciduria
Hydroxykynurenimuria	Kynureninase	Stomatitis, sensitivity to light; some response to nicotinamide and pyridoxine
Formiminoglutamic aciduria	Formininotransferase	Microcephaly, cortical atrophy; genetically heterogeneous; occasionally benign
Sulfite oxidase deficiency	Sulfite oxidase	Dystonia and dyskinesia; dislocation of lenses
Lowe's syndrome	?	Renal aminoaciduria; cataracts, buphthalmos, rickets; dwarfism
No causal relationship to mental defect		
Histidinaemia	Histidase	Usually benign; enhanced vulnerability of CNS?
Sarcosinaemia	Sarcosine oxidase	Benign trait
Hyperprolinaemia type I	Proline oxidase	Benign trait
Hyperprolinaemia type II	o-Pyroline-5-carboxylate dehydrogenate	Some cases mildly retarded with epilepsy
Hydroxyprolinaemia	Hydroxyproline oxidase	Benign trait?
Cystathioninaemia	Cystathioninase	Benign trait; may respond to pyridoxine; cystathionine also excreted in some malignancies and other disorders
Hydroxylysinuria	?	Fits, dystonia, hyperkinesis have been described, but causal link to mental retardation not established
Hartnup disease	Transport of monocarboxylic amino acids	Symptoms of pellagra occasionally seen

defect in *β-alaninaemia* is the enzyme β-alanine α-oxoglutarate transaminase (Stanbury *et al.*, 1983). In this rare disorder excess GABA, an inhibitory transmitter at a number of synapses, is found in brain and body fluids. Symptoms described include somnolence, hypotonia, diminished reflexes, fits and early death, a pattern not unlike that in neonatal nonketotic hyperglycinaemia. In both disorders failure to deal with accumulation of a neurotransmitter can result in rapid and irreversible neurological deterioration.

Mental retardation has been a feature of three patients so far described with deficiency of *γ-glutamyl transpeptidase*, one of five enzymes forming the γ-glutamyl cycle (see Table 5.31). It has been postulated that this cycle has a role in the transport of amino acids across cell membranes (Stanbury *et al.*, 1983). No generalized defect of amino acid transport has been observed in kidney or fibroblasts from patients with γ-glutamyl transpeptidase deficiency. However the cycle, and particularly γ-glutamyl transpeptidase, could have a more restricted but essential function in the nervous system, for example in the transport or metabolism of biologically active peptides. Two of the three patients with the disorder had severe behaviour problems, but positive evidence of any abnormality in neuropeptide metabolism is lacking. Disease-related changes in neuropeptides have been reported in *carnosinaemia* in which elevated levels of carnosine (β-alanyl histidine) are found in the body fluids and brain, and in *homocarnosinosis* in which elevated levels of homocarnosine (γ-aminobutyryl histidine) are found in CSF. The nervous system has been severely affected in most patients with these two disorders. In the brain, peptides probably function as neurotransmitters or as modulators of synaptic processes. In the future, investigation of their role in neurological disease may be expected to assume major importance. Recent clinical and pathological findings have been reviewed by Edwardson and McDermott (1982).

TABLE 5.31   Disorders involving the γ-glutamyl cycle

Deficient enzyme	*Clinical signs*
γ-Glutamyl transpeptidase	Mental retardation, behaviour disorders
γ-Glutamylcyclotransferase	Not yet described
5-Oxoprolinase	? Mental retardation in some patients
γ-Glutamylcysteine synthetase[1]	Late onset spinocerebellar degeneration, low red cell glutathione
Glutathione synthetase[1]	Acidosis, mental retardation and neurological deterioration in some patients

Note: 1 In some patients the defect is confined to red cells, when the disorder is characterized by haemolytic anaemia but absence of neurological deterioration.

ORGANIC ACIDURIAS

Disorders of pyruvate and lactate metabolism

Pyruvate occupies a key position in the metabolism of all animal cells. Even moderate impairment of its metabolism often results in profound biochemical abnormalities in associated pathways, neurological symptoms and mental handicap.

The major pathways of pyruvate utilization are: (1) transamination to alanine; (2) reduction to lactate; (3) carboxylation to oxaloacetate; and (4) oxidative decarboxylation to acetyl-CoA and CO_2. The transamination and reduction are reversible, and alanine and lactate may become a source of glucose provided the gluconeogenic pathway is intact. Not only is pyruvate carboxylase the first step in the gluconeogenic pathway but its product, oxaloacetate, is a precursor of aspartate, which is necessary to prime the Krebs tricarboxylic acid cycle and is also of importance as a neurotransmitter. Oxidative decarboxylation is affected by the pyruvate dehydrogenase multi-enzyme complex. There is relatively little excess of this enzyme system, particularly in the brain. Even a small reduction in activity is therefore dangerous.

Deficiency of *pyruvate dehydrogenase* may be acquired, for example, because of thiamine deficiency or heavy metal poisoning, or to the action of any toxin or metabolite which causes mitochondrial damage and a general decrease of mitochondrial enzyme activity.

A number of patients with hereditary deficiency of pyruvate dehydrogenase have been described, mutations affecting one or other of the components of the enzyme complex. Severe deficiency is associated with infantile lactic acidosis, severe mental and motor retardation, fits, hypotonia, poor co-ordination and sometimes optic atrophy. Milder cases have a later onset and milder course, with ataxia as a prominent clinical sign. The findings in *pyruvate carboxylase deficiency* are again retarded mental and motor development, fits, hypotonia, lactic acidosis and in some cases hypoglycaemia. In a variant there is additionally hyperammonaemia and the blood level of citrulline and other amino acids is elevated (Robinson and Sherwood, 1984).

Deficient oxidation of pyruvate leads to impaired production of acetyl-CoA, lactic acid and pyruvic acid accumulation and, eventually, lack of ATP. Partial impairment of pyruvate oxidation can compromise brain function long before there is a drop in high-energy compounds by affecting the synthesis of acetyl choline and other neurotransmitters. Deficient carboxylase activity may also interfere with oxidation by impaired priming of the Krebs cycle, and possibly with the synthesis of aspartate and glucose from alanine.

Elevation of lactate and of pyruvate may only be intermittent, even in severely affected patients, but pyruvate is always abnormally high one hour after a standard glucose load. Urinary lactate may be markedly increased, particularly during acute episodes. Blood and urine levels of alanine are elevated in some patients. It must be remembered that lactic acidosis is not at all uncommon in sick infants (see Table 5.32). At postmortem examination some patients with disorders of lactate and pyruvate metabolism have shown the neuropathological features of *Leigh's encephalopathy* (subacute necrotizing encephalomyelopathy). However, this pattern of lesions probably represents no more than a common abnormal pathway which can be triggered by several hereditary and possibly also environmental factors. The pathogenetic process in pyruvate carboxylase deficiency probably operates via the Krebs cycle rather than gluconeogenesis. Attempts have therefore been made to increase the 4-carbon carboxylic acid pool by giving glutamic and aspartic acid with vitamin B_6 supplements to ensure adequate transamination. Thiamine in high doses has also been used with or without glutamate or aspartate. Beneficial effects have been reported in some but not in other cases.

TABLE 5.32   Aetiological factors in lactic acidosis

Environmental	Hereditary
Shock, cardiopulmonary disease	Disorders of pyruvate dehydrogenase complex
Uraemia, liver disease	
Acute infections, septicaemia	Deficiency of pyruvate carboxylase, or other enzymes of gluconeogenesis
Diabetic ketoacidosis	
Drugs (e.g. phenformin)	Methylmalonic acidaemia, propionic acidaemia, other organic acidurias
	Mitochondrial myopathies
	Idiopathic

Pyruvate dehydrogenase deficiency has been treated by a high fat diet to bypass the metabolic block. This may slow down but does not arrest or reverse the neurological deterioration. Cholinergic agonists such as physostigmine have been used in an attempt to counteract the inhibition of acetyl choline synthesis. Thiamine and lipoic acid, cofactors, and dichloroacetate, an activator of pyruvate dehydrogenase, have also been used but with no sustained benefit. One patient responded dramatically to thiamine. He appears to have had a true thiamine dependency. This field has recently been reviewed by Robinson and Sherwood (1984).

Other organic acidurias

Organic acidurias are characterized by the excessive excretion in urine of aromatic or aliphatic carboxylic acids. Often hereditary, they may or may not be associated with overt metabolic acidosis and abnormalities of amino acid or carbohydrate metabolism. Most frequently they present as life-threatening emergencies soon after birth, less frequently later in the first year of life with failure to thrive, vomiting, hypotonia and delayed milestones. Some patients develop apparently normally, then an infection or other stress precipitates a metabolic crisis with involvement of the CNS. Clinical signs include fits, dystonia, ataxia and athetosis, neutropenia and thrombocytopenia, neurological deterioration, and the symptom cluster of Reye's encephalopathy (Brett, 1983; Cohn and Roth, 1983; Brandt, 1984).

Organic acidurias do not lend themselves readily to screening by the time-honoured methods of paper or thin-layer chromatography; often the more sophisticated techniques of gas chromatography and mass spectrometry have to be employed (Chalmers and Lawson, 1982). Using these techniques Watts *et al.* (1980) examined urine from 2000 severely retarded patients living in institutions. Virtually all observed abnormalities were attributable to drugs, diet or other environmental factors, or were artefacts produced by bacteria. Perhaps because of the high mortality among those affected, organic acidurias do not contribute substantially to the prevalence of severe mental handicap. An organic aciduria should, nevertheless, be considered in the differential diagnosis when the physician is confronted by a critical illness in a mentally retarded child which is of sudden onset and accompanied by a refractory metabolic acidosis, sometimes also by hypoglycaemia and ketonuria, and by neurological signs. More often than not meningitis, septicaemia or a cerebral catastrophe will provide the explanation for the symptoms, but a screen for organic acidurias should be done for such patients. This will include blood gases, glucose, ammonia and lactate, urine ketones and urine spot tests and amino acid chromatography, and will help to decide if advice from a specialized centre should be sought.

Selected organic acidurias are listed in Table 5.33. Few generalizations may be made about pathogenesis in these disorders, but impairment of mito-chondrial function plays an important part. Acyl-CoA derivatives can compet-itively inhibit reactions involving acetyl-CoA, a 'cross-roads metabolite' with a pivotal role in several metabolic pathways. For example, in propionic acidaemia propionyl-CoA inhibits pyruvate carboxylase for which acetyl-CoA is a critical positive effector. The malate shuttle essential for making oxaloacetate available for gluconeogenesis is also inhibited. Gluconeogenesis is therefore seriously impaired and patients are prone to hypoglycaemia. In the same disorder, inhibition of N-acetyl glutamate synthesis and of carbamoyl phosphate synthetase reduces the effectiveness of the urea cycle and results in toxic levels of ammonia, while inhibition of the glycine cleavage system leads to hyperglycinaemia. Accumulation of ketoacids such as ketoisocaproic acid in branched chain ketoaciduria may interfere with mitochondrial pyruvate transport and lead to a secondary disorder of pyruvate metabolism. Decreased production of acetyl-CoA in carnitine deficiency or acyl-CoA dehydrogenase deficiency results in reduced pyruvate carboxylase activity and in reduced ketone body formation. The risks of hypoglycaemic brain damage are enhanced when there is failure to utilize ketone bodies, potentially an alternative fuel, as in the Tildon–Cornblath syndrome, failure to form ketone

TABLE 5·33   Selected organic acidurias

Disorder	Enzyme affected	Comments
(1) Involving gluconeogenesis and pyruvate metabolism		
Von Gierke's disease	Glucose-6-phosphatase	Hypoglycaemia, acidosis, hepatomegaly; mental retardation preventable by control of hypoglycaemia
Hereditary fructose intolerance	Fructose-1, 6-diphosphatase	Hypoglycaemia, hepatomegaly; responds to exclusion of fructose from diet
Pyruvate carboxylase deficiency	Pyruvate carboxylase	Fits, acidosis, psychomotor retardation; neuropathological findings of Leigh's encephalopathy in some cases
Phosphoenol pyruvate carboxykinase deficiency	Phosphoenol pyruvate carboxykinase	Hypoglycaemia, hypotonia, hepatomegaly, mental retardation
Pyruvate decarboxylase deficiency	Pyruvate dehydrogenase, PDH-E_1	Acidosis, hypotonia, fits, hypoglycaemia, psychomotor retardation; severity related to any residual enzyme activity
Lipoate acetyltransferase deficiency	Pyruvate dehydrogenase, PDH-E_2	Acidosis, psychomotor retardation, fits
Dihydrolipoyl dehydrogenase deficiency	Pyruvate dehydrogenase PDH-E_3	Ketoglutarate and branched chain ketoacid dehydrogenase activity also deficient; lethargy, dystonia, fits, mild hypoglycaemia
Pyruvate dehydrogenase phosphatase deficiency	Pyruvate dehydrogenase regulating enzyme	Acidosis, hypotonia, fits, coma, death; enzyme present in brain

TABLE 5·33 cont.

Disorder	Enzyme affected	Comments
(2) Involving amino acid derivatives		
Maple syrup urine disease (branched chain amino acids)	Branched chain ketoacid decarboxylase	Acute neonatal, milder and intermittent presentation; results of treatment mostly disappointing
Isovaleric acidaemia (leucine)	Isovaleryl-CoA dehydrogenase	Neonatal emergency or later onset often with mental retardation; treatment with glycine encouraging; characteristic odour
3-Methylcrotonylglycinuria (leucine)	3-Methylcrotonyl-CoA carboxylase deficiency	Acidosis inconstant; variable neurological signs, infantile spasms in some cases; several variants; characteristic odour.
3-Methylglutaconic aciduria (leucine)	3-Methylglutaconyl-CoA hydratase?	Progressive neurological deterioration, choreoathetosis; acidosis not prominent; few cases, no enzyme studies
3-Hydroxy-3-methylglutaric aciduris (leucine)	3-Hydroxy-3-methyl-glutaryl-CoA lyase	Severe acidosis, vomiting, hypoglycaemia; resembles Reye's syndrome; similar urinary excretion patterns may be produced by secondary enzyme inhibition
2-Ketothiolase deficiency (isoleucine)	3-Ketoacyl-CoA thiolase	Isoenzyme affected is mitochondrial and of high substrate specificity; episodic severe acidosis with vomiting, diarrhoea; mostly of normal intelligence

TABLE 5.33   cont.

Disorder	Enzyme affected	Comments
3-Hydroxyisobutyric aciduria (valine)	3-Hydroxyisobutyryl-CoA deacylase	Multiple physical malformations, early onset; so far only one case described
Propionic acidaemia (valine, isoleucine)	Propionyl-CoA carboxylase	Usually acute neonatal onset; some cases respond to biotin but prognosis generally poor; in the past, sometimes described as ketotic hyperglycinaemia
Methylmalonic acidaemias (valine, isoleucine)	Methylmalonyl-CoA mutase (5 variants) Methylmalonyl-CoA racemase	Some variants respond to vitamin B_{12}; ketotic hyperglycinaemia; methylmalonic aciduria also seen in vitamin B_{12} deficiency
2-Ketoadipic aciduria (lysine, tryptophan)	2-Ketoadipic acid dehydrogenase	Mental retardation in some cases; clinical presentation variable
Glutaric aciduria (type I) (lysine)	Glutaryl-CoA dehydrogenase	Onset in early childhood, progressive dystonia and athetosis; severe acidosis in many cases; some patients mentally normal
2-Oxoprolinuria (glutathione)	Glutathione synthetase	Acidosis, jaundice, haemolytic anaemia; risk of neurological deterioration increased if untreated
4-Hydroxybutyric aciduria (glutamic acid)	Succinic semialdehyde dehydrogenase	Hypotonia, ataxia, mild retardation
(3) Miscellaneous Multiple carboxylase deficiency	Holoenzyme deficiency, biotinidase deficiency or biotin transport defect	Early or late onset variants, symptoms of biotin deficiency, ketoacidosis, lactic acidosis, response to biotin therapy

TABLE 5.33 cont.

Disorder	Enzyme affected	Comments
Acyl CoA dehydrogenase defects ('glutaric aciduria type II')	Medium, long or short chain or combined acyl CoA dehydrogenases; electron transferring flavoprotein (ETF) defective	Neonatal onset sometimes with congenital malformations, or later onset; hypoglycaemia without ketonuria, acidosis; some patients respond to riboflavin
Mitochondrial myopathies	Defects in one or more components of the respiratory chain, e.g. cytochrome oxidase	Involvement of many systems including CNS; lactic acidosis; prognosis often poor, e.g. in Kearns–Sayre syndrome
Systemic carnitine deficiency	Defect of carnitine transport in kidney and at other sites	Encephalopathic episodes, muscle weakness, hypoglycaemia, lipid excess in muscle, dicarboxylic aciduria; high mortality
D-glyceric acidaemia	D-glycerate kinase?	Variable clinical presentation; may be associated with hyperglycinaemia, acidosis
Acetoacetyl-CoA thiolase deficiency	Cytosolic acetoacetyl-CoA thiolase	Hypotonia, psychomotor retardation, acidosis; defective cholesterol and sterol synthesis
Tildon–Cornblath syndrome	Succinyl-CoA: 3-ketoacid CoA-transferase	Intermittent severe ketoacidosis and hypoglycaemia; mostly not mentally retarded

bodies, as in β-hydroxy-β-methylglutaric aciduria, or a reduced rate of gluconeogenesis, as in defective β-oxidation of fatty acids.

More generally, it is not just the levels of toxic metabolites which matter, but also the rate at which they build up and their site of action. For example, impairment of the mitochondrial function of the endothelial cells of the brain capillaries may result from the combined effects of toxic metabolites, acidosis and infection, and result in failure of the blood brain barrier, brain oedema and irreversible brain damage (Goldstein, 1979).

Advances in treatment have not been insignificant. In isovaleric acidaemia, treatment with glycine to form isovaleryl glycine from toxic isovaleryl CoA has been advocated, as has the use of carnitine supplements. Some patients with carboxylase deficiencies improve when given biotin; they are 'cofactor responsive'. Patients with multiple carboxylase deficiency respond well; however, two patients with biotinidase deficiency were left with a hearing loss and optic atrophy (Leonard *et al.*, 1984). Four of the six known genotypes of methylmalonic acidaemia have a defect in cobalamin metabolism and may respond to B_{12} therapy; treatment with riboflavin may benefit some patients with dicarboxylic aciduria due to acyl-CoA dehydrogenase deficiency. Carnitine supplements may help the excretion of toxic acyl-CoA intermediates.

A diet low in branched chain amino acids is life-saving in branched chain ketoaciduria. Cofactor-nonresponsive propionic acidaemia and methylmalonic acidaemia have been treated by protein restriction, exchange transfusion, peritoneal dialysis and forced diuresis. In general, the outcome for these, the most common organic acidurias, has been disappointing; the mortality is high and many of the survivors are mentally handicapped (Leonard *et al.*, 1984; Rousson and Guibaud, 1984).

Prenatal diagnosis is possible for many organic acidurias, either by assay for deficient activity in cultured amniocytes or by measurement of the increased concentration of the organic acids in amniotic fluid by stable isotope dilution analysis (Sweetman, 1984).

OTHER NEUROMETABOLIC DISORDERS

Galactosaemia

Most affected infants have life-threatening symptoms by the end of the first week of life. They include failure to thrive, vomiting, jaundice and liver disease progressing to cirrhosis. Cataracts usually develop over a period of weeks, but some infants show signs of cataracts and cirrhosis at birth and these lesions are then not fully reversible. Mortality is high, even in early-diagnosed cases, as the metabolic defect is often aggravated by infection, typically *escherichia coli* septicaemia. The disorder may be milder, patients presenting at a later age with cataracts and mental retardation, while some stay virtually symptom-free and intellectually normal. The gene coding for galactose-1-phosphate uridyl transferase, the enzyme affected in galactosaemia, exhibits extensive polymorphism. Genetic heterogeneity accounts, at least to a major extent, for the wide range of severity observed in this disorder.

The metabolic block in galactosaemia results in the accumulation of galactose and at least two toxic derivatives, galactitol and galactose-1-phosphate. Galactitol produces osmotic swelling of the lens leading to cataract formation but by itself probably does not produce neuropsychiatric deficits. In contrast, galactose-1-phosphate is neurotoxic and nephrotoxic. Many cases of galactosaemia have been detected when the finding of a nonglucose-reducing substance in the urine of a sick neonate was followed up. The disorder is readily detected in blood collected on filter paper by a microbiological inhibition test for excess galactose, or by a fluorescence test which detects deficiency of galactose-1-phosphate uridyl transferase. It does not safely distinguish between complete and partial enzyme deficiency. Quantitative assay of the enzyme and study of its stability and electrophoretic mobility are required to establish the genotype of the patient, as enzyme variants differ in overall activity, stability and electrophoretic mobility.

Treatment with a diet free from galactose is life-saving and usually results in the reversal of acute symptoms, but it is very difficult to maintain a diet which contains no lactose, galactose or galactosides (from soya beans) once mixed feeding is introduced. At present, it is uncertain to what extent treatment can ensure normal intellectual development. In surviving infants, delays of up to four months before starting treatment do not appear to affect intelligence appreciably. Even competently treated patients tend to have visiospatial difficulties, intellectual deficits of up to 15 IQ points compared to their parents or unaffected siblings, and sometimes tremor and ataxia (Lo *et al.*, 1984). Emotional and behavioural problems are common even in patients of normal intelligence, but this may be due, at least in part, to stress in the family caused by a serious disease and its onerous treatment. Treatment is monitored by assaying galactose-1-phosphate in red cells. The correlation between dietary control and intellectual progress is imperfect. Homozygous galactosaemics have elevated cord blood galactose-1-phosphate levels, suggesting that the fetus is at risk. Again the relationship between cord blood galactose-1-phosphate levels and intelligence is not clear cut. In contrast, the heterozygous fetus of a treated galactosaemic mother has an excellent chance of normal development.

In man, there is ample evidence for the biosynthesis of galactose from glucose via the so-called pyrophosphorylase pathway. Galactosaemics are thus able to synthesize the essential galactolipids of the nervous system but also galactose-1-phosphate. There exists, therefore, a potential mechanism for self-intoxication which might limit the effectiveness of the galactose-free diet. In vitro, galactose-1-phosphate inhibits a number of enzymes of carbohydrate metabolism, but the in vivo pathogenetic mechanism has not been established. Of related disorders, *galactokinase deficiency* is characterized by elevated galactose and galactitol levels but normal galactose-1-phosphate uridyl transferase activity. Patients develop cataracts but are essentially free from central nervous system signs. One patient with generalized *uridine diphosphate-4-epimerase deficiency* was severely affected and developmentally retarded (Henderson *et al.*, 1983).

Antenatal detection and heterozygote detection are possible in galactosaemia. In view of the uncertain outlook for affected infants, even if treated from birth, informed counselling must be offered to parents at risk of having an affected child, preferably before they embark on a pregnancy. For recent reviews on galactose metabolism and its disorders see Burman *et al.* (1980), Komrower (1982, 1983) and Stanbury *et al.* (1983).

Disorders of purine and pyrimidine metabolism

The *Lesch–Nyhan syndrome* is characterized by compulsive self-mutilation, choreoathetosis, spasticity, gout and severe mental retardation. The enzyme affected in this X-linked recessive disorder is hypoxanthine-guanine phosphoribosyl transferase. This enzyme plays a vital part in the feedback control of intracellular purine levels; its deficiency results in overproduction and increased urinary excretion of purines (notably uric acid), urolithiasis and ultimately renal failure. Stone formation can be prevented by treatment with allopurinol. Unsolved problems of this disorder are the pathogenesis and alleviation of the neurological symptoms. Of all tissues, the brain has the highest level of the phosphoribosyl transferase, particularly in the basal ganglia. Many of the symptoms are related to basal ganglia dysfunction and this has been attributed to dysfunction of the dopaminergic and adrenergic neurotransmitter systems, as formation of the dopamine and serotonin precursors, dopa and 5-hydroxytryptophan, requires a purine-derived pteridine cofactor (see also p. 173). Results of clinical trials of these neurotransmitter precursors, supplemented by pteridine cofactor and the peripheral decarboxylase inhibitor carbidopa, are awaited with interest. Treatment with diazepam has also been proposed.

The disorder is genetically heterogeneous and the severity of symptoms correlates with the extent of the enzyme defect. Patients with activity a few per cent of normal develop gout at a comparatively early age. Lower enzyme levels have been found in patients with choreoathetosis and spasticity but without self-mutilation and with near-normal intelligence, while enzyme deficiency is almost complete in the full-blown syndrome. Assay of the phosphoribosyl in blood collected on filter paper, fibroblasts and amniotic cells is offered by specialized centres which also provide services for carrier detection and antenatal diagnosis. A useful screening test is measurement of the uric acid/creatinine ratio in urine. The blood uric acid level is usually elevated. The syndrome has recently been reviewed by Nyhan (1982), Watts *et al.* (1982) and in Stanbury *et al.* (1983).

Purines and pyrimidines play an important part in the immune systems. In *purine nucleoside phosphorylase deficiency* severe immune deficiency may be associated in a minority of patients with developmental delay, tremor, ataxia or tetraparesis, possibly as sequelae of frequent severe infections. In contrast to the Lesch–Nyhan syndrome, blood and urine uric acid is low in this disorder. In patients with *xeroderma pigmentosum* (p. 248), pigmented skin lesions are produced by ultraviolet light and there is a high incidence of malignancies. Abnormalities of the CNS occur in 20–30 per cent of patients. The underlying defect is absence of an endonuclease involved in the repair of DNA molecules damaged, for example, by ionizing radiation. Microcephaly and mental retardation occur in up to half the patients with *Fanconi's anaemia* (p. 249).

An important disorder involving defective DNA repair is *ataxia telangiectasia* (p. 249), which combines cerebellar ataxia, choreoathetosis, mental retardation and telangiectases (dilatation of the capillaries in the conjunctiva, skin and other organs). Complex immunodeficiency occurs in most cases and there is a high incidence of malignancies attributed to spontaneous chromosome abnormalities arising from defective DNA repair. The serum α-fetoprotein level is persistently raised, suggesting that the liver is not fully developed. The mechanism of the pathological changes in the brain, which include atrophy of the cerebellum and posterior columns, is unknown.

Orotic aciduria, a disorder of pyrimidine metabolism, is of theoretical interest because it is apparently caused by a mutation affecting a protein with two enzymatic activities on the pathway from orotic acid to uridine-5-phosphate, namely orotidine-5-monophosphate pyrophosphorylase and orotidine-5-decarboxylase. One case has been described in which only the decarboxylase was affected. Patients are usually referred because of slow mental and physical development, severe anaemia refractive to treatment, and megaloblastic changes in the bone marrow. Immune defences may be impaired, as in patients with disorders of purine metabolism. An unusual feature is a high incidence of congenital malformations. In the laboratory, orotic acid can be identified in crystalline deposits which separate when freshly voided urine is passed. The disorder is expressed in fibroblasts. Those from affected children have only a few per cent of normal activity, but this can be stimulated to near-normal levels by pyrimidine analogues such as allopurinol or atauridine. The interruption of pyrimidine nucleotide synthesis creates a requirement in patients for pyrimidines which can be met by supplements of uridine in some patients. Disorders of purine and pyrimidine metabolism have been reviewed in Bondy and Rosenberg (1980) and Stanbury *et al.* (1983).

Endocrine disorders

In the mentally retarded, endocrine disorders are more often than not the consequence of impairment of the nervous system rather than its cause. Exceptions are *congenital hypothyroidism* and *hypoparathyroidism*. Cretinism was once regarded as the main cause of backwardness. In French and German the words 'cretin' and 'idiot' were used synonymously. Congenital hypothyroidism may be caused by maldevelopment or maldescent of the thyroid, inborn errors of the metabolism of thyroid hormones, iodine deficiency, pituitary or hypothalamic disorders, and ingestion of goitrogens. In severe cases symptoms include feeding difficulties, constipation, lethargy and prolonged jaundice, later short stature and a characteristic facies. Affected neonates may show few signs, if any, and the diagnosis is often missed by even experienced paediatricians.

Endemic cretinism has largely disappeared in developed countries. It is thought to be due to severe maternal iodine deficiency at an early stage of fetal development, but other factors are probably involved. Goitrous cretinism with mental retardation has been described in offspring of mothers who had excessive intake of iodine during pregnancy and in offspring of thyrotoxic mothers overtreated with antithyroid drugs. Mental retardation has also occurred in patients with several of the rare inborn errors of hormonogenesis, particularly those with iodide peroxidase defects, also those with dehalogenase defects, and in some cases involving deficits in thyroglobulin synthesis or disposal. Most frequent is nongoitrous cretinism associated with an absent hypoplastic or ectopic gland. The overall incidence of congenital hypothryoidism is 1 in 4000 to 1 in 7000 births, making it the most common endocrine disorder in infants and an important treatable cause of mental handicap.

Work on rats has established that thyroid deficiency in utero or early postnatal life leads to a reduction in brain growth and defective myelination. Cell acquisition, dendritic arborization, synaptic organization and the development of neurotransmitter systems are adversely affected, resulting in distortion of the 'chemical wiring' of the brain (Patel *et al.*, 1980). In man, hypothyroidism is uncommon among the severely retarded. Hulse (1984), in a retrospective study, found a mean IQ of 80 for 141 hypothyroid children; 25 out of 99 children had an IQ below 75 on the WISC-R test. Delay in diagnosis was associated with reduced intellectual performance, but other factors are also involved. Thus IQ was strongly positively correlated with parental social class, and there is some evidence that inadequate replacement therapy (serum thyroxine levels maintained in the lower rather than the recommended upper half of the reference range) results in suboptimal intellectual development (New England Congenital Hypothyroidism Collaborative, 1984). During pregnancy, maternal hormones cannot compensate for fetal thyroid deficiency. This results in morbidity in many aspects of cerebral function. Fortunately, the adverse effects of prenatal hypothyroidism are largely, though often not completely, reversible in early-treated cases (McFaul *et al.*, 1978). On the other hand, late-treated patients who are clearly retarded when entering school may show marked improvement in performance on intelligence tests into adolescence and adulthood (Money *et al.*, 1978). In the past few years neonatal screening for congenital hypothyroidism has been introduced in many countries. Early detection and vigorous replacement therapy should dramatically reduce the contribution of this disorder to the prevalence of mental handicap.

Mental retardation is not uncommon in *hypoparathyroidism* and *pseudohypo-parathyroidism*. It is tempting to attribute the mental handicap to hypocalcaemia, a salient feature of both syndromes, in view of the key role of this cation not only in normal neuronal activity but also in epileptogenesis and 'epileptic brain damage' (see p. 159; Rose, 1983). However, in some late-onset cases of pseudohypoparathyroidism mental retardation and epilepsy appear to precede the hypocalcaemia. In others, hypocalcaemia and the morphological features of the syndrome such as short stature, round face, short neck and brachydactyly may be present without mental retardation. It is thus not yet clear if the mental retardation is a consequence of the biochemical defect (lack of end-organ sensitivity to parathormone), or of an associated heritable defect. The pattern of inheritance is unclear, but contrary to some statements in the literature it is not X-linked recessive. The disorder is reviewed in Stanbury *et al.* (1983).

The association of hypercalcaemia with mental handicap, a characteristic facies and supravalvular aortic stenosis or peripheral pulmonary aortic stenosis has been known for over thirty years. To distinguish the disorder from the hypercalcaemia due to excessive vitamin D intake the condition is referred to as *Fanconi-type idiopathic infantile hypercalcaemia*. Correction of the hypercalcaemia by a diet low in calcium and vitamin D is not followed by improved intellectual progress. Mean IQs on the Stanford–Binet or Wechsler tests fall within the range 55–66. In Britain, the incidence of the disorder is about 1 in 50,000 births. Its aetiology is obscure, although inadequate parathormone suppression by plasma calcium may play a part in pathogenesis. The disorder has recently been reviewed by Martin *et al.* (1984).

Hereditary disorders of trace metal metabolism

Wilson's disease (hepatolenticular degeneration) is a rare autosomal recessive disorder of copper transport of insidious onset. Patients may present with hepatic or neurological symptoms. The latter include ataxia, tremor and intellectual deterioration. Copper accumulates in the brain, liver, kidney and cornea, where it produces the characteristic Kayser–Fleischer rings. Biochemically, the levels of caeruloplasmin, the major copper-binding protein, are nearly always low, as is caeruloplasmin-bound copper, while noncaeruloplasmin, which is much more loosely bound to protein, is raised. This loose binding favours tissue deposition of the metal and produces effects of heavy metal toxicity. The basic defect in the transport of copper remains unknown.

Early diagnosis is important as effective treatment with copper-chelating agents is available. There are few diagnostic problems once symptoms have become established, but early and presymptomatic diagnosis poses problems. Unexplained failure at school may be an early sign in neurological cases. Differentiation of presymptomatic cases from heterozygotes is difficult, as up to 25 per cent of these also have low levels of caeruloplasmin and copper and are about a hundred times more common in the general population than affected homozygotes. Studies with radiocopper or a liver biopsy may be necessary for a firm diagnosis.

Menkes' syndrome, an X-linked disorder, is also caused by a defect in copper transport. Clinical signs include abnormal hair, rapid neurological deterioration, changes in bone and blood vessels, hypopigmentation and hypothermia. Serum copper and serum caeruloplasmin tend to be low. In general, however, there is maldistribution rather than deficiency of copper, with excess in some tissues and deficits in others. Most of the manifestations, such as changes in hair, bones and blood vessels, and the neurological signs, are largely explained by failure of the copper-containing enzymes lysyloxidase, dopamine-β-hydroxylase and cytochrome oxidase. There is evidence that the pathogenetic process is already active in utero. Attempts at replacement therapy have had very limited success. Milder variants have been described. The disorder is expressed in fibroblasts and amniotic cells. Antenatal diagnosis and carrier detection can be offered to families at risk. Wilson's disease has recently been reviewed by Walshe (1983), and Wilson's and Menkes' disease in Stanbury *et al.* (1983).

Five patients have been described with a combined deficiency of the enzymes xanthine dehydrogenase, sulphite oxidase and aldehyde dehydrogenase (Wadman *et al.*, 1983). All three enzymes share a pterin-derived molybdenum cofactor. *Molybdenum cofactor deficiency* is responsible for the observed lack of activity of the enzymes, in the presence of normal plasma molybdenum levels. Absence of this cofactor has been demonstrated in liver biopsies from three affected children. Patients are severely mentally retarded with dystonia, myoclonus, fits, xanthine stones and dislocated lenses. The signs are a combination of those seen in xanthinuria (xanthine dehydrogenase deficiency) and in sulphite oxidase deficiency (Bremer *et al.*, 1981). So far, attempts at treatment have been unsuccessful. The defect is expressed in fibroblasts and amniotic cells so that antenatal diagnosis is possible.

Down's syndrome

Following the discovery of the chromosomal basis of this disorder, interest has focused on factors causing nondisjunction (Tuck *et al.*, 1984; see also Chapter 6) and the effect of the extra chromosome on the metabolism of cells and organs. The search for specific biochemical abnormalities has not been rewarding. Early work, summarized by Smith and Berg (1976), produced evidence of quantitative abnormalities and defective homeostasis rather than of specific changes attributable to the aneuploidy. Several studies have produced evidence of impaired cellular and humoral immune capacity, but the underlying cause of the increased rate of infection in Down's syndrome patients remains unknown. To complicate matters, the deficiencies are only partial and vary from patient to patient (Björksten *et al.*, 1979).

Adults and older children with Down's syndrome have an increased incidence of auto-immune disease affecting the thyroid, pancreas, adrenals and gastric mucosa (Burgio *et al.*, 1978). Congenital hypothyroidism in infancy is nearly thirty times commoner than in the general population (Fort *et al.*, 1984). In 10–17 per cent of older patients some evidence of biochemical hypothyroidism is found, but only a minority require treatment. The incidence of goitre, thyroid antibodies and hyperthyroidism is also greatly increased. Regular monitoring of thyroid function is desirable (Sare *et al.*, 1978; Ziai *et al.*, 1984). There is also evidence in the syndrome of defective end-organ response to ACTH, FSH and LH (Murdoch, 1981).

Statistically significant deficiencies in trace metals and vitamins have been found, but their clinical significance is uncertain. Improving the nutritional state of these patients is beneficial but is no substitute for optimizing all aspects of their environment (Begab, 1984). Dietary supplementation has been disappointing (Smith *et al.*, 1984), but results of long-term controlled studies in children have not yet been reported.

The crucial question of how the presence of an additional set of genes on the extra chromosome affects brain development remains unanswered. Of considerable interest is the observation that patients with Down's syndrome show signs of premature ageing and that the incidence of the Alzheimer type of dementia is much higher than in the normal population. Another recent development which has given fresh impetus to research in this field is the identification of individual genes located on chromosome 21. Evidence is accumulating of a link between one of these enzymes and the premature ageing process. One of the genes identified on chromosome 21 codes for the cytoplasmic superoxide dismutase (SOD-I) which catalyses the formation of hydrogen peroxide from superoxide radicals. Its level is elevated by about 50 per cent in blood cells and fibroblasts, and also in the fetal brain, in Down's syndrome (Balázs and Brooksbank, 1985). In most tissues there is an adaptive response by the enzyme glutathione peroxidase, but this protective mechanism does not operate in the brain. This suggests that the uncompensated perturbation of the metabolism of oxygen derivatives may render the brain vulnerable to oxidative damage.

Lipoperoxidation of polyunsaturated fatty acids is increased in preparations of Down's syndrome brain. Polyunsaturated fatty acids are the major substrates of lipoperoxidation and the polyunsaturated fatty acid composition of brain phospholipids in Down's syndrome fetal brain tissue is abnormal. The changes are similar to those which occur during ageing. The potential for lipoperoxidative damage thus appears increased in Down's syndrome brains. Such damage may affect the structure and function of cellular membranes. It is also suggested that the products of lipoperoxidation may, via their action on the regulators guanilate cyclase and cyclic GMP, affect neurotransmitter function, notably the cholinergic system. Pyruvate dehydrogenase, the rate-limiting enzyme of glucose oxidation with its close links to acetylcholine synthesis, is also reduced in cells from Down's syndrome patients. Some of the genes, including SOD-I, located in man on chromosome 21 are located in the mouse on chromosome 16. It is now possible to produce mouse embroys with trisomy 16 (Gropp, 1982); this should greatly help research on the bio-chemistry of trisomies. A review of this complex field will be found in a recent symposium (Sinex and Merril, 1982).

CONCLUSIONS – THE CHANGING OUTLOOK

Excess or deficiency of endogenous or exogenous metabolites can overwhelm the adaptive capacity of the brain and result in mental retardation. Not many years ago, biochemical causes of mental retardation had to be inferred from scanty data recorded at irregular intervals. Today we have comprehensive biochemical profiles and frequent, sometimes continuous, monitoring of the metabolism of the patient. The new imaging techniques permit us to follow the evolution and sometimes the regression of lesions in the brain.

Only exceptionally is it possible to interpret pathogenesis by reference to 'abnormal' levels of a single metabolite in the body fluids; often it is even impossible to define such a level. The rate at which a metabolic disturbance

TABLE 5.34   Fetal therapy

Prevention
    Pre-pregnancy advice
    Antenatal care
    Management of pregnancy complications
    Prevention of prematurity
Dietary intervention
    Restriction
        Phenylalanine in maternal PKU
        ? Galactose in galactosaemic fetus
    Supplementation
        Vitamins to prevent neural tube defects
        Vitamin B_{12} in some variants of methylmalonic acidaemia
        Biotin in multiple carboxylase deficiency
Endocrine therapy
    Intra-amniotic thyroxine in some cases of hypothyroidism
Drugs
    Glucorticoids for pulmonary maturation
    Digoxin for hydrops fetalis in rhesus immunization
    ? Phenobarbitone for prevention of neonatal jaundice
    ? Albumin and frusemide in unexplained hydrops fetalis
Avoidance
    Tobacco
    Alcohol
    Teratogens

Source: adapted from Rodeck and Nicolaides (1984).

develops, the integrity of the blood brain barrier, the developmental stage of the brain and the selective vulnerability of its formations, and not least the quality of the environment in which the patient is reared, can enhance or soften the impact of a metabolic insult to the brain. Poor correlation between observed biochemical abnormalities and ultimate outcome has often been due to failure to take into account synergistic and antagonistic factors. The question 'Has this patient's mental retardation a metabolic cause?' should be rephrased as 'To what extent do metabolic factors contribute to this patient's retardation?' It is the responsibility of all those dealing with retarded patients, in whatever capacity, to be alert to the possibility of a metabolic disturbance and to know where to turn for help.

The techniques of cell culture and molecular biology have greatly increased the scope for early diagnosis (see p. 149) and paved the way to antenatal therapeutic intervention (see Table 5.34). Given present knowledge and techniques of diagnosis, treatment and prevention, we can look forward to a substantial reduction in the prevalence of mental retardation provided society will make available the necessary resources.

REFERENCES

ADAMS, R.D. and LYON, G. (1982) *Neurology of Hereditary Metabolic Diseases of Children*, New York, McGraw-Hill.

ADINOLFI, M., AKLE, C., MCCOLL, I., FENSOM, A.H. and BODMER, W.F. (1982) 'Expression of HLA antigens, β_2 microglobulin and enzymes by human amniotic epithelial cells', *Nature*, 295, 325–7.

AIRD, R.B., MASLAND, R.L. and WOODBURY, D.M. (1984) *The Epilepsies: a Critical Review*, New York, Raven Press.

AYNSLEY-GREEN, A. (1981) 'Nesidioblastosis of the pancreas in infancy', *Dev. Med. Child Neurol.*, 372–9.

AZIZ, A.A., BLAIR, J.A., LEEMING, R.J. and SYLVESTER, P.E. (1982) 'Tetrahydrobiopterin metabolism in Down's syndrome and in non-Down's syndrome mental retardation', *J. Ment. Defic. Res.*, 26, 67–71.

BALÁZS, R. and BROOKSBANK, B.W.L. (1985) 'Current topics: neurochemical approaches to the pathogenesis of Down's syndrome', *J. Ment. Defic. Res.*, 29, 1–14.

BALÁZS, R., LEWIS, P.D. and PATEL, A.J. (1979) 'Nutritional deficiencies and brain development', in F. FALKNER and J.M. TANNER (eds), *Human Growth*, vol. 3, New York, Plenum, 415–79.

BARSON, A.J., TASKER, M., LIEBERMAN, B.A. and HILLIER, V.F. (1984) 'Impact of improved perinatal care on the causes of death', *Arch. Dis. Childh.*, 59, 199–207.

BARTLETT, K. (1983) 'Vitamin-responsive inborn errors of metabolism', *Adv. Clin. Chem.*, 23, 141–98.

BEGAB, M.J. (1984) 'Surgical and cognitive intervention in Down's syndrome – a critique', in J.M. BERG (ed.), *Perspectives and Progress in*

Mental Retardation, vol. II, Baltimore, University Park Press, 373–80.

BICKEL, H. (1980) 'Phenylketonuria: past, present, future', *J. Inher. Metab. Dis.*, 3, 123–32.

BICKEL, H., GUTHRIE, R. and HAMMARSEN, G. (eds) (1980) *Neonatal Screening for Inborn Errors of Metabolism*, Heidelberg, Springer.

BJÖRKSTEN, B., BACK, O., HAGLOFF, B. and TARNVIK, A. (1979) 'Immune function in Down's syndrome', in F. GUTTLER, J.W.T. SEAKINS and R.A. HARKNESS (eds), *Inborn Errors of Immunity and Phagocytosis*, Lancaster, MTP Press, 189–98.

BLASS, J.P. (1979) 'Disorders of pyruvate metabolism', *Neurology*, 29, 280–6.

BLASS, J.P. (1980) 'Pyruvate dehydrogenase deficiencies', in D. BURMAN, J.B. HOLTON and C.A. PENNOCK (eds), *Inherited Disorders of Carbohydrate Metabolism*, Lancaster, MTP Press, 252–7.

BLOOM, B.S. (1984) 'Changing infant mortality: the need to spend more while getting less', *Pediatrics*, 73, 862–6.

BONDY, P.K. and ROSENBERG, L.E. (1980) *Metabolic Control and Disease*, Philadelphia, Saunders.

BRANDT, N.J. (1984) 'Symptoms and signs in organic acidurias', *J. Inher. Metab. Dis.*, 7, Suppl. 1, 23–7.

BREMER, J.J., DURAN, M., KAMERLING, J.P., PRZYREMBEL, H. and WADMAN, S.K. (1981) *Disturbances of Amino Acid Metabolism: Clinical Chemistry and Diagnosis*, Munich, Urban & Schwarzenberg.

BRETT, E.M. (ed.) (1983) *Paediatric Neurology*, Edinburgh, Churchill Livingstone.

BURGIO, G.R. and UGAZIO, A.G. (1978) 'Immunity in Down's syndrome', *Eur. J. Pediat.*, 127, 293–4.

BURMAN, D., HOLTON, J.B. and PENNOCK, C.A. (eds) (1980) *Inherited Disorders of Carbohydrate Metabolism*, Lancaster, MTP Press.

CAMPBELL, D.M. and GILLMER, M.D.G. (eds) (1983) *Nutrition in Pregnancy*, London, Royal College of Obstetricians and Gynaecologists.

CARSON, N.A.J. (ed.) (1982) 'Selected reviews from the "Workshop on Nonketotic Hyperglycinaemia", Leeds, UK, 1979', *J. Inher. Metab. Dis.*, 5, Suppl. 2, 105–28.

CEDERBAUM, S.D., KOCH, R. and DONNELL, G.N. (1984) 'Symposium on genetic engineering and phenylketonuria', *Pediatrics*, 74, 406–27.

CHALMERS, R.A. and LAWSON, A.M. (1982) *Organic Acids in Man*, London, Chapman & Hall.

CHITHAM, R.G., STARR, D.J.T. and STERN, J. (1976) 'Hereditary disease: screening and detection', in J. WORTIS (ed.), *Mental Retardation and Developmental Disabilities*, New York, Brunner/Mazel, 8, 58–94.

COHN, R.M. and ROTH, K.S. (1983) *Metabolic Disease: A Guide to Early Recognition*, Philadelphia, Saunders.

CORBETT, J.A. and CAMPBELL, H.S. (1981) 'Causes of severe self-injurious behaviour', in P. MITTLER (ed.), *Frontiers of Knowledge in Mental Retardation*, vol. II, Baltimore, University Park Press, 285–92.

CRAWFURD, M.D'A., GIBBS, D.A. and WATTS, R.W.E. (1982) *Advances in the Treatment of Inborn Errors of Metabolism*, Chichester, Wiley.

CROME, L. and STERN, J. (1972) *Pathology of Mental Retardation*, 2nd edn, Edinburgh, Churchill Livingstone.

DELONG, G.R. and GLICK, T.H. (1982) 'Encephalopathy of Reye's syndrome: a review of pathogenetic hypotheses', *Pediatrics*, 69, 53–63.

DHONDT, J.-L. (1984) 'Tetrahydrobiopterin deficiencies: preliminary analysis from an international survey', *J. Pediat.*, 104, 501–8.

DOBBING, J. (1981) 'The later development of the brain and its vulnerability', in J.A. DAVIS and J. DOBBING (eds), *Scientific Foundations of Paediatrics*, 2nd edn, London, Heinemann Medical.

DOBBING, J. (ed.) (1983) *Prevention of Spina Bifida and other Neural Tube Defects*, London, Academic Press.

DOBBING, J., CLARKE, A.D.B., CORBETT, J.A., HOGG, J. and ROBINSON, R.O. (1984) *Scientific Studies in Mental Retardation*, London, Macmillan.

DUBOWITZ, L.M.S., DUBOWITZ, V., PALMER, T., MILLER, G., FAWER, C.-L. and LEVENE, M.I. (1984) 'Correlation of neurologic assessment in the preterm newborn infant with outcome at one year', *J. Pediat.*, 105, 452–6.

DUBOWITZ, V. (1978) *Muscle Disorders in Childhood*, Philadelphia, Saunders.

EADIE, M.J. and TYRER, J.H. (1983) *Biochemical Neurology*, Lancaster, MTP Press.

Editorial (1984) 'Honeybees, energy supply, and birth defects', *Lancet*, 1, 886–7.

EDWARDS, G. and OWENS, R.G. (1984) 'The clinical ecology debate: some issues arising', *Bull. Brit. Psychol. Soc.*, 37, 325–8.

EDWARDSON, J.A. and MCDERMOTT, J.R. (1982) 'Neurochemical pathology of brain peptides', *Brit. Med. Bull.*, 38, 259–64.

EGGER, J., CARTER, C.M., WILSON, J., TURNER, M.W. and SOOTHILL, J.F. (1983) 'Is migraine food allergy? A double-blind controlled trial of oligoantigenic diet treatment', *Lancet*, 2, 865–9.

EISENBERG, L. (1977) 'Development as a unifying concept in psychiatry', *Brit. J. Psychiat.*, 131, 225–37.

EISENBERG, L. (1984) 'Prevention: rhetoric and reality', *Proc. Roy. Soc. Med.*, 77, 268–80.

FORT, P., LIFSHITZ, F., BELLISARIO, R., DAVIS, J., LANES, R., PUGLIESE, M., RICHMAN, R., POST, E.M. and DAVID, R. (1984) 'Abnormalities of thyroid function in infants with Down's syndrome', *J. Pediat.*, 104, 545–9.

FRANCIS, D.E.M. (1986) *Diets for Sick Children*, 4th edn, Oxford, Blackwell.

GALJAARD, H. (1980) *Genetic Metabolic Diseases*, Amsterdam, Elsevier/North Holland.

GARROD, A.E. (1909) *Inborn Errors of Metabolism*, London, Oxford University Press.

GAULL, G.E., TALLAN, H.H., LAJTHA, A. and RASSIN, D.K. (1975)

'Pathogenesis of brain dysfunction in inborn errors of amino acid metabolism', in G.E. GAULL (ed.), *The Biology of Brain Dysfunction*, vol. 3, New York, Plenum, 47–143.

GIBBS, D.A., SPELLACY, E., TOMPKINS, R., WATTS, R.W.E. and MOWBRAY, J.F. (1983) 'A clinical trial of fibroblast transplantation for the treatment of mucopolysaccharidoses', *J. Inher. Metab. Dis.*, 6, 62–81.

GLEW, R.H. and PETERS, S.P. (eds) (1977) *Practical Enzymology of the Lipidoses*, New York, Alan R. Liss.

GOLDSTEIN, G.W. (1979) 'Pathogenesis of brain edema and haemorrhage: role of the brain capillary', *Pediatrics*, 64, 357–60.

GROPP, A. (1982) 'Value of an animal model for trisomy', *Virchows Arch. (Pathol. Anat.)*, 395, 117–31.

HAAN, E.A. and DANKS, D.M. (1981) 'Clinical investigations of suspected metabolic disease', in A.J. BARSON (ed.), *Laboratory Investigation of Fetal Disease*, Bristol, Wright, 410–28.

HAGBERG, B., KYLLERMAN, M. and STEEN, G. (1979) 'Dyskinesia and dystonia in neurometabolic disorders', *Neuropaediat.*, 10, 305–20.

HAMMOND, J.E. and STERN, J. (1984) 'The mentally subnormal child', in B.E. CLAYTON and J.M. ROUND (eds), *Chemical Pathology and the Sick Child*, Oxford, Blackwell, 405–42.

HARVEY, P.G. (1984) 'Lead and children's health: recent research and future questions', *J. Child Psychol. Psychiat.*, 25, 517–22.

HENDERSON, M.J., HOLTON, J.B. and MCFAUL, R. (1983) 'Further observations in a case of uridine diphosphate galactose-4-epimerase deficiency with a severe clinical presentation', *J. Inher. Metab. Dis.*, 6, 17–20.

HOLTON, J.B. (1982) 'Diagnosis of inherited metabolic diseases in severely ill children', *Ann. Clin. Biochem.*, 19, 389–95.

HULSE, J.A. (1984) 'Outcome for congenital hypothyroidism', *Arch. Dis. Childh.*, 59, 23–30.

KOCH, R. (ed.) (1981) *Urea Cycle Symposium, Pediatrics*, 68, 271–97 and 446–59.

KOCH, R., AZEN, C.G., FRIEDMAN, E.G. and WILLIAMSON, M.L. (1982) 'Preliminary report on the effect of diet discontinuation in PKU', *J. Pediat.*, 100, 870–5.

KOMROWER, G.M. (1982) 'Galactosaemia – thirty years on: the experience of a generation', *J. Inher. Metab. Dis.*, 5, Suppl. 2, 96–104.

KOMROWER, G.M. (1983) 'Clouds over galactosaemia', *Lancet*, 1, 190.

KRIVIT, W., RAMSAY, N.K.C., WOODS, W., NESBIT, M., FILIPOVICH, A.H., KIM, T. and KERSEY, J. (1983) 'Bone marrow transplantation in paediatrics', *Adv. Paediat.*, 30, 549–93.

KRONICK, J.B., SCRIVER, C.R., GOODYER, P.R. and KAPLAN, P.B. (1983) 'A perimortem protocol for suspected genetic disease', *Pediatrics*, 71, 960–3.

LEEMING, R.J., BARFORD, P.A., BLAIR, J.A. and SMITH, I. (1984) 'Blood spots on Guthrie cards can be used for inherited tetrahydrobiopterin deficiency screening in hyperphenylalaninaemic infants', *Arch. Dis. Childh.*, 59, 58–61.

LEEMING, R.J., HARPEY, J.-P., BROWN, S.M. and BLAIR, J.A. (1982) 'Tetrahydrofolate and hydroxocobalamine in the management of dihydropteridine reductase deficiency', *J. Ment. Defic. Res.*, 26, 21–5.

LEJEUNE, J. (1982) 'Is the fragile-X syndrome amenable to treatment?', *Lancet*, 1, 273–4.

LENKE, R.R. and LEVY, H.L. (1980) 'Maternal phenylketonuria and hyperphenylalaninaemia', *New Engl. J. Med.*, 303, 1202–8.

LEONARD, J.V. (1984a) 'Recurrent post-natal hypoglycaemia', in B.E. CLAYTON and J.M. ROUND (eds), *Chemical Pathology and the Sick Child*, Oxford, Blackwell, 73–95.

LEONARD, J.V. (1984b) 'Hyperammonaemia in childhood', in B.E. CLAYTON and J.M. ROUND (eds), *Chemical Pathology and the Sick Child*, Oxford, Blackwell, 96–119.

LEONARD, J.V., DAISH, P., NAUGHTON, E.R. and BARTLETT, K. (1984) 'The management and long-term outcome of organic acidaemias', *J. Inher. Metab. Dis.*, 7, Suppl. 1, 13–17.

LESSOF, M.H. (1983) 'Food intolerance and allergy – a review', *Quart. J. Med.*, 52, 111–19.

LEVY, H.L. and WAISBREN, S.E. (1983) 'Effects of untreated maternal phenylketonuria and hyperphenylalaninaemia on the fetus', *New Engl. J. Med.*, 309, 1269–74.

LEWIS, E.O. (1933) 'Types of mental deficiency and their social significance', *J. Ment. Sci.*, 79, 298–304.

LINGAM, S., WILSON, J. and OBERHOLZER, V.G. (1984) 'Neurological features in children with ornithine carbamoyltransferase deficiency – a rare preventable cause of mental retardation', in J.M. BERG (ed.), *Perspectives and Progress in Mental Retardation*, vol. II, Baltimore, University Park Press, 231–9.

LLOYD, J.B. (ed.) (1984) *The Lysosome and its Membrane. Biochem. Soc. Trans.*, 12, 899–915.

LO, W., PACKMAN, S., NASH, S., SCHMIDT, K., IRELAND, S., DIAMOND, I., NG, W. and DONNELL, G. (1984) 'Curious neurologic sequelae in galactosaemia', *Pediatrics*, 73, 309–12.

LUCEY, J.F. (1982) 'Bilirubin and brain damage – a real mess', *Pediatrics*, 69, 381–2.

LUCEY, J.F. and DANGMAN, B. (1984) 'A reexamination of the role of oxygen in retrolental fibroplasia', *Pediatrics*, 73, 82–96.

MCFAUL, R., DORNERS, S., BRETT, E.M. and GRANT, D.B. (1978) 'Neurological abnormalities in patients treated for hypothyroidism from early life', *Arch. Dis. Childh.*, 53, 611–18.

MCILWAIN, H. and BACHELARD, H.S. (1985) *Biochemistry and the Central Nervous System*, 5th edn, Edinburgh, Churchill Livingstone.

MCKUSICK, V.A. (1983) *Catalogs of Mendelian Inheritance in Man*, 6th edn,

Baltimore, Johns Hopkins University Press.

MAGOS, L. (1981) 'Synergism and antagonism of metal toxicology', in D.F. WILLIAMS (ed.), *Systemic Aspects of Biocompatibility*, Boca Raton, CRC Press, 87–100.

MARTIN, N.D.T., SNODGRASS, G.J.A.I. and COHEN, R.D. (1984) 'Idiopathic infantile hypercalcaemia – a continuing enigma', *Arch. Dis. Childh.*, 59, 605–13.

MONEY, J., CLARKE, F.C. and BECK, J. (1978) 'Congenital hypothyroidism and IQ increase, a quarter century follow up', *J. Pediat.*, 93, 432–4.

MOSER, H.W. (1981) 'Recent advances in certain disorders of lipid metabolism', in P. MITTLER (ed.), *Frontiers of Knowledge in Mental Retardation*, vol. II, Baltimore, University Park Press, 239–49.

MULLER, D.P.R., LLOYD, J.K. and WOLFF, O.H. (1983) 'Vitamin E and neurological function', *Lancet*, 1, 225–8.

MURDOCH, J.C. (1981) 'Hypothalamopituitary target organ function in adults with Down's syndrome', in P. MITTLER (ed.), *Frontiers of Knowledge in Mental Retardation*, vol. II, Baltimore, University Park Press, 159–65.

NEEDLEMAN, H.L., GUNNOE, C., LEVITON, A., REED, R., PERESIE, H., MAHER, C. and BARRETT, P. (1979) 'Deficits in psychologic and classroom performance of children with elevated dentine lead levels', *New Engl. J. Med.*, 300, 689–95.

NEW ENGLAND CONGENITAL HYPOTHYROIDISM COLLABORATIVE (1984) 'Characteristics of infantile hypothyroidism discovered on neonatal screening', *J. Pediat.*, 104, 539–44.

NYHAN, W.L. (1982) 'Inborn errors of purine metabolism', in F. COCKBURN and R. GITZELMANN (eds), *Inborn Errors of Metabolism in Humans*, Lancaster, MTP Press, 13–36.

PATEL, A.J., SMITH, R.M., KINGSBURY, A.E., HUNT, A. and BALÁZS, R. (1980) 'Effects of thyroid state on brain development: muscarinic, acetyl-choline and GABA receptors', *Brain Res.*, 198, 389–402.

PATRICK, A.D. (1984) 'Prenatal diagnosis of inherited metabolic disease', in C.H. RODECK and H.K. NICOLAIDES (eds), *Prenatal Diagnosis*, London, Royal College of Obstetricians and Gynaecologists, 121–32.

PEARSON, D.J., RIX, K.J.B. and BENTLEY, S.J. (1983) 'Food allergy: how much in the mind?', *Lancet*, 1, 1259–61.

PRATT, O.E. (ed.) (1984) *Mechanisms of Alcohol Damage in Utero*, Ciba Foundation Symposium 105, London, Pitman.

ROBINSON, B.H. and SHERWOOD, W.G. (1984) 'Lactic acidaemia', *J. Inher. Metab. Dis.*, 7, Suppl. 1, 69–73.

RODECK, C.H. and NICOLAIDES, K.H. (eds) (1984) *Prenatal Diagnosis*, London, Royal College of Obstetricians and Gynaecologists.

ROSE, F.C. (ed.) (1983) *Research Progress in Epilepsy*. London, Pitman.

ROSENBERG, L.E. and SCRIVER, C.R. (1980) 'Disorders of amino acid metabolism', in P.K. BONDY and L.E. ROSENBERG (eds), *Metabolic Control and Disease*, 8th edn, Philadelphia, Saunders.

ROTH, M. (1969) 'Seeking common ground in contemporary psychiatry', *Proc. Roy. Soc. Med.*, 62, 765–72.

ROUSSON, R. and GUIBAUD, P. (1984) 'Long-term outcome of organic acidurias: survey of 105 French cases (1967–83)', *J. Inher. Metab. Dis.*, 7, Suppl. 1, 10–12.

RUNDLE, A.T. (1979) 'The use and abuse of the laboratory', in M. CRAFT (ed.), *Tredgold's Mental Retardation*, 12th edn, London, Baillière Tindall, 163–9.

SANDLER, M., RUTHVEN, C.R.J., GOODWIN, B.L., FIELD, H. and MATTHEWS, R. (1978) 'Phenylethylamine overproduction in aggressive psychopaths', *Lancet*, 2, 1269–70.

SARE, Z., RUVALCABA, R.H.A. and KELLEY, V.C. (1978) 'Prevalence of thyroid disorder in Down's syndrome', *Clin. Genet.*, 14, 154–8.

SCRIVER, C.R. and LEVY, H.L. (1983) 'Histidinaemia. Part I: Reconciling retrospective and prospective findings', *J. Inher. Metab. Dis.*, 6, 51–3.

SHERWOOD, A.J. and SMITH, J.F. (1983) 'Bilirubin encephalopathy', *Neuropathol. Appl. Neurobiol.*, 9, 271–85.

SIEGEL, L.S. (ed.) (1982) 'Low birth weight infants', *Sem. Perinatol.*, 6, 265–389.

SINEX, F.M. and MERRIL, C.R. (eds) (1982) 'Alzheimer's disease, Down's syndrome and aging', *Ann. NY Acad. Sci.*, 396, 1–197.

SMITH, G.F. and BERG, J.M. (1976) *Down's Anomaly*, 2nd edn, Edinburgh, Churchill Livingstone.

SMITH, G.F., SPIKER, D., PETERSON, C.P., CHICCHETTI, D. and JUSTICE, P. (1984) 'Use of megadoses of vitamins with minerals in Down's syndrome', *J. Pediat.*, 105, 228–34.

SMITH, I., LOBASCHER, M.E., STEVENSON, J.E., WOLFF, O.H., SCHMIDT, H., GRUBELL-KAISER, S. and BICKELL, H. (1978) 'Effect of stopping low-phenylalanine diet on intellectual progress of children with phenylketonuria', *Brit. Med. J.*, 2, 723–6.

STAHLMAN, M.T. (1984) 'Newborn intensive care: success or failure?', *J. Pediat.*, 105, 162–7.

STANBURY, J.E., WYNGAARDEN, J.B., FREDRICKSON, D.S., GOLD-STEIN, J.L. and BROWN, M.S. (eds) (1983) *The Metabolic Basis of Inherited Disease*, 5th edn, New York, McGraw-Hill.

STERN, J. (1983) 'Hereditary and acquired mental deficiency', in D.L. WILLIAMS and V. MARKS (eds), *Biochemistry in Clinical Practice*, London, Heinemann Medical, 489–523.

STEVENSON, J.E., HAWCROFT, J., LOBASCHER, M., SMITH, I., WOLFF, D.H. and GRAHAM P.J. (1979) 'Behavioural deviance in children with early treated phenylketonuria', *Arch. Dis. Childh.*, 54, 14–18.

SWEETMAN, L. (1984) 'Prenatal diagnosis of organic acidurias', *J. Inher. Metab. Dis.*, 7, Suppl. 1, 18–22.

SZYMANOWICZ, W., YU, K.Y.H. and WILSON, F.E. (1984) 'Antecedents of periventricular haemorrhage in infants weighing 1250 g or less at birth',

Arch. Dis. Childh., 59, 13–17.

TADA, K., TATEDA, H., ARASHIMA, S. and SAKAI, K. (1982) 'Intellectual development in patients with untreated histidinaemia', *Pediatrics*, 101, 562–3.

TAYLOR, A. (1984) 'Diet and behaviour', *Arch. Dis. Childh.*, 59, 97–8.

THORLEY, G. (1984) 'Pilot study to assess behavioural and cognitive effects of artifical food colours in a group of retarded children', *Dev. Med. Child Neurol.*, 26, 56–61.

TUCK, C.M., BENNETT, J.W. and VARELA, M. (1984) 'Down's syndrome and familial aneuploidy', in J.M. BERG (ed.), *Perspectives and Progress in Mental Retardation*, vol. II, Baltimore, University Park Press, 167–83.

VINKEN, P.J. and BRUYN, G.W. (eds) (1976) *Handbook of Clinical Neurology*, vol. 28, Amsterdam, North-Holland.

WADMAN, G.K., DURAN, M., BEEMER, F.A. and CATS, B.P. (1983) 'Absence of hepatic molybdenum factor: an inborn error of metabolism leading to a combined deficiency of sulphite oxidase and xanthine dehydrogenase', *J. Inher. Metab. Dis.*, 6, Suppl. 1, 78–83.

WALKER, V., CLAYTON, B.E., ERSSER, R.S., FRANCIS, D.E.M., LILLY, P., SEAKINS, J.W.T., SMITH, I. and WHITEMAN, P.D. (1981) 'Hyperphenylalaninaemia of various types among three-quarters of a million neonates tested in a screening programme', *Arch. Dis. Childh.*, 56, 759–64.

WALSHE, J.M. (1983) 'Hudson Memorial Lecture: Wilson's disease: genetics and biochemistry – their relevance to therapy', *J. Inher. Metab. Dis.*, 6, Suppl. 1, 51–8.

WARNER, J. and HATHAWAY, M.J. (1984) 'Allergic form of Meadow's syndrome (Munchausen by proxy)', *Arch. Dis. Childh.*, 59, 151–6.

WATTS, R.W.E., BARAITSER, M., CHALMERS, R.A. and PURKISS, P. (1980) 'Organic acidurias and aminoacidurias in the aetiology of long-term mental handicap', *J. Ment. Defic. Res.*, 24, 257–70.

WATTS, R.W.E., SPELLACY, E., GIBBS, D.A., ALLSOP, J., MCKERAN, R.O. and SLAVIN, G.E. (1982) 'Clinical, post-mortem, biochemical and therapeutic observations on the Lesch–Nyhan syndrome with particular reference to the neurological manifestations', *Quart. J. Med.*, 51, 43–78.

WILSON, M.M.G. and JUNGNER, G. (1968) *Principles and Practice of Screening for Disease*, Geneva, World Health Organization.

WRIGHT, E.C., STERN, J., ERSSER, R. and PATRICK, A.D. (1979) 'Glutathionuria: γ-glutamyltranspeptidase deficiency', *J. Inher. Metab. Dis.*, 2, 3–7.

ZIAI, F., RHONE, D., JUSTICE, P. and SMITH, G.F. (1984) 'Thyroid function studies in children and adolescents with Down's syndrome', in J.M. BERG (ed.), *Perspectives and Progress in Mental Retardation*, vol. II, Baltimore, University Park Press, 243–50.

6
Chromosomal anomalies

Jane A. Evans and John L. Hamerton

INTRODUCTION

Chromosome anomalies play a significant role in the aetiology of mental retardation (Hamerton, 1971; de Grouchy and Turleau, 1977; Vogel and Motulsky, 1979; Smith, 1982). Studies prior to 1969 were reviewed extensively by Hamerton (1971), and thus we concentrate in this chapter on more recent research in which the cytogenetic anomalies have been well defined by chromosome banding.

Very early in the history of human cytogenetics it became clear that most unbalanced chromosomal abnormalities are associated with varying degrees of mental retardation. These include autosomal trisomies, unbalanced rearrangements and some sex chromosome anomalies as well as smaller deletions and duplications (see Hamerton (1971) for review). Prior to 1970, however, many anomalies could not be precisely defined because no easy means were available for the identification of all human chromosomes or chromosome regions. The advent of banding techniques (ISCN, 1978) has radically improved the identification of anomalies, even those which approach the limits of resolution of the light microscope.

In the present chapter we discuss first the ways in which chromosome anomalies arise and their frequency in both the general and the mentally impaired populations. This is followed by a review of chromosomal syndromes, including chromosome breakage syndromes and fragile sites, and we conclude with a brief discussion of potential prevention of chromosome anomalies by genetic counselling and prenatal diagnosis.

MECHANISMS OF CHROMOSOME DEFECT

Cell division

The number of chromosomes in somatic cells is constant and is termed the diploid (2n) number. Each gamete, however, has only half the *diploid* number and is said to be *haploid* (n). In order to maintain regularity two types of cell division occur: *mitosis*, occurring in somatic tissues during growth and repair, and *meiosis*, which is the specialized form of cell division leading to genetic formation of gametes. Mitosis serves to distribute and maintain the continuity of the genetic material in every cell of the body, while meiosis, which occurs only during the formation of the gametes, results in four daughter cells each with the haploid chromosome number. In males each primary spermatocyte forms four functional spermatids which develop into spermatozoa, while each oocyte forms only one ovum, the remaining products of meiosis being nonfunctional polar bodies.

The major functions of meiosis are threefold: (1) a halving of the number of chromosomes in the gametes; (2) the regular distribution of chromosomes to the daughter cells; and (3) the random distribution of genetic material resulting both from crossing over and the independent assortment of the maternal and paternal homologous chromosomes. This process is fundamental to sexual reproduction and ensures genetic variability of the species. These processes have been reviewed in detail by Hamerton (1971, 1984).

Examination of the chromosomes

Dividing cells are required for chromosome analysis. The cells most commonly used are mitogenically stimulated peripheral blood lymphocytes. Skin fibroblasts, amniotic fluid cells and bone marrow cells may be used for special tests. Dividing cells are accumulated at metaphase. Colcemid added to the culture medium towards the end of the culture period is most commonly used to accomplish this. The cells are then subjected to hypotonic treatment followed by fixation and spreading on microscope slides. The slides are then stained.

Staining techniques may result in either a nonbanded or a banded appearance of the chromosomes. The use of one or more banding techniques is routine today, since this provides much additional information. These methods allow precise identification of an extra or missing chromosome and the accurate localization of breakpoints in chromosome rearrangements (Plate 6.1).

Recent developments have expanded the number of visible bands from between 200 and 300 to between 1000 and 2000, allowing the recognition of small deletions and duplications. Most laboratories today work with chromosomes in which between 400 and 800 bands can be recognized.

Human chromosome nomenclature

The 46 human chromosomes consist of 23 distinct homologous pairs, each of which can be recognized by appropriate banding techniques. These are numbered from 1 to 22 in descending order of length. In the female the two sex chromosomes, designated X chromosomes, are identical while in the male the sex chromosomes designated X and Y are morphologically different.

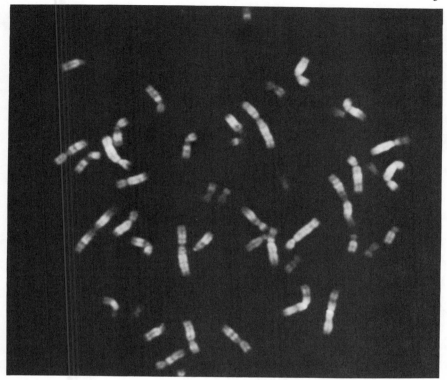

PLATE 6.1   Q-banded metaphase spread of chromosomes from a normal human female: 46, XX

Chromosome variants

Consistent minor chromosome changes, often involving the short arms of the acrocentric chromosomes, the long arm of the Y chromosome or the constitutive heterochromatin near to the centromere of chromosomes 1,9 and 16, are termed variants. These apparently have little obvious clinical significance. However, they can be useful as genetic markers as they are more common than major chromosome abnormalities and often segregate in families in a Mendelian fashion. Recent studies suggest that about 70 per cent of newborn infants carry one or more variant chromosomes.

Nomenclature

The nomenclature used to describe chromosomes, chromosome bands, variants and rearrangements is given in detail in ISCN (1978, 1981). A shorthand notation is used to describe the chromosome complement of an individual. In this notation the number of chromosomes is specified first, followed by the listing of the sex chromosomes. Thus a normal female karyotype is designated 46, XX and a normal male 46, XY. Any deviations from a normal karyotype are written after the sex chromosomes. An individual autosome is referred to by its number, its short arm by the letter 'p' and its long arm by the letter 'q'. A '+' or '−' sign after the p or q indicates an increase (+) or decrease (−) in the length of the arm. When written before a designated chromosome the sign indicates that the chromosome is extra (+) or missing (−). The following are examples: 46, XY, 18q− describes a male with 46 chromosomes including one chromosome 18 whose long arm is shortened; 47, XX, +21 describes a female with 47 chromosomes, including an extra chromosome 21 in addition to the 46 chromosomes of the normal karyotype.

Chromosome abnormalities

Chromosome abnormalities can be divided into two classes:

1. Abnormalities of chromosome number – these result from nondisjunction; that is, from the failure of two homologous chromosomes in the first division of meiosis or of two sister chromatids in mitosis or the second division of meiosis to pass to opposite poles of the cell. This results in cells with abnormal chromosome numbers. If these cells are gametes, fertilization will result in a zygote with an abnormal chromosome number. If nondisjunction occurs during an early cleavage division of a zygote, then a chromosome mosaic may result. This is an individual with two or more cell lines differing in chromosome complement.

2. Abnormalities of chromosome structure – these result from chromosome breakage and reunion. When a chromosome breaks it can rejoin in its old form (restitution) or it can rejoin at another breakpoint (reunion). Reunion leads to structural rearrangements which can be *balanced* or *unbalanced*. If a structural rearrangement is balanced the amount of genetic material is presumed to be identical to that found in a normal cell and there is a simple redistribution of this material. Types of balanced rearrangements include the balanced reciprocal translocation, Robertsonian translocations and inversions. Unbalanced rearrangements usually result in changes in the clinical phenotype and often a greater or lesser degree of mental impairment. Balanced rearrangements do not usually lead to clinical change (see p. 241).

Chromosome deletions involve the loss of a chromosome segment following chromosome breakage. Deletions may be terminal, interstitial or may result in ring chromosomes.

Inversions result from two breaks on the same chromosome and inversion of the intervening segment, and can be detected only by banding studies which show a changed banding sequence. Inversions result in disturbances in chromosome pairing and in the formation of unbalanced as well as balanced gametes.

Balanced reciprocal translocations result from exchange of chromosome segments between nonhomologous chromosomes. Individuals carrying such a rearrangement will have a higher frequency of abnormal gametes as the result of a disturbance in chromosome pairing at meiosis; thus they are at higher risk of having children with abnormalities or of increased fetal wastage.

Robertsonian translocations are a specific type of translocation which occurs between acrocentric chromosomes resulting in the formation of a new metacentric chromosome from two acrocentric ones. Such rearrangements may be important in the transmission of Down's syndrome when one of the chromosomes involved is chromosome 21, the other usually being chromosome 14.

POPULATION CYTOGENETICS

About 6 per 1000 or 1:160 newborn babies have a major chromosome abnormality which may result in some degree of morbidity or mortality at some time (see Hook and Hamerton (1977) for review). The frequency of the different types of chromosome abnormalities found among consecutive newborns is given in Table 6.1.

TABLE 6.1   Frequency of chromosome abnormalities among live births

Sex chromosomes	Frequency
Male	
47, XYY	1 : 1022
47, XXY	1 : 1022
Other	1 : 1277
Female	
45, X	1 : 9586
47, XXX	1 : 958
Other	1 : 2739
Autosomal trisomics	
+D	1 : 18,984
+E	1 : 8136
+G	1 : 802
Balanced structural	1 : 517
Unbalanced structural	1 : 1675
Total	1 : 1675

Note: Based on 56,952 babies: 35,779 males, 19,173 females.

Chromosome abnormalities among newborn infants represent only a small proportion of the total load of chromosome abnormalities at conception (see Creasy (1982) and Hamerton (1982) for reviews). Most such abnormalities are lethal and cause very early spontaneous abortions, failure of implantation or recognized spontaneous abortions and perinatal deaths. This group includes most trisomies, triploids (3n), tetraploids (4n) and X-monosomy. Between 40 and 50 per cent of all spontaneous abortions (Creasy, 1982; Hamerton, 1982) and about 6 per cent of stillbirths and perinatal deaths (Sutherland *et al.*, 1978; Angell *et al.*, 1984) have an abnormal chromosome complement.

There are also data on the large numbers of mothers who had received amniocentesis because of advanced maternal age. A recent study of 50,000 amniocenteses showed that about 2 per cent of mid-trimester pregnancies of mothers aged thirty-five and above have a chromosome abnormality (Ferguson-Smith and Yates, 1984).

Some idea of the quantitative significance of chromosome abnormalities in the aetiology of mental retardation may be obtained from studies of defined populations of retarded patients. There are major difficulties, however, in comparing studies because of differences in the definition of mental retardation and variable methods of patient selection.

Earlier studies (see Hamerton (1971) for review) used sex chromatin analysis to determine the frequency of chromatin positive males in mentally subnormal populations. These study populations were arbitrarily divided by IQ, and among patients with higher IQs (roughly 50–100) about 9 per 1000 were chromatin positive and thus presumably had an additional X chromosome or an X chromosome abnormality. Among patients with a lower IQ (roughly <75) about 7.5 per 1000 were chromatin positive. These figures compare with a frequency of 1–2 per 1000 chromatin positive males among newborn babies of which 1 : 1000 are XXY males (Hook and Hamerton, 1977). Several studies have examined the frequency of females with two sex chromatin bodies in the newborn (Taylor and Moores, 1967) and in institutions for the mentally retarded or mentally ill (Maclean *et al.*, 1968). Taylor and Moores summarized the results from sex chromatin surveys of 23,229 live-born females and gave a frequency of double chromatin positive females of 0.6 per 1000 live births. This compares with a frequency of triple-X females among karyotyped newborns of about 1 : 1000. Maclean *et al.* found frequencies of chromatin double positive females in institutions for the mentally retarded to be about 4 per 1000 and in mental hosptials to be about 2.5 per 1000. This represents an increase of between 4 and 7 times the newborn frequency.

Several studies have attempted to determine the overall frequency of chromosome anomalies among fully ascertained populations of the mentally subnormal. Speed *et al.* (1976) conducted a cytogenetic survey of the retarded in the north-east of Scotland ascertained through a register for the subnormal for that health region. Out of a total population of 3020 persons, 2770 patients were karyotyped, 297 had a chromosome abnormality and 250 of these had Down's syndrome. The remaining autosomal abnormalities were either supernumerary chromosomes (9) or deletions (7). Sex chromosome anomalies were found in 31 patients. The overall frequency of chromosome anomalies in this population was 10.7 per cent with a slight excess of males (11.9 per cent) over females (9.2 per cent). The excess among males was accounted for not only by an excess of sex chromosome anomalies but also, surprisingly, by an excess of males with Down's syndrome.

A similar study was carried out on an unselected group of mentally retarded persons in the county of Aarhus in Denmark (Rasmussen *et al.*, 1982). The study group comprised all patients registered with the Danish National Mental Retardation Service on 1 June 1976 and included both institutionalized and noninstitutionalized patients. The total number of patients was 2157 of whom 1905 were karyotyped; 359 or 18.8 per cent had a chromosome anomaly. Of these 281 (14.7 per cent) had Down's syndrome, 45 (2.4 per cent) another autosomal anomaly and 33 (1.8 per cent) a sex chromosome anomaly.

Table 6.2 summarizes the cytogenetic data from twelve studies. Ten of these were studies on institutionalized patients, some selected according to IQ or age, while two were based on completely ascertained patients in defined geographic regions. The overall prevalence of chromosome abnormalities was 13.2 per cent; one Japanese study (Fujita and Fujita, 1974) showed a very low prevalence, while both Danish studies showed higher prevalence (Nielsen *et al.*, 1983). These differences no doubt reflect differences in ascertainment and patient selection. In all investigations the largest category was Down's syndrome which comprised about 9 per cent or more patients in nine studies and nearly 15 per cent in the Danish study.

None of the above studies included any discussion of the population frequency of the fragile site at Xq28 which is associated with some forms of X-linked mental retardation among males and may be the most common single cause of mental retardation among males (see p. 243)

In conclusion, it is clear that chromosome abnormalities play a significant role in the aetiology of mental retardation and that the commonest type is trisomy 21 which has a prevalence of between 8 per cent and 15 per cent among populations of the mentally retarded. Other autosomal anomalies account for somewhere between 1 and 2 per cent of all mentally retarded persons, while sex chromosome anomalies occur in approximately 1 per cent of mentally retarded individuals with a somewhat higher frequency among males than among females.

CHROMOSOMAL SYNDROMES

Aneuploidy: autosomal trisomies

The commonest and most easily recognized chromosomal syndromes involve trisomy of chromosomes 13, 18 and 21. *Down's syndrome* or trisomy 21 remains the commonest single chromosome abnormality in live-born infants and occurs with a frequency of 1.25/1000 live births in most populations (Hook and Hamerton, 1977).

First clearly described by Langdon Down in 1866, children with Down's syndrome form a well-recognized group with classic phenotypic findings. The

TABLE 6.2 Chromosome surveys of mentally retarded persons

Authors	Type of population	No. studied	Sex chr. abm.		Down's syndrome		Other autosomal		Total	
			No.	%	No.	%	No.	%	No.	%
Sutherland and Wiener (1971)	Institution	159	0	0	17	10.7	3	1.9	20	12.6
Newton et al. (1972 a and b)	Institution < 15 years	1,255	10	0.8	103	8.2	15	1.2	128	10.1
Fujita and Fujita (1974)	Institution	59	2	3.4	1	1.7	1	1.7	4	6.8
Cassiman et al. (1975)	Institution children IQ<50	857	3	0.3	111	12.9	15	1.8	129	15.0
Sutherland et al. (1976)	Institution	588	4	0.7	73	12.4	13	2.2	90	15.3
Speed et al. (1976)	NE Scotland	2,770	31	1.1	250	9.0	16	0.6	297	10.7
Jacobs et al. (1978)	Institution	475	3	0.6	40	8.4	14	2.8	57	12.0
Ally and Grace (1979)	Institution	512	5	1.0	42	8.2	10	2.0	57	11.1
Faed et al. (1979)	Institution	756	6	0.8	91	12.0	6	0.8	103	13.6
Rasmussen et al. (1982)	Co. Aarhus, Denmark	1,905	33	1.8	281	14.7	45	2.4	359	18.8
Kondo et al. (1980)	Institution	449	1	0.2	33	7.3	3	0.7	37	8.2
Nielsen et al. (1983)	Institution	476	4	0.8	58	12.2	13	2.7	76	16.0
Total		10,261	102	1.00	1100	10.72	154	1.50	1357	13.22

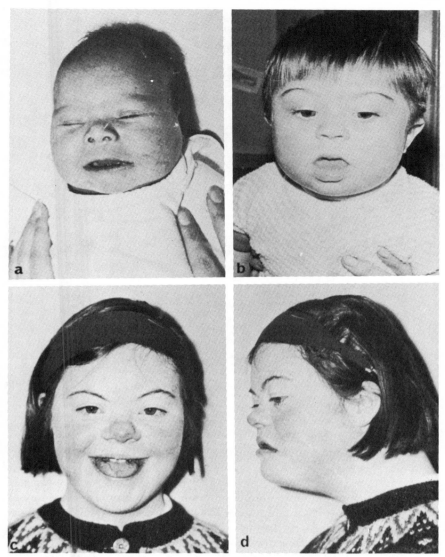

PLATE 6.2   Children with Down's syndrome at various ages: (a) newborn male; (b) male at twelve months; (c) and (d) girl at sixteen years (reproduced by permission of Professor P.E. Polani and the Academic Press)

characteristic facies is one of microbrachycephaly, epicanthic folds, flat nasal bridge, Brushfield's spots in the irides, flat malar area, small mouth with an often protruding fissured tongue and simple ears (Plate 6.2). Additional common dysmorphic signs include brachydactyly, clinodactyly of the fifth fingers, transverse single palmar creases (Plate 6.3), wide-spaced first and

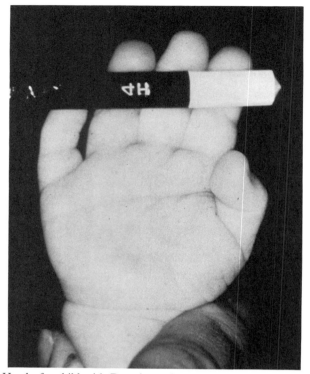

PLATE 6.3   Hand of a child with Down's syndrome showing brachydactyly, short fifth finger with clinodactyly and single palmar crease

second toes, and unusual dermatoglyphics (e.g. distal palmar axial triradii and arch tibial hallucal patterns). These findings, though varying from child to child, have been used to develop diagnostic indices that can be used to diagnose Down's syndrome clinically with a high degree of accuracy (Jackson *et al.*, 1976; Preus, 1977; Fried, 1980). The major clinically significant findings in Down's syndrome are the high incidence of cardiovascular anomalies (especially septal and endocardial cushion defects) and bowel malformations (especially duodenal atresia), the marked reduction in stature, the predisposition to infections and leukaemia, and the almost universal impairment of mental function. For a detailed review of clinical features see Smith and Berg (1976).

Mental development in Down's syndrome individuals is variable with a mean IQ around 40. Some children, however, function at a higher level, and intelligence within the low normal range has occasionally been noted in children subjected to intensive infant stimulation programmes (Carlin *et al.*, 1978; Kousseff, 1978). There is evidence of correlation between parental intelligence levels and those of their Down's syndrome children (Fraser and Sadovnick, 1976).

There is a reluctance now to institutionalize Down's syndrome children and thus their relative contribution to populations of institutionalized severely retarded individuals is apparently falling (Moser and Wolf, 1971; Hunter *et al.*, 1980). However, Down's syndrome accounts for about 19–35 per cent of children in most population-based surveys of *severe* retardation (McDonald, 1973; Gustavson *et al.*, 1977 a, b; Fryers and MacKay, 1979).

Cytogenetically the most common finding in Down's syndrome is trisomy 21, which is found in approximately 94 per cent of cases, while 5 per cent have a structural rearrangement and 1 per cent have mosaic karyotypes. Of the structural rearrangements, Robertsonian translocations are by far the the most common with the 14;21 translocation most often seen, especially in familial cases. Translocations involving only G group chromosomes are usually sporadic, though families with segregating 21;22 translocations have been reported (Yang and Rosenberg, 1969). Low-grade mosaicism is occasionally observed in the parents of Down's syndrome children with both trisomy 21 and 21;21 Robertsonian translocations (Richards, 1974; Priest *et al.*, 1977). Rarer cytogenetic aberrations have included isochromosome 21, tandem duplications (Pfeiffer and Loidl, 1982), partial trisomy 21 (21q22) (Cervenka *et al.*, 1977) and tetrasomy 21 (usually in mosaic form) (Fryns *et al.*, 1982; Hunter *et al.*, 1982; Jabs *et al.*, 1982). Also, trisomy 21 can occur with other cytogenetic abnormalities including Klinefelter syndrome (Hamerton *et al.*, 1965), XYY (Neu *et al.*, 1971; Leary *et al.*, 1975) and Turner syndrome (Townes *et al.*, 1975; Martsolf *et al.*, 1977).

Demographically the most pertinent single finding in Down's syndrome is the correlation with maternal age. Incidence at birth rises gradually from around 1 in 2000 at maternal age 20 to 1 in 1000 at 30. There is then a sharp upward turn in the incidence rate giving figures of 1 in 500 at 35 years, 1 in 200 at 38 years, 1 in 80 at 40 years and 1 in 18 at 45 years (Hook and Lindsjo, 1978). Even higher rates are noted from analysis of amniotic fluid samples taken at 15–16 weeks gestation, implying a significant fetal loss rate (Schreine-machers *et al.*, 1982; Hook, 1983a). The strong maternal age effect implies that the incidence of Down's syndrome will be influenced by changing patterns of age-specific fertility. The generally downward trend in age-specific fertility over 30 years of age has led to a reduction in the incidence of the syndrome. However, it has also meant that the majority of Down's syndrome infants are now born to mothers under 35 years of age who are not routinely offered prenatal diagnosis, and thus such programmes, while benefiting individual families, at present have little impact on the prevention of Down's syndrome births (Evans *et al.*, 1978b; Sadovnick and Baird, 1982; Mikkelsen *et al.*, 1983). It appears, however, that age-specific fertility rates over 30 years are now increasing; thus we may again observe changes in the maternal age distribution of Down's syndrome infants.

The mechanism for the maternal age effect observed in Down's syndrome and several other trisomies (Hassold *et al.*, 1980) is not known. Different hypotheses include increasing accumulation of radiation (Uchida *et al.*, 1968) or other environmental effects, ageing of the ovum and delayed fertilization (Juberg and Mailhes, 1976), hormonal influences (Janerich and Jacobson, 1977; Crowley *et al.*, 1979) and viral infection (Robinson and Puck, 1965). However, these hypotheses can rarely explain the still relatively high incidence of Down's syndrome in young mothers. It is well recognized that the causes of nondisjunction may be different at different maternal ages, and that Down's syndrome in the infants of younger mothers may be more related to intrinsic or extrinsic risk factors in those women rather than to their age. This concept is reinforced by the high recurrence risk (1 per cent) observed in young women who have had a Down's syndrome child (Mikkelsen, 1982a).

Paternal age effects independent of maternal age have also been postulated, but the data are controversial (Matsunaga *et al.*, 1978; Erickson and Bjerkedal, 1981; Stene *et al.*, 1981). It is unlikely that a significant increase in risk occurs at paternal ages less than forty-five years.

The importance of parental age effects in Down's syndrome has led to considerable interest in the origin of the additional chromosome in trisomy 21. Although not all families are informative, in many cases the origin of the extra chromosome can be determined from study of chromosome variants. Such investigations have revealed that approximately 75–85 per cent of nondisjunction is maternal and 15–25 per cent paternal in origin. Errors at meiosis I are considerably more common than at meiosis II in oogenesis. In spermatogenesis errors at meiosis I are still more common, but the relative frequency of meiosis II errors is more variable (Magenis *et al.*, 1977; Mikkelsen *et al.*, 1980; Mikkelsen, 1982b; del Mazo *et al.*, 1982). An interesting finding in these studies has been the lack of parental age differences in cases derived from maternal *v.* paternal meiosis errors, suggesting that maternal age *per se* may not only have an effect on the rate of nondisjunction but also on the spontaneous loss rates of chromosomally abnormal fetuses. This concept of altered embryonic selection is a controversial one (Ayme and Lippman-Hand, 1982; Hook, 1983b) and needs to be investigated further.

Obviously, because of its frequency, Down's syndrome has been intensively studied and can be considered the 'model' of a chromosomal syndrome. In this regard it is one of the few conditions which has allowed some consideration of the mechanisms which influence physical and mental abnormalities in chromosomal defects. Although one can postulate that chromosome imbalance will lead to abnormality, the precise nature of its influence is unknown. The primary effect of chromosomal defects is observed in gene dosage, and detailed studies on several proteins in both monosomic and trisomic states indicate that, for autosomal genes, there are no mechanisms to compensate for abnormal synthesis at the gene level. Thus the trisomic individual produces 1.5 times the normal gene product and the monosomic 0.5 times. The secondary effects of these unbalanced karyotypes is presumably through the influence of altered amounts of gene products either directly or indirectly. In

Down's syndrome and in animal models extensive alterations in protein synthesis are not observed, indicating that aneuploidy need not lead to widespread changes in gene expression (or is lethal if it does), but more limited variation may occur. These might have pathogenetic effects by altering the flux of metabolites through critical pathways, changing the composition of proteins made of several subunits or by influencing cell surface components including receptors. Initial studies on interferon synthesis in Down's syndrome patients suggest that some of these mechanisms may be working (Epstein *et al.*, 1982). An alternative, or rather complementary, concept is that chromosome imbalance leads to a generalized disruption of homeostasis and leaves the developing organism less able to adapt to genetic and environmental effects. In this sense, traits which are under tight genetic control would be less susceptible to change in an aneuploid organism while those usually less buffered, including most multifactorial and anthropometric traits such as height and intelligence, will be more severely affected (Shapiro, 1983). Rather than having exhausted the possibilities of common chromosomal anomalies as tools for improving our understanding of biological mechanisms, whole new areas of research are now opening up with the introduction of sophisticated molecular genetics techniques.

The other common autosomal trisomies are *trisomy 18* or Edwards syndrome and *trisomy 13* or Patau's syndrome. Trisomy 18 was first described by Edwards *et al.* in 1960. The incidence in live births is about 1 in 3000 (Hook and Hamerton, 1977). However, this abnormality is much more common in children dying in the perinatal period, where it accounts for about 1.5 per cent of such deaths (Machin and Crolla, 1974; Sutherland *et al.*, 1978). This is an important diagnosis to make in a stillbirth or neonatal death as the recurrence risk for an aneuploid child is 1 per cent, and may involve Down's syndrome in a subsequent pregnancy. The diagnosis may not be suspected on clinical grounds (Cassidy *et al.*, 1981).

In most cases the infant with trisomy 18 presents with a classical though subtle phenotype. These infants are growth retarded and often postmature. The craniofacies is characterized by a dolichocephalic skull with prominent occiput; low-set, large, malformed ears; and a small face with microphthalmia, microstomia and micrognathia (Plate 6.4). The hands frequently exhibit unusual fixed positioning of the fingers with the second finger overlapping the third and the fifth overlapping the fourth (Plate 6.5). The distal finger creases may be hypoplastic and there is a high frequency of arches on the fingertips. The toes are short with dorsiflexed halluces and toe- and fingernails are hypoplastic. Frequently the feet are rocker-bottomed with a prominent heel. The sternum is short with a reduced number of ossification centres. Males are usually cryptorchid and there is a high incidence of inguinal and umbilical herniae.

More severe external malformations including radial hypoplasia, meningomyelocele and omphalocele may occur. Internal malformations frequently involve the heart (including septal defects and patent ductus arteriosus) or the

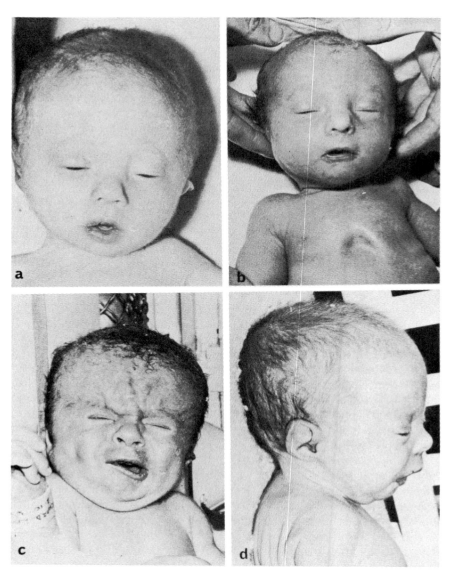

PLATE 6.4 Some clinical features of trisomy 18 showing: (a) round face, microphthalmia and microstomia; (b) abnormally short sternum; (c) low-set ears and unilateral facial palsy; (d) micrognathia, primitive ears, and redundant nuchal and back skin (reproduced by permission of Dr A. Taylor and the Academic Press)

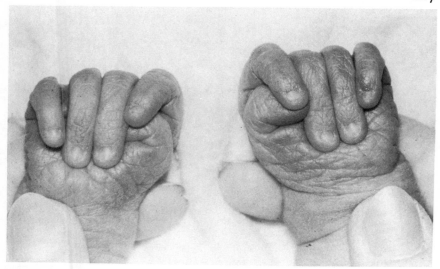

PLATE 6.5 Hands of an infant with trisomy 18 showing hypoplasia of the nails and unusual positioning of the fingers

kidneys (horseshoe kidney, renal ectopia). For detailed reviews of clinical findings see Gibson *et al.* (1963) and Taylor (1968).

The prognosis is poor. Those babies that are liveborn are usually feeble and have poor sucking ability, necessitating tube feeding. Fifty per cent die by two months of age and less than 10 per cent survive the first year. These children are profoundly mentally retarded and make little physical or mental progress. Long-term survival has been documented. For example, Smith *et al.* (1978) reported an eleven-year-old girl with apparently nonmosaic trisomy 18. Although severely retarded, she could sit unaided and feed herself with a spoon. However, long-term survival is usually seen only in patients with mosaicism and a normal cell line. It has been suggested that approximately 10 per cent of trisomy 18 patients are mosaics, 10 per cent are due to translocations or have double aneuploidy and 80 per cent are full trisomics (Bass *et al.*, 1982). The mosaic cases frequently show hemiatrophy with the normal cell line being found with greater frequency on the better-developed side of the body (Rao *et al.*, 1978; Rockman-Greenberg *et al.*, 1982). These children may do much better than full trisomics in terms of growth and mental development and have fewer major birth defects. Long-term survival and unexpected progress in a trisomy 18 child should lead to a suspicion of mosaicism, and skin fibroblasts should be studied especially if there is body assymetry. Trisomy 18 cases have a skewed sex ratio with females outnumbering males 3 to 1. This may be due to increased fetal loss of males. Mosaic cases have a more normal sex ratio. As with Down's syndrome, maternal age is elevated in trisomy 18 but this is not as marked.

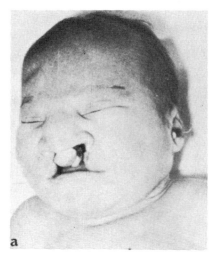
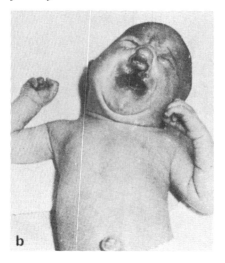
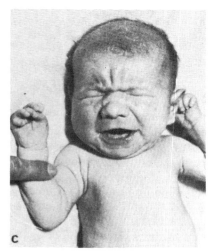

PLATE 6.6 Children with trisomy 13 showing: (a) microcephaly, cleft lip and palate, malformed pinna; (b) microcephaly, cleft lip and palate, and umbilical hernia; (c) long, thin mouth, low-set, primitive ears and polydactyly (reproduced by permission of Dr A. Taylor and the Academic Press)

Trisomy 13 was reported as a chromosomal syndrome in 1960 by Patau *et al.* The incidence in live births is about 1 in 5000 with again a higher incidence seen in perinatal deaths. In many cases the diagnosis of trisomy 13 is made clinically before the karyotype has been determined due to the distinct phenotype seen in this syndrome. In the craniofacial region the most classic finding is hypotelorism and microphthalmia associated with an underlying

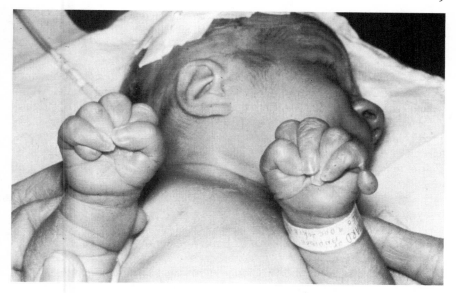

PLATE 6.7   Infant with trisomy 13 showing polydactyly of the hands

holoprosencephaly (Plate 6.6). In 60–80 per cent of cases there is clefting of the lip and/or palate. An unusual and characteristic finding is localized scalp defects in the occipito-parietal regions. The hands and feet frequently show an unusual form of postaxial polydactlyly with bulbous accessory digits attached by thin pedicles (Plate 6.7). Internal malformations include congenital heart defects, renal abnormalities and genital defects, especially bicornuate uterus in females. Meningomyelocele and omphalocele may occasionally occur. For a further review of clinical findings see Lazyuk *et al.* (1974).

As with trisomy 18, the prognosis for these infants is poor. Less than 30 per cent of live-born patients survive to 6 months of age. Long-term survival is rare and such children show severe physical and mental retardation and frequently develop seizure disorders. One child of 5 years reported by Mankinen and Sears (1976) had a social age of 5–6 months but could roll over and pull to sit.

Trisomy 13 is found in pure form in about 73 per cent of Patau's syndrome patients; 17 per cent have translocations and the rest are mosaics. Maternal age is elevated in trisomic patients and a recurrence risk of 1 per cent for aneuploidy is usually given in genetic counselling.

Rarer trisomic conditions involving autosomes occasionally occur. *Trisomy 8* has been reported in over seventy patients. Most cases show a mosaic karyotype with approximately 60 per cent trisomic cells in blood and 70 per cent in fibroblasts (Riccardi, 1977). First reported as a C group trisomy by Stadler *et al.* (1963), this syndrome is characterized by a distinctive facies with prominent forehead, broad-based upturned bulbous nose, dysplastic ears, short philtrum and everted lower lip. Skeletal abnormalities are common including absent or dysplastic patellae, broad ribs, abnormal vertebrae sometimes causing scoliosis, narrow pelvis and joint restrictions. The nipples may be wide spread and abnormal. There are unusually deep palmar and hallucal creases (Anneren *et al.*, 1981; Casey *et al.*, 1981). Although most patients are mentally retarded, the degree of intellectual impairment is variable and presumably related to the proportion of trisomic cells. Some have intelligence within the borderline normal range (Smith, 1982). This condition reinforces the need to karyotype all children with dysmorphic findings and retardation and the necessity of looking at many cells if mosaicism is suspected. In a large series of trisomy 8 patients reported by Riccardi (1977), only 43 per cent were diagnosed before one year of age and 50 per cent were two years old or more at diagnosis. There is a slight excess of males. Parental age is not increased and this probably reflects the postzygotic origin of nondisjunction in the vast majority of these patients. Recurrence risks are considered to be low.

Trisomy 9 is also predominantly found in mosaic form though patients with full trisomy have been reported (Feingold and Atkins, 1973). As with trisomy 8 the severity of clinical findings and mental retardation varies with the percentage of trisomic cells. However, several have died in infancy with multiple anomalies (Katayama *et al.*, 1980) or survive with severe retardation.

Children with trisomy 9 display growth deficiency and an unusual facies with proportionate microcephaly, high, sloping forehead, microphthalmia, broad nasal bridge, anteverted nares with bulbous nose tip, small simple ears, prominent upper lip and micrognathia. The neck may be short and broad with some webbing. Skeletal anomalies are common, including joint anomalies such as congenital hip dysplasia, dislocation and fixation of elbows and knees, kyphoscoliosis and sacral hypoplasia. Internal anomalies include congenital heart defects, renal anomalies and various structural brain malformations. Parental ages are not increased in this condition and recurrence risks in most cases are considered low. Cases with apparently pure trisomy 9 may be due to meiotic nondisjunction. Thus the parents may be at increased risk for aneuploidy in subsequent pregnancies and should be offered prenatal diagnosis (see Katayama *et al.*, 1980; Frohlich, 1982; and Sanchez *et al.*, 1982, for further details). Other autosomal trisomies such as trisomy 22 have been reported but are very rare.

Occasionally children are found to have additional chromosomal fragments which cannot always be identified. These small supernumerary or marker chromosomes may be ascertained fortuitously in newborn studies or detected in abnormal children. In newborns the incidence of fragments is approximately 1 in 6000 (Hook and Hamerton, 1977), but among mentally retarded populations this rises to 1 in 300. When mental retardation and congenital anomalies are present, it is probable that the additional chromosome contains some euchromatic material. However, often when these chromosomes are found in normal individuals they are dark-staining metacentric markers and presumably represent inactive heterochromatin. Passage of these markers from normal parents to their normal children has been reported (Yip *et al.*, 1982). Decisions as to the significance of these markers in a child should therefore be correlated with physical and mental findings and only after parental studies have been carried out.

Sex chromosome aneuploidy

Aneuploidy involving the X and Y chromosomes is relatively common. Phenotypic males may be found with 47, XXY or 47, XYY karyotypes while phenotypic females may have trisomy X (47, XXX) or monosomy X (45, X).

These abnormal karyotypes are associated with significantly less mortality and morbidity than autosomal aneuploidy and frank mental retardation is not a common finding. However, these children manifest a somewhat lower mean IQ and may have poor academic achievement. In addition they may have co-ordination problems, speech delay or behavioural disorders.

Klinefelter syndrome (47, XXY) was described initially in 1942 before its chromosomal aetiology was recognized. Occurring in approximately 1 in 1000 males it is one of the commonest causes of hypogonadism and infertility. No distinctive phenotype is recognized though there is a tendency for increased height and weight, especially in adulthood when obesity may occur. Hypogonadism is usual with inadequate testosterone production to allow full virilization. Gynaecomastia frequently occurs. These symptoms may be ameliorated by testosterone therapy at eleven to twelve years though infertility remains the rule except in mosaic cases.

There is a tendency towards dull mentality though few children are actually mentally retarded. They tend, however, to have increased problems with auditory perception, as well as receptive and expressive language (Walzer *et al.*, 1982; Bender *et al.*, 1983; Walzer, 1985). Distractability and poor attention span also lead to a general tendency to poorer school performance than intellectual levels would suggest. These children are also relatively passive and insecure.

The *47, XXX* karyotype occurs in about 1 in 1000 females. They also have some intellectual and behaviour problems. Again, no characteristic phenotype can be recognized, though these girls are tall. They too have increased problems with auditory perception and language. However, they tend to do relatively well in school despite somewhat lower mean IQ levels, often in the 80s (Haka-Ikse, 1982). In addition they may have problems in fine or gross motor co-ordination and behavioural difficulties including immaturity and lack of confidence (Nielsen *et al.*, 1981). Fertility is usually maintained.

Initially it was considered that the *47,XYY* karyotype might predispose males to aggressive behaviour. It has now been shown that these boys, in general, have fewer problems than those with additional X chromosomes. This karyotype is found in approximately 1 in 1000 males. No clinical phenotype has been recognized though they tend to be tall. Intelligence is usually within normal limits though they may have mild cognitive deficits or behavioural disorders (Haka-Ikse, 1982). Fertility is not impaired. There is an excess of 47,XYY males reported among incarcerated or institutionalized populations, reflecting their tendencies to decreased frustration tolerance and possible dull mentation. However, follow-up studies on unselected newborns ascertained with 47,XYY suggest that many individuals with this chromosome complement do well.

Turner syndrome or 45,X is a common karyotype in spontaneous abortions but rarely comes to live birth. Probably 95 per cent of such individuals are lost prenatally. Approximately 1 in 5000 females has this chromosome complement while others may have mosaicism for 45,X/46,XX or 45,X/46,XY. Turner syndrome is usually associated with a female phenotype and is characterized by short stature, sexual infantilism, a short webbed neck, shield chest, cubitus valgus and congenital lymphoedema giving puffiness of the hands and feet (Plate 6.8). There is an increased incidence of major anomalies including cardiac defects, especially coarctation of the aorta, and renal abnormalities. Fertility is usually drastically reduced though successful pregnancies in 45,X women have been reported. Oestrogen replacement therapy may not allow fertility but is indicated for normal secondary sexual development. Intellectual functioning is usually good though the mean IQ is slightly reduced at 95. Several have perceptive hearing loss and there is an increase in speech problems, in part due to structural abnormalities of the face and palate and there may also be problems with spatial concepts (Haka-Ikse, 1982; Bender *et al.*, 1983; Walzer, 1985). Behavioural problems do not usually occur. Individuals with 45,X/46,XY mosaicism may range phenotypically from females with Turner syndrome through children with ambiguous genitalia to normal males, depending on the relative proportion of the cell lines in different tissues. These children should be carefully followed as they are at increased risk for gonadoblastoma.

While these degrees of aneuploidy of the sex chromosomes are relatively benign in surviving children, higher levels of sex chromosome anomaly including 48,XXXY; 49,XXXXY; 48,XXXX; and 49,XXXXX are associated with more severe defects. These include hypotonia, growth deficiency, hypogonadism and multiple major and/or minor anomalies including radio-ulnar synostosis. IQ levels usually are within the severe-to-moderate mental retardation range and behavioural problems may be present.

Another entity which should be mentioned in regard to numerical chromosome anomalies is *triploidy*. This condition, where a whole extra set of chromosomes is present (69,XXX; 69,XXY; or 69,XYY), is usually lethal prenatally. Most infants surviving to live birth are mosaics with a normal diploid cell line. These children have multiple major and minor congenital anomalies and mental retardation. Hydatidiform degeneration of the placenta is a clue to the diagnosis in the perinatal period. In older children, especially

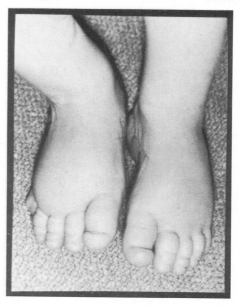

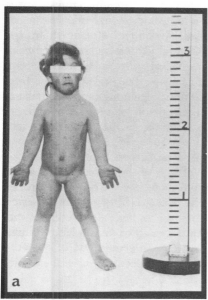

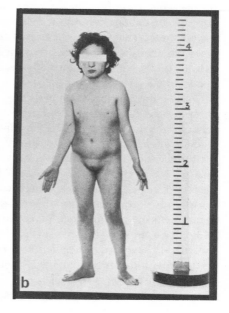

PLATE 6.8 Clinical features of patients with Turner syndrome, 45, X. *Top*: feet of a child showing dorsal oedema and small upturned nails. *Below*: (a) girl aged four years with webbing of the neck, unusual facies and short stature; (b) girl aged fourteen years with webbing of the neck, short stature, cubitus valgus and absent secondary sexual characteristics (reproduced by permission of Professor P.E. Polani and the Academic Press)

mosaics, mental retardation with or without body or facial asymmetry may be the primary presenting symptom (Blackburn *et al.*, 1982).

Structural abnormalities

The range of structural chromosome abnormalities reported in humans is extremely varied. In most cases an unbalanced structural rearrangement leads to physical and mental abnormalities. Individuals with apparently balanced rearrangements, such as translocations or inversions, are usually normal though they have a higher incidence of minor anomalies and retardation (see p. 241). The detailed documentation of recognized chromosomal syndromes due to structural rearrangements is beyond the scope of this chapter. Readers are referred to one of the atlases of chromosomal anomalies, for example that of de Grouchy and Turleau (1977). However, mention is made below of two of the relatively common syndromes occurring in children with mental retardation: cri du chat syndrome and Wolf–Hirschhorn syndrome.

Cri du chat syndrome, named for the characteristic cry of the newborn, is due to terminal deletion of the short arm of chromosome 5. In most cases this is a sporadic event and not associated with increased risk of recurrence. It results from parental translocation in 10–15 per cent of cases.

First described by Lejeune *et al.* in 1963, these children have a characteristic phenotype with microcephaly, round face, hypertelorism, epicanthus, down-slanting palpebral fissures and low-set ears. Major congenital anomalies include heart defects. These children are usually small at birth and show poor postnatal growth. They may be hypotonic and all exhibit mental retardation, usually in the severe range (IQ 20–40). Survival into the fifties has been documented.

Wolf–Hirschhorn syndrome is due to a terminal deletion of the short arm of chromosome 4. These children have a clinical phenotype quite distinct from cri du chat syndrome (5p −). They tend to be microcephalic with a prominent glabella, high arched eyebrows, downslanting fissures, iris anomalies, a broad malformed nose, large simple low-set ears, downturned mouth and micro-gnathia. Major malformations, especially cleft lip and/or palate and congenital heart defects, are common. These children show poor pre- and postnatal growth and frequently hypotonia (Wilson *et al.*, 1981). They exhibit severe mental retardation and usually have onset of seizures before two years of age. Most (two-thirds) do not survive beyond three to four years, though individuals have lived into their twenties (Fryns *et al.*, 1981). Most cases are sporadic with low recurrence risk, though 10–15 per cent are due to parental translocations (Gonzalez *et al.*, 1981; Wilson *et al.*, 1981).

In summary, although many chromosomal syndromes are associated with distinct clinical phenotypes, in others the diagnosis may be more difficult. Abnormalities in growth, body symmetry and personality or behavioural traits may indicate a chromosome anomaly even if major anomalies or frank mental retardation are not present. A karyotypic investigation should be carried out in all cases of mental retardation and major or minor congenital malformations unless the diagnosis of a clear-cut nonchromosomal syndrome can be made. Chromosomal studies, however, may be carried out as part of the selective work-up of other children and care should be taken to look for mosaicism or to utilize special banding techniques when appropriate.

NEW CHROMOSOMAL SYNDROMES: 'MICROCYTOGENETICS'

A new area of extreme interest and importance in cytogenetics has resulted from the development of techniques for banding chromosomes earlier in cell division, when they are less condensed and therefore longer. Prophase or prometaphase (high resolution) banding (Yunis, 1976; Francke and Oliver, 1978; Yunis, 1981) has allowed considerably greater definition of banding patterns. This development of microcytogenetics has reawakened interest in mental retardation–malformation syndromes of previously unknown aetiology and several have been found to have a cytogenetic basis in some patients.

Retinoblastoma

Retinoblastoma, an ocular tumour present in childhood, is interesting from a genetic perspective as it may show an autosomal dominant pattern of inheritance, an apparently multifactorial pattern, or occur as a sporadic case in a family. In 1963 Lele *et al.* noted that a child with retinoblastoma had a deletion involving the short arm of chromosome 13. Since then the association of retinoblastoma with anomalies of chromosome 13 in some patients has been well recognized. For example, Howard (1982) found that 14 (5 per cent) of 259 patients with retinoblastoma had abnormalities of chromosome 13, usually deletions involving the common segment 13q14. Children with such chromosomal anomalies differed from others with retinoblastoma in that they were usually sporadic cases and often had additional abnormalities. Although no characteristic phenotype has been described, there may be microcephaly, micrognathia, high- arched palate, low-set ears, abnormal nipples, abnormal digits with clinodactyly, abnormal palmar creases, abnormal genitalia, and musculoskeletal defects (Vogel, 1979; de Grouchy, 1982; Howard, 1982). Other eye abnormalities include microphthalmia, colobomata and strabismus. Hypotonia with inguinal herniae has been reported. Mild to severe mental retardation is common, though intelligence may be normal. Growth retardation may also be present. These children commonly have both mental retardation and major and minor congenital anomalies which are consistent with an autosomal deletion. In addition, the mortality rate is high (20 per cent) compared to that seen in isolated retinoblastoma. However, some children with deletions have few manifestations of a chromosomal defect and no doubt the severity of the disorder depends on the extent of the deleted segment (Vogel, 1979). It has been suggested that this deletion involves a gene for normal retinal function though the relationship between the tumour formation and the deletion is not clear (Wilson *et al.*, 1977). Gene dosage studies involving the esterase D locus which is mapped to 13q14 indicate a gene deletion in patients with obvious chromosomal deletions and in some in whom the deletion is submicroscopic (Sparkes *et al.*, 1980; Murphree *et al.*, 1982). Possibly deletion of this chromosome segment may produce functional hemizygosity for genes in this region and thus may allow the expression of recessive alleles for retinoblastoma. The fact that abnormalities of chromosome 13 have been documented in tumour cells from some retinoblastomas, even in patients whose karyotypes from blood lymphocyte and fibroblast cultures are normal, may indicate a more basic association of chromosomal deletion and tumour formation, though the pathogenetic mechanisms involved are not known (Hashem and Khalifa, 1975; Vogel, 1979).

Although most familial retinoblastoma cases do not show chromosomal abnormalities outside the tumour cells themselves, familial retinoblastoma has been reported in families where chromosomal anomalies involving 13q are segregating (Ferrell and Sparkes, 1981). For example, Strong *et al.* (1981) reported a family where retinoblastoma had occurred in four generations and had been transmitted by at least eight unaffected relatives. It was found that the unaffected carriers were heterozygotes for a balanced insertional translocation of 13q13 to 13q14.5 into the short arm of chromosome 3. Those individuals with the derivative chromosome leading to a deletion of 13q had retinoblastoma, mental retardation and failure to thrive, but no consistent congenital malformations. Their esterase D levels were 50 per cent of normal. Some other individuals in the pedigree had an unbalanced karyotype with duplication of the segment 13q13 to 13q14.5. Although their levels of esterase D were 1.5 times normal, these individuals had no phenotypic abnormalities.

Obviously, detailed investigations including prometaphase banding of chromosomes and gene dosage studies of esterase D may be indicated in children with retinoblastoma, especially when mental retardation or somatic anomalies occur.

Aniridia–Wilm's tumour association

Over fifty patients have been reported in whom aniridia is associated with Wilm's tumour. Although isolated aniridia usually shows an autosomal dominant mode of inheritance with variable expressivity, about 1 in 40–70 patients with Wilm's tumour may also have aniridia (Shannon *et al.*, 1982; Smith, 1982). These patients differ from others with Wilm's tumour in that other defects are frequently present and most such patients have moderate to severe mental retardation. Again, as with the retinoblastoma association, these patients with multiple defects in addition to Wilm's tumour have been found to have a high incidence of chromosomal deletions, in this case involving 11p (Anderson *et al.*, 1978; Riccardi *et al.*, 1978). Although not all patients with aniridia and Wilm's tumour have detectable deletions, in those where it has been observed the deletions have consistently involved the band 11p13 (Francke *et al.*, 1979). No characteristic phenotype is known for this association and presumably the variability of clinical findings reflects differences in the size of the deleted segment. Although most cases with chromosome deletion have been sporadic, familial recurrence due to transmission of a deleted chromosome derived from a parental balanced insertional translocation has been reported (Yunis and Ramsay, 1980). Patients with 11p deletions have variable clinical findings with a high incidence of genitourinary abnormalities such as ambiguous genitalia, hypospadias and cryptorchidism. Gonadal defects including streak gonads and gonadoblastoma have been reported. Many patients have growth deficiency, microcephaly and cardiopathy in addition to mental retardation. The patients also differ from other Wilm's tumour patients. For example, the Wilm's tumour presents earlier, the incidence of bilateral tumour is high, and there is an excess of males. As with retinoblastoma, a genetic marker for this deletion is known and catalase activity is reduced in these patients. It is obvious that detailed cytogenetic studies should be done on patients presenting with Wilm's tumour and/or aniridia, especially if mental retardation or other anomalies are present. Patients with aniridia and other defects who are found to have the 11p13 deletion must be followed closely for development of Wilm's tumour though this is not a universal complication (Gilgenkrantz *et al.*, 1982; Evans, unpublished data).

Prader–Willi syndrome

The Prader–Willi syndrome is another malformation–mental retardation syndrome which has been shown to be associated with chromosomal aberrations in a high proportion of cases. Unfortunately this situation has not proved as clear cut as the retinoblastoma 13q deletion or aniridia–Wilm's tumour association.

Prader *et al.* (1956) first described a pattern of hypotonia, obesity, hypogonadism and mental retardation in nine children. Since then this syndrome has become well recognized. The findings of severe hypotonia in infancy with feeding difficulties and failure to thrive, followed by improved muscle tone and the onset of obesity in early childhood, are well documented. The obesity is not due to excessive caloric intake but rather to bizarre eating habits. Dysmorphic findings include almond-shaped palpebral fissures, small hands and feet and hypogenitalism with cryptorchidism in males. Moderate mental retardation is usually present. The aetiology of Prader–Willi syndrome is unknown. The disorder follows no recognized pattern of inheritance and empiric recurrence risks are low. It has been suggested that this syndrome is the result of a de novo dominant mutation which is genetically lethal due to the mental retardation and hypogonadism. Conversely, it may represent a localized defect of morphogenesis influencing hypothalamic or midbrain development (Smith, 1982).

Interest in the aetiology of Prader–Willi syndrome was renewed when cytogenetic abnormalities in patients with this disorder were reported. In 1976 Hawkey and Smithies first noted the high incidence of anomalies of chromosome 15 in patients with Prader–Willi syndrome. Since then over 50 patients with this syndrome and an anomalous chromosome 15 have been reported. The proportion of Prader–Willi patients with anomalies of chromosome 15 varies from study to study. For example, Ledbetter *et al.* (1982) found that 21 of 40 cases (53 per cent) had anomalies of 15 while Cassidy *et al.* (1984) found that all 12 of their patients had such defects. The differences in the proportions of patients with chromosome defects may be due to many factors, including the heterogeneity of the patients' clinical findings, the level of chromosome resolution available (i.e. prometaphase *v.* metaphase banding) and the index of suspicion. In most cases the karyotypes have not been studied 'blind' in conjunction with karyotypes from normal individuals.

Regardless of the proportion of patients involved, the majority of cases with chromosome defects have had an interstitial deletion of 15q usually involving bands q11 to q13 in either complete or mosaic form. However, many other anomalies of 15 have been described including balanced Robertsonian translocations, reciprocal translocations, and isodicentric chromosome 15 (Wisniewski *et al.*, 1980; Ledbetter *et al.*, 1982; Cassidy *et al.*, 1984). There has been, therefore, no easily detected common segment of 15 implicated in all cases of Prader–Willi syndrome with chromosomal anomalies. The association of the syndrome with anomalies of chromosome 15 seems well proven. However, the precise relationship between them is not known. It has been suggested (Kousseff and Douglass, 1982) that the cytogenetic anomalies may be a secondary pleiotropic effect of a major gene influencing the development of Prader–Willi syndrome which also has an effect on the fragility of this chromosome. It is also possible that considerable genetic heterogeneity exists in this syndrome and that different pathogenetic mechanisms including major genes, chromosomal deletions or other factors may be responsible for similar phenotypes. Detailed analysis of Prader–Willi cases looking for precise phenotypic–karyotypic correlations may confirm genetic heterogeneity, with some cases due to chromosomal defects and others due to major gene defects or sporadic morphogenetic abnormalities. Until then it would seem appropriate to karyotype all infants who manifest signs of Prader–Willi syndrome, especially severe hypotonia. In one such screening study of floppy infants with signs suggestive of Prader–Willi syndrome, Berry *et al.* (1981) found that 3 out of 26 (12 per cent) had chromosome abnormalities, so the importance of such investigations should be emphasized as earlier identification of the syndrome may allow for more appropriate management of later problems.

The cat-eye syndrome

The obvious and rare malformation of iris colobomata occurring in patients with this malformation–mental retardation syndrome has given it the name of the cat-eye syndrome. However, this is a very variable syndrome and only a minority of cases have ocular colobomata. Other relatively common findings include anal atresia with rectovesicular fistula, congenital heart disease, unilateral renal agenesis and preauricular pits and/or tags. Many cases have a downslant to the palpebral fissures and mild hypertelorism. Growth is usually normal but most patients have mild mental retardation.

In 1972 Buhler *et al.* first described a chromosomal anomaly in these patients. This abnormality involved an extra marker chromosome which was acrocentric but half the size of a normal G group chromosome. Buhler *et al.* considered this marker to represent a deleted chromosome 22 and thus the patients could be considered to have partial trisomy 22. However, karyotypic analysis of eleven patients with cat-eye syndrome led Schinzel *et al.* (1981) to suggest that this extra chromosome was a bisatellited isodicentric one derived from chromosome 22 and representing a duplicated segment including the satellites, the short arm, the centromere and a small piece of the long arm. This would then represent tetrasomy for 22q11–22pter. In part this interpretation was suggested by comparison of anomalies in patients with cat-eye syndrome and those with trisomy 22pter–q11 or q12 due to the unbalanced segregation of familial translocations. In general the patients with the unbalanced translocations were more severely affected both physically and mentally, did not necessarily resemble those with the cat-eye syndrome and rarely had colobomata. They considered that the cat-eye syndrome was more benign than usually thought and that mental retardation was relatively uncommon. The severity of symptoms in the reported cases would then appear to reflect a bias of ascertainment. This hypothesis is also suggested by direct transmission of the marker from parent to child which has been reported in several families. In these cases variability in symptoms between family members was apparent, but possession of the marker chromosome did not preclude relatively normal development and fertility.

The diGeorge malformation complex

The diGeorge anomaly is a developmental field defect involving structures derived from the fourth branchial arch and derivatives of the third and fourth pharyngeal pouches. Faulty morphogenesis in these developing tissues can lead to hypoplasia or aplasia of the thymus and parathyroids and aortic arch anomalies. These children tend to have hypertelorism, downslanting palpebral fissures and a short philtrum. Other major congenital defects, including oesophageal atresia, choanal atresia, diaphragmatic hernia and imperforate anus may occur in association with the diGeorge anomaly (Smith, 1982).

Most patients have died in the first few months of life from infections secondary to impaired immune response, hypocalcaemic seizures or cardiac failure, all as a direct result of the malformations. Those who have survived for longer have shown mild to moderate mental retardation.

The aetiology of this condition is unknown and most cases have been sporadic. However, de la Chapelle *et al.* (1981) reported that four individuals in one family had anomalies typical of the diGeorge malformation complex. These patients were found to be monosomic for part of chromosome 22 (22pter-22q11) and trisomic for part of chromosome 20 (pter-q11) secondary to a familial translocation. Since then several other diGeorge patients have been found to have chromosomal anomalies, usually due to familial or de novo translocations. In all these cases the consistent finding has been a deletion of 22pter-q11 (Kelley *et al.*, 1982).

Langer–Giedion syndrome

The Langer–Giedion syndrome was first considered to be a form of tricho-rhino-phalangeal syndrome but is now realized to be a separate entity. It is characterized by short stature, unusual facies with a large bulbous nose and large protruding ears, thin scalp hair and eyebrows, redundant loose skin in infancy, cone-shaped epiphyses and multiple exostoses. Mild to moderate mental retardation is usually present (Hall *et al.*, 1974; Smith, 1982). The aetiology of the syndrome is not known and cases are sporadic within families. This first suggested that Langer–Giedion syndrome could be an autosomal dominant mutation which was genetically lethal due to mental retardation. However, some patients have now been reported to have deletions of chromosome 8q. This situation is not clear cut, as there is absence of overlap of the purported deletion segment in different patients. Deletions of 8q22 appear relatively common though 8q13–22, 8q24 and 8q21 deletions have been reported (Frontali *et al.*, 1982; Zaletajev and Marincheva, 1983). Also, other patients with partial deletions of 8q involving this area have not necessarily shown features of the Langer–Giedion syndrome. The cytogenetic situation in Langer–Giedion syndrome seems similar to that in Prader–Willi syndrome with some patients having normal chromosomes (Gorlin *et al.*, 1982), some having a similar chromosome deletion (8q22) and others having different but potentially related chromosomal defects. Again, further detailed micro-cytogenetic analysis and phenotypic–karyotypic correlation will be required before the nature of the relationship between the observed chromosomal defects and the Langer–Giedion syndrome can be elucidated.

Miller–Dieker syndrome

The Miller–Dieker syndrome is a multiple malformation–mental retardation syndrome characterized by lissencephaly and a characteristic facial appearance with bitemporal hollowing, upslanting palpebral fissures, small nose with anteverted nares, thin upper lip, micrognathia and ear anomalies. The high forehead may show vertical soft tissue ridging when the baby cries. Other congenital malformations including cardiac defects and cryptorchidism may be present. Postnatal growth in these infants is poor and they have profound mental retardation and seizures. Death usually occurs within the first three months though survival into early childhood has been noted. First described by Miller (1963) in siblings, the lissencephaly syndrome has been considered to be due to an autosomal recessive gene as affected siblings born to normal parents have been noted in at least five families (Smith, 1982; Dobyns *et al.*, 1983). Recently, however, some patients with Miller–Dieker syndrome have been found to have abnormalities of chromosome 17. Although the types of anomalies have varied (e.g. ring 17, unbalanced structural rearrangements), the band 17p13 has been absent in these patients. In addition Dobyns *et al.* (1983), when reporting their studies, indicated that a review of patients with ring 17 had detected one with undiagnosed Miller–Dieker syndrome. High-resolution banding of chromosome 17 has also revealed that one of the families reported with similarly affected siblings has a chromosomal rearrangement. It is possible, therefore, that the apparent autosomal recessive pattern of inheritance in Miller–Dieker syndrome is rather the result of abnormal segregation of structural rearrangements in some cases. Miller–Dieker syndrome therefore represents another example of a condition where specific chromosome observations have been documented in some patients while others have apparently normal chromosomes at the present level of banding resolution. Further studies on these patients will hopefully determine if genetic heterogeneity exists. Meanwhile, the finding of a chromosomal defect in a condition such as Miller–Dieker syndrome which was previously presumed to be a single gene disorder suggests that other malformation–mental retardation syndromes, whose pattern of inheritance is still not proven, may benefit from microcytogenetic investigations.

THE SIGNIFICANCE OF 'BALANCED' STRUCTURAL REARRANGEMENTS

A recent area of concern in the interpretation of chromosomal observations both in children with mental retardation and in individuals karyotyped for other reasons is the significance of apparently balanced structural rearrangements. The large newborn studies of consecutive live births showed an incidence of balanced structural rearrangements of approximately 0.2 per cent. About half of these were reciprocal translocations and half Robertsonian translocations, with occasional inversions seen. Approximately 80 per cent of these rearrangements were familial in origin (Hamerton *et al.*, 1975; Hook and Hamerton, 1977).

Many of the children with familial and de novo translocations who were ascertained through newborn studies have been followed up and have shown no excess of physical or mental abnormalities (Friedrich and Nielsen, 1974; Evans *et al.*, 1978a; Nielsen and Krag-Olsen, 1981). There have been reports of increased fetal wastage in some of these families presumably due to the production of unbalanced conceptuses (Nielsen and Rasmussen, 1976; Evans *et al.*, 1978a). This is in marked contrast to those families where a translocation was ascertained through an unbalanced proband with multiple anomalies and where the incidence of fetal wastage and abnormal infants in sibships is high (Ford and Clegg, 1969; Lejeune *et al.*, 1970).

It is to be expected that children with unbalanced karyotypes will suffer from mental retardation and congenital anomalies. It is less easy to understand, especially in view of the newborn studies, why children with balanced rearrangements should be at increased risk for such problems. There have been several reports, however, of mental retardation and congenital anomalies in children with apparently balanced rearrangements (Skovby and Niebuhr, 1974; Tharapel *et al.*, 1977; Fryns and van den Berghe, 1979; Dockery *et al.*, 1982) and other studies have suggested a significant increase in the incidence of apparently balanced translocations among retarded individuals. For example, Aurias *et al.* (1978) found 20 (0.9 per cent) balanced structural rearrangements in 2341 abnormal children in whom no known chromosomal syndrome was suspected. Funderburk *et al.* (1977) found 7 (1.5 per cent) balanced rearrangements in 455 children referred for chromosomal evaluation because of retardation and Jacobs *et al.* (1978) found 5 (1.1 per cent) balanced translocations among 435 institutionalized retarded patients (after Down's syndrome patients were excluded). Also of significance was the fact that the majority of these rearrangements were reciprocal translocations (70 per cent) and many were de novo (48 per cent).

The increased incidence of de novo translocations among the retarded population has led to speculation concerning the basis of their deleterious effects. Postulated mechanisms include submicroscopic chromosomal deletions, breakpoints that may interrupt a unique genetic sequence (a structural Mendelian gene) or position effects (Funderburk *et al.*, 1977; Hecht *et al.*, 1978). Although abnormal gene function due to position effect has not been demonstrated in man, it is possible that chromosome rearrangements may result in breakage or repositioning of heterochromatic segments and potential activation or suppression of euchromatic material. This is suggested by *Drosophila* and mouse models and from investigation on human Burkitt's lymphoma cells carrying a translocation between chromosomes 8 and 14. In this case heterochromatic material on 8q may become euchromatic when translocated to 14q allowing activation of a previously suppressed oncogene (Hecht *et al.*, 1978). In this regard it is interesting to note that such rearrangements frequently occur at breakpoints of evolutionary significance in the genome (Skovby and Niebuhr, 1974). These mechanisms potentially can explain deleterious effects of de novo translocations. However, it is more difficult to explain abnormalities in a child with a familial translocation in these ways. Several reports document mental retardation and congenital anomalies in children with apparently balanced rearrangements which have been inherited from a phenotypically normal parent (Bargman *et al.*, 1970; Ayme *et al.*, 1979). It is possible, however, that minute deletions at the breakpoints of a translocation or inversion may give rise to functional hemizygosity for several genes, in which case expression of those gene products will be influenced by the alleles on the homologous chromosomes which could differ in parent, child or sib. It is also possible that the egg or sperm carrying translocated chromosomes may be functionally abnormal and so predispose the embryo to faulty morphogenesis. In addition, the finding of a familial balanced translocation in a retarded child should not preclude other diagnostic investigations as the translocation may be coincidental (Ying *et al.*, 1982).

There appears to be good evidence, therefore, that the incidence of mental retardation in balanced carriers of structural rearrangements is increased, though the pathogenetic mechanisms are not yet clear. Although the majority of children with such rearrangements develop normally, especially if the translocation or inversion is familial, the increased risk of abnormality makes counselling of families difficult especially if the translocation is detected fortuitously by prenatal diagnosis. The difficulties in counselling are compounded by the fact that balanced translocation carriers may be at increased risk for other chromosomal anomalies, especially aneuploidy in their offspring due to potential interchromosomal effects (Stoll *et al.*, 1978). The safest course at this time would seem to be to offer prenatal diagnosis to all families where a balanced rearrangement is known to be segregating.

CHROMOSOME FRAGILITY AND CHROMOSOME BREAKAGE SYNDROMES

One of the major recent discoveries concerning chromosomal abnormality and mental retardation was the detection of heritable fragile sites on human chromosomes. These sites have not been easily recognized in the past due to their inhibition by normal lymphocyte culture media. However, they may be expressed in media low in folic acid, thymidine or bromodeoxyuridine and can be induced by methotrexate (Sutherland, 1979a). Heritable fragile sites involving 2q11, 10q23, 11q13, 15p12.4, 16q22 and 20p11 have been described (Sutherland, 1979b). However, the commonest and most important site involves Xq27 or Xq28 as it is now recognized as a marker for a specific form of X-linked mental retardation. First described by Lubs in 1969, the fragile X, as it is frequently known, is associated with a distinct clinical phenotype. This phenotype is characterized by above-average growth parameters, an unusual facies, moderate to severe mental retardation and, in many cases, macroorchidism. These individuals tend to be large at birth and have an accelerated growth rate. They have large, dolichocephalic heads, prominent foreheads with supraorbital fullness, a long nose, prominent chin and large protruding ears. The hands are somewhat brachydactylous. Neurological signs are variable even within families, but patients may be hyperreflexic and have mild co-ordination difficulties. Mental retardation is usually present in the hemizygous males with IQ values commonly in the 30–65 range. Speech is disproportionately delayed. Behavioural abnormalities including hyperactivity or autism may occur and occasionally also grand mal seizures. The macro-orchidism is a frequent sign with testicular volume in postpubertal males being approximately twice the average value for ethnic origin. Although prepubertal males often have normally sized testes they may also be slightly enlarged. The testicular histology is normal and hormone levels are usually within normal limits. However, mild reductions in serum testosterone and elevations in serum LH have been noted (Turner and Jacobs, 1983).

This classical phenotype with mental retardation and macroorchidism was recognized as an X-linked disorder before the identification of the fragile X chromosome in affected individuals. It had been postulated for some time that the excess of males with moderate mental retardation might be due, in part, to X-linked genes. For example Turner and Turner (1974) found a 32.2 per cent excess of males with retardation at IQ levels 30–55, when they studied the sex ratio in pairs of retarded sibs. They hypothesized that, if this male excess in familial retardation was due to X-linked forms of retardation, the prevalence of such conditions was at least 0.74 per 1000 males. With the advent of specialized culture techniques for detecting the fragile X syndrome, more specific studies were carried out and it was realized that X-linked retardation with macroorchidism and the fragile X syndrome were frequently synonymous (Sutherland and Ashforth, 1979). Turner *et al.* (1978) restudied 16 original families with X-linked retardation and found 6 where the fragile X was segregating. In these 6 families the probands were all macroorchid. A further 2 families with X-linked retardation and macroorchidism were also fragile X positive. Among 2533 karyotyped retarded patients Venter and Op't Hof (1982) found 22 with fragile X. Jacobs *et al.* (1983) studied 274 unselected retarded males living in the community and found 5 (1.8 per cent) with fragile X. In the 4 families available for study the fragile site was shown to be inherited. Among an institutionalized population, Froster-Iskenius *et al.* (1983) found 15 (6.2 per cent) with fragile X including one with Klinefelter syndrome. It would appear, therefore, that this syndrome occurs in at least 2 per cent of retarded males and that its prevalence in the total population is probably not less than 1 in 2000 males, making it one of the commonest genetic forms of mental retardation (Herbst and Miller, 1980; Turner, 1982).

Although the fragile X syndrome is now well recognized as an important contributor to mental retardation, especially in males, there are still several unanswered questions. It is still not clear, for example, what the relationship is between the fragile site and the mental retardation syndrome. It is not yet known if the fragile site in some way causes the clinical phenotype, or if it is a pleiotropic effect of the X-linked gene, or if it is due to another closely linked gene in linkage disequilibrium. Considerable interest has arisen, therefore, in the mechanism of fragile site expression as this may hold the clue to the precise molecular defect and its effects. It is known that folic acid and thymidine concentrations are crucial in fragile site expression. Glover (1981) found that the fragile site could be induced by FUdR with normal (i.e. normally inhibitive) folate levels if thymidine levels were low. He suggested that the fragile site was expressed because of depletion of deoxythymidine monophosphate which was needed for DNA synthesis. Certainly, although folic acid is important in determining the expression of the fragile site, its relationship to the syndrome is not clear. Folate metabolism has been studied in several families with the fragile X syndrome and to date no abnormalities have been detected (Wang and Erbe, 1984). Nevertheless, because of the decreased expression of the fragile site in high folate medium, attempts have been made to treat the syndrome with folic acid therapy. Lejeune (1982) first reported amelioration of behavioural aberrations in fragile X patients on folate treatment. Recently Brown *et al.* (1984) reported a double blind crossover trial of folate in two affected brothers. While the children were on treatment improved speech, attention span and motor co-ordination were documented and hyperactivity was reduced. One child also showed an improvement in mental function and regressed again when placed on the placebo. The expression of the fragile site in low folic acid medium was reduced when the boys were on therapy but no changes were observed in FUdR induction. These findings offer some hope for potential treatment of affected boys. However, in the light of normal findings concerning folate metabolism in such patients, there is still a considerable amount of investigation to be done before the precise mechanisms involved are understood.

A further area of investigation in the fragile X syndrome has concerned the level of expression of the marker chromosome in both affected males and heterozygous females. Even in affected males rarely do 50 per cent or more of cells exhibit the marker X, even under ideal culturing conditions, and it may be seen in less than 5 per cent (Turner and Jacobs, 1983). There is debate concerning the relationship of intelligence and patient age to percentage of marker positive cells. It appears that the percentage of fragile X cells diminishes with age and may show a weak negative correlation with intelligence. However, these findings have been more marked among carrier females than affected males. Although many obligate carriers of the X-linked gene have been normal, it appears that some heterozygous females express the disorder as mild mental retardation or borderline normal intelligence. There is debate as to the significance of the correlation between frequency of positive marker cells and intellect in carriers. There appears to be a significant negative correlation of intellect and marker frequency in carriers who express the marker frequency and intelligence in marker-positive women. They felt that a potential age effect in carriers, with older women less likely to show the marker, might be due to overrepresentation of marker-negative women among those 88 with a range of 57–119. Other at risk females in the families studied who did not express the fragile site had a mean IQ of 100 (range 78–126). Turner and Jacobs (1983) also found that the marker was more often seen in carriers with reduced intelligence. However, they found no correlation between marker frequency and intelligence in marker-positive women. They felt that a potential age effect in carriers, with older women less likely to show the marker, might be due to overrepresentation of marker-negative women among those who reproduce and thus are detected at older ages through their affected sons. Regardless of the potential effects of age on expression of the fragile site it appears that the fragile X is difficult to detect in many carriers, especially over the age of thirty-five years (Sutherland, 1978), and carrier studies on at risk females should be carried out when they are young and using the most appropriate medium, ideally with FUdR (Chudley *et al.*, 1983).

With respect to the contribution of the fragile X syndrome to retardation in females, it is unlikely that heterozygous females would be as severely affected as males. However, due to random X inactivation and thus Lyonization, some females may express mild symptoms and this no doubt contributes to the reduced mean intelligence quotients seen in carriers. In one study of mildly retarded females, Turner *et al.* (1980) found that 4 per cent had the marker X and thus extrapolated that about 2–3 per 10,000 women would be abnormal heterozygotes for the marker X gene. A much larger proportion would be normal carriers. Although theoretically possible, females homozygous for the gene would be rare due to the reduced reproductive potential of the affected males. An apparently homozygous female was reported by Nielsen *et al.* (1982). This phenotypically normal woman was an obligate carrier of the X-linked gene with 7 per cent marker-positive cells. In each of two separate cultures there was also one cell that showed identical breaks on each X chromosome. It was considered unlikely that this represented true homozygosity as her father was normal, but it was felt that this could indicate some transposition of X chromosome material during culture or possibly artificially induced breaks.

The difficulty in interpreting this type of case and other unusual findings in families where the fragile X syndrome is segregating has been compounded by apparent nonpenetrance of the gene in hemizygous males. Although initially passage of the mutant allele through normal males was considered extremely unlikely, the documentation of several families with such transmission has led to increased caution in counselling of such families (Fryns and van den Berghe, 1982). In one family reported by Daker *et al.* (1981) a fragile X positive male was detected during investigation of infertility and reproductive wastage. The man had no dysmorphic findings or macroorchidism and was of normal intelligence. He exhibited the fragile X in 15 per cent of cells. His habitus was somewhat eunuchoid and testosterone levels were low, so it was considered that he might be a Klinefelter mosaic (46, XY/47, XXY) and thus his fragile X symptoms were ameliorated by a cell line with a normal X chromosome. However, discovery of 8 per cent fragile X positive cells in his brother, who was also of normal intelligence and who had fathered four normal daughters, suggested that nonpenetrance of the gene could be occurring in this family. Webb *et al.* (1981) described another family where the fragile X had been transmitted by a normal male to his daughter who in turn had a son with classic fragile X syndrome. In addition two of her daughters expressed fragile sites. Although the carrier mother had some learning disabilities, her father was considered of normal intelligence. His personality was said to be somewhat bizarre and this might indicate a mild expression of the fragile X gene. In the past this had been ascribed to war neurosis.

The apparent nonpenetrance of the gene in males has led to renewed interest in segregation analysis of affected families. Sherman *et al.* (1984) reanalysed 110 pedigrees and found a 20 per cent deficit of affected males, suggesting a penetrance of 80 per cent. Approximately 30 per cent of carrier females showed reduced intelligence levels, and 56 per cent had the marker X and/or retardation. It was extrapolated that sisters of affected males who are of normal intelligence and do not express the marker still have a 10–20 per cent chance of being carriers for the gene. In addition there was no evidence in these families for sporadic cases and thus all affected males appeared to get the mutant gene from carrier mothers. This suggests that the mutation rate (which must be high considering the high selection against the gene in affected males) may be much higher in males than in females and that many isolated carrier females may represent sperm mutations. Evidence is now being sought for an increased paternal age effect in such women.

These data have made the counselling of families with the fragile X syndrome problematic. It is obvious that all family members, including apparently normal males, should have marker studies carried out. Although prenatal diagnosis of the marker X syndrome is difficult, the condition has been successfully detected by amniocentesis (Hogge *et al.*, 1984). The discovery, however, of the relatively high degree of nonpenetrance of the gene will only make the decisions of these families concerning childbearing all the more difficult.

In addition to heritable fragile sites certain other aspects of chromosome instability should be considered with respect to mental retardation. Although nonspecific increases in chromosome breakage have been observed in some patients studied because of increased fetal wastage (Kim *et al.*, 1975; Nordenson, 1981), these individuals are usually phenotypically normal. However, there are several single gene disorders which exhibit high levels of chromosome breakage or other manifestations of chromosome fragility. These include Fanconi's anaemia, Bloom's syndrome, incontinentia pigmenti, ataxia telangiectasia, xeroderma pigmentosum and Roberts syndrome–SC phocomelia. With the exception of incontinentia pigmenti these are autosomal recessive disorders with distinct clinical phenotypes. Frequently there is clinical evidence of abnormal DNA repair mechanisms such as chromosome breakage, increased sister chromatid exchange, immune deficiencies or increased risk of malignant neoplasia (Kaiser-McCaw, 1982; Ray, 1982). Although retardation is not a universal finding in most of these syndromes, there is an increase in the incidence of mental retardation in them all.

Roberts syndrome

Roberts syndrome or the pseudothalidomide syndrome (Freeman *et al.*, 1974) has a high incidence of severe mental retardation in the few children who survive infancy. This syndrome is characterized by growth retardation, hypomelia, and frequently midfacial defects including cleft lip and palate and capillary haemangioma. It is unclear whether the cases reported as SC phocomelia (Herrmann and Opitz, 1977; Waldenmaier *et al.*, 1978; da Silva and Bezerra, 1982) are examples of Roberts syndrome or whether they represent a separate entity. As early as 1973, it was suggested that chromosomal aberrations existed in Roberts syndrome. A distinctive centromeric puffing of the chromatids was described (Judge, 1973; Freeman *et al.*, 1974) and these findings have now been reported in several other patients with both the Roberts and SC phocomelia syndromes (Tomkins *et al.*, 1979; Ray, 1982). The relationship between the cytogenetic findings and the clinical phenotype is not clear. However, the gene may have effects on centromeric structure or function (Tomkins *et al.*, 1979).

Xeroderma pigmentosum

Xeroderma pigmentosum is characterized by hypersensitivity to sunlight, skin pigmentation changes, growth retardation and ataxia. There is an increased risk of basal and squamous cell carcinoma. Although inherited as an autosomal recessive disorder, it is evident from complementation studies that more than one nonallelic form exists (McKusick, 1983). In some cases there is severe dwarfism, mental retardation and gonadal hypoplasia. As these findings are not restricted to any one complementation group, it is likely that they reflect severe manifestations of the disease rather than a distinct syndrome. The cytogenetic anomaly in xeroderma pigmentosum involves a high degree of inducibility of sister chromatid exchange by ultraviolet light and it is felt that the primary defect involves defective repair of DNA damage induced by ultraviolet radiation. The prognosis is poor with progressive disfigurement, development of skin tumours in early childhood and death from neoplasia by twenty years of age. Prenatal diagnosis is possible (Ray, 1982).

Bloom syndrome

Another syndrome characterized by a high incidence of sister chromatid exchange is Bloom syndrome. This autosomal recessive syndrome is more common among Ashkenazi Jews. The clinical phenotype consists of growth retardation, an erythematous facial rash which is exacerbated by sunlight and an increased risk of malignancy (Kaiser-McCaw, 1982). Mild mental retardation may occur, though many patients are of normal intelligence. Cytogenetic findings include an increase in chromosome breakage with chromosome rearrangements, especially quadrivalent formation. In particular there is a tendency for exchanges between homologous chromosomes with breaks occurring at the same sites. The very high spontaneous increase in sister chromatid exchange from about 10 per cell in normal controls to 90 per cell in homozygous patients appears specific for Bloom syndrome but the primary defect is not known (Ray, 1982).

Fanconi's anaemia

In Fanconi's anaemia, there is also evidence of increased chromosome fragility with excessive chromosome breakage and formation of quadrivalents. The spontaneous sister chromatid exchange rate is not increased in this syndrome. Patients with this autosomal recessive disorder, as with several other chromosome fragility syndromes, display growth retardation, unusual skin pigmentation changes and propensity to develop leukaemia. In addition they have a high frequency of congenital malformations, especially radial ray hypoplasia, craniofacial anomalies and renal defects. They have a characteristic haemopoietic abnormality with marrow failure and pancytopenia. Onset of bleeding problems or recurrent infections often occur by late childhood, and normal lifespan is reduced with most children dying from infection or complications of their anaemia. Mental retardation occurs in over 20 per cent of patients. The basic defect appears to be an abnormality in repair of DNA crosslinks, possibly related to defects in enzyme transport across the nuclear membrane (Wunder *et al.*, 1981) and at least two distinct genetic forms have been described (McKusick, 1983). Both carrier detection and prenatal diagnosis are potentially feasible (Auerbach *et al.*, 1981).

Ataxia telangiectasia

This bears some similarity to Fanconi's anaemia and Bloom syndrome in that chromosomal fragility, predisposition to malignancy, increased immune deficiency and skin pigmentation changes occur. Mental retardation is not considered a classic finding in this syndrome but there is a progressive disparity between mental age and chronological age in these patients, with approximately one-half ultimately falling into the mildly retarded range (Hosking, 1982). Neurologically there is progressive ataxia and choreoathetosis beginning in early childhood, accompanied by unstable gait, drooling, aberrant eye movements, speech defects and occasionally seizures. The skin changes involve development of telangiectasia in the conjunctiva and midfacial skin. The impaired immune response is on the basis of a deficiency in cellular immunity involving thymic, tonsillar and adenoidal tissue, lymphopenia and often reduced gamma IgA and IgE. This leads to frequent respiratory infection and progressive bronchiolectasis. Children rarely survive past twenty years of age and death is usually due to respiratory complications, though approximately 10 per cent develop malignancies, especially lymphomas, sarcomas and leukaemia. As with many other chromosomal instability syndromes, the basic defect may involve defects in DNA repair mechanisms and genetic heterogeneity is suggested by complementation studies.

The cytogenetic abnormalities seen in ataxia telangiectasia resemble most closely those observed in Fanconi's anaemia with an increase in chromosome breakage and in the formation of dicentric and nonhomologous quadrivalents. The incidence of sister chromatid exchanges is not increased. An unusual

finding in ataxia telangiectasia patients is the increased incidence of chromosome breakage involving chromosome 14, including paracentric inversions of
14, tandem duplications of 14 and 7;14 translocations. Frequently the
breakpoints involved are at 14q12 or q32 (Kohn *et al.*, 1982). Chromosome 14
aberrations have been implicated in certain tumours, including Burkitt's
lymphoma, and it is suggested that such rearrangements may involve
activation of an oncogene. This may in part explain the high incidence of
malignancy in ataxia telangiectasia patients.

Incontinentia pigmenti

The last single gene disorder in which chromosomal aberrations have been
reported is incontinentia pigmenti. This is an unusual condition in that it is
found almost exclusively in females. The pattern of inheritance is of an X-
linked dominant condition which is lethal in males. Females affected by the
condition have normal sons, affected daughters and normal daughters in equal
proportions. These women also have an increased rate of spontaneous
abortions which may represent affected male fetuses. The clinical findings in
incontinentia pigmenti primarily involve tissues of ectodermal origin. The
most consistent features are changes in the skin including vesciculation,
verrucous changes, atrophy and brown pigmentation in swirling patterns
on the trunk and extremities. Other ectodermal defects include hypodontia
or delayed tooth eruption, conical teeth and patchy alopecia. Abnormal
ocular findings including strabismus, uveitis, cataract and retinal dysplasia are
common. Musculoskeletal findings include hemivertebrae, extra ribs,
kyphoscoliosis and hemiatrophy. About one-third of patients are mentally
retarded and may have microcephaly, spasticity and/or seizures (Smith,
1982). Although chromosome anomalies are not common in these patients, in
some cases there has been evidence of increased chromosomal breakage
(Kaiser-McCaw, 1982).

Although these syndromes are relatively rare, it is important that clinicians
are aware of their phenotypic features and can carry out appropriate clinical
investigations. Accurate diagnosis here is imperative both for appropriate
management and follow-up of these patients, most of whom are at increased
risk for malignancy, and for proper counselling of parents and siblings.

PREVENTION OF CHROMOSOME ANOMALIES

It is unlikely in the foreseeable future that it will be possible to prevent
nondisjunction or chromosome rearrangement prior to conception, so that we
will continue to be faced with the problems of detecting and preventing
chromosome abnormalities during gestation and prior to the birth of an
abnormal and mentally retarded child.

The offering of amniocentesis in the second trimester for the detection of
chromosome abnormalities is now routine in certain pregnancies (see also
Chapter 11). It involves the aspiration of a small sample of amniotic fluid,

culturing of the fetal cells contained in the fluid and determination of the karyotype of these cells and thus of the fetus. The major indications for the use of this technique for the detection of chromosome abnormalities are:

1. Maternal age – it is usually offered to all mothers over the age of thirty-four at the time of delivery.
2. The detection of the presence of a parental chromosome abnormality (i.e. one parent is a balanced translocation or inversion carrier, particularly if the rearrangement was detected as the result of the birth of a previously clinically abnormal infant).
3. Birth of a previous child with chromosomal trisomy (i.e. those cases in which the mother has had a previous trisomic infant or possibly a previous spontaneous abortion or perinatal death in which the abortus or neonate was trisomic).

The safety and reliability of amniocentesis as a diagnostic technique has now been well established and it is generally accepted that it increases the risk of spontaneous abortion by between 1 in 250 and 1 in 500 over the risk without any intervention. Other risks of the test, including fetal and maternal morbidity, are very low. In competent hands the test has been shown to have a near 100 per cent reliability for the detection of chromosome abnormalities.

The major disadvantage of the test is that it allows secondary prevention only, and thus can prevent the birth of only a relatively small proportion of infants with a chromosome anomaly, namely those cases of Down's syndrome or other anomalies born to mothers who are over thirty-five or who have had previous abnormal infants. It is therefore of great importance to develop a means of identifying couples at risk for nondisjunction irrespective of maternal age and prior to conception. If this could be done such couples could then selectively be offered prenatal diagnosis. Studies are in progress to examine the reproductive histories of couples who have had a child with Down's syndrome at a maternal age of less than thirty-five to determine whether clues as to their risk status might be found retrospectively (Evans, in preparation). If such risk factors are identified, these will need to be tested in large prospective studies. Additional studies on chromosome variants and acrocentric associations may also provide clues as to whether there might be an increased risk in some families (Wang and Evans, in preparation). However, it is unlikely that such studies will provide any means of clearly identifying all couples at increased risk for nondisjunction. At best, they can provide an indication of possible increased risk on which a decision as to whether an amniocentesis should be offered might be based.

The possibility of an earlier prenatal diagnostic test now exists. Chorion villus sampling (CVS) (see also Chapter 11) involves transcervical sampling of the villi of the chorion frondosum between seven and ten weeks of gestation (Rodeck *et al.*, 1983). Simple direct chromosome studies within twenty-four hours of sampling are possible (Simoni *et al.*, 1983). Such a test, if it proves to be safe and reliable in clinical trials, and if it is acceptable to a wide segment of the population, may become available to a much larger group of mothers than can at present be offered amniocentesis. This would allow the rapid testing of large numbers of pregnancies early in gestation with a possibility of terminating abnormal pregnancies early in the first trimester. Such early terminations are likely to be much more socially acceptable than termination late in the second trimester of pregnancy. Such terminations would take place at a time when the natural rate of loss is much higher and the risk of maternal morbidity associated with pregnancy termination much lower. Such an early test carries with it many fewer problems related to the emotional, psychological and social trauma of late second trimester terminations of pregnancy. CVS may, as it develops, and if adequate resources are available, become a screening test available to all couples who so desire. If so, it would go a long way towards the prevention of the birth of children with chromosome abnormalities.

THE FUTURE

Developments in molecular biology and recombinant DNA will make a great impact on clinical medicine over the next decade. Already DNA probes are available which are potentially useful for diagnosis of several different diseases. Isolation of chromosome-specific DNA probes recognizing specific base changes in the DNA is now routine. Such changes are often polymorphic and inherited in a Mendelian fashion. They can thus be used as markers for the study of genetic linkage with disease states. The fragile X condition may serve as a model for this approach. As indicated earlier, a significant proportion of males with X-linked mental retardation demonstrate a fragility at Xq27–28. A polymorphic DNA marker linked to this fragile site is recognized by the cloned gene for Factor IX when genomic DNA is digested with the restriction enzyme Taq I. Such a marker may be useful both for detection of carrier females and for prenatal diagnosis using fetal DNA extracted from amniocytes or chorionic villi. DNA markers linked to other conditions leading to mental retardation will no doubt become available shortly. Chromosome-specific markers are now readily obtained and several such markers for chromosome 21 are already available. DNA markers which recognize appropriate polymorphisms will be used to identify more reliably the origin of nondisjunction in Down's syndrome and perhaps, as DNA probes, to identify the trisomic state in fetal cells more rapidly and economically than with a cytogenetic study.

Many other areas of study into the causes and prevention of mental retardation will become possible as a direct result of basic studies in molecular biology. Already, close linkage has been demonstrated between a molecular probe G-8 and Huntington's chorea (Gusella *et al.*, 1983); in the future this may form the basis for a presymptomatic clinical test. As studies on the human gene map progress, other linkages of clinical importance will be revealed, some of which will be associated with conditions leading to mental retardation, thus making carrier detection and prenatal diagnosis possible. Wide-ranging and exciting possibilities have been opened by advances in molecular biology which will no doubt lead to new approaches to the study of many conditions causing mental retardation.

CONCLUSIONS

In the less than thirty years since the confirmation of the human chromosome number as 46, there have been massive developments in the field of human cytogenetics. New banding techniques have allowed detection and accurate delineation of many different chromosomal anomalies and the phenotypic manifestations associated with them. This has led to the understanding that chromosomal abnormalities contribute significantly to the genetic load in man, especially in fetal and neonatal life. In addition, there has been increasing awareness of the importance of chromosomal defects in the causation of mental retardation. The commonest single genetic type of moderate retardation, Down's syndrome, is a chromosomal anomaly. Many other numerical and structural abnormalities are well recognized and, with the advent of increasingly precise methods of chromosomal analysis, many mental retardation syndromes of unknown aetiology are proving to have a chromosomal basis.

The potential exists through prenatal diagnosis to detect chromosomal anomalies before birth, and this has proved of considerable benefit to individual families. Newer techniques such as chorion biopsy will have considerable impact in this area. However, greater advances towards the primary prevention of chromosomal defects and their deleterious effects will be made only when there is a clear understanding of both the underlying causes of nondisjunction and structural chromosomal defects and of the pathogenetic mechanisms which lead to mental and physical abnormalities in children with abnormal karyotypic findings.

REFERENCES

ALLY, F.E. and GRACE, H.J. (1979) 'Chromosome abnormalities in South African mental retardates', *S. Afr. Med. J.*, 55, 710–12.

ANDERSON, S.R., GEERTINGER, P., LARSON, H.W., MIKKELSEN, M., PARVING, A., VESTERMARK, S. and WASBURG, M. (1978) 'Aniridia, cataract and gonadoblastoma in a mentally retarded girl with deletion of chromosome 11', *Ophthalmology*, 176, 171–7.

ANGELL, R.R., SANDISON, A. and BAIN, A.D. (1984) 'Chromosome variation in perinatal mortality: a survey of 500 cases', *J. Med. Genet.*, 21, 39–44.

ANNEREN, G., FRODIS, E. and JORULF, H. (1981) 'Trisomy 8 syndrome', *Helv. Paediat. Acta*, 36, 465–72.

AUERBACH, A.D., ADLER, B. and CHAGANTI, R.S.K. (1981) 'Prenatal and postnatal diagnosis and carrier detection of Fanconi anemia by a cytogenetic method', *Pediatrics*, 67, 128–34.

AURIAS, A., PRIEUR, M., DUTRILLAUX, B. and LEJEUNE, J. (1978)

'Systematic analysis of 95 reciprocal translocations of autosomes', *Hum. Genet.*, 45, 259–82.

AYME, S. and LIPPMAN-HAND, A. (1982) 'Maternal age effect in aneuploidy: does altered embryonic selection play a role?', *Amer. J. Hum. Genet.*, 34, 538–65.

AYME, S., MATTEI, M., MATTEI, J.F. and GIRAUD, F. (1979) 'Abnormal childhood phenotypes associated with the same balanced chromosome rearrangements as in the parents', *Hum. Genet.*, 48, 7–12.

BARGMAN, G.J., NEU, R.L., POWERS, H.O. and GARDNER, L.I. (1970) 'A 46, XX, t(Cp+;Cq−) translocation in a girl with multiple congenital anomalies and in her phenotypically normal father 46, XY, t(Cp+;Cp−)', *J. Med. Genet.*, 7, 77–80.

BASS, H.N., FOX, M., WULFSBERG, E., SPARKES, R.F. and CRANDALL, B.F. (1982) 'Trisomy 18 mosaicism: clues to the diagnosis', *Clin. Genet.*, 22, 237–330.

BENDER, B., FRY, E., PENNINGTON, B., PUCK, M., SALBENBLATT, J. and ROBINSON, A. (1983) 'Speech and language development in 41 children with sex chromosome anomalies', *Pediatrics*, 71, 262–7.

BERRY, A.C., WHITTINGHAM, A.J. and NEVILLE, B.G.R. (1981) 'Chromosome 15 in floppy infants', *Arch. Dis. Childh.*, 56, 882–5.

BLACKBURN, W.R., MILLER, W.P., SUPERNEAU, D.W., COOLEY, N.R., ZELLWEGER, H. and WERTELECKI, W. (1982) 'Comparative studies of infants with mosaic and complete triploidy: an analysis of 55 cases', *Birth Defects Original Article Series*, 18 (3B), 251–74.

BROWN, W.J., JENKINS, E.C., FREEDMAN, E., BROOKS, J., COHEN, I.L., DUNCAN, C., HILL, A.L., MALIK, M.N., MORRIS, V., WOLF, E., WISNIEWSKI, K.A. and FRENCH, J.H. (1984) 'Folic acid therapy in the fragile X syndrome', *Amer. J. Med. Genet.*, 17, 289–98.

BUHLER, E.M., MEKES, K., MULLER, H. and STALLER, G.R. (1972) 'Cat-eye syndrome, a partial trisomy 22', *Hum. Genet.*, 15, 150–62.

CARLIN, M.E., LEON, S. and GILBERT, J.D. (1978) 'A comparison between a trisomy 21 child (probably mosaic) with normal intelligence and a mosaic Down's syndrome population', *Birth Defects Original Article Series*, 14 (6C), 327–41.

CASEY, P.A., CLARK, C.E. and COWELL, H.R. (1981) '46, XY/48, XXY, +8 in a male with clinical and dermatoglyphic features of mosaic trisomy 8 syndrome', *Clin. Genet.*, 20, 60–3.

CASSIDY, S.B., BENEDETTI, I.J. and SYBERT, V.P. (1981) 'Unsuspected trisomy 18: a case for an examination protocol in stillborn infants', *Amer. J. Obstet. Gynec.*, 139, 221–2.

CASSIDY, S.B., THULINE, H.C. and HOLM, V.A. (1984) 'Deletion of chromosome 15 (q11–13) in a Prader–Labhart–Willi syndrome clinic population', *Amer. J. Med. Genet.*, 17, 485–95.

CASSIMAN, J.J., FRYNS, J.P., DEROOVER, J. and VAN DEN BERGHE, H. (1975) 'Sex chromatin and cytogenetic survey of 10,417 adult males and 357 children institutionalized in Belgian institutions for mentally retarded patients', *Hum. Genet.*, 28, 43–8.

CERVENKA, J., GORLIN, R.J. and DJAVADI, G.R. (1977) 'Down's syndrome due to partial trisomy 21q', *Clin. Genet.*, 11, 119–21.

CHUDLEY, A.E., KNOLL, J., GERRARD, J.W., SHEPEL, L., MCGAHEY, E. and ANDERSON, J. (1983) 'Fragile (X) X-linked mental retardation 1: relationship between age and intelligence and the frequency of expression of fragile (X) (q28)', *Amer. J. Med. Genet.*, 14, 699–712.

CREASY, M.R. (1982) 'Chromosome aberrations as a cause of prenatal death', in M. ADINOLFI, P. BENSON, F. GIANNELLI and M. SELLER (eds), *Paediatric Research: A Genetic Approach*, London, Heinemann, 122–35.

CROWLEY, P.H., GULATI, D.K., HAYDEN, T.L., LOPEZ, P. and DYER, R. (1979) 'A chiasma–hormonal hypothesis relating Down's syndrome and maternal age', *Nature*, 280, 417–19.

DAKER, M.G., CHIDIAC, P., FEAR, C.N. and BERRY, A.C. (1981) 'Fragile X in a normal male: a cautionary tale', *Lancet*, 1, 780.

DA SILVA, E.O. and BEZERRA, H.G.E. (1982) 'The Roberts syndrome', *Hum. Genet.*, 61, 372–4.

DE GROUCHY, J. (1982) 'Towards clinical microcytogenetics: the aniridia and the retinoblastoma stories', *Prog. Clin. Biol. Res.*, 103B, 359–67.

DE GROUCHY, J. and TURLEAU, C. (1977) *Clinical Atlas of Human Chromosomes*, New York, Wiley.

DE LA CHAPELLE, A., HERVA, R., KOIVISTO, M. and AULA, P. (1981) 'A deletion in chromosome 22 can cause diGeorge syndrome', *Hum. Genet.*, 57, 253–6.

DEL MAZO, J., CASTILLO, A.P. and ABRISQUETA, J.A. (1982) 'Trisomy 21: origin of nondisjunction', *Hum. Genet.*, 62, 316–20.

DOBYNS, W.B., STRATTON, R.F., PARKE, J.T., GREENBERG, F., NUSSBAUM, R.L. and LEDBETTER, D.H. (1983) 'Miller–Dieker syndrome: lissencephaly and monosomy 17p', *J. Pediat.*, 102, 552–8.

DOCKERY, H.E., NEALE, H.C. and FITZGERALD, P.H. (1982) 'Gross congenital abnormality associated with an apparently balanced chromosomal translocation t(9;17)(q34;q11)', *J. Med. Genet.*, 19, 380–3.

EDWARDS, J.H., HARNDEN, D.G., CAMERON, A.H., CROSSE, V.M. and WOLFF, O.H. (1960) 'A new trisomic syndrome', *Lancet*, 1, 787–90.

EPSTEIN, C.J., EPSTEIN, L.B., WEIL, J. and COX, D.R. (1982) 'Trisomy 21: mechanisms and models', *Ann. NY Acad. Sci.*, 392, 107–8.

ERICKSON, J.D. and BJERKEDAL, T. (1981) 'Down's syndrome associated with father's age in Norway', *J. Med. Genet.*, 18, 22–8.

EVANS, J.A., CANNING, N., HUNTER, A.G.W., MARTSOLF, J.T., RAY, M., THOMPSON, D.R. and HAMERTON, J.L. (1978a) 'A cytogenetic survey of 14,069 newborn infants: III. An analysis of the significance and cytologic behaviour of the Robertsonian and reciprocal translocations', *Cytogenet. Cell Genet.*, 20, 96–123.

EVANS, J.A., HUNTER, A.G.W. and HAMERTON, J.L. (1978b) 'Down's syndrome and recent demographic trends in Manitoba', *J. Med. Genet.*, 15, 43–7.

FAED, M.J.W., ROBERTSON, J., FIELD, M.A.S. and MELLON, J.P. (1979) 'A chromosome survey of a hospital for the mentally subnormal', *Clin. Genet.*, 16, 191–204.

FEINGOLD, M. and ATKINS, L. (1973) 'A case of trisomy 9', *J. Med. Genet.*, 10, 184–7.

FERGUSON-SMITH, M.A. and YATES, J.R.W. (1984) 'Maternal age-specific rates for chromosome aberrations and factors influencing them: report of a Collaborative European Study of 52,965 amniocenteses', *Prenatal Diagnosis*, 4, 5–44.

FERRELL, R.E. and SPARKES, R.S. (1981) 'Familial retinoblastoma and chromosome 13 deletion transmitted by an insertional translocation', *Science*, 213, 1501–3.

FORD, C.E. and CLEGG, H.M. (1969) 'Reciprocal translocations', *Brit. Med. Bull.*, 25, 110–14.

FRANCKE, U., HOLMES, L.B., ATKINS, L. and RICCARDI, V.M. (1979) 'Aniridia–Wilm's tumor association: evidence for specific deletion of 11p13', *Cytogenet. Cell. Genet.*, 24, 185–92.

FRANCKE, U. and OLIVER, N. (1978) 'Quantitative analysis of high-resolution trypsin-Giemsa bands on human prometaphase chromosomes', *Hum. Genet.*, 45, 137–65.

FRASER, F.C. and SADOVNICK, A.D. (1976) 'Correlation of IQ in subjects with Down's syndrome and their parents and sibs', *J. Ment. Defic. Res.*, 20, 179–82.

FREEMAN, M.V.R., WILLIAMS, D.W., SCHIMKE, R.N., TEMTAMY, S.A., VACHIER, E. and GERMAN, J. (1974) 'The Roberts syndrome', *Clin. Genet.*, 5, 1–16.

FRIED, K. (1980) 'A score based on eight signs in the diagnosis of Down's syndrome in the newborn', *J. Ment. Defic. Res.*, 24, 181–5.

FRIEDRICH, U. and NIELSEN, J. (1974) 'Autosomal reciprocal translocations in newborn children and their relatives', *Hum. Genet.*, 24, 133–44.

FROHLICH, G.S. (1982) 'Delineation of trisomy 9', *J. Med. Genet.*, 19, 316–17.

FRONTALI, M., RAMENGHI, M., TRABACE, S. and DALLAPICCOLA, B. (1982) '"Microcytogenetics" and Langer–Giedion syndrome', *J. Med. Genet.*, 19, 390–1.

FROSTER-ISKENIUS, U., FELSCH, G., SCHIRREN, C. and SCHWINGER, E. (1983) 'Screening for fra(X)(q) in a population of mentally retarded males', *Hum. Genet.*, 63, 153–7.

FRYERS, T. and MACKAY, R.I. (1979) 'The epidemiology of severe mental handicap', *Early Hum. Develop.*, 3, 277–94.

FRYNS, J.P., DE MUELENAERE, A. and VAN DEN BERGHE, H. (1981) 'The 4p− syndrome in a 24-year-old female', *Ann. Genet.*, 24, 110–11.

FRYNS, J.P., PETIT, P., VINKEN, L., GEIYENS, J., MARIEN, J. and VAN

DEN BERGHE, H. (1982) 'Mosaic tetrasomy 21 in severe mental handicap', *Eur. J. Pediat.*, 139, 87–9.

FRYNS, J.P. and VAN DEN BERGHE, H. (1979) 'Possible excess of mental handicap and congenital malformations in autosomal reciprocal translocations', *Ann. Genet.*, 22, 125–7.

FRYNS, J.P. and VAN DEN BERGHE, H. (1982) 'Transmission of fragile (X) (q27) from normal male(s)', *Hum. Genet.*, 61, 262–3.

FUJITA, H. and FUJITA, K. (1974) 'A cytogenetic survey on mentally retarded children', *Jap. J. Hum. Genet.*, 19, 175–6.

FUNDERBURK, S.J., SPENCE, M.A. and SPARKES, R.S. (1977) 'Mental retardation associated with "balanced" chromosome rearrangements', *Amer. J. Hum. Genet.*, 29, 136–41.

GIBSON, D.A., UCHIDA, I.A. and LEWIS, A.J. (1963) 'A review of the 18 trisomy syndrome', *Med. Biol. Illust.*, 13, 80–8.

GILGENKRANTZ, S., VIGNERON, C., GREGOIRE, M.J., PERNOT, C. and RASPILLER, A. (1982) 'Association of del (11) (p15.1 p12), aniridia, catalase deficiency and cardiomyopathy', *Amer. J. Med. Genet.*, 13, 39–49.

GLOVER, T.W. (1981) 'FUdR induction of the X chromosome fragile site: evidence for the mechanism of folic acid and thymidine inhibition', *Amer. J. Hum. Genet.*, 33, 234–42.

GONZALEZ, C.H., CAPELOZZI, V.L. and WAJNTAL, A. (1981) 'Brief clinical report: pathologic findings in the Wolf–Hirschhorn (4p −) syndrome', *Amer. J. Med. Genet.*, 9, 183–7.

GORLIN, R.J., CERVENKA, J., BLOOM, B.A. and LANGER JR, L.O. (1982) 'No chromosome deletion found on prometaphase banding in two cases of Langer–Giedion syndrome', *Amer. J. Med. Genet.*, 13, 345–7.

GUSELLA, J.F., WEXLER, N.S., CONNEALLY, P.M., NAYLOR, S.L., ANDERSON, M.A., TANZI, R.E., WATKINS, P.C., OTTINA, K., WALLACE, M.R., SAKAGUCHI, A.Y., YOUNG, A.B., SHOULSON, I., BONILLA, E. and MARTIN, J.B. (1983) 'A polymorphic DNA marker genetically linked to Huntington's disease', *Nature*, 306, 234–8.

GUSTAVSON, K.H., HAGBERG, B., HAGBERG, G. and SARS, K. (1977a) 'Severe mental retardation in a Swedish county: II. Etiologic and pathogenetic aspects of children born 1959–70', *Neuropadiatrie*, 8, 293–304.

GUSTAVSON, K.H., HOLMGREN, G.R., JONSELL, R. and BLOMQUIST, H.K.: SON (1977b) 'Severe mental retardation in children in a northern Swedish county', *J. Ment. Defic. Res.*, 21, 161–79.

HAKA-IKSE, K. (1982) 'Early psychomotor development of children with sex chromosome aneuploidies', in T.V.N. RERSAUD (ed.), *Advances in the Study of Birth Defects*, vol. 5, Lancaster, MTP Press, 89–101.

HALL, B.D., LANGER, L.O., GIEDION, A., SMITH, D.W., COHEN, M.M., BEALS, R.K. and BRANDNER, M. (1974) 'Langer–Giedion syndrome', *Birth Defects Original Article Series*, 10 (12), 147–64.

HAMERTON, J.L. (1971) *Human Cytogenetics*, vols I and II, New York and London, Academic Press.

HAMERTON, J.L. (1982) 'Population cytogenetics: a perspective', in M. ADINOLFI, P. BENSON, F. GIANNELLI, and M. SELLER (eds), *Paediatric Research: a Genetic Approach*, London, Heinemann, 99–121.

HAMERTON, J.L. (1984) 'Chromosomes and their disorders', in J.B. WYNGAARDEN and L.H. SMITH (eds), *Cecil's Textbook of Medicine*, 17th edn, Philadelphia, Saunders, in press.

HAMERTON, J.L., CANNING, N., RAY, M. and SMITH, J. (1975) 'A cytogenetic survey of 14,069 newborn infants: I. Incidence of chromosome abnormalities', *Clin. Genet.*, 8, 223–43.

HAMERTON, J.L., GIANNELLI, F. and POLANI, P.E. (1965) 'Cytogenetics of Down's syndrome (mongolism): I. Data on a consecutive series of patients referred for genetic counselling and diagnosis', *Cytogenetics*, 4, 181–5.

HASHEM, N. and KHALIFA, S. (1975) 'Retinoblastoma, a model of hereditary fragile chromosomal regions,' *Hum. Hered.*, 25, 35–49.

HASSOLD, T., JACOBS, P., KLINE, J., STEIN, Z. and WARBURTON, D. (1980) 'Effect of maternal age on autosomal trisomies', *Ann. Hum. Genet.*, 44, 29–36.

HAWKEY, C.J. and SMITHIES, A. (1976) 'The Prader–Willi syndrome with a 15/15 translocation', *J. Med. Genet.*, 13, 152–63.

HECHT, F., KAISER-MCCAW, B., PATIL, S. and WYANDT, H.E. (1978) 'Are balanced translocations really balanced? Preliminary cytogenetic evidence for position effect in man', *Birth Defects Original Article Series*, 14, 281–6.

HERBST, D.S. and MILLER, J.R. (1980) 'Non-specific X-linked mental retardation: II. The frequency in British Columbia', *Amer. J. Med. Genet.*, 7, 461–9.

HERRMANN, J. and OPITZ, J.M. (1977) 'The SC phocomelia syndrome and the Roberts syndrome: nosologic aspects', *Europ. J. Pediat.*, 125, 117–34.

HOGGE, W.A., SCHONBERG, S.A., GLOVER, T.W., HECHT, F. and GOLBUS, M.S. (1984) 'Prenatal diagnosis of fragile (X) syndrome', *Obstet. Gynec.*, 63, 19S–21S.

HOOK, E.B. (1983a) 'Chromosome abnormalities and spontaneous fetal death following amniocentesis: further data and associations with maternal age', *Amer. J. Hum. Genet.*, 35, 110–16.

HOOK, E.B. (1983b) 'Down's syndrome rates and relaxed selection at older maternal ages', *Amer. J. Hum. Genet.*, 35, 1307–13.

HOOK, E.B. and HAMERTON, J.L. (1977) 'The frequency of chromosomal abnormalities detected in consecutive newborn studies – differences between studies – results by sex and by severity of phenotypic involvement', in E.B. HOOK and I.H. PORTER (eds), *Population Cytogenetics*, New York, Academic Press, 63–79.

HOOK, E.B. and LINDSJO, A. (1978) 'Down's syndrome in live births by single year maternal age interval in a Swedish study: comparison with results from a New York State study', *Amer. J. Hum. Genet.*, 30, 19–27.

HOSKING, G. (1982) 'Ataxia telangiectasia', *Dev. Med. Child Neurol.*, 24, 77–80.

HOWARD, R.O. (1982) 'Chromosome errors in retinoblastoma', *Birth Defects Original Article Series*, 18(6), 703–27.

HUNTER, A.G.W., CLIFFORD, B., SPEEVAK, M. and MACMURRAY, S.B. (1982) 'Mosaic tetrasomy 21 in a liveborn male infant', *Clin. Genet.*, 21, 228–32.

HUNTER, A.G.W., EVANS, J.A., THOMPSON, D.R. and RAMSAY, S. (1980) 'A study of institutionalized mentally retarded patients in Manitoba: I. Classification and preventability', *Develop. Med. Child Neurol.*, 22, 145–62.

ISCN (1978) 'An international system for human cytogenetic nomenclature (1978)', *Birth Defects Original Article Series*, XIV, no. 8.

ISCN (1981) 'An international system for human cytogenetic nomenclature: high resolution banding (1981)', *Birth Defects Original Article Series*, XVII, no. 5.

JABS, E.W., STROMBERG, J. and LEONARD, C.O. (1982) 'Tetrasomy 21 in an infant with Down's syndrome and congenital leukemia', *Amer. J. Med. Genet.*, 12, 91–5.

JACKSON, J.F., NORTH III, E.R. and THOMAS, J.G. (1976) 'Clinical diagnosis of Down's syndrome', *Clin. Genet.*, 9, 483–7.

JACOBS, P.A., MATSUURA, J.S., MAYERS, M. and NEWLANDS, I.N. (1978) 'A cytogenetic survey of an institution for the mentally retarded: I. Chromosome abnormalities', *Clin. Genet.*, 13, 37–60.

JACOBS, P.A., MAYER, M., MATSUURA, J., RHOADS, F. and YEE, S.C. (1983) 'A cytogenetic study of mentally retarded males with special reference to the marker (X) syndrome', *Hum. Genet.*, 63, 139–48.

JANERICH, D.T. and JACOBSON, H.I. (1977) 'Seasonality in Down's syndrome. An endocrinological explanation', *Lancet*, 1, 515–16.

JUBERG, R.C. and MAILHES, J.B. (1976) 'Origin of chromosomal abnormalities: evidence for delayed fertilization in meiotic nondisjunction', *Pediat. Res.*, 10, 367A.

JUDGE, C. (1973) 'A sibship with the pseudothalidomide syndrome and an association with Rh incompatibility', *Med. J. Austr.*, 2, 280–1.

KAISER-MCCAW, B. (1982) 'Sorting out the heterogeneity in the chromosome instability syndromes', *Prog. Clin. Biol. Res.*, 103B, 349–58.

KATAYAMA, K.P., WILKINSON, J., HERRMANN, J., GLASPEY, J.C., AGARWAL, A.B., ROESLER, M.R. and MATTINGLY, R.F. (1980) 'Clinical delineation of trisomy 9 syndrome', *Obstet. Gynec.*, 56, 665–8.

KELLEY, R.I., ZACKAI, E.H., EMANUEL, B.S., KISTENMACHER, M., GREENBERG, F. and PUNNETT, H.H. (1982) 'The association of the diGeorge anomalad with partial monosomy of chromosome 22', *J. Pediat.*, 101, 197–200.

KIM, H.J., HSU, L.Y.F., PACIUC, S., CRISTIAN, S., QUINTANA, A. and HIRSCHHORN, K. (1975) 'Cytogenetics of fetal wastage', *New Engl. J. Med.*, 293, 844–7.

KOHN, P.H., WHANG-PENG, J. and LEVIS, W.R. (1982) 'Chromosomal instability in ataxia telangiectasia', *Cancer Genet. Cytogenet.*, 6, 289–302.

KONDO, I., HAMAGUCHI, H., NAKAJIMA, S. and HANEDA, T. (1980) 'A cytogenetic survey of 449 patients in a Japanese institution for the mentally retarded', *Clin. Genet.*, 17, 177–82.

KOUSSEFF, B.G. (1978) 'Trisomy 21 with average intelligence?!', *Birth Defects Original Article Series*, 14 (6C), 323–5.

KOUSSEFF, B.G. and DOUGLASS, R. (1982) 'The cytogenetic controversy regarding the Prader–Willi syndrome', *Birth Defects Original Article Series*, 18 (3B), 301–4.

LAZYUK, G.I., KRAVTSOVA, G.I., KULAZHENKO, V.P., USOVA, Y.I. and USOEV, S.S. (1974) 'Analysis of 137 cases of the trisomy-D syndrome', *Sov. Genet.*, 7, 1338–49.

LEARY, P.M., WEBB, P.M., MELZER, C.W. and CLOSE, H.G. (1975) 'Down's syndrome with additional XYY aneuploidy', *Clin. Genet.*, 8, 55–8.

LEDBETTER, D.H., MASCARELLO, J.T., RICCARDI, V.M., HARPER, V.D., AIRHART, S.D. and STROBEL, R.J. (1982) 'Chromosome 15 abnormalities and the Prader–Willi syndrome: a follow-up report of 40 cases', *Amer. J. Hum. Genet.*, 34, 278–85.

LEJEUNE, J. (1982) 'Is the fragile X syndrome amenable to treatment?', *Lancet*, I, 273.

LEJEUNE, J., DUTRILLAUX, B. and DE GROUCHY, T. (1970) 'Reciprocal translocations in human populations: a preliminary analysis', in P.A. JACOBS, W.H. PRICE and P. LAW (eds), *Human Population Cytogenetics*, Edinburgh, Edinburgh University Press, pp. 81–7.

LEJEUNE, J., LAFOURCADE, J., BERGER, R., VIALETTE, J., BOESWILL-WARD, M., SERINGE, P. and TURPIN, R. (1963) 'Trois cas de délétion partielle du bras court d'un chromosome 5', *Compt. Rend.*, 257, 3098–102.

LELE, K.P., PENROSE, L.S. and STALLARD, H.B. (1963) 'Chromosome deletion in a case of retinoblastoma', *Ann. Hum. Genet.*, 27, 171–4.

LUBS, H.A. (1969) 'A marker-X chromosome', *Amer. J. Hum. Genet.*, 21, 231–44.

MCDONALD, A.D. (1973) 'Severely retarded children in Quebec: prevalence, causes and care', *Amer. J. Ment. Defic.*, 78, 205–15.

MACHIN, G.A. and CROLLA, J.A. (1974) 'Chromosome constitution of 500 infants dying during the perinatal period', *Hum. Genet.*, 23, 183–98.

MCKUSICK, V.A. (1983) '*Mendelian Inheritance in Man. Catalogs of Autosomal Dominant, Autosomal Recessive and X-linked Phenotypes*', 6th edn, Baltimore, Johns Hopkins University Press.

MACLEAN, N., COURT BROWN, W.M., JACOBS, P.A., MANTLE, D.J. and STRONG, J.A. (1968) 'A survey of sex chromatin abnormalities in mental hospitals', *J. Med. Genet.*, 5, 165–72.

MAGENIS, R.E., OVERTON, K.M., CHAMBERLIN, J., BRADY, T. and LOVRIEN, E. (1977) 'Parental origin of the extra chromosome in Down's syndrome', *Hum. Genet.*, 37, 7–16.

MANKINEN, C.B. and SEARS, J.W. (1976) 'Trisomy 13 in a female over 5 years of age', *J. Med. Genet.*, 13, 157–61.

MARTSOLF, J.T., RAY, M., BAUDER, F., BOYCHUK, R. and ARMSTRONG, J.D. (1977) 'Down's and Turner syndromes in a female infant with 47, X, del (X) (p11), +21', *Hum. Genet.*, 39, 103–8.

MATSUNAGA, E., TONOMURA, A., OISHI, H. and KIKUCHI, Y. (1978) 'Re-examination of paternal age effect in Down's syndrome', *Hum. Genet.*, 40, 259–68.

MIKKELSEN, M. (1982a) 'Down's syndrome: current stage of cytogenetic epidemiology', *Prog. Clin. Biol. Res.*, 103B, 297–309.

MIKKELSEN, M. (1982b) 'Parental origin of the extra chromosome in Down's syndrome', *J. Ment. Defic. Res.*, 26, 143–51.

MIKKELSEN, M., FISCHER, G., HANSEN, J., PILGAARD, B. and NIELSEN, J. (1983) 'The impact of legal termination of pregnancy and of prenatal diagnosis on the birth prevalence of Down's syndrome in Denmark', *Ann. Hum. Genet.*, 47, 123–31.

MIKKELSEN, M., POULSEN, H., GRINSTED, J. and LANGE, A. (1980) 'Non-disjunction in trisomy 21: study of chromosomal heteromorphisms in 110 families', *Ann. Hum. Genet.*, 44, 17–28.

MILLER, J.Q. (1963) 'Lissencephaly in two siblings', *Neurology*, 13, 841–50.

MOSER, H.W. and WOLF, P.A. (1971) 'The nosology of mental retardation', *Birth Defects Original Article Series*, 7(1), 117–34.

MURPHREE, A.L., GOMER, C.J., DOIRON, D.R. and BENEDICT, W.F. (1982) 'Recent developments in the genetics and treatment of retino-blastoma', *Birth Defects Original Article Series*, 18(6), 681–7.

NEU, R.L., SCHEUER, A.Q. and GARNER, L.I. (1971) 'A case of 48, XYY, 21+ in an infant with Down's syndrome', *J. Med. Genet.*, 8, 533–5.

NEWTON, M.S., CUNNINGHAM, C., JACOBS, P.A., PRICE, W.H. and FRASER, I.A. (1972a) 'Chromosome survey of a hospital for the mentally subnormal. Part 2: Autosome abnormalities', *Clin. Genet.*, 3, 215–25.

NEWTON, M.S., JACOBS, P.A., PRICE, W.H., WOODCOCK, G. and FRASER, I.A. (1972b) 'A chromosome survey of a hospital for the mentally subnormal. Part 1: Sex chromosome abnormalities', *Clin. Genet.*, 3, 226–48.

NIELSEN, K.B., DYGGVE, H.V., KNUDSEN, H. and OLSEN, J. (1983) 'A chromosomal survey of an institution for the mentally retarded', *Dan. Med. Bull.*, 30, 5–13.

NIELSEN, J. and KRAG-OLSEN, B. (1981) 'Follow-up of 32 children with autosomal translocations found among 11,148 consecutively newborn children from 1969 to 1974', *Clin. Genet.*, 20, 48–54.

NIELSEN, J. and RASMUSSEN, K. (1976) 'Autosomal reciprocal translocations and 13/14 translocations: a population study', *Clin. Genet.*, 10, 161–77.

NIELSEN, J., SORENSEN, A.M. and SORENSEN, K. (1981) 'Mental development of children with sex chromosome abnormalities', *Hum. Genet.*, 59, 324–32.

NIELSEN, K.B., TOMMERUP, N., POULSEN, H. and MIKKELSEN, M. (1982) 'Apparent homozygosity for the fragile site at Xq28 in a normal female', *Hum. Genet.*, 61, 60–2.

NORDENSON, I. (1981) 'Increased frequencies of chromosomal abnormalities in families with a history of fetal wastage', *Clin. Genet.*, 19, 168–73.

PATAU, K., SMITH, D.W., THERMAN, E., INHORN, S.L. and WAGNER, H.P. (1960) 'Multiple congenital anomaly caused by an extra autosome', *Lancet*, 1, 790–3.

PFEIFFER, R.A. and LOIDL, J. (1982) 'Mirror image duplications of chromosome 21. Three new cases and discussion of the mechanisms of origin', *Hum. Genet.*, 62, 361–3.

PRADER, A., LABHART, A. and WILLI, H. (1956) 'Ein Syndrome von Adipositas, Kleinwuchs, Kryptorchismus und Oligophrenie nach myatonieartigem Zustand in Neugeborenenalter', *Schweiz. Med. Wschr.*, 86, 1260–1.

PREUS, M. (1977) 'A diagnostic index for Down's syndrome', *Clin. Genet.*, 12, 47–55.

PRIEST, J.H., BRANTLEY, K.E. and BLACKSTON, R.D. (1977) 'Parental mosaicism as a cause of Down's syndrome. A report of 46, XX/46, XX, −21, +t(21q 21q) mother and 46, XY, +21, +t(21q 21q) child', *J. Pediat.*, 90, 786–8.

RAO, K.W., BUCHANAN, P.D. and AYLSWORTH, A.S. (1978) 'Asymmetric clinical and cytogenetic findings in a 4-year-old girl with trisomy 18 mosaicism', *Birth Defects Original Article Series*, 14(6C), 349–54.

RASMUSSEN, K., NIELSEN, J. and DAHL, G. (1982) 'The prevalence of chromosome abnormalities among mentally retarded persons in a geographically delimited area of Denmark', *Clin. Genet.*, 22, 244–55.

RAY, M. (1982) 'Chromosomal abnormalities in single gene disorders', in T.V.N. PERSAUD (ed.), *Advances in the Study of Birth Defects*, vol. 5, Lancaster, MTP Press, 1–13.

RICCARDI, V.M. (1977) 'Trisomy 8: an international study of 70 patients', *Birth Defects Original Article Series*, 13(3C), 171–84.

RICCARDI, V.M., SUJANSKY, E., SMITH, A.C. and FRANCKE, U. (1978) 'Chromosomal imbalance in the aniridia–Wilm's tumor association: 11p interstitial deletion', *Pediat.*, 61, 604–10.

RICHARDS, B.W. (1974) 'Investigation of 142 mosaic mongols and mosaic parents of mongols: cytogenetic analysis and maternal age at birth', *J. Ment. Defic. Res.*, 18, 199–208.

ROBINSON, A. and PUCK, T.T. (1965) 'Sex chromatin in newborns: presumptive evidence for external factors in human nondisjunction', *Science*, 148, 82–5.

ROCKMAN-GREENBERG, C., HERVO, P., RAY, M., SCHULZ, D., MAC-DONALD, N. and EVANS, J.A. (1982) 'A unique case of trisomy 18 mosaicism', *Amer. J. Hum. Genet.*, 34, 140A.

RODECK, C.H., MORSMAN, J.M., NICOLAIDES, K.H., MCKENZIE, C.,

GOSDEN, C.M. and GOSDEN, J.R. (1983) 'A single operator technique for first trimester chorion biopsy', *Lancet*, 2, 1340.

SADOVNICK, A.D. and BAIRD, P.A. (1982) 'Impact of prenatal chromosomal diagnosis in older women on population incidence of severe mental retardation', *Amer. J. Obstet. Gynec.*, 143, 486–7.

SANCHEZ, J.M., FIJTMAN, N. and MIGLIORINI, A.M. (1982) 'Report of a new case and clinical delineation of mosaic trisomy 9 syndrome', *J. Med. Genet.*, 19, 384–7.

SCHINZEL, A., SCHMID, W., FRACCARO, M., TIEPOLO, L., ZUFFARDI, O., OPITZ, J.M., LINDSTEN, J., ZETTERQUIST, P., ENELL, H., BACCICHETTI, C., TENCONI, R. and PAGON, R.A. (1981) 'The "cat-eye syndrome": dicentric small marker chromosome probably derived from a No. 22 (tetrasomy 22 pter – q11) associated with a characteristic phenotype', *Hum. Genet.*, 57, 148–58.

SCHREINEMACHERS, D.M., CROSS, P.K. and HOOK, E.B. (1982) 'Rates of trisomies 21, 18, 13 and other chromosome abnormalities in about 20,000 prenatal studies compared with estimated rates in live births', *Hum. Genet.*, 61, 318–24.

SHANNON, R.S., MANN, J.R., HARNDEN, D.G., MORTEN, J.E.N. and HERBERT, A. (1982) 'Wilm's tumour and aniridia: clinical and cytogenetic features', *Arch. Dis. Childh.*, 57, 685–90.

SHAPIRO, B.L. (1983) 'Down's syndrome – a disruption of homeostasis', *Amer. J. Med. Genet.*, 14, 241–69.

SHERMAN, S.L., MORTON, N.E., JACOBS, P.A. and TURNER, G. (1984) 'The marker (X) syndrome: a cytogenetic and genetic analysis', *Ann. Hum. Genet.*, 48, 21–37.

SIMONI, G., BRAMBATI, B., DANESINO, C., ROSSELLA, F., TERZOLI, G.L., FERRARI, M. and FRACCARO, M. (1983) 'Efficient direct chromosome analysis and enzyme determinations from chorionic villi samples in the first trimester of pregnancy', *Hum. Genet.*, 63, 349–57.

SKOVBY, F. and NIEBUHR, E. (1974) 'Presumably balanced translocations involving the same band of chromosome 4 found in two mentally retarded, dysmorphic individuals', *Ann. Genet.*, 17, 243–9.

SMITH, A., SILINK, M. and RUXTON, T. (1978) 'Trisomy 18 in an 11-year-old girl', *J. Ment. Defic. Res.*, 22, 277–86.

SMITH, D.W. (1982) *Recognizable Patterns of Human Malformation*, 3rd edn, Philadelphia, Saunders.

SMITH, G.F. and BERG, J.M. (1976) *Down's Anomaly*, 2nd edn, Edinburgh, Churchill Livingstone.

SPARKES, R.S., SPARKES, M.C., WILSON, M.G., TOWNER, J.W., BENEDICT, W., MURPHREE, A.L. and YUNIS, J.J. (1980) 'Regional assignment of genes for human esterase and retinoblastoma to chromosome band 13q14', *Science*, 208, 1042–4.

SPEED, R.M., JOHNSTON, A.W. and EVANS, H. J. (1976) 'Chromosome survey of total population of mentally subnormal in north-east of Scotland',

J. Med. Genet., 13, 295–306.

STADLER, G.R., BUHLER, E.M. and WEBER, J.R. (1963) 'Possible trisomy in chromosome group 6–12', *Lancet*, 1, 1379.

STENE, J., STENE, E., STENGEL-RUTKOWSKI, S. and MURKEN, J.D. (1981) 'Paternal age and Down's syndrome. Data from prenatal diagnoses (DFG)', *Hum. Genet.*, 59, 119–24.

STOLL, C.G., GLORI, G. and BESHARA, D. (1978) 'Interchromosomal effects in balanced translocations', *Birth Defects Original Article Series*, 14(6C), 393–8.

STRONG, L.C., RICCARDI, V.M., FERRELL, R.E. and SPARKES, R.S. (1981) 'Familial retinoblastoma and chromosome 13 deletion transmitted via an insertional translocation', *Science*, 213, 1501–3.

SUTHERLAND, G.R. (1978) 'Carrier detection in X-linked mental retardation', *Med. J. Austr.*, 2, 624.

SUTHERLAND, G.R. (1979a) 'Heritable fragile sites on human chromosomes: I. Factors affecting expression in lymphocyte culture', *Amer. J. Hum. Genet.*, 31, 125–35.

SUTHERLAND, G.R. (1979b) 'Heritable fragile sites on human chromosomes: II. Distribution, phenotypic effects and cytogenetics', *Amer. J. Hum. Genet.*, 31, 136–48.

SUTHERLAND, G.R. and ASHFORTH, P.L.C. (1979) 'X-linked mental retardation with macroorchidism and the fragile site at Xq27 or 28', *Hum. Genet.*, 48, 117–20.

SUTHERLAND, G.R., CARTER, R.F., BAULD, R., SMITH, I.I. and BAIN, A.D. (1978) 'Chromosome studies at the paediatric necropsy', *Ann. Hum. Genet.*, 42, 173–81.

SUTHERLAND, G.R., MURCH, A.R., GARDINER, A.J., CARTER, R.F. and WISEMAN, C. (1976) 'Cytogenetic survey of a hospital for the mentally retarded', *Hum. Genet.*, 34, 231–45.

SUTHERLAND, G.R. and WIENER, S. (1971) 'Chromosome studies in a mental deficiency hospital: total ascertainment', *Aust. J. Ment. Retard.*, 1, 246–7.

TAYLOR, A.I. (1968) 'Autosomal trisomy syndromes: a detailed study of 27 cases of Edwards' syndrome and 27 cases of Patau's syndrome', *J. Med. Genet.*, 5, 227–52.

TAYLOR, A.I. and MOORES, E.C. (1967) 'A sex chromatin survey of newborn children in two London hospitals', *J. Med. Genet.*, 4, 258–9.

THARAPEL, A.T., SUMMITT, R.L., WILROY, R.S. and MARTENS, P. (1977) 'Apparently balanced de novo translocations in patients with abnormal phenotypes: report of 6 cases', *Clin. Genet.*, 11, 255–69.

TOMKINS, D., HUNTER, A. and ROBERTS, M. (1979) 'Cytogenetic findings in Roberts–SC phocomelia syndrome(s)', *Amer. J. Med. Genet.*, 4, 17–26.

TOWNES, P.L., WHITE, M.R., STIFFLER, S.J. and GOH, K. (1975) 'Double aneuploidy – Turner–Down syndrome', *Amer. J. Dis. Child.*, 129, 1062–5.

TURNER, G. (1982) 'Fragile X-linked mental retardation', *Prog. Clin. Biol.*

Res., 103B, 311–14.

TURNER, G., BROCKWELL, R., DANIEL, A., SELIKOWITZ, M. and ZILIBOWITZ, M. (1980) 'Heterozygous expression of X-linked mental retardation and the marker X:fra (X) (q27)', *New Engl. J. Med.*, 303, 662–4.

TURNER, G. and JACOBS, P. (1983) 'Marker (X)-linked mental retardation', *Advances Hum. Genet.*, 13, 83–112.

TURNER, G., TILL, R. and DANIEL, A. (1978) 'Marker X chromosomes, mental retardation and macroorchidism', *New Engl. J. Med.*, 299, 1472.

TURNER, G. and TURNER, B. (1974) 'X-linked mental retardation', *J. Med. Genet.*, 11, 109–13.

UCHIDA, I.A., HOLUNGA, R. and LAWLER, C. (1968) 'Maternal radiation and chromosomal aberrations', *Lancet*, 2, 1045–9.

VENTER, P.A. and OP'T HOF, J. (1982) 'Cytogenetic abnormalities in patients with severe mental retardation', *S. Afr. Med. J.*, 62, 947–50.

VOGEL, F. (1979) 'Genetics of retinoblastoma', *Hum. Genet.*, 52, 1–54.

VOGEL, F. and MOTULSKY, A.G. (1979) *Human Genetics: Problems and Approaches*, New York, Springer-Verlag.

WALDENMAIER, C., ALDENHOFF, P. and KLEMM, T. (1978) 'The Roberts syndrome', *Hum. Genet.*, 40, 345–9.

WALZER, S. (1985) 'X chromosome abnormalities and cognitive development: implications for understanding normal human development', *J. Child Psychol. Psychiat.*, 26, 177–84.

WALZER, S., GRAHAM, J.M., BASHIR, A.S. and SILBERT, A.R. (1982) 'Preliminary observations on language and learning in XXY boys', *Birth Defects Original Article Series*, 18(4), 185–92.

WANG, J.-C.C. and ERBE, R.W. (1984) 'Folate metabolism in cells from fragile X syndrome patients and carriers', *Amer. J. Med. Genet.*, 17, 303–10.

WEBB, G.C., ROGERS, J.G., PITT, D.B., HALLIDAY, J. and THEOBALD, T. (1981) 'Transmission of fragile (X) (q27) site from a male', *Lancet*, 2, 1231–2.

WILSON, M.G., EBBIN, A.J., TOWNER, J.W. and SPENCER, W.H. (1977) 'Chromosomal anomalies in patients with retinoblastoma', *Clin. Genet.*, 12, 1–8.

WILSON, M.G., TOWNER, J.W., COFFIN, G.S., EBBIN, A.J., SIRIS, E. and BRAGER, P. (1981) 'Genetic and clinical studies in 13 patients with the Wolf–Hirschhorn syndrome [del (4p)]', *Hum. Genet.*, 59, 297–307.

WISNIEWSKI, L.P., WITT, M.E., GINSBERG-FELLNER, F., WILNER, J. and DESNICK, R.J. (1980) 'Prader–Willi syndrome and a bisatellited derivative of chromosome 15', *Clin. Genet.*, 18, 42–7.

WUNDER, E., BURGHARDT, U., LANG, B. and HAMILTON, L. (1981) 'Fanconi's anaemia: anomaly of enzyme passage through the nuclear membrane? Anomalous intracellular distribution of topoisomerase activity in placental extracts in a case of Fanconi's anaemia', *Hum. Genet.*, 58, 149–55.

YANG, S.-J. and ROSENBERG, H.S. (1969) '21/22 translocation Down's syndrome: a family with unusual segregating patterns', *Amer. J. Hum. Genet.*, 21, 248–51.

YING, Z., ZAIYU, C., CHUNYUN, L., HWEI-YUEN LO, W. and OPITZ, J.M. (1982) 'Phenotypic effects of inherited balanced translocation', *Amer. J. Med. Genet.*, 11, 177–84.

YIP, M.-Y., MARK, J. and HULTEN, M. (1982) 'Supernumerary chromosomes in six patients', *Clin. Genet.*, 21, 397–406.

YUNIS, J.J. (1976) 'High resolution of human chromosomes', *Science*, 191, 1268–70.

YUNIS, J.J. (1981) 'Mid-prophase human chromosomes. The attainment of 2000 bands', *Hum. Genet.*, 56, 293–8.

YUNIS, J.J. and RAMSAY, N.K.C. (1980) 'Familial occurrence of the aniridia–Wilm's tumor syndrome with deletion 11p13–14.1', *J. Pediat.*, 96, 1027–30.

ZALETAJEV, D.V. and MARINCHEVA, G.S. (1983) 'Langer–Giedion syndrome in a child with complex structural aberration of chromosome 8', *Hum. Genet.*, 63, 178–82.

7
Polygenic and environmental interactions
Ann M. Clarke

INTRODUCTION

To argue that anything as complex as human behaviour has multifactorial origins demanding a systems analysis is today almost a statement of the obvious. This does not, however, mean that a search for significant main effects in populations is unwarranted, provided that these can be shown in replicated studies across place and time.

In the various reviews we have offered in successive editions of this text we have consistently argued for both nature and nurture in combination as factors determining individual differences in intelligence, and although our thinking has matured over the years, taking account of new, often very sophisticated research findings, our attitude was well expressed by Zigler (1968):

> Not only do I insist that we take the biological integrity of the organism seriously, but it is also my considered opinion that our nation has more to fear from unbridled environmentalists than . . . from those who point to such integrity as one factor in the determination of development.

In 1969 an article was published in the *Harvard Educational Review* which raised a storm not only in the USA but throughout the English-speaking world and beyond. Arthur Jensen, addressing himself to the problem of 'How much can we boost IQ and scholastic achievement?', concluded that intelligence as measured in standardized tests is highly heritable, a composite value for it being given as 0.77 'which becomes 0.81 after correction for unreliability (assuming an average test reliability of 0.95)'. He further suggested that prenatal influences might well contribute the largest environmental influence, and discussed evidence which persuaded him that social class and racial variations in intelligence could not be accounted for by differences in the social environment but must be attributed partially to genetic differences. Jensen offered this as a major reason for the failure of the Head Start programme significantly to improve the learning abilities of children at risk of retardation on entry into school. A very large number of these children were black, and the implication was apparently clear: their IQs and scholastic attainment could not be substantially boosted. In a country such as the USA, with a strong egalitarian tradition, having painfully gone through the process of desegregating their education establishments, and believing they were in the process of building a great society, Jensen's conclusions resulted in a furious response particularly from those concerned with the education of disadvantaged children. 'Jensenism' became a term of abuse, and some investigators started to look very critically at the quality of the empirical evidence on which his conclusions were based. In this connection the extensively cited researches of the late Sir Cyril Burt were (belatedly) pronounced fraudulent to an extent not as yet fully established (Gillie, 1976; Hearnshaw, 1979; Clarke and Clarke, 1980). Kamin (1974), whose excavations into the researches underpinning the genetic contribution to variation in intelligence have been explosively influential, felt able to offer a perhaps incautiously extreme conclusion.

While maintaining that 'to assert that there is no genetic determination of IQ would be a strong and scientifically meaningless statement' he did, however, conclude that 'there exist no data which should lead a prudent man to accept the hypothesis that IQ scores are in any degree heritable'. Further, although apparently making a distinction between IQ scores and intelligence, Kamin felt able to end his book with a long quotation from Watson (1930) which included the statement:

> Give me a dozen healthy infants, well-formed, and my own specified world to bring them up in and I'll guarantee to take anyone at random and train him to become any type of specialist I might select – doctor, lawyer, artist, merchant-chief and, yes, even beggar-man and thief, regardless of his talents, penchants, tendencies, abilities, vocations, and race of his ancestors.

Since 1974 a large number of important studies bearing directly upon the nature–nurture issue have been published which, taken together with earlier work, point to the following conclusions with respect to intelligence test scores:

1. In the words of R.S. Wilson (1983) 'that there is a strong developmental thrust in the growth of intelligence that continues through adolescence, and is guided by an intrinsic template or ground plan. The template is rooted in genetic processes that operate all through childhood and adolescence.' This may be conceived as a biological trajectory which both underlies normal maturational processes from conception to maturity and also to an unknown extent accounts for individual differences.
2. No current investigator in the field of behavioural genetics denies the importance of the environment, and many are working hard to discover which environmental variations are helpful in potentiating development and which are disruptive. However, the precise effects of environmental events or by what processes they operate remain little understood except in environments of fairly severe disadvantage.
3. The environment can be shown to have deleterious effects where circumstances are exceptionally disadvantageous.

4. Removal of children from disadvantaged environments to favourable circumstances generally results in improvement in cognitive functioning.
5. As yet no early period in development has been identified which can be considered critical in the sense that the demonstrated effects of social disadvantage are irreversible, provided there is total ecological change.

Some scholars argue with Hebb (1949) that in normal circumstances nature and nurture are interlocked to such an extent in the development of intelligence and individual differences that to seek to establish which might be more important is scientifically meaningless. We disagree with this view, and suggest that research which might illuminate the nature and degree of the range of reaction to different environments is important not only in its own right but also for its general social implications. It must, however, be emphasized that, granted an assumption of a genotype interacting with various environments, it is useful to think in terms of a range of reaction within which the phenotype will be formed. It should come as no surprise, therefore, that heritability indices vary from study to study; the h^2 statistic is only characteristic of a given population, not a fixed value for a given trait (Vandenberg, 1971). Among the factors which will affect the expression of heritability are age (Scarr and Weinberg, 1983; Wilson, 1983), race and probably type of test, those with a predominantly verbal content being more likely to be influenced by the social environment than nonverbal and numerical tests.

A review of recent literature on polygenic factors will of necessity be brief, since so large and specialized a topic, mostly based on studies of nonretarded individuals, would be inappropriate in a book of this kind. Investigations of the heritability of IQ are based on a fairly simple, but very clear model of how genetic factors might work. For excellent expositions the reader is referred to Plomin *et al.* (1980) and to Jensen (1981), who also discuss elaborations of the model. It should be borne in mind that while there are biological patterns of inheritance originating with Mendel's work over a century ago which are capable of making precise predictions such as are discussed in other parts of this book, a parallel environmental model is not as yet available, leading to occasional difficulties in interpretation and agreement among researchers. Furthermore, in the real world allowance has to be made for the fact that many of the conditions underlying predictions for the polygenic model do not apply precisely.

GENETIC FACTORS RELATING TO INDIVIDUAL DIFFERENCES IN THE GENERAL POPULATION

Were we to assume *perfect* reliability of measurement, *no* effect of environmental variables, before, during or after birth, no dominance or epistasis, random mating, *and* a representative sample of a population, the polygenic model would predict that the correlation among different classes of kinship would depend upon the number of genes the relatives had in common, thus:

MZ twins	1.0
DZ twins	0.5
Siblings	0.5
Single parent/offspring	0.5
Midparent/offspring	0.7071
Grandparent/grandchild	0.25
Uncle, aunt/niece, nephew	0.25
Half-siblings	0.25
First cousins	0.125
Unrelated persons	0.00

In all cases, of course, the correlations should be the same whether the biological relatives are reared together or apart, since in this hypothetical (and totally unlikely) model the environment is assumed to have no effect whatever.

Erlenmeyer-Kimling and Jarvik (1963) were the first researchers systematically to collate data to test the hypothesis that there would be a relationship between degree of biological kinship and IQ. They presented median correlations based on 52 studies (30,000 correlational pairings) and found that the hypothesis was substantiated, although some of the kinship categories in those far-off days yielded no or few studies, and the extensive kinship data published by Burt had yet to be declared fraudulent and were therefore included. Moreover, studies demonstrating midparent/offspring correlations and single parent/offspring correlations were treated as equivalent although the predicted correlations differ (0.7071 and 0.50 respectively; see McAskie and Clarke, 1976). As might be expected, the correlations within each category of kinship varied, presumably reflecting differences in testing procedures and the nature of the samples. For a very detached review of Erlenmeyer-Kimling and Jarvik's work the reader is referred to Kamin (1974), who makes a number of substantial criticisms.

More recently Bouchard and McGue (1981) have performed, in the light of Kamin's attack, the difficult and exacting task of updating the material, providing a comprehensive contemporary summary of the world literature on IQ correlation between relatives. Recent studies are included, according to strict and explicit criteria, and some of the original ones deleted (among them Burt's) which did not meet important methodological requirements. The 111 studies, including 59 reported in the 17 years subsequent to the Erlenmeyer-Kimling and Jarvik summary, yielded 526 familial correlations based upon 113,942 pairings. In general the pattern of average correlations is consistent with the pattern predicted on the basis of polygenic inheritance. Although the overall trend in the data was strong, the individual data points were heterogeneous, as they were in the original collation. Bouchard and McGue attempted to discover the basis for the variations in outcome of studies, without any great success. Furthermore, there were clear indications of environmental effects, in addition to the genetic influences on IQ to an extent unascertainable from this particular meta-analysis.

Two factors which are likely to have affected some of the correlations, and hence the heterogeneity are: (1) the SES range (correlated with IQ) within each sample; and (2) where children are concerned, the age at testing. Reed and Rich (1982) illustrate the former point with reference to the data collected by Reed and Reed (1965) which included several thousand persons whose IQs had been determined when they were schoolchildren and later collated, making possible kinship correlations on an exceptionally large and representative sample of the US population. From this source 1029 pairs of parents with one or more offspring were identified, all tested when they were in their teens. Correlations and regression coefficients are presented for each offspring's IQ on the midparental average IQ and a demonstration made of the effect of truncation on each statistic. Thus, the midparent/offspring correlation for the whole sample was 0.531; for a subsample where the midparent IQ was one standard deviation above the mean (IQ 114 and above, N = 259) it was 0.218; for the middle range (IQ 74 to 114, N = 1664) it was 0.327, and for the low IQ range (IQ 74 and below, N = 106) the correlation was 0.419. The authors argue, correctly we believe, that a correlation as low as 0.08 between 559 gifted parents and 1027 offspring in Terman's study of the gifted, included in McAskie and Clarke's (1976) analysis, would be explained by truncation rather than by a lack of transmission of favourable genetic and environmental factors.

The effect of age on certain kinship correlations for IQ is illustrated by Wilson's (1983) study, which also highlights the related issue of heritability being to some extent age dependent. In a well-designed longitudinal study of a very large sample of MZ and DZ twins and their younger singleton siblings it has been shown that on age-appropriate tests of development very young MZ twins are not substantially different in concordance from DZ twins, but around the age of 18 months significantly greater concordance for MZ than DZ emerges, and heritability is seen to increase. By contrast DZ correlations reached a high point at 36 months, then progressively declined to an intermediate level by school age, ultimately reaching the level predicted by the polygenic model at 15 years of age, at which point in time the singleton/DZ twin correlations converged. (The WISC or WISC-R was used at ages 7, 8, 9 and 15.)

These factors are likely to have affected some of the individual correlations collated by Bouchard and McGue, but the paper is recommended for its careful and fair-minded weighing of evidence. The detailed findings are not incorporated into this chapter; instead, a few of the average correlations (in each case representing several studies and, with the exception of monozygotic twins reared apart, large samples) are presented. These are as follows: monozygotic twins reared together, 0.86; monozygotic twins reared apart, 0.72; dizygotic twins reared together, 0.60; siblings reared together, 0.47; siblings reared apart, 0.24; cousins, 0.15; adopting midparent/offspring, 0.24; biological midparent/midoffspring, reared together, 0.72.

Among the important new data included in this review are two adoption studies by Scarr and Weinberg (1976, 1978, 1983), which deserve special albeit brief attention. The Transracial Adoption Study provided a very large amount of data on 101 white families who generally had children of their own but decided to adopt predominantly black or interracial infants. The hypothesis to be tested was that these children would perform as well on IQ and school achievement tests as white adoptees by virtue of being reared 'in the culture of the tests and the schools'. This was found to be the case, the interracial adoptees scoring above the national average, although below their adopted siblings.

The Adolescent Adoption Study was designed to assess the cumulative impact of differences among family environments at the end of the childrearing period. A total of 104 adoptive white families and 120 biological families, representing a wide range of parental occupations and educational status, was studied. In the case of the adopting families a criterion for inclusion was that there were at least two unrelated children adopted in early infancy in each. Once again a wealth of data was obtained concerning this large sample of families, ranging from working to upper middle class, of particular importance since the adoptees were between 16 and 22 years, as were the offspring in the biological families. Furthermore, comparisons could be made across the two studies.

It was evident in both that parent/offspring correlations were higher for the biologically related than socially related, the results showing significant heritability for IQ. The adopted children's IQ scores were more closely correlated with the educational levels of their natural mothers than with the IQs of their adoptive mothers and fathers. The results of these large-scale new studies replicate the findings of earlier workers (Burks, 1928; Leahy, 1935) while providing evidence for changes in the pattern of sibling correlations as age increases. The young siblings in the transracial study were quite similar, whether genetically related or not; however, there was a zero correlation among the adolescent adopted siblings, strikingly different from the equivalent correlation in the biological families. The authors' interpretation of these results is that younger children are more influenced by differences among their family environments than older adolescents, who are freer to choose their own niches.

Many of the research articles published by Scarr and her colleagues, covering much wider territory than the two adoption studies, have been assembled in an important book, *Race, Social Class and Individual Differences in IQ* (Scarr, 1981), together with critical evaluations by others. Here Scarr states (p. 458):

> Going straight to the heart of the matter, I think that most evidence points to 'heritability' of about 0.4 to 0.7 in the US white population and 0.2 to 0.5 in the black, given that 'heritability' here means the proportion of genetic variance among individuals sampled in twin and family studies, which as I have repeatedly noted, are not representative of bad environments. If one could include people with really poor environments, the proportion of

environmental variance might rise; on the other hand, the genetic variance might also be increased. It is hard to predict whether or not the proportions of variance would change, and in which direction.

It is important to note here the small effects of environmental differences on IQ scores among the people in our white family samples. This suggests that within the range of 'humane environments', from an SES level of working to upper middle class, there is little evidence for differential environmental effects within the whole group. The average level of these environments is such that the black and white children reared by these families perform intellectually somewhat above the population average, even though they have average biological parents. Thus, the environments sampled in family studies are better than average at fostering intellectual development. But why are the relatively poor families rearing black and white *adopted* children whose IQ scores are nearly as high as those in professional families? It must be that all of these seeming environmental differences that predict so well to outcome differences among biological children are not primarily environmental differences, but indices of genetic differences among the parents and their biological offspring.

This statement serves as a summary of a consensus view on genetic factors influencing the development of intelligence and individual differences across a broad range of environments within an advanced society; implies a range of reaction within which the phenotype will be formed; and indicates certain limitations in our knowledge concerning those born and reared in disadvantaged environments. Before moving on to a discussion of the effects of depriving social conditions, a brief review will be presented of a few studies concerning the relatives of individuals identified as having low IQs or being administratively dealt with as handicapped.

GENETIC FACTORS IN THE FAMILIES OF CONTRASTING TYPES OF SUBNORMAL PERSONS

Much of this book is concerned with advances in our understanding of the effects of specific, and in some cases identifiable single genes, and chromosomal abnormalities and the consequences of severe traumata or noxious substances before, during and after birth, each of which is likely to cause fairly severe (rather than mild) retardation. For an introduction to this topic the reader is referred to the section on aetiological delineation and classification in Chapter 1. The results of numerous prevalence studies are in broad agreement that these catastrophes are fairly evenly distributed across social classes (see, for example, Birch *et al.*, 1970) and account for a small proportion of pupils with learning problems, or mildly retarded children and adults with IQs not greatly below 70–75. More often than not these mentally handicapped persons have IQs below 50, although it should always be remembered that there can be no single point in the distribution of IQ which will yield clearly dichotomous populations. We have already seen that behavioural geneticists agree about the importance of the environment interacting with the genetic template as it becomes activated over time, and that in severely disadvantaged environments development may be considerably retarded. One of the predictions which follows from the polygenic model is that of intergenerational regression towards the mean, which will, however, be attenuated with assortative mating which in many human populations is rather high, correlations among mates averaging 0.4 to 0.6. By the same token there should be substantial regression among the siblings of a person retarded by reason of polygenic inheritance.

It should, therefore, be possible to identify by means of kinship data two populations among the mentally retarded, those whose retardation appeared to arise from a specifically identifiable (biomedical) cause and those whose retardation is the result in part at least of polygenic inheritance, representing the lowest end of the normal distribution of intelligence. A distinction between 'pathological' and 'subcultural' types of mental deficiency was made by Lewis (1933) and explored by Penrose (1939) and Fraser Roberts (1952) whose studies contrasted the siblings of children with very low IQs and those who were backward or mentally retarded with IQs above 50. The hypothesis stated that the siblings of severely retarded children (that is, persons with a presumed pathological condition) should be of approximately normal intelligence, while the siblings of the normal variants in intelligence, assumed to be extreme deviants in the same way as the intellectually brilliant, should (1) not be of average intelligence, but (2) on the whole be more intelligent than the identified person. Despite the handicap of poor intelligence tests and (in the case of Fraser Roberts) an attempt to fit the data within predetermined IQ limits (which was not altogether successful) the hypothesis, was, broadly speaking, confirmed, or at least not disconfirmed.

The ever-vigilant Kamin (1974) strongly criticized Jensen's (1969) reporting of the Roberts study, and in addition made a number of criticisms of his own which served to cast doubt upon the validity of the findings and their interpretation. It is thus important that the study has been replicated in a manner which takes account of most of the criticisms.

Johnson *et al.* (1976) used data reported by Reed and Reed (1965) in order to determine whether siblings and parents of persons of varying degrees of retardation differ systematically from each other. Reed and Reed traced the ancestors and descendants of 289 persons who were residents in an American colony for the mentally retarded some time between 1911 and 1918, resulting in information on 82,217 persons. The original probands were classified on the basis of contemporary clinical notes and other examinations into: (1) a primarily genetic category which included diagnosed genetic anomalies and children of consanguineous marriages; (2) probably genetic (cultural-familial); (3) environmental, i.e. the result of perinatal trauma or early illness severe enough to account for their retardation; and (4), the largest category of all, 123 probands with no definite physical anomalies, no evidence of early trauma and no familial history of mental defect.

For Johnson *et al.*'s purposes it was obviously necessary for an original proband to have an IQ score and also at least one sibling, which criteria eliminated 47 of them, leaving 242 probands who could be used for their analysis. These were divided into six categories of IQ (1–19, 20–29, 30–39, 40–49, 50–59 and 60–79, only one person being above 69 in the last category) and the number of dead, mentally retarded or normal (or of unknown ability) siblings recorded, the total being 1499. There was a highly significant relationship between the IQ level of the proband and the percentage of retarded siblings and their mean IQs. The mean IQ of the 106 retarded siblings of probands who themselves had IQ scores was 45.32. Siblings of probands in the 0–39 range were below this mean in 35 cases, above in 12. Siblings of probands in the 40 + range were below the mean 8 times, above 51 times. A comparison of those siblings above and below the mean, by probands' ability levels, yielded a highly significant chi-square value while analysis of variance of the IQs of siblings in the six proband ability groups yielded a highly significant F value. Retarded persons lower in ability were less likely to have retarded siblings than probands of higher ability. However, if they did, these were less likely to be of lower ability than the retarded siblings of the more intelligent probands.

Parental occupational level significantly differentiated between the low- and high-ability retarded persons, as did their IQ scores (when available). Parents of the higher-level retarded persons were more likely themselves to be retarded than those of lower levels. Despite the statistical confirmation of the original hypothesis, the authors point out that the overlap between relatives of high- and low-level retarded persons was substantial, and that the 'clinical' and 'familial' groups are not as distinct as has sometimes been suggested.

Obtaining a statistically significant trend from these data is surely all that would have been possible, granted the nature of the original diagnostic system and proportion of probands of unknown origin. Moreover, it should again be emphasized that boundaries in nature are very seldom as distinct as the classifications we seek to impose on phenomena. Thus, in the unlikely event of obtaining new data conforming in every respect to agreed methodological criteria, there is every reason to suppose that categories would overlap. If such classification is to be maximally useful, it must seek minimal misclassification. Dichotomies, in particular, often polarize what are effectively adjacent and insignificantly different points on continua. Because of the complexity of aetiology and its environmental interactions, it is probable that subdividing criteria still further will better reflect reality than a simple dichotomous assessment.

It may well be, as we have suggested in Chapter 2, that a tripartite classification into pathological, subcultural (polygenic factors interacting with social environmental adversity) and normal variants without social adversity would do less injustice if applied to new data. Even so, anomalies would remain; Birch *et al.* (1970), in their careful clinical and epidemiological study of a total child population, point to the probable amplifying effects on pathological retardation of poor social circumstances and the ameliorating effects of good conditions on a similar degree of central nervous system damage. An individual might descend into, or move out of, a psychometric or administrative classification of retardation as a result.

We have already indicated (Chapter 2) that there is a considerable difference between administrative and 'IQ' prevalence. Thus in the Birch *et al.* study the administrative prevalence of subnormality was 1.26 per cent during childhood. The association of mild retardation with lower social class was amply confirmed, and related to a combination of large families, drawn from areas of poor housing where crowding was frequent. However, another group comprising 1.48 per cent of the population was identified psychometrically as having IQs below 75. It is our surmise that such children may have been drawn from less adverse conditions, therefore exhibiting fewer behavioural problems and thus no special need for identification; it seems more likely that their low IQs primarily reflected the operation of normal polygenic variation arising from parentage which was itself below average intellectually.

While we believe a tripartite classification of causes may be more helpful than a dichotomous one, it is also obvious that in individual cases a combination of influences is likely to be responsible for a given level of functioning.

ENVIRONMENTAL DISADVANTAGE

It would be unwise to accept low heritability estimates as the sole, or even the most important, evidence for the effects of the physical and/or social environment in the absence of *direct* indicators. In a book addressed to problems of mental retardation, particular attention should be paid to studies showing the effects of environmental disadvantage, provided they are not readily amenable to alternative interpretations in terms of genetic covariates, or open to methodological criticism. It has been surprisingly difficult to identify many studies which meet these criteria; however, the following summaries should suffice to indicate the potential power of adverse environments upon development.

The first are case-studies which demonstrate the devastating effects of severely depriving environments in producing mental retardation, and also the potentiality in some children at least for its reversal.

Kingsley Davis (1947) contrasted two children, both of whom suffered exceptionally abnormal rearing situations until the age of six and whose later outcome after rescue differed, one showing but little, and the other substantial improvement. Both were illegitimate children who had been kept in isolation; both were rachitic upon discovery, having been malnourished and sheltered from sunlight; both were unable to talk, in one case owing to total neglect, and in the other because she had been locked in an attic with her deaf-mute mother. This latter child, given the pseudonym Isabelle, had the advantage of an active rehabilitation programme undertaken by Mason (1942). Her wild, fearful behaviour improved and she rapidly learned to speak; her IQ trebled in a year and a half. At the age of fourteen she had passed sixth grade in a public school and was apparently progressing normally.

More recently a very fully documented account has been given of severely deprived twin boys born in Czechoslovakia in 1960 (Koluchova, 1972, 1976). Their mother died shortly after their birth, and they were placed in a children's home for a year. They then proceeded to the home of an aunt who kept them for six months. When they were eighteen months old their father, a simple inarticulate man, married a psychopathic woman who had no feelings for young children yet took them into the home. They had reached the age of seven before it was discovered that for most of the intervening period the boys had been kept isolated in a cellar, and had been cruelly treated and malnourished.

Experts who examined them found that they were severely rachitic and mentally handicapped. They could barely speak, they could hardly walk, were terrified of ordinary household objects and quite unable to recognize the meaning of pictures. It is not surprising that they were very emotionally disturbed. The twins were admitted to hospital for medical treatment after which they were placed in a children's home. Their physical and mental condition improved; they learned to walk, run, jump, ride a scooter and gradually to show less fear of strangers. During this time Dr Koluchova, a psychologist, was active in the supervision of the rehabilitation programme. The boys were placed in a school for the mentally retarded and simultaneously were fostered (and later adopted) by two unmarried sisters who had previously undertaken the care of children from deprived homes. They have provided the long-term security, stimulation and love which has ensured an entirely normal and happy outcome for the twins, who are now twenty-four. Their progress in the school for the subnormal was rapid and they began to outstrip their classmates. In spite of the risk involved they were placed in a normal school where, of course, they were at first a long way behind their age peers in attainment.

With special coaching they were later able to skip a class at school while still leaving time for hobbies such as sport and piano playing. They loved reading and showed signs of technical talent, which is now helping them in the first stages of their careers. They are entirely normal socially and emotionally, and above average in intellectual competence. It is important to note, however, that when they were first discovered a number of experts considered that, in view of their terrible condition and the extraordinary way they had been treated, they had been damaged beyond hope of recovery.

Their IQs, which were about 40 when first discovered, rose to 80 and 72 (WISC Full Scale) at the age of 8 years 4 months; 95 and 93 at the age of 11; 100 and 101 at 14 and were said at the age of 20 to be in the range of 115 (Koluchova, 1981, personal communication). Both are in further technical education, specializing in electronics; their social and emotional development as young adults is described as excellent.

Another case of early severe adversity has been reported by Angela Roberts, lately of Manchester University (Clarke, 1982). She had spent a period in Bogota, Colombia, associated with a missionary orphanage which catered for a small group of abandoned illegitimate babies, or infants given up because their parents could not cope. The illegitimate were usually the babies of young teenage servants and were sometimes literally foundlings. One little boy, Adam, was abandoned at 4 months and first received into a reformatory for girls. Our colleague visited him there and described the conditions as appalling. His main diet was a watery vegetable soup and porridge, and he remained in a bleak, bare, windowless room in perpetual darkness, unless the door was open. On admission to the mission orphanage Adam, aged 16 months, weighed only 5.809 kg. He had the physical signs of nutritional marasmus, his head was infested, he had scabies, a fungal rash and numerous sores. Emotionally he was completely withdrawn; he could not sit, crawl or walk. His development appeared similar to that of a 3-month-old infant. A local doctor diagnosed him as an extremely malnourished, mentally retarded spastic. By the age of 23 months his weight was 10.433 kg, he could sit up from a prone position, could stand holding furniture, could imitate two words together and could feed himself with a spoon. A month later he could stand without support for a few seconds, and could walk around his cot holding on with one hand. At 26 months, 10 months after admission, he weighed 11.794 kg, took his first independent steps, had improved emotionally and in other ways, and at 32 months was adopted by a North American family. There were, of course, problems; Adam was doubly incontinent and frequently bit his sister. However, by the age of 5 he was essentially average both mentally and physically. At the age of 8 years 8 months Adam was found to have a Full Scale WISC IQ of 113. His adopted sister from the same orphanage, who had also been clinically diagnosed as malnourished but had not experienced the same degree of deprivation, has at the age of 8 years 5 months an IQ of 102. Both children are doing well at school and neither has a serious emotional problem.

A further two cases of extreme early deprivation have been reported by Skuse (1984a). The sisters had been reared in infancy and early childhood by a microcephalic, mentally retarded and psychiatrically disturbed mother. Social services had asked a physician to visit when the children were aged 3.6 and 2.4 years respectively. He reported that they took no notice of anyone or anything except to scamper up and sniff strangers, grunting and snuffling like animals. Later a health visitor found them tied to the bed with leashes, partly because the mother insisted on keeping the flat spotlessly clean, and partly because she feared they might fall off the balcony.

The two children commenced playgroup attendance, the elder making tremendous strides and the younger little progress, her behaviour being decidedly odd. In her case, head circumference was below the third percentile, and she had a flattened occiput. There was partial bilateral syndactyly of the second and third toes and they lacked distal phalanges.

Nine months later assessments were carried out at 4 years 11 months and 3 years 9 months, respectively. The elder was well grown and lively, but still had practically no comprehensible language. Her social skills were at the $2\frac{1}{2}$-year level. The younger was described as miserable, withdrawn and as smelling and mouthing objects. She avoided eye contact and rocked persistently when alone. Pica was a great problem, she slept poorly, wandering at night in search of food and showing no fear of the dark. By now the children had been taken into care in a children's home because of persistent maltreatment.

The elder girl made rapid progress in this institution and was ready to start school full time at 6 years. By then her social skills were only 9–15 months below age norms; physically she was at the 50th percentile. The younger child began to attend a special school for retarded children at age 5, but at $7\frac{1}{2}$ her behaviour caused her to be sent to an autistic unit. Incidentally, an albino, severely retarded, autistic half-brother has been traced.

The elder girl has demonstrated a consistent trend towards recovery in virtually all aspects of cognitive functioning, emotional adjustment and social relationships. There remain some articulatory difficulties and relative social disinhibition but she is regarded as having excellent potential for normal development. She has been happy in her children's home for some nine years and continues to attend school.

The author suggests that the younger child is the subject of congenital vulnerability and supports our contention that grossly deprived children without such constraints have a good prognosis after removal from adversity. A second and equally useful paper (Skuse, 1984b) reviews the whole field of severe deprivation in early childhood, offering a detailed analysis of six studies in an endeavour to elucidate what unusual experiences during childhood are sufficient and necessary for normal development. He also assesses the extent to which critical periods of development exist, and suggests what minimal compensatory influences are necessary to alleviate psychological handicaps arising from early adversity. He concludes that, in the absence of genetic or congenital anomalies, or a history of gross malnourishment, victims of such deprivation have an excellent prognosis, although some subtle deficits in social adjustment may persist. Most human characteristics, with the possible exception of language, are virtually resistant to obliteration even by the most dire early environments.

Case-histories such as these and others of a similar kind illustrate in a tragic but dramatic way the effect of physical and social deprivation on developing humans, together with later recovery granted special help and complete removal from the depriving circumstances. Skeels's (1966) classic study is critically evaluated in Chapter 1, and will therefore be omitted here. The 'experimental group' provides case-studies of the advantageous effects of late adoption for children who appeared to be subnormal in infancy.

The second category of studies concerns an important phenomenon known as cumulative deficit, and in this connection two research papers have been chosen for presentation here because of the involvement of A.R. Jensen, a hereditarian not known for his sympathy with environmental hypotheses. Cumulative deficit is intended to explain the increasing decrement in IQ relative to population norms as a function of age in groups considered environmentally deprived. According to the hypothesis the decrement is a result of the cumulative effects of environmental disadvantages on mental development.

Jensen (1974) provides a critical review of the literature, faulting the cross-sectional and longitudinal methods used by many of those investigating the tendency for some disadvantaged children to decrease in IQ across the years of schooling, a phenomenon first noticed by Gordon (1923) in England who recorded that among children brought up on canal boats, leading a nomadic existence with little or no schooling, the mean Binet IQ of the youngest child in the family was 90, of the second youngest 77, of the third youngest 73 and of the oldest 60.

To overcome the many methodological criticisms raised in connection with many of the published researches, Jensen proposed as the unit of measurement differences in standardized test scores between older and younger siblings, the older being expected to have lower scores. He found a small but significant decrement in verbal but not nonverbal IQ among black but not white school-children in California, and concluded that cumulative deficit was not a problem in that state.

But in a large sample of black and white children in rural Georgia there was a substantial linear decrement in blacks between ages 5 and 16, of 1.62 verbal IQ points *per year* and 1.19 points of nonverbal. The overall IQ decreased 1.42 points per year, cumulatively 14 to 16 points over the whole time range. There was no similar effect in white children living in the same area. Jensen (1977) concluded that his findings demanded an environmental interpretation, at least in part. The loss in relative status which Jensen demonstrated among children from a particularly disadvantaged community could occur in certain families within a community, as suggested by Heber *et al.* (1968) who studied 586 children of 88 mothers from the same slum area, 40 of whom had IQs of 80 and above, while the remaining 48 had IQs of below 80. Cross-sectional testing within these families showed a marked disparity between the groups. Children from families with the more intelligent mothers showed a normal pattern of average IQs between 90 and 95; children of retarded mothers declined to an average of below 65 at age 14. The possibility of some genetic input into this sorry state of affairs does not, in the light of Jensen's more recent work, invalidate the conclusion that certain children are at risk for mental retardation by virtue of exceptionally disadvantaged environments.

Finally we present a study which amplifies the results of the few authentic researches concerning separated identical twins (Newman *et al.*, 1937; Shields, 1962; Juel-Nielsen, 1965), despite the lack of immediate connection with mental retardation.

Schiff *et al.* (1978) employed an entirely novel method which could usefully be followed by others. They searched the files of six public adoption agencies in France to find children of two lower-class parents adopted early into upper-middle-class homes who also had a sibling or half-sibling reared by the biological mothers. There are some problems with the presentation of the data, which inspire caution in interpreting the findings. However, 32 adopted children were located, born to mothers and fathers who were unskilled workers; only 20 biological half-siblings were found, reared by their own mothers. The 20 home-reared children of varying ages were reported as having average IQs of 94.5 and the 32 adoptees 110.6, while on another test the scores were 95.4 and 106.9, respectively. In terms of school attainment the authors state that the two groups were typical of their rearing environments. Certainly the home-reared children were very much more likely than their adopted siblings to have presented educational problems. Only 4 out of 32 adopted children had repeated a grade or been in a special class, whereas 13 out of 20 home-reared siblings had. A fuller version of this research project has been published (Schiff *et al.*, 1982) giving a table of IQ scores for the 20 children reared by their natural mothers. WISC IQ data for 18 children and scores provided by the school on the remaining two reveal that three children were borderline retarded with IQs of 69, 71 and 78; the remainder lay between 86 and 111, 7 having IQs over 100. Only 6 of the adopted children had WISC IQs below 100, the lowest being 81. It is pertinent to add that no child was offered for adoption who had been 'organically deficient at birth' (Schiff *et al.*, 1982, p. 182). However, SES-matched controls selected from the classmates of the adoptees had significantly higher average IQs (see also Dumaret, 1985).

An extension of this project has been undertaken by one of Schiff's collaborators, Dumaret (1985). She made a detailed study of all the progeny of 28 mothers, one of whose children was adopted. These subjects were divided into three groups:

1. Children abandoned before the age of 1 month and placed for adoption before 7 months in a privileged social environment.
2. Children remaining with the mother or another member of the family and raised in a disadvantaged social environment.
3. Children abandoned, left or taken away from the family and raised in foster homes or children's homes.

The results – increases in IQ and diminution of scholastic failures for the adopted children, by contrast with the home- or institution-reared – show that the social environment has important effects. Adoption played a dynamic role, permitting these children to develop their intellectual resources thanks to a favourable social, cultural and familial environment. The difference between groups 1 and 2 was similar to the average difference between the corresponding social groups in the general population. The children reared in institutions appeared to be at a particular disadvantage, many being mentally retarded. Even in the case of those with IQs of 100 or above, educational problems were normal occurrences. The author's interpretation is that 'the effects of long-term emotional deprivation are superimposed on the effects of the social environment; the fate of these children is the combined result of these two effects.'

It is important to emphasize that Schiff *et al.*'s demonstration of an environmental effect on IQ and achievement differences between half-siblings reared in different social contexts does nothing to invalidate studies showing high heritability for intelligence. Rather, it adds to the limited evidence indicating in a direct way the effects of differing social environments, which are also indicated by adoptive studies and studies of identical twins reared together or apart, referred to earlier in this chapter. As McNemar (1938) commented in connection with Newman *et al.*'s sample of nineteen pairs of monozygotic twins reared apart:

> it appears that the only evidence which approaches decisiveness is that for separated twins, and this rests ultimately upon the fact that four pairs reared in really different environments were undoubtedly different in intelligence. This fact can neither be ignored by the naturite nor deemed crucial by the nurturite.

The long-term outcomes of psychosocial intervention in early life designed to prevent mental retardation in children born into families 'at risk' are examined in Chapter 12 and will not be discussed here. Suffice it to say that there is no evidence that intervention confined to the pre-school period among children who remain in their deprived families results in the maintenance of IQ increments through adolescence. Nevertheless, some gain in educational status from atypical programmes has been demonstrated. Jensen (1981), in a commentary on attempts to raise the IQ of disadvantaged children, has expressed the position as follows:

> Even with heritability in the range of 0.70 to 0.80, the magnitude of environmental effects can be considerable. With a standard deviation of 7.5 IQ points, for example, and assuming that existing environmental effects on IQ are normally distributed (for which there is good evidence), the total range of environmental influences would be about six σ, or 45 IQ points. Intervention that produces IQ changes within that range is not in the least incompatible with present estimates of the broad heritability of IQ.
>
> The real problem, however, has been in bringing the environmental influences on IQ under experimental control. Even though evidence on the genetic analysis of IQ leaves considerable latitude for nongenetic influences, psychologists have not yet discovered more than a fraction of the nongenetic factors that contribute to IQ variance or how they can be experimentally harnessed to raise IQ markedly and permanently. Although it may come as a surprise to many psychologists, at present, we know more about the genetics of IQ than we know about environmental influences on

IQ, except for extreme deprivations and traumas that are too rare to contribute importantly to the IQ variance of the general population. My hunch is that the nongenetic variance in IQ is the result of such a myriad of microenvironmental events as to make it extremely difficult, if not impossible, to bring more than a small fraction of these influences under experimental control. The results of all such attempts to date would seem to be consistent with this interpretation.

Similarly Plomin and DeFries (1980) commented:

In fact, we know of no specific environmental influences nor combinations of them that account for as much as 10 per cent of the variance in IQ. For example, the longitudinal Collaborative Perinatal Project (Broman, Nichols and Kennedy, 1975) reported correlations between prenatal/neonatal factors and 4-year-old IQ scores for over 26,000 children. Even at 4 years of age, all the prenatal and neonatal measures combined explain less than 4 per cent of the variance in IQ scores. Another example is the relationship between IQ and birth order/family size (Zajonc and Marcus, 1975). Earlier born children and children in smaller families tend to have higher IQs on the average. However, birth order and family size account for less than 2 per cent of the variance of IQ in a population. (Grotevant, Scarr and Weinberg, 1977)

With this perhaps slightly pessimistic statement in mind we turn now to a consideration of two environmental variables, each of which has been promoted in the context of a wide audience of professionals and the general public as depressing intellectual functioning and contributing to mental handicap.

TWO POTENTIAL HAZARDS: MALNUTRITION AND EXPOSURE TO LEAD[1]

The first serious studies of malnutrition in relation to brain growth and mental development began in the 1960s. As many writers have indicated, unravelling the specific effects of malnutrition is exceedingly difficult for it exists in a web of other adversities which in combination are associated with backwardness and failure to thrive. Hence if it is found that children's development, and indeed their subsequent adult status, are below cultural norms, any one or more of these adversities could be either causally related or mere correlates. A masterly review of some of the problems has recently been provided by Richardson (1984) who draws attention to the climate of opinion which stimulated research in this field. First, 'the conceptual model underlying most of the research was that malnutrition caused damage to the central nervous system which was then reflected in intellectual impairment, and further that

1. These two problems have also been discussed in Chapters 4 and 5.

the brain's vulnerability was related to the speed of growth of the brain'. It had been shown by Dobbing (1964) that the main growth spurt occurred in the last trimester of pregnancy and during the first two years of postnatal life (Dobbing and Sands, 1973). Richardson notes that this model, which focused on physical development, may have led to scant attention being paid to correlated social environmental factors and their effects. Moreover, he indicates that this theory was reinforced by the long-held belief, challenged by Clarke and Clarke (1976), that early development exercises a critically important influence on later development. He argues that because of the inadequacies of the experimental controls in many studies, the association between malnutrition and retarded intellectual development either could be a spurious one, or could represent one of many factors which together might be responsible.

Richardson summarizes and critically evaluates a wide range of evidence from many parts of the world, emphasizing the methodological problems connected with empirical research with humans in this field, concluding that it is 'still an open question of what forms of malnutrition under what conditions have long-term effects on impairing intellect and at present there is no clear evidence that such effects exist'.

The more recent research shows that malnutrition must be considered among an array of social and biological variables over time which influence intellectual development and, further, there is evidence that the effects of malnutrition can be overcome by later favourable experiences. It is now clear that primary prevention of malnutrition cannot be achieved by shipments of food but must attend to the social and economic needs of those who are impoverished.

Commenting on Richardson's chapter, an additional point has been made by Sartorius (1984), who regards research on the effects of malnutrition on mental development as unjustifiably in the centre of many research agendas. Malnutrition is a consequence of many factors and is thoroughly undesirable, regardless of its effects on mental development.

In a commentary upon Richardson's evaluation of the effects of malnutrition, Yule (1984) 'was struck by the parallels in conceptual and methodological problems facing research into supposed effects of malnutrition with that into the supposed effects of lead on development'. Both sets of researches began with a reasonable but simple hypothesis. A lot of malnutrition or lead ingestion is clearly harmful; can a bit less do a bit less harm? The issues surrounding this question are, as indicated, much more complex than perhaps they sound. For example, the alleged central nervous system impairment is difficult to test, social factors are difficult to measure and to control, and

> sloppy concepts of 'subclinical' effects obscured the issues. Pressure groups and politicians quickly took 'sides' making rational discussion even more difficult. . . . Some of the studies underline the basic resilience of human infants. Others underline the wide individual differences which are the

essence of our humanness. All point to the complex interactions between children and their effective social environments.

Rutter (1980) has provided a careful and comprehensive account of research into raised lead levels as it relates to cognitive and social-behavioural functioning, which stresses the methodological problems often overlooked or ignored by researchers in this area. These include biased samples, problems in reliably determining the body lead burden, difficulties in the assessment of psychological and behavioural impairment, inadequate statistical control for the possible confounding effects of other variables (particularly genetic factors and social disadvantage), and small sample sizes. He concluded that clinic-type studies of children with high lead levels provide good evidence that blood lead levels persistently raised above 60 µg/100 ml are probably associated with an average reduction of some three to four IQ points, even in asymptomatic children. The more difficult issue is how far there may be cognitive impairment with blood lead levels in the 20 to 40 µg/100 ml range. Rutter cautiously concluded that, although the findings are somewhat contradictory, the evidence suggests that persistently raised blood lead levels in the range above 40 µg/100 ml may cause cognitive impairment (a reduction of one to five IQ points on average) and less certainly may increase the risk of behavioural difficulties.

The use of shed deciduous teeth to examine the body lead burden appears to be a more reliable method than blood levels, a method pioneered by Needleman and colleagues (1972, 1974, 1979), who showed that children with high levels of dentine lead scored significantly below children with low dentine lead on the WISC-R, and that lead level was correlated with teachers' ratings of classroom behaviour.

Yule (1984) reported that his own pilot study tended to parallel Needleman's results, but that studies by Winneke and colleagues in Germany and by Smith in England both indicated that when social factors were statistically controlled the effect was statistically nonsignificant (see Winneke, 1983; Smith, 1983). Two important additional points were made by Yule. First, that where the data are reported it is generally noted that the relationship between lead and IQ is stronger in working-class than in middle-class groups; in one of his most recent studies in a predominantly middle-class area no relationship could be found with either IQ or teachers' behaviour ratings. Second, Yule argues that an overall average difference of only 2 to 5 IQ points has considerable implications for the prevalence of mild handicap, since a significant increase in children with IQs below 70 would be expected.

CONCLUSIONS

Recent twin and adoption studies have confirmed earlier findings of the high heritability of intelligence in a wide range of environments which, however, usually exclude disadvantaged minority groups. It is, furthermore, increasingly evident that the genetic programme unfolds over time. If it is conceded that a proportion of the between-family variance is accounted for by genetic/environmental interaction within families, then it must follow that children with relatively poor heredity for intelligence may have the additional disadvantage of being reared in suboptimal environments. If the social environment is important, a proposition accepted by all behaviour geneticists, then these children must rely on chance events or the chance effects of intergenerational regression to the mean as a way out of the cycle of disadvantage, unless they are provided with superior rearing environments. In some areas of extreme disadvantage cumulative deficit may occur.

Consideration of the evidence leads to the likelihood of complex multi-factorial origins of mental retardation in an unknown, albeit probably relatively small proportion of an advanced nation's population. The demonstration of genetic factors as an important determinant in individual differences in IQ in the general population leads to the assumption that on occasion these will be the major cause of mild mental retardation in children reared in circumstances which cannot be considered disadvantageous, while many who might in other environmental contexts become victims are, in fact, protected.

Some genetic contributions in families subject to social disadvantage place a group of children at risk during the developmental period. The risk becomes exacerbated if there is in addition a lack of consistent intellectual stimulation, parental cruelty or chronic neglect, chaotic social relationships, poor nutrition, exposure to pollution, infections and irregular attendance at school, or combinations of some of these.

No planned intervention study to date has succeeded in substantially and permanently raising the IQ and scholastic achievement of children at risk for mental retardation, a subject discussed fully in Chapter 13. There are as yet no satisfactory research findings concerning outcomes for children of this kind were they to be adopted into advantaged homes. However, case-studies exist, some reviewed in this chapter, of children who had exhibited mental retardation following exceptional environmental adversity, attaining normal development upon removal.

The study by Schiff *et al.* (1978, 1982), although not of children identified as being at risk for retardation, is at least suggestive of what might happen if the 'myriad of microenvironmental events' so eloquently expressed by Jensen (1981) were positive rather than negative. It will, however, be recalled that the lower-class social environment in which the children were reared was not sufficient to render them mentally retarded, although many had been retained in grade (repeating a school year) or received special educational provision.

Nor is it likely that adoption into high-status families offers a viable solution to the problem of so-called 'subcultural subnormality' in a free society. As indicated in Chapter 12, consideration of lifespan development of mildly retarded persons, who have been administratively identified as in need of special services as children, suggests that the outcome for them as adults is not seriously disadvantageous compared with peers who have never been identified. It should, perhaps, also be borne in mind that in any society, perhaps particularly those which increasingly rely on complex cognitive skills, there will always be those whose individual qualities appear less adequate than others'. Until a more humane social organization evolves, these persons may experience discrimination. Although schools cannot compensate for society, it seems likely to this author that some educational establishments are already protecting pupils from the worst consequences of social disadvantage, and that others could be enabled to do more. There is increasing evidence, some of it summarized by Rutter (1983), that teachers, preferably working in partnership with parents, can offer children at risk for developmental retardation substantial support both cognitively and socially. Perhaps compensatory education across the years of schooling need not necessarily fail.

REFERENCES

BIRCH, H.G., RICHARDSON, S.A., BAIRD, D., HOROBIN, G. and ILL-SLEY, R. (1970) *Mental Subnormality in the Community: A Clinical and Epidemiologic Study*, Baltimore, Md., Williams & Wilkins.

BOUCHARD JR, T.J. and MCGUE, M. (1981) 'Familial studies of intelligence: a review', *Science*, 212, 1055–9.

BROMAN, S.H., NICHOLS, P.L. and KENNEDY, W.A. (1975) *Preschool IQ: Prenatal and Early Developmental Correlates*, Hillsdale, NJ, Lawrence Erlbaum.

BURKS, B. (1928) 'The relative influence of nature and nurture upon mental development: a comparative study of foster parent/foster child resemblance and true parent/true child resemblance', *Yearbook of the National Society of the Study of Education*, part 1, 27, 219–316.

CLARKE, A.M. (1982) 'Developmental discontinuities: an approach to assessing their nature', in L.A. BOND and J.M. JOFFE (eds), *Facilitating Infant and Early Child Development*, Hanover, NH, University Press of New England, 58–77.

CLARKE, A.M. and CLARKE, A.D.B. (eds) (1976) *Early Experience: Myth and Evidence*, London, Open Books; New York, Free Press.

CLARKE, A.M. and CLARKE, A.D.B. (1980) 'Comments on Professor Hearnshaw's "Balance Sheet on Burt"', in H. BELOFF (ed.), *A Balance Sheet on Burt: Supplement to the Bulletin of the BPS*, 33, 17–19.

DAVIS, K. (1947) 'Final note on a case of extreme isolation', *Amer. J. Sociol.*, 52, 432–7.

DOBBING, J. (1964) 'The influence of early nutrition on the development and myelination of the brain', *Proc. Roy. Soc.*, 159, 503–9.

DOBBING, J. and SANDS, J. (1973) 'Quantitative growth and development of the human brain', *Arch. Dis. Childh.*, 48, 757–67.

DUMARET, A. (1985) 'IQ, scholastic performance and behaviour of sibs raised in contrasting environments', *J. Child Psychol. Psychiat.*, 26, 553–80.

ERLENMEYER-KIMLING, L. and JARVIK, L.F. (1963) 'Genetics and intelligence: a review', *Science*, 142, 1477–9.

GILLIE, O. (1976) 'Crucial data faked by eminent psychologist', *Sunday Times*, London, 24 October.

GORDON, H. (1923) *Mental and Scholastic Tests among Retarded Children* (Education Pamphlet 44, Board of Education, London), London, HMSO.

GROTEVANT, H.D., SCARR, S. and WEINBERG, R.A. (1977) 'Intellectual development in family constellations with adopted and natural children: a test of the Zajonc and Marcus model', *Child Develop.*, 48, 1699–703.

HEARNSHAW, L.S. (1979) *Cyril Burt: Psychologist*, London, Hodder & Stoughton.

HEBB, D.O. (1949) *Organization of Behaviour*, New York, Wiley.

HEBER, R., DEVER, R. and CONRY, J. (1968) 'The influence of environmental and genetic variables on intellectual development', in H.J. PREHM, L.A. HAMERLYNCK and J.E. CROSSON (eds), *Behavioral Research in Mental Retardation*, Eugene, Oreg., University of Oregon, 1–22.

JENSEN, A.R. (1969) 'How much can we boost IQ and scholastic achievement?', *Harvard Educ. Rev.*, 39, 1–123.

JENSEN, A.R. (1974) 'Cumulative deficit: a testable hypothesis?', *Develop. Psychol.*, 10, 996–1019.

JENSEN, A.R. (1977) 'Cumulative deficit in IQ of blacks in the rural south', *Develop. Psychol.*, 13, 184–91.

JENSEN, A.R. (1981) 'Raising the IQ: the Ramey and Haskins Study', *Intelligence*, 5, 29–40.

JOHNSON, C.A., AHERN, F.M. and JOHNSON, R.C. (1976) 'Level of functioning of siblings and parents of probands of varying degrees of retardation', *Behav. Genet.*, 6, 473–7.

JUEL-NIELSEN, N. (1965) 'Individual and environment: a psychiatric-psychological investigation of monozygotic twins reared apart', *Acta Psychiat. Scandinav.*, 30, 325–32.

KAMIN, L.J. (1974) *The Science and Politics of IQ*, Hillsdale, NJ, Lawrence Erlbaum.

KOLUCHOVA, J. (1972) 'Severe deprivation in twins: a case study', *J. Child Psychol. Psychiat.*, 13, 107–14.

KOLUCHOVA, J. (1976) 'A report on the further development of twins after severe and prolonged deprivation', in A.M. CLARKE and A.D.B. CLARKE (eds), *Early Experience: Myth and Evidence*, London, Open Books; New York, Free Press, 56–66.

LEAHY, A.M. (1935) 'Nature–nurture and intelligence', *Genet. Psychol. Monogr.*, 17, 241–305.

LEWIS, E.O. (1933) 'Types of mental deficiency and their social significance', *J. Ment. Sci.*, 79, 298–304.

MCASKIE, M. and CLARKE, A.M. (1976) 'Parent–offspring resemblances in intelligence: theories and evidence', *Brit. J. Psychol.*, 67, 243–73.

MCNEMAR, Q. (1938) 'Newman, Freeman and Holzinger's Twins: a study of heredity and environment', *Psychol. Bull.*, 35, 237–49.

MASON, M. (1942) 'Learning to speak after six and one half years of silence', *J. Speech Disord.*, 7, 295–304.

NEEDLEMAN, H.L., DAVIDSON, I., SEWELL, E.M. and SHAPIRO, I.M. (1974) 'Subclinical lead exposure in Philadelphia schoolchildren: identification by dentine lead analysis', *New Engl. J. Med.*, 290, 245–8.

NEEDLEMAN, H.L., GUNNOE, C., LEVITON, A., REED, R., PERESIE, H., MAHER, C. and BARRETT, P. (1979) 'Deficits in psychologic and classroom performance of children with elevated dentine lead levels', *New Engl. J. Med.*, 300, 689–95.

NEEDLEMAN, H.L., TUNCAY, O.C. and SHAPIRO, I.M. (1972) 'Lead levels in deciduous teeth of urban and suburban American children', *Nature*, 235, 111–12.

NEWMAN, H.H., FREEMAN, F.M. and HOLZINGER, K.J. (1937) *Twins: A Study of Heredity and Environment*, Chicago, University of Chicago Press.

PENROSE, L.S. (1939) 'Intelligence test scores of mentally defective patients and their relatives', *Brit. J. Psychol.*, 30, 1–18.

PLOMIN, R. and DEFRIES, J.C. (1980) 'Genetics and intelligence: recent data', *Intelligence*, 4, 15–24.

PLOMIN, R., DEFRIES, J.C. and MCCLEARN, G.E. (1980) *Behavioral Genetics: A Primer*, San Francisco, Freeman.

REED, E.W. and REED, S.C. (1965) *Mental Retardation: A Family Study*, Philadelphia and London, Saunders.

REED, S.C. and RICH, S.S. (1982) 'Parent/offspring correlations and regression for IQ', *Behav. Genet.*, 12, 535–542.

RICHARDSON, S.A. (1984) 'The consequences of malnutrition for intellectual development', in J. DOBBING, A.D.B. CLARKE, J. CORBETT, J. HOGG and R.O. ROBINSON (eds), *Scientific Studies in Mental Retardation*, London, Macmillan.

ROBERTS, J.A. FRASER (1952) 'The genetics of mental deficiency', *Eugenics Rev.*, 44, 71–83.

RUTTER, M. (1980) 'Raised lead levels and impaired cognitive behavioural functioning: a review of the evidence', *Develop. Med. Child Neurol.*, 22, Suppl. 42.

RUTTER, M. (1983) 'School effects on pupil progress: research findings and policy implications', *Child Develop.*, 54, 1–29.

SARTORIUS, N. (1984) 'Critique of "The consequences of malnutrition for intellectual development" by S.A. Richardson', in J. DOBBING, A.D.B. CLARKE, J. CORBETT, J. HOGG and R.O. ROBINSON (eds), *Scientific Studies in Mental Retardation*, London, Macmillan.

SCARR, S. (1981) *Race, Social Class and Individual Differences in IQ*, Hillsdale, NJ, Lawrence Erlbaum.

SCARR, S. and WEINBERG, R.A. (1976) 'IQ test performance of black children adopted by white families', *Amer. Psychol.*, 31, 726–39.

SCARR, S. and WEINBERG, R.A. (1978) 'The influence of "family background" on intellectual attainment', *Amer. Sociol. Rev.*, 43, 674–92.

SCARR, S. and WEINBERG, R.A. (1983) 'The Minnesota Adoption Studies: genetic differences and malleability', *Child Develop.*, 54, 260–7.

SCHIFF, M., DUYME, M., DUMARET, A., STEWART, J., TOMKIEWICZ, S. and FEINGOLD, J. (1978) 'Intellectual status of working-class children adopted early into upper-middle-class families', *Science*, 200, 1503–4.

SCHIFF, M., DUYME, M., DUMARET, A. and TOMKIEWICZ, S. (1982) 'How much *could* we boost scholastic achievement and IQ scores? A direct answer from a French adoption study', *Cognition*, 12, 165–96.

SHIELDS, J. (1962) *Monozygotic Twins Brought Up Apart and Brought Up Together*, London, Oxford University Press.

SKEELS, H.M. (1966) 'Adult status of children with contrasting early life experiences', *Monogr. Soc. Res. Child Develop.*, 31 (3), no. 105.

SKUSE, D. (1984a) 'Extreme deprivation in early childhood: I. Diverse outcomes for three siblings from an extraordinary family', *J. Child Psychol. Psychiat.*, 25, 523–41.

SKUSE, D. (1984b) 'Extreme deprivation in early childhood: II. Theoretical issues and a comparative review', *J. Child Psychol. Psychiat.*, 25, 543–72.

SMITH, M. (1983) 'Lead, intelligence and behaviour', paper presented to Association for Child Psychology and Psychiatry, London, January.

VANDENBERG, S. (1971) 'What do we know today about the inheritance of intelligence and how do we know it?', in R.C. CANCRO (ed.), *Intelligence*, New York, Grune & Stratton, 182–218.

WATSON, J.B. (1930) *Behaviorism*, Chicago, University of Chicago Press.

WILSON, R.S. (1983) 'The Louisville Twin Study: developmental synchronies in behavior', *Child Develop.*, 54, 298–316.

WINNEKE, G. (1983) 'Neurobehavioural and neuropsychological effects of lead', in M. RUTTER and R. RUSSELL JONES (eds), *Lead versus Health: Sources and Effects of Low Level Lead Exposure*, Chichester, Wiley.

YULE, W. (1984) 'Critique of "Exposure to lead as an environmental factor in mental retardation" by H.A. Waldron', in J. DOBBING, A.D.B. CLARKE, J. CORBETT, J. HOGG and R.O. ROBINSON (eds), *Scientific Studies in Mental Retardation*, London, Macmillan.

ZAJONC, R.B. and MARCUS, G.B. (1975) 'Birth order and intellectual development', *Psychol. Rev.*, 82, 74–88.

ZIGLER, E. (1968) 'The nature–nurture issue reconsidered', chap. 5 in H.C. HAYWOOD (ed.), *Social-Cultural Aspects of Mental Retardation*, New York, Appleton-Century-Crofts, 81–106.

8

Psychiatric disorders

Andrew H. Reid

INTRODUCTION

Over the past twenty years there has been a change in concepts of care for mentally handicapped people (see Chapter 2). It is widely held that it is preferable for them to remain in the community, within either their natural or their foster families, and if this is not possible then residence within a small group or community home or hostel environment is considered preferable to institutionalization. Some advocates of community care policies maintain that all retarded people can be provided for in this way. The reality is that whereas most can be managed in the community, there are a substantial number who, by reason of physical dependency, psychiatric or behaviour disorder, require the resources and facilities of medical and nursing care in a hospital unit (Day, 1983). This whole question of appropriate services for the mentally retarded is discussed at length in Chapter 19. The diagnosis of psychiatric and behaviour disorders has, therefore, assumed a much greater significance, since they are a potential source of distress both to the patient and to his or her family, they may determine residential placement and they often give rise to major problems of management. Moreover, these disorders are frequently treatable and occasionally preventable. Their identification is, therefore, of considerable clinical importance (Reid, 1982).

For various reasons, mentally retarded people have an increased vulnerability to psychiatric illness. First, there is the factor of structural brain pathology. Nearly all severely and profoundly mentally retarded people have major structural brain abnormality, and substantial numbers of mildly retarded people may be similarly affected (Crome and Stern, 1972). The abnormality can be determined by a wide variety of agencies (see Chapters 1 and 4), including genetic causes as in tuberous sclerosis, infective causes as in the rubella syndrome, toxic causes as in the fetal alcohol syndrome, or related to trauma as in child abuse. Brain damage has effects on behaviour, personality, affect, memory, language and intellectual function, as well as on motor and sensory function, depending on the site, the developmental period at which damage was sustained and the nature of the process concerned. It may predispose to disturbances in levels of activity, irritability and noisiness, and to defects in social and emotional control. Given the present state of knowledge, some of the most pressing and intractable behaviour and personality problems one encounters, particularly among severely mentally retarded patients, can only be categorized as brain damage syndromes.

Second, brain damage also predisposes to epilepsy and it has been shown very clearly that the prevalence rate of epilepsy is increased in mentally retarded people, particularly among the most severely retarded and multiply handicapped groups where rates in excess of 50 per cent can be found (Corbett *et al.*, 1975). The overall relationship between neurological abnormality, intellectual retardation, epilepsy and psychiatric disorder has been demonstrated very clearly by Rutter *et al.* (1970). They showed that in the total child population in the Isle of Wight the overall prevalence rate of psychiatric morbidity was 6.6 per cent; where there were physical disorders not affecting the brain the rate rose to 11.6 per cent, but where brain disorders were present the rate rose to 34.3 per cent. The effect of epilepsy was shown by a further study of two groups, both with lesions above the brain stem. In the group without seizures the prevalence rate of psychiatric disorder was 37.5 per cent, whereas in the one with seizures it was 58.3 per cent.

Finally, there are the problems associated with the fact of handicap and its effect on lifestyles and interpersonal relationships. Retarded children and adults are vulnerable to the adverse social consequences of educational failure and social rejection. In childhood they may not be accepted as playmates by other children, and as they grow up they tend to be denied status and satisfaction. In adult life their employment prospects are poor and they are less likely to marry than their more gifted contemporaries (see Chapters 10 and 12). These social factors summate with organic brain dysfunction and family stresses to bring about a high prevalence rate of psychiatric disorder in mentally retarded people of all ages.

CONCEPTS AND SYMPTOMS OF PSYCHIATRIC DISORDER

There are, however, problems in formulating concepts of psychiatric disorder in mentally retarded people.

Psychiatric diagnosis and symptomatology are very substantially language based, but language development and vocabulary are usually limited in mentally retarded people, and more severely retarded patients frequently have no spoken language at all. There are difficulties, therefore, in gaining access to their thought processes, and to their ways of perceiving and interpreting events. All too often we attribute to them motivations and intentions which may seem logical in the light of our understanding of human behaviour, but which are, and remain, no more than inferences and assumptions. We also tend to overlook the insights into a severely retarded person's behaviour which are to be gained from sociology and other sciences such as ethology.

At the level of psychiatric symptomatology, phenomena such as thought disorder, hallucinations, delusions, ideas of influence and of significance, all of which are key concepts in the identification of psychotic illness, are entirely language bound and rely on a reasonable level of verbal fluency. As such it is virtually impossible to identify their presence in many severely retarded patients. This limitation of language also renders it very difficult for them to convey the nuances of meaning involved in such symptoms as obsessional phenomena, with the various aspects of the feeling of subjective compulsion together with a resistance to it and the retention of insight. On the other hand, symptoms such as change of mood in the direction of elation or depression can usually be picked up by a sensitive observer, even when the patient is unable to speak about it.

There may also be problems in evaluating the significance of items of behaviour which, in a normally intelligent person, would be construed as suggestive of mental illness, but which in a retarded person may be either developmentally determined or susceptible to an entirely different explanation. Symptoms such as self-injury and repetitive, stereotyped and manneristic behaviours can be particularly difficult in this respect.

Finally, there are often problems in interviewing mentally retarded people. They may not take easily to the interview situation with a complete stranger, and limitations in their powers of attention and concentration may mean that repeated short periods of contact are more productive than longer interviews. There may be difficulties in interpreting and comprehending rudimentary speech and language patterns, and family or care staff may be much more adept at interpreting. It is often necessary, therefore, to use media such as play, and it is important to make a longitudinal appraisal and to note changes in such observable parameters as facial appearance, social responsiveness, levels of activity, sleep and feeding patterns. It is also essential to complement the account from, and observation of, the retarded patient with an account from another outside informant who knows the patient well.

PREVALENCE

One of the main dilemmas in establishing prevalence rates for psychiatric disorder in mentally retarded people arises from the difficulty in defining what constitutes a case (see Chapters 2 and 10). Whereas it is possible to agree on the presence of disorder in the more florid examples of psychiatric illness, such as acute mania for example, it becomes far harder to reach a consensus in the milder forms of neurotic, personality and behaviour problems, where the patient would probably not be regarded as a case of psychiatric illness were it not for the fact that he or she is dependent on others as a result of mental and/or physical handicap. Many strange and eccentric ways of behaving pass without comment in the community and are never regarded as indicating psychiatric illness, provided that the person concerned is of normal intelligence and manages to live independently.

It is, however, important to attempt to establish prevalence rates since these

TABLE 8.1 Reported prevalence rates for psychiatric disorder in mentally handicapped patients

	Age range	Location	Percentage prevalence rate of psychiatric disorder
Leck et al. (1967)	All ages	Hospital	37
Williams (1971)	All ages	Hospital	58.8
Primrose (1971)	All ages	Hospital (admissions)	58
DHSS (1972)	All ages	Hospitals	32 (16% severe, 16% milder)
Ballinger and Reid (1977)	Over 16	Hospital	52 (31% significant)
		Community (ATC)	41 (13% significant)
Reid et al. (1978)	Over 16	Hospital	49 (severe and profound mental retardation)
Richardson et al. (1979)	Up to 22	Total Aberdeen population	46
Corbett (1979)	Under 15	Total London district population	47 (all severely mentally retarded)
	Over 15	Total London district population	46 (mild and severe mental retardation)

determine the range, type and extent of services required. Various investigators have accordingly tried, some of them using standardized definitions of psychiatric disorder. Studies have been carried out on populations of retarded people of various age ranges and degrees of retardation, both in hospital and in the community. The results of these surveys are summarized in Table 8.1. There seems to be a consensus that prevalence rates of psychiatric disorder are high in mentally retarded people, particularly among those living in hospital as opposed to nonhospital accommodation, and in those with the more severe degrees of mental retardation. Prevalence rates of around 50 per cent are reported in this population and among this 50 per cent are to be found some patients with functional illness such as manic depressive and schizophrenic psychoses, acute and/or chronic brain syndromes (delirium and dementia), and many more with neurotic, personality or behavioural problems, sometimes associated with epilepsy. A brief classification of these syndromes is provided in Table 8.2 and prevalence rates for the individual syndromes are noted in the appropriate sections of this chapter.

TABLE 8.2 Classification of the major psychiatric syndromes in mentally handicapped patients

---

Childhood psychosis (early childhood autism)
Hyperkinetic syndromes
Affective psychoses
Schizophrenic and paranoid psychoses
Delirium
Dementia: childhood disintegrative psychosis
           psychoses of senescence
Neurotic, conduct and personality disorders

RELATIONSHIP BETWEEN BEHAVIOURAL PATTERNS AND MENTAL RETARDATION SYNDROMES

Research has also been directed at the possibility of a direct relationship between individual mental retardation syndromes and specific behavioural patterns. Attention has focused in particular on Down's syndrome, tuberous sclerosis, phenylketonuria and the sex chromosomal abnormalities.

Down's syndrome

The public stereotype of persons with Down's syndrome as friendly, sociable and fond of music does probably have some basis in fact. There are, however, many exceptions and these children are quite likely to show conduct disorders in childhood, sometimes as a result of psychopathological problems within the family consequent on the presence of a mentally handicapped child (Reid, 1980). For unknown reasons they seem less vulnerable than ordinary children to early childhood autism. In adult life they may develop affective or paranoid disorders but these often turn out to be prodromal features of a dementing process. This association between Down's syndrome and premature dementia is an interesting and wholly unexplained phenomenon. All, or nearly all, Down's syndrome patients over the age of thirty-five show Alzheimer-type neuropathological change in the brain at autopsy, including dense senile plaques and neurofibrillary tangles in the cerebral cortex and hippocampus (Burger and Vogel, 1973). They also show associated neurochemical and neurophysiological changes, including reductions in the cerebral neurotransmitter substances choline acetyl transferase and acetyl cholinesterase (Yates *et al.*, 1983). These changes are found in both trisomic and translocation Down's syndrome patients, but the presence of a normal cell line in mosaicism seems to protect the patient against their development. Less than half the Down's syndrome patients with neuropathological evidence at autopsy of Alzheimer-type neuropathological change will, however, have shown a clinical picture of a dementing syndrome in life (Ropper and Williams, 1980). This may to some extent reflect difficulty in identifying the presence of intellectual deterioration in patients who are originally severely mentally retarded, but equally it calls into question the assumption that there is a linear relationship between plaque and tangle count at autopsy, and severity of dementia. The presence of these Alzheimer-type neuropathological changes in the brain is reflected in a rising prevalence rate of epilepsy in Down's syndrome patients as they get older; large-scale surveys of epilepsy in Down's syndrome have shown an overall prevalence rate of around 6 per cent with a marked trough in early adult life rising to a peak of over 12 per cent over the age of fifty-five (Veall, 1974).

Tuberous sclerosis

Tuberous sclerosis was once considered to be associated with a particular behavioural syndrome suggestive of catatonic schizophrenia (Critchley and Earl, 1932), but the behavioural patterns in question are widespread among severely and profoundly mentally retarded adults in general, and bear no relationship clinically to schizophrenia.

Phenylketonuria

Phenylketonuria has been linked with a tendency towards persistent hyperkinesis, but again this behavioural pattern is nonspecific and widespread in severely and profoundly mentally retarded adults. Hopefully, with further progress in primary prevention of phenylketonuria, the question will become of academic interest only (see Chapter 5 for further details).

Sex chromosomal abnormalities

The other area in which there has been considerable interest is that of the gonosomal abnormalities. Unfortunately the results of research to date have also tended to be inconclusive.

In the field of intelligence, the consensus view at present is that the XXY chromosome constitution carries an increased risk of mild mental retardation and the XYY constitution likewise but to a lesser extent. In general, the greater the degree of genetic abnormality the greater the severity of mental retardation.

In connection with the psychiatric associations of gonosomal abnormalities it did seem likely, following the discovery in the 1960s of a high prevalence rate of the XYY syndrome among males at some top-security hospitals, that men with XYY chromosomal constitution carried a genetically determined increased liability to criminality. It has since been shown, however, that the XYY genotype is widely distributed in the general population and is fully compatible with normal development and socially acceptable behaviour patterns (Hook, 1973; Pitcher, 1975). There may be an association with slightly increased impulsivity but nothing more specific than that (Clark and Johnston, 1974).

Finally, the XO (Turner's) syndrome, which was previously thought to be frequently associated with mental retardation and anorexia nervosa, has now been shown to be of much less direct psychiatric significance (Nielsen *et al.*, 1977). See Chapter 6 for further details on sex chromosome disorders.

EPILEPSY AND PSYCHIATRIC DISORDER

As mentioned earlier (and in Chapter 5), epilepsy is particularly common in mentally retarded patients. In such persons it acts as an important but again mainly nonspecific factor contributing to the high rates of psychiatric disorder.

Once epilepsy is diagnosed the type of disorder should be established from the history, clinical features and electroencephalographic findings. A simple classification of the epilepsies is provided in Table 8.3, along with anticonvulsants of choice (Davidson, 1983). In general it is preferable, where possible, to control seizures with a single drug and polypharmacy is to be avoided. Control can often be facilitated by monitoring serum anticonvulsant levels, a procedure which is now widely available. With phenytoin there may be trouble with gum hyperplasia, a megaloblastic anaemia and neurological side effects including ataxia, which may become chronic. Hirsutism, acne and facial coarsening can make phenytoin unacceptable to younger female patients. Valproate is relatively free of side effects although oesophageal discomfort, nausea and diarrhoea can occur. Platelet numbers and adhesiveness may be reduced, resulting in a tendency towards bleeding, but the drug is relatively free of unwanted sedative side effects. The principal side effects limiting its usefulness are the rare idiosyncratic responses producing severe or fatal hepatotoxicity,

TABLE 8.3 Classification of the epilepsies with anticonvulsants of choice

Type	Anticonvulsant	
	1st choice	2nd choice
Generalized epilepsy	Valproate	Clonazepam
Grand mal (tonic/clonic)	Phenytoin	Phenobarbitone
	Carbamazepine	Primidone
Petit mal (absence)	Ethosuximide	Valproate
		Clonazepam
Myoclonus	Valproate	Nitrazepam
	Clonazepam	
Combined grand mal and	Valproate	Clonazepam,
petit mal/myoclonus		Ethosuximide,
		plus Phenytoin
		Carbamazepine
		or Nitrazepam
Partial seizures (including	Carbamazepine	Clonazepam
temporal lobe and Jacksonian)	Phenytoin	Valproate
		Phenobarbitone
		Primidone
Status epilepticus	Intravenous	Intravenous
	Diazepam or	Chlormethiazole
	Clonazepam	or Phenytoin
		Intramuscular
		Paraldelyde
		Intravenous
		Thiopentone

particularly in children with pre-existing neurological disorders. The barbiturates (phenobarbitone and primidone) may bring about increased irritability and restlessness, are sometimes implicated in childhood behaviour disorders and may significantly impair learning ability in younger patients. The main adverse side effects of carbamazepine are on the central nervous system and include drowsiness, dizziness, ataxia and nystagmus.

For status epilepticus intravenous diazepam or clonazepam are the treatments of choice. In the event of control not being achieved with these drugs, intravenous chlormethiazole or phenytoin are alternatives. Refractory status epilepticus can be treated with intravenous thiopentone but this is a drastic remedy requiring artificial ventilation and the back-up of an intensive care unit.

Looking more closely at the association between epilepsy and psychiatric disorder, we can identify first those disorders which are associated with the fit itself. These can be further subdivided into pre-ictal, ictal and post-ictal phenomena. Pre-ictal disturbances include prodromes. Some epileptics experience and can describe prodromal feelings of mounting tension and irritability over the day or so prior to a fit, and the seizure when it comes may act to 'clear the air'. Auras properly constitute the preliminary part of the fit itself and may or may not lead to a major generalized seizure with tonic/clonic progression. They may include complex hallucinatory phenomena, déjà vu and déjà vécu experiences, paroxysmal disturbances of speech, and occasionally states of acute anxiety, depression, fear and even ecstasy. In temporal lobe epilepsy seizures are characterized by clouding rather than by loss of consciousness, and complex automatic actions including fugues for which the patient has impaired or absent subsequent recollection may occur. Petit mal status can present with a picture suggestive of a confusional state. Confusional symptoms and disturbed behaviour including aggressiveness are occasionally encountered in the post-ictal state.

There are, second, persistent or chronic disorders which are present in the inter-ictal period. Among these are abnormalities of personality which have been linked in particular with temporal lobe epilepsy: rigidity and egocentricity, moodiness and irritability, a proclivity towards outbursts of rage and resentment, pedantry, circumstantiality, argumentativeness and religiosity. The existence of the so-called epileptic personality has been challenged as an artefact of institutionally based studies (Tizard, 1962), but even so the evidence cannot be entirely dismissed (Geschwind, 1979). There seems to be an association between schizophreniform psychosis and epilepsy (especially temporal lobe epilepsy) but there is still some doubt over whether the relationship is coincidental or causal, particularly in the field of mental handicap. The association is said to be usually with left-sided temporal lobe lesions in patients in whom the onset of epilepsy is in the second and third decades (Taylor, 1971, 1975; Perez and Trimble, 1980). Severe and uncontrolled grand mal epilepsy can also produce in adults a state of epileptic dementia; when this occurs in children the dementia so produced is equivalent to a state of severe mental retardation. Epilepsy may be associated with aggressiveness (Betts *et al.*, 1976) and with depression, and we know that there is a fourfold increase in the rate of suicide in epileptics as compared with the general population (Leading Article, 1980).

CHILDHOOD PSYCHOSIS (EARLY CHILDHOOD AUTISM)

Early childhood autism was identified by Kanner (1943), although there had been previous descriptions of children who were almost certainly autistic. Originally it was considered to be caused by abnormalities in the parent/child interaction, and it was believed that autistic children were potentially of normal intelligence. This laid a terrible burden of guilt and responsibility on parents, but it is now widely accepted that over 70 per cent of these children are indeed mentally retarded, often severely so, and that IQ scores obtained by them on testing in childhood are reasonably consistent through time and have considerable predictive validity (Rutter, 1983). It seems likely, therefore, that many of the observed abnormalities in the parent/child interaction are the result of the immense difficulties inherent in attempting to relate to an autistic child (Rutter, 1968), and there is no convincing evidence that any kind of deviant family functioning leads to autism (Cantwell *et al.*, 1978).

Early childhood autism can be defined as a pervasive developmental disorder which starts before thirty months of age, characterized by an autistic-type failure to develop interpersonal relationships, delay in the development of speech and language, ritualistic and compulsive phenomena, and the absence of delusions, hallucinations and schizophrenic-type thought disorder (Rutter, 1985). In most cases the child's development will have been abnormal from the outset, but in a few cases there may have been a brief period in which development proceeded apparently normally. The condition is therefore quite distinct from childhood schizophrenia which arises much later in childhood and presents with symptoms akin to those seen in schizophrenia with onset in adult life (Kolvin, 1971).

According to strict diagnostic criteria, the prevalence rate of childhood autism among the general child population is around 2–4 per 10,000, with boys being affected some three times as frequently as girls (Wing *et al.*, 1976). However, it is becoming increasingly apparent that early childhood autism represents a spectrum of conditions with relatively few children showing the nuclear syndrome and many more showing features of early childhood autism such as social impairments, repetitive behaviour and abnormalities of language and symbolic activities, either alone or in combination (Wing and Gould, 1979).

Early childhood autism may be associated with organic brain damage as found, for example, in infantile spasms (Riikonen and Amnell, 1981), rubella embryopathy (Chess *et al.*, 1978), and severe perinatal complications, but no specific neuropathological or biochemical associations have yet been identified (Coleman, 1976; Darby, 1976). The possible influence of organic factors is suggested by the development of epilepsy in approximately 30 per cent of autistic children at around the age of adolescence (Rutter, 1970; Deykin and MacMahon, 1979), with a higher percentage in more severely retarded individuals (Rutter, 1983). Recent research by Folstein and Rutter (1977) and Minton *et al.* (1982) has suggested that there are, moreover, important genetic influences in the causation of childhood autism, and family studies have shown a significantly increased prevalence of language and cognitive abnormalities in nonautistic siblings of autistic children.

When the diagnosis is made in infancy, the failure to develop preverbal and social communication can be very evident to an experienced observer or mother. During babyhood the lack of eye contact and failure to cuddle or come for comfort are apparent. In childhood there are abnormalities in the comprehension and expression of speech. Many autistic children are, and remain, mute, while others show pronominal reversal, echolalia and abnormalities in the intonation and timing of speech. This central language impairment extends to understanding and thinking, and lies behind the abnormal patterns of social interaction and the marked deficits in creative and imaginative play so evident in these children. The autistic child may show strange fears and fascinations; for example, fears of open stairs, or fascinations with the smell or texture of hair, or mirror-gazing. Insomnia, restlessness and screaming may occur. There may be abnormalities in visual perception which lead the autistic child to focus on the periphery of a picture or environment rather than on the whole. Autistic children also show complex, manneristic and stereotypic movements which are of absorbing interest to them and which are performed in preference to normal imaginative play. These stereotypes include finger-posturing, hand-flapping, rocking and twirling, rituals involving spinning and stereotyped play with such objects as a piece of wool or a strip of paper. In addition, autistic children show a resistance to change and a drive towards the preservation of sameness. Pain sensation may be dulled and self-injury such as hand-biting, head-banging or eye-poking may occur. Many autistic children have feeding difficulties and extreme food fads. Autistic adolescents may have normal sexual feelings, but their lack of social awareness may bring problems with inappropriate sexual behaviour.

A few patients show an apparent intellectual, language and behavioural deterioration in adolescence, although this tends not to be progressive (Le Couteur, 1984). More usually, in adult life, some of the most pressing problems tend to fade, including hyperkinesis, screaming, insomnia and self-injury, although the language impairment, resistance to change, abnormal preoccupations and stereotyped phenomena may prove persistent. The abnormalities in social relationships also tend to persist although there may be some improvement with increased social awareness, often towards late adolescence. Few patients progress to the point where marriage becomes feasible, however.

Follow-up studies (Rutter, 1970; De Myer *et al.*, 1973; Lotter, 1978) show that overall about two-thirds of patients with early childhood autism will remain severely handicapped and unable to lead an independent life, with many eventually being cared for in a long-stay sheltered residential environment. Around 10 per cent are able to cope with some degree of independence and regular paid employment, but very few become completely normal, socially integrated adults. There have been moving accounts of occasional patients with such a happy outcome, however (Copeland and Hodges, 1973). In general the most powerful predictor of outcome in adult life is childhood IQ and speech development by the age of five, with an IQ on performance tests of below around 50 suggesting that the child is likely to remain severely handicapped throughout life.

There is no reliably effective medical treatment for early childhood autism. Hyperkinesis, screaming or self-injury may respond partially to pheno-thiazines or butyrophenones, and a few patients seem to derive benefit from treatment with lithium (Campbell *et al.*, 1972). Stimulants are contra-indicated for the treatment of hyperactivity, however, as they may promote stereotypy (Aman, 1982). Insomnia may require night sedation. Good control of fits is essential and there is some evidence to suggest that the newer anticonvulsants such as carbamazepine can exert a beneficial effect on symptoms such as aggressiveness and overactivity (Reid *et al.*, 1981).

There has been some progress over recent years with educational and behavioural methods of treatment (Schopler, 1976; De Myer *et al.*, 1981). Structured and organized teaching programmes have been shown to be more effective than permissive approaches and regressive techniques, and Browning (1974) has drawn attention to the need to tailor communication to the level of the child's understanding (Kiernan, 1983). Behavioural techniques may also be directed towards promoting planned periods of structured social interaction, and to the reduction of rigidity and stereotypy (Murphy, 1982).

Finally, the importance of keeping parents and families fully informed and involved, and encouraging and enabling them to participate in their child's treatment, cannot be overemphasized (Mittler and McConachie, 1983). Families will also need practical help in such matters as baby-sitting, holiday and respite care, and with appropriate educational and recreational activities.

HYPERKINETIC SYNDROMES

Over the last forty years the concept of a hyperkinetic syndrome characterized by a chronic, sustained, excessive level of motor activity relative to the age of the child has gained popularity. It has been said to be more common in boys and to be accompanied in many cases by distractability, short attention span, disturbed sleep, excitability, temper tantrums and low frustration tolerance (O'Malley and Eisenberger, 1973). More recently the attention-deficit component of the disorder has been increasingly emphasized in diagnosis by the American Psychiatric Association. Aggressive and antisocial behaviour, specific learning problems and emotional lability have often been considered as part of the syndrome. Premature birth, perinatal abnormalities, temporal lobe epilepsy and diencephalic abnormalities have all been implicated as possible causes (Leading Articles, 1975, 1979a), and the hyperkinetic syndrome has come to be identified with the rather elusive concept of minimal brain dysfunction (Clements, 1966).

This concept of the hyperkinetic syndrome has latterly been challenged, however (Sandberg *et al.*, 1978). Attention has focused on the wide disparity in reported prevalence rates between the US and the UK (Rutter *et al.*, 1976), and Taylor (1985) has commented that the conceptual problems of terminology and diagnostic criteria are such as to require caution in interpreting any account of hyperactivity. It has been pointed out that the phenomenon of hyperactivity is continuously distributed throughout the child population, and that it is frequently a situational phenomenon with a motivational component. Sandberg *et al.* (1978) see hyperkinetic syndromes as more akin to conduct disorders. There is some consensus now, however, that there is a small group of children who show the phenomenon of pervasive overactivity in home, school and clinic settings. In these children the symptoms appear to start at an earlier age. They show more behavioural disturbance and cognitive impairment, they are more likely to come from families of low social class and the disorder is more likely to prove persistent (Sandberg *et al.*, 1980; Schachar *et al.*, 1981). Although claims for an overall association between hyperactivity and minimal brain damage have not been sustained (Taylor, 1985), the work of Ounsted (1955) has suggested that the symptoms of hyperactivity are sometimes associated with brain damage and temporal lobe epilepsy in severely retarded children.

The outcome of childhood hyperactivity is uncertain, particularly in retarded patients. Normally intelligent children probably remain rather impulsive and accident-prone, and Weiss *et al.*'s (1979) study showed that the commonest adult psychiatric diagnosis in such children turned out to be 'impulsive' and 'immature dependent' types of personality disorder. In a more retarded population, however, Reid *et al.* (1978) found that hyperkinesis sometimes persisted for many years, although it did fluctuate in intensity. In some patients it was accompanied by elevation of mood and presented with a clinical picture resembling chronic hypomania. In other patients the hyperkinesis waned during adolescence to be replaced by inactivity in adult life, whereas in others the restlessness gave way to aggression and antisocial behaviour.

A variety of treatment approaches may be tried. Stimulants are certainly effective in reducing restlessness and impaired attention but there is little evidence to suggest that they are effective in promoting normal social adjustment in the longer term (Taylor, 1985). Aman and Singh (1982) found that these drugs were ineffective in severely intellectually retarded children and Aman (1982) reported that they may increase stereotypic behaviour. Stimulants may also produce dysphoria and there is concern about their longer-term effect on growth. Tricyclic drugs in small doses may be effective in reducing overactivity, and likewise phenothiazines and butyrophenones, but the usefulness of phenothiazines and butyrophenones tends to be limited by drowsiness (Aman *et al.*, 1984) and by neurological side effects including Parkinsonian rigidity and tremulousness, dystonias and tardive dyskinesias. Lithium preparations and the newer anticonvulsants, in particular carbamazepine, may be of use when overactivity in mentally retarded patients is accompanied by mood elevation and aggressiveness (Worrall *et al.*, 1975; Reid *et al.*, 1981). More recently some success has been claimed for behavioural approaches aimed at increasing the attention and concentration span (Bidder *et al.*, 1978), and in children these techniques can be carried into the classroom setting. There is currently a great deal of interest in the possible role of food additives in promoting overactivity (Feingold, 1975), and various dietary approaches have been advocated. Their efficacy is hard to assess, since double-blind trials are hard to construct and placebo effects difficult to eliminate (Leading Article, 1979b). Additive-free diets may well be useful in some cases, however. Finally, environmental change and manipulation with the provision of space, suitable outlets, structured activities and recreation can be of very considerable help.

AFFECTIVE PSYCHOSIS

Affective disorders occur in mentally handicapped patients (Sovner and Hurley, 1983) and there may be an increased vulnerability, and an earlier age of onset, in them as compared with the general population. Point prevalence rates of around 1.5 per cent for an episode of affective psychosis in retarded patients have been reported from hospital surveys by Reid (1972) and Heaton-Ward (1977).

Episodes of affective disorder may be related to such apparent precipitating events as childbirth, bereavement, viral infections including influenza and hepatitis, glandular fever, brain pathology and cerebral arteriosclerosis. In some patients there seems to be a psychogenic precipitant, but in many the illness seems endogenously determined. An affective disorder may occur once only or the illness may run a relapsing course with recurrent episodes of depression, mania or both. Depression is more common than mania, although this tendency may not be as marked as in patients of normal intelligence. In severely retarded patients the disorder may run a regularly cyclical course. Fig. 8.1 shows such a pattern in the psychosis in a profoundly mentally retarded female with arrested Schilder's disease, in whom alternating episodes of mania and of depression occurred at regular eight-week intervals, and were associated with fluctuations in temperature, pulse rate and sleep patterns (Reid and Naylor, 1976).

Diagnosis is based on the usual clinical grounds of change in mood accompanied by corresponding alterations in psychomotor activity and thought processes. In mentally retarded patients who are verbally fluent the diagnosis should present few problems; in more severely mentally retarded patients who may have little or no language the diagnosis is more difficult and relies on careful observation by relatives or care staff who know the patient well and who can sense abnormalities of affect. These observations must be backed up by information about changes in such parameters as sleep, appetite, level of activity and social responsiveness.

Mentally retarded patients who are depressed may find it difficult to verbalize their mood state; they may complain more of being fed up than depressed, or they may present with aggressive or irritable behaviour, with regression or with prominent somatic and hysterical symptoms. In mildly mentally retarded patients who are depressed there may be florid, affectively loaded delusions and hallucinations, ideas of guilt or failure leading to suicide or attempted suicide, diurnal variation of mood and sleep disturbance, usually in the direction of decrease but occasionally of increase.

Mentally handicapped patients suffering from mania may present with an unusual clinical picture. As a result of the limitation in verbal ability, wit and humour may be conspicuously lacking, and flight of ideas, clang associations

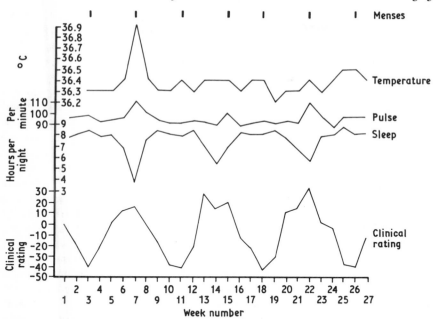

FIGURE 8.1   Regularly cyclical affective psychosis in a profoundly mentally retarded adult female

and rhyming may be rudimentary. Mood elation may be poorly sustained and replaced by excitement, irritability and restlessness. Some patients may behave in an assaultive manner. Delusions and hallucinations may be grandiose and wish-fulfilling, and there may be increased or inappropriate sexual activity.

Sometimes patients show a combination of manic and depressive symptomatology and in the resulting mixed affective state there may be an abundance of delusions and hallucinations together with some perplexity, suggestive of a confusional state.

Affective disorders may occur in patients with a wide variety of physical and neurological disorders, including epilepsy, but there does not seem to be any specific liability. The frequency with which affective disorders occur in mentally retarded patients with these conditions merely reflects the multiple physical pathology so often encountered in this population.

Affective disorders usually respond reasonably satisfactorily to appropriate psychiatric treatment, although the outcome depends to some extent on previous personality strengths and weaknesses. Depression usually responds to treatment with an antidepressant drug of the tricyclic group such as imipramine or amitriptyline. Side effects such as dry mouth, glaucoma, urinary retention in men, or drowsiness with amitriptyline, may pose problems and the dose needs to be titrated against response and side effects. Occasionally a manic swing can be precipitated by antidepressant medication. Other drugs which may be prescribed for depression include the newer tricyclics which have no clear advantages over the older preparations, tetracyclic drugs such as mianserin and, occasionally in appropriate cases, monoamine oxidase inhibitors such as phenelzine. In selected cases of severe depression, particularly where there is much anguish and suffering, or danger to life from food refusal or suicide ideation, electroconvulsive therapy may be the most effective and speedy way of bringing relief. Mania is treated in the usual way by drugs of the phenothiazine group such as chlorpromazine, or of the butyrophenone group such as haloperidol. These drugs have a rapid onset of action and are particularly useful in enabling quick control of manic overactivity. They are usually well tolerated in mentally handicapped patients but they can precipitate such neurological side effects as dystonic reactions, akathisia, rigidity, tardive dyskinesia and other Parkinsonian symptoms. Mania can also be treated with lithium, but this drug takes time to be effective and it is customary to combine it with chlorpromazine or haloperidol in the early stages. There has been anxiety in the past over the combination of lithium with haloperidol and there have been sporadic reports of irreversible brain damage precipitated by the combination. Although the association is by no means proven it is probably prudent not to prescribe lithium to patients receiving more than 20 mg haloperidol per day, and to ensure that blood lithium levels are not allowed to rise above 1.0 nmol/l in patients on combined therapy.

Along with specific drug treatment for mania and depression it may also be necessary to promote sleep through the judicious use of such sedatives as chloral hydrate, or a benzodiazepine such as oxazepam. Attention also needs to be given to the maintenance of an adequate nutritional state. In depressed patients, constipation may be a problem.

In the longer term, lithium is a useful prophylactic against recurrent attacks of bipolar manic depressive psychosis, and possibly also of unipolar recurrent depressive psychosis, in mentally handicapped patients. Unfortunately the response to lithium is frequently only partial and patients with rapidly cyclical affective disorders in whom episodes occur with great frequency rarely seem to gain satisfactory relief. Drug levels of lithium need to be carefully monitored and some brain-damaged mentally handicapped patients may not be able to tolerate a full therapeutic dose. The usually quoted therapeutic range is around 0.8–1.2 nmol/l but it seems increasingly likely that reasonably satisfactory control can be obtained at levels below this, of around 0.4–0.6 nmol/l, and these lower levels are often tolerated much better in brain-damaged mentally handicapped patients. Acute intoxication with lithium can give rise to alarming and dangerous side effects including nausea, vomiting, tremulousness, polyuria and polydipsia, weight gain, oedema, disturbance of consciousness, coma and even death. Possible longer-term side effects of prolonged treatment with lithium include hypothyroidism and renal damage. Notwithstanding these limitations, lithium can be a valuable drug in the management of recurrent affective disorders in mentally handicapped patients, if it is carefully monitored (Naylor *et al.*, 1974; Rivinus and Harmatz, 1979).

SCHIZOPHRENIC AND PARANOID PSYCHOSES

The interrelationship of schizophrenia or dementia praecox to mental retardation has been of interest to clinicians and research workers for many years. Originally it was considered that the onset of schizophrenia in the first few years of life could of itself bring about severe mental retardation and the term 'pfropfschizophrenia' was coined. The word was later used to denote a particular form of schizophrenia occurring in mentally handicapped patients and running its own distinctive course. It eventually came to have different meanings to different investigators and it has now been finally abandoned. There has also been controversy about the feasibility of diagnosing the various subtypes of schizophrenia (simple, hebephrenic, catatonic and paranoid) in mentally retarded patients. Some research workers have maintained that simple schizophrenia is particularly common, while others have stated that it is quite impossible to identify such a featureless and ill-defined illness in a mentally retarded population. Most now incline to the latter view.

There is some evidence from Swedish general population surveys to suggest that there is a modestly increased liability to schizophrenia in people of mildly subnormal intelligence (Larsson and Sjögren, 1954; Hallgren and Sjögren, 1959). Surveys of in-patient populations of mental handicap hospitals in the United Kingdom by Reid (1972) and Heaton-Ward (1977) have found prevalence rates of around 3.5 per cent, and it is clear that schizophrenia is a significant problem in the field of mental handicap.

Schizophrenic disorders may be of acute onset, perhaps with some clouding of consciousness as in the so-called oneiroid state, but more usually the psychosis seems to develop insidiously out of a previously unusual personality. It is sometimes possible to identify what seems to be a clear precipitating event but more often this is not the case. The age at onset of schizophrenia in mentally handicapped patients is similar to that in patients of normal intelligence (Hucker *et al.*, 1979), and is usually during the second and third decades of life. There is nothing distinctive about the natural history and it may run a chronic and persisting course or there may be prolonged remissions. It is to some extent responsive to environmental change and manipulation, and relapses are frequently related to emotional stress and tension, often within the family circle. With the passage of time patients may show a varying combination of hebephrenic and catatonic symptoms, or a residual defect state with impairment of volition and emotional blunting.

The diagnosis of schizophrenia is clinical and based on various symptoms which tend to be language based. The significance of these symptoms has to be evaluated against the background of previous personality, the mode of onset of the disability and the course of the illness. The main symptoms include ideas of influence, 'made' experiences, auditory hallucinations, thought disorder, primary delusions and abnormalities of affect and of motility (Batchelor, 1964). A degree of verbal fluency is required for patients to describe these diagnostic features and it is impossible to identify the condition in mentally retarded patients with an IQ below about 40. Schizophrenia may occur in more profoundly retarded patients who have no language, but in the absence of a convincing biological test the diagnosis cannot be sustained.

Mentally retarded patients with schizophrenia may show abnormalities of affect including incongruity or inappropriate cheerfulness. Some are socially withdrawn but others are surprisingly warm and accessible. Thought disorder is expressed in abnormalities of speech, but the significance of these abnormalities has to be assessed in the light of the patient's level of speech development. Ideas of influence and of self-reference may be dramatic, and delusions naïve and wish-fulfilling. Hallucinations tend to be of auditory type but may extend to visual, tactile and olfactory modalities. Some patients may be noisy, restless and impulsively aggressive (Reid, 1972).

Paranoid syndromes may be of various types. They may be of acute onset and associated with such precipitating factors as operations, infections or intoxication with alcohol or drugs. Under these circumstances the paranoid syndrome is more appropriately seen as originating in a toxic confusional state. An acute paranoid state may also be precipitated by intense stress in a vulnerable personality. Persistent paranoid schizophrenic syndromes, however, more usually develop slowly and progressively out of a previously abnormal personality and affect an older age group. In the early stages they may be characterized by anger, irritability and a sense of grievance and there may be marked depressive symptoms. Delusions may involve relatives, friends, neighbours or caring staff and be forcibly held. Voices may criticize, accuse, taunt or discuss, and there may be assaultive behaviour.

There are no proven associations between physical pathology and schizophrenia in mentally retarded persons. Schizophrenic disorders occur in patients with a wide range of neurological disabilities including epilepsy, and it is not clear whether the association between epilepsy and schizophrenia in mentally retarded patients is causal or coincidental. Paranoid syndromes are, however, known to be often associated with deafness (Cooper, 1976).

The differential diagnosis of schizophrenia in mentally retarded persons can be difficult. Isolated symptoms such as catalepsy may occur in the absence of other schizophrenic phenomena and should not be taken as indicative of schizophrenia; Plate 8.1 shows a severely mentally retarded female who would adopt strange cataleptic postures for long periods in the absence of any other symptoms suggestive of major psychiatric disorder. Some retarded patients seem to have a sustained and vivid fantasy life and these fantasies are recounted to the interviewer with a conviction suggestive of delusions. They may be derived from remnants of childhood thinking patterns or relationships, or they may have a clearly wish-fulfilling component: they should not be interpreted as psychotic phenomena (Heaton-Ward, 1977).

Schizophrenia usually responds in some degree to treatment with the

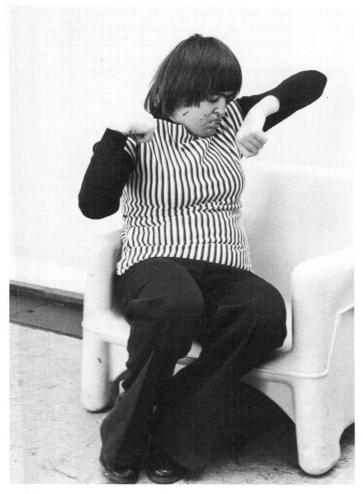

PLATE 8.1 Cataleptic posture in a profoundly mentally retarded adult female with no other symptoms of schizophrenia

phenothiazine group of drugs. Those most commonly in use are probably chlorpromazine and thioridazine, the longer-acting oral preparations such as pimozide, and the longer-acting injectable preparations such as fluphenazine decanoate and flupenthixol (Craft and Schiff, 1980). Chlorpromazine is usually effective in enabling rapid control of acute schizophrenic excitement. Butyrophenones have also been used, with varying success, in the treatment of schizophrenia. The management of the acutely disturbed schizophrenic also involves the use of a night sedative such as oxazepam, perhaps prescribed along with a phenothiazine to control nocturnal restlessness and induce sleep.

Phenothiazine and butyrophenone drugs carry the risk of side effects including skin photosensitivity, blood dyscrasias, liver disorders and such neurological sequelae as acute dystonic reactions, Parkinsonism, rigidity, akathisia and oculogyric crises. Tardive dyskinesias consisting of bucco-linguo-masticatory movements, and occasionally tardive dystonias, are emerging as troublesome and persistent side effects of longer-term phenothiazine treatment. Anticholinergic drugs which may be helpful in the Parkinsonian syndromes may actually be implicated in the genesis of tardive dyskinesias and dystonias. A further possible risk of phenothiazines, and particularly of the injectable preparations, is the development through time of depressive symptoms, and the clinician should be alert to this.

The treatment of schizophrenia also requires sustained and intensive efforts at rehabilitation once drug control of acute symptomatology has been gained. Patients are often subsequently left with defects in volition and social skills training, and behaviour modification programmes may help.

The outlook for schizophrenia has improved substantially over recent years, and many schizophrenic patients can now be maintained in the community, either in a family setting or, when the emotional involvement in such a setting is too high, in a small group home or hostel environment. Some patients will eventually be able to resume a completely independent life and cope with the demands of society, including a job under conditions of open employment. Others will require sheltered employment or day-care services. The successful maintenance of schizophrenics in the community demands support and sustained follow-up. This can best be achieved by outpatient clinics specializing in the aftercare and maintenance of schizophrenics in the community. Community psychiatric nurses are usually attached to these clinics and play a key role in them, monitoring progress, encouraging compliance, supporting families and other caring agencies, identifying early signs of relapse and maintaining contact with defaulters.

DELIRIUM

Delirium is usually the result of a temporary, toxic, biochemical process affecting brain function as in the deliria of fever or alcoholism. It is particularly common at the extremes of life. Clinically it is characterized by clouding of consciousness, which is usually worse at night, disorientation, impairment of memory, illusions, hallucinations (especially in the visual modality) and an affective change, usually of fear, although occasionally of euphoria. Attention and concentration are impaired. Paranoid misinterpretations and transient fleeting delusions are common. Behaviour may be severely disturbed and the patient is usually restless. There are often accompanying physical symptoms such as tremulousness, tachycardia, profuse sweating, dehydration, and chest and renal complications. Fits are not uncommon and the condition can be life-endangering.

There is nothing distinctive about delirious reactions in mentally retarded patients, the content of the delirium reflecting the patient's innate intellectual endowment (Wolff and Curran, 1935). Delirium can be precipitated in retarded patients by the usual factors including drugs, dehydration, uraemia, hypothyroidism, cardiac failure and chest infection (Reid, 1971). With the increasing tendency towards integrating retarded patients into the community, it is expected that a few mildly retarded people will manifest such alcohol-related problems as delirium tremens.

Treatment of delirium begins with treatment of the underlying cause such as chest infection and cardiac failure. In the delirium of alcoholism, vitamin B_1 by injection as parentrovite is widely believed to promote recovery. Treatment is otherwise symptomatic. Sleep should be encouraged by a sedative such as chloral hydrate or a benzodiazepine such as oxazepam. Daytime restlessness and excitement may need to be controlled by a tranquillizing agent such as chlormethiazole or chlordiazepoxide. The presence of fits may necessitate prescription of an anticonvulsant and nutritional and fluid balance need to be carefully monitored.

DEMENTIA

Dementia is characterized by a deterioration and disintegration in the intellectual, affective and behavioural spheres. It is nearly always progressive and occurs in the setting of clear consciousness. It is usually thought of in connection with the elderly but it can occur at any age, including childhood, when it is sometimes known as childhood disintegrative psychosis.

Among the progressive brain disorders which may be associated with the childhood disintegrative psychoses are the lipidoses, the leucoencephalopathies, the leucodystrophies and subacute sclerosing panencephalitis. Huntington's chorea, a hereditary neurodegenerative disorder combining a progressive dementia with choreiform movements, usually has its onset in adult life but may occasionally develop in childhood. Severe and uncontrolled epilepsy with frequent grand mal seizures and anoxic brain damage can be associated with a childhood disintegrative psychosis, although uncontrolled epilepsy may itself be a symptom of progressive brain disease. Some conditions, such as severe dehydration with gross electrolyte imbalance, lead poisoning, brain trauma or tumour, and measles, herpes, vaccinial and rubella encephalitis, can also produce catastrophic deterioration in intellectual function, behaviour, personality and loss of developmental skills. The dementia is not usually progressive once the underlying pathology is corrected or subsides, and in essence these nonprogressive disorders leave behind a condition of static childhood mental retardation.

Dementia is more usually considered in relation to the psychoses of senescence, in particular arteriosclerotic dementia and Alzheimer's senile and presenile dementia. The subject of dementia in retarded patients is important and becoming more so as the life expectation of mentally handicapped people increases. Community- and hospital-based surveys so far tend to suggest that,

TABLE 8.4 Mean age at death (years) of mentally handicapped patients in Stoke Park Hospital, Bristol

	All patients		Down's syndrome	
	Male	Female	Male	Female
1931–5	14.9	22.0	9.9	12.0
1976–80	58.3	59.8	55.3	52.7

Source: Carter and Jancar (1983).

with the exception of Down's syndrome, mentally retarded patients are about as likely as the rest of the population to develop a dementing process (Reid and Aungle, 1974; Tait, 1983). Table 8.4 suggests a marked increase in life expectation of mentally retarded patients in Stoke Park Hospital, Bristol, between the periods 1931–5 and 1976–80 although there may be other intervening variables, and Table 8.5 shows the prevalence rates of dementia identified in two surveys of mentally handicapped populations compared with one major general population survey in Newcastle-upon-Tyne.

Diagnosis is made on the usual clinical grounds including failure of grasp and comprehension, progressive deterioration in orientation, and failure to elaborate new impressions or to think in conceptual terms. Deterioration in thinking is reflected in loss of vocabulary, nominal dysphasia and perseveration. Eventually speech becomes grossly disorganized with both expressive and receptive dysphasia. Memory failure is initially most marked for recent events but progresses to involve more remote ones. Attention and concentration are impaired and the patient may fatigue readily. In the early stages there may be affective changes including anxiety, depression, agitation and hypochondriacal preoccupations. Organic lability tends to occur in dementias of vascular origin. There are changes in behaviour with the emergence of new and alien behaviour patterns such as disinhibited sexual activity, aggressiveness and attention-seeking hypochondriasis (Reid and Aungle, 1974). Hygiene and personal appearance are neglected, feeding habits deteriorate and incontinence of urine and faeces may supervene. There is a progressive loss of self-care skills in such fields as washing, bathing and shaving. Sleep patterns may be severely disrupted with some patients turning night into day. Awareness is impaired and judgement and insight are progressively lost.

The diagnosis of dementia in mentally retarded patients depends on eliciting a history of decline. For the diagnosis to be established, therefore, it is necessary to know the patient's premorbid levels of intellectual functioning, social competence and self-care skills. There may be difficulties in this, particularly in more severely mentally retarded patients whose previous level of ability may have been very modest.

The differential diagnosis and investigation of dementia in mentally retarded patients involves a good clinical history with particular attention to

TABLE 8.5 Prevalence rates for dementia in mental handicap

	Population studies	Prevalence rates (%) for dementia among patients aged over 65
Kay et al. (1964)	General population: institutional and community sample in Newcastle-upon-Tyne	5.6 (severe) 5.7 (mild)
Reid and Aungle (1974)	Total adult mentally handicapped hospital population in Dundee	13.6
Tait (1983)	Hospital and community survey of mentally handicapped adults in Aberdeen	10.0 (definite) 7.0 (possible)

the evolution of the disorder, backed up by careful physical examination to identify any neurological signs and such other manifestations as high blood pressure, uraemia and hepatic insufficiency. Chest and skull X-ray, full blood examination with folic acid and vitamin B_{12} assays, urea, electrolytes and liver function tests, precipitation tests and thyroid function tests should all be carried out. EEG examination, particularly if repeated over a period of time, may help establish the diagnosis: increasing and generalized slow-wave activity including delta frequency components is highly suggestive of a dementing process. Cerebral angiography may identify unilateral lesions such as a subdural haematoma, or clarify the vasculature of a tumour. Many of these neuroradiological investigations have been superseded by CT scanning which is noninvasive and which can identify with considerable accuracy the presence of brain atrophy.

Where a treatable cause of dementia can be established, treatment is directed in the first instance to the underlying condition, for example, hypothyroidism or conditions such as cerebral tumour or subdural haematoma. More usually no treatable pathology can be identified and treatment is then symptomatic and aimed at controlling insomnia through the use of sedatives such as chloral hydrate, oxazepam or chlormethiazole, and daytime restlessness through tranquillizing agents such as thioridazine. The maintenance of good physical health and the treatment of anaemia and urinary or chest infections may be helpful, and may sometimes serve to minimize the level of confusion. There is little point in attempting to reduce blood pressure in a patient with hypertension and established multi-infarct dementia.

NEUROTIC, CONDUCT AND PERSONALITY DISORDERS

It is uncommon to find conventional anxiety, obsessional and hysterical neuroses in mentally handicapped patients. Disturbances of conduct based on psychodynamic and interpersonal conflicts in the family, school or residential setting abound, however, and require elucidation and understanding. Classical psychoneurosis as observed in general adult psychiatry occurs rarely if at all (Forrest, 1979).

In the matter of obsessional neurosis it requires a degree of intellectual sophistication to experience and describe the various components of true obsessional symptomatology, including the feeling of subjective compulsion, the struggle against compulsion and the retention of insight. This sophistication is beyond all but very marginally mentally handicapped people and it is very uncommon to come across obsessional neurosis as such in a patient with a significant degree of intellectual retardation. On the other hand rituals, resistance to change and stereotyped patterns of behaviour frequently occur in mentally retarded people. These rituals should not be confused with obsessions. They are often deeply engrained, pleasurable, actively sought after and there is no component of distress or struggle.

Hysterical symptoms are common and sometimes gross in retarded patients. This is probably a function of increased suggestibility. In day-to-day clinical practice the meaning and gain of hysterical symptomatology is usually readily apparent. Often hysterical symptoms, including trivial hypochondriasis, are simply attention-seeking. This can be a difficult problem in the setting of a living environment which may be overcrowded, understaffed, unstimulating and lacking in the opportunity for privacy. Sometimes florid hysterical symptoms, including regression to an infantile level of development, occur in the setting of stress and threat to feelings of inner security. Hysterical symptoms may also arise on the basis of an underlying affective disorder.

Treatment of hysterical symptoms should be directed in the first instance towards eliciting their meaning and significance to the patient, and modifying and relieving any precipitating and perpetuating factors when that is possible. Where hysterical symptomatology is arising on the basis of an underlying affective disorder, treatment should be directed towards relieving that disorder through appropriate antidepressant medication.

Neurotic disorders characterized by states of disproportionate anxiety, fearfulness, depression and phobias are also common in mentally retarded people (Novosel, 1984). Phobias may be situation-specific as, for example, in school phobias. There is nothing distinctive about school phobia in a retarded as compared to a nonretarded child. The symptomatology is usually secondary to separation anxiety and may include a whole range of somatic symptoms such as stomach pains and morning headaches which miraculously disappear later in the day when school attendance has been avoided. Sometimes a phobia may be a very circumscribed phenomenon as, for example, in dog phobias; such phobias usually respond rapidly to a behaviour therapy approach using desensitization.

Adults with anxiety-based neurotic disorders may present with depression of mood, self-injury or with various types of acting-out behaviour related to an inability to verbalize their difficulties. Anxiolytic drugs of the benzodiazepine group may be helpful in cases where anxiety is a prominent feature, although the benzodiazepines can generate dependency problems and it is prudent to use them in small doses and for limited periods of time.

Retarded patients of all ages frequently present with, for want of a better term, a conduct or behaviour disorder. These disorders are often related to conflicts or problems in the family, school or residential setting. The psychogenesis may be apparent to the observer but can prove very hard to modify. They are often the outcome of attitudes and ways of relating and handling of many years' duration, and they may be very deeply engrained. Sometimes it is possible to intervene effectively, but there are times when admission to residential care is the outcome of a severe behaviour disorder.

Personality and temperament are important aspects of mental handicap about which little is known, and there are major problems in defining what is meant by personality disorder in mentally retarded people. One form which is fairly widely recognized, however, is that of psychopathic or antisocial personality disorder. Psychopathy is defined in terms of total disregard for social obligations, lack of feeling for others, impetuous violence or callous unconcern. The behaviour pattern should be such as to be regarded as abnormal within the peer or cultural group, and is not susceptible to modification through experience or punishment. Psychopathy is regarded as predominantly, but not exclusively, a male problem and this is probably so in the field of mental retardation also (Reid, 1980). By definition the term cannot be applied to patients with more than a mild degree of mental retardation since a certain quantum of intelligence is inherent in the diagnostic criteria. Some mildly mentally retarded psychopathic men may present major problems through sustained and seriously aggressive antisocial behaviour, sometimes including deviant sexual activities. They can give rise to serious management problems in any residential setting, be it home, hostel, mental handicap hospital, prison, secure unit or state hospital.

Personality disorders in retarded patients are not susceptible to curative treatment. Time may exert a beneficial effect, however, and many personality problems become less intrusive as the patient gets older. Management of personality disorders is difficult and demanding, and calls for qualities of insight into personal relationships, consistency, firmness or flexibility as appropriate, and imagination. Some nursing or residential care staff have an almost intuitive ability to handle patients with personality problems. Drugs have a relatively modest role, although phenothiazines may take the edge off irritability and aggressiveness. Good anticonvulsant drug control in patients who are epileptic is obviously important. Appropriate social and recreational outlets are required, and structured, interesting and worthwhile activity can go a long way to minimize management problems. Conversely boredom can result in the exacerbation of tensions and difficulties. For some patients a limit-setting approach may be necessary, with rewards and privileges tied to acceptable behaviour. There are times when containment is the only realistic goal, although more positive aims should be substituted as soon as possible.

FORENSIC PSYCHIATRY AND MENTAL HANDICAP

It is difficult to be precise about the nature of any relationship between mental retardation and criminality. Mentally retarded people tend to be suggestible and may, as a result, be led into petty criminality. They may be exploited by their partners in crime and led into taking the most risky role. They are probably less successful in concealing their actions, less effective in getting away and hence more likely to be caught than their fellow criminals. These factors would tend to overemphasize the connection between mental retardation and criminality. On the other hand the police may well choose not to charge a person who is obviously mentally abnormal and frequently take such a person home or even direct to hospital. Likewise, courts tend preferentially to seek a hospital admission. Against this background it is hard to assess the significance of reported prevalence rates for criminality among retarded persons. The situation is further complicated by ambiguities and uncertainties about the diagnosis of retardation at the borderline level of intelligence, and by lack of precision and consistency in many of the intelligence tests presently in use (see Chapters 2 and 3). Ostensibly it would seem that there is little direct link between defectiveness of intelligence and crime beyond sexual offences and arson in which it does seem clear from wideranging criminological surveys that mentally retarded persons are comparatively frequently implicated (Walker, 1968; Walker and McCabe, 1973; Gibbens and Robertson, 1983).

The explanation of the association between sex offences, arson and mental retardation is perhaps relatively simple. Sexual offences by retarded males are probably related to difficulty in finding suitable sexual partners, coupled with a reduced awareness and appreciation by the retarded person of the significance of his behaviour. A mildly retarded male is, for example, likely to have a normal sexual drive but to be an unattractive sexual partner for a normally intelligent female. He may find a retarded female partner and such relationships can be stable and supportive. Failing this, however, children may seem a more attainable and less daunting object of his sexual drive. Retarded women may be suggestible and gullible. They may be manipulated and exploited sexually and be vulnerable to casual sexual encounters and prostitution. Fireraising may be related to the combination of thrill and childlike fascination with fire, allied to a similar lack of awareness and insight into the potentially appalling consequence of arson. Sex offences and fire-raising in mentally retarded patients may prove persistent and repetitive and require careful monitoring. Most such offences are fortunately trivial, some cause significant distress or damage and a few are attended by disastrous consequences.

The other forensic aspect of mental handicap which has recently aroused interest is that of the retarded person's ability to cope with normal police interrogation and custody procedures. It is well known that many retarded people are compliant, anxious to please and will agree to almost any suggestion if the retarded person thinks this is the response wanted. This suggestibility can be a major problem in the legal/judicial setting where it is not uncommon for a retarded person to confess to an offence he has not committed so as to terminate a stressful interview situation, or in a naïve endeavour to please. It is imperative that there should be recognized safeguards for retarded people in the matter of court procedures involving them, and that these safeguards should be honoured.

TREATMENT APPROACHES

There are some fairly well-established psychopharmacological treatment approaches to the main functional and organic psychoses in mentally handicapped patients: these are in the main unremarkable and have been outlined in the appropriate sections of this chapter.

Psychotropic drugs may be helpful in the management of certain problem behaviours, for example, abnormal aggressiveness, in the absence of a recognized psychiatric illness. The phenothiazine group of drugs including chlorpromazine, and the butyrophenones such as haloperidol, can be of significant value in this respect. Lithium may also exert a nonspecific effect on aggressiveness and irritability (Worrall *et al.*, 1975; Dale, 1980), and there is some evidence to suggest that the newer anticonvulsant drugs including carbamazepine may have a place in treatment (Reid *et al.*, 1981). The danger lies in the temptation to use drugs of these groups to control behaviour problems which are related to unsatisfactory living conditions and an unstimulating environment. In such circumstances the main thrust of treatment should be towards the improvement of these living conditions, but this is not always possible within the constraints of limited resources. In general terms it is good practice in the field of mental retardation to use psychotropic drugs sparingly, at minimal dose levels, and to keep their continuing prescription under regular review (Kirman, 1975).

There is also scope for far more psychotherapeutic input than has previously been considered possible. Individual in-depth analytical psychotherapy is probably inappropriate in view of the limitation in intellectual capacity, but simple group therapy, and the harnessing of peer-group pressures, can go a long way to minimizing socially unacceptable behaviour. It is also possible in the group setting to explore a wide range of topics related to independent living, such as financial management, housing, sexuality and the use of leisure time. Psychodynamic insights in the family setting may complement behaviour therapy, whereas each in isolation may be ineffective.

Behavioural treatments are also making a significant contribution to the management of disturbed behaviour in mentally retarded patients. Among the behaviour problems which can be approached through behaviourally based techniques are aggression, hyperactivity, stereotypy, self-injury and pica. The techniques used include identifying behaviour for acceleration and deceleration, enhancing attention span, rewarding an alternative activity, withdrawing socially rewarding responses to inappropriate behaviour, overcorrection, obliging a patient to perform an incompatible response, isolation and the use of time-out and aversion (Yule and Carr, 1980). Helpful though these techniques are, none has proved reliable in all cases. The problem behaviour is rarely eliminated completely in the training situation and the improvement may fail to generalize satisfactorily to the less structured living environment. There are also ethical problems in the use of aversion techniques (Corbett, 1975). Even so, behavioural insights have made a valuable contribution to the understanding and management of psychiatric and behaviour problems in mentally handicapped people (see Chapter 13).

Any treatment approach has to be set against the context of the residential environment and the degree to which the mentally retarded person's rights as a human being are respected. All too often the residential environment falls short of acceptability and, far from enabling and promoting normal behaviour patterns, some living situations are positively antitherapeutic (Day *et al.*, 1974). It is against this background that the philosophies of normalization and personalization, and the advocacy movement, have taken root. These have been admirable developments and have contributed much to progress over the last ten years. At times, however, these philosophies have tended to become items of faith and unconstructively adversarial (see Chapter 1), but they have served to draw attention to the imperative need for a civilized living environment which is conducive to personal development and socially acceptable behaviour. In the absence of such an environment the impact of any treatment approach will be substantially diminished (Evans, 1983; Reid *et al.*, 1984).

The specialist therapist professions also have an important contribution to make to the management of psychiatric and behaviour problems in retarded people. Frequently retardation is accompanied by defective development of speech and language. Speech defects may serve to identify a retarded person as abnormal and can lead to ridicule and ostracism with much resulting unhappiness. Communication problems can generate frustration and tension which can be acted out in socially unacceptable behaviour. Speech therapy can sometimes help with these problems by enhancing communicative abilities, either directly or through the use of such nonverbal means of communication as Makaton and Blissymbolics (see Chapter 17), and through fostering a residential milieu which is communication based. Likewise, physiotherapy and the provision of suitable aids to mobility may enable a retarded person to partake of a wider circle of activities and social outlets, thereby relieving frustration and enhancing the quality of life. The specialist therapist professions have a direct and valuable contribution to make to the prevention and treatment of psychiatric and behaviour problems in mentally retarded people.

CONCLUSIONS

For various reasons, including the presence of brain pathology, epilepsy and pressures from both the family and society, mentally handicapped people have an increased vulnerability to psychiatric disorder. These disorders include the childhood psychoses, hyperkinetic syndromes, the main categories of functional and organic psychosis, and a much larger number of neurotic, conduct and personality disorders of varying degrees of severity. In the functional psychoses in particular there are reasonably well-defined psychopharmacological treatment implications, and in many of the other disorders clinical psychiatry has a contribution of varying significance to make to treatment and rehabilitation. It is important, therefore, to develop diagnostic criteria for psychiatric illness in mentally handicapped people. Psychiatric treatment must be informed by insights derived from other professional disciplines, including education, social work and psychology. Treatment cannot be divorced from the residential milieu in which it is delivered, and it is important for specialist hospital units to offer their residents a living environment which is conducive to normal, socially acceptable behaviour.

REFERENCES

AMAN, M.G. (1982) 'Stimulant drug effects in developmental disorders and hyperactivity: towards a resolution of disparate findings', *J. Autism Devel. Dis.*, 12, 385–98.

AMAN, M.G. and SINGH, N.N. (1982) 'Methylphenidate in severely retarded residents and the clinical significance of stereotypic behaviour', *Appl. Res. Ment. Retard.*, 3, 345–58.

AMAN, M.G., WHITE, A.J. and FIELD, C. (1984) 'Chlorpromazine effects on stereotypic and conditioned behaviour of severely retarded patients – a pilot study', *J. Ment. Defic. Res.*, 28, 253–60.

BALLINGER, B.R. and REID, A.H. (1977) 'Psychiatric disorder in an adult training centre and a hospital for the mentally handicapped', *Psychol. Med.*, 7, 525–8.

BATCHELOR, I.R.C. (1964) 'The diagnosis of schizophrenia', *Proc. Roy. Soc. Med.*, 57, 417–19.

BETTS, T.A., MERSKEY, H. and POND, D.A. (1976) 'Psychiatry', in J. LAIDLAW and A. RICHENS (eds), *A Textbook of Epilepsy*, London, Churchill Livingstone.

BIDDER, R.T., GRAY, O.P. and NEWCOMBE, R. (1978) 'Behavioural treatment of hyperkinetic children', *Arch. Dis. Childh.*, 53, 574–9.

BROWNING, E.R. (1974) 'The effectiveness of long and short verbal commands in inducing correct responses in three schizophrenic children', *J. Autism Child. Schiz.*, 4, 293–300.

BURGER, P.C. and VOGEL, F.S. (1973) 'The development of the pathological changes of Alzheimer's disease and senile dementia in patients with Down's syndrome', *Amer. J. Path.*, 73, 457–68.

CAMPBELL, M., FISH, B., KOREIN, J., SHAPIRO, T., COLLINS, P. and KOH, C. (1972) 'Lithium and chlorpromazine: a controlled crossover study of hyperactive severely disturbed young children', *J. Autism Child. Schiz.*, 2, 234–63.

CANTWELL, D., RUTTER, M. and BAKER, L. (1978) 'Family factors', in M. RUTTER and E. SCHOPLER (eds), *Autism: A Reappraisal of Concepts and Treatment*, New York, Plenum.

CARTER, G. and JANCAR, J. (1983) 'Mortality in the mentally handicapped: a fifty-year survey at the Stoke Park group of hospitals', *J. Ment. Defic. Res.*, 27, 143–56.

CHESS, S., FERNANDEZ, P. and KORN, S. (1978) 'Behavioural consequences of congenital rubella', *J. Paediat.*, 93, 699–703.

CLARK, D.F. and JOHNSTON, A.W. (1974) 'XYY individuals in a special school', *Brit. J. Psychiat.*, 125, 390–6.

CLEMENTS, S. (1966) *Minimal Brain Dysfunction in Children*, NINDB Monograph no. 3, Washington, DC, US Public Health Service.

COLEMAN, M. (ed.) (1976) *The Autistic Syndrome*, Amsterdam, North-Holland.

COOPER, A.F. (1976) 'Deafness and psychiatric illness', *Brit. J. Psychiat.*, 129, 216–26.

COPELAND, J. and HODGES, J. (1973) *For the Love of Ann*, London, Arrow Books.

CORBETT, J.A. (1975) 'Aversion for the treatment of self-injurious behaviour', *J. Ment. Defic. Res.*, 19, 79–95.

CORBETT, J.A. (1979) 'Psychiatric morbidity and mental retardation', in F.E. JAMES and R.P. SNAITH (eds), *Psychiatric Illness and Mental Handicap*, London, Gaskell Press.

CORBETT, J.A., HARRIS, R. and ROBINSON, R.G. (1975) 'Epilepsy', in J. WORTIS (ed.), *Mental Retardation and Development Disabilities*, vol. VII, New York, Brunner/Mazel.

CRAFT, M.J. and SCHIFF, A.A. (1980) 'Psychiatric disturbance in mentally handicapped patients', *Brit. J. Psychiat.*, 137, 250–5.

CRITCHLEY, M. and EARL, C.J.C. (1932) 'Tuberose sclerosis and allied conditions', *Brain*, 55, 311–46.

CROME, L. and STERN, J. (1972) *Pathology of Mental Retardation*, 2nd edn, Edinburgh, Churchill Livingstone.

DALE, P.G. (1980) 'Lithium therapy in aggressive mentally subnormal patients', *Brit. J. Psychiat.*, 137, 469–74.

DARBY, J.K. (1976) 'Neuropathologic aspects of psychosis in children', *J. Autism Child. Schiz.*, 6, 339–52.

DAVIDSON, D.L.W. (1983) 'Anticonvulsant drugs', *Brit. Med. J.*, 286, 2043–5.

DAY, K.A. (1983) 'A hospital-based psychiatric unit for mentally handicapped adults', *Mental Handicap*, 11, 137–40.

DAY, K.A., GORMAN, V., GWYN-WILLIAMS, R.H. and THOMAS, D. (1974) 'Subnormality at the crossroads', *Lancet*, 1, 622.

DE MYER, M.K., BARTON, S., DE MYER, W.E., NORTON, J., ALLEN, J. and STEELE, R. (1973) 'Prognosis in autism: a follow-up study', *J. Autism Child. Schiz.*, 3, 199–246.

DE MYER, M.K., HINGTGEN, J.N. and JACKSON, R.K. (1981) 'Infantile autism reviewed: a decade of research', *Schizo. Bull.*, 7, 388–451.

DEYKIN, E.Y. and MACMAHON, B. (1979) 'The incidence of seizures among children with autistic symptoms', *Amer. J. Psychiat.*, 136, 1310–12.

DHSS (1972) *Census of Mentally Handicapped Patients in Hospital in England and Wales at the End of 1970*, London, HMSO.

EVANS, D.P. (1983) *The Lives of Mentally Retarded People*, Colorado, Westview Press.

FEINGOLD, B.F. (1975) 'Hyperkinesis and learning disabilities linked to artificial food flavors and colors', *Amer. J. Nursing*, 75, 797–803.

FOLSTEIN, S. and RUTTER, M. (1977) 'Infantile autism: a genetic study of 21 twin pairs', *J. Child Psychol. Psychiat.*, 18, 297–321.

FORREST, A.D. (1979) 'Neurosis in the mentally handicapped', in F.E. JAMES and R.P. SNAITH (eds), *Psychiatric Illness and Mental Handicap*, London,

Gaskell Press.

GESCHWIND, N. (1979) 'Behavioural changes in temporal lobe epilepsy', *Psychol. Med.*, 9, 217–19.

GIBBENS, T.C.N. and ROBERTSON, G. (1983) 'A survey of the criminal careers of hospital order patients', *Brit. J. Psychiat.*, 143, 362–9.

HALLGREN, B. and SJÖGREN, T. (1959). 'A clinical and genetico-statistical study of schizophrenia and low-grade mental deficiency in a large Swedish rural population', *Acta Psychiat. Neurol. Scand.*, Supplement 140, Copenhagen, Munksgaard.

HEATON-WARD, A. (1977) 'Psychosis in mental handicap', *Brit. J. Psychiat.*, 130, 525–33.

HOOK, E.B. (1973) 'Behavioural implications of the XYY genotype', *Science*, 179, 139–50.

HUCKER, S.J. DAY, K., GEORGE, S. and ROTH, M. (1979) 'Psychosis in mentally handicapped adults', in F.E. JAMES and R.P. SNAITH (eds), *Psychiatric Illness and Mental Handicap*, London, Gaskell Press.

KANNER, L. (1943) 'Autistic disturbances of affective contact', *Nerv. Child*, 2, 217–50.

KAY, D.W.K., BEAMISH, P. and ROTH, M. (1964) 'Old age mental disorders in Newcastle-upon-Tyne: I. A study of prevalence', *Brit. J. Psychiat.*, 110, 146–58.

KIERNAN, C. (1983) 'The use of non-social communication techniques with autistic individuals', *J. Child Psychol. Psychiat.*, 24, 339–76.

KIRMAN, B. (1975) 'Drug therapy in mental handicap', *Brit. J. Psychiat.*, 127, 545–9.

KOLVIN, I. (1971) 'Psychoses in childhood – a comparative study', in M. RUTTER (ed.), *Infantile Autism: Concepts, Characteristics and Treatment*, London, Churchill Livingstone.

LARSSON, T. and SJÖGREN, T. (1954) 'A methodological psychiatric and statistical study of a large Swedish rural population', *Acta Psychiat. Neurol. Scand.*, Supplement 89, Copenhagen, Munksgaard.

Leading Article (1975) 'Hyperactivity in children', *Brit. Med. J.*, 4, 123–4.

Leading Article (1979a) 'Is there a hyperkinetic syndrome?', *Brit. Med. J.*, 1, 506–7.

Leading Article (1979b) 'Feingold's regimen for hyperkinesis', *Lancet*, 2, 617–18.

Leading Article (1980) 'Suicide and epilepsy', *Brit. Med. J.*, 2, 530.

LECK, I., GORDON, W.L. and MCKEOWN, T. (1967) 'Medical and social needs of mentally subnormal patients', *Brit. J. Prev. Soc. Med.*, 21, 115–21.

LE COUTEUR, A. (1984) Cited by M. RUTTER (1985).

LOTTER, V. (1978) 'Follow-up studies', in M. RUTTER and E. SCHOPLER (eds), *Autism: A Reappraisal of Concepts and Treatment*, New York, Plenum.

MINTON, J., CAMPBELL, M., GREEN, W.H., JENNINGS, S. and SAMIT, C. (1982) 'Cognitive assessment of siblings of autistic children', *J.*

Amer. Acad. Child Psychiat., 21, 456–61.

MITTLER, P. and MCCONACHIE, H. (eds) (1983) *Parents, Professionals and Mentally Handicapped People: Approaches to Partnership*, London, Croom Helm.

MURPHY, G. (1982) 'Sensory reinforcement in the mentally handicapped and autistic child: a review', *J. Autism Dev. Dis.*, 12, 265–78.

NAYLOR, G.J., DONALD, J.M., LE POIDEVIN, D. and REID, A.H. (1974) 'A double-blind trial of long-term lithium therapy in mental defectives', *Brit. J. Psychiat.*, 124, 52–7.

NIELSEN, J., NYBORY, H. and DAHL, G. (1977) *Turner's Syndrome – A Psychiatric-Psychological Study of 45 Women with Turner's Syndrome and a Control Group*, *Acta Jutlandica*, XLV, Medicine Series 21, Aarhus, Denmark.

NOVOSEL, S. (1984) 'Psychiatric disorder in adults admitted to a hospital for the mentally handicapped over a six-month period', *Brit. J. Ment. Subnorm.*, 30, 54–8.

O'MALLEY, J.E. and EISENBERGER, L. (1973) 'The hyperkinetic syndrome', *Sem. Psychiat.*, 5, 95–103.

OUNSTED, C. (1955) 'The hyperkinetic syndrome in epileptic children', *Lancet*, 2, 303–11.

PEREZ, M.M. and TRIMBLE, M.R. (1980) 'Epileptic psychosis – diagnostic comparison with process schizophrenia', *Brit. J. Psychiat.*, 137, 245–9.

PITCHER, D.R. (1975) 'The XYY syndrome', in T. SILVERSTONE and B. BARRACLOUGH (eds), *Contemporary Psychiatry*, *Brit. J. Psychiat.*, Special Publication no. 9, Ashford, Headley Brothers.

PRIMROSE, D.A. (1971) 'A survey of 502 consecutive admissions to a subnormality hospital from the 1st January, 1968 to 31st December, 1970', *Brit. J. Ment. Subnorm.*, 17, 25–8.

REID, A.H. (1971) 'Mental illness in adult mental defectives with special reference to psychosis', MD thesis, University of Dundee.

REID, A.H. (1972) 'Psychoses in adult mental defectives: I. Manic-depressive psychosis; II. Schizophrenic and paranoid psychoses', *Brit. J. Psychiat.*, 120, 205–12 and 213–18.

REID, A.H. (1980) 'Psychiatric disorders in mentally handicapped children: a clinical and follow-up study', *J. Ment. Defic. Res.*, 24, 287–98.

REID, A.H. (1982) *The Psychiatry of Mental Handicap*, London, Blackwell Scientific.

REID, A.H. and AUNGLE, P.G. (1974) 'Dementia in ageing mental defectives: a clinical psychiatric study', *J. Ment. Defic. Res.*, 18, 15–23.

REID, A.H., BALLINGER, B.R. and HEATHER, B.B. (1978) 'Behavioural syndromes identified by cluster analysis in a sample of 100 severely and profoundly retarded adults', *Psychol. Med.*, 8, 399–412.

REID, A.H., BALLINGER, B.R., HEATHER, B.B. and MELVIN, S.J. (1984) 'The natural history of behavioural symptoms among severely and profoundly mentally retarded patients', *Brit. J. Psychiat.*, 145, 289–93.

REID, A.H. and NAYLOR, G.J. (1976) 'Short-cycle manic depressive psychosis in mental defectives: a clinical and physiological study', *J. Ment. Defic. Res.*, 20, 67–76.

REID, A.H., NAYLOR, G.J. and KAY, D.S.G. (1981) 'A double-blind placebo-controlled crossover trial of carbamazepine in overactive severely mentally handicapped patients', *Psychol. Med.*, 11, 109–13.

RICHARDSON, S.A., KATZ, M., KOLLER, H., MCLAREN, J. and RUBINSTEIN, B. (1979) 'Some characteristics of a population of mentally retarded young adults in a British city. A basis for estimating some service needs', *J. Ment. Defic. Res.*, 23, 275–86.

RIIKONEN, R. and AMNELL, G. (1981) 'Psychiatric disorders in children with earlier infantile spasms', *Devel. Med. Child Neurol.*, 23, 747–60.

RIVINUS, T.M. and HARMATZ, J.S. (1979) 'Diagnosis and lithium treatment of affective disorder in the retarded: five case-studies', *Amer. J. Psychiat.*, 136, 551–4.

ROPPER, A.H. and WILLIAMS, R.S. (1980) 'Relationship between plaques, tangles and dementia in Down's syndrome', *Neurol.*, 30, 639–44.

RUTTER, M. (1968) 'Concepts of autism: a review of research', *J. Child Psychol. Psychiat.*, 9, 1–25.

RUTTER, M. (1970) 'Autistic children: infancy to adulthood', *Sem. Psychiat.*, 2, 435–50.

RUTTER, M. (1983) 'Cognitive deficits in the pathogenesis of autism', *J. Child Psychol. Psychiat.*, 24, 513–31.

RUTTER, M. (1985) 'Infantile autism and other pervasive developmental disorders', in M. RUTTER and L. HERSOV (eds), *Child and Adolescent Psychiatry: Modern Approaches*, 2nd edn, London, Blackwell Scientific.

RUTTER, M., TIZARD, J. and WHITMORE, K. (eds) (1970) *Education, Health and Behaviour*, London, Longman.

RUTTER, M., TIZARD, J., YULE, W., GRAHAM, P. and WHITMORE, K. (1976) 'Research report: Isle of Wight studies, 1966–74', *Psychol. Med.*, 6, 313–32.

SANDBERG, S.T., RUTTER, M. and TAYLOR, E. (1978) 'Hyperkinetic disorder in psychiatric clinic attenders', *Develop. Med. Child Neurol.*, 20, 279–99.

SANDBERG, S.T., WIESELBERG, M. and SHAFFER, D. (1980) 'Hyperkinetic and conduct-problem children in a primary school population: some epidemiological considerations', *J. Child Psychol. Psychiat.*, 21, 293–311.

SCHACHAR, R., RUTTER, M. and SMITH, A. (1981) 'The characteristics of situationally and pervasively hyperactive children: implications for syndrome definition', *J. Child Psychol. Psychiat.*, 22, 375–92.

SCHOPLER, E. (1976) 'Towards reducing behaviour problems in autistic children', in L. WING (ed.), *Early Childhood Autism*, 2nd edn, Oxford, Pergamon Press.

SOVNER, R. and HURLEY, A.D. (1983) 'Do the mentally retarded suffer from affective illness?', *Arch. Gen. Psychiat.*, 40, 61–7.

TAIT, D. (1983) 'Mortality and dementia among ageing defectives', *J. Ment. Defic. Res.*, 27, 133–42.

TAYLOR, D.C. (1971) 'Ontogenesis of chronic epileptic psychoses: a re-analysis', *Psychol. Med.*, 1, 247–53.

TAYLOR, D.C. (1975) 'Factors influencing the occurrence of schizophrenia-like psychosis in patients with temporal lobe epilepsy', *Psychol. Med.*, 5, 249–54.

TAYLOR, E. (1985) 'Syndromes of overactivity and attention deficit', in M. RUTTER and L. HERSOV (eds), *Child and Adolescent Psychiatry: Modern Approaches*, 2nd edn, London, Blackwell Scientific.

TIZARD, B. (1962) 'The personality of epileptics', *Psychol. Bull.*, 59, 196–200.

VEALL, R.M. (1974) 'The prevalence of epilepsy among mongols related to age', *J. Ment. Defic. Res.*, 18, 99–106.

WALKER, N. (1968) *Crime and Insanity in England*, vol. I, *The Historical Perspective*, Edinburgh, Edinburgh University Press.

WALKER, N. and MCCABE, S. (1973) *Crime and Insanity in England*, vol. II, *New Solutions and New Problems*, Edinburgh, Edinburgh University Press.

WEISS, G., HECHTMAN, L., PERLMAN, T., HOPKINS, J. and WENER, A. (1979) 'Hyperactives as young adults: a controlled prospective 10-year follow-up of 75 children', *Arch. Gen. Psychiat.*, 36, 675–81.

WILLIAMS, C.E. (1971) 'A study of the patients in a group of mental subnormality hospitals', *Brit. J. Ment. Subnorm.*, 17, 29–41.

WING, L. and GOULD, J. (1979) 'Severe impairments of social interaction and associated abnormalities in children: epidemiology and classification', *J. Autism Develop. Dis.*, 9, 11–29.

WING, L., YEATES, S.R., BRIERLEY, L.M. and GOULD, J. (1976) 'The prevalence of early childhood autism: comparison of administrative and epidemiological studies', *Psychol. Med.*, 6, 89–100.

WOLFF, H.G. and CURRAN, D. (1935) 'Nature of delirium and allied states: the dysergastic reaction', *Arch. Neurol. Psychiat.*, 33, 1175–215.

WORRALL, E.P., MOODY, J.P. and NAYLOR, G.J. (1975) 'Lithium in non-manic depressive: antiaggressive effect and red blood cell lithium values', *Brit. J. Psychiat.*, 126, 464–8.

YATES, C.M., SIMPSON, J., GORDON, A., MALONEY, A.F.J., ALLISON, Y., RITCHIE, I.M. and URQUHART, A. (1983) 'Catecholamines and cholinergic enzymes in presenile and senile Alzheimer-type dementia and Down's syndrome', *Brain Res.*, 280, 119–26.

YULE, W. and CARR, J. (eds) (1980) *Behaviour Modification for the Mentally Handicapped*, London, Croom Helm.

9

Neuropaediatric aspects of prevalence, aetiology, prevention and diagnosis

Bengt Hagberg and Gudrun Hagberg

INTRODUCTION

Mental retardation (MR) is one of the gravest and most common major handicaps in childhood and adolescence. It is often associated with other neurological impairments, thus underlining its close link with nervous system dysfunctions, defects and damage. MR is not a disease entity but a symptom with a broad range of aetiologies. Biomedical causes have long been known to be responsible for the vast majority of cases of severe mental retardation (SMR), defined here as an $IQ < 50$. That such causes are highly relevant also for mild mental retardation (MMR), defined as an IQ of 50–70, has recently been indicated from Swedish population-based studies (Hagberg *et al.*, 1981b).

This chapter considers neuropaediatric aspects of epidemiology, briefly surveys the panorama of biomedical causes and their distribution, draws conclusions about preventive measures, and provides some guidelines for a structured diagnostic approach in routine clinical work. Five Swedish studies, three on SMR and two on MMR, constitute the basis for the data presented here (Gustavson *et al.*, 1977a, b, c; Blomquist *et al.*, 1981; Hagberg *et al.*, 1981a, b). Related aspects are also considered in Chapters 4, 5, 6, 10 and 11.

PREVALENCE

True prevalence rates of a disease or a handicap are dependent on two important criteria – a strict and objective definition of the condition and a complete identification of cases in the population studied. Both criteria are difficult to meet when investigating MR, especially MMR.

Definition

When delineating MR, research workers aiming principally at scientific precision have different purposes and approaches from social workers in daily practical life. Consequently, different definitions and identification procedures are applied. We have chosen a definition based on the IQ as being the most objective, and providing possibilities for comparison between different populations, geographical areas and time periods. For research on school-age children, this approach to the classification of MR follows World Health Organization (1968) recommendations. Accordingly, MMR is defined here as being associated with an IQ range of -3.3 to -2.0 standard deviations (SD) from the mean of 100 $\pm$ 15, i.e. an IQ of 50–70. IQs below 50 are classified as SMR.

Ascertainment

To identify a condition completely, every individual in the population has to be examined. This is, with a frequency as low as that of MR, hardly feasible. More useful is to sort out, through a screening programme applied to all, those requiring further assessment. A third approach is that of the household survey, involving interviews. Its validity depends on the sampling of households, the competence of the interviewer and the set of questions asked. A fourth method is administrative ascertainment, the one commonly used when studying MR. It gives minimal figures and its value is dependent on the intensity of the search procedures. Multiple sources, not only registers for the mentally retarded but also hospital and other suitable settings, should be approached for information. We have found a combination of the screening and administrative methods to be the best applicable, taking into account available time and costs (Hagberg *et al.*, 1981a).

IQ distribution

The generally accepted basis for the IQ distribution in 10–14-year-old children has one normal and one pathological component (Penrose, 1963). The normal one has a Gaussian distribution with a mean IQ of 100 and an SD of 15. The pathological one, that due to organic impairment, falls mainly below -3 SD from the normal one. The two components give a theoretical prevalence of 0.3 per cent in the IQ range below 50 and 2.3 per cent for IQs of 50–70.

Consequences as to prevalence and ascertainment

It is important to emphasize that the problems of definition and ascertainment differ between SMR and MMR.

SMR

SMR is generally accepted to refer to IQs < 50. Its recognition, delineation and ascertainment should not, in the large majority of cases, be a major problem. SMR mainly comprises a pathological population, has little re-levance for the general IQ distribution and is predominantly independent of social class.

The prevalence rate and the main groups of known aetiologies have been delineated and are widely accepted. Many reports on causes have been presented through the years. However, most of these have dealt with institution-based series which tend to give an unrepresentative distribution. A

TABLE 9.1 Severe mental retardation: prevalence rate per 1000 by aetiology

	Drillien et al. (1966) Edinburgh, UK, n = 211	McDonald (1973) Quebec, Canada, n = 507	Laxova et al. (1977) Hertfordshire, UK, n = 146	Gustavson et al. (1977b) Uppsala, Sweden, n = 122	Gustavson et al. (1977c) Umeå, Sweden, n = 161	Hagberg et al. (1981b) Gothenburg, Sweden, n = 73
IQ	<55	<50	≤50	<50	<50	<50
Birth years	1950–6	1958	1965–7	1959–70 alive at 1 year of age	1959–70 alive at 1 year of age	1966–70
Ages	7½–14½ years old	8–12 years old	5–8 years old			8–12 years old
Origin						
Prenatal						
Genetic						
Chromosomal	1.7 (32)	0.9 (23)	1.0 (33)	1.0 (36)	1.4 (35)	0.9 (29)
Others	0.2 (4)	0.8 (21)	0.5 (17)	0.2 (7)	0.7 (17)	0.2 (5)
Unknown	1.1 (20)			0.6 (20)	0.3 (7)	0.4 (12)
Acquired				0.3 (10)	0.3 (8)	0.3 (11)
Perinatal (0–7 days of life)	0.7 (13)	0.4 (10–14)	0.1 (5)	0.3 (10)	0.3 (8)	0.3 (10)
Postnatal	0.5 (9)	0.4 (9–12)	0.1 (3)	0.1 (3)	0.1 (1)	0.4 (14)
Psychotic	0.1 (2)	0.1 (2)		0.1 (2)	0.1 (1)	<0.1 (1)
Untraceable						
With Ep/CP[1]	0.4 (8)	{1.2 (33)	0.3 (10)	0.2 (7)	0.4 (11)	0.3 (11)
Without Ep/CP[1]	0.7 (12)		0.4 (12)	0.1 (5)	0.4 (11)	0.2 (7)
Total	5.3 (100)	3.8 (100)	3.1 (100)	2.9 (100)	3.9 (100)	3.0 (100)

Source: Adapted to the classification used by Gustavson *et al.* (1977b).
Notes: 1 Ep = epilepsy; CP = cerebral palsy.
Figures in brackets = % of the series.

rather small number of population-based series have been published and largely comparable ones are shown in Table 9.1. There is general agreement on a prevalence in childhood of about 4 per thousand (3–5 per thousand) in developed countries, and that biomedical factors are the predominant aetiologies.

MMR

MMR is traditionally considered mainly to be of sociocultural origin and highly dependent on social class. To obtain complete ascertainment raises large practical and theoretical problems. The practical ones concern time, economy and labelling philosophy. There are different opinions between countries and at different times on whether labelling a person as MMR is of potential harm or value.

The theoretical problems concern definition. Should this be based on a fixed IQ range (where small changes in the general IQ distribution make a large difference in the prevalence) or on fixed SDs with a static prevalence of, say, 23 per thousand? Should IQ fluctuation over time be taken into consideration? Continuous changes in the mean IQ as well as in the SD have been demonstrated. Test restandardization of Terman and Merrill (1973) has shown increasing mental performance over time, especially in pre-schoolers. White Americans have been found to have gained almost a full SD over forty-two years and Japanese over twenty-four years (Flynn, 1982, 1984). Whether a measured IQ should be compared to earlier norms or later ones must be decided by each investigator, depending on the aims of each study. It is essential, however, to state the test used, when and where norms were established, and the year the testing was performed – so that comparisons can be made for time and place.

Prevalence figures for MMR differ markedly due to differences in criteria, search procedures and geographical variations. There are few population-based studies (Table 9.2), and the accuracy of ascertainment is often questionable. Our Swedish series gave a much lower prevalence rate than expected, 4 as opposed to 23 per thousand. Nevertheless, we consider the low prevalence found to be reasonably accurate. It would be fully explained by a shift of the IQ mean to 110–112. Such a shift would be compatible with the above-mentioned findings of a secular IQ trend, as the Swedish tests applied were standardized between ten and forty years ago. Terman and Merrill (1973) attributed the positive IQ shift to the impact of cultural changes. Our high proportion of biomedical origin, 40 per cent, would reflect a lowered prevalence of cases of sociocultural origin.

AETIOLOGY

System for classification of origin

From a neuropaediatric viewpoint it is logical first to classify origins of early neuroimpairments on the basis of when the defect or damage was judged to

TABLE 9.2 Mild mental retardation: prevalence per 1000

	Drillien et al. (1966) Edinburgh, UK	Birch et al. (1970) Aberdeen, UK	Hagberg et al. (1981a) Gothenburg, Sweden	Blomquist et al. (1981) Umeå, Sweden
IQ range	50–69	50–69	50–70	50–69
Tests used[1]	T, W	W	T, W	Not reported
Year standardized	Not reported	1949	1936, 1968	–
Search procedure[2]	A (multiple sources) S (test)	A (registry)	A (multiple sources) S (enquiry)	A (registry)
Prevalence date	July 1964	December 1962	December 1978	January 1979
Age (years)	$7\frac{1}{2}$–$14\frac{1}{2}$	8–10	8–12	8–19
Prevalence				
Minimum	5.3	5.4	3.7	3.8
Best estimate	6.3 (calculated)	23.7 (50–74 on screening test)[3]		

Notes: 1 T = Terman–Merrill; W = Wechsler Intelligence Scale for Children.
2 A = Administrative; S = Screening.
3 Moray House Picture Test of Intelligence. Year for standardization not reported.

have occurred, i.e. before, around or after birth (pre-, peri- and postnatal periods). The period limits used should be well defined as criteria quite often differ between obstetricians, neonatologists, neuropaediatricians and others. After that, groupings within each pathogenetic period by aetiology and according to strict criteria are appropriate. A description of the criteria for classifying cases in different aetiologic groups should also be given.

This kind of classification procedure is exemplified by the following model recently used by us (Hagberg *et al.*, 1981b) and found effective and simple. Five pathogenic groups were defined: I. prenatal, i.e. before the 28th week of gestation; II. perinatal, i.e. from the 28th week of gestation to the end of the 4th week postpartum; III. postnatal, i.e. after the age of 4 weeks; IV. psychotic; V. untraceable. A detailed aetiologic subgrouping was undertaken and the cases were referred to one or other of the groups according to a constructed ranking list (Table 9.3), in which any given factor had precedence over factors lower on the list. Data concerning the pregnancy, delivery and neonatal period were obtained from obstetric and paediatric case-records. Full details are given elsewhere (Hagberg *et al.*, 1981b).

Distribution of origin

Research concerning causes of MR has been performed mainly on institution-

TABLE 9.3   Ranking list of pathogenetic factors in mild mental retardation

Pathogenetic factor	*Pathogenetic group*
(1) Prenatal genetic	I
(2) Recognized syndrome	I
(3) Prenatal stigmata	I
(4) Embryo-/fetopathy caused by infection or toxic agent	I
(5) Defined postnatal cause	III
(6) Perinatal risk factors[1] and abnormal neurological syndrome/signs[2]	II
(7) Psychosis	IV
(8) Untraceable	
(a) with familial disposition to subnormal intelligence	V
(b) without familial disposition to subnormal intelligence	V

Source: Hagberg *et al.* (1981b).
Notes: 1 Fetal deprivation of supply, low birth weight, asphyxia, hypoxia, hyper-bilirubinaemia, polycythaemia, infection of central nervous system.
2 Cerebral palsy, hydrocephalus, clumsiness, severe visual loss, neurogenic hearing loss.

based series of SMR cases. Such surveys tend to give biased distributions of aetiologies. Analyses should be based on series representative of the *total* population. All cases traced should be adequately investigated with modern diagnostic techniques. The classification procedure must be detailed enough for differentiation between groups, yet simple enough to make allocation of a case to a particular group unequivocal. These requirements are difficult to fulfil, and a few surveys that do so are summarized in Tables 9.1 and 9.4 for SMR and MMR respectively. Parallel to the relative frequency of specific groups of origin, the prevalence per 1000 in the actual child population is stated. This makes it easier to compare these with other surveys even if the total prevalence rate differs substantially. As seen from Tables 9.1 and 9.4, the total prevalence of MR with a known or likely biomedical origin was 4.1 per 1000 in the Gothenburg series, which is more than double the prevalence of cerebral palsy in the same birth cohorts. Of the 4.1 per 1000, 2.5 had SMR, constituting 81 per cent of the SMR series. Two-thirds of them were grouped to the prenatal, a good one-sixth to the perinatal, and slightly less than one-sixth to the postnatal period. The remaining 1.6 per 1000 had MMR, constituting 43 per cent of the MMR cohort. In origin, a good half of these cases were prenatal, two-fifths were perinatal and a few remaining ones were postnatal. Associated major neurological impairments are well known to occur in about half of SMR children and were found in one-fourth of those with MMR in the Swedish series (Table 9.5). This emphasizes the importance of pre-, peri- and postnatal brain pathology as underlying not only SMR but also MMR. Interesting was the high rate of more 'soft' (minor) neurological findings in the Gothenburg MMR series, where a 'clumsy child' syndrome bordering on minimal cerebral palsy was observed in 23 per cent. Screening was also performed for behavioural, neurotic or psychotic deviations, and such psychiatric disturbances were found in 31 per cent.

ANALYSIS OF SPECIFIC BIOMEDICAL CONDITIONS

Identifiable chromosomal syndromes

Mental retardation originating from chromosomal aberrations diagnosed with original routine techniques (banding not regularly performed) had a prevalence of 1 per 1000 in the Gothenburg series, the majority having SMR. Children with diagnosed chromosomal abnormalities constituted 29 per cent of the SMR series in agreement with the approximately 30 per cent found in other comparable series (Table 9.1). Trisomy 21 (Down's syndrome) was the predominant chromosomal error and also the largest single variety of SMR. As the risk of having a Down's syndrome baby rises with maternal age and as there has been a successive change in distribution of maternal age towards fewer older mothers, a decreasing incidence of the syndrome can be expected and has occurred (Gustavson *et al.*, 1977c; Fryers and Mackay, 1979). However, owing to increased survival, a corresponding fall in the pre-

TABLE 9.4 Mild mental retardation: distribution of origin

Pathogenetic period	Drillien et al. (1966) Edinburgh, UK IQ 55–69		Blomquist et al. (1981) Umeå, Sweden IQ 50–69		Hagberg et al. (1981b) Gothenburg, Sweden IQ 50–70	
	% of series	per 1000 7½–14½ years old	% of series	per 1000 alive at 1 year of age	% of series	per 1000 8–12 years old
Prenatal						
Genetic	6	0.3	16	0.7	5	0.2
Unknown	}26	}1.2	8	0.3	10	0.4
Acquired			4	0.2	8	0.3
Perinatal	11[1]	0.5[1]	7[1]	0.3[1]	18[2]	0.7[2]
Postnatal	3	0.2	5	0.2	2	0.1
Psychotic	–	–	2	0.1	2	0.1
Untraceable						
with Ep/CP[3]	9	0.4	5	0.2	5	0.2
without Ep/CP[3]	45	2.1	53	2.2	49	1.8
Total	100	4.6	100	4.2	100	3.7
Total number	180		171		91	

Notes: 1 Perinatal period: birth to 7 days of life.
2 Perinatal period: 28th week of gestation to 28th day of life.
3 Ep = epilepsy; CP = cerebral palsy.

TABLE 9.5 Percentages of associated neurologic impairments in five Swedish series of children with mental retardation

	SMR Uppsala (1977)	SMR Umeå (1977)	SMR Gothenburg (1981)	MMR Gothenburg (1981)	MMR Umeå (1981)
Cerebral palsy	18	19	21	9	7
Epilepsy	30	36	37	12	18
Hydrocephalus	6	Not reported	5	2	Not reported
Severe impairment of vision	10	6	8	1	9
Severe impairment of hearing	3	10	15	7	2
One or more major impairments	42	52	40	24	30
Clumsy child syndrome				23	
Psychiatric disturbance				31	

valence among school-age children has not taken place (Fryers and Mackay, 1979).

The fragile X characteristic, with an X-linked recessive mode of inheritance (Lubs, 1969), has recently been revealed as an important marker of MR, particularly in boys (Sutherland, 1979). Blomquist *et al.* (1982, 1983) found that fragile X accounted for 4.5 per cent of MMR and 6 per cent of SMR in Swedish boys. Also 20–30 per cent of female carriers are considered to present with MR, usually MMR (Turner *et al.*, 1980). (See also Chapter 6.)

Refined techniques would probably have revealed additional chromosomal abnormalities. With present knowledge, chromosomal errors hence may be the underlying cause in 40 per cent of SMR or 1.2 per 1000 children, and in about 20 per cent of MMR with a biomedical origin or 0.4 per 1000 children.

Other multiple congenital anomalies/mental retardation syndromes (MCA/MR)

It has long been recognized that all series of MR contain a considerable number of various syndromes, more or less rare. These children have deviating physiognomies, which are peculiar and sometimes very characteristic; they also have other multiple stigmata of their hands, feet, ears or palates, and an increased rate of overt malformations. Opitz (1977) and his colleagues coined the term MCA/MR as a label for this whole group, which includes Down's syndrome and other now recognized chromosomal abnormalities such as cri du chat syndrome. The very broad panorama has been well illustrated in many detailed clinicogenetic syndrome reports from Wisconsin (Kaveggia *et al.*, 1975; Opitz, 1977). In fact, practically every series of SMR can be expected to include at least one so-called 'private syndrome', undoubtedly a previously undescribed MCA/MR condition.

Among the ever-increasing group of recognized MCA/MR syndromes, those of Cornelia de Lange, Prader–Willi, Sotos and Rubinstein–Taybi are examples repeatedly met in the literature. They have all been more or less suspected to have as yet undetected chromosomal defects as aetiology. In fact, Prader–Willi syndrome was recently shown to be associated with abnormality of chromosome 15 in about half the cases (Ledbetter *et al.*, 1981).

The proportion of aetiologically unknown MCA/MR cases in the population-based Swedish series comprised 12–20 per cent of all SMR. In the Hertfordshire series (Laxova *et al.*, 1977) the corresponding figure was 16 per cent. Among MMR children, such conditions are thought to be much rarer. However, in the Swedish Gothenburg MMR series, they constituted 10 per cent (0.4 per 1000).

Cerebral developmental abnormalities have been found in 25 per cent of autopsy series of SMR (Freytag and Lindenberg, 1967; Jellinger, 1972). Even if many such cases can be included in the clinically defined MCA/MR group, such percentages probably represent an overestimate of the actual proportions. One explanation of the high autopsy figures may be that malformations predispose to early death. On the other hand, developmental pathologies, particularly structural one, such as heterotopies, are underdiagnosed clinically. They may represent a proportion of 'silent' cases now defying classification.

Hydrocephalus and spina bifida as a cause

Hydrocephalus is due to different pre-, peri- and postnatal causes and is only to a limited extent associated with MR. The chronic hydrocephalic condition can, however, *per se* secondarily cause MR independently of its own original aetiology. By and large, this is valid also for *spina bifida cystica* which, through the connected Arnold–Chiari malformation, is associated with clinically obvious hydrocephalus in two-thirds of cases. The number of such secondary MR cases has decreased markedly with modern shunting operations. This, together with the low incidence of spina bifida cystica in Sweden, probably explains why no case of myelomeningocele was found in any of the Swedish SMR and MMR series.

Mutant gene conditions

Mutant gene conditions may show a more or less progressive deteriorating clinical course or be nonprogressive and nondegenerative. The predominating progressive subgroup is the one comprising inborn errors of metabolism.

Inborn errors of metabolism

The total number of known neurometabolic disorders is now confusingly large (see Chapter 5). Their contribution to SMR (4–5 per cent) and MMR (< 1 per cent) in recent Swedish series was, however, modest. Different metabolic diseases vary considerably in range and frequency between ethnic groups and countries, and also between different areas of a single country. Local concentration in certain geographic areas of Sweden is characteristic of, for example, the Norrbottnian type III Gaucher's disease, Sjögren–Larsson's ichthyosis-spastic diplegiaoligophrenia, and late infantile metachromatic leucodystrophy. A more even distribution is characteristic for other conditions: Rett's disease, globoid cell leucodystrophy, phenylketonuria, the mucopolysaccharidoses, and Spielmeyer–Sjögren–Vogt's juvenile amaurotic idiocy (Hagberg, 1981). By contrast, Tay–Sachs disease, a GM_2-gangliosidosis, and the predominating degenerative neurometabolic condition among infants in the United States with a heterozygote frequency of 1:24–30 in the Jewish population (O'Brien, 1983), is only exceptionally found in the Scandinavian countries.

Other mutant gene conditions

Nonprogressive conditions with classical Mendelian inheritance constitute 1–2 per cent among SMR children and less than that among MMR children. Examples are autosomal recessive microcephaly and X-linked hydrocephalus with MR. Corresponding progressive conditions occur with approximately the same frequency, about 1 per cent. The 'phakomatoses', particularly tuberous sclerosis, dominate this group.

Toxic embryo-/fetopathies

Fetal alcohol syndrome (FAS)

The complete FAS includes growth retardation, central nervous system involvement, characteristic facial dysmorphology and a history of maternal alcohol abuse during pregnancy. In incomplete FAS the children have clear damage but not the full syndrome. Most children are borderline retarded (IQ 70–85) but a wide IQ range is reported (Olegård *et al.*, 1979; Aronsson 1984). In the Gothenburg MMR series, complete FAS was found in 7 per cent or 0.2 per 1000 (Hagberg *et al.*, 1981b). The prevalence of incomplete FAS was less certain. It was estimated, however, that at least 10 per cent of Swedish city children with MMR – or 0.4 per 1000 children – would have the syndrome, complete or incomplete. Other experiences indicate that the prevalence is lower outside large city areas in Sweden (Blomquist *et al.*, 1981).

Anti-epileptic drug syndromes

Fetal exposure to hydantoins (phenytoin being by far the most frequently used) may result in the fetal hydantoin syndrome. This is characterized by a peculiar facial dysmorphism, specific craniofacial and skeletal malformations, retarded growth and MR. Such a full syndrome affects about 10 per cent of exposed infants. Three times as many may be partially affected (Smith, 1980). Similar prenatal teratogenic syndromes with MR as one of the key components have also been said to occur after phenobarbitone, primidone and trimethadione usage. In population-based SMR and MMR studies, cases with anti-epileptic drug syndromes are rare. No case was found in any of the Swedish series or in the Hertfordshire study (Laxova *et al.*, 1977).

Other exogenous fetal syndromes

Fetal syndromes with MR from chronic maternal abuse of various drugs, e.g. psychopharmacological ones and narcotics, may sometimes occur and appear in the literature mainly as anecdotal reports.

Fetal syndromes from intrauterine exposure to extensive radiation for maternal abdominal malignancy were seen in earlier days. There is one such third-trimester-damaged microcephalic girl in the Umeå SMR series (Gustavson *et al.*, 1977c).

Intrauterine infections

Only fragmentary and inexact epidemiologic data are available regarding this group of causes of MR. In the Swedish studies there were altogether nine diagnosed cases, all but two with SMR, of congenital toxoplasmosis, rubella, cytomegalovirus (CMV) or herpes simplex, the so-called ToRCH group. In a recent prospective study from the south of Sweden, Ahlfors (1982) calculated that 0.06 per cent of Swedish newborns, or some sixty Swedish infants a year, develop neurological sequelae from congenital CMV infection. The majority of these have isolated hearing impairments. Ahlfors's studies in Sweden and Peckham's (1983) in England indicate that CMV as an agent underlying mental retardation is probably a less frequent cause than previously believed.

Perinatal brain damage syndromes

Perinatal brain damage has often been overemphasized as a cause of mental retardation and has been a subject of much debate, particularly among neonatologists (Roberton, 1978). In the Gothenburg studies, the prevalence of perinatal risk factors in a broad sense – i.e. referrable to the period from the 28th week of gestation to the 28th postnatal day – as a cause of MR was about 1 per 1000 children. In low-birth-weight babies without complications, the risk of mental retardation seems to be low if there is good, basic neonatal care (Hagberg, 1979).

Postnatal conditions

Acute postnatal encephalopathy after extensive exposure to lead has been well documented. Permanent impairment of the central nervous system leading to MR may result (Perlstein and Attala, 1966). The risks of long-term moderate lead exposure are particularly high for newborn babies who absorb proportionally much more lead from their food than older children and adults. Where concentrations of lead in domestic water supplies are high, infants are at considerable risk of adverse toxic effects, particularly on rapidly developing cells, like those of the brain, during the first months of life. Reports of insidious effects on mental performance of long-term low levels of lead exposure are controversial and conflicting (Damstra, 1977; Moore, 1980).

A postnatal cause in terms of central nervous system infection or trauma was found in 0.4 per 1000 children in the Gothenburg series. The majority had SMR (0.33 per 1000 or 11 per cent of the SMR series). The proportion of postnatal causes in the SMR group was much higher in Gothenburg than in the other population-based Swedish series characterized by a combination of average urban and rural populations. It can be expected that accidents, the battered child syndrome and severe infections will be relatively more frequent in large city populations. Chapter 4 reviews environmental hazards in detail.

'Untraceable' conditions

In all SMR studies there are some cases where the pre-, peri- and postnatal history, as well as clinical and other examination, is unrevealing. The size of this 'untraceable' heterogeneous cohort of unknown aetiology depends on the extent of the diagnostic biomedical 'work-up' of each case, as well as on the criteria chosen for classification. In many surveys of SMR, proportions of 40–50 per cent have been given (cf. Moser *et al.*, 1983, and Chapter 1). With the criteria used by us, corresponding figures for the Swedish SMR series were less than 20 per cent, similar to the 22 per cent in the Hertfordshire study.

Part of this group probably includes undiagnosed genetic types of 'pure' MR (Becker *et al.*, 1977), such as autosomal recessive and X-linked recessive forms. The latter may partly explain the male preponderance in most MR series. Other 'untraceable' MR cases may be the result of noxious agents producing nondeforming brain deficits in a period of intrauterine life (6–11 weeks after conception) when the human brain is particularly prone to such a teratogenic tissue reaction. The agents known to cause deficits at this stage include viruses, radiation and probably also heat (fever > 39°). There are certainly other agents also, so far undetected (Hetzel and Smith, 1981).

Also in favour of biomedical factors causing MR in this untraceable group are the high rates of clinical symptomatology. Major associated neurohandicaps in the Swedish series were present in about half of the SMR, and in 10–15 per cent of the MMR, cases, i.e. about fifty times greater than in the general population.

ASPECTS OF PREVENTION

Some general biologic differences between SMR and MMR should be remembered as important for preventive approaches.

Severe mental retardation

SMR mainly comprises a pathological population. Changes in its prevalence have very little relevance for the general IQ distribution. Preventive projects have to be individually designed for specific aetiological groups. In this IQ category the greatest potential for prenatal prevention lies within the cytogenetic, inborn error, exogenous-toxic and intrauterine-infectious groups. Perinatally caused SMR is nearly always combined with cerebral palsy and preventive efforts should be related to the causes of that condition. SMR of postnatal origin ought to be accessible to further preventive measures. The role of traumatic injuries in city children deserves particular attention.

Mild mental retardation

The situation for prevention of MMR is somewhat different from that for SMR. Corresponding specific biologic brain pathology is represented to a much lesser extent. Nonspecific pre- and perinatal prejudicial factors may play a more important role than previously thought. It is reasonable to believe that biologic mechanisms for brain damage are of all grades of severity and operate throughout the whole scale of the genetic IQ potential. Each decrease in the severity or frequency of these mechanisms will therefore cause a shift towards better mental performance in the general population. Nonbiologic factors also contribute to the same shift. Terman and Merrill (1973) have shown an increasing mental performance over time, especially in pre-schoolers, and attribute this increase to the impact of cultural changes and increased parental literacy and education. Thompson (1977) found that this improvement occurs throughout the whole IQ range with the exception of the lowest levels (IQ < 50). MMR is known to be strongly associated with low social class. A combination of factors through all social classes such as family planning, good maternal preconceptional health, well-organized pregnancy supervision, good obstetric and neonatal care throughout the country and a general high socioeconomic level are all likely to contribute to a positive IQ shift. The most effective preventive factors are probably nonspecific related programmes for good medical, social and economic progress.

PREVENTIVE APPROACH TO SPECIFIC ORIGINS

The main MR groups of pre-, peri- and postnatal origin and the corresponding measures for prevention are summarized in Table 9.6.

Chromosomal errors and MCA/MR syndromes

Chromosomal errors are in principle preventable. However, with present-day techniques, it is not acceptable ethically or economically to screen all pregnant women for chromosomal aberrations of the fetus. A prenatal cytogenetic diagnosis – through amniocentesis or chorion villi biopsy – should be offered to selected groups, particularly older ones. Pregnancies where the father is over 55 years of age should also be considered, as older fathers may have a significantly increased risk of producing trisomy 21 offspring (Stene *et al.*, 1977). Even wideranging prenatal diagnosis would, however, not eradicate MR of chromosomal origin. Tizard and Lindenbaum (1984) calculated that a rate of amniocentesis of 70 per cent for mothers aged 40 +, 50 per cent for those aged 35–9 and 25 per cent for those aged 30–4 would result in a reduction in incidence of Down's syndrome by 23 per cent. A more effective early screening for trisomy 21 might be possible through development of a simple maternal blood test before the end of the first trimester. This is hypothetical at present, but an urgent subject for future research.

All MR cases with prenatal stigmata and MCA/MR syndromes should be regarded as potential index cases for further family investigations. When chromosomal errors are found, the mothers can be offered prenatal examinations in further pregnancies. Any finding of familial MR, especially in the absence of dysmorphic features, should lead to suspicion of the 'fragile X syndrome'.

TABLE 9.6 Pathology underlying mental retardation and preventive approaches

Origin	Preventive approach
Prenatal	
(− 28 weeks gestation)	
Genetic	Prenatal cytogenetic screening
Chromosomal errors	Index case diagnosis
	Prenatal diagnosis
Biochemical inborn errors	Neonatal screening
	Index case diagnosis
	Prenatal diagnosis
Unknown 'syndrome'	(Research)
Exogenous – toxic	
Alcohol/drug/chemical fetopathy	Education – school programmes
	Preconceptional information
	Tracing programmes
	Supporting programmes
	Pregnancy supervision
Intrauterine infection	
ToRCH group	Vaccination programmes
	Counselling
Fetal deprivation of supply	
Placental dysfunction	Pregnancy supervision
Perinatal	
(28 weeks gestation to 1 month of age)	
Asphyxia/hypoxia/infection	Pre-term birth prevention
	Fetal growth supervision
	Optimal delivery for actual state
	Optimal neonatal care
Postnatal	
(1 month of age +)	
Hypoxia/infection/	Child health supervision
brain injury traumata	Child abuse prevention
	Child accident prevention

Inborn errors of metabolism

Biochemically derived conditions associated with MR are in general more likely than others to have available some sort of *preventive therapy*. Dietary treatment of PKU cases from early infancy to mid-school age and the very early institution of hormone treatment for hypothyroid babies are classical examples. Other possible methods have been developed recently. Early-diagnosed cases of certain lysosomal diseases should be considered for enzyme substitution through transplants from a matching sibling. Successful results have been reported in mucopolysaccharidoses and Gaucher's disease (Svennerholm *et al.*, 1984).

Recent analysis of the Swedish *neonatal screening* programme for biochemical diseases, for the period 1965–79, showed that screening for PKU, galactosaemia and congenital hypothyroidism has preventive consequences and is thus justifiable (Alm and Larsson, 1981). Screening for histidinaemia, homocystinuria and tyrosinaemia was, however, shown not to be worthwhile, in either medical or cost–benefit terms. It is reasonable to expect that in the future more conditions will prove suitable for neonatal screening. Before such procedures are introduced routinely in any country, it is essential to know the incidence, the natural course and the possibility of treatment of the disease in question.

When the deficient enzyme in inherited biochemical defects is known, accurate *prenatal diagnosis* is now possible for many different diseases. A diagnosis followed by abortion of affected fetuses has long been invaluable for individual families. Such programmes cannot, however, influence the general prevalence of MR more than marginally until screening for heterozygotes is undertaken among selected populations in whom such recessive disorders occur with sufficiently high frequency. Nevertheless, a careful diagnostic work-up of the index case is essential as the background for advice on future family planning, i.e. prevention for the individual family.

Intrauterine infections

Effectively performed, mass vaccination programmes for this group are superior to all other preventive measures.

Congenital rubella infection

It ought to be possible to eradicate congenital rubella infection, with general vaccination of schoolchildren. General vaccination of schoolgirls (age 12 – grade 6) was introduced in Sweden in 1975. This programme, with 90 per cent vaccinated and 1 per cent loss of immunity/year, was expected within 20 years to reduce rubella embryopathy by two-thirds but not to eradicate it. Recently, therefore, a more effective programme for both sexes with a combined vaccine (measles–mumps–rubella), including a first injection at $1\frac{1}{2}$ and a second one at 12 years of age, was started (Jonsell *et al.*, 1981). A successful introduction of the programme, with 91.2 per cent coverage, has been achieved in Gothenburg (Taranger *et al.*, 1982).

Congenital cytomegalovirus infection (CMV)

This is much more problematic for a preventive approach. Vaccination against CMV is today considered of questionable value. Available vaccines cannot be expected to prevent secondary infections. Furthermore, they may have certain negative, particularly oncogenic, properties and may also result in latent maternal infections (Ahlfors, 1982). New approaches to vaccines, using DNA technology, may in the future improve prospects for effective preventive programmes.

Perinatal origin

MR of perinatal origin is usually associated with cerebral palsy (CP). In Sweden the incidence of CP increased during the 1970s, in contrast to an ongoing reduction in perinatal mortality (Hagberg *et al.*, 1984). Although this increase mainly comprised mentally normal CP children, the prevalence of perinatally caused MR cannot be expected to decrease until a fall in the incidence of CP has been achieved. At present, gains from advances in intensive neonatal care can be counted in an increasing number of surviving nondamaged babies, especially those born pre-term. For babies born at term, further progress in the prevention of prejudicial associated pre- and perinatal factors, such as fetal deprivation and intra- as well as extrauterine asphyxia, are essential.

Postnatal origin

Gains through prevention of early infections seem to be marginal in developed countries. In underdeveloped countries, however, postnatal infections are likely to account for a much higher proportion of mental retardation than is acceptable with present-day therapeutic possibilities. Traffic accidents, suspected 'battered baby syndrome' (subdural haematomata) and other violent head traumata tend to be relatively frequent in city populations. Preventive efforts should be devised accordingly.

EARLY IDENTIFICATION (DEVELOPMENTAL SCREENING) AND NEURODEVELOPMENTAL ASSESSMENT

For an accurate diagnosis of MR at the earliest possible age, three principal levels of medical attention are desirable:

1. *Early identification*, i.e. how to distinguish MR cases from other infants.
2. More detailed *neurodevelopmental assessment*, i.e. how to elucidate the quality and degree of delay.
3. Detailed neuropaediatric and *aetiological diagnosis*.

In this section the first two of these levels are discussed.

Early identification

The first step in understanding, effective handling and good care of children with handicapping conditions is early identification. Evident or suspected

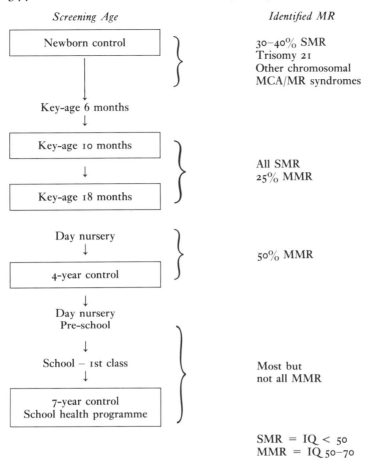

Screening Age   *Identified MR*

Newborn control   30–40% SMR
                             Trisomy 21
                             Other chromosomal
Key-age 6 months   MCA/MR syndromes

Key-age 10 months   All SMR
                             25% MMR
Key-age 18 months

Day nursery   50% MMR

4-year control

Day nursery
Pre-school

School – 1st class   Most but
                             not all MMR

7-year control
School health programme

                             SMR = IQ < 50
                             MMR = IQ 50–70

FIGURE 9.1   Cumulative proportions of identified children with mental retardation related to 'key-ages' suitable for developmental screening (B. Hagberg, unpublished observations)

cases of MCA/MR syndromes, due to peculiar and characteristic phenotypic deviations, can often be recognized in neonates. Others are successively found in an effectively organized well-baby service with rationally structured neurodevelopmental programmes.

Early detection procedures, commonly referred to as screening for handicap, imply simple yet reliable techniques routinely applied to large numbers of children in the general child health service (Rogers, 1971). Screening of infants for handicap differs markedly from traditional medical screening (Touwen, 1982) by being much more than just a positive or negative 'rapid slide test'. It is rather a quick but complex process of analysing developmental milestones and a systematic registering of deviating patterns of motor and developmental performance. This requires training and experience in developmental medicine. Comprehensive reviews and textbooks have dealt extensively with this important sector of paediatrics and child health (Illingworth, 1966, 1973; Egan *et al.*, 1969; Holt, 1977; Drillien and Drummond, 1977, 1983). Deviant findings in developmental patterns and a failure to pass relevant milestones mainly serve the purpose of 'drawing attention' and initiating referral for further diagnostic elucidation.

Ideally, all SMR infants should be identifiable before the end of the first year of life, and the lower IQ range of MMR children before the end of the second year (Fig. 9.1). To reach this goal, the use of well-chosen key-ages for intensive developmental screening is recommended (Egan *et al.*, 1969). In our opinion, 9–10 months and 18 months are particularly suitable key-ages for identification of major neuroimpairments.

Identification of MMR children in the upper IQ range is a later-presenting, more time-consuming and more difficult task. An approximate schedule for identification is shown in Fig. 9.1.

Standardized developmental screening tests for rapid structured evaluation have been devised. The test results are usually scored as normal, questionable or abnormal. One widely used is the Denver Developmental Screening Test (Frankenburg *et al.*, 1971). This contains many developmental items for the first year of life in percentile frames.

Neurodevelopmental assessment

For the paediatrician, the next diagnostic step is to perform a detailed neurodevelopmental assessment of the delayed infant referred after identification at screening. Such an assessment is a combination of a systematic developmental and neurological examination. The younger the infant is the more often traditional neurological techniques fail and one has to rely on developmental paramenters, because neurological manifestations may still be too undifferentiated and dependent on the stage of immaturity of the central nervous system.

A neurodevelopmental paediatric assessment is mainly based on:

1. Observations of spontaneous motor and other activities, with the infant undressed for inspection.
2. Registration and evaluation of how movements and motor developmental tasks are performed ('motoscopy').
3. Examination of neurological functions and reflexes by conventional means.
4. Screening of vision, hearing, speech and perceptional abilities.

Neuropaediatric developmental diagnostic assessment aims: to map neuromotor abilities and to relate them to chronological age; to elucidate deviations in the patterns of movement and to correlate abnormalities to neurological findings; and finally to give a synthesis of the whole impairment complex specified in its various components. The main components are tabulated in

TABLE 9.7   Key components of a neuropaediatric developmental assessment schema for infants and small children

I Motor function	Gross motor
	  ability – activity
	  pattern – performance
	Fine motor
	  ability – activity
	  pattern – performance
	  precision

II Neurology	Muscle strength and mass
	  (pareses; atrophies)
	Muscle tonus
	  (floppiness; spasticity; dystonia)
	Co-ordination
	  (ataxia; tremor)
	Movement dimension
	  (athetosis; hypokinesia; dyskinesia)
	Reflex pattern
	  (primitive remaining; age specific
	  attained)

III Language	'Inner language'
	  understanding
	Communication
	  activity – performance
	Own speech
	  ability
	Speech pattern

IV Social development	Play pattern ADL level
V Organ of sense function	Vision Hearing Perception

Table 9.7. Penetrating neuropaediatric analyses of infants' and children's developmental progress, anomalies and abnormalities have been given by Illingworth (1966), Holt (1977) and Egan (1978).

Standardized developmental testing for the early ages, performed by clinical psychologists, supplement the neurodevelopmental examination but do not replace it. Such tests give the age level of developmental achievements more exactly, while the neuropaediatric examination preferably elucidates the abnormal patterns of performance in relation to attained developmental levels.

EARLY NEURODEVELOPMENTAL PROFILE OF MENTALLY RETARDED INFANTS

Infants with a 'pure' MR syndrome, i.e. those without additional neurological impairments such as cerebral palsy, have a nonspecific generalized type of neurodevelopmental delay. The early profile is characterized by an even distribution over all developmental sectors: gross motor, fine motor, postural adjustment, perception, language and intellectual functions. This is in contrast to the profile of neuromotor disorders where dissociated patterns are usually prominent.

Illingworth (1968) showed, from a prospectively studied series, that only a minority of SMR infants could sit and walk at expected ages. A less marked delay was also found among MMR infants, less than one-fourth of whom were able to walk unsupported by seventeen months. Neligan and Prudham (1969) concluded, from a population-based study of four developmental milestones, that the combination of late walking and talking in sentences was a reliable early indicator of MR. Schmitt and Erickson (1973) emphasized combined delay in smiling and sitting as a most sensitive early predictor. Molnar (1978), in a series of SMR and MMR infants with no evidence of frank neuromuscular deficit, showed that the evolution of postural adjustment reactions was significantly and consistently delayed and of great temporal variability. This was in contrast to the primitive reflex pattern which largely did not persist beyond the expected age. Shapiro *et al.* (1979) stated, from their SMR study, that cognition is a less important determinant of the ability to walk than is basic neurological integrity.

GUIDELINES FOR APPROACHING AETIOLOGICAL DIAGNOSIS

The aim of this section is to provide general guidelines for *structuring* the diagnostic work-up in routine clinical practice.

It is essential to start with a thorough appraisal of the general clinical picture. A detailed history systematically covering genetic aspects and the pre-, peri- and postnatal periods, as well as the developmental course, can give rewarding clues for choice of diagnostic pathway. Particular importance should be attached to the 'profile' of the disorder. Is it of stationary type? Are there suspicions of deterioration and, if so, is this occurring continuously or stepwise? Have previously unnoticed neurological symptoms/signs, probably not explained by developmental maturation, been added?

The physical examination should start with a detailed inspection, especially concentrated on the presence or absence of deviations in general physical appearance (such as prenatal stigmata of the face, the ears, the hands and the feet), as well as obvious malformations. Together with a standard paediatric examination, this is usually adequate for recognizing about half of the SMR population, Down's syndrome included. Most of them will be found to belong

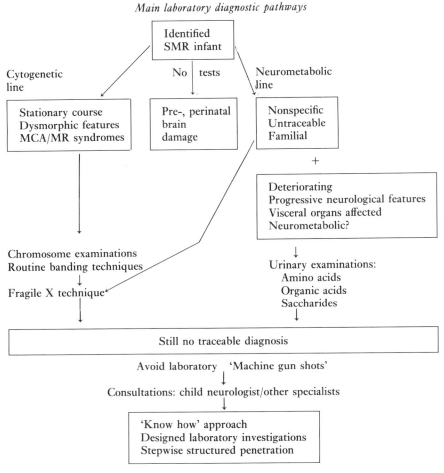

Main laboratory diagnostic pathways

FIGURE 9.2 A schematic model for a stepwise structured laboratory approach to reaching an aetiological diagnosis of severe mental retardation (modified from Hagberg, 1981)

to the MCA/MR category. In that case, one should proceed with cytogenetic investigation (Fig. 9.2). Batteries of neurochemical examinations are generally in vain in these cases and should be avoided.

Children who are not malformed and do not have prenatal stigmata but present with a coarse face and stunted stature do not belong to the MCA/MR category. They are more likely to suffer from biochemical storage diseases (e.g. the mucopolysaccharidoses). Together with other obviously deteriorating cases, and those with additional new neurological changes, they should be evaluated for neurodegenerative processes. Many neurometabolic disorders are generalized diseases. Symptoms and signs from tissues other than the central nervous system (e.g. eyes, liver, spleen, kidneys, skeleton) should therefore always be looked for, as characteristic features can sometimes give immediate diagnostic clues. Examples are the 'dancing eye lenses' of homocystinurics, and the osteolytic Erlenmeyer-flask skeletal X-ray changes in juvenile Gaucher's disease. Degenerative conditions should be considered for neurometabolic investigation (Fig. 9.2) but do not require extensive cytogenetic examinations.

A correct diagnosis of cases within the category of neurodegenerative conditions is now not just of academic interest. In certain situations, therapy which will at least prevent further deterioration can be instituted. In others, specific diagnosis may be vital for family planning through genetic counselling, prenatal diagnosis or preventive measures for younger siblings.

The design of a neurometabolic examination to reach a precise diagnosis is often quite intricate and differs between groups of biochemical disorders, and even between conditions within the same group. As there are many hundreds of such rare conditions known, most of them with MR as a major symptom, we suggest that the diagnostic procedure be performed stepwise and at rising levels of professional experience and 'know-how' (Fig. 9.2). Examination of amino acids in the urine and plasma, and of organic acids and saccharides in the urine, is recommended as the first step in the laboratory routine. Broadly ranging laboratory test requests, without knowing what to ask for, should be avoided. They are more expensive and less informative than the use of experienced clinical 'know-how'. Systematic exclusion of groups of disorders and, on the basis of clinical suspicion, direct questions to the clinical biochemist to pinpoint particular diseases are recommended. Neurodegenerative conditions which are not of neurometabolic origin are a small and complex group and need specific approaches tailored to the specific diagnostic problems of each case.

Late prenatally (third trimester) and perinatally brain-damaged MR cases are usually associated with other nonprogressive neurological features, mainly cerebral palsy syndromes. Many such cases have already been problems at delivery and in the newborn ward, and were extensively investigated with modern technology (e.g. evoked responses, ultrasound, CAT scans) by neonatologists. There is no merit in undertaking extensive biochemical and cytogenetic analyses in infants in this category.

In most 'unknown' cases of MR, without any clinical suspicion of a progressive disorder, urinary multicomponent analyses as in step one of the neurometabolic line in Fig. 9.2 are adequate. For this category, one should also bear in mind the possibility of an X-linked recessive form of MR and review the family history accordingly. When suspicion arises, a cytogenetic examination using marker X techniques is indicated.

Finally, a few remarks are made here on standard examinations in neurophysiology and neuroradiology. *Electroencephalography* contributes substantially to an aetiologic diagnosis only in special groups of cases (e.g. certain ceroidlipofuscinoses). However, when epilepsy is present, it is recommended as a routine procedure. *Evoked response examinations* – auditory, visual and somatosensory – are new, valuable tools for early tracing of neurodevelopmental abnormalities but rarely contribute to revealing aetiology. *Computerized tomography* (CAT scan) is abnormal in some cases, mostly showing nonspecific and relatively uninformative changes consistent with atrophic encephalopathy. CAT scan may, however, reveal cerebral malformations (e.g. agenesis of the corpus callosum) in MCA/MR cases and characteristic cerebral changes in certain neurodegenerative conditions, e.g. the leucodystrophies. Furthermore, it is certainly of considerable research interest when delineating new entities.

CONCLUSIONS

Mental retardation is defined in this chapter as severe (SMR) for IQs below 50 and mild (MMR) for the IQ range 50–70.

Prevalence

The prevalence of SMR in childhood is generally stated to be 3–5 per 1000. The true prevalence of MMR in childhood is more difficult to state because it is difficult to attain full ascertainment. Assuming that intelligence is normally distributed, with a mean of 100 $\pm$ 15 and with recently normed tests for the actual population, it should be 23 per thousand. Differences in definitions applied, type of tests used and year of test standardization all contribute to conflicting results.

Aetiology

In SMR, biomedical factors predominate strongly. About 40 per cent are chromosomal errors, trisomy 21 being by far the commonest aberration. About 15 per cent have undetected causes but with indications of early prenatal origin. About 20 per cent of SMR originates late in pregnancy, at delivery or during the first week of extrauterine life. Some 5–10 per cent have later-occurring pathology. The aetiology of MMR was formerly thought to be predominantly due to combined constitutional and sociocultural factors. In recent studies, however, a considerable proportion with biomedical origin has been found, larger in populations with a relatively low prevalence of MMR. The biomedical preventive approach to MR should be individually designed for the actual specific aetiologic group.

Early identification

This is the first diagnostic step. It requires training and experience in developmental medicine. Deviant findings should lead to referral for a detailed diagnostic 'work-up'. All SMR infants ought to be identified before the end of their first year of life, and the lower IQ range of MMR children before the end of the second.

Neurodevelopmental assessment

This is the second diagnostic step and is a combination of systematic developmental observations and neurological examination. It aims to map neuromotor abilities, to correlate these to neurological findings and to make a synthesis of the whole handicap pattern. MR infants without additional neurological problems are characterized by a nonspecific and even type of neurodevelopmental delay. This is in contrast to infants with isolated neuromotor abnormalities where dissociated patterns of development are prominent.

Diagnostic investigations

It is essential to proceed from a thorough appraisal of the general clinical picture. Infants with a stationary course and dysmorphic features should be investigated for potential cytogenetic errors. Infants with a stationary course and having known intrauterine or perinatal brain damage factors do not usually need extensive biochemical or cytogenetic investigations. In most 'untraceable' cases, analyses excluding main groups of neurometabolic conditions are adequate. An X-linked recessive form of MR should, however, be considered and cytogenetic examination performed accordingly. When developmental deterioration is obvious and/or additional neurological problems have supervened, a neurometabolic approach should be considered. Such a diagnostic procedure is recommended to be stepwise in structure, and performed at rising levels of professional experience and knowledge.

REFERENCES

AHLFORS, K. (1982) *Epidemiologic Studies of Congenital Cytomegalovirus Infection*, thesis, University of Lund, Sweden.

ALM, J. and LARSSON, A. (1981) 'Evaluation of a nation-wide neonatal metabolic screening programme in Sweden, 1965–1979', *Acta Paediat. Scand.*, 70, 601–7.

ARONSSON, M. (1984) *Children of Alcoholic Mothers*, thesis, University of Göteborg, Sweden.

BECKER, J.M., KAVEGGIA, E.G., PENDLETON, E. and OPITZ, J.M. (1977) 'A biologic and genetic study of 40 cases of severe pure mental retardation', *Eur. J. Pediat.*, 124, 231–56.

BIRCH, H.G., RICHARDSON, S.A., BAIRD, D., HOROBIN, G. and ILLSLEY, R. (1970) *Mental Subnormality in the Community. A Clinical and Epidemiologic Study*, Baltimore, Williams & Wilkins.

BLOMQUIST, H.K.:SON, GUSTAVSON, K.-H. and HOLMGREN, G. (1981) 'Mild mental retardation in children in a northern Swedish county', *J. Ment. Defic. Res.*, 25, 169–86.

BLOMQUIST, H.K.:SON, GUSTAVSON, K.-H., HOLMGREN, G., NORDEN-SON, I. and PÅLSSON-STRÅE, U. (1983) 'Fragile X syndrome in mildly mentally retarded children in a northern Swedish county. A prevalence study', *Clin. Genet.*, 24, 393–8.

BLOMQUIST, H.K.:SON, GUSTAVSON, K.-H., HOLMGREN, G., NORDEN-SON, I. and SWEINS, A. (1982) 'Fragile site X chromosomes and X-linked mental retardation in severely retarded boys in a northern Swedish county. A prevalence study', *Clin. Genet.*, 21, 209–14.

DAMSTRA, T. (1977) 'Toxicological properties of lead', *Environ. Hlth Perspect.*, 19, 297–307.

DRILLIEN, C.M. and DRUMMOND, M.B. (1977) *Neurodevelopmental Problems in Early Childhood: Assessment and Management*, Oxford, Blackwell Scientific.

DRILLIEN, C.M. and DRUMMOND, M.B. (1983) *Development Screening and the Child with Special Needs. A Population Study of 5000 Children*, Clinics in Developmental Medicine, no. 86, London, Heinemann Medical.

DRILLIEN, C.M., JAMESON, S. and WILKINSON, E.M. (1966) 'Studies in mental handicap. Part 1: Prevalence and distribution by clinical type and severity of defect', *Arch. Dis. Childh.*, 41, 528–38.

EGAN, D.F. (1978) 'Developmental assessment', in J. APLEY (ed.), *Clinics in Developmental Medicine*, no. 67, London, Heinemann Medical, 66–73.

EGAN, D., ILLINGWORTH, R.S. and MACKEITH, R. (1969) *Developmental Screening, 0–5 Years*, Clinics in Developmental Medicine, no. 30, London, Heinemann Medical.

FLYNN, J.R. (1982) 'Lynn, the Japanese, and environmentalism', *Bull. Brit. Psychol. Soc.*, 35, 409–13.

FLYNN, J.R. (1984) 'The mean IQ of Americans: massive gains 1932 to 1978', *Psychol. Bull.*, 95, 29–51.

FRANKENBURG, W.K., GOLDSTEIN, A.D. and CAMP, B.C. (1971) 'The revised Denver Developmental Screening Test: its accuracy as a screening instrument', *J. Pediat.*, 79, 988–95.

FREYTAG, E. and LINDENBERG, R. (1967) 'Neuropathological findings in patients in a hospital for the mentally deficient. A survey of 359 cases', *Johns Hopkins Med. J.*, 121, 379–93.

FRYERS, T. and MACKAY, R.I. (1979) 'Down syndrome: prevalence at birth, mortality and survival. A 17-year study', *Early Hum. Devel.*, 3, 29–41.

GUSTAVSON, K.-H., HAGBERG, B., HAGBERG, G. and SARS, K. (1977a) 'Severe mental retardation in a Swedish county: I. Epidemiology, gestational age, birth weight and associated CNS handicaps in children born 1959–70', *Acta Paediat. Scand.*, 66, 373–9.

GUSTAVSON, K.-H., HAGBERG, B., HAGBERG, G. and SARS, K. (1977b) 'Severe mental retardation in a Swedish county: II. Etiologic and pathogenetic aspects of children born 1959–1970', *Neuropädiatrie*, 8, 293–304.

GUSTAVSON, K.-H., HOLMGREN, G., JONSELL, R. and BLOMQUIST, H.K.:SON (1977c) 'Severe mental retardation in children in a northern

Swedish county', *J. Ment. Defic. Res.*, 21, 161–81.

HAGBERG, B. (1979) 'Epidemiological and preventive aspects of cerebral palsy and severe mental retardation in Sweden', *Eur. J. Pediat.*, 130, 71–8.

HAGBERG, B. (1981) 'Biochemical aspects of mental handicaps in infancy and childhood. A review with special emphasis on mental retardation', *Inserm*, 105, 93–106.

HAGBERG, B., HAGBERG, G., LEWERTH, A. and LINDBERG, U. (1981a) 'Mild mental retardation in Swedish school children: I. Prevalence', *Acta Paediat. Scand.*, 70, 441–4.

HAGBERG, B., HAGBERG, G., LEWERTH, A. and LINDBERG, U. (1981b) 'Mild mental retardation in Swedish school children: II. Etiologic and pathogenetic aspects', *Acta Paediat. Scand.*, 70, 445–52.

HAGBERG, B., HAGBERG, G. and OLOW, I. (1984) 'The changing panorama of cerebral palsy in Sweden: IV. Trends in epidemiology, 1959–78', *Acta Paediat. Scand.*, 73, 433–40.

HETZEL, B.S. and SMITH, R.M. (1981) *Fetal Brain Disorders – Recent Approaches to the Problem of Mental Deficiency*, Amsterdam, Elsevier.

HOLT, K.S. (1977) *Developmental Paediatrics. Perspectives and Practice*, London, Butterworth.

ILLINGWORTH, R.S. (1966) *The Development of the Infant and Young Child, Normal and Abnormal*, 3rd edn, Edinburgh, Churchill Livingstone.

ILLINGWORTH, R.S. (1968) 'Delayed motor development', *Pediat. Clin. N. Amer.*, 15, 569–80.

ILLINGWORTH, R.S. (1973) *Basic Developmental Screening 0–2 Years*, Oxford, Blackwell Scientific.

JELLINGER, K. (1972) 'Neuropathological features of unclassified mental retardation', in J.B. CAVANAGH (ed.), *The Brain in Unclassified Mental Retardation*, Edinburgh, Churchill Livingstone.

JONSELL, R., BROBERGER, O., BRZOKOUPIL, K., NORÉN, C.-E. and RABO, E. (1981) 'Vaccination against measles, mumps and rubella', *Läkartidningen (Sw.)*, 78, 767–9.

KAVEGGIA, E.G., DURKIN, M.V., PENDLETON, E. and OPITZ, J.M. (1975) 'Diagnostic/genetic studies on 1224 patients with severe mental retardation', in D.A.A. PRIMROSE (ed.), *Proceedings of the Third International Association for the Scientific Study of Mental Deficiency*, Warsaw, Polish Medical Publishers, 82–93.

LAXOVA, R., RIDLER, M.A.C. and BOWEN-BRAVERY, M. (1977) 'An etiological survey of the severely retarded Hertfordshire children who were born between January 1, 1965 and December 31, 1967', *Amer. J. Med. Genet.*, 1, 75–86.

LEDBETTER, D.H., RICCARDI, V.M., AIRHART, S.D., STROBEL, R.J., KEENAN, B.S. and CRAWFORD, J.D. (1981) 'Deletions of chromosome 15 as a cause of the Prader–Willi syndrome', *New Engl. J. Med.*, 304, 325–9.

LUBS, H.A. (1969) 'A marker X-chromosome', *Amer. J. Hum. Genet.*, 21, 231–3.

MCDONALD, A.D. (1973) 'Severely retarded children in Quebec: prevalence, causes and care', *Amer. J. Ment. Defic.*, 78, 205–15.

MOLNAR, G.E. (1978) 'Analysis of motor disorder in retarded infants and young children', *Amer. J. Ment. Defic.*, 83, 213–22.

MOORE, M.R. (1980) 'Exposure to lead in childhood: the persisting effects', *Nature (Lond.)*, 283, 334–5.

MOSER, H.W., RAMEY, C.T. and LEONARD, C.O. (1983) 'Mental retardation', in A. EMERY and D. RIMOIN (eds), *Principles and Practice of Medical Genetics*, New York, Churchill Livingstone, 1, 352–66.

NELIGAN, G.E. and PRUDHAM, D. (1969) 'Potential value of four early developmental milestones in screening children for increased risk of later retardation', *Develop. Med. Child Neurol.*, 11, 423–31.

O'BRIEN, J.S. (1983) 'The gangliosidoses', in J.B. STANBURY, J.B. WYNGAARDEN, D.S. FREDRICKSON, J.L. GOLDSTEIN and M.S. BROWN (eds), *The Metabolic Basis of Inherited Disease*, 5th edn, New York, McGraw-Hill, 945–69.

OLEGÅRD, R., SABEL, K.-G., ARONSSON, M., SANDIN, B., JOHANSSON, P.R., CARLSSON, C., KYLLERMAN, M., IVERSEN, K. and HRBEC, A. (1979) 'Effect on the child of alcohol abuse during pregnancy', *Acta Paediat. Scand.*, Suppl. 275, 112–21.

OPITZ, J.M. (1977) 'Diagnostic/genetic studies in severe mental retardation', in H.A. LUBS and F. DE LA CRUZ (eds), *Genetic Counselling*, New York, Raven Press.

PECKHAM, C.S. (1983), personal communication.

PENROSE, L.S. (1963) *The Biology of Mental Defect*, 3rd edn, London, Sidgwick & Jackson.

PERLSTEIN, M.A. and ATTALA, R. (1966) 'Neurologic sequelae of plumbism in children', *Clin. Pediat.*, 5, 292–8.

ROBERTON, N.R.C. (1978) 'Discussion', in K. ELLIOTT and M. O'CONNOR (eds), *Major Mental Handicap: Methods and Costs of Prevention*, Ciba Foundation Symposium 59 (new series), Amsterdam, Elsevier/Excerpta Medica, 42–3.

ROGERS, M.G.H. (1971) 'The early recognition of handicapping disorders in childhood', *Develop. Med. Child Neurol.*, 13, 88–101.

SCHMITT, R. and ERICKSON, M.T. (1973) 'Early predictors of mental retardation', *Ment. Retard.*, 11(2), 27–9.

SHAPIRO, B.K., ACCARDO, P.J. and CAPUTE, A.J. (1979) 'Factors affecting walking in a profoundly retarded population', *Develop. Med. Child Neurol.*, 21, 369–73.

SMITH, D.W. (1980) 'Hydantoin effects on the fetus', in T. HASSELL, M. JOHNSTON and K.-H. DUDLEY (eds), *Phenytoin-Induced Teratology and Gingival Pathology*, New York, Raven Press, 35–40.

STENE, J., FISCHER, G., STENE, E., MIKKELSEN, M. and PETERSEN, E. (1977) 'Paternal age effect in Down's syndrome', *Ann. Hum. Genet.*, 40, 299–308.

SUTHERLAND, G.R. (1979) 'Fragile sites on chromosomes: II. Distribution, phenotypic effects and cytogenetics', *Amer. J. Hum. Genet.*, 31, 136–48.

SVENNERHOLM, L., MÅNSSON, J.-E., NILSSON, O., TIBBLIN, E., ERIKSON, A., GROTH, C.-G., LUNDGREN, G. and RINGDÉN, O. (1984) 'Bone marrow transplantation in the Norrbottnian form of Gaucher disease', in R.O. BRADY and J.A. BARRANGER (eds), *The Molecular Basis of Lysosomal Storage Disorders*, New York, Academic Press, in press.

TARANGER, J., SEDVALL, A., KYLLERMAN, M. and GARTON, M. (1982) 'Experiences of combined vaccinations against measles, mumps and rubella in the 6th grade of school', *Läkartidningen (Sw.)*, 79, 3430–1.

TERMAN, L.M. and MERRILL, M.A. (1973) *Stanford–Binet Intelligence Scale: 1972 Norms Edition*, Boston, Houghton-Mifflin, 359.

THOMPSON, R.J. (1977) 'Consequences of using the 1972 Stanford–Binet Intelligence Scale norms', *Psychology in the Schools*, 14, 444–8.

TIZARD, P. and LINDENBAUM, R. (1984) 'Commentary', in J. DOBBING, A.D.B. CLARKE, J.A. CORBETT, J. HOGG AND R.O. ROBINSON (eds), *Scientific Studies in Mental Retardation*, London, Heinemann and the Royal Society of Medicine.

TOUWEN, B.C.L. (1982) 'Development neurology', in F.C. ROSE (ed.), *Paediatric Neurology*, Oxford, Blackwell Scientific, 86–97.

TURNER, G., BROOKWELL, R., DANIEL, A., SELIKOWITZ, M. and ZILIBOWITZ, M. (1980) 'Heterozygous expression of X-linked mental retardation and X-chromosome marker Fra (X) (q27)', *New Engl. J. Med.*, 303, 662–4.

WORLD HEALTH ORGANIZATION (1968), Expert Committee on Mental Health, Fifteenth Report 'Organization of services for the mentally retarded', *WHO Technical Report*, ser. 392, Geneva, WHO.

10

Epidemiology

Stephen A. Richardson
and Helene Koller

INTRODUCTION

The purposes of epidemiology are to investigate the distribution and determinants of a disease, disorder or condition. Examination of distribution includes identifying the size, nature and location of the disorder, the components of the problem, the population at risk for the disorder or the relevant base population, and the provision of estimates that may aid in the planning and conduct of treatment and special services. Examination of determinants of the disorder includes the search for clues to cause and opportunities for preventive intervention. The mode of approach in epidemiology has been well described by Frost (1936):

> Epidemiology at any given time is more than the total of its established facts. It includes their orderly arrangement into chains of inference which extend more or less beyond the bounds of direct observation. Such of these chains as are well and truly laid, guide investigation to the facts of the future; those that are ill made fetter progress.

The starting point of epidemiology is definition of the entity to be studied in order to identify who should and should not be included as having the disorder. The problems of definition are particularly difficult in the study of mental retardation, because the disorder varies widely in its range of manifestations and aetiology. The criteria included in current definitions of mental retardation are:

1. Evidence of significant subaverage intellectual functioning.
2. Impaired social adaptation, inability to satisfy expectations which society has for its members based on age and sex; a lack of social competence; poor adaptive behaviour; and a variety of like terms.
3. That the disorder is manifest during the developmental period, the end point of which is somewhat arbitrary but generally is around the age of leaving school.

Epidemiological studies have varied both in the weight given to the first and second criteria and in the ways they are defined.

The most common means of identification used by epidemiologists are administrative, i.e. to define as mentally retarded any person who has been so classified by some authority, usually by local departments of health and education. To understand the administrative definition requires examining how authorities reach decisions on each case and the variations in the process. The process is different for pre-school, school and post-school years. In the pre-school years there have, until recently, been few community-wide services for children identified as mentally retarded, so there has been little need for comprehensive administrative classification. A second problem in the pre-school years has been the difficulty of making a clear diagnosis, except for children with certain visible stigmata, or through chromosome, biochemical or other tests. Even when it is clear that a child has some developmental disability, it may be difficult to determine the extent to which mental retardation is present. For these reasons few epidemiological studies have focused on the pre-school years. More complete administrative data are available for the school years because of the requirement in western industrial societies of universal compulsory education for children.

At school-entry age the most severely retarded children are identified, but the majority of retarded children become classified at some time after school entry. For these children the first step in administrative classification is generally taken by the classroom teacher, who identifies a child who is not performing at some minimal level of expectations. Whether this leads to reporting the child to the school authorities depends on what special and remedial services are available, how well the teacher can cope with the child, and the teacher's view of whether placement in special services will help or hurt the child. Teacher identification is based, then, on the second definitional criterion of unsatisfactory performance in a role society regards as having central importance, i.e. the role of student. If recommended by a teacher, the child is then usually assessed psychometrically and, if the results are within the range covered by the definition used in the local school system and a special placement is available, the child will be classified as mentally retarded.

The prevailing opinion for many years about the use of IQ in defining mental retardation was well stated in an earlier edition of this volume:

> The IQ must, like the concept of social incompetence, be rejected as a possible sole criterion for the diagnosis of mental defect. Although intelligence tests have the advantage of being precise, objective, and standardized on a cross-section of the whole population, yet even the most perfect are subject to a certain degree of error, and the use of an arbitrary dividing line between the mentally defective and the 'subnormal normal' would classify in the former category some who were socially competent, and in the latter some who were quite incompetent. Nevertheless, a considerable degree of intellectual subnormality as measured on reputable

and appropriate intelligence tests should be a *sine qua non* of certification as a mental defective. (Clarke, 1965, p. 60)

IQ testing procedures influence who is classified as mentally retarded and, depending on the cut-off point used, the type of test, when it was standardized, and the similarity between the population tested and the population on whom the test was standardized, the numbers classified will vary from one community to another. The IQ level defining mental retardation is based on the assumption of a normal distribution with a mean IQ of 100 for the total population. Two standard deviations below the mean, or an IQ of 70, has general acceptance now as the upper limit of mental retardation, although some flexibility around this limit is understood to be necessary (Grossman, 1983). Different grades of mental retardation are sometimes used to classify those with IQs below 70 but, for epidemiological purposes, those with IQs between 50 and 70 are classified as mildly retarded, and those with IQs below 50 are classified as severely retarded (see Chapters 2 and 3).

The second criterion of mental retardation is poor adaptive behaviour, or social inadequacy. Only recently have attempts been made to give this criterion systematic attention. It is well known that some children whose IQs are within the mentally retarded range remain in regular classes, and there are children with IQs well above 70 in special classes for the mentally retarded. In the past, in some school systems, all children in regular classes were given a group IQ test, and those below a given cut-off point were then assessed further to determine whether they should be classified as mentally retarded (see, for example, Birch *et al.*, 1970). The use of IQ tests for screening is now far less common. Although school authorities are expected to take into account both the results of intelligence tests and impaired social adaptation based on the child's performance in school, and sometimes in different roles outside the school, the weighting given to the two criteria varies from one community to another and is rarely documented.

IQ testing was originally developed to provide a way of predicting school performance, so it is hardly surprising that there is a fairly high level of agreement between teacher assessment of school role performance and the results of IQ tests. Clearly the most difficult decisions in classification are those around the borderline area. The number of children who are administratively classified in any community is influenced by the kinds and numbers of special placements available for children with special needs. While special education facilities initially develop in response to demand, once established the number of places may influence the number of children later classified, and the number of places available may vary with the economic resources of the education system. There is also variation depending on the number of alternative special resources available in the schools for different types of disability. Clarke and Clarke (Chapter 2) note that ten types of disability were distinguished as requiring special educational treatment in England and Wales in the 1959 regulations. Because multiple classifications were not used, some mentally retarded children were placed in another disability category, and this would influence the numbers of children identified as retarded.

Another factor which influences who is classified in the school years is the weight given to parental opinion about whether their child should or should not be placed in some special facilities because of mental retardation. This again will vary depending on the time and location of the study.

Studies of adult populations are less common than those of children. As will be shown, epidemiological studies consistently show a sharp drop in prevalence after the school years, due largely to declassification of mildly retarded young people. In the adult years, adaptive behaviour takes precedence over IQ as a means of identifying mental retardation, and because of the problems of identification of mildly retarded adults not in services, studies are almost always limited to those who are administratively classified.

For any given investigative definition of mental retardation it is likely that, if administrative classification is used as the sole basis for identifying cases, some individuals classified as mentally retarded will not meet the investigator's definition, and there will be others who have not been classified as mentally retarded but would meet the investigator's definition. To deal with the false positives, investigators in some studies have independently examined all those who have been administratively classified. To deal with false negatives, investigators have obtained the co-operation of people who hold positions that enable them to make some judgement on intellectual incompetence, e.g. heads of schools, teachers, doctors, nurses, social and welfare workers, and ministers. In some studies records on the individual are used to form a judgement. In two studies (New York State Department of Mental Hygiene, 1955; Mercer, 1973) prevalence rates were given of those suspected of being mentally retarded. In two others (Imre, 1967; Rutter *et al.*, 1970) everyone in the population studied was screened for mental retardation, and all cases that were possibly mentally retarded were individually examined.

For most purposes it is necessary to know the frequency with which mental retardation occurs in the population being studied. The prevalence is expressed as a rate which is the number who are mentally retarded divided by the total relevant (denominator) population, of which they are a part. In order for prevalence rates to be accurate, it is necessary not only to enumerate carefully those in the population who are mentally retarded, but also to calculate the denominator population. In school populations the schools generally have an accurate census which can be used to provide the denominator data. In studies of adults, national census data may be used, but unless the census was recent there may be some error. For some study purposes, the total prevalence of mental retardation must be broken down by such characteristics as age, year(s) of birth, sex and social class, so it is necessary to know the distribution of these characteristics for the total relevant population as well as for the mentally retarded cases. The populations selected for study and the definitions of mental retardation used are influenced by the kinds of practical problems which have been outlined.

THE USE OF INCIDENCE AND PREVALENCE IN STUDIES OF MENTAL RETARDATION

Incidence refers to the number of new cases of a disorder arising in a population in a stated period of time, while prevalence is the number of cases, old and new, existing in a population at a given point in time or over a specified period. Incidence rates are valuable for making inferences about cause, but the determination of true incidence rates for mental retardation is prevented by insuperable problems. To determine biomedical causes which extend back to conception and may occur at different times during fetal growth and the perinatal period, a count is needed of every conceptus including those lost. It would be necessary to determine whether mental retardation would have occurred had each conceptus lived. While there have been studies of fetal loss, and identification of some with disorders that would have resulted in mental retardation through neuropathological, chromosome and biochemical studies, an unknown number of fetal losses are missed. For those who survive the perinatal period but die in the first few years of life, a determination of intellectual functioning cannot always be made. For these reasons true incidence studies of mental retardation are not possible, and studies dealing with older children yield prevalence rates. Prevalence rates can be used for two main purposes. First, extrapolations can be made with which to make inferences about incidence and cause. Second, useful information can be given to service planners and providers. Examples of the use of prevalence rates for these purposes are given later in the chapter.

STUDIES OF THE PREVALENCE OF MENTAL RETARDATION IN CHILDHOOD

The various methodological issues that have been discussed in using epidemiology for the study of mental retardation provide a basis for understanding the wide range of prevalence rates found in the research literature. We give below some examples of studies, primarily of children, where the prevalence rates reported range from approximately 80:1000 in Onondaga County (New York State Department of Mental Hygiene, 1955) to 9:1000 in Gothenburg, Sweden (Gillberg *et al.*, 1983), and show why it would be incorrect, on the basis of these findings, to conclude that mental retardation is almost nine times more frequent in the United States than Sweden, or that a drastic reduction has occurred in the twenty-eight years between these studies. Some additional studies are described to illustrate the variety of approaches.

Onondaga County, New York

The purpose of the study was to 'measure the extent of the socially recognized retardation in the community' (New York State Department of Mental

Hygiene, 1955, p. 84). The initiative 'arose from a committee of the State Legislature which wanted the information for planning purposes' (Gruenberg, 1964, p. 272). To identify cases, 'responsible child care agencies were requested to report all children under 18 years of age and residents of Onondaga County on March 1, 1953 identified as definitely mentally retarded, or suspected of mental retardation on the basis of developmental history, poor academic performance, IQ score, or social adaptation when contrasted with their age peers.' Commenting on the method used, the authors (New York State Department of Mental Hygiene, 1955, p. 87) noted: 'In practice the interpretation of the definition of a "case" undoubtedly differed with the reporting agency. It is believed that reporting errors ... resulted in a greater inclusion of false positives than exclusion of false negatives.' The maximum prevalence rate of 80:1000 was obtained for children in the 10–15-year age range. The rates increased sharply to this plateau with age-specific rates of 6:1000 at age 3–4, 22:1000 at age 5 and 39.1:1000 at age 6. The rate dropped sharply to 28:1000 at ages 16–17. Gruenberg suggested that the sharp initial rise at age 5 was due to school referrals and that the drop after age 15 was due to children leaving school at age 16, the legal school-leaving age.

A conclusion of that study was that 'these data strongly suggest that behavior leading to the social suspicion of "mental retardation" is not necessarily a fixed characteristic of individual children but is rather a complex set of manifestations of some children's relationship to their social environment' (p. 127).

This study did not use any systematic psychometric testing or other forms of individual examination, nor did it depend fully on administrative classification of mental retardation made by the educational authorities. Given the nature of the study, a high prevalence rate was to be expected.

Gothenburg, Sweden

A study of mental retardation in Gothenburg children was carried out by Gillberg *et al.* (1983). They used a screening test given to all children living in Gothenburg in 1977 and born in 1971 in order to estimate the prevalence of various neurodevelopmental disorders. Data were obtained from questionnaires filled out by the children's teachers. Criteria were developed for screening children at high risk of mental retardation, and all seven-year-old children were examined by the research team. They also conducted a search of registers of the Board for Provisions and Services to the Mentally Retarded (BPSMR). Sixty-seven children were identified as unequivocally mentally retarded, and a further eight cases were detected from the neurodevelopmental screening procedure. Their final result was a prevalence rate of 9.1:1000 for mental retardation defined as IQ < 70. An additional 9.3:1000 were considered borderline mentally retarded.

Isle of Wight, England

This was a pioneer study which, rather than being confined to a single disability, examined mental retardation as one of a set of disablements. Rutter *et al.* (1970) gave as their purpose 'an attempt to survey the total problem of handicapping conditions in a population of children'. The children were all the 9–12-year-olds resident in the Isle of Wight. In examining intellectual disability the investigators avoided the term mental retardation and instead used 'intellectual retardation', which they defined as follows:

> A child was designated as showing intellectual retardation if, having been selected for individual testing by means of group screening procedures, he was found to have a WISC scale score which was at least two standard deviations below the mean (average) WISC scale score for [a random sample of the total population of children]. (p. 28)

The first step in the study was the administration to all 9–12-year-old children of a number of group tests for screening purposes. In addition, teachers in all schools were asked to note children who were markedly backward. The screening procedures were designed to identify for individual examination many more children than the investigators expected to, or did, classify as intellectually retarded. A shortened version of the WISC was used in testing. To establish a cut-off point for the upper limits of retardation the investigators established their own norms. Instead of an IQ of 70, which has been used because it is two standard deviations below the usual mean of 100, they estimated the mean IQ for Isle of Wight children (111) and used as a cut-off point two standard deviations below that mean to define intellectual retardation. With this procedure, the prevalence rate was 25.3:1000. An estimated 15:1000 would have had scores below 70. They pointed out that the WISC had been standardized twenty years earlier and the Isle of Wight mean IQ of 111 showed the upward drift in performance. The investigators were not primarily interested in finding the prevalence of mental retardation. By using two standard deviations below the mean of the population studied, they identified children who could reasonably be called intellectually retarded.

Any study that establishes the mean WISC score for the population tested will find that approximately 25–30 per 1000 will fall two standard deviations or more below the mean, given a normal distribution.

Aberdeen, Scotland

A study which used administrative classification was conducted in Aberdeen, Scotland (Birch *et al.*, 1970). The population at risk was all children residing in Aberdeen in 1962 who had been born between 1 January 1952 and 31 December 1954. The designation of mental retardation was applied to any child who had been so classified by the local health and educational authorities. Clearly the number was dependent on the ways in which local authorities selected cases. They are described in detail in the report (pp. 17–19). Unless a child was severely retarded he or she entered school at five in a regular class. At ages seven and nine all children in regular classes were given standard IQ tests. A child would be considered for placement in special educational facilities either because a teacher noted poor school performance, or because of a score of less than 75 on the IQ test given at age seven. Those identified through low IQ scores were individually tested by a school psychologist and the finding and recommendation forwarded to the school medical officer. Evaluation also included a general report from the school. For those identified by teachers a similar evaluation was made. The information resulting from the evaluation and the recommendation of the school medical officer were sent to the director of education who reviewed the case, discussed it with the parents and made a recommendation to the education committee. Their decision was then communicated to the parents who had the right to appeal for a review by representatives of the Secretary of State for Scotland. In addition, there was a procedure of voluntary referral whereby parents could send their child to a special school on a trial basis, and if the parents were not satisfied, they could insist that their child be returned to regular school.

All classification is for a purpose, and in Aberdeen the purpose of administrative classification was to provide special education and care. The number of children classified could be influenced by the number of places open in the special facilities. At the time of the study the special services had recently been expanded, and there were places available for all children in need.

For the purposes of the research, each child administratively classified as mentally retarded by the local authorities and those in voluntary placement were independently assessed by a research team for intellectual level, clinical neurological findings and psychiatric status. This was done in part to check on the local psychological testing. The independent team felt that the placement of all the children had been appropriate.

Notably, the city was a single political unit with its own governmental structure. Had different local authorities been within the geographic area under consideration, problems could have arisen through lack of a uniform system for identification of mental retardation. The school census included private and parochial schools, and because these schools had no facilities for special education, children who were mentally retarded all attended the government-run schools.

Administrative classification, corroborated by the assessment of the research team, identified 104 children aged 8–10 as mentally retarded. In addition, 123 children of the same age were found to have scored below 75 on the group IQ test given to all seven-year-old children in regular classes. These children were considered mentally retarded on psychometric grounds alone. We recently reviewed the 104 administratively classified cases as part of a follow-up study we are conducting. Using the current definition of mental retardation of an IQ below 70, we eliminated 26 children with IQs of 70 and above. There remained 78 children who met that definition. To calculate prevalence rates, the total number of 8–10-year-old children (8274) was obtained from the 1962 school census. The following figures indicate that the same study population provides several different prevalence rates, depending on the definition used:

Administratively classified, IQs < 70	9.4 : 1000
All administratively classified	12.6 : 1000
All administrative + psychometric	27.4 : 1000

The combined prevalence rate of 27.4:1000 is close to the Isle of Wight rate of 25.3:1000, and this is hardly surprising. Both are based on psychometric data and both used two standard deviations from the mean of the populations studied as a cut-off point. Both figures are lower than the Onondaga rate which, it is suspected, included many false positive cases. When the administrative prevalence in Aberdeen is reduced by excluding cases with IQs of 70 and above, the resulting prevalence rate of 9.4 is similar to that found by Gillberg *et al.* (1983) in the Swedish study.

The four studies reviewed illustrate the ways in which the study definitions and methods yield wide variations in overall prevalence rates. Studies based on administrative prevalence alone would also yield variation from one community to another. Classification is the end point in a complex interaction between social, economic, political and organizational factors. For example, the ability of a teacher to help a less able child depends on the skill and experience of the teacher, class size, teaching methods used, and physical facilities and equipment available. Administrative classification is for the purpose of providing the child with special help. It therefore depends on the forms of help available for those with intellectual limitations and whether there are openings, and this in turn depends on the size and scope of the special facilities. The minimal level of expectation for school performance depends on the goals of the school, which in turn are influenced by the parents whose children are in the school. Difficulty in learning in school is usually considered the fault of the child. An old friend and colleague, Herbert Birch, who was trained in animal behaviour and psychology, told of a famous animal trainer who had once remarked somewhat ruefully that he was blamed if an animal did not learn, whereas in schools, if the child does not learn, the blame is not placed on the teacher but on the child. Clearly the factors we have discussed vary widely in the schools both between and within the areas where epidemiological studies have been undertaken.

The problems arising out of the use of different definitions and methods in studies of the overall prevalence of mental retardation are lessened somewhat when data are broken down by, or restricted to, populations with mild and severe retardation. Moreover, in general, the terms mild and severe retardation describe people with very different abilities and levels of functioning, and examining them as a single population does not provide the most useful information. The following sections examine issues relating to the prevalence of mental retardation for different groups.

THE PREVALENCE OF SEVERE MENTAL RETARDATION IN CHILDHOOD

Until recently, reviewers of studies of severe mental retardation have emphasized the similarity between the prevalence rates for children. Kushlick and Blunden (1974) cited eleven studies and concluded that 'in England and Wales about 3.7:1000 of the people who survive to the age of 15–19 are likely to be severely subnormal' (p. 32). Abramowicz and Richardson (1975), after reviewing twenty-seven studies, concluded:

> The best approximation of the 'true' prevalence of severe mental retardation is 3.7 per thousand and the average 'true' prevalence is 3.96 per thousand. Since cases of severe mental retardation in a community can be missed and because there may be a tendency to overestimate a child's potential by classifying him as mildly rather than severely mentally retarded, the average figure of 4 per 1000 age-specific population is probably a fair estimate of the number of severely retarded children who require services in the community. (p. 29)

The use of the term 'true' prevalence implies that the variation in the prevalence rates in the studies reviewed is largely caused by the methods used.

The expectation of a single 'true' prevalence rate of around 4:1000 that will be found across communities has been questioned. Fryers (1984) points out that prevalence studies are of survivors, and their numbers are 'determined by a very wide range of factors affecting the incidence of specific aetiologies, the mortality of different clinical groups, and the ascertainment of different types of child. It would be very surprising if they were all to operate to the same degree, in a similar manner, over the same period of time, in different communities' (chapter 4, p. 3). Adding to the complexity of the situation, there are problems of defining and consistently applying criteria for classification, temporal changes which affect particular cohorts differently, changes in aetiologies within the study population, demographic characteristics of the population and differential migration.

Sorel (1974) expressed similar concerns and pointed out that the prevalence of severe mental retardation may be influenced by the state of the health services in general and the perinatal care in particular, air and water pollution in the area, average age at marriage, average number of children per family and dietary customs.

In addition to the factors mentioned by Fryers and Sorel as possibly influencing the prevalence of severe retardation, the social environment in which a child is raised may also be important. While this has often been noted in the development of mild retardation, less attention has been paid to the effect the environment can have on the level of functioning of children with more severe retardation. Increasing emphasis on keeping retarded children with their families, and the growth of programmes for early intellectual stimulation of children, may alter the IQ test performance upward sufficiently to move some children above the cut-off IQ level for severe retardation.

In comparing results of surveys of severe mental retardation since 1945, Sorel found far less consistency than would be expected for a 'supposedly' stable characteristic of school-age populations, a characteristic that is 'supposedly' easily traced because it is 'supposedly' easily recognized. The rates varied from 1.9 to 7.3 per 1000, the latter for Sorel's own study in Amsterdam. Sorel further objected to the suggestions or implications by investigators of the representativeness of their surveys, without making clear the ways their communities are supposed to be representative, and whether the variables that make them representative 'can be regarded as the *special* factors which are connected with the prevalence of mental retardation: that is to say, whether they can explain the differences in prevalence at all' (p. 110).

This point was illustrated by Gruenberg (1964):

> Epidemiology makes a contribution to what can be determined 'community diagnosis' . . . [which] is directed at a particular community; it is obvious that the diagnosis which fits one community cannot be expected to fit every other community. . . . This point is sometimes obscured in practice because those needing a community diagnosis are often in no position to employ the proper procedures and must make the best judgment they can with inadequate information. They tend to look for another community which they have reason to think is like their own and which has been studied diagnostically and then to guess that, if similar studies were made in their own community, the results would be similar. While the conclusions may be either right or wrong, the inference is sensible in that it uses the best data available to the decision-maker; but the nature of the inference should be remembered and community uniqueness should be expected. (p. 260)

As with mildly retarded children, classification of a child as severely retarded is based on both IQ testing and administrative considerations. Whereas with children at the upper limit of mild retardation the choice is between regular and special school placement, with children at the upper limit of severe retardation, the choice is between classification as severely or mildly retarded. The question of whether children around the borderline IQ of 50 should be classified as mild or severe is often difficult, and how it is answered from one study to another can contribute to variation in prevalence. Whether a child with an IQ around 50 receives a score above or below that figure is influenced by the intelligence test used and the time that has elapsed since the test was last standardized. Administrative decisions are made about whether to place a child in services organized for those with mild or severe retardation, and these decisions take into account a more general set of factors than IQ alone. These include the characteristics of the child, such as other disabilities, and the range of facilities available for meeting the child's overall needs. For a disorder with a low prevalence, how decisions are made around the borderline between severe and mild mental retardation, although they affect only a few children in either direction, can have a marked effect on the prevalence rates.

With the understanding that real differences probably exist across communities, and that these differences may be exacerbated by differences in classification procedures as well as by methods and definitional criteria introduced by epidemiological investigators, we nevertheless considered it useful to examine the prevalence rates in recent studies in developed countries to see if any patterns emerged. We confined the examination to studies of 10–14-year-olds because it is a narrow enough age band to be meaningful, ascertainment by that age should be complete, and schooling should have sorted the mildly retarded from the more severely retarded children. Moreover, it is an age before entrance into adult services, which may include mildly retarded multiply handicapped people in their registers without differentiating them by intellectual level. Fortunately, 10–14 is an age band given in many studies. We used all the studies considered by Abramowicz and Richardson (1975) to be reliable, beginning with 1960, and which give rates for the 10–14 age group, and then added studies published after completion of that review. The data in Table 10.1, which lists the studies and the prevalence rates obtained, suggest that in Britain, the Republic of Ireland, Holland and Denmark there was a near twofold increase in prevalence over the last two decades. We will come back to this issue later when we consider temporal changes in studies that have examined successive cohorts in the same geographic area over time using the same methods. By doing so, the variation introduced by community and methodological differences is greatly reduced.

THE PREVALENCE OF MILD MENTAL RETARDATION IN CHILDHOOD

Because mild mental retardation accounts for most of the overall prevalence and because it includes all cases adjacent to whatever cut-off point is used to differentiate those with and without retardation, it may be expected that much of the variation between studies of overall prevalence will be found within the mildy retarded IQ range of approximately 50 and above.

The studies summarized in Table 10.2 illustrate that, whether or not an IQ limit is set, the demographic characteristics of the community and the methods of case-finding used will result in vastly different prevalence rates. In the Salford and Wessex studies the majority of the mildly retarded children were given special services within the school system and were not the responsibility of the health authorities or on their registers. This accounts for the very low rates from ages 5–14. In both these studies the rates rise after age 15, when mildly retarded school leavers who could not meet societal expectations for fulfilling adult roles were added to the registers of the health authorities. The very high rates found throughout the age bands in the Rose County study were

TABLE 10.1 Prevalence rates per 1000 population for severe mental retardation in 10–14-year-olds[1]

Year	Place	Prevalence rate per 1000 population
(1) 1960	NE Scotland	2.30
(2) 1960	London	2.81
(3) 1960	Salford	2.66
(4) 1960	Middlesex	2.83 (administrative)
		3.61 (individual assessment)
(5) 1963	Wessex	3.01
(6) 1964	Northern Ireland	3.60
(7) 1966	Amsterdam	5.20 (administrative)
	(ages 10 and 15)	7.30[2] (individual assessment)
(8) 1967	Camberwell	3.66
(9) 1968	Sheffield	3.66
(10) 1970[3]	Aarhus	4.50
(11) 1974[4]	Republic of Ireland	5.45
(12) 1975[5]	Sheffield	4.24
(13) 1978[6]	Salford	5.38
(14) 1980[6]	Salford	5.27
(15) 1981[4]	Republic of Ireland	4.70

Sources: 1 Studies 1–9 from Abramowicz and Richardson (1975).
2 This rate from Sorel (1974).
3 Bernsen (1976).
4 Mulcahy *et al.* (1983).
5 Martindale (1977).
6 Fryers (1984).

probably due to a combination of factors – the study was conducted in a rural area with a large preponderance of poor families, about 40 per cent of whom were black (Imre, 1967), and testing of every person suspected of being retarded in a house-to-house survey was bound to uncover large numbers who could not perform well on the tests.

Details about the 1978 Gothenburg study (Hagberg *et al.*, 1981; see also Chapter 9) are helpful in understanding why, despite inclusion of children known to the education authorities, the prevalence rate found was unusually low. Mild mental retardation was defined as an IQ of 50–70. The children studied were 8–12 years of age living in Gothenburg in 1978. In order to ascertain cases several search procedures were used. The registers of the Board for Provisions and Services to the Mentally Retarded (BPSMR) and of the Children's Hospital were examined. All school nurses and psychologists were asked to name children in ordinary schools suspected of being mentally retarded. All children identified were examined by a paediatrician, and tested

TABLE 10.2 Prevalence rate per 1000 population for mild mental retardation by age group for selected studies

Year	Place	Age group 5–9	10–14	15–19	Upper IQ limit	Type of community	Case-finding method
1957[1]	Maine	16.30	35.14	16.12	75	Predominantly rural; SES lower than for USA in general	Mail questionnaires to all schools and children's institutions requesting reports of all children known or believed to be retarded
1961[2]	Salford	0.36	0.29	8.65	None	Urban	All cases registered and known to the local health authority
1963[2]	Wessex	0.57	0.48	2.97	None	Urban	All cases known to mental health depts, hospitals, in private homes and hostels
1966[3]	Rose County	67.13	80.11	77.91	70	Rural, low SES	Every family in the county interviewed. Every child over age one, every adult <35 who had not completed high school and every adult >35 who had not completed 8th grade tested
1966[4]	Amsterdam		14.25 (age 10) 16.50 (age 13)		70	Urban	Tracing of all children attending special schools through education authorities, followed by individual assessments of all children traced
1978[5]	Gothenburg	3.7 (ages 8–12)			70	Urban	Registers of MR Provision and Services Board, case-records of special schools and institutions for motor handicapped children and Children's Hospital. School nurses and psychologists asked for suspected children in ordinary schools

Sources: 1 Levinson (1962). 2 Kushlick and Blunden (1974). 3 Imre (1967). 4 Sorel (1974). 5 Hagberg et al. (1981).

using the Wechsler Intelligence Scale for Children (WISC) standardized for Swedish children or the Terman–Merrill test. IQ tests were not given to all children in the city, so that some with IQs below 70 may have been missed. A small-scale attempt was made to check this by testing five children with the poorest school performances in one school district where there were great social problems. None of the five cases had an IQ score below 70. The results of the search yielded a prevalence rate of 3.7:1000 for the IQ range of 50–70 and 1.4:1000 for children with IQs 71–75. The Swedish revisions of the Terman–Merrill and the WISC have not been restandardized for some years and a general upward drift in test performance has been found in other Scandinavian countries. Hagberg *et al.* report this and give a qualified guess for the Gothenburg population aged 8–12 of a mean IQ score of 110–112. If this is, in fact, the case, Hagberg *et al.* calculate that this would theoretically imply a prevalence rate of 30:1000 in the IQ range 50–70 and a rate of 50:1000 for the 70–75 IQ range. Gillberg *et al.* (1983), discussing the results of their own study in Gothenburg, identify another factor which may influence IQ scores:

> Twenty years ago a 'wrong' answer to a question was almost always considered 'wrong'. These days with more negative attitudes toward IQ testing among many psychologists a 'wrong' answer is often 'interpreted positively' and a 'try again' answer allowed! This would lead to a 'false' increase in IQ not attributable to any real change in the child population, but to changing opinions among psychologists. (p. 217)

As shown, not only can the prevalence rates for mild mental retardation in childhood be expected to vary according to the demographic characteristics of the community and the case-finding methods used, but vagaries of testing and of classification practices may also contribute to variations across places and time.

MENTAL RETARDATION IN ADULTHOOD

Many studies have shown that the prevalence of mental retardation increases until it reaches a peak in the late school years. It then drops off sharply around school-leaving to approximately one-half, and the rate then flattens out (Gruenberg, 1964; Innes, 1975; Richardson *et al.*, 1984a). A few studies apparently contradict these findings, showing an increase around school-leaving age (Kushlick, 1964; Susser, 1968; Bayley, 1973). These studies are based on the records of mental health departments and do not include all children classified by education authorities. Had these additional children been added to those known to the mental health department, the apparent contradiction between the two sets of studies would have been resolved.

The sharp drop in prevalence around school-leaving age is almost entirely accounted for by the mildly retarded. This is shown in Figure 10.1 from a study by Innes *et al.* (1978) for the population of north-east Scotland, where the overall prevalence reaches a peak of 14.8:1000 at ages 10–14, and in the

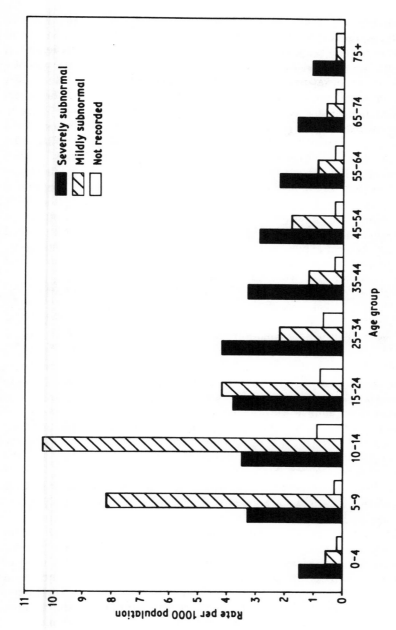

FIGURE 10.1   Age distribution by grade of subnormality in north-east Scotland (Innes *et al.*, 1978, reprinted with permission)

two following age groups of 15–24 and 25–34 drops to 8.8 and 7.1:1000 respectively. These rates include some mildly retarded persons with IQs of 70 and above. From age 25 on, even though the severely retarded predominate, the figure shows that some who are mildly retarded are also in services. In a study of mentally retarded young adults in Aberdeen, we have shown that virtually all mildly retarded adults receiving services had other disabilities, and primary among these was behaviour disturbance (Richardson *et al.*, 1984b).

Clearly the sharp drop in prevalence would not have occurred had IQ been the sole criterion used to define mental retardation. There is evidence that there is some rise in IQ test performance and increase in social competence for some of the mildly retarded in adolescence and early adulthood. This would account for some decrease in prevalence. Another reason is the changes in the roles available to young people before and after leaving school. They were initially classified as children because they were unable to meet the minimal expectations for school work. The adult world provides a far wider range of roles. The greater the diversity of roles for adults, the greater the opportunity for persons with intellectual limitations to avoid roles in which they are unable to meet the minimal expectations of society.

Virtually all those who are severely retarded in childhood will need special care and supervision as adults. This is apparent to their parents and to professionals who make judgements about admission to adult services. These young people will largely come into adult services from mental retardation hospitals, institutions or classes for severely retarded children. In a study of the career paths of mentally retarded young people through mental retardation services, almost all those with IQs of less than 50 made such a move (Richardson *et al.*, 1984a). Some less severely retarded young people attempt to manage in the adult world and are considered for adult mental retardation services only after they have failed. The numbers administratively classified as mentally retarded in the adult years are influenced by the kinds of mental retardation services available, the numbers the services can accommodate and the type of service in which a person with multiple disabilities is placed. A long-standing unresolved issue is whether those with mild mental retardation and behaviour disturbance are better cared for in mental retardation or psychiatric facilities.

Another factor influencing the prevalence of adult mental retardation is the availability of informal supervision, care and support from parents, relatives and others who may play a benefactor role. For example, a severely retarded adult may assist parents in a family business or in housekeeping, without the help of any mental retardation services. With the passage of time the parents will become unable to care for their child because of infirmity or death. At this time some will re-enter mental retardation services, generally residential, and again become administratively classified.

Another shift with age occurs within mental retardation services, with reduced numbers in day services and increased numbers in residential services. This is shown by Innes (1975) in Fig. 10.2. This shift probably

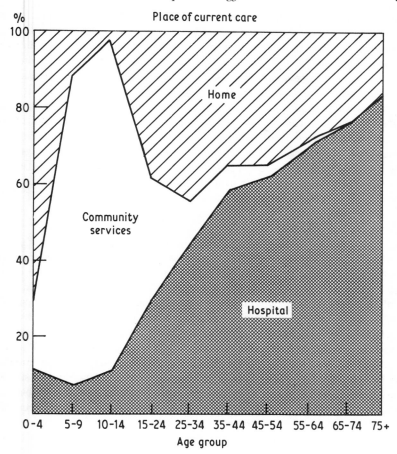

FIGURE 10.2 Place of current care for different age groups in north-east Scotland (Innes 1975, reprinted with permission)

occurs because of the break-up of the homes of mentally retarded adults who were attending day services until their parents died or became infirm. With the increasing longevity of severely retarded adults, there will be need for increased facilities for various forms of residential care.

The third criterion required for mental retardation is that it becomes manifest in the developmental period. For older people who need services because of intellectual disability, it would be unreasonable to refuse services because none was received in childhood. Adults may have come from areas where there were few children's mental retardation services, or their special needs were met informally by their families. Studies of adult prevalence of mental retardation generally ignore this criterion of when the condition developed.

Studies of the prevalence of adult mental retardation have been undertaken primarily to assist local authorities in the planning and evaluation of services. For example, Kushlick (1975), through epidemiological studies of administrative prevalence in Wessex, worked out plans for developing small residential facilities near the homes of the residents rather than building traditional large mental retardation hospitals. Studies of adults are of limited value in exploring the causes of mental retardation because of the long timespan since the inception of the disorder. Retrospectively it is often difficult to obtain the data needed for causal analysis. Apart from very general estimates of service needs, the value of adult prevalence rates outside the community where the study is undertaken is limited because results obtained will be so dependent on the particular forms of service that have developed in each community.

FOLLOW-UP AND LONGITUDINAL STUDIES

What happens to the people identified in epidemiological studies of mental retardation during their life course and what accounts for differences in their lives are two broad sets of questions encompassing important issues of social policy and causation. To answer these general questions requires following a population over time. A 'what happens' question arose in the previous section, where it was shown that there is a marked drop in the prevalence of mental retardation after the school years. The drop was inferred from cross-sectional studies that subdivided the population by age and severity of mental retardation. A study which followed a cohort of five birth years of mentally retarded children into adulthood (Richardson *et al.*, 1984a) looked at their paths through mental retardation services, the administrative total prevalence for each year from ages 5 to 22, and the history of the services they experienced. School-leaving age was 15–16 years, and the prevalence of those in mental retardation services as they reached each age level shows a drop by more than half when school-leaving occurs (Fig. 10.3). It also shows that the drop is accounted for by those who attended the school for mildly (educable) retarded children, there being no change for those coming from a placement designed for severely retarded children.

With the exception just referred to, follow-up studies have not used total populations but have dealt with those who were in institutions or those who attended special classes or schools for the mentally retarded during their childhood. The earliest of the follow-up studies were of persons who had been in mental retardation institutions in the United States and had been released or had escaped.

Earlier in this century there was widespread belief in the dominant role of hereditary factors in the aetiology of mental retardation (see Chapter 11). Stemming from this viewpoint, social policies developed for 'treating' mental retardation by segregating the retarded into large isolated institutions giving custodial care. Widespread legislation was enacted permitting sterilization of the mentally retarded. There seemed little point in providing any programmes

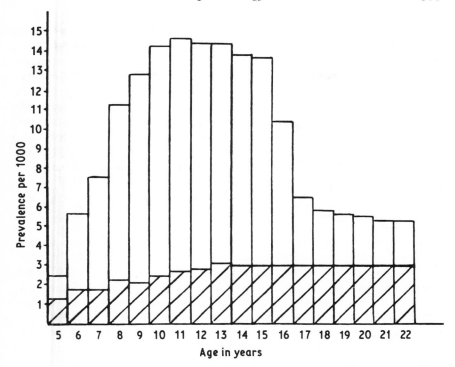

Level of functioning during school years based on placement

☐ EMR

▨ TMR or lower (post-school level of functioning based on final school-age placement)

FIGURE 10.3 Prevalence rates at different age levels for educable mentally retarded (EMR) and trainable mentally retarded (TMR) children and young adults in Aberdeen, Scotland (Richardson *et al.*, 1984a, reprinted with permission)

of social habilitation when genetic factors were considered so overbearing. This strongly held 'conventional wisdom' was slowly brought into question by studies which found that inmates of mental retardation institutions who escaped or were released were often able to function in the community, find and hold jobs, marry and raise families. They did not exhibit the social pathological behaviours expected of those who were retarded, and those who raised families did not produce large numbers of severely retarded children.

The results of these studies contributed to changes in the 'conventional wisdom' about the mentally retarded. From a scientific viewpoint there are major difficulties in interpreting these studies. There is an absence of data on the level of functioning of the subjects when they were children, on the social and physical environments which influenced their development, and on whether they were representative of the population in residential institutions.

Admission to institutions did not involve meeting specific evaluation criteria from which careful judgements were made about level of functioning. Placement in institutions occurred for many reasons other than clear evidence of mental retardation, and included placement of people judged to be nuisances or troublemakers by families, courts or influential members of the community; many were orphans, or persons for whom no other placement could be found. There is no way of knowing to what extent the follow-up studies were of people who should never initially have been placed in the institutions. Another difficulty in interpreting results is lack of information on the kind of socialization the subjects received before and after entering the institution. In most institutions, little attention was paid to developing social and intellectual potential. Some of the behaviour seen in the follow-up studies may have been influenced by the experience of living in the institution and lack of familiarity with the outside world. Nearly fifty years later, a new ideology of deinstitutionalization, mainstreaming and normalization came into prominence, in protest against the inhumane conditions existing in many mental retardation institutions. The ideology sparked a major movement to relocate people into a variety of smaller residences in communities. Studies which followed up relocated residents found that the new conditions did not uniformly meet the expectations of community integration based on the deinstitutionalization ideology, and some small residences had environments as restrictive and inhumane as the large institutions from which the residents had come.

A second kind of study has followed into adulthood young people who had been in special classes for the mentally retarded. These studies found that many were able, as young adults, to live in the community away from their parents' homes; a proportion found employment and some married, raised families and functioned in the adult society. Others experienced problems in achieving satisfactory living conditions. Among the problems, trouble with the law was examined in some studies. Ferguson and Kerr (1960) conducted two follow-up studies of children who left schools for educable mentally handicapped children and had reached their mid-twenties. 'The police records of these youths can only be viewed with grave concern; it is obvious that many of our young criminals are recruited from the ranks of high-grade mental defectives.' Ferguson and Kerr used no nonretarded comparison group, so there is no way of telling whether their findings may have been due to retardation, or the kinds of environments in which the subjects were raised.

Kennedy (1966) conducted a follow-up study of mentally retarded persons with IQs between 45 and 75 who had lived in a Connecticut community. She found that they had a higher frequency of arrests than a comparison group, and they were more likely to receive penalties from the courts.

A follow-up by Baller *et al.* (1967), of children with IQs below 70 in 'opportunity rooms' in Lincoln, Nebraska, showed a higher frequency of minor breaches of the law than in a control group selected by matching on sex, age, race and ethnic origin. Without data on other environmental influences, which may have contributed to their delinquent behaviour, however, it is difficult to assess the role of mental retardation as one of many variables that may cause such behaviour.

Stein and Susser (1960) followed a sample of mildly retarded children and studied their careers when they were between 20 and 24 years of age. The results 'suggest that the high delinquency rates and poor employment records of the subnormal in the community and especially in [mental retardation] hospitals may be largely a consequence of family disruption and homelessness' (pp. 87–8).

There are two general questions which only longitudinal studies can examine: what happens to children who are classified as mentally retarded?; why, as adults, do some fare better than others? Gruenberg (1964) addressed the first question:

> For this drop in prevalence to occur, a large group of people regarded as retarded at fourteen must improve in their functioning to the point where people no longer regard them as retarded. . . . Either these individuals are continuing to be extremely handicapped in later life and are unknown because the services they need are unavailable to them (in which case society is failing to do its duty toward them and ought to learn how to find and help them), or they have stopped being retarded in any real sense at all and do not need any special protection, help or services, in which case one had better change one's concept of what 'real' retardation 'really' is. (p. 274)

On the basis of the sketchy evidence now available, it appears that some who disappear from mental retardation services manage without any special protection, help or services, while others encounter difficulties, but little is known about the quality of their lives. For example, in the early stages of vocational careers, many young people hold unskilled jobs, so a young mildly retarded person holding such a job may manage to conceal his or her intellectual limitations. At later ages, however, if most people move to jobs making more intellectual demands which mildly retarded people cannot meet, the discrepancy between the jobs they and others hold may become more apparent. The lower wages they earn may lead to difficulties. If the mildly retarded person loses jobs because of inadequate performance, this will have different meanings in times of high and low unemployment rates. There is not only the question of how distinguishable mentally retarded persons are from others in jobs, friends, marriage, being a parent and in spare-time activities, but how they feel about themselves. Are there stresses associated with avoiding roles where their incompetence will become apparent?

While the least is known about those who disappear from services, there is also much that is not known about the lives of those who remain in services, in terms of what they experience, how they feel about their experiences, and what roles their families play. In addition to those who disappear from services and those who consistently remain within mental retardation services, there are mentally retarded adults who receive services intermittently and who apparently manage without services for varying periods. They may have needs that services are not meeting and may be misfits in existing forms of service. Learning about them may be valuable in reviewing the adequacy of present services.

For the second general question of why some children with similar characteristics do better than others as adults, there is almost no research which provides answers. We need to know more about the factors in a person's history, both biomedical and behavioural, as well as environmental experiences, that may be significant in predicting later outcomes.

MONITORING SUCCESSIVE AGE-SPECIFIC COHORTS OVER TIME IN THE SAME GEOGRAPHIC AREA

The question of whether there are changes over time in the prevalence rates of mental retardation is important, but difficult to answer. As discussed earlier, the variability in the methods used and in the ecological conditions of the populations in different studies makes comparisons extremely difficult. Much of the variability can be removed if studies monitor the prevalence of mental retardation in the same geographic area in successive cohorts of children of the same age using uniform methods throughout the enquiry.

The most notable example of this approach has been the Salford Mental Handicap Case Register in Salford, England, initiated by Susser and Kushlick. Fryers (1984) studied twenty successive annual cohorts of severely retarded children (1961–80) from this register. The overall prevalence rates for children aged 5–9 rose from 1.98:1000 in 1961 to a high of 5.54:1000 in 1971, then fell to 3.86:1000 by 1980. Fryers related the data to factors which may have contributed to the initial rise in prevalence rates and concluded that, while other factors may have contributed slightly, increased survival was probably the major cause. As to the decline in prevalence after 1971, Fryers suggests that this may largely be due to the reduction in Down's syndrome as a function of a dramatic fall in the birth rate at higher maternal ages. He also suggests that the reduced incidence of specific disorders must have had an impact on the prevalence. These include phenylketonuria, kernicterus due to rhesus incompatibility, congenital syphilis, tuberculosis and congenital hypothyroidism. An additional factor may be improved perinatal care.

A second register has been developed and maintained in Camberwell (Wing, 1971, 1976). Fryers examined the prevalence rates of the Camberwell register from 1967 to 1977. No obvious trend was found in the rates for the 5–9 age group, but for the 10–14 group there was evidence of a rise from 1970, reaching a peak in 1975, and then falling slightly. The Camberwell study suffers from not having an accurate census of the total population of children. There is also evidence of differential migration, with families with mentally retarded children remaining in the area and additional families with such children moving into the area, because of the superior reputation of the mental retardation services. These two studies illustrate the complexity of teasing out factors that may account for changes in prevalence over time. For a better understanding of the issues surrounding the dynamics of prevalence, Fryers (1984) provides an excellent and comprehensive review.

A prevalence study of successive cohorts was undertaken in Västerbotten, Sweden (Gustavson *et al.*, 1977) for the birth cohorts 1959–62, 1963–6 and 1967–70. The prevalence rates per 1000 of severely retarded children alive at age one year were 5.3, 3.4 and 3.1 for the three respective cohorts, and the investigators suggested that the *incidence* may have been declining. Moreover, this decline in prevalence took place in spite of the fact that it occurred prior to the introduction of prenatal diagnosis and other measures to prevent congenital disorders in Sweden and during a period when perinatal mortality declined. A similar decline for Down's syndrome occurred, falling from 2.2 per 1000 for the period 1959–62 to about 0.8 per 1000 for 1963–70, a decline correlated with a simultaneous reduction in maternal age at childbirth.

Stein and Susser (1975) showed the rates of Down's syndrome in successive cohorts of children from 1920 to 1980. These indicated that, while the prevalence of Down's syndrome at birth dropped during that time by almost half, the prevalence at older ages increased several fold, due to increased survival.

The cohort studies cited above lead to the conclusion that the incidence of severe mental retardation has probably been declining in recent years. In recent periods, when the prevalence rates of successive cohorts have increased, this has almost certainly been due to a decrease in mortality.

No monitoring of successive cohorts of mildly retarded children has been carried out that we are aware of. Such studies would be valuable in clearing up some of the problems relating to the widely discrepant rates found in different communities.

An excellent opportunity for monitoring changes in the prevalence of mental retardation, as well as changes that occur within mentally retarded populations, is available from data collected for three British cohort studies. All children born in England, Scotland and Wales during one week in 1946, 1958 and 1970 were selected for study (Atkins *et al.*, 1981; Fogelman and Wedge, 1981). Such studies provide an excellent framework for examining these issues. In addition, they have the unique ability of cohort studies to follow infants prospectively to learn who will and will not become mentally retarded, without the background data being contaminated, as they are in retrospective studies. Unfortunately, very little attention has as yet been paid to mental retardation by the investigators in these studies.

DISORDERS OTHER THAN INTELLECTUAL ONES

Since a purpose of epidemiological studies is to determine the needs for special help for the mentally retarded person and his or her family, additional information is needed about other disorders the person may have. The needs of a person with a given degree of mental retardation vary greatly depending on the presence or absence of other disorders (e.g. behavioural, motor, sensory and seizures) which may occur singly or multiply and at various levels of severity. This more comprehensive view of the attributes of a mentally retarded person also provides information on the relative frequency with which associated disorders are likely to be found in a population, and whether their occurrence is related to the severity of the retardation.

Increasingly, epidemiological studies of mental retardation are obtaining such information. There is inconsistency, however, in the classifications used, some researchers employing medical diagnostic terms such as are used in the International Classification of Diseases (ICD), e.g. epilepsy, whereas others use more descriptive terms of disorders, e.g. nonambulatory or incontinent. For purposes of ascertaining needs and planning services, classifications such as epilepsy and cerebral palsy are too general to be of much value. The classification of epilepsy does not indicate the frequency of seizures, whether they occur presently or whether medication is effective in controlling them. The classification of cerebral palsy does not tell what forms or degrees of disability are present.

One of the first researchers to acknowledge and deal with the need to examine a broader functional profile than just degree of retardation was Kushlick (1964). In a survey of mildly and severely retarded children and adults in Wessex, social and physical incapacity measures were examined. Table 10.3 is derived from data presented by Kushlick and Blunden (1974, p. 45). It is not clear from these data, but presumably some overlap existed among the three categories of nonambulant, severe behaviour disorders and severely incontinent. 'Other aspects of incapacity and ability studied in

TABLE 10.3 Mildly and severely retarded children and adults with and without other disorders in Wessex, England

| | Under age 16 | | | | Over age 16 | | | |
| | IQ<50 | | IQ⩾50 | | IQ<50 | | IQ⩾50 | |
	N	%	N	%	N	%	N	%
Mental retardation (MR) alone	25	53	8	73	98	76	114	93
MR + severe incontinence	5	11	1	9	7	5	1	1
MR + severe behaviour disturbance	9	19	1	9	16	12	4	3
MR + nonambulant	8	17	1	9	8	6	3	2
Total	47		11		129		122	

Source: from Kushlick and Blunden (1974).

Wessex include speech, self-help skills, literacy, and vision and hearing defects' (p. 45), but the data are not presented except to indicate that of 81 severely retarded adults in residential care, 39 were continent, ambulant, without severe behaviour disorders, and able to feed, wash and dress themselves. The corresponding numbers for mildly retarded adults in residential care were 42 out of 55. Thus far, to our knowledge, only Kushlick and researchers who have used his definitions (e.g. Mitchell and Woodthorpe, 1981) have attempted to examine the abilities as well as the disabilities of mentally retarded people.

With the move toward a more co-ordinated set of services to deal with developmental disabilities, it becomes essential to learn more about patterns of disorders as they occur in the individual. While the need for this is clear, it is difficult to devise a form of presentation of group data that provides such information.

In a study of all 9–11-year-olds in the Isle of Wight, Rutter *et al.* (1970) showed combinations of disorders, which they defined in terms of handicap. They 'classified as physically handicapped any child with a physical disorder which was chronic (lasting more than one year), present during the twelve months preceding assessment, and associated with persistent or recurrent handicap of some kind' (p. 348). The physical disorders included asthma, eczema, uncomplicated epilepsy, cerebral palsy, other brain disorders, orthopaedic conditions, heart disease, deafness, diabetes mellitus, neuromuscular disorders and miscellaneous disorders. Similarly, the investigators judged psychiatric disorder to be present if 'sufficiently marked and sufficiently prolonged to cause handicap to the child himself and/or distress or disturbance in the family or community which was continuing up to the time of assessment' (p. 176). The way in which intellectual retardation was defined for this study has been described earlier in this chapter. The ways in which these three disorders combined in the Isle of Wight children is shown in Table 10.4, which is based on data presented by Rutter *et al.* on page 349.

TABLE 10.4 Intellectual retardation (all grades) with and without other disorders in 9–11-year-old children on the Isle of Wight, England

	N	%
Intellectual retardation (IR) alone	33	57
IR + psychiatric handicap	5	9
IR + physical handicap	12	21
IR + physical and psychiatric handicap	8	14
Total	58	

Source: from Rutter *et al.* (1970).

TABLE 10.5 Severely retarded children with and without other disorders in Aarhus, Denmark

	N	%
Mental retardation (MR) alone	28	18
MR + cerebral palsy (CP)	6	4
MR + epilepsy	11	7
MR + hearing impairment	4	3
MR + vision impairment	39	25
MR + CP + epilepsy	9	6
MR + CP + hearing impairment	1	1
MR + CP + vision impairment	3	2
MR + epilepsy + hearing impairment	1	1
MR + epilepsy + vision impairment	13	8
MR + hearing + vision impairment	6	4
MR + 3 disorders	26	17
MR + 4 disorders	7	5
Total	154	

Source: from Bernsen (1981).

For a population of severely retarded children in Denmark, Bernsen (1981) showed multiplicity of disorders using the classifications of cerebral palsy, epilepsy, hearing impairment and vision impairment. Here the ICD classifications are mixed with disorders. No indication of level of severity is given. The author states that, in addition to these classifications, 6 per cent of the children had heart disease, 14 per cent had psychiatric disorders, and 13 per cent had contractures that made daily care difficult. These disorders are not included in Table 10.5, which is based on Bernsen's table (p. 60).

In a study of young adults with all grades of mental retardation in Aberdeen, Richardson *et al.* (1984b) examined the frequency with which various disorders combined. These were defined in terms of the degree to which they interfered with the functioning of the individual, and only those considered to be moderately to severely disabling were included. The data in Table 10.6 were taken from the data on page 31 of Richardson *et al.* These data show a marked excess of multiplicity of disability among the severely retarded as compared to the mildly retarded young adults.

It is clear that comparisons across Tables 10.3–10.6 are difficult. The only category that is comparable, mental retardation alone, shows a good deal of variability, even when comparisons are restricted to the same age group and the same grade of mental retardation. In other categories, comparability is limited by the different ways disorders are defined, if they are defined at all.

TABLE 10.6 Mildly and severely retarded young adults with and without other disorders in Aberdeen, Scotland

	IQ < 50 N	IQ < 50 %	IQ ≥ 50 N	IQ ≥ 50 %
Mental retardation (MR) alone	5	14	64	41
MR + epilepsy			2	1
MR + behaviour disturbance	4	11	42	27
MR + communication disorder	9	26	21	13
MR + limb disability			1	<1
MR + incontinence			1	<1
MR + epilepsy + behaviour disturbance	1	3	2	1
MR + epilepsy + communication disorder	1	3	2	1
MR + epilepsy + limb disability	1	3	1	<1
MR + epilepsy + incontinence	1	3	1	<1
MR + behaviour disturbance + communication disorder	1	3	12	8
MR + behaviour disturbance + limb disability			1	<1
MR + behaviour disturbance + incontinence			1	<1
MR + communication disorder + limb disability	4	11	2	1
MR + 3 disabilities	6	17	2	1
MR + 4 disabilities	2	6	1	<1
Total	35		156	

Source: from Richardson *et al.* (1984b).

DETERMINANTS OF MENTAL RETARDATION

It has become clear that the biomedical and socioenvironmental factors that influence intelligence are inseparably intertwined in a dynamic process that occurs throughout the growth of the individual. Other chapters (1, 4, 5, 6, 8, 11 and 12) deal extensively with these factors. Here we will deal primarily with reports from studies that focus on the interactive nature of the determinants.

Social deprivation, when severe, can clearly be a determinant of mental retardation, but the proportion of cases for whom this is the sole cause may be smaller than previously thought. Increasingly, researchers in a variety of areas have pointed to the interactive effects of the social environment with biomedical factors. Examples follow of studies that have found social variables to be associated with developmental outcomes for children considered to be at risk of mental retardation for biomedical reasons.

In a follow-up study of pre-term infants (gestational age < 37 weeks, birth weight < 2500 grams), Cohen *et al.* (1982) found that care-giving was the critical factor that separated those children whose scores were normal on the

Stanford–Binet at age 5 from those whose scores were below normal. Care-giving was assessed on the basis of the responsiveness of the care-giver to the child, the reciprocity of the relationship and the provision of autonomy to the child's activities.

Drillien *et al.* (1980) followed low-birth-weight infants to age $6\frac{1}{2}$–7. They divided the study population into the following social grades: (1) middle class; (2) superior working class with child-rearing practices and aspirations very similar to the middle class; (3) average working-class homes which fit into neither categories (2) or (4); (4) poor working class, with standards of care well below acceptable levels. An impairment score, consisting of low IQ, educational failure relative to IQ, and significant problems of behaviour, motor abilities, perceptual skills and speech, was used as the dependent variable in a multiple regression. The only predictors demonstrating inde-pendent influence on the impairment score were social grade, evidence of early intrauterine insult and neurologic abnormality, with social grade having the maximum influence.

Siegel (1982) used the Home Observation for Measurement of the Environment (HOME) scale at age 12 months, in addition to biologic and demographic variables, to examine the predictability of developmental delay at age 3 years for pre-term infants with birth weights < 1501 grams. The HOME scale consists of six subscales: (1) emotional and verbal responsivity of mother; (2) a lack of restriction and punishment; (3) organization of physical and temporal environment; (4) provision of appropriate play materials; (5) maternal involvement with child; and (6) opportunities for variety in daily stimulation. All but one of the six subscales, organization of the environment, were significantly correlated with the Stanford–Binet IQ score at age 3, and these significant correlations remained when SES was controlled for. These relationships were much weaker for a full-term control group.

Research into the long-term effects of perinatal complications on pre-term infants was reviewed by Sameroff (1981), who concluded that the major impact on developmental outcomes was that made by social environmental factors.

SOME TAXONOMIC CONSIDERATIONS

Thus far the definitions and classifications of mental retardation we have used come primarily from the mental retardation literature. Because the field has developed under heavy medical influence it is natural that the definitions and classifications used reflect the mode of medical thought. Before going on to consider mental retardation in a more international perspective, we examine here whether there are forms of classification which may be helpful in future studies.

An important contribution was made in the *International Classification of Impairments, Disabilities and Handicaps*, published for trial purposes by the WHO in 1980. In the introduction, the limitations of the International Classification of Diseases (ICD) were discussed:

Although in everyday practice, the medical model of illness ... provides a very efficient approach to disorders that can be prevented or cured – the impact is illness is relieved secondarily as the underlying condition is brought under control – it is incomplete because it stops short of the consequences of disease. It is the latter, particularly, that intrude upon everyday life and some framework is needed against which understanding of these experiences can be developed; this is especially true for chronic and irreversible disorders. The sequence underlying illness-related phenomena thus needs extension.

This can be presented as:

disease → impairment → disability → handicap.   (pp. 10–11)

The terms are defined as follows:

Impairment: any loss or abnormality of psychological, physiological, or anatomical structure or function. (p. 46)
Disability: any restriction or lack (resulting from an impairment) of ability to perform an activity in the manner or within the range considered normal for a human being. (p. 143)

This is further defined in another publication:

It involves tasks, skills and behavior. An abnormality which interferes with function to a significant degree.

The process through which a functional limitation expresses itself as a reality in everyday life in physical and psychological and social terms. (Wood and Badly, 1980, p. 15)

Handicap: A disadvantage for a given individual resulting from an impairment or a disability, that limits or prevents the fulfillment of a role that is normal (depending on age, sex, and social and cultural factors) for that individual. (WHO, 1980, p. 183)

This was also further defined:

Some value is attached to departure from (some) norm. The valuation is dependent on cultural norms.

It is relevant to other people and depends on existing societal values and institutional arrangements. (Wood and Badly, 1980, p. 16)

Wood and Badly also suggest the term *disablement* as: 'A collective description referring to any experience identified variously by the terms impairment, disability and handicap' (p. 17).

The distinction between disability and handicap was made by Wright (1960), and between impairment and disability by Stein and Susser (1971) who also considered impairments to be organic, disability to be functional and handicap to be social.

The distinctions between the concepts of impairment, disability and handicap to some extent fit the components of the definition of mental retardation. 'Evidence of significant subaverage intellectual functioning', usually derived from performance on IQ tests, may be considered the disability, while 'impaired social adaption' may be considered the handicap. If there is clear evidence of a related organic abnormality, there is an impairment. The distinction between impairment and disability becomes difficult when there is no apparent organic basis for the disability or handicap, as occurs in some forms of behaviour disturbance and mental retardation. Possibly the inferred abstraction of mental retardation may be the impairment, while the poor performance on an IQ test or in other tasks requiring intellectual ability are examples of disability.

The disability definition uses the term 'activity' and does not distinguish between specific skills and roles, which may be thought of as clusters of skills, organized for a societal purpose. Items on IQ tests examine specific skills while the mental retardation concept of social competence deals with clusters of skills including roles. It is not clear whether the activities referred to in the definition of disability are restricted to those which are common to all societies, as is suggested by the wording 'considered normal for a human being', or to the activities of a particular society or culture. The cultural context is specified only in the definition of handicap.

IQ tests are the result of years of experience in developing test items which tap specific skills required in western industrial society. Many of the items are clearly inappropriate in other societies, and the identification of a set of skills which can form the basis for making inferences about intelligence in a particular society is a major task which can be carried out only by people with knowledge of the society in which they work.

The symbolic depiction of impairment → disability → handicap can be misleading because it is easy to infer that handicap is a social consequence of a single disability and that a disability is the consequence of a single impairment. In reality, handicap, the inability to meet minimal societal expectations in playing roles, performing activities and engaging in social relationships, is an assessment of the total person by others in the society and takes into account all impairments and disabilities. Moreover, assessment of handicap also takes into account abilities and attributes, such as physical appearance, which may cause others to react in ways that lead to appearance being either an asset or a barrier to interpersonal relations (Richardson *et al.*, 1985). The perception of a disability is judged in the overall context of handicap which is the result of a combination of both abilities and disabilities.

At any point in a person's life, his/her degree of disability and handicap are due to the interaction between the impairment or disability from its inception and the overall physical and social ecological conditions a person experiences. This developmental and ecological component is especially important to keep in mind when trying to understand mental retardation in a crosscultural perspective. At this time it is more practical to develop methods for identifying people judged by their society to be handicapped and then work backwards attempting to determine the nature of the person's disabilities, abilities and impairments.

SOME ISSUES IN THE USE OF EPIDEMIOLOGY IN INTERNATIONAL STUDIES OF MENTAL RETARDATION

In this section consideration is given to the use of epidemiological studies in countries other than western industrial ones. So far, only a few exploratory studies have been carried out. Rather than reviewing each study, the emphasis below is on factors that will have to be considered in the planning of studies and whether some of the premises that have underlain previous mental retardation studies will need to be reconsidered in the light of cultural differences.

Epidemiological studies of mental retardation have largely been restricted to industrial countries, most having been conducted in Europe, the United Kingdom and the United States. The existence of universal compulsory education and some commonality in what constitutes adaptive behaviour have provided some basis for using definitions and measures that give a degree of comparability in methods and results. Earlier in this chapter we discussed some of the difficulties in comparing results across studies because of both methodological and cultural differences. The same difficulties exist to a vastly greater degree in societies that differ from the western industrial countries.

The use of IQ tests in many countries is impractical and meaningless. Tests developed for western industrial societies are based on assumptions of background experiences and knowledge which are invalid for persons coming from cultures other than the one for which the test was developed. Where only some children have schooling and there is variation in the amount of school experience, the resulting difference in experience also poses problems for using tests. There may be several languages used and differences in dialect within a country, and this raises problems of translation. While any crosscultural comparisons on IQ tests are senseless, Vernon (1969) has suggested that comparisons *within* a culture on a test standardized in another setting are appropriate so long as the results discriminate within the population tested. It is difficult however, to interpret test differences when the experiences of those within the population may differ widely. These issues are not only relevant in non-western industrial societies, but also in any country where there are minority groups with experiences and language usage different from the majority culture. With the inapplicability or limited use of the IQ test as a criterion of mental retardation, any assessment must be based on social competence, or adaptive behaviour, and this can be assessed only from the viewpoint of the values, practices, customs and expectations for behaviour held in the population being assessed.

Our concept of mental retardation heavily emphasizes the characteristics of the individual, with little attention being given to the environment. Edgerton (1970) has pointed out:

> If we are to examine incompetence – mental retardation – in comparative perspective we must go beyond a simple functional view to a more ecological one that permits us to attend to the environment, the social system, the culture and the possible relationships between them. In speaking of the environment we must be aware of the influence of human and animal systems outside the social system under analysis as well as the physical habitat. (p. 539)

In two reviews Edgerton (1970, 1981) illustrates from anthropological studies the ways in which different cultures vary regarding whom they perceive as incompetent, how societies hold people accountable for what they do, the demands made for social competence, the role of marriage and who may play the role, the influence of religious beliefs and the supernatural in shaping attitudes and behaviour toward those seen as incompetent, and the extent to which incompetence is stigmatized. The illustrations he gives demonstrate the enormous variation across cultures.

There has been growing interest in developing studies of disability and handicap at an international level. The United Nations named 1981 as the International Year for Disabled Persons. A reflection of this interest was a 'Workshop on Severe Mental Retardation Across the World: Epidemiological Studies' held in the Netherlands in 1980 under the aegis of the Bishop Bekkers Institute. Reports from the workshop were compiled and edited by Belmont (1981a). They include descriptions of very different approaches to research in non-western societies. Belmont (1981b) describes a rationale for a method of screening for severe mental retardation that might be used for children aged 4–9 years, assuming 'that severe retardation is recognized in all cultures because the child is markedly deviant compared to age mates and because the delays in development pose serious problems in the care of the child'. The screening instrument, which focuses on aspects of development that are present in children in all cultures, is used to obtain information such as time of sitting, walking and talking, whether the mother feels that the child is slow in growing up, whether there are abnormalities in behaviour, speech, vision, hearing, whether the child has seizures, and school performance if the child attends school. The information is obtained by questioning the mother and by observations made by the interviewer. The child is given some simple tests of performance such as clapping hands and identifying parts of the body, and is asked questions about numbers. Te interviewer notes evidence of small head and stature, weak limbs, strange movements, inability to sit still and aggressive behaviour. The test screens broadly for developmental disabilities. It has been piloted in a number of countries, and the result are being compared. The data obtained from the screening instrument provide evidence that some forms of developmental disability exist and give an indication of severity. Further examinations would be needed to learn what types of disability account for the developmental lags and abnormalities noted. It would also be useful if screening could be supplemented with information on how others react to the child and how the presence of the developmental disability influences the socialization experiences of the child. In other words, how are different disabilities perceived, what meaning are they given, and how do they cause others to change their behaviour toward the disabled child?

Epidemiology is used both to seek clues to cause and to provide information of value in planning services. Without systematic knowledge on reactions to disability, we cannot know to what extent the disability may be exacerbated or ameliorated by the behaviour of others. For planning services we also need to know the needs and forms of help which the parents see as important, and how help can be given which is acceptable within the culture and does not alienate the child from his or her family and community. These issues are salient in any community, society or culture but, whereas researchers working in their own communities are likely to have some understanding of these matters, investigators coming to an area foreign to them must make special efforts in order to learn about and take account of local conditions.

Hasan and Aziz (1981) report on a population survey of mental retardation in Karachi using interviewing and observation. For young children they use a similar approach to Belmont's, of identifying delays in reaching developmental milestones. For schoolchildren and adults they use evidence of poor role performance in education, jobs, being a housewife, and the somewhat unspecific criterion of skills and achievements (educational and technical) of individual adults compared with those of other members of the family. On the basis of the overall evidence the research team arbitrarily assign categories: 'severe' (IQ roughly less than 50) and 'mild' (IQ above 50). Apart from early childhood, the basis for assessment in the study is adaptive behaviour as evidenced by inability to meet role standards customarily expected within the society for a person of a given age and sex. The individuals identified by the study have some degree of handicap, but the particular disability or disabilities are unclear. Inability to perform may be for reasons other than intellectual limitations, such as behaviour disturbance or communication disorders. Low earning capacity may be due to conditions that are no fault of the individual. The study is valuable in pointing the way toward the use of role inadequacy as a basis for screening a population for mental retardation, but further steps are needed to assess the basis for the poor role performance of those identified in the screening.

An alternative method for identifying mental retardation, or more broadly developmental disabilities, is suggested in Edgerton's writings (1970, 1981). He points out that in some societies almost all adults marry, and marriage is viewed as an entry into adulthood and the assumption of economic responsibility. In such societies one way of screening for disabilities is to identify those individuals who do not contract or maintain marriages.

Another form of screening may be used in societies which assign special roles to persons with particular disablements. Edgerton (1970) describes how a supernatural or saint-like role is assigned to those with epilepsy, and they are accorded special care and revered. In other societies the special role may be that of scapegoat, or someone who is the butt of jokes and is laughed at, jeered at or derided. These forms of screening and identification of disablement depend on knowledge of the local culture.

Screening devices using developmental lags to identify those who cannot meet minimal role requirements or are accorded special roles can identify disability, but not necessarily mental retardation. The developmental lag approach seeks out impairments and disabilities, while the role approach gets at degree of handicap or the interaction between the person with the impairment or disability and the people in the society in which he or she lives. Neither deals with the question of how mental incompetence is thought of within a particular society.

In planning an epidemiological study in any country, a useful first step is to find out whether their language has words that in some way describe what we think of as mental retardation, and we should not assume that a ready translation is available. Richardson (1983) encountered difficulty in finding a local term for mental retardation during a two-month visit to remote areas in Nepal. He travelled with Nepalese who were bilingual, and his companions suggested as translations of mental retardation *lato* and *latebro*. The former meant 'no speech and hearing', while the latter meant 'speaks and hears a little, works slowly'. When asked for examples of people who fitted these terms they included persons who were not intellectually impaired. In a study of disability carried out during the trip, speech and hearing problems were the most common disabilities identified. These may be especially burdensome handicaps to people in a nonliterate society where the alternative form of communication through writing is not available. It was only toward the end of the trip that the translators came up with the term *murkka*, which they said meant 'limited in abilities'. Clearly the word was not in common use or it would have been thought of earlier.

On a visit to the People's Republic of China, Robinson (1978) experienced similar difficulty in obtaining a translation for mental retardation. She

> made repeated enquiries about special services provided for retarded children and their families. The consistent answer was that mental retardation affects so few people that it is not considered a problem in China. It was, in fact, difficult for the interpreters to find words to communicate our questions. . . . Eventually they adopted the term 'blunted child' which apparently best corresponds with local usage. (p. 295)

Where there is no generally understood translation of 'mental retardation', it may be possible to convey the meaning by developing a more general description of the concept through discussions with local people. Any study which uses local informants to identify cases must have some way of telling the informant who is to be identified. Although no details are given, this approach is suggested by Narayanan (1981) in studies of villages in south India. He used a questionnaire intended to identify any family member who might be mentally retarded and did a door-to-door survey using the head of the family as informant. It was then announced, through summoning people by traditional drum beating, that all mentally retarded children or adults should be brought to a meeting place. Unfortunately, the report does not include the way in which the concept of mental retardation was communicated to the people either in the questionnaire or by the drummer.

Richardson (1983), after several weeks of discussions with his bilingual companions, developed the following description of mental retardation:

> Some people learn easily and quickly. Others have great difficulty in learning even simple tasks. If they went to school, they would find it difficult to follow the lessons and do what is asked for, and this difficulty would increase as the children got older. They feel most at ease and comfortable in a well-established round of daily life and are worried and fearful about any new or unexpected situation. They especially have difficulty grasping ideas, and understanding and dealing with complex issues and problems would be impossible for them. They would have difficulty in the skills needed in barter, trading and buying and selling. They would have difficulty and probably would not be able to carry out the variety of tasks needed when they are adults in running a family and home.

The informants then named and described each individual in the village where they lived who fitted this description. Each case was then reviewed to see whether there was evidence of intellectual limitation. One case was reported of a man greatly respected for his strength who earned his living as a porter. He had difficulty in finding his way and could not function alone. He always travelled with other porters and his inability to find his way, which the describer of the case ascribed to incompetence, was of little importance as porters frequently travel with others, and his ability to carry heavy loads offset his inability to find the way. The process used led to a mutual increase in understanding. By determining the numbers of people identified in several villages and the size of each village, a prevalence rate was obtained for each village. Clearly a follow-up study and direct observation of each person nominated as mentally retarded would have been valuable. Unfortunately this was not possible at the time.

The restriction of international studies to severe mental retardation recommended by the Workshop at the Bishop Bekkers Institute is appealing because the correlation between severe mental retardation and being perceived as seriously handicapped will probably be very high in almost all cultures unless the individuals are ascribed a supernatural role. It remains an open question whether such a restriction will make the returns from the efforts at case-finding worthwhile. In western industrial societies we have shown the prevalence of severe mental retardation to range from 2.3 to 7.3 per 1000, with the lower prevalence rates from studies conducted at earlier dates.

In countries with high infant and childhood mortality rates, the chances of survival of a severely retarded child may be very low. Edgerton cites evidence from some cultures of killing severely damaged infants or allowing them to die. In Nepal, Richardson searched for severely retarded persons using both observation and the enquiries of his Nepalese companions. Based on western rates, somewhere between 20 and 35 cases might have been expected in a population of 7000. He found only one. Although he probably missed some cases, the prevalence rate is extremely low compared to western surveys.

Because severe mental retardation may be rare and because of the practical problems of sorting out the intellectual component from a totality of severe disablement, it appears more productive to broaden the scope of enquiries to severe disablement generally. This viewpoint was espoused by Fryers (1981) at the Bishop Bekkers Institute Workshop:

> we might do well to discard our conventional classification of severe mental retardation except in relatively sophisticated communities and, for primary screening, think much more broadly of gross developmental disabilities and disorders. . . . We must be clear about what intervention can be offered in particular communities. . . . Can we legitimately separate out mental retardation from all the other manifestations of high morbidity in small children in developing countries, and can it be justified as a separate priority? . . . Without sophisticated techniques and personnel, we are unlikely to be able to differentiate very clearly between severe mental retardation implying permanent cerebral impairment, physical impairments associated with communication difficulties and poor physical development, and reversible generalized retardation. Should we therefore define a wider group of impairments that give rise to gross deviation from developmental norms, expressed in simple and easily measured terms? (pp. 72–3)

As we pointed out earlier, the approaches of Belmont (1981a, b) and Hasan and Aziz (1981) both covered a wide range of disablements, not all of which are necessarily severe. One of the values of crosscultural comparisons will be to learn which particular disablements at varying levels of severity lead to a person being handicapped in one society and not in another. This will be influenced by the cultural context in which individuals are socialized. Some examples will be used as illustrations.

Mercer (1973) describes a summary of some of the characteristics of western industrial society:

> in a pluralistic, urban society characterized by geographic and social mobility, adults frequently find themselves in new social systems and must learn new roles and internalize new values. In American society, socialization to unfamiliar social roles is a life-long process. (p. 134)

Robinson (1978) relates some characteristics of Chinese society to mental retardation:

we came gradually to understand that mild mental handicap need not constitute a barrier to participation in society. From all we could gather, Chinese society makes limited demands for intellectual competence, and usually provides natural support within the family and commune or the workers' residential district. There is strong emphasis on helping one another, on minimizing individual differences (both positive and negative) and on group needs rather than those of the individual. (p. 295)

She describes the ways in which schools deal with intellectual impairment:

Our informants recognized that there were individual differences in preparation for school and in learning rate, but not basic differences in intelligence. Individual differences are not consistent with socialist teachings ... teachers are likely to blame a child's slowness on the parents' incomplete understanding of the importance of study, the child's lacking a sense of purpose or having missed basic preparatory work, or perhaps 'simply having difficulty learning'. In such cases, we were similarly told, the teachers give extra help on their own time and the quicker children are asked to tutor the slower ones. (p. 297)

Richardson (1983) was able to observe traditional villages in Nepal where the style of life was based largely on subsistence agriculture. In these villages the parents and the extended family possess the skills their children will need in adult life and are confident that the same skills will be needed in the next generation. There appears to be a relationship between the proportion of children attending school and the rate of social change. In the traditional villages only approximately 5 per cent attend school. Without universal schooling there is no assessment of children's level of ability in the kinds of intellectual demands required by the subjects taught.

Children at an early age are initiated into the wide range of tasks and roles that they will have to play as adults. They serve a long, gradual apprenticeship with parents who demonstrate, year after year, the annual cycle of tasks needed for everyday living and the social skills expected of adults in the village. The role models for learning are parents, adult relatives and older siblings, with whom the children have a strong emotional tie. There is an almost complete absence of any form of mechanical power and an enormous need for manpower of all kinds. Apart from a few specialized occupations, such as blacksmith, miller and the priesthood, a wide range of tasks and skills are needed to gain a livelihood from an agricultural form of life, so there is a wide range of activities in which children can engage. Because parents are the teachers of these activities, they have an excellent opportunity to assess their children's performance in a variety of tasks, and they can identify and encourage those skills in which the children demonstrate promise. They can also avoid making demands that their children will have difficulty in meeting, because of disability. The parents recognize the disabilities of their children but, by utilizing their abilities, minimize the extent to which the disabilities lead to handicap. Work, leisure activities and socializing intermingle, and children participate with their families in all these activities. In the villages there was an absence of abrupt discontinuities in activities, social relations and geographic location. Under these conditions, children's learning experiences may be particularly appropriate for those who are intellectually limited.

With adulthood there are changes in the expected behaviours and roles. Rather than carrying out single tasks, marriage and parenthood entail organizing the family in the variety of tasks needed in the agricultural society, including the skills required for barter, trade, using money and the handling of human relations problems.

These observations of a traditional society suggest that intellectual incompetence will be more apparent in adults than children, which is the reverse of the situation in western industrial society. In the enquiry mentioned, in which Richardson asked informants to name people in Nepalese villages who were mentally retarded, everyone named was an adult. In another traditional society, the Semai of the Highlands of Malaya, Dentan (1967) told of four mentally retarded persons in two villages. Three were adults and the fourth a teenager, who was noteworthy more because of aggressive behaviour than lack of intellectual ability.

In many parts of the world people live in a state of cultural change and in societies where subcultural differences exist side by side. In some cases there is a clear majority culture and one or more minority cultures; in other cases there may be several different cultures with communication between them. Stein (1981) suggests that with rapid social change there will be a rise in the prevalence of mental retardation, which families will become less able to support:

> For those with a minimum of resources, migration to the towns and the pressure on housing and jobs make almost impossible the maintenance of family networks capable merely of providing material support for kin. . . .
> To rear numerous children, to support the aged, and to care for the handicapped is to attempt more than can be done. (p. 16)

These illustrations of the widely different conditions that may be encountered in trying to understand what mental retardation is and how it can be studied bring us back to the cautionary conclusion of Gruenberg (1964) cited earlier, based on his research in the United States: 'behavior leading to the social suspicion of "mental retardation" is not necessarily a fixed characteristic of individual children but is rather a complex set of manifestations of some children's relationship to their social environment.' His conclusion is insightful for international studies.

Mental retardation has received attention in western industrial societies because of the problems experienced by people with intellectual limitation. We must not assume that intellectual limitation is seen as having such importance in all societies. We should attempt to learn, within any society where studies of disability are being planned, what, from their viewpoint, constitute the impairments and disabilities which are more or less handicapping. Other societies may have modes of thought and classificatory systems for evaluating people which are very different from those to which we are accustomed.

Although we have linked epidemiology to the provision of services throughout this chapter, we have not attempted to review the innovative service programmes in developing countries. Anyone interested in this topic would benefit from reading the review by Fryers (1984) as well as Chapter 19.

In crosscultural studies of mental retardation and in any development of programmes it is essential to work with professional leaders within the country where the studies are being carried out and with people with a concern for mental retardation. Through contact with westerners, and often through their education, indigenous leaders have become familiar with western thought and may have lost close touch with the customs, practices, values and modes of thought of the majority of people in their own country who are less urbanized and retain more traditional patterns of thought.

At the Bishop Bekkers Workshop on mental retardation in developing countries, there appeared to be agreement that it was unethical to conduct studies without following them up with actions. If the dictum of 'do no harm' is to be followed, then studies must be far broader in conception than in the past and take into account how the communities studied react to and deal with people who have various forms of disability, and whether there are belief systems which support their actions. It should not be assumed that there will always be some forms of intervention which have a net benefit for the person with a disability.

CONCLUSIONS

Research into the epidemiology of mental retardation spanned a period when services for the disabled were organized under a variety of categories, mainly stemming from medical classifications. The shortcomings of this fragmentation of services have become apparent, and efforts are being made to develop diagnostic and evaluation centres and a system of care directed toward the concept of developmental disabilities. The future evolution of this approach will be best served by epidemiological studies that encompass a broad spectrum of disabilities. The Isle of Wight study of Rutter *et al.* (1970) was a pioneer venture in this direction. Such studies, if they are to be comparable, require the further development and consistent use of classifications such as have been proposed by WHO for disablements. The need for a broader approach in epidemiology also becomes apparent in the review of mental retardation in international perspective.

Present criteria used to identify mental retardation have led to a reduction in the numbers of children who were wrongly classified (false positives), but may have led to an increase in the number of children whose needs for special help have been neglected (false negatives). The removal of the category of borderline mentally retarded may have had the unintended consequence of deflecting research attention from the children who remain in regular classes and may experience frequent failure and few rewards in their school careers, and may encounter difficulties after leaving school. They may have special needs that are not being fully recognized.

Epidemiological studies of the causes of mental retardation have customarily dealt mainly with biomedical factors for severe mental retardation and with social-environmental factors for mild mental retardation. There is increasing evidence of the interaction between biological and social factors for all grades of mental retardation, and future studies need to take this into account. Because it may be more difficult to develop measures and classifications of social than biological factors, this should not prevent a major effort to do so. Mental retardation, and more generally disablement, are dynamic factors which change over time, and there is need to adopt a more longitudinal and ecological view for their study. There is increasing interest in lifespan research and recognition that, in each stage of life, different circumstances and conditions are encountered. Yet there is almost no research on mental retardation or disablement that has examined these different adult stages, the demands they make, and how persons with disablements influence and are influenced by these varied conditions.

REFERENCES

ABRAMOWICZ, H.K. and RICHARDSON, S.A. (1975) 'Epidemiology of severe mental retardation in children: community studies', *Amer. J. Ment. Defic.*, 80, 18–39.

ATKINS, E., CHERRY, N., DOUGLAS, J.W.B., KIERNAN, K.E. and WADSWORTH, M.E.J. (1981) 'The first British birth cohort: an account of the origins, progress and results of the National Survey of Health and Development', in S.A. MEDNICK and A.E. BAERT (eds), *Prospective Longitudinal Research*, London, Oxford University Press, 25–9.

BALLER, W.R., CHARLES, D.C. and MILLER, E.L. (1967) 'Mid-life attainment of the mentally retarded: a longitudinal study', *Genet. Psychol. Monogr.*, 75, 235–9.

BAYLEY, M.J. (1973) *Mental Handicap and Community Care: A Study of Mentally Handicapped People in Sheffield*, London and Boston, Routledge & Kegan Paul.

BELMONT, L. (1981a) 'International studies of severe mental retardation', *Int. J. Ment. Hlth*, 10, 3–7.

BELMONT, L. (1981b) 'The development of a questionnaire to screen for severe mental retardation in developing countries', *Int. J. Ment. Hlth*, 10, 85–99.

BERNSEN, A.H. (1976) 'Severe mental retardation among children in the county of Aarhus, Denmark', *Acta. Psychiat. Scand.*, 54, 43–66.

BERNSEN, A.H. (1981) 'Severe mental retardation among children in a Danish urban area: assessment and aetiology', in P. MITTLER (ed.), *Frontiers of*

Knowledge in Mental Retardation, vol. II, Baltimore, University Park Press, 53–62.

BIRCH, H., RICHARDSON, S.A., BAIRD, D., HOROBIN, G. and ILLSLEY, R. (1970) *Mental Subnormality in the Community: A Clinical and Epidemiologic Study*, Baltimore, Williams & Wilkins.

CLARKE, A.M. (1965) 'Criteria and classification of mental deficiency', in A.M. CLARKE and A.D.B. CLARKE (eds), *Mental Deficiency: The Changing Outlook*, 2nd edn, London, Methuen, 47–70.

COHEN, S.E., PARMELEE, A.H., SIGMAN, M. and BECKWITH, L. (1982) 'Neonatal risk factors in pre-term infants', *Appl. Res. Ment. Retard.*, 3, 265–78.

DENTAN, R.K. (1967) 'The response to intellectual impairment among the Semai', *Amer. J. Ment. Defic.*, 71, 764–6.

DRILLIEN, C.M., THOMSON, A.J.M. and BURGOYNE, K. (1980) 'Low birthweight children at early school age: a longitudinal study', *Develop. Med. Child Neurol.*, 22, 26–47.

EDGERTON, R.B. (1970) 'Mental retardation in non-western societies: toward a cross-cultural perspective on incompetence', in H.C. HAYWOOD (ed.), *Sociocultural Aspects of Mental Retardation*, New York, Appleton-Century-Crofts, 523–59.

EDGERTON, R.B. (1981) 'Another look at culture and mental retardation', in M.J. BEGAB, H.C. HAYWOOD and H.L. GARBER (eds), *Psychosocial Influences in Retarded Performance*, vol. I, Baltimore, University Park Press, 309–24.

FERGUSON, T. and KERR, A.W. (1960) *Handicapped Youth*, London, Oxford University Press.

FOGELMAN, K. and WEDGE, P. (1981) 'The national child development study (1958 British cohort)', in S.A. MEDNICK and A.E. BAERT (eds), *Prospective Longitudinal Research*, London, Oxford University Press, 30–42.

FROST, W.H. (1936) Introduction to *Snow on Cholera*, New York, Commonwealth Fund.

FRYERS, T. (1981) 'Problems in screening for mental retardation in developing countries', *Int. J. Ment. Hlth*, 10, 64–75.

FRYERS, T. (1984) *The Epidemiology of Severe Intellectual Impairment: The Dynamics of Prevalence*, London, Academic Press.

GILLBERG, C., SVENSON, B., CARLSTRÖM, G., WALDENSTRÖM, E. and RASMUSSEN, P. (1983) 'Mental retardation in Swedish urban children: some epidemiological considerations', *Appl. Res. Ment. Retard.*, 4, 207–18.

GROSSMAN, H.J. (ed.) (1983) *Classification in Mental Retardation*, Washington, D.C., American Association on Mental Deficiency.

GRUENBERG, E.M. (1964) 'Epidemiology', in H.A. STEVENS and R. HEBER (eds), *Mental Retardation. A Review of Research*, Chicago and London, University of Chicago Press, 259–306.

GUSTAVSON, K.H., HOLMGREN, G., JONSELL, R. and BLOMQUIST,

H.K.:SON(1977) 'Severe mental retardation in children in a northern Swedish county', *J. Ment. Defic. Res.*, 21, 161–80.

HAGBERG, B., HAGBERG, G., LEWERTH, A. and LINDBERG, U. (1981) 'Mild mental retardation in Swedish school children', *Acta Paediat. Scand.*, 70, 441–4.

HASAN, Z. and AZIZ, H. (1981) 'Report on a population survey of mental retardation in Pakistan', *Int. J. Ment. Hlth*, 10, 23–7.

IMRE, P.D. (1967) 'The epidemiology of mental retardation in a south-east rural USA community', in B.W. RICHARDS (ed.), *Proceedings of the First Congress of the International Association for the Scientific Study of Mental Deficiency*, London, Michael Jackson, 655–60.

INNES, G. (1975) 'A multi-disciplinary study of mental subnormality in north-east Scotland', in D.A.A. PRIMROSE (ed.), *Proceedings of the Third Congress of the International Association for the Scientific Study of Mental Deficiency*, Warsaw, Polish Medical Publishers, 195–200.

INNES, G., JOHNSTON, A.W. and MILLAR, W.M. (1978) *Mental Subnormality in North-East Scotland: A Multi-Disciplinary Study of Total Population*, Scottish Home and Health Department, no. 38, Edinburgh, HMSO.

International Classification of Impairments, Disabilities and Handicaps (1980) Geneva, World Health Organization.

KENNEDY, R.J. (1966) *A Connecticut Community Revisited: A Study of the Social Adjustment of a Group of Mentally Deficient Adults in 1948 and 1960*, Hartford, Connecticut State Department of Health, Office of Mental Retardation.

KUSHLICK, A. (1964) 'The prevalence of recognized mental subnormality of IQ under 50 among children in the south of England, with reference to the demand for places for residential care', in J. OSTER (ed.), *Proceedings of the International Copenhagen Conference on the Scientific Study of Mental Retardation*, Copenhagen, unknown publisher, 550–6.

KUSHLICK, A. (1975) 'Epidemiology and evaluation of services for the mentally handicapped', in M.J. BEGAB and S.A. RICHARDSON (eds), *The Mentally Retarded and Society*, Baltimore, University Park Press, 325–44.

KUSHLICK, A. and BLUNDEN, R. (1974) 'The epidemiology of mental subnormality', in A.M. CLARKE and A.D.B. CLARKE (eds), *Mental Deficiency: The Changing Outlook*, 3rd edn, London, Methuen, 31–81.

LEVINSON, E. (1962) *Retarded Children in Maine*, Orono, University of Maine Press.

MARTINDALE, A. (1977) *Trends in the Prevalence of Mental Handicap since the Register was Set Up in 1975*, Report of the Sheffield Case Register, Ryegate Centre, Sheffield.

MERCER, J.R. (1973) *Labeling the Mentally Retarded*, Berkeley and London, University of California Press.

MITCHELL, S.J.F. and WOODTHORPE, J. (1981) 'Young mentally handicapped adults in three London boroughs: prevalence and degree of disability', *J. Epidem. Comm. Hlth*, 35, 59–64.

MULCAHY, M., O'CONNOR, S. and REYNOLDS, A. (1983) 'Census of the mentally handicapped in the Republic of Ireland, 1981', *Irish Med. J.*, 76, 71–5.

NARAYANAN, H.S. (1981) 'A study of the prevalence of mental retardation in southern India', *Int. J. Ment. Hlth*, 10, 28–36.

NEW YORK STATE DEPARTMENT OF MENTAL HYGIENE (1955) Mental Health Research Unit, 'A special census of suspected referred mental retardation, Onondaga County, New York', *Technical Report of the Mental Health Research Unit*, New York, Syracuse University Press.

RICHARDSON, S.A. (1983) 'Physical impairment, disability and handicap in rural Nepal', *Dev. Med. Child Neurol.*, 25, 717–26.

RICHARDSON, S.A., KOLLER, H., KATZ, M. and MCLAREN, J. (1984a) 'Career paths through mental retardation services: an epidemiological perspective', *Appl. Res. Ment. Retard.*, 5, 53–67.

RICHARDSON, S.A., KOLLER, H., KATZ, M. and MCLAREN, J. (1984b) 'Patterns of disability in a mentally retarded population between ages 16 and 22 years', in J.M. BERG (ed.), *Perspectives and Progress in Mental Retardation*, vol. II, Baltimore, University Park Press, 25–38.

RICHARDSON, S.A., KOLLER, H. and KATZ, M. (1985) 'Appearance and mental retardation. Some first steps in the development and application of a measure', *Amer. J. Ment. Defic.*, 89, 475–84.

ROBINSON, N.M. (1978) 'Mild mental retardation: does it exist in the People's Republic of China?', *Ment. Retard.*, 16, 295–8.

RUTTER, M., TIZARD, J. and WHITMORE, K. (1970) *Education, Health and Behaviour*, London, Longman; republished in 1981, Huntington, New York, Krieger.

SAMEROFF, A.J. (1981) 'Longitudinal studies of preterm infants: a review of chapters 17–20', in S.L. FRIEDMAN and M. SIGMAN (eds), *Preterm Birth and Psychological Development*, New York, Academic Press.

SIEGEL, L.S. (1982) 'Reproductive, perinatal and environmental factors in predictors of the cognitive and language development of preterm and full-term infants', *Child Develop.*, 53, 963–73.

SOREL, F.M. (1974) *Prevalences of Mental Retardation*, Tilburg, Netherlands, Tilburg University Press.

STEIN, Z. (1981) 'Why measure incidence and prevalence?', *Int. J. Ment. Hlth*, 10, 14–22.

STEIN, Z. and SUSSER, M. (1960) 'The families of dull children. A classification for predicting careers', *Brit. J. Prev. Soc. Med.*, 14, 83–8.

STEIN, Z. and SUSSER, M. (1971) 'Changes over time in the incidence and prevalence of mental retardation', in J. HELLMUTH (ed.), *Exceptional Infant*, vol. 2, *Studies in Abnormalities*, New York, Brunner/Mazel.

STEIN, Z. and SUSSER, M. (1975) 'Public health and mental retardation: new power and new problems', in M.J. BEGAB and S.A. RICHARDSON (eds), *The Mentally Retarded and Society: A Social Science Perspective*, Baltimore, University Park Press, 53–73.

SUSSER, M. (1968) *Community Psychiatry: Epidemiologic and Social Themes*, New York, Random House.

VERNON, P.E. (1969) *Intelligence and Cultural Environment*, London, Methuen.

WING, L. (1971) 'Severely retarded children in a London area: prevalence and provision of services', *Psychol. Med.*, 1, 405–15.

WING, L. (1976) 'Services for the mentally retarded in Camberwell', in J.K. WING and T. FRYERS (eds), *Psychiatric Services in Camberwell and Salford: Statistics 1964–1974*, London, Institute of Psychiatry, and Manchester, Department of Community Medicine, University of Manchester.

WOOD, P.H.N. and BADLY, E.M. (1980) *People with Disabilities*, New York, World Rehabilitation Fund.

WRIGHT, B.A. (1960) *Physical Disability – A Psychological Approach*, New York, Harper.

PART THREE
Prevention and amelioration

Biomedical amelioration and prevention

Joseph M. Berg

INTRODUCTION

Notions on amelioration and prevention of mental retardation often reflect not only the state of technical knowledge at a particular time but also prevailing societal attitudes and convictions about mentally handicapped persons. Following many centuries of what may be called therapeutic negativism and neglect, there has been advocacy, during the past 150 years or so, of a wide variety of interventions ranging from purported panaceas, recommended on dubious, misguided or even blatantly dishonest grounds, to well-founded undertakings of a generally desirable and ethically tenable nature.

In comparatively recent years, fairly extensive scope for rational biomedical amelioration and prevention has developed. Within the framework of advances in biological and medical science applicable to human disabilities in general, two particular trends have enhanced the prospects of effective ameliorative or preventive measures in mental retardation. There is increasing understanding of the multiple and varied environmental and genetical circumstances that result in mental deficit and associated manifestations, and a growing capacity to anticipate or recognize a large number of these influences early enough to allow for meaningful intervention.

Many of these considerations are referred to in other chapters, as would be expected in a book concerned with the changing outlook in mental retardation. It is perhaps further evidence of that changing outlook that, in addition, it seems appropriate to devote a chapter specifically to biomedical amelioration and prevention and that, in the penultimate decade of the twentieth century, it may even be inexcusable not to do so. Various aspects of the subject are presented here as an indication of earlier perceptions, current practices and future prospects.

HISTORICAL NOTE

In centuries gone by, retarded persons have variously been feared, despised, pitied, tolerated or respected, and dealt with accordingly with little if any attempt to alter their mental or physical characteristics in a therapeutic sense. Indeed, as Kanner (1964) noted, there are extremely few references to mental retardation as such (let alone to its treatment) in medical writings prior to the nineteenth century, although mental illness and epilepsy, for instance, were vividly described and debated. It is likely that such 'therapies' as were judged suitable for persons with these latter conditions were applied to those with mental handicap as well, and that measures which persisted for long years, such as trephination of the skull, blood letting and attempts to exorcize evil spirits, were equally ineffective and frequently disastrous for whoever the recipients might have been. It may well be, too, that various nonpharmacological concoctions, somewhat reminiscent of the witches' brew in Shakespeare's *Macbeth*, advised for seizures, for example, were sometimes also prescribed for those with mental handicap, equally without benefit. Thomas Willis (1621–75), in discussing medications for the mentally retarded over 300 years ago, was frank enough to indicate that amelioration was more likely than cure, and wise enough to recommend a multidisciplinary approach (joint efforts by physician and teacher) in achieving improvements (Cranefield, 1961).

Apart from the almost nonexistent pre-nineteenth-century medical ameliorative measures for mental retardation, a supposedly preventive component entered the outlook in circumstances where mental deficit was considered a punishment for parental sins or transgressions, with an implication therefore that avoidance of such deviations would eliminate or diminish prospects of producing retarded offspring. Empirically, too, it may have been recognized that certain practices such as alcoholism and, though seemingly not in ancient Egypt (Scheerenberger, 1983), incest did not augur well for the birth of healthy children, thus resulting in perceptions and regulations that could have somewhat reduced the frequency of occurrence of affected infants.

From about the middle of the nineteenth century, residential institutions, of which Guggenbühl's ill-fated one on the Abendberg in Switzerland was historically the major forerunner (Kanner, 1964), were founded in Europe and North America – with high hopes that they would be curative, or at least ameliorative, settings through the provision of mainly educational and training programmes in pleasant and healthy surroundings; though often under the jurisdiction of physicians, medically related undertakings were limited in these settings, as elsewhere, and consisted largely of greater or lesser attention to diet, hygiene and exercise.

A paucity of expected results dampened enthusiasm about curative prospects and, with a growth of ill-founded and often strident eugenic dogmas at the beginning of this century and well into it, institutionalization came to be seen less as a means of developing the potential of retarded persons and more as a method of protecting society from them. Hence it was argued that institutions constituted a valuable preventive measure by providing a barrier to parenthood and, by thus stopping retarded individuals from reproducing their kind, leading to a reduction in the frequency of retardation. Other ways of attempting to achieve this objective, such as sterilization, were by no means abandoned, though most (but not all!) advocates of eugenic safeguards stopped short of recommending legalized death sentences. Prohibition of marriage of retarded persons, though advocated by some to attain the objective mentioned, was thought inadequate by those who believed that, as such persons were by nature promiscuous and not law-abiding, they would have children anyway. In this connection it is interesting to note that many years earlier the papal physician Paulus Zacchias (1584–1659), though opposed to marriage of the congenitally deaf partly for eugenic reasons, considered that the mildly retarded should be allowed to marry and, though debarring marriage for the severely retarded, he did so on religious grounds (inability to understand the sacraments) and not eugenic ones (Cranefield and Federn, 1976).

In addition to the 'preventive' concepts mentioned above, therapeutic ones were also gradually introduced. From the latter part of the last century onwards, there was growing realization that mental retardation was not a unitary entity, and individual biomedical varieties of retardation became increasingly recognized. Early examples are Little's disease (Little, 1862), Down's syndrome (Down, 1866) and tuberous sclerosis (Bourneville, 1880–1), and many more followed. Nevertheless, supposedly ameliorative or curative medications and related therapies continued to be advocated, not as specific treatments for specific conditions, but as panaceas for mental deficit however caused. Thus, for example, 'brain foods' like glutamic acid had their protagonists, and still do to this day with alternatives like sicca cell treatment (see p. 407).

Increasingly, more rational approaches are being developed and adopted, and continue to grow in sophistication as knowledge of the aetiology and characteristics of the multiple biomedical types of mental retardation, and of means of intervention, advances. Most of this chapter is concerned with these developments.

TREATMENT

Medication

Medical treatment of mental retardation and commonly associated abnormalities can be divided into several categories consisting primarily of: (1) medication (which might be called more or less 'universal') supposedly raising the level of mental function in a wide variety of conditions in which retardation is a feature; (2) specific medication for particular, mainly biochemical, forms of retardation; and (3) symptomatic medication for various manifestations frequently found in retarded individuals, such as behavioural disturbance and epilepsy, and which contribute to the further impairment of mental function. Observations on the second and third of these categories are presented in Chapters 5 and 8, respectively, so that the focus below is on the first.

The notion that chemical central nervous system stimulants can have a beneficial effect on intelligence and memory has a long history. Morris *et al.* (1954) noted that the climbing shrub, *Celastrus paniculata*, enjoyed repute in these respects among Hindu physicians for centuries and, indeed, that a preparation containing oil from the plant was (and presumably still is) sold in bazaars under a name which translates as 'brain polisher'. Morris *et al.* tested previous claims of the efficacy of *Celastrus paniculata* administration in retarded persons. They concluded, from a careful study of young adults (aged 18 to 34 years and with IQ ranging from 49 to 72), that the medication, which produced a euphoric effect, had little value in the treatment of mental retardation. The same authors (Morris *et al.*, 1955) subsequently conducted another trial with a pharmacologically better-known stimulant, amphetamine sulphate, also formerly considered by some to improve mental performance in retarded individuals. Their subjects, similar in age to those in the earlier study and with an IQ range of 60 to 74, showed no effect in terms of intelligence, learning capacity, attention, fluency or memory. Stimulants of this kind therefore do not appear to have a useful general application in the medical treatment of mental retardation.

Several decades ago, administration of large doses of glutamic acid was claimed by some to enhance intellectual functioning of retarded persons. A critical review of published studies pointed out serious methodological weaknesses in the relatively small number of controlled investigations reporting favourable results (Astin and Ross, 1960) rendering, as these authors cautiously stated, the conclusions 'difficult to accept'. Few, if any, now advocate this treatment.

Somewhat akin to earlier enthusiasm for glutamic acid is more recent advocacy of the purported benefits of so-called megavitamin therapy. Though, as the Committee on Nutrition of the American Academy of Pediatrics (1976) noted, increased intake of various vitamins clearly is indicated in particular conditions like the steatorrhoeas and several inborn errors of metabolism, the committee observed also that 'a cult developed in the use of large doses of water-soluble vitamins to treat a wide spectrum of disease states'. These states include mental retardation and a variety of learning disorders, as well as schizophrenia and other psychiatric illnesses in children and adults. In general, claims purporting to show improved mental function have been treated by scientifically minded observers with scepticism, if not outright condemnation, on theoretical and methodological grounds, and concerns about unpleasant and potentially dangerous side effects have also been raised (see, for instance, Golden, 1980). At least in so far as mental retardation is concerned, megavitamin therapy seemed to have fallen into abeyance. However, relatively recently an account was published by Harrell *et al.* (1981) on the administration of large doses of multiple (eleven) vitamins, combined with eight minerals and often with thyroid hormone, to a group of school-age retarded children (IQ range about 17–70). These children, most 'unclassified' and some with Down's syndrome, were reported to have shown IQ gains in an eight-month period ranging from about 5 to 25 points. Even more dramatically, similar earlier treatment by the senior author of a seven-year-old child with an estimated IQ of 25 to 30 was said to have resulted in an IQ of 90 two years later. Not surprisingly, these findings attracted considerable attention, not least of all in the lay press. Several studies published subsequently using similar therapy in retarded children and adults of various types, including some with Down's syndrome, showed no IQ gains or other apparent benefits (Bennett *et al.*, 1983; Coburn *et al.*, 1983; Ellis and Tomporowski, 1983; Weathers, 1983; Ellman *et al.*, 1984). Hence megavitamin treatment for mental retardation with or without mineral supplementation remains, at best, a proposition of very doubtful validity.

Another type of medication, often referred to as cellular or sicca cell therapy, calls for comment here because it still keeps on being revived with undiminished zeal in certain quarters. The concept, dating back to the 1930s, involves the injection of cell preparations derived from animals. According to Goldstein (1956) intramuscular injection into a patient of such cells obtained from a gland, tissue or organ 'will activate the cells of the corresponding gland, tissue, or organ to produce improved or normal function'. Thus many diseases and disorders are considered amenable to this treatment (Griffel, 1957). With regard to mental retardation of many varieties, sicca cells from animal central nervous system tissues and sometimes, for good measure, from other tissues combined with additional chemical substances have been used, with claims, essentially anecdotal, of remarkable mental and physical benefits (see, for example, Goldstein (1956) and Destunis (1957)). To say the least, it is very difficult to understand the rationale for such treatment and there is a woeful absence of scientifically acceptable data demonstrative of its supposed efficacy. By contrast, a well-conducted study with appropriate controls on a group of retarded children of different clinical types, most with IQ below 50, undertaken by Black *et al.* (1966) found no evidence of intellectual or behavioural improvement consequent on sicca cell treatment.

Interest in such therapy seemed to wane. However, judging personally from an increase of enquiries by parents of retarded children, it appears to have received a boost through enthusiastic advocacy from a few professional (see Schmid, 1978, 1980) and lay (see Bernhard, 1981) sources. Neither the rationale for the treatment nor the evidence of its purported effectiveness is more convincing than was previously the case. Readers can evaluate the favourable claims mentioned for themselves and are referred also, to help balance the perspective, to a recently published stinging critique by Karp (1983).

In view of the widespread and varied cerebral pathology usually present in those with severe mental retardation, it is difficult to envisage that any medications, singly or in combination, could have a significant beneficial effect on the intellectual performance of these persons in general. While, of course, a search for such remedies is in itself not objectionable, there are major and reasonable requirements of those who contemplate or propose them. In addition to the obvious need to consider possibly harmful physical side effects, great care must be taken not to publicize claims of efficacy without solid, scientifically tenable supporting evidence. To do otherwise is irresponsible or worse, as raising expectations of often receptive parents and other relatives can be emotionally very traumatic if the expectations prove to be unfounded and hence unmet. Bearing these reservations in mind, it should be added that considerable experimental work is in progress concerning the possibilities of central nervous system nerve cell regeneration and chemical enhancement of impaired neural function. This may have beneficial practical application in the future for various retarded individuals. Interested readers are referred to a recent series of presentations on the subject in a book edited by Menolascino *et al.* (1983).

Surgery

Though one hopes that such violent and irrational practices as trephination of the skull to release evil spirits supposedly causing mental and related problems (Guthrie, 1945) is no longer tolerable anywhere, other craniocerebral surgery concerning mental handicap, and not motivated by metaphysical beliefs, has been undertaken over the years.

Craniotomy for microcephalics on the assumption that this would permit beneficial growth of the brain had a vogue at one time. As early as 1894, Jacobi presented strong arguments, quite often unheeded subsequently, against unfounded and indiscriminate use of the procedure, noting also not only the lack of objective evidence of benefit but inclinations to proclaim success merely 'because the victim consented not to die of the assault'.

Among other radical procedures which have had only a limited application to mental retardation are prefrontal leucotomy (Engler, 1948; Mackay, 1948) and hemispherectomy (Brett, 1969). Neither was intended primarily as a measure to raise intellectual level but mainly to reduce concomitant manifestations in some retarded persons, in particular epilepsy and severe behaviour disorders and, with hemispherectomy, infantile hemiplegia as well. Engler (1948), who reported on 44 retarded patients aged 17 to 47 years, most epileptic and/or psychotic, who had a leucotomy was sufficiently disenchanted with the results to state that the operation had been abandoned on residents in his mental deficiency institution. Hemispherectomy in general, as Brett (1969) indicated, received some enthusiastic advocacy including claims of intellectual advancement, but his critical review, particularly with reference to postoperative complications, presented a distinctly less favourable outlook. With regard to specific types of mental retardation, Falconer and Rushworth (1960), who undertook hemispherectomy in several children with Sturge–Weber syndrome (encephalotrigeminal angiomatosis) thought from their experience and that of others that the operation was beneficial in carefully selected instances of the condition. More recently, gratifying results, including normal intellectual development as well as cessation of seizures and minimizing of hemiparesis, have been reported in Sturge–Weber syndrome children who had a hemispherectomy before they were a year old (Hoffman *et al.*, 1979).

The surgical treatment of hydrocephalus of different aetiologies, in particular cerebrospinal fluid shunt operations aimed at maintaining intracranial pressure within normal limits, has been a major development in the past several decades. As Jones and Stening (1981) observed, the many operative techniques and types of apparatus advocated over the years are an indication of the multitude of problems encountered. Though such technical considerations and their ramifications, as well as factors related to the nature and extent of the underlying pathology, significantly effect outcome (Raimondi and Soare, 1974; Dennis *et al.*, 1981), the development of shunting procedures has improved life expectancy and mental and physical prognosis for a large number of hydrocephalic individuals. An interesting historical account of the evolution of these procedures, based on interviews of some of the pioneers involved, was presented by Wallman (1982). An equally interesting and more detailed historical review of these and related approaches to the surgical management of hydrocephalus has been provided by Pudenz (1980).

The possibility of extending surgery for hydrocephalus to the fetus has been explored recently. Hopeful results were obtained in hydrocephalic fetal rhesus monkeys (Michejda and Hodgen, 1981) and the operative feasibility of decompression by means of ventriculo-amniotic shunting in human hydrocephalic fetuses has been demonstrated (Clewell *et al.*, 1982; Frigoletto *et al.*, 1982; Depp *et al.*, 1983). Such procedures are still essentially at an experimental stage and, as Avery (1982) observed, many technical and philosophical questions still require resolution so as not to 'excessively intrude technology into the quiet and privileged sanctuary of the womb'.

Craniofacial malformations, like those which occur in Apert's and Crouzon's syndromes (see Table 1. 2, p. 16), are relatively frequently associated with mental retardation. Surgical repair of such malformations is often a realistic proposition and can have not only advantageous cosmetic effects but also play a role in the improvement of mental function. An instructive account of the application of craniofacial surgery in the types of conditions mentioned has been provided by Hoffman *et al.* (1982). The valuable volume in which their observations were published also contains much other material on neurosurgery in a variety of circumstances (such as cerebral congenital anomalies, neoplasms, trauma and infections) in which timely operative intervention can improve the outlook in mental as well as other respects.

In the last few years a number of professionals have recommended facial plastic surgery for Down's syndrome. There have been two main interrelated considerations in this proposition, one concerned with improving appearances so that psychosocial benefits would ensue and the other directed towards enhancing physical functions like breathing, eating and speech development. To help achieve these objectives, such procedures as straightening slanting eyes, eliminating epicanthic folds, elevating the nasal bridge, advancing a receding chin and reducing tongue size have been advocated. In an account of one Down's syndrome child thus surgically treated in Frankfurt, West Germany, Höhler (1977) reported 'a remarkable change' in her and in the attitude of others towards her – so much so that a geneticist, when he saw the child presumably in her early teens, 'urgently recommended sterilization' in the belief that there was a very high probability that she would become the mother of affected children. Lemperle and Radu (1980) subsequently published a report on 67 other Down's syndrome individuals, ranging in age from 2 to 22 years, who had similar plastic surgery in the same city. The consequences of the surgical procedures were described essentially in anecdotal terms, but were sufficiently satisfactory, the authors felt, 'that no Down's syndrome child should be deprived of them'. So sweeping a recommendation was not made by Olbrisch (1982) or by Rozner (1983) who operated on 202 and 11 Down's syndrome children in Munich and in Victoria, Australia, respectively. Olbrisch's briefly described follow-up, partly with questionnaires, of those children in his series who had operations more than a year previously (about half of the total series) indicated favourable results in most, and Rozner stated that his findings were similar.

There is a need for more precise and long-term follow-up data, in comparison with suitably matched control groups, in order to evaluate adequately the claimed advantages of the surgery. Improvements in breathing, eating and speech, mainly following reduction of tongue size, should be relatively easy to confirm or disprove in this way. Psychosocial benefits because of the various cosmetic changes are less easily demonstrable and raise questions as to whether acceptance by society of persons with Down's syndrome could not be better achieved by changing public attitudes rather than, say, the slant of the eye or the lack of prominence of the chin. There are other concerns also – for example, how long-lasting are the supposedly beneficial aesthetic effects (repetition of surgery was thought necessary in some cases), and will unrealistic expectations be harboured by some Down's syndrome individuals and/or their parents to their eventual detriment ('Now I am perfectly normal' said one of the patients of Lemperle and Radu after she had had three surgical repairs)? It thus remains to be established whether all or some of the plastic surgical undertakings referred to do more good than harm and, if the former, how best to select appropriate recipients. It is perhaps not so much the idea of the plastic surgery *per se* that would be repugnant to many, as a leading article (1983) in the *Lancet* suggested, but vigorous claims for its benefits without adequate scientifically collected data supporting such claims.

Mentally retarded persons, particularly those with severe retardation, often have an increased incidence of concomitant physical abnormalities and impairments, present at birth or developing later, of the kind found also in the general population. When amenable to surgical correction such intervention is usually no less appropriate in those with mental retardation than in others. A growing interest in the welfare of the retarded in these terms is exemplified by a recent volume, emanating from a symposium, concerned with orthopaedic surgery and related considerations in individuals with mental handicap (Hoffer, 1981). A further illustration, in a different sphere, is a report on the role of operative treatment (fundoplication) for chronic vomiting associated with gastro-oesophageal reflux in severely retarded patients (Byrne *et al.*, 1982).

Other treatment

Various medically related treatments besides those involving medication and surgery have particular relevance to mental retardation because of the comparative frequency among the mentally handicapped of the abnormalities in question and because their presence can substantially impair further the functional capacities of those affected. Several examples are briefly referred to below.

Auditory and/or visual impairments rank high in this category and, indeed, can hamper progress to the extent of creating an impression of mental retardation or learning disability when such retardation or disability *per se* is not actually present. Useful comments on the recognition and significance of these sensory impairments in relation to mental retardation were made by Barlow (1978). Hearing aids and spectacles are obviously important components of treatment in many cases. In much more detailed terms, Hall's (1984) book on children with handicaps contains several chapters with helpful practical information on auditory and visual impairments and the testing for, and management of, these problems.

In severely, and particularly profoundly, retarded children with or without cerebral palsy, deformities involving muscles, bones and joints are common and likely to develop and progress in the absence of appropriate intervention. Scrutton (1978) has reviewed the different types of these deformities in such children and has offered helpful guidance on good postural care which, he noted, can reduce significantly progression of the physical handicaps. Physiotherapy has an important role in certain cases, especially when cerebral palsy is present. A particular approach, considered suitable for retarded persons with spasticity and/or athetosis, has been advocated by Bobath (1963); it involves techniques, not requiring the conscious participation of the patient, aimed at inhibiting abnormal postural reflex activity and facilitating normal postural reactions in their proper developmental sequence. Bobath (1980) has published a comprehensive monograph on the principles and methods concerned, and more recently he and his wife have elaborated further on their approach in a text edited by Scrutton (1984). Though this volume does not have a specific focus on mental retardation, it contains many useful observations, mainly by therapists, on various approaches to the management of motor disorders in children with cerebral palsy, applicable to affected persons whether they are also mentally retarded or not. An attractive feature of the book is the important emphasis in it that those with severe handicaps, to use a phrase from the editor's preface, 'have disorders to be treated'. With respect specifically to mentally retarded children with cerebral palsy, there is conflicting evidence, reviewed by Parette and Hourcade (1984), as to what extent different physiotherapeutic programmes are beneficial. As might be expected, they found that most available research suggests that intelligence is related to demonstrable gains subsequent to such programmes, though these gains, motoric and other, are by no means restricted to individuals of normal intelligence.

For many with various degrees of mental retardation, physical education programmes have been found to be advantageous as a means of improving motor proficiency and skills, as well as of enhancing physical fitness. Chasey and Wyrick (1971) reported on one such programme and its benefits to a group of children with IQs ranging from 50 to 85. The authors also reviewed the generally favourable findings of others in these spheres.

A form of treatment, often referred to as the Doman–Delacato 'patterning' method, requires mention here because, though highly controversial for years, it continues to be held out by some as valuable therapy for many types of mental retardation and other varieties of cerebral dysfunction. An account of the procedures used to achieve so-called 'neurological organization', including active and passive mobility exercises in set patterns and sensory stimulation, was provided by Doman *et al.* (1960). The exercises proposed for retarded children, as recently summarized in a plea for their abandonment (Zigler, 1981), involve repetitive manipulations of the limbs and head in patterns that allegedly simulate pre- and postnatal movements of nonretarded children; it is believed that repeated motions of these kinds will lead to previously unused brain cells taking over functions of damaged ones and that the acquisition of higher functions depends on successful mastery of lower ones. Despite the absence, or at least remarkable paucity, of scientifically tenable data showing effectiveness, and the availability of convincing scientific arguments and evidence to the contrary (e.g. Cohen *et al.*, 1970; Sparrow and Zigler, 1978), and despite devastating critiques by responsible organizations (e.g. American Academy for Cerebral Palsy and nine other national bodies, 1968; American Academy of Pediatrics, 1982), the procedures continue to appeal to some parents, not least of all because of the glowing enthusiasm of some articles in the lay press. As with other uncritically acclaimed treatments of unproven worth discussed earlier, disadvantages and dangers are not only that they will be ineffective but that unrealistic expectations of benefit could have serious consequences for hopeful parents.

PREVENTION OF ENVIRONMENTALLY DETERMINED MENTAL RETARDATION

A review of the multiple physical hazards of environmental origin which can result in mental deficit and associated abnormalities is presented in Chapter 4. The recognition of the existence and nature of these hazards, and of the circumstances in which they occur, is a crucial prerequisite for avoiding or counteracting them, and this can be done effectively and relatively readily in many instances. Thus, for example, protection of potential mothers against rubella and other infections, avoidance of teratogens, appropriate obstetric care during pregnancy and delivery, specialized perinatal monitoring and treatment of infants at high risk for disabilities, prompt attention to postnatal infective illness, and precautions to counteract cerebral damage from trauma or chemicals in vulnerable children are all known safeguards and often within practical reach.

As an indication of realistic current preventive scope, the study of Hunter *et al.* (1980) is instructive. These investigators made an analysis of the aetiology of mental retardation and of its preventability in 406 persons less than 20 years old and with IQs of 50 or below, living in institutions in Manitoba, Canada. They found that the defect could be attributed to acquired (i.e. environmentally determined) factors in 123 cases and that, in the current state of knowledge, prevention could have been achieved in 68 (55 per cent) of these. As many of the causal factors involved can result in mild, as well as severe, mental deficit, it is evident that the numbers of persons with acquired mental retardation can be much reduced.

The multitude of appropriate medical and related measures to attain such preventive objectives are well documented in standard present-day textbooks of obstetrics, neonatology, paediatrics and public health among others, and could not be done justice in anything like a comprehensive manner in the space available here. Many of these measures will be apparent from a reading of Chapter 4, and others are specifically referred to in that chapter and Chapters 5 and 9. Additional informative coverage of the subject during the past decade will be found in, for instance, the texts of Milunsky (1975), McCormack (1980) and Fotheringham *et al.* (1983), substantial portions of which are devoted particularly to prevention of mental retardation due to physical determinants of environmental origin. A striking example of technical progress is the actual and prospective development of effective and safe vaccines of various types (Sabin, 1981) as prophylaxis against infections which can result in complications including cerebral involvement with adverse mental consequences. An indication of the potential in these terms is the mass vaccination programme, using a combined vaccine, introduced in Sweden in 1982 aimed at eradicating measles, mumps and rubella in that country, an objective considered to be entirely practicable (Christenson *et al.*, 1983).

It is important to add that the scope for prevention of mental retardation due to factors of the kinds mentioned above is by no means dependent only on the existence of relevant medical and related knowledge, but is also significantly influenced by existing socioeconomic realities. In many parts of world, abysmal poverty associated with totally inadequate housing, hygiene and diet takes a great toll in terms of mortality and morbidity, including impairment of mental development. The potential for prevention of disease and disability in general and, in relation to the focus of this chapter, of mental deficits is enormous, through improvements of the living conditions of the populations concerned. Furthermore, even in affluent societies reasonably similar in socioeconomic terms and in professional and technical resources, historical differences in attitudes and outlooks concerning funding, organization and general provision of preventive health care facilities result in some differences in mortality and morbidity outcomes. An interesting comparison between Sweden and Ontario, Canada, of such outcomes in the perinatal period, and of the influences that determined them, was published recently by Ohlsson and Fohlin (1983).

GENETIC COUNSELLING

General

Genetic counselling clinics have now become a widespread feature of the health care system in a large number of countries. Many attending such clinics do so because of concerns related to the prospect of occurrence or recurrence of mental retardation in their families. The principles and practice of providing them with guidance are basically the same as those applying to other disabilities.

In general, genetic counselling with respect to mental retardation can be said to be concerned with the provision of information to the counsellee(s) about her/his/their chances of having a retarded child, about the likelihood or otherwise of associated abnormalities, about the anticipated severity and outlook in an affected individual, and about preventive or therapeutic measures which may be available. This requires not only close familiarity on the part of the counsellor with the relevant data but also an appreciation of the emotional stresses and conflicts which the particular counsellee(s) may face in the given circumstances. In the context of a discussion of the issues involved, some counsellors tend to be directive in the sense of firmly advocating or discouraging childbearing, whereas others, including the present writer, are inclined to present the facts and options without deliberately attempting to influence decisions. It seems judicious not to adhere rigidly to one or other of these positions but to be guided by perceptions, admittedly subjective to a considerable extent, of what appears to serve best the counsellees' interests. It is pertinent to add that there is some evidence to suggest that directive genetic counselling is no more effective than nondirective counselling in deterring high-risk couples from having children (Leading article, *Lancet*, 1982).

The large majority of persons seeking genetic counselling regarding mental retardation are parents who have previously had a retarded child or potential parents with such a relative in the family. Others are individuals who may consider themselves to be at increased risk of bearing retarded children for a variety of different reasons – for example, an Ashkenazi Jewish couple who had heard or read that they were statistically more likely than others to be heterozygous carriers of the gene for Tay–Sachs disease (see Chapter 5); or a consanguineous couple of any ethnic origin who wonder whether the consanguinity is likely to affect their chances of having normal children (see, for instance, Roberts and Pembrey (1978), Thompson and Thompson (1980), and Nora and Fraser (1981) for informative details); or a couple one or both of whom may have some degree of mental deficit (see p. 417).

Statistical risks

When there is a history of an affected person or persons in the family, an often crucial consideration is the precise aetiological diagnosis. When this is known, or can be established clinically or by special investigations such as biochemical ones, recurrence risks can often be provided with mathematical precision. Thus many types of mental retardation are autosomal recessive in nature (see Chapters 1 and 5), in which case heterozygous parents of the gene concerned have a 25 per cent recurrence risk for any pregnancy. A smaller number are X-linked recessive, resulting typically in a 50 per cent chance that any son of a carrier mother will be affected with the condition in question, and a 50 per cent chance that any daughter (though all clinically unaffected) will be a carrier like the mother. Still other types of mental retardation are autosomal dominant, either as a result of new mutation in the afflicted individual without increased risk of a sibling being affected, or as a result of transmission of the relevant gene from one of the parents with a 50 per cent chance of any of that parent's children, male or female, also having the condition.

Readers wishing to familiarize themselves, in greater detail than can suitably be provided here, with these classical Mendelian patterns of transmission (and their nuances) applicable to many specific varieties of mental retardation are referred to a growing number of comprehensive texts concerned mainly with genetic counselling; the following are examples published during the past ten years – Murphy and Chase (1975), Stevenson and Davison (1976), Lubs and de la Cruz (1977), Hsia *et al.* (1979), Kelly (1980), Harper (1981) and Fuhrmann and Vogel (1983). These texts also provide further elaboration on other genetic counselling considerations discussed below.

The kind of mathematically precise risks of recurrence or occurrence exemplified above cannot be provided where aetiology is obscure or uncertain. In these circumstances, predictions must be based on empirical data derived from subsequent pregnancy outcomes in families in which a similarly affected individual had been born. Even with chromosomal aberrations, despite the capacity to delineate them with increasing precision, the chances of their occurring or recurring usually have to be determined empirically (see Chapter 6). Other empiric risk estimates can be based on data from representative samples of families containing a person with an aetiologically undifferentiated but phenotypically characteristic mental retardation syndrome: de Lange syndrome is an example. On the basis of a review of a personal series and virtually all previously published instances of the syndrome, Berg *et al.* (1970) found that the overwhelming majority were sporadic (i.e. without recurrence in siblings). However, 16 out of 376 known siblings of index cases were reported also to be affected, not always convincingly, suggesting that the risk of recurrence in a sibship could be about 4 per cent; more recently, Smith (1982) quoted a somewhat lower recurrence risk, i.e. in the range of 1–3 per cent. Despite the definite possibility that even such clinically distinctive syndromes may be aetiologically heterogeneous, a consideration that could affect recurrence risk statistics, the type of empiric findings mentioned is helpful to parents as at least an educated guess of the likely outcome, regarding the syndrome in question, in a subsequent pregnancy.

Rather less satisfactory, generally speaking, are empiric recurrence risk data for what is often referred to as nonspecific mental retardation – i.e. the many instances which are causally obscure and which, though including among them some with various clinical features in common, are not clearly distinguishable as characteristic named syndromes. The problem of deriving reasonably accurate risk figures is not a reflection on the investigators, but largely inherent in the wideranging phenotypic characteristics of these 'nonspecific' cases. They differ, for instance, in mental levels and in the presence or absence of many common concomitant manifestations such as head size, epilepsy, and motor and sensory disorders; and, of course, they are also aetiologically very heterogeneous. Other methodological concerns, applicable also to some extent to empiric data collection for distinct syndromes of unknown causation such as the de Lange syndrome referred to above, are difficulties in representative ascertainment of index cases and in comprehensive follow-ups of subsequent parental reproductive outcomes.

Nevertheless, useful empiric information concerning recurrence of 'nonspecific' mental retardation has been compiled. A valuable recent study, which also includes a review of earlier investigations, is that of Herbst and Baird (1982). Overall risks (based on the whole sibship) to sisters and brothers of persons with 'nonspecific' retardation and recurrence risks (based on siblings born after the index case) were derived from a large population-based series of individuals with different degrees of mental retardation, and the risks were calculated in relation to the variables of mental level, sex, selected associated neurological disabilities and singleton versus multiple birth. It would be difficult to do justice to the extensive findings in a brief summary; interested readers are referred to the original paper for details. Suffice it to quote here from the authors' own synopsis:

> The overall risk of affected individuals among all sibs was 4.4 ± 0.6 per cent, which was about ten times greater than the minimum population incidence of nonspecific MR. The risk among subsequent sibs of the first affected case in a family was 3.7 ± 0.8 per cent. These risks varied depending on sex, MR level, and whether the mental retardation was associated with hydrocephalus, microcephalus, cerebral palsy or epilepsy. The recurrence risk after two affected individuals was 12 ± 7 per cent.

Additional studies of this kind will further improve precision in empiric risk figures which can be provided to families concerned about the recurrence of mental retardation of unknown aetiology and not distinguishable as a recognized syndrome.

The perceived burden of risk

In addition to the statistical odds conveyed during genetic counselling concerning the chances of occurrence or recurrence of a given type of mental retardation, a significant nonmetrical and subjective consideration is the burden of the disability as perceived by the counsellee. There is great variation in this respect, as illustrated by a few examples (the first not concerning mental retardation) from personal experience. One potential mother, born with a cleft lip but normal in all other respects, considered the approximately 4 per cent chance that a child of hers would be affected as a sufficiently serious prospect to conclude that she would rather adopt children than take that risk, despite the very favourable clinical and aesthetic outlook with modern surgical repair. By contrast another couple, one of whom was known to be the carrier of the gene for Bourneville disease (tuberous sclerosis) and had had a severely retarded, epileptic son with the disease, firmly opted to go ahead with a further pregnancy despite the 50 per cent recurrence risk involved; unfortunately, that child was also seriously affected. Yet another, who were parents of a daughter with Down's syndrome, chose not to have a diagnostic amniocentesis in a forthcoming pregnancy not, they explained, on religious or other moral grounds but because they did not mind having a second child with the syndrome; their next baby, as was statistically probable, was unaffected.

Whatever the actual or presumed motivations of such parents or potential parents, the present writer believes that they have the right to make choices of the kind indicated without pressure from a genetic counsellor to act otherwise, though discussion, if desired, of the pros and cons of a particular course of action is certainly appropriate. Some medical colleagues and others from various disciplines feel that there is a measure of responsibility to society as well as to the individual family in relation to increased risks of bearing children with mental retardation or other serious disabilities; perhaps so, but the argument does not seem persuasive in the genetic counselling context, not least of all because there is some chance that *any* child will during his/her life be a greater problem and wreak more havoc at home and in the wider world than persons with mental retardation such as those exemplified above.

A usually crucial component of the perceived burden of risk is a counsellee's perception of the seriousness or otherwise of the disabilities under consideration. Because of the substantial phenotypic variability in most types of mental retardation, it is essential to explain the range of such variability, so that the counsellee is aware that another child with the same diagnostic label as a previously affected one may be afflicted to a greater or lesser degree. The frequent difficulty of accurate prior prediction of the extent and severity of manifestations in a particular instance is a complicating factor.

Counselling for retarded potential parents

Increasingly, advice is being sought regarding childbearing prospects when one or both potential parents are retarded. In biomedical terms, the approach to determining or estimating risk of abnormality in offspring is essentially akin to that for any other couple, i.e. aetiological diagnosis in affected relatives (in this case the retarded potential parent(s)), or suitable empiric data as a less precise alternative, generally provide the basis for formulating expectations of pregnancy outcome. For example, there would be no increased biological

risk for a parent whose retardation was due to meningitis, a 50 per cent risk for a
parent with Bourneville disease (tuberous sclerosis), and an even higher risk for
an untreated phenylketonuric mother.

Frequently, however, the concern expressed, commonly by close relatives of
severely retarded persons (IQ below 50), is not specifically about the risks of
the latter having affected children but about procreation irrespective of the
outcome. In practice, few severely retarded individuals become parents for
various reasons including relatively early mortality and, in many reaching
reproductive age, infertility or sterility and/or psychosocial barriers to
parenthood. Thus, for example, this writer is unaware of any recorded
instance of a nonmosaic Down's syndrome male having fathered a child.
Nevertheless, the anxieties of relatives are understandable, especially with
respect to severely retarded females. Indeed, occasions are not rare when they
are uncomprehendingly enticed, or forced, to participate in sexual acts
resulting in unintended pregnancy in some cases. Some at least of the two
dozen or so reported births to fully affected Down's syndrome females (Smith
and Berg, 1976) resulted from such circumstances. No reasonable person
would dispute that protection of such individuals against unwanted pregnancy, though not necessarily against desired sexual relationships, is required,
though there is some debate about appropriate prophylactic measures (for
example, contraceptive chemicals or devices versus sterilization).

More than with the severely retarded, genetic counselling considerations for
the mildly retarded are intertwined with controversial questions related to the
biological desirability or otherwise of childbearing, and to the capacity of
affected parents to cope adequately with the responsibilities of parenthood and
the needs of their children. Mildly retarded individuals are often fertile, with
an interest in marriage and having children, and their views on these matters
deserve serious attention. In some, specific biomedical risks of abnormality in
offspring apply and therefore are a relevant consideration. In others, no such
specific hazards appear to be present and offspring are often healthy and
normal or near normal in intelligence. Though genes which lower intelligence
are considered to be transmitted to at least some of these children (see Chapter
7), Murphy (1974) made the pertinent point that, as a very conservative
estimate, 95 per cent of all people carry harmful genes and that figure is more
likely to be about 99.9 per cent; 'thus', he remarked, 'if the human race is to
reproduce from unsullied stock only, a minute portion of the population is
going to be very busy indeed.' To this may be added that anyone hoping for
such a role would be disappointed by the inability to determine accurately
membership of that relatively tiny genetically élite group. Furthermore, as
stated elsewhere (Berg, 1976):

> Intelligence is but one quality of potential benefit to society; very many
> persons who are mentally dull are entirely worthy citizens, competent and
> assets to their communities ... any overall attempt to proscribe a basic
> inclination to have children for whole classes of society is uncomfortably

reminiscent of atrocities committed in the name of mythologies such as 'race purity' and the like. Advice about child-bearing for mildly retarded persons, as for others, should therefore be based on the facts and circumstances directly applicable to the particular potential parents and not on preconceived judgments. In the case of many with mild retardation, the crucial and important considerations are likely to be social and psychological, rather than genetic, ones.

It is perhaps unnecessary to emphasize, particularly in the generally more open-minded atmosphere of the last decades of the twentieth century, that considerations about biological and/or social advisability or inadvisability of procreation by retarded persons are different from those concerning sexual activity. Proscription of sexual relationships is obviously not a necessary prerequisite for avoidance of pregnancy. Indeed, sexual behaviour by retarded individuals is no less natural, and should be no more frightful or reprehensible, than is ordinarily the case in the general population. A changing outlook towards the retarded in these respects is evidenced by an increasing array of enlightened observations on the subject, as exemplified for instance by contributions to the book edited by de la Cruz and La Veck (1974), and in a review by Craft and Craft (1981) on the topic of sexuality and mental handicap.

Preventive effects

Genetic counselling, whether viewed as a directive or as a more neutral informative procedure, has preventive implications and in that sense can be considered to some extent as eugenic in nature. Follow-ups of persons receiving counselling for a wide variety of disorders usually show some correlation between size of risk conveyed and reduction in subsequent births. In a survey of information published during the 1970s about genetic counselling follow-ups in relation to various disabilities, Evers-Kiebooms and van den Berghe (1979) found that parents with a risk of 10 per cent or greater generally decided against future pregnancies considerably more frequently than those with a risk of less than 10 per cent. Data of these kinds specifically concerning mental retardation are scanty. However, Carter *et al.*'s (1971) follow-up, three to ten years after initial counselling, of couples seeking advice on the risk of recurrence of serious disorders in their children involved substantial numbers in whom mental retardation was the concern. Their findings with respect to such retardation are shown here in Table 11.1.

There are, of course, any number of variables which influence couples in their decisions about childbearing. They include such factors as the desire for children, numbers of previous births, and attitudes towards, and availability of, an adoption alternative. Clearly, however, the size of risk and the perceived burden are often among these variables, so that genetic counselling can have a considerable preventive effect. An important development during the last

TABLE 11.1   Pregnancy decisions of couples following genetic counselling after birth of a child with severe mental retardation

Subsequent pregnancy intent	Couples with recurrence risk $\geqslant$ 10%		Couples with recurrence risk < 10%	
Deterred	25	(86%)	28	(24%)
Undeterred	4	(14%)	89	(76%)
Total	29	(100%)	117[1]	(100%)

Source: from data provided by Carter *et al.* (1971).

Note: [1]Includes 61 couples who had had a Down's syndrome child; of these, at a time prior to availability of diagnostic amniocentesis, 11 (18 per cent) were deterred from another pregnancy.

fifteen years in that regard has been the increasing capacity to identify various abnormalities (many directly linked with mental retardation) prenatally, at a stage in pregnancy when termination is legally available in many countries. That topic is considered in the next section.

PRENATAL DIAGNOSIS AND ITS IMPLICATIONS

The past fifteen years have witnessed major advances in the capacity to detect and accurately diagnose abnormality in the fetus. In particular, the diagnostic scope of ultrasonography, amniocentesis, fetoscopy and, most recently, chorionic villus sampling has developed apace (Ferguson-Smith, 1983a; Rodeck and Nicolaides, 1984). Many of the fetal abnormalities recognizable by these means are generally or relatively frequently associated with mental retardation in live-born children, so that the procedures mentioned are of much relevance to this field. They are briefly commented on from that perspective below. Extensive additional information on these procedures will be found in the texts referred to, which also provide further bibliographic sources about the many ramifications of this rapidly expanding area. Readers wishing to keep abreast of these topics are reminded that new developments and data are being reported very frequently, so that some observations current at the time may well seem dated after relatively short intervals.

Ultrasonography

The number of anomalies in the fetus which can be detected using this noninvasive, and seemingly safe (Stark *et al.*, 1984), procedure has grown steadily with the advances in ultrasound apparatus, allowing real-time (in contrast to static) scanning and better resolution (Campbell and Pearce, 1983; Hill *et al.*, 1983). The abnormalities connected with mental retardation most frequently recognized by ultrasonography have been neural tube defects involving cerebral and/or spinal pathology. A family history, particularly among close relatives, of these defects and, though nonspecific, elevation of maternal serum alphafetoprotein near the middle of the second trimester (Ferguson-Smith, 1983b) are very helpful in identifying pregnant women for whom high-resolution ultrasonography for neural tube defects is especially indicated. Other cerebral pathology not necessarily associated with neural tube defects can also be found in an increasing number of instances. Examples are hydro, micro-, hydranen-, holoprosen- and porencephaly, and cerebellar anomalies such as occur in Joubert's syndrome (Campbell and Pearce, 1983). Campbell and Pearce cautioned that the diagnosis of microcephaly can be particularly difficult prior to the end of the second trimester or even later.

The ability to diagnose certain abnormalities in parts of the body other than the brain and spine can also be helpful in detecting mental retardation syndromes in which such findings are a feature. Again, a family history of affected relatives can assist in pinpointing the presence of such syndromes, even though ultrasonography may reveal only a single manifestation. For example, a virtually certain diagnosis of tuberous sclerosis was made by Crawford *et al.* (1983) in a twenty-two-week-old fetus, in a family in which the father and two of his children had the disease, by demonstrating cardiac rhabdomyomata on echocardiography. Other detectable anomalies may raise suspicion of the presence of a chromosomal aberration. For instance, a demonstration of duodenal atresia or stenosis, because of its substantially increased frequency in Down's syndrome (Fonkalsrud *et al.*, 1969), may well justify fetal karyotyping to check for that syndrome, if the pregnancy is not too far advanced.

Amniocentesis

Amniotic fluid samples collected at about sixteen weeks of gestation by transabdominal amniocentesis for the purpose of diagnosing fetal abnormalities is now extensively undertaken in many countries. Based on a current international directory of genetic services (Lynch *et al.*, 1983), Kaback (1984) estimated that between 70,000 and 140,000 diagnostic amniocenteses per year are undertaken at present throughout the world. Cells from the sample, usually when cultured and sometimes when uncultured (Gosden, 1983), and the fluid itself provide an opportunity to detect chromosomal aberrations, an increasing array of metabolic disorders (many of which are linked with mental retardation), and biochemical evidence, in the form of elevated amniotic fluid alphafetoprotein often supplemented by acetylcholinesterase measurement (Brock, 1983), of the presence of an open neural tube defect (see Chapters 5 and 6).

Because amniocentesis is an invasive procedure and thus not entirely without risk, it is usually offered only to couples with an increased chance of having children with anomalies detectable by the means mentioned above.

TABLE 11.2   Criteria for amniocentesis commonly used to detect conditions associated with mental retardation

---

Maternal age of 35 years and over[1]
Parental chromosome anomaly, including balanced translocation and aneuploidy
Previous birth of a child with a chromosome aberration
Family history of neural tube defect, particularly in first- or second-degree relative of fetus
Elevated maternal serum alphafetoprotein
Increased risk for an inborn metabolic error recognizable in utero
Increased risk for an X-linked disorder unrecognizable *per se* in utero (to determine fetal sex)

Note: 1 There have been suggestions that relatively advanced paternal age (say over 40 years) might also constitute an indication for amniocentesis, but evidence in favour of this view seems inconclusive (Ferguson-Smith, 1984).

Commonly used indications, though with some variation between centres, are shown in Table 11.2. A possible additional indication is a finding on ultrasonography of certain fetal morphological abnormalities frequently associated with chromosomal syndromes (e.g. duodenal atresia/stenosis – see page 421); in more general terms, evidence in the fetus of retarded physical growth, or of abnormal movement patterns (Boué *et al.*, 1982), may also provide a rationale for prenatal karyotyping. One further indication for amniocentesis in the near future may be *reduced* maternal serum alphafetoprotein at about fourteen to twenty weeks of gestation, in view of very recent evidence of such reduction when the fetus has Down's syndrome or other types of chromosomal aneuploidy (Cuckle *et al.*, 1984; Merkatz *et al.*, 1984).

Fetoscopy

Examination of the fetus during the second trimester by means of percutaneous transabdominal fetoscopy using fibre-optic instruments (Rocker and Laurence, 1981) is now a well-established, though limited, diagnostic procedure in experienced hands. Undertaken both for the purpose of recognizing various anatomical abnormalities and in order to collect certain tissue samples (currently blood, skin and liver), it has been applied to date for the prenatal diagnosis of at least fifty congenital abnormalities (Rodeck and Nicolaides, 1983). Among these are some associated with mental retardation as exemplified in Table 11.3.

Safer, and hence preferable, methods exist for the in utero diagnosis of some of the conditions shown in Table 11.3. However, they may not be applicable or informative in a given instance, thus making the alternative of fetoscopy with or without tissue sampling appropriate. For example, direct visualization by

TABLE 11.3 Examples of conditions usually or relatively frequently associated with mental retardation for which diagnostic fetoscopy with or without fetal tissue sampling has been undertaken

Diagnostic approach	Suspected condition
Direct visualization	Syndromes with recognizable anatomical anomalies (e.g. de Lange, Laurence–Moon–Biedl, Smith–Lemli–Opitz, Treacher Collins)
Blood sampling	Metabolic disorders (e.g. galactosaemia, Hurler syndrome, Tay–Sachs disease) Chromosomal aberrations Blood group incompatibility Fetal infection (e.g. rubella, toxoplasmosis)
Skin sampling	Bloch–Sulzberger syndrome (incontinentia pigmenti) Sjögren–Larsson syndrome
Liver sampling	Ornithine carbamoyl transferase deficiency

Sources of examples: Filkins and Benzie (1983); Rodeck and Nicolaides (1983); Special Report (1984).

fetoscopy can be valuable for detecting anatomical anomalies of certain syndromes when these anomalies are not recognizable, or only equivocally so, on ultrasonography. Further, chromosomal aberrations and various metabolic disorders, though diagnosable from an amniotic fluid specimen, may require fetal blood sampling for rapid diagnosis in particular cases because of such considerations as failed amniotic cell cultures or a pregnancy that is too far advanced for such a culture to be of practical value; as Rodeck and Nicolaides (1983) indicated, results from a fetal blood sample can be obtained within hours or a few days of its collection, instead of what may be weeks if cells from the amniotic fluid are used.

Chorionic villus sampling

This recent development has great potential importance as a means for early (i.e. first trimester) diagnosis of various abnormalities in the fetus. For over a decade, but more effectively in the last few years, a number of methods have been tried for sampling chorionic villi, usually via the vaginal and cervical route, using aspiration or direct biopsy methods (Rodeck and Morsman, 1983). Despite remaining uncertainties, mainly concerning safety and reliability (Daker, 1983), there have been some notable diagnostic successes and undoubtedly more will follow.

In relation to mental retardation, accurate and rapid recognition of the fetal karyotype during the first trimester is increasingly being achieved, with reports appearing of selective abortion following detection of chromosomal aberrations – for example, trisomy 21 (Brambati and Simoni, 1983) and more subtle unbalanced structural rearrangements (Sachs *et al.*, 1983). In addition, diagnostic scope for conditions associated with mental retardation, using chorionic villi specimens among others, is likely to extend substantially in the near future through advances in enzyme determination techniques (Kazy *et al.*, 1982; Simoni *et al.*, 1983; Gustavii *et al.*, 1984) and in DNA technology (Humphries and Williamson, 1983; Gosden, 1984; Rosenberg, 1984).

There are obviously significant advantages in first- rather than second-trimester diagnosis of fetal abnormalities, including, as Ward (1984) noted, the reduced waiting period, less social and psychological stress, privacy (as pregnancy is not yet obvious to others), and earlier (hence safer) pregnancy termination where indicated. To this list may be added the prospect of more prompt, and therefore possibly more effective, fetal therapy if such therapy becomes available for any conditions recognizable from chorionic villus samples.

Implications of prenatal diagnosis

The usual rationale for the prenatal detection of fetal abnormality associated with subsequent mental retardation has been to provide potential parents with the option of pregnancy termination of affected fetuses. In some instances, where a diagnosis may be made at too late a stage in the pregnancy for selective abortion to be feasible, such a diagnosis still can be advantageous in providing the physicians concerned with information which may be helpful in the management of the birth and in subsequent neonatal care. A major hope for the future, however, is for the prenatal diagnosis of abnormality to provide scope for fetal therapy in a substantial proportion of instances. As exemplified below with regard to conditions linked with mental retardation, the first steps in that direction have already been taken.

A relatively early example of direct fetal treatment was initiated by the pioneering work of Liley (1963) involving in utero intraperitoneal Rh-negative red cell transfusion in the management of haemolytic disease due to rhesus sensitization. The procedure, or variants of it, has been used over the years with ultrasonography replacing X-rays for visualization purposes (Frigoletto *et al.*, 1981; Larkin *et al.*, 1982). Fetal intravascular transfusion with the aid of fetoscopy has recently been undertaken earlier in pregnancy for the management of severe isoimmunization (Rodeck *et al.*, 1981). Though the need for such treatments has been much reduced by the development of anti-D gammaglobulin prophylaxis, it still appears to have an application in carefully selected cases.

Apart from protection of potentially affected fetuses by maternal prophylactic measures as illustrated by anti-D gammaglobulin usage in relation to rhesus incompatibility risks mentioned above, or by control of the mother's diet if she has phenylketonuria (see Chapter 4), a few existing fetal disorders can be treated by therapy given to the mother. For instance, a fetus with vitamin B_{12}-

responsive methylmalonic acidaemia, diagnosed in utero by culture of amniotic fluid cells, appears to have benefited from maternal vitamin B_{12} medication in the last nine weeks of pregnancy (Ampola *et al.*, 1975).

One can reasonably anticipate, in the years immediately ahead, that the means not only for increasingly precise and more wideranging prenatal diagnosis but also for fetal treatment will extend considerably and perhaps even dramatically with further advances in the spheres of biochemistry and molecular biology (see above and also Chapters 5 and 6). Surgical intervention in utero, briefly discussed on page 409 in relation to hydrocephalus, may also attain greater applications in various circumstances. The fetal therapeutic vacuum, in a sphere of flourishing prenatal diagnostic procedures, to which the late Sir William Liley referred in his foreword to a recent instructive book on the unborn patient (Harrison *et al.*, 1984) seems unlikely to persist for very much longer.

ETHICAL, MORAL AND LEGAL CONSIDERATIONS

The observations here are concerned primarily with issues of life and death in the sphere of mental retardation. They are written with an acute awareness that the topic is not only highly controversial and emotional, but one in which views expressed are largely dependent on subjective value judgements not readily sustained by scientifically accumulated data.

The increasing technical capacity to prolong life, even when the mental and/or physical outlook is bleak, has evoked much debate about the sanctity of life in relation to its quality. It is convenient and may well also be important to make a distinction, as is done below, between active termination of pregnancy when the fetus is found to be abnormal and allowing death to occur at or after birth through the withholding or withdrawal of life-sustaining measures. Whether these distinctions in timing and action have ethical or moral force is perhaps an open question (Singer, 1983).

Prenatal aspects

As indicated in the previous section, the capacity to diagnose abnormality in the fetus is now well established and the scope for such diagnosis is steadily expanding. One can hope that these developments will in due course facilitate therapeutic intervention in a substantial proportion of recognizably affected fetuses. For the immediately foreseeable future, however, the practical rationale for prenatal diagnosis will usually remain that of providing parents with the option of pregnancy termination when fetal pathology is detected. In relation to the sensitive controversies impinging on this subject, it is necessary to recognize that practically all those working in this area take the position that legal availability of the relevant technology and of the associated abortion option makes it appropriate, and indeed essential, to provide the known facts in these regards to potential parents who wish to hear them. As in genetic counselling generally (see p. 414), some informants are inclined to be directive, whereas others (including this writer) consciously try to avoid either an anti- or pro-abortion stance in these circumstances and are supportive of the potential parents in whichever decision they choose to make.

Some regard prenatal diagnosis relating to a pregnancy termination option as unacceptable and even reprehensible. Many who do not, even when adopting the nondirective position mentioned above, are fully aware of philosophical dilemmas which remain. There is perhaps some irony in being engaged in this field of work and also being an advocate for retarded and other handicapped persons to be treated in a humane and dignified way and to be accorded opportunities to develop their potential. Nevertheless, there is a considerable body of opinion that the status of the fetus in terms of 'right to life' is not ethically and morally identical to that of the live-born individual. Interested readers are referred to a thought-provoking series of papers bearing on these delicate issues in Beauchamp and Walters's (1982) excellent book on bioethics. Additional religious perspectives on the subject have been provided by Fineman and Gordis (1982).

Besides that, there is the narrower but important question, often agonizing for parents, of the extent and degree of fetal abnormality which might be considered by them and/or their advisors as grounds for abortion. A problem here is that, although an exact biological diagnosis can often be made in the fetus, the phenotypic consequences in the live-born child can be variable and frequently imprecisely predictable.

Taking as an illustration the morphological chromosomal aberrations (see Chapter 6) which are readily detectable prenatally, a diverse phenotypic picture emerges. Thus, for example, fetuses with trisomy 13 or 18 have an almost uniformly grave outlook in terms of severity of malformations and survival prospects; those with trisomy 21 may be severely afflicted or have a reasonably favourable mental and physical prognosis; others with a sex chromosome abnormality can do even better, at least with regard to intellectual development – for instance, many males with an extra Y and females with an extra or a missing X. As the diagnosis of these errors in utero frequently does not provide clear evidence of severity of subsequent manifestations in a given instance, the only guidance available to parents has to be derived from empiric data based on outcomes in others with the same genotypic aberration. The prediction of outcome is further complicated when chromosomal mosaicism occurs, as this suggests that the fetus in question may be just partially affected clinically; here again, only empiric evidence can provide an indication of possible clinical prognosis in a particular case.

Perhaps the most stressful dilemma of all concerns a situation in which parents are at risk of having a seriously affected child with an X-linked recessive disorder not detectable as such in utero. In this circumstance, with a 50 per cent chance that males will be affected (see p. 415), terminating pregnancies of males would mean aborting unaffected fetuses in half the cases.

In the debate about the ethics and morality of prenatal diagnosis it is relevant to add that its elective abortion component (and unintended pregnancy loss consequent on the procedures themselves, currently averaging about 0.5 per cent following amniocentesis and about 5 per cent after fetoscopy) is but one facet of the issue. On the other side of the coin, the availability of the procedures can also be what might be termed life-creating and life-preserving. Some couples wishing to have children, but deterred because of an increased risk of mental and/or other abnormality in offspring, opt for pregnancy if prenatal diagnosis for the disability in question is available. Occasions arise as well, once pregnancy has occurred, when fear of the outcome would have led to termination in the absence of an opportunity for the prenatal testing. Furthermore, particularly as the large majority of prenatal diagnostic investigations yield normal results, the consequent frequent relief of parental anxiety and emotional stress months before birth must surely count for something.

As with legal decisions about life or death issues concerning handicapped children after birth (see p. 428), court rulings regarding termination of pregnancy have been varied and, indeed, sometimes in conflict with each other. Legal suits generally have been concerned with alleged wrongdoing, through nonfeasance or malfeasance, in not checking for or recognizing pregnancies of defective fetuses and hence the continuation of such pregnancies. Thus suits have been launched on the grounds of 'wrongful birth' (i.e. claims by parents related to denial of an available opportunity to detect and abort an abnormal fetus) and/or 'wrongful life' (i.e. claims on behalf of an abnormal child, the essence of which has been, as described by Milunsky (1983), 'that nonexistence would have been preferable to life with catastrophic defects and that a monetary award for damages should be paid for the individual having to live that life').

Shaw (1984) reviewed twenty-seven cases, often in one or both of these categories and most concerning mental retardation, heard in United States courts between 1973 and 1983. Court rulings differed, even in similar cases, with respect to guilt or otherwise for wrongful birth, and usually wrongful life claims were dismissed on various grounds, including that there is no legal right not to be born and judicial refusal to try to compare life with defects against no life at all. However, there were a few instances when claims for wrongful life against professional health care providers were upheld, though there may be some debate as to whether those rulings specifically meant that life with the abnormalities in question was worse than not being born. One case involved a Tay–Sachs disease child in California, where a laboratory had incorrectly diagnosed the parents as being noncarriers of the gene concerned, after the laboratory had not taken proper precautions following an earlier warning that their testing procedures were inaccurate. Another successful wrongful life claim, also in California, was by a deaf child whose older sibling's deafness had not been recognized by an audiologist, so that the parents went ahead with the second pregnancy. In yet another case, in Washington State, two siblings with fetal hydantoin syndrome (see Chapter 4 for comments on this syndrome) won their wrongful life suit on the grounds that the obstetricians had not accurately informed the mother of the teratogenic hazards of the anticonvulsant medication involved. A rather bizarre possibility is that, if wrongful life suits can be brought against health care professionals, they might in some instances, unless explicitly forbidden by law, also be launched against parents. No such suit appears to have occurred anywhere to date; apparently, also, a claim for wrongful life by a child against anybody is not recognizable in English law (Brahams, 1982).

A peculiar situation seems to exist currently in various places in which termination of pregnancy, considered immoral by some, can lead to successful punitive legal action if not undertaken. Conflicts between moral perceptions and the law's expectations are, of course, by no means limited to the circumstances under discussion, but their existence is a good illustration of persisting unresolved questions in this complex ethical, legal and emotional sphere.

Postnatal aspects

It may seem entirely admirable to maintain that all human life, at least after birth, is sacred to the point of meriting preservation at all costs. In reality, however, the situation is not so clear-cut. For instance, is an anencephalic infant to be kept alive for a few extra hours or days when technical resources to do so exist?; is the same to be done for years by elaborate artificial means for a grossly hydrocephalic, blind, essentially immobile child virtually unaware of his/her environment?; is a very tiny newborn's life to be sustained by prolonged complex intervention if his/her functional prognosis, as may well be the case (Schechner, 1980; Hunt *et al.*, 1982; Milligan *et al.*, 1984), is dismal? Decisions to the contrary are made daily by entirely honourable individuals as evidenced by surveys of the attitudes and practices of various medical specialists (Shaw *et al.*, 1977; Todres *et al.*, 1977; Singer *et al.*, 1983; Weir, 1984). A major dilemma for such persons does not usually arise in the context of the prognostically bleak examples mentioned above. Rather, because outlook in terms of quality of life is not simply disastrous or good, the dilemma which often occurs is where to draw the line, and who should be involved in drawing it, between active life-prolonging intervention and letting 'nature take its course'. With regard to such intervention, there is debate also as to when 'extra-ordinary' as opposed to 'ordinary' treatment measures are indicated. However, as Singer *et al.* (1983) found, there are different views among physicians concerning what these terms imply, even antibiotic administration being considered 'extra-ordinary' by some in certain circumstances.

Various people may feel able to offer unequivocal answers in relation to these questions but the law, in western society at least, does not seem at this stage to provide precise guidance. Singer (1983) gave two examples with reference to Down's syndrome infants in need of corrective, presumably life-saving, surgery. In one instance, in the United States, the court refused to intervene when the parents withheld permission for the surgery; in another, in the United Kingdom, the court ordered surgery to be performed but observed that in a case in which the infant's life would be 'demonstrably awful' there would have been grounds for allowing death to occur. In yet another instance in Britain of an infant with Down's syndrome not requiring surgery (Brahams, 1981), the paediatrician concerned, noting that the parents did not wish the baby to survive, ordered only nursing care and dihydrocodeine to alleviate any distress. The infant died within three days with the cause of death given as 'bronchopneumonia due to consequences of Down's syndrome'. The paediatrician, whose motives were considered even by the prosecution to be of the highest order, was charged with attempted murder and acquitted in a jury trial.

These kinds of issues arise with older individuals as well as infants. A widely publicized illustration is the case of Phillip Becker, a Down's syndrome child in California institutionalized soon after his birth in 1966 (Herr, 1984). He was found to have a congenital heart defect amenable to surgical correction, a procedure considered necessary for his continued health and, indeed, for the prolongation of his life. The parents repeatedly refused consent for this intervention and were able legally to prevent it for years until, finally, a new round of litigation awarded guardianship of the boy, against the parents' wishes, to a couple who had befriended him and who authorized the surgery; the operation, in 1983, was successful and Phillip appears to be doing well in the home of his guardians. A striking feature of this case, in terms of contemporary legal, social and ethical perceptions, is the length of time it took to achieve an end-result undoubtedly in the interests of the youth concerned and presumably one which most people would applaud, as does this writer.

The issue of applying advanced modern techniques and procedures for the prolongation of life in infants whose functional prognosis in mental and physical terms is grave has another facet which was touched on by the late Dr Ronald Mac Keith (1975) under the heading of 'Helping one or helping many'. That gentleman, devoted to the welfare of handicapped and other children, observed, using severe myelomeningocoele as an example, that the care given to such a child would involve 'much time' of various skilled professionals and 'heavy cost'. He added, 'As medical facilities are not infinite, giving care to this child means denying it to others.'

If that is so, it raises a dilemma about priorities in the allocation of health-related resources. The present writer posed it to colleagues and others during a recent invited visit to Karnataka State, India, for the purposes of making recommendations about the proposed establishment of genetic services with particular reference to mental retardation. Not surprisingly, responses were varied, ranging from statements that 'if such services exist in other countries, they should be provided here also' to comments that 'the funds involved could be used with greater benefit in other spheres such as meeting nutritional, hygienic and housing needs'.

Mac Keith's advice, with respect to the example he quoted, was that wise decisions on the ethical implications of such matters could only be made through discussions with philosophers, sociologists, priests, parents and physicians. That may well be, with a consensus perhaps emerging among many that limited funds and resources should be devoted, on the basis of a utilitarian ethic (Adams, 1984), where they would do the greatest good to the greatest number. A distinctly less likely consensus would be on where this latter phrase applies – for example, amniocenteses for mothers at increased risk of having various kinds of abnormal children versus special schools for the handicapped; medical evaluation and therapeutic clinics versus better housing; or, in wider terms, increased safeguards against accidents versus improved food production. Indeed, Childress (1982) posed the question much more broadly by asking whether hospitals should always have priority over museums and opera houses. These, of course, are not all-or-nothing alternatives or unrelated to each other but, with a wherewithal that is circumscribed, choices of priorities between desirable objectives must be made.

CONCLUSIONS

This chapter and several others in the present book provide evidence of considerable progress in the spheres of biomedical amelioration and prevention of mental retardation and associated disabilities or defects. Once cerebral pathology with resultant mental deficit has occurred, cure in the sense of restoring mental capacity to normal generally remains unrealistic, and claims to the contrary, particularly for wideranging panaceas, must be viewed with the utmost caution. Nevertheless, *appropriate* medical, surgical and related ameliorative treatments of the specific kinds described have a distinct and important role, together with suitable psychosocial and educational habilitative undertakings, in facilitating mental progress or in avoiding further deterioration.

Where curative measures for those already affected with mental retardation are nonexistent, or at best very limited, preventive objectives take on a special significance. As indicated earlier, teratogens and many other physical hazards to mental development in the environment are eminently preventable, and various treatments of maternal conditions before and during pregnancy, and of the child environmentally or genetically at increased risk for mental retardation at or after birth, have been considered in this book. At this stage, the capacity to recognize abnormality related to mental retardation pre- and postnatally is, in most instances, well ahead of the ability to provide a cure. Thus, preconception genetic counselling and, in selected cases, the option of pregnancy termination are at present major preventive approaches. Prevention by means of appropriate prophylactic or therapeutic measures, rather than by avoidance or termination of pregnancy, are obviously preferable alternatives.

Though there is a long way to go, advances in the biomedical amelioration or prevention of mental retardation in recent years have been substantial and new advances in the next few years are very likely. In addition to that challenge, the gaps (often great between known effective therapeutic and preventive measures and their availability and application in practice call for urgent attention.

REFERENCES

ADAMS, M. (1984) 'Socioethical issues in the management of developmental disability', in J.M. BERG (ed.), *Perspectives and Progress in Mental Retardation*, vol. I, Baltimore, University Park Press, 3–10.

AMERICAN ACADEMY FOR CEREBRAL PALSY, AND OTHERS (1968) 'The Doman–Delacato treatment of neurologically handicapped children', *Develop. Med. Child Neurol.*, 10, 243–6.

AMERICAN ACADEMY OF PEDIATRICS (1982) 'The Doman–Delacato treatment of neurologically handicapped children', *Pediatrics*, 70, 810–12.

AMPOLA, M.G., MAHONEY, M.J., NAKAMURA, E. and TANAKA, K. (1975) 'Prenatal therapy of a patient with vitamin B_{12}-responsive methylmalonic acidemia', *New Engl. J. Med.*, 293, 313–17.

ASTIN, A.W. and ROSS, S. (1960) 'Glutamic acid and human intelligence', *Psychol. Bull.*, 57, 429–34.

AVERY, G.B. (1982) 'Fetal surgery: some questions', *J. Amer. Med. Ass.*, 248, 2498.

BARLOW, C.F. (1978) *Mental Retardation and Related Disorders*, Philadelphia, F.A. Davis, 13–16, 126–8.

BEAUCHAMP, T.L. and WALTERS, L. (eds) (1982) *Contemporary Issues in Bioethics*, 2nd edn, Belmont, California, Wadsworth, 215–68.

BENNETT, F.C., MCCLELLAND, S., KRIEGSMANN, E.A., ANDRUS, L.B. and SELLS, C.J. (1983) 'Vitamin and mineral supplementation in Down's syndrome', *Pediatrics*, 72, 707–13.

BERG, J.M. (1976) 'Genetics and genetic counseling', in J. WORTIS (ed.), *Mental Retardation and Developmental Disabilities*, vol. VIII, New York, Brunner/Mazel, 41–57.

BERG, J.M., MCCREARY, B.D., RIDLER, M.A.C. and SMITH, G.F. (1970) *The de Lange Syndrome*, Oxford, Pergamon Press.

BERNHARD, M. (1981) *New Hope for the Retarded*, private publication, copyright, Marsha Bernhard, USA.

BLACK, D.B., KATO, J.G. and WALKER, G.W.R. (1966) 'A study of improvement in mentally retarded children accruing from siccacell therapy', *Amer. J. Ment. Defic.*, 70, 499–508.

BOBATH, K. (1963) 'The prevention of mental retardation in patients with cerebral palsy', *Acta Paedopsychiat.*, 30, 141–54.

BOBATH, K. (1980) *A Neurophysiological Basis for the Treatment of Cerebral Palsy*, Clinics in Developmental Medicine, no. 75, London, Heinemann Medical.

BOUÉ, J., VIGNAL, P., AUBRY, J.P., AUBRY, M.C. and MACALEESE, J.

(1982) 'Ultrasound movement patterns of fetuses with chromosome anomalies', *Prenat. Diagn.*, 2, 61–5.

BOURNEVILLE, D.M. (1880–1) 'Sclérose tubéreuse des circonvolutions cérébrales: idiotie et épilepsie hémiplégique', *Arch. Neurol. (Paris)*, 1, 81–91.

BRAHAMS, D. (1981) 'Acquittal of paediatrician charged after death of infant with Down syndrome', *Lancet*, 2, 1101–2.

BRAHAMS, D. (1982) 'No claim in English law for wrongful birth', *Lancet*, 1, 691–2.

BRAMBATI, B. and SIMONI, G. (1983) 'Diagnosis of fetal trisomy 21 in first trimester', *Lancet*, 1, 586.

BRETT, E. (1969) 'Second thoughts on hemispherectomy in infantile hemiplegia', *Develop. Med. Child Neurol.*, 11, 374–6.

BROCK, D.J.H. (1983) 'Amniotic fluid tests for fetal neural tube defects', *Brit. Med. Bull.*, 39, 373–7.

BYRNE, W.J., EULER, A.R., ASHCRAFT, E., NASH, D.G., SEIBERT, J.J. and GOLLADAY, E.S. (1982) 'Gastroesophageal reflux in the severely retarded who vomit: criteria for and results of surgical intervention in twenty-two patients', *Surgery*, 91, 95–8.

CAMPBELL, S. and PEARCE, J.M. (1983) 'Ultrasound visualization of congenital malformations', *Brit. Med. Bull.*, 39, 322–31.

CARTER, C.O., ROBERTS, J.A.F., EVANS, K.A. and BUCK, A.R. (1971) 'Genetic clinic: a follow-up', *Lancet*, 1, 281–5.

CHASEY, W.C. and WYRICK, W. (1971) 'Effects of a physical developmental program on psychomotor ability of retarded children', *Amer. J. Ment. Defic.*, 75, 566–70.

CHILDRESS, J.F. (1982) 'Priorities in the allocation of health care resources', in F.L. BEAUCHAMP and L. WALTERS (eds), *Contemporary Issues in Bioethics*, 2nd edn, Belmont, California, Wadsworth, 410–23.

CHRISTENSON, B., BÖTTINGER, M. and HELLER, L. (1983) 'Mass vaccination programme aimed at eradicating measles, mumps and rubella in Sweden: first experience', *Brit. Med. J.*, 287, 389–91.

CLEWELL, W.H., JOHNSON, M.L., MEIER, P.R., NEWKIRK, J.B., ZIDE, S.L., HENDEE, R.W., BOWES, W.A., HECHT, F., O'KEEFE, D., HENRY, G.P. and SHIKES, R.H. (1982) 'A surgical approach to the treatment of fetal hydrocephalus', *New Engl. J. Med.*, 306, 1320–5.

COBURN, S.P., SCHALTENBRAND, W.E., MAHUREN, J.D., CLAUSMAN, R.J. and TOWNSEND, D. (1983) 'Effect of megavitamin treatment on mental performance and plasma vitamin B_6 concentrations in mentally retarded young adults', *Amer. J. Clin. Nutrit.*, 38, 352–5.

COHEN, H.J., BIRCH, H.G. and TAFT, L.T. (1970) 'Some considerations for evaluating the Doman–Delacato "patterning" method', *Pediatrics*, 45, 302–14.

COMMITTEE ON NUTRITION, AMERICAN ACADEMY OF PEDIATRICS (1976) 'Megavitamin therapy for childhood psychoses and learning disabilities', *Pediatrics*, 58, 910–12.

CRAFT, A. and CRAFT, M. (1981) 'Sexuality and mental handicap: a review', *Brit. J. Psychiat.*, 139, 494–505.

CRANEFIELD, P.F. (1961) 'A seventeenth-century view of mental deficiency and schizophrenia: Thomas Willis on "stupidity or foolishness"', *Bull. Hist. Med.*, 35, 291–316.

CRANEFIELD, P.F. and FEDERN, W. (1976) 'Paulus Zacchias on mental deficiency and on deafness', in J. JARCHO (ed.), *Essays on the History of Medicine*, New York, Neale Watson, 118–36.

CRAWFORD, D.C., GARRETT, C., TYNAN, M., NEVILLE, B.G. and ALLAN, L.D. (1983) 'Cardiac rhabdomyomata as a marker for the antenatal detection of tuberous sclerosis', *J. Med. Genet.*, 20, 303–4.

CUCKLE, H.S., WALD, N.J. and LINDENBAUM, R.H. (1984) 'Maternal serum alpha-fetoprotein measurement: a screening test for Down syndrome', *Lancet*, 1, 926–9.

DAKER, M. (1983) 'Chorionic tissue biopsy in the first trimester of pregnancy', *Brit. J. Obstet. Gynaec.*, 90, 193–5.

DE LA CRUZ, F.F. and LA VECK, G.D. (eds) (1974) *Human Sexuality and the Mentally Retarded*, Baltimore, Penguin.

DENNIS, M., FITZ, C.R., NETLEY, C.T., SUGAR, J., HARWOOD-NASH, D.C.F., HENDRICK, E.B., HOFFMAN, H.J. and HUMPHRIES, R.P. (1981) 'The intelligence of hydrocephalic children', *Arch. Neurol.*, 38, 607–15.

DEPP, R., SABBAGHA, R.E., BROWN, J.T., TAMURA, R.K. and REEDY, N.J. (1983) 'Fetal surgery for hydrocephalus: successful in utero ventriculoamniotic shunt for Dandy–Walker syndrome', *Obstet. Gynec. Survey*, 38, 657–9.

DESTUNIS, G. (1957) 'Treatment of mental deficiency and encephalopathies in childhood by means of fresh tissue and sicca cell', *Arch. Pediat.*, 74, 285–90.

DOMAN, R.J., SPITZ, E.B., ZUCMAN, E., DELACATO, C.H. and DOMAN, G. (1960) 'Children with severe brain injuries: neurological organization in terms of mobility', *J. Amer. Med. Ass.*, 174, 257–62.

DOWN, J.L.H. (1866) 'Observations on an ethnic classification of idiots', *Lond. Hosp. Rep.*, 3, 259–62.

ELLIS, N.R. and TOMPOROWSKI, P.D. (1983) 'Vitamin/mineral supplements and intelligence of institutionalized mentally retarded adults', *Amer. J. Ment. Defic.*, 88, 211–14.

ELLMAN, G., SILVERSTEIN, C.I., ZINGARELLI, G., SCHAFER, E.W.P. and SILVERSTEIN, L. (1984) 'Vitamin–mineral supplement fails to improve IQ of mentally retarded young adults', *Amer. J. Ment. Defic.*, 88, 688–91.

ENGLER, M. (1948) 'Prefrontal leucotomy in mental defectives', *J. Ment. Sci.*, 94, 844–50.

EVERS-KIEBOOMS, G. and VAN DEN BERGHE, H. (1979) 'Impact of genetic counseling: a review of published follow-up studies', *Clin. Genet.*, 15, 465–74.

FALCONER, M.A. and RUSHWORTH, R.G. (1960) 'Treatment of encephalotrigeminal angiomatosis (Sturge–Weber disease) by hemispherectomy', *Arch. Dis. Childh.*, 35, 433–47.

FERGUSON-SMITH, M.A. (ed.) (1983a) 'Early prenatal diagnosis', *Brit. Med. Bull.*, 39, 301–408.

FERGUSON-SMITH, M.A. (1983b) 'The reduction of neural tube defects by maternal serum alpha-fetoprotein screening', *Brit. Med. Bull.*, 39, 365–72.

FERGUSON-SMITH, M.A. (1984) 'Prenatal diagnosis of chromosome anomalies: who is at risk?', in C.H. RODECK and K.H. NICOLAIDES (eds), *Prenatal Diagnosis*, London, Royal College of Obstetricians and Gynaecologists, 53–64.

FILKINS, K. and BENZIE, R.J. (1983) 'Fetoscopy', *Clin. Obstet. Gynec.*, 26, 339–46.

FINEMAN, R.M. and GORDIS, D.M. (1982) 'Jewish perspective on prenatal diagnosis and selective abortion of affected fetuses, including some comparisons with prevailing Catholic beliefs', *Amer. J. Med. Genet.*, 12, 355–60.

FONKALSRUD, E.W., DE LORIMIER, A.A. and HAYS, D.M. (1969) 'Congenital atresia and stenosis of the duodenum', *Pediatrics*, 43, 79–83.

FOTHERINGHAM, J.B., HAMBLEY, W.D. and HADDAD-CURRAN, H.W. (1983) *Prevention of Intellectual Handicaps*, Toronto, The Martin Group.

FRIGOLETTO, F.D., BIRNHOLZ, J.C. and GREENE, M.F. (1982) 'Antenatal treatment of hydrocephalus by ventriculoamniotic shunting', *J. Amer. Med. Ass.*, 248, 2496–7.

FRIGOLETTO, F.D., UMANSKY, I., BIRNHOLZ, J., ACKER, D., EASTERDAY, C.L., HARRIS, G.B.C. and GRISCOM, N.T. (1981) 'Intrauterine fetal transfusion in 365 fetuses during 15 years', *Amer. J. Obstet. Gynec.*, 139, 781–7.

FUHRMANN, W. and VOGEL, F. (1983) *Genetic Counseling*, 3rd edn, New York, Springer-Verlag.

GOLDEN, G.S. (1980) 'Nonstandard therapies in the developmental disabilities', *Amer. J. Dis. Child.*, 134, 487–91.

GOLDSTEIN, H. (1956) 'Sicca-cell therapy in children', *Arch. Pediat.*, 73, 234–49.

GOSDEN, C.M. (1983) 'Amniotic fluid cell types and culture', *Brit. Med. Bull.*, 39, 348–54.

GOSDEN, J.R. (1984) 'DNA analysis and its application to prenatal diagnosis', in C.H. RODECK and K.H. NICOLAIDES (eds), *Prenatal Diagnosis*, London, Royal College of Obstetricians and Gynaecologists, 31–48.

GRIFFEL, A. (1957) 'The latest developments in dry cell therapy (siccacell)', *Arch. Pediat.*, 74, 325–42.

GUSTAVII, B., CHESTER, M.A., EDVALL, H., IOSIF, S., KRISTOFFERSSON, U., LÖFBERG, L., MINEUR, A. and MITELMAN, F. (1984) 'First-trimester diagnosis on chorionic villi obtained by direct vision technique',

Hum. Genet., 65, 373–6.

GUTHRIE, D. (1945) *A History of Medicine*, London, Nelson, 5–11.

HALL, D.M.B. (1984) *The Child with a Handicap*, Oxford, Blackwell Scientific.

HARPER, P.S. (1981) *Practical Genetic Counselling*, Baltimore, University Park Press.

HARRELL, R.F., CAPP, R.H., DAVIS, D.R., PEERLESS, J. and RAVITZ, L.R. (1981) 'Can nutritional supplements help mentally retarded children? An exploratory study', *Proc. Nat. Acad. Sci.*, 78, 574–8.

HARRISON, M.R., GOLBUS, M.S. and FILLY, R.A. (1984) *The Unborn Patient: Prenatal Diagnosis and Treatment*, Orlando, Florida, Grune & Stratton.

HERBST, D.S. and BAIRD, P.A. (1982) 'Sib risks for nonspecific mental retardation in British Columbia', *Amer. J. Med. Genet.*, 13, 197–208.

HERR, S.S. (1984) 'The Phillip Becker case resolved: a chance for habilitation', *Ment. Retard.*, 22, 30–5.

HILL, L.M., BRECKLE, R. and GEHRKING, W.C. (1983) 'The prenatal detection of congenital malformations by ultrasonography', *Mayo Clin. Proc.*, 58, 805–26.

HOFFER, M.M. (ed.) (1981) *Orthopedic Surgery in the Mentally Retarded*, Orthopedic Clinics of North America, 12, no. 1, Philadelphia, Saunders.

HOFFMAN, H.J., HENDRICK, E.B., DENNIS, M. and ARMSTRONG, D. (1979) 'Hemispherectomy for Sturge–Weber syndrome', *Child's Brain*, 5, 233–48.

HOFFMAN, H.J., HENDRICK, E.B. and MUNRO, I.R. (1982) 'Craniosynostosis and craniofacial surgery', in *Pediatric Neurosurgery: Surgery of the Developing Nervous System* (editor not specified), New York, Grune & Stratton, 121–56.

HÖHLER, H. (1977) 'Changes in facial expression as a result of plastic surgery in mongoloid children', *Aesthet. Plast. Surg.*, 1, 245–50.

HSIA, Y.E., HIRSCHHORN, K., SILVERBERG, R.L. and GODMILOW, L. (eds) (1979) *Counseling in Genetics*, New York, Alan R. Liss.

HUMPHRIES, S.E. and WILLIAMSON, R. (1983) 'Application of recombinant DNA technology to prenatal detection of inherited defects', *Brit. Med. Bull.*, 39, 343–7.

HUNT, J.V., TOOLEY, W.H. and HARVIN, D. (1982) 'Learning disabilities in children with birth weights ⩽ 1500 grams', *Sem. Perinat.*, 6, 280–7.

HUNTER, A.G.W., EVANS, J.A., THOMPSON, D.R. and RAMSAY, S. (1980) 'A study of institutionalized mentally retarded patients in Manitoba: I. Classification and preventability', *Develop. Med. Child Neurol.*, 22, 145–62.

JACOBI, A. (1894) 'Surgical treatment of idiocy and microcephalus', *Arch. Pediat.*, 11, 423–37.

JONES, R. and STENING, W. (1981) 'Management of hydrocephalus in children', *Med. J. Austr.*, 1, 334–8.

KABACK, M.M. (1984) 'The utility of prenatal diagnosis', in C.H. RODECK and K.H. NICOLAIDES (eds), *Prenatal Diagnosis*, London, Royal College of Obstetricians and Gynaecologists, 1–12.

KANNER, L. (1964) *A History of the Care and Study of the Mentally Retarded*, Springfield, Illinois, C.C. Thomas, 7–8.

KARP, L.E. (1983) 'New hope for the retarded?', *Amer. J. Med. Genet.*, 16, 1–5.

KAZY, Z., ROSOVSKY, I.S. and BAKHAREV, V.A. (1982) 'Chorion biopsy in early pregnancy: a method of early prenatal diagnosis for inherited disorders', *Prenat. Diagn.*, 2, 39–45.

KELLY, T.E. (1980) *Clinical Genetics and Genetic Counseling*, Chicago, Year Book Medical Publishers.

LARKIN, R.M., KNOCHEL, J.Q. and LEE, T.G. (1982) 'Intrauterine transfusions: new techniques and results', *Clin. Obstet. Gynec.*, 25, 303–12.

Leading article (1982) 'Directive counselling', *Lancet*, 2, 368–9.

Leading article (1983) 'Plastic surgery in Down's syndrome', *Lancet*, 1, 1314.

LEMPERLE, G. and RADU, D. (1980) 'Facial plastic surgery in children with Down's syndrome', *Plast. Reconstr. Surg.*, 66, 337–42.

LILEY, A.W. (1963) 'Intrauterine transfusion of foetus in haemolytic disease', *Brit. Med. J.*, 2, 1107–9.

LITTLE, W.J. (1862) 'On the influence of abnormal parturition, difficult labours, premature births, and asphyxia neonatorum, on the mental and physical conditions of the child, especially in relation to deformities', *Trans. Obstet. Soc. Lond.*, 3, 293–344.

LUBS, H.A. and DE LA CRUZ, F. (eds) (1977) *Genetic Counseling*, New York, Raven Press.

LYNCH, H.T., KIMBERLING, W. and PELLETTERA, K.M. (1983) *International Directory of Genetic Services*, 7th edn, New York, March of Dimes Birth Defects Foundation.

MCCORMACK, M.K. (ed.) (1980) *Prevention of Mental Retardation and Other Developmental Disabilities*, New York, Marcel Dekker.

MACKAY, G.W. (1948) 'Leucotomy in the treatment of psychopathic feeble-minded patients in a state mental deficiency institution', *J. Ment. Sci.*, 94, 834–43.

MAC KEITH, R. (1975) 'Helping one or helping many', *Develop. Med. Child Neurol.*, 17, 419–20.

MENOLASCINO, F.J., STARK, J.A. and NEEMAN, R.J. (eds) (1983) *Curative Aspects of Mental Retardation: Biomedical and Behavioral Advances*, Baltimore, P.H. Brookes.

MERKATZ. I.R., NITOWSKY, H.M., MACRI, J.N. and JOHNSON, W.E. (1984) 'An association between low maternal serum alpha-fetoprotein and fetal chromosomal abnormalities', *Amer. J. Obstet. Gynec.*, 148, 886–94.

MICHEJDA, M. and HODGEN, G.D. (1981) 'In utero diagnosis and treatment of non-human primate fetal skeletal anomalies: I. Hydrocephalus', *J. Amer. Med. Ass.*, 246, 1093–7.

MILLIGAN, J.E., SHENNAN, A.T. and HOSKINS, E.M. (1984) 'Perinatal intensive care: where and how to draw the line', *Amer. J. Obstet. Gynec.*, 148, 499–503.

MILUNSKY, A. (ed.) (1975) *The Prevention of Genetic Disease and Mental Retardation*, Philadelphia, Saunders.

MILUNSKY, A. (1983) 'Genetics, law and obstetric practice', *Brit. J. Obstet. Gynaec.*, 90, 497–500.

MORRIS, J.V., MACGILLIVRAY, R.C. and MATHIESON, C.M. (1954) 'The experimental administration of *Celastrus paniculata* in mental deficiency practice', *Amer. J. Ment. Defic.*, 59, 235–44.

MORRIS, J.V., MACGILLIVRAY, R.C. and MATHIESON, C.M. (1955) 'The results of the experimental administration of amphetamine sulphate in oligophrenia', *J. Ment. Sci.*, 101, 131–40.

MURPHY, E.A. (1974) 'Effects of changing sexuality on the gene pool: a response to Sheldon Reed', in F.F. DE LA CRUZ and G.D. LA VECK (eds), *Human Sexuality and the Mentally Retarded*, Baltimore, Penguin, 126–37.

MURPHY, E.A. and CHASE, G.A. (1975) *Principles of Genetic Counseling*, Chicago, Year Book Medical Publishers.

NORA, J.J. and FRASER, F.C. (1981) *Medical Genetics: Principles and Practice*, 2nd edn, Philadelphia, Lea & Febiger.

OHLSSON, A. and FOHLIN, L. (1983) 'Reproductive medical care in Sweden and the province of Ontario, Canada: a comparative study', *Acta Paediat. Scand.*, suppl. 306, 1–15.

OLBRISCH, R.R. (1982) 'Plastic surgical management of children with Down's syndrome: indications and results', *Brit. J. Plast. Surg.*, 35, 195–200.

PARETTE, H.P. and HOURCADE, J.J. (1984) 'How effective are physio-therapeutic programmes with young mentally retarded children who have cerebral palsy?', *J. Ment. Defic. Res.*, 28, 167–75.

PUDENZ, R.H. (1980) 'The surgical treatment of hydrocephalus – an historical review', *Surg. Neurol.*, 15, 15–26.

RAIMONDI, A.J. and SOARE, P. (1974) 'Intellectual development in shunted hydrocephalic children', *Amer. J. Dis. Child.*, 127, 664–71.

ROBERTS, J.A.F. and PEMBREY, M.E. (1978) *An Introduction to Medical Genetics*, 7th edn, London, Oxford University Press.

ROCKER, I. and LAURENCE, K.M. (eds) (1981) *Fetoscopy*, Amsterdam, Elsevier/North-Holland.

RODECK, C.H., HOLMAN, C.A., KARNICKI, J., KEMP, J.R., WHITMORE, D.N. and AUSTIN, M.A. (1981) 'Direct intravascular fetal blood transfusion by fetoscopy in severe rhesus isoimmunization', *Lancet*, 1, 625–7.

RODECK, C.H. and MORSMAN, J.M. (1983) 'First-trimester chorion biopsy', *Brit. Med. Bull.*, 39, 338–42.

RODECK, C.H. and NICOLAIDES, K.H. (1983) 'Fetoscopy and fetal tissue sampling', *Brit. Med. Bull.*, 39, 332–7.

RODECK, C.H. and NICOLAIDES, K.H. (eds) (1984) *Prenatal Diagnosis*, London, Royal College of Obstetricians and Gynaecologists.

ROSENBERG, R.N. (1984) 'Molecular genetics, recombinant DNA techniques, and genetic neurological disease', *Ann. Neurol.*, 15, 511–20.

ROZNER, L. (1983) 'Facial plastic surgery for Down's syndrome', *Lancet*, 1, 1320–3.

SABIN, A.B. (1981) 'Immunization: evaluation of some currently available and prospective vaccines', *J. Amer. Med. Ass.*, 246, 236–41.

SACHS, E.S, VAN HEMEL, J.O., GALJAARD, H., NIERMEIJER, M.F. and JAHODA, M.G.J. (1983) 'First trimester chromosomal analysis of complex structural rearrangements with RHA banding on chorionic villi', *Lancet*, 2, 1426.

SCHECHNER, S. (1980) 'For the 1980s: how small is too small?', *Clin. Perinat.*, 7, 135–43.

SCHEERENBERGER, R.C. (1983) *A History of Mental Retardation*, Baltimore, Paul H. Brookes, 10–11.

SCHMID, F. (1978) 'Down's syndrome: treatment and management', *Cytobiologische Revue*, nr. 1, Thun, Ott Verlag.

SCHMID, F. (1980) 'Cell therapy – experimental basis and clinics', *Cytobiologische Revue*, nr. 2, Thun, Ott Verlag.

SCRUTTON, D. (1978) 'Developmental deformity and the profoundly retarded child', in J. APLEY (ed.), *Care of the Handicapped Child*, Clinics in Developmental Medicine, no. 67, London, Heinemann Medical, 83–91.

SCRUTTON, D. (ed.) (1984) *Management of the Motor Disorders of Children with Cerebral Palsy*, Clinics in Developmental Medicine, no. 90, London, Spastics International Medical Publications.

SHAW, A., RANDOLPH, J.G. and MANARD, B. (1977) 'Ethical issues in pediatric surgery: a national survey of pediatricians and pediatric surgeons', *Pediatrics*, 60, 588–99.

SHAW, M.W. (1984) 'To be or not to be? That is the question', *Amer. J. Hum. Genet.*, 36, 1–9.

SIMONI, G., BRAMBATI, B., DANESINO, C., ROSSELLA, F., TERZOLI, G.L., FERRARI, M. and FRACCARO, M. (1983) 'Efficient direct chromosome analyses and enzyme determinations from chorionic villi samples in the first trimester of pregnancy', *Hum. Genet.*, 63, 349–57.

SINGER, P. (1983) 'Sanctity of life or quality of life', *Pediatrics*, 72, 128–9.

SINGER, P., KUHSE, H. and SINGER, C. (1983) 'The treatment of newborn infants with major handicaps: a survey of obstetricians and paediatricians in Victoria', *Med. J. Austr.*, 2, 274–8.

SMITH, D.W. (1982) *Recognizable Patterns of Human Malformation: Genetic, Embryologic and Clinical Aspects*, 3rd edn, Philadelphia, Saunders, 76–7.

SMITH, G.F. and BERG, J.M. (1976) *Down's Anomaly*, 2nd edn, Edinburgh, Churchill Livingstone, 223–5.

SPARROW, S. and ZIGLER, E. (1978) 'Evaluation of a patterning treatment for retarded children', *Pediatrics*, 62, 137–50.

SPECIAL REPORT (1984) 'The status of fetoscopy and fetal tissue sampling', *Prenat. Diagn.*, 4, 79–81.

STARK, C.R., ORLEANS, M., HAVERKAMP, A.D. and MURPHY, J. (1984) 'Short- and long-term risks after exposure to diagnostic ultrasound in utero', *Obstet. Gynec.*, 63, 194–200.

STEVENSON, A.C. and DAVISON, B.C.C. (1976) *Genetic Counselling*, 2nd edn, London, Heinemann Medical.

THOMPSON, J.S. and THOMPSON, M.W. (1980) *Genetics in Medicine*, 3rd edn, Philadelphia, Saunders.

TODRES, I.D., KRANE, D., HOWELL, M.C. and SHANNON, D.C. (1977) 'Pediatricians' attitudes affecting decision-making in defective newborns', *Pediatrics*, 60, 197–201.

WALLMAN, L.J. (1982) 'Shunting for hydrocephalus: an oral history', *Neurosurg.*, 11, 308–13.

WARD, R.H.T. (1984) 'First trimester chorionic villus sampling', in C.H. RODECK and K.H. NICOLAIDES (eds), *Prenatal Diagnosis*, London, Royal College of Obstetricians and Gynaecologists, 99–103.

WEATHERS, C. (1983) 'Effects of nutritional supplementation on IQ and certain other variables associated with Down syndrome', *Amer. J. Ment. Defic.*, 88, 214–17.

WEIR, R. (1984) *Selective Nontreatment of Handicapped Newborns: Moral Dilemmas in Neonatal Medicine*, London, Oxford University Press, 59–90.

ZIGLER, E. (1981) 'A plea to end the use of the patterning treatment for retarded children', *Amer. J. Orthopsychiat.*, 51, 388–90.

Lifespan development and psychosocial intervention

Ann M. Clarke and Alan D.B. Clarke

INTRODUCTION

Much of this part of the book is devoted to description and assessments of various kinds of psychosocial intervention, including behaviour modification and education; a separate chapter on psychosocial intervention might therefore seem redundant. There are, however, certain issues mostly concerned with long-term patterns of social adjustment in the retarded which may best be reviewed together, in order to give a broad perspective within which the results of specific initiatives may be evaluated. The authors are aware of the dangers of claims for miracle cures in the field of mental handicap, as in other areas such as cancer and disseminated sclerosis, but are also aware of the positive effects of social environmental influences throughout the lifespan. The seriously deleterious effects of environmental disadvantage were reviewed in Chapter 7. It would be pleasant to be able to report that the constellations of adverse influences could readily be dispelled, or that children born into serious disadvantage could easily be helped, but however much researchers and practitioners can point to social factors as major or minor concomitants in the aetiology of retardation, their ability to improve the position for the mentally handicapped in society is strictly limited.

An important question is the extent to which the mentally retarded show behavioural consistency over time, requiring special support services of either a formal or an informal nature. This is part of the general issue of continuities and discontinuities in development, reviewed recently by several writers including Emde and Harmon (1985) and Clarke and Clarke (1984), whose evaluation of the evidence may be summarized as follows:

> Neither genetic programmes nor social influences necessarily unfold in a constant way, and their interactions are complex. The role of chance events adds a further and sometimes potent uncertainty in prediction equations. Both constancies and changes in ordinal position and/or level occur for most characteristics in normal circumstances, but following significant ecological improvement, personal changes among the disadvantaged can be much larger. Recent research emphasizes the inadequacy of considering either genetic or environmental effects during one period of development

outside the context of preceding and subsequent influences. It is to long-term consistent influences that importance must be ascribed.

Before turning to longitudinal studies of mentally retarded persons an important general point should be made, excellently expressed by the late Jack Tizard in the last edition of this book (1974, Chapter 9) concerning expectancies for different subsections of the retarded population:

> The differences between those with handicaps associated with severe (or low-grade) mental defect on the one hand and mild or high-grade mental handicap on the other have already been reviewed. The severely retarded tend to be stunted physically as well as mentally; their handicaps are often recognizable at birth or during early infancy; they are much more backward in development throughout childhood, and usually remain dependent upon others throughout life; they have a greatly reduced expectation of life; they are rarely fertile; almost all of them suffer from gross structural damage to the brain. However, their relatives tend either to be normal in development or to suffer from severe mental and physical handicaps. Parents of the severely retarded are drawn from all classes of the population and not mainly from one depressed social group.
>
> In all of these respects the mildly retarded differ from the severely retarded and there are indeed very strong reasons for the belief that the two classes of handicap are caused by different agents, and that they necessarily have very different outcomes.
>
> For present purposes the importance of these distinctions lies in the different prognosis of persons diagnosed as either mildly or severely retarded.

LONGITUDINAL STUDIES

It has been known for years that the prevalence of administratively defined mental retardation is at its peak during the later years of schooling and thereafter declines sharply, and that this is almost entirely due to the later community adjustment of the mildly subnormal. Follow-up studies of the severely subnormal, however, indicate that even in conditions of very full employment they remain dependent upon social agencies dealing with mental handicap (Tizard, 1958; Kushlick, 1961; Kushlick and Blunden, 1974). The conclusion to be drawn from longitudinal studies of the mildly retarded was put as follows by Cobb (1972):

> in terms of the criteria of employment, marriage and law abiding behaviour, studies over 50 years have shown that a high proportion of those identified as mildly retarded make satisfactory adjustments. Without any special service or treatment, they tend to disappear into the general lower class population from which they are hardly distinguishable as a social group. ... All of the major longitudinal studies report identifiable shifting from

early instability to relatively increased stability over time. Thus, as compared with a non-retarded control group, the retarded show a higher incidence of marital, civic and occupational failure, especially in the early stages. The difference, however, tends to diminish over time. The group identified as retarded still tends to retain a difference in frequency of unsatisfactory adaptations from non-retarded controls, but these frequencies are relatively small and decreasing.

One of the most interesting and important longitudinal studies of mentally subnormal persons across time was conducted by Edgerton and colleagues, who undertook intensive studies of a carefully selected sample of persons institutionalized in the USA in the 1930s at an average age of 14, remaining there for an average period of 20 years (Edgerton, 1967, p. 12).

During the period 1949 to 1958, 110 patients successfully graduated from a vocational training programme and were discharged from the hospital without any reservations about their freedom. At the time of the first follow-up this cohort included 55 men who were on average 33.7 years of age and had a mean IQ of 66.5, and 55 women who were 35.6 years old on average, with a mean IQ of 62.9. Of the 110 people, 53 were still living within a 50-mile radius of the hospital and thus could be studied without great difficulty. Twelve could not be traced, and the remaining 45, dispersed over a wide area, did not differ in any significant way from those included in the research sample, which finally numbered 48 with IQs ranging from 47 to 85 for each sex. Edgerton's method was 'anthropological', his material being gained through repeated non-structured interviews, the aim being a general description of the lives of mentally retarded persons in the community, the problems they face, 'and the techniques they employ in dealing with their stigma and their incompetence'.

Although at one time or another since their discharge 32 per cent of the ex-patients had received social welfare aid, three had been in prison and another six had minor brushes with the law, they had nevertheless achieved a measure of success in their return to the outside world from which they had been excluded over such a long period. Furthermore, their lives were remarkably varied and characterized by a fair degree of complexity. Two findings are emphasized and elaborated: first the great importance in the lives of these men and women of unofficial benefactors, normal persons in the community who helped them with their problems, typically a spouse, relative, professional person or employer; and second, the efforts made to obscure all traces of their past and to pass as normal, an activity in which the benefactors participated as part of a benevolent conspiracy. The present authors, who at one time were responsible for a vocational programme in a hospital for mentally retarded persons, can confirm these aspects of the lives of 'patients' discharged from care, and were themselves involved in a similar benevolent conspiracy.

Edgerton and Bercovici (1976) conducted a second field study of this group a decade later, during 1972–3, locating and gaining permission to interview 30 of the original 48. They concluded that 'the lives of these people offer inconclusive support for the idea that the passage of considerable amounts of time improves either the level or stability of community adjustment. Compared to 1960–1961, 8 of these 30 persons were judged to have a better level of community adjustment, but 10 were judged to have a lower level of adjustment, and 12 remained the same.' Attention was drawn, however, to the discrepancy between the scientists' assessments of competence and the subjects' views of their own adaptation. Competence appeared to be less important than confidence, with independence less vital than a sense of well-being. On this latter criterion 12 were happier than they had been a decade before; of these, 5 had been rated more adjusted and 7 the same by the researchers. Three people who appeared to have improved said they were less happy and 7 people who were rated unchanged said they were happier.

The authors, in an important discussion of criteria which might evolve to predict community adjustment of the mentally retarded, raise the possibility that this population 'may sometimes fluctuate markedly not only from year to year, but from month to month or even from week to week', rendering prognostic research difficult unless provision is made for 'sufficient continuity of measurement over time to permit assessment of microshifts in adaptation of a short-term, emergent nature'.

Ten years later 15 of these mildly retarded persons were studied again (Edgerton *et al.*, 1984) at a mean age of 56. The quality of their lives was re-examined with an emphasis on personal and social resources for coping with chronic or acute stress. They were found to be less dependent on others than previously, appearing relatively hopeful, confident and independent, despite ill health, stressful life events and the lack of assistance from mental retardation service agencies. The authors point out that sample attrition may have been selective, although there is some evidence against this. Once again the heterogeneity of the group and their individual methods of coping with the complexities of life emerges, as does the variety of personal characteristics other than their relatively poor mental development which has enabled them to stay afloat.

We turn now to another major prospective longitudinal study, using an impeccable scientific methodology. Richardson (1978) faulted many previous investigations of the long-term prospects for mentally retarded children on several important counts. These included their largely retrospective nature, sample biases, lack of appropriate comparison groups and lack of investigation of factors influencing later outcome. Richardson's study is based on an earlier large-scale project carried out in 1962 when the total population of children born in the city of Aberdeen during the years 1951 and 1952 was studied with particular reference to those identifiable as mentally retarded, by means of either IQ scores or administrative intervention (Birch *et al.*, 1970).

For the purposes of this study all of the 97 cases of children who at the age of 10 had been administratively identified as mentally retarded were regarded as index cases, and data were obtained on 88 of them. For each case a matched comparison was selected who had at no time during the years of schooling been dealt with as mentally retarded. The matching variables were age, sex, occupation of head of the household at the time the child was aged 8–10, and the type of housing at that time. No subject was included as a control who had at the ages of 7 and 9 scored less than 75 and 80, respectively, in group intelligence tests given to all children in the city.

The data collected when these young people were 22 years old were derived from a standardized interview, crosschecked whenever possible with parents of the mentally retarded and records from a variety of institutions. Two-thirds of the index cases were not receiving any special mental retardation services. Of these, 89 per cent of the males were in full-time jobs, with the remaining 11 per cent unemployed. For this subset of persons not receiving services, a comparison was made with the members of the control group. For employment there were no significant differences, although there was a tendency for higher unemployment in the retarded group. Three measures were used to examine the kinds of job held, in terms of degree of skill, take-home pay and whether the job dealt with objects only or persons as well. As might be guessed, the index cases had a high frequency of less skilled jobs. The male index cases averaged two-thirds of the pay of their matched comparisons. Finally, fewer held jobs that required interpersonal skills.

In discussing these and other data, Richardson indicates that classification as retarded does not have to be a one-way irrevocable process. The enthusiastic labelling theorists argue that once a child has been labelled retarded, declassification will not occur either because educational authorities might regard this as an admission of error or because, once classified, initial judgements are seldom revised. But some 18 per cent who in this study had been in special schools returned to regular schools, indicating a flexibility not always recognized by critics of services for the mentally retarded.

It is of interest that index cases appeared to have a lesser degree of discontent with their jobs, but of course such persons may be limited in their ability to imagine alternatives. Moreover, differences in careers between them and their comparisons may become more evident as the years pass. So far as interpersonal relations are concerned, index cases assess their situation less favourably than do their matched comparisons. Further reports of this study are awaited with interest.

In summary, longitudinal studies of the outcome in adulthood for mildly retarded persons are, as Cobb (1972) and Tizard (1974) have argued, unanimous in showing that the majority make more or less adequate adjustments to society and usually without official special help. Of course, as Edgerton has shown, unofficial help has often been available for such persons.

We have in the past suggested that three nonmutually exclusive processes may be at work in what appears to be a self-ameliorative tendency in the adolescent and adult retarded. First, *camouflage*: for many the most challenging intellectual demands of a lifetime may reside in the later years of schooling. Subsequently, with lessened strains, the essentially unchanged individual may be 'hidden' by virtue of an ability to undertake unskilled work and to function more or less adequately in society. Second, *prolonged social learning* of the means of meeting social demands may occur, such that at age 15 the individual is relatively much less able to cope than his age peers, than at 25 or 30. Modelling behaviour is implicit in this hypothesis. Third, *delayed intellectual maturation* in those from the most adverse backgrounds appears to be common and sometimes considerable (e.g. Clarke *et al.*, 1958; Balla and Zigler, 1975; Svendsen, 1982). The first of these processes involves no essential change in the individual, but the second and third involve incremental alterations in behaviour. While this picture is relatively hopeful for the majority of the mildly retarded in the long term, current economic problems in developed, industrial nations may substantially diminish these prospects.

There is also the larger group of persons never administratively labelled mildly retarded, but who in terms of IQ alone might have been thus identified, but were not. Next to nothing is known about their life-histories, but no doubt they share some of the problems of the identified group.

The 1950s and 1960s saw a substantial change in society's view of how best to provide for mentally retarded persons, with a shift of emphasis from incarceration in large institutions to various forms of community support for the mentally handicapped of all ages and levels of retardation. Three interlocking factors appear to have been responsible: first, a surge of sensitivity to the waste of potential among the handicapped, initiated in part by the researches of the late Jack Tizard and his colleagues both in Britain and elsewhere; second, the activities of parents' groups on behalf of their handicapped children; and third, protests by civil rights movements on behalf of those who had been 'put away'. Evaluation of the efficacy of settings in promoting development in the mentally handicapped became an important research topic, but also one demanding powerful statistical designs to overcome the effects of inevitable biases in populations allocated to various forms of care.

Eyman and Arndt (1982) have undertaken a particularly impressive review of the lifespan development of institutionalized and community-based mentally retarded persons using the semi-longitudinal method proposed by Fisher and Zeaman (1970). The methodological problems inherent in determining rates of development in various settings are clearly enunciated, given the considerable differences between the kinds of retarded individuals residing in alternative placements. Eyman and Arndt's purpose was to investigate 'lifespan development of retarded persons relative to their level of retardation, institution *v.* community placement, and for institutionalized residents, quality of environment'.

Lifespan development was assessed in terms of gains in adaptive behaviour performance across a 4-year period for groups of individuals of ages varying between 5 and 47 in 1974. The institution sample consisted of 3457 persons within 7 state institutions in western states of the USA. The 312 people in the community sample received state services through a regional centre for developmentally disabled individuals living in their own home, a family-care home, convalescent hospital or a board-and-care home in southern California. The average ages of the institutionalized and community-based groups was 20 and 21, respectively (SDs = 8 and 9). The average IQ of residents in institutions was 26 (SD = 17); and for the community residents was much higher, being 36 (SD = 19).

All subjects had been professionally assessed annually on the AAMD Adaptive Behavior Scale (see Chapter 2) between 1974 and 1978. For the purposes of this investigation a single total score was used, representing the three applicable domains: personal self-sufficiency, community self-sufficiency and personal–social responsibility. Readers are referred to the original paper for details of the sophisticated statistical design which employed an incomplete and nonorthogonal repeated measures analysis of variance using three independent variables: level of retardation, birth-year cohort group (nested in level of retardation) and age as the repeated measure. The analysis was performed upon cell means rather than individual scores, and data on the institutionalized and community samples were treated separately.

The results indicated that the patterns of adaptive growth were essentially similar across the levels of retardation for the age range examined. The effect of level of retardation (based on IQ) was, of course, highly significant, indicating that IQ was associated with adaptive behaviour ratings, and that the scores of those in the community were higher than those in institutions. As for the effect of age, there was significant growth in adaptive behaviour competence at all levels of retardation as a function of age.

The scores for adaptive behaviour were smoothed and plotted against age. The curves can be considered as lifespan curves because the effects of generational differences had been removed. The scores appeared far less stable after age 35 especially in the community sample, to some extent perhaps due to small numbers, but probably also reflecting real patterns of increment and decrement, implicitly supporting the findings of Edgerton and Bercovici (1976) reported earlier. There also seemed to be an overall decline in adaptive functioning for the older institutionalized individual in contrast to slight increases in competence for those in the community. Further analysis suggested that the quality of the environment did not have a differential effect on the groups studied. 'Rather, all groups demonstrated about the same pattern of growth regardless of whether the environment in which they resided was rated high or low.'

In summary, the authors indicate that both institutionalized and community groups demonstrated significant growth in adaptive behaviour over the early years of development. Indeed, the differing levels for these two groups are roughly parallel. The findings are also congruent with other research. The fact that differing environmental qualities in the institutionalized were not reflected in differences in competence was disappointing but consistent with previous work. The same may not apply to community residents. However, although there is a large amount of variation in adaptive behaviour among institutionalized residents overall, their competence within a specified level of the environment was relatively homogeneous. This fact could result, write the authors, in an 'unfair' test of environmental effects, since once the environment main effect is considered, there is limited client variation remaining that could be related to different developmental patterns.

The authors argue correctly that there is a need for more lifespan studies. The questions that should be raised concern the type of intervention needed to prevent the decline associated with growing old in an institution. What treatments, if any, might promote development, and why are there patterns of increment and decrement in midlife?

One of the most popular forms of residential care in the community is fostering, a method which in theory at least should provide the retarded person with a close approximation of life in an intact family, and act as a stimulus to adequate social development. However, Begab (1975) from America concluded that 'while heroic efforts were being launched to find suitable foster parents and to develop alternative patterns of care to institutions, there are little scientific data available to ensure constructive outcomes. Questions regarding the kind of retarded child most likely to profit from foster family care and the essential characteristics of foster parents await answers from research' (see Chapter 1).

Eyman and Begab (1981) sought answers to these questions, as part of the large-scale project discussed above. The sample consisted of 131 mentally retarded individuals below the age of 21 who had resided in 112 foster family-care homes for at least one year. In age they ranged from young children to adults, and in level from profound to mild retardation. Most homes were managed by 2 people who cared for up to 6 clients. All subjects had been rated at least twice over the 1–4-year interval by a social worker on a version of the AAMD Adaptive Behavior Scale. Improvement or regression in social competence was assessed in relation to client characteristics, IQ and initial adaptive behaviour level, and also characteristics of the caretaker, number of clients in the home and two measures of the home environment.

The Path analysis which had been planned to analyse the results was abandoned when it was found that: (1) the covariance structure of the variables differed for the moderately and severely retarded; and (2) that the characteristics of the foster parents showed no correlation with any of the environments or the initial or current levels of adaptive behaviour. The analysis was restricted to residents' level of retardation, post-interview environment ratings, and initial and current levels of adaptive behaviour measured in three domains. The correlations were rather low, but on the whole the relationship between environments and improvement in adaptive behaviour was higher for the more severely handicapped clients than for the moderately and mildly retarded. The authors conclude very cautiously that although there seems to be little question that specified environments offering supportive encounters with normal adults encourage psychological growth and greater autonomy in the retarded, further research is needed to indicate the extent to which retarded behaviour can be modified and how environments interact to produce desired behaviour. 'This exploratory investigation, if replicable, suggests at the very least the need for a significant commitment on the part of foster parents to provide growth-promoting opportunities for their clients.'

Early intervention for the severely retarded child

Various approaches to psychosocial intervention for the more severely retarded are discussed in Chapters 12–19. Here we shall be briefly concerned with longitudinal studies in which attempts are made to evaluate possible effects of intervention programmes.

The Down's syndrome group is a conveniently delineated one for study, although its members are far from homogeneous in behaviour, and not always biologically homogeneous. They have been frequently chosen, however, for follow-up studies. Cunningham (personal communication) has argued that there has been considerable agreement from earlier studies that the rate of intellectual growth rapidly declines during childhood, especially in the early years, and that development is nonlinear, characterized by stages and plateaux. There are considerable difficulties, he believes, in interpreting the results of cross-sectional studies and few researchers have been able to control for such factors as health history, secondary handicapping disorders and the nature of care regimes.

There could be several explanations for the decline in normal circumstances of Down's syndrome children. One such possibility, supported by the research of Glenn and Cunningham (1984), is that the crude developmental measures used in infancy are insensitive to subtle sensory-motor deficits and thus give a spurious measure of normality. Increasingly such deficits might prevent the acquisition of normal skills.

Whatever the reason for the relative deceleration of intellectual growth, an effective intervention might be expected to arrest this, or to enhance the growth rate towards more normal levels. Clinicians occasionally meet an unusually advanced Down's syndrome child, and often note the correlate of an unusually stimulating home situation with, for example, the mother's profession as a teacher. Moreover, some early work has made bold claims for the success of early, intensive intervention programmes.

Berry *et al.* (1984) also point to the widespread acceptance that intellectual growth decelerates during the development of Down's syndrome children, even though average levels at each age are thought to be higher than formerly. In their longitudinal study of children from birth to five years their data appear to confirm that average levels are improving, perhaps attributable to better services, including early intervention. But the authors add a point which we have also frequently made, that many such programmes directly teach test-taking skills, unwittingly, as we believe, because of the limited repertoire of early childhood behaviour. However, 'the extent to which this contemporary early intervention may influence much later development remains an open question.'

Cunningham's (1983) research indicated that relatively intense but fairly brief early stimulation had no greater long-term benefits than less intense, but structured activities. He has provided an overview of his important study of a cohort of Down's children followed from birth to five years. Various subsamples were studied under varying conditions of intervention or nonintervention. Among a variety of findings, the following may be picked out. First, within the first 12–18 months, the age of entering the home support programme is not critical for the child's early development; those who started later caught up with the early starters. Nevertheless, early counselling probably helps the parents. Second, no support was found for the view that the more frequent the home visits (weekly, two weekly or six weekly) the faster the rate of development during the first two years of life. Third, the intensity of the programme (number of times per day and number of repetitions of activities) was not a major variable in outcome. These findings are reminiscent of the results of Lazar and Darlington's (1982) review of much higher-level children, discussed on p. 452.

Cunningham goes on to argue that constitutional factors are highly influential in affecting the child's responsiveness to early intervention. Moreover, with the exception of early walking, none of the training appeared to have long-lasting effects; the earlier attainments do not automatically feed forward to later stages and, as noted earlier, there appear to be specific learning difficulties in these children. Since there are such difficulties the children and their parents will require continuous help throughout life to compensate for these. New conceptions of development are needed, based on a better understanding of its nature, together with the promotion of activities which more closely relate to specific areas known to be crucial. Finally, Cunningham urges that studies are needed which will illuminate the processes through which such knowledge is best mediated through the parent to the child.

Hayden and Haring (1977) report a more intensive programme which, as the authors note, yielded gains in Down's syndrome children quite different from those noted by other investigators. Using a Model Pre-school employing behavioural methods, and with contrast children in a further group, older children in the former had achieved higher levels than earlier in life, whereas exactly the opposite had occurred for the contrast children. However, the ages of the two groups were somewhat different, so an age match was made for a proportion of both groups. Both were then found to be accelerating, but the ex-Model Pre-school children more so, and at a higher level overall. The authors state that their results are very tentative, but if nothing else consider that there is now reason to believe that previous studies were in themselves pessimistic. They appear to attribute this to the differing results from cross-sectional as opposed to longitudinal studies but, necessarily in the space allowed, do not give sufficient data for the reader properly to evaluate their findings.

Investigations over the past thirty years have indicated that specific skills can often be substantially improved by direct training, and that initial performance in the more severely retarded is no necessary guide to trainability (e.g. Clarke and Clarke, 1974, pp. 369–86). However, the proponents of intervention programmes are naturally more interested in broader developmental perspectives, and outcome from these appears far less promising.

One of the major trends in the last decade has been an acceptance that parents can play a potent role in assisting their children's development. It seems clear from studies of psychosocial intervention both with disadvantaged children and with the mentally handicapped, that parents and teachers working together can both extend and enhance intervention effects. Carr (Chapter 14 in this volume) has reviewed the better of these studies, many of which, however, were of rather short duration. Hence the persistence or otherwise of gains, whether in IQ or social behaviour, awaits lengthier studies. As in other fields, behavioural change, whether in parents or their children, requires a continuation of the conditions from which it originated if it is to be maintained. Of course, in some cases, an acquisition by the parent of the principles of behaviour modification may solve both immediate and future problems, and in this sense perpetuates intervention effects.

Pre-school intervention for children at risk for mild retardation

The notion that early experience is in some sense critical for later development has an extensive history, but was a view which gained prominence in the 1950s, with John Bowlby's influential monograph (1951) and the conclusions of diverse researchers in the field of animal behaviour, particularly, but not exclusively, the ethologists. The idea that intervening in the lives of very young children in order to prevent the consequences of early adversity received a considerable stimulus from the work of the Iowa school which flourished between the early 1930s and the late 1940s, and was associated with the names of Beth Wellman, George Stoddard, Harold Skeels and Marie Skodak. Their studies were methodologically weak (McNemar, 1940; Clarke and Clarke, 1958; Longstreth, 1981; Clarke, 1982), and the results were often overstated or in some cases inappropriately interpreted (see Chapter 1), but the message captured the imagination of many developmental psychologists. Among the more influential contributors to the research literature in the 1960s were Hunt (1961), who suggested a greater modifiability of development than had earlier been accepted, and Bloom (1964), who undertook a marathon analysis of longitudinal correlations for physical characteristics, intelligence, achievement and personality, using ingenious statistical techniques which included comparisons across studies and with cross-sectional data. Bloom concluded that:

> Although there is relatively little evidence of the effects of changing the environment on the changes in intelligence, the evidence so far available suggests that marked changes in the environment in the early years can produce greater changes in intelligence than will equally marked changes in the environment at later periods of development. (p. 89)

Since infancy is a period of unusually rapid maturation and sensitivity, the conclusion appeared perfectly logical that a high degree of environmental stimulation is needed for the development of secure conceptual structures and social relationships in later life. Intervention during this earlier period should give children at risk for educational retardation a boost which should lead to permanent advantages during the years of schooling and later. Insufficient attention was given to the possibility that only total ecological change of an enduring nature would be likely to produce the desired benefits (Clarke and Clarke, 1976; Clarke, 1984), and to the work of Kirk (1958) which, in a controlled study, showed that the effects of early intervention 'washed out' during the first few years of regular schooling. Moreover, children's repertoires of behaviour are, of course, much more limited in the early years than later. Hence an unwitting 'teaching to the test' is almost inevitable in pre-school work, so that the ease with which early characteristics are apparently modified may reflect little more than a transfer of specific learning, as opposed to more pervasive cognitive changes.

Head Start programmes were hastily launched in the United States. Within a few years various official bodies identified a wash-out effect, and concluded that in the long term such programmes failed to raise levels of achievement. Edward Zigler, adviser to successive presidents, recently stated in the context of McV. Hunt's unrepentant assertions that the reaction range for the IQ is 70 points and the early environment is pre-potent: 'With such environmental sugar plums dancing in our heads, we actually thought that we could compensate for the effects of several years of impoverishment as well as inoculate the child against the future ravages of such impoverishment' (Zigler and Valentine, 1979).

With the initiation of Head Start programmes the possibility of proper evaluation became a reality, but many of them were designed in such a way that no assessment could be made. However, a sufficient number of children were appropriately allocated to 'treatment' and 'no treatment' conditions that in 1969 A.R. Jensen felt able to start his lengthy article on 'How much can we boost IQ and scholastic achievement?' with the statement 'Compensatory education has been tried and it apparently has failed' (p. 1). In support of this contention he quoted a statement by the US Commission on Civil Rights which concluded that 'none of the programs appear to have raised significantly the achievement of participating pupils, as a group, within the period evaluated by the Commission.' He went on to suggest that the major component in academic failure by minority children was genetic, thus provoking an outcry from which the social and educational sciences have not as yet fully recovered.

A watershed in evaluation research was Bronfenbrenner's (1974) review of the evidence into the early 1970s, not least because of the clear statements about the essential requirements of an experimental design, and the pitfalls into which some unwary researchers had stumbled, particularly the failure of random allocation of children to treatment and control conditions which in some cases resulted in demonstrable biases.

Recently evidence on the long-term effects of well-conducted researches involving exceptionally high-quality pre-school intervention has become available. The Consortium for Longitudinal Studies, a self-appointed group of researchers, pooled data from fourteen studies in which late childhood and adolescent follow-up data were analysed by sophisticated techniques. The overall findings include the following:

1. Before inception into the programmes, IQ scores of children in experimental and control groups did not differ.
2. At age six, on school entry, there was a substantial and significant IQ difference in favour of the experimentals, which lasted at least three years.
3. At follow-up in late childhood or adolescence there was no IQ difference between the groups, whether verbal, performance or full scale.
4. There was invariably a significant difference in allocation to special classes and a less powerful effect on grade retention, both of these indices being a reflection of teacher decision.
5. On standardized achievement tests all the children were in the lowest quartile but the intervention groups were significantly better at maths and showed some benefit in reading, which did not, however, reach significance. (Lazar and Darlington, 1982)

Careful exploration of the potential effects of differences among the early programmes yielded no single factor or combination of factors which accounted for better or worse outcome in later years. The effects remained when such factors as the sex, ethnic background, early IQ, type of programme, age of commencement, length of intervention, number of hours of instruction, presence or absence of language goals, degree of parental involvement, location of programme (centre versus home), training or nontraining of teachers, were controlled in the analysis.

This is a remarkable finding, suggesting that within the context of high-quality programmes neither what is done, nor by whom, nor when, nor where, nor for how long, affects outcome. Hence some general as well as post-programme influences seem to be involved, the latter perhaps triggered by the fact of pre-school intervention. As the authors point out, it seems probable that noncognitive aspects of development were affected. Of the four areas explored at follow-up, two yielded strong results. First, the mothers of pre-school children had higher vocational aspirations than the children had for themselves. Second, their children were more likely to mention achievement-related reasons for feeling proud of themselves.

The Perry Pre-school Project

One of the most carefully designed studies included in the Consortium analysis was the Perry Pre-school Project (Schweinhart and Weikart, 1980, 1981). Within this cluster of studies it was outstanding in providing the largest cohort of pre-school-educated children, followed up for the longest period of time, and contrasted with a randomly allocated control group.

The original sample comprised 123 black children who were 'born to fail', being the progeny of grossly disadvantaged and poorly educated parents, half of whom were single and a large proportion unemployed. The scientists responsible added an additional criterion for inclusion in the intervention experiment, namely that the children's IQ scores at entry on the Stanford–Binet scale had to be 85 or lower. They joined the project in successive waves, randomly allocated with adjustments to ensure that experimental and control groups were equated on such variables as sex and average SES score (Schweinhart and Weikart, 1981, p. 114). Intervention consisted of $2\frac{1}{2}$ hours' daily attendance by the children in the experimental group (5-day week) for a 2-year period (total of 60 weeks) and a weekly home visit by a teacher of about $1\frac{1}{2}$ hours. A cognitively oriented curriculum was employed.

The experimental group (N = 58) and the control group (N = 65) had pretest mean IQs of 79.6 and 78.5 respectively. Experimental children exceeded the controls by 12 IQ points at the end of pre-school, by 6 points at the end of kindergarten and by 5 points at the end of first grade (age 7). Contrary to earlier expectations the groups were equivalent by the end of second grade and thereafter. At the age of 14 each group had a mean WISC IQ of 81, virtually identical with their Binet scores at age 3.

There was thus no effect on IQ of the cognitively oriented programme within a few years of school entry, a finding which, with the possible exception of the Milwaukee project, has been replicated many times (see Bronfenbrenner, 1974; Lazar and Darlington, 1982). Nor does there appear to be much evidence of cumulative deficit (see Chapter 7), although Schweinhart and Weikart discuss this possibility (1980, p. 33).

Of greater importance perhaps is the fact that, despite the lack of disparity in IQ, there was a significant difference in standardized achievement scores (reading, arithmetic and language) which increased with age, although for this variable sample attrition was somewhat higher (11 per cent for the WISC and 23 per cent for the California Achievement Test). In view of the care with which these analyses have been undertaken, and the extent of detailed information available in published form, the authors' contention should perhaps be accepted that sample attrition is unlikely to have affected the achievement test means. These are, however, not recorded, despite many pages of the monograph devoted to analyses of the bases for the group educational differences, which amounted to 8 per cent (Schweinhart and Weikart, 1980, pp. 24–7). There was, of course, the usual advantage accruing to the experimental group in terms of fewer allocations to special classes: 39 per cent of the controls were thus allocated, but only 19 per cent of those who had attended pre-school. Painstaking reports are presented on many variables, including chronic delinquency, which was also significantly lower in the experimental (36 per cent) than the control (52 per cent) condition.

So far as the processes underlying these outcomes are concerned the authors state:

> As data accumulate, it is clear that we are viewing a complex network of causes and effects. The preschool intervention has been successful over the years because its effects became the causes of other effects as well.... Preschool education leads to increased commitment to schooling and increased cognitive ability at school entry (the latter after the effect of cognitive ability prior to preschool has been taken into account). Family socioeconomic status, even though restricted to impoverished families and unrelated to cognitive ability within this sample, is still an antecedent of school achievement. Cognitive ability at school entry is indeed a gateway to better school performance, with a higher cognitive ability at school entry leading to greater commitment to schooling, higher school achievement and fewer years spent receiving special education services. Commitment to schooling and fewer years in special education combined in leading to fewer delinquent offenses, while achievement led to more delinquent offenses. (p. 64)

Intervention effects on this model never became dormant; the triggering effect of a high-quality programme sets in motion ongoing consequences.

Commenting upon the discrepancy between the IQ measures (where on follow-up there was no difference) and scholastic achievement (where there was a difference), Schweinhart and Weikart have suggested the following:

> The disappearance of IQ gains has been taken to mean that the effects of compensatory preschool education are temporary at best. Yet, as IQ gains disappeared in the Perry Project, we found persistent and cumulative preschool effects on teacher ratings, grade placement and academic achievement.
>
> School achievement, particularly at eighth grade, cannot be affected directly by preschool experience – a mediating variable is logically necessary. It might be expected that IQ would be this mediating variable; apparently it is not.
>
> The environment of poverty, when it occurs, usually persists throughout childhood and seems to provide little opportunity to experience the domain measured by intelligence tests at any age. ... Yet intelligence theoretically refers to one's ability to adapt, cope with, and learn from one's environment, even when it is an environment of poverty. Our present intelligence tests simply do not have the scope of our theoretical definitions of intelligence. Until they do, it seems a dangerous expedient to equate the concept of intelligence with IQ.
>
> It is reasonable to state that intelligence encompasses both the IQ tests and adaptive functioning in one's actual environment. Using this definition, we can make the parsimonious assumption that quality preschool education positively affects intelligence. Its effect on IQ, however, is not supported by

the post-preschool environment of poverty, so that effect withers away with time.

At the same time, preschool may positively affect adaptive functioning in the actual school environment. This improved adaptive functioning creates a more positive social dynamic and thereby supports and maintains itself. Children who attended preschool actually do function better in school, are perceived and treated as functioning better, therefore continue to function better, and so on. All of the preschool benefits found in this study – achievement, IQ, classroom behavior, grade placement – may be taken as evidence of improved functioning in the school environment. We offer this interpretation not as a final answer, but as a line of thought worthy of pursuit. (p. 123)

Intensive pre-school intervention: the Milwaukee experiment

Some early researchers reasoned that it was unlikely that significant improvement in school-related behaviours could be induced in very high-risk children without massive intervention. One of the most imaginative and today controversial programmes was initiated in the mid-1960s in Milwaukee (see Heber, 1968; Heber *et al.*, 1972; Garber and Heber, 1977, 1978). This project was designed to provide maximum support, short of removing the children altogether from their families.

The sample was recruited following a survey undertaken of children in a slum area of Milwaukee with the greatest population density, lowest median family income and greatest rate of dilapidated housing. The major finding was that low maternal intelligence proved to be the best single predictor of low intelligence in the offspring. Mothers with IQs less than 80, comprising less than half the total, accounted for almost four-fifths of the children with IQs below 80. Moreover, children of low IQ mothers showed a decline in intelligence with increasing age, from an average of about 84 at age 5 to an average of 78 at age 10 and 66 at age 14; the progeny of mothers with IQs above 80 showed no commensurate decline. Although the data could permit of differing explanations it was concluded that, within the slum, mental retardation was neither randomly distributed nor randomly caused. Large families where maternal intelligence was low provided the context for mild retardation and provided the stimulus for a long-term intensive rehabilitation programme.

Trained interviewers visited all mothers in the area with newborn children, using the PPVT as an initial screening device, also collecting extensive data on family history. Scores of 70 or less were checked by a full administration of the WAIS. Forty black mothers, on the criterion of a WAIS Full Scale IQ of 75 or less, were assigned to experimental or control conditions and were invited to participate in the study, the experimental part of which comprised (1) an infant stimulation programme, and (2) a maternal rehabilitation programme.

The teachers were paraprofessional, language-facile, affectionate people who had had some experience with infants or young children and resided in the same general neighbourhood as the children. At 3 months of age the infant commenced attendance at the centre. Each was then assigned a teacher who remained with the child until he or she reached 12–15 months of age, at which time the child was gradually paired with other teachers and children. Each teacher of the 18 months and older group was responsible for 10 children, seen in groups of 2, 3 or 4 depending on age. Teachers had to familiarize themselves with one of three main academic areas (maths/problem solving, language and reading). They were expected to evaluate progress and to individualize instruction, as well as having a part to play in art, music, field trips and special holiday activities. They also had to establish as a major responsibility contact and rapport with the children's mothers.

The philosophy of pre-school education was, in the authors' words, 'to prevent from occurring those language, problem solving and achievement motivation deficits which are known to be common attributes of mild retardation'. Meanwhile, the mothers were involved in a rehabilitation programme which aimed to increase literacy and enable them to organize their domestic arrangements while also emphasizing work skills.

From 24 months to 72 months the experimental group maintained an advantage over the control subjects of between 20 and 34 IQ points. Intervention terminated at school entry, which was at the mean age of 72 months. At this point in time the experimental group's mean IQ was 120.7 (SD = 11.2) compared to the control group's mean IQ of 87.2 (SD = 12.8), a difference of over 30 IQ points.

Garber and Heber (1978, 1982) followed the children for nearly four years past intervention and in the last report the experimental group had a WISC mean IQ of 104 (SD = 11.5, range 93–138) as compared to the control group mean of 86 (SD = 9.8, range 72–106) (Garber and Heber, 1982, p. 126). Thus there still continued to be an 18-point gap in IQ, albeit reduced from an earlier maximum of over 30, and the experimental group continued to be a little above the national average.

The picture is very much less rosy for scholastic achievement. Although the experimental children show the usual advantage in special class placement, their status on standardized achievement tests is stated as follows:

> After a period of over four years, since the end of the pre-school program, we still had contact with more than three-quarters of the original families (Experimental N = 17; Control N = 17). Across the first four grades of school, the Experimental children are significantly superior to the Control group on total reading (p < 0.06) and total mathematics (p < 0.01) as measured by standard scores on the Metropolitan Achievement Test. The Experimental group's language-related subtest performance more consistently showed significant differences over the Control group across the four grades on the nine subtests of the MAT than performance on mathematics subtests.

When standard scores are converted to percentile and grade equivalent scores, there is a significant decline for both groups from first through fourth grade. Although the Experimental group remains superior to the Control group throughout the first four grades, the performance of both groups falls below national norms as they progress through the grades. For the first year, the distribution of the Experimental children as a group approximates the national profile on the MAT: while the Control group was already depressed. The performance of the Experimental group since then has further declined, first to the lower level of the city, and then to the still lower one of the inner-city schools, and the magnitude of differences between groups decreases. (p. 119)

Evidently, then, the relatively high IQs of the children who had enjoyed massive pre-school intervention did not protect them from poor scholastic performance after four years of ordinary schooling; in terms of advantage in this crucially important sphere, the differences between experimental and control groups appear similar to those obtained in the much less ambitious and much less costly programmes summarized by the Consortium. Furthermore, in view of their findings, it is likely that, had intelligence testing been undertaken in adolescence after the age of thirteen, the gap between the groups would have narrowed still further.

This study has been the subject of serious criticism (Page and Grandon, 1981; Sommer and Sommer, 1983), partly as a result of Heber's failure to respond to enquiries. The question of replication has been raised, and it must be evident that financial constraints would make this a difficult task. However, a somewhat similar experiment has been conducted as part of a long-term programme initiated by Ramey and colleagues at the University of North Carolina (Ramey and Haskins, 1981a, b).

A cohort of black babies from disadvantaged families was randomly allocated to treatment and control conditions, the educational programme once again commencing when the infants were between 6 and 12 weeks of age. The day-care centre was open 5 days per week, 50 weeks per year, from 7.15 am until the children left between 3.30 and 5.15 pm; transportation to and from home was provided. In order to avoid the potentially confounding influence of diet, nutritional supplements were offered to control children together with paediatric care (Ramey and Haskins, 1981a, pp. 10 and 11). At the age of 48 months the mean Stanford–Binet IQs were 96.48 (SD 10.43) for the 27 experimental children and 84.25 (SD 14.20) for the 24 controls. At 60 months the WISC mean IQs were 97.96 and 91.00 respectively (Ramey and Haskins, 1981b, p. 42). These results were manifestly different from those of the Milwaukee researchers so far as the experimental group was concerned, although the controls are not dissimilar, depending upon at which age the comparison is made. As yet the children in Ramey's study have not been followed up into adolescence, so no further comparison can be made.

A more recent report (Ramey and Campbell, 1984), however, outlines the results of a greatly augmented sample assessed up to age $4\frac{1}{2}$ years on a number of different tests. By this age the educationally treated and controls scored 101.7 and 89.2, respectively, on the Stanford–Binet. In general, these and other differences were due to a decline by the control children while the experimental group remained at or near the national average. Whether such gains will prove more or less durable than those reported in other programmes remains to be seen, write the authors, who, commenting on a comparison with the Milwaukee project, believe that the size of differences may reflect the differing intensities of intervention.

Psychosocial intervention and total ecological change

There are a number of documented cases of children discovered in circumstances so adverse as to demand their removal from the environments which appeared to be seriously deleterious to their development. These have been collated by Clarke and Clarke (1976), and more recently summarized by Clarke (1984). Within the advantageous environments to which these deprived children were removed, often by legal process, there was a generally favourable outcome, occasionally accompanied by dramatic improvements in intelligence, scholastic achievement and social adjustment. It may perhaps be assumed that more often than not the 'myriad of microenvironmental events' to which Jensen (1981) has referred combined to facilitate development, allowing a 'self-righting' tendency (Waddington, 1957, 1966) to operate.

The minutiae of the psychosocial processes which operate in these contexts are as yet unknown. However, it seems likely that in gross terms a combination of regular intimate social interaction with intelligent, caring, foster relatives, particularly in the period preceding and following puberty, as well as acceptance by members of a relatively secure and advantaged wider community, are among the necessary conditions for full personal and social development.

The work of Schiff and his colleagues has been described in Chapter 7. Dumaret and Duyme (personal communication) have designed a further project, the results of which when finally analysed are likely to add significantly to existing knowledge in the field of child development. A large cohort of children, all having suffered social deprivation by being abandoned and brought up in institutions or in foster families, was later adopted. Selection for entry to the project was determined by the following criteria: each child at the time of adoption should have an IQ below 85 and be above the age of four years. Length of time in the foster home was held constant at approximately six years, after which data were obtained on IQ, school achievement and emotional stability. Preliminary results on the educational attainments only of 89 children indicate that one-fourth of them had no school failure, while one-third had been retained in grade for one year, a common situation in France. Nearly one-half of all children's educational development is delayed by at least this amount when leaving primary school to enter sixth grade (Schiff *et al.*, 1982). The remaining project children (a little over 40 per cent) were to varying degrees educationally retarded. Again the context is important; some 18 per cent of all French children are placed in classes for slow learners. It should be emphasized that the scholastic status of the project sample was only marginally related to the social class of the adoptive family, unlike control children, selected as being present in the same classroom. These latter showed a very clear social class gradient, favouring middle–class homes. Age of placement was, however, a significant factor, those placed after the age of six being at greater risk of retardation.

CONCLUSIONS

So far as many of the more severely retarded are concerned early work, replicated many times, has indicated that increments in specific skills (e.g. perceptual–motor) can be achieved using simple learning principles, including breakdown of task, systematic reinforcement and one-to-one instruction. Behaviour modification, as one might expect, has had considerable success in enhancing particular behaviour, and extinguishing the undesirable. Overall development, however, may not be so modifiable.

There is a dearth of long-term studies of intervention for the more severely retarded. As with most programmes, at other levels, the aim of intervention is to produce an accelerated development, including IQ. Early intervention can, for example, have some effect and is anyway justified in terms of helping both parents and children at that particular period of their lives. But, as at higher levels, one cannot expect long-term gains unless there is some continuation of the extra attention these children have enjoyed. Even then, constitutional limits may prevent the maintenance of growth. In this case an intervention may have merely caused the child to reach these limits earlier. There are many such problems which await elucidation from careful longitudinal studies.

For the mildly retarded a very different picture emerges. The difference between IQ prevalence and administrative prevalence makes it clear that the possession of an IQ between 50 and 70 alone does not necessarily demand administrative action or, when it does, this may be confined to the school years. As indicated in Chapter 2, a low IQ together with problems in adaptation, existing in combination, lead to official action. Studies of administrative prevalence are unanimous in showing declining numbers from the early adolescent peak. This means that society has no longer found the need for action, either because the individual can survive socially without special help, or because there has been a change, an improved level of social and intellectual functioning. The other side of this coin can be found in longitudinal studies which are unanimous in showing that, on average, the individual increasingly merges into the community and becomes not markedly different from perhaps dull but not retarded peers. Such studies usually concern specified groups of ex-institutional or ex-special educational persons who have mostly received little official help but may enjoy considerable unofficial support. A combination of special educational facilities, vocational training programmes and delayed maturation serves to place the majority of mildly and moderately retarded above the level of community tolerance. However, the current unemployment crisis in developed nations may modify this hitherto quite hopeful picture.

Where deliberate attempts are made to intervene, either to prevent the emergence of mild retardation or to modify its course, the immediate effects can be considerable. The 'wash-out' effect of IQ gains, however, is found without exception some years after pre-school programme termination. However, atypically good programmes are associated in adolescence with significantly smaller numbers allocated to special education or to grade repetition, and some gain on standardized achievement tests. Motivational changes in both the children and their parents appear to be relevant. The effects of early programmes appear to become causes in their turn of other and later effects. Even so, the achievements of the children in adolescence are still quite modest, although better than their controls. This raises the question whether intervention can ever be fully successful within the context which gave rise to its need. As we once put it, life in such circumstances is an anti-Head Start programme. The implication here is that total ecological change might enhance levels of functioning.

There have been a few studies of this latter type, usually on individuals rescued from extreme adversity or isolation. It is impressive that, with few exceptions, they show rapid gains in IQ, scholastic attainment and emotional stability. Such environmental changes can be achieved for some children where parental rights have been removed by legal process. It has never been possible to replicate the same degree of change in the more typical cases of mild retardation where social influences have played some part in aetiology. In some senses, then, we do not know the extent to which levels of functioning can be altered, nor their limits. We can justifiably expect, however, that higher levels can theoretically be achieved than occur in the 'sink-or-swim' situation in which so many adolescent and adult mildly retarded persons find themselves.

REFERENCES

BALLA, D.A. and ZIGLER, E. (1975) 'Preinstitutional social deprivation, responsiveness to social reinforcement, and IQ change in institutionalized retarded individuals', *Amer. J. Ment. Defic.*, 80, 228–30.

BEGAB, M.J. (1975) 'The mentally retarded and society: trends and issues', in M.J. BEGAB and S.A. RICHARDSON (eds), *The Mentally Retarded and Society: A Social Science Perspective*, Baltimore, University Park Press, 3–32.

BERRY, P., GUNN, V.P. and ANDREWS, R.J. (1984) 'Development of Down's syndrome children from birth to five years', in J.M. BERG (ed.), *Perspectives and Progress in Mental Retardation*, vol. 1, Baltimore, University Park Press, 167–77.

BIRCH, H.G., RICHARDSON, S.A., BAIRD, D., HOROBIN, G. and ILLS-LEY, R. (1970) *Mental Subnormality in the Community: A Clinical and Epidemiologic Study*, Baltimore, Williams & Wilkins.

BLOOM, B. (1964) *Stability and Change in Human Characteristics*, New York, Wiley.

BOWLBY, J. (1951) *Maternal Care and Mental Health*, Geneva, World Health Organization.

BRONFENBRENNER, U. (1974) *A Report on Longitudinal Evaluation of Pre-school Programs*, vol. 2, *Is Early Intervention Effective?*, Washington, DC, DHEW Publication no. (OHD) 74–25.

CLARKE, A.D.B. and CLARKE, A.M. (1984) 'Constancy and change in the growth of human characteristics: the first Jack Tizard Memorial Lecture', *J. Child Psychol. Psychiat.*, 25, 191–208.

CLARKE, A.D.B., CLARKE, A.M. and REIMAN, S. (1958) 'Cognitive and social changes in the feeble-minded: three further studies', *Brit. J. Psychol.*, 45, 173–9.

CLARKE, A.M. (1982) 'Developmental discontinuities: an approach to assessing their nature', in L.A. BOND and J.M. JOFFE (eds), *Facilitating Infant and Early Child Development*, Hanover, NH, University Press of New England, 58–77.

CLARKE, A.M. (1984) 'Early experience and cognitive development', *Rev. Res. Educ.*, 11, 125–60.

CLARKE, A.M. and CLARKE, A.D.B. (eds) (1958) *Mental Deficiency: The Changing Outlook*, 1st edn, London, Methuen; Glencoe, Ill., Free Press, 101–5.

CLARKE, A.M. and CLARKE, A.D.B. (1974) 'Severe subnormality: capacity and performance', in A.M. CLARKE and A.D.B. CLARKE (eds), *Mental Deficiency: The Changing Outlook*, 3rd edn, London, Methuen; New York, Free Press, 369–86.

CLARKE, A.M. and CLARKE, A.D.B. (eds) (1976) *Early Experience: Myth and Evidence*, London, Open Books; New York, Free Press.

COBB, H.V. (1972) *The Forecast of Fulfilment*, New York, Teachers' College Press, Columbia University.

CUNNINGHAM, C.C. (1983) *Early Development and its Facilitation in Infants with Down's Syndrome*, Final Report to the Department of Health and Social Security, Manchester University, Hester Adrian Research Centre.

EDGERTON, R.B. (1967) *The Cloak of Competence: Stigma in the Lives of the Mentally Retarded*, Berkeley, University of California Press.

EDGERTON, R.B. and BERCOVICI, S.M. (1976) 'The cloak of competence: ten years later', *Amer. J. Ment. Defic.*, 80, 485–97.

EDGERTON, R.B., BOLLINGER, M. and HERR, B. (1984) 'The cloak of competence: after two decades', *Amer. J. Ment. Defic.*, 88, 345–51.

EMDE, R. and HARMON, R. (1985) *Continuities and Discontinuities in Development*, New York, Plenum, in press.

EYMAN, R.K. and ARNDT, S. (1982) 'Life-span development of institutionalized and community-based mentally retarded residents', *Amer. J. Ment. Defic.*, 86, 342–50.

EYMAN, R.K. and BEGAB, M.J. (1981) 'Relationship between foster home environment and resident changes in adaptive behavior', in P. MITTLER (ed.), *Frontiers of Knowledge in Mental Retardation*, vol. 1, *Social, Educational and Behavioural Aspects*, Baltimore, University Park Press, 327–36.

FISHER, M.A. and ZEAMAN, D. (1970) 'Growth and decline of retardate intelligence', in N.R. ELLIS (ed.), *International Review of Research in Mental Retardation*, New York and London, Academic Press, 4, 151–91.

GARBER, H. and HEBER, R. (1977) 'The Milwaukee project: indications of the effectiveness of early intervention in preventing mental retardation', in P. MITTLER (ed.), *Research to Practice in Mental Retardation*, vol. 1, Baltimore, University Park Press, 119–28.

GARBER, H. and HEBER, R. (1978) 'The efficacy of early intervention with family rehabilitation', paper delivered at the Conference on Prevention of Retarded Development in Psychosocially Disadvantaged Children, Madison, Wisconsin.

GARBER, H. and HEBER, R. (1982) 'Modification of predicted cognitive development in high-risk children through early intervention', in D.K. DETTERMAN and R. STERNBERG (eds), *How and How Much can Intelligence be Increased?*, Norwood, NJ, Ablex, 121–37.

GLENN, S. and CUNNINGHAM, C.C. (1984) 'Selective preferences to different speech stimuli in infants with Down's syndrome', in J.M. BERG (ed.), *Perspectives and Progress in Mental Retardation*, vol. 1, Baltimore, University Park Press, 201–10.

HAYDEN, A.H. and HARING, N.G. (1977) 'The acceleration and maintenance of developmental gains in Down's syndrome school-age children', in P. MITTLER (ed.), *Research to Practice in Mental Retardation*, vol. I, Baltimore, University Park Press, 129–41.

HEBER, R. (1968) 'The role of environmental variables in the etiology of cultural-familial mental retardation', in B.W. RICHARDS (ed.), *Proceedings of the First Congress of the International Association for the Scientific Study of Mental Deficiency*, Reigate, Michael Jackson, 456–65.

HEBER, R., GARBER, H., HARRINGTON, S., HOFFMAN, C. and FALENDER, C. (1972) *Rehabilitation of Families at Risk for Mental Retardation*, Madison, University of Wisconsin.

HUNT, J. MCV. (1961) *Intelligence and Experience*, New York, The Ronald Press.

JENSEN, A.R. (1969) 'How much can we boost IQ and scholastic achievement?', *Harvard Educ. Rev.*, 39, 1–123.

JENSEN, A.R. (1981) 'Raising the IQ: the Ramey and Haskins study', *Intelligence*, 5, 29–40.

KIRK, S.A. (1958) *Early Education of the Mentally Retarded*, Urbana, Ill., University of Illinois Press.

KUSHLICK, A. (1961) 'Subnormality in Salford', in M.W. SUSSER and A. KUSHLICK (eds), *A Report on the Mental Health Services of the City of Salford for the Year 1960*, Salford, Health Department.

KUSHLICK, A. and BLUNDEN, R. (1974) 'The epidemiology of mental subnormality', in A.M. CLARKE and A.D.B. CLARKE (eds), *Mental Deficiency: The Changing Outlook*, 3rd edn, London, Methuen; New York, Free Press, 31–81.

LAZAR, I. and DARLINGTON, R. (1982) *Lasting Effects of Early Education: A Report from the Consortium for Longitudinal Studies, Monographs of the Society for Research in Child Development*, 47, nos 2–3.

LONGSTRETH, L.E. (1981) 'Revisiting Skeels' final study: a critique', *Dev. Psych.*, 17, 620–5.

MCNEMAR, Q. (1940) 'A critical examination of the University of Iowa studies of environmental influences upon the IQ', *Psychol. Bull.*, 37, 63–92.

PAGE, E.B. and GRANDON, G.M. (1981) 'Massive intervention and child intelligence: the Milwaukee project in critical perspective', *J. Spec. Educ.*, 15, 239–56.

RAMEY, C.T. and CAMPBELL, F.A. (1984) 'Preventive education for high-risk children: cognitive consequences of the Carolina Abecedarian Project', *Amer. J. Ment. Defic.*, 88, 515–23.

RAMEY, C.T. and HASKINS, R. (1981a) 'The modification of intelligence through early experience', *Intelligence*, 5, 5–17.

RAMEY, C.T. and HASKINS, R. (1981b) 'Early education, intellectual development and school performance: a reply to Arthur Jensen and J. McVicker Hunt', *Intelligence*, 5, 41–8.

RICHARDSON, S. (1978) 'Careers of mentally retarded young persons: services, jobs and interpersonal relations', *Amer. J. Ment. Defic.*, 82, 349–58.

SCHIFF, M., DUYME, M., DUMARET, A. and TOMKIEWICZ, S. (1982) 'How much *could* we boost scholastic achievement and IQ scores? A direct answer from a French adoption study', *Cognition*, 12, 165–96.

SCHWEINHART, L.J. and WEIKART, D.P. (1980) *Young Children Grow Up: The Effects of the Perry Preschool Program on Youths Through Age 15*, Ypsilanti, Mich., High/Scope Press.

SCHWEINHART, L.J. and WEIKART, D.P. (1981) 'Perry preschool effects nine years later: what do they mean?', in M.J. BEGAB, H.C. HAYWOOD and H.L. GARBER (eds), *Psychosocial Influences in Retarded Performance*, vol. 2, Baltimore, University Park Press, 113–25.

SOMMER, R. and SOMMER, B.A. (1983) 'Mystery in Milwaukee', *Amer. Psychol.*, 38, 982–5.

SVENDSEN, D. (1982) 'Changes in IQ, environmental and individual factors: a follow-up study of EMR children', *J. Child Psychol. Psychiat.*, 23, 69–74.

TIZARD, J. (1958) 'Longitudinal and follow-up studies', in A.M. CLARKE and A.D.B. CLARKE (eds), *Mental Deficiency: The Changing Outlook*, 1st edn, London, Methuen; Glencoe, Ill., Free Press, 422–49.

TIZARD, J. (1974) 'Longitudinal studies: problems and findings', in A.M. CLARKE and A.D.B. CLARKE (eds), *Mental Deficiency: The Changing Outlook*, 3rd edn, London, Methuen; New York, Free Press, 223–56.

WADDINGTON, C.H. (1957) *The Strategy of Genes*, London, Allen & Unwin.

WADDINGTON, C.H. (1966) *Principles of Development and Differentiation*, New York, Macmillan.

ZIGLER, E. and VALENTINE, J. (eds) (1979) *Project Head Start: A Legacy of the War on Poverty*, New York, Free Press.

13

Behaviour modification

Chris Kiernan

INTRODUCTION

A very large amount of work with mentally handicapped people could be classified as involving the use of behaviour modification or principles derived from it. Many of the chapters in this book reflect the extent of this impact (see, for example, Chapters 14, 15 and 18). This situation presents two problems. First, it would be impossible to attempt a summary of such work within a single chapter, even if it were sensible in this context; consequently this review will be highly selective. Second, the extent of work which could be covered conceals the great diversity of theoretical orientations which are implied by the term behaviour modification. One of the tasks which will be attempted is to describe the various strands of theory which go to make up this agglomeration, and to point out where there appear to be differences which affect outcome.

The origins of the term behaviour modification are somewhat unclear. Although the conceptual roots lie firmly in the work of Skinner (1938, 1953), the actual term was used by Watson (1962) to relate to situations which involved studies of learning with a particular intent of 'the clinical goal of treatment'. Watson's situations included structured interviews, experimental neuroses and doctor–patient relationships. However, during the last quarter century, use of the term has narrowed in the sense that it is now normally taken to cover studies which involve techniques derived from Skinnerian and related work although, as already noted, this covers a multitude of strands.

Before describing this diversity it will be useful to list sources of research on the use of behavioural techniques with the mentally handicapped. Many major psychological journals, including the *Psychological Bulletin* and the *Psychological Review*, carry occasional important articles, and other general journals carry experimental or case-study papers. Specialist publications dealing with the mentally handicapped include a substantial number of articles within the behavioural tradition. Notable among these are the *American Journal of Mental Deficiency*, the *Journal of Mental Deficiency Research*, the *Journal of Special Education*, the *Journal of Autism and Developmental Disabilities* and *Mental Retardation*. For many years two specialist behavioural publications, the *Journal of Applied Behaviour Analysis* and *Behaviour Research and*

Therapy, published many of the major studies examining the impact of behavioural work with the mentally handicapped. These have been joined more recently by a large number of others, including *Behaviour Therapy*, *Behaviour Modification*, *Journal of Behaviour Therapy and Experimental Psychiatry*, *Analysis and Intervention in Developmental Disabilities*, *Child Behaviour Therapy*, *Behaviour Analysis and Intervention* and *Behavioural Assessments*. Those dealing with general and theoretical issues include *The Behaviour Therapist* and *Behaviourism*. The *Journal of the Experimental Analysis of Behaviour*, the major journal publishing empirical work in the Skinnerian tradition, carries occasional important articles on the use of these techniques with the mentally handicapped.

Behavioural work has also generated a large number of review texts and theoretical papers. The *International Review of Research in Mental Retardation* (edited by N.R. Ellis) has carried a number of chapters of central importance. Handbooks edited by Turner *et al.* (1981), Matson and McCarthy (1981) and Bellack *et al.* (1982), and texts by Kazdin (1980a) and Yule and Carr (1980) are representative of this literature.

BASIC PRINCIPLES

Behaviouristic analyses of human performance are based on the original principles which Skinner and others derived from work on infra-human organisms (Skinner, 1938; Keller and Schoenfeld, 1950; Ferster and Skinner, 1957). These were applied to human behaviour in general by Skinner himself (1953, 1957) and by Bijou and Baer (1961), and to the behaviour of the mentally handicapped in particular by Bijou (1966) and Spradlin and Giradeau (1966).

The fundamental assumption of the approach is that the control and explanation of behaviour is best accomplished in terms of environmental variables, there being two classes of these. They are antecedents, which may be stable or relatively stable features of the environment, such as a classroom environment, on the one hand, or more transient features, particular stimuli such as verbal instructions; and consequences, those events which follow the emission of a response. The analysis avoids explanation in terms of 'inner events' or theoretical devices such as hypothetical constructs or intervening variables. The heuristic value of this approach is outlined by Skinner (1950) as focusing attention on behaviour rather than on theoretical constructs. Bijou (1966) argues that this highlights the day-to-day behaviour of the mentally handicapped individual, and the variables which affect that behaviour, rather than 'retarded mentality' as an abstract entity.

The approach sees mental handicap as involving failure by the individual to learn appropriate responses. Several factors bear on this failure. These include biological variables affecting stimulus reception and potential for responding, the learning history of the individual and the current environment. However, behaviour is not 'caused by' these factors. They set the occasion for failure to learn or for anomalous learning. The attitudes of hospital staff do not affect the individual. It is the restriction on the behaviour of the inmates brought about by the behaviour of the staff which is critical. Attitudes and other factors are critical only in that they correlate with behaviour, the latter being the prime basis for analysis. A full analysis of behaviour in relation to both antecedents and consequences, termed a functional analysis, may reveal procedures which will indicate necessary changes in antecedents and consequences and also how biological and other limiting factors can be overcome.

Antecedents, behaviour and consequences

As already indicated, antecedents can be of two types, setting events (relatively stable features of the environment), and more transient events (discriminative stimuli). A setting event is defined as a stimulus–response interaction which affects a whole set of succeeding events. In addition to classrooms, home environments and the like, setting events include physical injury and drugs. Their unifying characteristic is that they affect a substantial number of subsequent behaviours which may be conveniently dealt with together. Discriminative stimuli reflect a more transient class of events, such as green lights or red lights at traffic junctions, and instructions such as 'do it if you like'. The crucial feature of setting events and discriminative stimuli is that they set the occasion for behaviour. They do not coerce behaviour in the sense of producing it 'automatically'.

This feature of antecedents relates to the definition of responses within the Skinnerian behavioural model. Skinner and subsequent theorists draw the distinction between respondents and operants. Respondents are responses which are elicited by preceding stimulation in a 'reflexive' or 'involuntary' manner. They include salivation, pupillary dilation and patellar responses. Respondents are, in this sense, controlled by antecedent events.

Operants, on the other hand, are in essence voluntary responses, behaviours which are goal-directed, purposeful or instrumental in attaining goals. Antecedent stimuli set the occasion for operants but they do not elicit them. Consequent events exert a controlling effect on operants. Individuals emit operants because of their consequences; we respond voluntarily one way or another because of the consequences of our actions.

This respondent–operant distinction is important. In practice, behaviour modification has been almost exclusively concerned with operants, especially in work with mentally handicapped people. Work with other groups has shown that the distinction between response classes is not hard and fast. Many autonomic functions such as heart rate and vasoconstriction, which would classify as respondents, may be brought under control of their consequences (e.g. Brener and Hothersall, 1967). The demonstration that respondents can behave like operants is theoretically and practically important, but possible implications for work with the mentally handicapped have not been developed.

It may be, for example, that the analysis of operant control of respondents has importance for self-injurious behaviour.

The consequences of responding within the operant framework are of two types. *Rewarding stimuli* represent positive events defined in terms of whether the individual will approach them or whether they will increase the probability of an operant response. *Aversive stimuli* are 'unpleasant' events, which the individual will avoid or which will lead to a decrease in the probability of responding when they are used as consequences.

The rewarding/aversive stimulus distinction is in practice a continuum. Premack (1959) pointed out that the rewarding and aversive aspects of consequences were relative to the alternatives available. A child may be rewarded by adult attention (event A) when he plays co-operatively (event B). Here A rewards B. The same child may perform an academic task (event C) in order to be allowed to play co-operatively, if the academic task is less preferred than co-operative play (event B now rewards event C). Therefore the same event (B) may be either rewarded or rewarding depending on the consequences available in the setting.

Four types of operant conditioning are specified by the consequences of behaviour. If a rewarding stimulus is presented following a response, the probability of responding will increase. This procedure is termed *positive reinforcement*. If an aversive stimulus follows a response, the probability of responding will decrease, at least in the short run. This procedure is termed *punishment*. Removal of a rewarding stimulus, a procedure called *extinction*, leads to the eventual decrease in the probability of responding. The term 'time-out' is used to refer to an extinction procedure in which a disruptive or otherwise inappropriate behaviour is treated by withdrawing the individual from sources of rewarding stimuli, for example by exclusion from a rewarding classroom or by withdrawing attention for a specified period of time. Finally, removal of an aversive stimulus leads to an increase in the likelihood of a response. If a child's cry to his mother whenever he is in pain or discomfort always leads to relief, then the likelihood of crying when in pain will increase. This procedure is called *negative reinforcement* or escape learning.

In summary there are two basic procedures for increasing or accelerating the probability of responding, positive reinforcement and negative reinforcement or escape training. These involve the presentation of a rewarding stimulus and the withdrawal of an aversive stimulus. The two basic procedures for decelerating or decreasing the probability of responding, punishment and extinction, involve the presentation of an aversive stimulus or the removal of a positive stimulus.

A further element in the behavioural framework considers the relationship between responses and their consequences, the *response–consequence contingency*. Specification of a contingency or schedule of reinforcement indicates when consequences for responses are to be delivered. The majority of Skinner's own studies concentrated on contingencies. In these studies responses (pecking or lever pressing) and consequences (grain or food pellets) were held constant and only the frequencies and timing of consequences were allowed to vary. These schedule effects were shown to have a dramatic impact. Acquisition was shown to be fastest when reinforcement always followed a response (continuous reinforcement or *crf*). Acquisition was slower when reinforcement was only delivered for a ratio of responses emitted (fixed ratios, FR, or variable ratios, VR, having different properties) or following fixed or variable time intervals (FI or VI). However, when consequences were withdrawn, decline in rate of responding was *fastest* following *crf* and slower with intermittent reinforcement. To a large extent the same relations hold with decelerative consequences. Punishment will be most effective on *crf* and less so following intermittent reinforcement. However, recovery of a punished response will be fastest following termination of *crf* and slower when it has been intermittently presented.

Other features of contingencies and consequences also influence responding. For example, magnitude or intensity of rewarding or aversive stimuli and the delay between responses and consequences are crucial factors. The stronger the stimulus, and the more immediately it is presented, the greater the effect will be.

Clearly consequences occur in particular settings in the presence of particular discriminative stimuli, the antecedent element. An individual may be punished for biting his hand only when a nurse is present in a workshop situation. This may lead to a reduction in biting, but only when the nurse is in the workshop and watching the person. Change in behaviour may fail to generalize to other people and other settings although it may be under complete stimulus control in the particular setting.

Antecedent stimuli can be classed together as in the same stimulus class if they all control the same response or responses. So, if hand-biting ceases whenever a nurse is present, regardless of which nurse it is, then 'nurses' represent the stimulus class resulting in a generalization of the response.

Generalization can also occur in terms of response classes. A response class is said to exist if rewarding one response, for example one instance of imitative behaviour, leads to an increase in the likelihood of the person imitating other responses.

Generalization of behaviour represents a major practical and theoretical issue for behaviour modification. The topic will be returned to on a number of occasions.

The principles just outlined represent a body of ideas which have formed the inheritance of behaviour modification from Skinnerian theory. Of these ideas the basic teaching paradigms and principles concerning magnitude and delay of reward have been most influential. In practice, the majority of programmes have used *crf* in developing new responses although, as will be seen later, more elaborate schedules have been used in dealing with inappropriate behaviour.

Methodology of the behavioural approach

The behavioural approach has its own characteristic methodology. Because it is centrally interested in the behaviour of individuals in context, the initial stage of analysis should be to analyse those antecedents and consequences which affect behaviour. This is called a 'functional analysis' (Kiernan, 1973). Intervention should begin from observation of 'baseline' behaviour, the effects of intervention being assessed through systematic introduction of changes in contingencies. These might involve introducing and withdrawing contingencies (reversal designs) or introducing the same contingency for successive behaviour in a set, for example rewarding different types of acceptable mealtime behaviour at successive times in treatment. Both strategies are designed to show the relationships between responding and contingencies (Baer *et al.*, 1968). The methodology of behavioural analysis has become increasingly sophisticated in the last decade and a wide range of designs are now available (see Hersen and Barlow, 1976; Kratochwill, 1978; Kazdin, 1982c, for reviews). These techniques have been developed to allow the assessment of the effects of treatments without interfering with clinical goals. They include methods for examining the effects of withdrawal of treatments (Rusch and Kazdin, 1981).

The approach to mental handicap

Behavioural theory is essentially optimistic about mental handicap. In essence it holds that the fundamental problem shared by mentally handicapped people is their failure to learn. If we can identify what such persons need to learn, and teach using effective methods, then mental handicap can in a real way be 'cured', or at least significantly ameliorated. It is undoubtedly this promise which accounted for much of the initial enthusiasm for behavioural work in the care and education of the mentally handicapped. Behaviour modification caught the mood of optimism in the western world during the 1960s and 1970s. This enthusiasm has been rewarded by substantial success in demonstrating the modifiability of the behaviour of the retarded. However, behavioural techniques also attracted fierce criticism, sometimes in principle and sometimes because of the use of particular procedures, specifically punishment involving electroshock. This 'bad press' has led some authors to suggest the need for behaviour modification actively to project a new image (O'Leary, 1984).

The 1980s have witnessed the emergence of what has been referred to as a 'new realism', accepting the difficulties in ameliorating the basic deficits of mentally handicapped people and of successfully integrating them into society. It is undoubtedly a part-manifestation of a general social and political mood which has little to do with scientific principles or teaching techniques. However, it is also partly a function of the failure of intervention techniques, primarily behavioural in nature, to produce radical change in the behaviour of mentally handicapped individuals.

Given this situation it is necessary to take stock in order to decide whether behavioural techniques have failed and, if so, why. It will, in fact, be argued that very considerable progress has been made in terms of techniques and the development of programmes. However, the successful use of techniques has raised other questions which need to be answered. Second, it will be suggested that the approach, taken in the round, offers a powerful methodology for analysis and intervention which has not yet been applied effectively in day-to-day living settings. The task for the next decade must be to develop personnel who are skilled and creative in its use.

THE CONTRIBUTION OF THE BEHAVIOURAL APPROACH

In this section the general format of behavioural programmes is described and a brief review is presented of the range of problems to which such techniques have been applied. Studies in which they have been used by nonprofessionals or paraprofessionals are then sampled. These developments have been particularly widespread, and account at least in part for their success in affecting practice.

Behaviour modification programmes are characterized by the use of a range of analytic devices and teaching techniques. Programme developers typically specify target behaviour to be developed prior to teaching. This specification is in terms of particular responses which the student will show, or not show, following teaching. A complete specification will include the stimulus and setting conditions, and the consequences which will maintain the behaviour. Specification of target behaviours in this way allows the breakdown of tasks into steps for teaching, the task analysis. Task analysis can reveal many facets of target behaviours which have been unrealized and can lead to revision of demands.

The main methods for teaching new responses involve physical guidance, often simply called prompting, the use of modelling by the teacher with the individual imitating the required response, or the use of verbal instructions. Prompting through physical guidance clearly requires less understanding or 'cognitive skill' on the part of students than other techniques and, although the occasional individual resists prompting, is possibly the most commonly used method with the more severely mentally handicapped. It will be seen later that firm physical guidance can itself have aversive properties which make the prompting procedure a form of punishment training, the individual learning appropriate responses in order to escape physical prompts.

Modelling or training through imitation is a less time-consuming method, given that the individual is able to imitate efficiently. Several studies have demonstrated that nonimitative severely mentally handicapped people can be taught to imitate novel responses (e.g. Striefel and Phelan, 1972). However, the time taken to train imitative responses may be very extended (Nelson *et al.*, 1976). In addition, the ability to imitate one class of responses, motor responses, may not generalize to acquisition of another class, for example speech sounds and vice versa (Garcia *et al.*, 1971).

The ability to follow verbal instructions, usually spoken, adds greater flexibility to training. Again, various studies have shown the acquisition of instruction-following behaviour by severely mentally handicapped people. Whitman *et al.* (1971b) showed acquisition of instruction-following after training using physical prompting and reward for correct responding. Striefel *et al.* (1976) have explored optimal methods for teaching instruction-following.

When using prompts, imitation training or instructions as teaching methods, a procedure for eliminating these aids to performance has to be developed. Added guidance may be 'faded' by successively reducing the extent or form of guidance. Alternatively, a time-delay procedure may be used in which once the individual has acquired a cued response (for example, asking for an object following a cue 'what do you want?'), the cue is delayed or provided only with increasing delays. Halle *et al.* (1979, 1981) have shown that the procedure is an effective and usable method of eventually eliminating supporting cues.

Some types of response are difficult to prompt or guide physically. This applies particularly to speech sounds where, if the individual cannot imitate or follow verbal instructions and demonstrations of tongue and lip placement, potential for teaching is limited. In these circumstances response shaping may be used. This technique involves initial reinforcement of virtually any broadly relevant behaviour, for example, any vocalization. Once rate of responding is high, only closer and closer approximations to the required response are rewarded and other responses ignored. This process may be slow and requires considerable skill on the part of the teacher or trainer. It is worth pointing out that, although it was for many years the sole method used in the initial stages of animal training, it is seldom used in behaviour modification studies. This represents an interesting divergence of applied work from the methods used in basic studies and highlights the emergence of problems, like the technology of imitation training, which do not exist in the infra-human literature.

Having identified target behaviours, broken them down into steps and decided on appropriate teaching methods, the behaviour modifier needs to identify the sequence in which steps are to be taught. Trainers may use either forward or backward chaining. In forward chaining the first step in a task is taught first, followed by the second and so on until the final response in the chain is the only one rewarded. So an individual might be rewarded for picking up a sock and then prompted through the remaining steps in putting the sock on. At the second stage in teaching, reward would follow picking up and successfully positioning the sock, the third, pulling the sock over the foot.

The alternative method, backward chaining, involves initial prompting throughout the chain except for the last component, say pulling the sock up from the heel. After initial physical guidance, prompts are faded from this last component as a *first* step in teaching. The next would require the individual to draw the sock over the heel and pull it up, the third, to pull the sock on to the foot. Reward is always given after the sock has been pulled up.

The two types of chaining procedure contrast in several ways. Forward chaining often appears to be more logical but involves continuously changing the point at which the individual obtains reward. If strong expectation of reward at particular points in a sequence is built up this could be a problem.

Both forward and backward chaining have been used in successful programmes. For example van Wagenen *et al.* (1969) report a toilet training programme which uses forward chaining, and Azrin and Foxx (1971) a toilet training programme using backward chaining. However, Azrin *et al.* (1976) chose to use a forward chaining procedure in teaching dressing and undressing skills. The rationale for choice between forward and backward chaining is seldom discussed and there are only occasional investigations in which the two methods of organizing teaching are compared.

Finally, programmes need to include some technique to ensure the generalization of learned responses in appropriate ways. Unfortunately many published studies have relied on what Stokes and Baer (1977) call 'train and hope', in other words generalization is not planned. More adequate studies may repeat training in a variety of settings in which the behaviour is appropriate in order to ensure that the stimulus class of antecedents is sufficient. Or a variety of responses which can serve the same function may be trained in the presence of particular stimuli, thereby ensuring the breadth of the response class. For instance, the child may be taught several different ways of asking for a drink. In its most thorough form the task analysis may use 'general case methodology', in which the full expected range of stimuli and responses which need to be taught in order to ensure generalization are analysed (Becker and Englemann, 1978).

One way in which generalization to the living environment can be maximized is by reorganizing it in order to ensure continuity of training and maintenance conditions. This notion is embodied in the 'token economy', first developed by Ayllon and Azrin (1968). The method derives its name from the use of tokens as rewards for appropriate behaviours. 'Tokens' (stars, plastic discs, points) can be earned according to prearranged individualized contingencies and, subsequently, exchanged for individualized rewards. Since 1968 a large number of token economies at various levels of sophistication have been described (cf. Kazdin, 1982b). Clearly these represent a way in which new behaviours can be shaped and stimulus and response classes developed and maintained.

Case-studies and programmes typically employ a package of techniques: reward for appropriate behaviour, time-out or mild punishment for inappropriate behaviour, a combination of prompting, imitation training and instructions as a teaching method and chaining where necessary and, in good programmes, planned generalization. Analyses of the impact of components of overall procedures are fairly rare. In what follows a range of programmes is described, and thereafter studies which have begun to take a more analytic approach.

Self-help skills

These have received a great deal of attention from behaviour modifiers, partly because a large amount of work has concentrated on the more severely handicapped in whom such skills are poorly developed. In addition, self-help skills lend themselves to task analysis and to the use of the various teaching methods outlined. As will be seen, a particular contribution in this field has derived from the work of Azrin and his colleagues.

(1) *Self-feeding skills.* Two types of problem have been tackled, the acquisition of self-feeding skills and the elimination of problem behaviours such as throwing, spilling and generally 'messy eating'. Acquisition of skills is potentially hampered by the infrequency of meals and by the fact that, at normal mealtimes, care-givers may have several individuals to oversee and teach. These problems were sidestepped by Azrin and Armstrong (1973) who developed a mini-meal approach in which a meal was divided into three, allowing more intensive and more frequent training sessions. Training for eleven mentally handicapped adults was completed within twelve days using the mini-meal procedure, with an average rate of acquisition of five days. A replication of this by Stimbert *et al.* (1977) with six children required, on average, longer periods of training. The problem of increasing the opportunities to run teaching sessions was tackled in a different way by Richman *et al.* (1980). They used simulated lunch sessions, in which children were trained to use a fork to pick up pieces of styrofoam rather than food. The authors found that the procedure produced generalization to the real food situation.

Several studies have considered the acquisition of more sophisticated skills concerned with eating. Matson *et al.* (1980b) taught a range of responses including eating, orderliness, use of utensils and table manners.

Inappropriate behaviours have been dealt with through the use of a range of procedures including time-out (Barton *et al.*, 1970, for finger feeding, food stealing and 'pigging'), mild punishment (Henriksen and Doughty, 1967, for stealing, finger feeding, hitting others, tray throwing) and various other decelerative procedures such as positive practice, overcorrection and restitution (see p. 490) (Stimbert *et al.*, 1977).

(2) *Toilet training.* Two of the major published toilet training programmes devised for use with the severely mentally handicapped have already been mentioned. These are the van Wagenen *et al.* (1969) forward chaining programme and the Azrin and Foxx (1971) backward chaining programme. Both procedures use devices to signal when the individual has urinated in his or her pants. Azrin and Foxx (1971) and Azrin *et al.* (1973b) used an additional device to signal successful toilet bowl use as well as employing increased fluid intake, frequency of toileting and frequent pants checks. The van Wagenen

and Azrin methods differ in that Azrin introduced time-out and other consequences following toileting accidents.

The Azrin and Foxx method has been widely copied, albeit often in a modified form (e.g. Song *et al.*, 1976), although fairly direct replications have shown that the procedure can be effective (Smith *et al.*, 1975). Smith (1979) compared three training methods, an individualized one close to the Azrin–Foxx procedure, another based on the van Wagenen method, and a group toileting method in which the general Azrin–Foxx approach was used but without, among other features, the use of the pants alarm. Using three small matched groups, Smith found that the two individual procedures did not differ, but were better than the group method.

Several studies have examined ways of dealing with nocturnal enuresis. Azrin *et al.* (1973b) developed a rapid method for reducing the frequency of bed-wetting. It involves the use of an alarm device to detect urination, increases in fluid intake, regular hourly trips to the toilet during the night and bed-cleaning and toileting following accidents. A modified version of the Azrin procedure, in which the bed-cleaning and toilet trips were omitted, was used successfully by Smith (1981). Although her programme took longer, it may well be more acceptable to trainers (see p. 495).

(3) *Other self-help skills*. Various studies have focused on other self-help skills. Azrin *et al.* (1976) described a programme for the teaching of dressing and undressing skills. Other successful or partly successful programmes have been described by Martin *et al.* (1971) and Colwell *et al.* (1973). Face- and/or handwashing programmes have been evaluated by Treffry *et al.* (1970) with severely mentally handicapped women, by Wehman (1974) within a token economy and by Doleys *et al.* (1981). The latter study also included other skills such as bathing, hairwashing and toothbrushing. A thorough task analysis of toothbrushing by Horner and Keilitz (1975) showed fifteen different component responses including brushing the outside of the teeth, the biting surfaces and the inside of the teeth. This analysis was completed with great care, involving observation by three staff members. It demonstrates the complexity of apparently 'simple' tasks. Other studies have included grooming skills such as haircombing, shaving and selection of appropriate clothing (e.g. Wehman, 1974; Doleys *et al.*, 1981; Thinesen and Bryan, 1981).

Language and communication skills

A number of examples of successful teaching of instruction-following were described on p. 472. The studies by Striefel, Wetherby and their colleagues have explored, in particular, optimal teaching strategies (Wetherby, 1978). Studies teaching expressive communication skills have had moderate success. Behaviourally based language programmes were among the first to be developed and evaluated. The work of Lovaas and his colleagues (Lovaas *et al.*, 1966, 1973) showed that severely mentally handicapped autistic children could acquire some language through behaviourally based teaching. Carrier and Peak (1975) have developed and evaluated an extremely well-documented programme to initiate use of syntax which is a model of its type (see Carrier, 1976, 1979). However, in these as well as later studies, the problem encountered has always been one of the generalization of skills learned in teaching settings to everyday use (see Harris, 1975; Goetz *et al.*, 1979, for reviews).

At least one reason why generalization of learned responses related to communication skills has been poor is that taught responses have not been functional, or that subjects have not been shown that they could be functional. All too often responses have been taught within a traditional question–answer format without ensuring that they will lead to meaningful consequences in real-life settings. The child may be taught that a picture of food is called 'dinner' and learn to produce the word in response to the question 'what is this?' However, there is no guarantee that the child will then generalize the use of the word to a setting in which he wants his dinner. In Skinner's terms the child has learned to use the word as a response to a question, a 'tact'. There is no reason to expect him to generalize the use of the response to asking for goods and services, Skinner's 'mand' response class (Skinner, 1957).

More recent behavioural studies have emphasized these distinctions. Goetz *et al.* (1983) have put forward a notion of *functional competence*. They suggest, among other postulates, that initial lexicons will be acquired more rapidly and efficiently when the items involve 'instrumental acts rather than passive discrimination responses' (p. 73). Similar notions of increasing the relevance of teaching to everyday interactions are outlined by Hart and Risley (1980). Schepis *et al.* (1982) describe a manual sign language programme in which, among other tactics, the physical environment was rearranged to produce a higher likelihood that signing would be required.

These developments within the behavioural approach are, arguably, thoroughly consistent with the basic behavioural model (Kiernan, 1981, 1985). They are certainly in line with recent thinking in nonbehavioural work with normal children and adults (see Chapter 16). In the light of these considerations, future work may yield more effective behaviourally based general language programmes.

Attending and behavioural control

Short attention span and hyperactivity are problems which affect general social interaction and academic activities. Several studies have used various combinations of positive reinforcement for appropriate behaviour, and extinction (time-out) and negative reinforcement for inappropriate behaviour. Using a differential reinforcement and shaping procedure, Maier and Hogg (1974) and Hogg and Maier (1974) showed an increase in eye fixation for ten boys with trained and untrained tasks in a classroom setting. Whitman *et al.* (1971a) increased sitting in a play situation with a severely mentally handicapped girl. Other studies routinely include attention training and appropriate sitting as an initial phase in teaching. This usually amounts to rewarding whatever activity the student is engaged in while sitting, rather than simply rewarding sitting and doing nothing.

More sophisticated procedures have been used with more able children. Burgio *et al.* (1980) describe the use of a self-instructional package for increasing attending behaviour with two children with IQs of 70 and 46. The package was aimed to develop on-task academic behaviour by questions and self-instructions: 'What does (the teacher) want me to do?' 'To draw this word'; etc. Children were also taught to self-reward. Transfer to untrained tasks was shown, but without consistent improvement in accuracy and quality of work.

Social interaction

Social interaction, including greeting (Gandhi, 1974), eye contact and basic interaction (Williams *et al.*, 1975), simple play behaviour, like ball rolling (Whitman *et al.*, 1970), and social play (Redd, 1969) have been successfully trained. Generalization effects were observed in several of the studies.

The importance of developing the social skills of mentally handicapped individuals has become paramount in recent years with the increasing pressure to integrate in normal living settings. In reviewing a substantial number of studies Gresham (1981) concludes that social skills training has potential for facilitating the integration of handicapped children and young people in schools. Many of these studies, however, fail to show generalization of effects across settings. Gresham notes that only two of thirty-three studies reviewed in one section of his paper assessed or demonstrated generalization.

Community living skills

Many of the studies mentioned earlier in the context of the training of self-help skills have been concerned primarily with facilitating community living. Other relevant ones have concentrated on recognition of coins (e.g. Wunderlich, 1972), the arithmetic skills necessary to use vending machines (Bellamy and Buttars, 1975) and the ability to give change (Cuvo *et al.*, 1978). Telephone skills were taught by Matson (1982a) and emergency phone use by Risley and Cuvo (1980).

A number of studies looked at various cooking skills (Johnson and Cuvo, 1981; Schleien *et al.*, 1981). In both of these, successful generalization of abilities involved in boiling, broiling or baking was shown in new settings. Van den Pol *et al.* (1981) taught three mentally handicapped adults to locate fast food restaurants, to order and pay for food and to clear utensils appropriately. Teaching of aspects of mobility in the community, such as pedestrian skills (Matson, 1980) and the ability to use buses (Coon *et al.*, 1981), have also been successfully illustrated.

A number of studies analysed preliminary academic skills such as basic number work (Grimm *et al.*, 1973), reading (Dorry and Zeaman, 1973, 1975), and writing (Konarski *et al.*, 1981). A substantial number of texts offering task analyses of academic and pre-academic work have been published (e.g. Bender and Valletutti, 1976). It is rare to find data relating to the appropriateness of these analyses.

Studies directed at vocational training have focused in part on examining the efficiency of different training procedures. For instance, Walls *et al.* (1981) found that backward and forward chaining procedures were both more effective than whole task training. Other studies have examined the effects of contingencies on performance of existing skills (e.g. Schroeder, 1972; Bellamy and Sontag, 1973). Hoover *et al.* (1981) examined how decreases in reaction time and movement times could be effected. Hoover *et al.* successfully used positive reinforcement and verbal feedback. Hall *et al.* (1980) taught mentally handicapped adults skills concerned with job finding including completion of application forms and interview behaviour. Acquisition and generalization were illustrated.

Various techniques for increasing on-task behaviour in vocational or leisure situations have been developed. These include 'room management' procedures, in which a member of care or teaching staff is made responsible for prompting and reinforcing appropriate behaviour of clients on a systematic basis. The positive effect of this on engagement in appropriate behaviour has been shown by Mansell *et al.* (1982) with mentally handicapped adults (see also Risley and Favell, 1979). These methods often involve prompting of appropriate use of equipment (McClannahan and Risley, 1975) and commonly result in decreases in stereotyped or self-injurious behaviours as well as increases in appropriate behaviours (Spangler and Marshall, 1983). The effectiveness of such programmes is enhanced if combined with environmental enrichment (Horner, 1980).

The studies just described are complemented by others which focus on teaching conversation skills. These often concentrate on less handicapped individuals and emphasize appropriate content of speech, intonation, number of words used and other features of conversation (e.g. Matson *et al.*, 1980a). Several treatment packages concerned with topic choice, eliciting information, self-disclosure and extending invitations have been published (Nelson *et al.*, 1973; Kelly *et al.*, 1979a, 1979b).

Despite the range of published studies directed at community living, coverage is curiously incomplete in concentrating mainly on the individual's skills. This restriction is offset to some degree by a few researches which examine the emotional problems of mentally handicapped individuals in community settings. For example, Matson (1981) reports a study in which behavioural techniques were used to reduce fear of shopping in adults. He also (1982b) indicates the outcome of treatment of behavioural characteristics of depression, including speech latency and number of words used, in mentally handicapped people. These studies, and case-studies using assertiveness training and related procedures, would appear to be important in indicating methods of dealing with the adjustment problems experienced by mentally handicapped young people and adults faced with the demands of community living. In addition, community placement will clearly create an increasing need to monitor performance and evaluate training needs which emerge in these settings. However, the current trend in development of skill teaching packages runs the danger of ignoring the difficulties experienced in creating suitable environments for use of such skills. The work of Edgerton (1967, 1983) and others which documents the life experiences of mentally handicapped individuals is an excellent antidote to a narrow skill-based conception of what is needed for successful adjustment. Teaching skills is of little purpose if the mentally handicapped are unable to use them or are chronically unhappy in their living environments.

Modification of inappropriate behaviour

Accounts of the day-to-day lives of mentally handicapped people illustrate the way in which a combination of skill deficiencies, emotional problems and inappropriate behaviours reduces their adaptation to their environment. In this respect the division between skill building and modification of inappropriate behaviours which is imposed in this chapter is artificial. In addition, as already noted, many of the studies and programmes concerned with skill building have had to include techniques for eliminating or modifying problem behaviours.

In this part of the chapter, however, consideration is given to studies of inappropriate behaviour with particular emphasis on techniques. One reason for taking this approach is that it allows an illustration of the way in which methods have been developed and of the way in which behavioural work can continue to benefit from basic research.

Modification of antecedents

Within the basic model, behaviour may be modified by changing either antecedents or consequences. Studies in the behavioural tradition have tended to concentrate on modification of consequences, but changes in antecedents may be equally or more effective.

At the simplest level, analysis of the stimuli which control behaviour may show discriminative stimuli which can be avoided. If shouting at someone provokes an aggressive response we can simply ensure that requests are given in a normal voice. Similarly, if distressed behaviour only occurs when a person known to have been aggressive to a child is present then the need is either to change that person's behaviour or to keep the two apart. However, where hostilities or tears hamper adaptation a more active approach may be necessary. Desensitization techniques or techniques of social skill training may be one way to tackle the problem.

Several reviewers argue that various types of problem behaviour, in particular stereotyped and self-stimulatory behaviour, occur because environments present too little stimulation (Baumeister and Forehand, 1973; Baumeister and Rollings, 1976; Carr, 1977). There is a good deal of evidence in these accounts to back the notion that problem behaviours decline in frequency once the person is offered the opportunity for more rewarding alternative activities. Certainly, making the environment more stimulating and improving the individual's general quality of life must be initial steps in remediating problem behaviours.

At a more specific level Bachman and Fuqua (1983) have shown that specific activities may affect subsequent problem behaviours. In this study controlled physical exercise led to a reduction in problem behaviours during subsequent classroom activities.

Modification of consequences

Two basic ways of reducing the frequency of responses through modifying sequences have already been described. These involved the failure to reward or the removal of reward as a consequence of responding, the *extinction* or *time-out* procedures, and the presentation of an aversive stimulus as a consequence of responding, *punishment*. Other techniques, some of them variants on these procedures and some involving complex contingencies, have been used to control inappropriate behaviour. Together they represent a theoretically and practically interesting body of work.

Choice of technique for intervention is often guided by the assumption that behaviours are learned operants maintained either by positive social reinforcement or by the sensory consequences of the response. This hypothesis indicates the use of extinction or time-out. Other behaviours, for example, self-injurious ones, may be so life-threatening that they require immediate reduction and so merit the use of punishment. Alternatively, behaviours may be maintained by negative reinforcement; the individual may respond in order to escape from a demand or setting.

The behaviours to be discussed in this section are mainly those which represent substantial or persistent problems in adaptation. They include self-injurious behaviour, vomiting and rumination, stereotyped acts and aggression and disruption. However, as will be seen, the techniques to be described are also of value and importance in dealing with less dramatic forms of inappropriate behaviour.

Extinction. This technique involves the elimination of potentially rewarding consequences for a response. Laboratory studies show that such elimination leads to the eventual disappearance of the response in the particular setting.

There are problems in applying the extinction model in daily living settings. Behaviour may, theoretically, be maintained by several different reinforcers and indeed could be maintained by negative and positive reinforcement. A self-injurious response may be instrumental in removing an individual from an aversive situation, being required to work, and also in obtaining a rewarding situation of being given added attention. Similarly, responses may be maintained through intermittent reinforcement, making rewards difficult to identify. In addition, many of the more extreme behaviours which may need modification cannot simply be 'left'. It is difficult to justify ignoring an aggressive or self-destructive child.

None the less, extinction procedures have been used with extreme behaviours. Jones *et al.* (1974) report a study in which the self-destructive behaviour of a nine-year-old autistic mentally handicapped girl was extinguished by ignoring the behaviour (self-mutilation through hitting her hand or wrist against her front teeth and jabbing herself forcefully with her fingers). The use of an extinction procedure was justified on the grounds that a previous programme using electroshock had met with increased self-destructive responding and other side effects. Although the intensity of the child's self-destructive behaviour decreased by week seven, the rate of jabbing did not reach zero until week twelve of the programme. However, this represented a decline from an estimated rate of well over 30,000 hits or jabs per week.

Jones *et al.* are unclear on the reasons for the effectiveness of the programme. They suggest that the eventual positive outcome had less to do with removal of attention for self-destruction than with adjustment to being without the physical restraining devices which were normally used to control the behaviour.

A heroic study by Martin and Foxx (1973) illustrates extinction of aggressive behaviour in a mentally handicapped twenty-two-year-old woman. A staff member acted as victim of the attacks and tried to ignore all aggressive behaviour, which did eventually extinguish. Although extinction is not necessarily the most appropriate treatment for aggressive behaviour, it avoids the possibility, indicated by studies on infra-human organisms, that punishment may lead to increased aggression (Azrin and Holz, 1966).

Carr *et al.* (1980) also treated aggressive behaviour. Their first study showed that attacks on the experimenter only occurred when demands were placed on the two children studied. They found also that attacks were reduced in frequency when the experimenter signalled the children that demands were to cease. From these data Carr *et al.* concluded that aggressive responses were being negatively reinforced because they led to the children being allowed to escape from demand situations. Their approach to modifying this behaviour was, first of all, to substitute a nonaggressive response, tapping, for the aggressive behaviour, both being reinforced by allowing escape. However, because rates of the two behaviours were so high, it was necessary to extinguish escape responding by preventing the child concerned from leaving the demand situation. At the beginning of extinction, rates were high (500 or more responses per hour) but fell to one or two acts per hour-long session after five hours of the treatment. Rates jumped to 1625 aggressive acts when they were again negatively reinforced but fell to near zero when extinction was reintroduced.

The Carr *et al.* study shows that unacceptable behaviours may be maintained by negative reinforcement resulting from being allowed to escape. It underscores the desirability of examining the contingencies which are maintaining problem behaviours before intervention.

Time-out. The essential feature of time-out is that the individual is removed from a rewarding situation for a fixed period of time as a consequence of a particular response. So, removal of food for a period of a minute or removal of the individual from the table at which he or she is eating can lead to decrease in unacceptable mealtime behaviours (e.g. Barton *et al.*, 1970). The same effect occurs in classroom or therapy situations in which unacceptable behaviours are timed-out through withdrawal of attention or exclusion from the classroom (e.g. Tyler and Brown, 1967).

However, if the overall level of reward provided by the setting in which behaviour is occurring is very low, time-out is unlikely to be effective. Birnbrauer *et al.* (1965) found that when rewards for good behaviour were withdrawn in a classroom situation, the subjects competed to be put into a time-out room separate from the classroom. Husted *et al.* (1971) found that aggressive and self-destructive behaviours were successfully controlled by time-out in training sessions where there was a high level of reward for acceptable behaviours. However, time-out was ineffective when the individuals were returned to ward situations in which the level of positive interaction was low. Similar results were shown by Solnick *et al.* (1977), who showed that the effectiveness of time-out depended on whether the living setting was impoverished or enriched. In practice, if environments are very unstimulating for the person, even the attention accruing from being put in a time-out area may sustain negative behaviours.

It is useful at this stage to introduce the concept of response co-variation. Responses or individual behaviours are part of a stream of reactions which consitute the overall behaviour of a person. When a response is eliminated from the stream of behaviour in any setting it will be replaced by another. At an extreme the response which emerges may be sitting and doing nothing, but it is more likely that another activity will emerge. The term response co-variation has been put forward by Kazdin (1982a) to refer to a situation in which two or more responses are related in such a way that changes in one affect others. This is similar to the notion of the response class, where changing the frequency of occurrence of one member of the class will affect the probability of all other members of the class (Spradlin *et al.*, 1976). However, the response class concept suggests that increasing the frequency of, say, an imitative response will lead to increases in the frequency of all imitative behaviours. Response co-variation may operate in other ways. Consequently, extinguishing aggressive behaviour toward other people may lead to an increase in the frequency of friendly approach behaviour; or it may lead to an increase in self-destructive behaviour.

Clearly this formulation relates to phenomena often covered by the concept of symptom substitution. Kazdin (1982a) points out that there is wide acceptance by behaviourally oriented therapists that 'negative' changes of the type just indicated do occur as a result of treatment. But he argues that the concept of symptom substitution is essentially untestable and needs to be replaced by one which can, among other things, encompass 'positive' and 'negative' changes in behaviour.

The notion of response co-variation would envisage the individual's behaviour as organized into clusters of co-varying responses within any setting. Such clusters have been identified by Wahler (1975) in deviant children. Observation of a child's behaviour showed that doing work in school was positively correlated with self-stimulation, fiddling with objects, staring into space and not interacting with others. Wahler found that clusters differed for different children, and across settings for the same child. The Wahler account provides an extension of the concepts of stimulus and response classes.

Response co-variation suggests that, if we are to understand and predict the effects of treatments, especially those involving the elimination of behaviours, we need to assess clusters of behaviours so that negatively and positively correlated responses can be identified. It definitely implies that several behaviours must be observed when any remedial procedure is used. In addition, it assumes that some changes will be positively valued by other people in the environment and others will be negatively valued. For instance, Sajwaj *et al.* (1972) found that using an extinction procedure for 'talking out' by a disturbed mentally handicapped pre-school child was effective. At the same time, initiation of conversations with other children and playing co-operatively with other children increased, but 'disruptive' behaviour at times of the day other than when the programme was conducted also increased.

As with extinction, several time-out studies show response co-variation effects. Jackson and Calhoun (1977) found that decreases in whining, shouting and crying by a ten-year-old mentally handicapped boy followed two-minute periods of time-out. These decreases in vocal behaviour were accompanied by reductions in hitting and out-of-seat activity, and increases in appropriate social interaction with other children.

Several studies have examined parameters of time-out, including duration of the time-out and interval and schedule effects. Longer durations, up to several minutes, appear to be more effective in controlling behaviour (Hobbs and Forehand, 1977). Low fixed and variable ratio schedules, i.e. contingencies in which only one out of every two or three occurrences of a response is subjected to time-out, appear to be as effective as *crf* in controlling behaviour (Clark *et al.*, 1973; Calhoun and Matherne, 1975). Higher ratios are not effective in gaining initial control of behaviour, but may be successful as maintenance conditions, once the frequency of responding has been brought under control (Hobbs and Forehand, 1977). The implication of these studies is that the overall proportion of 'missed' occurrences of inappropriate behaviours can be quite high and time-out still be an effective means of control. However, this is not equivalent to advocating poor vigilance in the observation of inappropriate behaviours, since this may well lead to the individual discriminating situations in which performance will not be timed-out.

It is normally argued that the person should not be 'released' from time-out until inappropriate behaviour has stopped and, if possible, appropriate behaviour has taken its place, in order to prevent inappropriate behaviour from being negatively reinforced, i.e. reinforced by leading to escape from time-out.

Punishment. It was noted earlier that the punishment procedure involves making an aversive stimulus consequent to an unacceptable behaviour. As with time-out, the effectiveness of a punishment procedure will depend on the context in which it occurs. It is quite conceivable that aversive stimulation for unacceptable behaviour may be positively reinforcing under certain circumstances. For instance, if the only attention an individual achieves is for 'inappropriate' behaviour, then such attention, even if it is 'aversive', for instance being shouted at, may be more rewarding than the alternative of being ignored. This argument reflects the Premack principle described earlier. For this reason the distinction between time-out and punishment as separate procedures is not clear-cut, to such a degree that some reviews classify time-out as a type of punishment (Murphy, 1980).

Early studies using punishment often employed contingent electroshock (e.g. Tate and Baroff, 1966; Baumeister and Forehand, 1972). Lovaas and Simmons (1969) found that, when self-destructive behaviour was allowed to extinguish, over 9000 self-hitting responses were recorded. This reduction did not generalize to other settings. In one of these, punishment by noninjurious electroshock was used. A total of twelve one-second shocks eliminated self-hitting completely and without other unacceptable behaviours emerging. Other studies showed similar effectiveness, but not all applications were successful and occasionally unacceptable side effects emerged (e.g. Jones *et al.*, 1974; see p. 481). Generalization of response suppression from one setting to another and from one trainer to another was often poor (e.g. Risley, 1968), and concern was expressed about the possible association, by the client, of the individual using the punishment with the aversive stimulus, generating fear and avoidance (cf. Skinner, 1953).

Concern about the use of electroshock on the part of practitioners, lawyers and the general public alike, especially in North America, led to an active search for more acceptable alternative aversive stimuli (Richards, 1975). The literature now contains a wide variety of examples of the successful use of nonshock procedures within the punishment paradigm. These include the use of mild physical and verbal punishment, the use of unpleasant sensory stimuli such as squirts of lemon juice (e.g. Sajwaj *et al.*, 1974; Marholin *et al.*, 1980, for rumination), inhalation of aromatic ammonia (Tanner and Zeiler, 1975; Baumeister and Baumeister, 1978, for self-injurious behaviour; Singh, 1979, for breath-holding; Singh *et al.*, 1980, for face-slapping and hitting), and water mist sprayed in the face (Dorsey *et al.*, 1980, for self-injury). Blount *et al.* (1982) describe the use of an 'icing' procedure, in which ice was applied to the lips or chin of two severely mentally handicapped individuals who showed bruxism (grinding, clenching or clicking their teeth). Contingent icing was shown to reduce the behaviour in treatment sessions, although generalization was imperfect. The authors suggest that the individuals discriminated 'time since treatment' as a means of identifying when it was 'safe to brux'.

Several studies have used a technique called 'facial screening'. This involves placing a terrycloth bib over the person's face contingent on unacceptable behaviour (Lutzker and Spencer, 1974, in Lutzker, 1978). It has been applied to a range of problems. Zegiob *et al.* (1976) found that facial screening was effective in reducing scratching, biting and other disruptive behaviour but was not effective in reducing bruxism. Lutzker (1978) used a procedure in which the subject, a twenty-year-old retarded man, wore a large terrycloth bib. Contingent on self-hitting, slapping his head and face with his hands and fists, a teacher quickly said 'no' and put the bib over the young man's face and head, holding it loosely at the back until hitting had stopped for three seconds. This resulted in a rapid reduction in the frequency of hitting to near-zero levels in three classroom settings, with some generalization to ward contexts and a healing of many of the subjects' bruises.

The 'appropriateness' of facial screening to responses in which there is contact between the individual's hands and head is also seen in a study by Barmann and Vitali (1982), in which trichotillomania (compulsive hair-pulling) was successfully treated. However, McGonigle *et al.* (1982) used a modified procedure in which a therapist put a hand over the person's eyes for five seconds. Self-destructive and self-stimulatory behaviours, hair-pulling, 'ear-bending', and visual and auditory self-stimulation were successfully treated in four subjects. Initial resistance to treatment was shown, but McGonigle *et al.* conclude that the method is an 'easily administered and quick procedure' (p. 467). Singh *et al.* (1982b) also used facial screening to suppress screaming. These studies suggest that facial screening does not operate simply by preventing responses.

The limits of effectiveness of facial screening across different types of behaviour have clearly not yet been established, a conclusion which appears to apply to other forms of punishment. For instance, it would seem reasonable to use lemon juice for reducing rumination, since the taste of the juice should prevent what are presumably sought-after sensory consequences. Although there may be an element of effects of this type in treatment, both specific and general responses appear to be present in most cases. The issue may be resolved around the question of whether the intervention interrupts the sequence of behaviour involved in the punished response.

In token economies individuals earn tokens for acceptable behaviours and may also lose them for unacceptable behaviours. Removal of tokens is termed 'response cost'. There are a number of individual studies of response cost with mentally handicapped individuals. Kazdin (1971) and Burchard and Barrera (1972) both report studies in which response cost was used to reduce inappropriate verbal behaviour and, in the latter research, aggressive and destructive behaviour. Salend and Kovalich (1981) report an ingenious study in which the inappropriate verbal behaviour of several members of a class of children was reduced using a simple group contingency. Others have used response cost to reduce lateness and off-task behaviour (Kaufman and O'Leary, 1972; Iwata and Bailey, 1974).

Once a token economy is established, response cost appears to be a valuable technique (e.g. Phillips, 1968). Lutzker *et al.* (1983) conclude that it 'is very simple to use, requires a minimum amount of time, and can be administered in a non-emotional manner while providing clients with concrete feedback on the inappropriateness of their behaviour' (p. 44).

Finally, the peculiar case of physical restraint is considered here. This is a fairly commonly used resort in the control of self-destructive and aggressive behaviours. As such it can clearly serve to prevent injury or damage to property, although it is ethically problematic and can interfere significantly with training goals. On the other hand, brief contingent restraint has been used with some success in the treatment of self-injury, but with some puzzling results.

Several studies report positive effects. Hamilton *et al.* (1967) showed reduction of aggressive, self-destructive and noncompliant behaviour in severely mentally handicapped women through physical restraint (being belted to a padded chair) for periods of between thirty minutes and two hours. Far briefer and more humane methods were used by Giles and Wolf (1966) in a toilet training programme, by Henriksen and Doughty (1967) in a self-feeding programme, and by Koegel *et al.* (1974) in reducing self-stimulation and stereotyped behaviours (in association with slapping).

Salzberg and Napolitan (1974) used two minutes of contingent physical restraint, being held at a table, for playing with doors and staring out of windows. The subject, a twelve-year-old severely mentally handicapped boy, showed a reduction from above 90 per cent to around 10 per cent in intervals during which the inappropriate behaviour was shown. Similar effects were shown by Rapoff *et al.* (1980) for self-injurious behaviour. Dorsey *et al.* (1982) produce evidence which suggests that protective equipment used to prevent head and hand injury can be successfully phased out. A similar example of long-term suppressive effects is given by Williams (quoted by Corbett, 1975). In this case a newspaper was used as an arm splint in order to prevent head-hitting. The newspaper was systematically removed, page by page, over a period of some weeks without recurrence of the behaviour. In a systematic study Singh *et al.* (1981a) showed positive effects of a soft restraining jacket and holding down hands on self-injurious behaviour. Singh *et al.* found that a one-minute restraint period was more effective than a three-minute period.

These relatively successful uses of restraint are compounded by phenomena described by Corbett (1975), whereby individuals can become 'addicted' to restraining apparatus, 'seeking it out and demanding more restraint with only greater restriction of activity' (p. 84). As Favell *et al.* (1981) point out, some clients 'appear to enjoy being restrained ... these individuals may appear calm when restrained, but extremely agitated when released, and they often attempt to restrain themselves' (p. 425). Favell *et al.* (1978) showed that restraint which had been used to prevent self-injury could be used to reinforce the *nonoccurrence* of this behaviour and also an arbitrary response (marble placement). Favell *et al.* (1981) describe similar evidence for three severely mentally handicapped adults who had been restrained, either contingently or noncontingently, as treatment for self-injury and aggression. They point out that, although the problem may be a minority one (their subjects were the only ones of twenty-one cases who were reported to enjoy restraint), the problem is serious because restraint may be rewarding self-injury.

The study reinforces the suggestion made by Dorsey *et al.* (1982) that it is important to understand 'the motivational variables responsible for clients' behaviour prior to attempting treatment' (p. 230). However, such understanding is likely to be very difficult to achieve and, in the current case, it is possible that the *treatment* led to physical restraint becoming rewarding. Subjects may become reliant on restraining devices as a means of controlling their own behaviour.

There has been a great deal of discussion of the supposed or actual side effects of the use of punishment, summarized by Balsam and Bondy (1983) as including anger, aggression, withdrawal, general suppression of behaviour, and ritualistic or inflexible behaviour. There is some evidence for such side effects in the literature on the use of punishment procedures with mentally handicapped individuals. The child treated by Jones *et al.* (1974) through extinction of self-injurious behaviours had received contingent electroshock for self-hitting in a previous treatment. During treatment, which was very prolonged, the child's repertoire of self-destructive behaviour expanded to include 'pinching and jabbing with her fingers of sufficient intensity to open lesions in her sides, stomach, thighs and the back of her neck' (p. 243). When this behaviour was also punished with shock, jabbing increased, hitting reappeared and increased, and she refused food. Eventually the child was being tube-fed and was restrained with a neck collar and arm tubes.

This dramatic case does not reflect a general situation. Indeed, Solomon (1964), Gardner (1969) and Corbett (1975) conclude that there is relatively little evidence to support the case for automatic adverse effects of punishment. Balsam and Bondy (1983) go so far as to argue that there is a symmetry between aversive and rewarding stimuli such that there are negative side effects for both. The response co-variation concept developed by Kazdin (1982a) would imply that punishment may have positive or negative side effects, depending on the repertoire of the individual. Certainly effects can be mixed. Balsam and Bondy quote a study by Becker *et al.* (1978) in which regurgitation was punished by squirting lemon juice into the mouth of the child. Rumination decreased, as did crying. Smiling and spontaneous social interaction increased, but so did stereotyped play with objects and head-slapping.

These arguments do not cover all of the objections to punishment. Particular aversive stimuli may have unacceptable side effects. For instance, Sajwaj *et al.* (1974) note that excessive use of lemon juice may lead to health problems, including irritation to the interior of the mouth. In addition, care staff and parents may find the use of punishment, especially in its more extreme forms, unacceptable or distressing.

Studies of the type reported in this section have led to questions being raised about the ethics of behaviour modification. The use of punishment has, on occasion, led to legal action and public enquiries on both sides of the Atlantic. Guidelines for the use of behavioural techniques have been developed on several occasions and by various professional groups.

Three general points relate to the controversy over the use of behavioural techniques. Quite frequently, offending practices represent misapplications of behavioural ideas in the name of behaviour modification. A major working party examining the ethics of behaviour modification was established in the UK as a result of complaints arising from such a misconception (HMSO, 1980). Second, behavioural techniques were often developed in institutional contexts where they were employed as ways through which the institutions could be run more effectively. With the radical shift in public opinion away from institutional provision, behavioural techniques tend to be rejected along with the pattern of care. However, the techniques themselves can be used to enhance the lives of mentally handicapped people. They can be used in the service of positive goals.

In practice, concern about the use of extreme forms of punishment has, as indicated, led to the development of more acceptable alternatives. There is general agreement that the use of stimuli such as electroshock is only acceptable under strict controls and for behaviours which threaten the life of the mentally handicapped individual (Corbett, 1975).

Differential reinforcement of acceptable behaviours. Several procedures have been developed from experimental literature which rely on the manipulation of the response–consequence contingencies. Three of these rely on the reinforcement of acceptable behaviours.

Differential reinforcement of other behaviours, DRO, is a schedule which requires the subject to withhold a response for a specified period of time. If this is withheld, reward is given; if it is not, the time period begins again from the termination of the response (Reynolds, 1961). Schroeder *et al.* (1979) point out that, if no specific incompatible response is to be reinforced, DRO becomes reinforcement of zero behaviour. As such it is procedurally similar to time-out, where reward is withheld for a specified period following inappropriate responding.

'Pure' DRO can be effective in controlling behaviour. Repp *et al.* (1975) showed that a DRO schedule was effective in reducing the stereotyped behaviour of three severely mentally handicapped individuals when mild verbal punishment ('no') was ineffective. In other studies, DRO schedules involve the positive reinforcement of a range of acceptable behaviours. Luiselli *et al.* (1981) used treats for 'good sitting' and for 'good talking' with their two subjects. They also used the principle of extending the DRO time interval as the behaviour of their subjects improved, the criteria for reward for not vocalizing irrelevantly being extended from one minute to six minutes during treatment. They reported generalization of improved behaviour to other, untreated responses, by one of their subjects. However, failure to find generalization across settings and responses has been highlighted by some authors (Homer and Peterson, 1980).

Several studies have compared DRO with other procedures. Results have been very mixed, but have usually shown DRO to be a relatively weak method. For example, Corte *et al.* (1971) found DRO to be only moderately effective when compared to time-out and punishment of self-injurious behaviour. Similar results were reported by Harris and Wolchik (1979) and by Foxx and Azrin (1973) for self-stimulation, and by Myers (1975) for finger-biting, where DRO was inferior to response-cost. However, Bostow and Bailey (1969) and Repp and Deitz (1974) found conjunction of DRO and time-out for inappropriate behaviour an effective combination. Other studies combining DRO with other methods have shown it to be effective (e.g. Barton and Madsen, 1980, with awareness training for drooling; Polvinale and Lutzker, 1980, with social restitution). Before dismissing pure DRO it is well to note that Repp *et al.* (1983) describe two types of DRO, momentary DRO where reward is given if the response is not occurring at the particular moment of observation, and whole-interval DRO, where reward follows if the response has not occurred within the interval. The authors found that the full-interval DRO procedure was more effective than momentary DRO.

A second method involves the differential reinforcement of responses which are alternatives to the inappropriate behaviour (DRA). DRA schedules require specification of the particular responses which are to be positively reinforced. It has been the most frequently used schedule since early studies, in that workers have typically specified desirable behaviours for reward. Several of these combined DRA with other methods, such as time-out or extinction. The importance of exploring the combination of DRA with other procedures is emphasized in a study by Cavalier and Ferretti (1980) in which DRA on its own was shown to be ineffective in suppressing finger-digging, tongue-protrusion and skin-sucking. When combined with a mild slap to the forearm, which had also been shown to be ineffective on its own, DRA was successful.

A third schedule uses the rationale that rewarding behaviour which is incompatible with the inappropriate behaviour, rather than just an alternative, will be more effective (differential reinforcement of incompatible behaviour, DRI). Evidence to support this suggestion is provided by Tarpley and Schroeder (1979) for self-injury. Young and Wincze (1974) found that reinforcing alternatives which were compatible with the self-injurious behaviours of a severely mentally handicapped woman increased *their* frequency, but did not reduce the rate of the self-injurious behaviours. Reinforcement of incompatible alternatives led to an increase in compatible self-injurious responses of a different topography. Only reinforcement of specific incompatible responses reduced specific self-injurious behaviours. In this study DRA did not reduce the frequency of target behaviours.

A further type of schedule has been used fairly frequently. In this, the individual is rewarded for whatever behaviour is in question, but only when it is produced at a low rate (differential reinforcement of low rate, DRL). For example Singh *et al.* (1981b) rewarded stereotyped responses in three individuals but only if, initially, they had not made the response for 12 seconds. This interval was then extended to 30, 60 and 80 seconds, the behaviour occurring at these increasingly low rates and being replaced by increased social behaviour such as smiling and communicating. The procedure has been used successfully in a number of studies by Deitz and his colleagues. Deitz (1977) has described several variants of the schedule: Spaced DRL in which reward follows a minimum time between responses, Interval DRL which requires an average time between responses, and Full-session DRL where reward follows if, at the end of a session, n or less than n responses have occurred. Deitz also suggests that it may be necessary to make DRL into a DRO schedule in order to effect complete suppression.

A study by Deitz *et al.* (1976) illustrates the effectiveness of whole-interval DRL, whole-interval DRO and DRI in controlling disruptive behaviour and sleeping in class. All three methods were found to be effective. Deitz points out that the choice of method will depend on the particular circumstances of treatment, including the other responses available to subjects.

Overcorrection. Discussion of overcorrection has been left until the end of the description of procedures because it is, in many ways, a combination of many of those which have already been considered. Overcorrection was first described by Foxx and Azrin (1972). It involves two components, *restitution*, or restoring the disrupted environment, whether it be the physical or social, and *positive practice*, being required to practise repeatedly an alternative behaviour which is appropriate in the situation. During the 1970s a large number of influential papers were published by Azrin and his colleagues, in which positive practice overcorrection (PPOC) was applied successfully to a range of very difficult problems. The Foxx and Azrin (1972) study used PPOC with aggressive and destructive behaviours. These authors (1973) extended its use to self-stimulation. Webster and Azrin (1973) used 'required relaxation', lying quietly, as the positive practice element in the treatment of agitative-disruptive behaviour. Azrin *et al.* (1973a) required practice of appropriate behaviour in the same topography as inappropriate stereotyped and self-stimulatory behaviour. PPOC was applied to stealing by Azrin and Wesolowski (1974), to classroom disruption by Azrin and Powers (1975), and to pica (eating non-nutritive substances) and coprophagy (eating faecal matter) by Foxx and Martin (1975). Azrin *et al.* (1975) treated self-injurious behaviour, Azrin and Wesolowski (1975) floor-sprawling, Foxx (1976) showed the value of PPOC in eliminating stripping by mentally handicapped women, Foxx *et al.* (1979) in eliminating rumination. If the many examples of the application of PPOC by other workers to other problems are added it is clear that the notion has been highly influential.

The parameters governing PPOC have been examined in a number of studies. Duration of overcorrection has been shown to be crucial in some settings, but not in others (e.g. Foxx and Azrin, 1973; Carey and Bucher, 1983). Ollendick and Matson (1976) argue that the subject must actively and vigorously perform the responses in positive practice before this will be an effective component. If this is the case, then longer periods of overcorrection would be likely to be more effective (cf. Foxx and Azrin, 1972). Durations of positive practice have varied from thirty seconds (e.g. Carey and Bucher, 1981) to two hours (Webster and Azrin, 1973).

The educative value of PPOC has been a matter for disagreement. Some authors have reported such effects, others not so (Wells *et al.*, 1977a, b; Cavalier and Ferretti, 1980; Carey and Bucher, 1981). Hung *et al.* (1979) have suggested that they may stem, at least in some cases, from negative reinforcement (escape learning) when firm physical prompts are used to teach instruction-following.

It is clear that, although effective, PPOC is not a single procedure, but a principle or set of guidelines which incorporates a whole series of other procedures. Indeed, Epstein *et al.* (1974) point out that there are two types of overcorrection, restitutional and positive practice overcorrection, and that the two can be used together. So a child who marks a wall may be required to wash the wall and the rest of the room as well, thereby restoring it to a 'better-than-normal' state (restitution), or to copy patterns or forms using a pencil and paper (positive practice), or to do both.

Overcorrection clearly involves elements of positive and negative reinforcement. Noncompliance is subject to punishment, and ongoing behaviour is interrupted, introducing an element of time-out. The subject is given verbal feedback on what is wrong with his or her behaviour, instructions on correct behaviour and, in some cases, physical guidance or prompting which is gradually faded. This instruction component may involve DRO, DRA or DRI, depending on the particular problems and tasks.

The possible confusion which these multiple components could bring about is emphasized by several authors. For instance, Murphy (1978) points out that overcorrection acts as a punishment procedure for many individuals, but that it does not need to act as such. She notes that, in empirical terms, rates in published studies may show no change (Azrin and Wesolowski, 1975) or actual increases in frequency of target behaviours (Azrin *et al.*, 1975; Measel and Alfieri, 1976). The effects shown are reminiscent of the consequences of use of restraint. Murphy concludes that a proper functional analysis before treatment begins may allow predictions to be made.

Several authors have called for component analysis, which would investigate the impact of the various components of PPOC, and some studies have appeared (e.g. Wesolowski and Zawlocki, 1982). Although this is clearly a desirable trend, the task is complicated because there are so many variants of the method, dependent on behaviours attacked. However, as Murphy emphasizes, given the complexity of the procedure, overcorrection should not be applied in any general 'cookbook' fashion to any and all undesirable behaviours.

As with other procedures involving punishment, the ethical aspects of PPOC are important. All elements of the method can be aversive to parents and practitioners. As with the general use of punishment, this has led to an interest in less aversive techniques. For instance, Azrin and Wesolowski (1980) have shown that stopping stereotyped behaviour and holding the subject's hands on his or her lap for two minutes is as effective as forced arm exercises.

Not surprisingly, PPOC studies have shown a wide variety of side effects. Epstein *et al.* (1974) found an increase in appropriate toy play, but also an increase in unwanted vocalization after suppressing self-stimulation. Rollings *et al.* (1977) reported increases in a variety of unacceptable behaviours such as self-hitting, self-pinching, screaming and self-scratching in two subjects being overcorrected for body-rocking and head-weaving. Similarly, Singh *et al.* (1982a) indicated a rise in stereotyped behaviours as a side effect of a programme treating rumination for one child, but a rise in appropriate behaviour for another. Carey and Bucher (1983) stated that incidents of aggression and disruptive behaviour occurred under a three-minute treatment duration, but not under a thirty-second duration. Doke and Epstein (1975) found that PPOC suppressed stereotypic behaviour but that threats of overcorrection led to an increase in rocking, noise-making, face-slapping and masturbation. Wells *et al.* (1977b) indicated mixed effects for different subjects and concluded that patterns of response co-variation may be highly idiosyncratic.

Conclusion

This section has reviewed selected studies concerned with the development of new behaviours and the elimination of unacceptable behaviour. Several general conclusions can be drawn in the context of the behavioural model of antecedents, behaviours and consequences.

There is a fair body of literature confirming that changes in setting and discriminative stimuli change behaviour. At a trivial but important level, if you do not ask someone to do something you may never know if he or she can do it. In broader terms, if an environment is unstimulating then unacceptable behaviours may emerge and be sustained. Simply improving the environment may be sufficient to reduce their rate and to allow new behaviours to take their place. This explanation underlies some of the effects shown in studies of time-out and also covers findings on reduction of stereotyped behaviours with improved environmental stimulation (Baumeister and Forehand, 1973).

The question of whether different behaviours require different approaches in order to modify them has not been fully considered. However, it seems likely that we need to plan the teaching of language and communication skills by taking greater account of the functions to which such skills are to be put in natural settings (Goetz *et al.*, 1979, 1983; see also Chapter 16). One of the keys to improving generalization clearly lies in tailoring the social setting of teaching to that in which skills will subsequently be used.

In terms of elimination of inappropriate responses the same basic question emerges. Are there responses which are functionally linked to their consequences in such a way that only particular types of consequence sustain them or can be used to eliminate them? Although consideration cannot be given here to the range of theories generated to explain behaviours such as stereotypy, rumination or self-injurious behaviours, it is clear that they tend to suggest specific treatments related to changes in consequences. In practice, the data suggest that aversive consequences, like lemon juice treatment, may have effects beyond specific responses. This possibility needs further investigation.

This takes us naturally to the question of elimination of responses. Overall we might argue that DRI coupled with punishment is likely to be *the* most effective procedure for eliminating responses. This may well underlie the strength of some versions of PPOC which involve required practice of appropriate responses following punishment of inappropriate responses. Alternative procedures, from DRO to DRA, both alone and coupled with punishment or time-out, will be likely to be effective if the individual readily produces alternative responses at a reasonably high rate and if these responses are consequated. Again, one returns to the need to examine response co-variation in the context of setting and discrimination stimuli and current and novel consequences in order to begin to formulate a theoretical model which can lead us to explain and predict the impact of particular techniques. One key to such a theory is provided by Premack's emphasis on the relativity of 'rewarding' and 'aversive' stimuli to settings and contingencies. Data from several groups of studies, including those on physical restraint, indicate the likely complexity of such a theory.

IMPLEMENTATION AND DISSEMINATION

We have seen that the behavioural approach emphasizes the importance of environmental variables in the understanding and modification of behaviour. It follows that the individual's living environments must be carefully considered when teaching or remediation are planned.

This proposition has led to two important developments in behaviour modification. First, great attention has been paid to the advice and training of parents and relatives of handicapped individuals. Numerous projects in all parts of the world have been reported. Possibly the most influential to date is the Portage Project (Shearer and Shearer, 1972). The Portage method involves a management structure in which an individual experienced in the use of behavioural techniques, and in work with parents and handicapped children, supervises a group of professionals or others who themselves assist individual families. The families teach the handicapped individual. The home visitors may be professionals such as physiotherapists, speech therapists or health visitors, or they may be volunteers who have little or no initial relevant knowledge. After training in behavioural techniques home visitors co-operate with parents in the assessment of their offspring, using assessment materials which are part of the package. Results of these assessments, and of the teaching programmes which are established on the basis of them, are discussed in weekly management meetings with the 'expert' in behavioural techniques and intervention. Parents are visited regularly, typically once a week, by home visitors. In these meetings progress achieved is discussed and new targets set.

Great care is taken to plan teaching in such a way that target behaviours can be taught by families within the space of a week in brief daily sessions. Teaching is planned in part through a pack of suggestions which is linked to the assessment framework. Families are asked to record their sessions and are given a great deal of positive feedback on their efforts. Similarly, Portage managers give home visitors positive feedback for their reports on home interventions. Managerial consultations also provide an essential structure for the development of relevant ideas, either with the manager or with the manager in conjunction with other home visitors.

The Portage method is a variant of procedures used widely prior to its inception. However, the Portage model and its materials have proved particularly flexible and acceptable in many countries. Certainly, so far as the UK is concerned, one crucial factor seems to have been the provision of attractive assessment materials and the linked package of teaching suggestions (Bluma *et al.*, 1976). During the last decade a large number of Portage and Portage-derived programmes have been established in the UK. Many of these have been described in Cameron (1982) and Bendall *et al.* (1984).

Behaviour modification principles have also provided the basis for interventions in residential and day-care settings. A large number of short staff training programmes have been established in which behavioural techniques have been taught to teachers, nurses, care workers and other professionals, often within a framework of guided practice with mentally handicapped individuals. Carr (1980) discusses issues arising in the organization of such courses.

Several packages have been developed to mediate teaching. McBrien and Foxen (1981) and Foxen and McBrien (1981) have published handbooks relating to a course entitled EDY (Education of the Developmentally Young). This was developed in the mid-1970s to provide a method of teaching behavioural methods through written materials and guided practice. It used a pyramid training structure through which McBrien and Foxen trained potential instructors from education departments and other agencies in the UK. These then trained working teachers and others in the use of the methods, using materials provided by the course organizers. Because teachers and others who were successfully 'EDYfied' were provided with course certificates through the centre which had fostered the initial development, it has been possible to keep track of at least a minimum number of trainees, now exceeding 2500 and continuing to rise.

Robson (1981) utilized a 'minicourse' approach to teaching behavioural principles within a structured language programme. This provides course participants with written and video materials which they can work through relatively independently. More emphasis is placed on self-evaluation than in the EDY course. As a consequence the method places relatively less of a load on the course co-ordinator than does EDY.

In addition to these types of material, behaviour modification has stimulated the development of a large number of criterion-referenced assessment procedures (e.g. Kiernan and Jones, 1982), often linked in to suggestions for teaching programmes (e.g. Bender and Valletutti, 1976).

Overall approaches to programme planning have evolved. These usually emphasize the development of new repertoires of behaviour rather than the elimination of behaviour (cf. Goldiamond, 1974).

Behavioural techniques have become incorporated into teaching and care practices through these means, and also through their inclusion in the content of initial and advanced courses. In the UK this has occurred in a wide range of professions including nursing, teaching, some social work courses and in the training of medical doctors, psychologists and others.

Behaviour modifiers realized early that simply teaching behaviour modification techniques to staff in agencies would not lead to changes in their work behaviour unless their working environments were also changed. These changes included the introduction of new feedback and job accountability structures (Panyan *et al.*, 1970) and the reorganization of ward and class timetables to build in teaching sessions (e.g. Kiernan *et al.*, 1975). The development of token economies represents a particular form of organization of settings which has increased in sophistication over the years. Kushlick (1975), among others, has presented a description of the need to consider whole organizations as systems controlled by behavioural principles. Kiernan and Jones (1980) point out that the effective use of any and all elements within agencies will depend on their compatibility with the organizational philosophy of the agency. One manifestation of this is the attempt to establish the 'social validity' of behavioural programmes, i.e. the extent to which they are felt by parents or staff in agencies to be of value to their clients or themselves (Wolf, 1978). In addition there are attempts being made to evaluate the acceptability of techniques. For instance Kazdin (1980b) found that time-out was judged as more acceptable when it was part of a programme encouraging positive behaviours than when simply used to eliminate behaviours.

Evaluation of these various attempts at dissemination and implementation has been uneven. The pressure has been to disseminate and to implement procedures and structures which appear to be valuable. A certain amount of evaluation of the effectiveness of programmes has nevertheless been undertaken (e.g. Ivancic *et al.*, 1981; Page *et al.*, 1982; Kissel *et al.*, 1983), but this clearly remains as a complex and important task for the next decade.

TAKING STOCK

This final section will try to draw some conclusions about the effectiveness of behaviour modification and indicate future directions for development.

The review of studies on the development of new skills and the elimination of unacceptable behaviours indicates considerable success in the use of behavioural techniques. Furthermore, the approach has been as well if not more effectively disseminated than other therapeutic or educational philosophies.

There are areas where the use of behavioural techniques has been less effective. In particular, their application to the development of communication skills may have suffered from initial limitations of the model of teaching. As indicated, newer approaches may be more fruitful in the next decade. In addition, the results of studies in which inappropriate behaviours are treated raises theoretical questions at several levels. It is suggested that the response co-variation concept requires further elaboration. At another level inappropriate behaviours may be seen as self-stimulatory, positively reinforced operants, negatively reinforced operants or, possibly, communicative behaviours (Carr and Durand, 1984). Understanding of the characteristics of these behaviours must represent a goal for future research if treatments are to become more precise and humane.

If behaviour modification is to become more sophisticated there is a need for it to draw more from related traditions. In particular there has been a separation from laboratory research in the operant tradition which has resulted in behaviour modification failing to benefit from relevant academic thinking. For example, the effect of verbal behaviour on response to contingencies of reinforcement is well recognized in laboratory studies and may be a crucial point for growth in behaviour modification, but it is virtually ignored in the practitioner literature (cf. Lowe, 1979, 1983).

Similarly, it could be argued that the traditional separation of operant and nonoperant research and thinking is unproductive (Krantz, 1972). There is some evidence of a greater awareness of work in different traditions, at least in some areas, for example language and communication, but an almost total theoretical divide in others.

Despite relatively successful efforts to implement and disseminate the behavioural approach the most worrying gap must still be between work in centres of development of theory and practice and field settings. Inevitably not only will there be temporal gaps between development and implementation and some distortion of basic ideas, but also a proportion of day-to-day practice will be alarming in its misinterpretation of ideas and in the thoughtless application of cookbook approaches. Poor practice will inevitably lead to good ideas being discredited and benefits which could be gained being lost.

It seems clear that the general pressure during the next decade should be to disseminate sophisticated behavioural techniques and, at the same time, to correct oversimplifications. This means that dissemination to direct care personnel must be complemented by an increase in the effort to develop management-level staff who are in direct touch with sophisticated ideas and who can be skilled and creative in using them with direct care staff in developing programmes.

CONCLUSION

In this chapter behavioural theory, methods and the outcome of a selected group of behavioural studies have been reviewed. The review would suggest that behavioural techniques and behaviour modification have made a substantial contribution and impact. Future directions for development might well be to improve dissemination, to develop contacts with other traditions and to develop theory, as well as to continue to exploit the potential of the approach in the analysis and planning of teaching and remediation.

REFERENCES

AYLLON, T. and AZRIN, N.H. (1968) *The Token Economy*, New York, Appleton-Century-Crofts.

AZRIN, N.H. and ARMSTRONG, P.M. (1973) 'The "mini-meal": a method for teaching eating skills to the profoundly retarded', *Ment. Retard.*, 11 (1), 9–13.

AZRIN, N.H. and FOXX, R.M. (1971) 'A rapid method of toilet training the institutionalized retarded', *J. Appl. Behav. Anal.*, 4, 89–99.

AZRIN, N.H., GOTTLIEB, L.H., HUGHART, L., WESOLOWSKI, M.D. and RAHN, T. (1975) 'Eliminating self-injurious behaviors by educative procedures', *Behav. Res. Ther.*, 13, 101–11.

AZRIN, N.H. and HOLZ, W.C. (1966) 'Punishment', in W.K. HONIG (ed.), *Operant Behavior: Areas of Research and Application*, New York, Appleton-Century-Crofts.

AZRIN, N.H., KAPLAN, S.J. and FOXX, R.M. (1973a) 'Autism reversal: eliminating stereotyped self-stimulation of retarded individuals', *Amer. J. Ment. Defic.*, 78, 241–8.

AZRIN, N.H. and POWERS, M. (1975) 'Eliminating classroom disturbances of emotionally disturbed children by positive practice procedures', *Behav. Ther.*, 6, 525–34.

AZRIN, N.H., SCHAEFFER, R.M. and WESOLOWSKI, M.D. (1976) 'A rapid method of teaching profoundly retarded persons to dress by a reinforcement–guidance method', *Ment. Retard.*, 14 (6), 29–33.

AZRIN, N.H., SNEED, J.J. and FOXX, R.M. (1973b) 'Dry-bed: a rapid method of eliminating bed-wetting (enuresis) of the retarded', *Behav. Res. Ther.*, 11, 427–34.

AZRIN, N.H. and WESOLOWSKI, M.D. (1974) 'Theft reversal: an overcorrection procedure for eliminating stealing by retarded persons', *J. Appl. Behav. Anal.*, 7, 577–81.

AZRIN, N.H. and WESOLOWSKI, M.D. (1975) 'The use of positive practice to eliminate floor-sprawling by profoundly retarded persons', *J. Appl. Behav. Anal.*, 6, 627–32.

AZRIN, N.H. and WESOLOWSKI, M.D. (1980) 'A reinforcement plus interruption method of eliminating behavioral stereotypy of profoundly retarded persons', *Behav. Res. Ther.*, 18, 113–19.

BACHMAN, J.E. and FUQUA, R.W. (1983) 'Management of inappropriate behaviors of trainable mentally impaired students using antecedent exercise', *J. Appl. Behav. Anal.*, 16, 477–84.

BAER, D.M., WOLF, M.M. and RISLEY, T.R. (1968) 'Some current dimensions of applied behavior analysis', *J. Appl. Behav. Anal.*, 1, 91–7.

BALSAM, P.D. and BONDY, A.S. (1983) 'The negative side effects of reward', *J. Appl. Behav. Anal.*, 16, 283–96.

BARMANN, B.C. and VITALI, D.L. (1982) 'Facial screening to eliminate trichotillomania in developmentally disabled persons', *Behav. Ther.*, 13, 735–42.

BARTON, E.J. and MADSEN, J.J. (1980) 'The use of awareness and omission training to control excessive drooling in a severely retarded youth', *Child Behav. Ther.*, 2, 55–63.

BARTON, E.S., GUESS, D., GARCIA, E. and BAER, D.M. (1970) 'Improvements in retardates' mealtime behaviors by time-out procedures using multiple baseline techniques', *J. Appl. Behav. Anal.*, 3, 77–84.

BAUMEISTER, A.A. and BAUMEISTER, A. (1978) 'Suppression of repetitive self-injurious behavior by contingent inhalation of aromatic ammonia', *J. Aut. Child. Schiz.*, 8, 71–7.

BAUMEISTER, A.A. and FOREHAND, R. (1972) 'Effects of contingent shock and verbal command on body-rocking of retardates', *J. Clin. Psychol.*, 28, 586–90.

BAUMEISTER, A.A. and FOREHAND, R. (1973) 'Stereotyped acts', in N.R. ELLIS (ed.), *International Review of Research in Mental Retardation*, 6, New York, Academic Press, 55–96.

BAUMEISTER, A.A. and ROLLINGS, A. (1976) 'Self-injurious behavior', in N.R. ELLIS (ed.), *International Review of Research in Mental Retardation*, 9, New York, Academic Press.

BECKER, W. and ENGLEMANN, S. (1978) 'Systems for basic instruction: theory and application', in A.C. CATANIA and T.A. BRIGHAM (eds), *Handbook of Applied Behavior Analysis*, New York, Wiley.

BECKER, J.V., TURNER, S.M. and SAJWAJ, T.E. (1978) 'Multiple behavioral effects of the use of lemon juice with a ruminating toddler-age child', *Behav. Mod.*, 2, 267–78.

BELLACK, A.S., HERSEN, M. and KAZDIN, A.E. (eds) (1982) *International Handbook of Behavior Modification and Therapy*, New York, Plenum Press.

BELLAMY, T. and BUTTARS, K.L. (1975) 'Teaching trainable level retarded students to count money: toward personal independence through academic instruction', *Educ. Tr. Ment. Retard.*, 10, 18–26.

BELLAMY, T. and SONTAG, E. (1973) 'Use of group contingent music to increase assembly line production rates of retarded students in a simulated sheltered workshop', *J. Mus. Ther.*, 10, 125–36.

BENDALL, S., SMITH, J. and KUSHLICK, A. (1984) *National Study of Portage-type Home Teaching Services*, vols 1–3, Southampton, HCERT Research Reports, University of Southampton.

BENDER, M. and VALLETUTTI, P.J. (1976) *Teaching the Moderately and Severely Handicapped*, vol. 1, *Behavior, Self-Care and Motor Skills*, Baltimore, University Park Press.

BIJOU, S.W. (1966) 'A functional analysis of retarded development', in N.R.

ELLIS (ed.), *International Review of Research in Mental Retardation*, New York, Academic Press.

BIJOU, S.W. and BAER, D.M. (1961) *Child Development 1: A Systematic and Empirical Theory*, New York, Appleton-Century-Crofts.

BIRNBRAUER, J.S., WOLF, M.M., KIDDER, J.D. and TAGUE, C.E. (1965) 'Classroom behavior of retarded pupils with token reinforcement', *J. Exp. Child Psychol.*, 2, 219–35.

BLOUNT, R.L., DRABMAN, R.S., WILSON, N. and STEWART, D. (1982) 'Reducing severe diurnal bruxism in two profoundly retarded females', *J. Appl. Behav. Anal.*, 15, 565–71.

BLUMA, S., SHEARER, J., FROHMAN, A. and HILLIARD, J. (1976) *Portage Guide to Early Education*, Portage, Wisconsin, Co-operative Educational Service Agency, 12.

BOSTOW, D.E. and BAILEY, J.B. (1969) 'Modification of severe disruptive and aggressive behavior using brief timeout and reinforcement procedures', *J. Appl. Behav. Anal.*, 2, 31–7.

BRENER, J. and HOTHERSALL, D. (1967) 'Heart rate control under conditions of augmented sensory feedback', *Psychophysiol.*, 4, 1–6.

BURCHARD, J.D. and BARRERA, F. (1972) 'An analysis of time-out and response cost in a programmed environment', *J. Appl. Behav. Anal.*, 5, 271–82.

BURGIO, L.D., WHITMAN, T.L. and JOHNSON, M.R. (1980) 'A self-instructional package for increasing attending behavior in educable mentally retarded children', *J. Appl. Behav. Anal.*, 13, 443–59.

CALHOUN, K.S. and MATHERNE, P. (1975) 'The effects of varying schedules of time-out on the aggressive behaviors of a retarded girl', *J. Behav. Ther. Exp. Psychiat.*, 6, 139–43.

CAMERON, R.J. (ed.) (1982) *Working Together*, Windsor, NFER/Nelson.

CAREY, R.G. and BUCHER, B. (1981) 'Identifying the educative and suppressive effects of restitutional overcorrection and positive practice overcorrection', *J. Appl. Behav. Anal.*, 14, 71–81.

CAREY, R.G. and BUCHER, B. (1983) 'Positive practice overcorrection: the effects of duration of positive practice on acquisition and response reduction', *J. Appl. Behav. Anal.*, 16, 101–10.

CARR, E.G. (1977) 'The motivation of self-injurious behavior: a review of some hypotheses', *Psychol. Bull.*, 84, 800–16.

CARR, E.G. and DURAND, V.M. (1984) 'The social-communicative basis of severe behavior problems in children', in S. REISS and R. BOOTZIN (eds), *Theoretical Issues in Behavior Therapy*, New York, Academic Press.

CARR, E.G., NEWSOM, C.D. and BINKOFF, J.A. (1980) 'Escape as a factor in the aggressive behavior of two retarded children', *J. Appl. Behav. Anal.*, 13, 101–17.

CARR, J. (1980) 'The organization of short courses', in W. YULE and J. CARR (eds), *Behaviour Modification for the Mentally Handicapped*, London, Croom Helm, 213–25.

CARRIER, J.K. (1976) 'Application of a nonspeech language system with the severely language handicapped', in L.L. LLOYD (ed.), *Communication Assessment and Intervention Strategies*, Baltimore, University Park Press, 523–48.

CARRIER, J.K. (1979) 'Application of functional analysis and a nonspeech response mode to teaching language', in R.L. SCHIEFELBUSCH and J.H. HOLLIS (eds), *Language Intervention from Ape to Child*, Baltimore, University Park Press, 363–418.

CARRIER, J.K. and PEAK, T. (1975) *Non-speech Language Initiation Programme*, Lawrence, Kansas, H. & H. Enterprises.

CAVALIER, A.R. and FERRETTI, R.P. (1980) 'Stereotyped behavior, alternative behavior and collateral effects. A comparison of four intervention procedures', *J. Ment. Defic. Res.*, 24, 219–30.

CLARK, H.B., ROWBURY, T., BAER, A.M. and BAER, D.M. (1973) 'Time-out as a punishing stimulus in continuous and intermittent schedules', *J. Appl. Behav. Anal.*, 6, 443–55.

COLWELL, C.N., RICHARDS, E., MCCARVER, R.B. and ELLIS, N.R. (1973) 'Education of self-help habit-training of the profoundly retarded', *Ment. Retard.*, 11 (6), 14–18.

COON, M.E., VOGELSBERG, R.T. and WILLIAMS, W. (1981) 'Effects of classroom public transportation instruction on generalization to the natural environment', *J. Assoc. Sev. Hand.*, 6, 46–53.

CORBETT, J. (1975) 'Aversion for the treatment of self-injurious behaviour', *J. Ment. Defic. Res.*, 19, 79–95.

CORTE, H.E., WOLF, M.M., and LOCKE, B.J. (1971) 'A comparison of procedures for eliminating self-injurious behavior of retarded adolescents', *J. Appl. Behav. Anal.*, 4, 201–13.

CUVO, A.J., VEITCH, V.C., TRACE, M.W. and KONKE, J.L. (1978) 'Teaching change computation to the mentally retarded', *Behav. Mod.*, 2, 531–48.

DEITZ, S.M. (1977) 'An analysis of programming DRL schedules in educational settings', *Behav. Res. Ther.*, 15, 103–11.

DEITZ, S.M., REPP, A.C. and DEITZ, D.E.D. (1976) 'Reducing inappropriate classroom behavior of retarded students through three procedures of differential reinforcement', *J. Ment. Defic. Res.*, 20, 155–70.

DOKE, L.A. and EPSTEIN, I.H. (1975) 'Oral overcorrection: side effects and extended applications', *J. Exp. Child Psychol.*, 20, 496–511.

DOLEYS, S., STACY, D.M. and KNOWLES, S. (1981) 'Modification of grooming behavior in the adult retarded', *Behav. Mod.*, 5, 119–28.

DORRY, G.W. and ZEAMAN, D. (1973) 'The use of a fading technique in paired-associate teaching of a reading vocabulary with retardates', *Ment. Retard.*, 11, 3–6.

DORRY, G.W. and ZEAMAN, D. (1975) 'Teaching a simple reading vocabulary to retarded children: effectiveness of fading and nonfading procedures', *Amer. J. Ment. Defic.*, 79 (6), 711–16.

DORSEY, M.F., IWATA, B.A., ONG, P. and MCSWEEN, T.E. (1980) 'Treatment of self-injurious behavior using a water mist: initial response suppression and generalization', *J. Appl. Behav. Anal.*, 13, 343–54.

DORSEY, M.F., IWATA, B.A., REID, D.H. and DAVIS, P.A. (1982) 'Protective equipment: continuous and contingent application in the treatment of self-injurious behavior', *J. Appl. Behav. Anal.*, 15, 217–30.

EDGERTON, R.B. (1967) *The Cloak of Competence*, Berkeley, University of California Press.

EDGERTON, R.B. (1983) 'Failure in community adaptation: the relativity of assessment', in K.T. KERNAN, M.J. BEGAB and R.B. EDGERTON (eds), *Environments and Behavior*, Baltimore, University Park Press, 123–43.

EPSTEIN, H., DOKE, L., SAJWAJ, T., SORELL, S. and RIMMER, B. (1974) 'Generality and side effects of overcorrection', *J. Appl. Behav. Anal.*, 7, 385–90.

FAVELL, J.E., MCGIMSEY, J.F. and JONES, M. (1978) 'The use of physical restraint in the treatment of self-injury and as positive reinforcement', *J. Appl. Behav. Anal.*, 11, 225–42.

FAVELL, J.E., MCGIMSEY, J.F., JONES, M.L. and CANNON, P.R. (1981) 'Physical restraint as positive reinforcement', *Amer. J. Ment. Defic.*, 85, 425–32.

FERSTER, C.B. and SKINNER, B.F. (1957) *Schedules of Reinforcement*, New York, Appleton-Century-Crofts.

FOXEN, T. and MCBRIEN, J. (1981) *Training Staff in Behavioural Methods: Trainee Workbook*, Manchester, Manchester University Press.

FOXX, R.M. (1976) 'The use of overcorrection to eliminate public disrobing (stripping) of retarded women', *Behav. Res. Ther.*, 14, 53–61.

FOXX, R.M. and AZRIN, N.H. (1972) 'Restitution: a method of eliminating aggressive-disruptive behavior of retarded and brain damaged patients', *Behav. Res. Ther.*, 10, 15–27.

FOXX, R.M. and AZRIN, N.H. (1973) 'The elimination of autistic self-stimulatory behavior by overcorrection', *J. Appl. Behav. Anal.*, 6, 1–14.

FOXX, R.M. and MARTIN, E.D. (1975) 'Treatment of scavenging behavior (coprophagy and pica) by overcorrection', *Behav. Res. Ther.*, 13, 153–62.

FOXX, R.M., SNYDER, M.S. and SCHROEDER, F. (1979) 'A food satiation and oral hygiene punishment program to suppress chronic rumination by retarded persons', *J. Aut. Dev. Disord.*, 9, 399–412.

GANDHI, J.S. (1974) 'The use of social feedback for training the mentally retarded', *Ment. Retard.*, 12 (3), 45–7.

GARCIA, E., BAER, D.M. and FIRESTONE, I. (1971) 'The development of generalized imitation with topographically determined boundaries', *J. Appl. Behav. Anal.*, 4, 101–12.

GARDNER, J.M. (1969) 'Behavior modification research in mental retardation: search for an adequate paradigm', *Amer. J. Ment. Defic.*, 73, 844–51.

GILES, D.K. and WOLF, M.M. (1966) 'Toilet training institutionalized, severe retardates: an application of behavior modification techniques', *Amer. J.*

Ment. Defic., 70, 766–80.

GOETZ, L., SCHULER, A. and SAILOR, W. (1979) 'Teaching functional speech to the severely handicapped: current issues', *J. Aut. Dev. Disord.*, 9, 325–43.

GOETZ, L., SCHULER, A. and SAILOR, W. (1983) 'Motivational considerations in teaching language to severely handicapped students', in M. HERSEN, V.B. VAN HASSELT and J.L. MATSON (eds), *Behaviour Therapy for the Developmentally and Physically Disabled*, New York, Academic Press, 57–77.

GOLDIAMOND, I. (1974) 'Toward a constructional approach to social problems: ethical and constitutional issues raised by applied behavior analysis', *Behaviorism*, 2, 1–84.

GRESHAM, F.M. (1981) 'Social skills training with handicapped children: a review', *Rev. Educ. Res.*, 51, 139–76.

GRIMM, J., BIJOU, S. and PARSONS, J. (1973) 'A problem-solving model for teaching remedial arithmetic to handicapped young children', *J. Abnorm. Child Psychol.*, 7, 26–39.

HALL, C., SHELDON-WILOGEN, J. and SHERMAN, J.A. (1980) 'Teaching job interview skills to retarded clients', *J. Appl. Behav. Anal.*, 13, 433–42.

HALLE, J.W., BAER, D.M. and SPRADLIN, J.E. (1981) 'Teachers' generalized use of delay as a stimulus control procedure to increase language use in handicapped children', *J. Appl. Behav. Anal.*, 14, 389–409.

HALLE, J.W., MARSHALL, A.M. and SPRADLIN, J.E. (1979) 'Time delay: a technique to increase language use and facilitate generalization in retarded children', *J. Appl. Behav. Anal.*, 12, 431–9.

HAMILTON, J., STEPHENS, L. and ALLEN, P. (1967) 'Controlling aggressive and destructive behavior in severely retarded institutionalized residents', *Amer. J. Ment. Defic.*, 71, 852–6.

HARRIS, S.L. (1975) 'Teaching language to nonverbal children – with emphasis on problems of generalization', *Psychol. Bull.*, 82, 565–80.

HARRIS, S.L. and WOLCHIK, S.A. (1979) 'Suppression of self-stimulation: three alternative strategies', *J. Appl. Behav. Anal.*, 12, 185–98.

HART, B. and RISLEY, T.R. (1980) 'In vivo language intervention: unanticipated general effects', *J. Appl. Behav. Anal.*, 13, 407–32.

HENRIKSEN, K. and DOUGHTY, R. (1967) 'Decelerating undesired mealtime behavior in a group of profoundly retarded boys', *Amer. J. Ment. Defic.*, 72, 40–4.

HERSEN, M. and BARLOW, D.H. (1976) *Single-case Experimental Designs*, New York, Pergamon Press.

HMSO (1980) *Behaviour Modification: Report of a Joint Working Party*, London, HMSO.

HOBBS, S.A. and FOREHAND, R. (1977) 'Important parameters in the use of time-out with children: a re-examination', *J. Behav. Ther. Exp. Psychiat.*, 8, 365–70.

HOGG, J. and MAIER, I. (1974) 'Transfer of operantly conditioned visual fixation in hyperactive severely retarded children', *Amer. J. Ment. Defic.*, 79, 305–10.

HOMER, A.L. and PETERSON, O. (1980) 'Differential reinforcement of other behavior: a preferred response elimination procedure', *Behav. Ther.*, 11, 449–71.

HOOVER, J.H., WADE, M.G. and NEWELL, K.M. (1981) 'Training moderately and severely mentally retarded adults to improve reaction and movement times', *Amer. J. Ment. Defic.*, 85, 389–95.

HORNER, R.D. (1980) 'The effects of an environmental "enrichment" program on the behavior of institutionalized profoundly retarded children', *J. Appl. Behav. Anal.*, 13, 473–91.

HORNER, R.D. and KEILITZ, I. (1975) 'Training mentally retarded adolescents to brush their teeth', *J. Appl. Behav. Anal.*, 8, 301–9.

HUNG, D.W., COSENTINO, A. and HENDERSON, E. (1979) 'Teaching autistic children to follow instructions in a group by a firm physical prompting procedure', *J. Behav. Ther. Exp. Psychiat.*, 10, 329.

HUSTED, J.R., HALL, P. and AGIN, B. (1971) 'The effectiveness of time-out in reducing maladaptive behavior of autistic and retarded children', *J. Psychol.*, 79, 189–96.

IVANCIC, M.T., REID, D.H., IWATA, B.W., FAW, G.D. and PAGE, T.J. (1981) 'Evaluating a supervision program for developing and maintaining therapeutic staff–resident interactions during institutional care routines', *J. Appl. Behav. Anal.*, 14, 95–107.

IWATA, B.H. and BAILEY, J.S. (1974) 'Reward versus cost token systems: an analysis of the effects on students and teachers', *J. Appl. Behav. Anal.*, 7, 567–76.

JACKSON, J.L. and CALHOUN, K.S. (1977) 'Effects of two variable-ratio schedules of time-out: changes in target and non-target behaviors', *J. Behav. Ther. Exp. Psychiat.*, 8, 195–9.

JOHNSON, B.F. and CUVO, A.J. (1981) 'Teaching mentally retarded adults to cook', *Behav. Mod.*, 5, 187–202.

JONES, F.H., SIMMONS, J.G. and FRANKEL, F. (1974) 'Case-study: an extinction procedure for eliminating self-destructive behavior in a 9-year-old autistic girl', *J. Aut. Child. Schiz.*, 4, 241–50.

JONES, R.R., VAUGHT, R.S. and WEINROTT, M. (1977) 'Time-series analysis in operant research', *J. Appl. Behav. Anal.*, 10, 151–66.

KAUFMAN, K.F. and O'LEARY, K.D. (1972) 'Reward, cost and self-evaluation procedures for disruptive adolescents in a psychiatric hospital school', *J. Appl. Behav. Anal.*, 5, 293–309.

KAZDIN, A.E. (1971) 'The effect of response cost in suppressing behavior in a prepsychotic retardate', *J. Behav. Ther. Exp. Psychiat.*, 2, 137–40.

KAZDIN, A.E. (1980a) *Behavior Modification in Applied Settings*, Homewood, Ill., Dorsey.

KAZDIN, A.E. (1980b) 'Acceptability of time-out from reinforcement procedures for disruptive child behavior', *Behav. Ther.*, 11, 329–44.

KAZDIN, A.E. (1982a) 'Symptom substitution, generalization and response covariation: implications for psychotherapy outcome', *Psychol. Bull.*, 91, 349–65.

KAZDIN, A.E. (1982b) 'The token economy: a decade later', *J. Appl. Behav. Anal.*, 15, 431–45.

KAZDIN, A.E. (1982c) *Single-case Research Designs*, New York, Oxford University Press.

KELLER, F.S. and SCHOENFELD, W.N. (1950) *Principles of Psychology*, New York, Appleton-Century-Crofts.

KELLY, J.A., FURMAN, W., PHILLIPS, J., HATHORN, S. and WILSON, T. (1979a) 'Teaching conversational skills to retarded adolescents', *Child. Behav. Ther.*, 1, 85–97.

KELLY, J.A., WILDMAN, B.G., UREY, J.R. and THURMAN, C. (1979b) 'Group skills training to increase the conversational repertoire of retarded adolescents', *Child Behav. Ther.*, 1, 323–36.

KIERNAN, C.C. (1973) 'Functional analysis', in P. MITTLER (ed.), *Assessment for Learning in the Mentally Handicapped*, London, Churchill Livingstone, 263–83.

KIERNAN, C.C. (1974) 'Behaviour modification', in A.M. CLARKE and A.D.B. CLARKE (eds), *Mental Deficiency: The Changing Outlook*, 3rd edn, London, Methuen, 729–803.

KIERNAN, C.C. (1981) 'Behaviour modification and the development of communication', in P. MITTLER (ed.), *Frontiers of Knowledge in Mental Retardation*, 1, Baltimore, University Park Press, 171–9.

KIERNAN, C.C. (1985) 'The behavioural approach to language development', in D. FONTANA (ed.), *Behaviourism and Learning Theory in Education*, Edinburgh, Scottish Academic Press, 150–69.

KIERNAN, C.C. and JONES, M.C. (1980) 'The Behaviour Assessment Battery for use with the profoundly retarded', in J. HOGG and P.J. MITTLER (eds), *Advances in Mental Handicap Research*, 1, New York, Wiley, 27–53.

KIERNAN, C.C. and JONES, M.C. (1982) *Behaviour Assessment Battery: Assessment of the Cognitive, Communicative and Self-Help Skills of Severely Handicapped Children*, 2nd edn, Windsor, NFER.

KIERNAN, C.C., WRIGHT, E.C. and HAWKS, G.D. (1975) 'The word-wide application of operant training techniques', in D.A. PRIMROSE (ed.), *Proceedings of the Third Congress of the International Association for the Scientific Study of Mental Deficiency*, vol. 1, Warsaw, Polish Medical Publishers, 233–40.

KISSEL, R.C., WHITMAN, T.L. and REID, D.H. (1983) 'An institutional staff training and self-management program for developing multiple self-care skills in severely/profoundly retarded individuals', *J. Appl. Behav. Anal.*, 16, 395–415.

KOEGEL, R.L., FIRESTONE, P.B., KRAMME, K.W. and DUNLAP, G. (1974) 'Increasing spontaneous play by suppressing self-stimulation in autistic children', *J. Appl. Behav. Anal.*, 7, 521–8.

KONARSKI, E.A., CROWELL, C.R. and DUGGAN, L.M. (1981) 'Application of the response deprivation hypothesis to improve the handwriting of EMR students', paper to the 14th Gatlinberg Conference.

KRANTZ, D.L. (1972) 'Schools and systems: the mutual isolation of operant and non-operant psychology as a case-study', *J. Hist. Behav. Sci.*, 8, 86–102.

KRATOCHWILL, T.R. (ed.) (1978) *Single Subject Research: Strategies for Evaluating Change*, New York, Academic Press.

KUSHLICK, A. (1975) 'Improving the services for the mentally handicapped', in C.C. KIERNAN and F.P. WOODFORD (eds), *Behaviour Modification with the Severely Retarded*, Amsterdam, Elsevier, 263–91.

LOVAAS, O.I., BERBERICH, J.P., PERLOFF, B.F. and SCHAEFFER, B. (1966) 'Acquisition of speech by schizophrenic children', *Science*, 151, 705–7.

LOVAAS, O.I., KOEGEL, R., SIMMONS, J.Q. and LONG, J.S. (1973) 'Some generalizations and follow-up measures on autistic children in behavior therapy', *J. Appl. Behav. Anal.*, 6, 131–65.

LOVAAS, O.I. and SIMMONS, J.W. (1969) 'Manipulation of self-destruction in three retarded children', *J. Appl. Behav. Anal.*, 2, 143–57.

LOWE, C.F. (1979) 'Determinants of human operant behavior', in M.D. ZEILER and P. HARZEM (eds), *Reinforcement and Organization of Behavior*, Chichester, Wiley, 159–92.

LOWE, C.F. (1983) 'Radical behaviourism and human psychology', in G.C.L. DAVEY (ed.), *Animal Models of Human Behavior*, New York, Wiley, 71–93.

LUISELLI, J.K., POLLOW, R.S., COLOZZI, G.A. and TEITELBAUM, M. (1981) 'Application of differential reinforcement to control disruptive behaviours of mentally retarded students during remedial instruction', *J. Ment. Defic. Res.*, 25, 265–73.

LUTZKER, J.R. (1978) 'Reducing self-injurious behavior in three classrooms by facial screening', *Amer. J. Ment. Defic.*, 82, 510–13.

LUTZKER, J.R., MCGIMSEY-MCRAE, S. and MCGIMSEY, J.F. (1983) 'General description of behavioral approaches', in M. HERSEN, V.B. VAN HASSELT and J.L. MATSON (eds), *Behavior Therapy for the Developmentally and Physically Disabled*, New York, Academic Press, 25–56.

MCBRIEN, J. and FOXEN, T. (1981) *Training Staff in Behavioural Methods: Instructor's Handbook*, Manchester, Manchester University Press.

MCCLANNAHAN, L.E. and RISLEY, T.R. (1975) 'Design of living environments for nursing home residents: increasing participation in recreational activities', *J. Appl. Behav. Anal.*, 8, 261–8.

MCGONIGLE, J.J., DUNCAN, D., CORDISCO, L. and BARRETT, R.P. (1982) 'Visual screening: an alternative method for reducing stereotyped behaviors', *J. Appl. Behav. Anal.*, 15, 461–7.

MAIER, I. and HOGG, J. (1974) 'Operant conditioning of sustained visual fixation in hyperactive severely retarded children', *Amer. J. Ment. Defic.*, 79, 696–701.

MANSELL, J., FELCE, D., DEKOCK, U. and JENKINS, J. (1982) 'Increasing purposeful activity of severely and profoundly mentally handicapped adults', *Behav. Res. Ther.*, 20, 593–604.

MARHOLIN, D., LUISELLI, J.K., ROBINSON, M. and LOTT, I.T. (1980) 'Response-contingent taste-aversion in treating chronic ruminative vomiting of institutionalized retarded children', *J. Ment. Defic. Res.*, 24, 47–56.

MARTIN, G.L., KEHOE, B., BIRD, E., JENSEN, V. and DARBYSHIRE, M. (1971) 'Operant conditioning in dressing behavior of severely retarded girls', *Ment. Retard.*, 9 (3), 27–31.

MARTIN, P.L. and FOXX, R.M. (1973) 'Victim control of the aggression of an institutionalized retardate', *J. Behav. Ther. Exp. Psychiat.*, 4, 161–5.

MATSON, J.L. (1980) 'A controlled group study of pedestrian skill training for the mentally retarded', *Behav. Res. Ther.*, 18, 99–106.

MATSON, J.L. (1981) 'A controlled outcome study of phobias in mentally retarded adults', *Behav. Res. Ther.*, 19, 101–7.

MATSON, J.L. (1982a) 'Independence training *v.* modeling procedures for teaching phone conversation skills to the mentally retarded', *Behav. Res. Ther.*, 20, 505–11.

MATSON, J.L. (1982b) 'The treatment of behavioural characteristics of depression in the mentally retarded', *Behav. Ther.*, 13, 209–18.

MATSON, J.L., KAZDIN, A.E. and ESVELDT-DAWSON, K. (1980a) 'Training interpersonal skills among mentally retarded and socially dysfunctional children', *Behav. Res. Ther.*, 18, 419–27.

MATSON, J.L. and MCCARTHY, J.R. (eds) (1981) *Handbook of Behavior Modification with the Mentally Retarded*, New York, Plenum Press.

MATSON, J.L., OLLENDICK, T.H. and ADKINS, J. (1980b) 'A comprehensive dining program for mentally retarded adults', *Behav. Res. Ther.*, 18, 107–12.

MEASEL, J. and ALFIERI, P.A. (1976) 'Treatment of self-injurious behavior by a combination of reinforcement for incompatible behavior and over-correction', *Amer. J. Ment. Defic.*, 81, 147–53.

MURPHY, G. (1978) 'Overcorrection: a critique', *J. Ment. Defic. Res.*, 22, 161–74.

MURPHY, G.D. (1980) 'Decreasing undesirable behaviours', in W. YULE and J. CARR (eds), *Behaviour Modification for the Severely Handicapped*, London, Croom Helm, 80–115.

MYERS, D.V. (1975) 'Extinction, DRO and response-cost procedures for eliminating self-injurious behaviors: a case study', *Behav. Res. Ther.*, 13, 189–91.

NELSON, R.O., GIBSON, F. and CUTTING, D.S. (1973) 'Video taped modeling: the development of three appropriate social responses in a mildly retarded child', *Ment. Retard.*, 11 (2), 24–8.

NELSON, R.O., PEOPLES, A., HAY, L.R., JOHNSON, T. and HAY, W. (1976) 'The effectiveness of speech training techniques based on operant conditioning: a comparison of two methods', *Ment. Retard.*, 14 (3), 34–8.

O'LEARY, K.D. (1984) 'The image of behavior therapy: it is time to take a stand', *Behav. Ther.*, 15, 219–34.

OLLENDICK, T.H. and MATSON, J.L. (1976) 'An initial investigation into the parameters of overcorrection', *Psychol. Rep.*, 39, 1139–42.

PAGE, T.J., IWATA, B.A. and REID, D.H. (1982) 'Pyramidal training: a large-scale application with institutional staff', *J. Appl. Behav. Anal.*, 15, 335–51.

PANYAN, M., BOOZER, H. and MORRIS, N. (1970) 'Feedback to attendants as a reinforcer for applying operant techniques', *J. Appl. Behav. Anal.*, 3, 1–4.

PHILLIPS, E.L. (1968) 'Achievement place: token reinforcement procedures in a home-style rehabilitation setting for "predelinquent" boys', *J. Appl. Behav. Anal.*, 1, 213–23.

POLVINALE, R.A. and LUTZKER, J.R. (1980) 'Elimination of assaultive and inappropriate sexual behavior by reinforcement and social restitution', *Ment. Retard.*, 18, 27–30.

PREMACK, D. (1959) 'Toward empirical behavior laws: 1. Positive reinforcement', *Psychol. Rev.*, 66, 219–33.

RAPOFF, M.A., ALTMAN, K. and CHRISTOPHERSEN, E.R. (1980) 'Elimination of a blind child's self-hitting by response-contingent brief constraint', *Educ. Treat. Child.*, 3, 231–6.

REDD, W.H. (1969) 'Effects of mixed reinforcement contingencies on adult's control of children's behavior', *J. Appl. Behav. Anal.*, 2, 249–54.

REPP, A.C., BARTON, L.E. and BRULLE, A.R. (1983) 'A comparison of two procedures for programming the differential reinforcement of other behaviors', *J. Appl. Behav. Anal.*, 16, 435–45.

REPP, A.C. and DEITZ, S.M. (1974) 'Reducing aggressive and self-injurious behavior of institutionalized retarded children through reinforcement of other behaviors', *J. Appl. Behav. Anal.*, 7, 313–25.

REPP, A.C., DEITZ, S.M. and SPEIR, N.C. (1975) 'Reducing stereotypic responding of retarded persons through the differential reinforcement of other behavior', *Amer. J. Ment. Defic.*, 79, 279–84.

REYNOLDS, G.S. (1961) 'Behavioral contrast', *J. Exp. Anal. Behav.*, 4, 57–71.

RICHARDS, B.W. (1975) 'Editorial: the ethics of aversion therapy', *J. Ment. Defic. Res.*, 19, 1–2.

RICHMAN, J.S., SONDERBY, T. and KAHN, J. (1980) 'Prerequisite *v.* in vivo acquisition of self-feeding skill', *Behav. Res. Ther.*, 18, 327–32.

RISLEY, T.R. (1968) 'Effects and side effects of punishing autistic behaviors of an autistic child', *J. Appl. Behav. Anal.*, 1, 21–34.

RISLEY, T.R. and CUVO, A. (1980) 'Training mentally retarded adults to make emergency telephone calls', *Behav. Mod.*, 4, 513–26.

RISLEY, T.R. and FAVELL, J. (1979) 'Constructing a living environment in an institution', in L. HAMMERLYNCK (ed.), *Behavioral Systems for the Developmentally Disabled: Institutional, Clinic and Community Environments*, New York, Brunner/Mazel.

ROBSON, C. (1981) *Language Development through Structured Teaching*, Cardiff, Drake Educational Associates.

ROLLINGS, J.P., BAUMEISTER, A. and BAUMEISTER, A. (1977) 'The use of overcorrection procedures to eliminate stereotyped behaviors in retarded individuals', *Behav. Mod.*, 1, 29–46.

RUSCH, F.R. and KAZDIN, A.E. (1981) 'Toward a methodology of withdrawal designs for the assessment of response maintenance', *J. Appl. Behav. Anal.*, 14, 131–40.

SAJWAJ, T., LIBET, J. and AGRAS, S. (1974) 'Lemon juice therapy: the control of life-threatening rumination in a six-month old infant', *J. Appl. Behav. Anal.*, 7, 557–63.

SAJWAJ, T.E., TWARDOSZ, S. and BURKE, M. (1972) 'Side effects of extinction procedures in a remedial pre-school', *J. Appl. Behav. Anal.*, 5, 163–76.

SALEND, S.J. and KOVALICH, B. (1981) 'A group response-cost system mediated by free tokens: an alternative to token reinforcement', *Amer. J. Ment. Defic.*, 86, 184–7.

SALZBERG, B. and NAPOLITAN, J. (1974) 'Holding a retarded boy at a table for two minutes to reduce inappropriate object contact', *Amer. J. Ment. Defic.*, 78, 748–51.

SCHEPIS, M.M., REID, D.H., FITZGERALD, J.R., FAW, G.D., VAN DEN POL, R.A. and WELTY, P.A. (1982) 'A program for increasing manual signing by autistic and profoundly retarded youth within the daily environment', *J. Appl. Behav. Anal.*, 15, 363–79.

SCHLEIEN, S.J., ASH, T., KIERNAN, J. and WEHMAN, P. (1981) 'Developing independent cooking skills in a profoundly retarded woman', *J. Assoc. Sev. Hand.*, 6, 23–9.

SCHROEDER, S.R. (1972) 'Parametric effects of reinforcement frequency, amount of reinforcement, and required response force on sheltered workshop behavior', *J. Appl. Behav. Anal.*, 5, 431–42.

SCHROEDER, S.R., MULICK, J.A. and SCHROEDER, C.S. (1979) 'Management of severe behavior problems of the retarded', in N.R. ELLIS (ed.), *Handbook of Mental Deficiency, Psychological Theory and Research*, Hillsdale, Lawrence Erlbaum, 341–66.

SHEARER, M.S. and SHEARER, D.E. (1972) 'The Portage Project: a model for early childhood education', *Excep. Child.*, 39, 210–17.

SINGH, N.N. (1979) 'Aversive control of breath-holding', *J. Behav. Ther. Exp. Psychiat.*, 10, 147.

SINGH, N.N., DAWSON, M.J. and GREGORY, P.R. (1980) 'Self-injury in the profoundly retarded: clinically significant versus therapeutic control', *J. Ment. Defic. Res.*, 24, 87–97.

SINGH, N.N., DAWSON, M.J. and MANNING, P.J. (1981a) 'The effects of physical restraint on self-injurious behavior', *J. Ment. Defic. Res.*, 25, 207–16.

SINGH, N.N., DAWSON, M.J. and MANNING, P.J. (1981b) 'Effects of spaced responding DRL on the stereotyped behavior of profoundly retarded persons', *J. Appl. Behav. Anal.*, 14, 521–6

SINGH, N.N., MANNING, P.J. and ANGELL, M.J. (1982a) 'Effects of an oral hygiene punishment procedure on chronic rumination and collateral behaviors in monozygotic twins', *J. Appl. Behav. Anal.*, 15, 309–14.

SINGH, N.N., WINTON, A.S. and DAWSON, M.J. (1982b) 'Suppression of antisocial behavior by facial screening using multiple baseline and alternating treatment designs', *Behav. Ther.*, 13, 511–20.

SKINNER, B.F. (1938) *The Behaviour of Organisms*, New York, Appleton-Century-Crofts.

SKINNER, B.F. (1950) 'Are theories of learning necessary?', *Psychol. Rev.*, 57, 193–226.

SKINNER, B.F. (1953) *Science and Human Behavior*, New York, Macmillan.

SKINNER, B.F. (1957) *Verbal Behavior*, New York, Appleton-Century-Crofts.

SMITH, L.J. (1981) 'Training severely and profoundly mentally handicapped nocturnal enuretics', *Behav. Res. Ther.*, 19, 67–74.

SMITH, P.S. (1979) 'A comparison of different methods of toilet training the mentally handicapped', *Behav. Res. Ther.*, 17, 33–43.

SMITH, P.S., BRITTON, P.G., JOHNSON, M. and THOMAS, D.A. (1975) 'Problems involved in toilet training profoundly mentally handicapped adults', *Behav. Res. Ther.*, 13, 301–7.

SOLNICK, J.V., RINCOVER, A. and PETERSON, C.R. (1977) 'Some determinants of reinforcing and punishing effects of timeout', *J. Appl. Behav. Anal.*, 10, 415–24.

SOLOMON, R.L. (1964) 'Punishment', *Amer. Psychol.*, 19, 237–53.

SONG, A.Y., SONG, R.H. and GRANT, P.A. (1976) 'Toilet training in the school and its transfer in the living unit', *J. Behav. Ther. Exp. Psychiat.*, 7, 281–4.

SPANGLER, P.R. and MARSHALL, A.M. (1983) 'The unit play manager as facilitator of purposeful activities among institutionalized profoundly and severely retarded boys', *J. Appl. Behav. Anal.*, 16, 345–9.

SPRADLIN, J.E. and GIRADEAU, F.L. (1966) 'The behavior of moderately and severely retarded persons', in N.R. ELLIS (ed.), *International Review of Research in Mental Retardation*, 1, New York, Academic Press.

SPRADLIN, J.E., KARLAN, G.R. and WETHERBY, B. (1976) 'Behavior analysis, behavior modification, and developmental disabilities', in L.L. LLOYD (ed.), *Communication, Assessment and Intervention Strategies*, Baltimore, University Park Press, 225–63.

STIMBERT, V.E., MINOR, J.W. and MCCOY, J.F. (1977) 'Intensive feeding training with retarded children', *Behav. Mod.*, 1, 517–29.

STOKES, T.F. and BAER, D.M. (1977) 'An implicit technology of generalization', *J. Appl. Behav. Anal.*, 10, 349–67.

STREIFEL, J.S. and PHELAN, J.G. (1972) 'Use of reinforcement of behavioral similarity to establish imitative behavior in young mentally retarded children', *Amer. J. Ment. Defic.*, 77, 239–41.

STRIEFEL, S., WETHERBY, B. and KARLAN, G.R. (1976) 'Establishing generalized verb–noun instruction-following skills in retarded children', *J. Exp. Child Psychol.*, 22, 247–60.

TANNER, B.A. and ZEILER, M. (1975) 'Punishment of self-injurious behavior using aromatic ammonia as the aversive stimulus', *J. Appl. Behav. Anal.*, 8, 53–8.

TARPLEY, H.D. and SCHROEDER, S.R. (1979) 'Comparison of DRO and DRI and rate of suppression of self-injurious behavior', *Amer. J. Ment. Defic.*, 84, 188–94.

TATE, B.G. and BAROFF, G.S. (1966) 'Aversive control of self-injurious behavior in a psychotic boy', *Behav. Res. Ther.*, 4, 281–7.

THINESEN, P.J. and BRYAN, A.J. (1981) 'The use of sequential pictorial cues in the initiation and maintenance of grooming behaviors with mentally retarded adults', *Ment. Retard.*, 19, 247–50.

TREFFRY, D., MARTIN, G., SAMELS, J. and WATSON, C. (1970) 'Operant conditioning of grooming behavior of severely retarded girls', *Ment. Retard.*, 8, 29–33.

TURNER, S.M., CALHOUN, K.S. and ADAMS, H.E. (eds) (1981) *Handbook of Clinical Behavior Therapy*, New York, Wiley.

TYLER, V.O. and BROWN, G.D. (1967) 'The use of swift, brief isolation as a group control device', *Behav. Res. Ther.*, 5, 1–9.

VAN DEN POL, R.A., IWATA, B.A., IVANCIC, M.T., PAGE, T.M., NEEF, N.A. and WHITLEY, P. (1981) 'Teaching the handicapped to eat in public places: acquisition, generalization and maintenance of restaurant skills', *J. Appl. Behav. Anal.*, 14, 61–9.

VAN WAGENEN, R.K., MEYERSON, L., KERR, N.J. and MAHONEY, K. (1969) 'Field trials of a new procedure for toilet training', *J. Exp. Child Psychol.*, 8, 147–59.

WAHLER, R.G. (1975) 'Some structural aspects of deviant child behavior', *J. Appl. Behav. Anal.*, 8, 27–42.

WALLS, R.T., SIENICKI, D.A. and CRIST, K. (1981) 'Operations training in vocational skills', *Amer. J. Ment. Defic.*, 85, 357–67.

WATSON, R.I. (1962) The experimental tradition and clinical psychology', in A.J. BACHRACH (ed.), *Experimental Foundations of Clinical Psychology*, New York, Basic Books.

WEBSTER, O.R. and AZRIN, N.H. (1973) 'Required relaxation: a method of inhibiting agitative-disruptive behavior of retardates', *Behav. Res. Ther.*, 11, 67–78.

WEHMAN, P. (1974) 'Maintaining oral hygiene skills in geriatric retarded women', *Ment. Retard.*, 12 (4), 20.

WELLS, K.C., FOREHAND, R. and HICKEY, K. (1977a) 'Effects of a verbal warning and overcorrection on stereotyped and appropriate behaviors', *J. Abnorm. Child Psychol.*, 5, 387–403.

WELLS, K.C., FOREHAND, R., HICKEY, K. and GREEN, K.D. (1977b)

'Effects of a procedure derived from the overcorrection principle on manipulated and nonmanipulated behaviors', *J. Appl. Behav. Anal.*, 10, 679–87.

WESOLOWSKI, M.D. and ZAWLOCKI, R.J. (1982) 'The differential effects of procedures to eliminate an injurious self-stimulatory behavior (digito-ocular sign) in blind retarded twins', *Behav. Ther.*, 13, 334–45.

WETHERBY, B. (1978) 'Miniature languages and the functional analysis of verbal behavior', in R.L. SCHIEFELBUSCH (ed.), *Bases of Language Intervention*, Baltimore, University Park Press, 397–448.

WHITMAN, T.L., CAPONIGRI, Y. and MERCURIO, J. (1971a) 'Reducing hyperactive behavior in a severely retarded child', *Ment. Retard.*, 9 (3), 17–19.

WHITMAN, T.L., MERCURIO, J.R. and CAPONIGRI, V. (1970) 'Development of social responses in two severely retarded children', *J. Appl. Behav. Anal.*, 3, 133–8.

WHITMAN, T.L., ZAKARAS, M. and CHARDOS, S. (1971b) 'Effects of reinforcement and guidance procedures on instruction-following behavior of severely retarded children', *J. Appl. Behav. Anal.*, 4, 283–90.

WILLIAMS, L., MARTIN, G.L., MCDONALD, S., HARDY, L. and LAMBERT, S.L. (1975) 'Effects of a backscratch contingency on reinforcement for table serving or social interaction with severely retarded girls', *Behav. Ther.*, 6, 220–9.

WOLF, M.M. (1978) 'Social validity: the case for subjective measurement', *J. Appl. Behav. Anal.*, 11, 203–14.

WUNDERLICH, R.A. (1972) 'Programmed instruction: teaching coinage to retarded children', *Ment. Retard.*, 10 (5), 21–3.

YOUNG, J.A. and WINCZE, J.P. (1974) 'The effects of the reinforcement of compatible and incompatible alternative behaviors on the self-injurious and related behaviors of a profoundly retarded female adult', *Behav. Ther.*, 5, 614–23.

YULE, W. and CARR, J. (eds) (1980) *Behaviour Modification for the Mentally Handicapped*, London, Croom Helm.

ZEGIOB, L.E., JENKINS, J., BECKER, J. and BRISTOW, A. (1976) 'Facial screening: effects on appropriate and inappropriate behaviors', *J. Behav. Ther. Exp. Psychiat.*, 7, 355–7.

14

The effect on the family of a severely mentally handicapped child

Janet Carr

INTRODUCTION

Over the past quarter of a century a wealth of data has accumulated showing that severely mentally handicapped children brought up in their own homes are more forward in their development than are those reared in institutions (Tizard, 1962; Lyle, 1960; Centerwall and Centerwall, 1960; Stedman and Eichorn, 1964; Shipe and Shotwell, 1965; Bayley *et al.*, 1966; Carr, 1975). Partly as a result, there has been increased pressure on parents to keep their mentally handicapped child at home, and the question arises as to what effect this may have on the child's family, and in particular on the parents and siblings.

Wolfensberger (1967) pointed out that to read the literature of the previous twenty years was hardly to be aware that parents existed: 'Very little mention was made of parents, of their feelings and sensibilities, or of the impact of the diagnosis on them.' This was followed in the mid-1940s–1950s by a 'trickle' and later 'almost a flood . . . of armchair papers', discussing parent dynamics. Later studies became more research-oriented, while currently the emphasis has shifted towards studies of the effect on families of programmes enabling them to teach and help their own children, and of changing patterns of services.

Socioeconomic factors

In contrast with the families of the mildly retarded, who have been found predominantly in working-class populations (Stein and Susser, 1960; Saenger, 1962; Rutter *et al.*, 1970), families of the severely mentally handicapped are 'evenly distributed among all the social strata in society' (Kushlick, 1966).

In the study by Tizard and Grad (1961), families with a severely mentally handicapped child at home were significantly worse off in terms of housing and income than were those with such a child in an institution. Twice as many in the 'home' group were judged to be overcrowded (40 per cent, compared with 20 per cent of the 'institution' group), and poor (25 per cent, compared with 13 per cent). However, in each case the differences between the two groups disappeared if the variables were recalculated for the institution group as if the retarded child were at home. The differences seemed to be due entirely to the fact that the 'institution' families were one member short, so that available resources such as living space and income could be spread more generously among the remaining members. In a more recent study of 120 families, there were no consistent differences in living standards between those who were and were not seeking long-term care for a mentally handicapped child (Wilkin, 1979).

THE EFFECT ON THE FAMILY

How the parents were told

Initial counselling is generally regarded, by parents as well as professionals, as of crucial importance. Raech (1966), himself the father of a mentally handicapped child, writes:

> Of particular importance, in my view, is the *initial* counselling experience. Usually this is given by a medical person untrained for the task. Yet, this interview is likely to be the source of the parents' greatest single emotional trauma in what is commonly a life-long struggle. Since this is true, it is important that the experience be handled as skillfully as possible. ... I submit that, in many cases, being told that one's child is retarded may well be the most severe shock that one may experience in a normal lifetime full of trying experiences.

Perhaps the three major aspects of this initial interview are its timing, what is told and how it is told. Since many forms of mental handicap do not become apparent at any particular period of the child's life, the timing of the interview and the parents' reactions to this are best studied in relation to Down's syndrome children, whose handicap is discoverable at birth. Table 14.1 summarizes the data on time of telling from eight studies. It should be noted that the method of enquiry in these varied somewhat: most were by personal interviews, but one was by telephone interview (Springer and Steele, 1980) and one by postal questionnaire with an 81 per cent response rate (Pueschel and Murphy, 1976).

Of those told by one month, 78 per cent in Drillien and Wilkinson's (1964) study and 68 per cent in Carr's (1970) study were satisfied with the telling compared with one-third of those who were told later. Of those told early who were dissatisfied, most felt that they should have been informed earlier still ('When I asked'). In more recent studies about half were dissatisfied with the way they were told, the most common complaint being that they should have been told sooner (Pueschel and Murphy, 1976; Gath, 1978; Reynolds, 1979). It is, then, reassuring that the trend shown in Table 14.1 is towards earlier telling, while in some obstetric departments a delay of even four days is now thought unacceptable and the policy is to inform mothers, of babies with any

TABLE 14.1   Time of breaking the news to mothers of babies with Down's syndrome

Authors	Publication date	N	Child's age at enquiry	Told by 1 week %	Told by 1 month %	Told by 1 year %
Tizard and Grad	1961	80	<45 years	–	–	55
Drillien and Wilkinson	1964	70	<14 years	22.5[1]	25	72
Carr	1970	46	< 2 years	41	60	96
Pueschel and Murphy	1976	414	<19 years	55	64	90
Reynolds	1979	79	<17 years	53[2]	–	90
Springer and Steele	1980	37	< 4 years	70	–	100[3]
Berry *et al.*	1981	31	< 2 months	84	–	–
Murdoch	1983	123	<10 years	88	93	–

Notes: 1 = by 10 days.
        2 = 'at birth'.
        3 = by 6 months.

disability, as soon as possible within the first twenty-four hours (Dr Elaine Lynch, personal communication).

If parents want to be told of their child's condition early, they also want to hear the truth. 'The truth must be expressed. No purpose can possibly be served by concealing the truth, and indeed a great deal of damage may be done in not stating the facts clearly yet gently' (Raech, 1966). 'The fact that it was hidden did us more harm than the fact of her condition' (Carr, 1970). Other studies, too, have noted the bitterness that mothers experience when they feel that they have been fobbed off with reassurances, or that information that they urgently asked for was withheld, or that they were told lies (Tizard and Grad, 1961; Drillien and Wilkinson, 1964; Hutton, 1966; Lonsdale, 1978).

Much has been made of the question of who should tell the parents, especially in relation to the view that they will feel resentful towards the doctor who breaks the news (Cowie, 1966; Pueschel and Murphy, 1976), but these fears seem unfounded (Drillien and Wilkinson, 1964). Half the parents in Carr's (1970) study said they would be glad to see the teller again to discuss the baby and only four mothers (9 per cent) seemed antagonistic towards the person who informed them. Some parents were concerned when the news was not given to them by the obstetrician, but by a paediatrician who was 'a complete stranger' (Pueschel and Murphy, 1976; Reynolds, 1979; Berry *et al.*, 1981). Of far greater importance than who does the telling is how it is done. All studies agree that the informant should take trouble and, if need be, time over the telling, be sympathetic towards the parents and answer their questions fully. Resentment arises when the teller seems unfeeling (worse still, facetious – cf. Tizard and Grad, 1961) or informs the parents briefly or abruptly – what Raech calls the 'get-it-over-with' school. Where prognosis is concerned, doctors are often warned against over-optimism and raising false hopes, but in many cases it seems that they have gone too far in the opposite direction and have been unnecessarily discouraging, with parents being given the impression that their child would never walk, talk, feed himself or become toilet-trained (Tizard and Grad, 1961; Raech, 1966; Berg *et al.*, 1969; Berry *et al.*, 1981). To engender such feelings of hopelessness is probably at least as unkind as it is to overestimate the child's future potential. A more appropriate approach would be to indicate to the parents that, for their baby as for all newborn babies, his future development cannot be precisely predicted; and, where this is known, as in Down's syndrome, to outline the range of developmental levels with an emphasis on the possibilities of positive achievement such as in walking, speaking, toilet-training, and so on.

Family adjustment

While there undoubtedly are families who suffer from the strain of caring for a mentally handicapped child (Holt, 1958a), most studies suggest that the majority are not seriously impaired and cope well with the problems they meet (Schipper, 1959; Caldwell and Guze, 1960; Cleveland and Miller, 1977; Dunlap and Hollinsworth, 1977; Gath, 1978), and 'the great majority of parents wish to keep their mentally subnormal children at home' (Tizard and Grad, 1961). Reynolds (1979) points out that 'This impression is perhaps contrary to that which is gained by clinicians working in the field', and feels this may be because they see families who have problems while 'the coping family generally does not attract attention' – a point made previously (Carr, 1976).

Effect on the marriage

Several studies have investigated the effect of a mentally handicapped child on the relationship between the parents. Tizard and Grad (1961) found a higher proportion of families with a child at home to have good relationships compared with the institution sample (62 per cent as against 42 per cent); and fewer to be disturbed (3 per cent as against 13 per cent). They concluded that it was not possible to show that keeping a retarded child at home had an adverse effect on family life but that, on the contrary, the better-adjusted families seemed better able to cope with the problems of an abnormal child. Farber (1959), in a much quoted study, suggested that mentally handicapped boys living at home affected 'marital integration', especially in lower-class families, more than did girls, and his effect increased as the boys grew older. However, these results were not confirmed (Fowle, 1968) and Farber's study has been criticized on methodological grounds (Wolfensberger, 1967). Nihira *et al.* (1980) found that where there was marital disharmony families were more likely to report feeling affected by the mentally handicapped child, but which was cause and which effect could not be determined. In the small number of cases where parents volunteered their views, just over half indicated adverse effects on the marriage (Lloyd-Bostock, 1976; Dunlap and Hollinsworth, 1977; Lonsdale, 1978). In other studies of parents with or without a handicapped child, indices of marital satisfaction were lower where the child was handicapped (Friedrich and Friedrich, 1981) or showed no significant differences (Waisbren, 1980). The former study was based on a postal survey with only a two-thirds response rate, and this may have had unknown effects on the validity of the results. Another difference between the two studies was in the age of the handicapped child, being $9\frac{1}{2}$ years and less than 18 months, respectively, and it may be that more harmful effects are seen with an older child. In a study of families of $2\frac{1}{2}$-year-olds, the marriage was more likely to be rated as poor where there was a Down's syndrome rather than a normal baby, but equal numbers of marriages were rated as good (Gath, 1978).

Effect on parents' reactions to the child

Many early writers took it as self-evident that parents of mentally handicapped children would feel guilty, reject their children, and/or overprotect them (Wardell, 1947; Holt, 1958a). Walker (1949) writes:

> Probably every woman bearing a defective child develops some sense of guilt . . . [which may] be very openly expressed by such statements as the child is 'her cross to bear' . . . [or] projected towards the institution in a spirit of fault-finding solicitation for the patient's welfare, or shown by an overt attempt to make up to the child by frequent visitations.

It is difficult to imagine how any woman who did not feel guilty could demonstrate the fact.

Hutchison (1966) and Illingworth (1966) speak of 'pathological attachment' of the mother as a source of damage to the family, but Wright (1960) believes that in some cases overprotection may be the result of real love and concern for the child, and advises parents to do whatever they feel will benefit their child, as no matter what they do they will be criticized; this seems realistic advice.

Other writers consider that 'the general tendency to characterize parents of handicapped children as guilt-ridden, anxiety-laden, overprotective and rejecting beings' is unfortunate. While it is true that such cases exist, 'the majority of parents are unduly stigmatized by this generalization' (Barsch, 1968). In Saenger's (1962) study, with the exception of a few cases of severe rejection, the proportion of devoted and affectionate parents was equal among those with the child at home or in an institution. Roith (1963) sent questionnaires to 120 mothers of mentally handicapped patients in Monyhull Hospital, and received a 60 per cent response rate; 94 per cent of these said that they did not feel guilty or that they had somehow brought the child's condition about. Despite the low response rate to the questionnaire, the figures show that even if all the nonresponders had felt guilty there would still have been a majority who said that they did not. Roith points to the frequent use of the words 'guilt', 'shame' and 'hostility' in articles, and feels that their usage in relation to parents of handicapped children is copied from one textbook to another, commenting: 'no matter what the parents did, they were construed as guilty'.

Wolfensberger (1967) takes a novel approach to the role of guilt, suggesting that it may be beneficial. Perhaps a little guilt may go a long way in motivating a parent to provide the extra attention, effort and even love a retarded child may need. Perhaps it may prevent premature institutional placement, thus serving the welfare of the child, society and even the family, and instead of being alleviated, some parents may need to be helped to a realistic and manageable amount of it.

Although this begs the question of whether guilt has a distorting effect on the person's actions and emotions and so might undermine their value to the object of them, there is no denying that this is a refreshing view of the place of guilt in parents of the mentally handicapped. On the whole, however, the reported studies of the subject are unsatisfactory. On the one hand, there are a number of intuitive, subjective reports which infer from a wide variety of parental behaviour, or even from armchair reasoning, the guilt parents must feel. On the other, there are a few studies where parents have been asked point-blank whether they feel guilty and have said they did not. Until a more objective assessment instrument becomes available perhaps we should be less hasty in ascribing guilt to the parents or in invoking it to explain their behaviour, and indeed such concerns are seldom found in the contemporary literature.

Social restriction

Social isolation is often thought to be part of the penalty parents must suffer for having a handicapped child. Lonsdale (1978) writes of 'many' families feeling socially restricted and 'several' isolated, but gives no figures. Lloyd-Bostock (1976) writes that 'Almost all the parents caring for a child at home reported that they had little or no social life.' This study, however, is based on results of a postal questionnaire with only a 24 per cent response rate and a strong bias among those who did respond towards the middle class (only two respondents were manual workers), so the findings cannot be regarded as representative. Wilkin (1979) interviewed 120 mothers of severely mentally handicapped children aged 2–16, over half of whom (58 per cent) said they would like to go out more in the evenings. Carr (1975) reported that although mothers of Down's syndrome children went out significantly less than did mothers of normal children, this was to some extent due to the difference in age between the two groups of mothers, and an equal proportion in each group (about two-thirds) felt they went out as much as they wished.

No differences were found regarding holidays: 92 per cent of parents of Down's syndrome and 85 per cent of control children had had at least one holiday during the four years of the child's lifetime. Only 21 per cent of the mothers in this and in Hewett's (1970) study said that having a handicapped child had made them lonely. In a later study, Reynolds (1979) interviewed 80 families of mentally handicapped children under 16, of whom just under one-third felt that the child had restricted their ability to visit friends and relatives, and 14 per cent that they had lost friends because of the child; but over half (like the quarter in Carr's survey) felt they had gained friends because of the mentally handicapped child.

In general, then, in these and other studies (Schipper, 1959; Barsch, 1968; Dunlap and Hollinsworth, 1977; Waisbren, 1980) most families did not feel isolated on account of the child. Tizard and Grad found families with the child at home to be significantly more isolated than those where the child was institutionalized. Since the subjects in this research were older (two-fifths were over sixteen, compared with none in the Schipper, Barsch and Waisbren studies) this problem may increase with age; alternatively the situation for the family may have improved over the years. Comparison of two earlier studies – Tizard and Grad, and Holt – with those of Hewett and of Carr suggests that families nowadays feel that handicapped children are more accepted and understood by the general public than they were; 74 per cent of Holt's families found their neighbours objectionable or reserved, compared with the 45 per cent of families of Down's syndrome and 18 per cent of cerebral palsied children who received little support from friends and neighbours. Tizard and Grad say: 'There were few families who did not comment on the sense of humiliation they felt, or had felt on occasion in the past, when strangers stared at their child, or made comments.' Similar remarks were relatively rarely encountered in the studies of Hewett and Carr, and over 70 per cent of the mothers in each said they welcomed the interest of strangers when they took the child out. As Hewett says, 'Genuine, sensible, and nonadvisory approaches are likely to be welcome. Tactless comment and gratuitous advice are not.' Although some mothers disliked 'noseyness' and 'remarks', most were glad of a friendly interested attitude from strangers. It seems that there has been some real and welcome progress in public attitudes to handicapped children which may do much to help their parents.

Genetic counselling and family limitation

Much has been written about the need for genetic counselling for parents of handicapped children (Illingworth, 1966; Hutchison, 1966; see also Chapter 11), but, as in other areas, awareness of need may outstrip the provision made for it. Only one-third of the mothers in Tizard and Grad's (1961) study had had medical advice about the risks to further children; 45 per cent of the mothers in Hewett's (1970) and in Carr's (1975) studies had discussed with a doctor the question of future children. In a study of almost 433 children with major disorders which usually lead to genetic referral, only 1.5 per cent of the case-notes showed that genetic counselling had been considered, offered or given (Riccardi, 1981). Since that research was hospital-based it was unknown whether home-based doctors might have provided genetic counselling; but in a second investigation of 100 children with serious genetic disorders at least 60 per cent had had no genetic counselling either within or outside the hospital (Riccardi, 1981).

Amniocentesis and the consequent possibility of elective abortion offer another approach by which mothers can avoid giving birth to certain handicapped babies. The proportion of pregnant women aged forty or more who were referred for prenatal diagnosis has been steadily rising, reaching almost 50 per cent in 1977 in some places (Alberman *et al.*, 1979). Other data suggest that although the antenatal detection programme is important, the availability of abortion on demand has an even greater effect in limiting the birth of Down's syndrome babies to older women (Luthy *et al.*, 1980).

Some writers believe that parents have tended to limit their families after the birth of a mentally handicapped child (Holt, 1958b; Tips *et al.*, 1963). Holt found that nearly two-thirds of the mothers did not want more children and estimated that further pregnancies in this group were reduced by 21 per cent, but as age and parity of the mother appear not to have been taken into account the validity of this estimate is uncertain. On the other hand, Fraser and Latour (1968), comparing the reproductive history of mothers, aunts and aunts-in-law of Down's syndrome children (N = 45) and of children with cleft lip and palate (N = 62) and with hay fever (N = 104), found a decline in birth rate which began well before the birth of the index child and which was similar for the three groups. The authors conclude that the decline in the birth rate following the birth of an affected child is largely due to the normal decline in fertility with advancing age, and that there is little reason to think that relatives of affected children will be discouraged from having babies. Similar results were obtained by Sigler *et al.* (1967), who studied 216 mothers of Down's syndrome and of normal children, matched for sex, race, place of birth and age of mother. No differences were found between the groups in the number of pregnancies either before or after the birth of the index child.

It seems, then, that the proportion of mothers receiving genetic counselling is increasing, and that although some parents may be deterred by the birth of a handicapped child from adding to their families, this effect may not be as great as has been suggested.

Parental stress

Studies have been made of parents' reactions to having a handicapped child, and the stages that most go through – including shock, denial and adaptation –

have been described (Drotar *et al.*, 1975). More recently, attention has turned to the difficulties of living with and caring for a handicapped child, and how this affects the parents. Dupont (1980) found that in a population sample of thirty-nine severely mentally handicapped children the families were spending an average of seven hours a day in the care and training of the children (there were no comparable data for families of normal children). Holroyd and McArthur (1976) 'contrasted' the effect of a Down's syndrome or an autistic child and compared these with a sample of mothers of children attending a psychiatric clinic. Using sophisticated statistical techniques the study purported to show that mothers of Down's syndrome children reported fewer problems than did those of autistic children and were no more stressed than were mothers of the clinic sample. However, the report contains numerous design faults: parents of autistic and clinic children were apparently interviewed personally, while those of the Down's syndrome children were sent a postal questionnaire; sex and social class distribution differed markedly between the groups, no attempt being made in the analysis to allow for these factors; and the clinic sample, which was contrasted with 'the two retarded groups', contained 25 per cent retarded children. Hence little confidence can be placed in the findings.

Ferguson and Watt (1980) studied 87 mothers of school-age children, 30 of severely and 27 of moderately handicapped children, and 30 of children attending ordinary schools, matched for the social class, sex and age of the children. Mothers were interviewed in their own homes and completed the Rutter Malaise Inventory (Rutter *et al.*, 1970). Mothers of handicapped children reported more family problems than did those of nonhandicapped children (as did also working-class compared with middle-class mothers). Scores on the Malaise Inventory, however, showed no effect of degree of handicap but a significant social class correlate, the mean score of working-class mothers of nonhandicapped children surpassing that of middle-class mothers of severely handicapped children (6.1 and 5.2 respectively). Further, neither problems nor Malaise scores were related 'in any straightforward way' to the degree of the child's handicap. The authors comment, 'It need not follow that a parent who denies that his whole family is a handicapped family is seeking refuge from hostility, anxiety or guilt in a neurotic refusal to face reality.' The finding that mothers of more severely handicapped children do not necessarily report greater levels of stress echoes those from studies of mothers of physically handicapped children (Dorner, 1975; Bradshaw, 1980; Carr *et al.*, 1983).

In Bradshaw's (1980) study, mothers doing unrestricted paid work had lower Malaise scores (6.26) than had the whole group (9.02) and than those who wanted to work and could not (10.32). Although in some investigations there has been little difference in employment between mothers of normal and of mentally handicapped children (Carr, unpublished), in Bradshaw's study only 27 per cent of mothers of handicapped children had paid work, compared with 41 per cent of all mothers with dependent children. Out of 53 interviewed mothers of children on the Camberwell Register, just over half (28) said that they had been prevented from working as they wished to because of the handicapped child (Wing, personal communication), and similar results were obtained by Wilkin (1979).

Effect on the fathers

In most family studies the main emphasis has been on mothers, but recently some attention has been given to fathers. Waisbren (1980) investigated 30 couples with a developmentally disabled child and 30 with a nonhandicapped child, mean age 13.5 months. Half of each group lived in the United States and half in Denmark, and the parents were interviewed and given a written questionnaire. For both parents 'the relationship between supports and coping is complicated', and fathers who felt that their own parents were highly supportive had more positive feelings about, and did more with, the child, although they also listed more symptoms of stress and were more likely to feel that the effect of the child on the marriage was a negative one.

Cummings (1976) studied sixty families each of mentally retarded, chronically ill and healthy children, the groups being matched for socioeconomic status and sex and age of the children. Co-operation was markedly more difficult to obtain from fathers than from mothers. Those fathers who did participate completed four self-administered personality tests, returning these by mail. From the results Cummings concludes that, compared with fathers of healthy children, those with a mentally retarded child express more depression, less enjoyment not only of the retarded child but also of their other children, lower self-esteem (at the 10 per cent level of significance) and sense of paternal competence, and 'a pattern of neurotic-like constriction' shown by an increased stress on orderliness and dominance, and less expressed interest in the opposite sex. Most of these traits were also shown by parents of chronically ill children. McConachie (1982) points out that the figures on which Cummings bases this 'pattern of neurotic-like constriction' could equally well be interpreted as showing that fathers of handicapped children express 'a need for routine to cope with the strain of everyday caring for a handicapped child, and a more relaxed, accepting view of the important things in life'.

Cummings concludes that the research will be of value to those helping families of handicapped children: 'We must recognize and deal with these fathers' efforts to avoid painful contact with inner feelings of loss and lowered self-esteem.' Whether such intervention is either necessary, or would be to the benefit of the fathers, awaits demonstration.

In a review of both the research literature and parents' own writings, McConachie (1982) found no simple pattern of paternal response to a handicapped child. A research project on nineteen fathers showed that their interaction with their children varied widely, but 'mothers are more likely than fathers to engage in a high level of interaction with their children . . . [and] the increased burden of caring for a severely handicapped child tends to fall on the mother's shoulders', a conclusion also reached by Wilkin (1979). She suggests that services which concentrate on mother and child may aggravate this situation and further isolate the fathers, and pleads for a flexible service structure that would allow fathers greater involvement with their handicapped children.

Studies of the effect of the child on the father's career have shown either no difference between fathers of handicapped and nonhandicapped children (Waisbren, 1980; Piachaud *et al.*, 1981) or that only a minority – 15 per cent – felt that their careers had been affected (Dunlap and Hollinsworth, 1977). These findings, of a minimal effect on the father's career, are supported by evidence from families of spina bifida children in whom the pattern of upward social mobility is similar to that shown by the general population (Carr *et al.*, 1983).

Effect on the siblings

Many parents are worried that the presence of a severely retarded child will have a harmful effect on their other children. They are concerned that the normal siblings will be disturbed by the retarded child's behaviour, and ashamed of him or her so that they may be unwilling to bring their friends home, or that the retarded child will take so much of the parents' time that the normal children will be neglected.

Perhaps the most serious problem recorded was that reported by Holt (1958a), in whose study 12 per cent of the siblings had suffered physical attacks by the retarded child. Compared with this the disadvantages found in other surveys were minor. Siblings were found to be affected by a young, very dependent child living at home; normal sisters, especially the eldest, were more likely to be affected than normal brothers (Farber, 1959; Fowle, 1968). Simeonsson and McHale (1981) point out that complex interactions between various factors, such as gender, sex and age of both the handicapped child and the sibling, birth order, social class and parental attitudes may affect the findings on any single variable. They discuss studies indicating more adverse effects on younger siblings which, they suggest, result from their being supplanted in their 'younger' role by the slower-developing handicapped child. However, other surveys have found older siblings, especially older and eldest sisters, to be more adversely affected (Gath, 1974; Cleveland and Miller, 1977) and this may in part be due to demands which are put on these girls to care for the child, especially in large, and predominantly lower-class, families.

Other studies have shown fewer and less adverse effects on siblings who, in general, are said to love and accept the handicapped child (Dunlap and Hollinsworth, 1977; Lonsdale, 1978). Schipper (1959) felt that three-quarters of the siblings of Down's syndrome children in her investigation were happily adjusted and that, of those who were disturbed, in only about half the cases (six out of a total of forty-three families) did the retarded child appear to be the cause of the maladjustment. In another study (Barsch, 1968) the majority of parents of different types of handicapped children thought the child was well accepted by his siblings, of whom only a minority (12 per cent) were considered to show predominantly negative attitutdes.

In a series of investigations of the influence of a Down's syndrome child on the siblings, Gath found no significant effect (1972), a small (10 per cent) increase in deviance reported by parents and teachers of siblings of Down's syndrome children compared with those of controls (1973), and no significant difference between siblings of Down's syndrome and control babies (1978). In a larger sample than those discussed above Tizard and Grad (1961) indicated that, contrary to expectation, significantly fewer siblings of the severely retarded living at home than of those in institutions had mental health problems, the proportions being 12 per cent (home) and 26 per cent (institution). The authors comment:

> This interesting difference does not support the view that keeping a defective in the family upsets the other children; but it does suggest that parents who have more than one difficult child to cope with are more likely to seek institutional care for a mental defective.

All the preceding studies were based on interviews with parents, but a number of workers have directly interviewed the siblings themselves. Graliker *et al.* (1962) interviewed 21 teenage siblings of severely retarded children who gave high ratings to their relationship with their parents and their home life, showed minimal reluctance about their friends meeting the retarded child, and minimal signs of feeling overburdened. These findings are closely similar to those of Caldwell and Guze (1960). Hart and Walters (1979a) interviewed 40 teenage siblings of mentally handicapped children, the 27 families comprising a wide variety of ethnic backgrounds. Social class was skewed towards the lower end, 48 per cent being from social classes 4 and 5 (compared with 29 per cent in general London samples), and the majority of the siblings were older than the handicapped child. Most did not feel embarrassed by having a handicapped child in the family, had their friends around freely and did not feel stigmatized when they were out with the handicapped child, although behaviour problems, especially when the sibling was in charge of the child and did not know how to control him, were often cited as a source of embarrassment. They did not feel that their lives were restricted, were interested in trying to teach and play with the handicapped children, and missed them when they went on holiday. They appeared concerned about the handicapped child, to an extent underestimated by the parents, and might have benefited from more information about aetiology, management and the future provision available for handicapped people.

In a smaller study using a control group, McConachie and Domb (1983) interviewed 10 older siblings of mentally handicapped and 10 of nonhandicapped children, matched for age (from 8 to 15, mean 11 years) and age difference from the younger child (approximately 7 years), and for sex and social class. Siblings of the mentally handicapped children were found to be no more embarrassed than were those of the nonhandicapped, nor were there differences in jealousy, playing with, teaching or enjoying being with the younger child, or in the amount of housework done. Siblings of handicapped children were, however, significantly more likely to say that the younger child disturbed them at night and interfered with their activities. A number of sex and age differences were found: girls, although somewhat more negative towards the younger child than boys, played with and taught the child more and enjoyed doing so, while older children (12–15 years) had more negative attitudes to the younger child, but these findings applied regardless of whether or not the younger child was handicapped.

Training

The studies discussed above suggest that siblings are in general not devastated by having a mentally handicapped child in the family, but that they may benefit from a chance to express their feelings and to gain practical information and advice. Counselling groups have been conducted for siblings (Hart and Walters, 1979b; Chinitz, 1981; Ellington, 1982), and on an anecdotal level seem to have been successful. Participants in these groups were eager to help and teach the handicapped child and a number of projects have set out to enable them to do so more effectively. Weinrott (1974) provided a one-week training for 18 siblings, aged 10–18 years, of mentally handicapped children attending a summer camp. The siblings first observed the campers' classes and were taught behavioural principles, 'one of the most worthwhile' being to ignore inappropriate behaviour, though this was especially difficult to do with their own brother or sister. From the third day they were involved in teaching the mentally handicapped campers, both their own brother or sister and the other campers. Two months after the end of the camp a follow-up questionnaire to the parents revealed that, with one exception, siblings were said to have improved the 'quality' of their interaction with the mentally handicapped child, spent more time with him and were continuing to make use of the skills they had learned, albeit in a more informal and less intensive manner.

   Miller and Cantwell (1976) describe two cases where siblings were able to participate with their parents to increase language and to decrease problem behaviours in the handicapped child, following teaching using didactic materials, role-play and videotape feedback. They were able to modify their behaviours towards the handicapped child and, through restructuring the time they spent with him, were freed of some of the restrictions he had previously put on them. The authors identify some problems in training siblings, some of which (the need for short teaching sessions and to ensure that assignments are carried out) seem similar to those involved in the teaching of any nonprofessionals. Others are more specific to the family situation: on occasion it was necessary for the therapist to ensure equal participation of all family members where, for example, parents may 'talk for' the children; similarly, following an incident where a child 'blurted out' details of some inappropriate behaviour of a parent who then denied it, it became apparent that among the rules to be established at the beginning of the programme should be one stating that 'all behaviour in the family that is observed by anyone is subject to discussion in the meetings'. Nevertheless, the siblings were seen to be effective aides to the parents and teachers of the mentally handicapped child, and to enjoy this constructive interaction with him. One major benefit seen in these programmes was improvement in the siblings' own behaviours, especially where there was some concordance between problems in the retarded and nonretarded siblings (an effect also seen with normal siblings; Lavigeur, 1976). It may be that, if children who seek to modify behaviours in their siblings improve their own behaviours, then problems in mildly or moderately retarded children might be tackled by asking them to modify similar (possibly enacted) behaviours in their siblings.

SUPPORT FOR FAMILIES

Parent counselling and family therapy

Although at one time the diagnostic session contained all the counselling that the parents were likely to get, increasingly it has come to be realized that parents cannot absorb in one interview all that they need to know. Many writers (Richards, 1964; Wolfensberger, 1967; Pinkerton, 1970; Pueschel and Murphy, 1976) have stressed the need for repeated interviews with the parents. The more contact they had had with a clinic, the higher was their expressed satisfaction (Caldwell *et al.*, 1961), while Drillien and Wilkinson (1964) stated that mothers were more satisfied with the way they had been told if 'they were encouraged to return to the family doctor or paediatrician with any further queries or problems' (though no figures are given). Out-patient follow-up appointments may be seen as serving the purpose of repeated interviews, but well over half the mothers in Hewett's (1970) and Carr's (1975) studies found their hospital visits very unhelpful, complaining of a long wait for a short interview, lack of discussion or advice, and a perfunctory attitude on the part of the doctor. Unless these visits are carefully designed to allow for adequate discussion and exchange of information they are likely to be seen by the parents as a waste of time.

Much of the early literature on counselling, reviewed in full in Wolfensberger (1967), is concerned with the need for ways of dealing with the parents' own psychodynamic problems. 'The parents are often viewed as being problem-ridden, anxious and maladjusted ... and ... the source of their problems as residing within them' (Wolfensberger, 1967). A parent of a mentally handicapped child (personal communication) reacted to a paragraph in a White Paper (Department of Health and Social Security, 1971, paragraph 140) which discusses the parents' need for help with emotional problems, which may lead to rejection or overprotection of the child and the neglect of the other children. He commented:

My reaction to this paragraph is that it is impertinent in the extreme. It gives the impression that the parents can do nothing right, but that if they are lucky they might get some professional worker to help them cope with the worst emotional problems that they have got themselves into.

Similar feelings of frustration and irritation have probably been felt by other parents who, asking for information or practical advice, have received psychotherapy instead (cf. Yates and Lederer, 1961; Cummings and Stock, 1962). Undoubtedly in many cases parents do want the chance to talk and to express their feelings, and they should be given the opportunity to do so, but this should not be all that they get. Wing (1975) feels that a family counsellor should be able to advise on behavioural management programmes, to recognize when families can or cannot cope with these, to help sort out difficulties for the other children and to liaise with other workers (e.g. teachers, speech therapists), always on a basis of 'precise knowledge of the nature of [the child's] handicap and the techniques for dealing with them. No other kind of expertise can substitute for this basic knowledge.'

Although the volume of literature on parent counselling has declined over the years, the topic is still seen as important by professionals (Drotar *et al.*, 1975) and by parents (Marks, 1980). A relatively recent development is that of family therapy for families of mentally handicapped children (Ballard, 1982), which aims to increase acceptance of the child, identify family roles and give practice in relating to the child's problems (Turner, 1980). Typically the whole family, including the deviant member, is involved in therapy sessions and it has been suggested that the mentally handicapped child should participate through the use of drawing, music, clay modelling and so on in place of verbal communication (Gomersall, 1981). It is difficult to imagine how the profoundly handicapped child could be expected genuinely to participate except as a focus for discussion. Black (1982) advocates family therapy at times of crisis, and gives examples of successful interventions, some of which combine such therapy with behavioural methods, resulting in what appears to be an appropriate model of help for parents who wish for this type of approach. These accounts are, however, anecdotal, and no research has been published showing the value of a family therapy approach for families of mentally handicapped children.

Experience of services

Studies of the services parents require have found them dissatisfied with the facilities available (Upshur, 1982), especially older parents (Suelzle and Keenan, 1981), or unaware that services they needed in fact existed (Goddard and Rubissow, 1977). Dunlap and Hollinsworth (1977) indicated that in a poor rural area of Alabama where very few services for the mentally handicapped existed, little demand for them was expressed, and they suggested either that these families had no idea of what services might have done for them, or else that their past experience of them had been unsatisfactory. Families in ethnic minority groups showed a higher percentage who had had no help from or knowledge of state resources than did white American families (Justice *et al.*, 1971). These findings are confounded by the higher IQs of the children in the ethnic minority groups, suggesting that these children may be identified as mentally handicapped although actually relatively able, and the markedly lower level of reported problems, especially in the black group. Median IQs for the Anglo-American, Mexican-American and black families were 62, 68 and 74 respectively, while the proportion of children with learning, health, supervision and physical disability problems in the black group was approximately half that in the Anglo-American group.

Services are intended and expected to ease the burden for parents, but two studies investigating their effectiveness have produced unexpectedly negative results. Wing (1971), reviewing the expanded provision of services in Camberwell, London, found no corresponding reduction in the demand for residential places. In Waisbren's (1980) study of families in California and in Denmark, despite the markedly higher level of services in Denmark (Dupont, 1980), the strain on families of retarded children appeared similar in the two countries, as was their use of services, which in any case did not figure prominently in parents' reports. On the other hand, a facility designed especially to meet the expressed needs of parents, which offers an uninterrupted emergency service plus short- or long-term care, home- or hospital-based treatment as required, appears to offer an ideal source of help (Brimblecombe, 1979). Institution bed occupancy in the district served by this facility is extremely low, 2.3 per 100,000 population, compared with 9.0 per 100,000 for England and Wales as a whole, but the absence of figures for bed occupancy before the inception of the service makes it impossible to determine how far this low figure is due specifically to the service. The author himself says that the facility may not be the sole reason, and that other factors may include the existing well-developed educational and social services facilities 'but it is believed that the direct contribution of Honeylands is substantial'.

Extra monetary allowances are designed to alleviate the burdens of families with handicapped children, but how far these allowances are seen as conveying positive benefits is questionable. Mothers who had applied to the Family Fund completed the Malaise Inventory (Rutter *et al.*, 1970) before and after receiving substantial assistance (averaging £173). Malaise scores showed on the second occasion 'a hardly discernible improvement' of 0.19, with no correlation between score and the amount, type or value of items given (Bradshaw, 1980). A study of the effect of the mobility allowance showed that it eased the practical problems families face in taking their handicapped children out, but made little difference to the children's outdoor mobility (Cooke, 1980). These and related problems are discussed in Chapter 19.

Alternative care

Early studies, especially those in the United States, focused on the family's decision on whether, or when, the child should be sent to an institution

(Wardell, 1947; Walker, 1949; Jolly, 1953). Later, attention turned to the factors making institutionalization of a child more or less likely. Graliker *et al.* (1965) showed that although social class, religion and educational level and age of the parents could not be shown to have had an effect, first-born children, those from larger families, those with brain defects and more severe mental handicap, were the more likely to be institutionalized. In a study by Stone (1967), families with the most favourable social conditions were less likely to be actively seeking placement for their children, while families of older children (over five years), especially boys, were more likely to be seeking placement. Saenger (1962), studying 1050 families of institutionalized and noninstitutionalized people, found that degree of mental, and to a lesser extent physical, handicap was associated with institutionalization, while, when all other predisposing factors had been allowed for, severely mentally handicapped people remaining at home had received a significantly higher level of services, such as speech and occupational therapy, compared with the institution sample. In their classic study, Tizard and Grad (1961) interviewed 150 families with a mentally handicapped child or adult living at home, and 100 with a child or adult in hospital. The hospital cases included many more with numerous problems (e.g. of degree of retardation, health, temperament, management) while, as in other studies (Graliker *et al.*, 1965), Down's syndrome persons were less often institutionalized than were other mentally handicapped people.

Whereas the earlier literature was often concerned with reasons for and effects of admission to an institution, more attention is now paid to the effects of deinstitutionalization on both mentally retarded people and their parents. In a thoughtful review of the literature on community living, Landesman-Dwyer (1981) concludes that no one pattern of care has been shown to be appropriate for all mentally handicapped people; that the belief that 'smaller is better' is not invariably correct but that, on the contrary, 'theoretically and practically, the advantages of having a range in the size of community-based programs are considerable'; and that higher staffing ratios do not necessarily result in a higher quality of care. Willer *et al.* (1981) interviewed forty-three families of mentally retarded people who had been discharged two years previously, after a minimum of one year in an institution. Fifteen had returned to their own families, and the remainder were placed in other families or in group homes. Almost half the families had experienced guilt, or anxiety related to the retarded person's future, which had been seen as secure while she/he was in the institution but less so in the community.

Meyer (1980) sent questionnaires to 538 parents or guardians of all current residents of a state institution for mentally handicapped people; 273 (50.7 per cent) were returned, and since the replies were anonymous it was not possible to follow up those who had not responded. Age and sex distributions were closely similar to those of the total population; functioning levels indicated by the respondents were somewhat higher than those of the total population, which may have been the result of a higher response rate from parents of higher-functioning individuals, or due to parents somewhat overestimating their child's level of functioning. Community living arrangements, in either small group homes or supervised apartments, were described and assumed in each case to be run by qualified staff and located in a desirable neighbourhood. Parents were asked whether they would prefer one of these alternative arrangements or that their relative remain in the state institution. Over 80 per cent of those responding felt that they would prefer their retarded relative to remain in the institution where she/he now was, mainly because of the kind and amount of care they felt it afforded. None of the factors of age, ability or presence or absence of behaviour problems in the retarded person was related to parents' preferences, nor was dissatisfaction with the institution, but younger respondents were significantly more likely to choose community placement, both in the present and in the future. The author suggests that some of the support for the institution may represent a fear of the unknown, and there is evidence that attitudes may change as the result of experience. Two-thirds of families whose adult child was moved from an institution to a community placement were unhappy about it, whereas a year later only 8 per cent responded in a similar way (Landesman-Dwyer, 1981); while hostility expressed by local residents before the opening of a hostel for mentally handicapped adults had virtually disappeared three years later (Locker *et al.*, 1981). It seems that more favourable attitudes to community living came about in each case because the dire consequences envisaged as a result of the proposed changes had not materialized.

The participation of parents in their child's education and training: effect on intellectual levels

Many parents wish to be involved in the teaching of their own children, and programmes designed to help them to do so began to appear in the 1960s and have proliferated over the past decade. In one of the first studies, de Coriat *et al.* (1967) described a programme of written and verbal instruction for daily activities given to mothers of Down's syndrome infants. Gesell tests were administered every 3–6 months to both the 'educated' group and a control group, those 'left alone to spontaneous evolution'. The programme appears to have been applicable to the child's first year, but test results are given for 10 semesters (5 years). Median IQs and standard deviations are reported for a maximum of 80 'educated' children, declining to 9 at 5 years, compared with a maximum of 182 controls, declining to 15 at 5 years. The IQs of the 'educated' group were consistently higher, roughly 17 points above those of the control group, and the authors say the difference is significant. However, no details are given as to the social class composition or sex distribution of the groups, or how the children were allocated to either group, so it is not possible to be sure that the two were comparable.

Brinkworth (1973) reports on a comparison between 5 'experimental' Down's syndrome babies whose parents had advice on ways of stimulating their child and were given worksheets to follow, and 12 controls. Tests were given at 6 months for the experimental group and at ages varying between 7 and 13 months for the controls, and again 6 months later. At the first test there was a significant difference between the mean DQs (experimental group = 101.8, controls = 75.0) but not at the second test (experimental group = 81.07, controls = 75.0). The study suffers from serious drawbacks in that, first, it seems that the testing was done by the author who was also solely responsible for the remedial programme, and second that, given the well-documented decline in IQ with increasing age in Down's syndrome infants, the difference in the DQs between the two groups might well have been due to this factor alone. So there is no conclusive evidence on whether or not the author's methods made any significant difference to the developmental progress of the children. This does not, however, detract from the importance of his pioneering work in giving help to parents of retarded children.

In a study carried out in Kent (Ludlow and Allen, 1979), mothers of Down's syndrome children from one geographical area attended a developmental clinic where the children were engaged in nursery-type activities, each being allocated an individual helper. The mothers and children attended twice a week for between two and eight years, mothers participating in the activities, being given talks by professionals and sharing experiences with other mothers. The children were tested at varying ages on the Griffiths and Stanford–Binet scales, and results were compared with those from children from a neighbouring geographical area whose mothers did not have access to developmental clinics. Those in the experimental group had an average of 5.6 tests and those in the control group 4.1 tests over the survey period, and where a child had not been assessed in any one year a score was interpolated from the graph of his or her scores. Numbers tested varied between 25 and 72 for the experimental group, and 9 and 62 for the controls. Mean scores of the experimental group were consistently above those of the controls, from 79.8 and 69.4 respectively, in the first year, to 48.9 and 42.6 in the tenth year. The graph of scores for the two groups are almost parallel, with a slightly larger gap between four and six years and a noticeable narrowing towards the end of the period. Mean scores declined in the experimental group by 30.9 points and in the control group by 26.8 points (Carr, 1985). Given that the experimental children were not composed of initially higher-grade children (which seems unlikely), this suggests that they gained from the extra stimulation an advantage which they largely maintained until after the eighth year, but that the stimulation was not, in this group, able to affect the rate of decline of the scores. At the end of the study, just over one-quarter of the experimental group, compared with about 5 per cent of the controls, were attending normal primary schools or schools for the mildly educationally subnormal, ESN(M). This difference was highly significant and held to provide independent evidence of the effectiveness of the intervention (Ludlow, 1980). However, it is possible that other factors, such as a more ready acceptance of a child into schools not catering for the severely retarded, consequent upon the author's work in that part of Kent, may have had some effect.

In the Toddler Project (Bricker and Bricker, 1971), parents of 10 handicapped children (7 of them with Down's syndrome) were given intensive training in the teaching of their children by operant techniques. Over a period of 10 months the average mental age gain for 9 children was 7.3 months. This may be compared with an average gain, for children of roughly comparable age over a period of 12 months, of about 4 months (Carr, 1975), while the most advanced ten children in that study had an average gain of about 5 months. Hence the results reported by Bricker and Bricker are impressive, and probably not only due to higher-grade children having been selected for their study.

In another investigation (Bidder *et al.*, 1975), mothers of 8 Down's syndrome children attended 12 sessions of group training in behaviour modification techniques while a comparison group of 8 mothers of children matched for sex and for chronological and mental age received no extra training. Mean CAs for the two groups were 23.8 and 24.5 months respectively; mean MAs were 16.6 and 14.8, indicating that the experimental children were initially somewhat more advanced than were the controls. Both groups were pre- and post-tested on the Griffiths scale, showing significant gains for the experimental group children, of 6.56 months on language and 7 months on the performance scale, compared with the control group's 2.56 and 4.37 months respectively.

In contrast to these studies, reporting at least short-term advantage to the experimental children, the investigation by Piper and Pless (1980) found no significant differences. Thirty-seven infants attended a centre for biweekly one-hour sessions of stimulation when their parents also received training, and 21 received no such training. The children were tested at the outset and at the end of the 6 months on the Griffiths scale, by a specially appointed psychologist 'who was kept unaware of the group status ·:ᶜ the subjects and of the basic design of the study'. Pre-intervention scores of the two groups were closely similar (CA = 9 months, GQ = 79). Following the 6 months' intervention the scores of both groups had declined by about 6 points; on 4 out of the 6 Griffiths scales, scores of the experimental group had declined more than had those of the controls, although the differences were small and none was significant. This study has been criticized by Bricker *et al.* (1981) on the grounds that the 6-month intervention period was very short, that the Griffiths scale may have been insufficiently sensitive to show significant effects, and that the authors did not assess how far the instructions to the parents were carried out at home. These criticisms, however, could equally well be applied to the study by Bidder *et al.* (1975), which showed significant advantages in the experimental group, while the major difference of the Piper and Pless study lies in the use of an independent assessor.

Cunningham (1982), as part of a major series of studies of intervention with Down's syndrome infants, investigated two groups of families, one of 32 infants whose mothers were given advice from the age of 6 weeks, and another group of 13 whose families came into the study when the child was 6–12 months old. Developmental quotients of the group receiving intervention from birth showed the least decline, and scores of the delayed treatment group were similar to those of Carr's (1975) home-reared cohort up to the age of one year, after which they caught up with the early treatment group. In a further study (Cunningham, 1983), a group of 8 infants whose parents received intensive training and 10 in a comparison group were, from 12 weeks of age, visited at 2-weekly intervals, and were assessed at 6-weekly intervals on the Bayley scales, these assessments being carried out by three 'independent' workers (members of the research team other than the main experimenter), while 15 per cent of assessments were carried out by 'blind' assessors. Comparison of assessments by the 'blind' and the 'independent' assessors did not reveal any bias. Training continued to around 48 weeks, during which time the intensive group of children were significantly advanced in their mental age scores, but by 54–60 weeks no significant differences could be found. Over this period of comparatively short intervention 'there is little evidence that the initial intensive training maintains long-term advantages'.

In a 3-year intervention programme, 32 pre-school, severely subnormal children (mean CA, 2 years 6 months; mean MA, 1 year 3 months) were visited at home, 16 at 2-week and 16 at 2-month intervals (Sandow and Clarke, 1978; Sandow et al., 1981). Mothers discussed with the visiting therapist the gaps in the child's performance, based on assessment on Gunzburg's Progress Assessment Charts, and a behaviourally based programme was devised for the parents to carry out. A matched group of 15 children in a different geographical area received no intervention. The children were assessed at the start of the project and thereafter at annual intervals on the Cattell Infant Intelligence Scale and the Vineland Social Maturity Scale. The expectation was that the more frequently visited group would make the greater developmental gains. However, a different opinion, by Dr C.C. Cunningham, that this would be true for the first year but that subsequently the less frequently visited group (Group B) would surpass Group A and that differences would finally be insignificant, was recorded. Results are reported in terms of direction of IQ change, which show a nonsignificant advantage to Group A in year one, a reversal to advantage significant at less than 0.025 to Group B in year two, and a general decline in all three groups in year three, thus largely fulfilling Cunningham's predictions. It was concluded that frequent visiting, which may lead the parents into undue dependence on outside help, does not necessarily represent the most helpful approach; visiting may be most useful if it is frequent in the early stages and gradually diminishes as the parents become more competent: 'We are committed to a policy of gradual self-effacement for the therapist' (Sandow et al., 1981).

Teaching skills and managing problem behaviours

In other studies, the aim was to enable mothers to teach a variety of skills, and to manage or eliminate behaviour problems in their children. Mothers were visited individually at home, discussed objectives with the therapists who demonstrated methods, and were asked to carry out training sessions and to keep records of progress until the therapist's next visit (Howlin *et al.*, 1973; Burden, 1978).

Firth (1983) reports the results of a home-visiting service for 33 families with children aged between 3 and 15 years, 85 per cent over the age of 6. A variety of problems were tackled, but 28 out of the 33 families chose socially unacceptable behaviour as at least one of these problems. They were visited every 3–4 weeks for periods varying between 3 and 27 months, until the targets set were reached or parents felt that they had done as much as they could. Forty-one per cent of the problems tackled were dealt with successfully, and a further 28 per cent partially successfully, and programmes to deal with socially unacceptable behaviour were as successful as those dealing with other areas (e.g. incontinence, feeding, communication).

In a review of the effectiveness of a home-visiting service (Callias and Carr, 1975), parents' success was found to be unaffected by social class; behavioural problems were better dealt with where marital relationships were satisfactory and the family a small one; learning skills were more successfully taught to brighter children (IQ 36–51) but IQ did not relate to success with behaviour problems; parents receiving more home visits were more successful than those visited less.

A number of studies have reported the implementation of the Portage model (Shearer and Shearer, 1972), a highly structured and systematized approach to parent teaching in the home which makes use of developmental checklists, curriculum cards and activity charts on which parents record the results of their teaching. Typically, the service is delivered by a team of specially trained home advisers who meet on a regular basis with one or more supervisors, usually clinical psychologists. On the first visit the home adviser completes the Portage checklist on the child and, with the parent, selects a suitable task for the parent to teach the child during the coming week, takes a baseline on this task and completes an activity chart setting out in behavioural terms how, and how often, the skill is to be practised. At the weekly visits the home adviser checks on progress and advises on any changes necessary. Once a week the home advisers meet the supervisors to discuss cases in progress, problems and successes. Partly, perhaps, because tasks are selected so that they are attainable in one week, a high success rate is reported.

Revill and Blunden (1979) discuss the first 4 months of a Portage service to 19 families, and show that of a total of 306 tasks set (an average of 1.08 per week per child), 270 (88 per cent) were trained to criterion and less than 5 per cent abandoned. Children also acquired skills at about twice the rate found during the baseline that were not being specifically taught. In this study the two home advisers were full-time workers, but Holland (1981) describes how health visitors were able to give a Portage service to one family apiece as part of their normal duties. The model may be an expensive one in terms of training time related to the service provided – the health visitors had four half-days of training and felt that they should have had more – but they seem to have appreciated this extension of their role, and felt that it enabled them to work in similar ways with other families on their caseload.

Cameron (1979) reports that after a three-day training, three home teachers were able to visit between them approximately twenty families each week with almost 90 per cent of targets attained within one week. Reservations have been expressed about the Portage model, that the teaching of the minimal self-help and educational skills contained in the checklist may not always fulfil the parents' most pressing needs. Home advisers have sometimes also offered advice on behaviour difficulties and other family and service problems (Cameron, 1979), and this dual approach has considerable potential for helping parents on an individual basis.

Parent training groups

The early 1970s saw the first publications of reports of group training for parents. In the Parents' Workshop (Cunningham and Jeffree, 1971), forty-one parents contacted through the National Society for Mentally Handicapped Children (now MENCAP) enrolled for an eight-week course of lectures, discussions and tutor groups. The parents assessed their child's present level of functioning and were then helped to find ways to stimulate the child to the next appropriate stage of activity. It was emphasized that this was not a research project, but tutors' records and parents' responses to a post-course questionnaire showed that in general the parents felt the course to have been useful, that at least 50 per cent had successfully applied the teaching model to a wide variety of tasks, and that success 'did not appear to correlate with the parents' educational background'. On the negative side, the course was felt to have been least helpful to the parents of very severely retarded children.

Other workers have also run parent groups and the essential model is described by Callias (1980). Groups have met at varying intervals, from weekly (McCall and Thacker, 1977) to monthly (Holland and Hattersley, 1980); and in a variety of venues, such as hospital (Holland and Hattersley, 1980), university (Jeffree *et al.*, 1977) and school (Attwood, 1977; McCall and Thacker, 1977; Tennant and Hattersley, 1977). Parents were helped to assess their children, to identify problems or targets, and were taught principles and/or techniques of behaviour modification. Between meetings they worked on specific objectives with their children, reporting progress at the next meeting. Many of the projects saw the need to include both parents, but in practice mothers predominated in most groups. Attendance, where this was reported, was between 72 and 82 per cent (McCall and Thacker, 1977; Tennant and Hattersley, 1977; Holland and Hattersley, 1980; Firth, 1982). Most of the projects included home visits or individual sessions with the parents, but where this is impracticable the use of videotape equipment, passed round from parent to parent, and films then exhibited at group meetings, is suggested as a useful alternative (Harris, 1978). Notes on the course content, which parents can take home with them, have been found valuable (Carr, 1980a; Holland and Hattersley, 1980). Some groups had sessions given over to taks by other professionals, such as speech therapists and physiotherapists (Attwood, 1977), while contact between the parents themselves has been seen as an advantage of the group approach (Harris, 1978).

Evaluation of group training

Evaluation of parent group training is difficult. Most studies report the results of post-course questionnaires which were circulated to parents, and in the main comments from these were very positive, respondents saying that they had been helped to approach their handicapped child more positively, to be more objective and constructive, and that they felt more confident and more able to cope with the problems associated with handicapped children (Attwood, 1977; McCall and Thacker, 1977; Tennant and Hattersley, 1977; Holland and Hattersley, 1980; Firth, 1982). While these undoubtedly represent a genuine response from the parents, caution has been advised in attributing the positive effect to the particular kind of course concerned, when they may simply have been grateful to be given any help and teaching at all (Carr, 1980b). Other evaluative efforts have examined the success rate in targets tackled: in 16 families, Tennant and Hattersley (1977) reported complete success with 57 per cent of targets and 6 per cent showing no progress, while in a larger group of 40 parents, Firth (1982) found that 46 per cent were completely successful and 28 per cent showed no progress. In one group of parents, Firth (1982) observed that videotapes showed that they seemed to learn how to organize their teaching and to use appropriate prompting, but did not improve their skills at reinforcing their children. Holland and Hattersley (1980) assessed the children of the parents in their group on the Alpern and Boll Developmental Schedule and found no significant differences overall in pre- and post-test scores, although the parents themselves assessed improvement in the behaviour of their children on the teaching targets; on a 10-point scale the mean improvement score was 6.

Problems and advantages of parent groups

Many of the studies discussed problems that arise in the running of parent groups, which may be summarized as follows:

1. Stress is laid on the importance of including both parents in the teaching sessions, and almost all projects found difficulty in attracting fathers to the groups, especially when these were run during working time (Attwood, 1977; McCall and Thacker, 1977; Tennant and Hattersley, 1977). Evening groups offer a better chance of attracting both parents, despite the possibility of baby-sitting problems.
2. Difficulties have arisen when the children of the parents in the group present a great diversity of problems, abilities and age. Two studies have

commented that it was mothers of younger children who gained the most from the group (Attwood, 1977; Firth, 1982), and the latter author states that 'parent workshops did not appear to be particularly effective in treating the problems of the older children'. Similarly, Harris (1978) suggests that parents with more able children get most out of the group meetings, while those of children with low ability feel discouraged and embarrassed and may be unwilling to attend further meetings, thus perpetuating their problems.

3. Problems have also arisen when the skills that parents learn bring them into conflict with other professionals, such as teachers, who have not had experience of similar methods, and parents then may become critical of these other professionals (Attwood, 1977). One solution may be to organize groups of both teachers and parents together, or to train teachers to run school-based groups themselves (Harris, 1978).

The advantages of group training may be that behavioural principles can be more systematically covered in this way; that parents are glad of the opportunity to meet others in a similar position, and to exchange ideas and experiences with them; and that they may be stimulated and supported in their work with their children by their contacts with these others. One advantage propounded is that groups may be more economical of professional time. However, this has been disputed for families of nonhandicapped children (Mira, 1970), while Firth (1983) found that a home-visiting service was equally efficient in terms of therapist time and resulted in rather higher levels of behaviour change in the children.

A number of studies have found that parents of low socioeconomic or educational status were less able to benefit from training in behavioural methods (Salzinger *et al.*, 1970; Rinn *et al.*, 1975) although this was not confirmed by Callias and Carr (1975). Clark *et al.* (1982) describe an alternative form of training in which parents taught children alongside experienced staff members, receiving supervision and videotaped feedback. This programme was used predominantly with lower socioeconomic status parents who had gone through a group training programme, and had not been able to use the principles effectively, but by these means attained the same levels as most achieved in the standard training format. This represents an interesting and positive approach to a problem which most workers have simply noted.

Maintenance of training effects

That parents can learn methods to help them teach their own children has been well established, but a further question concerns the extent to which they can maintain and extend the changes brought about in their children once professional supervision has ended. Doleys *et al.* (1976) followed up a group of five mothers of learning-disabled children who had attended a course of eight weekly meetings consisting of lectures and role-playing. The importance of contingent positive reinforcement and of decreasing commands and questions was emphasized. Later, parents were videotaped with their own children and received feedback on their performance. Changes following the role-playing phase were slight, with an increase in reinforcement and no decrease in the rate of commands, but following the videotaped feedback phase reinforcements increased and commands and questions dropped dramatically. Five follow-up observations showed this picture modified somewhat, with a decrease in reinforcement and an increase in commands and questions, but at the end of a thirty-week follow-up phase reinforcement and questions were still significantly different from baseline, showing that parents were able to maintain their teaching skills.

Baker *et al.* (1980) report a follow-up of 95 families who had been assigned to one of four teaching conditions: (1) given a written manual only; (2) given a written manual and 8 biweekly phone calls; (3) given a written manual and 9 biweekly group meetings; and (4) given a written manual, 9 biweekly group meetings and 6 home visits. The average cost of these conditions rose from $38 for (1) to $211 for (4). Mothers in all four groups had learned to teach their children more effectively than had a control group who were on the waiting list to receive training. Follow-up 14 months later showed that initial gains, in both mothers and children, were largely maintained, with group (1) doing as well as groups (3) and (4), and group (2) somewhat lower (as they had been immediately following training). About half the families had continued systematically teaching skills (51 per cent) and working on behaviour problems (69 per cent). However, when incidental teaching ('the incorporation of behaviour modification principles into daily routine, to help a child to learn skills without formal teaching sessions') was considered, 76 per cent of the families reported this for at least one skill, and overall 86 per cent of families reported the continuation of 'some scorable teaching efforts'. The most usually perceived obstacle to continuing teaching was limited time, followed by problems related to the child (e.g. behaviour problems, lack of skills), mothers' lack of confidence in themselves and their need for outside support, and finally their feeling that teaching was not really their job, but that of the school. There was no difference between the four groups in the obstacles that they identified. Although mothers in group (1) equalled those in the other groups in teaching skills, they were less likely to begin and carry through programmes for managing behaviour problems, and when parents were asked what training condition they would have preferred, all put group (4) first and group (1) last. The authors conclude that those embarking on group training should encourage formal teaching first, so that principles may be effectively learned, but should then 'encourage shifting to incidental teaching and . . . might teach ways to analyse and modify the usual daily routine to make incidental teaching more likely', as this was more likely to endure.

The stress of parental involvement

In some cases services intended to help families have themselves been seen as causing stress. Large numbers of interventionists may be involved – 'frequently five or more professionals in daily contact' (Lacoste, 1978) involving the mother as 'therapist, teacher, trainer or, at the least, transporter' (Doernberg, 1978), so that it is as much as she can do to keep up with her child's treatment, let alone function as wife, mother to her other children, or as a human being in her own right. The result, especially where heroic efforts are demanded as in the Doman–Delacato programmes (see Chapter 11), may be to damage the whole family (Zigler, 1981). Doernberg questions whether 'a small improvement in the child is worthwhile in terms of its cost to the family'.

Parents, too, have commented that they felt looked down on by professionals (Berry *et al.*, 1981) and that professionals have undervalued parents' achievements: 'They always tell us how well we are doing, but then go on to say, *but* if you do this it will be more helpful' (Black, 1978). Some parents react to a switch in the views of professionals who, having found that parents can teach their own children, now see it as almost obligatory that they should do so. Turnbull and Turnbull (1982), discussing legislation in the United States extending parents' rights to participate in educational decision-making, make a strong plea for this right not to become an inescapable duty for all parents. They quote the professional view as to the skills parents need to acquire ('No less is required of every Master's level special education teacher'), and the contrasting views of some parents ('I leave him off in the mornings and I feel like – phew – people more competent than me are taking him and that's a great feeling'). They point to the need to consider other members of the family as well as the handicapped child, and to the conflict that may exist between the interests of the child and of the rest of the family, and urge the adoption of 'a model that takes into account the diverse needs and perspectives of parents', so that they could choose either not to be involved, or to be as involved as they themselves wish, in their child's education. Parents who do not wish to be committed to teaching their children may still, if the child remains at home, need to deal with difficult behaviour, and they may need help with this. Furthermore, as Mittler (1979) says, in urging moderation in the pressure professionals put on parents: 'No matter how successfully a child is taught in school, the effort is largely wasted unless systematic steps are taken to help the child use and apply his learning in his own home and in all the real-life settings in which he moves.' The need, then, is for professionals to arrive at ways of helping parents that are acceptable to them, that recognize and value the skills that they already possess, and the importance of other family members, and to acknowledge that, while involvement in teaching the child will vary from one family to another, so it may also vary in any one family from one time to another.

CONCLUSIONS

With the increasing emphasis in recent years on the benefits of home care for the mentally handicapped has come an increasing concern with the effect that this may have on their families. In general, most families want to keep their mentally handicapped child at home, and most adjust to doing so. The situation is more difficult for them where the child is severely handicapped and presents more problems of behaviour and management, and where families are larger and already beset by many other problems. That most parents manage to cope should be a cause for admiration of them, rather than of the existing services and facilities, but some progress has been made. There are welcome signs that those responsible for conveying the news that a child is mentally handicapped are doing so earlier and more compassionately, and research might now aim at showing in what other ways parents could best be helped at this time. For example, there is little evidence that a mentally handicapped child will do serious harm to other children in the family, although parents should also be made aware of the need not to overburden older children, especially girls. In this connection, however, there may be a real conflict between the needs of parents and of siblings, and siblings who take over part of the care of the mentally handicapped child may be performing a real service for the parent.

The pattern of services for parents has been changing, with a move away from custodial to educational approaches, and from institutional to community care. It is recognized that no one kind of provision will be suitable for all mentally handicapped people, and there is a need to examine what will best serve a widely differing population of handicapped people, at different times in their lives, and their parents, and to ensure that those who require them are aware of the availability of these services.

Over the past decade parent training has been a major growth area in mental handicap. Those offering this training need, perhaps, to consider whom they are hoping to benefit, the child or the family. If the answer, predictably, is 'both', it may be that trainers will have to accept that many parents who want to help their child do not want to do so at the expense of themselves and the rest of the family (indeed, if they did this they would risk being categorized as hyperpaedophiliac – Lonsdale, 1978). Especially, they may not want to gear their lives rigidly to regular sessions of teaching and the paraphernalia of charts and recording. Parent trainers are anxious to demonstrate the value of their work in terms of measured effects, and they are right to do so if this effort is not to be easily dismissed. Nevertheless, in order to help the largest number of families, they will have to seek measures which are manageable in family life, and teaching methods that can reach the most, and the most needy, families, such as those outlined by Clark *et al.* (1982). In other cases workers may have to accept that they must balance real help for the families with limited objectives for the child. Parents are now in many cases working as partners with professionals, but as Mittler (1979) says, 'We must allow them to choose *not* to be involved at the level of detailed collaboration that some professionals are now demanding.' With that caution in mind we may yet acknowledge that many parents welcome the opportunity to help their children and the teaching that enables them to do so. Much progress has been made over the last decade: in the next we should look still more urgently for methods by which they can be more effectively enabled to help their children in whatever way they wish.

REFERENCES

ALBERMAN, E., BERRY, A.C. and POLANI, P.E. (1979) 'Planning an amniocentesis service for Down syndrome', *Lancet*, 1, 50.

ATTWOOD, T. (1977) 'The Priory parents' workshop', *Child: Care, Hlth Develop.*, 3, 81–91.

BAKER, B.L. (1977) 'Support systems for the parent as therapist', in P. MITTLER (ed.), *Research to Practice in Mental Retardation*, vol. 1, *Care and Intervention*, Baltimore, University Park Press.

BAKER, B.L., HEIFETZ, L.J. and MURPHY, D.M. (1980) 'Behavioral training for parents of mentally retarded children: one-year follow-up', *Amer. J. Ment. Defic.*, 85, 31–8.

BALLARD, R. (1982) 'Taking the family into account', *Ment. Handicap*, 10, 75–6.

BARSCH, R.H. (1968) *The Parent of the Handicapped Child*, Springfield, Ill., C.C. Thomas.

BAYLEY, N., RHODES, L. and GOOCH, B. (1966) 'A comparison of the development of institutionalized and home-reared mongoloids', *Calif. Ment. Hlth Res. Digest*, 4, 104–5.

BERG, J.M., GILDERDALE, S. and WAY, J. (1969) 'On telling parents of a diagnosis of mongolism', *Brit. J. Psychiat.*, 115, 1195–6.

BERRY, P., GUNN, P., ANDREWS, R. and PRICE, C. (1981) 'Characteristics of Down syndrome infants and their families', *Aust. Paed. J.*, 17, 40–3.

BIDDER, R.T., BRYANT, G. and GRAY, O.P. (1975) 'Benefits to Down's syndrome children through training their mothers', *Arch. Dis. Child.*, 50, 383–6.

BLACK, D. (1982) 'Handicap and family therapy', in A. BENTOVIM, G. GORELL BARNES and A. COOKLIN (eds), *Family Therapy – Complementary Framework of Theory and Practice*, London, Academic Press.

BLACK, J.M.M. (1978) 'Families with handicapped children – who helps whom and how?', *Child: Care, Hlth Develop.*, 4, 239–45.

BRADSHAW, J. (1980) *The Family Fund*, London, Routledge & Kegan Paul.

BRICKER, D. and BRICKER, W. (1971) 'Toddler research and intervention project: report – year 1', *IMRD Behavioral Science Monograph*, no. 20, Nashville, Tenn., George Peabody College.

BRICKER, D., CARLSON, L. and SCHWARTZ, R. (1981) 'A discussion of early intervention for infants with Down syndrome', *Pediatrics*, 67, 45–6.

BRIMBLECOMBE, F.S.W. (1979) 'A new approach to the care of handicapped children', *J. Roy. Coll. Phys.*, London, 13, 231–6.

BRINKWORTH, R. (1973) 'The unfinished child. Effects of early home training on the mongol infant', in A.D.B. CLARKE and A.M. CLARKE (eds), *Mental Retardation and Behavioural Research*, London, Churchill Livingstone; Baltimore, Williams & Wilkins.

BURDEN R.L. (1978) 'An approach to the evaluation of early intervention projects with mothers of severely handicapped children: the attitude dimension', *Child: Care, Hlth Develop.*, 4, 171–81.

CALDWELL, B.M. and GUZE, S. (1960) 'A study of the adjustment of parents and siblings of institutionalized and non-institutionalized retarded children', *Amer. J. Ment. Defic.*, 66, 845–61.

CALDWELL, B.M., MANLEY, E.J. and SEELYE, B.J. (1961) 'Factors associated with parental reaction to a clinic for retarded children', *Amer. J. Ment. Defic.*, 65, 590–4.

CALLIAS, M.M. (1980) 'Teaching parents, teachers and nurses', in W. YULE and J. CARR (eds), *Behaviour Modification for the Mentally Handicapped*, London, Croom Helm.

CALLIAS, M.M. and CARR, J. (1975) 'Behaviour modification programmes in a community setting', in C.C. KIERNAN and F.P. WOODFORD (eds), *Behaviour Modification with the Severely Retarded*, Amsterdam, Associated Scientific Publishers.

CAMERON, R.J. (1979) 'A lot can happen at home too', *Remed. Educ.*, 14, 173–8.

CARR, J. (1970) 'Mongolism: telling the parents', *Dev. Med. Child Neurol.*, 12, 213–21.

CARR, J. (1975) *Young Children with Down's Syndrome*, London, Butterworth.

CARR, J. (1976) 'Effect on the family of a child with Down's syndrome', *Physiotherapy*, 62, 20–4.

CARR, J. (1980a) *Helping Your Handicapped Child: A Step-by-Step Guide to Everyday Problems*, Harmondsworth, Penguin.

CARR, J. (1980b) 'The organization of short courses', in W. YULE and J. CARR (eds), *Behaviour Modification for the Mentally Handicapped*, London, Croom Helm.

CARR, J. (1985) 'The development of intelligence', in D. LANE and B. STRATFORD (eds), *Current Approaches to Down's Syndrome*, New York, Holt, Rinehart & Winston.

CARR, J., PEARSON, A. and HALLIWELL, M. (1983) *The GLC Spina Bifida Survey: Follow-up at 11 and 12 Years*, obtainable from the Information Section, Research and Statistics Branch, Addington Street Annexe, London SE1 7UY.

CENTERWALL, S.A. and CENTERWALL, W.H. (1960) 'A study of children with mongolism reared in the home compared to those reared away from home', *Pediatrics*, 25, 678–85.

CHINITZ, S.P. (1981) 'A sibling group for brothers and sisters of handicapped children', *Children Today*, Nov.–Dec., 21–3.

CLARK, D.B., BAKER, B.L. and HEIFETZ, L.J. (1982) 'Behavioral training for parents of mentally retarded children: prediction of outcome', *Amer. J. Ment. Defic.*, 87, 14–19.

CLEVELAND, D.W. and MILLER, N. (1977) 'Attitudes and life commitments of older siblings of mentally retarded adults: an exploratory study', *Ment. Retard.*, 15 (3), 38–41.

COOKE, K.R. (1980) 'An evaluation of the mobility allowance for families with handicapped children', *Child: Care, Hlth Develop.*, 6, 279–89.

COWIE, V. (1966) 'Genetic counselling', *Proc. Roy. Soc. Med.*, 59, 15–16.

CUMMINGS, S.T. (1976) 'The impact of the child's deficiency on the father', *Amer. J. Orthopsychiat.*, 46, 246–55.

CUMMINGS, S.T. and STOCK, D. (1962) 'Brief group therapy of mothers of retarded children outside the speciality clinic setting', *Amer. J. Ment. Defic.*, 66, 739–48.

CUNNINGHAM, C.C. (1982) 'Psychological and educational aspects of handicap', in F. COCKBURN and R. GITZELMAN (eds), *Inborn Errors of Metabolism*, Lancaster, MTP Press.

CUNNINGHAM, C.C. (1983) *Early Development and Its Facilitation in Infants with Down's Syndrome*, Final Report, Part 1, London, DHSS.

CUNNINGHAM, C.C. and JEFFREE, D.M. (1971) *Working with Parents: Developing a Workshop Course for Parents of Young Mentally Handicapped Children*, Manchester, National Society for Mentally Handicapped Children, NW Region.

DE CORIAT, L.F., THESLENCO, L. and WAKSMAN, J. (1967) 'The effects of psychomotor stimulation on the IQ of young children with trisomy 21', in B.W. RICHARDS (ed.), *Proc. 1st Cong. International Assoc. for the Scientific Study of Mental Deficiency*, Reigate, Michael Jackson.

DEPARTMENT OF HEALTH AND SOCIAL SECURITY (1971) *Better Services for the Mentally Handicapped*, Command Paper 4383, London, HMSO.

DOERNBERG, N.L. (1978) 'Some negative effects on family integration of health and educational services for young handicapped children', *Rehab. Lit.*, 39, 107–10.

DOLEYS, D.M., DOSTER, J. and CARTELLI, L.M. (1976) 'Parent training techniques: effects of lecture–roleplaying followed by feedback and self-recording', *Behav. Ther. Exper. Psychiat.*, 7, 359–62.

DORNER, S. (1975) 'The relationship of physical handicap to stress in families with an adolescent with spina bifida', *Dev. Med. Child Neurol.*, 17, 765–76.

DRILLIEN, C.M. and WILKINSON, E.M. (1964) 'Mongolism: when should parents be told?', *Brit. Med. J.*, 2, 1306–7.

DROTAR, D., BASKIEWICZ, A., IRVIN, N., KENNELL, J. and KLAUS, M. (1975) 'The adaptation of parents to the birth of an infant with a congenital malformation: a hypothetical model', *Pediatrics*, 56, 710–17.

DUNLAP, W.R. and HOLLINSWORTH, J.S. (1977) 'How does a handicapped child affect the family? Implications for practitioners', *The Family Co-ordinator*, 26, 286–93.

DUPONT, A. (1980) 'A study concerning the time-related and other burdens when severely handicapped children are reared at home', *Acta Psychiat. Scand.*, supplement 285, 62, 249–57.

ELLINGTON, S. (1982) 'Children in the shadows. Working with siblings of handicapped children', paper presented to the Thirteenth International Study Group on Child Neurology and Cerebral Palsy, St Edmund Hall, Oxford.

FARBER, B. (1959) *Effects of a Severely Mentally Retarded Child on Family Integration*, Monogr. Soc. Res. Child Develop., no. 71, 24.

FERGUSON, N. and WATT, J. (1980) 'The mothers of children with special educational needs', *Scottish Educ. Rev.*, 12, 21–31.

FIRTH, H. (1982) 'The effectiveness of parent workshops in a mental handicap service', *Child: Care, Hlth Develop.*, 2, 77–91.

FIRTH, H. (1983) 'Difficult behaviour at home. A domiciliary service for handicapped children', *Ment. Handicap*, 11, 61–4.

FOWLE, C.M. (1968) 'The effect of the severely mentally retarded child on his family', *Amer. J. Ment. Defic.*, 73, 468–73.

FRASER, F.C. and LATOUR, A. (1968) 'Birth rates in families following birth of a child with mongolism', *Amer. J. Ment. Defic.*, 72, 883–6.

FRIEDRICH, W.N. and FRIEDRICH, W.L. (1981) 'Psychosocial assets of parents of handicapped and non-handicapped children', *Amer. J. Ment. Defic.*, 85, 551–3.

GATH, A. (1972) 'The mental health of siblings of congenitally abnormal children', *J. Child Psychol. Psychiat.*, 13, 211–18.

GATH, A. (1973) 'The school-age siblings of mongol children', *Brit. J. Psychiat.*, 123, 161–7.

GATH, A. (1974) 'Sibling reactions to mental handicap: a comparison of the brothers and sisters of mongol children', *J. Child Psychol. Psychiat.*, 15, 187–98.

GATH, A. (1978) *Down's Syndrome and the Family: The Early Years*, London, Academic Press.

GODDARD, J. and RUBISSOW, J. (1977) 'Meeting the needs of handicapped children and their families. The evolution of Honeylands: a family support unit, Exeter', *Child: Care, Hlth Develop.*, 3, 261–73.

GOMERSALL, J.D. (1981) 'Family psychotherapy and mental handicap', paper presented at pre-conference workshop, Combined Asian and Regional Commonwealth Congress on the Scientific Study of Mental Deficiency, Bromley.

GRALIKER, B.V., FISHLER, K. and KOCH, R. (1962) 'Teenage reaction to a mentally retarded sibling', *Amer. J. Ment. Defic.*, 66, 838–43.

GRALIKER, B.V., KOCH, R. and HENDERSON, R.A. (1965) 'A study of factors influencing placement of retarded children in a state residential institution', *Amer. J. Ment. Defic.*, 69, 553–9.

HARRIS, J. (1978) 'Working with parents of mentally handicapped children on a long-term basis', *Child: Care, Hlth Develop.*, 4, 121–30.

HART, D. and WALTERS, J. (1979a) 'Brothers and sisters of mentally handicapped children', unpublished manuscript.

HART, D. and WALTERS, J. (1979b) 'A group work project with siblings of mentally handicapped children', unpublished manuscript.

HEWETT, S. (1970) *The Family and the Handicapped Child*, London, Allen & Unwin.

HOLLAND, J.M. (1981) 'The Lancaster Portage project. A home-based service for developmentally delayed young children and their families', *Hlth Visitor*, 54, 486–8.

HOLLAND, J.M. and HATTERSLEY, J. (1980) 'Parent support groups for the families of mentally handicapped children', *Child: Care, Hlth Develop.*, 6, 165–73.

HOLROYD, J. and MCARTHUR, D. (1976) 'Mental retardation and stress on parents: a contrast between Down's syndrome and childhood autism', *Amer. J. Ment. Defic.*, 80, 431–6.

HOLT, K.S. (1958a) 'The home care of severely retarded children', *Pediatrics*, 22, 744–55.

HOLT, K.S. (1958b) 'The influence of a retarded child upon family limitation', *J. Ment. Defic. Res.*, 2, 28–36.

HOWLIN, P., MARCHANT, R., RUTTER, M., BERGER, M., HERSOV, L. and YULE, W. (1973) 'A home-based approach to the treatment of autistic children', *J. Aut. Child. Schiz.*, 3, 308–36.

HUTCHISON, A. (1966) 'Stress on families of the mentally handicapped', in *Stress on Families of the Mentally Handicapped*, 3rd Int. Cong., Int. League of Societies for the Mentally Handicapped.

HUTTON, LADY V. (1966) 'Breaking the news', in *Stress on Families of the Mentally Handicapped*, 3rd Int. Cong., Int. League of Societies for the Mentally Handicapped.

ILLINGWORTH, R.S. (1966) 'Counselling', in *Stress on Families of the Mentally Handicapped*, 3rd Int. Cong., Int. League of Societies for the Mentally Handicapped.

JEFFREE, D.M., MCCONKEY, R. and HEWSON, S. (1977) 'A parental involvement project', in P. MITTLER (ed.), *Research to Practice in Mental Retardation*, vol. 1, *Care and Intervention*, Baltimore, University Park Press.

JOLLY, D.H. (1953) 'When should the seriously retarded infant be institutionalized?', *Amer. J. Ment. Defic.*, 57, 632–6.

JUSTICE, R.S., O'CONNOR, G. and WARREN, N. (1971) 'Problems reported by parents of mentally retarded children – who helps?', *Amer. J. Ment. Defic.*, 75, 685–91.

KUSHLICK, A. (1966) 'Subnormality – the size of the problem', *Mental Handicap*, Basle, Switzerland, Geigy.

LACOSTE, R. J. (1978) 'Early intervention: can it hurt?', *Ment. Retard.*, 16 (3),

266–8.

LANDESMAN-DWYER, s. (1981) 'Living in the community', *Amer. J. Ment. Defic.*, 86 (3), 223–34.

LAVIGEUR, H. (1976) 'The use of siblings as an adjunct to the behavioral treatment of children in the home with parents as therapists', *Behav. Ther.*, 7, 602–13.

LLOYD-BOSTOCK, s. (1976) 'Parents' experiences of official help and guidance in caring for a mentally handicapped child', *Child: Care, Hlth Develop.*, 2 (6), 325–38.

LOCKER, D., RAO, B. and WEDDELL, J.M. (1981) 'The impact of community care on the public response to the mentally handicapped', *Comm. Med.*, 3 (2), 98–107.

LONSDALE, G. (1978) 'Family life with a handicapped child: the parents speak', *Child: Care, Hlth Develop.*, 4, 99–120.

LUDLOW, A.R. (1980) 'Early intervention in Down's syndrome' (letter), *Brit. Med. J.*, 281, 1143.

LUDLOW, J.R. and ALLEN, L.M. (1979) 'The effect of early intervention and pre-school stimulus on the development of the Down's syndrome child', *J. Ment. Defic. Res.*, 23, 29–44.

LUTHY, D.A., EMANUEL, I., HOEHN, H., HALL, J.G. and POWERS, E.K. (1980) 'Prenatal genetic diagnosis and elective abortion in women over 35: utilization and relative impact on the birth prevalence of Down's syndrome in Washington State', *Amer. J. Med. Genet.*, 7, 335–81.

LYLE, J.G. (1960) 'The effect of an institution environment upon the verbal development of imbecile children. III: The Brooklands residential family unit', *J. Ment. Defic. Res.*, 4, 14–23.

MCCALL, C. and THACKER, J. (1977) 'A parent workshop in the school', *Spec. Ed.*, 4 (4), 20–1.

MCCONACHIE, H. (1982) 'Fathers of mentally handicapped children', in N. BEAIL and J. MCGUIRE (eds), *Fathers: Psychological Perspectives*, Thomas Coram Research Unit, University of London Institute of Education.

MCCONACHIE, H. and DOMB, H. (1983) 'An interview study of 20 older brothers and sisters of mentally handicapped and non-handicapped children', *Ment. Handicap*, 11, 64–6.

MARKS, L. (1980) 'Parents' needs and how to meet them', in G.B. SIMON (ed.), *Modern Management of Mental Handicap*, Lancaster, MTP Press.

MEYER, R.J. (1980) 'Attitudes of parents of institutionalized mentally retarded individuals towards deinstitutionalization', *Amer. J. Ment. Defic.*, 85 (2), 184–7.

MILLER, N.B. and CANTWELL, D.P. (1976) 'Siblings as therapists: a behavioral approach', *Amer. J. Psychiat.*, 133, 447–50.

MIRA, M. (1970) 'Results of a behavior modification training program for parents and teachers', *Behav. Res. Ther.*, 8, 309–11.

MITTLER, P. (1979) 'Patterns of partnership between parents and professionals', *Teaching and Training*, 17, 111–16.

MURDOCH, J.C. (1983) 'Communication of the diagnosis of Down's syndrome and spina bifida in Scotland, 1971–1981', *J. Ment. Defic. Res.*, 27 (4), 247–53.

NIHIRA, K., MEYERS, C.E. and MINK, I.T. (1980) 'Home environment, family adjustment and the development of mentally retarded children', *Appl. Res. Ment. Retard.*, 1, 5–24.

PENROSE, L.S. (1938) 'A clinical and genetic study of 1280 cases of mental defect', *Spec. Rep. Ser. Med. Res. Coun.*, no. 229, London, HMSO.

PIACHAUD, D., BRADSHAW, J. and WEALE, J. (1981) 'The income effect of a disabled child', *J. Epidemiol. Comm. Hlth*, 35, 123–7.

PINKERTON, P. (1970) 'Parental acceptance of the handicapped child', *Dev. Med. Child Neurol.*, 12, 207–12.

PIPER, M.C. and PLESS, I.B. (1980) 'Early intervention for infants with Down syndrome: a controlled trial', *Pediatrics*, 65, 463–8.

PUESCHEL, S.M. and MURPHY, A. (1976) 'Assessment of counseling practices at the birth of a child with Down's syndrome', *Amer. J. Ment. Defic.*, 81 (4), 325–30.

RAECH, H. (1966) 'A parent discusses initial counseling', *Ment. Retard.*, 2, 25–6.

REVILL, S. and BLUNDEN, R. (1979) 'A home training service for pre-school developmentally handicapped children', *Behav. Res. Ther.*, 17, 207–14.

REYNOLDS, A.R. (1979) 'Some social effects of the mentally retarded child on the family: a third survey', *Aust. J. Ment. Retard.*, 5, 214–18.

RICCARDI, V.M. (1981) 'Understanding clinical genetics and family counseling', in S.R. APPLEWHITE, D.L. BUSBEE and D.S. BORGAONKAR (eds), *Genetic Screening and Counseling: A Multi-disciplinary Perspective*, Springfield, Ill. C.C. Thomas.

RICHARDS, B.W. (1964) 'Mental subnormality in the general hospital', *J. Ment. Sub.*, 10, 19–22.

RINN, R.C., VERNON, J.C. and WISE, M.J. (1975) 'Training parents of behaviorally disordered children in groups: a three-year's program evaluation', *Behav. Ther.*, 6, 378–87.

ROITH, A.I. (1963) 'The myth of parental attitudes', *J. Ment. Sub.*, 9, 51–4.

RUTTER, M., TIZARD, J. and WHITMORE, K. (eds) (1970) *Education, Health and Behaviour*, London, Longman.

SAENGER, G. (1962) 'Social factors in the institutionalization of retarded individuals', in B.W. RICHARDS (ed.), *Proc. London Conf. on the Scientific Study of Mental Deficiency* (1960), Dagenham, May & Baker, 642–9.

SALZINGER, K., FELDMAN, R.S. and PORTNOY, S. (1970) 'Training parents of brain injured children in the use of operant conditioning procedures', *Behav. Ther.*, 1, 4–32.

SANDOW, S. and CLARKE, A.D.B. (1978) 'Home intervention with parents of severely subnormal, pre-school children. An interim report', *Child: Care, Hlth Develop.*, 4, 29–39.

SANDOW, S.A., CLARKE, A.D.B., COX, M.V. and STEWART, F.L. (1981)

'Home intervention with parents of severely subnormal pre-school children: a final report', *Child: Care, Hlth Develop.*, 7, 135–44.

SCHIPPER, M.T. (1959) 'The child with mongolism in the home', *Pediatrics*, 24, 132–44.

SHEARER, M. and SHEARER, D.E. (1972) 'The Portage project: a model for early childhood education', *Excep. Child.*, 36, 210–17.

SHIPE, D. and SHOTWELL, A. (1965) 'Effect of out-of-home care on mongoloid children: a continuation study', *Amer. J. Ment. Defic.*, 69, 649–52.

SIGLER, A.T., COHEN, B.H., LILIENFELD, A.M., WESTLAKE, J.E. and HETZNECKER, W.H. (1967) 'Reproductive and marital experience of parents of children with Down's syndrome (mongolism)', *J. Pediat.*, 70, 608–14.

SIMEONSSON, R.J. and MCHALE, S.M. (1981) 'Review: research on handi-capped children: sibling relationships', *Child: Care, Hlth Develop.*, 7, 153–71.

SPRINGER, A. and STEELE, M.W. (1980) 'Effects of physicians' early parental counselling on rearing of Down's syndrome children', *Amer. J. Ment. Defic.*, 85 (1), 1–5.

STEDMAN, D.J. and EICHORN, D.H. (1964) 'A comparison of the growth and development of institutionalized and home-reared mongoloids during infancy and early childhood', *Amer. J. Ment. Defic.*, 69, 381–401.

STEIN, Z. and SUSSER, M. (1960) 'Families of dull children', *J. Ment. Sci.*, 106, 1296–319.

STONE, N.D. (1967) 'Family factors in willingness to place the mongoloid child', *Amer. J. Ment. Defic.*, 72, 16–20.

SUELZLE, M. and KEENAN, V. (1981) 'Changes in family support networks over the life cycle of mentally retarded persons', *Amer. J. Ment. Defic.*, 86 (3), 267–74.

TENNANT, L. and HATTERSLEY, J. (1977) 'Working together: a progress report on parent workshops', *Apex*, 5 (3), 7–8.

TIPS, R.L., SMITH, G.S., PERKINS, A.L., BERGMAN, E. and MEYER, D.L. (1963) 'Genetic counseling problems associated with trisomy 21, Down's disorder', *Amer. J. Ment. Defic.*, 68, 334–9.

TIZARD, J. (1962) 'The residential care of mentally handicapped children', in B.W. RICHARDS (ed.), *Proc. London Conf. on the Scientific Study of Mental Deficiency*, Dagenham, May & Baker, 659–66.

TIZARD, J. and GRAD, J.C. (1961) *The Mentally Handicapped and their Families*, London, Oxford University Press.

TURNBULL, A.P. and TURNBULL, H.R. (1982) 'Parent involvement in the education of handicapped children. A critique', *Ment. Retard.*, 20 (3), 115–22.

TURNER, A.L. (1980) 'Therapy with families of a mentally retarded child', *J. Mar. Fam. Ther.*, April, 167–70.

UPSHUR, C.C. (1982) 'Respite care for mentally retarded and other disabled populations: program models and family needs', *Ment. Retard.*, 20, 2–6.

WAISBREN, S.E. (1980) 'Parents' reactions after the birth of a developmentally disabled child', *Amer. J. Ment. Defic.*, 84, 345–51.

WALKER, G.H. (1949) 'Some considerations of parental reactions to institutionalization of defective children', *Amer. J. Ment. Defic.*, 54, 108–14.

WARDELL, W. (1947) 'Casework with parents of mentally deficient children', *Amer. J. Ment. Defic.*, 52, 91–7.

WEINROTT, M.R. (1974) 'A training program in behavior modification for siblings of the retarded', *Amer. J. Orthopsychiat.*, 44, 362–75.

WILKIN, D. (1979) *Caring for the Mentally Handicapped Child*, London, Croom Helm.

WILLER, B.S., INTAGLIATA, J.C. and ATKINSON, A.C. (1981) 'Deinstitutionalization as a crisis event for families of mentally retarded persons', *Ment. Retard.*, 19, 28–9.

WING, L. (1971) 'Severely retarded children in a London area: prevalence and provision of services', *Psychol. Med.*, 1, 405–15.

WING, L. (1975) 'Practical counselling for families with severely mentally retarded children living at home', *REAP*, 1 (3), 113–27.

WOLFENSBERGER, W. (1967) 'Counselling parents of the retarded', in A. BAUMEISTER (ed.), *Mental Retardation*, London, University of London Press, 329–400.

WRIGHT, B.A. (1960) *Physical Disability – A Psychological Approach*, New York, Harper & Row. Quoted by M. TRETAKOFF (1969), 'Counselling parents of handicapped children: a review', *Ment. Retard.*, 7, 31–4.

YATES, M.L. and LEDERER, R. (1961) 'Small, short-term group meetings with parents of children with mongolism', *Amer. J. Ment. Defic.*, 65, 467–72.

ZIGLER, E. (1981) 'A plea to end the use of the patterning treatment for retarded children', *Amer. J. Orthopsychiat.*, 51, 388–90.

15

Microelectronic and computer-based technology

Steven Lovett

INTRODUCTION

The aim of this chapter is to explore the ways in which microelectronic and computer-based technology can be employed with people who are mentally handicapped to enhance their abilities to cope effectively with the environment. The use of such technology is no panacea and few of its advocates would claim this. But it is the writer's contention that, with careful, considered applications, which take account both of the specific needs of the individual and also of our knowledge of mental handicap and normal cognitive growth, significant gains can take place. If this technology is used to design and develop applications within a broadly developmental theoretical framework, it is believed that it has a role to play and can benefit even the most profoundly multiply handicapped. The examples of work recorded herein will attempt to validate this assertion.

Over the past three decades there have been major advances in the field of microelectronic and computer-based technology. Because of the speed at which this has occurred and the profound effect the results of this new technology is having on our lives, many have argued that we have entered a second industrial revolution, or a 'new age' of man – the computer age. In expressing this general feeling, the US National Academy of Science (1979) has indicated that this new industrial revolution will have an even greater impact on society than did the first. It has also been predicted that during the next ten years many areas of our lives will be transformed, such that we will have greater access to information, and that our main method of communication will move away from paper to the development of international computer-controlled networks (Evans, 1979). These developments in technology, together with those already available, particularly with respect to the microprocessor, will have an increasing impact upon all our lives. Indeed, it is likely that such technological advances will ultimately change the very nature of the constraints placed upon us as human beings. It has already made us begin to reformulate certain expectations we have concerning the handicapped person in society and, as Goldenberg (1979) has indicated, 'Such technology can provide the kind of flexibility that can so thoroughly enrich the experiences and communication abilities of certain handicapped people.' He further suggests that activities and learning previously believed impossible can become well established and part of the normal daily routine.

Up to ten years ago the use of microelectronic and computer-based applications clearly lagged behind educational use, due to technological limitations and the prohibitive cost. However, this situation has now been reversed such that our ideas about how technology can best be applied in the educational sphere actually lag behind the technology itself. These advances are difficult to conceptualize for those unfamiliar with the area and it is not easy to think of any suitable analogies in other fields. In one advertisement, in *Computerworld* (1979), it was claimed that if, during the last thirty years, the automobile industry had made the same progress as the computer industry, a Rolls Royce would cost about $2.50 and do 1 million miles per gallon. Constant miniaturization of components has meant that increasingly powerful microelectronic devices have been produced which have become smaller and smaller with time. In 1946 one of the earliest computers, the ENIAC, occupied 15,000 square feet of floor space, consisted of 18,000 vacuum tubes, cost several million dollars and required a full-time staff of technicians to keep it running for just ten minutes per day. This device contrasted with a modern microcomputer which takes up no more space than an average-sized typewriter, uses small amounts of energy and is considerably more powerful and flexible, not to mention completely portable, leaves one in no doubt about the magnitude of these advances.

We have this tremendously powerful technology, therefore, which continues to fall in price even in the midst of deep world recession. However, how we harness this for the benefit of the handicapped is by no means clear. Often those in the best position to work with the technology itself in producing applications are not necessarily the best to provide the most creative and effective ways of using these ideas in the educational context. It is of great importance that the technological possibilities are understood by as wide a range of professionals as possible and not just those specializing in computer and electronic engineering. However, a common complaint from teachers, Adult Training Centre (ATC) staff and nurses, after being supplied with a microcomputer, is that they are so unfamiliar with its use that they do not know how to incorporate it in daily activities. This also applies to the employment of individual microelectronic aids to a certain extent. Because of this problem, the computer experts' lack of understanding of the nature of mental handicap, and the computer-illiteracy of most other groups, there is a real need to develop interdisciplinary links between education, psychology and the microelectronics sciences. Where these links have been made, the quality and usefulness of applications have been of benefit to their client group. That these important developments cannot be carried out by individuals or single disciplines working in isolation is sadly true and the results of such attempts are all too evident.

Within the limits of this chapter it is not possible to give an exhaustive review of the many hundreds of applications of the new technology, nor is it necessary. An attempt will be made, rather, to give broad illustrations of general points considered to be essential if the potentials that 'flexibility' and 'portability' of microelectronic and computer-based technology can offer can be realized in practical terms. The reader unfamiliar with the concepts and nomenclature of behaviour modification procedures is referred to Chapter 13 as an aid to understanding the present text.

The remainder of this chapter is split into two main sections. The first considers the utility of using microelectronic learning aids with profoundly and multiply handicapped people to enable them to interact with their environment. It will be argued that it is only through such learning aids that these individuals can interact and gain control over their surroundings in any meaningful way, and must therefore be seen as an essential prerequisite in their education and training. However, it is not suggested that this type of aid cannot be used to great effect with more able mentally handicapped people, or that one cannot use more sophisticated computer-based systems (one of these will be described); it merely reflects current application. The second section concerns the use of microcomputer-based learning aids with the mildly, moderately and severely mentally handicapped. It is here where there is so much needed research to be done. A smaller number of evaluated programmes will be discussed, together with a suggested overall rationale.

THE USE OF MICROELECTRONIC LEARNING AIDS

Numerous electronic-based devices have been used for the mentally handicapped in the past. For example, the equipment called 'Playtest' developed by Friedlander *et al.* (1967) can be seen as a direct forerunner of the types of aids developed in the last five years. Playtest was a piece of equipment designed for use with children who were functioning developmentally below twelve months. It consisted of a modified crib in which a wide variety of sensory reinforcers could be obtained by the operation of one of a number of 'switches'. The equipment was designed to be flexible, so that both reinforcement given and type of switch used were based upon the characteristics of the individual child. In one study using Playtest, two large plastic knobs, in which small red lights flickered, acted as the switches to be operated. If a knob was lightly pressed a chime would sound once. If the second knob was then pressed, the subject received auditory stimulation in the form of a scale of organ notes. Every three minutes the function of these two switches alternated. The results showed that, of the four children tested, two presented a clear preference and pattern in responding. An automated system for sensory reinforcement delivery based upon Playtest, developed by Glenn *et al.* (1979) for use with profoundly mentally handicapped children, will be discussed later.

The general usefulness of sensory reinforcement with profoundly and multiply handicapped people has been repeatedly emphasized (Murphy and

Doughty, 1977; Haskett and Hollar, 1978; Jones, 1979). Other studies have found that more traditional forms, such as consumables, appear to be ineffective at maintaining components of behaviour in the profoundly mentally handicapped (Rice *et al.*, 1967; Kiernan, 1974b). Therefore, a great number of devices have been made in a general attempt to stimulate both profoundly and multiply handicapped people by the automatic presentation of some form of sensory stimulation. This section attempts to survey some of these, with a main emphasis on pointing out what they can offer in terms of increased controllability of the environment. It should be stressed that a common theme of all devices described is their ability to enable the constraints of severe disabilities to be modified in order that the individual can have some level of interaction with his or her environment, a prerequisite for development to take place. All those described rely upon the modern integrated circuit and can be very complex in their design and construction. They all administer some form of sensory stimulation (visual, auditory or tactile) automatically to the handicapped person on the completion of a predefined task. As such there is no possibility of rewarding an inappropriate response, a problem often encountered with the group in question using normal techniques of administration. Responses required from individuals using such microelectronic aids may be a simple raising of an arm or the completion of a complex shape-sorting task. Some systems now available allow subjects to start with very simple tasks and then gradually work through a series of more complicated ones until the responses required to gain reinforcement become very complex and/or multiple.

The cost of microelectronic components has fallen dramatically over the past fifteen years and many devices have been made which claim to be beneficial to the mentally handicapped. In the main, most of this work is excellent and does have many easily identifiable applications. However, any successful aid must take account of the specific learning requirements of people who are mentally handicapped. It is not acceptable for a producer to suggest that a particular aid develops hand–eye co-ordination simply because it requires the individual to touch a switch which then activates the onset of various visual effects. Therefore, whether all the microelectronic aids presently produced are as useful as some manufacturers suggest remains to be shown and one should be very careful when purchasing them. The vast majority of commercially available aids have not been scientifically evaluated, a position similar to that of commercially available software for microcomputers. However, there is a small but growing body of research showing the usefulness of the types of aids to be described. Much of this is carried out on easily made equipment which is often extremely inexpensive but which nevertheless has large and significant effects. Before describing this research in some detail, a brief description of some of the better commercially available applications will be given. This is by no means an exhaustive list, but should give a brief idea of the range of aids available. It must be stressed once again, however, that these pieces of equipment have not been evaluated for their usefulness with mentally handicapped people.

Pethna toys

Pethna is a toy system for the profoundly and multiply handicapped and was developed in response to the lack of suitable play equipment commercially available. The project was started in 1979 at Broughton Hospital in Cheshire, and concerned the design and production of toys which would stimulate and engage even the profoundly and multiply handicapped. This project was multidisciplinary in nature and was directed by Dr Peter Woods, a clinical psychologist. Pethna is a reactive toy system which consists of two interchangeable components known as in-boxes and out-boxes. A major aim of the programme, which is still ongoing, was to overcome the facts that:

1. The severely and profoundly mentally handicapped child does not seem to derive the same intrinsic satisfaction or pleasure from toys that most children do (a point to be discussed later).
2. The skills needed to activate the toy are too complex for the child to play with independently and hence someone else usually operates it.

The in-boxes, which are essentially switches to be operated, consist of a vast range of manipulative devices. These vary in complexity from simple touch switches to manipulanda which require complex manipulative and discriminative skills. Many can be gradually adjusted to increase task difficulty. They are connected to one of many out-boxes which deliver sensory stimulation of various sorts. Stimulation can be of one discrete form or a combination of modalities.

Many examples of in-boxes and out-boxes are given by Woods and Parry (1981). Among the easiest to operate in-boxes are those where the child has simply to touch any part of a large surface area, or squeeze a device that is placed in the hand. For more profoundly and multiply handicapped persons, in-boxes may be constructed so that any minimal movement that a child might make would operate an out-box (switch on some form of sensory reinforcement). Out-boxes contain a cassette-player on to which any piece of auditory stimulation can be recorded. Therefore, if a particular piece of music is found to be reinforcing for an individual child, it can be used as a form of reinforcement in the Pethna. For instance, Woods reports using music, TV advertisement jingles and familiar voices to act as the reinforcing event. Out-boxes also provide visual stimulation, usually from a series of flashing lights, or in spinning objects.

Vibrotactile stimulation can be used by connecting a small vibrating cushion to the system.

Reports from centres which have used this equipment have been very favourable in that Pethna does engage severely and profoundly mentally handicapped people who are usually uninterested in normal toys. Pethna toys probably represent the best microelectronic aids for severely and profoundly mentally handicapped people presently available commercially. They have been carefully designed and are portable and very flexible. Another advantage is that they are constantly being augmented. Once a basic system has been purchased it is obviously possible for individual groups to begin to design their own in-boxes. Unfortunately, as with all commercially produced equipment, Pethna is relatively expensive, costing approximately £300 per system. In fact, this price is probably very good value when one considers that large numbers of people can use it. Such expenditure is, however, likely to be prohibitive for many.

The Handicapped Persons Research Unit (HPRU)

The microelectronic-based toys and learning aids produced by the HPRU at Newcastle Polytechnic under the direction of Sandhu are based upon an analysis of the relationship between motor and cognitive development. Sandhu and his colleagues have attempted to produce a series of individual devices whose operation progresses from very simple to complex. They see the use of microelectronic aids as a means of inducing that initial engagement in children who are otherwise difficult to stimulate, considering that this will facilitate the developmental process and increase control and communication. This view is based on a strong developmental theoretical framework.

From this rationale, HPRU have developed numerous aids for mentally and physically handicapped children and adults. As with Pethna toys no formal evaluations have been carried out and therefore one must be cautious concerning their application. In general, the electronic aids produced by HPRU do not form an interactive toy system as does Pethna. However, they do attempt to give a range of 'toys' with which large groups of handicapped people can interact and thus gain pleasure, while in a learning environment.

HPRU produce a vast range of devices designed for the handicapped child. Many are shown in detail in one of their publications (Sandhu, 1983). From their description and design, together with reports from a number of centres using the equipment, it would appear that many seem more appropriate for those with varying degrees of physical disability or sensory handicap. However, some have obvious potential for the mentally handicapped.

Other microelectronic aids

There are many other producers of microelectronic toys and learning aids for mentally handicapped people. Of particular note is the work of Jones and Ketteridge (1979) and Kitchen (1982, 1983). However, there exist, in addition to these larger producers, many individuals who make aids in an attempt to give some level of stimulation to clients. Many of these are similar to those described above, others differ.

A major problem with many aids produced, whether by the larger groups or by the individual, is that they fail to build in the requirement that the mentally handicapped person should be actively involved in activating the toy. It is sad to see well-made equipment that either requires nothing from the mentally handicapped user or has a response impossible for him or her to make. Many staff members have commented on their pleasure at being able to sit with multiply handicapped children and switch on and off variously produced microelectronic aids which present sensory stimulation. However, if the onset of such stimulation does not involve the subject then the likelihood is that such children will be in no better a position than their normally passive and inactive state. Some would argue that specific individuals are so grossly multiply handicapped that no method can be found to enable them to respond. However, using microelectronic aids can reduce the overall response requirement necessary, so that even a finger movement can activate devices. The next section examines the research and evaluative work carried out on aids for the profoundly and multiply handicapped. Although there are only a small number of studies, the results are very clear and show the general usefulness of such devices.

EVALUATIVE STUDIES

Numerous demonstrations of the general usefulness of sensory reinforcement can be found in the operant literature over the past twenty years. Unfortunately, such research knowledge has only very recently been employed in the practical setting, in the form of microelectronic learning aids. Several studies now exist showing the usefulness of these when tailored to meet the specific needs of the individual. Research has been undertaken by investigators interested in various theoretical and practical issues, related to the behaviour of profoundly and multiply handicapped people. In such areas as stereotypes, the relationship between cognitive development and early motor behaviour, and an analysis of the role of early simple and constructive toy play, the design and production of microelectronic equipment has subsequently been assessed for its value.

Simple and constructive play

An example of microelectronic equipment developed as a direct result of research into play and the profoundly mentally handicapped can be offered from the work of Murphy and her colleagues (Murphy *et al.*, 1983a, 1983b). It is well established that the profoundly mentally handicapped, as a group, show an overall absence of interest in toy play, of the type seen in both normal and less handicapped children, a problem discussed by a number of writers (Kiernan, 1974a; Wehman and Marchant, 1978; Carr and Wilson, 1980; Howlin, 1980), reflecting the group's general lack of involvement and interaction with their environment. This problem directly resulted in the development of the two toy systems described earlier.

In discussing the whole question of play and the profoundly and multiply handicapped, Kiernan (1974a) has put forward two possible explanations for its absence. First, he suggests that since a characteristic of these individuals is their inability to acquire skills and learn from observation and modelling, they will necessarily require a very structured form of training in order to acquire the skill of toy play. Second, he argues that the problem may concern the reinforcing properties of toys and play. For example, the reinforcers (whatever these are?) which maintain play in normal and less handicapped children may be ineffective for profoundly mentally handicapped children. These two hypotheses are clearly not mutually exclusive, but do suggest different methods of intervention and amelioration: in the first, some form of structured behaviour modification and, in the second, the addition of 'effective' reinforcers for toy play. These methods were systematically investigated by Murphy and her colleagues in two studies.

In the first of these, Murphy *et al.* (1983a) investigated toy play in 20 profoundly mentally handicapped children, whose average chronological age was 14 years and mental age was 9.0 months. The aim was to increase overall constructive play and interaction with normal toys, using a structured behaviour modification approach. The 20 subjects were split into two groups, one receiving operant-based training, the second receiving none (the control group). The experiment consisted of 30 sessions and a follow-up after 12 weeks. Although those exposed to operant procedures had some increased interaction with toys during the experimental phase, the use of a structured training approach to the problem of play did not produce significant improvements in terms of the amounts of manipulations and interactions with toys, compared to the control group. The authors indicated that:

> Very few children appear to find toys reinforcing in themselves . . . and rarely appear to be 'engrossed' in a toy. . . . There was little evidence to support the hypothesis that profoundly retarded children show little constructive play with toys simply because they need structured training in constructive play skills.

Their overall conclusion was that the most effective method of increasing simple and constructive play with toys would probably involve making the reinforcement part of the toy itself. That is, the overall problem is more concerned with the identification of suitable reinforcers for the group, which can effectively initiate behaviour.

In a second study, Murphy *et al.* (1983b) investigated Kiernan's second hypothesis, with the use of three toys which delivered some form of additional sensory reinforcement. These were:

1. A panda (92 cm tall). When the panda's stomach was lightly pressed, loud electronic music of variable frequency was produced. This was held on a continuous cassette fitted inside the panda.
2. A car (45 cm long, 18 cm wide and 23 cm off the ground). Sensory stimulation in this case was in the form of vibration from the small car seat which, when pressed by the subject, would vibrate.
3. A wooden train (27 cm long, 13 cm wide and 27 cm high). On the front of the train was an 8-cm-diameter light which flashed when the train was pushed or pulled along.

The 20 subjects were the same as those in the first study. Their selection for the experiment was based upon the observation that they showed less than 25 per cent of the time engaged in active toy manipulations. All had use of their upper limbs, but were not excluded on the basis of visual and auditory impairment. The group was observed for 33 sessions, each lasting 5 minutes.

The first three sessions constituted the baseline period in which subjects were observed with the toys without additional sensory stimulation. This was followed by 30 sessions in which sensory stimulation was made available to subjects. Throughout the study several classes of behaviour were monitored, using a time-sampling approach. These behaviours included: active manipulation of the toys; stationary toy contact; number and frequency of stereotypes exhibited by subjects; imaginative play with the toys; and whether the toy was actually turned on by the subject. Each of these behaviours was precisely defined for the purposes of the experiment.

The results showed significant differences between control sessions (in which sensory reinforcement was not available) and experimental sessions (with sensory reinforcement). Specifically it was found that subjects:

1. Made more toy contacts when sensory reinforcement was available to them, compared to its nonavailability ($p < 0.05$).
2. Showed active manipulation of toys when sensory reinforcement was available to them ($p < 0.05$).
3. Exhibited fewer stereotyped behaviours while exposed to sensory stimulation ($p < 0.05$), a result found recently by one investigator using Pethna toys (Sturmey, 1983, personal communication).

This study used a group design which yielded large and significant individual differences between subjects. For example, it was found that one spent 94 per cent of the time in contact with toys when sensory reinforcement was available, as compared to 12 per cent with the same toys when reinforcement was not available. Other subjects showed no differences between experimental and control conditions. This problem clearly demonstrates the difficulties and general inappropriateness of using group designs when studying such heterogeneous individuals.

In general, the results from this study give strong support to the use of microelectronic technology, which automatically offers some form of sensory stimulation.

Reducing stereotyped behaviours

One piece of apparatus which has been evaluated for its usefulness with severely and profoundly mentally handicapped people is the 'sensory reinforcement table', developed by Goodall, and described by her and her colleagues elsewhere (Goodall *et al.*, 1981). Its design and development arose directly from research into sensory stimulation and stereotyped behaviour

(Goodall and Corbett, 1982). From this work it was found that sensory stimuli could reduce stereotypes in severely and profoundly mentally handicapped people. However, of the four sensory stimuli used (constant light, flashing lights, vibration and sounds), large individual differences were seen in terms of preferences.

It was on the basis of this result that the 'sensory reinforcement table' was developed, a device which could produce various types of sensory stimulation and which could be tailored to meet the individual's preferences. The table is of normal classroom size and has a central recess into which a tray of teaching equipment can be fitted, linked to the stimulus-emitting apparatus. This automatically provides various sensory stimuli following correct responses made by a child. For example, one tray is made up of five different-shaped holes and correspondingly shaped blocks. When one is fitted into the correct hole, a magnetic contact is made, triggering the administration of sensory reinforcement. The types built into the table were:

1. Visual stimulation from a 12V car reversing light which either could provide constant illumination, or could flash four times per second.
2. Auditory stimulation provided by a door bell chime unit with variable speed and volume.
3. Vibration from a vibrating motor, fixed under the table, causing the top to vibrate.

A control unit at the back of the table allowed both sensory stimulation and task difficulty to be varied. In addition, sensory stimulation can be given from between 0.5 and 15 seconds, singly or in combinations of two or three. There is also a manual override control, so that a 'good' attempt can be reinforced.

To date, two types of evaluations have been carried out:

1. A comparison of the effectiveness of sensory stimulation, provided by the table, with conventional reinforcers, in occupying four children working singly at the table, using skills they had already gained.
2. An investigation of the value of sensory reinforcement in teaching *new* form-board skills.

The results of these two studies are reported by Goodall *et al.* (1982). In their first study 'edible', 'social' and 'sensory' reinforcement were compared in 4 profoundly mentally handicapped children whose ages ranged from 5 to 13 years and whose mental ages ranged from 6 to 14 months. The experiment consisted of 30 10-minute sessions (10 sessions for each type of reinforcer). Reinforcement would only be given on successful completion of a form-board task. From the results it was shown that the time spent in placing or attempting to place blocks was increased when sensory reinforcement was available in 2 of the 4 children tested.

In their second study, which investigated teaching 'new' skills to 6 severely and profoundly mentally handicapped children, it was clearly demonstrated that a combination of social and sensory reinforcement was more effective than social reinforcement alone.

In conclusion, Goodall *et al.* (1982) suggest that their results show the utility of using microelectronic technology in the educational context. They further argue that its use may have an important time-saving effect for staff.

The relationship between cognitive development and early motor behaviour

Investigations of various developmental issues in the profoundly multiply handicapped have shown how microelectronic learning aids can benefit the individual user to become more independent of others. Studies which have taken a strongly developmental theoretical position, or which have looked at the use of automated equipment and developmental level (Friedlander *et al.*, 1967; Accrino and Zuromski, 1976; Glenn and Cunningham, 1983; Lovett, 1982, 1984a, b, 1985), have shown how increased activity can result when individuals are exposed to microelectronic technology.

Three studies by Glenn and Cunningham, using the Playtest equipment described earlier, have shown its usefulness, even when working with very multiply handicapped children. Their aim was to establish whether pro-foundly mentally handicapped children with an apparent developmental age below 12 months could show auditory preference using the modified Playtest equipment. An additional question was whether patterns of responding in the most profoundly mentally handicapped were similar to those found in less handicapped infants.

The results with a total of 15 severely, profoundly and multiply handi-capped children, showed that:

1. Contingency learning was established in 13 children.
2. Six could discriminate between the two manipulanda in order to receive 'preferred' auditory reinforcement. When an additional visual cue was added it was found that a further three were then able to show a preference, thus enabling them to identify which manipulandum was the one control-ling their preferred auditory stimulation.
3. At developmental levels above 10.7 months, subjects made similar patterns of preferential responding to rhythmical speech stimuli as was seen in more able handicapped children. On the other hand, at developmental ages below 4–8 months, although contingency learning together with preferen-tial responding was seen, this was much less consistent. This result is similar to that found by Lovett (1984a), although he found that variability in responding was greatly reduced as children (developmentally all below 4 months) were exposed more to contingent reinforcement.

Glenn and Cunningham concluded that automated equipment 'under the child's control' appeared to be highly motivating for these multiply handi-capped children, and suggest that the results clearly demonstrate that they sought auditory stimulation when they were given the opportunity to control its onset. In addition, the authors suggest that at around the 5-months level of development the children have difficulty in locating auditory stimuli on the basis of spatial cues alone, whereas by 9 months they can do this easily. One very interesting finding was that the most profoundly mentally handicapped children did not show any signs of response termination which had been previously shown in less handicapped and normal infants (Glenn *et al.*, 1979). This result has been confirmed by others (Remington *et al.*, 1977; Haskett and Hollar, 1978; Murphy *et al.*, 1979; Lovett, 1982, 1984a, b, 1985) and is directly contradictory to the proposed hypothetical 'spontaneous extinction' phenomenon reported to operate when working with such low-functioning children (Rice *et al.*, 1967). Glenn and Cunningham (1983) indicate that this result may be explained by two possible factors:

1. That subjects of very low developmental level suffer from extreme stimulus deprivation, or lack of ability to control their own environment.
2. It may simply take longer for the group to habituate to perceptual input.

Some of the most detailed evaluative research concerning the utility of microelectronic learning aids has been carried out on individuals who represent the lowest level of adaptive functioning found. These children are very profoundly multiply handicapped, typically functioning between the 0–6 months level of development.

The work was carried out from the Department of Psychology at the University of Hull and involved the design and evaluation of microelectronic learning aids for nonambulatory, profoundly mentally retarded (NPMR), multiply handicapped children. This series of experimental investigations, carried out by Lovett, was multidisciplinary in nature, aids being constructed on the basis of psychological, developmental, educational and technological knowledge. In order that this could be achieved, a psychologist, teachers, and electronic and mechanical engineers all contributed from their expert knowledge. The initial goals for the series of studies were set at the start of the project and modified throughout its three-year course by the present writer and the two teachers responsible for the children.

Little information existed concerning this type of multiply handicapped, highly dependent children, prior to the 1970s. Before the 1960s, the vast majority died before they reached school age as did the majority of the profoundly mentally handicapped (Conley, 1973). Since this time, increasing numbers of children have survived, some now living until early adulthood, although their mortality rate is still considerably higher than other groups of mentally handicapped people (Landesman-Dwyer and Sackett, 1978). The trend in increasing longevity is currently causing a number of problems for adult training and education centres in developing suitable environments for such low-functioning people. It is likely that their numbers will continue to rise, particularly with advances in both medical science and patterns of environmental care.

The first long-term study of this group was observational, noting activity levels in different environments. It was carried out by Landesman–Dwyer (1974), who identified a number of defining group characteristics, as follows:

1. Extreme limited responsiveness to external stimulation.
2. Obvious severe neuromuscular dysfunction.
3. Inability to move through space by any means other than simple turning.
4. Inability to achieve or maintain a seated position.
5. Poor head control.
6. Abnormally small body size for chronological age.
7. Records indicating a 'hopeless' prognosis for behavioural and physiological development, even with treatment.

In addition to these characteristics, the group showed signs of severe epilepsy, which usually presented from birth and was often cited as a major cause of the profound brain damage. As a result, various combinations of anti-epileptic drugs were prescribed to try to control seizure frequency. However, current animal research has shown that the use of such toxic medication with immature organisms itself carries with it the risk of producing brain damage (Diaz and Schain, 1978). Although one must always be cautious when trying to draw comparisons between animals and humans, it is felt that the closeness of the behavioural changes observed in both, at similar drug levels, is sufficient cause seriously to question the emphasis placed upon the control of seizures when the amount of anti-epileptic drug required is high. Clearly, once the dose is beyond the therapeutic threshold, the risk of drug-induced side effects becomes considerable. In addition, there is now much evidence showing the harmful effects anti-epileptic drugs have on a large number of bodily systems, especially blood, liver and kidney functions (Reynolds, 1975). There is also growing concern over the potentially harmful effects of anti-epileptic drugs on the behavioural and cognitive abilities of epileptic people (Stores, 1975, 1978). However, relatively little work has been carried out in this area with the mentally handicapped. The general findings from research with people of normal intelligence has indicated that anti-epileptic drugs have detrimental effects upon the following: overall reaction time and general vigilance (Dekanban and Lehman, 1975), perceptual and motor tasks (Matthews and Hartley, 1975) and short-term memory (MacLeod *et al.*, 1978). It has also been suggested that prolonged use of drugs can lead to progressive mental deterioration (Trimble and Reynolds, 1976). In conclusion, although anti-epileptic drug treatment is seen as a necessary treatment for epileptic people, it should be viewed with caution, possessing potential additional handicapping effects. (For a brief review of anti-epileptic drugs see Gadow, 1979, and also Chapter 8.)

Since the group's inclusion into the educational system, professionals have had to investigate closely the methods to be used to create an appropriate learning environment for children whose effect upon, and control over, their surroundings is practically zero. A number of authors indicated that the only realistic approach for dealing with the educational needs of the multiply handicapped is some method of microelectronic intervention (Gardner and Murphy, 1980; Lovett, 1982).

The design and development of microelectronic and electromechanical aids at Hull came about from a direct invitation from a local ESN(S) school. The equipment produced and the studies carried out by Lovett were based upon a developmental psychology analysis in which learning and manipulation of the person's environment were conceived in terms of making interaction possible between the child and the surroundings. Clearly, from the characteristics outlined above, the extent of the constraints placed upon these children is so great that this interactive process was not normally realizable. The rationale for using microelectronic learning aids, therefore, was to modify the child's environment and thereby enable him or her to interact with surroundings in a meaningful way. As with other studies described in this section, some form of sensory reinforcement was given automatically for 'on-target' behaviour. However, the aim of using such technology was not simply to increase operant rate of responding, but to aid primary care staff to initiate activity and develop an 'awareness' for the child of his/her own control over aspects of the environment. From such increased activity it was hypothesized this could then be used to develop adaptive skills.

During a three-year period a number of devices were produced which included:

1. An ultrasonic switch device, operated by the child, to turn on any piece of battery or electrical equipment.
2. A rotating chair in which the child could sit and, by means of activating one of a number of switches, rotate his/her position by 180° at a time.
3. A battery-operated car, in which the child could sit and travel on a predetermined path, for several seconds.
4. A rocking cradle.
5. A number of small devices designed to give visual reinforcement through large coloured lights.
6. A modified slide projector, in which a child could control the presentation of visual material.
7. A device for training limb movements.

While other devices were designed, the seven listed were actually built, but only the ultrasonic switch, the car and the modified slide projector were fully evaluated. A common feature of *all* was the importance placed upon the child's own active participation in operating them and thereby receiving positive reinforcement. It is only through active control and manipulation of the environment that overall development can take place (Piaget, 1952; Bruner, 1964; Fischer, 1980).

The first two studies carried out involved the use of the ultrasonic switch. This type of device is one in which sound of very high frequency is passed between transducers. If the sound beam is broken by an object, it produces an electrical contact similar to any switch and thereby turns on or off whatever equipment with which it is connected. The ultrasonic switch was built on to a wooden framework which could be placed underneath a mattress on which a child was laid. By adjusting the height of the beam, one could arrange that even the smallest movement of the hands, legs or even a finger could break the sound beam and thereby turn on a piece of battery-operated equipment. For the purposes of the experimental investigation into the usefulness of this device, music was used, played by a battery-operated tape-recorder, in the form of continuous nursery rhyme music.

In these studies an ABA design was employed with a yoked treatment control condition in the form of noncontingent reinforcement. Numbers of practical questions were asked, such as 'When was the most suitable time to work with the children?', 'Would their previous activity rate influence their test performance?', 'What was the most suitable type of environment to enhance activity?', 'How did the children's response rates fluctuate over time?' In order to try to answer these questions experimental sessions were carried out during periods throughout the day and in two treatment conditions: with other children and staff present, and alone in a quiet room. When reinforcement was available to the children it lasted for six seconds, after which the ultrasonic beam had to be broken once again for more music.

Participants in these studies were 7 children aged between 2 and 12 years whose mental ages were below 4 months. Most scored below the 2-months level of development in both mental and motor ability. They were all severely physically handicapped, epileptic and had some level of sensory deficit. The results showed that:

1. All children tested learned the association between breaking the ultrasonic beam and the administration of music during contingent reinforcement (CR) periods.
2. Response rate during baseline periods (sensory reinforcement not available) showed large fluctuations but remained essentially a straight line.
3. On the application of CR, response rate showed an immediate doubling over baseline sessions, even on trial one.
4. Over the 80 sessions making up the CR condition, overall response rate increased by more than four times that of baseline.
5. When CR was removed during the extinction phase, response rate showed a fast decline back down to a baseline level.
6. Noncontingent reinforcement (NCR) sessions initially resulted in a doubling of response rate. However, this showed decline over sessions reverting to a baseline level.
7. No differences were found during testing throughout different periods in the day.
8. A large increase in responding was seen when children were tested 'alone' in a quiet environment. This was found to be stable across conditions and approximated to being one-third more active when in a quiet environment. This result is consistent with that found by Landesman-Dwyer (1974).
9. Previous activity level appeared to have no effect upon test performance.

Mental Deficiency

During the first study the children were tested for only ten minutes at a time as it was felt by teaching staff that a longer period might fatigue them. However, this question was specifically addressed in the second study, which used a session length of forty minutes. From this it was found that, both between and within sessions, response rates increased during CR periods, whereas both showed rapid decline during NCR periods. This result indicates that, even with such low-functioning children, providing they are able to gain active control over the onset of reinforcement, their behaviour is maintained and shows a steady increase. In addition, throughout both studies the frequency of vocalizations and smiling was recorded. The results from this showed that all of the seven children increased their vocalizations and smiling during CR periods, suggesting a general awareness and pleasure from the learning environment.

As a major problem for NPMR, multiply handicapped children is their severe lack of mobility, any technique to give them some means of movement in the environment has important implications. Thus, a small battery-operated car was designed, in which a child could sit and have a short ride. The car was developed by the writer to be the basic component of a broader learning environment in which various other components (switches) could be added. The design was not for sole use with the most profoundly mentally handicapped but, with the attachment of a series of graded switching devices, could also be employed with the most able severely mentally handicapped. In this sense, this particular aid is constructed in a similar manner to the Pethna equipment, i.e. it possesses a central reinforcement device on to which various 'to-be' operated switches can be attached. In addition, the car was designed to have computer-controlled steering, consisting of a light sensor which followed a black line on a floor (for further details see Lovett, 1985).

The initial evaluation of this equipment involved the same group of children as in the first two studies. A multi-element design was used in which both periods of reinforcement (either CR or NCR) and no reinforcement are given in the same session.

During this evaluative study, subjects had to break an ultrasonic beam switch, similar to the one described in the first two studies. The results clearly showed the usefulness of the car. Children's response rate increased substantially during periods of CR, compared to either no reinforcement or NCR. As with the other studies, children smiled and vocalized more when using the car and teachers were able to make use of this device as part of their standard equipment for working with the group in question.

A major part of this evaluative study investigated whether NPMR, multiply handicapped children could discriminate between differences in their environment and thus alter their behaviour accordingly. If so, this has far-reaching consequences for the provision of training in terms of curriculum and the level to which this can go. By using nursery rhyme music as discriminative stimuli, indicating either the presence or absence of contingent reinforcement, clear supportive evidence was found to suggest that these children can show discrimination learning. Previous work by Haskett and Hollar (1978) and Murphy *et al.* (1979) found similar results. However, their data did not so clearly show how response rate can be dramatically increased with the use of an S^D. As a whole this study demonstrated that NPMR, multiply handicapped children can learn both simple associations and also to use information in their environment to modify their own behaviour. It is only in the kind of highly controlled environment offered by the car that this ability can be shown experimentally (for further details see Lovett, 1985).

Overall, the car had very dramatic effects upon the children's behaviour and activity levels. For example, even using a multi-element design without any form of S^D produced threefold increases in response rates during CR periods. This rate was increased to approximately eightfold when an S^D was used. Staff were also clearly affected by the children's use of the car and definite changes in opinion occurred regarding what individual children could achieve. For example, those taking part in the study who had been initially thought 'unteachable', particularly in conventional ways, were reassessed in the light of the results as quite active. Teachers could use the type of aid described to begin planning programmes which catered for the individual needs of their most multiply handicapped children. This could not be done using more conventional methods of stimulation.

In a further study using the car it was found that adaptive behaviours could be initiated and enhanced via the use of microelectronic technology. In this particular experiment, a specially designed grip-switch was built, which could be connected to the child's hand. A major problem with the members of this sub-group is their general inability to grasp objects. Although numerous attempts had been tried to teach such skills, these were unsuccessful. By the use of this grip-switch, connected to the car, the problem became far simpler. In a study which investigated the use of the grip-switch it was found that over 20 sessions, each lasting 20 minutes, overall grasp response increased from approximately 2 minutes to 12 minutes per session during CR periods. In one particular case, the child learned to keep the switch activated almost continuously. In addition, teaching staff noted that individual children were beginning to pick up objects in the normal classroom situation. This is a very important result which shows not only that adaptive behaviour skills can be trained using this type of microelectronic technology, but that it actually generalizes to other settings.

Conclusions

There appears to be impressive evidence for the continued employment of microelectronic technology in the form of individualized learning aids for the more severely and profoundly mentally handicapped. Its correct use, which should aim to give these persons the active control over their surroundings which their handicap normally denies them, can have major effects upon their interactions with others. In addition, it would appear that if we want to develop appropriate curricula for such individuals, we cannot begin until we initiate the process of environmental manipulation seen in normal and less handicapped children. Microelectronic technology can begin this process by enabling handicapped persons to make meaningful responses to their environment. Once these have been initiated, the same type of technology can gradually increase the response demands and thereby increase the repertoire of adaptive skills.

COMPUTER-AIDED LEARNING (CAL)

The usefulness of microcomputers in the education and training of mentally handicapped people of all levels appears to be widely accepted. However, many of the basic educational questions still remain unanswered concerning how new skills can be trained via this new technology. Numerous questions regarding computer-aided applications require close investigation and scientific evaluation. The remainder of this section will attempt to identify these.

Because of the complexity and level of expertise required to develop CAL applications, their design has often been left up to specialists in the field of computing. However, many now argue that this has been unfortunate and has tended to reduce the overall appropriateness of such applications. For example, in discussing the poor quality of software available for handicapped children, Stallard (1982), a teacher, suggests that this is a direct consequence of relying upon people outside the field of handicap.

In reviewing the present literature, and surveying many of the microelectronic systems presently being employed, it is very disappointing to find so little formal evaluation of their usefulness being undertaken. The considerable amount of time spend in developing such systems and the degree of enthusiasm shown by those engaged in this work need the support of those directly involved with the mentally handicapped and the advantages of formal evaluation of what they are producing. Much work presently under way runs a risk of failure because professionals in the field are not fully involved and/or evaluative measures are not being carried out. The type of enthusiasm being shown for the new technology, not properly guided, may ultimately lead to a conclusion that it has little to offer, a view far from the truth. In addition, there has been a tendency in the past for people to accept, too uncritically, many aids and applications which were said to be microelectronic- or microcomputer-based. There existed, and still does to a lesser extent, a danger of giving devices an assumed status and validation that they simply may not have. A similar point is made by Griffin (1982) in suggesting that a dangerous intoxication with technology exists within special education. More specifically she states: 'Too much energy is going into pushing the microcomputer as a prosthetic device and little into using the technology for developing the curriculum for special education.' In this, she is drawing attention to the fact that if we do not use technology in sensible ways then potential gains will be lost.

Although the situation is beginning to change, particularly with the moves made in Britain by the government-funded Microelectronics in Education Programme (MEP) and the development from this of the four Special Education Microelectronics Resource Centres (SEMERC), few evaluative studies are presently available. This problem is particularly acute for people with learning disabilities, as any devices produced need not only to take into account the numerous associated problems faced by the group, but also to be shown to fulfil their learning needs. In discussing the four regional SEMERCs, Hogg (1984) suggests that they are 'busily acquiring . . . locally generated software oriented towards the child with special educational needs'; however, he adds that 'little attempt at classification is being made, no constructive evaluation attempted (in educational terms) and no generalized overview of the curriculum effect offered'. This whole problem appears to be a reflection of the unwillingness of professionals with knowledge of the mentally handicapped to become involved at all levels of development of such technology. However, if we are to achieve the maximum potential from this form of intervention there needs to be considerably more emphasis placed upon planning and then careful evaluation directly from those professions closest to the mentally handicapped. It has only been through such careful and detailed experimental research in the field of mental handicap over the past three decades that we are now able to offer so much. It would certainly be the case that in the absence of research and evaluation into such areas as learning processes, gross and fine motor behaviour, self-help skills, language and communication, overall provisions for the mentally handicapped in our society would be very much poorer than they are today. Evaluation identifies new avenues for involvement, new questions to be answered, possible modifications to be made to new learning environments, together with helping to identify those who might gain most from a particular technique. There is a clear need to carry out scientific research into the construction of computer-based learning aids and into their suitability for various groups of handicapped people. As Weddell and Roberts (1981) suggest, because of the wide availability of new technology, its use must be developed and this should be done on a sound research basis.

Ways in which microcomputers can be used

That CAL has a place in mainstream education is becoming well established, its usefulness being shown in a small but significant number of studies (Schneider, 1980; Sevcik and Sevcik, 1980; Milsop, 1981; Saltinski, 1981). In addition, for those people with educational difficulties, CAL has been found to be valuable when it is used as a supplementary component (Burns and Bozeman, 1981). For example, Caldwell (1979) investigated the use of CAL to teach reading skills to nonliterate adults and found it a very useful additional component in the wider educational package offered.

There is presently much optimism concerning the employment of microcomputers in the education and training of handicapped people, its use being advocated by many (Goldenberg, 1979; Hart and Staples, 1980; Bennett, 1982; Green *et al.*, 1982; Hannaford and Taber, 1982; Hofmeister, 1982; Stallard, 1982; Goldenberg *et al.*, 1984; Hogg, 1984; Rostron and Sewell, 1984). However, unlike CAL in mainstream education, only a small amount of evaluation has been attempted with the handicapped (Goldenberg, 1979; Sewell *et al.*, 1980) and almost none with people who are mentally handicapped. A number of important factors need to be considered before appropriate microcomputer learning environments can be developed for persons with mental handicap which are unique to them. These will be discussed later.

The general rationale for employing such technology remains the same as for the use of microelectronic aids with the profoundly multiply handicapped: to reduce the constraints placed upon individuals due to their handicap, thus giving them the opportunity to interact and gain some level of control over their environment. It is only when CAL allows the user some degree of active control over the environment that increased skill acquisition is likely to be seen. It is suggested that the absence of such control in many educational software programs accounts for the slow progress and disappointing findings in the field of handicap generally. The use of CAL is no different from any other technique in education and should be seen within the broader curriculum framework if it is to be most effective, a view strongly held by Green *et al.* (1982). Surveying the field, there presently appears little concern for producing CAL programmes either which take account of the learning needs of the mentally handicapped in a developmental framework, or which are based upon the curriculum needs. For example, in discussing the production of educational software, Rostron and Sewell (1984) indicate that 'computer programs are being written . . . many . . . without . . . concern for educational philosophy or for the principles which govern human intellectual growth'. They add that if CAL is to be successful in the long term, it is essential that we do not lose sight of these principles because these will ultimately influence the scope of future work.

The way in which the microcomputer is used in a learning situation will be determined to a great extent by the client's severity of mental handicap. However, its ability to present information in the same or slightly modified ways, while monitoring the behaviour of the user and adjusting task difficulty accordingly, giving feedback and reinforcement in various modalities, makes it a potentially powerful tool. Its ability to reduce the complexity of environmental demands because of its own flexibility and power, its ability to control a number of peripheral devices and its small size account for the popularity and speed of its development. With regard to the microcomputer's teaching potential, Hannaford and Taber (1982) emphasize its flexibility but also suggest that CAL can provide a one-to-one learning environment, be interactive, offer a nonthreatening learning environment and maintain interest and motivation. These characteristics will be outlined in the review of the evaluation work below.

Because of the flexibility of modern microcomputers there is no unitary approach advocated by CAL workers. However, Watkins and Webb (1981) have identified six modes which they believe may be of benefit to the handicapped: drill and practice; tutorial; games; simulations; problem-solving; and computer-managed instruction (CMI).

By far the most common form of CAL mode with the mentally handicapped has been drill-and-practice programs, these being a direct translation of one traditional teaching style. The majority of programs being produced have not been evaluated for their usefulness with the client group for which they are intended, and many simply lack any understanding of the needs of a mentally handicapped person. A common error in a number of programs seen by the present writer has been to require from the user a greater degree of skill than the program is intended to teach. For example, in one simple program to teach moderately and severely mentally handicapped children to discriminate between a 'square' and a 'circle', the response required from the child was to press the 'S' key when a square appeared on the VDU, or press the 'C' key if a circle appeared. Although many recently produced programs appear not to make the above mistake, their overall effectiveness in achieving what they set out to do can be questioned. It is likely that over 50 per cent of programs written to be used with the mentally handicapped are simply pitched at the wrong developmental level or do not fit in with the broader curriculum requirements.

Alternatives to the conventional QUERTY keyboard

One of the most important factors to take into account when considering using microcomputers is their design, which is not appropriate to most handicapped people. A computer which has not been designed specifically for the handicapped will have to be physically modified before it can be used. This is a quite separate issue from the development of appropriate software, but should be viewed as important. Numerous attempts have been made to simplify the method by which the user can input information. These have included the development of a variety of 'modified keyboards' which functionally replace the standard QUERTY one.

One of the earliest attempts to do this, when working with the severely mentally handicapped, was in the mid-1970s at Hull University. Here a number of pilot CAL programs were produced to teach basic concepts to severely mentally handicapped schoolchildren. These included a coin-matching program and one which attempted to teach the concept of direction (up and down, left and right). However, with a minicomputer based in the Department of Psychology, it was clearly inappropriate to use a conventional keyboard with such children. A simpler keyboard with fewer alternatives was required so a small keyboard, consisting of just six 4 × 4 cm square keys, was constructed on to which pictures, words, letters or symbols could be attached. This modified keyboard thus effectively reduced the complexity of the normal one and made it possible for the children to respond to the computer. The system comprised a PDP8 minicomputer, a modified keyboard and a computer-controlled slide projector. It proved very successful, but was never systematically evaluated for its usefulness in the educational context. However, it did form the basis of work using CAL on a microcomputer carried out by Farnell (1983).

Another attempted modification of the conventional keyboard has been the production of the 'concept keyboard', made commercially by Staar Microterminals. This is a flat plate of approximately A4 size, which is connected to the microcomputer and contains 128 touch-sensitive switches covering its surface. Paper overlays are placed on the concept keyboard which correspond with the program being used. A particularly good feature is that it can be programmed via the conventional keyboard so that new overlays can be produced.

Alternatively, the perspex screen overlay device developed by Agar (1982) is much more able to facilitate user–computer instructions. In this modification, known as the 'microcube system', which was developed for the PET microcomputer, a perspex screen is connected to the VDU screen. This 'additional' screen is split into a series of panels which, when lightly pressed, activate concealed microswitches and thus enable interaction between user and machine to take place. Agar has used this system to teach concepts such as size. Typically, two rectangles would be presented on the VDU, one larger than the other. If the larger of the two rectangles were pressed, the individual user would receive reinforcement in the form of a flashing screen or a sweet.

Selection of the panel containing the small rectangle would result in a blank screen. An interesting finding from this work was that until the larger rectangle was seen to increase in size and the smaller to decrease in size, over successive trials, discrimination was difficult to achieve. Once size was *seen* to change in the given direction, users were able to discriminate large from small rectangles. This result is very similar to that found by Lally in trying to teach handwriting skills to the mentally handicapped, using a CAL technique.

Farnell (1983) developed a modified keyboard which could be used on almost all microcomputers, because it did not rely on any electrical connection to the machine. In essence, it was a large box into which the microcomputer was placed. Over the conventional keyboard was a perspex grid which held large keys (as many as required). When the keys were pressed by the user, they hit the conventional keyboard keys and thus simplified the standard keyboard layout. This apparatus was used to investigate coin recognition and the use of money with severely mentally handicapped children, and will be described later.

A final type of modified keyboard should be mentioned. It is one developed by EDC in Walsall and is described by Blagg (1982). This is called the 'adventure' keyboard. It is commercially available from Holloway Plastics and can be used with a TRS 80 Model I and III microcomputer; it is not really a keyboard at all. In one of its forms it is a model village board, on which objects can be moved around. Objects are moved via slots in the board, which pass over microswitches which feed back to the microcomputer. Thus the microcomputer is able to display on the VDU words and phrases, as well as graphics, about its journey. This is a much more interactive type of modification and use of the microcomputer. Although originally designed to make reading more interesting, it has great potential in many areas related to the mentally handicapped. It is this type of use of the microcomputer which is likely to have the greatest impact upon the mentally handicapped person, that is, programs which allow the user to take limited control over their environment and explore that environment, being given constant feedback about what he or she is doing. This approach is a long way away from the traditional drill-and-practice programs, but is nevertheless the direction in which CAL must advance.

One of the major problems with modified keyboards, and with software production, is the incompatibility of products. Apart from Farnell's work, most will only work on specific machines. However, it is likely that this problem will be overcome in time, but it should be considered when thinking about purchasing equipment.

EVALUATIVE STUDIES OF CAL

Although there are only a very small number of evaluated microcomputer-based applications for use with the mentally handicapped, their results collectively indicate possible directions for the future. Additionally, this work shows the versatility of such systems when developed appropriately. Only four studies will be reviewed, but each indicates different areas in which CAL can have benefits for mentally handicapped people. All the work presently available has been carried out with children, but the need to evaluate the utility with adults is desperately required.

One of the earliest identified applications of CAL was as a drill-and-practice machine to enable parts of the curriculum to be taught more effectively. A most successful area in mainstream education has been mathematics instruction and it is therefore not surprising that many CAL programs are involved in training such skills to mentally handicapped people. However, only one study to date has attempted to evaluate the use of CAL compared with more traditional methods, this having been undertaken with children diagnosed as learning disabled. The findings by Trifiletti *et al.* (1984) do, however, have clearly identifiable implications for such applications with the mildly mentally handicapped.

Twenty-one subjects took part in the study, their ages ranging from 9 to 15 years. They were randomly assigned to one of two groups: a computer group (N = 12) and a remedial–resource room group (N = 9). Subjects in the former group received 40 minutes of computerized instruction per day, whereas those in the resource room group were provided with 40 minutes of mathematics instruction from their teachers.

The computer package used in this study was the SPARK-80 run on four Radio Shack Model III computers with disc drives. The SPARK-80 program included 112 basic skills in various areas of mathematics, such as addition, multiplication, division and fractions. Each skill has 5 delivery modes. These are:

1. Computerized Tutorial Instruction
2. Computerized Drill Instruction
3. Computerized Skill Games
4. Computerized Assessment
5. Computerized Word Problems.

Throughout the study a continuous measure of speed and accuracy was kept. At the end of each daily session subjects were given worksheets as homework which corresponded to their computerized instruction. If this was completed, they were allowed 5 minutes of computer games (a highly motivating factor in this study). Of course, the availability of computer games was not given to the resource room group.

The children were compared with respect to number of skills learned, number of skills lost, number of skills gained and yearly achievement gains. The results clearly showed that subjects in the computerized instruction group learned almost twice the number of new maths skills as the resource group over a period of 5 months. It was found that the mean number of skills gained by the computerized instruction group was 15.33 compared to 8.33 skills acquired by the resource group ($p < 0.05$). In addition, in looking at the yearly gain in mathematics skills, it was found that the computer group improved by an average of 8 months over the resource group, who only gained 3 months.

Trifiletti *et al.* suggest that these results clearly support the use of computerized instruction for students with learning disability as a viable alternative to existing instructional methods. In conclusion, they indicated that the increased skill acquisition could be attributed to four main factors: reduced fear of failure using the computer, the availability of computer games for additional work on mathematics, daily feedback from teachers, and the detailed nature of the program giving the teacher information of subjects' performance. The efficacy of this type of program needs to be demonstrated with the mentally handicapped before any conclusions can be drawn, but there does appear good reason to develop CAL systems of this kind for people with mild retardation.

A completely different CAL application has been demonstrated for use with moderately and severely mentally handicapped infants. In this study the microcomputer was used as a control device operating a number of reinforcing events. The work was carried out over a two-year period by Brinker and Lewis (1982), who used an APPLE II (48K) microcomputer in order to control the relationship between movements made by the children and their consequences. Throughout the study the microcomputer automatically recorded the frequency and duration of the infant's movements.

Because of the ability of microcomputers to process large amounts of information, the equipment used was able to monitor eight separate components of behaviour from children. Specifically, the experimenters identified classes of behaviour the frequency of which needed to be increased or shaped. These behaviours, when emitted by a subject, would be reinforced automatically by the microcomputer. For example, movements of the foot against a small panel, movement of the arm to which a ribbon is tied, reaching for a ball, were all able to be programmed and linked to contingencies of reinforcement. In addition, the type of reinforcement available to the infants could be switched automatically within sessions, depending on the infant's behaviour. For example, in the case where an infant who had learned to turn on a tape-recorder by moving an arm begins to habituate to the music, then arm movements would begin to decrease. However, the program was designed to detect such decreases in responding and then switch to another form of reinforcement, perhaps in a different modality. In addition, contingencies of reinforcement could be monitored and constantly modified. Thus the experimenters suggest that they had produced 'a sophisticated, portable interactive system . . . transforming the simple movements which infants make into more complex exploratory actions'. Because a microcomputer was used, this system is completely portable and can be taken into the home of the handicapped infant.

When working with individual children the experimenters established those movements which an infant could make, responses which were quite specific, and selected appropriate consequent events (i.e. suitable reinforcers).

Brinker and Lewis (1982) describe the results on four children between the ages of three months and four years. Their major characteristic was that they did not seem to be interested in physical objects in their environment and did not consistently reach for them. The results showed that using such a system produced clear differential responding when contingent reinforcement was available. The experimenters indicated that over time subjects clearly developed expectancies about controlling the environment and 'systematically varied their behaviour to explore specific contingencies'.

In conclusion, Brinker and Lewis suggest that this procedure requires no social interactions and is therefore an important addition to the normal range of experiences. It is interesting to note the similarity of the aims of this study and the series carried out by the present writer with NPMR, multiply handicapped children. It is suggested that this form of flexible and interactive use of the microcomputer is the logical progression with the very low-functioning individual, i.e. the computer as environmental controller.

A major difficulty for many mentally handicapped people is their handwriting inability. In one study carried out by Lally (1981), a CAL approach to this problem was used with moderately and severely mentally handicapped children. Although this study was carried out on a PDP 11/20 minicomputer it is being designed to be used with an APPLE II.

Because of the speed of handwriting, the feedback to the writer must be given extremely quickly. Therefore, as speed of information processing is one of the main characteristics of a computer, it would appear logical that it could be used to help develop and train such a skill. Therefore, Lally (1981) developed such a system, based upon a prototype originally produced by Macleod and Lally (1981). The apparatus consisted of a display screen, laid flat on a school desk, and a specially designed light-pen with which subjects could write. Both display screen and light pen were controlled by a PDP 11/20 computer. The display screen measured 22 × 22 cm and consisted of a 512 × 512 matrix of neon orange light points, each able to be lit independently by the light-pen. The size of the light-pen approximated to that of a thick pencil. It was kept in place (on the display screen) using two fine strings, lightly tensioned. The tip of the pen was spring loaded and operated a switch when sufficient pressure was being exerted. This then caused one of the neon lights to light up and in this way lines could be drawn, just as if the pen was a real one.

During the experiment the computer would display incomplete outlines of lower-case letters (3–4 cm high). Subjects were required to trace around each letter correctly. The sensitivity of the light-pen could be adjusted so that each subject's handwriting could be shaped. For example, initially all that was required was to place the pen on the outline of a letter and it would then be filled in by the computer. However, over sessions, subjects were required to make closer and closer approximations to the specific shape of the letter in order for it to light up. In this way, the work can be seen as a computer-aided shaping programme.

Each subject attended four 20-minute sessions per week. During the first session of the experiment, subjects were familiarized with the equipment, being required to carry out some simple tracking exercises. Sessions were carried out over a 4-week period (i.e. 16 sessions in all). Samples of handwriting before and after this experimental period were taken and analysed by two independent raters on a 10-point scale. The scoring was based upon correct formation of letters, hand control, confidence and care displayed, and the position of letters on a page.

The initial results for 6 children, 2 with mild and 4 with moderate mental handicap, showed that all improved their handwriting skills. The greatest improvement was seen in the roundness of letters, and the smoothness and size of individual letters. For example, with one of the mentally handicapped children, the size of handwriting reduced from 12 cm to 3 cm in the classroom situation.

In a further study Lally (1981) investigated this technique with 9 mentally handicapped children between the ages of 9 and 16 years and with a mean IQ of 61 (range 41–81). All were selected on the basis of having the poorest handwriting skills in the special school. Subjects were exposed to three treatment conditions related to the sensitivity of the light-pen. These were a wide sensitivity (15 mm), a narrow sensitivity (5 mm) and a changing sensitivity over sessions (15–5 mm). As with the previous subjects, samples of handwriting before and after the experimental period were taken. The results showed that the largest improvement occurred within those three subjects exposed to the variable sensitivity treatment condition.

In two studies the utility of CAL for teaching coin recognition and the skill of counting money were investigated. Farnell (1984) aimed to develop and evaluate software which could fit into an educational framework. The goals set were that the children using the programs would:

1. Be able to use the computer.
2. Show evidence of learning in terms of increased success over time.
3. Be able to transfer any learning to other situations, so that its real educational value could be shown.

The work was carried out at a special school for severely mentally handicapped children in North Humberside, using an APPLE II computer with pupils from the middle and senior classes. Thirty subjects were initially assessed for the two studies whose ages ranged from 12 to 15 years. As pointed out by Farnell, the group was heterogeneous, ranging from the upper end of the severely mentally handicapped to others who had no language ability and few skills. Unfortunately, no intellectual or social assessments were carried out but the subjects represented a cross-section of children found in such schools.

The first program written concerned coin recognition, based on the earlier work in the Department of Psychology at Hull University using a PDP8 minicomputer, described on p. 569. As much of the normal classroom activities concerns the development of basic discriminatory skills, Farnell considered the computer to be a potentially useful 'additional' component in this. His reason for choosing coin recognition and counting money was because of its obvious practical value to the mentally handicapped person.

Coin recognition is a simple perceptual learning task which is suitable for a wide range of children in schools. For the study, coin recognition was defined as the ability to learn the association between an auditory stimulus and the perceptual–tactile sensation of the coin. As such the first program gave verbal commands to children using it, and the child had then to press a key.

Thirty children were assessed initially to ascertain whether they were able to discriminate between 1p, 2p, 5p, 10p and 50p coins and if they were able to name them. All could discriminate the 5 coins, i.e. match them, but 11 could not reliably pick up a particular coin on request. It was these 11 children who took part in the study.

The program was very straightforward. Through the use of a cassette recorder controlled by the computer, together with visual displays of the coins required, subjects had to press a key on the modified keyboard (described on p. 569). Fixed to each key were the actual coins themselves. In the experimental setting the tape would ask the child 'Can you give me 5p?' There were 11 tapes used and these ranged in complexity until all 5 coins were asked for randomly.

The reinforcement used in this experiment was both social praise (at the start of the study) and computer graphics in the form of a colour character which walked across the screen and put a 'tick' on it. Farnell found that once the children were used to the 'system' they could be left independently of supervision.

In the experiment a voice would request the subject to press a coin and a visual facsimile would appear on the colour monitor, thus giving visual feedback. This information was gradually removed and, by tape 11, subjects were receiving only auditory requests.

Of the 11 children who started this experiment, 2 were found to be too anxious and were therefore not tested further. Of the remaining 9, 6 were successful in increasing their coin-recognition abilities. The 3 who failed to discriminate did so with the 1p and 2p coins.

Having established coin recognition in 6 children who had previously been unable to discriminate between coins, Farnell established some evidence to indicate that this was transferable to real-life situations. This was tested in two ways:

1. A child was given a handful of coins and asked to give back particular coins, e.g. 'Can I have a 10p please?'
2. The child was then sent to the school tuck shop to get specific items.

The results showed that there was good performance when children were simply asked for coins, but somewhat poorer performance when buying items.

Farnell concluded that the use of CAL in this area of skill training and with this group of subjects was effective. However, he indicated:

1. Initial assumptions about the computer being a basic teaching medium should be seriously questioned.
2. It was important how the subjects using the equipment perceived the task, i.e. is it a learning task or a game?
3. The best ways to label success and failure: he suggested that for those who succeeded, the very fact that they were able to press the 'correct coin' on the keyboard appeared enough reward in itself to maintain their interest and behaviour.
4. For those who did not succeed this may have been due to numerous problems such as motivation, lack of understanding of the situation, or anxiety.

Farnell added: 'In the teaching situation it would not be advisable, nor would I wish to see, the microcomputer become an isolated part of the education of the mentally handicapped for teaching normal coin usage.'

The second program Farnell designed was one which aimed to develop the skill of counting money correctly. Again, this is a skill which is particularly important and one which is made more difficult by some traditional educational approaches. For example, there is an assumption that counting money cannot begin until the child has acquired the concept of number. However, this may not be the case as many children who do not have this concept still possess a high degree of adaptive skills. In addition, Farnell suggests that much time is spent in the classroom counting coins which are functionally useless, i.e. 1p and 2p coins, with which one can hardly buy single items. Farnell also argues that coin equivalence is seen as being important. However, this is a very complex skill to acquire.

The aim of the program, therefore, was to develop a technique of coin usage which did not rely upon the concept of coin equivalence, or the concept of number. The study was split into four stages:

1. Counting in 10p coins (from 10p to 40p).
2. 50p coin introduced (counting from 50p to £1.00)
3. 5p introduced (counting 35p–75p)
4. 1p and 2p coins introduced.

Some of the children tested got to stage (3) but no further.

Again, the experimental situation was as before, with the computer giving visual feedback and controlling a tape-recorder. A verbal request from the tape would be given such as 'Can you give me 20p?' When the subject pressed the various keys on which the coins were fixed, visual facsimiles would appear on the monitor. In addition, a running total was displayed of the total coins they had pressed. *Two* buttons were used, one to signal that they had finished, the second to delete the full sum to enable subjects to start again.

Again 11 tapes were used which ranged from values of 10, 20, 30, 40p to tape 11 which asked for random amounts made up of all 5 coins. *Six* subjects were selected for this study (one from the original sample, i.e. a child who originally could not even discriminate between the 5 coins). At the start, 3 children had understanding of the order of the coins, and 3 did not. All children could count from 1 to 10 and do simple sums. In addition, all could count out small amounts of money in 1p coins.

After 4 weeks of use with this program, all subjects had shown some improvements. They were then tested in a real-life shopping situation. In this, children had to visit 4 shops with the experimenter and had target values – each based upon the child's success on the computer. The results of this post-experimental evaluation were that 58 per cent of children were able to achieve targets in shops; 34 per cent required an initial prompt, and only 8 per cent failed to achieve target. Unfortunately, no control group was used to compare these results, although it is clear that these figures do represent an improvement in the level of skill in the individual children.

In his general conclusions concerning both programs, Farnell indicated that:

1. The computer was of value to the children.
2. The computer was used independently.
3. There was high motivation to use the computer.
4. There was evidence to show that the computer could be used as part of the education of children.
5. Learning and transfer did take place.

CONCLUSIONS

Although many would argue that the microcomputer can be used as a very effective learning aid for mentally handicapped people, there is only a small amount of evaluative research to support this claim. However, the four projects summarized in this section do show specific areas of use.

In many ways the modern microcomputer is so obviously inappropriate to meet the learning requirements of the mentally handicapped user that many professionals are dissuaded before they begin. The main point discussed was that microcomputers are not built or designed with the handicapped in mind. Their reliance for inputting information using the QUERTY keyboard is not suitable for the vast majority, nor is the output of information via a VDU. If information is displayed in the form of letters and words it obviously requires that the individual user can understand and act upon that type of information. However, once this hardware problem is overcome, appropriate software has to be developed which both meets the specific learning needs of the user and fits into the broader curriculum objectives. This is no simple matter and is clearly the major problem in the effective demonstration of CAL as a component of the wider education and training of the mentally handicapped. At present, most facilities are finding themselves in possession of highly sophisticated microcomputer systems but cannot use them because of the lack of good-quality software. As a final point, it should be remembered that the eventual failure of teaching machines was not because applications could not be found, but because their software was either inappropriate for the group or simply undeveloped. One should really ask whether history could possibly repeat itself for our mentally handicapped citizens?

REFERENCES

ACCRINO, S. and ZUROMSKI, E.S. (1976) 'Simple discrimination learning with sensory reinforcement by profoundly retarded children', unpublished paper presented at the EPA Convention, Washington, DC.

AGAR, A.K. ST C. (1982) 'The development of a microcomputer-based teaching system for mentally handicapped individuals. The computer as an aid for those with special needs', Sheffield City Polytechnic, Conference Proceedings.

BENNETT, R.E. (1982) 'Applications of microcomputer technology to special education', *Except. Child.*, 49, 106–13.

BLAGG, T. (1982) 'Learning should be fun. Learning to cope', *Educ. Comput. Spec.*, 32–3.

BRINKER, R.P. and LEWIS, M. (1982) 'Making the world work with microcomputers: a learning prosthesis for handicapped infants', *Except. Child.*, 49, 163–70.

BRUNER, J.S. (1964) 'The course of cognitive growth', *Amer. Psychol.*, 19, 1–15.

BURNS, P.K. and BOZEMAN, W.C. (1981) 'Computer-assisted instruction and mathematics achievement: is there a relationship?', *Educ. Technol.*, 21, 32–9.

CALDWELL, R.B. (1979) 'The effects of selected strategies for teaching reading to non-literate adult learners using computer-based education', paper presented at the annual meeting of the American Educational Research Association, San Francisco, April.

CARR, J. and WILSON, B. (1980) 'Self-help skills: washing, dressing and feeding', in W. YULE and J. CARR (eds), *Behaviour Modification for the Mentally Handicapped*, London, Croom Helm.

CONLEY, R.W. (1973) *The Economics of Mental Retardation*, Baltimore, Johns Hopkins University Press.

DEKANBAN, A.S. and LEHMAN, E.J. (1975) 'Effects of different dosages of anticonvulsant drugs on mental performance in patients with chronic epilepsy', *Acta Neurol. Scand.* 52, 319–30.

DIAZ, J. and SCHAIN, R. (1978) 'Phenobarbital: effects of long-term administration on behaviour and brain of artificially reared rats', *Science*, 199, 90–1.

EVANS, C. (1979) *The Mighty Micro: The Impact of the Micro-chip Revolution*, London, Gollancz.

FARNELL, B. (1983) 'Using microcomputers with severely mentally handicapped children', paper presented at the British Institute of Mental Handicap conference, Using Microelectronic Aids with Mentally Handicapped People, University of Hull, April.

FARNELL, B. (1984) Assessment of Computer-Aided Learning with Severely Mentally Handicapped Children, MSc. thesis (in preparation), University of Hull.

FISCHER, K.W. (1980) 'A theory of cognitive development: the control and construction of hierarchies of skills', *Psychol. Rev.*, 84, 477–531.

FRIEDLANDER, B.Z., MCCARTHY, J.J. and SOFORENKO, A.Z. (1967) 'Automated psychological evaluation with severely retarded, institutionalized infants', *Amer. J. Ment. Defic.*, 71, 909–19.

FULLER, P.R. (1949) 'Operant conditioning in a vegetative human organism', *Amer. J. Psychol.*, 62, 587–90.

GADOW, K. (1979) *Children on Medication*, Virginia, Council for Exceptional Children.

GARDNER, J.M. and MURPHY, J. (1980) 'The development of toys for the multiply handicapped', in the report by Walsall Education Authority 'Teaching the multiply handicapped'.

GLENN, S.M. (1983) 'The application of an automated system for the assessment of profoundly mentally handicapped children', *Internat. J. Rehab. Res.*, 6.

GLENN, S.M. and CUNNINGHAM, C.C. (1983) 'Selective auditory preferences and the use of automated equipment by severely, profoundly and multiply handicapped children', working paper, March, Hester Adrian Research Centre, University of Manchester.

GLENN, S.M., CUNNINGHAM, C.C., JOYCE, P.F. and CREIGHTON, W.T. (1979) 'An automated system for the study of auditory preferences in infants', Infants Project Paper 10, Manchester, Hester Adrian Research

Centre, University of Manchester.

GOLDENBERG, E.P. (1979) *Special Technology for Special Children*, Baltimore, University Park Press.

GOLDENBERG, E.P., RUSSELL, S.J., CARTER, C.J., STOKES, S., SYLVESTER, M.J. and KELMAN, P. (1984) *Computers, Education and Special Needs*, Reading, California, Addison-Wesley.

GOODALL, E. and CORBETT, J. (1982) 'Relationship between sensory stimulation and stereotyped behaviour in severely retarded children', *J. Ment. Defic. Res.*, 26, 163–75.

GOODALL, E., CORBETT, J., MURPHY, G. and CALLIAS, M. (1981) 'Sensory Reinforcement Table for severely retarded and multiply handicapped children', *Apex: J. Brit. Inst. Ment. Handicap*, 9, 96–7.

GOODALL, E., CORBETT, J., MURPHY, G. and CALLIAS, M. (1982) 'Sensory Reinforcement Table – an evaluation', *Ment. Handicap*, 10, 52–5.

GREEN, F., HART, R., MCCALL, C. and STAPLES, I. (1982) *Microcomputers in Special Education*, London, Longman, for the Schools Council.

GRIFFIN, P. (1982) 'A powerful servant, nothing more', *Times Educ. Suppl.*, 10 September, 41–2.

HANNAFORD, A.E. and TABER, F.M. (1982) 'Microcomputer software for the handicapped: development and evaluation', *Except. Child.*, 49, 137–42.

HART, B. and STAPLES, I. (1980) 'Microcomputers in special schools', *Spec. Educ.: Forward Trends*, 1, 22–5.

HASKETT, J. and HOLLAR, W.D. (1978) 'Sensory reinforcement and contingency awareness in profoundly retarded children', *Amer. J. Ment. Defic.*, 83, 60–8.

HOFMEISTER, A.M. (1982) 'Microcomputers in perspective', *Except. Child.*, 49, 115–21.

HOGG, R. (1984) *Microcomputers and Special Educational Needs: A Guide to Good Practice*, Developing Horizons in Special Education Series 5, Stratford-upon-Avon, National Council for Special Education.

HOWLIN, P. (1980) 'Language training', in W. YULE and J. CARR (eds), *Behaviour Modification for the Mentally Handicapped*, London, Croom Helm.

JONES, C. (1979) 'The use of mechanical vibration with the severely mentally handicapped. Part I: Clinical effects', *Apex: J. Brit. Inst. Ment. Handicap*, 7, 81–2.

JONES, M. and KETTERIDGE, K. (1979) *Meldreth Manor Occasional Papers: Meldreth Electronic Aids*, Book 1, London, The Spastics Society.

KIERNAN, C.C. (1974a) 'Experimental investigation of the curriculum for the profoundly retarded', in J. TIZARD (ed.), *Mental Retardation: Concepts of Education and Research*, London, Butterworth.

KIERNAN, C.C. (1974b) 'Behaviour modification', in A.M. CLARKE and A.D.B. CLARKE (eds), *Mental Deficiency: The Changing Outlook*, 3rd edn, London, Methuen.

KITCHEN, T. (1982) 'Independence and its interaction. Learning to cope',

Educational Computing Special Issue.

KITCHEN, T. (1983) 'Simple additions. Learning to cope', *Educational Computing Special Issue.*

LALLY, M. (1981) 'Computer-assisted handwriting instruction for retarded children and the role of visual/kinaesthetic feedback process', in W. GLADSTONES (ed.), *Ergonomics and the Disabled Person*, Canberra, Commonwealth Government Printer.

LALLY, M. (1982) 'Computer-assisted handwriting instruction and visual/kinaesthetic feedback process', *Appl. Res. Ment. Handicap*, 3, 397–405.

LANDESMAN-DWYER, S. (1974) 'A description and modification of the behaviour of nonambulatory, profoundly mentally retarded children', unpublished doctoral thesis, University of Washington.

LANDESMAN-DWYER, S. and SACKETT, G. (1978) 'Behavioural change in nonambulatory, profoundly mentally retarded individuals', in C. MEYERS (ed.), *Quality of Life in Severely and Profoundly Mentally Retarded People: Research Foundations for Improvements*, Washington, DC, AAMD Publications.

LOVETT, S. (1982) 'The use of electromechanical and computer-based aids to increase activity and develop learning potential in nonambulatory, profoundly mentally retarded, multiply handicapped children', paper presented at the BPS annual conference held at the University of York; abstract published in the *BPS Bulletin*, 35, A13.

LOVETT, S. (1984a) 'An experiment to investigate discrimination learning in NPMR, multiply handicapped children using an electromechanical car', paper presented at the symposium, Organizing Environments for Mentally Handicapped People, Hester Adrian Research Centre, University of Manchester.

LOVETT, S. (1984b) 'An experiment to investigate the use of microelectronic technology in developing increased grasp responses on nonambulatory, profoundly mentally retarded, multiply handicapped children', unpublished M. Clinical Psychology thesis, University of Liverpool.

LOVETT, S. (1985) 'Using microelectronic and electromechanical aids to increase activity in NPMR, multiply handicapped children', PhD thesis (in preparation), University of Hull.

MACLEOD, C.M., DEKANBAN, A.S. and HUNT, E. (1978) 'Memory impairment in epileptic patients: selective effects of phenobarbital concentration', *Science*, 202, 1102–4.

MACLEOD, I. and LALLY, M. (1981) 'The effectiveness of computer-controlled feedback in handwriting instruction', in R. LEWIS and E.D. TAGG (eds), *Computers in Education*, Amsterdam, North-Holland.

MATTHEWS, C.G. and HARTLEY, J.P. (1975) 'Cognitive and motor-sensory performance in toxic and non-toxic epileptic subjects', *Neurology*, 25, 184–8.

MILSOP, M.P. (1981) 'So you've got a microcomputer in physics class – now what?', *Physics Teacher*, 7, 142–51.

MURPHY, G., CALLIAS, M. and CARR, J. (1983a) 'Increasing simple toy play in the profoundly mentally handicapped: I. Training to play', unpublished experiment, Institute of Psychiatry, University of London.

MURPHY, G., CARR, J. and CALLIAS, M. (1983b) 'Increasing simple toy play in the profoundly mentally handicapped child: II. Designing special toys', unpublished paper: data presented at the BPS annual conference, York.

MURPHY, R.J. and DOUGHTY, N.R. (1977) 'Establishment of controlled arm movements in profoundly retarded students using response contingent vibratory stimulation', *Amer. J. Ment. Defic.*, 82, 212–16.

MURPHY, R.J., DOUGHTY, N.R. and NUNES, D. (1979) 'Multielement designs: an alternative to reversal and multiple baseline evaluation strategies', *Ment. Retard.*, 17, 23–7.

NATIONAL ACADEMY OF SCIENCE (1979) *Microstructure Science, Engineering and Technology*, Washington, DC, National Academy of Science.

PIAGET, J. (1952) *The Origins of Intelligence in Children*, New York, International University Press.

REMINGTON, R.E., FOXEN, T.H. and HOGG, J. (1977) 'Auditory reinforcement in profoundly retarded multiply handicapped children', *Amer. J. Ment. Defic.*, 82, 299–304.

REYNOLDS, E.H. (1975) 'Chronic antiepileptic toxicity: a review', *Epilepsia*, 16, 319–52.

RICE, H.K., MCDANIEL, M.W., STALLINGS, V.D. and GATZ, M.J. (1967) 'Operant conditioning in vegetative patients, II', *Psychol. Record*, 17, 449–60.

ROSTRON, A.B. and SEWELL, D.F. (1984) *Microtechnology in Special Education*, London, Croom Helm.

SALTINSKI, R. (1981) 'Microcomputers in social studies: an innovation technology for instruction', *Educ. Technol.*, 21, 29–32.

SANDHU, J. (1983) 'The use of microelectronics in education of ESN(S) children', Handicapped Persons Research Unit, Newcastle Polytechnic.

SCHNEIDER, M.S. (1980) 'Computer-assisted skill assessment in secondary math curriculum', *Technol. Horizons Educ.*, 7, 34–5.

SEVCIK, E. and SEVCIK, J. (1980) 'PET reading room program: a learning program for problem readers', *Recreational Computing*, 8, 25–8.

SEWELL, D.F., CLARK, R.A., PHILIPS, R.J. and ROSTRON, A.B. (1980) 'Language and the deaf: an interactive microcomputer-based approach', *Brit. J. Educ. Technol.*, 11, 57–68.

STALLARD, C.K. (1982) 'Computers and education for exceptional children: emerging applications', *Except. Child.*, 49, 102–4.

STORES, G. (1975) 'Behavioural effects of antiepileptic drugs', *Dev. Med. Child Neurol.*, 17, 646–58.

STORES, G. (1978) 'Antiepileptics (anticonvulsants)', in J.S. WERRY (ed.), *Pediatric Psychopharmacology: The Use of Behaviour Modifying Drugs in Children*, New York, Brunner/Mazel.

TRIFILETTI, J.J., FRITH, G.H. and ARMSTRONG, S. (1984) 'Microcomputers versus resource room for LD students: a preliminary investigation of the effects of maths skills', *Learning Disab. Quart.*, 7, 69–76.

TRIMBLE, M.R. and REYNOLDS, E.H. (1976) 'Anticonvulsant drugs and mental symptoms: a review', *Psychol. Med.*, 6, 169–78.

WATKINS, M. and WEBB, C. (1981) 'Computer-assisted instruction with learning disabled students', *Educ. Computer Mag.*, 4, 24–7.

WEDDELL, K. and ROBERTS, J. (1981) 'Survey of current research in the UK on children with special educational needs', unpublished research, University of London, Institute of Psychiatry.

WEHMAN, P. and MARCHANT, J.A. (1978) 'Improving free play skills of severely retarded children', *Amer. J. Occup. Ther.*, 32, 100–4.

WOODS, P. and PARRY, R. (1981) 'Pethna: tailor-made toys for the severely retarded and multiply handicapped', *Apex: J. Brit. Inst. Ment. Handicap*, 9, 53–4.

16

Communication

Chris Kiernan

INTRODUCTION

In this chapter a selection of studies on the communication and language skills of mentally handicapped people will be described, and important trends in remediation will be discussed. Few areas of research relevant to mental handicap can have undergone the radical transformation which has been wrought in this area during the past decade. In particular, empirical studies of normal development have given rise to fertile linking of language to cognitive development and of the evolution of language to social context and social development.

The decade has also seen a substantial increase in work on the growth of the communication and language skills of mentally handicapped people. Remedial techniques have been developed, both from research bases and from practitioner-led innovation. The introduction of microprocessors into research and remedial contexts may mean that we are entering a further period of rapid growth in knowledge and skills.

The chapter will outline the main theoretical changes which have stemmed from the study of normal infants and children. The extent to which mental handicap research has built on the work will then be examined. Its purpose will be to air a number of issues and to suggest lines of research which may be fruitful for the next decade. A selective overview of remedial techniques and programmes will then be provided. This survey will allow us to highlight a number of issues relating to research in remediation and again to suggest lines for future work.

STUDIES IN NORMAL DEVELOPMENT

Research and theory concerned with the development of language and communication skills in normal children have passed through several phases during the past few decades. Prior to the mid-1950s, language development was a largely neglected field; published studies were conceptually thin, often concentrating on the development of vocabulary or the simplest aspects of grammar. Although there were exceptions (e.g. de Laguna, 1963), the absence of a general theoretical model in terms of which to conceptualize work in the field resulted in an arid and incoherent picture.

During the mid-1950s Chomsky (1957) and Skinner (1957) produced widely differing accounts of language development. Chomsky's analysis concentrated heavily on syntax as the central phenomenon of language and sought to explain how it was developed and codified. Skinner, on the other hand, placed much more emphasis on functional aspects. He recognized that spoken responses could serve a variety of social functions, in particular 'mands', which included asking, requesting, demanding or commanding, and 'tacts' which covered naming and describing. Skinner's other two categories were 'echoic' responses, in essence direct repetitions or imitations, and a problematic category called 'intra-verbals', which included elaborations, comments and other responses which related to the context of exchange.

Skinner's orientation relates to much contemporary thinking in its emphasis on the social function of language. However, the theory stimulated virtually no research. This was partly because it was not explored by behaviourally oriented workers and partly because Chomsky produced a very influential, harshly critical review of Skinner's book (Chomsky, 1959). This, combined with Chomsky's own theory, killed the influence of Skinner on the development of language theory in the 1960s and 1970s.

Chomsky's theory saw the acquisition and use of syntax as the central phenomena to be explained in language theory. One might caricature it by saying that Chomsky was, and is, centrally impressed by the young child's ability to learn appropriate syntactic structures at a rate which almost defies belief. The learning theory available in the 1950s and 1960s could not explain this rapid acquisition of complex skills and, as a consequence, he postulated that language learning represented an unfolding of preprogrammed abilities. One consequence is that if the physiological structures mediating language development are damaged, as they might well be in the severely mentally handicapped, language development will be inherently limited.

Chomsky's views remain important. There is no doubt that the development of syntax represents a crucial thread in language study, and one where the phenomena identified by Chomsky are still a mystery. However, from 1970 onward, two other threads have been identified and have become increasingly important.

One thread reflects the argument that spoken utterances encode meaning. This thesis, embodied in what has been called the 'semantic revolution', emphasized two points. On the one hand, the work of Bloom (1970) and others showed that it was not possible to understand the speech of young children (or much adult speech for that matter) without taking context into account. The same utterance, e.g. 'mommy sock', could mean a variety of things depending on the context in which it emerged.

On the other hand, there was increasing emphasis on the argument that language reflected what the person knew. Or, in other terms, that the developing child's language was closely related to his or her level of cognitive development. Piaget's theoretical model has been particularly influential as a structure in terms of which language evolution is explored (e.g. Morehead and Morehead, 1974).

One feature of the semantic analysis is of particular interest. Chomsky's thesis argues that syntax is central to language development and that the child's ability to use language results from maturing abilities to employ syntactic structures. The approach from semantics sees language as dependent, at least in part, on the development of cognitive abilities. In terms of remediation, the Chomsky approach suggests that the way to enhance language development would be to encourage or possibly to teach syntactic rules. The semantic view envisages another intervention strategy. The child, or adult for that matter, would be taught about the world; his cognitive development would be treated as prior to syntax. Once this knowledge is available it can be encoded in various syntactic forms. Consequently the focus of initial attack changes from syntax to cognition.

The other thread in work on normal development emerged in the early to mid-1970s. It involved a distinction between language, seen broadly as a system through which the world is represented, and communication, the use of language as a means of social interaction. The differentiation is important. Language can be used in an asocial way, for example in self-regulation or imagination. On the other hand, communication skills may not involve language as such, and certainly communication can be nonverbal or nonvocal, as in the case of facial expression, gesture or body language.

Beginning with the work of Bates (1976), Bruner (1975) and others, a series of studies has focused on the communicative skills of young babies. They have shown that these are developed well before speech emerges and before language as such is evident. These preverbal phenomena encode a series of intentions, including attention-seeking, requesting, greeting, protesting or rejecting, and informing (cf. Halliday, 1973; Dore, 1974). Studies of children at the single-word level and at later stages of development have produced similar lists (e.g. Dore, 1977). Atkinson (1982) points out that these various classification systems do not agree with one another in several respects. In practice, this limits their value, but there is none the less what Atkinson terms 'a fairly solid core of agreement on early appearing functions' (p. 153).

The really important point about this stream of work is that it embeds language within the context of communication and social behaviour. From this perspective expressive language can be seen as developing because it allows the child to influence his or her world more effectively. In other words, language develops not because it is preprogrammed, or as a side product of cognitive growth, but because the child needs it in order to relate to his or her social milieu (cf. Moerk 1977; Bates and MacWhinney, 1979). The child learns language at least in part as a social response, a way of relating to other people. And his sophisticated use of language, the acquisition of semantics and syntax, is again a part-result of a need to encode the increasingly sophisticated or precise messages which he wants to transmit and which his social context expects of him.

These notions have clear implications for remediation. Aside from the need to assess the individual's abilities in these various areas, the approach would suggest that progress will depend, in part, on the social relationship between the handicapped individual and other people. Put bluntly, if the individual gains no satisfaction from communicating, in terms of either material gain or enjoyment of the interaction for its own sake, he or she is unlikely to communicate and *pari passu* unlikely to develop language. Consequently, social development and the social environment become central in remediation.

Other fields of research and theory have emerged from the emphasis on communication. Interest in the analysis of discourse, including conversational skills, is growing rapidly (cf. Coulthard, 1977). These studies introduce important ideas. It is argued that successful discourse involves the ability to take the part of the other person, to understand what the other person needs to know, needs to have pointed out, in order to understand the speaker. This ability to 'presuppose' will entail the individual in talking to different people in different ways in different contexts. In addition, there are rules governing how topics for conversation are agreed upon, how conversation proceeds in terms of turn-taking and length of individual contributions, how breakdowns in conversation, caused by misunderstanding, or failure to hear, are to be 'repaired', and how topics are to be changed and conversations terminated (cf. Grice, 1975). Within this framework the importance of such features as intonation needs to be appreciated.

Conversational exchanges also define relationships among individuals in terms of social roles. Both content and style of utterances define dominant and submissive status. Again, rules about what can be said to whom and how have to be learned (cf. Mischler, 1975).

The findings from these relatively new areas of study of language and communication have potentially important implications for research on mental handicap and its remediation.

Conclusion

In this section the broad outlines of development of work on language and communication have been indicated, but with some areas, for example studies on articulation, having been omitted completely (see Ingram, 1976, for a useful discussion). What should be clear from this account is that there is considerable diversity of opinion in the field and a very active growth of knowledge and theory. In particular, it is obvious that language and communication skills are not to be explained by any one simple theory. In fact, we may never evolve a single theory which will cover all aspects of development. This argument has obvious implications for studies on mentally handicapped people and for the theory and practice of remediation. Among other considerations we need to develop theories and strategies for conceptualizing the impact of poor development in one area of functioning on others.

STUDIES ON MENTALLY HANDICAPPED PEOPLE

In this section a selective review of studies of the language and communication skills of mentally handicapped individuals will be provided. Readers are referred to other texts for more exhaustive consideration of particular areas (e.g. Bloom and Lahey, 1978; McLean and Snyder-McLean, 1978).

Guiding hypotheses

The majority of studies to be reported have been guided by the comparison of the delay hypothesis and the difference hypothesis. The delay hypothesis suggests that mentally handicapped people develop language and communication skills in the same sequence as do normal people and that, by inference, factors underlying development are the same. However, the argument runs, mentally handicapped people develop skills more slowly and they have a lower ceiling of development than normal individuals. The difference hypothesis suggests that the sequence, and possibly the final pattern of developed skills, is different in normal and handicapped people. Underlying mechanisms may be different and the concept of a lower 'ceiling' would not hold.

The delay–difference model has been used widely in mental handicap research. Weisz and Zigler (1979), in reviewing studies examining the relationship between Piagetian sequences of development in normal and handicapped populations, conclude that there is general support for the delay model because similar stages of development occur in the two populations and ceilings of development are lower. In fact, as will be seen shortly, the same conclusion can be drawn from studies of language development.

However, in considering this material two points should be borne in mind. First, it is really quite surprising that similar sequences do occur. Most severely mentally handicapped people are brain damaged, and one might expect the cerebral problems to affect their evolving abilities. Rather than being the end of the story, as often seems to be implied, support for the delay or similar sequence hypothesis should be the beginning of questioning why this should be. One explanation may lie in the suggestion that sequences are socially determined, another that studies have obscured differences through averaging over groups. Certainly one can argue that most studies explain what happens and not what fails to happen. Thus, studies of syntax examine how it develops, but do not ask about individuals who do not develop it.

Second, even though the sequences of development of a particular set of skills may be similar to those shown by normal children, the pattern across them may differ. Hence syntax may lag behind semantic knowledge and skills in the social use of language may be ahead of or behind both. These and other points are discussed on p. 604.

Phonology

Defective articulation is a common feature of the speech of mentally handicapped individuals (Fawcus and Fawcus, 1974). Although there are difficulties in equating the results of various surveys because of differences in samples, there is general agreement that mentally handicapped children produce errors of articulation which are consistent with a delay rather than a difference or deviance model (Ingram, 1976).

Several other hypotheses have been explored. Dodd (1975) has argued that the articulatory problems of Down's syndrome children reflect a 'disability in the motor programming of the speech act' (p. 306). This study has been extensively criticized by Rosenberg (1982), whose analysis casts substantial doubt on the validity of the conclusions. Similarly Hogg (1984) has shown that predictions from Dodd's hypothesis to other aspects of motor programming are not borne out.

Dodd (1976) compared 10 normal and 10 Down's syndrome children and reported that, although 23 rules accounted for the errors of normal children and a number of the errors made by Down's children, not all of the Down's children's errors were accounted for. Stoel-Gammon (1980) concluded from her sample of 4 mildly retarded Down's syndrome children that patterns were consistent with those shown by normal children. This study also suggests that the rate of development of the phonological system in Down's children does not lag behind the evolution of other aspects of their linguistic development. Smith and Stoel-Gammon (1983) compared normal and Down's syndrome children of similar developmental level and concluded that there were 'no major qualitative differences' (p. 117), but that more extensive analyses should be pursued before drawing firm conclusions. Hogg's data suggest that, while 11 out of 15 Down's syndrome children simply showed immature phonological deviations, 4 displayed aberrant phonology, possibly connected with some disorder of motor function. However, there was no relationship between these latter disorders and a measure of motor programming ability.

It is well to remember in this connection that common observation suggests that some mentally handicapped individuals either fail to develop any marked articulatory system or appear to develop highly deviant ones. They present a problem of initial elicitation and development of ranges of sound. Beyond this, the literature suggests that both delayed and deviant patterns may be identified, requiring careful individual analysis and consideration for remediation.

Syntax

Two sets of questions emerge in considering syntactic behaviour: what normally happens in the development of syntactic behaviour by mentally handicapped individuals? and can acquisition be hastened? The second takes point from Chomsky's critique of the applicability of learning theory to language learning.

Virtually all studies of syntactic development support the delay model in showing similar patterns of difficulty and error in mentally handicapped and normal children. This conclusion holds for use of vocabulary (Lozar *et al.*, 1973), use of syntactic structures (McLeavey *et al.*, 1982), understanding of syntactic structures (Wheldall, 1976), understanding different levels of transformation (Cromer, 1975), and ability to master morphological structures. This last topic has been investigated in several studies using Berko's (1958) test in which subjects are asked to produce appropriate inflections of various types. The results here show similar patterns of mastery in mentally handicapped and nonhandicapped children with, in general, poorer performance when nonsense words are to be inflected as opposed to real words (e.g. Dever and Gardner, 1970).

Several researchers have suggested that the grammatical skills of mentally handicapped children lag behind their mental age levels. For example McLeavey *et al.* (1982), using an elicited imitation task, found that performance of a mentally handicapped group with a mean MA of 5 years was equivalent to that of nonhandicapped children with a mean MA of just over 3 years. This finding concurs with studies by Lovell and Bradbury (1967) and Semmel *et al.* (1968). Mastery of morphological inflections appears to be an area of especial difficulty for mentally handicapped children.

This point adds edge to research which has sought to teach grammatical morphemes. Beginning in the late 1960s behaviourally oriented researchers rose to Chomsky's challenge and showed that mentally handicapped individuals could learn to understand and use a variety of grammatical morphemes when taught through imitation and reinforcement techniques (cf. Welch, 1981). An early study by Guess *et al.* (1968) is typical of this stream of work. They took as their starting point the fact that individuals typically show language behaviour which goes beyond what has been taught directly. In other words, a feature of normal language acquisition is its 'generative' nature: the developing child will 'spontaneously' produce language which suggests that he or she has learned and is using the rules governing language. The Guess study involved teaching a severely mentally handicapped girl to use plural forms, s and z (e.g. cups and cars), through an imitation training procedure. She was initially asked to name objects when presented singly, then to use the plural form when shown more than one example. At this stage prompting and reinforcement for correct imitation was necessary. The most stringent criterion for generative use was the production of the plural form on the first presentation of two objects. Guess *et al.* showed the successful acquisition of this type of generative use and also demonstrated control over the responses through reversing the use of plural forms, before finally reverting to correct plural usage in the last phase of the study. The use of imitation as a training procedure was seen as significant since both Chomsky (1957) and Lenneberg (1967) had expressed scepticism about its role in language development, questioning whether imitative learning could lead to acquisition of generative structures.

A large number of studies paralleling the above accumulated in the early 1970s. Possibly the most thorough series of investigations was concerned with instruction-following (e.g. Striefel *et al.*, 1978). In these the subjects were taught to respond to verbs such as 'push' or 'lift', in combination with nouns such as 'car' or 'block'. Striefel and his colleagues explored ways of teaching with the overall aim of finding methods which led as quickly as possible to subjects understanding instructions when first presented, i.e. learning the rule underlying pair formation. The optimal method emerged as one in which subjects were initially taught the meanings of nouns, verbs (and adjectives when used) and then to respond to a single verb–noun combination (V_1-N_1). Following attainment of criterion they were shifted to a second noun with the first verb (V_1-N_2) and, again, once criterion was achieved, to a second verb with the second noun (V_2-N_2). This stepwise procedure was used throughout a 12 by 12 matrix, or until the subject followed instructions without further training. Wetherby (1978) has provided a significant theoretical analysis of these and other studies in terms of conditional discrimination learning.

It seems clear from published research that mentally handicapped individuals show slow development of syntax and have particular problems with morphological inflections. However, their problems are substantially understandable within a delay rather than a difference model. Experimental teaching data demonstrate that inflections can be taught using suitable procedures. Whether their impact is sufficient to raise the level of syntactic function to that anticipated by MA levels has not been explored.

Semantics

The above conclusions concerning syntactic development also apply to semantic development. In general, studies suggest that semantic development in mentally handicapped individuals follows the same patterns as in normal development but is delayed relative to that of normally developing individuals. Given the potential importance of semantic development there are surprisingly few studies in the literature. In this section a selection of these are reviewed.

Many of the early investigations examined the development of vocabulary in mentally handicapped individuals. Mein and O'Connor (1960) studied the oral vocabularies of mentally handicapped children and adults in a subnormality hospital. The authors aimed to record words used in spontaneous conversation, but found that conversational themes were exhausted by about the third or fourth interview. Consequently they fell back on eliciting conversation through the use of pictures employed by Burroughs (1957) in a study of vocabulary of normal children of approximately equal mental age to the handicapped sample. This led to serious anomalies in the findings, with high frequencies of occurrence of words represented in pictures of zoos, supermarkets and the like, which presumably did not figure overmuch in a hospital vocabulary.

Papania's (1954) study reflects another common thread in early literature. He examined the types of definition given by handicapped children (MA 6–10 years, IQ around 70) for Stanford–Binet vocabulary items. Papania found that the proportion of abstract definitions increased with increasing MA and that, overall, the proportion given by mentally handicapped children was lower than that for a CA matched group.

More recent work has brought newer conceptualizations to bear. Several studies have investigated the distinction between availability of semantic information and its accessibility. Availability relates to what the individual has 'stored' in memory and is assessed through his or her ability to recognize events, words, objects or pictures as instances of one class or another. Accessibility refers to the ability of the person to recall (retrieve) information. An individual may 'possess' information, may have it available, but be unable to retrieve it (recall it) from memory because of a lack of appropriate recall strategies. In relation to studies of the mentally handicapped it is clearly important to investigate whether poor performance reflects problems with storage (availability) or with retrieval (accessibility).

Several studies using subjects of normal intelligence have suggested that age of acquisition of words relates to accessibility as assessed by the speed with which they are retrieved from memory from the 'lexical store' (Carroll and White, 1973a, b). Winters and Brzoska (1975) compared groups of normal children with a home-based mentally handicapped group (mean CA 11.89 years, mean IQ 71.61) on the speed of naming 480 pictured common objects. The results suggested that size of lexical store was related more closely to MA than to CA but that, for the mentally handicapped group, it lagged behind their MA matched normal group, a result reminiscent of the findings on syntactic levels. Winters and Brzoska also found that the lexical store for the mentally handicapped group was most deficient in the easiest words, i.e. those which were assumed to have been acquired earliest, but later studies have produced results which suggest that accuracy is related to age of acquisition in ways similar to those shown for normal subjects (e.g. Winters *et al.*, 1978).

Understanding and use of language involves employment of the conceptual categories expressed in its structure. One strategy for investigating these capacities is to examine the extent to which subjects associate or cluster items in memory (Bousfield and Sedgewick, 1944). These studies show that items which are clustered together will be recalled by adults more easily when required as a set than will disparate items. Clustering and recall are not as closely related in children or mentally handicapped individuals (Gerjuoy and Winters, 1970; Jablonski, 1974) but clustering develops during childhood and is subsequently an important ability.

The development of clustering ability was investigated by Winters and Brzoska (1976) through a task which explored the availability of category information to mentally handicapped and normal populations. Apparently the same groups were used as in the study mentioned on p. 592. The results suggest that classification of the pictures shown was a function of both MA and IQ levels, but that the mentally handicapped group performed at a lower level than their MA matched group, i.e. they underfunctioned in terms of MA prediction. The form of classification was also related to MA. As MA increased, so there was an increased likelihood that the superordinate classes given, the clusters, would correspond to normal adult criteria.

These data are reflected by several studies on word association. For example, Harrison *et al.* (1975) showed that, although the number and variety of associations were equivalent between normal and handicapped groups (mean IQs 70), the handicapped produced fewer superordinate and subordinate responses as associations.

The concept of clustering also underlies work on 'semantic priming', in which subjects are asked to name pairs of pictures. The priming effect emerges in the finding that the second picture in a related pair is named faster than the second picture in an unrelated pair (McCauley *et al.*, 1976). Studies by Sperber *et al.* (1976) and Glidden and Mar (1978), among others, have demonstrated this effect with mentally handicapped individuals (with IQs averaging in the 60s), again suggesting that organization of category knowledge is similar in retarded and normal individuals. Sperber's and Glidden's data suggest that subjects did not retrieve many of the relationships which were available to them, i.e. they did not verbalize what was recognized. This failure to use category information has also been found by others, e.g. Davies *et al.* (1981). More recently, Sperber and McCauley (in Brooks and McCauley, 1984) have argued that these and other results point to deficits in attentional allocation.

The studies described indicate the general importance of work on memory for an understanding of the development of language. Others have approached semantic aspects of language growth more directly.

Duchan and Erickson (1976) examined the understanding of four types of semantic relation – agent–action, action–object, possessive and locative – under a variety of conditions. Three groups of children, mentally handicapped, language-disordered and nonhandicapped were matched in terms of mean length of utterance (MLU). The results show an ordering of difficulty from possessive, the easiest form, to action–object and locative, the most difficult. There were no differences among groups, again supporting a delay or similar sequence hypothesis. Broadly similar conclusions were drawn by Bilsky *et al.* (1983), in the context of comprehension and recall of sentences, and by Luftig and Johnson (1982) and Luftig and Greeson (1983) in respect of recall of longer units of material. The Bilsky study is of interest in showing better performance by nonhandicapped than MA matched handicapped groups in recall of sentences (68 per cent as opposed to 43 per cent), but use of similar inferential processes. However, the authors argue that the differences between the groups may be traced to the tendency of the mentally handicapped subjects to produce the 'first response that came to mind' rather than checking and editing potential responses. This type of explanation is clearly more constructive than those which simply attribute differences to MA since it suggests ways in which performance might be improved through teaching.

Other studies have explored the expressive skills of mentally handicapped children. Layton and Sharifi (1979) used Chafe's (1970) classification of semantic features to analyse samples of the spontaneous language of Down's syndrome and nonhandicapped children. It showed that the structures used by the two groups were different in detail but that 'for the most part [there was] more similarity than difference' (1979, p. 444) between children with comparable MA or MLU. It also suggested that the Down's syndrome group's utterances were limited to basic 'here and now' features of pictures, objects and events.

Broadly similar conclusions were reached by Coggins (1979) who recorded language samples from four Down's syndrome children. The data suggest that these children, at the level of combining two words, tend to concentrate on the same small set of relational meanings as normal children. These include meanings concerned with ongoing or intended action, properties of objects, and existence, recurrence and location of objects and people.

Taken together these studies support a delay rather than a difference theory of development. They suggest, in particular, that the way in which information is encoded and retrieved from memory is basically similar in mentally handicapped and normal individuals. However, there is some evidence pointing to deficiencies in strategies of dealing with information which suggest possible methods of remediation.

A word of special caution is necessary in considering these results. The majority of relevant studies deal with more able mentally handicapped individuals (with IQs in the 60s and 70s). It is an open question whether the findings would be mirrored for less able individuals. Clearly, when considering profoundly mentally handicapped people who have no speech at all, considerations about size of lexical stores, clustering and knowledge of superordinates and subordinates become inapplicable. There is, however, a substantial gap in the literature relating to the severely handicapped who use some speech, but who are not as sophisticated as the subjects in many of the studies described here.

Social function

Data suggesting delayed development of syntax and semantic aspects of language need to be explained. One possibility is that they may reflect general cognitive delay although, as has been shown, there is evidence of delay over and above what would be anticipated from this source. A further possibility is that the retardation observed reflects delayed social development. Given that language develops, at least in part, as an aspect of this and in response to a need to relate to other individuals, anomalies in social relationships may explain delayed emergence.

From the start such hypotheses would provide only a partial explanation of delayed development. There is no evidence to suggest that mentally handicapped people, as a group, are antisocial or asocial; in fact the opposite holds for at least a proportion of the retarded. Studies of institutionalized populations (e.g. Zigler, 1964) and of the social interaction of mentally handicapped people in day facilities (Romer and Berkson, 1980) show high levels of social responsiveness and interaction. However, data on attachment formation do suggest that mental handicap can be accompanied by delayed or deviant attachment formation (Blacher and Meyers, 1983). Finally, sociability as such does not necessarily lead to productive social relationships in terms of learning.

Studies on language and communication skills approached from the viewpoint of social function fall into two groups. There are a substantial number of studies in which the interaction of mentally handicapped individuals and parents or caretakers has been examined. In addition, there is a body of literature examining the communicative behaviour of mentally handicapped people within the context of investigations of the social function of language.

Early studies of mothers' speech to their handicapped children suggested that they were being more directive in interchange and were using more 'primitive' forms of speech, thereby possibly inhibiting their children's language development. Later authors have argued that these conclusions were a result of CA matching rather than matching on MA or measures of linguistic development. When groups are matched appropriately, very few differences emerge. For example, Rondal (1978) matched in terms of mean length of utterance (MLU), and found very few differences between the language of mothers of Down's syndrome children and normal controls. The studies suggest that mothers are sensitive to features of their children's language behaviour and respond accordingly. As such they reflect a large body of data from studies of normal development which show that mothers adjust their speech according to the linguistic abilities of their children, possibly in order to maintain effective conversational interchange, and that these adjustments serve to facilitate language acquisition (e.g. Nelson, 1973).

A few studies have analysed the behaviour of children in cueing their parents. For examples, Jones (1977) studied six Down's syndrome and six normal children, matched for developmental age, in interaction with their mothers. She concluded that the former were more often 'supported' in their communicative role by their mothers, did not initiate as frequently and showed poor timing in turn-taking interactions with their mothers. Jones argues that the Down's syndrome children had a lack of sensitivity to their mothers which resulted in less opportunity for enriched feedback and a more directive and less stimulating environment. Similarly, Terdall *et al.* (1976) report that mentally handicapped children were less responsive to maternal social interaction, questions and commands than normal children of comparable developmental levels.

The Jones and Terdall studies suggest that conversation with handicapped children may be difficult to maintain because of lack of fine tuning on the part of the child, a conclusion consistent with suggestions made by Condon (1975). The studies can be interpreted within the proposition that mothers try to maintain 'conversation' with their offspring. For a variety of reasons, maintaining conversation with handicapped children by 'normal' means can be difficult. This in turn leads to adjustments in style of parent input toward being more directive and to structuring interactions more deliberately in order to establish initial contact and to maintain interaction. Interestingly, Guralnick and Paul-Brown (1980) found that nonhandicapped five-year-old children responded differentially to those with severe, moderate and mild handicaps. The normal children were more directive and provided less information the more handicapped the other child. The authors see these adjustments as increasing the likelihood that messages would be understood and responded to.

The quantity and quality of talk from care-givers to mentally handicapped children and adults have been examined in a number of studies of the impact of institutional rearing. Earlier research emphasized the overall detrimental effects of institutional environments on cognitive functioning, including language development (Lyle, 1959, 1960). In 1972 Tizard and her colleagues reported on the quality of adult talk to normal children in institutional environments. Their main conclusions were that level of language comprehension of the children was related to the frequency of informative talk by staff (as opposed, for example, to instructions) and also to the frequency with which adults responded to child-initiated verbal interaction.

A number of studies on environments for mentally handicapped people have followed the Tizard framework of analysis. Prior and her colleagues (1979) observed staff interaction with two groups of older people who had been institutionalized for a considerable period, and with a group of younger, more recently institutionalized individuals. They found that the most frequently occurring staff initiation was instruction and the least was conversation (e.g. 'What did you do today?'). However, it was conversation which elicited more verbal responses from the mentally handicapped residents than the other three types of staff initiation – comments, questions and instructions. This conclusion reflects that reached by Paton and Stirling (1974) who found that the most effective way of eliciting vocalization from mentally handicapped individuals was to converse with them. Prior *et al.* also found that staff initiation of interaction was higher in structured than in unstructured settings where frequency of verbal interaction was low. They ignored approximately one-third of all resident initiatives (92 responses) and responded yes/no (34), with an instruction (18), question (45), comment (60), and with a conversational response (36) to the rest. Interaction with the younger, less institutionalized group was higher than with the other groups, a finding which Prior and her colleagues relate to covert staff attitudes.

Raynes and her colleagues (1979) developed an informative speech index (ISI) based on five-minute observation periods. It classified staff talk as informative speech, i.e. 'statements which explain, give new information, or ask residents for information' (p. 28), controlling speech, subdivided into positive and negative control, 'other talk' and 'no talk'. The index was obtained by computing the average proportion of all observations which included speech classified as informative with periods where there were no residents present.

In a study of twenty-one buildings in residential institutions, Raynes and her colleagues found marked variation between residencies on the ISI (2.6–62.8 with a possible range from 0 to 100). In part this related to the likelihood of staff speaking at all but, of greater interest, buildings which housed similar groups of residents showed marked variations on the ISI. For instance, two residences which housed profoundly mentally handicapped men showed marked differences in ISI (26 and 18) with widely varying patterns of instruction giving and likelihood of replies by residents (Raynes *et al.*, 1979, p. 75). Like Tizard, Raynes *et al.* found significant correlations between informative talk and measures of language performance, in their case correlations with measures of comprehension and expressive abilities.

The Pratt and Raynes studies examine further the variables associated with ISI scores. The data described by Pratt *et al.* (1976) show a correlation between IQ and ISI which leads them to conclude that less competent residents provide different 'environments' for the staff care-takers and that these are related to provision of care which is 'characteristically unstimulating, undifferential, de-personalized, and rigid' (Raynes *et al.*, 1979, p. 97). Staff–resident ratios did not affect the ISI, but the presence of more than one staff member decreased the frequency of informative remarks. Raynes *et al.* suggest that this may be explained by staff talking to each other rather than to residents, an explanation backed by observations reported by Blindert (1975). Staff attitudes also affected informative talk, attitudes of general concern being associated with more frequent informative remarks. Long service was associated with *less* informative use of speech than service under a year, a finding which is, at least in part, interpreted in relation to 'staff institutionalization'.

The Raynes *et al.* study contains other significant and interesting findings which demonstrate the importance of examining the impact of attitudinal and organizational variables on staff–resident interaction. It goes some way to explaining how the interaction patterns observed in simple one-to-one situations are potentiated or distorted within wider frameworks of interaction.

The two groups of studies so far described examine the overall patterns of interaction between care-givers and mentally handicapped individuals. A further series of studies has focused on the detail of development of functional responding by handicapped individuals, usually against the background of normal development.

Several authors have examined the vocal and nonvocal behaviour of preverbal or minimally verbal mentally handicapped children using social function (or pragmatic) categories derived from developmental studies. These have, in general, provided data which are consistent with a normal developmental model in suggesting the emergence of precommunicative skills (attention and vocal responses to adults), followed by the use of 'proto-imperatives' (e.g. asking for objects) (McLean and Snyder-McLean, 1984). Kiernan and Reid (1985a) classified the reported nonvocal and vocal communicative behaviour of ninety severely mentally handicapped children and young people, most of whom lived in their own homes. They found that responses subserving three functions – attention-getting for its own sake, asking for objects or services (proto-imperative responses), and simple negation – occurred most frequently. The other three groups of responses – those promoting general positive interaction (proto-conversational responses), responses functioning to draw attention to objects or events (proto-declaratives) and responses based on negative interaction, including behaviours which functioned purely to provoke anger or irritation in the other individual – occurred less frequently.

The data showed that responses in the first three categories were normally present whenever those in the second group of categories occurred. This pattern of cross-sectional data led Kiernan and Reid to suggest that the attention-seeking, asking-for and simple negation behaviours probably emerged earlier than the other categories. The responses sampled in the study included vocal, gestural, manipulative and other types of communicative behaviour. Factor analysis of the data suggested that vocal and nonvocal behaviours were not differentially grouped. The bulk of variance was accounted for by a single factor of 'general communicative ability' (Reid and Kiernan, 1985a).

Owens and MacDonald (1982) developed a speech act taxonomy based on the observation of mentally handicapped and nondelayed children. Their taxonomy consists of nine categories: answer, question, reply, declaration, practice, name (labelling), continuant (wanting the other person to continue or repeat), a single category of suggestion, command, demand and request, and an other/inappropriate category. Although their study involved only six Down's syndrome and six nondelayed children, the authors suggest that there appears to be little difference between the delayed and nondelayed groups.

Studies so far mentioned examine gross patterns of interaction with an emphasis on the characteristics of input from the nonhandicapped care-givers and studies on the social functions shown by handicapped individuals. A handful have explored the process of interaction between handicapped persons and others.

Price-Williams and Sabsay (1979) recorded conversations among nine severely mentally handicapped Down's syndrome men who lived and worked together in an institution. Their prime interest was in examining the communicative competence of their subjects, which was defined as the ability to perform speech acts, to shape responses to satisfy one's obligations as a conversational partner and to structure discourse through turn-taking, topic-shifting and other strategies. On the basis of fifteen hours of conversation, observed in natural settings, the authors concluded that there was a 'great deal of communication' which was a 'great deal more complex than previous clinical studies ... would suggest' (p. 57). They found evidence of a wide range of communicative strategies including methods for securing the attention of the hearer, for establishing referents and propositions, and for repairing breakdowns in communication. They point out that sometimes this repair work can be surprisingly complex, and that at least some of the men were not only capable of responding to 'repair' initiated by another person but also of being aware of their own failure to communicate and initiating repair on their own utterances. Price-Williams and Sabsay conclude that these strategies may be 'occasioned less by communicative or cognitive incompetence than by communicative distress arising from the retardates' *linguistic* impairment' (p. 57).

In a subsequent study, Sabsay and Kernan (1983) examined the communicative competence of forty-eight mildly mentally handicapped adults. They suggest that the syntactic and lexical deficits of the severely mentally handicapped, in addition to physical problems in speech production, are so extensive that difficulties in other areas of competence go unnoticed. They analysed transcripts of tape-recorded conversations between handicapped individuals and researchers or counsellors. Their results show failure on the part of the retarded in giving either too little information concerning referents or of giving too much or irrelevant information. So 'he' would be referred to without saying who 'he' was; parts of narratives or whole narratives would be left out, the hearer being told only the outcome or given a comment on the omitted story; or irrelevant side issues would be developed at length. However, Sabsay and Kernan also found that individuals could form perfectly understandable discourse. They conclude that 'the skill exists but, whether through neglect, false assumptions regarding knowledge available to interlocutors, or inability to recognize that the speech situation requires its use, the skill is sometimes not employed by the speaker' (p. 292).

Sabsay and Kernan argue that this reliance on the other person to seek the information they need in order to understand may reflect the particular type of situation studied, i.e. one where the mentally handicapped person is interacting with a powerful nonretarded person, who is controlling the conversation. This explanation is necessary to reconcile the apparent discrepancies between this study, in which failures of awareness of the other were identified, and the Price-Williams and Sabsay study in which considerable sensitivity appeared to be exercised by less able subjects. It also links with data quoted earlier, which show that parents of mentally handicapped children regulate the form and direction of conversations more than those of nonhandicapped children

(Marshall *et al.*, 1973; Buium *et al.*, 1974). The topic of regulation will be returned to in a few paragraphs.

Abbeduto and Rosenberg (1980) also studied the skills of mildly mentally handicapped adults. They set up conversation groups involving seven men. Their focus was on the ability of their subjects in conversational turn-taking and in expressing and responding to speech acts such as assertion, agreement or disagreement, various types of acknowledgement, requests for information or clarification, and questions and answers. Abbeduto and Rosenberg found that subjects used turn-taking rule systems which were like those used by normal individuals, and that they made few turn-taking errors. The commonest types of initiatives were assertions and questions. They conclude that the pattern of turn-taking indicates that all groups were involved in information exchange. There were substantial individual differences among subjects which were consistent across time and groups. One subject showed a high number of turn-taking errors and a 'passive' conversational style. IQ was not related to differences observed.

Coggins and Stoel-Gammon (1982) studied one aspect of the conversational skills of four mildly handicapped Down's syndrome children with a mean CA of 5.4 years in a range of everyday activities. These authors were particularly interested in the children's responses to requests for clarification on the part of adults. The data show that all requests were heeded, i.e. in all cases they were aware that their communication attempt had failed and they tried to repair the breakdown. The most common type of clarification was to revise the communication, either phonetically by saying the word again but more clearly or correctly, or by expansion, adding more information.

This small group of studies presents some interesting conclusions. They show the interrelation of impairment of linguistic function and relative communicative competence. They also suggest that mentally handicapped people can show sophisticated awareness of the dynamics of discourse. As will be shown shortly, the social setting in which conversations occur may be crucial in determining whether these skills are exhibited.

A small group of studies provide experimental analyses of variables which might underly some of the skills described in naturalistic research. Beveridge and Mittler (1977) showed that their three mentally handicapped subjects could make use of positive and negative feedback from a speaker to correct choices. Longhurst (1974) and Longhurst and Berry (1975) examined the ability of mentally handicapped individuals to describe objects to other individuals and to correct their descriptions in order to make their communication more successful. The main conclusions from these studies were that success in the basic task was related to IQ level, as was ability to adjust descriptions on the basis of feedback which showed communicative failure. This relationship to IQ is inconsistent with the Abbeduto and Rosenberg findings quoted earlier. The Longhurst paradigm was extended by Beveridge and Tatham (1976), who examined descriptive and listening skills when the task was a more controlled one of describing and identifying pictures. The authors found that subjects who were good speakers were also good listeners, but that the ability to produce and comprehend a sentence did not guarantee its appropriate use in the communicative setting explored. Specific characteristics of descriptive speech were examined by Naremore and Dever (1975). They found that mentally handicapped children with an IQ range from 74 to 84 tended to repeat themselves more and to be more prone to hesitation than normal children.

Hoy and McKnight (1977) used a situation in which high- and low-ability speakers and listeners, assessed in terms of MA and IQ, were required to teach and learn a board game. They found that low-level speakers took longer to explain the game than high-level speakers, and that they tended to use verbal-manipulative means rather than the purely verbal means used by high-level speakers. Speech-styles differed in complexity between the groups in ways which would be anticipated. Both shifted styles depending on listener abilities, with the verbal-manipulative channel being used more frequently for low-level listeners. Communicative success depended on ability levels of both members of the dyad, and also on age. High-level individuals were not uniformly better understood. On some measures, low-level listeners did better with low-level speakers than with high.

The results of the Hoy and McKnight study indicate the complexity of data which can emerge from settings in which the roles of individuals (teachers–learners) are defined by external factors, in this case participation in an experiment. A further dimension of analysis examines the ways in which social roles define and are defined by patterns of interaction.

Bedrosian and Prutting (1978) examined the communicative and social interaction of four mentally handicapped adults in four conversational settings, with parents, peers, the persons' speech-language pathologist (SLP) and a normal child of equivalent mental age. Interactions were analysed in terms of a number of categories of response with central interest in style of interaction assessed in terms of dominance–submission, the extent to which control over the interchange was achieved and methods used to attain and maintain control.

The data showed that three of the mentally handicapped individuals did not hold the dominant position overall in any of the conversational settings. The remaining subject was dominant only with her peers and the child. Dominance–submission was defined in terms of a majority of 'bids' or attempts to control being in one direction or another. At the level of skills in expressing control all the subjects showed ability to use several methods. These included strategies such as 'arching', answering a question with another question, or 'chaining', in which the speaker, having had a question answered, asks another in the context of confirming his understanding. The data show variation across conversations and individuals which are only partly explained by differences between settings. Although the dominant position of the SLP reflected the clinical situations studied, the reasons for many of the other relationships which emerged are less clear.

Clearer predictions concerning the appropriateness of different types of response were made by Owings and McManus (1980) in a study of an adult mentally handicapped man in a group home. They showed that features such as use of questions, information-giving, imitation, commands and other classes of response differed, depending on the person with whom he was conversing With some exceptions, use was appropriate in terms of the expectations of the group home setting.

Bedrosian and Prutting (1978) make a plea for an 'ethnography of communication', the description of communicative behaviours within a range of social contexts. The importance of this enterprise is clearly related to the need to match the hoped-for outcome of a placement with the behaviour which is likely to be occasioned by the setting. This remark takes us back to the studies already described on the impact of institutional settings on communicative behaviour and to the studies by Sabsay, Abbeduto and their colleagues in which part of the subjects' performances can be understood as reflecting the social context of communication.

The studies lead to a further line of investigation, the examination of the impact of the 'personality', or personal characteristics of the mentally handicapped individual, on the quality and quantity of interaction.

Evans and Hogg (1975) found that children rated as more excitable on a scale of excitation–inhibition were more reward-seeking in learning situations, and Beveridge and Evans (1978) showed that frequency of initiation of interaction, amount of speech, number of approaches and likelihood of interaction with a teacher were also positively related to teachers' ratings of excitability. Beveridge and Hurrell (1980) have shown that teachers' responses to child-initiated interactions were related to both child and teacher personality. They found that teachers tended not to respond to child-initiated interactions, this tendency being less pronounced for inhibitable children. Teachers high on a neuroticism scale were more likely to respond negatively to excitable children and to change the content of the child initiation when maintaining an interaction. Other studies suggest that characteristics such as self-blame for communication failure may affect aspects of performance (Beveridge *et al.*, 1979).

The data described under the heading of social function support a 'delay' theory, to the degree that they show that mentally handicapped individuals can use their communication skills in a variety of ways which correspond to normal use. However, the area is clearly under-researched, especially from a developmental viewpoint. In addition, there are a number of studies which suggest that the mentally handicapped child may not relate to his or her parents 'normally' in turn-taking settings, thereby disrupting the communicative link. This deficit may arise from idiosyncratic attentional processes, the child attending to unusual features of the environment, or not being as tuned to adult behaviour as the normal child. We do not have enough data to say whether the social functions expressed in language emerge in the same order or, in the case of some functions, emerge at all in handicapped individuals. Data on discourse do, however, suggest that, although they may be hampered by poor syntactic and semantic skills, mentally handicapped individuals can acquire and employ rules of discourse. Use appears to be determined by the social setting individuals find themselves in and by the 'personality' of the handicapped person.

This account is clearly neither full enough nor well enough backed by evidence. However, it does suggest that this and related areas, such as social development and personality, are crucial to the understanding of the development of communication skills and possibly also to the development of language.

Conclusion

It seems clear that, overall, the delay or similar sequence hypothesis gains more support from published data than the deviance or difference hypothesis. Consequently, it can be expected that a mentally handicapped person will show the same pattern of development as a normal person within particular areas of language functioning, but with slower progression through stages and a lower ceiling of development. However, there are differences between the performance of MA matched normal and handicapped groups. Even allowing for the difficulties in interpreting studies employing MA matching, these differences suggest possible fundamental problems in information processing. The same conclusion seems to follow from studies on availability and accessibility of information. These raise familiar problems of difficulty in the use of strategies for correcting recall – Bilsky *et al.*'s (1983) suggestion that their subjects were producing 'the first response that came to mind'.

Acceptance of the delay hypothesis also needs to be tempered by recognition that studies are often limited to subjects who show the particular type of behaviour of interest. No differential analysis of those who have not acquired skills is undertaken. The present author suspects that the extent of deviance in the development of language and communication skills is underestimated in the current literature. Nor does the support for the delay hypothesis mean that there are no different patterns across areas of development. Data relevant to this point are described in the next section.

There is clearly still room for a great deal of research work across all fields. The study of semantic development, especially among the less able, and of development of social function are also in clear need of investigation. In this brief review the distinction between comprehension and expression has not been emphasized. For many years these were seen as directly linked (Jones and Robson, 1979) but, increasingly, the relative independence of the two sets of skills is emerging (Chapman and Miller, 1975; Lee, 1981).

In terms of priorities the investigation of social function, of both language use and discourse analysis, offers exciting avenues for future research. It will already have become apparent that this is seen as a priority area. In addition, related areas of the development of social responsiveness and of 'personality' merit further study.

REMEDIATION

The first section of this chapter concluded by indicating that one cannot expect that there will ever be one single theory of the development of communication and language. By the same token, this section can begin by asserting that we cannot expect to find one theory or one type of programme which will meet the challenge of remediating all language and communication problems of the mentally handicapped. Programmes or teaching strategies will be needed which will take account of individual patterns of delay (or deviance) in sound production, the cognitive underpinning of language development, semantic aspects of performance, syntactic problems, problems of acquisition of social functions, and actual use of communicative skills in particular environments. Much of the discussion in the last section makes it clear that acquisition and use of language and communication skills can be critically affected by the social and physical environment of the handicapped person. There are strong reasons for encouraging intervention programmes which approach remediation from the viewpoint of environmental manipulation, in addition to specific programming.

The previous section concluded by pointing out that the overall support for the delay hypothesis in particular areas of functioning does not necessarily imply that mentally handicapped people will show the same overall profiles of ability as normal individuals. Miller *et al.* (1981; see also Miller and Chapman, 1984) have presented data suggesting three patterns of ability in the mentally handicapped. These are expressive ability equal to comprehension with both below cognitive level, expressive ability below comprehension with the latter equivalent to cognitive ability, and expressive ability equivalent to comprehension with both equivalent to cognitive level. This analysis is useful but probably oversimplified. A substantial number of severely mentally handicapped individuals are affected by deafness or partial deafness, blindness or partial sight, and varying degrees of gross physical handicap which may affect the reception and production of speech. There seems no reason to expect that the centrally determined communication and language disorders of mentally handicapped individuals should not be as complex as those of people with specific language disabilities. In this case we would expect delayed development (and possibly deviant development resulting from differential delays) to occur routinely (cf. Bloom and Lahey, 1978).

Other differences have emerged in research in which language relevant cognitive skills have been examined. Two groups of studies have suggested that although *sequence* of development may be normal, *patterns* of development at any given time may not be equivalent to those in normal development. Studies of Piagetian sensorimotor progression in handicapped children suggest a general correspondence to a normal developmental model (Greenwald and Leonard, 1979), but specific deficits in ability to imitate both verbally and motorically (Kiernan and McMinn, 1985).

These arguments have important implications for assessment for remediation. Clearly we need to have assessment procedures which can analyse cognitive skills, if possible independent of formal communication skills. A few such procedures exist, including those based on Piagetian work (Uzgiris and Hunt, 1975). However, because of the rapid evolution of theory in the field, older assessment methods such as the Reynell Developmental Language Scales (Reynell, 1977) and the Illinois Test of Psycholinguistic Abilities (Kirk *et al.*, 1968) have become outdated (Muller *et al.*, 1981). Other procedures are being developed which reflect more up-to-date taxonomies and which, although often complex, provide a sounder basis for programme development. Procedures developed by Crystal *et al.* (1976) for assessing syntax and other methods for assessing semantics and other aspects of language are discussed by Miller (1980), Muller *et al.* (1981), Crystal (1982) and Lund and Duchan (1983).

Ways of assessing social function are beginning to emerge. Roth and Spekman (1984a, b) provide a valuable discussion of nonstandardized approaches derived from the work of linguists. Coggins and Carpenter (1981) describe a Communicative Intention Inventory which was tested on 16 normally developing children between 15 and 16 months of age. Kiernan and Reid (1985b) present a Preverbal Communication Schedule with reliability data based on a sample of 48 severely and profoundly mentally handicapped children and young people.

There is a clear need to develop a wider range of assessment procedures than currently exist. In particular, devices for assessing less able mentally handicapped people who may not score on procedures for assessing syntactic skills need to be evolved. The form which these should take must depend in part on who is seen as the consumer. This question reflects considerations of programme development, in particular whether package programmes with associated assessments can be used in order to tackle communication and language skills. These considerations are taken up on p. 610.

The remainder of this chapter will be presented under three heads. First, evidence from studies in which specific remedial procedures have been used will be briefly reviewed and related to the question of programme development. Second, the use of nonvocal communication systems with mentally handicapped individuals will be discussed. The chapter will end with a general conclusion relating to future directions of research and practice.

Teaching communication and language skills

The majority of published studies on the teaching of communication and language skills to severely mentally handicapped individuals reflect a strong influence of the behavioural tradition. In addition, as Rogers–Warren *et al.*

(1983) point out, techniques deriving from other traditions have converged with behavioural studies in their use of particular methods. As a consequence, the typical programme strategy involves a phase during which attending is brought under control (attention training), a phase in which imitative behaviour is taught as a means through which new responses can be prompted, followed by the teaching of syntactic or other forms (Harris, 1975).

Procedures for bringing attention under control through the use of extrinsic reinforcers are well developed. However, a preferable strategy would be to use objects or events to which the child or adult will attend spontaneously as a basis for the development of communication. This reflects the emphasis on the need to provide adequate motivation to communicate, though ensuring that the individual, once he or she has acquired vocabulary or forms, is more likely to want to use them (Rogers-Warren *et al.*, 1983).

Procedures for teaching imitative behaviour are also well developed (Harris, 1975). The 'classical' approach is to teach motor imitation prior to trying to shape vocal imitation. However, the transfer from motor to vocal imitation is difficult to ensure and teaching vocal imitation can be a very prolonged exercise. Nelson *et al.* (1976) compared two methods of teaching, one derived from Lovaas *et al.* (1966) and one from Nelson and Evans (1968). The methods differ mainly in the inclusion of kinaesthetic cues from the face or larynx by Nelson and Evans. The two methods were equally effective but around twelve months was needed to train children to imitate twenty-four verbal stimuli.

Failure to transfer and time are lesser problems since manual sign languages have been used. Now a communication system based on signs can be taught even though little or no progress may be made in teaching vocal imitation. In addition, teaching functional sign language is, in effect, teaching generalized motor imitation. There is evidence for the development of functional speech within sign language programmes. This suggests that motor to vocal or verbal transfer may take place at some level (see p. 622).

Several studies have described the modification of articulation errors (e.g. Murdock *et al.*, 1977; Ravers *et al.*, 1978). In general, programme priorities often appear to lie in improving other aspects of language and communication, despite the frequency of occurrence of such problems in relevant populations. It is often held that problems of articulation can be unravelled more effectively after communication skills are established.

As already shown, the teaching of expressive use of specific syntactic forms can be successful (see Welch, 1981, for a review). Striefel, Wetherby and their colleagues have developed optimal techniques for teaching comprehension of specific syntactic structures (Striefel *et al.*, 1978). Carrier has evolved and standardized procedures for teaching understanding and use of what he and his colleagues see as a core syntactic structure (Carrier and Peak, 1975). Robson (1981) has produced a video-based minicourse which uses as its programme framework increasingly complex syntactic structures.

Other workers, in particular Miller and his associates, emphasize the cognitive basis for language development in their programmes for remedial training (Miller and Yoder, 1972, 1974). The sequence proposed by Miller and Yoder was designed to teach relations such as recurrence and nonexistence, agent and action, agent and object and possession. The semantic approach is also taken by MacDonald and his colleagues in a programme package (MacDonald *et al.*, 1974; Horstmeier and MacDonald, 1978). Other programmes, for example the one developed by Guess and his colleagues (1976a, b) and by Schaeffer *et al.* (1980), originated in behavioural work but reflect an emphasis on the knowledge base underpinning communication.

There is a great diversity of studies relating to remediation of the social use of language and communication skills. A number of studies deal with 'mutism', or the unwillingness of individuals to use existing skills (e.g. Halle *et al.*, 1979) or to the elimination of echoic responding (e.g. Risley and Wolf, 1967). Voice loudness was modified by Fleece *et al.* (1981). Group programmes to raise the general level of conversational interchange have been reported by van Biervliet *et al.* (1981) and Kleitsch *et al.* (1983). Similar initiatives have been used with handicapped individuals using sign language (e.g. Schepis *et al.*, 1982).

Specific functions such as requesting objects or services (Simic and Bucher, 1980; Kiernan and Jones, 1985; Reid and Kiernan, 1985b) have been taught successfully to severely handicapped individuals. In practice such responses represent a natural extension of a behavioural approach in which they are rewarded with reinforcement appropriate to the word or sign emitted. Goetz *et al.* (1979, 1983) have argued strongly for the teaching of responses which are functional in producing an immediate effect as the first stage in teaching. Other studies have taught subjects to ask or answer questions (e.g. Twardosz and Baer, 1973; Leeming *et al.*, 1979), to increase descriptive skills (Longhurst, 1972), or to engage in 'conversation' at levels of complexity depending on the ability of subjects (e.g. Garcia, 1974; Kelly *et al.*, 1979). Studies have also focused on particular skills such as telephone use (Matson, 1982), verbalization about current events (Keilitz *et al.*, 1973), and job interview behaviour (Hall *et al.*, 1980). Matson *et al.* (1980) describe a study in which content of speech, number of words used and intonation were treated as aspects of an interpersonal skills programme.

In addition to skill deficiencies, mentally handicapped people can also manifest a range of unacceptable behaviours including swearing, screaming, nonsense talk and constant repetitive questioning. Kiernan and Reid (1985a), in the development of the PVC schedule, found that preverbal or minimally verbal children and young people would not infrequently show a range of provocative or hurting behaviours. These were clearly 'communicative' in the sense that the individuals concerned were trying to affect the behaviour of other people in particular ways. Such behaviours would tend to be treated normally as unacceptable social behaviours but clearly indicate a style of interaction.

Several studies have shown the modifiability of bizarre vocalizations (e.g.

Mental Deficiency

Barton, 1970; Herdman, 1979). The most favoured procedure for reducing such responses is either extinction or time-out.

Much recent theorizing and practice has increasingly recognized the social nature of early communicative behaviour, especially as it bears on the teaching of the severely or multiply handicapped individual. Van Dijk (1965) and Sternberg (1982) have evolved techniques for teaching deaf–blind mentally handicapped children through stages of joint and reciprocal movements up to imitation and natural gesture. Methods of establishing basic social contact are embodied in 'intrusive therapy', in which initially avoiding and resistive children are more or less coerced into accepting and eventually deriving enjoyment from normal social interaction (Bell, 1975).

Unfortunately, reports of specific intervention studies (e.g. Lovaas *et al.*, 1973), and successive reviews of the impact of programmes, tend to show limited effectiveness (e.g. Goetz *et al.*, 1979). These all conclude that there is evidence for the effective teaching of specific responses or syntactic forms, but that taught behaviour fails to generalize to new settings unless mediated through training of care-givers in these new settings. Even when parents are used as therapists, long-term effectiveness of intervention is disappointing (Howlin, 1984).

There are several possible explanations for this relatively poor outcome. The first lies in the very broad definition of the term generalization. In both teaching and research contexts, generalization of learned responses is often seen almost as the student's 'responsibility'. For example, a child may be taught to name a ball when it is held up in front of him with the question 'what's this?' The child is likely to have been prompted, 'say ball' – 'ball' – 'good boy, it's a ball!' The child is then expected to use the word (or sign) 'spontaneously', i.e. to generalize its use to other settings, people and, more critically, to other pragmatic functions such as asking for a ball which he or she wants, or drawing attention to a ball. The point of this example is not that generalization must always be taught but that failure to 'generalize' is often left as an unanalysed issue tacitly felt to reflect the inherent limitations of the handicapped individual.

This line of argument suggests that the problems with much published work may lie in a weakness in the analysis of generalization. This approach was advanced forcefully by Stokes and Baer (1977) for behavioural technology in general. They describe nine techniques for enhancing generalization, all of which can apply to the teaching of communication and language skills. Since the publication of the Stokes and Baer article there has been a clear increase in the number of studies which depart from the format of individual training with generalization being 'up to the individual', the Train and Hope procedure described by Stokes and Baer. Many studies within behavioural tradition have relied on systematic training of the individual across a sufficient range of settings and people to ensure generalization. Others have taught parents or a range of staff to use specific techniques (e.g. Faw *et al.*, 1981). These techniques include 'incidental teaching', a format developed by Hart and

Risley (1980) in which naturally occurring interactions are used as a basis for increasing communication and language behaviours. This approach is clearly in line with other traditions, in particular the implications of teaching using motivation arising from social interaction.

There are two problems with this general orientation as it relates to the teaching of language and communication skills. The first is that, in order to achieve a sufficiently high number of instances of the targeted communicative behaviour to allow learning to occur, we cannot simply rely on 'natural' events. In essence, one problem with handicapped individuals is that they have not learned from incidental occurrences. Consequently we need to analyse the potential of different environmental settings for producing settings in which the learning of language and communication skills is likely to occur. We then need to establish such settings, but with a clear idea of how teaching is to take place within those settings.

This approach may be generally categorized as ecological or ecobehavioural. It has been developed by Brinker and his colleagues (Brinker, 1978; Brinker and Goldbart, 1981) using settings like a tea party or putting a doll to bed. What is crucial is that, once the child or adult has learned the structure of the activity, *particular* appropriate phrases are used and expected. In this way the lack of specificity, which can bedevil play-based teaching, can be overcome. Strategies such as role-reversal or peer modelling can also be used to encourage motivated use of skills.

The ecobehavioural approach has been developed by Warren and Rogers-Warren (1983). They have focused attention on the need to examine settings in terms of their support for generalization of learned skills. Kiernan and Willis (1985) have used a similar method in analysing the type of interaction occasioned by various classes in an educational institution where severely mentally handicapped adults were integrated. Some classes, like swimming, occasioned mainly instructions to the handicapped students. Others, for example, dressmaking, involved a broader range of talk to the students.

The second problem with incidental teaching, and one which it shares with the ecological or ecobehavioural approaches, lies in the relation between teaching forms and teaching function. Teaching the student forms, such as subject, verb, object or agent, action, object structures, is likely to lead to drills, the learning of which will be functionless – the individual will not be using them to communicate – to such a degree that he or she will have to be extrinsically rewarded. However, if the focus is primarily on functional communication, the organization of the curriculum from the viewpoint of form becomes problematic, since it may be difficult to predict with confidence the recurrence of situations which will allow the repetition and consolidation of particular forms.

This issue has, to date, received scant discussion in the literature on programme development for the mentally handicapped. In this and other respects research on teaching English as a second language (ESL, otherwise referred to as communicative language teaching, CLT, or English for special purposes, ESP) has much to offer. Workers within this field face many of the problems experienced by those in mental handicap, in considering how to motivate learners who may be adults and to teach them English in a restricted space of time. Groups of potentially valuable teaching techniques have been evolved, many of which could be adopted for use with the handicapped (e.g. Brumfit and Johnson, 1979; Littlewood, 1981). Of particular interest are discussions concerned with the development of the syllabus. Here a central issue is how it can reflect specific needs, but with a more general reference which will allow the learner to utilize learned forms appropriately in new contexts (cf. Johnson and Porter, 1983). Again, much of the thinking within this stream of work and some of the materials produced are of potential value in teaching the handicapped.

Discussion

So far it has been shown that there are a large number of demonstrations of successful teaching of communication and language-related skills. It was also suggested that there are approaches which are of value in structuring teaching of particular skills. From the point of view of the practitioner this account may appear rather daunting. It would be valuable if published package programmes could be used to help in the teaching of relevant skills.

A large number of programmes have been developed and produced (see McLean and Snyder-McLean, 1978; and Harris, 1984, for partial reviews). However, on nearly any criteria which can be selected, these fall short of being satisfactory. Many have poor rationales in terms of their theoretical bases, they are often poorly specified in terms of programme steps and expected outcomes, and they fail almost universally to provide evidence of effectiveness (Harris, 1984; Kiernan, 1984b). Because of the rapid evolution of the field over the last decade, authors of programmes who have tried to evaluate their work before publishing have run into the problem of being out of date before their programmes are available. Under these circumstances they need either constant updating, a procedure used in the maintenance of the Derbyshire Language Programme (Knowles and Masidlover, 1982), or to be seen as 'ideas books' with a very short life.

Leeming and his colleagues (1979) suggest that programmes can still provide a structure for teaching and a source of objectives and methods to be fitted into other lessons rather than set recipes to be followed. As Harris (1984) points out, packages represent one way in which theory is transmitted to teachers and other practitioners. In this light programmes become more ways in which inservice training can be undertaken rather than formulae to be adhered to slavishly.

Rogers-Warren *et al.* (1983) have summarized a number of suggestions derived from literature on the development of language and communication skills. They suggest that teachers or care-givers should follow the child's lead by focusing attention on the objects and events which the child finds of interest, should assume that the child (or adult) is trying to communicate and should treat utterances with attention and support. They suggest that corrective feedback should be provided in a gentle, positive way with an emphasis on what is correct and appropriate. Finally, they suggest that caregivers talk *with* the child, limiting instructions and directives, but offering alternatives that maintain activity and responsiveness and encourage exploration of the environment.

The use of nonvocal systems

Virtually all surveys of communicative skills in mentally handicapped individuals show that a large proportion have seriously deficient speech. For example, Kiernan *et al.* (1982), in a survey of schools for the severely mentally handicapped (ESN(S)), asked about the numbers of pupils who could use 'only three or fewer than three spoken words with which to express needs or requests'. They found that 31 per cent of pupils in day schools and 65 per cent of those in subnormality hospital schools fell into this category. Leeming *et al.* (1979) found that 26.5 per cent of their sample were not even imitating single words and a further 7.0 per cent were only able to produce single meaningful words.

The reasons for poor use of speech are complex and, in some cases, clearly related to physical abnormalities (cf. Fawcus and Fawcus, 1974). However, in many cases, failures to use speech cannot be traced to causes which are remediable. Nor does attribution of limited ability to low overall cognitive level provide much in the way of guidelines for a direct attack on communication problems.

Against this background it is not surprising that the discovery that nondeaf severely mentally handicapped individuals could learn to use nonverbal means of communication was enthusiastically welcomed by practitioners. From slow beginnings in the late 1960s and early 1970s in North America and the United Kingdom, the employment of various forms of sign language and graphic symbol systems has become very common. Reid *et al.* (1983) found that 92.5 per cent of ESN(S) schools reported using some form of nonvocal system. There are no systematic data for adult facilities in the UK or for usage in North America, but the dominating impression is of very widespread use.

An exhaustive account of the accumulating literature or of issues arising from the field is not presented here. Several extended reviews have appeared recently and the interested reader is referred to these (Kiernan *et al.*, 1982; Lloyd and Karlan, 1984). In this chapter a brief overview of the main methods in use is offered, incorporating a general comparison of the systems in terms of likely underlying processing, a discussion of the outcome of studies employing them with mentally handicapped individuals, and a consideration of the problems of selection.

The systems in use

Nonvocal systems divide themselves into two groups, those employing manual sign, often referred to as 'unaided systems' (Fristoe and Lloyd, 1979), and 'aided systems', which require equipment of some sort in order that they can be utilized. The category thus includes graphic symbol systems and other methods of aiding communication such as speech synthesizers or typewriters.

Unaided and aided systems have been used with a wide range of handicapped individuals, including the mentally handicapped, both deaf and hearing, and with and without minimal speech, autistic individuals, physically handicapped children and adults, and stroke and surgery patients. In all groups several general conclusions emerge from case-studies.

First, individuals who have been unable to communicate through speech, often after extended speech therapy or education, can learn to use nonvocal methods to communicate effectively. Second, there is some evidence to suggest that some mentally handicapped persons can attain unexpected levels of linguistic sophistication. Third, learning to use nonvocal systems is frequently accompanied by improvement in speech, sometimes to the degree that speech eventually supplants the nonvocal system as a means of communication (Kiernan *et al.*, 1982).

In the next sections the systems will be discussed and the factors which may facilitate their acquisition will be examined.

Sign

This term applies to any language or system in which information is primarily transmitted through the use of hand postures and movements of the hands and arms. Typically, a given configuration of postures and movements can be translated as a 'word' in spoken English. Fingerspelling, in which each letter of a world from a spoken language is represented by a different configuration, is often used to complement manual signing but is distinct from sign language.

Sign languages have been evolved by large groups of people who, for one reason or another, are unable or unwilling to use speech. The most sophisticated communicative use of sign is in communities of deaf people. Within these, the systems have evolved to the level of being definable as distinct languages, with lexicons and syntax systems which are distinct from those of spoken languages. By far the best documented and studied deaf sign language is American Sign Language (ASL) (cf. Wilbur, 1979), although British Sign Language (BSL) is now being researched with increasing interest (cf. Kyle and Woll, 1981; Deuchar, 1984).

Surveys of the use of ASL and BSL in North America and the United Kingdom show that these languages are employed rarely, if at all, with mentally handicapped individuals (Goodman *et al.*, 1978; Kiernan *et al.*, 1982). As noted, sign language has its own syntactic rules but practitioners working with the mentally handicapped typically follow spoken English word order and accompany signing with speech. In addition, for the most part, practitioners do not use morphological markers to indicate tense and other features of signs. If these are utilized they are drawn from systems developed to render ASL and BSL more suitable for pedagogic usage.

Several pedagogic systems are available in North America (Wilbur, 1979) and a pedagogic variant of BSL has been developed in schools for the deaf in the UK (Sayer, 1984). The pedagogic approaches typically emphasize lip-reading and the use of residual hearing. The various systems add morphological features, sometimes based on fingerspelling of spoken English markers. This produces a fairly direct translation into sign of all features of spoken English with the aim of augmenting the spoken word with sign as completely as possible.

The Paget-Gorman Sign System (PGSS) (Wilbur, 1979) was devised specifically as a pedagogic method with the features outlined above. The form of signs for the basic lexicon and the form of morphological markers are distinct from that in other systems. However, in a study comparing various pedagogic systems in terms of their ability to represent spoken English, Crystal and Craig (1978) show that PGSS was the most successful system of those available at that time.

Several other schemes have been devised and have from time to time had some currency with mentally handicapped people (cf. Kiernan *et al.*, 1982). Of these, Amerind (Skelly, 1979) is the most important since it has been seen by a number of speech pathologists and instructors as being of particular value with adults. It is based on American Indian Hand Talk but was devised with the needs of adult stroke patients in mind. Consequently, efforts were made to keep sign forms simple and close to gestures used conventionally in normal settings. The programme makes no attempt to represent syntax other than through the use of spoken word order. As with PGSS, Amerind sign forms are sufficiently different from those found in ASL and BSL for it to represent a quite distinct system.

All of the methods described achieve criteria for utility for basic communication. All are reasonably well codified, have reasonably large vocabularies, and have methods for generating new lexical items. However, in addition to the broad contrasts already mentioned, they differ in a variety of ways which bear on the extent to which they have been taken up for use by practitioners working with the mentally handicapped.

Who uses what?

Several surveys of use have been completed in North America and the United Kingdom. Fristoe (1975) found that 'over 10 per cent' of 689 professionals responding to a national survey in the United States said that they employed some form of nonspeech communication. Fristoe and Lloyd (1978) report the results from a follow-up questionnaire sent to 86 respondents to the original survey. Some 61.9 per cent of the respondents stated that they were using ASL or one of its pedagogic variations. However, they doubted whether *any* respondents were using ASL syntax, a supposition backed by a complementary study by Goodman *et al.* (1978). Fristoe and Lloyd (1978) also found that around 28 per cent of respondents used gesture, mime or esoteric sign methods, one Amerind and nine fingerspelling.

A series of surveys completed in 1978, 1979, 1980 and 1982 gathered information on the use of systems from all schools for mentally handicapped, physically handicapped, autistic pupils and other nondeaf groups in England, Wales and Scotland (Kiernan *et al.*, 1982; Reid *et al.*, 1983; Kiernan and Reid, 1984). For mentally handicapped pupils the story of adoption and use is fairly simple. The surveys show a rapid growth in the utilization of systems, to around 92 per cent of schools in 1982. This rapid increase in signing coincided with the active dissemination of a 'language programme' embodying BSL signs, the Makaton Vocabulary (Walker, 1976a, 1978). This is a series of signs arranged in 11 supposedly developmentally based 'stages', each comprising around 35–40 signs. Signs are depicted by line drawings, and 'language programmes' corresponding to the stages are also available (Walker, 1976b).

The Makaton Vocabulary was developed in practical settings with mentally handicapped individuals. It has been offered to speech therapists and teachers in brief, inexpensive workshops, as of particular value in meeting the communication needs of the mentally handicapped (Walker, 1978). There is no published evidence on which to assess its value, either as a language programme (Byler, 1985; Kiernan, 1984b), or as a set of BSL signs. The only published evidence on acquisition by mentally handicapped individuals comes from the 1978 survey (Kiernan *et al.*, 1982). These data suggest that pupils learning PGSS acquire signs as readily as those in BSL Makaton Vocabulary programmes.

None the less, the surveys trace an increasing dominance of the field by BSL Makaton Vocabulary (BSL(M)) programmes in ESN(S) schools. In 1978, 70.3 per cent of schools employing sign used BSL(M) and 27.9 per cent PGSS. In 1980 these values were BSL(M) 91.2 per cent, PGSS 4.8 per cent and in 1982 BSL(M) 95.0 per cent and PGSS 3.7 per cent. In 1982 only 17 ESN(S) schools used PGSS. The remainder employed BSL independent of the Makaton Vocabulary or Amerind.

These shifts can be explained by several factors. Kiernan *et al.* (1982) conclude that the perceived image, ease of use of systems, availability of instruction (which Goodman *et al.* (1978) identify as a crucial variable), and pressures to use the same systems in all schools in an authority, have all played their part. These factors can also be seen in operation in other sectors of the education system, for example in schools for autistic and aphasic pupils (Kiernan and Reid, 1984). The data suggest that, given reasonable perceived success, selection of system is partly a result of chance and partly explained by social psychological factors, rather than being a choice based on empirical evaluation. However, in fairness to schools, virtually no information was available in the late 1970s when they were deciding on the introduction of sign systems.

There are no formal data available on the employment of systems in facilities in the UK catering for adult mentally handicapped people. The impression created is of reasonably frequent use, although probably less often than in schools. Again BSL(M) appears to dominate, but there are not infrequent reports of use of Amerind.

Comparisons of the systems

As indicated, BSL(M) dominates ESN(S) school provision in the UK and probably also adult provision. In North America ASL, or one of the pedagogic modifications, is pre-eminent. Second, there are self-evident arguments for maintaining one scheme, with suitable variants to deal with the specific needs of subgroups of the population of handicapped users, rather than proliferating systems.

Consequently, studies comparing systems are largely of academic value since, except in limited circumstances, change would not be recommended. However, such comparisons can be helpful in identifying variables which are likely to be important in acquisition, regardless of method. In addition, given the popularity of Amerind in use with adults, there is a case for comparing it with other systems.

Forms of signs

Several studies have examined the form of signs across systems and in relation to their acquisition. Kiernan (1983a) reports a study comparing signs in ASL, BSL and PGSS in terms of hand postures used and other characteristics. He found that the two 'natural' sign languages, ASL and BSL, were very similar in their use of postures. Three types of postures – flat hands, fist hands and index finger hands – accounted for 55.1 per cent of all postures used in ASL, 54.1 per cent of those used in BSL, but only 39.0 per cent of postures in PGSS. Developmental data suggest that these three types of posture emerge early in development (Halverson, 1940), and data from studies on imitation and expressive learning by mentally handicapped children show that these types are easier to imitate and to learn expressively (Kiernan, 1984a). However, in these studies, type of posture did not affect receptive learning, suggesting an explanation of data in terms of motor difficulty rather than perceptual problems. It can be concluded that hand posture needs to be taken into account in selecting expressive vocabulary, but not necessarily receptive vocabulary, for mentally handicapped people.

Similar data emerge in studies on the employment in signs of one hand, two hands maintaining the same posture, and two hands maintaining different ones. Again, the two 'natural' languages were similar in employing one-hand or two-hand same signs more frequently than two-hand different signs. In the samples examined, ASL used two-hand different signs in 16.4 per cent of signs and BSL in 14.0 per cent, as opposed to PGSS where two-hand different signs were used in 49.1 per cent of signs. Learning studies (Kiernan, 1984a) show that one-hand and two-hand same signs were learned expressively equally easily, with two-hand different signs being significantly more difficult. Again, the result suggests that one or two-hand same signs should be selected for expressive vocabulary over two-hand different. In addition, both this and the previous result suggest an interesting parallel between ASL and BSL in which both naturally evolving languages have selected similar types of sign. The rules underlying the construction of PGSS have led to the system adopting more difficult sign forms.

Data bearing on receptive learning come from studies by Lane *et al.* (1976), and Griffith and Robinson (1980). The Lane study examined the effect of image degeneration on the ability of subjects of normal intelligence to discriminate between hand postures, such as fists and flat hands. The study extracted eleven 'features' of sign postures which, along with other distinctive features analyses of sign languages, should bear on perceptual aspects of acquisition (cf. Wilbur, 1979).

Griffith and Robinson (1980), using moderately to severely mentally handicapped subjects, examined the effect on receptive learning of phonological similarity, i.e. the degree to which pairs of signs contrasted in terms of hand posture, movement and other aspects. The results show that learning was more rapid when pairs were dissimilar. As the authors point out, these data suggest that 'students should initially be taught widely dissimilar signs'. However, it is also clear that, as the receptive sign lexicon is built up, they will have to learn signs which are increasingly similar in feature.

Iconicity

Signs differ in the extent to which a gesture is 'perceived by signers, or potentially perceived by them, as visually related to its referents' (Mandel, 1977, p. 94). In practice the concept is complex and this has caused some confusion in experimental studies. These problems are outlined and examined by Mandel (1977) and Kiernan (1983a).

Iconicity clearly reflects a 'meaning' dimension in signs and consequently, in line with a large amount of data from learning studies, iconicity should facilitate learning. This assumption is widely adopted by practitioners and researchers, although Kiernan (1983a), after reviewing available studies employing mentally handicapped subjects, concluded that there was little evidence to suggest a positive effect on expressive learning. One study (Griffith and Robinson, 1980), however, suggests a positive effect on receptive learning.

Several explanations can be offered for these results. The expressive learning studies failed to control for differences in form of signs, as defined above. They also failed to show that the signs used were perceived as related to their referents *by the students who learned the signs* (Konstantareas *et al.*, 1978; Kohl, 1981). In both cases, signs were rated as iconic by students of normal intelligence and no evidence of the ability of the handicapped students to perceive their iconicity was gathered. There is also some reason to suppose that mental age may have an impact on facilitative effects of iconicity (cf. Kiernan, 1983a). It might be hypothesized that the latter will have a positive effect on learning only when the child is able to represent objects symbolically (cf. Morehead and Morehead, 1974).

Given the equivocal status of data on the effects of iconicity on learning, comparisons among systems have little point. Clearly more research is needed.

Translucency and transparency

The term translucency refers to the extent to which nonsigners can describe the basis for connection of the meaning of the sign to the sign form. Transparency refers to the extent to which nonsigners can guess the meaning of signs, without cues, under multiple-choice conditions. The BSL sign for 'book' is made with two hands, both flat, held palms together and then 'opened' with hands still touching along the little finger and the side of the hand. This sign would probably be rated high on *both* translucency and transparency. The BSL sign for 'man', the miming of a beard on the chin, would be high on translucency but lower on transparency, since uninstructed viewers usually guess the meaning as 'beard'. Finally a sign such as BSL 'sugar', in which the signer draws a 'clawed' hand down the cheek, would be rated as low on both dimensions. The supposed etymology of this sign refers to the time when deaf workers in sugar factories contracted sugar dermatitis. This connection could hardly be inferred from knowledge of the form of the sign and its meaning, giving low translucency. Similarly, it seems most unlikely that nonsigners could guess the meaning of the sign given only its form.

Studies of translucency and transparency have typically used subjects of normal intelligence. None the less, the studies are of interest here for several reasons. Transparency and translucency are likely to relate to the acceptability and ease of learning of signs by practitioners and relatives of handicapped individuals. Luftig and Lloyd (1981) show that high translucency is related to ease of such learning signs by college students. Given that this is in effect a second language for most normal adults, the variables are of clear importance.

A number of studies have approached the question of translucency and transparency of ASL, BSL, PGSS and Amerind. Klima and Bellugi (1979) found that around 50 per cent of 90 ASL signs were rated as translucent but that only 10 per cent were guessed, i.e. were transparent. Skelly (1979) reports a study in which 110 uninstructed viewers were asked to guess the meaning of 100 Amerind signs. The median score for the viewers was between 80 and 84 signs, an amazingly high transparency score. The methods used in this and related studies by Skelly and her colleagues are not clear. In one study, signs were presented 'in context' and it is not clear in any of them how responses were scored, e.g. whether strict correspondence with listed words was required. Data supporting Skelly, albeit more conservative, are provided by Kirschner *et al.* (1979), who found that an average 11 of 20 Amerind signs were guessed before learning as opposed to an average of 2.8 ASL signs. Similarly, Daniloff *et al.* (1983) obtained transparency ratings of around 42 to 50 per cent for Amerind signs. These levels are considerably lower than those reported by Skelly (80 to 88 per cent), but still well above those for ASL.

Feinmann (1982) compared the translucency and transparency of 50 PGSS and BSL signs employing 64 junior school children as raters. No differences emerged overall between the two systems.

Outcome

Given the large investment of time and effort by practitioners in the teaching of sign to mentally handicapped individuals, the amount of case-study evidence demonstrating efficacy is disappointingly small. The earliest studies were published in the late 1960s and early 1970s, and from these investigations onward several outcomes have been recorded quite consistently. Reviews by Kiernan (1983b) and Kiernan *et al.* (1982) provide detailed critiques. As noted already, the studies show acquisition of signs by individuals hitherto unable to communicate. Speed and outcome are not closely related to variables such as developmental level. Other subject characteristics which might predict performance are either not measured, imperfectly assessed or not related to outcome. The level of description of programmes used in teaching is seldom adequate to allow replication of research. Multisign utterances are often reported, but few studies provide either analyses in terms of syntax or social function, or enough data to permit an independent assessment to be undertaken. Again, as already noted, development of speech is often reported within the context of teaching programmes, but recording of this phenomenon tends to be fairly informal, rendering it impossible to infer causal mechanisms. However, it is important that none of the studies indicates a *decline* in the use of speech.

These conclusions are a matter of concern, given the wide use of sign with mentally handicapped individuals. There is a clear need for studies which document subject characteristics and methods of teaching, and which describe outcome in terms of students' ability to use sign communicatively in social settings. The possible impact of language and cognitive development needs to be explored. Without such studies, teaching cannot be guided into more effective modes. Furthermore, lack of empirical evaluation will make the use of sign subject to fluctuations in 'fashion' in teaching method.

Graphic symbol systems

Graphic symbols represent a subgroup of aided systems in which the symbols are permanently displayed or can be called up in a fixed form, for example on a TV screen. Typical examples include pictures, pictograms, Blissymbols and the printed or written word (traditional orthography or TO).

A wide variety of graphic symbols is available (Kiernan *et al.*, 1982; Lloyd and Karlan, 1984). In practice only a small number of such systems are commonly used in schools, at least in the UK. Reid *et al.* (1983) found that two systems predominated in 1982. These were Blissymbols (Bliss, 1965; Bailey and Jenkinson, 1982) and variants of Rebus systems (Clark and Woodcock, 1976; van Oosterum and Devereux, 1982). Over the period from 1978 to 1982, during which surveys in the UK were completed, Blissymbol use grew relatively slowly in ESN(S) schools. Respondents to surveys often noted that the symbols were felt to be too complex for mentally handicapped pupils. Consequently, it is not surprising that use of the less complex Rebus-type method expanded rapidly during this period. Reid and her colleagues estimated that around 900 pupils were using Rebus systems in ESN(S) schools in 1982, as opposed to around 300 Blissymbol users (Reid *et al.*, 1983).

The Blissymbol system was developed initially in an attempt to provide a universal method of communication (Bliss, 1965). Its employment with handicapped populations began with physically handicapped children and young people. It is well documented and a substantial number of resources are available (e.g. Hehner, 1980).

The system is developed from a number of basic line forms within a fixed framework, a square. These have basic meanings, for example, an inverted V at the top of the square signifies protection, at the bottom creation, a heart-shape represents emotion. The basic line forms are combined to produce symbols, for example, the creation element is combined with the person element to produce the symbol for female, the person of creation. Adding in the protection element creates the mother symbol, the female who protects.

In practice Blissymbols are often pictographic, i.e. their form reflects the visual appearance of their referents. Others, for example, those relating to emotions, are ideographic, form reflecting concepts. More complex symbols require an element of conceptualization in which several ideas are aggregated. For example, the television symbol involves an enclosure (box), and the symbols for ear, eye and electricity. Still others are more abstract in form.

The other commonly used 'system' is more difficult to characterize. Rebus methods have their origin in a variety of reading schemes published or used in educational provision for nonhandicapped children, the most widely known being the Peabody Rebus system (Clark and Woodcock, 1976). The symbols follow a variety of forms. In most systems many of the symbols are explicit pictograms, i.e. they are close in form to direct pictorial representatives of objects. Rebus systems typically have problems with representing verbs, because they try to concretize representation. So, a system may use a stick figure lying down to represent 'lie'. However, when this representation of the verb is used in combination with a picture of a dog to describe a dog lying down, there are clearly problems in justifying the method, especially for use with mentally handicapped individuals.

Rebus systems also include ideographic elements. For example, in representing prepositions, several methods use a framework in which an abstract entity, for example a black blob, is shown in appropriate relationships 'on', 'in', 'under' or 'beside' a box or container-like object.

Other principles embodied in expanded Rebus systems include the direct representation of the syllables constituting a word by pictures. The word 'cannot' is represented by a picture of a tin can and a knot in Peabody Rebus. At least one system, Sigsymbols (Cregan, 1982), includes symbols which depict the sign form relevant to its referent. Such graphic symbols may aid by linking referents through signs known by the student to graphic symbols.

The discussion makes the point that the two most commonly used graphic symbol systems in fact embody several different principles of derivation of symbol form. Systems can try to ensure that visual representation is clear. This reflects a feature of Blissymbols, where inference from pictographic form to referent is typically more difficult that with Rebus systems. However, series of enhanced Blissymbols, where basic symbols are made more pictorial by the addition of forms related to meanings, have been published recently (McNaughton and Warrick, 1984). All methods have to include items which are more abstract, in order to reflect even basic vocabulary. We are faced with a number of principles underlying the construction of symbols, systems varying in the degree to which they employ these differing principles. Given this situation what is important is whether the handicapped person can decode items reflecting these principles rather than a system as a whole.

Two further graphic symbol systems require comment. Carrier and Peak (1975) describe a language-initiation programme based on the work of Premack (1970). This uses abstract symbols, usually plastic cut-out plaques. It has been employed successfully with mentally handicapped students by Carrier and Peak, and in a modified form by Deich and Hodges (1977). Occasional use in schools has been described (Kiernan *et al.*, 1982).

The other graphic symbol system is traditional orthography (TO), employed as a medium for teaching receptive skills, modified reading, and expressive skills through the use of word cards.

Comparisons of the systems

Two studies which compare the systems in controlled teaching situations throw useful light on differences in the impact of graphic symbols at different levels. Clark (1981) compared the rate of learning of TO, Rebus, Blissymbols and Carrier symbols by pre-school children (4.3 to 5.4) of normal intelligence. Children were shown a set of graphic symbols, told the corresponding words and then shown a response page and asked to name the symbols. Rebus symbols were significantly easier to learn than Blissymbols, and both Rebus and Bliss easier than Carrier symbols. TO was more difficult than the other symbol systems.

Kuntz *et al.* (1978) compared acquisition of matching of Carrier-type symbols and Rebus symbols to pictures by fourteen severely mentally handicapped youngsters. The Rebus group achieved criterion more rapidly than the Carrier group, but Kuntz and her colleagues interpret their data as showing that transfer from Carrier symbols to TO was faster than from Rebus to TO. These data suggest that the Carrier group had practice in dealing with 'a level of abstraction' which benefited them when they came to dealing with TO.

Evaluation of graphic symbol systems

Systematic evidence on the use of graphic symbols by mentally handicapped individuals is sparse. The surveys provide few clear data, since they do not define the characteristics of students using the systems. Published case material on teaching of Blissymbols and Rebus methods is of limited value in clarifying the impact of systems on communication. The clearest study is reported by Harris-Vanderheiden *et al.* (1975), with a follow-up report by Harris *et al.* (1979). Although the papers describe performance relatively briefly, they illustrate that the severely and profoundly mentally handicapped can learn to use Blissymbols and to employ them in a variety of contexts, for a variety of social functions, and to utilize them in multi-element utterances.

Data on the impact of Rebus system teaching is similarly sparse at the case-study level. Reid and Hurlbut (1977) describe a study in which multiply handicapped adults were taught to use pictures as a means of communication. Carrier (1976, 1979) has described extensive data on students taught through the Carrier and Peak programme (abstract symbols). However, little detail of the characteristics of subjects or the progress of teaching and generalization is provided. Deich and Hodges (1977) and Hodges and Deich (1979) report a pilot and a partially completed main study which show progress through a number of steps in their programme. Massive individual differences, unrelated to CA, MA or IQ, emerged in the early stages of the main project.

A study by House *et al.* (1980) involved the teaching of symbol use to ten severely mentally handicapped adults. Symbols were line forms, not unlike Blissymbols. The learning task involved 'describing' pictures through the construction of sentences of up to four items from the taught set. The results are of interest from several viewpoints. First, they showed that severely mentally handicapped people could learn this task, despite showing little evidence of syntactic skills in normal communication. Second, the strategies used were of interest. They typically broke the task down into two steps, initially selecting the correct symbols in nonstandard order, and then ordering them syntactically. This two-stage breakdown illustrates a possible advantage of graphic symbols over manual signs. It is clear that, using manual sign, the process of sentence construction cannot be dichotomized.

This study represents a clear illustration of the possible value of symbol teaching. Several experiments involving mentally handicapped autistic children have documented the ability of those students to use symbols in meaningful combinations (see Kiernan, 1983b, for review). Coupled with data from the Carrier studies they suggest that one particular strength of graphic symbols may be in the teaching of syntactic rules for mentally handicapped individuals.

Discussion

In this section several of the manual sign and graphic symbol systems in use with mentally handicapped individuals have been described. Given the size of the population of nonspeaking mentally handicapped people, it is clear that any method which can offer help in increasing their communication skills is to be welcomed. Survey data show that systems are being widely used and published case data suggest that their employment by handicapped individuals can make a significant difference to their lives.

However, use of nonvocal systems brings with it particular problems. Because they are not the normal means by which people communicate, they are novel and strange and, in the case of manual sign, they have to be learned as new systems. Learning by care-givers or teachers may in itself be difficult, but particular problems are met in generalized use. This is especially the case where the speech-handicapped are integrated with users of speech. Faw *et al.* (1981) and Schepis *et al.* (1982) both describe programmes designed to increase the use of sign across environments.

As already indicated the development of speech within programmes using nonvocal systems is commonly reported, but these reports give little clear guidance on why speech develops. In some cases it seems likely that it has developed because, for the first time, the individual is being involved in a systematic training programme. A study by Kahn (1981) is the only one which controls for this impact of teaching. Kahn found an almost complete overlap between his speech training and sign training groups in words or signs learned. Both groups did better than a placebo control. There were some differences between the speech and sign groups in that all of the sign group learned some signs, whereas two of the four speech group children failed to learn any words. Speech may develop in the context of sign and speech programmes because of the enhancement of imitative skills and a transfer from motor to vocal imitation. Evidence gathered by Carr and Dores (1981) and Carr *et al.* (1984) suggests that mentally handicapped autistic children with relatively good verbal imitative skills acquired receptive speech more readily than those with less good skills. It is possible, however, that enhancement of speech results from more specific linking of signs to particular spoken words (Reich, 1978).

Evidence exists to support each of these propositions, but it is sparse and we are a long way from being able to predict and ensure speech production in individual cases. It is clearly important that skills in identifying crucial characteristics and strategies are developed. Through such endeavours the central problem of the possible isolation of individuals through sign use could be overcome.

Several schemes have been evolved which allow decisions across systems, i.e. between sign languages and symbol systems (Ferrier and Shane, 1983). Although thoroughly evolved in clinical practice, such methods really represent theories of development and, as such, need to be tested.

It can be questioned whether the exclusive use of sign language or graphic symbol systems should be advocated for particular individuals. The discussion of their relative merits suggests that they have differing potential; as suggested above, graphic symbol systems may have particular value in encouraging the development of syntax. In this view manual sign and graphic symbols should be used as teaching aids rather than as communication systems. Clearly a great deal of research and development remains to be done.

CONCLUSIONS

In this chapter a very diverse literature has been considered, the single unifying element being its concern with communication and language skills in the mentally handicapped. One of the dominating impressions from this review is its lack of coherence, particularly between experimental studies (in which the capacities of the handicapped are investigated) and programmes and studies concerned with remediation. There is little evidence that the findings of experimental research were utilized as bases for remediation.

The reasons for this gap probably lie in the oft-discussed failure of researchers to affect practice, either because they do not communicate their findings effectively or because practitioners do not read research reports. This is especially unfortunate in the area of communication and language, since it appears that changing conceptions have clear indications for the style and content of practice. In particular, the emphasis on social function, language use, and the analysis and remediation of discourse skills within natural environments have very substantial implications.

The separation of experimental and remedial literatures has other unfortunate consequences. These are highlighted by the relatively poor response by research workers to the discovery of the value and potential of sign languages and symbol systems. Here it is not the practitioners who are failing to take account of what the researchers are saying, but researchers not absorbing and investigating what practitioners are revealing.

It is instructive to consider the reasons for this failure. One is certainly that researchers need time to observe phenomena, draft research applications, complete studies and publish them. Hence, a thin literature early in the development of a field does not necessarily reflect a lack of ongoing work. Second, what appears to be a single problem at a practical level may, when conceptualized in research teams, emerge as multifaceted and requiring very extensive investigation. For example, there is the question of transfer from sign use to speech where there are at least a dozen possible mechanisms ranging from physical through social to cognitive explanations. All of these may be valid given the diversity of cases. Consequently, a research project investigating transfer would need to be both extensive and, if intervention was involved, extremely time-consuming.

The research–practice gap clearly needs to be bridged more effectively. Part of this bridging can be effected if researchers and other academics interact more with practitioners in workshops or joint conferences, which allow a two-way exchange of ideas. What does seem clear is that the production of language programme packages as a route for research dissemination is inappropriate. This is partly because they are often outdated by the time they are published, a consequence of the rapid growth of knowledge in the field, and partly because, by their very nature, language and communication skills need to be based on transactions between individuals in real-life settings. Although there is clearly still a place for such packages as teaching aids, it seems clear that effective instruction will only evolve if practitioners are able to apply principles which they themselves understand thoroughly, in a flexible, student-based programme context. Such a goal requires greater efforts towards two-way communication on the part of both researchers and practitioners.

REFERENCES

ABBEDUTO, L. and ROSENBERG, S. (1980) 'The communicative competence of mildly retarded adults', *Appl. Psycholing.*, 1, 405–26.

ATKINSON, M. (1982) *Explanations in the Study of Child Language Development*, Cambridge, Cambridge University Press.

BAILEY, P. and JENKINSON, J. (1982) 'The application of Blissymbolics', in M. PETER and R. BARNES (eds), *Signs, Symbols and Schools*, Stratford, NCSE, 18–21.

BARTON, E.S. (1970) 'Inappropriate speech in a severely retarded child: a case study in language conditioning and generalization', *J. Appl. Behav. Anal.*, 3, 299–307.

BATES, E. (1976) *Language and Context*, New York, Academic Press.

BATES, E. and MACWHINNEY, B. (1979) 'A functionalist approach to the acquisition of grammar', in E. OCHS and B.B. SCHIEFFLIN (eds), *Developmental Pragmatics*, New York, Academic Press, 167–211.

BEDROSIAN, J.L. and PRUTTING, C.A. (1978) 'Communicative performance of mentally retarded adults in four conversational settings', *J. Speech Hear. Res.*, 21, 79–95.

BELL, V. (1975) 'A therapeutic approach through intrusive play', in M.P. CREEDON (ed.), *Appropriate Behavior Through Communication: A New Program in Simultaneous Language for Nonverbal Children*, Chicago, Michael Reese Medical Center.

BERKO, J. (1958) 'The child's learning of English morphology', *Word*, 14, 150–77.

BEVERIDGE, M.C. and EVANS, P. (1978) 'Classroom interaction: two studies of severely educationally subnormal children', *Res. Educ.*, 18, 39–48.

BEVERIDGE, M.C. and HURRELL, P. (1980) 'Teachers' responses to severely mentally handicapped children's initiations in the classroom', *J. Child Psychol. Psychiat.*, 21, 175–81.

BEVERIDGE, M.C. and MITTLER, P. (1977) 'Feedback, language and listener performance in severely retarded children', *Brit. J. Dis. Comm.*, 12, 149–57.

BEVERIDGE, M.C., SPENCER, J. and MITTLER, P. (1979) 'Self-blame and communication failure in retarded adolescents', *J. Child Psychol. Psychiat.*, 20, 129–38.

BEVERIDGE, M.C. and TATHAM, A. (1976) 'Communication in retarded adolescents: utilization of known language skills', *Amer. J. Ment. Defic.*, 81, 96–9.

BILSKY, L.H., WALKER, N. and SAKALES, S.R. (1983) 'Comprehension and recall of sentences by mentally retarded and nonretarded individuals', *Amer. J. Ment. Defic.*, 87, 558–65.

BLACHER, J. and MEYERS, C.E. (1983) 'A review of attachment formation and disorder of handicapped children', *Amer. J. Ment. Defic.*, 87, 359–71.

BLINDERT, H.D. (1975) 'Interactions between residents and staff', *Ment. Retard.*, 13, 38–40.

BLISS, C. (1965) *Semantography*, Sydney, Australia, Semantography Publications.

BLOOM, L. (1970) *Language Development: Form and Function in Emerging Grammars*, Cambridge, Mass., MIT Press.

BLOOM, L. and LAHEY, M. (1978) *Language Development and Language Disorders*, New York, Wiley.

BOUSFIELD, W.A. and SEDGEWICK, C.G.W. (1944) 'An analysis of sequences of restrictive associative responses', *J. Gen. Psych.*, 30, 149–65.

BRINKER, R.P. (1978) 'Teaching language in context: a feasibility study', *La Revue de phonétique appliquée*, 46–7.

BRINKER, R.P and GOLDBART, J.L. (1981) 'A problem of reliability in the study of early communication skills', *Brit. J. Psychol.*, 72, 27–41.

BROOKS, P.H. and MCCAULEY, C. (1984) 'Cognitive research in mental retardation', *Amer. J. Ment. Defic.*, 88, 479–86.

BRUMFIT, C. and JOHNSON, K. (eds) (1979) *The Communicative Approach to Language Teaching*, London, Oxford University Press.

BRUNER, J.S. (1975) 'The ontogenesis of speech acts', *J. Child Lang.*, 2, 1–20.

BUIUM, N., RYNDERS, J. and TURNURE, J. (1974) 'Early maternal linguistic environment of normal and Down's syndrome language-learning children', *Amer. J. Ment. Defic.*, 79, 52–8.

BURROUGHS, G.E.R. (1957) *A Study of the Vocabulary of Young Children*, Birmingham University Institute of Education (Educational Monographs no. 1), Edinburgh, Oliver & Boyd.

BYLER, J. (1985) 'The Makaton Vocabulary: an analysis based on recent research', *Special Education–Forward Trends* (in press).

CARR, E.G. and DORES, P.A. (1981) 'Patterns of language acquisition following simultaneous communication with autistic children', *Anal. Intervent. Develop. Disab.*, 1, 1–15.

CARR, E.G., PRIDAL, C. and DORES, P.A. (1984) 'Speech versus sign comprehension in autistic children: analysis and prediction', *J. Exp. Child Psychol.*, 37, 587–97.

CARRIER, J.K. (1976) 'Application of a nonspeech language system with the severely language handicapped', in L.L. LLOYD (ed.), *Communication Assessment and Intervention Strategies*, Baltimore, University Park Press, 523–48.

CARRIER, J.K. (1979) 'Perspectives on nonspeech symbol systems', in R.L. SCHIEFELBUSCH and J.H. HOLLIS (eds), *Language Introduction from Ape to Child*, Baltimore, University Park Press, 493–511.

CARRIER, J.K. and PEAK, T. (1975) *Non-Speech Language Initiation Programme*, Lawrence, Kansas, H. & H. Enterprises.

CARROLL, J.B. and WHITE, W.N. (1973a) 'Word frequency and age of acquisition as determiners of picture-naming latency', *Quart. J. Exp. Psychol.*, 25, 85–95.

CARROLL, J.B. and WHITE, W.N. (1973b) 'Age of acquisition norms for 220 picturable nouns', *J. Verb. Learn. Verb. Behav.*, 12, 563–76.

CHAFE, W.L. (1970) *Meaning and the Structure of Language*, Chicago, University of Chicago Press.

CHAPMAN, R.S. and MILLER, J.F. (1975) 'Word order in early two and three word utterances: does production precede comprehension?', *J. Speech Hear. Res.*, 18, 355–71.

CHOMSKY, N. (1957) *Syntactic Structures*, The Hague, Mouton.

CHOMSKY, N. (1959) 'Review of *Verbal Behaviour* by B. F. Skinner', *Language*, 35, 26–58.

CLARK, C.R. (1981) 'Learning words using traditional orthography and the symbols of Rebus, Bliss and Carrier', *J. Speech Hear. Dis.*, 46, 191–6.

CLARK, C.R. and WOODCOCK, R.W. (1976) 'Graphic systems of communication', in L.L. LLOYD (ed.), *Communication, Assessment and Intervention Strategies*, Baltimore, University Park Press, 549–605.

COGGINS, T.E. (1979) 'Relational meaning encoded in the two-word utterances of Stage 1 Down's syndrome children', *J. Speech Hear. Dis.*, 22, 166–78.

COGGINS, T.E. and CARPENTER, R.L. (1981) 'The Communicative Intention Inventory: a system for coding children's early intentional communication', *Appl. Psycholing.*, 2, 235–52.

COGGINS, T.E. and STOEL-GAMMON, C. (1982) 'Clarification strategies used by four Down's syndrome children for maintaining normal conversational interaction', *Educ. Trg. Ment. Retard.*, 17, 65–7.

CONDON, W.S. (1975) 'Multiple response to sound in dysfunctional children', *J. Autism Child Schizophren.*, 5, 37–56.

COULTHARD, M. (1977) *An Introduction to Discourse Analysis*, Harlow, Longman.

CREGAN, A. (1982) *Signsymbols*, Cambridge, LDA.

CROMER, R.F. (1975) 'Are subnormals linguistic adults?', in N. O'CONNOR (ed.), *Language, Cognitive Deficits and Retardation*, London, Butterworth.

CRYSTAL, D. (1982) *Profiling Linguistic Disability*, London, Edward Arnold.

CRYSTAL, D. and CRAIG, E. (1978) 'Contrived sign language', in I.M.

SCHLESINGER and L. NAMIR (eds), *Sign Language of the Deaf*, New York, Academic Press, 147–68.

CRYSTAL, D., FLETCHER, P. and GARMAN, M. (1976) *The Grammatical Analysis of Language Disability*, London, Edward Arnold.

DANILOFF, J.K., LLOYD, L.L. and FRISTOE, M. (1983) 'Amer-Ind transparency,' *J. Speech Hear. Dis.*, 48, 103–10.

DAVIES, D., SPERBER, R.D. and MCCAULEY, C. (1981) 'Intelligence related differences in semantic processing speed', *J. Exp. Child Psychol.*, 3, 387–402.

DEICH, R.F. and HODGES, P.M. (1977) *Language Without Speech*, London, Souvenir Press.

DE LAGUNA, G.A. (1963) *Speech: Its Function and Development*, Bloomington, University of Indiana Press (first published 1927).

DEUCHAR, M. (1984) *British Sign Language*, London, Routledge & Kegan Paul.

DEVER, R. and GARDNER, W.I. (1970) 'Performance of normal and retarded boys on Berko's test of morphology', *Lang. Speech*, 13, 162–81.

DODD, B. (1975) 'Recognition and reproduction of words by Down's syndrome and non-Down's syndrome retarded children', *Amer. J. Ment. Defic.*, 80, 306–11.

DODD, B. (1976) 'A comparison of the phonological systems of mental age matched normal, severely subnormal and Down's syndrome children', *Brit. J. Dis. Comm.*, 11, 27–42.

DORE, J. (1974) 'A pragmatic description of early language development', *Psycholing. Res.*, 3, 343–50.

DORE, J. (1977) '"Oh them Sheriff": a pragmatic analysis of children's responses to questions', in S. ERVIN-TRIPP and C. MITCHEL-KERNAN (eds), *Child Discourse*, New York, Academic Press, 139–63.

DUCHAN, J.F. and ERICKSON, J.G. (1976) 'Normal and retarded children's understanding of semantic relations in different verbal contexts', *J. Speech Hear. Dis.*, 19, 767–76.

EVANS, P. and HOGG, J.H. (1975) 'Individual differences in severely retarded children in acquisition, stimulus generalization and extinction in go/no go discrimination learning', *J. Exp. Child Psychol.*, 20, 377–90.

FAW, G.D., REID, D.H., SCHEPIS, M.M., FITZGERALD, J.R. and WELTY, P.A. (1981) 'Involving institutional staff in the development and maintenance of sign language skills with profoundly retarded persons', *J. Appl. Behav. Anal.*, 14, 411–23.

FAWCUS, M. and FAWCUS, R. (1974) 'Disorders of communication', in A.M. CLARKE and A.D.B. CLARKE (eds), *Mental Deficiency: The Changing Outlook*, 3rd edn, London, Methuen, 592–627.

FEINMANN, J.L. (1982) 'The visuo-motor complexity, transparency and translucency of the Paget Gorman Sign System and British Sign Language', unpublished MSc. thesis, University of Manchester, Faculty of Education.

FERRIER, L.J. and SHANE, H.C. (1983) 'A description of a nonspeaking population under consideration for augmentative communication systems', in J. HOGG and P.J. MITTLER (eds), *Advances in Mental Handicap Research*, vol. 2, *Aspects of Competence in Mentally Handicapped People*, Chichester, Wiley, 95–137.

FLEECE, L., GROSS, A., O'BRIEN, T., KISTNER, J., ROTHBLUM, E. and DRABMAN, R. (1981) 'Elevation of voice volume in young developmentally delayed children via an operant shaping procedure', *J. Appl. Behav. Anal.*, 14, 351–5.

FRISTOE, M. (1975) *Language Intervention Systems for the Retarded*, Montgomery, State of Alabama Dept of Education.

FRISTOE, M. and LLOYD, L.L. (1978) 'A survey of the use of non-speech systems with the severely communication impaired', *Ment. Retard.*, 16, 99–103.

FRISTOE, M. and LLOYD, L.L. (1979) 'Non-speech communication', in N.R. ELLIS (ed.), *Handbook of Mental Deficiency: Psychological Theory and Research*, 2nd edn, New York, Lawrence Erlbaum, 401–30.

GARCIA, E. (1974) 'The training and generalization of a conversational speech form in nonverbal retardates', *J. Appl. Behav. Anal.*, 7, 137–49.

GERJUOY, I.R. and WINTERS, J.J. (1970) *Word Association Norms: Adolescent Retardates*, Bordentown, NJ, Edward Johnstone Training and Research Centre.

GLIDDEN, L.M. and MAR, H.H. (1978) 'Availability and accessibility of information in the semantic memory of retarded and nonretarded adolescents', *J. Exp. Child Psychol.*, 25, 33–40.

GOETZ, L., SCHULER, A. and SAILOR, W. (1979) 'Teaching functional speech to the severely handicapped: current issues', *J. Autism Devel. Dis.*, 9, 325–43.

GOETZ, L., SCHULER, A. and SAILOR, W. (1983) 'Motivational considerations in teaching language to severely handicapped students', in M. HERSEN, V.B. VAN HASSELT and J.L. MATSON (eds), *Behavior Therapy for the Developmentally and Physically Disabled*, New York, Academic Press, 57–77.

GOODMAN, L., WILSON, P.S. and BORNSTEIN, H. (1978) 'Results of a national survey of sign language programmes in special education', *Ment. Retard.*, 16, 104–6.

GREENWALD, C.A. and LEONARD, L.B. (1979) 'Communicative and sensorimotor development of Down's syndrome children', *Amer. J. Ment. Defic.*, 84, 296–303.

GRICE, H. (1975) 'Logic and conversation', in D. DAVIDSON and G. HARMON (eds), *The Logic of Conversation*, Encore, Calif., Dickenson.

GRIFFITH, P.L. and ROBINSON, J.H. (1980) 'Influence of iconicity and phonological similarity on sign learning by mentally retarded children', *Amer. J. Ment. Defic.*, 85, 291–8.

GUESS, D., SAILOR, W. and BAER, D.M. (1976a) *Functional Speech and Language Training for the Severely Handicapped* (Part 1), Lawrence, Kansas, H. & H. Enterprises.

GUESS, D., SAILOR, W., KEOGH, W. and BAER, D.M. (1976b) 'Language development programs for severely handicapped children', in N. HARING and L. BROWN (eds), *Teaching the Severely Handicapped – A Yearly Publication*, vol. 1, New York, Grune & Stratton.

GUESS, D., SAILOR, W., RUTHERFORD, G. and BAER, D.M. (1968) 'An experimental analysis of linguistic development: the productive use of the plural morpheme', *J. Appl. Behav. Anal.*, 1, 297–306.

GURALNICK, M.J. and PAUL-BROWN, D. (1980) 'Functional and discourse analyses of nonhandicapped preschool children's speech to handicapped children', *Amer. J. Ment. Defic.*, 84, 444–54.

HALL, C., SHELDON-WILDGEN, J. and SHERMAN, J.A. (1980) 'Teaching job interview skills to retarded clients', *J. Appl. Behav. Anal.*, 13, 433–42.

HALLE, J.W., MARSHALL, A.M. and SPRADLIN, J.E. (1979) 'Time delay: a technique to increase language use and facilitate generalization in retarded children', *J. Appl. Behav. Anal.*, 112, 431–9.

HALLIDAY, M.A.K. (1973) *Explorations in the Function of Language*, London, Edward Arnold.

HALVERSON, H.M. (1940) 'Motor development', in A. GESELL (ed.), *The First Five Years of Life*, New York, Harper, 65–107.

HARRIS, D., LIPPERT, J.C., YODER, D.E. and VANDERHEIDEN, G.C. (1979) 'Blissymbolics: an augmentative symbol communication system for nonvocal severely handicapped children', in R.L. YORK and E. EDGAR (eds), *Teaching the Severely Handicapped*, vol. IV, Seattle, Washington, American Association for the Education of the Severely/Profoundly Handicapped, 238–62.

HARRIS, J. (1984) 'Early language intervention programmes: an update', *Association for Child Psychology and Psychiatry Newsletter*, 6 (1).

HARRIS, S.L. (1975) 'Teaching language to nonverbal children – with emphasis on problems of generalization', *Psychol. Bull.*, 85, 565–80.

HARRISON, R.H., BUDOFF, M. and GREENBERG, G. (1975) 'Differences between EMR and nonretarded children in fluency and quality of verbal associations', *Amer. J. Ment. Defic.*, 79, 583–91.

HARRIS-VANDERHEIDEN, D.H., BROWN, W.P., MACKENZIE, P., REINED, S. and SCHEIBEL, C. (1975) 'Symbol communication for the mentally handicapped', *Ment. Retard.*, 13, 34–7.

HART, B.J. and RISLEY, T.R. (1980) 'In vivo intervention: unanticipated general effects', *J. Appl. Behav. Anal.*, 13, 407–32.

HEHNER, B. (1980) *Blissymbols for Use*, Toronto, Blissymbolics Communication Institute.

HERDMAN, M.A. (1979) 'Reduction of inappropriate verbalization in an emotionally disturbed adolescent', *Ment. Retard.*, 17, 251–2.

HODGES, P. and DEICH, R.G. (1979) 'Language intervention strategies with manipulable symbols', in R.L. SCHIEFELBUSCH and J.H. HOLLIS (eds), *Language Intervention from Ape to Child*, Baltimore, University Park Press, 419–40.

HOGG, J.H. (1984), personal communication.

HORSTMEIER, D.S. and MACDONALD, J.D. (1978) *The Environmental Language Intervention Programme*, Columbus, Ohio, Bell & Howell.

HOUSE, B.J., HANLEY, M.J. and MAGID, D.F. (1980) 'Logographic reading by TMR adults', *Amer. J. Ment. Defic.*, 85, 161-70.

HOWLIN, P. (1984) 'Parents as therapists: a critical review', in D.J. MULLER (ed.), *Remediating Children's Language*, London, Croom Helm.

HOY, E.A. and MCKNIGHT, J.R. (1977) 'Communication style and effectiveness in homogeneous and heterogeneous dyads of retarded children', *Amer. J. Ment. Defic.*, 81, 587-98.

INGRAM, D. (1976) *Phonological Disability in Children*, New York, Elsevier.

JABLONSKI, E.M. (1974) 'Free recall in children', *Psychol. Bull.*, 81, 522-39.

JOHNSON, K. and PORTER, D. (eds) (1983) *Perspectives in Communicative Language Teaching*, New York, Academic Press.

JONES, A. and ROBSON, C. (1979) 'Language training the severely mentally handicapped', in N.R. ELLIS (ed.), *Handbook of Mental Deficiency, Psychological Theory and Research*, 2nd edn, Hillsdale, NJ, Lawrence Erlbaum, 367–400.

JONES, O.H.M. (1977) 'Mother–child communication with prelinguistic Down's syndrome and normal infants' in H.R. SCHAFFER (ed.), *Studies in Mother–Infant Interaction*, London, Academic Press, 175–95.

KAHN, J.W. (1981) 'A comparison of sign and verbal language training with nonverbal retarded children', *J. Speech Hear. Res.*, 46, 113–19.

KEILITZ, I., TUCKER, D.J. and HORNER, R.D. (1973) 'Increasing mentally retarded adolescents' verbalizations about current events', *J. Appl. Behav. Anal.*, 6, 621–30.

KELLY, J.A., FURMAN, W., PHILLIPS, J., HATHORN, S. and WILSON, T. (1979) 'Teaching conversational skills to retarded adolescents', *Child Behav. Ther.*, 1, 85–97.

KIERNAN, C.C. (1983a) 'The exploration of sign and symbol effects', in J. HOGG and P.J. MITTLER (eds), *Aspects of Competence in Severely Mentally Handicapped People*, vol. II of *Advances in Mental Handicap Research*, Chichester, Wiley, 27–68.

KIERNAN, C.C. (1983b) 'The use of nonvocal communication techniques with autistic individuals', *J. Child Psychol. Psychiat.*, 24, 339–75.

KIERNAN, C.C. (1984a) 'Imitation and learning of hand postures', in J.M. BERG (ed.), *Perspectives and Progress in Mental Retardation*, vol. 1, *Social, Psychological and Educational Aspects*, Baltimore, University Park Press, 251–60.

KIERNAN, C.C. (1984b) 'Language remediation programmes: a review', in D.J. MULLER (ed.), *Remediating Children's Language: Behavioural and Naturalistic Approaches*, London, Croom Helm.

KIERNAN, C.C. and JONES, M.S. (1985) 'The Heuristic Programme: a combined use of signs and symbols with severely mentally handicapped children', *Aust. J. Hum. Comm. Disords*, in press.

KIERNAN, C.C. and MCMINN, K. (1985) 'Cognitive development in the sensorimotor period and the emergence of communication skills', *J. Ment. Defic. Res.*, in press.

KIERNAN, C.C. and REID, B.D. (1984) 'The use of augmentative communication systems in schools and units for autistic and aphasic children in the United Kingdom', *Brit. J. Dis. Comm.*, 19, 47–56.

KIERNAN, C.C. and REID, B.D. (1985a) 'Patterns of communicative abilities in severely mentally handicapped individuals', *J. Ment. Defic. Res.*, in press.

KIERNAN, C.C. and REID, B.D. (1985b) *The Pre-verbal Communication Schedule (PVC)*, Windsor, NFER, in press.

KIERNAN, C.C., REID, B.D. and JONES, L.M. (1982) *Signs and Symbols: A Review of Literature and Survey of Use of Non-vocal Communication Systems*, London, University of London Institute of Education Studies in Education, no. 11, London, Heinemann.

KIERNAN, C.C. and WILLIS, P. (1985) 'The influence of subject settings on patterns of interaction', submitted for publication.

KIRK, S.A., MCCARTHY, J.J. and KIRK, W.D. (1968) *The Illinois Test of Psycholinguistic Abilities*, Urbana, University of Illinois Press.

KIRSCHNER, A., ALGOZZINE, B. and ABBOTT, T.B. (1979) 'Manual communication systems: a comparison and its implications', *Educ. Trg. Ment. Retard.*, 14, 5–10.

KLEITSCH, E.C., WHITMAN, T.L. and SANTOS, J. (1983) 'Increasing verbal interaction among elderly socially isolated mentally retarded adults: a group language training program', *J. Appl. Behav. Anal.*, 16, 217–33.

KLIMA, E.S. and BELLUGI, U. (1979) *The Signs of Language*, Cambridge, Mass., Harvard University Press.

KNOWLES, W. and MASIDLOVER, M. (1982) *Derbyshire Language Scheme*, Ripley, Derbyshire, private publication.

KOHL, F.L. (1981) 'Effects of motoric requirements on the acquisition of manual sign responses by severely handicapped students', *Amer. J. Ment. Defic.*, 85, 396–403.

KONSTANTAREAS, M.M., OXMAN, J. and WEBSTER, C.D. (1978) 'Iconicity: effects on the acquisition of sign language by autistic and other severely dysfunctional children', in P. SIPLE (ed.), *Understanding Language Through Sign Language Research*, New York, Academic Press, 218–37.

KUNTZ, J.B., CARRIER, J.K. and HOLLIS, J.H. (1978) 'A nonvocal system for teaching retarded children to read and write', in C. MEYERS (ed.), *Quality of Life in Severely and Profoundly Retarded People: Research Foundations for Improvements*, Washington, American Association on Mental Deficiency, 145–91.

KYLE, J. and WOLL, B. (eds) (1981) *Language in Sign: An International Perspective on Sign Language*, London, Croom Helm.

LANE, H., BOYES-BREAM, P. and BELLUGI, U. (1976) 'Preliminaries to a distinctive feature analysis of handshapes in American Sign Language', *Cog. Psychol.*, 8, 263–89.

LAYTON, T.L. and SHARIFI, H. (1979) 'Meaning and structure of Down's syndrome and nonretarded children's spontaneous speech', *Amer. J. Ment. Defic.*, 83, 439–45.

LEE, V.L. (1981) 'Prepositional phrases spoken and heard', *J. Exp. Anal. Behav.*, 35, 227–42.

LEEMING, K., SWANN, W., COUPE, J. and MITTLER, P. (1979) *Teaching Language and Communication to the Mentally Handicapped*, London, Evans/Methuen.

LENNEBERG, E. (1967) *Biological Foundations of Language*, New York, Wiley.

LITTLEWOOD, W. (1981) *Communicative Language Teaching*, London, Cambridge University Press.

LLOYD, L.L. and KARLAN, G. (1984) 'Nonspeech communication symbols and systems: where have we been and where are we going?', *J. Ment. Defic. Res.*, 28, 3–20.

LONGHURST, T.M. (1972) 'Assessing and increasing descriptive communication skills in retarded children', *Ment. Retard.*, 10 (2), 42–5.

LONGHURST, T.M. (1974) 'Communication in retarded adolescents: sex and intelligence level, *Amer. J. Ment. Defic.*, 78, 607–18.

LONGHURST, T.M. and BERRY, G.W. (1975) 'Communication in retarded adolescents: response to listener feedback', *Amer. J. Ment. Defic.*, 80, 158–64.

LOVAAS, O.I., BERBERICH, J.P., PERLOFF, B.F. and SCHAEFFER, B. (1966) 'Acquisition of imitative speech by schizophrenic children', *Science*, 151, 705–7.

LOVAAS, O.I., KOEGEL, R., SIMMONS, J.Q. and LONG, J.S. (1973) 'Some generalization and follow-up measures on autistic children in behavior therapy', *J. Appl. Behav. Anal.*, 6, 1–36.

LOVELL, K. and BRADBURY, B. (1967) 'The learning of English morphology in educationally subnormal special school children', *Amer. J. Ment. Defic.*, 72, 609–15.

LOZAR, B., WEPMAN, J.M. and HASS, W. (1973) 'Syntactic indices of language use of mentally retarded and normal children', *Lang. Speech*, 16, 22–3.

LUFTIG, R.L. and GREESON, L.E. (1983) 'Effects of structural importance and idea saliency on discourse recall of mentally retarded and nonretarded pupils', *Amer. J. Ment. Defic.*, 87, 414–21.

LUFTIG, R.L. and JOHNSON, R.E. (1982) 'Identification and recall of structurally important units in prose by mentally retarded learners', *Amer. J. Ment. Defic.*, 86, 495–502.

LUFTIG, G. and LLOYD, L.L. (1981) 'Manual sign translucency and referential concreteness in the learning of signs', *Sign Lang. Stud.*, 30, 49–60.

LUND, N.J. and DUCHAN, J.F. (1983) *Assessing Children's Language in Naturalistic Contexts*, Englewood Cliffs, NJ, Prentice-Hall.

LYLE, J.G.. (1959) 'The effect of an institution environment upon the verbal development of imbecile children: I. Verbal intelligence', *J. Ment. Defic. Res.*, 3, 122–8.

LYLE, J.G. (1960) 'The effect of an institution environment upon the verbal development of imbecile children: II. Speech and language', *J. Ment. Defic. Res.*, 4, 1–13.

MCCAULEY, C., WEIL, C.M. and SPERBER, R.D. (1976) 'The development of memory structures as reflected by semantic-primary effects', *J. Exp. Child Psychol.*, 22, 511–18.

MACDONALD, J., BLOTT, J., GORDON, K., SPIEGEL, B. and HARTMAN, M. (1974) 'An experimental parent-assisted treatment program for pre-school language-delayed children', *J. Speech Hear. Dis.*, 39, 395–415.

MCLEAN, J.E. and SNYDER-MCLEAN, L.K. (1978) *A Transactional Approach to Early Language Training*, Columbus, Ohio, Merrill.

MCLEAN, J.E. and SNYDER-MCLEAN, L.K. (1984) 'Recent developments in pragmatics: remedial implications', in D.J. MULLER (ed.), *Remediating Children's Language*, London, Croom Helm, 55–82.

MCLEAVEY, B.C., TOOMEY, J.F. and DEMPSEY, P.J.R. (1982) 'Non-retarded and mentally retarded children's control over syntactic structures', *Amer. J. Ment. Defic.*, 86, 485–94.

MCNAUGHTON, S. and WARRICK, A. (1984) 'Picture your Blissymbols', *Canad. J. Ment. Retard.*, 34, 1–9.

MANDEL, M. (1977) 'Iconic devices in American Sign Language', in L.A. FRIEDMAN (ed.), *On the Other Hand: New Perspectives on American Sign Language*, New York, Academic Press, 57–107.

MARSHALL, N.R., HEGRENES, J.R. and GOLDSTEIN, S. (1973) 'Verbal interactions: mothers and their retarded children *v.* mothers and their nonretarded children', *Amer. J. Ment. Defic.*, 77, 415–19.

MATSON, J.L. (1982) 'Independence training *v.* modeling procedures for teaching phone conversation skills to the mentally retarded', *Behav. Res. Ther.*, 20, 505–11.

MATSON, J.L., KAZDIN, A.E. and ESVELDT-DAWSON, K. (1980) 'Training interpersonal skills among mentally retarded and socially dysfunctional children', *Behav. Res. Ther.*, 18, 419–27.

MEIN, R. and O'CONNOR, N. (1960) 'A study of the oral vocabularies of severely subnormal patients', *J. Ment. Defic. Res.*, 4, 130–43.

MILLER, J. (1980) *Assessing Language Production in Children*, Baltimore, University Park Press.

MILLER, J.F. and CHAPMAN, R.S. (1984) 'Disorders of communication: investigating the development of language of mentally retarded children', *Amer. J. Ment. Defic.*, 88, 536–45.

MILLER, J.F., CHAPMAN, R. and MACKENZIE, H. (1981) 'Individual differences in the language acquisition of mentally retarded children', paper to the Society for Research in Child Development, Boston, USA.

MILLER, J.F. and YODER, D.E. (1972) 'A syntax teaching program', in J.E. MCLEAN, D. YODER and R.L. SCHIEFELBUSCH (eds), *Language Interven-*

tion with the Retarded, Baltimore, University Park Press, 191–211.

MILLER, J.F. and YODER, D.E. (1974) 'An ontogenetic lanaguage teaching strategy for retarded children', in R.L. SCHIEFELBUSCH and L.L. LLOYD (eds), *Language Perspectives: Acquisition, Retardation and Intervention*, Baltimore, University Park Press, 505–28.

MISCHLER, E. (1975) 'Studies in dialogue and discourse: II, types of discourse initiated by and sustained through questioning', *J. Psycholing. Res.*, 4, 99–121.

MOERK, E. (1977) *Pragmatic and Semantic Aspects of Early Language Development*, Baltimore, University Park Press.

MOREHEAD, D.M. and MOREHEAD, A. (1974) 'From signal to sign: a Piagetian view of thought and language during the first two years', in R.L. SCHIEFELBUSCH and L.L. LLOYD (eds), *Language Perspectives: Acquisition, Retardation and Intervention*, Baltimore, University Park Press.

MULLER, D.J., MUNRO, S.M. and CODE, C. (1981) *Language Assessment for Remediation*, London, Croom Helm.

MURDOCK, J.Y., GARCIA, E.E. and HARDMAN, M.L. (1977) 'Generalized articulation training with trainable mentally retarded subjects', *J. Appl. Behav. Anal.*, 10, 717–33.

NAREMORE, R.C. and DEVER, R.B. (1975) 'Language performance of educable mentally retarded and normal children at five age levels', *J. Speech Hear. Res.*, 18, 82–95.

NELSON, K.E. (1973) 'Structure and strategy in learning to talk', *Monographs of the Society for Research in Child Development*, 38 (1–2, serial no. 149).

NELSON, R.O. and EVANS, I.M. (1968) 'The combination of learning principles and speech therapy techniques in the treatment of noncommunicating children', *J. Child Psychol. Psychiat.*, 9, 111–24.

NELSON, R.O., PEOPLES, A., HAY, L.R., JOHNSON, T. and HAY, W. (1976) 'The effectiveness of speech training techniques based on operant conditioning: a comparison of two methods', *Ment. Retard.*, 14 (3), 34–8.

OWENS, R.E. and MACDONALD, J.D. (1982) 'Communicative uses of early speech of nondelayed and Down syndrome children', *Amer. J. Ment. Defic.*, 86, 503–10.

OWINGS, N.O. and MCMANUS, M.D. (1980) 'An analysis of communication functions in the speech of a deinstitutionalized adult mentally retarded client', *Ment. Retard.*, 18, 309–14.

PAPANIA, N. (1954) 'A qualitative analysis of vocabulary responses of institutionalized mentally retarded children', *J. Clin. Psychol.*, 10, 361–5.

PATON, X. and STIRLING, M.A. (1974) 'Frequency and type of dyadic nurse–patient verbal interactions in a mental subnormality hospital', *Int. J. Nurs. Stud.*, 11, 135–45.

PRATT, M.W., BUMSTEAD, D.C. and RAYNES, N.V. (1976) 'Attendant staff speech to the institutionalized retarded: language use as a measure of the quality of care', *J. Child Psychol. Psychiat.*, 17, 133–43.

PREMACK, D. (1970) 'A functional analysis of language', *J. Exp. Anal. Behav.*,

14, 107–25.

PRICE-WILLIAMS, D. and SABSAY, S. (1979) 'Communicative competence among severely retarded persons', *Semiotica*, 26, 35–63.

PRIOR, H., MINNES, P., COYNE, T., GOLDING, B., HENDY, J.E. and MCGILLIVRAY, J. (1979) 'Verbal interactions between staff and residents in an institution for the young mentally retarded', *Ment. Retard.*, 17, 65–70.

RAVERS, S.A., COOKE, T.P. and APOLLONI, T. (1978) 'Generalization effects from intratherapy articulation training: a case study', *J. Appl. Behav. Anal.*, 11, 436.

RAYNES, N.V., PRATT, M.W. and ROSES, S. (1979) *Organizational Structure and the Care of the Mentally Retarded*, London, Croom Helm.

REICH, R. (1978) 'Gestural facilitation of expressive language in moderately/severely retarded preschoolers', *Ment. Retard.*, 16, 113–17.

REID, B.D., JONES, L.M. and KIERNAN, C.C. (1983) 'Signs and symbols – the 1982 survey of use', *Spec. Educ. – Forward Trends*, 10, 27–8.

REID, B.D. and KIERNAN, C.C. (1985a) 'The Pre-verbal Communication Schedule (PVC): a method of assessing non-verbal communicative behaviours', *J. Ment. Defic. Res.*, in press.

REID, B.D. and KIERNAN, C.C. (1985b) 'Non-verbal communication behaviour and measures of cognitive and symbolic functioning', *Brit. J. Dis. Comm.*, in press.

REID, D.H. and HURLBUT, B. (1977) 'Teaching nonvocal communication skills to multihandicapped retarded adults', *J. Appl. Behav. Anal.*, 10, 591–603.

REYNELL, J. (1977) *Reynell Developmental Language Scales*, Windsor, NFER.

RISLEY, T.R. and WOLF, M.M. (1967) 'Establishing functional speech in echolalic children', *Behav. Res. Ther.*, 5, 73–88.

ROBSON, C. (1981) *Language Development Through Structured Teaching*, Cardiff, Drake Educational Associates.

ROGERS-WARREN, A.K., WARREN, S.F. and BAER, D.M. (1983) 'Interactional basis of language learning', in K.T. KERNAN, M.J. BEGAB and R.B. EDGERTON (eds), *Environments and Behavior*, Baltimore, University Park Press, 239–66.

ROMER, D. and BERKSON, G. (1980) 'Social ecology of supervised communal facilities for mentally disabled adults: III. Predictors of social choice', *Amer. J. Ment. Defic.*, 85, 243–52.

RONDAL, J.A. (1978) 'Maternal speech to normal and Down's syndrome children matched for mean length of utterance', in C.E. MEYERS (ed.), *Quality of Life in Severely and Profoundly Mentally Retarded People: Research Foundations for Improvement*, Washington, DC, AAMD, 193–265.

ROSENBERG, S. (1982) 'The language of the mentally retarded: development, processes and intervention', in S. ROSENBERG (ed.), *Handbook of Applied Psycholinguistics: Major Thrusts of Research and Theory*, Hillsdale, NJ, Lawrence Erlbaum, 329–92.

ROTH, F.P. and SPEKMAN, N.J. (1984a) 'Assessing the pragmatic abilities of children: Part 1. Organizational framework and assessment parameters', *J. Speech Hear. Dis.*, 49, 2–11.

ROTH, F.P. and SPEKMAN, N.J. (1984b) 'Assessing the pragmatic abilities of children: Part 2. Guidelines, considerations and specific evaluation procedures', *J. Speech Hear. Dis.*, 49, 12–17.

SABSAY, S.L. and KERNAN, K.T. (1983) 'Communicative design in the speech of mildly retarded adults', in K.T. KERNAN, M.J. BEGAB and R.B. EDGERTON (eds), *Environments and Behavior*, Baltimore, University Park Press, 283–94.

SAYER, D.J. (ed.) (1984) *Signed English for Schools*, vol. 1, *Structural Language*, Surrey, Working Party on Signed English.

SCHAEFFER, B., MUSIL, A. and KOLLINZAS, G. (1980) *Total Communication: A Signed Speech Program for Nonverbal Children*, Champaign, Ill., Research Press.

SCHEPIS, M.M., REID, D.H., FITZGERALD, J.R., FAW, G.D., VAN DEN POL, R.A. and WELTY, P.A. (1982) 'A program for increasing manual signing by autistic and profoundly retarded youth within the daily environment', *J. Appl. Behav. Anal.*, 15, 363–79.

SEMMEL, M.I., BARRITT, L.S., BENNETT, S.W. and PERFETTI, C.A. (1968) 'A grammatical analysis of word associations of educable mentally retarded and normal children', *Amer. J. Ment. Defic.*, 72, 567–76.

SIMIC, J. and BUCHER, B. (1980) 'Development of spontaneous wording in language deficient children', *J. Appl. Behav. Anal.*, 13, 523–8.

SKELLY, M. (1979) *Amerind Gestural Code Based on Universal American Indian Hand Talk*, New York, Elsevier.

SKINNER, B.F. (1957) *Verbal Behavior*, New York, Appleton-Century-Crofts.

SMITH, B.L. and STOEL-GAMMON, C. (1983) 'A longitudinal study of the development of stop consonant production in normal and Down's syndrome children', *J. Speech Hear. Dis.*, 48, 114–18.

SPERBER, R.D., RAGAIN, R.D and MCCAULEY, C. (1976) 'Reassessment of category knowledge in retarded individuals', *Amer. J. Ment. Defic.*, 81, 227–34.

STERNBERG, L. (1982) 'Communication instruction', in L. STERNBERG and G.L. ADAMS (eds), *Educating Severely and Profoundly Handicapped Students*, Rockville, Md, Aspen Systems.

STOEL-GAMMON, C. (1980) 'Phonological analysis of four Down's syndrome children', *Appl. Psycholing.*, 1, 31–48.

STOKES, T.F. and BAER, D.M. (1977) 'An implicit technology of generalization', *J. Appl. Behav. Anal.*, 10, 349–67.

STRIEFEL, S., WETHERBY, B. and KARLAN, G. (1978) 'Developing generalized instruction-following behavior in severely retarded people', in C.E. MEYERS (ed.), *Quality of Life in Severely and Profoundly Mentally Retarded People: Research Foundations for Improvement*, Washington, DC, AAMD, 267–326.

TERDALL, L.E., JACKSON, R.H. and GARNER, A.M. (1976) 'Mother–child interactions: a comparison between normal and developmentally delayed groups', in E.J. MASH, L.A. HAMMERLYNCK and L.C. HANDY (eds), *Behavior Modification and Families*, New York, Brunner/Mazel.

TIZARD, B., COOPERMAN, O., JOSEPH, A. and TIZARD, J. (1972) 'Environmental effects on language development: a study of young children in long-stay residential nurseries', *Child Develop.*, 43, 337–58.

TWARDOSZ, S. and BAER, D.M. (1973) 'Training two severely retarded adolescents to ask questions', *J. Appl. Behav. Anal.*, 6, 655–61.

UZGIRIS, I. and HUNT, J. MCV. (1975) *Assessment in Infancy: Ordinal Scales of Psychological Development*, Urbana, University of Illinois Press.

VAN BIERVLIET, A., SPANGLER, P.F. and MARSHALL, A.M. (1981) 'An ecobehavioural examination of a simple strategy for increasing mealtime language in residential facilities', *J. Appl. Behav. Anal.*, 14, 295–305.

VAN DIJK, J. (1965) 'The first steps of the deaf/blind child toward language', *Proceedings of the Conference on the Deaf/Blind, Refsnes, Denmark*, Boston, Perkins School for the Blind.

VAN OOSTERUM, J. and DEVEREUX, K. (1982) 'Rebus at Rees Thomas School', in M. PETER and R. BARNES (eds), *Signs, Symbols and Schools*, Stratford, NCSE, 22–4.

WALKER, M. (1976a) *The Makaton Vocabulary*, revised edn, London, RADD.

WALKER, M. (1976b) *Language Programmes for Use with the Revised Makaton Vocabulary*, Chertsey, Surrey, private publication.

WALKER, M. (1978) 'The Makaton Vocabulary', in T. TEBBS (ed.), *Ways and Means*, Basingstoke, Globe Education, 174–84.

WARREN, S.F. and ROGERS-WARREN, A.K. (1983) 'Because no one asked. Setting variables affecting the generalization of trained vocabulary within a residential institution', in K.T. KERNAN, M.J. BEGAB and R.B. EDGERTON (eds), *Environments and Behavior*, Baltimore, University Park Press, 267–81.

WEISZ, J.R. and ZIGLER, E. (1979) 'Cognitive development in retarded and nonretarded persons: Piagetian tests of the similar sequence hypothesis', *Psychol. Bull.*, 88, 831–51.

WELCH, S.J. (1981) 'Teaching generative grammar to mentally retarded children: a review and analysis of a decade of behavioural research', *Ment. Retard.*, 19, 277–84.

WETHERBY, B. (1978) 'Miniature languages and the functional analysis of verbal behavior', in R.L. SCHIEFELBUSCH (ed.), *Bases of Language Intervention*, Baltimore, University Park Press, 397–448.

WHELDALL, K. (1976) 'Receptive language development in the mentally handicapped', in P. BERRY (ed.), *Language and Communication in the Mentally Handicapped*, London, Edward Arnold, 36–55.

WILBUR, R.B. (1979) *American Sign Language and Sign Systems*, Baltimore, University Park Press.

WILKINS, D.A. (1976) *Notional Syllabuses*, London, Oxford University Press.

WINTERS, J.J. and BRZOSKA, M.A. (1975) 'Development of lexicon in normal and retarded persons', *Psychol. Rep.*, 37, 391–402.

WINTERS, J.J. and BRZOSKA, M.A. (1976) 'Development of the formation of categories by normal and retarded persons', *Devel. Psychol.*, 12, 125–31.

WINTERS, J.J., WINTER, L. and BURGER, A.L. (1978) 'Confidence in age-of-acquisition estimates and its relationship to children's labelling performance', *Bull. Psychom. Soc.*, 12, 361–4.

ZIGLER, E. (1964) 'Research on personality structure in the retardate', in N.R. ELLIS (ed.), *International Review of Research in Mental Retardation*, vol. 1, New York, Academic Press.

17

Education

Ronald Gulliford

INTRODUCTION

Theory and practice in the education of the mentally retarded can be traced to the nineteenth century, but the intention of making comprehensive provision began to develop only during the postwar period and is still in a formative stage. Although the first British educational legislation was passed in 1899 it was merely permissive, and it was not until 1914 that authorities were required to make provision for educable mentally defective children in special schools. There was, however, little increase in provision during the next quarter century as a result of the First World War, the economic difficulties of the interwar years and perhaps also a lack of serious intent. There were 13,000 'mentally defective' children in special schools in 1913 and only 17,000 in 1939, dropping to 11,000 in 1946. Special schools were mainly in large towns, with little provision in ordinary schools except for the backward class or repeating the class of a lower level. There was no special training for teachers. The mentally handicapped were excluded from schools and were either at home or in institutions.

The development of British educational practice for the retarded is therefore mainly a postwar one, with a trend towards increasing acceptance into the main educational system. The 1944 Education Act was the first major legislation to include clauses relating to children with disabilities of mind or body; a broad definition of educationally subnormal was given in order to avoid a sharp distinction between the 1.2 per cent of pupils estimated as requiring special school placement and the 8–9 per cent who needed special help in ordinary schools. It led to a wider interpretation of the need for special schooling than the below IQ 70 criterion which had obtained pre-war, and to an increase in special school provision but rather little special provision in ordinary schools.

The Act detailed the procedure to be followed if it was considered that a child could not be educated at school, either because he was deemed ineducable or because it was inexpedient that he should be associated with other children. A pamphlet on special educational treatment (Ministry of Education, 1946) explained why a child might be considered ineducable. The negative character of that account enables one to appreciate why it took another quarter of a century before the severely retarded, after a period of debate, were accepted as an educational responsibility by the Education Act of 1970. Since then these children have been included in the education system, considerable progress has been made and the research in and development of practice has had a stimulating effect on the rest of special education.

By contrast, the special provision for mildly/moderately retarded children ran into problems of definition and how facilities should be organized – which retarded children should be given special education? how effective is it? how can arrangements be made in ordinary schools? – problems which have not been convincingly resolved yet on either side of the Atlantic. In England the number of special schools for the educationally subnormal rose from 166 in 1950 to 478 in 1970; the number of pupils from 15,000 to over 50,000 – about 0.6 per cent of the total school population. New buildings and an influx of new staff effected a break with the tradition of pre-war schools, and the approach became more broadly educational.

The 1946 Ministry of Education pamphlet stated that how provision could best be made in ordinary schools 'must be found by experiment . . . for there is as yet no unanimity of views on how schools can make the best arrangements for their retarded children'. Unfortunately, arrangements for educationally retarded children in ordinary schools did not expand significantly, and at first relied on the traditional method of streaming and occasionally on a special or area class. Remedial teaching services began to develop from the 1950s, but they were mainly seen as short-term help for educationally retarded children and increasingly as performing advisory and inservice training functions. In 1961, the Ministry of Education suggested to local educational authorities various ways in which special help for educationally retarded children could be organized in ordinary schools.

However, a survey in 1967–8 of provision for slow learners in 158 secondary schools revealed a depressing picture (Department of Education and Science, 1971). Fourteen per cent of pupils were deemed by schools to be needing some form of special educational help but only half were judged to be receiving it. The curriculum for slow learners was characterized as showing uncertainty of aims and methods, and only one-third of schools had a special department. Of the 90,000 pupils in the secondary schools surveyed, 0.75 per cent were considered by their teachers to need placement in a special school – in addition to those already there. As Brennan (1982) has pointed out, when the main school system is under pressure there is a tendency to isolate minority problems, and there was a period of pressure for schools during the 1960s: secondary school reorganization; curriculum reform; preparation for raising the school leaving age; and social changes, especially in large cities.

Similar trends occurred in the USA and the special class ran into controversy. An influential article by Dunn (1968) questioned whether much of the special education for the mildly retarded was justifiable. He referred to children from low-status background, including certain ethnic and nonstandard English-speaking-ones. The latter were also a concern in England where, in certain towns, there was an overrepresentation of West Indian children in ESN schools (Townsend, 1971). Dunn was not opposed to special education programmes for the moderately retarded and other handicapped children but, arguing for 'doing something better for slow learning children', he mentioned a range of possibilities for more effective instruction and provision. He supported his argument by referring to the failure of research into the effects of special education to show any clear difference between the progress of retarded children in special and ordinary classes. A review of these efficacy studies by Kirk (1964) had pointed out their methodological weaknesses, for example, in the selection of control and experimental groups; and in the failure to specify the special curriculum and teaching methods employed. Subsequent studies tried to avoid the pitfalls and a four-year study by Goldstein *et al.* (1965) randomly assigned children with low IQs to special and regular classes; the teaching in the special classes was based on the Illinois Curriculum Guide (Goldstein and Seigle, 1958). The teachers had special education training and were given support and advice during the experiment. There were no major differences in the achievements of the two groups, although there were some indications that pupils with low IQ did better in special classes. Even this carefully planned study can be criticized on the grounds that children were assessed as retarded and allocated to classes before the school entry age of six; the need for special placement is usually determined later, with reference to the degree of observed difficulty in learning in school. Many other studies and reviews of studies at that time contributed to the prevalent disquiet about special school and class placement (Kaufman and Alberto, 1976).

Although separate education was increasingly being questioned in Britain, it was not the only or even the major factor which led to the setting up of the Warnock Committee, a government committee of enquiry into educational provision for handicapped children (Department of Education and Science, 1978). It came about because of a growing consensus that the system set up in 1944 was due for change, in order to match current understanding of the nature of handicap and changing concepts about the needs for services and provision. Moreover, two major research projects, the National Child Development Study (Kellmer Pringle *et al.*, 1966) and the Isle of Wight study (Rutter *et al.*, 1970), had presented data about the prevalence and nature of handicaps in schoolchildren which showed the inadequacy of existing arrangements. The Warnock Report made comprehensive recommendations about the special help needed from pre-school to the post-school period. Some of its main principles were soon incorporated in legislation.

The Education Act, 1981, which came into force in April 1983, required local education authorities to provide for children with special educational needs. A child is deemed to have such needs if he has a learning difficulty significantly greater than most children of his age, or has a physical or mental disability which prevents or hinders him from making use of the educational facilities generally provided. A learning difficulty arising solely because the language of the home is different from the language of instruction in the school is specifically excluded.

The concept of special educational needs replaces the 1944 Education Act's system of special educational treatment based on classification of handicapped children into ten categories according to their major disability (see Chapter 2). Dissatisfaction with the categorization had been growing for many years, since emphasis on the major disability tended to lead to a restricted view of children's other needs. The Isle of Wight study (Rutter *et al.*, 1970) had shown how frequently children have more than one handicap; a multidisciplinary working party on the education and care of handicapped children had emphasized the personal, social and family needs (Younghusband *et al.*, 1970). Rutter *et al.* (1970) had suggested that 'special schooling should be reconsidered from the point of view of the actual needs of children.' The Warnock Committee also recognized that there is no simple relationship between degree of disability and degree of educational handicap, since the latter depends on the child's personal characteristics and resources, the quality of support and encouragement from the family and, importantly, the outlook, expertise and resources in his school. Special educational need is seen not in terms of a particular disability but in relation to all the factors which have a bearing on progress.

Since 'special educational needs' could easily come to be used simply as a synonym for 'handicapped' it is worth noting that the Warnock Report defined this term as demanding: (1) provision of special means of access to the curriculum through special equipment, facilities or resources, modification of the physical environment or specialist teaching techniques; (2) the provision of a special or modified curriculum; (3) particular attention to the social structure and emotional climate in which education takes place. Special education, which in the past has been equated with the system of special provision in special schools, classes and units, was redefined in terms of its essential functions wherever they are performed: access to appropriately qualified or experienced teachers and to other trained professional personnel, and an educational and physical environment appropriate to the child's requirements.

The accumulation of evidence of the frequency of special needs, from the National Development Study, the Isle of Wight survey and other sources, led to the Warnock recommendation that services should be planned on the assumption that up to 20 per cent of children require some form of special provision. The administrative circulars which interpreted the Act and gave guidance on its implementation reflected these views.

The majority of the large number of children with special educational needs are to be assessed and provided for within the normal resources of ordinary schools. For a smaller percentage (perhaps 2 per cent) of children with more severe and complex difficulties, whose education is likely to require additional resources, it is necessary for local education authorities themselves to determine the appropriate provision to be made, i.e. to institute a formal assessment procedure in order to protect the child, with a statement of his needs. The circulars suggested that the factors leading to a decision on whether to initiate a formal procedure are likely to vary, depending on the range of provision normally available in an authority's schools. Parents have the right to make representations about the proposal to assess and to be consulted at each stage of the process; they may also request an assessment.

The circulars stress that a clear distinction should be made in the assessment process between (1) the analysis of the child's learning difficulties, (2) the specification of his special needs for different kinds of approach, facilities and resources, and (3) the determination of the special educational provision to meet those needs. A checklist is offered as advice to professionals for description of the child's functioning, the aims of provision and the required facilities and resources. These are the basis for the local education authority's formulation of the child's special educational needs and specification of the type of provision needed.

The translation of the statement of needs and its supporting information into the detailed goals and objectives of the child's education is clearly the responsibility of the school, based upon advice from relevant professionals. Authorities must review statements at least once a year, drawing upon reports from schools and including the views of parents wherever possible.

Perhaps the greatest challenge of this Act lies in the area of assessment. There is the necessity for co-ordination of the contributions of several professions – medical, social, psychological, educational – and for a balance in psychoeducational assessment between traditional methods of monitoring children's development and needs and the more recent emphasis on curriculum-based assessment. Moreover, the concept of special needs implies continuous monitoring with periodic reappraisals.

In the context of a chapter for a multidisciplinary international readership it should be emphasized that neither the English legislation nor the related regulations and administrative circulars make any reference to particular disabilities, or use any terminology for the different degrees of intellectual retardation. In practice, the terms mild, moderate and severe learning difficulties suggested by the Warnock Report have become current, associated at present with the kind of curriculum required. Pupils with mild learning difficulties can be helped successfully to follow a normal curriculum; they should not be confused with the internationally recognized category of mild mental retardation, although some pupils with mild learning difficulties will, of course, have IQs below 70. Pupils with moderate educational difficulties are the equivalent of those previously described as ESN(M), the IQ range being *approximately* 50–70; they will require a modified curriculum. Those with severe learning difficulties will need a developmental curriculum which promotes personal development, independence and social skills. Fig. 2.1 on page 40 shows, in relation to IQ levels, how these terms correspond to others which were formerly or are currently used. Warnock's nomenclature, though cumbersome, is used in this chapter. One may hope that, in the future, it will be possible to do without terminologies and simply provide appropriate education for children.

There are obvious similarities between the 1981 Act's statement of special educational needs and the USA's individualized education program (the IEP) required under Public Law 94–142. A major difference appears to be that the IEP is more detailed and prescriptive. It requires a statement of annual goals, including short-term instructional objectives, and also projected dates for initiation and anticipated duration of special educational services as well as indicating objective criteria and evaluation procedures for determining on an annual basis whether instructional objectives are being achieved. Welton *et al.* (1982) conclude that a statement cannot provide detailed prescriptive information and argue that the Act's procedures make their main contribution by requiring services to children with special needs to be accountable in terms of both process and expenditure. They specify accountability for provision, first to the child and his parents; second, to the local authority and through it to the community and the taxpayer; and, third, the accountability of one service to another with respect to formulation of the child's need, the appropriateness of the specification of services and resources and of the chosen provision and its effectiveness. The definition of needs should be sufficiently detailed to derive practical indications for provision. They suggest, however, that these will not have to be limited by facilities actually available since there would in this case be no impetus for the improvement of resources. Time will show whether this element of accountability – far less than there is in PL 94–142 – is effective and also what results there are of the increased rights given to parents.

INTEGRATION: CONCEPTS AND PROVISIONS

The 1981 Act established the principle that children for whom a statement is maintained are to be educated in ordinary schools, so far as is reasonably practicable. Those providing special education in ordinary schools must ensure that children engage in its activities together with those who do not have special educational needs. The principle is subject to account being taken of the views of the child's parents, the ability of the school to meet the child's special educational needs, the provision of efficient education for others in the school, and the efficient use of resources by the local education authority.

The comparable concept in the American Public Law 94–142 is that of 'the least restrictive environment'. Larsen and Poplin's (1980) commentary on its implementation points out that the term is sometimes thought to imply that there must be some degree of education in regular class, whereas it really means placement on a continuum of alternatives (ranging from separate special education through part-time regular class or resource teacher through to full-time regular class) which permits achievement of the goals and objectives stated in the IEP. Successful progress at one level may indicate the feasibility of a move to 'a less restrictive' placement on the continuum. Hegarty and Pocklington (1981) give a similar priority to education:

> Integration is a means not an end in itself. Pupils with special needs do not need integration. What they need is education. Integrated placement may well turn out to be important in achieving goals or facilitating certain aspects of development and to that extent become important. The primary concern, however, must be individual development and other considerations such as where education takes place have relevance only in relation to it.

The integration principle does not mean a stark choice between ordinary and special school. The Warnock Committee expressed the conviction that special schools would continue to be necessary for children with severe and complex disabilities (including children with severe, and some with moderate, learning difficulties), but outlined a continuum of alternative forms of provision increasing in proximity to ordinary schooling – examples of which are already operating. Essentially these are:

1. Full-time education in an ordinary class with support.
2. Education in an ordinary class with periods of withdrawal to a supporting base.
3. Education in a special class or unit with periods of attendance at an ordinary class and full involvement in the general community life and extracurricular activities of the school.
4. Full-time education in a special class or unit with social contact with the main school.
5. Education in a special school with some shared lessons with a neighbouring ordinary school.
6. Full-time education in a special school with social contact with an ordinary school.

This scheme of types of organization was usefully supplemented in the Warnock Report by distinctions between locational, social and functional integration.

Locational refers to the placement of special classes or centres in ordinary schools or of a special school on the campus of an ordinary school. A minimum benefit is that children are seen to be going to a neighbourhood school (not always their own) rather than being transported some distance to an isolated special school. Physically, at least, they remain part of the community of schoolchildren, which is usually welcomed by parents and, as the Warnock Report suggests, 'There is opportunity for children in ordinary classes to be aware of children with special needs and for those with disabilities to be able to observe the behaviour of their contemporaries.' A research into integration of children with moderate and severe difficulties in Sweden (Söder, 1981) showed that a reduction of the physical distance between special and ordinary children was the main outcome. In 13 per cent of all schools which had been integrated, the special school's classrooms were in separate buildings; 7 per cent of the others had some of their rooms outside the main school. There was virtually no functional and little social integration of pupils.

Locational integration may – indeed should – lead to *social* integration when children participate in assemblies, mealtimes, playground and extracurricular activities. Whether *functional* or academic integration, full-time or part-time, is feasible depends on the special needs of the children and the nature of the ordinary school's curriculum and ethos.

The three concepts are useful in planning and evaluating schemes of integrated education. For example, it is important to consider the effects, and therefore the value, of different kinds of location. A special class or unit in the grounds of a school or even at the end of a remote corridor is less likely to be integrated than one placed centrally in a school where it is more likely to be visited by other staff and pupils. An isolated location may lead to isolation of the unit's staff, who may not share the same common room. Clearly, location is not simply a geographical matter. If isolated in most senses, one might question whether locational integration is any better than being on separate sites, especially since a special class or unit may have the disadvantage of catering for fewer pupils over a wider age range than a special school. There may also be constraints in the use of equipment, hall, gym and other resources. While there are many potential benefits for the special unit and the main school being together, problems for the unit and additional management ones for the school may arise.

One of the advantages of locational integration is the possibility of social integration. This may not 'just happen' but requires positive steps from both sides to promote social interaction between handicapped and nonhandicapped pupils. Likewise, there are procedures to be adopted to involve and integrate staff. Rose (1981) reported a peer-tutoring programme in which normal primary children were paired with a mentally handicapped child for a period of constructive play and activities. Observational records of interaction in the playground before and after the programme showed a significant increase in co-operative play between normal and handicapped pupils. Unfortunately the permanence of this effect was not assessed, but the experiment indicates one way of promoting social interaction.

Research into integration

It is important to evaluate the integration of handicapped children in order to be assured that their educational progress is satisfactory and to identify the critical factors of the integration process. Earlier American studies of the efficacy of special provisions frequently employed an experimental paradigm comparing educable retarded children in special and mainstream classes, using measures of ability, attainment, social adjustment and self-concept. As Meyers *et al.* (1980) concluded, the efficacy studies pointed out the need to examine what goes on *within* the programmes being compared – their assumptions, curricula and methods, time allocations, teacher skills and attitudes. Programme evaluation, however, has not been a strong feature of research in special education. Crowell (1980) reports that over a four-year period only 18 of 822 articles in three journals devoted to the education and training of mentally retarded people were concerned with programme evaluation. He argues for what he terms multiple perspective evaluation of integration schemes (i.e. the perspectives of teachers, other professionals, the public and parents) in which quantitative and qualitative aspects of evaluation would be regarded as complementary.

The first British integration studies (Anderson, 1973; Cope and Anderson, 1977) provided data about the attainments and sociometric status of physically handicapped children being integrated individually or in units, which yielded evidence of satisfactory progress and adjustment. Some of the most useful features of those studies were qualitative, which enabled them to make recommendations for future integration schemes. Descriptive studies by teachers and others of the inception and development of integrated provision are useful for the same reason – they reveal problems about organization, co-operation between teachers and with parents, resources, services and management, which are a guide to other practitioners as well as researchers. A more systematic form of qualitative evaluation was given cogent expression in the appendix to a report on the integration of visually handicapped children (Jamieson *et al.*, 1977). Experimental methodologies would have been difficult with the small and heterogeneous visually handicapped population and an approach was developed from methods applied earlier in the evaluation of curriculum. The qualitative research draws upon the experience and ways of thinking of people involved – pupils, parents, teachers, administrators – and the methods of operation of school, classrooms and services. The nub of the evaluative process is the unbiased researcher capable of weighing up the evidence objectively.

Hegarty and Pocklington's (1981) research into seventeen integration schemes in fourteen local education authorities is an example. Another approach which should now become more common is action-research, involving interaction between the monitoring process and the development of the integration scheme. There is also great scope, and there could be considerable value, in observational studies of interactions between handicapped and nonhandicapped children in integrated settings (Guralnick, 1978; Sackett, 1978) and of teacher–child interactions in the classroom (Gunstone *et al.*, 1982).

An important review of studies concerned with 'mainstreaming' students with mild handicaps and their academic and social outcomes was published by Madden and Slavin (1983). They conclude tentatively that there is evidence to support placement in normal classes, provided individualized instruction is available, or well-designed resource programmes for the achievement, self-esteem, behaviour and emotional adjustment of academically handicapped pupils. Furthermore, empirical research indicates that co-operative learning and individualized instructional programmes can improve the self-perceptions and behaviour of pupils with learning difficulties and acceptance by their nonhandicapped class-mates. Some essential educational prerequisites for successful integration are presented. For an extensive discussion of the issues surrounding integration within an international perspective, the reader is referred to Chapter 19.

Integration of children with severe and moderate learning difficulties

The English Department of Education and Science statistics for January 1982 show that 27,252 children with severe learning difficulties were being educated in special schools, 235 in special classes and 110 registered in ordinary classes. The second and third figures will probably increase in the coming years. In any such developments, the well-organized teaching with progression and continuity required by these children should not be jeopardized and positive steps should be taken to help them and their normal peers to interact socially. The needs of staff should also be recognized by ensuring links with a special school and the appropriate support services. It is most important to evaluate such developments so that the lessons learnt can be applied in other schemes.

There are already many signs of social integration whereby young children with severe difficulties spend time in activity periods in nearby primary schools, and adolescents join others in residential courses, outdoor pursuits and physical activities. The ability of the new generation of pupils to respond to these wider opportunities is a measure of the progress that has been made in their education and the normalization of their lives in recent years. Unfortunately many special schools are in isolated locations so that social integration is not facilitated, although locational integration itself does not necessarily lead to social interaction.

There are a few arrangements whereby children with severe learning difficulties are educated in ordinary schools. Young handicapped children commonly attend nursery schools or classes or pre-school playgroups, but in one borough there is a unique policy of placing children with severe learning difficulties (ages 3–8) in special classes in ordinary infant schools (Hegarty and Pocklington, 1982). There are 5 classes, each catering for a maximum of 10 children, and each staffed by a teacher and 2 welfare assistants. At 8 years children move on to a school for those with severe difficulties or to some other appropriate placement. The main benefit is the possibility of association with others in a normal infant school environment, although there are no nursery classes matching the pre-fives in the special class. There is some selective participation in infant classes including creative work, storytime and television. The scheme seems well accepted by staff and parents, and specialist advisory support and inservice training are available. Integrating a small class in a school has some advantages for children, but may be a disadvantage for teachers who need the exchange of experience and information with others. Links with local special school staff are important.

A scheme in another area consists of a centre for 35 children aged 2–11 in a primary school, including a 'special care' class. The school also has a special centre for 40 children aged 7–11 with moderate learning difficulties, the two centres liaising, but running independently. Each has a teacher in charge but the headteacher of the school has overall responsibility. There is some classroom integration of children with moderate learning difficulties; a few have eventually transferred to ordinary classes and there is some participation of children from both centres in mealtimes and assemblies. Initially, active promotion of social integration was not seen as a priority by the centres or the staff of the main school, but recently various integrative measures have been instituted.

The children from both units may transfer at eleven to the nearby secondary school in which a department is responsible for two units: one for pupils with severe learning difficulties in purpose-built accommodation adjacent to the main school, the other for those with moderate learning difficulties within the main building. The department staff also provide remedial teaching for about 100 pupils needing additional help in learning basic skills, a service which has helped to bring about the reciprocal teaching in the unit by specialist teachers who also show readiness to integrate unit children in mainstream classes. This ranges from 20 per cent of the timetable in the first year to 50 per cent by the fifth year. Another feature is the extent to which the department has become a focus for a multidisciplinary team. Like many special schools, it organizes a carefully planned programme of work experience and leavers' preparation which may include selected pupils with severe learning difficulties. According to Roberts and Williams (1980), the latter spend most of their time in their special unit, but may join pupils in the main school for physical education, lunch and corporate activities such as youth club ones. Some senior pupils from the main school visit the unit for various purposes. The inception and development of this department has been reported by Fisher (1977), Roberts and Williams (1980), and Hegarty and Pocklington (1982).

The provision for moderate learning difficulties and the role of the department as a resource for 'remedial' work appear to be highly appropriate and successful. The location of the unit for pupils with severe difficulties in a secondary school, leading to opportunities for social integration and some degree of joint participation in activities, is not easily evaluated in comparison with a special school. Brennan (1982) questions whether the modest degree of integration, socially and educationally, justifies this type of provision, a cogent argument being that a small unit of 20 pupils aged 12–18 can have problems in grouping pupils and has limited staff resources for the breadth of educational activity now increasingly common for those with severe learning difficulties. There may also be problems for a small unit with its specialized needs within a large organization with different preoccupations and with a management structure designed for a different type of education. As in the case of peripatetic advisory services, the links with – and possibly a base in – a special school have advantages. One type of solution is suggested by the example of a special school for children with severe learning difficulties which took advantage of two empty classrooms in a nearby secondary school and moved in two senior classes. They remained part of the special school but had some of the benefits, locationally and socially, of the ordinary school.

In January 1982, 55,561 children ascertained as educationally subnormal under the 1944 Act were in special schools, 7644 in designated special classes or units in ordinary schools and 2399 registered in ordinary classes. Information about the number of children being given other forms of help in ordinary schools has been limited, although the Warnock Report quoted the figure of 458,087 children (4.7 per cent of the school population) spending at least part of their time in special classes set up on the initiative of individual schools. Eighty-two per cent of those children spent less than half their time in those classes and 12 per cent more than three-quarters. Clunies-Ross and Wimhurst (1983) obtained information from 698 secondary and middle schools about their use of various forms of organization, either singly or in combination, for helping slow learners: special classes; dividing age groups into sets according to ability and attainment for certain subjects; provision of a variety of optional courses, particularly in the fourth and fifth years, to suit the range of ability and attainment; and withdrawal for individual remedial help. Two-thirds of schools organized some special classes but in only 3 per cent was this the sole form of provision. The advantages of these were seen as providing a stable learning environment, giving emotional security and promoting slow learners' confidence. The small group permitted individual teaching in a well-resourced classroom with trained or experienced teachers. Generally, the classes were available for the first three years. A major disadvantage was considered to be the restricted curriculum which created difficulties for return to mainstream and limited the choice of options in the fourth and fifth years. The possible effect of labelling pupils as members of a special group was a further concern, as was the limited number who could be catered for in this way. In fact, most schools organized special arrangements in a variety of combinations.

The findings of this survey indicate that during the last decade progress has been made in developing various strategies of provision in ordinary schools for educationally retarded children. What the survey does not indicate is whether pupils who might otherwise be placed in special schools can be assured of the special help they need, as well as access to a mainstream curriculum.

Although 7000 children with moderate learning difficulties are recorded as being educated in special classes or units (designated as such, not part of the informal arrangements in schools previously referred to), there have been few accounts of their operation and little evaluation. More attention has been given to the special units for physically handicapped, delicate and hearing-impaired children and, although the special needs of these children are different, the problems of resources provision and management are similar. Cope and Anderson (1977) studied six special units in primary schools and obtained evidence from matched samples of unit and special school children which allays the commonly stated fear that physically handicapped children will do less well academically in ordinary school. Carr *et al.* (1983) also provide evidence on this point in respect of children with spina bifida and showed, furthermore, that those in ordinary schools do better in number work. Cope and Anderson also found that handicapped children benefited from the opportunities for social contact with ordinary pupils but that there was no consensus in schools that integration was something which all teachers should be aiming towards – this goal had not been thoroughly discussed either when the units were first planned or later.

One of the few reports on special units for children with moderate learning difficulties indicates a similar finding (Lowden, 1984). Fifty-three special units for educationally subnormal pupils in primary schools were included in the investigation. Attitudes of teachers, and especially parents, to this form of provision were generally positive but teachers were less favourable to the idea of actually having a retarded child in their class. There was little attempt at academic integration of children from the units and, in general, integration was not seen as requiring a definite policy. On the whole the special classes functioned as separate units. The integration of special classes into a school involves numerous organizational matters, especially in secondary schools, as Bailey (1982) found in a study of six units for pupils with a variety of special needs. The constraints of school timetabling, class sizes, needs for additional resources, communication in a large staff, and relationships between special education and other staff are some of the management issues which require further research. It is interesting to note, for example, that in this study it was the practical subjects (e.g. crafts, home economics) which presented greatest difficulty of placement for children from the unit because of safety factors and the need for small teaching groups.

Garnett (1976) described a unit for fifteen retarded children aged eleven and twelve. Initially it was located in the grounds of a comprehensive school, its contacts with the main school being for administration, registration, assemblies, school meals and certain creative and practical subjects. The unit staff did not feel part of the main school or have access to facilities that would have been available in a special school. The pupils tended to be rejected by mainstream pupils and were sometimes teased and bullied. Subsequently, it was moved to a central position in the main school, pupils spending an average of 50 per cent of their time in mainstream. They returned to the unit for small group work in mathematics and English, but increasingly felt attached to their mainstream base. Recently Garnett (1983) described the development of her role as co-ordinator, which had three aspects: (1) identification of pupils with special needs in co-operation with senior staff; (2) management of a resource base for meeting special needs; (3) support and advice within the mainstream curriculum, key teachers being appointed in departments to liaise with the co-ordinator in making the curriculum accessible.

Jones and Berrick (1980) have described a special resources department which has similarities with the American resource room model (Hawisher and Calhoun, 1978; Wiederholt *et al.*, 1978). Essentially it is a base from which, as far as possible, children are integrated in ordinary classes and tutor groups. They may be withdrawn for special help or aided in their classes; their teachers may be assisted with suitable teaching materials. The department is responsible for educational assessment, individual programmes, and liaison with parents and visiting professionals. In evaluations of this kind of approach, its effectiveness for children with moderate learning difficulties is particularly important.

Sayer (1983) describes the development of a resources approach in a comprehensive school. There was existing special class provision for educationally retarded children but it was realized that there were many others with comparable needs for special help. The special class provision and the remedial department were combined into a new special needs department as a resource for the whole school, and at the same time the secondary school *and* its feeder primary schools developed as a 'sector' providing a multiprofessional servicing resource for all teachers and pupils. The potentialities for early recognition and intervention and for continuity of special help are obvious. Jones (1983) has examined some of the management issues in this type of approach to provision for special needs and agrees with Meisgeir (1976) that mainstreaming is not only a philosophy but also a management system. It should receive more attention in the academic study of educational management.

Another form of resource, as the Warnock Report pointed out, is special schools provided that their facilities and expertise can be made more widely available through links with ordinary schools. Hallmark and Dessent (1982) described the inception and development of a scheme whereby four or five teachers from a special school for children with moderate learning difficulties visit certain local primary schools once a week in order to help the class teacher assess the needs of a nominated child and to plan a programme for the following week. An important feature was that the teachers had all been involved in developing the special school's curriculum and could assist the primary teacher with suitable materials. The scheme appears to have been highly successful. Some of the pupils concerned certainly would have been transferred to the special school, and a further result was that some special school pupils were able to be returned to the ordinary school, presumably the result of an inservice training effect of the scheme. Issues in a project of this kind are discussed by Hegarty and Pocklington (1982).

Another town with fifteen special schools and several special units has attempted a wider involvement of these resources and their staff in a scheme to provide support to pupils with special needs in all schools. It involves the designation of an appropriate teacher in each ordinary school as co–ordinator for special needs, who is given specialist inservice training so that he can become a tutor in his own right and disseminate ideas and practice in his own school. Among the aims are the early identification of learning difficulties and the support and continuous monitoring of pupils with special needs (Muncey and Ainscow, 1983).

In summary, the present situation may be viewed as one of cautious, rather than hasty, implementation of the integration principle, the effects of which have been documented by Meyers *et al.* (1980) in some instances of the American experience of mainstreaming. There is evidence from the surveys that schools are developing forms of organization and more suitable curricula for the many children with moderate and mild learning difficulties, and the innovative schemes already noted provide models and experience on which further development can be based. As Hegarty (1982) has argued, the presence of children with special needs can be a challenge and a positive opportunity to 'stretch' the ordinary school, by examining goals and objectives, and developing its provision so as to cater more appropriately for its pupils. It is also a matter of 'stretching' the training of teachers (Gulliford, 1984) and developing the systems in which administrators and professionals operate, as Jones (1983) has pointed out. For children with severe learning difficulties, it is a matter of exploring further ways in which they may become integrated into school and out-of-school communities at all ages and the methods of developing skills for social interaction between ordinary and retarded individuals.

EDUCATING CHILDREN WITH SEVERE LEARNING DIFFICULTIES

The education of the mentally handicapped child begins with the process of informing parents that their child is affected, the immediate measures of support and the continuation of measures to assist them in helping the child's development. In Hughes's (1975) survey of 88 special schools, interviews with a sample of parents showed that 60 per cent had been informed of their child's handicap within one year, 23 per cent between one and three years of age. Smith and Phillips (1978) found that in cases with no recognized specific pathology, 30 per cent of the parents did not learn of their child's handicap until after the fourth birthday. Cunningham and Sloper's (1977a) account of the early needs of parents of Down's syndrome babies includes a vivid picture of a mother's reactions to the birth of the child. Pugh (1981) gives examples of schemes in which immediate support to parents is organized by other parents of mentally handicapped children or by a combined professional and parent group. The importance of that early support as part of the base for continuing help in the pre-school years cannot be overestimated. The reader is referred to Chapter 14 for a detailed account of research in this area.

Various methods of assisting parents have emerged, using health visitors, visiting teachers and other professionals, some approaches being prescriptive, and others encouraging parents to develop their own understanding and resources. Some have had a group or workshop format. Cunningham and Sloper (1977b) describe a scheme whereby health visitors were given additional training with a view to six-weekly visits to parents of Down's syndrome children, starting as soon as possible after birth and reducing to six-monthly visits after the child had commenced attendance at a pre-school group. A particular feature was that parents observed an assessment on the Bayley Infant Development Scale and were helped in discussion with the health visitor to think how they might promote the sequences of development. Importantly, an opportunity was also provided to discuss the many other problems which concern parents.

Sandow and Clarke (1978) considered this point and also the different dynamics of the situation when visits take place at shorter or longer intervals. They also discussed the relative advantage of parent involvement based on visiting, workshops and clinics and their suitability for different social groups. A good example of how parents can be involved in the process of assessment as members of the team has been described by Newson (1976) and is relevant to assessments under the 1981 Act. Television and video are other resources which merit greater use as a means of showing parents how they can observe and provide appropriate materials and tasks. Parents always ask 'What can we do?'

Workshops have been organized for parents of children in different age groups and with varying aims and different locations – sometimes in conjunction with a school and sometimes separately (Cunningham and Jeffree, 1975; Tennant and Hattersley, 1977; Pugh, 1981). One benefit of being in a school is that it can be a first step towards mutual co-operation, which should continue during the pre-school and school period.

Home-visiting teachers of the mentally handicapped have been increasingly appointed by local education authorities. A widely used scheme is based on the materials and approach developed in Portage, a small town in Wisconsin, as a means of serving the needs of a rural area (Shearer and Shearer, 1972). The materials consist of a behavioural checklist, charts and a collection of cards each suggesting how a particular objective might be taught. The teacher visits the family once a week and chooses, with parent(s), one or two behaviours as the target for learning during the week. The teaching procedure is modelled by the teacher and practised by the parent who records progress during the following week (see also Chapter 14). British pilot schemes were set up by the Wessex Health Care Evaluation Research Team (Smith *et al.*, 1977), the home teachers coming from either health, social services or education departments, and also by clinical psychologists in Glamorgan (Revill and Blunden, 1979) who used various personnel including two nursery nurses. A success rate of 80–90 per cent for achieving objectives was recorded and parents' responses to the schemes were positive. Among the benefits, with a week's training and with supervision from a psychologist, a variety of personnel can deliver the service since the material provides the structure and sequence. The approach has attracted much interest and has been applied in various ways and settings (Cameron, 1982). Teachers have made their own evaluation of the materials, identified sequences which are insufficiently defined (e.g. early language) and have used Portage as a basis for further development.

Pre-school provision

Recent English statistics (Department of Education and Science, 1982) show that there were 261 children aged 2 years in attendance at special schools for children with severe learning difficulties. At 3 years there were 628, and at 4, 1034. The numbers in later age groups rise to 2000 at 12 years. Bearing in mind that others attend ordinary nursery schools, pre-school playgroups and pre-school classes in other kinds of special school, it appears possible that a fair proportion of children have some form of pre-school experience. The researches of Clark and Cheyne (1979) and Chazan *et al.* (1980) indicate that children with special needs in ordinary pre-school settings do not get sufficient specific help and that their parents are insufficiently involved. Teachers and assistants need to realize that it is not enough to rely on spontaneous interaction; specific steps can be taken to assist participation in activities and social contacts, as Gunstone *et al.* (1982) and others have shown. Guralnick (1978), for example, refers to measures designed to promote frequent and productive interactions between handicapped and nonhandicapped children (careful selection of curricula and of social play activities; arrangements of rooms and equipment), and to the need actively to promote the skills of handicapped children in observation, imitation, social interaction and group involvement. There is also a role for nonhandicapped peers in learning to prompt others, to serve as models and to provide for interpersonal behaviours.

Education in school

The development of a distinctive form of schooling for the mentally handicapped in Britain has been virtually telescoped into the last thirty years. In the 1950s, those children not in hospital were in occupation centres, the responsibility of health departments, often in makeshift accommodation, and there were few opportunities for staff training. In the 1960s, centres became junior training centres, many of them in purpose-built accommodation, and the establishment of a training council for teachers of the mentally handicapped increased the number of trained staff (Department of Health and Social Security, 1974). When centres became schools in 1971, the training of teachers was undertaken within the teacher education system and schools and teachers could draw upon the advisory and other resources of the education services. In 1982 there were 383 schools with an average enrolment of 60.

The small size of schools makes for a secure and supportive community for pupils and a unity of purpose in the staff, although there is some limitation in their range of expertise and special teaching interests. In a few instances (about 30), special schools provide for both severe and moderate learning difficulties, either in one school or by merging two on separate sites. A combined one has benefits in terms of staffing and as a focus for support and specialist services, and can be helpful to children who are on the borderline of the two groups. Although teaching the two groups is generally organized in separate classes, there are opportunities for the severely retarded to join the moderately retarded in school and in extracurricular activities. Those with severe difficulties appear to gain most. The benefits of merging two schools on separate sites may not outweigh the disadvantages of physical separation. In an evaluation of one such scheme, Jones *et al.* (1979) found that the teachers on one site, which was the primary department with mixed teaching groups, were in favour. The secondary department on the other site did not favour this procedure, the differences in learning, maturity and social competence creating disadvantages for both groups and difficulties for the teachers in catering for the wide range of learning ability. The real need of each is for some interaction with nonhandicapped children rather than with each other.

The school buildings deserve mention. Many were purpose-built in the 1960s but to a different standard from ordinary schools, often with insufficient space and flexibility for individual and small group work. Many, particularly the former centres, are isolated, thus limiting opportunities for interaction with nonhandicapped children and co-operation between schools and staff. Placement on a campus with others, however, does not guarantee interaction and there may be a mismatch of age ranges. Organizing schools as separate primary and secondary, rather than all-age, occurs in some areas, but since most have less than 100 pupils, any division may create other problems of size, staffing, resources and travelling distance from a wide catchment area.

The special needs of mentally handicapped children are, of course, extremely diverse. A survey of schools by Mittler and Preddy (1981) involving 2500 children of all ages, mostly 5–16 years, showed that about one-fifth had very limited language comprehension and between one-third and one-fifth had not started to speak even in single words. Half of those with some expressive language had largely unintelligible speech. In their sample, 12 per cent were unable to walk, 8 per cent had little use of arms and hands, 16 per cent had some degree of visual impairment and 7 per cent had hearing impairments. One-quarter had a history of epilepsy and 20 per cent were incontinent daily. Some 20–25 per cent of children required special care and individual attention on account of severe and multiple handicaps. The problem for the teacher was eased by a ratio of one for 7.2 children and one classroom assistant for 6.8 children, a ratio of one adult to 3.5 children.

An enquiry by Colborne Brown and Tobin (1982) obtained information nationally about the number of visually handicapped children who were not being educated in schools for the blind or partially sighted. Whereas about 1000 blind and 2000 partially sighted children are in such schools, the survey located another 999 visually handicapped ones in England and Wales. Of these, 588 were in special schools for severe learning difficulties in the community or in hospitals, most of the remainder being in other special or ordinary schools. Overlapping this survey was another one by Best (1983) aimed at locating deaf-blind children. With a response rate of 58 per cent of schools 228 deaf-blind children were recorded, 60 per cent of whom were partially sighted and partially hearing, the remainder having various combinations and degrees of impairment. Of the 60 per cent, less than 50 per cent were ambulant, only 36 per cent could use a communication system and 69 per cent had additional handicaps. As yet the special approaches, which require something more than a mere summation of methods for the visually and mentally handicapped, are not sufficiently developed nor is there special training available for teachers in the UK.

The frequency of additional disabilities in mentally handicapped children underlines the importance of regular assistance from a range of specialists. Mittler and Preddy (1981) reported that 14 per cent of children in their survey were treated weekly and 9 per cent monthly by a physiotherapist, 13 per cent were taught weekly or monthly by a speech therapist, but 70 per cent were never visited by either. Half were never seen by an educational psychologist (though such input might have been through teachers). Seven per cent were seen by a teacher of the deaf, which matched the number of hearing-impaired children. Only 2 per cent of children were visited by a teacher of the visually handicapped, although 5 per cent had no useful vision and 11 per cent had some impairment. At the time of the study in 1977, peripatetic services for the visually handicapped were only in the process of being established. Medical surveillance of children in varying degrees of frequency was recorded as: paediatric 64 per cent; orthopaedic 20 per cent; neurological 4.2 per cent.

The central issues in the education of mentally handicapped children are the construction of a curriculum and the development of teaching procedures adapted to their learning deficits. 'Deficits' refers not only to their retarded development, particularly in communication, but to their difficulties in attention, learning and in transfer of learning. In essence, it means that their learning should be carefully structured, whether the tasks are educational or social ones. In both respects there are distinct differences from methods in normal teaching, although their education as a whole should be as normal as possible.

At the time of the transfer to education in 1971, schools which had been first occupation, then training centres not surprisingly looked towards methods with ordinary children, based on developmental notions and the importance of children's active and spontaneous learning. This was in some respects beneficial, especially when combined with the close observation of children's responses to learning situations displayed by teacher trainers such as Stevens (1978), but there was, as Clarke and Clarke (1975) pointed out, insufficient recognition of the specific learning needs of the mentally handicapped. A pamphlet on the education of the mentally handicapped (Department of Education and Science, 1975b) reflected something of the normal developmental approach, but gave excellent guidance on the organization and nature of school learning and also stressed the importance of objectives in teaching. Since then schools have increasingly employed behavioural methods and have been encouraged to define the curriculum in terms of behavioural or teaching objectives. They have also been made aware of a range of psycholinguistic information and of practice which has some basis in Piagetian and other cognitive psychology. The range of theory relevant to the teaching of the mentally handicapped is wide.

Teachers are essentially practitioners rather than theorists, yet every practitioner has some kind of theoretical framework, even if vaguely formulated. Attention might be given to clarifying the changed conceptual framework so that, for example, they do not see unnecessary conflict between the various approaches to which they are exposed. A discussion of strategies and models made in the context of pre-school programmes by Anastasiow (1978) suggests a possible starting point. He distinguishes four models. He perceives the *normal developmental* model as based on a maturational theory; children learn through spontaneous activity, with skills acquired according to age expectancy. He sees the *cognitive developmental* model in terms of a Piagetian view of the development of cognitive structures through the assimilation of and accommodation to new experience. The *behavioural model* emphasizes techniques which derive from Skinner and are termed applied behaviour analyses or functional analyses of behaviour. The strategies involve assessment of the child's current level of attainment and teach further steps by the use of task analysis and appropriate reinforcers. The *cognitive learning* model uses operant procedures for teaching and remediation while drawing upon cognitive, psycholinguistic and perceptual theories to diagnose levels of development and to plan intervention. The author ascribes this to Bricker and Bricker (1974), but it is more clearly articulated in Bricker *et al.* (1980), where it is referred to as a developmental-interactive model. In essence, Piagetian and other work on cognitive development provides knowledge of the sequences and prerequisites of early mental development as a basis for teaching steps in mental activity. Other examples with which teachers have become familiar are the concept of the symbolic function and the development of 'pretend' play (McConkey and Jeffree, 1979, 1980). Much other work in a Piagetian framework (e.g. Woodward, 1962; Uzgiris and Hunt, 1975; Smith, 1982) can illuminate (though not prescribe for) educational practice as can other cognitive theories. A model for teachers should also, of course, encompass the idea of the child's development and learning being influenced by the environment and expectations of school and home, and the effects of interactions with adults and peers.

An explicit formulation of the theory underlying practice would be an advantage in the initial and inservice training of teachers of the mentally handicapped. McMaster (1973) made an early attempt to examine the contributions of several disciplines to an educational theory – medicine, psychology, history, philosophy, sociology, social science – and ended with a proposal for systematic planning of the curriculum involving aims, objectives, methods, skills, assessment and evaluation; in short, a curriculum theory for mentally handicapped students.

It is regrettable that curriculum specialists and educational philosophers have fought shy of the special education field, no doubt deterred by what they see as specialist territory, unknown to them (Aspin, 1982). Schools nevertheless have attempted to plan the curriculum more deliberately. The aims of education for the mentally handicapped are not so easily stated as those in ordinary schools and it is difficult to avoid statements which are vague and general. Leeming *et al.* (1979) found that teachers often referred to 'reaching potential' or 'developing as fully as possible'. As Hughes (1975) indicated, 'social competence' has often been given as a prime aim. Although – or perhaps because – such statements have doubtful value, the attempt to state aims should be made so that they can be subject to scrutiny and discussion. The expressed aims may conceal low or unrealistic expectations; may implicitly be rejecting the concept of normalization; or may be saying something quite different from what goes on in practice. Parents' perceptions of the aims of educating their children also should be taken into account. The discussion of aims is where a clear-headed educational philosopher should have something to offer.

As McMaster pointed out, aims provide answers to *why* certain items should be in the educational programme. Objectives state *what* will have been achieved when they have been taught. General objectives may be stated for particular areas of the curriculum or for particular age levels or special groups, which are then specified in greater detail as a programme or sequence of teaching. These specific objectives need to be worded unambiguously and are frequently regarded as behavioural objectives (i.e. precise statements of the performance which is the target of teaching) with the learning task being broken down into smaller steps by the process of task analysis (Klein *et al.*, 1979; Gardner and Murphy, 1980; Perkins *et al.*, 1980). There are many published sources which can be drawn upon in developing a curriculum in this way (Bender and Valletuti, 1976; Crawford, 1980). The Portage materials (Bluma *et al.*, 1976) have been used as a guide in some schools (Cameron, 1982), and books for teachers and parents provide guidance on activities and their sequence in teaching skills (Jeffree *et al.*, 1977; Kiernan *et al.*, 1978; Cunningham and Sloper 1978). The Behaviour Assessment Battery (Kiernan and Jones, 1982) was designed as a basis for planning programmes for the severely mentally handicapped.

A carefully planned school curriculum is valuable in providing a structure for teaching, and defining a 'syllabus' in an area in which there was little established tradition. The actual process of developing the various strands is equally valuable since staff discussion and enquiry create understanding of what is involved in teaching particular skill sequences rather than simply following a published guide. Planning the curriculum also helps teachers to realize how work at one level prepares a basis for learning at later levels. It also directs attention to the need for different methods of organizing teaching groups and individual tutoring, in order to cater for the range of ability and development in age groups and the uneven development in individuals. A particular benefit is that a curriculum provides a basis for assessment of learning as skills are achieved to a level according to a specified criterion. While normative tests and schedules of development may have utility for certain purposes, criterion-referenced assessment becomes part of the process of monitoring learning and the effects of teaching. A further benefit is that communications between school and home can include more precise information about progress in learning and how new skills can be practised and used.

A 'structured' curriculum does not – or should not – imply a limited or constricted educational programme. 'Structured' implies some organizing principles for the curriculum and that, where appropriate, there is an order and sequence in the skills and concepts which it is hoped to teach. As Kiernan and Jones (1982) pointed out, a distinction between core aspects of the curriculum (such as cognitive and communication skills, self-help, physical skills, social education) as opposed to the noncore areas of art, pottery, music and dance is inappropriate. The 'core' skills, which can be specified and in most cases sequenced, may have to be elicited or taught in the context of a variety of activities. They also need to be generalized within the child's total experience at school and home.

In some areas, such as self-help and motor skills, sequences can be defined with reasonable confidence; in others, such as language, it is more problematic. Leeming *et al.* (1979), in an excellent study of the teaching of the language curriculum, offer a framework rather than a complete outline since 'we are still a long way from an exact knowledge of the development of language and communication skills either in normal or in mentally handicapped children', and also because the precise objectives must depend on the characteristics and abilities of the child. The importance of the language curriculum is underlined by their study of over 1000 children in which 42 per cent of 16-year-olds did not use grammatical constructions, 22 per cent did not use two-word utterances and 17 per cent were at the pre-one-word stage. There was considerable growth in language production between 3 and 6 years of age, and to a lesser extent in the 9–11 age group. The effect of this growth pattern was interestingly reflected in the increases in verbal and social interaction in classrooms (Beveridge *et al.*, 1978). It is also of interest that Smith and Phillips (1981) found indications of a spurt in cognition, language and social competence around 11–12 years.

While Leeming *et al.*'s investigation indicates the complexity of language and the breadth of knowledge and understanding which teachers might need, it is perhaps most valuable for its exploration of the teaching process through study of six teachers implementing a lesson plan and also of the teachers' use of language and questioning in the classroom. Although teachers should always monitor their language to suit the audience, the way communication is initiated can limit or encourage responses. Mittler (1976) proposed a classification of questions in seven types which have relevance not only to teachers but to other professions and parents – questions leading to naming of things or actions, choice of alternatives, and open-ended, facilitatory, maintenance and rhetorical questions. Jones and Robson (1979) show how questioning and prompting strategies have similarities with behaviour procedures such as modelling, prompting and chaining. They have also demonstrated in the

TASS (Teaching and the Severely Subnormal) project (Robson, 1981) how small groups of teachers can be trained to use teaching objectives in language and to be sensitive to the interplay between teacher and child language in individual or small group sessions, the effectiveness of which have been well demonstrated by Fenn (1976). Blank's (1973) work on the teacher's role and Tough's (1977) classification of the functions of language in young children also are relevant to teacher–pupil verbal interaction. The rapid growth in the use of nonvocal communication systems such as the British Sign Language, Paget-Gorman or symbols (Blissymbolics) testifies to the value that teachers find in them; these are discussed in Chapter 16. As one headteacher remarked, 'I don't know what we did before we had them.'

Reading for the normal child is a complex skill in which he interprets the words and sentences symbolized in print through his understanding of their meaning and his competence in the language used. For most children with severe learning difficulties, therefore, reading in this sense has its limits, though recognition of words, signs and labels might be achieved. Some Down's syndrome children, for example, learn quite a large vocabulary of words that they can recognize visually and sometimes at an early age (Buckley, 1984). Reading should be seen as part of enjoyable language work and, indeed, may help language development. Gillham (1981, 1983) has described a sound tutorial method which can be used when the child has a vocabulary of fifty words. Thatcher (1984) has produced a useful guide to practice.

The development of language may require careful teaching to individuals or small groups, but language and communication are involved in every aspect of the curriculum. Physical education and movement provide opportunities for practising or learning words, naming parts of the body and actions. Creative activities in art, music, practical skills and leisure skills all provide opportunities for comprehending and producing language (Upton, 1979). These need to be 'structured' in the teacher's (or parents') mind just as much as other parts of the curriculum.

The same point may be made about the cognitive curriculum. In a sense, the teacher of normal children can 'get by' without concepts about cognitive development since the school curriculum is based on and matches changes in cognitive processes. For the teacher of the mentally handicapped, recognizing and assisting cognitive processes are more explicit aims and elements of the curriculum through the development of sensorimotor patterns, symbolic play, perceptual discrimination, discrimination of similarities and differences, and the beginnings of classification, ordering and seriating. McConkey (1981) warned of the danger of concentrating on behaviour as products with insufficient attention to the *processes* through which children develop new patterns or schemas.

Though the cognitive level which mentally handicapped children reach is limited, there is potential for enhancing the cognitive strategies which they employ. Smith *et al.* (1983) suggest that such activities are nearly always provided in special schools, but often divorced from meaning. They give examples of situations, such as out-of-school visits, through which recall can be facilitated by senior pupils by the use of imagery and verbal elaboration, monitoring by auditory rehearsal, and checking carried out against a verbal description. Rectory Paddock School (1981) includes many examples in its published school curriculum.

A study of mentally handicapped adolescents by Cheseldine and Jeffree (1982) also provides pointers for the curriculum. Assessment of social competence in relation to visiting friends and other social activity outside the home showed that 70–80 per cent had basic competence for mealtimes, dressing and hygiene, and 41 per cent had sufficient language (16 per cent were understood only by the parents). In relation to social table games, 75 per cent could recognize pictures and 46 per cent could count up to twelve. Most were not capable of catching a familiar bus, or going beyond the immediate neighbourhood, or getting a meal in a café, and 77 per cent were not competent in handling money. Their limited independence was related to parental attitudes, lack of local friends and limited social and travelling skills, reflecting the sheltered life which most of them experience at home and the way their schooling is provided. The increasing contact with nonhandicapped pupils and the general activity in the environment need to be supported by specific teaching of key activities such as making a purchase in shops and travel.

Profoundly and multiply handicapped children

The needs of the 20–25 per cent of children with profound mental handicap, often with physical and sensory disabilities, have increasingly been provided in settings which have improved the quality of their lives and in which opportunities for experience, including, for example, the resources of micro-electronics (Rostron and Sewell, 1984), have been considerably extended (see also Chapter 15). The aims of making them less dependent, of developing their behavioural repertoire and their interaction with others, require knowledge by the teacher of how the simplest levels of functioning can be assessed and developed by, for example, the Behaviour Assessment Battery (Kiernan and Jones, 1982). The teacher also needs to understand and learn from the contribution of physiotherapists, occupational therapists, speech therapists, physicians, psychologists and specialist teachers of the visually handicapped, hearing impaired and physically handicapped. It might be argued that all these are still learning what their contribution can be and that the teacher, as the permanent team member, is not simply a co-ordinator but an agent with a multidisciplinary rationale for his or her work with children – as well as having a role in relation to the needs of parents. As in the case of the deaf-blind, the methodology and the training for teachers need to be further developed. Presland (1980, 1982) has reviewed the considerable literature on the topic of children with profound and multiple handicaps.

The place of these children in schools is becoming less separate; opportunities for association with others and school activities are increasingly being sought (Myland and Thurlow, 1982). The same is true of those with disordered and difficult behaviour for whom a special setting is seen as a step to integration in other groups, as behaviour comes more under control.

EDUCATING CHILDREN WITH MODERATE LEARNING DIFFICULTIES

It is not possible to distinguish precisely those children whose learning difficulties may be termed moderate rather than mild and who need some form of special educational provision. Research has identified the numerous interrelated and interacting factors associated with their educational retardation – retarded cognitive development, speech and language difficulties, mild physical and sensory disabilities, motivational and behavioural characteristics, and adverse family circumstances (Rutter *et al.*, 1970). These cluster in different ways in individuals and, in most cases, it is not easy to predict at the beginning of schooling which children will have the greatest and most persistent educational difficulty. It depends partly on teachers' ability to provide appropriate educational experiences in pre-school or infant school years, and the extent to which schools can individualize teaching and organize a thorough approach to children's personal as well as educational needs. In the Isle of Wight survey, Rutter *et al.* (1970) showed that a quarter of the ESN school pupils had IQs above 70, but more of the children identified as intellectually handicapped (IQs below 70 on a short form of WISC) were in ordinary schools than in the special school. Of those with IQs above 70 at the ESN school, all had reading levels more than $2\frac{1}{2}$ years below their age and most of them $3\frac{1}{2}$ years below, whereas, of those with IQs below 70 but in ordinary school, the majority were less retarded educationally ($1-1\frac{1}{2}$ years). They also showed fewer features such as clumsiness, difficulty with left–right differentiation and neurological abnormalities. Nor was there any evidence for a social factor in relation to placement in a special school rather than in an ordinary school. Their findings illustrate the multiple admission criteria generally employed. The researchers concluded that in the Isle of Wight selection for special schooling had been conducted with care and was appropriate. The need for special provision is seen to be more frequent for boys than girls, special school placement being in the ratio of 2 to 1 mainly as a result of boys' greater difficulty in reading. In the Isle of Wight study, the number of boys and girls with IQs below 70 was approximately equal but severe educational retardation occurred in the ratio of 2 to 1 and specific reading retardation in the ratio of 3.3 to 1. It is also of some educational significance that Williams (1964) reported a disproportionate number of children with summer birthdays in his special school sample. Bookbinder (1967) confirmed this trend in special classes for educationally subnormal children in ordinary primary schools and suggested that, even if younger children commenced school early enough to ensure nine full terms instead of six in the infant school, the disadvantage of being younger and less mature would still be present. Educational implications are further discussed by Williams *et al.* (1970).

Tomlinson (1981) studied how decisions are made to refer a child for assessment with a view to special education placement. In 40 cases, head-teachers' reasons for referral were solely on account of educational backwardness in 11, difficult behaviour or home problems were additional reasons in 23 cases, with medical and speech/language problems in 6 cases. Clearly, schools and teachers perceive pupils' problems and needs differently according to their own conceptions of learning difficulties, comparison with the level of achievement in their school and the available resources. The need for the future is to develop more satisfactory provision in ordinary schools and to consider whether children with multiple difficulties could be given early help with a view to return to suitable provision in ordinary schools. The sector organization and the special school as a resource centre (see p. 652) point the way to new practice.

That the degree of special need usually cannot be assessed until the child has been exposed to teaching in school is reflected in the numbers of children in different age groups in special schools and classes. In 1982, there were 509 such children below the age of 5. At age 7 there were 2453, rising to 6273 at age 11 and to 7704 at 15. It could be argued that those with developmental and severe educational difficulties deemed to require special and separate education should be recognized early in the primary school, and that later referral in the secondary school should not be needed. It could also be argued that it should be possible to transfer some children back to ordinary school at the end of the primary period. There is little information about the frequency and results of such transfers. Fleeman (1984) followed up 33 pupils from 3 urban special schools who had been transferred to ordinary secondary schools over a 7-year period, an annual rate of transfer of 1.1 per cent of the special school numbers. The mean age at which they had been placed in special schools was 8.6 years; the mean age of transfer was 13.2 years. In 40 per cent of the cases, the pupils were judged to be academically and socially ready; in 10 per cent parental wishes were a major factor; in 20 per cent the existence of a special unit in the receiving school was an important consideration; and in 30 per cent there were a number of factors of expediency. Transfer was judged to be successful in 20 per cent of the cases – they took a range of courses for the Certificate of Secondary Education, adapted reasonably well socially and were not over-dependent on teacher support. In another 50 per cent transfer was reasonably beneficial; they stayed the course, though with some adjustment difficulties and without full benefit from the curriculum. In 30 per cent the transfer was unsuffessful owing to social and emotional problems, poor attendance and lack of parental support.

The problem of deciding which children need special placement is obviously a difficult one. Rutter *et al.* (1970) concluded that the selection of children for the special school on the Isle of Wight was rational and highly successful in choosing the most severely handicapped children as well as those with multiple handicaps who most needed the relevant services. Presland (1970) discussed thirteen criteria, based on a study of research evidence, which he applied to his consideration of recommendations about placement. He gave greatest weight to the child's level of attainment, intelligence and adjustment in school. Phillips (1979) has argued well the case for criteria which ensure attention to the special educational needs of children from very disadvantaged families.

Tomlinson (1981) studied the decision-making processes whereby moderately retarded children are placed in special schools, the perceptions of the referring schools, educational psychologists, medical officers and headteachers of special schools being explored by interviews. She did not disagree that the professionals attempt to do the job with concern for individual children but asserted that they are unaware that 'the educationally subnormal' child is a social construct 'who comes into existence through the judgements and decisions of professional people who have vested career interests in defining ESN children'. She interprets the social construct of 'educationally subnormal' as a control mechanism to assist the orderly working of normal education and as part of a wider social process whereby dominant groups in society need to control inferior groups.

An alternative interpretation is that there are a few children who need more individual help and a more supportive environment than can be assured at present in most schools. As methods of organization, individual teaching and support develop in ordinary schools on the lines described earlier, it may be expected, and hoped, that they will provide for more, if not all, of their retarded pupils.

The immediate problem for schools and teachers is how methods and curricula can be improved and school organization modified to be more effective for educationally and intellectually retarded children. Education as a whole has to consider a broad strategy for: (1) early recognition and intervention; (2) continuity of special help during the school years; (3) continuing help in the post-school years; and (4) availability of educational assistance and other forms of support in adult life.

Pre-school

Possibilities for intervention before the age of five are limited by the small proportion of the pre-school population in nursery schools, classes or playgroups. The Warnock Report recorded that in 1977 only 15 per cent of three-year-olds were in nursery schools and classes.

Several studies show the need for a more active policy in pre-schools, involving both the programme and the advisory help available to teachers. Chazan *et al.* (1980) surveyed children with special needs in all nursery schools and classes, day nurseries and playgroups in two local education authorities. Although teachers were more likely than parents and other professionals to recognize difficulties in language, co-ordination and emotional and social development, there was little systematic assessment of children's needs, nor much evidence of individual programmes and recording. While there was frequent contact with parents, little use was made of this to develop parents' co-operation in their child's education. There was also scanty involvement of the school psychological service and other professional advisers. Similar conclusions were reached by Clark and Cheyne (1979) and Clark *et al.* (1982) in studies of pre-school provision in Scotland and the West Midlands, retarded speech and language being particularly frequent problems. In contrast with ordinary pre-school units, they found that nursery classes in special schools usually had well-planned individual programmes and that their location resulted in more advice and assistance from psychologists and speech therapists. There is clearly a need for dissemination of recent developments in the practice of pre-school education and parent co-operation (Pugh, 1981) as well as for wider professional involvement.

The limited availability of pre-school education means that the infant school years are the first at which whole age groups can be observed in school. There has been considerable interest in screening for early identification of children with special educational needs. Cornwall and Spicer (1982) revealed that 85 per cent of school psychological services employed some form of screening procedure, most commonly for third-year infants and first-year juniors (aged 7+ and 8+) and in the final year in junior school (age 11). With infants, a simple checklist can be used to record teachers' observations; for example, the Croydon Checklist (Wolfendale and Bryans, 1980) has items covering communication, perceptual-motor, emotional-social and response to learning. Lindsay (1980) prepared an infant rating scale of twenty-five items including behaviour, expressive and receptive language, motor skills, early learning abilities and general development. Leach (1981) rightly emphasized that such procedures have low predictive value and that the main benefits of screening are improved teacher vigilance and the stimulus it provides for an inservice training programme. Gray and Reeve (1978) described a programme of inservice training of infant teachers which was associated with additional staff and teaching resources. The Bullock Report on language teaching was less than enthusiastic about screening, and put more emphasis on teachers' own skills in observing and assessing children's difficulties (Department of Education and Science, 1975a). In fact, Moses (1982) showed that teachers do not find it difficult to identify children with special needs. In ten classes spread over six schools, teachers noted an average of 18 per cent of such pupils, which tallies with the Warnock Report's estimate. Three-quarters of these were recorded as having learning difficulties and 43 per cent as having behaviour problems. In an observational study, it was shown that the least intelligent spent less time on learning activities and were more isolated. Southgate *et al.* (1981), in a study of the teaching of reading in first- and second-year junior classes, found that the teachers' attempts to hear many children reading resulted in an average time for each child of thirty seconds. Fourteen per cent of teachers' time was spent on listening to reading and only 4 per cent on direct teaching. Children spent between one-third and half their time on activities which were not task-orientated.

The problem which a teacher faces in trying to cater for the learning needs of 25 to 30 children (or 15 to 20 in a special school or class) is obvious. As Corman and Gottlieb (1978) commented in a review of mainstreaming research: 'Critics of special school/class placement assume that the regular class teacher is able to individualize instruction and cater for a wide diversity of ability though the extent to which teachers can accomplish this feat is largely unexplored.'

The curriculum

In pre-1939 schools, special methods advocated for retarded children included sensory training; emphasis on the practical rather than the verbal; and learning through centres of interest to promote motivation and through units of experience to assist understanding. In practice, a reduced or 'watered-down' curriculum was what most retarded children received. Later, Kirk and Johnson (1951) outlined a curriculum from pre-school to adolescent level which had the clear purpose of preparation for living in the community through learning, aiming to develop personal, social and vocational adequacy. It was based on a recognition of the limitations and immaturities of retarded children and of their post-school difficulties, about which follow-up studies provided evidence (Baller, 1939; Collman and Newlyn, 1956; Mathew, 1963, 1964; Jackson, 1968). The Illinois Curriculum Guide (Goldstein and Seigle, 1958) organized a curriculum in terms of ten life functions (citizenship, communication, home and family, leisure, management of materials and money, occupational adequacy, health, safety, social adjustment, travel). Traditional subject areas (language, number, creative and practical work) were seen as contributing to the main life function areas through appropriate learning and experience at different age levels. A further development was the Social Learning Curriculum (Goldstein, 1974) and a social emphasis was reflected in many other publications. Kolstoe (1976) was concerned to provide retarded youngsters with 'those skills which make it possible for them to live independently and to work effectively', and identified instructional objectives at pre-school, intermediate, pre-vocational and vocational levels for communication, arithmetic, social competence, motor and recreational skills, aesthetics, health and safety. Klein *et al.* (1979) proposed a Functional Life Curriculum in a way which they believed would enable mainstream teachers to appreciate the contribution of subject areas to four 'curriculum centres': gaining insight into contemporary life; understanding oneself and others; becoming a responsible adult; and education for independence.

In recent years, the general concern in schools about curriculum development has resulted in a movement towards planning the curriculum more thoroughly and comprehensively. General statements of aims and content in schemes of work have been replaced by specification of sequences of objectives in the teaching of basic educational skills and of social and motor competencies. The process whereby staff concerned with particular age groups, helped by teachers with responsibility for particular curriculum fields, examined and defined their aims and objectives was productive. It was assisted by the increasing availability of teaching programmes and kits in which the sequence and methods of teaching were well structured. Among the best known are those produced by Science Research Associates and the Direct Instruction programmes (DISTAR) for language, reading, arithmetic and spelling (Englemann and Osborn, 1969; Englemann and Carnine, 1975). Teachers are normally exposed to various theoretical viewpoints in areas such as language, reading and mathematics, but the translation of these into teaching sequences and procedures is often uncertain. Well-prepared materials not only assist the teaching of children, but also teach the teachers.

The advantages of a curriculum based on the specification of objectives have been stated by Burman *et al.* (1983) as being that new teachers know exactly where to start with each child; that assessment of progress is continuous; and that teachers know what they should teach next and have more time to prepare individual programmes for children having difficulties. Co-operation with parents and sharing information is also easier. The approach is, furthermore, optimistic, with emphasis on success. One drawback is the volume of paper involved in writing a curriculum and recording children's progress. Ainscow and Tweddle (1979) delineated a behavioural objectives approach developed in a school for children with moderate learning difficulties. They distinguished between the 'closed' curriculum and the 'open', the former being derived from a statement of Bloom's (1975): 'Subjects which are required, sequential, closed and which emphasize convergent thinking should, in so far as possible, employ mastery learning strategies'. They elaborated a 'closed' curriculum in arithmetic, gross motor development, handwriting, language, early reading and spelling, social competence, based on the specification of behavioural objectives, the employment of task analysis and criterion-referenced assessment. This approach has the advantage of making explicit the goals of teaching, the sequences of instruction and the intimate relationship between teaching and the assessment of pupils' progress. It also provides for individualization in terms of pupils' learning rather than by references to assumptions about abilities and disabilities.

One of the major advantages of using behavioural objectives, in common with applied behaviour analysis techniques in general, is that the assessment is made by the teacher. The method, being by criterion-referenced assessment (i.e. whether the specified objective has been learnt to a specified criterion level) rather than by a norm-referenced test, provides close monitoring of learning – a contrast to termly or yearly normative tests of attainment which may or may not be relevant to the learning and are not sensitive to small changes and increments in learning.

A related procedure used increasingly is precision teaching. Raybould and Solity (1982) point out that the techniques of precision teaching are not so much a method of teaching as a way of finding out by means of brief tests or probes what is most effective, so that the amount and rate of learning can be charted and monitored over several days, and modifications made to instruction (Lovitt, 1977). This combination of systematic teaching, checks on progress and suitable reinforcement seems appropriate to the problem of literacy failure, the degree of which is a major factor distinguishing retarded children placed in special education from those who are not. Moreover, limited reading and writing skills require a large expenditure of time in pupils' school life and also impede their learning in other ways. The levels of attainment at school leaving are, nevertheless, very low. Chazan (1964) referred to 'the formidable task of teachers in trying to improve the scholastic attainments of ESN pupils'. In his sample, over half the boys and 45 per cent of the girls aged 13–14 years had reading ages below 7 years.

The use of a behavioural objectives framework for teaching basic educational skills is too recent a development to permit an assessment of outcomes at school leaving age. Benefits of a systematic approach there must be. There are, however, some difficulties in accepting the validity of attempts to reduce even basic educational learning to behavioural objectives. While this may be a sound procedure in connection with motor and self-competence skills, the itemization of reading in terms of letters, phonic elements and sight words runs counter to much current understanding of learning to read, which presents the process as one in which the child uses his own language and experience to develop various strategies for attending to relevant detail in print, for detecting and correcting errors, and for making use of the syntactic and semantic context. Clay (1979) believes that reading failures are produced by allowing children to build inefficient systems of functioning which keep them crippled in this process throughout their school careers: 'As older readers they are difficult to help because they are habituated in their inefficiency'. How to teach the young child in such a way that he is helped to develop effective strategies is difficult enough, but teaching the older child who has cognitive, linguistic and motivational inadequacies is even more problematic. Similar issues arise in the teaching of mathematics, in which the heart of the teaching problem, accentuated in teaching the less intelligent, is the relationship between understanding and skills. Teaching objectives should be well defined but not necessarily as behavioural ones. Macdonald-Ross (1975) has provided an informed critique of behavioural objectives in education.

The difficulties of the retarded in basic skills – language, reading, mathematics and social competence – require a well-organized programme in these areas. The contribution of other curriculum components to their cognitive and personal development is of equal importance but less easy to specify and, in the case of special schools, the smaller number of staff commonly reduces the amount of expertise in teaching the range of possible subjects. In ordinary schools (especially at the secondary level) the wider range of specialist teaching expertise in theory should provide a broader curriculum for the slow learner. The issue of mainstreaming suggests the need for a bridge between the special and normal curriculum. There have always been children in ordinary schools who need considerable modifications in the normal curriculum, and the number may be expected to increase with the integration trend. It is also desirable to seek more opportunity for transfer from special school or class to mainstream, and this can be inhibited by very different curricular approaches. In trying to create a bridge, it is notable that the mainstream curriculum for less academic pupils has changed during a decade or so of reform. Courses have been developed which attempt to match the needs and interests of less able pupils, often providing specially planned components of integrated study and, in the final years of school, offering leavers' courses and work experience. Gulliford and Widlake (1974) showed that some curriculum materials and approaches well suited to the least able pupils were little used in secondary and special schools.

The report of a Schools Council study (Brennan, 1979) indicated that successful courses for slow learners in secondary schools were most frequently in English, leavers' courses, parenthood courses and environmental studies. The humanities and science did not fare well, no doubt because subject specialists do not see their areas as being relevant for or teachable to the least able. However, the specialist teacher, with his knowledge of the content and methods of teaching his subject, can, if ready to accept the challenge of adapting to the difficulties of retarded children, make a valuable contribution. Cowie (1979) provided a useful account of the problems and possibilities of teaching history, and Tate (1979) demonstrated the benefits which a history specialist can bring to the learning and experience of pupils in special schools for children with moderate learning difficulties. Hinson (1978) and Hinson and Hughes (1982) are useful sources about developments across the curriculum, including science, history, geography and life skills programmes. Appropriate work in geography is discussed by Boardman (1982).

Even when content and teaching methods are well adapted to the needs of slow learners, the most retarded are likely to gain less from a modified mainstream curriculum – though lower expectations should not be assumed automatically. Brennan (1974) has pointed out the dilemma between a curriculum limited to the basic skills and knowledge, which the retarded can master during the years of formal education, and the wider curriculum which may generate interest, but contributes little to learning basic skills nor results in any depth of understanding in other areas. He suggests a useful distinction between learning to a level of mastery and to a level of familiarity or awareness. The need for mastery learning of literacy, numeracy and social competence skills is well understood. In some curriculum fields there are concepts, information of practical value and skills which deserve to be thoroughly learned. There are others where awareness or familiarity is desirable, even essential, if the young person is to relate adequately to his fellows, to human experience and his social framework. Brennan suggests that these areas are no less important. The teacher needs to be clear about their purpose and to cultivate interaction between the two to motivate and reinforce learning and to generate transfer. There are, for example, some ideas in the topic of electricity that the retarded person should master, if only in relation to using electrical apparatus safely. In many other aspects of the topic some awareness is desirable. In geography, learning which enables the retarded person to use a simple plan or town map might be considered appropriate for mastery learning, whereas acquaintance with more complex maps might not be thought necessary, beyond the level of familiarity. Likewise, in health education, home economics and other subjects, essential knowledge or skills need to be identified within the broad experience which might be offered.

There are other curriculum areas where the distinction between mastery and awareness is inappropriate. For example, McPhail's (1972) Moral Education curriculum materials use simple pictorial stimuli (or everyday situations) to prompt children and young people to think of the consequences of actions, the significance of situations and to be sensitive to the viewpoints of others. The responses hoped for are more open-ended and aim to promote ways of thinking and feeling about common human situations rather than precise instruction, and as such are relevant to the child's future interactions in the community. Other approaches combine this type with more specific social skills training. Goldstein (1979) has reported a procedure for improving pupils' reasoning about social situations; and a methodology for assessing adolescent thinking in a variety of contexts was developed by Peel (1971).

One essential view of the purpose of special education is that it should aim to improve cognitive functioning. For example, the amount of time given to a mathematics curriculum might be thought excessive in view of the limited use of mathematical skills in adult life (some of which, such as the handling of money, retarded adolescents are likely to learn quickly anyway) were it not that the mathematics curriculum develops numerical, spatial and time concepts as well as reasoning processes for ordering and classifying experience – and the related language. There are justifications also for appropriate experience in other areas of the curriculum. Feuerstein's (1980) Instrumental Enrichment programme is attractive for similar reasons, and because it is relatively free from association with the conventional curriculum on which the retarded have failed. The programme consists of structured materials through which pupils learn to perceive patterns, to categorize and see relationships, and to contrast and compare objects, events and ideas. An essential feature is the mediation through dialogue and discussion, the lack of which Feuerstein sees as a fundamental source of retarded performance. An exploratory study was undertaken in five local regions in England (Weller and Craft, 1983).

A critical appraisal of the Feuerstein model and the research reported so far has been made by Bradley (1983). While he views the model as an attractive alternative to some of the poorly structured programmes often provided, he is, rightly, wary of a repetition of the over-optimism aroused during the 1960s and early 1970s by diagnostic-remedial approaches to the training of abilities and remediation of learning disabilities. The crucial aspect of his critique is, however, a careful appraisal of the research reported so far from which he concludes that results in terms of improved intellectual and school subject performances and measures of attitudes, classroom behaviour and motivation are 'very modest, perhaps promising but, more likely, at best clouded'. Even if other evaluations are not more conclusive, Feuerstein's ideas will have been worthwhile if they provoke specialist teachers to examine how their subject can be used to improve the performance and motivation of retarded learners – as some good teachers have always done, and as has been reported from some schools in respect of microcomputers.

The needs of post-school life give a coherence and purpose to the final years at school which have led to successful leavers' courses with an outward-looking orientation. In addition to pre-vocational aspects, including work experience, it is an opportunity to bring to a focus previous learning and to develop such areas as health, sex education, parenthood, the management of money, leisure and holidays, social and life skills, and to consolidate reading, writing and numeracy skills in relation to everyday needs. Many will have another opportunity, not superfluous, for further learning in these areas when they move into further education.

FURTHER EDUCATION AND VOCATIONAL PREPARATION

No educator accepts that education of young people at any level of ability should cease at the end of compulsory schooling at age sixteen. A move into a college of further education or, as in some countries, a senior high school, is desirable partly to mark a stage in the transition to adulthood (which in itself provides a stimulus to maturing) and partly to begin a phase of education in which vocational preparation and education are combined and reinforce each other.

In the past few decades it has been usual in many countries for pupils with moderate learning difficulties to leave school at sixteen. About 60–70 per cent obtained employment (Brennan, 1974, chapter 4), and most adjusted to work and living in the community without undue difficulty (Atkinson, 1984). Over a long period, special schools have paid particular attention to preparation for leaving school with early involvement of the Careers Advisory Service, and well-planned leavers' courses including work experience. In some schools, leavers in their final year are accommodated in a separate unit with courses orientated to work and living, and with greater scope for independence and responsibility. At least one school established a workshop, separate from the school, where less mature pupils aged sixteen plus had a year's realistic preparation for working life (Jerrold and Fox, 1968). 'Link' courses whereby pupils in their final year attended a local college of further education for one or two days a week have been common.

In a survey of handicapped school leavers, Tuckey *et al.* (1973) found that only 4 per cent of those with moderate learning difficulties progressed on to further education, though 16 per cent went on to adult training centres, employment rehabilitation centres or other training. In recent years, however, further educational opportunities have increased, partly in response to the high rate of unemployment among young people.

During the 1970s some colleges began to provide courses for young people with special needs. One of the earliest, the North Nottinghamshire College at Worksop, has developed into a model of its kind (Hutchinson and Clegg, 1975). In 1978–9 its Work Orientation Unit was providing assessment, work preparation and further education for 147 students with special needs, 71 of them with moderate or severe learning difficulties in courses of 1–3 years' duration. Some are placed and supported on normal or modified further education courses, but most follow specially designed courses in which the vocational element includes a programme in a purpose-built operative's training workshop, sample vocational courses, limited skills vocational courses and work experience. All students include in their programme training in basic educational skills, social and life skills, and recreational and leisure skills. The department, which has 33 technical and 13 special teaching staff, is an integral part of the college. There is good medical, nursing and therapy support in the college to cater for the range of disability, appropriate resources for sensory and physical handicaps and close relationships with the Careers Advisory Service, social and employment services and with local industry (Hutchinson, 1982).

The unit may be viewed as following the recommendations of both the Thomas Report (1964) and the Warnock Report (DES, 1978) that there should be a special unit in each region providing assessment, vocational training and further education for young people with disabilities. Panckhurst (1980) and Bradley and Hegarty (1982) indicate that a number of colleges of further education have developed as special centres offering courses for young people with sensory, physical and learning handicaps; that some residential colleges have widened the range of intake; and that some new ones have been set up.

It is even more important to increase the amount, variety and quality of local provision. Courses for those with moderate learning difficulties have a base in the experience of link courses between colleges and schools in the final school years. Full-time ones have been increasingly offered, usually run in departments of general education or community studies but making use of other college facilities, e.g. practical and creative activities (Browne, 1979). They vary in duration and in the time allocated to literacy and numeracy, social and life skills, vocational preparation and work experience, and creative and recreational skills (Bradley and Hegarty, 1982). The courses which most frequently provide for students with learning difficulties are those which stem from the Holland Report, *Young People and Work* (Manpower Services Commission, 1977), which led to the development by the Commission of the Youth Opportunities Programme, replaced in 1983 by the Youth Training Scheme. An investigation of work introduction courses at 32 colleges of further education found that, of 359 students aged between 16 and 19, 77 had attended special schools (McDaid, 1982). Most of their 32 tutors had moved from traditional areas of college work, though 8 held a special education qualification. The need for inservice training of staff is very clear and is currently the subject of a research project at the National Bureau of Handicapped Students. Further education staff are increasingly enrolling for relevant courses in special education and a City and Guilds qualification is also available. Valuable contributions to staff development have been made by the Further Education Curriculum Review and Development Unit (FEU) which has produced a series of discussion documents on the curriculum and on assessment and recording procedures relevant to the teaching of students with special needs in further education (FEU, 1982).

Courses for students with severe learning difficulties are less common. Smith and Phillips (1981), following up 128 pupils, found that between 16 and 19 years 41 per cent were still at school, 4 per cent were on courses, 39 per cent were at adult training centres, 8 per cent were at home and 8 per cent in hospital. Dean and Hegarty (1984) showed that nationally about 50 per cent remained in school to 17 years and 25 per cent to 18, and that the trend is towards an annual increase in the percentage staying at school in each age group to 19 years. They suggest several reasons for this trend: lack of other alternatives; parental wishes; local policies for developing further provision in special schools; and co-operative arrangements involving links between school, adult centres and colleges. In their enquiry in 111 local education authorities, they identified 47 colleges making some type of provision. Thirty-four arranged link courses with schools, adult training centres and sometimes hospitals. Twenty colleges offered full-time, two-year courses, ten of them including a residential component.

Aldridge (1982) described a special course for students with severe learning difficulties at Kingsway College, London. They attend a part-time link course during their last year at school, primarily to assess their suitability for proceeding to a two-year full-time course. During the part-time year, a teacher and an assistant spend the day with the students, gradually withdrawing their support for lunchtimes in the canteen and in moving round the college, for instance to the gym, and for home economics. In the full-time course, their timetables include educational and life skills, travel, movement, yoga, home economics and a choice of physical, craft and recreational activities alongside students from other courses. Dean and Hegarty (1984) provide examples of various approaches in other colleges.

Bradley and Hegarty (1982) refer to a significant and developing contribution by further and adult education centres in the form of outreach provision, whereby staff move into adult training centres, day centres, hospitals, homes and employment rehabilitation centres to provide recreational basic education courses (see Chapter 18).

Although there are many gaps and insufficiencies in existing provisions, particularly in further education for young people with severe learning difficulties between the ages of 16 and 19 or 21, the movement to organize further education and vocational training for those with intellectual handicaps has commenced. Experience is beginning to be acquired in the methods of teaching, the devising of curricula and the organization of training in skills relevant to work or to living. The opportunities for further learning, cognitive development and personal/social maturing should be regarded as essential continuations of the efforts begun in the infancy and childhood of the retarded, which already show evidence of success.

AFTER FURTHER EDUCATION – WHAT?

The future of young people after school or further education is obviously a matter of concern to teachers and tutors. Having invested much effort in individuals and having encouraged them to look towards their future after education, teachers inevitably have a personal involvement and are frustrated when employment or suitable adult provision is lacking or inadequate. There is encouragement in the developing work in adult centres and other forms of provision, and in the fact that some young people with moderate difficulties obtain employment following good leavers' programmes and work experience.

The opening up of discussion about alternatives to work for severely handicapped people by the OECD paper prepared by Tizard and Anderson (1983) raises the question whether there are implications for the curricula of schools and colleges of a life without work or, as Massie (1982) termed it, 'without formal employment'. Massie suggested that some may be lulled into the view that disabled people may have to accept that they cannot realistically expect to obtain employment and that they should consider a life outside the sphere of economic activity. He argued that this attitude should be vigorously resisted. It would certainly be unwise to assume too readily that training in work skills is inappropriate. Work marks the transition from school towards adulthood, often with enhanced effort and motivation. Training develops mental and physical skills which can have a broad application in life.

Tizard and Anderson proposed that schools should do more to prepare young people for the idea that they might not be able to find employment and to discuss with them the possible alternatives. They considered that such preparation had both practical and psychological aspects. The former includes visits to centres in the community, the development of awareness of community activities in which they might become involved, and greater attention to recognizing and fostering aptitudes and interests. On the psychological aspect, they referred to the need for discussion and counselling in order to assist coming to terms with the situation and to consider such aspects as isolation, boredom and depression (Anderson and Clarke, 1982). Cheseldine and Jeffree (1982) surveyed the abilities of mentally handicapped teenagers relevant to independent living, social skills and acceptance. While most were quite competent in basic self-help skills and in everyday living skills at home, they lacked many of the abilities for getting round the neighbourhood, meeting people and using public facilities. There are implications for schools and parents and particularly, perhaps, for further and adult education when the widening experience of the environment creates both the need and the opportunities for extending those competencies.

CONCLUSIONS

The basic achievement of the past three decades in some countries has been the provision of education during the school years for all mentally retarded children. In the pre-school years, appropriate programmes and methods of parent involvement have developed but need to be comprehensively available. In the post-school years, further education and vocational preparation need to be more soundly based and organized, especially for those with severe learning difficulties. A major aim in the immediate future should be to decrease further the separation of children with learning difficulties from ordinary experiences of living, recreation and education. Understanding of the issues involved has been increased by evaluations of integrated forms of provision and of the practical steps which should be taken by teachers and educational administrators. The nature and planning of curricula in special education have profitably been the focus of attention, alongside methods of instruction which are more systematic and which emphasize the teacher's role in monitoring learning. In this and other ways, the gap between research and practice has narrowed and the time-lag between research findings and implementation has been shortened. There are, however, no grounds for complacency, since the resourcing of research, and particularly of the inservice training of teachers through which new concepts and practice are disseminated, at present remain inadequate.

REFERENCES

AINSCOW, M. and TWEDDLE, D.A. (1979) *Preventing Classroom Failure*, Chichester, Wiley.

ALDRIDGE, H. (1982) 'The Gateway 2 Course at Kingsway – Princeton College', *Educare*, 14, 23–5.

ANASTASIOW, N.T. (1978) 'Strategies and models for early childhood intervention programs in integrated settings', in M.J. GURALNICK (ed.), *Early Intervention and the Integration of Handicapped and Nonhandicapped Children*, Baltimore, University Park Press, 85–111.

ANDERSON, E. (1973) *The Disabled School Child*, London, Methuen.

ANDERSON, E.M. and CLARKE, L. (1982) *Disability in Adolescence*, London, Methuen.

ASPIN, D. (1982) 'Towards a concept of human being as a basis for a philosophy of special education', *Educ. Rev.*, 34 (2), 113–24.

ATKINSON, E. (1984) 'The adaptation of educationally subnormal school leavers thirty years on', *Spec. Educ.: Forward Trends*, 11 (4), 17–24.

BAILEY, J. (1982) 'Special units in secondary schools', *Educ. Rev.*, 34 (2),

107–12.

BALLER, W.R. (1939) 'A study of the behaviour records of adults who when they were in school, were judged to be dull in mental ability', *J. Genet. Psychol.*, 55, 365–79.

BENDER, M. and VALLETUTI, P.J. (1976) *Teaching the Moderately and Severely Handicapped*, Baltimore, University Park Press.

BEST, C. (1983) 'The "new" deaf–blind?', *Brit. J. Vis. Impairment*, 1 (2), 11–13.

BEVERIDGE, M., SPENCER, J. and MITTLER, P. (1978) 'Lanuage and social behaviour in severely educationally subnormal children', *Brit. J. Soc. Clin. Psychol.*, 17, 75–83.

BLANK, M. (1973) *Teaching Learning in the Pre-school*, Columbus, Ohio, Merrill.

BLOOM, B.S. (1975) 'Mastery learning and its implications for curriculum development', in M. GOLBY, J. GREENWARD and R. WEST (eds), *Curriculum Development*, London, Croom Helm, 334–50.

BLUMA, S.M., SHEARER, M.S., FROHMAN, A.H. and HILLIARD, J.M. (1976) 'Portage guide to early education', *CESA-12*, Portage, Wisconsin.

BOARDMAN, D. (1982) *Geography with Slow Learners*, Sheffield, The Geographical Association.

BOOKBINDER, G.E. (1967) 'The preponderance of summer-born children in ESN classes: which is responsible, age or length of schooling?', *Educ. Res.*, 9 (3), 213–18.

BRADLEY, J. and HEGARTY, S. (1982) *Stretching the System*, London, Further Education Curriculum Review and Development Unit.

BRADLEY, T.B. (1983) 'Remediation of cognitive deficits: a critical appraisal of the Feuerstein model', *J. Ment. Defic. Res.*, 27, 79–82.

BRENNAN, W.K. (1974) *Shaping the Education of Slow Learners*, London, Routledge & Kegan Paul.

BRENNAN, W.K. (1979) *Curricular Needs of Slow Learners*, London, Methuen.

BRENNAN. W.K. (1982) *Special Education in Mainstream Schools*, Stratford-on-Avon, National Council for Special Education.

BRICKER, D., SEIBERT, J.M. and CASUSO, V. (1980) 'Early intervention', in J. HOGG and P. MITTLER (eds), *Advances in Mental Handicap*, vol. 1, Chichester, Wiley, 225–63.

BRICKER, W.A. and BRICKER, D.D. (1974) 'An early language training strategy', in R.L. SCHIEFELBUSCH and L.L. LLOYD (eds), *Language Perspectives – Acquisition, Retardation and Intervention*, Baltimore, University Park Press, 431–68.

BROWNE, G. (1979) *Continuing Education: A Programme for the Less Able in Colleges of Further Education*, Manchester, National Elfrida Rathbone Society.

BUCKLEY, S. (1984) *Reading and Language Development in Children with Down's Syndrome*, Portsmouth Polytechnic.

BURMAN, L., FARRELL, P., FEILER, A., MEFFERMAN, M. and MITTLER, P. (1983) 'Redesigning the school curriculum', *Spec. Educ.*, 10 (2), 33–6.

CAMERON, R. (1982) *Working Together: Portage in the UK*, Windsor, NFER/Nelson.

CARR, J., HALLIWELL, M.D. and PEARSON, M. (1983) 'Educational attainments of spina bifida children attending ordinary schools', *Spec. Educ.*, 10 (3), 22–4.

CHAZAN, M. (1964) 'The incidence and nature of maladjustment among children in schools for the ESN', *Brit. J. Educ. Psychol.*, 34 (3), 292–304.

CHAZAN, M., LAING, A.F., BAILEY, M.S. and JONES, G. (1980) *Some of our Children*, Shepton Mallet, Open Books.

CHESELDINE, S.E. and JEFFREE, D.M. (1981) 'Mentally handicapped adolescents: their use of leisure', *J. Ment. Defic. Res.*, 25, 45–59.

CHESELDINE, S.E. and JEFFREE, D.M. (1982) 'Mentally handicapped adolescents: a survey of ability', *Spec. Educ.*, 9 (1), 19–22.

CLARK, M.M. and CHEYNE, W.M. (1979) *Studies in Pre-school Education*, London, Hodder & Stoughton.

CLARK, M.M., ROBSON, R. and BROWNING, M. (1982) *Pre-school Education and Children with Special Needs*, University of Birmingham, Dept of Educational Psychology.

CLARKE, A.D.B. and CLARKE, A.M. (1975) *Recent Advances in the Study of Subnormality*, London, MIND, National Association for Mental Health.

CLAY, M.M. (1979) *Reading: The Patterning of Complex Behaviour*, 2nd edn, London, Heinemann.

CLUNIES-ROSS, L. and WIMHURST, S. (1983) *The Right Balance*, Windsor, NFER/Nelson.

COLBORNE BROWN, M. and TOBIN, M.J. (1982) 'Integration of the educationally blind', *New Beacon*, 1 May, 113–17.

COLLMAN, R.D. and NEWLYN, D. (1956) 'Employment success of educationally subnormal ex-pupils in England', *Amer. J. Ment. Defic.*, 60, 733–43.

COPE, C. and ANDERSON, E. (1977) *Special Units in Ordinary Schools*, Windsor, NFER.

CORMAN, L. and GOTTLIEB, J. (1978) 'Mainstreaming mentally retarded children: a review of research', in N.R. ELLIS (ed.), *International Review of Research in Mental Retardation*, vol. 9, New York, Academic Press, 251–75.

CORNWALL, K. and SPICER, J. (1982) 'The role of the educational psychologist in the discovery and assessment of children requiring special education', *Brit. Psychol. Soc., DECP Occasional Papers*, 6 (2), 3–11.

COWIE, E.E. (1979) *History and the Slow Learning Child*, London, The Historical Association.

CRAWFORD, N.B. (ed.) (1980) *Curriculum Planning for the ESN(S) Child*, Kidderminster, British Institute of Mental Handicap.

CROWELL, F.A. (1980) 'Evaluating programs for educating mentally retarded persons', in J. GOTTLIEB (ed.), *Educating Mentally Retarded Persons in the Mainstream*, Baltimore, University Park Press, 47–72.

CUNNINGHAM, C.C. and JEFFREE, D. (1975) 'The organization and structure of workshops for parents of mentally handicapped children', *Bull. Brit. Psychol. Soc.*, 28, 405–11.

CUNNINGHAM, C.C. and SLOPER, P. (1977a) 'Parents of Down's syndrome babies: their early needs', *Child: Care, Health, Dev.*, 3 (5), 325–47.

CUNNINGHAM, C.C. and SLOPER, P. (1977b) 'Down's syndrome infants: a positive approach to parent and professional collaboration', *Health Visitor*, 50 (2), 32–7.

CUNNINGHAM, C.C. and SLOPER, P. (1978) *Helping Your Handicapped Baby*, London, Souvenir Press.

DEAN, L. and HEGARTY, S. (1984) *Learning for Independence*, Windsor, NFER.

DEPARTMENT OF EDUCATION AND SCIENCE (1971) *Slow Learners in Secondary Schools*, London, HMSO.

DEPARTMENT OF EDUCATION AND SCIENCE (1975a) *A Language for Life* (The Bullock Report), London, HMSO.

DEPARTMENT OF EDUCATION AND SCIENCE (1975b) *Educating Mentally Handicapped Children*, London, HMSO.

DEPARTMENT OF EDUCATION AND SCIENCE (1978) *Special Educational Needs* (The Warnock Report), London, HMSO.

DEPARTMENT OF EDUCATION AND SCIENCE (1982) *Statistics of Education (Schools)*, London, HMSO.

DEPARTMENT OF HEALTH AND SOCIAL SECURITY (1974) *A Decade of Progress: A History of the Training Council for Teachers of the Mentally Handicapped*, London, HMSO.

DUNN, L.M. (1968) 'Special education for the mildly retarded: is much of it justified?', *Excep. Child.*, 35, 5–22.

ENGLEMANN, S. and CARNINE, D. (1975) *DISTAR Arithmetic*, 1, 2nd edn, Chicago, Science Research Associates.

ENGLEMANN, S. and OSBORN, J. (1969) *DISTAR Language*, Henley-on-Thames, Science Research Associates.

FENN, G. (1976) 'Against verbal enrichment', in P.L. BERRY (ed.), *Language and Communication in the Mentally Handicapped*, London, Edward Arnold, 84–96.

FEUERSTEIN, R. (1980) *Instrumental Enrichment: An Intervention Program for Cognitive Modifiability*, Baltimore, University Park Press.

FISHER, G. (1977) 'Integration at Pingle School', *Spec. Educ.*, 4 (1), 8–11.

FLEEMAN, A.M.F. (1984) 'From special to secondary school', *Spec. Educ.: Forward Trends*, 11, 23–6.

FURTHER EDUCATION CURRICULUM REVIEW AND DEVELOPMENT UNIT (1982) *A Basis for Choice: Report of a Study Group on Post-16 Pre-employment Courses*, 2nd edn, London, Further Education Unit, Honeypot Lane.

GARDNER, J.M. and MURPHY, J. (1980) 'A curriculum model', in N.B. CRAWFORD (ed.), *Curriculum Planning for the ESN(S) Child*, Kidderminster, British Institute for Mental Handicap, 25–39.

GARNETT, J. (1976) 'Special children in a comprehensive', *Spec. Educ.*, 3 (1), 8–12.

GARNETT, J. (1983) 'Providing access to the mainstream curriculum in secondary schools', in T. BOOTH and P. POTTS (eds), *Integrating Special Education*, Oxford, Blackwell, 125–37.

GILLHAM, B. (1981) *The First Words Language Programme*, London, Allen & Unwin.

GILLHAM, B. (1983) *Two Words Together*, London, Allen & Unwin.

GOLDSTEIN, H. (1974) *The Social Learning Curriculum*, Columbus, Ohio, Merrill.

GOLDSTEIN, H. (1979) 'Reasoning abilities of mildly retarded children', in P. MITTLER (ed.), *Research to Practice in Mental Retardation*, vol. 2, *Education and Training*, Baltimore, University Park Press.

GOLDSTEIN, H., MOSS, J.W. and JORDAN, L.J. (1965) *The Efficacy of Special Class Training on the Development of Mentally Retarded Children*, Urbana, University of Illinois.

GOLDSTEIN, H. and SEIGLE, D. (1958) *The Illinois Curriculum Guide*, Springfield, Ill., Office of the Superintendent of Public Instruction.

GRAY, D. and REEVE, J. (1978) 'Ordinary schools: some special help', *Spec. Educ.*, 5 (1), 25–8.

GULLIFORD, R. (1984) *Integration and the Training of Teachers*, Paris, OECD.

GULLIFORD, R. and WIDLAKE, P. (1974) *Teaching Materials for Disadvantaged Pupils*, London, Evans/Methuen.

GUNSTONE, C., HOGG, J., SEBBA, J., WARNER, J. and ALMOND, S. (1982) *Classroom Organization for Integrated Pre-school Provision*, Paper 2, Ilford, Dr Barnardo Publications.

GURALNICK, M.J. (1978) *Early Intervention and the Integration of Handicapped and Nonhandicapped Children*, Baltimore, University Park Press.

HALLMARK, N. and DESSENT, T. (1982) 'A special education service centre', *Spec. Educ.*, 9 (1), 6–8.

HAWISHER, M.F. and CALHOUN, M.L. (1978) *The Resource Room*, Columbus, Ohio, Merrill.

HEGARTY, S. (1982) 'Integration and the comprehensive school', *Educ. Rev.*, 34 (2), 99–106.

HEGARTY, S. and POCKLINGTON, K. (1981) *Educating Pupils with Special Needs in the Ordinary School*, Windsor, NFER/Nelson.

HEGARTY, S. and POCKLINGTON, K. (1982) *Integration in Action*, Windsor, NFER/Nelson.

HINSON, M. (1978) *Encouraging Results*, London, Macdonald Educational.

HINSON, M. and HUGHES, M. (1982) *Planning Effective Progress*, Amersham, Hulton Educational.

HUGHES, J.M. (1975) 'The educational needs of the mentally handicapped', *Educ. Res.*, 17 (3), 228–33.

HUTCHINSON, D. (1982) *Work Preparation for the Handicapped*, London, Croom Helm.

HUTCHINSON, D. and CLEGG, N. (1975) 'Orientated towards work', *Spec. Educ.*, 2 (1), 22–5.

JACKSON, R.N. (1968) 'Employment adjustment of mentally handicapped ex-pupils in Scotland', *Amer. J. Ment. Defic.*, 72, 924–30.

JAMIESON, M., PARLETT, M. and POCKLINGTON, K. (1977) *Towards Integration*, Windsor, NFER.

JEFFREE, D.M., MCCONKEY, R. and HEWSON, S. (1977) *Teaching the Handicapped Child*, London, Souvenir Press.

JERROLD, M.A. and FOX, R. (1968) 'Pre-jobs for the boys', *Spec. Educ.*, 57 (2), 15–17.

JONES, A. and ROBSON, C. (1979) 'Do we ask the right questions?', *Spec. Educ.*, 6 (1), 11–14.

JONES, E. and BERRICK, S. (1980) 'Adopting a resourceful approach', *Spec. Educ.*, 7 (1), 11–14.

JONES, L., REID, B. and KIERNAN, C.C. (1982) 'Signs and symbols: the 1980 survey', *Spec. Educ.*, 9 (2), 34–7.

JONES, N. (1983) 'The management of integration, the Oxfordshire experience', in A. BOOTH and P. POTTS (eds), *Integrating Special Education*, Oxford, Blackwell, 62–73.

JONES, N., BURNHAM, M. and COLES, C. (1979) 'An appraisal of mixed ability teaching', *Spec. Educ.*, 6 (3), 28–31.

KAUFMAN, M.E. and ALBERTO, P.A. (1976) 'Research on efficacy of special education for the mentally retarded', in N.R. ELLIS (ed.), *International Review of Research in Mental Retardation*, 8, 225–55.

KELLMER PRINGLE, M.L., BUTLER, N.R. and DAVIE, R. (1966) *11,000 Seven Year Olds: First Report of the National Child Development Study*, London, Longman.

KIERNAN, C.C. and JONES, M.C. (1982) *Behaviour Assessment Battery*, 2nd edn, Windsor, NFER/Nelson.

KIERNAN, C.C., JORDAN, R. and SAUNDERS, C. (1978) *Starting Off: Establishing Play and Communication in the Handicapped Child*, London, Souvenir Press.

KIRK, S.A. (1964) 'Research in education', in H.A. STEVENS and R. HEBER (eds), *Mental Retardation: A Review of Research*, Chicago, University of Chicago Press, 57–99.

KIRK, S.A. and JOHNSON, D. (1951) *Educating the Retarded Child*, Boston, Houghton Mifflin.

KLEIN, N.K., PASCH, M. and FREW, T.W. (1979) *Curriculum Analysis and Design for Retarded Learners*, Columbus, Ohio, Merrill.

KOLSTOE, O.P. (1976) *Teaching Educable Mentally Retarded Children*, New York, Holt, Rinehart & Winston.

LARSEN, S.C. and POPLIN, M.S. (1980) *Methods for Educating the Handicapped*, Boston, Allyn & Bacon.

LEACH, D.J. (1981) 'Early screening for school learning difficulties', *Brit. Psychol. Soc., DECP Occasional Papers*, 5 (2), 46–59.

LEEMING, K., SWANN, W., COUPE, J. and MITTLER, P. (1979) *Teaching Language and Communication to the Mentally Handicapped*, London, Evans/Methuen.

LINDSAY, E.A. (1980) 'The infant rating scale', *Brit. J. Educ. Psychol.*, 50 (2), 97–104.

LOVITT, T.C. (1977) *In Spite of my Resistance – I've Learned from Children*, Columbus, Ohio, Merrill.

LOWDEN, G.D. (1984) 'Integrating slow learners in Wales', *Spec. Educ.: Forward Trends*, 11 (4), 25–6.

MCCONKEY, R. (1981) 'Education without understanding', *Spec. Educ.*, 8 (3), 8–10.

MCCONKEY, R. and JEFFREE, D. (1979) 'First steps in learning to pretend', *Spec. Educ.*, 6 (4), 13–16.

MCCONKEY, R. and JEFFREE, D. (1980) 'Developing children's play', *Spec. Educ.*, 7 (2), 21–3.

MCDAID, M.M. (1982) 'Young people with learning difficulties in work introduction courses', *Educ. Rev.*, 34 (2), 155–66.

MACDONALD-ROSS, M. (1975) 'Behavioural objectives: a critical review', in M. GOLBY, J. GREENWALD and R. WEST (eds), *Curriculum Design*, London, Croom Helm.

MCMASTER, J. MCG. (1973) *Towards an Educational Theory for the Mentally Handicapped*, London, Edward Arnold.

MCPHAIL, P. (1972) *Moral Education Curriculum Project*, Harlow, Longman.

MADDEN, N.A. and SLAVIN, R.E. (1983) 'Mainstreaming students with mild handicaps: academic and social outcomes', *Rev. Educ. Res.*, 53, 519–69.

MANPOWER SERVICES COMMISSION (1977) *Young People and Work* (The Holland Report), London, HMSO.

MASSIE, B. (1982) 'Significant living without Warnock', *Spec. Educ.*, 9 (3), 27–9.

MATHEW, G.C. (1963) 'The post-school adaptation of educationally subnormal boys', unpublished MEd. thesis, University of Manchester.

MATHEW, G.C. (1964) 'The social competence of the subnormal school leaver', *J. Ment. Subnorm.*, 10 (2), 83–8.

MEISGEIR, C. (1976) 'A review of critical issues underlying mainstreaming', in L. MANN and D.A. SABATINO (eds), *The Third Review of Special Education*, vol. 8, New York, Grune & Stratton, 225–53.

MEYERS, C.E., MACMILLAN, D.L. and YOSHIDA, R.K. (1980) 'Regular class education of EMR students, from efficacy to mainstreaming', in J. GOTTLIEB (ed.), *Educating Mentally Retarded Persons in the Mainstream*, Baltimore, University Park Press, 176–206.

MINISTRY OF EDUCATION (1946) *Special Educational Treatment*, London, HMSO.

MITTLER, P. (1976) 'Assessment for language learning', in P. BERRY (ed.), *Language and Communication in the Mentally Handicapped*, London, Edward Arnold, 5–35.

MITTLER, P. and PREDDY, D. (1981) 'Mentally handicapped pupils and school leavers: a survey in north-west England', in B. COOPER (ed.), *Asssessing the Handicaps and Needs of Mentally Retarded Children*, London, Academic Press, 33–51.

MOSES, D. (1982) 'Special educational needs: the relationship between teacher assessment, test scores and classroom behaviour', *Brit. J. Educ. Res.*, 8 (2), 111–16.

MUNCEY, J. and AINSCOW, M. (1983) 'Launching SNAP in Coventry', *Spec. Educ.*, 10 (3), 8–10.

MYLAND, E. and THURLOW, O. (1982) 'Integrating the special care class', *Ment. Handicap*, 10 (4), 114–15.

NEWSON, E. (1976) 'Parents as a resource in diagnosis and assessment', in T.E. OPPÉ and F.P. WOODFORD (eds), *Early Management of Handicapping Disorders*, Amsterdam, Elsevier, 105–17.

PANCKHURST, J. (1980) *Focus on Physical Handicap*, Windsor, NFER.

PEEL, E.A. (1971) *The Nature of Adolescent Judgement*, London, Staples.

PERKINS, F.A., TAYLOR, P.D. and CAPIE, A.C.M. (1980) *Helping the Retarded*, Kidderminster, British Institute for Mental Handicap.

PHILLIPS, C.J. (1979) 'Children from socially disadvantaged families and special education', *Res. Educ.*, 21, 25–40; 22, 24–36.

PRESLAND, J.L. (1970) 'Who should go to ESN schools?', *Spec. Educ.*, 59 (1), 11–16.

PRESLAND, J.L. (1980) 'Educating "special care" children: a review of the literature', *Educ. Res.*, 23 (1), 20–3.

PRESLAND, J.L. (1982) *Paths to Mobility in 'Special Care'*, Kidderminster, British Institute for Mental Handicap.

PUGH, G. (1981) *Parents as Partners*, London, National Children's Bureau.

RAYBOULD, E. and SOLITY, J. (1982) 'Teaching with precision', *Spec. Educ.*, 9 (2), 9–14.

RECTORY PADDOCK SCHOOL (1981) *In Search of a Curriculum*, Sidcup, Robin Wren Publications.

REVILL, S. and BLUNDEN, R. (1979) 'Home training service for pre-school developmentally handicapped children', *Behav., Res. Ther.*, 17, 207–14.

ROBERTS, L. and WILLIAMS, I. (1980) 'Three years on at Pingle School', *Spec. Educ.*, 7 (2), 24–8.

ROBSON, C. (1981) 'A minicourse in structured teaching', *Spec. Educ.*, 8 (2), 26–7.

ROSE, C. (1981) 'Social integration of ESN(S) school age children in a regular school', *Spec. Educ.*, 8 (4), 17–21.

ROSTRON, A. and SEWELL, D. (1984) *Microtechnology in Special Education*, London, Croom Helm.

RUTTER, M., WHITMORE, K. and TIZARD, J. (1970) *Education, Health and Behaviour*, London, Methuen.

SACKETT, G.P. (1978) *Observing Behaviour*, vol. 1, *Theory and Applications in Mental Handicap*, Baltimore, University Park Press.

SANDOW, S. and CLARKE, A.D.B. (1978) 'Home intervention with parents of severely subnormal, pre-school children: an interim report', *Child: Care, Health, Dev.*, 4 (1), 29–39.

SAYER, J. (1983) 'A comprehensive school for all', in A. BOTH and P. POTTS (eds), *Integrating Special Education*, Oxford, Blackwell.

SCIENCE RESEARCH ASSOCIATES (various dates) *Reading Laboratories*, Henley-on-Thames, Science Research Associates.

SHEARER, M.S. and SHEARER, D. (1972) 'The Portage Project: a model for early childhood education', *Excep. Child.*, 39, 210–17.

SMITH, B. (1982) 'A study of mental growth in young severely subnormal children', unpublished PhD thesis, University of Birmingham.

SMITH, B., MOORE, Y. and PHILLIPS, C.J. (1983) 'Education with understanding', *Spec. Educ.*, 10 (2), 21–4.

SMITH, B. and PHILLIPS, C.J. (1978) 'Identification of severe mental handicap', *Child: Care, Health, Dev.*, 4, 195–203.

SMITH, B. and PHILLIPS, C.J. (1981) 'Age related progress among children with severe learning difficulties', *Develop. Med. Child Neurol.*, 23, 465–76.

SMITH, B. and PHILLIPS, C.J. (1982) 'Eight years later in Birmingham', *Ment. Handicap*, 10 (2), 48–51.

SMITH, J., KUSHLICK, A. and GLOSSOP, C. (1977) *The Wessex Portage Project*, Winchester, Health Care Evaluation Research Team.

SÖDER, M. (1981) 'School integration of the mentally retarded', in *The Education of the Handicapped Adolescent: Integration in the School*, Paris, OECD.

SOUTHGATE, V., ARNOLD, H. and JOHNSON, S. (1981) *Extending Beginning Reading*, London, Heinemann.

STEVENS, M. (1978) *Observe – Then Teach*, 2nd edn (1st edn, 1968), London, Edward Arnold.

TATE, N. (1979) 'How can we re-create the past?', *Spec. Educ.*, 6 (3), 22–7.

TENNANT, L. and HATTERSLEY, J. (1977) 'Working together – a progress report on parent workshops', *Apex*, 5 (3), 7–8.

THATCHER, J. (1984) *Teaching Reading to Mentally Handicapped Children*, Beckenham, Croom Helm.

THOMAS, E. (1964) *The Handicapped School Leaver*, London, British Council for Rehabilitation of the Disabled.

TIZARD, J. and ANDERSON, E. (1983) 'The education of the handicapped adolescent, alternatives to work for severely handicapped people', in A.D.B. CLARKE and B. TIZARD (eds), *Child Development and Social Policy*, Leicester, British Psychological Society.

TOMLINSON, S. (1981) *Educational Subnormality – A Study in Decision Making*, London, Routledge & Kegan Paul.

TOUGH, J. (1977) *Talking and Learning: A Guide to Fostering Communication Skills in Nursery and Infant Schools*, London, Ward Lock.

TOWNSEND, H.E.R. (1971) *Immigrant Pupils in England*, Slough, NFER.

TUCKEY, L., PARFIT, J. and TUCKEY, R. (1973) *Handicapped School*

Leavers: Their Further Education and Training, Slough, NFER.

UPTON, G. (ed.) (1979) *Physical and Creative Activities for the Mentally Handicapped*, Cambridge, Cambridge University Press.

UZGIRIS, I.C. and HUNT, J. MCV. (1975) *Assessment in Infancy*, Urbana, University of Illinois Press.

WELLER, K. and CRAFT, A. (1983) *Making up our Minds*, London, Schools Council.

WELTON, J., WEDELL, K. and VORHAUS, G. (1982) *Meeting Special Educational Needs*, Bedford Way Papers, 12, London, Heinemann.

WIEDERHOLT, J.L., HAMMILL, D.D. and BROWN, V. (1978) *The Resource Teacher: A Guide to Effective Practice*, Boston, Allyn & Bacon.

WILLIAMS, P. (1964) 'Date of birth, backwardness and educational organization', *Brit. J. Educ. Psychol.*, 34, 247–55.

WILLIAMS, P., DAVIES, P., EVANS, R. and FERGUSON, N. (1970) 'Season of birth and cognitive development', *Nature*, 228, no. 5276, 1033–6.

WOLFENDALE, S. and BRYANS, T. (1980) *Identification of Learning Difficulties*, Stafford, National Association of Remedial Education.

WOODWARD, M. (1962) 'The application of Piaget's theory to the training of the subnormal', *J. Ment. Subnorm.*, 8, 17–25.

YOUNGHUSBAND, E., BIRCHALL, D., DAVIE, R. and KELLMER PRINGLE, M.L. (1970) *Living with Handicap*, London, National Bureau for Cooperation in Child Care.

18

The habilitation of adults

Edward Whelan

INTRODUCTION

This chapter draws upon American, Canadian and British research and aims to show how these findings should contribute to practice in the further education of the adult mentally handicapped. It thus forms a sequel to Chapter 17. In particular, research in the University of Manchester's Hester Adrian Research Centre is outlined, and the development of a comprehensive approach to the problems is described. Although the context of these endeavours is British, it is suggested that the philosophy and components of action are equally relevant to other developed nations. Chapter 19, however, offers a more international perspective, with special reference to the developing world.

The next few years will see the first of a new generation of mentally handicapped adults to emerge having completed a full period of entitlement within the educational system. They are the individuals who attained school age shortly after the implementation of the English Education (Handicapped Children) Act, 1970. Many of their parents are already expressing very positive views about the need for an adult provision which is capable of sustaining and enhancing the personal development which they perceive their sons/daughters to have achieved during their school years.

The expectations of such parents have been influenced by the considerable shift in public attitudes towards mental handicap which has taken place during the 1970s, elaborated in Chapters 1, 19 and elsewhere in this book. This has included the Declaration of General and Specific Rights by the United Nations, the enactment of supportive legislation in many countries and the growth of numerous programmes of implementation, from 'Head Start' to 'normalization'. Of particular relevance to adults has been the growth of the 'self-advocacy' movement and a greater awareness of the rights of individuals to be consulted and involved in decisions concerning their lives. All this is consistent with the important findings of Cobb (1969), who ushered in the previous decade by his review of the international literature concerned with the prediction of adjustment by mentally handicapped adults to opportunities for independent life in the community: 'The most consistent and outstanding finding of all follow-up studies is the high proportion of the adult retarded who achieve satisfactory adjustments, by whatever criteria are employed.'

There is now an urgent need to update the philosophy of provision for mentally handicapped adults, if only to match that which has been accepted for mentally handicapped children. Both were once believed to be capable only of being 'occupied' and later, as a result of the Mental Health Act (1959), to be suitable for 'training'. Since 1970, while children have been recognized as 'educable', the main forms of community day provision for mentally handicapped adults continue to be known as 'training centres'. This is why the National Development Group (NDG) in England recommended that these centres should be renamed 'social education' centres, and that their clients should be known as 'students' rather than trainees.

Current government policy concerning the nature of day service provision for mentally handicapped adults is to be found in Circular LAC(80)2 which clearly endorsed the contents of NDG *Pamphlet 5* (1977) and commended this to local authorities. *Pamphlet 5* states, for example:

> We see the work of day services as educational in the broadest sense of the word ... and its staff as ... specialists whose services should be made available to the widening range of community agencies who are now working with mentally handicapped people....
>
> It follows that an educational approach is common to all who work with them, whether they are teachers, day-centre staff, therapists, nurses or care staff. They may differ in their methods but the goal of working for development is common to all.

Such assertions are supported by studies spanning several years which have consistently concluded that mentally handicapped people can and do continue to develop well beyond the normal statutory age for school attendance (Brand *et al.*, 1969; Parmenter, 1976; Salagaras and Nettlebeck, 1984). Most would agree, in fact, that adults pose greater challenges than children in terms of their size, emotional and sexual needs, and problems associated with ageing parents and the need to make more permanent forms of provision available.

The recommendations in NDG *Pamphlet 5* took full account of the findings of the first National Survey of Adult Training Centres (Whelan and Speake, 1977), which clearly indicated the willingness of staff to move from the former occupation and training models of provision, with their great reliance on 'industrial' activities, towards a more appropriate emphasis on providing the individual with the knowledge and skills needed in the activities of daily living. Despite this willingness of staff, however, there is currently a danger that 'day care', which prevails as the generic term for provision during the day by many social services departments for numerous groups of individuals, could become widely accepted as appropriate also for mentally handicapped adults. The effect of adopting such a philosophy, which responds primarily to the perception of a need to provide respite care for families, would be to set back by some twenty-five years the advances made in responding to the needs and potential of mentally handicapped adults.

THE HABILITATION PHILOSOPHY

Several authors have pointed out the suitability of the term 'habilitation' to describe the work with adults which continues the process of education, still regarded by some as having primarily a child and school connotation. Rosen *et al.* (1977), for example, say:

> The term 'rehabilitation' usually connotes the restoration of a former capacity. However, training of the developmentally disabled is geared toward teaching new skills rather than restoring skills lost by illness or injury. The term 'habilitation' is gaining increasing acceptance as a better word for describing this endeavour.

Habilitation essentially involves building upon the individual's strengths and, by a process of sequential evaluation and systematic teaching, preparing him or her to function comfortably within a particular setting. In contrast, the earlier medical model, while having great strength in its recognition of the importance of specialist services, tended to view mental handicap as primarily a problem of 'deficit', with a consequent emphasis on remediation. The emergence of special schools shifted the emphasis to a developmental one which, none the less, in seeking to promote progress in accordance with developmental stages, often failed to identify unusual strengths or to become sufficiently prospective to the needs of the adult world.

A good example of the habilitation strategy may be found in 'goal planning' (Houts and Scott, 1975), in which the instructor draws up two lists, one of the client's strengths and the other of the client's needs. After a training goal has been selected from the needs list, a programme is devised to achieve this, using any item(s) appearing on the strengths list as a lever. A particular advantage of the habilitation approach is its ability to identify 'functional' objectives, knowledge and skills needed in particular environments, including those of the 'next environment' (Marlett, 1984) for which the individual is being prepared.

Another example of an attempt to facilitate building upon strengths is the suggestion that staff using the Scale for Assessing Coping Skills (SACS) (Whelan and Speake, 1979) for the purpose of selecting a training objective should choose an item ticked under the heading 'can do, but only with help', rather than one ticked under the heading 'cannot yet do' in order to be more likely to achieve some discernible progress. This is important for staff morale, particularly in the case of a new and relatively inexperienced member of staff. Indeed, for this reason, Houts and Scott recommend that a selected goal should be capable of being achieved in no more than one week.

In conclusion, it can be seen that the habilitation approach is capable of sustaining a positive expectation of progress on the part of both client and staff while enabling the person's individuality to be realized in terms of specific strengths rather than limitations. From this positive standpoint it can subsume other supportive medical and care philosophies should they be found to be applicable to certain individuals at certain times in their lives. The prospective nature of the philosophy enables it to respond more flexibly to changes in the functional requirements of new and more demanding environments.

THE TECHNOLOGY OF HABILITATION

There can be no doubt, in the light of research during the past decade, that the technology available for teaching mentally handicapped people is very powerful. In his comprehensive review of the literature on vocational evaluation and training, Gold (1973a) emphasized the contrast which exists between the potential of retarded adults to respond to strong training methods and the inadequate opportunities which they receive as a result of low levels of expectation of them. As a culmination of several years of fruitful research, Gold (1978) demonstrated the effectiveness of some of these techniques in a way which enabled many practitioners to learn of them by his film *Try Another Way* and its associated publications. During the same period, Bellamy (1976) and his colleagues carried out a programme of parallel research in Oregon, exploring factors which influence work rates as well as reporting many examples of achieved competence on complex tasks following the use of behavioural techniques of training coupled with due regard for the work environment.

The demonstration by Bellamy *et al.* (1975) that severely and profoundly retarded adults could achieve standard rates of production was confirmed by Tomlinson and Whelan (1978), using time allowances derived from both factory rates and the application of a predetermined motion–time system, MTM, widely used in industry. In a series of related experiments, Tomlinson (1976) showed the feasibility of teaching complex industrial tasks to groups of up to ten mentally handicapped adults in a time comparable to one-to-one teaching. She also demonstrated the potential applications of 'peer-group' or 'pyramid' teaching, of teaching involving videotape presentation, and the value of programmed pictorial presentation as an almost errorless teaching technique. An excellent review of vocational habilitation curriculum and technology is provided by Wehman and McLaughlin (1980).

A very important parallel set of studies concerned with the acquisition of self-help and interpersonal skills was conducted by others throughout this period, for example by Clark *et al.* (1968), Eaton and Brown (1974), and Elias-Burger *et al.* (1981). These served to demonstrate that, where tasks could be defined as a series of steps, the same technology as used with vocational tasks may be applied and that, where this is not so, additional techniques, such as role-play, modelling and behaviour rehearsal may be used effectively.

The ability of mentally handicapped adults to respond to systematic teaching in the area of 'social education', as reported by Gunzburg (1974), is fully supported by these other studies. Indeed, some of the emerging concepts from this work, such as 'acquiescence' (Rosen *et al.*, 1974/1975; Shaw and Budd, 1982) and 'helplessness' (Floor and Rosen, 1975) serve to underline the consequences of prolonged dependency on others, itself a result of prevailing underexpectation and its relation, overprotection.

Perhaps the most important factor to counter this has been the growth of self-advocacy (Schaaf *et al.*, 1977; Crawley, 1980, 1983; Williams and Shoultz, 1982; Herr, 1983), and the apparent greater readiness of professionals to listen to what handicapped or disabled people want (see also Chapter 19). Sometimes this can be achieved by interview (e.g. Birenbaum and Seiffer, 1976; Reiter and Whelan, 1976; Schlesinger and Whelan, 1979), although there are often considerable difficulties in eliciting responses by this method. Sigelman *et al.* (1982) explored alternative approaches, particularly the substitution of open-ended questions by multichoice ones (sometimes accompanied by pictures) in order to achieve valid responses. Sometimes, special tools have been produced to help individuals to express choices or opinions (e.g. Parnicky *et al.*, 1971; Whelan and Reiter, 1980; Whelan and Speake, 1980).

One certain outcome of listening to handicapped or disabled individuals is the discovery that they do not want always to remain on the receiving end of services. They wish to make a contribution, particularly to be of help to others. When given an opportunity, for example, to indicate relative strength of preference among eleven job domains on the Illustrated Vocational Inventory (Whelan and Reiter, 1980), the most popular choice among females was 'patient care' and among males was 'horticulture', both choices involving dependent living things. The BBC reported that the most popular of their twenty programmes in the series 'Let's Go', specifically produced for mentally handicapped viewers, was the programme 'Let's Go and Lend a Hand'.

Many opportunities present themselves for mentally handicapped adults to experience being of service to others, and habilitation programmes should seek to take full advantage of these, creating such opportunities where necessary. An excellent example, involving the identification of individual strengths, was provided by the study by Hayes-Light (1983). In this, a small group of mentally handicapped men and women, having performed exceptionally well on a specially designed Creative Abilities Test (CAT), were given the opportunity to operate as a 'design team'. They visited a school for physically handicapped children and, in consultation with teachers, responded to the difficulties of selected individual children by designing appropriate aids which they proceeded to manufacture first in a prototype and then in a final form. This study is notable also for the finding that some mentally handicapped individuals had exhibited performances on the test elements of the CAT which were far superior to those achieved by nonhandicapped adolescents, including some attending sixth form college.

In addition to their wish to be of service, many mentally handicapped adults also wish for the chance to show that they can respond to a challenge. This may, in part, explain the popularity of, and the growing participation in, the Special Olympics. In the work setting, Gold (1973b), in an experiment involving a fourteen-piece bicycle brake assembly, showed that production figures soared and errors decreased over a ten-day period under conditions which excluded external rewards. Indeed, those who chose to undertake the task did so instead of a simple repetitive paid alternative. Gold attributed the finding to the intrinsic satisfaction derived from completion of a complex task and stated that this has implications for traditionally held views about the necessity of external reinforcers, as used by operant trainers, for example. This insight into the needs of retarded individuals, together with the powerful technology which unlocked individual skills, enabling many to experience the dignity of real and often complex work, should stand as a fitting epitaph to the memory of that great researcher.

THE TECHNOLOGY NEEDS TO BE APPLIED

Although research and demonstration projects have shown what is *feasible*, a major task facing those engaged in the habilitation of mentally handicapped adults must be to close the wide gap which exists between research and practice. Unfortunately, the most effective technologies for teaching and training have so far been applied to only a small fraction of those who could benefit from them. In part, this may be a consequence of the relatively low proportion of national budgets spent on supporting such applications research compared with the large sums spent actually providing services.

Serious misgivings are now being expressed by parents at the discovery that relatively few places exist in further education colleges or other forms of continuing education. Moreover, many local authorities offer day centre places which fail to reflect the advances in knowledge which have been made concerning the continued potential of mentally handicapped adults to respond to systematic teaching/training (see also Chapters 17 and 19).

The research fraternity has become increasingly aware and concerned that a large gulf still exists between research and practice. This was the theme of the Fourth Congress of the International Association for the Scientific Study of Mental Deficiency (IASSMD) (Mittler, 1977a) at which, in concluding his presidential address, Clarke (1977) urged that: 'more of us must be involved in seeing that our discoveries are field tested and applied. If we do not, who will?' It should be recalled that much of the knowledge of what can be achieved by mentally handicapped people, given systematic teaching, was learned from research with adults (rather than with children) using selected work tasks which established that they could contribute substantially to their financial independence. This is a further reason why it would be inappropriate to withhold from adults the best that is now available in effective teaching technologies.

An indication of the *scope* for applying effective habilitation technology was provided by the results of the National Survey of Adult Training Centres (Whelan and Speake, 1977). Table 18.1, based on the responses of 305 adult training centres (ATCs), provides data on the abilities of over 24,000 trainees.

TABLE 18.1   Summary of educational and social attainments of 24,251 trainees in ATCs

	Able	Not able	Not known
		(percentages rounded)	
Talks in sentences	69	14	17
Counting and measuring	38	41	21
Reading	26	53	21
Recognition of colours	59	20	21
Telling time	34	43	23
Use of money, including budgeting	28	54	18
Use of telephone	23	55	22
Writing	29	48	23
Signature	41	37	22
Public transport	28	50	22
Post Office procedures	21	53	26
Prepares basic meals, including shopping	24	51	26
Personal hygiene	52	23	26
Health hazards	28	38	34
Honesty	53	11	37
Normal courtesies	62	12	26
Use of medical, dental, social services	17	49	34
Sexual responsibility	19	28	54
Could live on own	6	63	31
Can take own medicine	18	46	36

Source: from the *National Survey of Adult Training Centres* (Whelan and Speake, 1977).

The very high percentages of 'not known' responses shows the extent to which assessment needs to be carried out in the centres.

In a more recent study, the same researchers (Whelan and Speake, 1983) present the results of the application by staff of the Scale for Assessing Coping Skills to over 1500 trainees. In addition to providing more reliable data on attainments, this tool enabled staff to indicate the extent to which these were actually being used. Once again, it was found that many trainees lack precisely those skills which are most needed for independent functioning in the community (eg. shopping, use of transport), while many others have not yet even been assessed in those areas.

The national survey highlighted the need for a massive increase in the throughput achieved by ATCs. The population, though relatively young (74 per cent below the age of thirty-five years), was almost static. In addition to the problems of staff shortages and a generally inadequate proportion of relevantly trained staff, a major reason for the low attainments of trainees seemed to be insufficient application of systematic teaching and a reliance instead on teaching 'as the opportunity arose'. The survey also highlighted the shortage of adequate records, particularly of those transferred from special school. If there was to be a pro-active approach to the development of habilitation programmes (Bernstein *et al.*, 1981) then it was necessary for a partnership to be formed between the special schools and the adult centres in which a further assessment of the attainments of school leavers would be carried out. The value of this to the schools themselves, in obtaining information about the success of their programmes, had been illustrated earlier by Marshall (1967).

When invited to indicate the obstacles which they perceived as standing in the way of an increased application of habilitation technology, ATC staff perceived the greatest problems to be the lack of suitable placements beyond the centre for trainees, poor staff-to-trainee ratios, and inadequate opportunities for staff training, for attending conferences, or for participation in research. Their perceptions were in accord with those of the researchers made some ten years earlier. Thus it is appropriate to give some consideration to alternative strategies for applying research to practice. This is then followed by a description of the strategy adopted by the Habilitation Technology Project, the products of which are described later.

VARIOUS STRATEGIES FOR APPLYING RESEARCH TO PRACTICE

There have been numerous attempts to make practitioners aware of the powerful habilitation technology which is now available and to encourage them to use it in their day-to-day work. There continues to be scope for new approaches, including combined strategies, and it is considered that this presents one of the greatest challenges of the present decade. The problems are complex and some papers have been written about them (for example, Brown, 1972; Mittler, 1977b; Whelan, 1980). A brief summary of the types of approach is given here together with some of the conclusions which may be drawn:

Improving written communication

Recent years have seen the appearance of a number of practitioner-orientated journals which invite contributions from both researchers and practitioners written in a plain jargon-free style. There is some evidence, however, that front-line staff prefer to learn about new concepts by demonstration rather than by reading about them (Hall, 1974), and that many staff do not have access even to practitioner journals (Whelan and Speake, 1977).

Improving spoken communication

Several new umbrella organizations have been established to promote meetings, conferences, forums and workshops at which researchers and practitioners can meet face to face and exchange ideas. While these, particularly the short specialized workshops, are often highly acclaimed, only a relatively small proportion of those for whom they are designed are able to attend and a 'conference-going' élite sometimes emerges.

Demonstrations in field settings

These serve the useful purpose of raising awareness and often the level of expectation of what can be achieved, and they are usually welcomed by practitioners as more valid than work carried out in 'laboratory' settings. The value of any demonstration is likely to be increased if it includes an opportunity for the practitioner to try out the new technique himself and to gain confidence in its application. However, the short duration of many site visits, and lack of opportunities to change prevailing management practices, often means that the interest and enthusiasm engendered in practitioners during the visit soon dissipates under the pressure of a return to normal daily routines.

Model or demonstration facilities

Perhaps the most ambitious attempts to create an interface between research activity and service provision have been the mental retardation centres in the USA. As university-affiliated facilities, in most cases, they interface also with the process of professional training across a range of disciplines relevant to mental retardation and developmental disability. They have provided powerful demonstrations of what may be achieved and often have 'outreach' projects in a variety of community settings. The main problem associated with most demonstration projects of this type is that of translating what is feasible within typical local agencies which usually enjoy far less resources.

Direct training of practitioners

While perhaps the most important single means of increasing the knowledge and skills of individual practitioners, it is clear that such training *by itself* is not sufficient to have a major impact upon the adoption of the habilitation philosophy and technology within the field. Newly qualified members of staff usually have low status and are produced at a rate which may reduce the impact of new ideas or attitudes. Indeed, there is evidence (Klaber, 1971) that such individuals may quickly be absorbed by the prevailing *Zeitgeist* of the organization.

Based on the experience of these various approaches, five criteria are proposed for improving future success:

1. In selecting their research objectives, researchers should take some account of practical problems and priority issues identified by practitioners.
2. The results of ensuing research should be communicated in clear and unambiguous language and possible applications should be jointly explored.

3. Researchers should provide practical demonstrations where possible within the field setting of the applications concerned.
4. Practitioners themselves should try out the applications, under guidance where necessary.
5. Having established the usefulness and feasibility of the applications, the researcher and practitioner should jointly co-operate with local management in procuring agreements and any necessary organizational changes to enable the application to continue into long-term practice.

THE HABILITATION TECHNOLOGY PROJECT (HTP)

The methodology of the HTP is briefly described here as an example of 'research to practice', within the habilitation philosophy. Its methodology took account of the five criteria outlined and consisted essentially of a *partnership* between researcher and practitioner working to ensure that the outcomes of this partnership would be durable and built into long-term practice.

The project provided an opportunity for innovation and it was considered that this could be achieved methodologically by a combination of 'action research' with 'lattice theory'.

Action research commences with the establishment of an action research group (Cunningham, 1976). This should include representatives of the particular service or organization concerned who are able to identify issues of common concern, to set agreed objectives, and to produce and evaluate pilot solutions. This process may consist of the sharing of good ideas (building upon strengths) in addition to the identification of problems (expressed as needs). In order to organize the work of the action research group, in terms of both content and sequencing of its activities, a programme methodology lattice was designed.

Lattice theory was clearly described, in an early application to mental retardation by Budde and Menolascino (1971), as:

a network of interrelated and interdependent elements or components which are graphically illustrated by cells, containing verbal description. These cells are ranged sequentially left to right and bottom to top, so that they provide a flow and hierarchical structure leading to the attainment of a major objective.

The lattice is presented elsewhere (Whelan, 1980), but its agreed goal, formulated by the action research group, was 'a comprehensive set of habilitation packages available, thoroughly evaluated, and in use in the field by practitioners'. The 'habilitation packages' represent the tangible end products of the partnership and refer to agreed content, resource materials and techniques, to be built into long-term habilitation practice.

The action research group consisted of ten managers of adult training centres, all of whom were elected by colleagues to represent their local authority area. The group met once a month with the research team over a period of five years, becoming highly skilled in the specification of operational objectives (related to the habilitation of trainees) and contributing to the design of pilot solutions to these (teaching packages).

Within each local authority area, a number of voluntary 'field trials' centres assisted the action research group by carrying out an independent application of the teaching packages with trainees selected on the basis of assessment. In addition to the completion of an evaluation questionnaire, record forms were completed recording the response of individual trainees to exposure to the packages. These data enabled the action research group to make decisions concerning the readiness of individual packages for wider distribution or to identify specific ways in which improvements were needed.

It may be seen that the overall process in which researchers and practitioners were engaged could be likened to that of 'creative problem-solving' described by Treffinger (1983) as consisting of: fact finding, problem finding, idea finding, solution finding and acceptance finding. Certainly, all taking part valued this experience of teamwork and the results achieved, and felt that this same strategy could be extended to other areas of concern.

To enable the results of the HTP to be easily recognized, the resulting habilitation materials were named the 'Copewell System'. This is briefly described below.

THE COPEWELL SYSTEM

Following a pooling of perceived priorities for training, it was decided at an early stage in the meetings of the action research group that the first step should be the development of a comprehensive habilitation curriculum. Some of the influences upon curriculum content had been identified previously (Whelan, 1976) and a review of the content of social education programmes had also been completed (Speake and Whelan, 1977). These were available as background materials, together with other relevant publications (e.g. Bender and Valletuti, 1976).

Each objective within the curriculum would then become the topic of a teaching package and the overall system would also incorporate criterion-referenced assessment and forms for recording individual response to training.

The content of the 'Copewell Curriculum' is presented in Table 18.2, and this is followed by a brief description of the *format* which is common to the associated teaching packages. Table 18.2 shows that there is a total of 174 objectives, distributed over the four sections of the curriculum. Within each section, areas are defined and these are broken down into specific objectives. The latter are identified by a decimal component within the particular area, so that any additional objectives may be added within that area without having to renumber the whole curriculum.

For easy reference, each objective is printed on a separate card, in one of four colours (depending upon its section), and these are held in a file box easily accessible to staff. In the individual's records, therefore, it is possible to denote his/her current training objectives (and thus the teaching packages through

TABLE 18.2   Contents of the Copewell Curriculum

Self-help. The basic skills that an individual must acquire in order to care for and maintain him/herself both at home and in the community. These also include skills which allow a person to seek out and use community resources.

Self-help

1.   *Hygiene*
1.1   Washing hands
1.2   Washing face, neck and ears
1.3   Bathing
1.4   Taking a shower
1.5   Washing feet
1.6   Washing and drying hair
1.7   Cleaning teeth
1.8   Use of toilet (domestic)
1.9   Use of toilet (public)
1.10 Menstrual hygiene
1.11 Washing clothes (by hand)
1.12 Washing clothes (by machine)
1.13 Using a launderette

2.   *Dress*
2.1   Selection of clothing
2.2   Dressing (male)
2.3   Dressing (female)
2.4   Undressing (male)
2.5   Undressing (female)

3.   *Appearance*
3.1   Hair grooming
3.2   Shaving (males) using a dry razor
3.3   Shaving (males) using a wet razor
3.4   Shaving (females)
3.5   Care of nails – hands and feet
3.6   Use of make-up
3.7   Posture
3.8   Use of iron
3.9   Repair of clothing
3.10 Awareness of fashion and accessories

4.   *First aid/health*
4.1   Handling emergencies

4.2   Dealing with simple injuries
4.3   Dealing with minor ailments
4.4   Use of, and co-operation with, medical services
4.5   Recognition of health hazards
4.6   Recognition of physical danger
4.7   Correct use and storage of noxious substances
4.8   Attention to balanced diet and weight
4.9   Sensible use of intoxicants

5.   *Domestic skills*
5.1   Preparation of shopping list
5.2   Storage of food and drink
5.3   Use of utensils/gadgets for food preparation
5.4   Preparation of cold drinks
5.5   Preparation of hot drinks
5.6   Preparation of simple snacks (no cooking required)
5.7   Using a cooker
5.8   Preparation of simple snacks (involving cooking)
5.9   Preparing a typical meal (not requiring a recipe)
5.10 Setting a table
5.11 Use of correct cutlery
5.12 Acceptable table habits
5.13 Clearing a table
5.14 Washing up
5.15 Changing and making the bed
5.16 Simple housework
5.17 Use of electrical equipment in the home
5.18 Maintenance of home environment

TABLE 18.2 cont.

6. *Community skills*
6.1 Road safety
6.2 Knowledge of neighbourhood
6.3 Recognition of function of different types of shop
6.4 Shopping
6.5 Use of bus
6.6 Use of rail services
6.7 Use of hire services for transport
6.8 Recognition of function of different types of community services and amenities
6.9 Use of post office
6.10 Use of bank
6.11 Use of community amenities
6.12 Use of café or restaurant (self-service)
6.13 Use of café or restaurant (waiter service)
6.14 Seeking help or advice

7. *Leisure*
7.1 Use of leisure in the home
7.2 Knowledge of local leisure facilities
7.3 Use of local leisure facilities
7.4 Club membership

Social academic. Aspects of the more traditional educational or academic skills, geared to functioning in the community.

Social academic

8. *Communication*
8.1 Communication by signs or symbols
8.2 Speech production
8.3 Linguistic ability
8.4 Conversational ability
8.5 Expression of feelings
8.6 Expression of opinions
8.7 Discussion of current affairs

9. *Numeracy*
9.1 Pre-numeracy skills
9.2 Number recognition and printing
9.3 Counting
9.4 Measuring
9.5 Weighing
9.6 Addition
9.7 Subtraction
9.8 Multiplication
9.9 Division

10. *Literacy*
10.1 Pre-literacy skills
10.2 Recognition of alphabet
10.3 Recognition of useful words
10.4 Functional reading
10.5 Reading for pleasure and interest

11. *Writing*
11.1 Pre-writing skills
11.2 Printing own name
11.3 Printing address
11.4 Printing the alphabet
11.5 Signature
11.6 Completing simple forms
11.7 Writing from dictation
11.8 Writing messages
11.9 Creative writing

12. *Money*
12.1 Recognition of coins
12.2 Recognition of notes
12.3 Knowledge of monetary values
12.4 Knowledge of coin and note equivalence
12.5 Money (spending, and checking change)

TABLE 18.2 cont.

12.6 Understanding a budget
12.7 Following a budget
12.8 Saving

13. *Time*
13.1 Telling the time
13.2 Association of time with events
13.3 Estimation of time intervals
13.4 Knowledge of calendar

14. *Telephone*
14.1 Using domestic telephone
14.2 Using public telephone

15. *Colour*
15.1 Colour discrimination and matching
15.2 Colour identification
15.3 Use of colour

Interpersonal. Those skills which enable a person to enter into meaningful and fulfilling relationships with individuals or groups in the community.

Interpersonal

16. *Bodily awareness*
16.1 Knowledge of body parts (male)
16.2 Knowledge of body parts (female)
16.3 Knowledge of body measurements and clothing sizes (male)
16.4 Knowledge of body measurements and clothing sizes (female)
16.5 Sexual knowledge

17. *Personal knowledge*
17.1 Knowledge of personal details
17.2 Role awareness
17.3 Self-esteem and aspirations

18. *Social interaction skills*
18.1 Greeting behaviour

18.2 Good manners
18.3 Spatial behaviour
18.4 Visual contact
18.5 Bodily contact
18.6 Facial expression
18.7 Awareness of, and response to, feelings of others
18.8 Friendship

19. *Social responsibility*
19.1 Knowledge of socially acceptable behaviour
19.2 Knowledge of sexual behaviour
19.3 Helping others
19.4 Knowledge of law-abiding behaviour
19.5 Moral judgement
19.6 Discrimination between situations.

Vocational. The work-related skills, habits and attitudes which are critical to successful adjustment to work.

Vocational

20. *Work skills*
20.1 Work terms
20.2 Knowledge of tools
20.3 Understanding instructions

20.4 Discrimination skills
20.5 Quality and accuracy
20.6 Memory
20.7 Co-ordination

TABLE 18.2 cont.

20.8	Dexterity	23.2	Adaptability
20.9	Speed	23.3	Response to pressure
20.10	Use of basic tools and machinery	24.	*Work independence*
		24.1	Concentration
21.	*Work habits*	24.2	Work without supervision
21.1	Time keeping	24.3	Decision-making
21.2	Safety	24.4	Exercise of foresight and initiative
21.3	Clothing at work		
21.4	Adherence to rules and regulations	24.5	Problem-solving and originality
21.5	Care of tools	24.6	Leadership
21.6	Consistency of performance	25.	*Job seeking*
22.	*Work relationships*	25.1	Vocational exploration
22.1	Response to authority	25.2	Job-seeking procedures
22.2	Response to criticism	25.3	Completion of job application forms
22.3	Relations with co-workers		
23.	*Work attitudes*	25.4	Behaviour at interview
23.1	Job satisfaction		

which he/she is working) using only the number of the objectives concerned. Although assigned to particular groups, objectives are often closely related between sections. Certain work-related interpersonal skills, for example, appear in the vocational section and it is recognized that failures in adjustment are likely to be related more frequently to inadequate self-help and interpersonal skills than to work skills *per se* (Cohen, 1961). Other important themes, such as recreation and leisure (Beck *et al.*, 1977), are covered by numerous objectives throughout the curriculum, rather than by a separate section.

The format of teaching packages

The teaching packages within the Copewell System are intended to act as structured resource material to be used by practitioners. While offering teaching suggestions and often providing visual material, they are not as detailed as certain 'scripted' systems (e.g. DISTAR) and users are *encouraged* to supplement and adapt the materials according to the needs of their own situation and in the interests of their own job satisfaction.

All packages conform to a *standard format*, containing the same six headings. These headings, with a brief description, are:

Objective

This restates the objective which appears on the curriculum card; it states what the student will be able to do upon successful completion of the package.

Prerequisite knowledge and skills

In this section, there is a two-column format: the left-hand column lists the prerequisite knowledge and skills and the right-hand column, headed 'relevant packages', lists the packages by the number and name which cover these knowledge and skills. Under this heading, packages are linked to each other, where appropriate, in a logical sequence. Experience in use, together with suggestions from elsewhere concerning the sequencing of skills (for example, Allen and Cortazzo, 1970), as well as a knowledge of the functional requirements of a particular environment, may enable a more appropriate selection to be made of the next objective(s) to be taught.

Preparation

This section provides notes of guidance enabling the user, before applying a package, to collect the necessary resources, consider the vocabulary to be used while teaching, and to become familiar in advance with the task analysis and/or exercises outlined within the package. The user is encouraged to supplement the pictures provided with other visual material, as some studies have indicated the importance of the visual modality in mentally handicapped people (for example, Holden and Corrigan, 1983).

Application of the teaching package

This section consists of a number of suggested teaching sessions, including teaching methods and the use of resource materials provided within the package and by the user. In general, sessions involve groups of up to six people, in twenty-minute periods. Both 'teacher activity' and 'student activity' are suggested, including group participation in the student's review of his/her performance. Group-based training appears to be more successful in helping individuals to develop personal responsibility for their success or failure at a task (Zoeller *et al.*, 1983). During the 'self-evaluation', the student's record form is completed by the staff member, as this is more reliable and more convenient than having to complete records later. A repertoire of teaching techniques, e.g. modelling (Stephan *et al.*, 1973), is suggested to provide variety and maintain interest levels across the teaching sessions.

Reviewing and recording students' progress

Under this heading, suggestions are given concerning the best use of the individual record forms for recording progress, from the pre-test session through to the follow-up session. Criterion levels of performance are suggested and forms are suitable for individual filing.

Creating opportunities for student(s) to apply knowledge and skills

This section suggests activities or assignments to be carried out *as part of the training* to ensure that transfer and generalization of skills to different settings and individuals are achieved. These important considerations continue to receive attention in the research literature (for example, Matson, 1981; Borkowski and Varnhagen, 1984).

'Probes' must be built into the overall teaching plan, involving observing the individual in other settings, in order to ensure that transfer of skills is taking place. Similarly, care must be taken that any extraordinary techniques used in teaching (for example, verbalized self-instruction) have been success- fully faded out in order that the resulting behaviour blends appropriately into normal activities.

The format of the teaching packages, described above, has evolved during field-trials evaluation and it has been found acceptable to staff, who report that it fits in satisfactorily with the staffing and organizational framework of the ATC. The format can be seen to be similar to that evolved by other workers (e.g. Matson and Andrasik, 1982). In addition, packages evaluated within the self-help section were shown to be effective as a teaching strategy, as indicated in Fig. 18.1 in which the three 'error-reduction' curves show the mean rate of learning (each based on ten different ATC trainees) of three skills relevant to independent functioning in the community. Of particular interest is the large improvement observed between the pre-test (which was not preceded by any demonstration) and the first teaching trial. This finding was common to most individual performances on most packages evaluated. The discontinuity occurring typically between trials 5 and 8 during the acquisition of these sequential skills is also of interest, possibly representing a consolidation phase or a change in response strategy (Whelan and Speake, 1983).

In a broad sense, the Habilitation Technology Project has demonstrated both the ability and the willingness of staff in ATCs to use structured teaching methods and to keep systematic records which can enable them to discover for themselves whether their teaching is proving effective. One surprising outcome was the wish by several members to use even more detailed methods of recording, including, for example, inserting a code letter to denote the form of their intervention.

In addition to producing a large quantity and range of teaching materials, the HTP has enabled practitioners to discover the feasibility of teaching certain objectives to a small group which was previously thought to require one-to-one teaching and thus frequently omitted from programmes. They have discovered that methods are available for teaching more difficult, for example interpersonal, skills (e.g. using role-play and behaviour re- hearsal) where it is not appropriate to follow a sequential task analysis. A closer involvement of the learner in the overall process, and in selecting future goals, has been linked to providing opportunities for him/her to con- solidate newly acquired knowledge/skills by contributing to the teaching of others.

The project provided the opportunity to study the effectiveness of certain teaching techniques (e.g. the use of anticipation) and, from an analysis of the relative frequency with which different types of learning difficulty were encountered (e.g. discriminations compared with manipulations), staff began

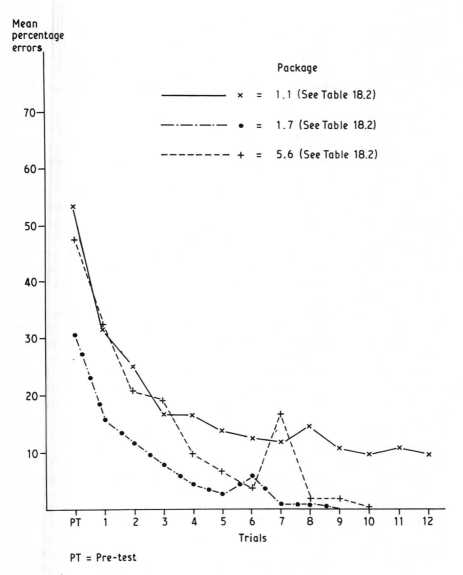

FIGURE 18.1   Sample learning curves, based on mean percentage rates

to identify 'core' skills common to many activities. The higher percentage of errors made at 'decision points', for example, considered in the light of other studies (e.g. Spradlin and Saunders, 1984) suggests that the development of decision-making skills should come early in the sequence of packages undertaken. When combined with the selection of objectives dealing with knowledge and skills important to certain environments (e.g. Foss and Peterson, 1981; Isett *et al.*, 1983), it may be seen that the identification of 'core' skills should make the habilitation process more efficient.

One of the difficulties of identifying critical skills relevant to successful functioning at different ecological levels is the absence of normative guidelines for much of the behaviour concerned. Many of the interpersonal skills, for example, learned 'incidentally' by normal youngsters (and not forming any part of any formal school curriculum) are not spontaneously learned by mentally handicapped people. In selecting such ability areas for structured teaching (e.g. appropriate personal space during a conversation), staff need to develop skills of observation, to take some account of the methods used by ethologists in describing behaviour patterns, and at the same time to make appropriate allowances for individual differences when teaching what is acceptable to others.

A useful concept to emerge from consideration of the most effective use of limited staff resources has been that of 'marginality', in which a series of boundaries, or margins, is defined, possibly corresponding to the different skill levels necessary for an individual to operate successfully within increasingly independent living situations. Staff could then 'target' specific objectives to be taught to different individuals whose current ability placed them close to *several* boundaries, thereby enabling individuals over a wide range of attainment to experience some movement upwards.

One attempt to produce a taxonomy of skills related to different levels of independent functioning in living and working was reported in *Getting to Work* (Whelan and Speake, 1981). The residential component was subsequently examined by Strickland (1983) who reported on the different attainments (as measured by the Scale for Assessing Coping Skills (SACS)) of individuals currently living in local authority hostels, group homes, sheltered housing, landlady schemes and in private tenancies. The results are sufficiently encouraging to indicate that a more extensive study along these lines should be carried out. It is already apparent that, provided their interpersonal behaviour is acceptable, approximately one in three of the individuals included in the study by Strickland have skill levels which would enable them to live at a more independent level than at present (by comparing their SACS score with the mean SACS score of individuals already functioning at a higher level). Several other studies may be seen to have relevance to future attempts to draw up skill levels needed for different environments and the 'margins' between these (Berkson, 1981; Thiel, 1981; Vitello *et al.*, 1983).

A NEW ROLE FOR THE ADULT TRAINING CENTRE

The groundwork for developing a new and more relevant role for the adult training centre was laid by the first national survey, cited on p. 687, the results of which were incorporated in *Pamphlet 5* (NDG, 1977). Although it is now considered by many that the unit size suggested in the *Pamphlet* was too large, and that insufficient emphasis was placed therein on the process of achieving 'throughput', none the less, the ingredients of a multidisciplinary team were clearly identified, with a core of specially trained and experienced staff operating as a resource to others.

This view of the role of the ATC as a 'focal point of expertise' for mentally handicapped adults living in the community should be seen in the context of suggestions made by the National Development Group (1976) for the establishment of 'Community Mental Handicap Teams' in which both National Health Service and local authority staff come together to act as a source of expert advice. In referring to the establishment of 'Community Units', providing a base for such activities, the National Development Group identified a need which the author believes could be readily met by the existing network of over 500 ATCs.

As mental handicap is a problem that greatly affects families, the service to be provided must be one in which there is a close working partnership with the family and, in the case of those trainees/students resident in local authority or health provision, the partnership must be with the staff of the residential establishment concerned. There is evidence of a significant shift in the readiness of staff of ATCs to work more closely with families and with 'external' professionals. In addition, a greater awareness on the part of such staff of the advantages of adopting certain more standardized practices, such as record systems, should facilitate greater inter-agency co-operation in the future. The climate is right for a change to a more dynamic service model.

As a result of enlightened policies, many mentally handicapped people who were formerly resident in large hospitals are now taking their place in the community. But so far, little has been done to educate the community about mental handicap and to prepare adequately for the absorption of such individuals. There is clearly an important place for ATC staff in community education but, if this is to be achieved, then new and more imaginative roles must be created. Essentially, the new service must make maximum use of the local community and neighbourhood as a resource for learning, and this may be achieved by a dramatic increase in the use of 'peripatetic' staff, operating from the centre as their base, but spending up to four-fifths of their time outside it, providing training and support for their clients and, particularly in relation to their overall knowledge of the individual and his needs, acting as a specialist resource to others (e.g. those providing occasional specialist medical services). In such a role, ATC staff may be seen to be acting as a 'named person', as described in the Warnock Report (1978), or as a 'key worker', in more recent terminology.

If efficient use is to be made of staff and material resources within the improved service, the latest technology must be fully utilized, including microcomputers (see Chapter 15), for filing and retrieving information, for rapid communications, and for improved decision-making concerning client needs and progress. In addition, there must be sound application of management and organizational knowledge in the interests of effective staff deployment and utilization (Olsen, 1968; Moore, 1974).

In addition to employing the powerful habilitation technology described earlier, more use should also be made of associated (e.g. industrial) technology. There are considerable advantages, for example, in the use of predetermined motion–time systems within the vocational training part of the programme, enabling skills acquisition and performance rates to be compared to the standards acceptable to employers (Grant *et al.*, 1973; Wilcock, 1983).

Perhaps the biggest change in the direction of services provided by the ATC/SEC should be in the higher level of *throughput* which is achieved. The low level (less than 10 per cent) reported in the national survey of ATCs was clearly a cause for low morale in some staff. Although it will not be possible for all, or perhaps even the majority of clients, to progress permanently beyond the centre to other form(s) of provision, a move from the static model to a dynamic one in which the centre becomes more a base for community and inter-agency programmes should partly overcome this problem. The goal of 'productivity' which formerly referred to the accumulation of finished goods on a Friday afternoon, while still being partly justified in the context of work-training programmes, should generally be redefined to connote objectively measurable degrees of personal development in the clients.

Some essential ingredients of an improved service to clients by the ATC/SEC may be listed as:

1. An effective staff team.
2. Availability of basic space and material resources.
3. Clear overall *agreed* aims.
4. A comprehensive programme – an overall curriculum.
5. Assessment tools for overall trainee assessment.
6. A timetabling system to provide teaching within programme areas.
7. Teaching packages (including pre-test and ongoing assessment methods).
8. A sytem of personal records on all trainees, standardized across centres.
9. Links with external supportive professionals/organizations.
10. Working links with families/residential staff.
11. A system for overall review of organization and programmes.
12. A suitable programme of staff development.

The Copewell System, described on pp. 696–704, through its curriculum, teaching materials and record forms, provides an example of one contribution to items (4), (5), (7) and (8) on the list. Thus considerable scope remains for the ATC and those responsible for its development to make provision for the other eight items on the list, in the absence of which input such as that provided by the Copewell System will be largely ineffective.

SUPPORT NEEDED BY PRACTITIONERS

If staff working with mentally handicapped adults are to respond appropriately to the challenges and privileges which this involves, they must acquire the necessary level of specialist skills for the work. The national survey of ATCs clearly showed the aspirations of the majority of staff to do so, to be provided with a two-year full-time course of specialist training and to be known as 'teacher-instructors'.

In addition to the arguments for such training which apply to the preparation of any other professional group (e.g. social workers, nurses, psychologists), an important consequence of providing training for staff working with mentally handicapped people is its effect on the level of expectation concerning what such individuals are capable of achieving (Grant, 1974). This is particularly relevant in view of the increasing challenges to be faced by staff as a result of the policy of providing more places in the community for mentally handicapped adults with additional special needs (profound and multiple handicap, often including severe behaviour disorder). The former one-year Diploma in the Training and Further Education of Mentally Handicapped Adults (DTMHA) included little on these topics, unlike the new two-year Certificate in the Further Education and Training of Mentally Handicapped People (Joint Consultative Group, 1980), which has been designed to replace it as a relevant specialist qualification alongside the more generic Certificate in Social Service which was its official successor.

A further consequence of providing an appropriate level of staff training is the confidence with which they are able to enter into interdisciplinary activities. A mutual respect and understanding of the different contributions made by related disciplines, including the acceptance of some areas of overlap, is crucial for establishing effective teamwork. These needs are also shared by staff working in local authority residential provision for mentally handicapped adults, the majority of whom have so far received no special training for their work (Strickland, 1983), although many have similar aspirations to adopt a more professional approach.

Practitioners have identified a need for a national level of support, in the form of approved guidelines, not merely support from local management. Suggestions have been made for the establishment of a regional advisory service to staff, similar to that which operates within the special education sector. In view of the earnest requests for external comment upon the quality of their work, there is some evidence that the introduction of an 'accreditation system' (possibly on a voluntary basis at first) would be welcomed by many.

As indicated on p. 693, the practitioner also needs the continued support of research activity which involves him and enables particular issues/problems to be subjected to the discipline, and benefit from the insights, of the large volume of research literature. The rewards of such a partnership to both the researcher and practitioner are only beginning to be realized.

One value of a link with the wider body of knowledge is its power to attenuate the effects of transitory and sometimes attractively packaged 'panaceas' which may fail to tackle the real issues or address the needs of mentally handicapped people and their families. At present, for example, many of those who claim to operate within a 'normalization philosophy' fail to recognize that this had its origins in 'deinstitutionalization' (Nirje, 1970), and that merely to provide mentally handicapped individuals with a normal environment and opportunities is to do them a *disservice* (Kleinberg and Galligan, 1983; Flynn, 1984). In an important contribution relating to the current recognition of the rights of mentally handicapped people to exercise choices (e.g. of friends) and express views concerning their future, Hendrix (1981) has pointed out several fallacies in the concept of normalization which often overlooks their needs and, in the case of some individuals, contravenes their own wishes.

CONCLUSIONS

There is good reason to believe that, if present opportunities are grasped and the obvious pitfalls avoided, a new and more responsive pattern of services to mentally handicapped people and their families will be developed. It is hoped that the habilitation philosophy will serve to guide practitioners and planners who must chart the most appropriate course forward through strong, sometimes opposing, currents. Improvements in the quality of health care and in the general standard of living in many countries have contributed to the almost normal life expectancy of most mentally handicapped people. Those at the ATC show an exceptionally high attendance record (over 98 per cent) and most are in good physical health. There are clearly good economic, as well as humane, reasons for enabling the large percentage of individuals who are capable and wish to be employed to do so. One estimate of the overall annual benefit of providing employment for approximately 12,700 ATC trainees was £63 million (if in sheltered employment) or £77 million (if in open employment). These were the numbers estimated to be capable of employment and the benefit is the result of adding savings made (especially the cost of an ATC place, unnecessary in such instances) to gross earnings in employment (Whelan and Speake, 1981).

There can be few parallels to the benefits expected from a change in outlook which recognizes the appropriateness of applying the habilitation philosophy, compared with the costs in both human and economic terms of preventing individuals from experiencing their right to growth and to make a contribution within our interdependent society.

REFERENCES

ALLEN, R. and CORTAZZO, A. (1970) *Psychosocial and Educational Aspects and Problems of Mental Retardation*, Springfield, Ill., C.C. Thomas.

BECK, V., POSSBERG, E. and BROWN, R.I. (1977) 'Recreation and leisure time as an integral part of rehabilitation programming for the mentally handicapped adult', *Research Exchange and Practice in Mental Retardation*, 3 (3), 153–68.

BELLAMY, G.T. (ed.) (1976) *Habilitation of the Severely and Profoundly Retarded: Reports from the Specialized Training Program*, Eugene, Center on Human Development, University of Oregon.

BELLAMY, G.T., PETERSON, L. and CLOSE, D. (1975) 'Habilitation of the severely and profoundly retarded: illustration of competence', *Educ. Train. Ment. Retard.*, 10, 174–86.

BENDER, M. and VALLETUTI, P.J. (1976) *Teaching the Moderately and Severely Handicapped Curriculum Objectives, Strategies and Activities*, vols I, II, III, Baltimore, University Park Press.

BERKSON, G. (1981) 'Social ecology of supervised communal facilities for mentally disabled adults: V. Residence as a predictor of social and work adjustment', *Amer. J. Ment. Defic.*, 86, 39–42.

BERNSTEIN, G.S., ZIARNIK, J.P., REDRUD, E.H. and CZAJKOWSKI, L.A. (1981) *Behavioural Habilitation through Proactive Programming*, Baltimore, Paul H. Brookes.

BIRENBAUM, A. and SEIFFER, S. (1976) *Resettling Retarded Adults in a Managed Community*, New York, Praeger.

BORKOWSKI, J.J. and VARNHAGEN, C. (1984) 'Transfer of learning strategies: contrasts of self-instructional and traditional training formats with EMR children', *Amer. J. Ment. Defic.*, 88, 369–79.

BRAND, J., SHAKESPEARE, R. and WOODS, G.E. (1969) 'Psychological development of the severely subnormal after 16 years of age', *Dev. Med. Child Neurol.*, 11 (6), 783–5.

BROWN, R.I. (1972) 'Research to practice', in *International Research Seminar on Vocational Rehabilitation of the Mentally Retarded*, Washington, DC, AAMD, Special Publication Series, no. 1.

BUDDE, J.F. and MENOLASCINO, F.J. (1971) 'Systems technology and retardation: applications to vocational habilitation', *Ment. Retard.*, 9, 11–16.

CLARK, G., KIVITZ, M. and ROSEN, M. (1968) *A Transitional Programme for Institutionalized Adult Retarded*, Elwyn, Pa., Elwyn Institute.

CLARKE, A.D.B. (1977) 'Presidential address', in P. MITTLER (ed.), *Research to Practice in Mental Retardation*, vol. I, Proceedings of the Fourth Congress of the International Association for the Scientific Study of Mental Deficiency, Baltimore, University Park Press.

COBB, H.V. (1969) *The Predictive Assessment of the Adult Retarded for Social and Vocational Adjustment*, Part 2, Vermillion, Psychology Department,

University of Dakota.

COHEN, J. (1961) 'An analysis of vocational failures of mental retardates placed in the community after a period of institutionalization', *Amer. J. Ment. Defic.*, 65, 371–5.

CRAWLEY, B. (1980) *Report of a Survey of Trainee-Committees in Adult Training Centres in England and Wales*, Manchester, Hester Adrian Research Centre, University of Manchester.

CRAWLEY, B. (1983) *Self-advocacy Manual: An Overview of the Development of Self-advocacy by Mentally Handicapped People and Recommendations for the Development of Trainee Committees*, Manchester, Hester Adrian Research Centre, Habilitation Technology Project, University of Manchester.

CUNNINGHAM, B. (1976) 'Action research: toward a procedural model', *Hum. Relat.*, 29 (3) 215–38.

DEPARTMENT OF HEALTH AND SOCIAL SECURITY (1980) *Adult Training Centres*, Circular LAC 80(2), London, HMSO.

EATON, P. and BROWN, R.I. (1974) 'The training of mealtime behaviour in the subnormal', *Brit. J. Ment. Subnorm.*, 20 (2), 78–85.

ELIAS-BURGER, S.F., SIGELMAN, C.K., DANLEY, W.E. and BURGER, D.L. (1981) 'Teaching interview skills to mentally retarded persons', *Amer. J. Ment. Defic.*, 85, 655–7.

FLOOR, L. and ROSEN, M. (1975) 'Investigating the phenomenon of helplessness in mentally retarded adults', *Amer. J. Ment. Defic.*, 79, 565–72.

FLYNN, M. (1984) 'Community backlash', *Parents Voice*, 34, 16–17.

FOSS, G. and PETERSON, S. (1981) 'Social-interpersonal skills relevant to job tenure for mentally retarded adults', *Ment. Retard.*, 19, 103–6.

GOLD, M.W. (1973a) 'Research on the vocational habilitation of the retarded: the present, the future', in N.R. ELLIS (ed.), *International Review of Research in Mental Retardation*, vol. 6, New York, Academic Press.

GOLD, M.W. (1973b) 'Factors affecting production by the retarded: base rate', *Ment. Retard.*, 11, 41–5.

GOLD, M. (1978) *Try Another Way*, training manual, National Institute of Mental Retardation, Austin, Marc Gold and Assoc.; *Try Another Way*, film series, National Film and Videotape Library.

GRANT, G.W.B. (1974) 'An examination of care patterns in subnormality hospitals with differing resource levels', unpublished PhD thesis, Manchester, Dept of Management Sciences, UMIST.

GRANT, G., MOORES, B. and WHELAN, E. (1973) 'Assessing the work needs and work performance of mentally handicapped adults', *Brit. J. Ment. Subnorm.*, 19, 71–9.

GUNZBURG, H.C. (1974) 'Further education for the mentally handicapped', in A.M. CLARKE and A.D.B. CLARKE (eds), *Mental Deficiency: The Changing Outlook*, 3rd edn, London, Methuen.

HALL, J. (1974) 'Survey of behaviour modification training in UK hospitals', paper given to IRMMH Action Workshop no.2, *Training and Reorgani-*

zation for Behaviour Modification in Hospital and Community Settings, held at the Ciba Foundation, London, 24–5 October 1974.

HAYES-LIGHT, J. (1983) 'Creativity and problem-solving in mentally handicapped adults', unpublished PhD thesis, Hester Adrian Research Centre, University of Manchester.

HENDRIX, E. (1981) 'The fallacies in the concept of normalization', *Ment. Retard.*, 19 (6), 295–6.

HERR, S.S. (1983) *Right and Advocacy for Retarded People*, Lexington, Lexington Books, D.C. Heath.

HOLDEN JR, E.A. and CORRIGAN, J.G. (1983) 'Decision-time measures of sequential processing by mentally retarded and nonretarded adolescents and MA-matched children', *Amer. J. Ment. Defic.*, 87, 640–8.

HOUTS, P. and SCOTT, R. (1975) *Goal Planning with Developmentally Disabled Persons*, Hershey, Pa., The Mitton Hershey Medical Center.

ISETT, R., ROSZKOWSKI, M., SPREAT, S. and REITER, S. (1983) 'Tolerance for deviance: subjective evaluation of the social validity of the focus of treatment in mental retardation', *Amer. J. Ment. Defic.*, 87, 458–61.

JOINT CONSULTATIVE GROUP (1980) *A New Specialist Training for Adult Training Centre Staff*, press conference held on 17 November, London.

KLABER, M.M. (1971) *Retardates in Residence: A Study of Institutions*, Hartford, Connecticut, University of Hartford.

KLEINBERG, J. and GALLIGAN, B. (1983) 'Effects of deinstitutionalization on adaptive behavior of mentally retarded adults', *Amer. J. Ment. Defic.*, 88, 21–7.

MARLETT, N. (1984) 'Development of assessment and training alternatives for dependent handicapped persons: implications of recent theory and research', paper given to the *Summer Workshop in Habilitation*, Winchester, King Alfred's College.

MARSHALL, A. (1967) *The Abilities and Attainments of Children Leaving Junior Training Centres*, London, National Association for Mental Health.

MATSON, J.L. (1981) 'Use of independence training to teach shopping skills to mildly mentally retarded adults', *Amer. J. Ment. Defic.*, 86, 178–83.

MATSON, J.L. and ANDRASIK, F. (1982) 'Training leisure-time social-interaction skills to mentally retarded adults', *Amer. J. Ment. Defic.*, 86, 542–53.

MITTLER, P. (ed.) (1977a) *Research to Practice in Mental Retardation*, vol. I, Proceedings of the Fourth Congress of the International Association for the Scientific Study of Mental Deficiency, Baltimore, University Park Press.

MITTLER, P. (1977b) 'Research workers as practitioners', in T. FRYERS and E. WHELAN (eds), *North-West Forum on Research in Mental Handicap*, Manchester, North-West Regional Health Authority.

MOORE, M. (1974) 'The measurement of differentiation: a study of the organizational processes and activities of a welfare service unit (Adult training centre)', unpublished MSc. thesis, Dept of Management Sciences, UMIST.

NATIONAL DEVELOPMENT GROUP (1976) *Mental Handicap: Planning Together*, London, HMSO.

NATIONAL DEVELOPMENT GROUP (1977) *Pamphlet No. 5: Day Services for Mentally Handicapped Adults*, London, HMSO.

NIRJE, B. (1970) 'The normalization principle – implications and comments', *J. Ment. Subnorm.*, 16 (2), no. 31, 62–70.

OLSEN, M. (1968) *The Process of Social Organization*, London, Holt, Rinehart & Winston.

PARMENTER, T.R. (1976) 'The vocational development of the learning disabled: implications for lifelong learning', *Austr. J. Ment. Retard.*, 4, 8–14.

PARNICKY, J.J., KAHN, H. and BURDETT, A.B. (1971) 'Standardization of the (VISA) Vocational Interest and Sophistication Assessment technique', *Amer. J. Ment. Defic.*, 75, 442–8.

REITER, S. and WHELAN, E. (1976) 'The needs of young mentally retarded adults', *Apex*, 3, 2022.

ROSEN, M., CLARK, G.R. and KIVITZ, M.S. (1977) *Habilitation of the Handicapped*, Baltimore, University Park Press.

ROSEN, M., FLOOR, L. and ZISFEIN, L. (1974/1975) 'Investigating the phenomenon of acquiescence in the mentally handicapped: I. Theoretical model, test development and normative data', *Brit. J. Ment. Subnorm.*, 20 (2), 58–68; 'II. Situational determinants', *Brit. J. Ment. Subnorm.*, 21 (1), 6–9.

SALAGARAS, S. and NETTELBECK, T. (1984) 'Adaptive behaviour of mentally retarded adults in work-preparation settings', *Amer. J. Ment. Defic.*, 88, 437–41.

SCHAAF, V., HOOTEN, T., SCHWARTZ, T., YOUNG, C., KERRON, J. and HEATH, D. (1977) 'People first: a self-help organization of the retarded', in J. WORTIS (ed.), *Mental Retardation and Developmental Disabilities*, vol. IX, New York, Brunner/Mazel.

SCHLESINGER, H. and WHELAN, E. (1979) *Industry and Effort: A Study of Work Centres in England, Wales and Northern Ireland for Severely Disabled Adults*, London, The Spastics Society in association with Heinemann Medical.

SHAW, J.A. and BUDD, E.C. (1982) 'Determinants of acquiescence and naysaying of mentally retarded persons', *Amer. J. Ment. Defic.*, 87, 108–10.

SIGELMAN, C.K., BUDD, E.L., WINER, J.L., SHOENROCK, C.J. and MARTIN, P.W. (1982) 'Evaluating alternative techniques of questioning mentally retarded persons', *Amer. J. Ment. Defic.*, 86, 511–18.

SPEAKE, B.R. and WHELAN, E. (1977) 'Social education: definition, content and organization', Appendix to *Report of Special Interest Conference for ATC Managers*, Cardiff, Welsh Office.

SPRADLIN, J.E. and SAUNDERS, R.R. (1984) 'Behaving appropriately in new situations: a stimulus class analysis', *Amer. J. Ment. Defic.*, 88, 574–9.

STEPHAN, C., STEPHANO, S. and TALKINGTON, L. (1973) 'Use of

modelling in survival skill training with educable mentally retarded', *Trg Sch. Bull.*, 70 (2), 63–8.

STRICKLAND, H.T. (1983) 'The attainments of mentally handicapped adults in different types and levels of residential accommodation', unpublished M Ed. thesis, University of Manchester.

THIEL, G.W. (1981) 'Relationship of IQ, adaptive behaviour, age, and environmental demand to community placement success of mentally retarded adults', *Amer. J. Ment. Defic.*, 86, 208–11.

TOMLINSON, E. (1976) 'Evaluating the relative effectiveness of different methods of developing the work skills of retarded adults', unpublished PhD thesis, Hester Adrian Research Centre, University of Manchester.

TOMLINSON, E. and WHELAN, E. (1978) 'Acquisition and performance difference between normal and mentally handicapped adults on a complex assembly task', *Brit. J. Psychol.*, 69, 385–91.

TREFFINGER, D.J. (1983) 'George's group: a creative problem-solving facilitation case-study', *J. Creative Behav.*, 17 (1), 39–48.

VITELLO, S.J., ATTHOWE, J.M. and CADWELL, J. (1983) 'Determinants of community placement of institutionalized mentally retarded persons', *Amer. J. Ment. Defic.*, 87, 539–45.

WARNOCK REPORT (1978) *Special Educational Needs: Report of the Committee of Enquiry into the Education of Handicapped Children and Young People*, London, HMSO.

WEHMAN, P. and MCLAUGHLIN, P.J. (1980) *Vocational Curriculum for Developmentally Disabled Persons*, Baltimore, University Park Press.

WHELAN, E. (1976) 'The needs of mentally handicapped adults: methods of developing a curriculum of training', in R.J. KEDNEY and E. WHELAN (eds), *Educating Mentally Handicapped Young Adults*, Bolton, College of Education (Technical).

WHELAN, E. (1980) 'Research to practice in mental handicap', taken from *Recent Developments in Special Education: Proceedings of the Professional Seminar in Special Education held at Macquarie University in 1979*, to commemorate the International Year of the Child, edited by James Ward and Sandra Bochner, Macquarie University Special Education Centre, August 1980, 264–77.

WHELAN, E. and REITER, S. (1980) *The Illustrated Vocational Inventory*, Manchester, Copewell Publications.

WHELAN, E. and SPEAKE, B. (1977) *Adult Training Centres in England and Wales: Report of the First National Survey*, Manchester, National Association of Teachers of the Mentally Handicapped.

WHELAN, E. and SPEAKE, B. (1979) *Learning to Cope*, London, Souvenir Press, Human Horizons Series.

WHELAN, E. and SPEAKE, B. (1980) *Me at Work*, Manchester, Copewell Publications.

WHELAN, E. and SPEAKE, B.R. (1981) *Getting to Work*, London, Souvenir Press, Human Horizons Series.

WHELAN, E. and SPEAKE, B. (1983) 'Final report to the DHSS on the Habilitation Technology Project', Manchester, Hester Adrian Research Centre, University of Manchester.

WILCOCK, R. (1983) 'Introducing MAST: a vocational assessment and man/job matching system', *International MTM Directorate Rehabilitation Project*, Sunderland Polytechnic.

WILLIAMS, P. and SHOULTZ, B. (1982) *We Can Speak for Ourselves*, London, Souvenir Press.

ZOELLER, C., MAHONEY, G. and WEINER, B. (1983) 'Effects of attribution training on the assembly task performance of mentally retarded adults', *Amer. J. Ment. Defic.*, 88, 109–12.

(*Note*: Edward Whelan is a director of Copewell Publications which publishes various assessment scales.)

Services: an international perspective

Peter Mittler and Robert Serpell

INTRODUCTION: SOME COMMON ELEMENTS IN INTERNATIONAL DEVELOPMENTS

Most people with intellectual disability* live in rural areas of the Third World. Very few receive any form of training or services designed to meet their needs. Of the small minority who live in Europe, North America and Australia, the majority attend schools, or receive some form of specialized, though not necessarily appropriate, service.

At first sight, such contrasts of scale seem to rule out any possibility of comparisons between richer and poorer nations. But closer examination of international trends makes it possible to discern some common features affecting all countries. These include a commitment to an attempt to provide for the needs of intellectually disabled people within their local communities, to mobilize local resources through working with families and community agencies, to develop better partnership and collaboration between voluntary organizations and professional groups, and to work through existing programmes of community development, including primary health care and universal primary education. In many countries, it is also possible to detect the beginning of an attempt to meet the unique needs of the handicapped person with some form of individual programme plan.

By and large in the Third World, intellectual disability has not been perceived as a problem, far less a priority deserving serious consideration. Compared with the struggle for sheer survival facing the population of many countries, and the overwhelming scale of poverty, malnutrition, inadequate sanitation and water supply, and the consequences of continuing infections and ill health, the problems of the disabled seem secondary.

Yet it is precisely because many countries are beginning to tackle these major challenges to survival that the problems of disability are becoming more prominent. For example, more disabled children, who would previously have died at a very early age, are now surviving as a direct consequence of improved health care, just as in western countries children with Down's syndrome now have a much longer life expectancy as a result of improvements in health care.

*See Note on Terminology on pp. 772–3 for an explanation of our choice of terminology.

The numbers who survive in Third World countries are probably still very small; for example, a community survey of handicapped children in a population of 6000 in Nigeria (Saunders, 1982; Fryers, 1984) failed to reveal a single child with Down's syndrome – certainly they are nowhere as common as in western countries, where they generally constitute about one-third of all intellectually disabled children living in community settings (Mittler and Preddy, 1981). Nevertheless, it is becoming apparent that measures taken to improve the health and economic well-being of the community will result in the survival of larger numbers of individuals who previously would have died at an early age, and hence in a demand for basic services.

On the other hand, a relatively higher proportion of children in Third World countries become disabled after a period of apparently normal development. Illnesses such as meningitis, viral encephalitis and measles are far more common and also more damaging if untreated. The effects of severe malnutrition, domestic accidents and injury (including nonaccidental injury) will also add to the numbers with a later onset of a disabling condition. These account for a comparatively smaller proportion of intellectually disabled children in richer nations.

The vast majority of the world's disabled people are already living (however uncomfortably) in the communities into which they were born. For them, the question is quite simply: will *any* significant services reach them during their lifetime? If they are to receive any services, this generation at least (and probably the next two generations likewise) will *have* to receive them in the community setting. As it happens, this may not be bad, since the experience of the rich, industrialized nations of the world with institutional care has been far from satisfactory.

In this sense, it may be said that Third World countries have an opportunity to avoid some of the worst mistakes made in the development of formal provision for the disabled over the past hundred years in Europe and North America. But this opportunity should not be mistaken as implying that Third World planners are in a position to impose an ideal 'blueprint' on to a 'blank slate'.

First, it is clear that in virtually every country a cadre of concerned professionals and committed volunteers has existed for some time, many of them experimenting on a small scale with voluntary services for one or more categories of disabled persons. Their moral commitment, specialized skills and local experience are invaluable resources for the development of effective services on a larger scale. National governments will be well advised to enlist their supportive participation in such efforts, even if this calls for protracted and difficult negotiations.

Second, each disabled client is already embedded in a network of family and neighbourhood relationships, the structure and dynamics of which arise from a complex of cultural traditions, community activities and personal needs. Conventionally the advocates of public services concentrate on the restrictive and/or understimulating aspects of these contextual factors, but they are also likely to include many instances of supportive care. The mobilization of local resources is more likely to generate long-term growth of community acceptance if official interventions seek to build on what is positive in the existing social system than if they are confined to direct confrontation with undesirable practices, or propose idealized solutions, as if in a vacuum. Popular participation in working out a development strategy is an essential step towards the acceptance of responsibility by local communities, especially those in impoverished, rural areas of the Third World (Korten, 1980).

THE PHILOSOPHICAL BASIS OF SERVICE PROVISION

What are the origins of the benevolent support which people with disabilities need to live in the community? In some societies, a more or less universal religion prescribes the giving of alms to the poor, while in others this behaviour is actively discouraged and begging in public is prohibited by the civil law. There is some evidence to suggest that certain small-scale subsistence societies have a cultural tradition of infanticide for all those visibly deformed, while in others the severely impaired individual is traditionally revered as a protégé of the gods (Edgerton, 1970). Not long ago, a leading western democracy was practising 'eugenic' sterilization of adults certified as mentally defective, and people are still alive to resent bitterly the effect that this policy has had on their lives (Edgerton, 1967; Edgerton *et al.*, 1984).

There are several ways of approaching the motivation for benevolent support. It may be regarded as spontaneously altruistic behaviour inspired by compassion for one's disadvantaged neighbour; as a religious duty; as a political obligation; or as a professional occupation sustained by a sense of vocation and by extrinsic rewards. From a less optimistic perspective, some analysts point to emotional and social rewards for the person rendering such support, such as feelings of power, fulfilment or righteousness. Then there is the unique situation of family members (including the person's parents, siblings and in some societies grandparents) who, by virtue of chance biological relationships, find themselves expected to develop a long-lasting social bond with a person with intellectual disabilities. Rose-Ackerman (1982) has provided a thoughtful and provocative analysis of the conflicts which may arise in this field among different principles, interests and political realities (see Chapter 1).

Social policy serves to legitimate some forms of support more than others. The western world has seen a shift of perspective over the past fifty years away from protecting society, through protecting the individual with intellectual disability, to enabling society to accommodate the person in its midst, and assisting the individual to participate fully in social affairs. The role of the family has received increasing emphasis in recent years, perhaps reflecting in part the important contribution to this phase of policy development made by a number of middle-class families with an intellectually disabled child, but also arguably arising from an objective analysis of the unique contribution which the family is in a position to make to the social and intellectual development of the child (Mittler and Mittler, 1983). Families which accept this responsibility have become a significant political pressure group in several western countries (Mittler and McConachie, 1983), demanding a major role in the definition of priorities and in the design of services.

The declaration of the year 1981 as the International Year of the Disabled Person (IYDP) precipitated a number of political initiatives in many countries, including a process in which specialist professional groups displayed and sought to justify to the general public their normally rather invisible activities. In countries which had already experienced a considerable amount of institutional development of specialized services for people with various disabilities, a major outcome of this public display was a growth in pressure for accountability by professionals towards the community of their client families. Where very little public institutional development had taken place (that is, most of the countries in the Third World) the emphasis was more on the small numerical coverage achieved to date by those services. Although the feelings of dependence on, and special need for, professional help may be crossculturally universal among parents of children with intellectual disability, the ways in which these needs are expressed tend to vary greatly, reflecting both different levels of general expectation of public assistance (in the light of the prevailing economic and political climate) and also specific cultural values attached to particular facets of family life.

Implementing rights

Radical changes of emphasis have occurred in the ways in which planners and professionals have been thinking about the planning of services for intellectually disabled people. These changes have not been evident in all countries; nor are published plans or official statements by governments or policy-makers necessarily translated into services 'on the ground'. Nevertheless, there are growing signs of a serious concern with the needs of disabled people in general, which sometimes, though not always, extends to those who are intellectually disabled.

These concerns were reflected in and by the 1981 IYDP which, despite certain misgivings arising from earlier international years on other themes, seems to have been a catalyst for action lasting well beyond the year itself, particularly in the United Nations commitment to a 'Decade for the Disabled', which clearly includes those who are intellectually disabled. Many countries undertook a systematic examination of their services for disabled people, often prompted by disabled people themselves, who worked to ensure that IYDP resulted in something more permanent than speeches, resolutions and exhibitions (UN, 1983).

1981 was itself the culmination of a good deal of international activity during the previous decade. This began in 1971 with the adoption by the

General Assembly of the United Nations of a Declaration of the Rights of Mentally Retarded Persons which stated:

1. The mentally retarded person has, to the maximum degree of feasibility, the same rights as other human beings.

2. The mentally retarded person has a right to proper medical care and physical therapy and to such education, training, rehabilitation and guidance as will enable him to develop his ability and maximum potential.

3. The mentally retarded person has a right to economic security and to a decent standard of living. He has a right to perform productive work or to engage in any other meaningful occupation to the fullest possible extent of his capabilities.

4. Wherever possible the mentally retarded person should live with his own family or with foster parents and participate in different forms of community life. The family with which he lives should receive assistance. If care in an institution becomes necessary, it should be provided in surroundings and other circumstances as close as possible to those of normal life.

5. The mentally retarded person has a right to a qualified guardian, when this is required, to protect his personal well-being and interests.

6. (a) The mentally retarded person must be protected from every kind of exploitation, degrading treatment and abuse.

6. (b) If prosecuted for any offence, he shall have a right to due process of law with full recognition being given to his degree of mental responsibility.

7. Whenever mentally retarded persons are unable, because of the severity of their handicap, to exercise for themselves all their rights in a meaningful way, or it should become necessary to restrict or deny some or all of these rights, the procedure to be used for that restriction or denial of rights must contain proper legal safeguards against every form of abuse. This procedure must be based on an evaluation of the social capability of the mentally retarded person by qualified experts and must be subject to periodic review and the right of appeal to higher authorities.

This 1971 UN Declaration was a major advance at the time, but although its basic philosophy is still accepted, some organizations of parents and professionals might today wish to express some of those rights somewhat differently. For example, qualifying phrases such as 'to the maximum extent possible' are notoriously subjective; similarly, there is less ready acceptance today of institutionalization as an appropriate form of care.

The 1971 Declaration, and many similar international and national pronouncements, are inevitably couched in terms of general principles and long-term goals. Desirable as these may be, they need to be translated into more specific short-term objectives which can be implemented and evaluated in concrete form at local level. Accordingly, some organizations have tried to provide guidelines for local use. For example, the International League of Societies for Persons with Mental Handicap (ILSMH, 1978a) published a document called *Step by Step* for the use of its member societies throughout the world; this poses specific questions concerning the extent to which each of the rights in the UN Declaration is being implemented at local level.

Countries seeking guidance on the development of services for disabled people in general and for intellectually disabled people in particular can now draw on a number of guidance documents produced by major international organizations in close consultation with representatives of Third World countries. For example, the World Health Organization (WHO, 1985) has published a substantial booklet prepared by the Joint Commission on International Aspects of Mental Retardation, which is composed of senior officers from the two principal international nongovernmental organizations in the field of mental handicap – the International League of Societies for Persons with Mental Handicap (ILSMH) and the International Association for the Scientific Study of Mental Deficiency. This document, which was the subject of an extensive consultation process in relation to the needs of developing countries, summarizes current knowledge concerning prevention, teaching and rehabilitation, policy development, implementation and service delivery.

It stresses that the means of preventing and intervening to help intellectually disabled people are already available within existing knowledge and skills, and that an immediate priority is to ensure that this information is much more effectively disseminated. Many of the measures which can be taken to help disabled people are inexpensive, and can be incorporated into basic measures to improve the health and social conditions of the population as a whole. Others, which aim to ensure that disabled people are included in services available to the rest of the population, may call for a change of attitude in the direction of willingness to try to make such provision, and acceptance that many intellectually disabled people are, contrary to previous beliefs, capable of benefiting.

One aim of the document was to encourage national organizations to formulate their own guidelines, since international documents cannot be sensitive to local needs. In the United Kingdom, for example, the main voluntary organization, the Royal Society for Mentally Handicapped Children and Adults, has published a series of *Stamina* documents, specifying minimum standards for specific services, such as special schools, adult training centres and residential services (NSMHC, 1977). These are intended to provide the basis of a dialogue between local parent organizations and service providers. Similarly, the National Development Group for the Mentally Handicapped (NDGMH, 1980), which was set up by the government to give independent advice to ministers, published a detailed checklist of standards in the form of some 220 questions on specific components of local services. These were distributed free of charge to all health and local authorities in order to provide a self-assessment tool which could enable them to monitor the quality of their own service provision and planning. In the United States, the Accreditation Council for Services for Mentally Retarded and Other Developmentally Disabled Persons has been publishing detailed guidelines for the public accreditation of services (ACMRDD, 1983). The Program Analysis of Service Systems (PASS) (Wolfensberger and Glenn, 1975) is also an increasingly well-known approach to the evaluation of services in relation to principles of normalization; this system has recently been simplified (Wolfensberger and Thomas, 1983).

Community attitudes

Local attitudes to disabled people in general, and to those with intellectual disability in particular, are clearly fundamental to their community acceptance and to their chances of integration. Unfortunately, few systematic comparative studies of community attitudes have been undertaken, and most of the information is anecdotal. Edgerton (1970, 1981) has attempted a synthesis of the information scattered in the anthropological literature on attitudes to intellectual disability in nonwestern societies, while Miles (1983a) has prepared a valuable review concerning attitudes to the disabled from ancient times and in the major religions of the world. Although providing a wealth of material and relevant quotations, he emphasizes the paucity of well-conducted scientific studies and the reliance on experience and anecdote. Miles's review precedes a systematic attempt to assess the impact of the International Year of Disabled Persons by means of interviews with 286 men, women and children in both urban and rural areas of the North-West Frontier Province of Pakistan, and is one of the most ambitious attempts to document public attitudes to disabled people in a Third World country. An important conclusion to emerge from this literature is the danger of generalization. Community attitudes vary not only across societies but also within them, between adjacent neighbourhoods.

A very useful discussion of public attitudes is reported by McConkey and McCormack (1983), in a book which summarizes four recent major opinion polls conducted in the United Kingdom and in the Irish Republic, with particular reference to mental handicap. They then provide an illuminating account of several attempts to influence public attitudes, particularly among schoolchildren and sales assistants. As a result of these experiences, the authors offer helpful guidelines to others wishing to gauge and possibly modify community attitudes. Their conclusions on the results of the four opinion polls are worth summarizing:

1. Most members of the public associate disability with physical impairments, in particular with the need to use a wheelchair. Less than one-third of those polled mentioned mental handicap.
2. When mental handicap was mentioned, it was frequently confused with mental illness.

3. The majority of those polled were in favour of increased community services for disabled people, and were prepared to pay additional rates and taxes.

4. Even so, it was clear that close contact was not favoured, in the neighbourhood, at work, in social life and certainly not in marriage. This conclusion applied to some disabled people more than others, but particularly to the mentally handicapped. Approximately half of those polled personally knew someone who was mentally handicapped.

5. In general, it seems true to summarize the results of this and most surveys by saying that both positive and negative attitudes to disabled people exist side by side.

Obviously, community attitudes are fundamental to any attempt to improve the quality of life or provide better services for handicapped persons. On the other hand, it is all too easy to seek to postpone proposals for change on the grounds that 'the community is not yet ready', or that there may be a public backlash against, say, a plan to relocate large numbers of people from residential institutions into community services. A balance needs to be struck between moving too fast and moving too slowly, between being responsive to local needs and providing leadership and initiative. Fortunately, publications are now available which document various approaches to the process of securing community acceptance for people who are intellectually disabled (e.g. Begab and Richardson, 1975; Baker *et al.*, 1977; Willms, 1981; Seltzer and Litchfield, 1984). The last study, for example, indicated that in the United States at least, opposition to a proposed community residence programme was less likely if local people were informed of the proposal either at a very early stage or shortly after residents have moved in. Furthermore, initial opposition often gave way to expressions of support and positive offers of assistance.

MEETING INDIVIDUAL NEEDS

Much of the earlier literature on service delivery has been based on the working assumption that the needs of intellectually disabled people could be considered in broad groupings: i.e. severity or grade of disability (mild, moderate, severe, profound, multiple); the nature of the primary impairments (e.g. chromosome anomalies, central nervous system damage, inborn errors of metabolism); place of residence (home, hospital, hostel); type of school (ordinary or special); or even the type of agency best suited to meeting needs (health dependency, local government dependency). In many countries, planning and policy development are still based on perceptions of the intellectually disabled as a single, relatively homogeneous group or series of subgroups.

In sharp contrast to this approach is the increasing tendency to try to assess and meet the unique needs of each individual to the maximum possible extent. This has come about for a variety of reasons. In the first place, rapid advances in behavioural methods of teaching have helped professionals to set short-term goals for single persons, and to work through parents and staff members to help the individual to reach those goals. At a broader level, the trend represents an attempt to overcome some of the disadvantages of providing for large groups by trying to recognize that each intellectually disabled person has unique special needs. Ideally, this is realized in pro-grammes of individual teaching and rehabilitation based on a thorough assessment of needs, seen not only through professional eyes but also with the active contribution of the individual disabled person. In more ordinary settings, staff do what they can to make some provision for the vast range of individual differences and needs found even within a small group of intellect-ually disabled people. For example, some recognition needs to be given to individual preferences in clothes, food and recreational interests, as well as in the more fundamental areas of choice, such as human relationships and housing.

Taking the service to the client

One expression of the movement towards community services is reflected in an increasing tendency to take services to the handicapped person, rather than to insist that the person comes to the service. The balance between centre-based and community-based services varies not only from country to country but from locality to locality. In countries with virtually no specialized services or where such services as do exist are inaccessible to all but a very small minority, the disabled person and his family will in any case be dependent on whatever help and support they can find locally. The community-based approach therefore tries to mobilize whatever resources are available to the whole local population, but works to extend this help to disabled people and their families.

The outstanding example here is the tendency to use primary health care workers who live in the local community and have received training in the basics of health care, including nutrition, sanitation, childbirth and child care, the treatment of minor illness and the recognition of more serious health problems. Such personnel are now beginning to extend their role to basic work with disabled children and their families. The World Health Organization's drive for the training of primary health care workers embodied in the Alma Ata declaration of 1978 has now been extended into the field of community-based rehabilitation, through the publication of a set of manuals, *Training Disabled People in the Community* (WHO, 1983). These are aimed at locally based primary health care workers and those involved in their training and support. They offer detailed examples of training activities, are written in simple language, and make liberal use of line drawings which illustrate the specific training activities discussed in the text. Separate manuals are available for people with difficulties in learning, moving, seeing, hearing and speaking, those who have fits and those who show 'strange behaviour'. There are also manuals for disabled adults, as well as guidelines for teachers, supervisors of training activities and community leaders. They have been extensively field tested in several Third World countries, but are still in the process of revision.

The community-based approach to rehabilitation (CBR) is clearly a development of the greatest importance, but it remains to be seen whether it will win the support of national governments and health professionals. Its success is to some extent bound up with that of the earlier initiative of training primary health care workers at local level; although this has worked well in some countries, it has often failed to arouse much interest at government level, and has run counter to strongly entrenched professional interests and concerns. A wideranging critique of the WHO manuals has recently been published by Miles (1984c), warning against the premature formalization of a new orthodoxy and pointing out that the principle of responsiveness to locally felt needs is more central to the philosophy of CBR than any single formula for the response.

Home-based education

An early example of a community-based approach is the Portage programme of home education, originally developed in a rural area of the United States (Bluma *et al.*, 1976), but now extensively adapted and translated for use in the Caribbean and parts of South America and Asia. The essence of the Portage approach is that a home visitor visits the family regularly, works with the parent to assess the child's current level of functioning in crucial areas of development (socialization, language, self-help, cognitive and motor skills) and uses these as the basis of a programme for helping the child to reach the immediate next stage of development. The task of the home visitor is to help the parent to help the child to learn the skill, and to ensure that the targets set are realistic and can be attained within a very short period, before the next visit. Home visitors have been trained to use the Portage materials after as little as a one-week intensive course, but it is essential to provide at least one day a week's continuous inservice training, so that the problems can be shared among a group of workers and they can continue to learn from one another. The interest of the Portage programme is that it supports rather than supplants parents (see Chapter 14).

Despite the importance attached to participation in the experience of mainstream schooling, the concept of home-based education should not be construed as a last resort or as a second-class service. As Dessent (1984) observed, a major contribution of schemes like the Portage Project consists in their 'celebrating' for the parent of a child with intellectual disability 'the inescapable role' of teacher. The technical advantages of teaching in the home arise in large part from the frequency with which family life presents opportunities for a child to address the demands of tasks of practical importance for his or her future life, and to practise their performance. This 'naturalistic' opportunity structure tends to cut through or attenuate some of the constraints experienced by schools, such as the difficulty of ensuring generalization of skills to real-life situations, of capturing the child's attention and motivation, and of individualizing instruction. Understandably, these advantages and techniques for their maximal exploitation are stressed in the training manual for the Portage Project.

Both Dessent (1984) and Sandow (1984), however, argue from experience with the scheme in England that the importance of the service it provides may reside as much, or perhaps even more, in its contribution to the more 'fuzzy' goals of a supportive, caring and befriending relationship with parents, regarded as consumers in their own right. As Sandow puts it, 'there is more to family life than training children', and strict adherence to the formal tasks identified in the manual could lead to an 'educalization' effect analogous to the 'medicalization' which has so often been deplored by educators. A particularly poignant dilemma arising from the emphasis on observation and measurement of the child's progress towards specific goals is: 'Should a child's performance be an index of individual success or failure as a parent?' (Sandow, 1984, pp. 19–20).

Another problem area noted also by Gulliford (Chapter 17) is the emphasis on written record-keeping by the family. Activity charts and rating scales greatly assist professionals to clarify their ideas to themselves and to certain audiences, as well as providing in principle an objective basis for monitoring the activities of the family and the child on periodic home visits. But their effective and reliable use by parents presupposes skills and attitudes which may not be present, especially in communities where literacy is marginal to the affairs of daily life. Insistence on such records when these preconditions are not met may lead to meaningless documentation, generated simply to satisfy an externally imposed expectation. Worse still, it may actually undermine the parents' confidence in their own competence to meet the needs of their child, which the scheme is designed to promote. An important need for research and development in this respect concerns the effectiveness and acceptability in various sociocultural settings of different styles and methods of communication, explanation and instruction (cf. Greenfield and Lave, 1982).

Advocacy of home-based education has often been linked to the principle of diffusing technical knowledge, or 'learning to give away skills' (Mittler, 1982). Particular importance has been attached to the short duration (and hence the cost-effectiveness) of the training required for a home trainer or home visitor to implement these schemes. On the other hand, the necessity for sensitivity to the multiple needs of families suggests that the careful selection of personnel for these roles may be of considerable significance.

The importance of interpersonal skills is illustrated by the observation of Cunningham (1983) that in England 'often the issue which was really worrying the parent was raised as one was about to leave' (p. 104). In this sociocultural setting the health visitor was encouraged during her three-week training course to 'talk with the parent about more general areas, e.g. difficulties in acceptance of the condition, the future, effects on sibling or relatives, parent groups, feeding, etc. . . . . in a relaxed and informal fashion, usually over a cup of tea or coffee' and 'not to appear to hurry away from the visit once the assessment/training phase was complete'. Such skills and strategies can only be effectively applied if they are modulated to reflect the cultural expectations of the family.

Edgerton (1981) has reviewed two illuminating studies designed to explore the reasons for apparent under-utilization of existing services for people with handicap in a large US city by specific communities: American Indians and Chinese Americans. In both cases, a plausible explanation was the dissonance in cultural orientation between the service providers and a group of their potential clients, who might otherwise have benefited greatly from services they felt unwilling or unable to obtain. Contrasting social and cultural expectations are found not only between ethnic groups in multicultural societies, but also among different socioeconomic strata in both industrialized and Third World countries. Cunningham (1983) and Chapter 1 of this volume point to evidence that the regular clients of social services are often disproportionately drawn in England from middle-class families with higher levels of formal education. Reports from several Third World countries (Busnello, 1983; Climent, 1983; Serpell, 1983) have recognized that senior health professionals often rely, for the more sensitive, 'psychosocial' aspects of health care, on their less well-paid 'ancillary' colleagues who lack professional training. Generally these members of staff are recruited locally from the community served by a rural health centre and can bring to bear on the tasks of diagnosis, explanation and persuasion a repertoire of relevant cultural knowledge, skills and intuitions which lie beyond the grasp of their more socially mobile professionally trained colleagues. The importance of this kind of sociocultural competence led Werner and Bower (1982) to contend that in the Third World countries the role of highly trained physicians should be construed as ancillary or supportive to front-line workers, rather than supervisory and directive as the administrative structure conventionally states.

Another context in which the need has been stressed for professionals to adopt a less 'know-all' attitude is that of partnership with parents (Ingstad, 1983; Mittler and Mittler, 1983; Onarheim, 1983). Indeed, it is arguable that many social and emotional needs of parents can be more effectively served by participation in an informal, voluntary association with other parents of children with disabilities than by explicit counselling from professionals. This concept is sadly missing from the latest edition of the WHO manual on CBR's 'Guide to local supervisors' (WHO, 1983). It is to be hoped that it will receive attention in their forthcoming supplementary publication on 'the role disabled people and their family members must play in order to promote and control the programme' (p. 3). Professionals can play a valuable catalytic but nondirective role by suggesting to appropriate members of a local community a 'menu' of concrete, but incompletely defined, activities which a group of parents can undertake without external guidance, which are likely to yield an outcome valuable to the group, which afford opportunities for creativity, which have not all been tried locally before, and in which local professionals could participate on an equal footing without compromising their professional standards. The ILSMH (1983) has published guidelines for the formation of a new parent association.

Relevant assessment

We have noted above that in western societies the philosophy of services for people with disabilities has increasingly emphasized the objectives of social integration and participation. Professionals in this context have become advocates of the disabled person's 'right to be different' and right to expect society to understand and accept that difference. Nevertheless, a major theme of services for people with disabilities, especially during their childhood years, remains that of stimulating, teaching and guiding them towards as great a degree of skill and independence as possible, with a view to their responsible participation in the life of their local community.

The type of service most appropriate to these dual goals of social acceptance and individual autonomy will vary in the light of a complex of interacting considerations. Specific opportunities and constraints are implied both by the current abilities and dispositions of the individual and by the resources of the immediate family, the local neighbourhood and the wider society. The function of assessment is to identify these resources and constraints as a basis for planning action to promote the growth of both autonomy and acceptance. At an earlier stage in the development of services, such actions were classified in terms of placement of the individual in one of various institutional settings, each of which was designed, in principle, to provide a comprehensive package of services. Current plans in the west aim for a much more 'finely graded continuum of support' (Heron and Myers, 1983), in which various contributions are organized from several different sources to respond to each individual's changing needs.

Such a fine gradation requires a form of assessment which is both multidimensional and action-oriented. Unfortunately, the public image of psychological assessment which has been projected in the curriculum of many medical schools around the world is heavily biased towards a unidimensional intelligence test. As a result, modern psychiatry as practised in many parts of the world begins and ends in its use of psychological assessment for disabled clients with a request for an IQ. And yet the current definition of the condition to be diagnosed, propounded by the WHO and the two major international bodies specializing in this field, includes 'two essential components: first, intellectual functioning which is significantly below average; second, marked impairment in the ability to adapt to the demands of the society' (WHO, 1985, and Chapter 2 in this book).

A recent consultation among psychiatrists and psychologists with a special interest in disabilities at ten centres widely dispersed across nine Third World countries revealed a high degree of consensus about the major dimensions of assessment for arriving at a diagnosis of disability (Serpell, 1984a). Their use of systematic (and in some cases standardized) assessment scales or tests was almost entirely confined to the dimensions of learning, understanding, communication and physical co-ordination. Yet eight of the ten centres reported that they also included among their assessment criteria the dimensions of social co-operation and of self-help maintenance habits and skills. Behaviour in these domains was, however, assessed predominantly on the basis of a report from the child's family, supplemented by minimal direct observations of a rather unsystematic and intuitive nature. Since at least some, if not most, major contributions of service interventions to the welfare of these clients are likely to be in these domains, there is clearly a need for greater attention to the development, selection and use of systematic scales for their assessment.

A second assessment problem in many Third World countries arises from the tendency to rely on tests which have not been adequately adapted or standardized for the population from which clients are drawn. It sometimes has been assumed that the translation of verbal instructions is the only significant step required for making an imported western test suitable for use in other sociocultural settings. But crosscultural research has shown the importance of other factors in determining the level of performance on many structured cognitive tasks. These include the testee's repertoire of perceptual and motor skills, and the extent to which these are matched by appropriate nonverbal test materials, as well as a wide range of subtle aspects of social interaction. Children in some cultures seldom engage in prolonged, intensive, structured dyadic play with an adult, and are not encouraged to display their intellectual competence to strangers; nor are they familiar with the experience of interaction with strangers or with the conventions of verbal elicitation of information outside the context of practical activities.

Many clinicians are aware of these and other differences in opportunity for learning relevant to test performance and make *ad hoc* allowances for them in arriving at an assessment of a client's intelligence. Thus, (1) some adjust the scores they require a child to attain as evidence of 'normality'; (2) some give extra practice on introductory items; (3) some omit selected items as inappropriate; (4) some modify certain items to make them more appropriate to the child's prior experience; and (5) some actually teach the main task and assess the rate at which the child learns. Recourse to the first four of these strategies can be criticized as violating essential assumptions on which the standardization of the test depends (cf. Newland, 1980). Learning ability tests have been developed along the lines of strategy (5), but their measured validity is unfortunately little or no higher than that of clearly inappropriate tests (Haynes, 1971; Hegarty and Lucas, 1979); moreover, it is unclear whether this type of measure is appropriate for the children of communities which have not opted for a specific type of acculturation. More radical strategies include (6) to dispense with tests altogether and rely on unstructured observations combined with family reports; (7) systematically to adapt and restandardize foreign tests for local use; and (8) to develop new tests using concepts, methods and materials derived from the local culture. Both of these last two strategies are complex and long-term ventures, the merits and difficulties of which are discussed by Lansdown and Graham (1985) and Serpell (1984b).

Meanwhile, in most countries the task of psychological assessment has to be undertaken with the assistance of a rather motley collection of semi-standardized instruments. An important principle guiding the practice of assessment under these conditions must be a determined resistance to the temptation (indeed, sometimes, explicit pressure from families, administrators or professional colleagues) to simplify the diagnosis into a single concise label. The focus of assessment should be on the client's needs, and these should be construed in temporally and situationally specific terms. Since needs are a joint function of developmental status, life situation and goals, their assessment must necessarily yield a temporary and flexible classification. Often criterion-referenced scales will be more useful in this respect than norm-referenced tests, and for these the use of the simpler adaptation strategies ((1)–(4) above) is much less technically problematic. A checklist of behavioural items, such as those published by the Portage Project and the British Institute of Mental Handicap (Simon, 1981) can be used eclectically as a guide to intervention without any statement about the individual's global developmental status.

The prescriptive focus of the type of assessment we have advocated also carries the implication that it must include an analysis of the client's social environment. If placement in an institutional setting is envisaged, the resources of personnel and other distinctive features of the institution are liable to constrain the range of possible interventions. This is equally true of the client's home and neighbourhood. In a home-based teaching programme it may be as important to assess the impact of the prescribed activities on the designated 'agent' (e.g. a member of the family) as their impact on the client. The potential of the home environment for supporting a child's development is a function not only of that child's needs but also of the individual needs of the parents and of the siblings. The goal of services in a family setting must therefore be focused both on the individual and on 'helping the care unit to cope' (Ingstad, 1983, p. 3). The needs and behaviour of the core of immediate agents, likewise, cannot be effectively interpreted without reference to their wider community and cultural context. As Edgerton (1970, p. 556) put it, 'We need to look at retarded men as social men, as men-in-a-social-order, not simply as men with intellectual deficits.' And for this what is required is a socially embedded system of assessment and service design (cf. Dybwad, 1970).

EDUCATIONAL INTEGRATION

Given that most national governments now regard several years of schooling as a basic human right for all children, increasing emphasis is currently laid on the importance of providing within the school system for the integration of disabled children (see Chapter 17).

Integration always involves meeting needs at two levels: first, the child's ordinary needs which are shared with all other children – for acceptance and love, for new experiences, for praise and recognition, and for responsibility (Pringle, 1974). Special measures may be necessary to ensure that these basic needs are not overlooked in the case of those intellectually disabled children who are socially isolated in their own communities. But, second, they also have special educational needs – particularly for teaching which takes account of their particular difficulties in new learning and in using and generalizing what they have learned.

There is now general agreement with the goals of integration but each country approaches this aim from a different starting point. Even within western societies with a considerable history of services, there are substantial differences in philosophy, organization and practice. Some countries still exclude children with severe learning difficulties from the education system and assign responsibility to health or social welfare agencies. In other cases, voluntary organizations provide education, either with the help of state funding or from their own resources. In North America, there are relatively few special schools, most disabled children being either in special classes attached to ordinary schools or in the ordinary class with or without some form of support for them and for the class teacher.

In general, however, the tendency in most European countries is for the education authorities to accept responsibility for the education of children with severe learning difficulties, though the way in which they discharge this varies considerably. A survey of special education provision in eight European Economic Community (EEC) countries suggests that most 'mentally retarded' children attend special schools (Jorgensen, 1980), though definitions of categories vary slightly from country to country. For example, France and the German Federal Republic set an upper limit of IQ 65 or 60, whereas UK practice, while perhaps giving less emphasis to IQ, would place an upper limit of IQ 50 or possibly 55 to a categorization of 'severe learning difficulty'.

Within Europe, the most radical approach to integrated education has been developed recently in Italy. This is based on a wholesale commitment to closure of all special institutions for the mentally ill as well as for those with intellectual disabilities, and to substitute community-based treatment facilities for the former and integrated education in ordinary classes of regular schools for the latter. It is difficult to obtain detailed information on the development of this programme, particularly as implementation varies considerably in different parts of the country, but there is no doubt about the determination with which some areas are carrying out a commitment to close all their special schools (Posternak, 1979; Vislie, 1981a; Zelioli, 1982). It remains to be seen whether parents are satisfied with the new provision, whether outcomes for children can be assessed, and whether teachers in ordinary schools are satisfied with the support and advice which is being mobilized at local level.

In the United States, the Education of All Handicapped Children Act (1975) (Public Law 94–142) has mandated education in 'the least restrictive environment' on the basis of an individualized educational programme (IEP) drawn up in full consultation with parents. The full implementation of this Act has been beset with funding and administrative problems, and American parents, unlike their British counterparts so far, have made extensive use of the courts and 'due process'. There have been complaints that IEPs were not written in sufficiently clear language, and that 'what appears to be the least restrictive environment may indeed be the most restrictive, perhaps to an even greater extent than poor quality special educational programs' (Cruickshank, 1977). A useful description of one of the best-known and most visited programmes in Madison, Wisconsin, has been given by Gruenwald and Schroeder (1981). They note, however, that Wisconsin still maintains some special schools.

The development of policy in the UK since 1944 is described by Gulliford in Chapter 17, with detailed examples of the various specific forms of integration currently being practised, and a review of some evaluative studies pointing to problems of implementation. There is a growing acceptance in the UK and other western countries of the view that children with intellectual disabilities should be educated alongside other children, and that the present system of segregated education should be gradually phased out (DES, 1978). Special schools are under criticism not for what they do but for what they represent – a legacy from an earlier period when segregation was more easily accepted than it is today. On this view, special schools, by their very existence, fail to prepare children to live in an integrated adult society, and similarly deprive society of the experience of mixing with handicapped children. Some schools are also thought to overprotect and underestimate their children, and to provide too sheltered and too undemanding an environment. Many teachers employed in special schools are themselves critical of the system, and are actively working for change while trying to ensure that specialist skills and resources are not lost.

The Third World

The situation in Third World countries is very different, since most of them have few specialist services (cf. Table 19.1). At first sight, therefore, they appear to have an ideal opportunity to learn from what we now regard as the mistakes made by earlier twentieth-century planners in the more industrialized countries, by avoiding the erection of special schools and institutions and putting a high priority on the development of comprehensive locally based services available to all.

Such advice is understandable and well meaning but must be set against the background of local needs. For example, what happens in a country where only a small proportion of ordinary children attend school? Or where one teacher is working with up to 100 children in one classroom? In these

TABLE 19.1 Estimated coverage by special schooling of children with severe intellectual disability in some African countries

	Botswana	*Kenya*	*Nigeria*	*Zambia*	*Zimbabwe*
(1) Number of children with severe intellectual disability (CSID) receiving special schooling	33	648	458	150	543
(2) Number of institutions providing special schooling for CSID	1	27	9	5	10
(3) Estimated number of CSID in the country aged 5–15 (national population × 0.25 × 0.0035)	700	14,400	67,000	5,100	6,500
(4) Estimated percentage of CSID receiving special schooling	4.7%	4.5%	0.7%	2.9%	8.4%

Source: Serpell (1983).

situations, which are by no means unknown in some countries, it is understandable that both parents and professionals may opt for specialist provision which is better than that available for other children. It also has to be remembered that many state schools refuse to accept children with disabilities and that much of the existing provision is organized by voluntary and private bodies, including many religious and charitable ones. Unless the staff of such schools work very closely with ordinary schools, the integration of children with disabilities can be difficult to negotiate. Where there is no provision, there may be grounds for beginning with specialist provision, but building in safeguards to ensure that such schools do not isolate either the children or the staff, and that plans are made from the outset to transfer children to ordinary schools as soon as there is any possibility of their deriving benefit from them.

On the other hand, the contrary view would be that once special schools exist, the possibilities of achieving integrated education are correspondingly reduced (cf. Serpell, 1982, for a discussion of the Botswana case). Parents may be reluctant to expose their children to poorer conditions, and teachers will wish to strengthen special schools and therefore resist the integration of their children into ordinary ones.

The alternatives are obviously not as extreme or as clear cut as this. In practice, it should be possible to develop a local policy which combines the best features of both systems – for example, special classes attached to ordinary schools. This is certainly preferable to allowing provision to develop without adequate planning or by opting for a single approach which may not meet the needs of many of the children it is meant to serve. Special needs call for special measures; they do not have to be expensive or elaborate, but they require assessment and consideration in advance. The aim would then be both to help all children with disabilities to attend their local school, and also to provide a support system for local teachers. This could take the form of regular visits from itinerant teachers with experience of working with disabled children; these could be drawn from workers on home-visiting programmes such as Portage, or they could be teachers with some additional training and experience. Their task would be to support the local teacher in setting realistic short-term goals for the child, suggesting educational and other aids and appliances which might be made or adapted locally, helping carry out simple assessments of the child's level of functioning, and suggesting specialist assessment or treatment where this was considered essential. The peripatetic teachers should themselves be able to draw on the help of specialist workers wherever these were available – including physicians, therapists and more highly trained special educationalists. Various forms of 'distance teaching' also can be used, particularly direct radio transmission, audiotapes and correspondence texts, sometimes individualized for particular children and their families, as in Australia and New Zealand.

One way of providing help for the child in the local school, as well as general support for the teacher, is to enlist the services of an adult helper who will spend much of the day with the child and assist him to take as full a part as possible in the life and work of the school. The adult can be a parent, an older sibling or a volunteer. Another suggestion is that two or three nondisabled children in the school can take turns to accompany the child during the day, and to help him with school tasks and in the social life of the school.

An example of the planned use of peers to assist integration has been reported from the Philippines; some large urban primary schools include centres of special education which provide a temporary base from which each child's programme of gradual integration into one of the ordinary classes is systematically planned. Part of the process of introducing the child to an ordinary classroom involves the use of peers who befriend the child and help him to adapt to the academic and social demands of the classroom and the school. Other examples of support to assist the child's integration are briefly described in a UNESCO report (1979), summarizing programmes in Jamaica, Malawi and Algeria; similarly, a major international study sponsored by the Organization for Economic Co-operation and Development has brought together a number of case-reports of integration of older disabled children and young people (OECD, 1981) A detailed account of one integration project in Peshawar, in the North-West Frontier Province of Pakistan, has been provided by Miles (1984a).

However desirable the goal of integration, the recommendation that children with severe learning difficulties (as well as those with other disabilities) should have full access to whatever educational provision is available to other children in Third World countries has to confront some serious obstacles. These have been summarized by Gardner (1984), in a commentary designed to put proposals such as these in a wider context.

Between 1960 and 1980, global enrolments of children in primary education have increased by 142 per cent, of which at least half is constituted by the rapid rise in child population of school age. Although 73 per cent of the world's child population is now enrolled in some form of primary education, the proportion of those enrolled in the world's 31 'least developed countries' is only 45 per cent. Taking account of projected rises in world population between 1980 and 2000, there will have to be an increase in provision from just under 300 million to between 500 and 600 million children of school age. Furthermore, the proportion of primary teachers who are unqualified is still very high in many parts of the world.

Both in the short term and in the long term, teacher education is clearly a high priority. In the short term, serving teachers can be helped to adapt appropriate teaching methods with the support of specialist teachers. Ultimately, all new teachers in training should have some exposure to the needs of disabled children.

If severe problems are encountered in integrating and meeting individual needs in highly staffed special schools in the richer nations, the task is likely to be even more difficult in countries with less developed educational services. In both, progress is likely to come from a realization that integration is not merely a matter of placing disabled children in ordinary schools. It involves a development from within the ordinary school itself which questions the extent to which it is meeting the needs of less able children who are already attending. Consequently, examination and curriculum reform, coupled with reappraisal of styles of management, organization and classroom practice, are likely to result in positive benefits for less able as well as for disabled children. This in turn is based on a recognition of the principle that learning difficulties should not be construed as lying within the child but as stemming from an interaction of the child and the various environments in which the child is living and learning.

SERVICES FOR ADULTS

Most of the recent and current concern for meeting the needs of persons with intellectual disabilities seems to have been centred on children and young people. This is understandable for a variety of reasons, particularly in Third World countries where at least half the population is under sixteen, unlike industrialized societies where the proportion is nearer one-quarter. On the other hand, most people with severe intellectual disabilities will continue to have special needs for the whole of their lives, though the nature of these needs will vary with age and social circumstances (see also Chapter 18).

Few Third World countries make specific provision for adults with intellectual disabilities: they have to adapt as best they can to the demands of the local community, with support from relatives and friends; some of them are given work, though the level of pay is often too low to enable them to live above subsistence level. Others are reduced to begging and to dependence on charity. Although many live with their families, it is probable that many others are institutionalized, more or less permanently, either in prisons or in hospitals which make little or no distinction between the mentally ill and those with intellectual disabilities.

Goals of a service for adults: normalization

Many documents originating from the international organizations and from western Europe and North America are influenced by the 'normalization' philosophy. In simple terms, this states that the guiding principles of services for adults should be concerned with helping them to lead as ordinary a life as possible, making use of the range of services and facilities available to nondisabled people, but still being able to call on special services for special needs (Perske, 1977; O'Brien and Tyne, 1981). The principal 'special service' should result in the development of an individual programme plan, which normally will be concerned with ways of helping the individual to make the fullest possible use of ordinary community resources. The individual should be able to take a full part in the formulation of this goal plan, rather than have it superimposed from above by all-knowing 'wise' professionals and parents (Goffman, 1968).

The 'normalization' philosophy (see Chapter 1) is now accepted in many industrialized countries, and has developed its own specialized vocabulary and assessment tools; e.g. 'social role valorization' is now the preferred term to 'normalization' (Wolfensberger, 1983). But how far is it universally valid, and in particular how does it apply to Third World countries? Miles (1984b), on the basis of several years' experience of work with persons with intellectual disabilities in the North-West Frontier Province of Pakistan, provides a harsh critique of its irrelevance to the realities of day-to-day life in most of Asia. He argues, for example, that, for many Asians, 'The fact that a person is disabled is closely linked to notions of retribution or correction for actions taken in a previous incarnation.' It follows that 'There is less of the post Judaeo/Christian obsession with personal, individual fulfilment in the present life.'

As far as adults are concerned, therefore, there is room for doubt about the implementation of the International Year of the Disabled Person slogans of equality and participation. Miles points out that the slightest misdemeanour or violation of accepted conventional behaviour is likely to result in isolation and possible incarceration in gaol or in a closed psychiatric hospital. Disability and learning difficulties do not generally provide grounds for leniency, and even if this were the case, custodial institutions would be thought to be needed to protect the public and prevent misdemeanours.

Very few rehabilitation or social services for disabled people in general, and for persons with intellectual disabilities in particular, are available in most Third World countries, and there is little or no professional interest or opportunity for working with these populations. In such a context, the quality of an intellectually disabled adult's life depends on securing access to whatever is available to the rest of the population – basic health care, shelter and whatever work can be found. Day-to-day life depends to a great extent on the way they are treated by those with whom they come into occasional or frequent contact, and in particular by any help they may receive from people who aid or befriend them.

A qualitative account of how such informal social support operates has been provided for one society by Edgerton and his colleagues in their longitudinal ethnographic study of former residents of a large institution who have now been living in the community for over twenty years. Edgerton (1967) described the 'benevolent conspiracies' through which benefactors assisted adults with mild intellectual disabilities in California to cope with everyday practical problems and to 'pass' as normal behind a 'cloak of competence'. Such networks of benefactors may be much more likely to emerge from a childhood spent, however stressfully, in the company of abler peers than in the protective environment of special classes or schools.

Although the importance of benefactors was perceived by Edgerton's cohort as declining over the years, they may well have served as gatekeepers whose assistance at crucial junctures enabled the individual to secure access to major development opportunities, and also acted as buffers against some of life's adversities. At the ten-year follow-up, Edgerton and Bercovici (1976) observed that 'the majority seem to experience continued instability in their lives . . . maybe . . . because persons who have been institutionalized . . . have so few reliable resources that can stabilize them in times of crisis' (p. 489). And after twenty years, Edgerton *et al.* (1984) summarize the role of social and personal support resources by saying that the four persons whose quality of life worsened all suffered a major loss; and 'none had a strong benefactor, a network of supporters, or any agency aid' (p. 349).

Edgerton's (1967) detailed ethnographic account illustrates the many ways in which social interaction can substitute for individual action in the solution of problems posed by daily living. This phenomenon has been explored in some depth by Cole *et al.* (1978) in their analyses of cognitive work in naturalistic settings. For the planners of services, the implication of these observations is that neither mastery of the skills of self-reliance, physical prostheses, nor protective restrictions are essential in social settings where the disabled person's needs for self-esteem are recognized concurrently with his or her needs for help with specific components of life's tasks.

The importance of social support networks also emerge in Seed's (1981) study of the varying ways in which adults with intellectual disabilities were integrated into six rural communities in Scotland. Similarly, studies by Mattinson (1975) and by Craft and Craft (1981) indicated the ways in which marriage can provide a powerful form of support. In addition, we can note the special role of citizen advocates who provide not only practical help in gaining access to services but also friendship and emotional support (Wolfensberger and Zauha, 1973). Such support can also be given by relatives (even if they are no longer providing a home) and by other persons with intellectual disabilities, especially if they are already close friends. Hence it is particularly important for service planners and other professionals to take great care not to disrupt friendships when relocating people from institutional to community services. It is becoming increasingly clear that informal networks of friendship and mutual self-help may be at least as important as the provision of appropriate community services.

Against this background, we now list the principal services which can be mobilized to help adults with intellectual disabilities.

Continuing education

If education is construed as being concerned with ways of systematically fostering learning and development, it follows that education neither begins nor ends in school. In the case of children with severe learning difficulties, intervention can begin in the first weeks of life by supporting and working through the family in their own home (e.g. Cunningham and Sloper, 1978). Towards the end of the period of 'compulsory' education, plans need to be made for using whatever local resources are available to ensure that the continuing needs for new learning and development are made available, as far as possible. In the UK, an increasing number of young people with intellectual disabilities remain at school until the age of nineteen, and proceed from there to a college of further education. This is, by definition, a form of integrated provision, since it is open to all young people, though in practice students with certain special needs tend to attend courses and classes specifically designed to meet these, though mixing with other students in the college for various other purposes.

The major source of information about practice in other countries is the OECD study on the handicapped adolescent. OECD commissioned a substantial number of reports on various aspects of practice in the twenty-one OECD countries, mostly written by independent consultants. The study has so far produced two short publications, one concentrating on 'integration in school' (OECD, 1981) and the second on 'transition to work' (OECD, 1983). Even so, relatively little detailed information or evaluation seems to be available on further and adult education provision for adults with intellectual disabilities in other countries.

In many Third World countries, formal education extends beyond the primary age for relatively few children. Continuing education can therefore begin as early as eleven or twelve. The nature of the 'curriculum' and learning experiences provided for young people or adults beyond the age of basic education will obviously vary with the needs and resources of the local community, as well as those of the learner. In many urban settings, the main aims may be concerned with the acquisition and use of basic literacy and numeracy skills; many people with intellectual disabilities who fail to acquire these while they are at school (or who are not exposed to them as a consequence of school policy) do so more readily after leaving school, particularly if the methods of teaching capture their motivation by using age-appropriate materials which treat them as adult learners, rather than as children working on reading primers originally designed for five- or six-year-old children (Dean and Hegarty, 1984).

Apart from literacy skills, adult education for people with intellectual disabilities must also be concerned with helping them to learn and use the skills required to live successfully in the local community and to adapt to its needs. In industrialized societies, this includes a wide range of skills, including daily living and community living skills such as using public transport, shopping, budgeting, cooking and food preparation, use of household tools, purchase and care of clothes, and domestic tasks necessary to live as independently as possible but with appropriate support. 'Social education' curricula increasingly emphasize 'interpersonal skills' concerned with personal relationships, sometimes involving structured programmes to do with eye contact, smiling, physical distance, greeting, use of local social conventions, accepting criticism, but also help in self-assertiveness where appropriate, including the skills of self-advocacy (see Whelan and Speake, 1979, and Chapter 18). Helping adults to use their leisure and spare time both to develop their own interests and also to gain access to local leisure, recreational and sports facilities is receiving emphasis in adult education programmes not only for people with disabilities but for the population as a whole (see Jeffree and Cheseldine, 1984, for a recent example). Such a 'curriculum' for adults could be delivered by various agencies, professional or voluntary, and not least by parents and other relatives. It need not necessarily originate in a specialized facility for a specific group of disabled people, though this happens to have been the form in which such programmes have been traditionally delivered.

Day services

In many industrialized countries, day services for adults have been provided through various types of sheltered workshop, occupation training or day-care centres, sometimes exclusively for persons with intellectual disabilities, and sometimes for people with a wide range of disabilities and needs. Although day centres undoubtedly have provided an important service, they have been increasingly criticized in the recent past. This is partly because they provide a separate and segregated service within the community, and partly because there is a considerable lack of clarity about the aims of the service as a whole, coupled with an absence of planning for the individual, particularly in relation to an active programme of training and rehabilitation into less sheltered and more ordinary services. In several countries, day services are provided through voluntary organizations, usually with the help of public funds; for example in several European countries 'sheltered workshops' are run by national parent organizations but under local control (Gruenwald, 1984). A detailed analysis of current practice in UK adult training centres and plans for its improvement are provided by Whelan in Chapter 18. There is little evidence, either in the UK or elsewhere, of significant numbers of day-centre clients being discharged to other forms of community provision. Consequently, the centres are now generally full, partly because they have reached a natural saturation point and partly because, due to financial restrictions, no new centres are being built.

The embargo on the erection of further day centres provides an opportunity to reconsider the function of day services as a whole, and specifically the place of day centres within a more varied pattern of service provision. This can contain a number of components which can be considered separately merely for purposes of exposition, but which in practice should be integrated into an individual programme plan.

Training for work

In western countries, the long-established tradition of vocational training in day centres has for some time now been seriously discredited (Perske, 1979). Even in times of full employment, very few persons with intellectual disabilities were ever discharged from such centres into open or even sheltered employment. More fundamentally, the role of vocational training in what is now known as a post-industrial society requires reconsideration. While high levels of youth and adult unemployment are likely to be a permanent feature of western society for the foreseeable future, should one conclude from this that attempts to train persons with intellectual disabilities to find and keep a job are unjustified or a waste of scarce resources? This seems to be the assumption underlying the 'significant living without work' concept. While it is true that the whole social context of vocational training has been fundamentally changed, does this justify abandoning all attempts to find work for people with learning difficulties? After all, most people wish to enjoy significant living *and* work, though perhaps this goal is not attained by many.

Vocational training can be justified partly in terms of human rights and the principles of normalization, but also in the light of growing evidence that persons with intellectual disabilities can be helped to enter full employment. A number of innovative schemes have been reported in the last few years, some usefully summarized by Heron and Myers (1983).

In particular, the Pathway scheme pioneered by MENCAP (1981) in the UK provides for the placement into work of individual clients through a Pathway employment officer working in close liaison with employers and with staff of adult training centres, hospitals and hostels, as well as with staff of the ordinary and specialist employment services in the locality, including careers officers and disablement resettlement officers. Intensive preparation both for the work itself and for the social and personal demands involved in the job as a whole can be provided either at the adult training centre or in a work preparation course at a local college of further education. The scheme pays the employer twelve weeks' wages for the trainee, and asks him or her to find a suitable 'foster worker' who would befriend the new worker and guide him or her through the personal, social and occupational maze of tasks which confront any new employee, particularly one with a disability.

The Pathway scheme originally began in Cardiff, where there was a very high rate of unemployment, but has since been extended to many other regions in the UK, often with the support of public funding. The success of this scheme in what could hardly be a more unfavourable employment climate probably rests on three key elements: its emphasis on the unique needs of the individual; the use of a rehabilitation officer with local specialist knowledge; and the support and friendship of the foster worker. The last is perhaps the most innovative and imaginative element, which helps to ensure that the individual not only finds a job but achieves success in a way that enhances self-esteem. This parallels Edgerton's (1967) findings on the difference that personal support from 'benevolent benefactors' makes to the survival and quality of life of highly vulnerable people.

Attempts to place persons with intellectual disabilities directly into employment have also been made in Italy, in the context of the radical deinstitutionalization movement in that country (see Posternak, 1979, for an interim report). In some cases, groups of disabled workers have been placed under skilled supervision in 'work stations' or 'enclaves'; examples of this approach were reported in the UK as early as the 1960s and more recently in the ENCOR programmes in eastern Nebraska, USA (Thomas *et al.*, 1978). A more intensive direct training approach has been developed in the United States, following Gold's seminal studies (see Gold, 1973, for a review of earlier work), and the earlier pioneering British studies in which severely handicapped hospital residents were taught complex assembly tasks by the application of systematic teaching and training methods (Clarke and Clarke, 1965). Perhaps the most advanced work in this tradition is now taking place at the University of Oregon where Bellamy *et al.* (1979) have been providing intensive training programmes, first in sheltered workshops and then in a series of different environments – a form of operational replication. The workers are successfully producing subassemblies for electronic equipment, and are receiving training in their own work setting. They usually do not move on to more advanced training elsewhere. This is in contrast to a project in Seattle, Washington, where the emphasis was on individual placement in open employment, including jobs in the food industry and in student cafeteria services (Moss, 1979, cited by Heron and Myers, 1983; King's Fund, 1984).

At the international level, the International Labour Office (ILO) has recently been very active in promoting better employment opportunities for all disabled persons, including those with intellectual disabilities. In particular, the ILO (1983a, b) has adopted and promulgated two major instruments, Convention 159 and Recommendation 168, setting out detailed guidelines on the employment of disabled persons (ILO, 1984a, b). The Convention has been submitted to all national governments; its clauses are binding for ten years once they agree to ratification. The Convention calls for the adoption of a national policy on vocational rehabilitation and employment of all disabled persons, including those in rural areas; a policy of equal opportunity, involving vocational guidance training, placement and employment; and a parallel programme of training of rehabilitation counsellors or equivalent staff. Recommendation 168 provides more detailed suggestions for implementation but these are not legally binding.

These recommendations apply to all disabled persons but an earlier ILO conference had concluded that:

> The mentally retarded, even the most severe cases, are capable, with proper preparation and training, of undertaking a wide range of unskilled and semi-skilled work both in urban and rural areas. (ILO, 1978)

The occupations which they listed as suitable for intellectually disabled people included: janitorial and housekeeping; laundry; hotel and catering; office and shop work; messenger; general labouring/handyman; furniture-making; packaging; newspaper delivery; ceramics; electronics; garage work; poultry- and rabbit-raising; fishing; boat-building; silkscreen printing; garment-making; vegetable-growing; sugar industry; citriculture; banana-growing; car-washing; wood, metal and leather work.

Further detailed guidance on vocational preparation is included in the World Health Organization manuals *Training Disabled People in the Community* (WHO, 1983).

Within Europe, and particularly within the ten nations of the EEC, there has also been a marked revival of interest in the possibilities of mounting a major employment initiative for disabled people. As a direct consequence of the International Year for Disabled Persons, the EEC commissioned a factual statistical survey of provision in each of the (then) nine member states (Mangin, 1983). In addition, Croxen (1982) has produced a useful *Overview* which ranges from a conceptual analysis to operational issues. Furthermore, the EEC Bureau in Favour of the Handicapped has instituted demonstration programmes in ten areas designed to develop and disseminate good practice in the employment of disabled persons, some of which include provision for people with intellectual disabilities.

Turning to the Third World, Miles (1983b) makes some interesting proposals for rehabilitation in rural areas. These take the form of identifying a range of suitable handicrafts which could be produced, after a short period of training either at home or in small groups, and which would then be sold in the local markets. Although a small initial outlay would be needed and the income probably would not be enough to achieve economic subsistence, the disabled person could at least become a contributor to the family and marginally increase the chances of enhancing the attitudes of the family and the local community, as well as his own self-esteem. Miles reports that detailed illustrated manuals are being written by a local tradesman in Peshawar, setting out step-by-step instructions for making a range of goods, including clothes pegs, candles, raffia fans, ropes, prayer mats, rubber buckets, flowerpots, cardboard boxes, paper bags and many other items for which there is a ready market in the bazaar. A similar project is under way in Manchester with EEC funding in which a small group of young adults is being trained by community college staff to set up stalls in a local street market.

Since most persons with intellectual disabilities live in rural areas, it would be instructive to have more information on the range of ways in which they are helped to contribute to the local rural economy in various places. At present, very little factual information is available, apart from some descriptive accounts of particular projects. Here again, the extent to which intellectually disabled people are integrated into the employment patterns of their local community varies enormously from area to area, and from village to village, depending on local customs, experiences and attitudes. But it seems reasonable to assume that in many parts of the Third World the individual disabled person will be encouraged to contribute, as far as his or her disabilities allow, to the well-being, or indeed the survival, of the local community. In the formalized and systematized work structures of western societies, problems of access to employment are more likely to be found, partly because of the complex nature of the tasks to be performed, and partly because of the unduly low expectations of the work abilities of people with intellectual disabilities held not only by potential employers but also by some professional staff and parents. In a small village, local people will have got to know disabled persons from childhood, and acquired a rough working knowledge of the kind of tasks which might be entrusted to them, and of the kind of help or supervision that they might need. In larger, more complex societies, disabled people are more isolated and often not even given the chance to show their capabilities.

Residential services

In residential services, there are again contrasts between Third World and industrialized countries. In the former, the majority of people with intellectual disabilities are necessarily living in the community, mostly with their own, or within the extended, family. The alternatives would be gaol, a hospital for the mentally ill or some form of vagrancy. The situation in the latter countries is changing and complex: whereas a substantial number do live with their own families, or in some form of alternative supported accommodation in the community, many others still live more or less permanently in large institutions of varying quality.

A number of trends can be discerned in changing patterns of provision in western countries. In reviewing these, it is useful to make an initial distinction between the development of community services and the relocation of residents from large institutions.

Until comparatively recently, professional and official thinking has been dominated by what has been called 'the residential assumption', namely that nearly all adults would eventually require permanent residential institutional care. A corollary to this is the assumption that the family will continue to provide a home for the disabled relative until prevented from doing so by incapacity or death. Both assumptions are now being questioned, with the result that a significant attempt is being made in some countries to develop a wide range of alternative living arrangements in the community, each adapted to the needs of a particular individual or a very small group. The aim is to prevent the admission to long-term care of many or all of those who previously would have been sent to institutions. In addition, some countries, regions and areas are now engaged in a major strategic exercise designed to relocate hospital residents into appropriate community services, though this movement is still in its earliest stages.

Ideas and attitudes on appropriate residential provision within the community have changed considerably in the past ten years. In Britain, during the 1960s and early 1970s, there was a slow but steady expansion of hostels run by social services departments. In general, these provided accommodation for some two dozen adults, most of whom attended adult training centres during the day or were otherwise occupied; most were fairly independent in self-care and social independence skills, and very few had significant behaviour problems or required intensive help (see the survey carried out for the Jay Committee by the Office of Population Censuses and Surveys (DHSS, 1979)). Although remarkably few hard data exist to evaluate the work of hostels and their impact on residents, criticism of hostel provision has taken a number of forms. First, it seems that many people in hostels could live more independently, without need of the services provided by the hostel. Second, there is not enough information on the extent to which hostels provide active training and preparation for greater independence outside; indeed, some hostel staff believe that the hostel is the resident's home, and therefore not part of a training environment. Third, there is concern that hostel staff do not always work within the overall framework of an individual programme plan or of the local policy for people with intellectual disabilities. Finally, the increasing emphasis on principles of normalization led to criticisms of many hostels as too institutional in their regimes and by definition unnecessarily segregated from the mainstream of community activities and provision (Mittler, 1979).

These criticisms coincided with the dissemination of information from the ENCOR programme in eastern Nebraska (e.g. Thomas *et al.*, 1978; Libby, 1981). The ENCOR model, which has been highly influential in the UK, is based on the premise that all residential needs can be met in ordinary housing within the local community, and that there is therefore no need for specialist hospital provision. The ENCOR model has itself gone through some changes but now provides ordinary housing for all, with each house receiving the support services required by its residents. The nature of these needs is determined through the individual programme plan to which the client is a central contributor. The result is a very wide range of provision at variable cost. Some clients clearly require very high levels of staffing; others may be able to live independently, with only a weekly visit from a social worker or volunteer to assist with budgeting, or merely to provide general support and friendship. Adaptations of the ENCOR model are currently being introduced in parts of the UK, including Cardiff (e.g. the NIMROD scheme, Blunden, 1985), Sheffield and north-west England. An influential English publication has been the King's Fund's (1982) *Ordinary Life*, which summarizes various service options and provides clear guidelines on implementation (see also Ward, 1982).

Although it seems likely that more adults will in future live in ordinary housing with appropriate support, various other types of community provision also exist in most western countries, frequently somewhat larger than ordinary housing stock. Apart from 'classical' hostels of the kind found in the UK, many countries in Europe, and Japan, have residential services on one site for as many as 100 people, although they may be divided to provide much smaller living units. In Sheffield, for example, two 96-bedded hospital units were developed for more severely disabled residents, subdivided into subunits for 24 people; although offering far better services than large hospitals, these are now thought far too large and inevitably institutional, however good the physical amenities may be (Heron and Myers, 1983). Similarly, the 24-bedded local hospital units developed in the Wessex region of the UK from the mid-1960s were intended to provide long-term residential care for all who required this, with no provision made for continued admission to the larger hospitals.

The work of these small units has been exhaustively evaluated by Kushlick and his associates (Felce *et al.*, 1983). More recently, several 'community units' have been established, largely on the basis of recommendations made in the field by the Development Team for the Mentally Handicapped (DHSS, 1985). Large-scale national surveys in the United States have also indicated that 'more than half of mentally retarded persons in "community facilities" lived in settings with more than thirty residents' (Developmental Disabilities Project (1978), cited in Lakin *et al.*, 1981). There are also many who live in village-type communities of various kinds, generally run by voluntary or religious organizations (e.g. Segal, 1984).

Although the development of community residential provision is to be warmly welcomed, it is important to sound some cautionary notes. First, community provision is not *ipso facto* superior; it covers a wide range of housing and support, which varies in quality. Accordingly, it is essential to develop a system of discreet and nonobtrusive monitoring, designed to ensure that the needs of residents are being met as fully as possible, and which allows them to express their point of view. The individual programme plan, if it exists, provides a good foundation for such monitoring. On the other hand, it is difficult to monitor and keep under review the extent to which the needs of several hundred individuals are being met when these persons are deliberately 'scattered' across a whole city, particularly as some of them will not welcome what they might regard as visits of inspection, however well intended. It is also difficult to ensure that any special services which may be needed for a given person can continue to be provided.

It also should not be assumed that all the negative aspects of institutional life are automatically absent in hostels or staffed homes. Although there is reasonable evidence that the quality of care in community homes is in general superior to that found in institutions, there is obviously considerable within-group variation, with some homes being run along rigid institutional lines, sometimes by the same staff who have changed their job descriptions but not their care practices. Even people living in an unstaffed group home can be isolated and lonely, unless efforts are made to establish their own priorities (Baker *et al.*, 1977).

In the UK, the development of community residential services has until very recently largely been used to prevent admission to hospital. Both parents and professionals have begun to question the 'assumption' that parents would provide a home for their son or daughter indefinitely; instead, the aim is to prepare the young person to live more independently and to leave the family home in the late teens or early twenties, in the same way as young people who are not disabled.

THE DEINSTITUTIONALIZATION MOVEMENT

Although it has long been known that long-stay hospitals and other residential institutions housed many thousands of people who had no need of their services, it is only comparatively recently that serious attempts have been made significantly to reduce the size of hospitals and to relocate as many residents as possible into appropriate community provision. In the United States, this began towards the end of the 1960s and was substantially aided by a series of court actions forcing the closure of some of the largest institutions or mandating a much higher quality of care in others. At the same time, however, although the number of residents per public institution showed a sharp drop, there was a marked increase in the building of new smaller facilities, housing as many as 100 residents (Scheerenberger, 1981).

In Britain the development of community services in the 1970s benefited those already in the community and therefore had comparatively little impact on the discharge of hospital residents. Despite the fact that the government White Paper, *Better Services for the Mentally Handicapped* (DHSS, 1971), suggested a reduction in numbers from 52,000 to 26,000 adults in the period 1970–90, the actual rate of discharge has been much slower than this, with some 45,000 adults still in hospital in 1984, and most of the reductions accounted for by deaths rather than discharge. On the other hand, the number of children under sixteen living in hospital on the grounds of intellectual disability has fallen dramatically from over 6000 in 1971 to around 1000 in 1984; this is largely due to a policy of not admitting children for long-term care while providing better personal and financial support for families and a greatly enhanced quality of schooling (IDC, 1984). However, few of the intellectually disabled children in hospital were actually discharged to community provision in the 1970s and most are now living in adult wards.

In Britain, as in many other countries, relocation has been slow, partly because of the labyrinthine administrative and professional structures within which the services are organized. These make it extraordinarily difficult to achieve co-ordination across service boundaries, and for professionals working in hospitals and local authorities to work together to achieve the discharge and rehabilitation of an individual resident. Following publication of the report of the Jay Committee on Nursing and Care (DHSS, 1979) and the report of the National Development Group, *Helping Mentally Handicapped People in Hospital* (NDGMH, 1978), the government launched a new *Care in the Community* initiative (DHSS, 1981), designed to resolve some of these administrative and financial obstacles. In particular, specific sums of money have been earmarked to achieve relocation at local level, including money which passes from health to local authorities in the form of an annual grant to provide services for each individual who is discharged from hospital. With the help of this and earlier initiatives which had made it possible for health authorities to transfer money to local government, many hospitals are now beginning a dialogue with surrounding local government units in an effort to achieve the relocation of substantial numbers of hospital residents on an individual basis. Some hospitals, including some with over 1000 residents, are planning for total closure within a ten-year period of at least their ablest residents, perhaps one-third of all those in hospital.

Research implications

Against this background we can briefly consider some research evaluation issues which arise from the deinstitutionalization initiative. Some have been clearly identified in an important monograph from the American Association on Mental Deficiency edited by Bruininks *et al.* (1981).

In particular, it is important to emphasize the increasing consensus that the success of 'community adjustment' cannot be simplistically sought in the characteristics of the individual; indeed, several research reviews could not demonstrate anything other than the most modest relationships with some of the classical predictor variables, including intellectual level, academic ability, age at release, diagnosis and personality. Certainly, research evidence cannot be used to justify the inclusion or exclusion of particular groups of people from deinstitutionalization initiatives.

Although individual characteristics and behaviour are clearly important, they cannot be understood except in relation to the specific environments in which individuals are studied. In making a strong plea for more ecologically valid research, Brooks and Baumeister (1977) argue not only for a greater concern for environmental variables, but for research which studies interactions between persons and environments. In particular, the quality of community adjustment of a person leaving a residential institution is partly a function of the success of the 'match' between the individual and the nature of the environment into which he or she is moving, and especially the expectation and attitudes of care-givers in the new environment (Lei *et al.*, 1981; Sutter and Mayeda, 1981).

The current commitment to deinstitutionalization should not be allowed to obscure the need to monitor its effectiveness for individuals, nor should it inhibit research designed to identify the characteristics of individuals and environments and their interaction which are associated with relatively successful outcomes. For example, studies by Landesman-Dwyer (1983) and her associates in Washington State indicate that transfer of selected residents of long-stay institutions into small staffed houses did not necessarily result in a significant increase in adaptive skills or in social interaction with others. Such changes occurred only if carefully structured programmes of staff training were introduced, emphasizing ways in which a more demanding environment could be created, and ways in which residents could be helped to be more independent and to interact more with others. But similar results also were achieved with those who remained in the large hospital, whereas those left on wards with nothing to do were likely to deteriorate.

Equally disturbing are consistent research findings which suggest that simply increasing the number of direct care staff does not necessarily affect either the quantity or quality of staff–client interactions (e.g. Raynes *et al.*, 1979); indeed, increases in staff may actually decrease the number of interactions with residents, as staff may find it more congenial to interact with one another. In this context, studies of room management are important, since this approach contributes to a clearer identification of staff roles, where one staff member works with the group as a whole while a second works for a short period with a single individual (McBrien and Weightman, 1980). There is also evidence to suggest that staff in charge of small residential units may actually spend less time in direct interaction with residents than those in charge of wards in large institutions (Felce *et al.*, 1980).

The move towards community services represents both a moral and a policy imperative, based on human rights in general and those of disabled and handicapped persons in particular, and supported by innumerable reports reflecting intolerably poor conditions in large institutions. Although the role of research has been relatively insignificant in bringing about these changes, there is ample scope for research in helping to pinpoint policies and practices relevant to successful community adjustment in the future. The available literature on residential services and deinstitutionalization has highlighted some issues which urgently need investigation, and which are relevant to the interests of planners and policy-makers as well as to the research community. While there is much to be done in preparing people to live and work successfully in community settings, adjustment must be seen as a two-way process. The task is now to develop a more finely differentiated awareness of the ways in which various aspects of the environment impinge on the individual. For example, there is considerable research documenting the low levels of interaction between staff and residents both in large and in smaller facilities; it seems that staff initiate very little interaction themselves, and that most residents are ignored for most of the time unless their behaviour is severely disruptive. In fact, remarkably little information is available on the day-to-day interactions of professional staff and other care-givers in any service. This needs to be an essential component of any monitoring or evaluation of service provision; studies by Heron and Myers (1983) and by King *et al.* (1971) in the UK and subsequently by Baker *et al.* (1977) and by Raynes *et al.* (1979) in the USA provide useful examples.

Finally, there is a dearth of information on the perceptions of the consumers of the service. It is clear from recent studies that adults with intellectual disability can be reliably interviewed by open-ended methods, and that a range of more structured interviewing tools can be used (see Howie *et al.*, 1984).

Implications for Third World countries

Is there anything to be learned from the experience of the western industrialized countries with residential services that may be relevant to countries in the Third World? Although most western commentators would probably wish to advise their colleagues in the Third World to avoid all institutions and to concentrate on measures designed to achieve community integration, such advice may be simplistic set against the realities of life for disabled people in many countries. Indeed, some wealthier countries in the Arab region are building new institutions for both children and adults, sometimes with a high quality of care but often isolated from the mainstream of community life. In other regions, particularly in Asia, the demand for some form of residential service is irresistible, as the only alternatives to community living are gaol or a secure mental hospital, neither of which is likely to provide the kind of training and rehabilitation needed by intellectually disabled adults.

Each country and each community needs to work out its own solution to the challenge of providing a form of residential service consistent with local conditions and customs. However, the disadvantages of large institutions have been so repeatedly documented that advice to avoid them in favour of community alternatives seems justified. Such alternatives will take a wide variety of forms and will, in many countries, be provided by voluntary or religious organizations, sometimes with the support of public funds but only rarely provided directly by government agencies or their local counterparts. In many cases, residential services can be found in small hostels, often side by side with a sheltered workshop or local industry; some of the communities provide for small groups of disabled and nondisabled people to live together. There are also examples of rural co-operatives, particularly in eastern Europe and parts of South America, which remain self-sufficient through marketing their products to the local community.

Whatever the form taken by these services, thought needs to be given to the degree of permanence of these arrangements for any individual, and in particular whether the residential environment should provide some form of training in the skills needed to live more independently. Since facilities are likely to be very limited, it is important to ensure that they do not become blocked by people who could live in less sheltered settings. It may be necessary to develop a range of accommodation, with some houses providing such training, and others primarily providing a permanent home.

Planners should not assume that the forms which have been tried in the industrialized countries constitute either an exhaustive list of the possibilities, or necessarily the most promising types for different social and cultural settings. The existing forms of unplanned community provision in Third World countries deserve close examination and evaluation to ensure that alternative culturally acceptable models are not overlooked.

STRATEGIES FOR GROWTH

Following on from earlier sections which have reviewed past and present patterns of service delivery, what future trends can be discerned? How can strategies for growth of people and of services be planned and put into practice? What are the possibilities for progress at a time of world economic recession and where should the priorities lie?

Although these are questions which each country and each community must answer for itself, we believe that there are some common elements which are, to varying extents, relevant to any society that wishes to consider the needs of its disabled citizens. Since many basic assumptions concerning the rights and needs of intellectually disabled people have either already undergone a fundamental change in the last two decades or are at least in the process of modification, we suggest that all countries can reconsider the quality and quantity of their services, whether those services are already highly developed or still virtually nonexistent.

General goals and assumptions

Fundamental to all services and to all plans for development are the assumptions that are made concerning the place of intellectually disabled people in society. In particular, it is necessary to consider assumptions concerning their rights to whatever services are available to the majority of others in their local community, however limited those may be; the possibility of meeting additional special needs which arise from their particular disabilities and circumstances; and whether such special needs can be met from an adaptation of ordinary services or by providing additional ones. Much depends also on the extent to which people with intellectual disabilities are seen as able to learn, to benefit from opportunities to develop their skills and abilities, and perhaps to make some positive contribution to society, rather than being seen solely as recipients of charitable assistance.

Many western countries are currently confronted by multiple paradoxes.

They are trying to deliver a service that reflects a developmental and educational model of disability with some totally anachronistic buildings and services created at a time when assumptions concerning intellectually disabled people were very different from those current today. In particular, the building of large 'colonies' remote from centres of population reflected the concerns of a society obsessed with fears of a decline of national intelligence which might be brought about by the 'propagation of the unfit' at the very time that the 'educated classes' were beginning to limit their families through contraception (Barker, 1983). The rapid growth of special schools, particularly in the period following the Second World War, represents a more recent example of a policy which has, to some extent, been overtaken by later thinking on educational integration.

The momentous expansion in the UK of special educational provision for children classified as 'educationally subnormal' (ESN) has provided the stimulus for a radical sociological critique of the whole field of special education by Tomlinson (1981, 1982), but with an explicit emphasis on the category of children designated as ESN(M) (now generally known as children with moderate learning difficulties). There are three main strands to her argument, pertaining to the processes of classification, segregation and professionalism. Classification of children as disabled, she argues, following the phenomenological school of thought, is not so much a process of discovery as one of construction. Disabled children are segregated into special educational programmes not merely as a preliminary to providing them with assistance which they need, but as a form of social control. Professionals who classify children as disabled thus tend to legitimate a process of segregating children in ways which stigmatize them and restrict their opportunities for participation in society as adults. Moreover, the economic interests of people accredited as special education professionals are served by the definition of increasing numbers of clients deemed to be in need of the services they provide.

The first problem is, on Tomlinson's own admission, less pertinent to the severely disabled than to marginal cases. However, the mere assertion that children with mild learning difficulties 'are not handicapped in the sense of the other designated categories' of children in need of special education (Tomlinson, 1981, p. 348) does nothing to reduce the need for psychological assessment. On the contrary, the argument that behaviour indicative of learning difficulties can arise from a multiplicity of different causes must surely point to the real technical complexity of psychological assessment as well as its moral importance.

We have discussed at some length the importance, as well as the practical difficulties, of integrated education. Furthermore, although Tomlinson's critique is centred on educational services for children, many of the arguments apply forcefully to the assumptions and processes underlying the organization of services for intellectually disabled adults. Despite the increasing emphasis on community-based services, a large proportion are still living and working in highly segregated settings.

On the third topic, of professional interests, Tomlinson has shifted her position from the notion that professionals would regard it as 'doing themselves out of business by letting their clients go' (1981, p. 323), to the more realistic view that if the Warnock recommendations (DES, 1978) are implemented, 'professional interests will be catered for by more complex procedures for assessing, recording and reviewing children with special educational needs' (Tomlinson, 1982, p. 57). The principal messages we would derive from this aspect of the sociological analysis are: (1) that professionals who specialize in working with people with intellectual disability would do well to recognize that their relationship with their clients is one of mutual dependency; and (2) that they should invest their professional pride in a tradition of adapting the services which they provide to the individual and changing needs of their clients, rather than in the promotion of any self-sustaining traditions concerning the best way of doing so.

Another paradox confronting many countries arises from the fact that the ordinary community services which disabled people are being urged to use are under severe strain as a result of public expenditure restrictions. In particular, the brunt of expenditure cuts in many European countries is being borne by the very same local government social service and welfare departments that are being asked to take a lead in the provision of new-style comprehensive local services for intellectually disabled people.

In the Third World, although the attitudes of society towards disabled people in general and the intellectually disabled in particular vary enormously, most disabled people are already in the community, living as best they can with their families, without much prospect of special services to meet their individual needs. Many are, in effect, segregated and isolated from their own local community, and regard disability as their 'station in life' (Miles, 1983a). Governments and public bodies rarely place intellectual disability high on their priority list, and are understandably preoccupied with problems of providing basic health care, sanitation and nutrition to the population as a whole.

Participation and self-advocacy

Against this background, we should note a growing recognition in some western countries that the abilities of intellectually disabled people to participate in discussion and decision-making, and to have a right to a say about their own needs, have been significantly underestimated by many professionals and parents. People with physical and sensory disabilities have increasingly organized themselves into 'consumer groups' at local, national and international level, and have drawn a parallel between their struggle for civil rights and those of other groups which have campaigned, with varying success, against discrimination – in particular women, and ethnic and religious minorities. Although 'participation and equality' were the slogans of IYDP, very few governments have passed legislation against discrimination of people with disabilities.

The demands of disabled people take a number of forms. Some demand a say in decision-making concerning their own personal rehabilitation programmes, and wish to have access to all case-conferences and to their personal records. Others wish to be represented at all planning and policy meetings where decisions concerning services for disabled people are being made. In addition, there are demands that the disabled should be represented, or even in a majority, on executive boards of voluntary organizations purporting to represent their interests, e.g. associations concerned with particular disabilities. There is concern that representation could be conceded by all these bodies merely on a 'token' basis.

In the case of people whose disabilities are intellectual in nature, arguments can be advanced (which need not be either dehumanizing or disrespectful) to the effect that they are, by definition, disabled from contributing *as equals* to many discussions at each of these levels. For this reason, a preoccupation with their right to do so may be seen as unrealistic, and could sometimes even lead to injustices or to a decline in the quality of services. If, for instance, the advocates who emerge from some kind of electoral process turn out (because of their greater articulacy) to be consistently those individuals whose disabilities are relatively mild, their interest in the special problems and needs of mildly disabled people might divert attention and resources away from the somewhat different needs of the more severely disabled. On the other hand, although there must be limits to the quality of understanding and participation of which an intellectually disabled person is capable, history is replete with examples of the abilities of intellectually disabled people being considerably under-estimated, even (perhaps especially) by those who know them well. A study of statements in textbooks over the past fifty years would surely bear testimony to the changing outlook of professionals and families on their abilities to respond to education, to vocational training, to find and keep a job, to live in ordinary housing, to take part in competitive sport and in the arts. These achievements are by no means confined only to the 'most able'.

There is also a small research literature on self-advocacy. In particular, a number of studies have examined the reliability and validity of statements made by intellectually disabled people concerning the quality of the services they were using. Howie *et al.* (1984) compared their own observations and assessments of care practices in a range of small residential environments with comments made by the residents themselves and with their use of a number of assessment measures. (See also Howie and Cuming (1984) for a more detailed historical account of the development of self-advocacy in New Zealand, and studies by Sigelman (1981, 1983) and Wyngaarden (1981) using intellectually disabled clients as informants in the context of deinstitutionalization studies.) Clearly, clients can articulate both criticisms and appreciation of services being provided for them, and their views can be elicited by those who are willing to take the trouble to do so.

The growing self-advocacy movement among intellectually disabled people is particularly noteworthy in the context of service developments which emphasize individual needs. Starting in Sweden, several self-advocacy organizations are now actively working in North America, Australia, the UK and some other European countries. An account of their origins and aims was provided by Williams and Shoultz (1982). In the UK many of the developments have taken place through the establishment of student committees in adult training centres (Crawley, 1982), as well as through regional groupings, particularly in London and central Scotland. Self-advocacy groups run their own meetings, elect their own officers and discuss issues of central concern to them, including questions relating to housing, employment, leisure, discrimination, relationships with parents and with professionals, personal relationships, marriage and children. Some 'People First' groups in the USA have produced helpful guidance leaflets and documents, advising their members on how to organize meetings, stand up for their rights, obtain information and deal with discrimination. In the USA, a quarterly newsletter, *UT (United Together)*, collates information on the activities of all the self-advocacy groups in the country.

At the international level, Disabled Persons International (DPI) is regularly represented at international meetings and is an accredited 'nongovernmental organization' to the major United Nations agencies. However, its policy with respect to full membership for organizations directly representing intellectually disabled people is still a little uncertain. Initially, DPI appeared willing to include only organizations representing the parents of intellectually disabled people, but later discussions appeared to open the door to national organizations such as People First. Presumably, the earlier decision was based on the assumption that intellectually disabled people were unable to speak for themselves and could not therefore make a meaningful contribution to an international self-advocacy movement.

The International League of Societies for Persons with Mental Handicap (ILSMH) has published a position paper on self-advocacy (Elkin and Temby, 1984) outlining ways in which intellectually disabled people can be helped to participate in decision-making from an early stage, for example by being encouraged to make choices between alternatives: it quotes examples of ways in which self-advocacy groups have developed in different countries. The ILSMH also provides a forum for people with intellectual disabilities to contribute to international and regional meetings, and has invited several members to join league committees.

The role of voluntary organizations

In considering possibilities for progress, there are good arguments in favour of initiatives coming both from the centre and from the periphery; clearly, the relationship between them will vary from country to country. In western Europe and North America, although central governments have played a major part in the drive to develop national policies and local services, the initiatives have often come from the local level, frequently from parent groups which have either set up their own services or persuaded public bodies or professional associations to do so. This is also a common pattern of development in Third World countries: small groups of parents, families and interested professionals, initially established to provide mutual support and encouragement, have gradually become more effective as pressure groups, or as fundraisers for local services. These may take the form of a small nursery group or a special class, often taught by the parents themselves or by volunteers, sometimes helped by foreign expatriates or local professionals. As the children become older, the focus of concern often shifts towards vocational training facilities and sheltered employment schemes.

Many services in Third World countries are provided entirely through voluntary organizations, including religious and charitable groups. Some of them are single services provided in only one town or locality; others are networks of services across a country or region. The organizations may be local or international (e.g. L'Arche communities, Vanier, 1982), and do not necessarily have any affiliations with central or local government or with any of the international agencies. Their work is largely undocumented.

One decision facing voluntary societies concerns the extent to which they should campaign for services for a specific group of children with intellectual disabilities or whether they should join forces with other organizations such as those for children with motor, hearing or visual disabilities. Although the specific needs of each group may be seen as quite distinct by their own members and those who advocate for them, there are considerable advantages in organizations concerned with a wide range of disabilities speaking with a single voice when making representations to governments and decision-making bodies. An alternative arrangement is for separate groups to maintain their own identity in relation to the needs of their own members, but to combine in an umbrella organization when they wish to make a political or policy impact.

The relationship of voluntary organizations to government agencies raises many complex issues. Should voluntary bodies aim to persuade governments to assume direct responsibilities for services out of public funds (for example, set up schools for children with learning difficulties, or create special classes attached to ordinary schools), or should the aim be to induce governments to fund schools and other services provided directly by the voluntary organizations? Many parent groups doubt the interest of government or the capacity of the educational system to operate schools for 'their' children, and would prefer to do the job themselves, or to employ others to do so. After all, the slogan of 'parents as partners' assumes a certain force if parents are in fact employing the teachers (Mittler and McConachie, 1983). On the other hand, a permanent commitment to run a service is a heavy financial burden for most voluntary organizations, and prevents them from pursuing other objectives.

Parent societies in all countries face challenges in the course of their development. In addition to those already mentioned, they have to make difficult decisions concerning their relationship with professionals and service providers in general, including the extent to which their own boards should or can include interested and helpful professionals but without sacrificing the essential priorities of the parent organization. Some organizations insist that the majority of board members should be parents, others that no professionals should be on the board. The larger societies can resolve this question by appointing professionals to advisory committees, e.g. those concerned with education, vocational training and fundraising, but ensuring that these committees are responsible to an all-parent executive board.

A further challenge for societies is to ensure that their membership, and particularly their leadership, includes younger parents and represents their interests. Many societies are run by older parents who tend to be concerned with the needs of adolescents and young adults and, more recently, with those of older adults and even the elderly. These parents have won many battles to secure better services, but they do not necessarily represent the interests and priorities of younger parents, some of whom are inclined to take a somewhat militant stance if they do not agree with what professionals or politicians are doing (or not doing). Problems may also arise in relation to the growing self-advocacy movement. In some countries, 'People First' organizations are entirely independent of the national or local parent societies; indeed, some conflict of interest is almost inevitable on certain issues.

Voluntary societies also have a delicate role in relation to central and local government. In many cases, they have succeeded in gaining the confidence of individual ministers or politicians, and have learned how to press their case with influential public servants. Some of the larger societies even have an office in the legislature and ready access to officials, and are involved in policy-making through consultation and membership of influential committees. Nevertheless, they have to reserve the right to mobilize opposition and to protest vigorously against policies which threaten or are contrary to the major objectives of their association.

The role of central government

What, then, is the role of central government in the development of services? It can certainly take strong initiatives in laying down legislation, in setting guidelines on the principles of a good service and in disseminating information on good practice. It can also provide an advisory service, or an 'inspectorate'. In addition, it can set up national advisory committees and announce its commitment in principle to the ensuing recommendations. It can also appoint a minister with specific responsibility for disabled people, to act as a catalyst and mobilize resources. On the other hand, governments can exercise a negative influence by lack of interest in the needs of disabled persons, and by failing to provide resources to implement policies or to improve the quality of services.

A critical problem in most countries arises from the overlapping responsibilities of different government departments for service delivery to intellectually disabled people and their families, resulting in a lack of co-ordination and collaboration in delivering a viable service at local level. Responsibilities for different aspects of service provision can rest with ministries of health, social welfare, education, employment, housing and environment, and justice, to name just some. Each minister and each group of officials jealously guards its boundaries, and resists not only territorial infringement but attempts at co-ordination. Attempts to resolve this problem produce new difficulties: for example, the establishment of a nondepartmental office under a single minister responsible directly to the president, prime minister or head of state still has to compete for resources with the main government departments from which it is organizationally isolated, thus defeating the ideological commitment to an integrated service for disabled people. Allocating the major responsibility to one department, such as social welfare, runs the risk of reducing collaboration with the others.

Despite these problems, there is a key role for central government in national policy formation. The recent WHO pamphlet *Mental Retardation: Meeting the Challenge* (1985) recommends the establishment of a comprehensive consultative body with representatives from the main government departments, professional bodies and voluntary organizations. Such a body would develop general policies, advise on and review services, stimulate good practice, develop guidelines on the quality of services and undertake or at least encourage continuous monitoring of services and standards. Questions can be asked concerning incidence and prevalence, the numbers served by existing specialized and ordinary services, unmet needs, the extent to which families and consumers have been consulted, community attitudes, policies of relevant professional bodies and examples of innovative services.

The role of local government

Even in countries with a strong central government, implementation of national policies generally depends on local interest and initiatives. Moreover, many countries regard services for the disabled as entirely a local responsibility. In many, central government delegates responsibility for various services to units of government that may serve millions of people, as in North America or India, whereas in the UK a typical local authority provides services for around 300,000 people. The extent to which the general public has access to decision-making at local and regional level varies considerably, but in most democratic societies decisions about resource allocation and the setting of priorities between different groups and services are influenced by elected citizens. By definition, these lay persons cannot be expected to be knowledgeable about the needs of disabled people, except through personal or family experience, and organizations campaigning for better services will need to inform and influence such key decision-makers at local level.

Decentralization of services to the community level has made considerable progress in the field of health care, and has been strongly encouraged by the WHO; several countries are now beginning to incorporate programmes of early detection and intervention for disabled children into primary health care, delivered by locally trained workers, but with some support and technical and specialized back-up from the nearest centres. (See, for example, Kysela and Marfo (1984) for descriptions of developments in Ghana and other West African countries; Bayes *et al.* (1982) for several examples from Asian countries; and Thorburn (1981) for a description of community programmes in the Caribbean region.)

It is important to ensure that such local programmes adopt a developmental growth orientation within the framework of a health care approach; this does not stop short at screening and identification or even at offering diagnostic and treatment services, but considers ways in which the family and local community can be helped on a daily basis to foster the development of their child by assisting him or her to acquire and use skills needed for community living. At a later stage, special measures may be needed to help the child to attend the local school and, at adolescence and adulthood, to help him or her to contribute to the local community.

A key role for local government agencies in the future will be to help disabled people to use the whole range of general services provided for the population as a whole. This includes not only the obvious 'institutional' services, such as schools, general hospitals, further and adult education colleges and vocational training services, but also those provided by family doctors, community nurses, social workers, counsellors and those who administer welfare benefits. Even if disabled people are, in principle, entitled to these services, they may need help in learning how to use them, perhaps from a friend or volunteer. At the same time, staff of these agencies in most countries need some training to make them aware of the needs and difficulties of disabled people in using ordinary community facilities.

STAFF TRAINING

Giving away skills

Preparing staff to work effectively with intellectually disabled people is probably the main priority for the coming decades. Although different countries will need to face this challenge in different ways and from different starting points, the development and delivery of appropriate forms of staff and personnel training provide the key to the development of better services.

The task for the future lies in bringing training to those who need it, that is, to the majority of people who work with or come into contact with intellectually disabled people and have no formal qualifications or training. They include parents and family members, volunteers and people working in ordinary services, as well as paid staff who are in day-to-day contact with clients. If progress is to be made, it is this group of people who will need to implement change, and who will need to be helped to do so by direct training in their own work setting rather than in distant centres of learning. This calls for a planned and strategic approach to staff development which is a total reversal of present practice; fortunately, there are signs that progress towards such a goal is possible, though it demands some fundamental changes in current assumptions about staff training.

One element of a strategic approach to staff development involves a planned commitment to disseminate information and skills by those professionals with some claim to specialist knowledge. This in turn calls for special initiatives in 'training the trainers', in preparing them to train other staff not only to work more effectively with clients and families but also to become change agents in their own work settings. In the UK, for example, twenty-one intensive five-day workshops in behavioural techniques of teaching children with severe learning difficulties were provided for a total of 100 educational psychologists, each of whom undertook to provide extended training courses in their own localities. So far, they have trained more than 3000 staff to criteria of competence identified in the original workshops (McBrien, 1981). The training materials were later made available in self-instructional form (McBrien and Foxen, 1981).

Such courses provide examples of a 'giving away of skills' model, in this instance from educational psychologists to teachers and care staff in special schools, but later extended to staff working in other services including hospitals, hostels and adult training centres. Similarly, speech therapists, physiotherapists, clinical psychologists and, to some extent, physicians have tended increasingly to work through front-line staff by helping them to acquire and use skills which were traditionally confined to more highly trained but exceedingly scarce specialists. The latter work more on a consultancy than a clinical model – that is, they act as advisers and co-ordinators and as staff trainers with the aim of helping front-line staff to make the best use of their own skills and practical experience rather than in a one-to-one relationship with individual children. Psychologists, for example, have helped staff in both schools and residential settings to use relevant assessment scales, and to relate these to the planning of intervention programmes both for groups and for individuals, just as physiotherapists and speech therapists have done in their own fields.

The challenge of retraining

The speed and scale of change in the field of teaching and habilitation have been so rapid that it is not far-fetched to suggest that all staff are unqualified and ill equipped to meet the challenges of the coming decades (Mittler, 1981a).

The changing patterns of service delivery from an institution to a community-based model, and the change of professional philosophy from a custodial or caring model to one which emphasizes teaching, habilitation and adaptation not only to, but also by, the community, call for a corresponding reorientation of professional training. This applies both to the training syllabus for any single professional group and also to a reappraisal of the kind of multidisciplinary professional skills needed in emerging services.

Several established professional groups are beginning to respond to this challenge. In the field of long-term hospital care, many nurses who trained as specialists in the hospital care of intellectually disabled people are now taking advanced courses in community nursing and in behavioural methods of teaching. Their experience with severely disabled people is invaluable in a consultative or direct support role for families and staff who are working to provide appropriate services for such clients in the community. Similarly, teachers who have been trained to work in special schools are now seeking wider training and experience to equip them for a role as support specialists to their colleagues in ordinary schools. In addition to their expertise, such specialists will need to be particularly sensitive to their role as 'adult educators'. To be a skilled teacher of children is not the same as sharing those skills with a colleague in an ordinary school. Particular attention will, therefore, need to be given to the interpersonal aspects of such consultancy skills, especially listening and negotiating. They will also need to have a working knowledge of various ways of achieving organizational change (e.g. Bowers, 1984).

In preparing themselves for a wider community role, professionals will need to acquire competencies which they may not previously have required. Until recently, the emphasis in training and retraining courses has been largely on teaching and rehabilitation skills, particularly in the use of behavioural methods of helping intellectually disabled people to learn basic self-care (including feeding, washing, dressing and toileting), language and communication (including nonvocal alternatives to speech), community living, vocational and, more recently, social and interpersonal skills. In addition to these direct teaching skills, however, training courses are increasingly concerned with issues of orientation and philosophy, with the principles and goals underlying services and with a range of possible models of service delivery. In particular, emphasis is being laid on the principles of normalization, as this value system is frequently misunderstood (Wolfensberger, 1972, 1983). All levels of staff are also being encouraged to participate in monitoring and evaluation sessions in which they identify their own goals as well as their perceptions of the goals of their service.

In addition to disability professionals retraining to prepare themselves for a wider role in community services, staff working in ordinary community services will need to learn more about the ways in which they might meet the needs of disabled people. At the level of 'primary care', family doctors, health visitors, public health nurses, specialists in community medicine, as well as teachers in ordinary schools, social workers and psychologists are all examples of professions whose initial pre-service training is unlikely to have included more than the briefest introduction to the needs of disabled people in general or of the intellectually disabled in particular, but who will all need to become more familiar with recent developments in professional practice. At the referral level, the services of specialists in sensory and motor impairments and in psychiatric disorders are particularly required by intellectually disabled people, in whom these conditions are found much more frequently than among the general public. These include both medical and nonmedical personnel in these fields; for example, technical help is needed in the fitting, repair and appropriate use of spectacles, hearing aids, wheelchairs and prosthetic devices. Intellectually disabled people have in the past not always enjoyed access to such specialists; even when they did, their needs were not necessarily fully appreciated. For example, it was sometimes assumed that they would be 'unlikely to benefit from' aids or specialized treatment for these disorders because of their low intelligence.

Multidisciplinary training

Although it is widely recognized that work with intellectually disabled people calls for the skills of several different professions, many recent training initiatives have come from and been confined to single professions. It is to be hoped that training courses will in future be planned on a more interdisciplinary basis than in the past. In countries with a strong basis of initial single discipline professional training (e.g. in medicine, nursing, teaching, psychology and social work), some attempt can be made to provide pre-service students with awareness and, if possible, actual experience of working alongside other professionals. While this may help to provide the foundations for an appreciation of the contribution of other professions, it seems more realistic to emphasize the importance of interdisciplinary training at the post-experience level. Advances in the teaching and rehabilitation of intellectually disabled people are of equal interest and relevance to several professions, and rarely the exclusive concern of any single profession. It therefore makes sense to ensure that training courses are made available on a multidisciplinary basis, though this is difficult to achieve in countries where even short advanced courses tend to be organized within a single service.

Initial training

Initial training courses for health professionals, teachers, social workers and psychologists are now beginning to include an element of awareness of the needs of disabled people, and wherever possible to ensure that students encounter people with disabilities, their families and the professionals who work with them. Despite a crowded syllabus and many other priorities, students seem to show a high level of interest in the needs of disabled people, and take advantage of opportunities to gain experience in working with these populations, sometimes in a voluntary capacity. A UNESCO survey has indicated that an increasing number of initial teacher training courses now include a 'special education' element (Alinson *et al.*, 1984). In Britain, for example, such a special educational element is likely to become compulsory in all initial teacher training courses. As part of their response to IYDP some medical and other professional training schools have included more material on disability, but no detailed information is available on either the extent of such teaching or whether the needs of intellectually disabled people are included in the initial training curriculum. One obvious obstacle lies in the absence of teaching staff with sufficient knowledge and experience to provide even an introductory course.

Implications for Third World countries

Third World countries with limited trained manpower clearly face particular problems in making the most effective use of training facilities in their own countries and overseas. One model designed to provide a strategic approach to meeting this challenge was developed by the Canadian Association for the Mentally Retarded and adopted by the International League of Societies for Persons with Mental Handicap (ILSMH). It is summarized by Roeher (1978, 1982) and Mittler (1982, 1983). This Manpower Model distinguishes four categories of personnel and four corresponding levels of training:

Level 1 includes all those who are in continuous daily contact with handi-capped people – parents, volunteers and all direct care staff; their training needs are for short structured 'on the job' courses of skill training – for example, on methods of helping intellectually disabled people to acquire basic self-care and community competencies.
Level 2 are also mostly in direct contact with clients but have some supervisory responsibilities. Levels 1 and 2 combined contain as many as 80 per cent of the workforce who need to be reached by locally based training courses.
Level 3 consists of more highly trained supervisors and advisors, many of whom will have some higher education.
Level 4 consists of a small group of programme planners, administrators, research workers and professionals in key roles.

Unfortunately the WHO programme on CBR, which also distinguishes four levels of personnel in the organization of services, has chosen the reverse order for numbering the levels. In the WHO scheme, level 1 is entitled referral services, level 2 intermediate-level supervision (by teams which would normally include a trained rehabilitation therapist), level 3 comprises local supervisors (e.g. primary health care workers) and level 4 trainers (identified among the client's family and local community).

Roeher (1982) pointed out that many industrialized countries have large numbers of highly trained staff who are doing tasks which could be done by parents, volunteers and untrained staff working under supervision, whereas Third World countries have very few specialized personnel, not all of whom are training or supervising others. In particular, staff who have been on advanced training courses overseas may need to be encouraged to share their knowledge and skills with others; to this end, some form of pyramid training structure may have to be developed, which will allow those who have been trained to assume a contractual commitment to train others in their turn. Although such a model has been shown to work in the west, it may not be so readily applicable elsewhere. Staff with high-level training acquired overseas are not always prepared to share their skills with others, for reasons of status and prestige (see comments on the Manpower Model summarized by Mittler (1982)). In any case, their level 3 and 4 training may have been theoretical and academic, and has not necessarily equipped them with direct teaching and rehabilitative skills which they can pass on to others.

Level 3 and 4 staff have not been well used in either industrialized or Third World countries. Many have gone overseas and received training which did not prepare them to play a useful catalytic role on their return; nor was there any systematic plan to enable them to do so.

Management issues

Staff training cannot be seen in isolation from the goals and operations of the service as a whole. Training of level 3 and 4 workers, whether in their own countries or abroad, should be part of a systematic service development strategy which clearly identifies the goals of the training, its suitability to the needs of the service and of the seconded staff members, and which plans in advance for ways in which they will put their training to the most effective use on their return. Such planning is rare in any country. It becomes of even greater importance when a country is relying heavily on foreign institutions for the training of its professional personnel. Such personnel will often need encouragement and assistance to 'unpackage' the technology to which their foreign training has exposed them and identify appropriate ways of adapting it to local needs and resources (cf. Serpell, 1984b). Even the training of level 1 and 2 staff is unlikely to be effective unless there is involvement of the local supervisors and decision-makers without whom change will be impossible. One strength of the WHO community-based rehabilitation manuals is that they have begun to address these issues (WHO, 1983).

The literature on the effectiveness of staff training in industrialized countries gives grounds for concern and raises questions about the extent to which less developed countries can avoid some of the problems highlighted in the literature (for a brief summary, see Mittler, 1984a):

1. There is no necessary relationship between knowledge and application in the work setting.
2. Even when staff do try to use and apply training, the effects are not necessarily lasting and may 'wash out' after a short period.

3. Clients do not necessarily show measurable gains in skills and competencies.
4. Good managerial support and commitment to the implementation and evaluation of change are essential components of success. To this end, staff training must take managerial and organizational factors into account; staff training in isolation is of little value.
5. One of the key elements in considering staff performance concerns the number and nature of the interactions between staff and clients. There is evidence of rather low levels of interaction of any kind and that many attempts by clients to initiate interactions are not noticed or reciprocated by staff, even when staffing levels are relatively high (Raynes *et al.*, 1979; Landesman-Dwyer, 1983; Repp *et al.*, 1983).

ROLE OF INTERNATIONAL ORGANIZATIONS

International collaboration in the field of disability has been developing fairly rapidly during the past decade, and has been given considerable impetus by IYDP. Nevertheless, there is potential for a much more systematic approach to international collaboration, particularly in respect of practical activities. We do not refer here in any detail to the work of all the different organizations involved, but it may be useful to draw some simple distinctions between different levels of activity.

The United Nations family of organizations

Although much of the detailed work is done by specific UN agencies, the UN itself has developed major initiatives in the field of disability. The Secretary-General of the UN accepted significant responsibilities for IYDP, most of these being implemented through the Centre for Social Development and Humanitarian Affairs in Vienna, which co-ordinated many of the UN activities for IYDP, and produced the World Programme of Action Concerning Disabled Persons and the UN Decade of Disabled Persons (1983–1992) (UN, 1983). It reports to the General Assembly which determines policy and resource allocation.

Most of the specific organizations have a small section concerned with disability. Although the specific needs of intellectually disabled people are increasingly mentioned in their publications, disability is still frequently associated with physical and sensory impairments. Initiatives taken by the UN organizations have included publications, and international and regional seminars, in an effort to disseminate examples of good practice and provide international leadership. But UN organizations are entirely dependent on the support of member states for the implementation of changes at the national level. The UN can do nothing except by direct invitation of member states. A second level of activity concerns direct help to individual countries through visits of consultants and specialists, again at the request of member states. A brief account of UN activities has been provided by representatives of each of the main organizations (ILSMH, 1978b).

There are several examples of influential new initiatives which have originated with the UN organizations, perhaps the most significant being the WHO community-based rehabilitation programme resulting in the publication of the manual *Training Disabled People in the Community*. A pamphlet, *Mental Retardation: Meeting the Challenge*, commissioned by WHO from the Joint Commission on International Aspects of Mental Retardation, provides an overview of recent developments in prevention, rehabilitation and services, with particular reference to the needs of Third World countries (WHO, 1985).

UNESCO has also been active in the field of special education and has produced a substantial number of publications, some providing general guidelines on policy and implementation, others giving examples of good practice in particular countries.

In connection with IYDP, tape slides were commissioned illustrating innovative developments in some countries in different parts of the world. Some of UNESCO's publications are specifically concerned with the education of children and young people with severe learning difficulties. Among their more important recent ones are those concerned with general policies and principles of special education (1979), economic aspects (1978), a book of case-studies concerned with early detection, intervention and education (1981), the proceedings of a world conference (1982), a volume on terminology in four languages (1984a), and an international directory of development in special education in each of the member states (1984b). In addition, several reports are available on conferences and seminars in particular regions.

The ILO's work has displayed a specific interest in the vocational rehabilitation of people with intellectual disabilities. The publication *Vocational Rehabilitation of the Mentally Retarded* (ILO, 1978) provides detailed guidelines on advances in vocational training and work placement, as well as case-studies from different countries. Since then, the ILO has promulgated recommendations and conventions and provided a manual on implementation (ILO, 1984a).

UNICEF has not been active in the field of childhood disability until comparatively recently but, following the recommendations of a report from Rehabilitation International (1981), is now embarking on several projects in different regions, with particular emphasis on prevention and early intervention. Its journal, *Assignment Children*, devoted a special issue to the theme of childhood disability (UNICEF, 1981) which included accounts of the work of UNICEF and other international agencies, as well as detailed case-studies of intervention programmes in different countries (e.g. Algeria, Botswana, Jamaica, Philippines).

Regional organizations

Many regional and supranational organizations not necessarily connected with the United Nations have set up working parties, issued policy statements and in some cases launched action projects concerned with disability. Within Europe, for example, the EEC has established a special Bureau of Action in Favour of the Handicapped in Brussels which has been particularly active in launching demonstration projects in the field of vocational rehabilitation.

The Council of Europe and the European Parliament have also been active, particularly since IYDP. The OECD's Centre for Research and Innovation has undertaken a study of services for disabled adolescents and young people in their twenty-one member states, mainly in Europe, North America, Australia and New Zealand (OECD, 1981, 1983).

In the Americas, the Partners of the Americas, which have organized an exchange of people, materials and resources between specific regions within the American continent, have recently included disability services within its programme and is rapidly becoming a productive framework for development partnerships in Latin America and the Caribbean. The PATH (Partners Appropriate Technology for the Handicapped) disseminates information about low-cost aids and rehabilitation techniques.

International organizations and networks

Of the two major international organizations concerned with intellectual disability, the International Association for the Scientific Study of Mental Deficiency is primarily involved in the dissemination of information on research developments in all the major disciplines, and in rehabilitation work and the evaluation of services. International conferences are held every three years (e.g. Mittler, 1977, 1981b; Berg, 1984; Berg, in preparation). The International League of Societies for Persons with Mental Handicap (ILSMH) is a world-wide federation of 100 parent and professional societies in 67 countries. Strong links have been established between Canada and the Caribbean (Thorburn, 1981); New Zealand and the Pacific Islands; Norway and Bangladesh (Barua, 1983) and Kenya; and Germany and several Asian countries (Mutters, 1982). These partnerships are increasingly conceived on a basis of equality and sharing, rather than as means of richer countries providing aid to poorer ones. 'Partnership markets' have been arranged at international and regional conferences; these provide a forum for the exchange of people and materials not only between industrialized and Third World countries but also among less developed countries which have much to learn from one another's experience.

The ILSMH has organized a number of regional workshops. For example, a family/training workshop was held for teams of three people from each of thirteen countries in the Asian region – a parent, a teacher and a community worker. Participants, who were selected by their own organizations at local level, met for one week in Hong Kong in an intensive training workshop concerned with techniques designed to help intellectually disabled children to acquire specific skills, e.g. in walking, movement, self-care, play, language and in the management of behaviour problems (Mittler and Beasley, 1982). A similar workshop, concentrating on ways in which services for intellectually disabled persons could be developed from local resources, was organized by the League in Nairobi for two representatives from each of ten African countries, each team consisting of a parent and a professional or government official (Serpell, 1983). Within Europe, nine parent societies were asked to send a parent and a professional to discuss their experience of parent–professional relationships and to make recommendations (Mittler and McConachie, 1983).

The League has also established a number of working parties on specific issues and regularly publishes position papers and guidance documents (for a brief overview of its work, see Mittler, 1984b). These are concerned, *inter alia*, with the establishment of local societies (ILSMH, 1983); differences between mental illness and intellectual disability (Cobb and Mittler, 1980); rights and advocacy (Herr and Herr, 1984); participation and self-advocacy (Elkin and Temby, 1984); presenting a positive image of people with intellectual disabilities (Shearer, 1984); the needs of elderly people (Thomae and Fryers, 1982), as well as reports on conferences and seminars on various topics.

Stronger regional organizations are developing in Asia and Africa. In Asia, the Asian Federation for Persons with Mental Handicap is a regional federation of voluntary societies associated with the League which holds regional conferences every two years, and is active in promoting staff and service development (cf. Bayes *et al.*, 1982). Network Africa was launched in 1982 and is co-ordinated by the Kenya Society for the Mentally Handicapped following the recommendations of the local resources workshop in Nairobi; it issues regular newsletters in English and French and aims to promote services and encourage local initiatives in all African countries.

RESEARCH, EVALUATION AND MONITORING

Some of the stimulus for the changes we have described in the orientation of services in western industrialized countries came from evaluative studies of earlier forms of care. Many administrators and planners, however, remain profoundly sceptical about the usefulness of research, and especially about the relevance of basic research to the formulation of service policy. To a somewhat lesser degree, this scepticism tends to be shared by many direct care staff. Scientists are often regarded as having a contribution to make to the causal explanation of intellectual disability, but as being too abstract and theoretical to be of help with the practical tasks of education and rehabilitation. The remoteness of research from immediate needs is even more strongly felt by many families of a child with intellectual disability.

In some respects, however, this situation is changing. The demystification of scientific knowledge about intellectual disability has been of interest to a number of research centres in the past decade, and is well illustrated by such books as the Human Horizon series (e.g. Cunningham and Sloper, 1978; Whelan and Speake, 1979), many of which are written by research workers aiming to provide practical advice on various aspects of management and education to literate parents with an intellectually disabled child. As we have noted on p. 757, the current movement towards community-based care brings with it a need for professionals to diffuse their expertise, sharing knowledge and 'giving away' skills. Implicit in this formulation, however, is the premise that relevant knowledge and techniques will always originate from specialists. Even when direct care personnel are invited to participate in the generation of information, this is strictly within a framework specified by a centrally placed specialist.

The partnership between professionals, parents and paraprofessional service staff which we have advocated in respect of assessment, management and education also finds a parallel in the utilization of information. Family members and paraprofessional, direct care staff can derive immediate benefit from the information they record rather than merely reporting it to a specialist researcher for analysis and interpretation. 'Implementers' who observe the client, take stock of their own resources, set their own targets and monitor progress towards them have ceased to be passive reporters of information and become instead full participants in the search for knowledge and understanding. Detection of such progress is a demonstrable source of motivation for the implementer of a programme, and involvement in the interpretation of the recorded information greatly reduces the likelihood of casual disinterest in the accuracy of what is recorded.

On the other hand, the evaluation of a service calls for a greater degree of detachment than monitoring. The agents responsible for implementing a service can profitably participate in the determination of programme objectives and in the criteria for assessing progress towards them, but it is probably counterproductive to assign to them the full task of evaluation. Although the implementer may derive considerable insight from attempting a self-assessment, the incentives for detecting and reporting successful features at the expense of unsuccessful ones are too great for a balanced or 'objective' assessment to be likely. And if token, self-congratulatory inhouse evaluations are substituted for detached, critical enquiries, the long-term consequences are likely to be complacency and a decline in the quality of services. In general, therefore, an effective division of responsibilities among implementers and outside researchers will assign more monitoring to the former and more evaluation to the latter.

Research expertise can be brought to bear on the preparation of both types of exercise by training the various observers in techniques of coding, ordering and aggregating data, as well as in the co-ordination of the various perspectives on a problem favoured by different participants. Research centres which are willing to undertake these less academically conventional tasks as well as prospective investigations of a practical nature, such as studying the feasibility of a policy innovation or assessing the demand for a certain type of service, are then in a stronger position of credibility among practitioners and families of clients for gaining their co-operation in respect of longer-term, more basic investigations whose practical pay-off can only be dimly envisaged as an ultimate consequence of greater scientific understanding.

The development of written individual programme plans provides an opportunity for direct care staff and parents to monitor progress and assess the extent to which stated objectives are being achieved. This calls for closer attention to the clear specification of targets written in clear and unambiguous language, as well as some knowledge of simple but appropriate methods of recording the progress made by clients in specific areas of skill and functioning. If client progress is to be the final yardstick of the success of a service, more attention will need to be given to helping staff to develop and use clear records of learning and skill acquisition.

In addition, more could be done to encourage managers of agencies to make clearer statements about the goals of the services for which they are responsible, and to prepare annual reports, recording the extent to which stated targets have been achieved, obstacles and difficulties which have been encountered, and ways in which it is proposed to try to resolve these in the coming year. In the UK the 1980 Education Act requires all schools to issue a public statement concerning the nature of their curriculum and resources, whereas the 1981 Education Act mandates 'statements' of special educational needs for certain children and the plans of the authority for meeting those needs. It has been suggested that all adult training centres and hospitals should publish annual reports and ensure that their contents are widely disseminated and discussed (NDGMH, 1977, 1978).

Maintaining a balance of priorities between the needs perceived by administrators for immediate practical information and the more theoretical interests of the scientific community is particularly difficult in Third World societies (cf. Stifel *et al.*, 1982). On the one hand, the scale and severity of practical problems are often monumental in these countries, and the proportion of the population with sufficiently advanced formal education for the understanding of theoretical concerns is extremely small. The research community, on the other hand, is very small and has very limited local precedent which can be cited to legitimate basic research. And yet the need for basic descriptive information and for new theoretical concepts and imaginative innovations is probably greatest in these societies, since so much of the formal body of knowledge concerning intellectual disability derives from studies conducted in very different social conditions and interpreted in terms of a cultural system which is very remote from most of the local clientele (cf. Serpell, 1984a, 1984b).

At a more formal level, there is increasing evidence of greater interest among both research workers and administrators in evaluation both of existing services and, more particularly, of the effectiveness of innovative services. A much wider range of research methods is now in use, including both qualitative and quantitative research, and there is rather less reliance on comparisons between experimental and control groups and the use of comparisons between 'before and after' measures. While strict quantitative approaches certainly provide powerful analytic tools, they need to be supplemented by a wider range of evaluation methodologies which can at least try to incorporate some of the more qualitative aspects of service evaluation, including the views of the consumers and professionals most closely involved.

Interesting examples of studies evaluating an innovative service have been provided by Heron and Myers (1983) in Sheffield, as well as by Blunden (1985) in Cardiff and Felce *et al.* (1983) in the Wessex region of the UK. The main evaluation methods used in these and other studies are as follows (Mittler, 1984a):

1. Simple quantitative monitoring studies of the number of places provided, number of clients served, staffing ratios, measures of progress on an annual basis towards stated goals.
2. Descriptive, qualitative and observational studies of the operation of specific services, e.g. of a hospital in process of run-down, the effects of relocating residents into community services, the attitudes of staff in both settings; effects on an ordinary school of the arrival of a group of handicapped children.
3. Attitudes and attitude change to intellectually disabled people by members of a local community as a consequence of increased contact and media programmes.
4. Evaluation of specific components of a service by staff and by the consumers themselves.
5. Quantitative studies on the nature and frequency of interactions between clients and those around them.
6. Studies which experimentally manipulate features of the environment, including number of staff, nature of staff demands, size and homogeneity of client groupings, physical changes in environment such as room size, placement of furniture and use of space.
7. The effects of organizational and managerial change, e.g. delegating decision-making to direct care staff.
8. Individual differences in the reactions of clients to change, with a view to assessing whether effects differ between subgroups of clients.
9. Monitoring the short-term and long-term impact of staff training courses on participants, clients and management practices.
10. Assessing spontaneous and learned generalization of learned skills by intellectually disabled people and by care-givers across different settings, and in a variety of demand contexts.

CONCLUSION: OBSTACLES TO DEVELOPMENT

In considering strategies for growth in services, it seems useful in conclusion to identify a number of obstacles which have been encountered, some of which might be avoided by careful planning and by studying the experience of other societies. Although each country will need to interpret such experience in the light of its own situation, beliefs and priorities, some common elements are discernible in the range of national and international statements and policies which have been promulgated concerning the needs of intellectually disabled people.

Broadly speaking, these are concerned with the rights of access to ordinary services and resources of the community; the need to develop a wide range of locally accessible services to match the range of need; services which will achieve maximum social integration into the community in education, work and leisure; the right of individuals and families to participate in decision-making and to receive individualized services that match perceived needs, including any special help that may be needed to compensate for specific or general impairments and difficulties.

(1) Segregation within the community

The fact that an individual is using community services does not imply that he or she is accepted by or integrated into that community. It is possible to live in an ordinary house but to be totally isolated from the neighbourhood; to attend an ordinary school but to be effectively segregated from activities, peers and friendships. The fact that this is also the fate of many nondisabled persons is no reason for allowing such isolation to develop by default.

(2) Failure to provide necessary support

It is not enough to provide integrated facilities such as housing, schooling or work without ensuring that the individual receives the necessary support and help to enable him or her to make the best use of these local services. Simply placing a person in an ordinary house or school is only the first step to integration; the difficulty comes in providing whatever support is needed, and knowing when the time has come to reduce it and help the individual to take a further step in becoming autonomous and independent.

(3) Discontinuities

The needs of intellectually disabled people do not change when responsibility for their services passes from one agency to another. All too frequently, however, services which are available at one stage of a person's development suddenly disappear when responsibility for services passes from one agency to another. Examples of such discontinuities can be found in all countries. They include withdrawal of family support when children begin school; loss of specialist programming, the services of health care professionals and partnership with families when children leave school and enter adult services, or when adults are discharged from long-stay hospitals into community services; withdrawal of leisure outlets when young people are 'too old' for youth clubs; and absence of specialist help when older people are 'integrated' into community services for elderly people who are not intellectually disabled.

(4) Exclusions

Although a local service should be available to all local citizens, certain groups tend to be overlooked because their needs are complex and difficult to meet. These include people who are profoundly and multiply handicapped, those with severe behaviour disturbances, and the elderly. Even countries with highly integrated services still tend to exclude certain groups, sometimes only temporarily. But short-term arrangements can easily become permanent.

(5) Neglecting families and clients

Partnership between families and professionals is now widely agreed to be a hallmark of a good service, but many families are still involved only in token relationships. This is particularly so with families of adults.

Professionals too easily assume that the current ideology of community services must automatically be in the interests of all users of the service. Since individual needs vary, some people, if given a real choice, might prefer a lifestyle which was not envisaged by those who drew up the plan. In a pluralistic, tolerant society scope must be provided for flexible accommodation of such individual preferences, wherever possible.

(6) Excessive programming

Despite the advantages of individual programme planning, it is important to allow scope for individual choice, including the choice not to be constantly climbing developmental ladders or achieving the next step on the task analysis.

(7) Blaming lack of resources

In times of severe resource constraint, it is all too easy to use shortage of money/staff/buildings/equipment as an excuse for doing little or nothing. Experience of some Third World countries indicates that much can be achieved with very little, and that resources in industrialized countries are often deployed on the wrong services in the wrong place.

(8) Undefined aims and woolly planning

Many countries and local communities remain at the stage of rhetorical statements of principle without identifying processes and procedures for implementation. Principles of goal planning which have been developed for individuals can also apply to service development, i.e. clear specification of who will do what, when, how and with what result. Costs also need detailed consideration.

(9) Rigid planning

Too much planning can stultify flexibility for decades ahead. Buildings that seem to suit the needs of today will almost certainly be regarded as totally unsuitable a few years hence. Allocating responsibility for certain groups to specific professions or services (e.g. the more severely disabled to health professionals) can also inhibit flexibility.

(10) Failing to monitor

Complacency induced by erecting buildings or creating jobs can lead to neglect of the need to maintain a good quality of service. The needs of individuals should be reviewed regularly, with the participation of individual clients and of the family and staff who are in a direct service relationship with them.

(11) Neglecting the needs of staff

All levels of staff need to feel that their work is valued by others. Managers too often take the work of staff for granted, except when there is a problem, and forget to recognize and praise good-quality work. Continuous staff training and development are essential to maintain morale and growth in staff and service delivery.

(12) Excessive professionalization

Excessive professionalization occurs when highly trained staff carry out tasks which can be done by staff without formal qualifications, and when there is too much mystification concerning the skills required to work with intellectually disabled people. Many of these skills can be learned comparatively quickly by families, volunteers, community workers and staff without formal qualifications. Skilled professionals are needed to provide leadership, staff training and support.

NOTE ON TERMINOLOGY

We have chosen to use the expression *intellectual disability* in this chapter, in preference to the expression *mental deficiency* which appears in the title of the book, for the following reasons:

1. It seems to us important that those who are directly involved in the provision of services should be able to defend the terminology they use to a nonspecialist public in terms of its actual connotations in current usage.
2. The distinctive characteristic of the group to be defined is an *intellectual disability*. This intellectual disability is not a static or unchanging feature

of the individual, as the term *deficiency* appears to imply. Nor does it reflect a mere *retardation* of the processes of cognitive development, still less a global *mental* retardation. One of the advances in service orientation implicit in the 'normalization' principle is the recognition that intellectually disabled people do mature into adults, but without necessarily losing their intellectual disability.

3. Our objection to the use of *mental* is largely on two grounds. In the first place, the mental life of intellectually disabled people shows a great deal of variation in terms of personality, temperament and emotion, as well as in other dimensions of their experience. It is therefore not appropriate to invoke a global concept of mental impairment when only some mental functions are affected. Second, the use of the adjective *mental* has the grave disadvantage of confusing intellectual disability with *mental illness*. It is politically important to avoid such confusion at a time when attempts are being made to help the public to understand the distinctive needs of intellectually disabled people.

4. A further reason for considering the revision of terminology arises from the attempt made by the World Health Organization (1980, 1983) to effect a clearer distinction between *impairment, disability* and *handicap*. Although these terms do not necessarily translate well into other languages, they do have the advantage of emphasizing distinctions between words which are frequently confused in the English language. In particular, it is now increasingly accepted that handicap should be seen as residing not in the individual but in the interactions between the individual and the opportunities presented by the various environments in which he or she is living; in other words, handicap is seen as a social rather than as a personal phenomenon. Furthermore, the extent to which the disability results in a disadvantage or handicap in daily life must be extremely variable. Since the aim of services must be to reduce handicap, it follows that describing an individual as handicapped is circular, and perhaps a contradiction in terms.

5. Our preference for 'disability' as a term of choice is partly related to its growing acceptance in the population, and in particular to its more widespread use in the context of IYDP and later developments. Although the term disability has in the past been associated with physical and sensory impairments, the time now seems ripe for the inclusion of those with intellectual disabilities within the wider group of disabled people.

Our analysis is, of course, based on the connotations of the available terms in one language. A similar, but not literally parallel analysis needs to be made in each language used for the national planning of services. In some cases the language may be regarded as lacking in suitable vocabulary, and planners will prefer to coin new words or to borrow terms from another language. But if this is done it will still be necessary to compose a suitable explanatory glossary in the local language for introducing the new terminology.

APPENDIX: REPORTS ON REGIONAL AND NATIONAL DEVELOPMENTS

In preparing this chapter, we have drawn on a number of reports describing service and research developments in different regions and countries. Since we refer to only some of these in the main text, we thought it might be helpful to list some of these sources in an appendix. Although the list is necessarily incomplete and unrepresentative, readers may find it helpful to consult the *International Directory of Mental Retardation Resources* (Dybwad, 1979) or Sterner (1976) for a brief description of the services and principal organizations in a large number of countries. Both lists are being updated, but recent information can usually be obtained by writing to the addresses listed in these directories.

Useful sources of information for purposes of updating include the annual review volumes edited by Wortis (1966) and by Ellis (1966); the proceedings of international and regional conferences organized by IASSMD and ILSMH, the *International Journal of Rehabilitation Research, Assignment Children* (UNICEF), *World Health* (WHO), *Courier* (UNESCO), *Ideas Forum* (UNICEF) and *International Rehabilitation Review* (Rehabilitation International).

Reports are listed in alphabetical order of countries, preceded by a number of international and regional reports.

(1) International reports

Dybwad, R.F. (1974, 1979); Sterner (1976); Dixon and Davis (1981); UNICEF (1981); Kysela and Marfo (1984).

(2) Regional reports

Asia	Abad (1973); Yamaguchi (1975); Prabhu (1980); Smith *et al.* (1980); Stein and Susser (1980); Bayes *et al.* (1982).
Europe	Magne (1976); Jorgensen (1980).
Africa	Marfo *et al.* (1983); Serpell (1983); Dybwad and Mittler (1984).
Latin America	Sardi de Selle and Abadi (1977).

(3) Individual countries

Australia	Birnbrauer and Leach (1981).
Canada	Kysela *et al.* (1981).
France	Lafon and Chabenier (1966); Laury (1976).
Hungary	Szondy and Szentagothai (1981); Lanyi-Engelmayer *et al.* (1983).
India	Sen (1976, 1981); Sinclair (1981).
Italy	Jervis (1972); Posternak (1979); Vislie (1981a).

Japan	Takahashi (1973).
Nepal	Thaler (1982).
New Zealand	Mathews (1973); Singh (1981); Singh and Wilton (1984).
Norway	Bjorgen (1966); Vislie (1981b); Mellgren and Gotestam (1983).
Soviet Union	Vlasova (1973); Shennan (1977); Holowinsky (1984).
Sweden	Gruenwald (1975); Omsorgkomitten (1981); Soder (1981).
United States	President's Committee on Mental Retardation (PCMR, 1979); Schroeder and Schroeder (1981).
West Germany	Schmidt and Baltes (1971); Mutters (1973); Kane and Rojahn (1981).

REFERENCES

ABAD, C.M. (1973) *Hope for the Retarded in Asia*, proceedings of the Asian Conference on Mental Retardation, Manila, Philippines Association for the Retarded.

ACMRDD (Accreditation Council for Services to Mentally Retarded and Other Developmentally Disabled Persons) (1983) *Standards for Services for Developmentally Disabled Individuals*, 2nd edn, Washington, DC, ACMRDD.

ALLINSON, O., BOWMAN, I. and WEDELL, K. (1984) *Teacher Training and the Education of Handicapped Pupils in the Ordinary School*, Paris, UNESCO, mimeo.

BAKER, B.L., SELTZER, G.N. and SELTZER, M.M. (1977) *As Close as Possible: Community Residences for Retarded Adults*, Boston, Little, Brown.

BARKER, S. (1983) 'How to curb the fertility of the unfit: the feeble-minded in Edwardian Britain', *Oxford Rev. Educ.*, 9, 197–211.

BARUA, D.P. (1983) 'Report from Bangladesh', in R. SERPELL (ed.), *Mobilizing Local Resources in Africa for Persons with Learning Difficulties or Mental Handicap*, Oslo, NFPU; Brussels, ILSMH.

BAYES, K., CHAN, W., NG, W. and TANG, F.C. (eds) (1982) *Developing Resources for Mentally Retarded Persons*, Hong Kong, Joint Council for the Physically and Mentally Disabled.

BEGAB, M. and RICHARDSON, S. (eds) (1975) *The Mentally Retarded and Society*, Baltimore, University Park Press.

BELLAMY, G.T., HORNER, R.H. and INMAN, D.P. (1979) *Vocational Rehabilitation of Severely Retarded Adults*, Baltimore, University Park Press.

BERG, J.M. (ed.) (1984) *Perspectives and Progress in Mental Retardation*, 2 vols, Baltimore, University Park Press.

BERG, J.M. (ed.) (in preparation) *Science and Service in Mental Retardation*, London, Methuen.

BIRNBRAUER, J. and LEACH, D. (1981) 'A progress report on Australian practice and research in intellectual handicap', *Appl. Res. Ment. Retard.*, 2,

165–80.

BJORGEN, I.A. (1966) 'Some aspects of research on mental retardation in Norway; in N. ELLIS (ed.), *International Review of Research in Mental Retardation*, vol. 2, New York, Academic Press.

BLUMA, S., SHEARER, J., FROHMAN, A. and HILLIARD, J. (1976) *Portage Guide to Early Education*, Windsor, NFER/Nelson.

BLUNDEN, R. (1985) 'Behaviour analysis of services for mentally handicapped people', in S.E. BREUNING, J.L. MATSON and R.P. BARRETT (eds), *Advances in Mental Retardation and Developmental Disabilities*, Greenwich, Conn.: JAI press.

BOWERS, T. (ed.) (1984) *Management and the Special School*, London, Croom Helm.

BROOKS, P.H. and BAUMEISTER, A.A. (1977) 'A plea for consideration of ecological validity in the experimental psychology of mental retardation', *Amer. J. Ment. Defic.*, 81, 407–16.

BRUININKS, R., MEYERS, C.E., SIGFORD, B. and LAKIN, J.C. (eds) (1981) *Deinstitutionalization and Community Adjustment of Mentally Retarded People*, Washington, DC, Monograph 4, AAMD.

BUSNELLO, E. D'A. (1983) 'A mechanism for recording and reporting physical and psychosocial components of health in a Community Health System in Porto Alegre, Brazil', in M. LIPKIN and K. KUPKA (eds), *Psychosocial Factors Affecting Health*, New York, Praeger.

CLARKE, A.M. and CLARKE, A.D.B. (1965) 'The abilities and trainability of imbeciles', in A.M. CLARKE and A.D.B. CLARKE (eds), *Mental Deficiency: The Changing Outlook*, 2nd edn, London, Methuen.

CLIMENT, C. (1983) 'Challenges in the utilization of a triaxial classification of disease in a primary health care setting', in M. LIPKIN and K. KUPKA (eds), *Psychosocial Factors Affecting Health*, New York, Praeger.

COBB, H. and MITTLER, P. (1980) *Retardation and Mental Illness: Similarities and Differences*, position paper, Brussels, ILSMH.

COLE, M., HOOD, L. and MCDERMOTT, R. (1978) 'Ecological niche picking: ecological invalidity as an axiom of experimental cognitive psychology', in U. NEISSER (ed.), *Memory Observed*, San Francisco, Freeman.

CRAFT, M. and CRAFT, A. (1981) *Sex and the Mentally Handicapped*, London, Routledge & Kegan Paul.

CRAWLEY, B. (1982) 'The feasibility of trainee committees as a means of self-advocacy in adult training centres in England and Wales', unpublished PhD thesis, University of Manchester.

CROXEN, M. (1982) *Overview: Disability and Employment*, Brussels, EEC.

CRUICKSHANK, E. (1977) 'Least restrictive placement: administrative wishful thinking', *J. Learn. Disab.*, 10, 194–8.

CUNNINGHAM, C.C. (1983) 'Early support and intervention: the HARC infant project', in P. MITTLER and H. MCCONACHIE (eds), *Parents, Professionals and Mentally Handicapped People: Approaches to Partnership*, London, Croom Helm.

CUNNINGHAM, C.C. and SLOPER, P. (1978) *Helping Your Handicapped Baby*, London, Souvenir Press.

DEAN, A. and HEGARTY, S. (eds) (1984) *Learning for Independence: Post-16 Provision for People with Severe Learning Difficulties*, London, FEU, DES.

DES (Department of Education and Science) (1978) *Special Educational Needs*, Report of the Warnock Committee of Enquiry into the Education of Handicapped Children and Young People, Cmnd 7212, London, HMSO.

DESSENT, T. (ed.) (1984) *What is Important about Portage?*, Windsor, NFER.

DHSS (Department of Health and Social Security) (1971) *Better Services for the Mentally Handicapped*, Cmnd 4683, London, HMSO.

DHSS (Department of Health and Social Security) (1979) *Report of Committee of Enquiry into Mental Handicap, Nursing and Care*, 2 vols, London, HMSO.

DHSS (Department of Health and Social Security) (1981) *Care in the Community: A Consultative Document on Moving Resources for Care in England*, London, DHSS.

DHSS (Department of Health and Social Security) (1982) *A Third Report of the Development Team for the Mentally Handicapped*, London, HMSO.

DIXON, G. and DAVIS, K. (1981) *Peace Corps in Special Education and Rehabilitation*, Washington, DC, Partners of the Americas.

DYBWAD, G. (1970) 'Treatment of the mentally retarded: a cross-national view', in H.C. HAYWOOD (ed.), *Sociocultural Aspects of Mental Retardation*, New York, Appleton-Century-Crofts.

DYBWAD, G. and MITTLER, P. (eds) (1984) *L'Education des personnes handicapées mentales dans les pays francophones d'Afrique*, Séminaire organisé conjointement par l'UNESCO et ILSMH, Brazzaville, Congo; Brussels, ILSMH.

DYBWAD, R.F. (1974) 'The voluntary association on the international scene', in J. WORTIS (ed.), *Mental Retardation and Developmental Disabilities*, vol. V, Edinburgh and London, Churchill Livingstone.

DYBWAD, R.F. (ed.) (1979) *International Directory of Mental Retardation Resources*, 2nd edn, revised, Brussels, ILSMH.

EDGERTON, R.B. (1967) *The Cloak of Competence: Stigma in the Lives of the Retarded*, Berkeley, University of California Press.

EDGERTON, R.B. (1970) 'Mental retardation in non-western societies', in H.C. HAYWOOD (ed.), *Sociocultural Aspects of Mental Retardation*, New York, Appleton-Century-Crofts.

EDGERTON, R.B. (1981) 'Another look at culture and mental retardation', in M. BEGAB, H. HAYWOOD and H. GARBER (eds), *Psychosocial Influences on Retarded Performance*, Baltimore, University Park Press.

EDGERTON, R.B. and BERCOVICI, S. (1976) 'The cloak of competence: ten years later', *Amer. J. Ment. Defic.*, 80, 485–90.

EDGERTON, R.B., BOLLINGER, M. and HERR, B. (1984) 'The cloak of competence: after two decades', *Amer. J. Ment. Defic.*, 88, 345–51.

ELKIN, E. and TEMBY, E. (1984) *Participation and Self-Advocacy*, position paper, Brussels, ILSMH.

ELLIS, N. (ed.) (1966ff.) *International Review of Research in Mental Retardation*, New York, Academic Press.

FELCE, D., KUSHLICK, A. and SMITH, J. (1983) 'Planning and evaluating a community-based residential service for severely and profoundly mentally handicapped people', in J. MATSON (ed.), *Advances in Mental Retardation and Developmental Disabilities*, vol. I, Greenwich, Conn.: JAI Press.

FELCE, D., MANSELL, J. and KUSHLICK, A. (1980) 'Evaluation of residential facilities for the severely mentally retarded: staff performance', *Adv. Behav. Res. Ther.*, 3, 25–30.

FRYERS, T. (1984) *The Epidemiology of Severe Intellectual Impairment: The Dynamics of Prevalence*, London and New York, Academic Press.

GARDNER, R. (1984) 'The classroom implications of integrating handicapped children in ordinary schools in developing countries', in R. GARDNER (ed.), *Meeting Special Educational Needs in Developing Countries*, London, Institute of Education, mimeo.

GOFFMAN, M. (1968) *Stigma: Notes on the Management of Spoiled Identity*, Harmondsworth, Penguin.

GOLD, M. (1973) 'Research on the vocational rehabilitation of the retarded', in N. ELLIS (ed.), *International Review of Research in Mental Retardation*, New York, Academic Press.

GREENFIELD, P. and LAVE, J. (1982) 'Cognitive aspects of informal education', in D.A. WAGNER and M.W. STEVENSON (eds), *Cultural Perspectives on Child Development*, San Francisco, Freeman.

GRUENWALD, K. (1975) 'Sweden: services and developments', in J. WORTIS (ed.), *Mental Retardation and Developmental Disabilities*, vol. VII, New York, Grune & Stratton.

GRUENWALD, K. (1984) *Day Centres for Mentally Handicapped Adults*, 2nd edn, Stockholm, Socialstyren; Brussels, ILSMH.

GRUENWALD, L.J. and SCHROEDER, J. (1981) 'Integration of moderately and severely handicapped students in public schools: concepts and processes', in *Education of the Handicapped Adolescent: Integration in School*, Paris, CERI, OECD.

HAYNES, J. (1971) *Educational Assessment of Immigrant Children*, Windsor, NFER.

HEGARTY, S. and LUCAS, D. (1979) *Able to Learn – The Pursuit of Culture-Fair Assessment*, Windsor, NFER/Nelson.

HERON, A. and MYERS, M. (1983) *Intellectual Impairment: The Battle against Handicap*, New York and London, Academic Press.

HERR, S. and HERR, R. (1984) *Advocacy and Mental Handicap*, position paper, Brussels, ILSMH.

HOLOWINSKY, I.Z. (1984) 'Terminology, classification and educational services for the mentally retarded in the USSR', in J.M. BERG (ed.), *Perspectives and Progress in Mental Retardation*, Baltimore, University Park Press.

HOWIE, D. and CUMING, J. (1984) 'Self-advocacy by mentally retarded persons', mimeo.

HOWIE, D., CUMING, J. and RAYNES, J. (1984) 'Development of tools to facilitate participation by moderately retarded persons in residential evaluation procedures', *Brit. J. Ment. Subnorm.*, 30, 92–8.

IDC (Independent Development Council for People with Mental Handicap) (1984) *Next Steps: An Independent Review of Progress, Problems and Priorities in the Development of Services for People with Mental Handicap*, London, King's Fund and IDC.

ILO (International Labour Office) (1978) *Vocational Rehabilitation of the Mentally Retarded*, Geneva, ILO.

ILO (International Labour Office) (1983a) *Convention Concerning Vocational Rehabilitation and Employment (Disabled Persons)*, Convention 159, Geneva, ILO.

ILO (International Labour Office) (1983b) *Recommendation Concerning Vocational Rehabilitation and Employment (Disabled Persons)*, Recommendation 168, Geneva, ILO.

ILO (International Labour Office) (1984a) *ILO Standards on Vocational Rehabilitation: Guidelines for Implementation*, Geneva, ILO.

ILO (International Labour Office) (1984b) *Employment of Disabled Persons: Manual on Selective Placement*, Geneva, ILO.

ILSMH (International League of Societies for Persons with Mental Handicap) (1978a) *Step by Step: Implementation of the Rights of Mentally Retarded Persons*, Brussels, ILSMH.

ILSMH (International League of Societies for Persons with Mental Handicap) (1978b) 'International organizations in the field of mental handicap: reports from UNO, UNESCO, ILO, WHO, Council of Europe, IIN, CWOIH, IASSMD, OECD, PCMR', in H. SPUDICH (ed.), *Proceedings 7th World Congress on Mental Handicap*, vols 1 and 2, Brussels, ILSMH.

ILSMH (International League of Societies for Persons with Mental Handicap) (1983) *Starting a Local Society for Persons with Mental Handicap: Guidelines for Action*, Brussels, ILSMH.

INGSTAD, B. (1983) 'Activities to promote locally based services', in R. SERPELL (ed.), *Mobilizing Local Resources in Africa for Persons with Learning Difficulties or Mental Handicap*, Oslo, NFPU; Brussels, ILSMH.

JEFFREE, D. and CHESELDINE, S. (1984) *Let's Join In*, London, Souvenir Press.

JERVIS, R. (1972) 'Recent Italian literature', in J. WORTIS (ed.), *Mental Retardation and Developmental Disabilities*, vol. IV, New York, Grune & Stratton.

JORGENSEN, S. (1980) *Special Education in the European Community*, Brussels, Education Series, II, Commission of the European Communities.

KANE, J. and ROJAHN, J. (1981) 'Development of services for mentally retarded people in the Federal Republic of Germany: a survey of history, empirical research and current trends', *Appl. Res. Ment. Retard.*, 2,

195–210.

KING, R., RAYNES, N. and TIZARD, J. (1971) *Patterns of Residential Care*, London, Routledge & Kegan Paul.

KING'S FUND (1982) *An Ordinary Life: Comprehensive Locally Based Services for Mentally Handicapped People*, London, King's Fund Centre Paper no. 24.

KING'S FUND (1984) *An Ordinary Working Life: Vocational Services for People with Mental Handicap*, London, King's Fund Centre.

KORTEN, D. (1980) 'Community organization and rural development: a learning processes approach', *Publ. Admin. Rev.*, 40, 480–511.

KYSELA, G., ANDERSON, D. and MARFO, K. (1981) 'Issues in mental retardation in Canada: transitions', *Appl. Res. Ment. Retard.*, 2, 145–63.

KYSELA, G. and MARFO, K. (1984) 'Early handicapping conditions: detection and intervention in developing countries', in J. BERG (ed.), *Perspectives and Progress in Mental Retardation*, vol. 1, Baltimore, University Park Press.

LAFON, R. and CHABENIER, J. (1966) 'Research in mental retardation during the last decade in France', in N. ELLIS (ed.), *International Review of Research in Mental Retardation*, vol. 2, New York, Academic Press.

LAKIN, K.C., BRUININKS, R. and SIGFORD, B. (1981) 'Deinstitutionalization and community-based residential adjustment: a summary of research and issues', in R. BRUININKS, C.E. MEYERS, B. SIGFORD and J.C. LAKIN (eds), *Deinstitutionalization and Community Adjustment of Mentally Retarded People*, Washington, DC, Monograph 4, AAMD.

LANDESMAN-DWYER, S. (1983) 'The changing structure and function of institutions: a search for optimal group care environments', in S. LANDESMAN-DWYER and P. VIETZE (eds), *The Social Ecology of Residential Environments: Person* x *Setting Transactions in Mental Retardation*, Baltimore, University Park Press.

LANDSDOWN, R. and GRAHAM, P. (1985) *The Uses and Abuses of Psychological Tests in Childhood*, Geneva, WHO, mimeo.

LANYI-ENGELMAYER, A., KATONA, F. and CZEIZEL, A. (1983) 'Current issues in mental retardation in Hungary', *App. Res. Ment. Retard.*, 4, 123–38.

LAURY, G.V. (1976) 'Recent French literature', in J. WORTIS (ed.), *Mental Retardation and Developmental Disabilities*, vol. III, New York, Grune & Stratton.

LEI, T., NIHIRA, L., SHEEHY, N. and MAYERS, C.E. (1981) 'A study of small family care for mentally retarded people', in R. BRUININKS, C.E. MEYERS, B. SIGFORD and J.C. LAKIN (eds), *Deinstitutionalization and Community Adjustment of Mentally Retarded People*, Washington, DC, Monograph 4, AAMD.

LIBBY, M. (1981) *Meaning Well . . . and Thinking Right*, a report on a visit to North America on behalf of the Cheshire Foundation, mimeo.

MCBRIEN, J. (1981) 'Introducing the EDY Project', *Spec. Educ.: Forward Trends*, 8, 29–30.

MCBRIEN, J. and FOXEN, T. (1981) *Training Staff in Behavioural Methods: the EDY Inservice Courses for Mental Handicap Practitioners, Instructor's Handbook*, Manchester, Manchester University Press.

MCBRIEN, J. and WEIGHTMAN, J. (1980) 'The effect of room management procedures on the engagement of profoundly retarded children', *Brit. J. Ment. Subnorm.*, 26, 38–46.

MCCONKEY, R. and MCCORMACK, B. (1983) *Breaking the Barriers: Educating people About Disability*, London, Souvenir Press.

MAGNE, O. (1976) 'Survey of international research into special education', *Educ. Res.*, Uppsala, 4, 31–50.

MANGIN, G. (1983) *The Handicapped and their Employment*, Luxemburg, Office for Publications of the European Communities; London, HMSO.

MARFO, E., WALKER, S. and CHARLES, B. (eds) (1983) *Education and Rehabilitation of the Disabled in Africa*, vol. I, *Towards Improved Services*, Edmonton, Alberta, Centre for International Education and Development.

MATHEWS, R.G. (1973) 'Community service models: New Zealand', in J. WORTIS (ed.), *Mental Retardation and Developmental Disabilities*, vol. V, New York, Brunner/Mazel; London, Butterworth.

MATTINSON, J. (1975) *Marriage and Mental Handicap*, London, Tavistock Institute on Human Relations.

MELLGREN, S.I. and GOTESTAM, K.G. (1983) 'Reaserch on mental retardation in Norway 1970–1980: a review', *Appl. Res. Ment. Retard.*, 4, 103–12.

MENCAP (1981) *The Pathway Scheme*, London, Royal Society for Mentally Handicapped Children and Adults.

MILES, M. (1983a) 'Attitudes towards persons with disabilities following IYDP, with suggestions for promoting positive changes', Peshawar, Pakistan, Mission Hospital.

MILES, M. (1983b) 'Vocational rehabilitation: realities for the rural Asian disabled person', Peshawar, Pakistan, Mission Hospital, mimeo.

MILES, M. (1984a) 'Preliminary report on action study for integration of handicapped children', Peshawar, Pakistan, Mission Hospital, mimeo.

MILES, M. (1984b) 'Some questions about the "normalization principle" in an Asian context', Peshawar, Pakistan, Mission Hospital, mimeo.

MILES, M. (1984c) 'Where there is no Rehab Plan', Mental Health Centre, Peshawar, Pakistan, mimeo.

MITTLER, P. (ed.) (1977) *Research to Practice in Mental Retardation*, vol. I: *Care and Intervention*; vol. 2: *Education and Training*; vol. 3: *Biomedical Aspects*, Baltimore, University Park Press.

MITTLER, P. (1979) *People Not Patients: Problems and Policies in Mental Handicap*, London, Methuen.

MITTLER, P. (1981a) 'Training for the 21st century', *Spec. Educ.: Forward Trends*, 8, 8–11.

MITTLER, P. (ed.) (1981b) *Frontiers of Knowledge in Mental Retardation*, vol. I: *Social, Educational and Behavioural Aspects;* vol. 2: *Biomedical Aspects*, Baltimore, University Park Press; Lancaster, MTP Press.

MITTLER, P. (1982) 'The tasks ahead of us', in K. BAYES, W. CHAN, W. NG and F.C. TANG (eds), *Developing Resources for Mentally Retarded Persons*, Hong Kong, Joint Council for the Physically and Mentally Disabled.

MITTLER, P. (1983) 'New trends in community special education', *Assignment Children* (UNICEF), 63–4, 45–57.

MITTLER, P. (1984a) 'Evaluation of staff services and training', in J. DOBBING, A.D.B. CLARKE, J. CORBETT, J. HOGG and J. ROBINSON (eds), *Scientific Studies in Mental Retardation*, Basingstoke, Macmillan.

MITTLER, P. (1984b) *What is the International League of Societies for Persons with Mental Handicap?*, Brussels, ILSMH.

MITTLER, P. and BEASLEY, D. (1982) *A Multinational Family Training Workshop*, report to UN and UNESCO, Brussels, ILSMH.

MITTLER, P. and MCCONACHIE, H. (eds) (1983) *Parents, Professionals and Mentally Handicapped People: Approaches to Partnership*, London, Croom Helm.

MITTLER, P. and MITTLER, H. (1983) 'Partnership with parents: an overview', in P. MITTLER and H. MCCONACHIE (eds), *Parents, Professionals and Mentally Handicapped People: Approaches to Partnership*, London, Croom Helm.

MITTLER, P. and PREDDY, D. (1981) 'Mentally handicapped pupils and school leavers: a survey in north-west England', in B. COOPER (ed.), *Assessing the Handicaps and Needs of Mentally Retarded Children*, London and New York, Academic Press.

MUTTERS, T. (1973) 'Community service models: West Germany', in J. WORTIS (ed.), *Mental Retardation and Developmental Disabilities*, vol. V, New York, Brunner/Mazel; London, Butterworth.

MUTTERS, T. (1982) 'Interstate co-operation experiences gained in the Federal Republic of Germany with trainees from developing countries', in K. BAYES, W. CHAN, W. NG and F.C. TANG (eds), *Developing Resources for Mentally Retarded Persons*, Hong Kong, Joint Council for the Physically and Mentally Disabled.

NDGMH (National Development Group for the Mentally Handicapped) (1977) *Day Services for Mentally Handicapped Adults*, NDG, Pamphlet 5, London, DHSS.

NDGMH (National Development Group for the Mentally Handicapped) (1978) *Helping Mentally Handicapped People in Hospital*, London, DHSS.

NDGMH (National Development Group for the Mentally Handicapped) (1980) *Improving the Quality of Services for Mentally Handicapped People: A Checklist of Standards*, London, DHSS.

NEWLAND, T.E. (1980) 'Psychological assessment of exceptional children', in W. CRUIKSHANK (ed.), *Psychology of Exceptional Children and Youth*, 4th edn, Englewood Cliffs, NJ, Prentice-Hall.

NSMHC (National Society for Mentally Handicapped Children) (1977) *STAMINA: Minimum Standards for ESN(S) Schools, ATCs and Residential Homes*, London, MENCAP.

O'BRIEN, J. and TYNE, A. (1981) *The Principle of Normalization: A Foundation for Effective Services*, London, Campaign for Mentally Handicapped People.

OECD (Organisation for Economic Co-operation and Development) (1981) *The Education of the Handicapped Adolescent: Integration in School*, Paris, Centre for Educational Innovation and Research, OECD.

OECD (Organisation for Economic Co-operation and Development) (1983) *Education of the Handicapped Adolescent: Transition from School to Working Life*, Paris, CERI/OECD.

OMSORGKOMITTEN (1981) *Care and Service for Persons with Certain Handicaps in Sweden*, Stockholm, Omsorgkomitten.

ONARHEIM, K.J. (1983) 'Co-operation between parents, family members, government officials and professionals', in R. SERPELL (ed.), *Mobilizing Local Resources in Africa for Persons with Learning Difficulties or Mental Handicap*, Oslo, NFPU; Brussels, ILSMH.

PCMR (President's Committee on Mental Retardation) (1979) *Mental Retardation: The Leading Edge, Service Programs that Work*, Washington, DC, PCMR, US Dept HEW.

PERSKE, R. (1977) *Improving the Quality of Life: A Symposium on Normalization and Integration*, Arlington, Texas, Association of Retarded Citizens; Brussels, ILSMH.

PERSKE, R. (1979) *The Child with Retardation Today – The Adult of Tomorrow*, Arlington, Texas, Association of Retarded Citizens; Brussels, ILSMH.

POSTERNAK, Y. (1979) *Integration of Handicapped Children and Adolescents in Italy*, Paris, CERI/OECD.

PRABHU, G.G. (ed.) (1978) *The Mentally Retarded in a Changing Society: Proceedings of the 3rd Asian Conference on Mental Retardation*, New Delhi, Federation for the Welfare of the Mentally Retarded.

PRABHU, G.G. (1980) 'Developments in south-east Asia', in J. WORTIS (ed.), *Mental Retardation and Developmental Disabilities*, vol. XI, New York, Brunner/Mazel.

PRINGLE, M.L.K. (1974) *The Needs of Children*, London, Hutchinson.

RAYNES, N., PRATT, M. and ROSES, S. (1979) *Organizational Structure and the Care of the Mentally Retarded*, London, Croom Helm.

REHABILITATION INTERNATIONAL (1981) 'Childhood disability: its prevention and rehabilitation', *Assignment Children*, 53–4, 43–75.

REPP, A., FELCE, D. and DE KOCK, U. (1983) 'Observational studies of staff working with mentally retarded persons: a review', unpublished paper, Health Care Evaluation Research Team.

ROEHER, A. (1978) 'Models of staff training', in H. SPUDICH (ed.), *Proceedings of 7th World Congress on Mental Handicap*, Brussels, ILSMH.

ROEHER, A. (1982) 'Resources for personnel training', in K. BAYES, W. CHAN, W. NG and F.C. TANG (eds), *Developing Resources for Mentally*

Retarded Persons, Hong Kong, Joint Council for the Physically and Mentally Disabled.

ROSE-ACKERMAN, S. (1982) 'Mental retardation and society: the ethics and politics of normalization', *Ethics*, 93, 81–101.

SANDOW, S. (1984) 'The Portage Project: ten years on', in T. DESSENT (ed.), *What is Important about Portage?*, Windsor, NFER.

SARDI DE SELLE, M. and ABADI, A. (1977) 'Latin America: recent developments', in J. WORTIS (ed.), *Mental Retardation and Developmental Disabilities*, vol. IX, New York, Brunner/Mazel.

SAUNDERS, C.A. (1982) 'The epidemiology of handicap in the child population of Plateau State', in V. CURRAN (ed.), *The Developing Child: A Nigerian Perspective*, London, Routledge & Kegan Paul.

SCHEERENBERGER, R.C. (1981) 'Deinstitutionalization: trends and difficulties', in R. BRUININKS, C.E. MEYERS, B. SIGFORD and J.C. LAKIN (eds), *Deinstitutionalization and Community Adjustment of Mentally Retarded People*, Washington, DC, Monograph 4, AAMD.

SCHMIDT, L.P. and BALTES, P.D. (1971) 'German theory and research on mental retardation: emphasis on structure', in N. ELLIS (ed.), *International Review of Research on Mental Retardation*, vol. 5, New York, Academic Press.

SCHROEDER, C. and SCHROEDER, S. (1981) 'Mental retardation in the United States: assessment, program development and applied research', *Appl. Res. Ment. Retard.*, 2, 181–94.

SEED, P. (1981) *Mental Handicap: Who Helps in Rural and Remote Communities?*, Tonbridge, Costello.

SEGAL, S. (1984) *Society and Mental Handicap: Are We Ineducable?*, Tonbridge, Costello.

SELTZER, M. and LITCHFIELD, L. (1984) 'Community reaction to community residences: a study of factors related to community response', in J. BERG (ed.), *Perspectives and Progress in Mental Retardation*, Baltimore, University Park Press.

SEN, A.K. (1976) 'A decade of experimental research in mental retardation in India', in N. ELLIS (ed.), *International Review of Research in Mental Retardation*, vol. 8, New York, Academic Press.

SEN, A.K. (1981) 'Care, prevention and assessment of mental retardation in India', *Appl. Res. Ment. Retard.*, 2, 129–37.

SERPELL, R. (1982) 'Childhood disability in Botswana', report to government of Botswana, mimeo.

SERPELL, R. (1983) *Mobilizing Local Resources in Africa for Persons with Learning Difficulties or Mental Handicap*, Oslo, NFPU; Brussels, ILSMH.

SERPELL, R. (1984a) 'Assessment for severe intellectual handicap in various cultural settings', paper presented to Bishop Bekkers Institute, Utrecht, Holland.

SERPELL, R. (1984b) 'Applications of crosscultural psychology in the development of services for disabled children', paper presented to workshop on 'Applications of crosscultural psychology to the promotion of healthy human development', Instituto Mexicano de Psichiatria, Mexico City, August 1984, in press.

SHEARER, A. (1984) *Think Positive: Presenting a Positive Image of Persons with Mental Handicap*, Brussels, ILSMH, in press.

SHENNAN, V. (1977) *Russian Education for the Retarded*, London, MENCAP.

SIGELMAN, C.K. (1981), Issues in interviewing mentally retarded persons: an empirical study', in R. BRUININKS, C.E. MEYERS, B. SIGFORD and J.C. LAKIN (eds), *Deinstitutionalization and Community Adjustment of Mentally Retarded People*, Washington, DC, Monograph 4, AAMD.

SIGELMAN, C.K. (1983) *Communicating with Mentally Retarded Persons: Asking Questions and Getting Answers*, Lubbock, Texas, Texas Technical University.

SIMON, G.B. (1981) *Next Step on the Ladder: Assessment and Management of the Multi-Handicapped Child*, Kidderminster, British Institute for Mental Handicap.

SINCLAIR, S. (1981) *National Planning for the Mentally Handicapped*, New Delhi, All India Institute of Medical Sciences and WHO.

SINGH, N.N. (1981) 'Mental retardation: state of the field in New Zealand', *Appl. Res. Ment. Retard.*, 2, 115–27.

SINGH, N.N and WILTON, K.M. (eds) (1984) *Mental Retardation: Research and Services in New Zealand*, Wellington, Whitcoulls.

SMITH, G., DANIEL, D.R., THAMUTARAM, S. and BAILEY, D. (1980) *Proceedings of the 4th Asian Conference on Mental Retardation*, Kuala Lumpur, Selangor and Federal Territory for Retarded Children.

SODER, M. (1981) 'School integration of the mentally retarded', in *Education of the Handicapped Adolescent: Integration in the School*, Paris, CERI/OECD.

STEIN, Z. and SUSSER, M. (1980) 'The less developed world: south-east Asia as a paradigm', in J. WORTIS (ed.), *Mental Retardation and Developmental Disabilities*, vol. XI, New York, Brunner/Mazel.

STERNER, R. (1976) *Social and Economic Conditions of the Mentally Retarded in 48 Selected Countries*, Brussels, ILSMH.

STIFEL, L.D., DAVIDSON, R. and COLEMAN, J.S. (eds) (1982) *Social Sciences and Public Policy in the Developing World*, Lexington, Mass., Heath.

SUTTER, P. and MAYEDA, T. (1981) 'Matching developmentally disabled client characteristics to care-provider and employer preferences', in R. BRUININKS, C.E. MEYERS, B. SIGFORD and J.C. LAKIN (eds), *Deinstitutionalization and Community Adjustment of Mentally Retarded People*, Washington, DC, Monograph 4, AAMD.

SZONDY, M. and SZENTAGOTHAI, K. (1981) 'Assessment and management of mental retardation in Hungary', *Appl. Res. Ment. Retard.*, 2, 139–44.

TAKAHASHI, A. (1973) 'Japanese literature and developments', in J. WORTIS (ed.), *Mental Retardation and Developmental Disabilities*, vol. V, New York, Brunner/Mazel; London, Butterworth.

THALER, J. (1982) *Mental Retardation in Nepal: A Nationwide Study*, Kathmandu, Human and National Development Service.

THOMAE, I. and FRYERS, T. (1982) *Ageing and Mental Handicap*, position paper, Brussels, ILSMH.

THOMAS, D. FIRTH, H. and KENDALL, A. (1978) *ENCOR – A Way Ahead*, London, Campaign for the Mentally Handicapped.

THORBURN, M. (1981) 'Community aides for pre-school children in Jamaica', *Assignment Children*, 53–4, 117–34.

TOMLINSON, S. (1981) *Educational Subnormality: A Study in Decision-Making*, London, Routledge & Kegan Paul.

TOMLINSON, S. (1982) *A Sociology of Special Education*, London, Routledge & Kegan Paul.

UN (United Nations) (1983) *World Programme of Action Concerning Disabled Persons*, New York, UN.

UNESCO (United Nations Educational, Scientific and Cultural Organization) (1978) *Economic Aspects of Special Education (Czechoslovakia, New Zealand and USA)*, Paris, UNESCO.

UNESCO (1979) *Expert Meeting on Special Education, Final Report*, Paris, UNESCO.

UNESCO (1981) *Early Detection, Intervention and Education (Argentina, Canada, Denmark, Jamaica, Jordan, Nigeria, Sri Lanka, Thailand, United Kingdom)*, Paris, UNESCO.

UNESCO (1982) *World Conference on Actions and Strategies for Education, Prevention and Integration* (Sundberg declaration), Torremolinos, Paris, UNESCO.

UNESCO (1984a) *Terminology in Special Education (English, French, Russian, Spanish)* (revised edn), Paris, UNESCO.

UNESCO (1984b) *International Directory of Special Education*, 2nd edn, Paris, UNESCO.

UNICEF (United Nations Children's Fund) (1981) 'The disabled child: a new approach to prevention and rehabilitation', *Assignment Children*, 53–4, Geneva, UNICEF.

VANIER, J. (ed.) (1982) *The Challenge of L'Arche*, London, Darton, Longman & Todd.

VISLIE, L. (1981a) 'Integration of handicapped children in Italy: a view from outside', in *Education of the Handicapped Adolescent: Integration in the School*, Paris, CERI/OECD.

VISLIE, L. (1981b) 'Policies for basic education: Norway and the concept of integration', in *Education of the Handicapped Adolescent: Integration in the School*, Paris CERI/OECD.

VLASOVA, T. (1973) 'Recent advances in Soviet defectology', in J. WORTIS (ed.), *Mental Retardation and Developmental Disabilities*, vol. V, New York, Brunner/Mazel; London, Butterworth.

WARD, L. (1982) *People First: Developing Services in the Community for People with Mental Handicap*, London, King's Fund Centre Paper 37.

WERNER, D. and BOWER, B. (1982) *Helping Health Workers Learn: A Book of Aids and Ideas for Instructors at the Village Level*, Palo Alto, Calif., Hesperian Foundation (available in UK through TALC, Institute of Child Health, London).

WHELAN, E. and SPEAKE, B. (1979) *Learning to Cope*, London, Souvenir Press.

WHO (World Health Organization) (1980) *International Classification of Impairments, Disabilities and Handicaps*, Geneva, WHO.

WHO (World Health Organization) (1983) *A Manual on Training Disabled People in the Community: Community-Based Rehabilitation for Developing Countries*, Geneva, WHO.

WHO (World Health Organization (1985) *Mental Retardation: Meeting the Challenge*, Geneva, WHO; Brussels, ILSMH/IASSMD.

WILLIAMS, P. and SHOULTZ, B. (1982) *We Can Speak for Ourselves: Self-Advocacy by Mentally Handicapped People*, London, Souvenir Press.

WILLMS, J.D. (1981) 'Neighbourhood attitudes towards group homes for mentally retarded adults', in P. MITTLER (ed.), *Frontiers of Knowledge in Mental Retardation*, vol. 1, Baltimore, University Park Press.

WOLFENSBERGER, W. (1972) *The Principle of Normalization in Human Services*, Toronto, National Institute on Mental Retardation.

WOLFENSBERGER, W. (1983) 'Social role valorization: a proposed new term for the principles of normalization', *Ment. Retard.*, 21, 234–9.

WOLFENSBERGER, W. and GLENN, L. (1975) *Program Analysis of Service Systems*, 3rd edn, Handbook, Toronto, National Institute of Mental Retardation.

WOLFENSBERGER, W. and THOMAS, S. (1983) 'PASSING (Program Analysis of Service Systems)', in *Implementation of Normalization Goals, Normalization Criteria and Ratings Manual*, 2nd edn, Handbook, Toronto, National Institute of Mental Retardation.

WOLFENSBERGER, W. and ZAUHA, H. (eds) (1973) *Citizen Advocacy and Protective Services for the Impaired and Handicapped*, Toronto, National Institute for Mental Retardation.

WORTIS, J. (ed.) (1966ff.) *Mental Retardation: An Annual Review*, New York, Brunner Mazel.

WYNGAARDEN, M. (1981) 'Interviewing mentally retarded persons', in R. BRUININKS, C.E. MEYERS, B. SIGFORD and J.C. LAKIN (eds), *Deinstitutionalization and Community Adjustment of Mentally Retarded People*, Washington, DC, Monograph 4, AAMD.

YAMAGUCHI, K. (ed.) (1975) *Equal Rights for the Retarded: Report of 2nd Asian Conference on Mental Retardation*, Tokyo, Japan League for the Mentally Retarded.

ZELIOLI, A. (1982) 'The right to education', paper presented to 8th World Congress, International League of Societies for Persons with Mental Handicap, Nairobi, Kenya, November 1982, Brussels, ILSMH.

Name Index

Subject Index